THE HENRY ADAMS COLLECTION: 4 CLASSIC WORKS BY

Henry Adams

The Education of Henry Adams

Preface

JEAN JACQUES ROUSSEAU began his famous Confessions by a vehement appeal to the Deity: "I have shown myself as I was; contemptible and vile when I was so; good, generous, sublime when I was so; I have unveiled my interior such as Thou thyself hast seen it, Eternal Father! Collect about me the innumerable swarm of my fellows; let them hear my confessions; let them groan at my unworthiness; let them blush at my meannesses! Let each of them discover his heart in his turn at the foot of thy throne with the same sincerity; and then let any one of them tell thee if he dares: 'I was a better man!' "

Jean Jacques was a very great educator in the manner of the eighteenth century, and has been commonly thought to have had more influence than any other teacher of his time; but his peculiar method of improving human nature has not been universally admired. Most educators of the nineteenth century have declined to show themselves before their scholars as objects more vile or contemptible than necessary, and even the humblest teacher hides, if possible, the faults with which nature has generously embellished us all, as it did Jean Jacques, thinking, as most religious minds are apt to do, that the Eternal Father himself may not feel unmixed pleasure at our thrusting under his eyes chiefly the least agreeable details of his creation.

As an unfortunate result the twentieth century finds few recent guides to avoid, or to follow. American literature offers scarcely one working model for high education. The student must go back, beyond Jean Jacques, to Benjamin Franklin, to find a model even of self-teaching. Except in the abandoned sphere of the dead languages, no one has discussed what part of education has, in his personal experience, turned out to be useful, and what not. This volume attempts to discuss it.

As educator, Jean Jacques was, in one respect, easily first; he erected a monument of warning against the Ego. Since his time, and largely thanks to him, the Ego has steadily tended to efface itself, and, for purposes of model, to become a manikin on which the toilet of education is to be draped in order to show the fit or misfit of the clothes. The object of study is the garment, not the figure. The tailor adapts the manikin as well as the clothes to his patron's wants. The tailor's object, in this volume, is to fit young men, in universities or elsewhere, to be men of the world, equipped for any emergency; and the garment offered to them is meant to show the faults of the patchwork fitted on their fathers.

At the utmost, the active-minded young man should ask of his teacher only mastery of his tools. The young man himself, the subject of education, is a certain form of energy; the object to be gained is economy of his force; the training is partly the clearing away of obstacles, partly the direct application of effort. Once acquired, the tools and models may be thrown away.

The manikin, therefore, has the same value as any other geometrical figure of three or more dimensions, which is used for the study of relation. For that purpose it cannot be spared; it is the only measure of motion, of proportion, of human condition; it must have the air of reality; must be taken for real; must be treated as though it had life. Who knows? Possibly it had!

February 16, 1907

Chapter I. Quincy (1838-1848)

UNDER the shadow of Boston State House, turning its back on the house of John Hancock, the little passage called Hancock Avenue runs, or ran, from Beacon Street, skirting the State House grounds, to Mount Vernon Street, on the summit of Beacon Hill; and there, in the third house below Mount Vernon Place, February 16, 1838, a child was born, and christened later by his uncle, the minister of the First Church after the tenets of Boston Unitarianism, as Henry Brooks Adams.

Had he been born in Jerusalem under the shadow of the Temple and circumcised in the Synagogue by his uncle the high priest, under the name of Israel Cohen, he would scarcely have been more distinctly branded, and not much more heavily handicapped in the races of the coming century, in running for such stakes as the century was to offer; but, on the other hand, the ordinary traveller, who does not enter the field of racing, finds advantage in being, so to speak, ticketed through life, with the safeguards of an old, established traffic. Safeguards are often irksome, but sometimes convenient, and if one needs them at all, one is apt to need them badly. A hundred years earlier, such safeguards as his would have secured any young man's success; and although in 1838 their value was not very great compared with what they would have had in 1738, yet the mere accident of starting a twentieth-century career from a nest of associations so colonial, -- so troglodytic -- as the First Church, the Boston State House, Beacon Hill, John Hancock and John Adams, Mount Vernon Street and Quincy, all crowding on ten pounds of unconscious babyhood, was so queer as to offer a subject of curious speculation to the baby long after he had witnessed the solution. What could become of such a child of the seventeenth and eighteenth centuries, when he should wake up to find himself required to play the game of the twentieth? Had he been consulted, would he have cared to play the game at all, holding such cards as he held, and suspecting that the game was to be one of which neither he nor any one else back to the beginning of time knew the rules or the risks or the stakes? He was not consulted and was not responsible, but had he been taken into the confidence of his parents, he would certainly have told them to change nothing as far as concerned him. He would have been astounded by his own luck. Probably no child, born in the year, held better cards than he. Whether life was an honest game of chance, or whether the cards were marked and forced, he could not refuse to play his excellent hand. He could never make the usual plea of irresponsibility. He accepted the situation as though he had been a party to it, and under the same circumstances would do it again, the more readily for knowing the exact values. To his life as a whole he was a consenting, contracting party and partner from the moment he was born to the moment he died. Only with that understanding -- as a consciously assenting member in full partnership with the society of his age -- had his education an interest to himself or to others.

As it happened, he never got to the point of playing the game at all; he lost himself in the study of it, watching the errors of the players; but this is the only interest in the story, which otherwise has no moral and little incident. A story of education -- seventy years of it -- the practical value remains to the end in doubt, like other values about which men have disputed since the birth of Cain and Abel; but the practical value of the universe has never been stated in dollars. Although every one cannot be a Gargantua-Napoleon-Bismarck and walk off with the great bells of Notre Dame, every one must bear his own universe, and most persons are moderately interested in learning how their neighbors have managed to carry theirs.

This problem of education, started in 1838, went on for three years, while the baby grew, like other babies, unconsciously, as a vegetable, the outside world working as it never had worked before, to get his new universe ready for him. Often in old age he puzzled over the question whether, on the doctrine of chances, he was at liberty to accept himself or his world as an accident. No such accident had ever happened before in human experience. For him, alone, the old universe was thrown into the ash-heap and a new one created. He and his eighteenth-century, troglodytic Boston were suddenly cut apart -- separated forever -- in act if not in sentiment, by the opening of the Boston and Albany Railroad; the appearance of the first Cunard steamers in the bay; and the telegraphic messages which carried from Baltimore to Washington the news that Henry Clay and James K. Polk were nominated for the Presidency. This was in May, 1844; he was six years old ; his new world was ready for use, and only fragments of the old met his eyes.

Of all this that was being done to complicate his education, he knew only the color of yellow. He first found himself sitting on a yellow kitchen floor in strong sunlight. He was three years old when he took this earliest step in education; a lesson of color. The second followed soon; a lesson of taste. On December 3, 1841, he developed scarlet fever. For several days he was as good as dead, reviving only under the careful nursing of his family. When he began to recover strength, about January 1, 1842, his hunger must have been stronger than any other pleasure or pain, for while in after life he retained not the faintest recollection of his illness, he remembered quite clearly his aunt entering the sickroom bearing in her hand a saucer with a baked apple.

The order of impressions retained by memory might naturally be that of color and taste, although one would rather suppose that the sense of pain would be first to educate. In fact, the third recollection of the child was that of discomfort. The moment he could be removed, he was bundled up in blankets and carried from the little house in Hancock Avenue to a larger one which his parents were to occupy for the rest of their lives in the neighboring Mount Vernon Street. The season was midwinter, January 10, 1842, and he never forgot his acute distress for want of air under his blankets, or the noises of moving furniture.

As a means of variation from a normal type, sickness in childhood ought to have a certain value not to be classed under any fitness or unfitness of natural selection; and especially scarlet fever affected boys seriously, both physically and in character, though they might through life puzzle themselves to decide whether it had fitted or unfitted them for success; but this fever of Henry Adams took greater and greater importance in his eyes, from the point of view of education, the longer he lived. At first, the effect was physical. He fell behind his brothers two or three inches in height, and proportionally in bone and weight. His character and processes of mind seemed to share in this fining-down process of scale. He was not good in a fight, and his nerves were more delicate than boys' nerves ought to be. He exaggerated these weaknesses as he grew older. The habit of doubt; of distrusting his own judgment and of totally rejecting the judgment of the world; the tendency to regard every question as open; the hesitation to act except as a choice of evils; the shirking of responsibility; the love of line, form, quality; the horror of ennui; the passion for companionship and the antipathy to society -- all these are well-known qualities of New England character in no way peculiar to individuals but in this instance they seemed to be stimulated by the fever, and Henry Adams could never make up his mind whether, on the whole, the change of character was morbid or healthy, good or bad for his purpose. His brothers were the type; he was the variation.

As far as the boy knew, the sickness did not affect him at all, and he grew up in excellent health, bodily and mental, taking life as it was given; accepting its local standards without a dificulty, and enjoying much of it as keenly as any other boy of his age. He seemed to himself quite normal, and his companions seemed always to think him so. Whatever was peculiar about him was education, not character, and came to him, directly and indirectly, as the result of that eighteenth-century inheritance which he took with his name.

The atmosphere of education in which he lived was colonial, revolutionary, almost Cromwellian, as though he were steeped, from his greatest grandmother's birth, in the odor of political crime. Resistance to something was the law of New England nature; the boy looked out on the world with the instinct of resistance; for numberless generations his predecessors had viewed the world chiefly as a thing to be reformed, filled with evil forces to be abolished, and they saw no reason to suppose that they had wholly succeeded in the abolition; the duty was unchanged. That duty implied not only resistance to evil, but hatred of it. Boys naturally look on all force as an enemy, and generally find it so, but the New Englander, whether boy or man, in his long struggle with a stingy or hostile universe, had learned also to love the pleasure of hating; his joys were few.

Politics, as a practice, whatever its professions, had always been the systematic organization of hatreds, and Massachusetts politics had been as harsh as the climate. The chief charm of New England was harshness of contrasts and extremes of sensibility -- a cold that froze the blood, and a heat that boiled it -- so that the pleasure of hating -- one's self if no better victim offered -- was not its rarest amusement; but the charm was a true and natural child of the soil, not a cultivated weed of the ancients. The violence of the contrast was real and made the strongest motive of education. The double exterior nature gave life its relative values. Winter and summer, cold and heat, town and country, force and freedom, marked two modes of life and thought, balanced like lobes of the brain. Town was winter confinement, school, rule, discipline; straight, gloomy streets, piled with six feet of snow in the middle; frosts that made the snow sing under wheels or runners; thaws when the streets became dangerous to cross; society of uncles, aunts, and cousins who expected children to behave themselves, and who were not always gratified; above all else, winter represented the desire to escape and go free. Town was restraint, law, unity. Country, only seven miles away, was liberty, diversity, outlawry, the endless delight of mere sense impressions given by nature for nothing, and breathed by boys without knowing it.

Boys are wild animals, rich in the treasures of sense, but the New England boy had a wider range of emotions than boys of more equable climates. He felt his nature crudely, as it was meant. To the boy Henry Adams, summer was drunken. Among senses, smell was the strongest -- smell of hot pine-woods and sweet-fern in the scorching summer noon; of new-mown hay; of ploughed earth; of box hedges; of peaches, lilacs, syringas; of stables, barns, cow-yards; of salt water and low tide on the marshes; nothing came amiss. Next to smell came taste, and the children knew the taste of everything they saw or touched, from pennyroyal and flagroot to the shell of a pignut and the letters of a spelling-book -- the taste of A-B, AB, suddenly revived on the boy's tongue sixty years afterwards. Light, line, and color as sensual pleasures, came later and were as crude as the rest. The New England light is glare, and the atmosphere harshens color. The boy was a full man before he ever knew what was meant by atmosphere; his idea of pleasure in light was the blaze of a New England sun. His idea of color was a peony, with the dew of early morning on its petals. The intense blue of the sea, as he saw it a mile or two away, from the Quincy hills; the cumuli in a June afternoon sky; the strong reds and greens and purples of colored prints and children's picture-books, as the American colors then ran; these were ideals. The opposites or antipathies, were the cold grays of November evenings, and the thick, muddy thaws of Boston winter. With such standards, the Bostonian could not but develop a double nature. Life was a double thing. After a January blizzard, the boy who could look with pleasure into the violent snow-glare of the cold white sunshine, with its intense light and shade, scarcely knew what was meant by tone. He could reach it only by education.

Winter and summer, then, were two hostile lives, and bred two separate natures. Winter was always the effort to live; summer was tropical license. Whether the children rolled in the grass, or waded in the brook, or swam in the salt ocean, or sailed in the bay, or fished for smelts in the creeks, or netted minnows in the salt-marshes, or took to the pine-woods and the granite quarries, or chased muskrats and hunted snapping-turtles in the swamps, or mushrooms or nuts on the autumn hills, summer and country were always sensual living, while winter was always compulsory learning. Summer was the multiplicity of nature; winter was school.

The bearing of the two seasons on the education of Henry Adams was no fancy; it was the most decisive force he ever knew; it ran though life, and made the division between its perplexing, warring, irreconcilable problems, irreducible opposites, with growing emphasis to the last year of study. From earliest childhood the boy was accustomed to feel that, for him, life was double. Winter and summer, town and country, law and liberty, were hostile, and the man who pretended they were not, was in his eyes a schoolmaster -- that is, a man employed to tell lies to little boys. Though Quincy was but two hours' walk from Beacon Hill, it belonged in a different world. For two hundred years, every Adams, from father to son, had lived within sight of State Street, and sometimes had lived in it, yet none had ever taken kindly to the town, or been taken kindly by it. The boy inherited his double nature. He knew as yet nothing about his great-grandfather, who had died a dozen years before his own birth: he took for granted that any great-grandfather of his must have always been good, and his enemies wicked; but he divined his great-grandfather's character from his own. Never for a moment did he connect the two ideas of Boston and John Adams; they were separate and antagonistic; the idea of John Adams went with Quincy. He knew his grandfather John Quincy Adams only as an old man of seventy-five or eighty who was friendly and gentle with him, but except that he heard his grandfather always called "the President," and his grandmother "the Madam," he had no reason to suppose that his Adams grandfather differed in character from his Brooks grandfather who was equally kind and benevolent. He liked the Adams side best, but for no other reason than that it reminded him of the country, the summer, and the absence of restraint. Yet he felt also that Quincy was in a way inferior to Boston, and that socially Boston looked down on Quincy. The reason was clear enough even to a five-year old child. Quincy had no Boston style. Little enough style had either; a simpler manner of life and thought could hardly exist, short of cave-dwelling. The flint-and-steel with which his grandfather Adams used to light his own fires in the early morning was still on the mantelpiece of his study. The idea of a livery or even a dress for servants, or of an evening toilette, was next to blasphemy. Bathrooms, water-supplies, lighting, heating, and the whole array of domestic comforts, were unknown at Quincy. Boston had already a bathroom, a water-supply, a furnace, and gas. The superiority of Boston was evident, but a child liked it no better for that.

The magnificence of his grandfather Brooks's house in Pearl Street or South Street has long ago disappeared, but perhaps his country house at Medford may still remain to show what impressed the mind of a boy in 1845 with the idea of city splendor. The President's place at Quincy was the larger and older and far the more interesting of the two; but a boy felt at once its inferiority in fashion. It showed plainly enough its want of wealth. It smacked of colonial age, but not of Boston style or plush curtains. To the end of his life he never quite overcame the prejudice thus drawn in with his childish breath. He never could compel himself to care for nineteenth-century style. He was never able to adopt it, any more than his father or grandfather or great-grandfather had done. Not that he felt it as particularly hostile, for he reconciled himself to much that was worse; but because, for some remote reason, he was born an eighteenth-century child. The old house at Quincy was eighteenth century. What style it had was in its Queen Anne mahogany panels and its Louis Seize chairs and sofas. The panels belonged to an old colonial Vassall who built the house; the furniture had been brought back from Paris in 1789 or 1801 or 1817, along with porcelain and books and much else of old diplomatic remnants; and neither of the two eighteenth-century styles -- neither English Queen Anne nor French Louis Seize -- was cofortable for a boy, or for any one else. The dark mahogany had been painted white to suit daily life in winter gloom. Nothing seemed to favor, for a child's objects, the older forms. On the contrary, most boys, as well as grown-up people, preferred the new, with good reason, and the child felt himself distinctly at a disadvantage for the taste.

Nor had personal preference any share in his bias. The Brooks grandfather was as amiable and as sympathetic as the Adams grandfather. Both were born in 1767, and both died in 1848. Both were kind to children, and both belonged rather to the eighteenth than to the nineteenth centuries. The child knew no difference between them except that one was associated with winter and the other with summer; one with Boston, the other with Quincy. Even with Medford, the association was hardly easier. Once as a very young boy he was taken to pass a few days with his grandfather Brooks under charge of his aunt, but became so violently homesick that within twenty-four hours he was brought back in disgrace. Yet he could not remember ever being seriously homesick again.

The attachment to Quincy was not altogether sentimental or wholly sympathetic. Quincy was not a bed of thornless roses. Even there the curse of Cain set its mark. There as elsewhere a cruel universe combined to crush a child. As though three or four vigorous brothers and sisters, with the best will, were not enough to crush any child, every one else conspired towards an education which he hated. From cradle to grave this problem of running order through chaos, direction through space, discipline through freedom, unity through multiplicity, has always been, and must always be, the task of education, as it is the moral of religion, philosophy, science, art, politics, and economy; but a boy's will is his life, and he dies when it is broken, as the colt dies in harness, taking a new nature in becoming tame. Rarely has the boy felt kindly towards his tamers. Between him and his master has always been war. Henry Adams never knew a boy of his generation to like a master, and the task of remaining on friendly terms with one's own family, in such a relation, was never easy.

All the more singular it seemed afterwards to him that his first serious contact with the President should have been a struggle of will, in which the old man almost necessarily defeated the boy, but instead of leaving, as usual in such defeats, a lifelong sting, left rather an impression of as fair treatment as could be expected from a natural enemy. The boy met seldom with such restraint. He could not have been much more than six years old at the time -- seven at the utmost -- and his mother had taken him to Quincy for a long stay with the President during the summer. What became of the rest of the family he quite forgot; but he distinctly remembered standing at the house door one summer morning in a passionate outburst of rebellion against going to school. Naturally his mother was the immediate victim of his rage; that is what mothers are for, and boys also; but in this case the boy had his mother at unfair disadvantage, for she was a guest, and had no means of enforcing obedience. Henry showed a certain tactical ability by refusing to start, and he met all efforts at compulsion by successful, though too vehement protest. He was in fair way to win, and was holding his own, with sufficient energy, at the bottom of the long staircase which led up to the door of the President's library, when the door opened, and the old man slowly came down. Putting on his hat, he took the boy's hand without a word, and walked with him, paralyzed by awe, up the road to the town. After the first moments of consternation at this interference in a domestic dispute, the boy reflected that an old gentleman close on eighty would never trouble himself to walk near a mile on a hot summer morning over a shadeless road to take a boy to school, and that it would be strange if a lad imbued with the passion of freedom could not find a corner to dodge around, somewhere before reaching the school door. Then and always, the boy insisted that this reasoning justified his apparent submission; but the old man did not stop, and the boy saw all his strategical points turned, one after another, until he found himself seated inside the school, and obviously the centre of curious if not malevolent criticism. Not till then did the President release his hand and depart.

The point was that this act, contrary to the inalienable rights of boys, and nullifying the social compact, ought to have made him dislike his grandfather for life. He could not recall that it had this effect even for a moment. With a certain maturity of mind, the child must have recognized that the President, though a tool of tyranny, had done his disreputable work with a certain intelligence. He had shown no temper, no irritation, no personal feeling, and had made no display of force. Above all, he had held his tongue. During their long walk he had said nothing; he had uttered no syllable of revolting cant about the duty of obedience and the wickedness of resistance to law; he had shown no concern in the matter; hardly even a consciousness of the boy's existence. Probably his mind at that moment was actually troubling itself little about his grandson's iniquities, and much about the iniquities of President Polk, but the boy could scarcely at that age feel the whole satisfaction of thinking that President Polk was to be the vicarious victim of his own sins, and he gave his grandfather credit for intelligent silence. For this forbearance he felt instinctive respect. He admitted force as a form of right; he admitted even temper, under protest; but the seeds of a moral education would at that moment have fallen on the stoniest soil in Quincy, which is, as every one knows, the stoniest glacial and tidal drift known in any Puritan land.

Neither party to this momentary disagreement can have felt rancor, for during these three or four summers the old President's relations with the boy were friendly and almost intimate. Whether his older brothers and sisters were still more favored he failed to remember, but he was himself admitted to a sort of familiarity which, when in his turn he had reached old age, rather shocked him, for it must have sometimes tried the President's patience. He hung about the library; handled the books; deranged the papers; ransacked the drawers; searched the old purses and pocket-books for foreign coins; drew the sword-cane; snapped the travelling-pistols; upset everything in the corners, and penetrated the President's dressing-closet where a row of tumblers, inverted on the shelf, covered caterpillars which were supposed to become moths or butterflies, but never did. The Madam bore with fortitude the loss of the tumblers which her husband purloined for these hatcheries; but she made protest when he carried off her best cut-glass bowls to plant with acorns or peachstones that he might see the roots grow, but which, she said, he commonly forgot like the caterpillars.

At that time the President rode the hobby of tree-culture, and some fine old trees should still remain to witness it, unless they have been improved off the ground; but his was a restless mind, and although he took his hobbies seriously and would have been annoyed had his grandchild asked whether he was bored like an English duke, he probably cared more for the processes than for the results, so that his grandson was saddened by the sight and smell of peaches and pears, the best of their kind, which he brought up from the garden to rot on his shelves for seed. With the inherited virtues of his Puritan ancestors, the little boy Henry conscientiously brought up to him in his study the finest peaches he found in the garden, and ate only the less perfect. Naturally he ate more by way of compensation, but the act showed that he bore no grudge. As for his grandfather, it is even possible that he may have felt a certain self-reproach for his temporary role of schoolmaster -- seeing that his own career did not offer proof of the worldly advantages of docile obedience -- for there still exists somewhere a little volume of critically edited Nursery Rhymes with the boy's name in full written in the President's trembling hand on the fly-leaf. Of course there was also the Bible, given to each child at birth, with the proper inscription in the President's hand on the fly-leaf; while their grandfather Brooks supplied the silver mugs.

So many Bibles and silver mugs had to be supplied, that a new house, or cottage, was built to hold them. It was "on the hill," five minutes' walk above "the old house," with a far view eastward over Quincy Bay, and northward over Boston. Till his twelfth year, the child passed his summers there, and his pleasures of childhood mostly centred in it. Of education he had as yet little to complain. Country schools were not very serious. Nothing stuck to the mind except home impressions, and the sharpest were those of kindred children; but as influences that warped a mind, none compared with the mere effect of the back of the President's bald head, as he sat in his pew on Sundays, in line with that of President Quincy, who, though some ten years younger, seemed to children about the same age. Before railways entered the New England town, every parish church showed half-a-dozen of these leading citizens, with gray hair, who sat on the main aisle in the best pews, and had sat there, or in some equivalent dignity, since the time of St. Augustine, if not since the glacial epoch. It was unusual for boys to sit behind a President grandfather, and to read over his head the tablet in memory of a President great-grandfather, who had "pledged his life, his fortune, and his sacred honor" to secure the independence of his country and so forth; but boys naturally supposed, without much reasoning, that other boys had the equivalent of President grandfathers, and that churches would always go on, with the bald-headed leading citizens on the main aisle, and Presidents or their equivalents on the walls. The Irish gardener once said to the child: "You'll be thinkin' you'll be President too!" The casuality of the remark made so strong an impression on his mind that he never forgot it. He could not remember ever to have thought on the subject; to him, that there should be a doubt of his being President was a new idea. What had been would continue to be. He doubted neither about Presidents nor about Churches, and no one suggested at that time a doubt whether a system of society which had lasted since Adam would outlast one Adams more.

The Madam was a little more remote than the President, but more decorative. She stayed much in her own room with the Dutch tiles, looking out on her garden with the box walks, and seemed a fragile creature to a boy who sometimes brought her a note or a message, and took distinct pleasure in looking at her delicate face under what seemed to him very becoming caps. He liked her refined figure ; her gentle voice and manner; her vague effect of not belonging there, but to Washington or to Europe, like her furniture, and writing-desk with little glass doors above and little eighteenth-century volumes in old binding, labelled "Peregrine Pickle" or "Tom Jones" or "Hannah More." Try as she might, the Madam could never be Bostonian, and it was her cross in life, but to the boy it was her charm. Even at that age, he felt drawn to it. The Madam's life had been in truth far from Boston. She was born in London in 1775, daughter of Joshua Johnson, an American merchant, brother of Governor Thomas Johnson of Maryland; and Catherine Nuth, of an English family in London. Driven from England by the Revolutionary War, Joshua Johnson took his family to Nantes, where they remained till the peace. The girl Louisa Catherine was nearly ten years old when brought back to London, and her sense of nationality must have been confused; but the influence of the Johnsons and the services of Joshua obtained for him from President Washington the appointment of Consul in London on the organization of the Government in 1790. In 1794 President Washington appointed John Quincy Adams Minister to The Hague. He was twenty-seven years old when he returned to London, and found the Consul's house a very agreeable haunt. Louisa was then twenty.

At that time, and long afterwards, the Consul's house, far more than the Minister's, was the centre of contact for travelling Americans, either official or other. The Legation was a shifting point, between 1785 and 1815; but the Consulate, far down in the City, near the Tower, was convenient and inviting; so inviting that it proved fatal to young Adams. Louisa was charming, like a Romney portrait, but among her many charms that of being a New England woman was not one. The defect was serious. Her future mother-in-law, Abigail, a famous New England woman whose authority over her turbulent husband, the second President, was hardly so great as that which she exercised over her son, the sixth to be, was troubled by the fear that Louisa might not be made of stuff stern enough, or brought up in conditions severe enough, to suit a New England climate, or to make an efficient wife for her paragon son, and Abigail was right on that point, as on most others where sound judgment was involved; but sound judgment is sometimes a source of weakness rather than of force, and John Quincy already had reason to think that his mother held sound judgments on the subject of daughters-in-law which human nature, since the fall of Eve, made Adams helpless to realize. Being three thousand miles away from his mother, and equally far in love, he married Louisa in London, July 26, 1797, and took her to Berlin to be the head of the United States Legation. During three or four exciting years, the young bride lived in Berlin; whether she was happy or not, whether she was content or not, whether she was socially successful or not, her descendants did not surely know; but in any case she could by no chance have become educated there for a life in Quincy or Boston. In 1801 the overthrow of the Federalist Party drove her and her husband to America, and she became at last a member of the Quincy household, but by that time her children needed all her attention, and she remained there with occasional winters in Boston and Washington, till 1809. Her husband was made Senator in 1803, and in 1809 was appointed Minister to Russia. She went with him to St. Petersburg, taking her baby, Charles Francis, born in 1807; but broken-hearted at having to leave her two older boys behind. The life at St. Petersburg was hardly gay for her; they were far too poor to shine in that extravagant society; but she survived it, though her little girl baby did not, and in the winter of 1814-15, alone with the boy of seven years old, crossed Europe from St. Petersburg to Paris, in her travelling-carriage, passing through the armies, and reaching Paris in the Cent Jours after Napoleon's return from Elba. Her husband next went to England as Minister, and she was for two years at the Court of the Regent. In 1817 her husband came home to be Secretary of State, and she lived for eight years in F Street, doing her work of entertainer for President Monroe's administration. Next she lived four miserable years in the White House. When that chapter was closed in 1829, she had earned the right to be tired and delicate, but she still had fifteen years to serve as wife of a Member of the House, after her husband went back to Congress in 1833. Then it was that the little Henry, her grandson, first remembered her, from 1843 to 1848, sitting in her panelled room, at breakfast, with her heavy silver teapot and sugar-bowl and cream-jug, which still exist somewhere as an heirloom of the modern safety-vault. By that time she was seventy years old or more, and thoroughly weary of being beaten about a stormy world. To the boy she seemed singularly peaceful, a vision of silver gray, presiding over her old President and her Queen Anne mahogany; an exotic, like her Sevres china; an object of deference to every one, and of great affection to her son Charles; but hardly more Bostonian than she had been fifty years before, on her wedding-day, in the shadow of the Tower of London.

Such a figure was even less fitted than that of her old husband, the President, to impress on a boy's mind, the standards of the coming century. She was Louis Seize, like the furniture. The boy knew nothing of her interior life, which had been, as the venerable Abigail, long since at peace, foresaw, one of severe stress and little pure satisfaction. He never dreamed that from her might come some of those doubts and self-questionings, those hesitations, those rebellions against law and discipline, which marked more than one of her descendants; but he might even then have felt some vague instinctive suspicion that he was to inherit from her the seeds of the primal sin, the fall from grace, the curse of Abel, that he was not of pure New England stock, but half exotic. As a child of Quincy he was not a true Bostonian, but even as a child of Quincy he inherited a quarter taint of Maryland blood. Charles Francis, half Marylander by birth, had hardly seen Boston till he was ten years old, when his parents left him there at school in 1817, and he never forgot the experience. He was to be nearly as old as his mother had been in 1845, before he quite accepted Boston, or Boston quite accepted him.

A boy who began his education in these surroundings, with physical strength inferior to that of his brothers, and with a certain delicacy of mind and bone, ought rightly to have felt at home in the eighteenth century and should, in proper self-respect, have rebelled against the standards of the nineteenth. The atmosphere of his first ten years must have been very like that of his grandfather at the same age, from 1767 till 1776, barring the battle of Bunker Hill, and even as late as 1846, the battle of Bunker Hill remained actual. The tone of Boston society was colonial. The true Bostonian always knelt in self-abasement before the majesty of English standards; far from concealing it as a weakness, he was proud of it as his strength. The eighteenth century ruled society long after 1850. Perhaps the boy began to shake it off rather earlier than most of his mates.

Indeed this prehistoric stage of education ended rather abruptly with his tenth year. One winter morning he was conscious of a certain confusion in the house in Mount Vernon Street, and gathered, from such words as he could catch, that the President, who happened to be then staying there, on his way to Washington, had fallen and hurt himself. Then he heard the word paralysis. After that day he came to associate the word with the figure of his grandfather, in a tall-backed, invalid armchair, on one side of the spare bedroom fireplace, and one of his old friends, Dr.

Parkman or P. P. F. Degrand, on the other side, both dozing.

The end of this first, or ancestral and Revolutionary, chapter came on February 21, 1848 -- and the month of February brought life and death as a family habit -- when the eighteenth century, as an actual and living companion, vanished. If the scene on the floor of the House, when the old President fell, struck the still simple-minded American public with a sensation unusually dramatic, its effect on a ten-year-old boy, whose boy-life was fading away with the life of his grandfather, could not be slight. One had to pay for Revolutionary patriots; grandfathers and grandmothers; Presidents; diplomats; Queen Anne mahogany and Louis Seize chairs, as well as for Stuart portraits. Such things warp young life. Americans commonly believed that they ruined it, and perhaps the practical common-sense of the American mind judged right. Many a boy might be ruined by much less than the emotions of the funeral service in the Quincy church, with its surroundings of national respect and family pride. By another dramatic chance it happened that the clergyman of the parish, Dr. Lunt, was an unusual pulpit orator, the ideal of a somewhat austere intellectual type, such as the school of Buckminster and Channing inherited from the old Congregational clergy. His extraordinarily refined appearance, his dignity of manner, his deeply cadenced voice, his remarkable English and his fine appreciation, gave to the funeral service a character that left an overwhelming impression on the boy's mind. He was to see many great functions -- funerals and festival -- in after-life, till his only thought was to see no more, but he never again witnessed anything nearly so impressive to him as the last services at Quincy over the body of one President and the ashes of another.

The effect of the Quincy service was deepened by the official ceremony which afterwards took place in Faneuil Hall, when the boy was taken to hear his uncle, Edward Everett, deliver a Eulogy. Like all Mr. Everett's orations, it was an admirable piece of oratory, such as only an admirable orator and scholar could create; too good for a ten-year-old boy to appreciate at its value; but already the boy knew that the dead President could not be in it, and had even learned why he would have been out of place there; for knowledge was beginning to come fast. The shadow of the War of 1812 still hung over State Street; the shadow of the Civil War to come had already begun to darken Faneuil Hall. No rhetoric could have reconciled Mr. Everett's audience to his subject. How could he say there, to an assemblage of Bostonians in the heart of mercantile Boston, that the only distinctive mark of all the Adamses, since old Sam Adams's father a hundred and fifty years before, had been their inherited quarrel with State Street, which had again and again broken out into riot, bloodshed, personal feuds, foreign and civil war, wholesale banishments and confiscations, until the history of Florence was hardly more turbulent than that of Boston? How could he whisper the word Hartford Convention before the men who had made it? What would have been said had he suggested the chance of Secession and Civil War?

Thus already, at ten years old, the boy found himself standing face to face with a dilemma that might have puzzled an early Christian. What was he? -- where was he going? Even then he felt that something was wrong, but he concluded that it must be Boston. Quincy had always been right, for Quincy represented a moral principle -- the principle of resistance to Boston. His Adams ancestors must have been right, since they were always hostile to State Street. If State Street was wrong, Quincy must be right! Turn the dilemma as he pleased, he still came back on the eighteenth century and the law of Resistance; of Truth; of Duty, and of Freedom. He was a ten-year-old priest and politician. He could under no circumstances have guessed what the next fifty years had in store, and no one could teach him; but sometimes, in his old age, he wondered -

- and could never decide -- whether the most clear and certain knowledge would have helped him. Supposing he had seen a New York stock-list of 1900, and had studied the statistics of railways, telegraphs, coal, and steel -- would he have quitted his eighteenth-century, his ancestral prejudices, his abstract ideals, his semi-clerical training, and the rest, in order to perform an expiatory pilgrimage to State Street, and ask for the fatted calf of his grandfather Brooks and a clerkship in the Suffolk Bank?

Sixty years afterwards he was still unable to make up his mind. Each course had its advantages, but the material advantages, looking back, seemed to lie wholly in State Street.

Chapter II. Boston (1848-1854)

PETER CHARDON BROOKS, the other grandfather, died January 1, 1849, bequeathing what was supposed to be the largest estate in Boston, about two million dollars, to his seven surviving children: four sons -- Edward, Peter Chardon, Gorham, and Sydney; three daughters -- Charlotte, married to Edward Everett; Ann, married to Nathaniel Frothingham, minister of the First Church; and Abigail Brown, born April 25, 1808, married September 3, 1829, to Charles Francis Adams, hardly a year older than herself. Their first child, born in 1830, was a daughter, named Louisa Catherine, after her Johnson grandmother; the second was a son, named John Quincy, after his President grandfather; the third took his father's name, Charles Francis; while the fourth, being of less account, was in a way given to his mother, who named him Henry Brooks, after a favorite brother just lost. More followed, but these, being younger, had nothing to do with the arduous process of educating.

The Adams connection was singularly small in Boston, but the family of Brooks was singularly large and even brilliant, and almost wholly of clerical New England stock. One might have sought long in much larger and older societies for three brothers-in-law more distinguished or more scholarly than Edward Everett, Dr. Frothingham, and Mr. Adams. One might have sought equally long for seven brothers-in-law more unlike. No doubt they all bore more or less the stamp of Boston, or at least of Massachusetts Bay, but the shades of difference amounted to contrasts. Mr. Everett belonged to Boston hardly more than Mr. Adams. One of the most ambitious of Bostonians, he had broken bounds early in life by leaving the Unitarian pulpit to take a seat in Congress where he had given valuable support to J. Q. Adams's administration; support which, as a social consequence, led to the marriage of the President's son, Charles Francis, with Mr. Everett's youngest sister-in-law, Abigail Brooks. The wreck of parties which marked the reign of Andrew Jackson had interfered with many promising careers, that of Edward Everett among the rest, but he had risen with the Whig Party to power, had gone as Minister to England, and had returned to America with the halo of a European reputation, and undisputed rank second only to Daniel Webster as the orator and representative figure of Boston. The other brother-in-law, Dr. Frothingham, belonged to the same clerical school, though in manner rather the less clerical of the two. Neither of them had much in common with Mr. Adams, who was a younger man, greatly biassed by his father, and by the inherited feud between Quincy and State Street; but personal relations were friendly as far as a boy could see, and the innumerable cousins went regularly to the First Church every Sunday in winter, and slept through their uncle's sermons, without once thinking to ask what the sermons were supposed to mean for them. For two hundred years the First Church had seen the same little boys, sleeping more or less soundly under the same or similar conditions, and dimly conscious of the same feuds; but the feuds had never ceased, and the boys had always grown up to inherit them. Those of the generation of 1812 had mostly disappeared in 1850; death had cleared that score; the quarrels of John Adams, and those of John Quincy Adams were no longer acutely personal; the game was considered as drawn; and Charles Francis Adams might then have taken his inherited rights of political leadership in succession to Mr. Webster and Mr. Everett, his seniors. Between him and State Street the relation was more natural than between Edward Everett and State Street; but instead of doing so, Charles Francis Adams drew himself aloof and renewed the old war which had already lasted since 1700. He could not help it. With the record of J. Q. Adams fresh in the popular memory, his son and his only representative could not make terms with the slave-power, and the slave-power overshadowed all the great Boston interests. No doubt Mr. Adams had principles of his own, as well as inherited, but even his children, who as yet had no principles, could equally little follow the lead of Mr. Webster or even of Mr. Seward. They would have lost in consideration more than they would have gained in patronage. They were anti-slavery by birth, as their name was Adams and their home was Quincy. No matter how much they had wished to enter State Street, they felt that State Street never would trust them, or they it. Had State Street been Paradise, they must hunger for it in vain, and it hardly needed Daniel Webster to act as archangel with the flaming sword, to order them away from the door.

Time and experience, which alter all perspectives, altered this among the rest, and taught the boy gentler judgment, but even when only ten years old, his face was already fixed, and his heart was stone, against State Street; his education was warped beyond recovery in the direction of Puritan politics. Between him and his patriot grandfather at the same age, the conditions had changed little. The year 1848 was like enough to the year 1776 to make a fair parallel. The parallel, as concerned bias of education, was complete when, a few months after the death of John Quincy Adams, a convention of anti-slavery delegates met at Buffalo to organize a new party and named candidates for the general election in November: for President, Martin Van Buren; for Vice-President, Charles Francis Adams.

For any American boy the fact that his father was running for office would have dwarfed for the time every other excitement, but even apart from personal bias, the year 1848, for a boy's road through life, was decisive for twenty years to come. There was never a side-path of escape. The stamp of 1848 was almost as indelible as the stamp of 1776, but in the eighteenth or any earlier century, the stamp mattered less because it was standard, and every one bore it; while men whose lives were to fall in the generation between 1865 and 1900 had, first of all, to get rid of it, and take the stamp that belonged to their time. This was their education. To outsiders, immigrants, adventurers, it was easy, but the old Puritan nature rebelled against change. The reason it gave was forcible. The Puritan thought his thought higher and his moral standards better than those of his successors. So they were. He could not be convinced that moral standards had nothing to do with it, and that utilitarian morality was good enough for him, as it was for the graceless. Nature had given to the boy Henry a character that, in any previous century, would have led him into the Church; he inherited dogma and a priori thought from the beginning of time; and he scarcely needed a violent reaction like anti-slavery politics to sweep him back into Puritanism with a violence as great as that of a religious war.

Thus far he had nothing to do with it; his education was chiefly inheritance, and during the next five or six years, his father alone counted for much. If he were to worry successfully through life's quicksands, he must depend chiefly on his father's pilotage; but, for his father, the channel lay clear, while for himself an unknown ocean lay beyond. His father's business in life was to get past the dangers of the slave-power, or to fix its bounds at least. The task done, he might be content to let his sons pay for the pilotage; and it mattered little to his success whether they paid it with their lives wasted on battle-fields or in misdirected energies and lost opportunity. The generation that lived from 1840 to 1870 could do very well with the old forms of education; that which had its work to do between 1870 and 1900 needed something quite new.

His father's character was therefore the larger part of his education, as far as any single person affected it, and for that reason, if for no other, the son was always a much interested critic of his father's mind and temper. Long after his death as an old man of eighty, his sons continued to discuss this subject with a good deal of difference in their points of view. To his son Henry, the quality that distinguished his father from all the other figures in the family group, was that, in his opinion, Charles Francis Adams possessed the only perfectly balanced mind that ever existed in the name. For a hundred years, every newspaper scribbler had, with more or less obvious excuse, derided or abused the older Adamses for want of judgment. They abused Charles Francis for his judgment. Naturally they never attempted to assign values to either; that was the children's affair; but the traits were real. Charles Francis Adams was singular for mental poise -- absence of self-assertion or self-consciousness -- the faculty of standing apart without seeming aware that he was alone -- a balance of mind and temper that neither challenged nor avoided notice, nor admitted question of superiority or inferiority, of jealousy, of personal motives, from any source, even under great pressure. This unusual poise of judgment and temper, ripened by age, became the more striking to his son Henry as he learned to measure the mental faculties themselves, which were in no way exceptional either for depth or range. Charles Francis Adams's memory was hardly above the average; his mind was not bold like his grandfather's or restless like his father's, or imaginative or oratorical -- still less mathematical; but it worked with singular perfection, admirable self-restraint, and instinctive mastery of form. Within its range it was a model.

The standards of Boston were high, much affected by the old clerical self-respect which gave the Unitarian clergy unusual social charm. Dr. Channing, Mr. Everett, Dr. Frothingham. Dr. Palfrey, President Walker, R. W. Emerson, and other Boston ministers of the same school, would have commanded distinction in any society; but the Adamses had little or no affinity with the pulpit, and still less with its eccentric offshoots, like Theodore Parker, or Brook Farm, or the philosophy of Concord. Besides its clergy, Boston showed a literary group, led by Ticknor, Prescott, Longfellow, Motley, O. W. Holmes; but Mr. Adams was not one of them; as a rule they were much too Websterian. Even in science Boston could claim a certain eminence, especially in medicine, but Mr. Adams cared very little for science. He stood alone. He had no master -- hardly even his father. He had no scholars -- hardly even his sons.

Almost alone among his Boston contemporaries, he was not English in feeling or in sympathies. Perhaps a hundred years of acute hostility to England had something to do with this family trait; but in his case it went further and became indifference to social distinction. Never once in forty years of intimacy did his son notice in him a trace of snobbishness. He was one of the exceedingly small number of Americans to whom an English duke or duchess seemed to be indifferent, and royalty itself nothing more than a slightly inconvenient presence. This was, it is true, rather the tone of English society in his time, but Americans were largely responsible for changing it, and Mr. Adams had every possible reason for affecting the manner of a courtier even if he did not feel the sentiment. Never did his son see him flatter or vilify, or show a sign of envy or jealousy; never a shade of vanity or self-conceit. Never a tone of arrogance! Never a gesture of pride!

The same thing might perhaps have been said of John Quincy Adams, but in him his associates averred that it was accompanied by mental restlessness and often by lamentable want of judgment. No one ever charged Charles Francis Adams with this fault. The critics charged him with just the opposite defect. They called him cold. No doubt, such perfect poise -- such intuitive self-adjustment -- was not maintained by nature without a sacrifice of the qualities which would have upset it. No doubt, too, that even his restless-minded, introspective, self-conscious children who knew him best were much too ignorant of the world and of human nature to suspect how rare and complete was the model before their eyes. A coarser instrument would have impressed them more. Average human nature is very coarse, and its ideals must necessarily be average. The world never loved perfect poise. What the world does love is commonly absence of poise, for it has to be amused. Napoleons and Andrew Jacksons amuse it, but it is not amused by perfect balance. Had Mr. Adams's nature been cold, he would have followed Mr. Webster, Mr. Everett, Mr. Seward, and Mr. Winthrop in the lines of party discipline and self-interest. Had it been less balanced than it was, he would have gone with Mr. Garrison, Mr. Wendell Phillips, Mr. Edmund Quincy, and Theodore Parker, into secession. Between the two paths he found an intermediate one, distinctive and characteristic -- he set up a party of his own.

This political party became a chief influence in the education of the boy Henry in the six years 1848 to 1854, and violently affected his character at the moment when character is plastic. The group of men with whom Mr. Adams associated himself, and whose social centre was the house in Mount Vernon Street, numbered only three: Dr. John G. Palfrey, Richard H. Dana, and Charles Sumner. Dr. Palfrey was the oldest, and in spite of his clerical education, was to a boy often the most agreeable, for his talk was lighter and his range wider than that of the others; he had wit, or humor, and the give-and-take of dinner-table exchange. Born to be a man of the world, he forced himself to be clergyman, professor, or statesman, while, like every other true Bostonian, he yearned for the ease of the Athenaeum Club in Pall Mall or the Combination Room at Trinity. Dana at first suggested the opposite; he affected to be still before the mast, a direct, rather bluff, vigorous seaman, and only as one got to know him better one found the man of rather excessive refinement trying with success to work like a day-laborer, deliberately hardening his skin to the burden, as though he were still carrying hides at Monterey. Undoubtedly he succeeded, for his mind and will were robust, but he might have said what his lifelong friend William M. Evarts used to say: "I pride myself on my success in doing not the things I like to do, but the things I don't like to do." Dana's ideal of life was to be a great Englishman, with a seat on the front benches of the House of Commons until he should be promoted to the woolsack; beyond all, with a social status that should place him above the scuffle of provincial and unprofessional annoyances; but he forced himself to take life as it came, and he suffocated his longings with grim self-discipline, by mere force of will. Of the four men, Dana was the most marked. Without dogmatism or self-assertion, he seemed always to be fully in sight, a figure that completely filled a well-defined space. He, too, talked well, and his mind worked close to its subject, as a lawyer's should; but disguise and silence it as he liked, it was aristocratic to the tenth generation.

In that respect, and in that only, Charles Sumner was like him, but Sumner, in almost every other quality, was quite different from his three associates -- altogether out of line. He, too, adored

English standards, but his ambition led him to rival the career of Edmund Burke. No young Bostonian of his time had made so brilliant a start, but rather in the steps of Edward Everett than of Daniel Webster. As an orator he had achieved a triumph by his oration against war; but Boston admired him chiefly for his social success in England and on the Continent; success that gave to every Bostonian who enjoyed it a halo never acquired by domestic sanctity. Mr. Sumner, both by interest and instinct, felt the value of his English connection, and cultivated it the more as he became socially an outcast from Boston society by the passions of politics. He was rarely without a pocket-full of letters from duchesses or noblemen in England. Having sacrificed to principle his social position in America, he clung the more closely to his foreign attachments. The Free Soil Party fared ill in Beacon Street. The social arbiters of Boston -- George Ticknor and the rest -- had to admit, however unwillingly, that the Free Soil leaders could not mingle with the friends and followers of Mr. Webster. Sumner was socially ostracized, and so, for that matter, were Palfrey, Dana, Russell, Adams, and all the other avowed anti-slavery leaders, but for them it mattered less, because they had houses and families of their own; while Sumner had neither wife nor household, and, though the most socially ambitious of all, and the most hungry for what used to be called polite society, he could enter hardly half-a-dozen houses in Boston. Longfellow stood by him in Cambridge, and even in Beacon Street he could always take refuge in the house of Mr. Lodge, but few days passed when he did not pass some time in Mount Vernon Street. Even with that, his solitude was glacial, and reacted on his character. He had nothing but himself to think about. His superiority was, indeed, real and incontestable; he was the classical ornament of the anti-slavery party; their pride in him was unbounded, and their admiration outspoken.

The boy Henry worshipped him, and if he ever regarded any older man as a personal friend, it was Mr. Sumner. The relation of Mr. Sumner in the household was far closer than any relation of blood. None of the uncles approached such intimacy. Sumner was the boy's ideal of greatness; the highest product of nature and art. The only fault of such a model was its superiority which defied imitation. To the twelve-year-old boy, his father, Dr. Palfrey, Mr. Dana, were men, more or less like what he himself might become; but Mr. Sumner was a different order -- heroic.

As the boy grew up to be ten or twelve years old, his father gave him a writing-table in one of the alcoves of his Boston library, and there, winter after winter, Henry worked over his Latin Grammar and listened to these four gentlemen discussing the course of anti-slavery politics. The discussions were always serious; the Free Soil Party took itself quite seriously; and they were habitual because Mr. Adams had undertaken to edit a newspaper as the organ of these gentlemen, who came to discuss its policy and expression. At the same time Mr. Adams was editing the "Works" of his grandfather John Adams, and made the boy read texts for proof-correction. In after years his father sometimes complained that, as a reader of Novanglus and Massachusettensis, Henry had shown very little consciousness of punctuation; but the boy regarded this part of school life only as a warning, if he ever grew up to write dull discussions in the newspapers, to try to be dull in some different way from that of his great-grandfather. Yet the discussions in the Boston Whig were carried on in much the same style as those of John Adams and his opponent, and appealed to much the same society and the same habit of mind. The boy got as little education, fitting him for his own time, from the one as from the other, and he got no more from his contact with the gentlemen themselves who were all types of the past.

Down to 1850, and even later, New England society was still directed by the professions.

Lawyers, physicians, professors, merchants were classes, and acted not as individuals, but as though they were clergymen and each profession were a church. In politics the system required competent expression; it was the old Ciceronian idea of government by the best that produced the long line of New England statesmen. They chose men to represent them because they wanted to be well represented, and they chose the best they had. Thus Boston chose Daniel Webster, and Webster took, not as pay, but as honorarium, the cheques raised for him by Peter Harvey from the Appletons, Perkinses, Amorys, Searses, Brookses, Lawrences, and so on, who begged him to represent them. Edward Everett held the rank in regular succession to Webster. Robert C. Winthrop claimed succession to Everett. Charles Sumner aspired to break the succession, but not the system. The Adamses had never been, for any length of time, a part of this State succession; they had preferred the national service, and had won all their distinction outside the State, but they too had required State support and had commonly received it. The little group of men in Mount Vernon Street were an offshoot of this system; they were statesmen, not politicians; they guided public opinion, but were little guided by it.

The boy naturally learned only one lesson from his saturation in such air. He took for granted that this sort of world, more or less the same that had always existed in Boston and Massachusetts Bay, was the world which he was to fit. Had he known Europe he would have learned no better. The Paris of Louis Philippe, Guizot, and de Tocqueville, as well as the London of Robert Peel, Macaulay, and John Stuart Mill, were but varieties of the same upper-class bourgeoisie that felt instinctive cousinship with the Boston of Ticknor, Prescott, and Motley. Even the typical grumbler Carlyle, who cast doubts on the real capacity of the middle class, and who at times thought himself eccentric, found friendship and alliances in Boston -- still more in Concord. The system had proved so successful that even Germany wanted to try it, and Italy yearned for it. England's middle-class government was the ideal of human progress.

Even the violent reaction after 1848, and the return of all Europe to military practices, never for a moment shook the true faith. No one, except Karl Marx, foresaw radical change. What announced it? The world was producing sixty or seventy million tons of coal, and might be using nearly a million steam-horsepower, just beginning to make itself felt. All experience since the creation of man, all divine revelation or human science, conspired to deceive and betray a twelve-year-old boy who took for granted that his ideas, which were alone respectable, would be alone respected.

Viewed from Mount Vernon Street, the problem of life was as simple as it was classic. Politics offered no difficulties, for there the moral law was a sure guide. Social perfection was also sure, because human nature worked for Good, and three instruments were all she asked -- Suffrage, Common Schools, and Press. On these points doubt was forbidden. Education was divine, and man needed only a correct knowledge of facts to reach perfection:

"Were half the power that fills the world with terror,

  Were half the wealth bestowed on camps and courts,

Given to redeem the human mind from error,

  There were no need of arsenals nor forts."

Nothing quieted doubt so completely as the mental calm of the Unitarian clergy. In uniform excellence of life and character, moral and intellectual, the score of Unitarian clergymen about Boston, who controlled society and Harvard College, were never excelled. They proclaimed as their merit that they insisted on no doctrine, but taught, or tried to teach, the means of leading a virtuous, useful, unselfish life, which they held to be sufficient for salvation. For them, difficulties might be ignored; doubts were waste of thought; nothing exacted solution. Boston had solved the universe; or had offered and realized the best solution yet tried. The problem was worked out.

Of all the conditions of his youth which afterwards puzzled the grown-up man, this disappearance of religion puzzled him most. The boy went to church twice every Sunday; he was taught to read his Bible, and he learned religious poetry by heart; he believed in a mild deism; he prayed; he went through all the forms; but neither to him nor to his brothers or sisters was religion real. Even the mild discipline of the Unitarian Church was so irksome that they all threw it off at the first possible moment, and never afterwards entered a church. The religious instinct had vanished, and could not be revived, although one made in later life many efforts to recover it. That the most powerful emotion of man, next to the sexual, should disappear, might be a personal defect of his own; but that the most intelligent society, led by the most intelligent clergy, in the most moral conditions he ever knew, should have solved all the problems of the universe so thoroughly as to have quite ceased making itself anxious about past or future, and should have persuaded itself that all the problems which had convulsed human thought from earliest recorded time, were not worth discussing, seemed to him the most curious social phenomenon he had to account for in a long life. The faculty of turning away one's eyes as one approaches a chasm is not unusual, and Boston showed, under the lead of Mr. Webster, how successfully it could be done in politics; but in politics a certain number of men did at least protest. In religion and philosophy no one protested. Such protest as was made took forms more simple than the silence, like the deism of Theodore Parker, and of the boy's own cousin Octavius Frothingham, who distressed his father and scandalized Beacon Street by avowing scepticism that seemed to solve no old problems, and to raise many new ones. The less aggressive protest of Ralph Waldo Emerson, was, from an old-world point of view, less serious. It was naif.

The children reached manhood without knowing religion, and with the certainty that dogma, metaphysics, and abstract philosophy were not worth knowing. So one-sided an education could have been possible in no other country or time, but it became, almost of necessity, the more literary and political. As the children grew up, they exaggerated the literary and the political interests. They joined in the dinner-table discussions and from childhood the boys were accustomed to hear, almost every day, table-talk as good as they were ever likely to hear again. The eldest child, Louisa, was one of the most sparkling creatures her brother met in a long and varied experience of bright women. The oldest son, John, was afterwards regarded as one of the best talkers in Boston society, and perhaps the most popular man in the State, though apt to be on the unpopular side. Palfrey and Dana could be entertaining when they pleased, and though Charles Sumner could hardly be called light in hand, he was willing to be amused, and smiled grandly from time to time; while Mr. Adams, who talked relatively little, was always a good listener, and laughed over a witticism till he choked.

By way of educating and amusing the children, Mr. Adams read much aloud, and was sure to read political literature, especially when it was satirical, like the speeches of Horace Mann and the "Epistles" of "Hosea Biglow," with great delight to the youth. So he read Longfellow and Tennyson as their poems appeared, but the children took possession of Dickens and Thackeray for themselves. Both were too modern for tastes founded on Pope and Dr. Johnson. The boy Henry soon became a desultory reader of every book he found readable, but these were commonly eighteenth-century historians because his father's library was full of them. In the want of positive instincts, he drifted into the mental indolence of history. So too, he read shelves of eighteenth-century poetry, but when his father offered his own set of Wordsworth as a gift on condition of reading it through, he declined. Pope and Gray called for no mental effort; they were easy reading; but the boy was thirty years old before his education reached Wordsworth.

This is the story of an education, and the person or persons who figure in it are supposed to have values only as educators or educated. The surroundings concern it only so far as they affect education. Sumner, Dana, Palfrey, had values of their own, like Hume, Pope, and Wordsworth, which any one may study in their works; here all appear only as influences on the mind of a boy very nearly the average of most boys in physical and mental stature. The influence was wholly political and literary. His father made no effort to force his mind, but left him free play, and this was perhaps best. Only in one way his father rendered him a great service by trying to teach him French and giving him some idea of a French accent. Otherwise the family was rather an atmosphere than an influence. The boy had a large and overpowering set of brothers and sisters, who were modes or replicas of the same type, getting the same education, struggling with the same problems, and solving the question, or leaving it unsolved much in the same way. They knew no more than he what they wanted or what to do for it, but all were conscious that they would like to control power in some form; and the same thing could be said of an ant or an elephant. Their form was tied to politics or literature. They amounted to one individual with half-a-dozen sides or facets; their temperaments reacted on each other and made each child more like the other. This was also education, but in the type, and the Boston or New England type was well enough known. What no one knew was whether the individual who thought himself a representative of this type, was fit to deal with life.

As far as outward bearing went, such a family of turbulent children, given free rein by their parents, or indifferent to check, should have come to more or less grief. Certainly no one was strong enough to control them, least of all their mother, the queen-bee of the hive, on whom nine-tenths of the burden fell, on whose strength they all depended, but whose children were much too self-willed and self-confident to take guidance from her, or from any one else, unless in the direction they fancied. Father and mother were about equally helpless. Almost every large family in those days produced at least one black sheep, and if this generation of Adamses escaped, it was as much a matter of surprise to them as to their neighbors. By some happy chance they grew up to be decent citizens, but Henry Adams, as a brand escaped from the burning, always looked back with astonishment at their luck. The fact seemed to prove that they were born, like birds, with a certain innate balance. Home influences alone never saved the New England boy from ruin, though sometimes they may have helped to ruin him; and the influences outside of home were negative. If school helped, it was only by reaction. The dislike of school was so strong as to be a positive gain. The passionate hatred of school methods was almost a method in itself. Yet the day-school of that time was respectable, and the boy had nothing to complain of. In fact, he never complained. He hated it because he was here with a crowd of other boys and compelled to learn by memory a quantity of things that did not amuse him. His memory was slow, and the effort painful. For him to conceive that his memory could compete for school prizes with machines of two or three times its power, was to prove himself wanting not only in memory, but flagrantly in mind. He thought his mind a good enough machine, if it were given time to act, but it acted wrong if hurried. Schoolmasters never gave time.

In any and all its forms, the boy detested school, and the prejudice became deeper with years. He always reckoned his school-days, from ten to sixteen years old, as time thrown away. Perhaps his needs turned out to be exceptional, but his existence was exceptional. Between 1850 and 1900 nearly every one's existence was exceptional. For success in the life imposed on him he needed, as afterwards appeared, the facile use of only four tools: Mathematics, French, German, and Spanish. With these, he could master in very short time any special branch of inquiry, and feel at home in any society. Latin and Greek, he could, with the help of the modern languages, learn more completely by the intelligent work of six weeks than in the six years he spent on them at school. These four tools were necessary to his success in life, but he never controlled any one of them.

Thus, at the outset, he was condemned to failure more or less complete in the life awaiting him, but not more so than his companions. Indeed, had his father kept the boy at home, and given him half an hour's direction every day, he would have done more for him than school ever could do for them. Of course, school-taught men and boys looked down on home-bred boys, and rather prided themselves on their own ignorance, but the man of sixty can generally see what he needed in life, and in Henry Adams's opinion it was not school.

Most school experience was bad. Boy associations at fifteen were worse than none. Boston at that time offered few healthy resources for boys or men. The bar-room and billiard-room were more familiar than parents knew. As a rule boys could skate and swim and were sent to dancing-school; they played a rudimentary game of baseball, football, and hockey; a few could sail a boat; still fewer had been out with a gun to shoot yellow-legs or a stray wild duck; one or two may have learned something of natural history if they came from the neighborhood of Concord; none could ride across country, or knew what shooting with dogs meant. Sport as a pursuit was unknown. Boat-racing came after 1850. For horse-racing, only the trotting-course existed. Of all pleasures, winter sleighing was still the gayest and most popular. From none of these amusements could the boy learn anything likely to be of use to him in the world. Books remained as in the eighteenth century, the source of life, and as they came out -- Thackeray, Dickens, Bulwer, Tennyson, Macaulay, Carlyle, and the rest -- they were devoured; but as far as happiness went, the happiest hours of the boy's education were passed in summer lying on a musty heap of Congressional Documents in the old farmhouse at Quincy, reading "Quentin Durward," "Ivanhoe," and " The Talisman," and raiding the garden at intervals for peaches and pears. On the whole he learned most then.

Chapter III. Washington (1850-1854)

EXCEPT for politics, Mount Vernon Street had the merit of leaving the boy-mind supple, free to turn with the world, and if one learned next to nothing, the little one did learn needed not to be unlearned. The surface was ready to take any form that education should cut into it, though Boston, with singular foresight, rejected the old designs. What sort of education was stamped elsewhere, a Bostonian had no idea, but he escaped the evils of other standards by having no standard at all; and what was true of school was true of society. Boston offered none that could help outside. Every one now smiles at the bad taste of Queen Victoria and Louis Philippe -- the society of the forties -- but the taste was only a reflection of the social slack-water between a tide passed, and a tide to come. Boston belonged to neither, and hardly even to America. Neither aristocratic nor industrial nor social, Boston girls and boys were not nearly as unformed as English boys and girls, but had less means of acquiring form as they grew older. Women counted for little as models. Every boy, from the age of seven, fell in love at frequent intervals with some girl -- always more or less the same little girl -- who had nothing to teach him, or he to teach her, except rather familiar and provincial manners, until they married and bore children to repeat the habit. The idea of attaching one's self to a married woman, or of polishing one's manners to suit the standards of women of thirty, could hardly have entered the mind of a young Bostonian, and would have scandalized his parents. From women the boy got the domestic virtues and nothing else. He might not even catch the idea that women had more to give. The garden of Eden was hardly more primitive.

To balance this virtue, the Puritan city had always hidden a darker side. Blackguard Boston was only too educational, and to most boys much the more interesting. A successful blackguard must enjoy great physical advantages besides a true vocation, and Henry Adams had neither; but no boy escaped some contact with vice of a very low form. Blackguardism came constantly under boys' eyes, and had the charm of force and freedom and superiority to culture or decency. One might fear it, but no one honestly despised it. Now and then it asserted itself as education more roughly than school ever did. One of the commonest boy-games of winter, inherited directly from the eighteenth-century, was a game of war on Boston Common. In old days the two hostile forces were called North-Enders and South-Enders. In 1850 the North-Enders still survived as a legend, but in practice it was a battle of the Latin School against all comers, and the Latin School, for snowball, included all the boys of the West End. Whenever, on a half-holiday, the weather was soft enough to soften the snow, the Common was apt to be the scene of a fight, which began in daylight with the Latin School in force, rushing their opponents down to Tremont Street, and which generally ended at dark by the Latin School dwindling in numbers and disappearing. As the Latin School grew weak, the roughs and young blackguards grew strong. As long as snowballs were the only weapon, no one was much hurt, but a stone may be put in a snowball, and in the dark a stick or a slungshot in the hands of a boy is as effective as a knife. One afternoon the fight had been long and exhausting. The boy Henry, following, as his habit was, his bigger brother Charles, had taken part in the battle, and had felt his courage much depressed by seeing one of his trustiest leaders, Henry Higginson -- "Bully Hig," his school name -- struck by a stone over the eye, and led off the field bleeding in rather a ghastly manner. As night came on, the Latin School was steadily forced back to the Beacon Street Mall where they could retreat no further without disbanding, and by that time only a small band was left, headed by two heroes, Savage and Marvin. A dark mass of figures could be seen below, making ready for the last rush, and rumor said that a swarm of blackguards from the slums, led by a grisly terror called Conky Daniels, with a club and a hideous reputation, was going to put an end to the Beacon Street cowards forever. Henry wanted to run away with the others, but his brother was too big to run away, so they stood still and waited immolation. The dark mass set up a shout, and rushed forward. The Beacon Street boys turned and fled up the steps, except Savage and Marvin and the few champions who would not run. The terrible Conky Daniels swaggered up, stopped a moment with his body-guard to swear a few oaths at Marvin, and then swept on and chased the flyers, leaving the few boys untouched who stood their ground. The obvious moral taught that blackguards were not so black as they were painted; but the boy Henry had passed through as much terror as though he were Turenne or Henri IV, and ten or twelve years afterwards when these same boys were fighting and falling on all the battle-fields of Virginia and Maryland, he wondered whether their education on Boston Common had taught Savage and Marvin how to die.

If violence were a part of complete education, Boston was not incomplete. The idea of violence was familiar to the anti-slavery leaders as well as to their followers. Most of them suffered from it. Mobs were always possible. Henry never happened to be actually concerned in a mob, but he, like every other boy, was sure to be on hand wherever a mob was expected, and whenever he heard Garrison or Wendell Phillips speak, he looked for trouble. Wendell Phillips on a platform was a model dangerous for youth. Theodore Parker in his pulpit was not much safer. Worst of all, the execution of the Fugitive Slave Law in Boston -- the sight of Court Square packed with bayonets, and his own friends obliged to line the streets under arms as State militia, in order to return a negro to slavery -- wrought frenzy in the brain of a fifteen-year-old, eighteenth-century boy from Quincy, who wanted to miss no reasonable chance of mischief.

One lived in the atmosphere of the Stamp Act, the Tea Tax, and the Boston Massacre. Within Boston, a boy was first an eighteenth-century politician, and afterwards only a possibility; beyond Boston the first step led only further into politics. After February, 1848, but one slight tie remained of all those that, since 1776, had connected Quincy with the outer world. The Madam stayed in Washington, after her husband's death, and in her turn was struck by paralysis and bedridden. From time to time her son Charles, whose affection and sympathy for his mother in her many tribulations were always pronounced, went on to see her, and in May, 1850, he took with him his twelve-year-old son. The journey was meant as education, and as education it served the purpose of fixing in memory the stage of a boy's thought in 1850. He could not remember taking special interest in the railroad journey or in New York; with railways and cities he was familiar enough. His first impression was the novelty of crossing New York Bay and finding an English railway carriage on the Camden and Amboy Railroad. This was a new world; a suggestion of corruption in the simple habits of American life; a step to exclusiveness never approached in Boston; but it was amusing. The boy rather liked it. At Trenton the train set him on board a steamer which took him to Philadelphia where he smelt other varieties of town life; then again by boat to Chester, and by train to Havre de Grace; by boat to Baltimore and thence by rail to Washington. This was the journey he remembered. The actual journey may have been quite different, but the actual journey has no interest for education. The memory was all that mattered; and what struck him most, to remain fresh in his mind all his lifetime, was the sudden change that came over the world on entering a slave State. He took education politically. The mere raggedness of outline could not have seemed wholly new, for even Boston had its ragged edges, and the town of Quincy was far from being a vision of neatness or good-repair; in truth, he had never seen a finished landscape; but Maryland was raggedness of a new kind. The railway, about the size and character of a modern tram, rambled through unfenced fields and woods, or through village streets, among a haphazard variety of pigs, cows, and negro babies, who might all have used the cabins for pens and styes, had the Southern pig required styes, but who never showed a sign of care. This was the boy's impression of what slavery caused, and, for him, was all it taught. Coming down in the early morning from his bedroom in his grandmother's house -- still called the Adams Building in -- F Street and venturing outside into the air reeking with the thick odor of the catalpa trees, he found himself on an earth-road, or village street, with wheel-tracks meandering from the colonnade of the Treasury hard by, to the white marble columns and fronts of the Post Office and Patent Office which faced each other in the distance, like white Greek temples in the abandoned gravel-pits of a deserted Syrian city. Here and there low wooden houses were scattered along the streets, as in other Southern villages, but he was chiefly attracted by an unfinished square marble shaft, half-a-mile below, and he walked down to inspect it before breakfast. His aunt drily remarked that, at this rate, he would soon get through all the sights; but she could not guess -- having lived always in Washington -- how little the sights of Washington had to do with its interest.

The boy could not have told her; he was nowhere near an understanding of himself. The more he was educated, the less he understood. Slavery struck him in the face; it was a nightmare; a horror; a crime; the sum of all wickedness! Contact made it only more repulsive. He wanted to escape, like the negroes, to free soil. Slave States were dirty, unkempt, poverty-stricken, ignorant, vicious! He had not a thought but repulsion for it; and yet the picture had another side. The May sunshine and shadow had something to do with it; the thickness of foliage and the heavy smells had more; the sense of atmosphere, almost new, had perhaps as much again; and the brooding indolence of a warm climate and a negro population hung in the atmosphere heavier than the catalpas. The impression was not simple, but the boy liked it: distinctly it remained on his mind as an attraction, almost obscuring Quincy itself. The want of barriers, of pavements, of forms; the looseness, the laziness, the indolent Southern drawl; the pigs in the streets; the negro babies and their mothers with bandanas; the freedom, openness, swagger, of nature and man, soothed his Johnson blood. Most boys would have felt it in the same way, but with him the feeling caught on to an inheritance. The softness of his gentle old grandmother as she lay in bed and chatted with him, did not come from Boston. His aunt was anything rather than Bostonian. He did not wholly come from Boston himself. Though Washington belonged to a different world, and the two worlds could not live together, he was not sure that he enjoyed the Boston world most. Even at twelve years old he could see his own nature no more clearly than he would at twelve hundred, if by accident he should happen to live so long.

His father took him to the Capitol and on the floor of the Senate, which then, and long afterwards, until the era of tourists, was freely open to visitors. The old Senate Chamber resembled a pleasant political club. Standing behind the Vice-President's chair, which is now the Chief Justice's, the boy was presented to some of the men whose names were great in their day, and as familiar to him as his own. Clay and Webster and Calhoun were there still, but with them a Free Soil candidate for the Vice-Presidency had little to do; what struck boys most was their type. Senators were a species; they all wore an air, as they wore a blue dress coat or brass buttons; they were Roman. The type of Senator in 1850 was rather charming at its best, and the Senate, when in good temper, was an agreeable body, numbering only some sixty members, and affecting the airs of courtesy. Its vice was not so much a vice of manners or temper as of attitude. The statesman of all periods was apt to be pompous, but even pomposity was less offensive than familiarity -- on the platform as in the pulpit -- and Southern pomposity, when not arrogant, was genial and sympathetic, almost quaint and childlike in its simple-mindedness; quite a different thing from the Websterian or Conklinian pomposity of the North. The boy felt at ease there, more at home than he had ever felt in Boston State House, though his acquaintance with the codfish in the House of Representatives went back beyond distinct recollection. Senators spoke kindly to him, and seemed to feel so, for they had known his family socially; and, in spite of slavery, even J. Q. Adams in his later years, after he ceased to stand in the way of rivals, had few personal enemies. Decidedly the Senate, pro-slavery though it were, seemed a friendly world.

This first step in national politics was a little like the walk before breakfast; an easy, careless, genial, enlarging stride into a fresh and amusing world, where nothing was finished, but where even the weeds grew rank. The second step was like the first, except that it led to the White House. He was taken to see President Taylor. Outside, in a paddock in front, "Old Whitey," the President's charger, was grazing, as they entered; and inside, the President was receiving callers as simply as if he were in the paddock too. The President was friendly, and the boy felt no sense of strangeness that he could ever recall. In fact, what strangeness should he feel? The families were intimate; so intimate that their friendliness outlived generations, civil war, and all sorts of rupture. President Taylor owed his election to Martin Van Buren and the Free Soil Party. To him, the Adamses might still be of use. As for the White House, all the boy's family had lived there, and, barring the eight years of Andrew Jackson's reign, had been more or less at home there ever since it was built. The boy half thought he owned it, and took for granted that he should some day live in it. He felt no sensation whatever before Presidents. A President was a matter of course in every respectable family; he had two in his own; three, if he counted old Nathaniel Gorham, who, was the oldest and first in distinction. Revolutionary patriots, or perhaps a Colonial Governor, might be worth talking about, but any one could be President, and some very shady characters were likely to be. Presidents, Senators, Congressmen, and such things were swarming in every street.

Every one thought alike whether they had ancestors or not. No sort of glory hedged Presidents as such, and, in the whole country, one could hardly have met with an admission of respect for any office or name, unless it were George Washington. That was -- to all appearance sincerely -- respected. People made pilgrimages to Mount Vernon and made even an effort to build Washington a monument. The effort had failed, but one still went to Mount Vernon, although it was no easy trip. Mr. Adams took the boy there in a carriage and pair, over a road that gave him a complete Virginia education for use ten years afterwards. To the New England mind, roads, schools, clothes, and a clean face were connected as part of the law of order or divine system. Bad roads meant bad morals. The moral of this Virginia road was clear, and the boy fully learned it. Slavery was wicked, and slavery was the cause of this road's badness which amounted to social crime -- and yet, at the end of the road and product of the crime stood Mount Vernon and George Washington.

Luckily boys accept contradictions as readily as their elders do, or this boy might have become prematurely wise. He had only to repeat what he was told -- that George Washington stood alone. Otherwise this third step in his Washington education would have been his last. On that line, the problem of progress was not soluble, whatever the optimists and orators might say -- or, for that matter, whatever they might think. George Washington could not be reached on Boston lines. George Washington was a primary, or, if Virginians liked it better, an ultimate relation, like the Pole Star, and amid the endless restless motion of every other visible point in space, he alone remained steady, in the mind of Henry Adams, to the end. All the other points shifted their bearings; John Adams, Jefferson, Madison, Franklin, even John Marshall, took varied lights, and assumed new relations, but Mount Vernon always remained where it was, with no practicable road to reach it; and yet, when he got there, Mount Vernon was only Quincy in a Southern setting. No doubt it was much more charming, but it was the same eighteenth-century, the same old furniture, the same old patriot, and the same old President.

The boy took to it instinctively. The broad Potomac and the coons in the trees, the bandanas and the box-hedges, the bedrooms upstairs and the porch outside, even Martha Washington herself in memory, were as natural as the tides and the May sunshine; he had only enlarged his horizon a little; but he never thought to ask himself or his father how to deal with the moral problem that deduced George Washington from the sum of all wickedness. In practice, such trifles as contradictions in principle are easily set aside; the faculty of ignoring them makes the practical man; but any attempt to deal with them seriously as education is fatal. Luckily Charles Francis Adams never preached and was singularly free from cant. He may have had views of his own, but he let his son Henry satisfy himself with the simple elementary fact that George Washington stood alone.

Life was not yet complicated. Every problem had a solution, even the negro. The boy went back to Boston more political than ever, and his politics were no longer so modern as the eighteenth century, but took a strong tone of the seventeenth. Slavery drove the whole Puritan community back on its Puritanism. The boy thought as dogmatically as though he were one of his own ancestors. The Slave power took the place of Stuart kings and Roman popes. Education could go no further in that course, and ran off into emotion; but, as the boy gradually found his surroundings change, and felt himself no longer an isolated atom in a hostile universe, but a sort of herring-fry in a shoal of moving fish, he began to learn the first and easier lessons of practical politics. Thus far he had seen nothing but eighteenth-century statesmanship. America and he began, at the same time, to become aware of a new force under the innocent surface of party machinery. Even at that early moment, a rather slow boy felt dimly conscious that he might meet some personal difficulties in trying to reconcile sixteenth-century principles and eighteenth-century statesmanship with late nineteenth-century party organization. The first vague sense of feeling an unknown living obstacle in the dark came in 1851.

The Free Soil conclave in Mount Vernon Street belonged, as already said, to the statesman class, and, like Daniel Webster, had nothing to do with machinery. Websters or Sewards depended on others for machine work and money -- on Peter Harveys and Thurlow Weeds, who spent their lives in it, took most of the abuse, and asked no reward. Almost without knowing it, the subordinates ousted their employers and created a machine which no one but themselves could run. In 1850 things had not quite reached that point. The men who ran the small Free Soil machine were still modest, though they became famous enough in their own right. Henry Wilson, John B. Alley, Anson Burlingame, and the other managers, negotiated a bargain with the Massachusetts Democrats giving the State to the Democrats and a seat in the Senate to the Free Soilers. With this bargain Mr. Adams and his statesman friends would have nothing to do, for such a coalition was in their eyes much like jockeys selling a race. They did not care to take office as pay for votes sold to pro-slavery Democrats. Theirs was a correct, not to say noble, position; but, as a matter of fact, they took the benefit of the sale, for the coalition chose Charles Sumner as its candidate for the Senate, while George S. Boutwell was made Governor for the Democrats. This was the boy's first lesson in practical politics, and a sharp one; not that he troubled himself with moral doubts, but that he learned the nature of a flagrantly corrupt political bargain in which he was too good to take part, but not too good to take profit. Charles Sumner happened to be the partner to receive these stolen goods, but between his friend and his father the boy felt no distinction, and, for him, there was none. He entered into no casuistry on the matter. His friend was right because his friend, and the boy shared the glory. The question of education did not rise while the conflict lasted. Yet every one saw as clearly then as afterwards that a lesson of some sort must be learned and understood, once for all. The boy might ignore, as a mere historical puzzle, the question how to deduce George Washington from the sum of all wickedness, but he had himself helped to deduce Charles Sumner from the sum of political corruption. On that line, too, education could go no further. Tammany Hall stood at the end of the vista.

Mr. Alley, one of the strictest of moralists, held that his object in making the bargain was to convert the Democratic Party to anti-slavery principles, and that he did it. Henry Adams could rise to no such moral elevation. He was only a boy, and his object in supporting the coalition was that of making his friend a Senator. It was as personal as though he had helped to make his friend a millionaire. He could never find a way of escaping immoral conclusions, except by admitting that he and his father and Sumner were wrong, and this he was never willing to do, for the consequences of this admission were worse than those of the other. Thus, before he was fifteen years old, he had managed to get himself into a state of moral confusion from which he never escaped. As a politician, he was already corrupt, and he never could see how any practical politician could be less corrupt than himself.

Apology, as he understood himself, was cant or cowardice. At the time he never even dreamed that he needed to apologize, though the press shouted it at him from every corner, and though the Mount Vernon Street conclave agreed with the press; yet he could not plead ignorance, and even in the heat of the conflict, he never cared to defend the coalition. Boy as he was, he knew enough to know that something was wrong, but his only interest was the election. Day after day, the General Court balloted; and the boy haunted the gallery, following the roll-call, and wondered what Caleb Cushing meant by calling Mr. Sumner a "one-eyed abolitionist." Truly the difference in meaning with the phrase "one-ideaed abolitionist," which was Mr. Cushing's actual expression, is not very great, but neither the one nor the other seemed to describe Mr. Sumner to the boy, who never could have made the error of classing Garrison and Sumner together, or mistaking Caleb Cushing's relation to either. Temper ran high at that moment, while Sumner every day missed his election by only one or two votes. At last, April 24, 1851, standing among the silent crowd in the gallery, Henry heard the vote announced which gave Sumner the needed number. Slipping under the arms of the bystanders, he ran home as hard as he could, and burst into the dining-room where Mr. Sumner was seated at table with the family. He enjoyed the glory of telling Sumner that he was elected; it was probably the proudest moment in the life of either.

The next day, when the boy went to school, he noticed numbers of boys and men in the streets wearing black crepe on their arm. He knew few Free Soil boys in Boston; his acquaintances were what he called pro-slavery; so he thought proper to tie a bit of white silk ribbon round his own arm by way of showing that his friend Mr. Sumner was not wholly alone. This little piece of bravado passed unnoticed; no one even cuffed his ears; but in later life he was a little puzzled to decide which symbol was the more correct. No one then dreamed of four years' war, but every one dreamed of secession. The symbol for either might well be matter of doubt.

This triumph of the Mount Vernon Street conclave capped the political climax. The boy, like a million other American boys, was a politician, and what was worse, fit as yet to be nothing else. He should have been, like his grandfather, a protege of George Washington, a statesman designated by destiny, with nothing to do but look directly ahead, follow orders, and march. On the contrary, he was not even a Bostonian; he felt himself shut out of Boston as though he were an exile; he never thought of himself as a Bostonian; he never looked about him in Boston, as boys commonly do wherever they are, to select the street they like best, the house they want to live in, the profession they mean to practise. Always he felt himself somewhere else; perhaps in Washington with its social ease; perhaps in Europe; and he watched with vague unrest from the Quincy hills the smoke of the Cunard steamers stretching in a long line to the horizon, and disappearing every other Saturday or whatever the day might be, as though the steamers were offering to take him away, which was precisely what they were doing.

Had these ideas been unreasonable, influences enough were at hand to correct them; but the point of the whole story, when Henry Adams came to look back on it, seemed to be that the ideas were more than reasonable; they were the logical, necessary, mathematical result of conditions old as history and fixed as fate -- invariable sequence in man's experience. The only idea which would have been quite unreasonable scarcely entered his mind. This was the thought of going westward and growing up with the country. That he was not in the least fitted for going West made no objection whatever, since he was much better fitted than most of the persons that went. The convincing reason for staying in the East was that he had there every advantage over the West. He could not go wrong. The West must inevitably pay an enormous tribute to Boston and New York. One's position in the East was the best in the world for every purpose that could offer an object for going westward. If ever in history men had been able to calculate on a certainty for a lifetime in advance, the citizens of the great Eastern seaports could do it in 1850 when their railway systems were already laid out. Neither to a politician nor to a business-man nor to any of the learned professions did the West promise any certain advantage, while it offered uncertainties in plenty.

At any other moment in human history, this education, including its political and literary bias, would have been not only good, but quite the best. Society had always welcomed and flattered men so endowed. Henry Adams had every reason to be well pleased with it, and not ill-pleased with himself. He had all he wanted. He saw no reason for thinking that any one else had more. He finished with school, not very brilliantly, but without finding fault with the sum of his knowledge. Probably he knew more than his father, or his grandfather, or his great-grandfather had known at sixteen years old. Only on looking back, fifty years later, at his own figure in 1854, and pondering on the needs of the twentieth century, he wondered whether, on the whole the boy of 1854 stood nearer to the thought of 1904, or to that of the year 1. He found himself unable to give a sure answer. The calculation was clouded by the undetermined values of twentieth-century thought, but the story will show his reasons for thinking that, in essentials like religion, ethics, philosophy; in history, literature, art; in the concepts of all science, except perhaps mathematics, the American boy of 1854 stood nearer the year 1 than to the year 1900. The education he had received bore little relation to the education he needed. Speaking as an American of 1900, he had as yet no education at all. He knew not even where or how to begin.

Chapter IV. Harvard College (1854-1858)

ONE day in June, 1854, young Adams walked for the last time down the steps of Mr. Dixwell's school in Boylston Place, and felt no sensation but one of unqualified joy that this experience was ended. Never before or afterwards in his life did he close a period so long as four years without some sensation of loss -- some sentiment of habit -- but school was what in after life he commonly heard his friends denounce as an intolerable bore. He was born too old for it. The same thing could be said of most New England boys. Mentally they never were boys. Their education as men should have begun at ten years old. They were fully five years more mature than the English or European boy for whom schools were made. For the purposes of future advancement, as afterwards appeared, these first six years of a possible education were wasted in doing imperfectly what might have been done perfectly in one, and in any case would have had small value. The next regular step was Harvard College. He was more than glad to go. For generation after generation, Adamses and Brookses and Boylstons and Gorhams had gone to Harvard College, and although none of them, as far as known, had ever done any good there, or thought himself the better for it, custom, social ties, convenience, and, above all, economy, kept each generation in the track. Any other education would have required a serious effort, but no one took Harvard College seriously. All went there because their friends went there, and the College was their ideal of social self-respect.

Harvard College, as far as it educated at all, was a mild and liberal school, which sent young men into the world with all they needed to make respectable citizens, and something of what they wanted to make useful ones. Leaders of men it never tried to make. Its ideals were altogether different. The Unitarian clergy had given to the College a character of moderation, balance, judgment, restraint, what the French called mesure; excellent traits, which the College attained with singular success, so that its graduates could commonly be recognized by the stamp, but such a type of character rarely lent itself to autobiography. In effect, the school created a type but not a will. Four years of Harvard College, if successful, resulted in an autobiographical blank, a mind on which only a water-mark had been stamped.

The stamp, as such things went, was a good one. The chief wonder of education is that it does not ruin everybody concerned in it, teachers and taught. Sometimes in after life, Adams debated whether in fact it had not ruined him and most of his companions, but, disappointment apart, Harvard College was probably less hurtful than any other university then in existence. It taught little, and that little ill, but it left the mind open, free from bias, ignorant of facts, but docile. The graduate had few strong prejudices. He knew little, but his mind remained supple, ready to receive knowledge.

What caused the boy most disappointment was the little he got from his mates. Speaking exactly, he got less than nothing, a result common enough in education. Yet the College Catalogue for the years 1854 to 1861 shows a list of names rather distinguished in their time. Alexander Agassiz and Phillips Brooks led it; H. H. Richardson and O. W. Holmes helped to close it. As a rule the most promising of all die early, and never get their names into a Dictionary of Contemporaries, which seems to be the only popular standard of success. Many died in the war. Adams knew them all, more or less; he felt as much regard, and quite as much respect for them then, as he did after they won great names and were objects of a vastly wider respect; but, as help towards education, he got nothing whatever from them or they from him until long after they had left college. Possibly the fault was his, but one would like to know how many others shared it. Accident counts for much in companionship as in marriage. Life offers perhaps only a score of possible companions, and it is mere chance whether they meet as early as school or college, but it is more than a chance that boys brought up together under like conditions have nothing to give each other. The Class of 1858, to which Henry Adams belonged, was a typical collection of young New Englanders, quietly penetrating and aggressively commonplace; free from meannesses, jealousies, intrigues, enthusiasms, and passions; not exceptionally quick; not consciously skeptical; singularly indifferent to display, artifice, florid expression, but not hostile to it when it amused them; distrustful of themselves, but little disposed to trust any one else; with not much humor of their own, but full of readiness to enjoy the humor of others; negative to a degree that in the long run became positive and triumphant. Not harsh in manners or judgment, rather liberal and open-minded, they were still as a body the most formidable critics one would care to meet, in a long life exposed to criticism. They never flattered, seldom praised; free from vanity, they were not intolerant of it; but they were objectiveness itself; their attitude was a law of nature; their judgment beyond appeal, not an act either of intellect or emotion or of will, but a sort of gravitation.

This was Harvard College incarnate, but even for Harvard College, the Class of 1858 was somewhat extreme. Of unity this band of nearly one hundred young men had no keen sense, but they had equally little energy of repulsion. They were pleasant to live with, and above the average of students -- German, French, English, or what not -- but chiefly because each individual appeared satisfied to stand alone. It seemed a sign of force; yet to stand alone is quite natural when one has no passions; still easier when one has no pains.

Into this unusually dissolvent medium, chance insisted on enlarging Henry Adams's education by tossing a trio of Virginians as little fitted for it as Sioux Indians to a treadmill. By some further affinity, these three outsiders fell into relation with the Bostonians among whom Adams as a schoolboy belonged, and in the end with Adams himself, although they and he knew well how thin an edge of friendship separated them in 1856 from mortal enmity. One of the Virginians was the son of Colonel Robert E. Lee, of the Second United States Cavalry; the two others who seemed instinctively to form a staff for Lee, were town-Virginians from Petersburg. A fourth outsider came from Cincinnati and was half Kentuckian, N. L. Anderson, Longworth on the mother's side. For the first time Adams's education brought him in contact with new types and taught him their values. He saw the New England type measure itself with another, and he was part of the process.

Lee, known through life as "Roony," was a Virginian of the eighteenth century, much as Henry Adams was a Bostonian of the same age. Roony Lee had changed little from the type of his grandfather, Light Horse Harry. Tall, largely built, handsome, genial, with liberal Virginian openness towards all he liked, he had also the Virginian habit of command and took leadership as his natural habit. No one cared to contest it. None of the New Englanders wanted command. For a year, at least, Lee was the most popular and prominent young man in his class, but then seemed slowly to drop into the background. The habit of command was not enough, and the Virginian had little else. He was simple beyond analysis; so simple that even the simple New England student could not realize him. No one knew enough to know how ignorant he was; how childlike; how helpless before the relative complexity of a school. As an animal, the Southerner seemed to have every advantage, but even as an animal he steadily lost ground.

The lesson in education was vital to these young men, who, within ten years, killed each other by scores in the act of testing their college conclusions. Strictly, the Southerner had no mind; he had temperament He was not a scholar; he had no intellectual training; he could not analyze an idea, and he could not even conceive of admitting two; but in life one could get along very well without ideas, if one had only the social instinct. Dozens of eminent statesmen were men of Lee's type, and maintained themselves well enough in the legislature, but college was a sharper test.

The Virginian was weak in vice itself, though the Bostonian was hardly a master of crime. The habits of neither were good; both were apt to drink hard and to live low lives; but the Bostonian suffered less than the Virginian. Commonly the Bostonian could take some care of himself even in his worst stages, while the Virginian became quarrelsome and dangerous. When a Virginian had brooded a few days over an imaginary grief and substantial whiskey, none of his Northern friends could be sure that he might not be waiting, round the corner, with a knife or pistol, to revenge insult by the dry light of delirium tremens; and when things reached this condition, Lee had to exhaust his authority over his own staff. Lee was a gentleman of the old school, and, as every one knows, gentlemen of the old school drank almost as much as gentlemen of the new school; but this was not his trouble. He was sober even in the excessive violence of political feeling in those years; he kept his temper and his friends under control.

Adams liked the Virginians. No one was more obnoxious to them, by name and prejudice; yet their friendship was unbroken and even warm. At a moment when the immediate future posed no problem in education so vital as the relative energy and endurance of North and South, this momentary contact with Southern character was a sort of education for its own sake; but this was not all. No doubt the self-esteem of the Yankee, which tended naturally to self-distrust, was flattered by gaining the slow conviction that the Southerner, with his slave-owning limitations, was as little fit to succeed in the struggle of modern life as though he were still a maker of stone axes, living in caves, and hunting the bos primigenius, and that every quality in which he was strong, made him weaker; but Adams had begun to fear that even in this respect one eighteenth-century type might not differ deeply from another. Roony Lee had changed little from the Virginian of a century before; but Adams was himself a good deal nearer the type of his great-grandfather than to that of a railway superintendent. He was little more fit than the Virginians to deal with a future America which showed no fancy for the past. Already Northern society betrayed a preference for economists over diplomats or soldiers -- one might even call it a jealousy -- against which two eighteenth-century types had little chance to live, and which they had in common to fear.

Nothing short of this curious sympathy could have brought into close relations two young men so hostile as Roony Lee and Henry Adams, but the chief difference between them as collegians consisted only in their difference of scholarship: Lee was a total failure; Adams a partial one. Both failed, but Lee felt his failure more sensibly, so that he gladly seized the chance of escape by accepting a commission offered him by General Winfield Scott in the force then being organized against the Mormons. He asked Adams to write his letter of acceptance, which flattered Adams's vanity more than any Northern compliment could do, because, in days of violent political bitterness, it showed a certain amount of good temper. The diplomat felt his profession.

If the student got little from his mates, he got little more from his masters. The four years passed at college were, for his purposes, wasted. Harvard College was a good school, but at bottom what the boy disliked most was any school at all. He did not want to be one in a hundred -- one per cent of an education. He regarded himself as the only person for whom his education had value, and he wanted the whole of it. He got barely half of an average. Long afterwards, when the devious path of life led him back to teach in his turn what no student naturally cared or needed to know, he diverted some dreary hours of faculty-meetings by looking up his record in the class-lists, and found himself graded precisely in the middle. In the one branch he most needed --

mathematics -- barring the few first scholars, failure was so nearly universal that no attempt at grading could have had value, and whether he stood fortieth or ninetieth must have been an accident or the personal favor of the professor. Here his education failed lamentably. At best he could never have been a mathematician; at worst he would never have cared to be one; but he needed to read mathematics, like any other universal language, and he never reached the alphabet.

Beyond two or three Greek plays, the student got nothing from the ancient languages. Beyond some incoherent theories of free-trade and protection, he got little from Political Economy. He could not afterwards remember to have heard the name of Karl Marx mentioned, or the title of "Capital." He was equally ignorant of Auguste Comte. These were the two writers of his time who most influenced its thought. The bit of practical teaching he afterwards reviewed with most curiosity was the course in Chemistry, which taught him a number of theories that befogged his mind for a lifetime. The only teaching that appealed to his imagination was a course of lectures by Louis Agassiz on the Glacial Period and Paleontology, which had more influence on his curiosity than the rest of the college instruction altogether. The entire work of the four years could have been easily put into the work of any four months in after life.

Harvard College was a negative force, and negative forces have value. Slowly it weakened the violent political bias of childhood, not by putting interests in its place, but by mental habits which had no bias at all. It would also have weakened the literary bias, if Adams had been capable of finding other amusement, but the climate kept him steady to desultory and useless reading, till he had run through libraries of volumes which he forgot even to their title-pages. Rather by instinct than by guidance, he turned to writing, and his professors or tutors occasionally gave his English composition a hesitating approval; but in that branch, as in all the rest, even when he made a long struggle for recognition, he never convinced his teachers that his abilities, at their best, warranted placing him on the rank-list, among the first third of his class. Instructors generally reach a fairly accurate gauge of their scholars' powers. Henry Adams himself held the opinion that his instructors were very nearly right, and when he became a professor in his turn, and made mortifying mistakes in ranking his scholars, he still obstinately insisted that on the whole, he was not far wrong. Student or professor, he accepted the negative standard because it was the standard of the school.

He never knew what other students thought of it, or what they thought they gained from it; nor would their opinion have much affected his. From the first, he wanted to be done with it, and stood watching vaguely for a path and a direction. The world outside seemed large, but the paths that led into it were not many and lay mostly through Boston, where he did not want to go. As it happened, by pure chance, the first door of escape that seemed to offer a hope led into Germany, and James Russell Lowell opened it.

Lowell, on succeeding Longfellow as Professor of Belles-Lettres, had duly gone to Germany, and had brought back whatever he found to bring. The literary world then agreed that truth survived in Germany alone, and Carlyle, Matthew Arnold, Renan, Emerson, with scores of popular followers, taught the German faith. The literary world had revolted against the yoke of coming capitalism -- its money-lenders, its bank directors, and its railway magnates. Thackeray and Dickens followed Balzac in scratching and biting the unfortunate middle class with savage ill-temper, much as the middle class had scratched and bitten the Church and Court for a hundred years before. The middle class had the power, and held its coal and iron well in hand, but the satirists and idealists seized the press, and as they were agreed that the Second Empire was a disgrace to France and a danger to England, they turned to Germany because at that moment Germany was neither economical nor military, and a hundred years behind western Europe in the simplicity of its standard. German thought, method, honesty, and even taste, became the standards of scholarship. Goethe was raised to the rank of Shakespeare -- Kant ranked as a law-giver above Plato. All serious scholars were obliged to become German, for German thought was revolutionizing criticism. Lowell had followed the rest, not very enthusiastically, but with sufficient conviction, and invited his scholars to join him. Adams was glad to accept the invitation, rather for the sake of cultivating Lowell than Germany, but still in perfect good faith. It was the first serious attempt he had made to direct his own education, and he was sure of getting some education out of it; not perhaps anything that he expected, but at least a path.

Singularly circuitous and excessively wasteful of energy the path proved to be, but the student could never see what other was open to him. He could have done no better had he foreseen every stage of his coming life, and he would probably have done worse. The preliminary step was pure gain. James Russell Lowell had brought back from Germany the only new and valuable part of its universities, the habit of allowing students to read with him privately in his study. Adams asked the privilege, and used it to read a little, and to talk a great deal, for the personal contact pleased and flattered him, as that of older men ought to flatter and please the young even when they altogether exaggerate its value. Lowell was a new element in the boy's life. As practical a New Englander as any, he leaned towards the Concord faith rather than towards Boston where he properly belonged; for Concord, in the dark days of 1856, glowed with pure light. Adams approached it in much the same spirit as he would have entered a Gothic Cathedral, for he well knew that the priests regarded him as only a worm. To the Concord Church all Adamses were minds of dust and emptiness, devoid of feeling, poetry or imagination; little higher than the common scourings of State Street; politicians of doubtful honesty; natures of narrow scope; and already, at eighteen years old, Henry had begun to feel uncertainty about so many matters more important than Adamses that his mind rebelled against no discipline merely personal, and he was ready to admit his unworthiness if only he might penetrate the shrine. The influence of Harvard College was beginning to have its effect. He was slipping away from fixed principles; from Mount Vernon Street; from Quincy; from the eighteenth century; and his first steps led toward Concord.

He never reached Concord, and to Concord Church he, like the rest of mankind who accepted a material universe, remained always an insect, or something much lower -- a man. It was surely no fault of his that the universe seemed to him real; perhaps -- as Mr. Emerson justly said -- it was so; in spite of the long-continued effort of a lifetime, he perpetually fell back into the heresy that if anything universal was unreal, it was himself and not the appearances; it was the poet and not the banker; it was his own thought, not the thing that moved it. He did not lack the wish to be transcendental. Concord seemed to him, at one time, more real than Quincy; yet in truth Russell Lowell was as little transcendental as Beacon Street. From him the boy got no revolutionary thought whatever -- objective or subjective as they used to call it -- but he got good-humored encouragement to do what amused him, which consisted in passing two years in Europe after finishing the four years of Cambridge

The result seemed small in proportion to the effort, but it was the only positive result he could ever trace to the influence of Harvard College, and he had grave doubts whether Harvard College influenced even that. Negative results in plenty he could trace, but he tended towards negation on his own account, as one side of the New England mind had always done, and even there he could never feel sure that Harvard College had more than reflected a weakness. In his opinion the education was not serious, but in truth hardly any Boston student took it seriously, and none of them seemed sure that President Walker himself, or President Felton after him, took it more seriously than the students. For them all, the college offered chiefly advantages vulgarly called social, rather than mental.

Unluckily for this particular boy, social advantages were his only capital in life. Of money he had not much, of mind not more, but he could be quite certain that, barring his own faults, his social position would never be questioned. What he needed was a career in which social position had value. Never in his life would he have to explain who he was; never would he have need of acquaintance to strengthen his social standing; but he needed greatly some one to show him how to use the acquaintance he cared to make. He made no acquaintance in college which proved to have the smallest use in after life. All his Boston friends he knew before, or would have known in any case, and contact of Bostonian with Bostonian was the last education these young men needed. Cordial and intimate as their college relations were, they all flew off in different directions the moment they took their degrees. Harvard College remained a tie, indeed, but a tie little stronger than Beacon Street and not so strong as State Street. Strangers might perhaps gain something from the college if they were hard pressed for social connections. A student like H. H. Richardson, who came from far away New Orleans, and had his career before him to chase rather than to guide, might make valuable friendships at college. Certainly Adams made no acquaintance there that he valued in after life so much as Richardson, but still more certainly the college relation had little to do with the later friendship. Life is a narrow valley, and the roads run close together. Adams would have attached himself to Richardson in any case, as he attached himself to John LaFarge or Augustus St. Gaudens or Clarence King or John Hay, none of whom were at Harvard College. The valley of life grew more and more narrow with years, and certain men with common tastes were bound to come together. Adams knew only that he would have felt himself on a more equal footing with them had he been less ignorant, and had he not thrown away ten years of early life in acquiring what he might have acquired in one.

Socially or intellectually, the college was for him negative and in some ways mischievous. The most tolerant man of the world could not see good in the lower habits of the students, but the vices were less harmful than the virtues. The habit of drinking -- though the mere recollection of it made him doubt his own veracity, so fantastic it seemed in later life -- may have done no great or permanent harm; but the habit of looking at life as a social relation -- an affair of society -- did no good. It cultivated a weakness which needed no cultivation. If it had helped to make men of the world, or give the manners and instincts of any profession -- such as temper, patience, courtesy, or a faculty of profiting by the social defects of opponents -- it would have been education better worth having than mathematics or languages; but so far as it helped to make anything, it helped only to make the college standard permanent through life. The Bostonian educated at Harvard College remained a collegian, if he stuck only to what the college gave him. If parents went on generation after generation, sending their children to Harvard College for the sake of its social advantages, they perpetuated an inferior social type, quite as ill-fitted as the Oxford type for success in the next generation.

Luckily the old social standard of the college, as President Walker or James Russell Lowell still showed it, was admirable, and if it had little practical value or personal influence on the mass of students, at least it preserved the tradition for those who liked it. The Harvard graduate was neither American nor European, nor even wholly Yankee; his admirers were few, and his many; perhaps his worst weakness was his self-criticism and self-consciousness; but his ambitions, social or intellectual, were necessarily cheap even though they might be negative. Afraid of such serious risks, and still more afraid of personal ridicule, he seldom made a great failure of life, and nearly always led a life more or less worth living. So Henry Adams, well aware that he could not succeed as a scholar, and finding his social position beyond improvement or need of effort, betook himself to the single ambition which otherwise would scarcely have seemed a true outcome of the college, though it was the last remnant of the old Unitarian supremacy. He took to the pen. He wrote.

The College Magazine printed his work, and the College Societies listened to his addresses. Lavish of praise the readers were not; the audiences, too, listened in silence; but this was all the encouragement any Harvard collegian had a reasonable hope to receive; grave silence was a form of patience that meant possible future acceptance; and Henry Adams went on writing. No one cared enough to criticise, except himself who soon began to suffer from reaching his own limits. He found that he could not be this -- or that -- or the other; always precisely the things he wanted to be. He had not wit or scope or force. Judges always ranked him beneath a rival, if he had any; and he believed the judges were right. His work seemed to him thin, commonplace, feeble. At times he felt his own weakness so fatally that he could not go on; when he had nothing to say, he could not say it, and he found that he had very little to say at best. Much that he then wrote must be still in existence in print or manuscript, though he never cared to see it again, for he felt no doubt that it was in reality just what he thought it. At best it showed only a feeling for form; an instinct of exclusion. Nothing shocked--not even its weakness.

Inevitably an effort leads to an ambition -- creates it -- and at that time the ambition of the literary student, which almost took place of the regular prizes of scholarship, was that of being chosen as the representative of his class -- Class Orator -- at the close of their course. This was political as well as literary success, and precisely the sort of eighteenth-century combination that fascinated an eighteenth century boy. The idea lurked in his mind, at first as a dream, in no way serious or even possible, for he stood outside the number of what were known as popular men. Year by year, his position seemed to improve, or perhaps his rivals disappeared, until at last, to his own great astonishment, he found himself a candidate. The habits of the college permitted no active candidacy; he and his rivals had not a word to say for or against themselves, and he was never even consulted on the subject; he was not present at any of the proceedings, and how it happened he never could quite divine, but it did happen, that one evening on returning from Boston he received notice of his election, after a very close contest, as Class Orator over the head of the first scholar, who was undoubtedly a better orator and a more popular man. In politics the success of the poorer candidate is common enough, and Henry Adams was a fairly trained politician, but he never understood how he managed to defeat not only a more capable but a more popular rival.

To him the election seemed a miracle. This was no mock-modesty; his head was as clear as ever it was in an indifferent canvass, and he knew his rivals and their following as well as he knew himself. What he did not know, even after four years of education, was Harvard College. What he could never measure was the bewildering impersonality of the men, who, at twenty years old, seemed to set no value either on official or personal standards. Here were nearly a hundred young men who had lived together intimately during four of the most impressionable years of life, and who, not only once but again and again, in different ways, deliberately, seriously, dispassionately, chose as their representatives precisely those of their companions who seemed least to represent them. As far as these Orators and Marshals had any position at all in a collegiate sense, it was that of indifference to the college. Henry Adams never professed the smallest faith in universities of any kind, either as boy or man, nor had he the faintest admiration for the university graduate, either in Europe or in America; as a collegian he was only known apart from his fellows by his habit of standing outside the college; and yet the singular fact remained that this commonplace body of young men chose him repeatedly to express his and their commonplaces. Secretly, of course, the successful candidate flattered himself -- and them -- with the hope that they might perhaps not be so commonplace as they thought themselves; but this was only another proof that all were identical. They saw in him a representative -- the kind of representative they wanted -- and he saw in them the most formidable array of judges he could ever meet, like so many mirrors of himself, an infinite reflection of his own shortcomings.

All the same, the choice was flattering; so flattering that it actually shocked his vanity; and would have shocked it more, if possible, had he known that it was to be the only flattery of the sort he was ever to receive. The function of Class Day was, in the eyes of nine-tenths of the students, altogether the most important of the college, and the figure of the Orator was the most conspicuous in the function. Unlike the Orators at regular Commencements, the Class Day Orator stood alone, or had only the Poet for rival. Crowded into the large church, the students, their families, friends, aunts, uncles and chaperones, attended all the girls of sixteen or twenty who wanted to show their summer dresses or fresh complexions, and there, for an hour or two, in a heat that might have melted bronze, they listened to an Orator and a Poet in clergyman's gowns, reciting such platitudes as their own experience and their mild censors permitted them to utter. What Henry Adams said in his Class Oration of 1858 he soon forgot to the last word, nor had it the least value for education; but he naturally remembered what was said of it. He remembered especially one of his eminent uncles or relations remarking that, as the work of so young a man, the oration was singularly wanting in enthusiasm. The young man -- always in search of education -- asked himself whether, setting rhetoric aside, this absence of enthusiasm was a defect or a merit, since, in either case, it was all that Harvard College taught, and all that the hundred young men, whom he was trying to represent, expressed. Another comment threw more light on the effect of the college education. One of the elderly gentlemen noticed the orator's "perfect self-possession." Self-possession indeed! If Harvard College gave nothing else, it gave calm. For four years each student had been obliged to figure daily before dozens of young men who knew each other to the last fibre. One had done little but read papers to Societies, or act comedy in the Hasty Pudding, not to speak of regular exercises, and no audience in future life would ever be so intimately and terribly intelligent as these. Three-fourths of the graduates would rather have addressed the Council of Trent or the British Parliament than have acted Sir Anthony Absolute or Dr. Ollapod before a gala audience of the Hasty Pudding. Self-possession was the strongest part of Harvard College, which certainly taught men to stand alone, so that nothing seemed stranger to its graduates than the paroxysms of terror before the public which often overcame the graduates of European universities. Whether this was, or was not, education, Henry Adams never knew. He was ready to stand up before any audience in America or Europe, with nerves rather steadier for the excitement, but whether he should ever have anything to say, remained to be proved. As yet he knew nothing Education had not begun.

Chapter V. Berlin (1858-1859)

A FOURTH child has the strength of his weakness. Being of no great value, he may throw himself away if he likes, and never be missed. Charles Francis Adams, the father, felt no love for Europe, which, as he and all the world agreed, unfitted Americans for America. A captious critic might have replied that all the success he or his father or his grandfather achieved was chiefly due to the field that Europe gave them, and it was more than likely that without the help of Europe they would have all remained local politicians or lawyers, like their neighbors, to the end. Strictly followed, the rule would have obliged them never to quit Quincy; and, in fact, so much more timid are parents for their children than for themselves, that Mr. and Mrs. Adams would have been content to see their children remain forever in Mount Vernon Street, unexposed to the temptations of Europe, could they have relied on the moral influences of Boston itself. Although the parents little knew what took place under their eyes, even the mothers saw enough to make them uneasy. Perhaps their dread of vice, haunting past and present, worried them less than their dread of daughters-in-law or sons-in-law who might not fit into the somewhat narrow quarters of home. On all sides were risks. Every year some young person alarmed the parental heart even in Boston, and although the temptations of Europe were irresistible, removal from the temptations of Boston might be imperative. The boy Henry wanted to go to Europe; he seemed well behaved, when any one was looking at him; he observed conventions, when he could not escape them; he was never quarrelsome, towards a superior; his morals were apparently good, and his moral principles, if he had any, were not known to be bad. Above all, he was timid and showed a certain sense of self-respect, when in public view. What he was at heart, no one could say; least of all himself; but he was probably human, and no worse than some others. Therefore, when he presented to an exceedingly indulgent father and mother his request to begin at a German university the study of the Civil Law -- although neither he nor they knew what the Civil Law was, or any reason for his studying it -- the parents dutifully consented, and walked with him down to the railway-station at Quincy to bid him good-bye, with a smile which he almost thought a tear.

Whether the boy deserved such indulgence, or was worth it, he knew no more than they, or than a professor at Harvard College; but whether worthy or not, he began his third or fourth attempt at education in November, 1858, by sailing on the steamer Persia, the pride of Captain Judkins and the Cunard Line; the newest, largest and fastest steamship afloat. He was not alone. Several of his college companions sailed with him, and the world looked cheerful enough until, on the third day, the world -- as far as concerned the young man -- ran into a heavy storm. He learned then a lesson that stood by him better than any university teaching ever did -- the meaning of a November gale on the mid-Atlantic -- which, for mere physical misery, passed endurance. The subject offered him material for none but serious treatment; he could never see the humor of sea-sickness; but it united itself with a great variety of other impressions which made the first month of travel altogether the rapidest school of education he had yet found. The stride in knowledge seemed gigantic. One began a to see that a great many impressions were needed to make very little education, but how many could be crowded into one day without making any education at all, became the pons asinorum of tourist mathematics. How many would turn out to be wrong whether any could turn out right, was ultimate wisdom.

The ocean, the Persia, Captain Judkins, and Mr. G. P. R. James, the most distinguished passenger, vanished one Sunday morning in a furious gale in the Mersey, to make place for the drearier picture of a Liverpool street as seen from the Adelphi coffee-room in November murk, followed instantly by the passionate delights of Chester and the romance of red-sandstone architecture. Millions of Americans have felt this succession of emotions. Possibly very young and ingenuous tourists feel them still, but in days before tourists, when the romance was a reality, not a picture, they were overwhelming. When the boys went out to Eaton Hall, they were awed, as Thackeray or Dickens would have felt in the presence of a Duke. The very name of Grosvenor struck a note of grandeur. The long suite of lofty, gilded rooms with their gilded furniture; the portraits; the terraces; the gardens, the landscape; the sense of superiority in the England of the fifties, actually set the rich nobleman apart, above Americans and shopkeepers. Aristocracy was real. So was the England of Dickens. Oliver Twist and Little Nell lurked in every churchyard shadow, not as shadow but alive. Even Charles the First was not very shadowy, standing on the tower to see his army defeated. Nothing thereabouts had very much changed since he lost his battle and his head. An eighteenth-century American boy fresh from Boston naturally took it all for education, and was amused at this sort of lesson. At least he thought he felt it.

Then came the journey up to London through Birmingham and the Black District, another lesson, which needed much more to be rightly felt. The plunge into darkness lurid with flames; the sense of unknown horror in this weird gloom which then existed nowhere else, and never had existed before, except in volcanic craters; the violent contrast between this dense, smoky, impenetrable darkness, and the soft green charm that one glided into, as one emerged -- the revelation of an unknown society of the pit -- made a boy uncomfortable, though he had no idea that Karl Marx was standing there waiting for him, and that sooner or later the process of education would have to deal with Karl Marx much more than with Professor Bowen of Harvard College or his Satanic free-trade majesty John Stuart Mill. The Black District was a practical education, but it was infinitely far in the distance. The boy ran away from it, as he ran away from everything he disliked.

Had he known enough to know where to begin he would have seen something to study, more vital than the Civil Law, in the long, muddy, dirty, sordid, gas-lit dreariness of Oxford Street as his dingy four-wheeler dragged its weary way to Charing Cross. He did notice one peculiarity about it worth remembering. London was still London. A certain style dignified its grime; heavy, clumsy, arrogant, purse-proud, but not cheap; insular but large; barely tolerant of an outside world, and absolutely self-confident. The boys in the streets made such free comments on the American clothes and figures, that the travellers hurried to put on tall hats and long overcoats to escape criticism. No stranger had rights even in the Strand. The eighteenth century held its own. History muttered down Fleet Street, like Dr. Johnson, in Adams's ear; Vanity Fair was alive on Piccadilly in yellow chariots with coachmen in wigs, on hammer-cloths; footmen with canes, on the footboard, and a shrivelled old woman inside; half the great houses, black with London smoke, bore large funeral hatchments; every one seemed insolent, and the most insolent structures in the world were the Royal Exchange and the Bank of England. In November, 1858, London was still vast, but it was the London of the eighteenth century that an American felt and hated.

Education went backward. Adams, still a boy, could not guess how intensely intimate this

London grime was to become to him as a man, but he could still less conceive himself returning to it fifty years afterwards, noting at each turn how the great city grew smaller as it doubled in size; cheaper as it quadrupled its wealth; less imperial as its empire widened; less dignified as it tried to be civil. He liked it best when he hated it. Education began at the end, or perhaps would end at the beginning. Thus far it had remained in the eighteenth century, and the next step took it back to the sixteenth. He crossed to Antwerp. As the Baron Osy steamed up the Scheldt in the morning mists, a travelling band on deck began to play, and groups of peasants, working along the fields, dropped their tools to join in dancing. Ostade and Teniers were as much alive as they ever were, and even the Duke of Alva was still at home. The thirteenth-century cathedral towered above a sixteenth-century mass of tiled roofs, ending abruptly in walls and a landscape that had not changed. The taste of the town was thick, rich, ripe, like a sweet wine; it was mediaeval, so that Rubens seemed modern; it was one of the strongest and fullest flavors that ever touched the young man's palate; but he might as well have drunk out his excitement in old Malmsey, for all the education he got from it. Even in art, one can hardly begin with Antwerp Cathedral and the Descent from the Cross. He merely got drunk on his emotions, and had then to get sober as he best could. He was terribly sober when he saw Antwerp half a century afterwards. One lesson he did learn without suspecting that he must immediately lose it. He felt his middle ages and the sixteenth century alive. He was young enough, and the towns were dirty enough -- unimproved, unrestored, untouristed -- to retain the sense of reality. As a taste or a smell, it was education, especially because it lasted barely ten years longer; but it was education only sensual. He never dreamed of trying to educate himself to the Descent from the Cross. He was only too happy to feel himself kneeling at the foot of the Cross; he learned only to loathe the sordid necessity of getting up again, and going about his stupid business.

This was one of the foreseen dangers of Europe, but it vanished rapidly enough to reassure the most anxious of parents. Dropped into Berlin one morning without guide or direction, the young man in search of education floundered in a mere mess of misunderstandings. He could never recall what he expected to find, but whatever he expected, it had no relation with what it turned out to be. A student at twenty takes easily to anything, even to Berlin, and he would have accepted the thirteenth century pure and simple since his guides assured him that this was his right path; but a week's experience left him dazed and dull. Faith held out, but the paths grew dim. Berlin astonished him, but he had no lack of friends to show him all the amusement it had to offer. Within a day or two he was running about with the rest to beer-cellars and music-halls and dance-rooms, smoking bad tobacco, drinking poor beer, and eating sauerkraut and sausages as though he knew no better. This was easy. One can always descend the social ladder. The trouble came when he asked for the education he was promised. His friends took him to be registered as a student of the university; they selected his professors and courses; they showed him where to buy the Institutes of Gaius and several German works on the Civil Law in numerous volumes; and they led him to his first lecture.

His first lecture was his last. The young man was not very quick, and he had almost religious respect for his guides and advisers; but he needed no more than one hour to satisfy him that he had made another failure in education, and this time a fatal one. That the language would require at least three months' hard work before he could touch the Law was an annoying discovery; but the shock that upset him was the discovery of the university itself. He had thought Harvard College a torpid school, but it was instinct with life compared with all that he could see of the University of Berlin. The German students were strange animals, but their professors were beyond pay. The mental attitude of the university was not of an American world. What sort of instruction prevailed in other branches, or in science, Adams had no occasion to ask, but in the Civil Law he found only the lecture system in its deadliest form as it flourished in the thirteenth century. The professor mumbled his comments; the students made, or seemed to make, notes; they could have learned from books or discussion in a day more than they could learn from him in a month, but they must pay his fees, follow his course, and be his scholars, if they wanted a degree. To an American the result was worthless. He could make no use of the Civil Law without some previous notion of the Common Law; but the student who knew enough of the Common Law to understand what he wanted, had only to read the Pandects or the commentators at his ease in America, and be his own professor. Neither the method nor the matter nor the manner could profit an American education.

This discovery seemed to shock none of the students. They went to the lectures, made notes, and read textbooks, but never pretended to take their professor seriously. They were much more serious in reading Heine. They knew no more than Heine what good they were getting, beyond the Berlin accent -- which was bad; and the beer -- which was not to compare with Munich; and the dancing -- which was better at Vienna. They enjoyed the beer and music, but they refused to be responsible for the education. Anyway, as they defended themselves, they were learning the language.

So the young man fell back on the language, and being slow at languages, he found himself falling behind all his friends, which depressed his spirits, the more because the gloom of a Berlin winter and of Berlin architecture seemed to him a particular sort of gloom never attained elsewhere. One day on the Linden he caught sight of Charles Sumner in a cab, and ran after him. Sumner was then recovering from the blows of the South Carolinian cane or club, and he was pleased to find a young worshipper in the remote Prussian wilderness. They dined together and went to hear "William Tell" at the Opera. Sumner tried to encourage his friend about his difficulties of language: "I came to Berlin," or Rome, or whatever place it was, as he said with his grand air of mastery, "I came to Berlin, unable to say a word in the language; and three months later when I went away, I talked it to my cabman." Adams felt himself quite unable to attain in so short a time such social advantages, and one day complained of his trials to Mr. Robert Apthorp, of Boston, who was passing the winter in Berlin for the sake of its music. Mr. Apthorp told of his own similar struggle, and how he had entered a public school and sat for months with ten-year-old-boys, reciting their lessons and catching their phrases. The idea suited Adams's desperate frame of mind. At least it ridded him of the university and the Civil Law and American associations in beer-cellars. Mr. Apthorp took the trouble to negotiate with the headmaster of the Friedrichs-Wilhelm-Werdersches Gymnasium for permission to Henry Adams to attend the school as a member of the Ober-tertia, a class of boys twelve or thirteen years old, and there Adams went for three months as though he had not always avoided high schools with singular antipathy. He never did anything else so foolish but he was given a bit of education which served him some purpose in life.

It was not merely the language, though three months passed in such fashion would teach a poodle enough to talk with a cabman, and this was all that foreign students could expect to do, for they never by any chance would come in contact with German society, if German society existed, about which they knew nothing. Adams never learned to talk German well, but the same might be said of his English, if he could believe Englishmen. He learned not to annoy himself on this account. His difficulties with the language gradually ceased. He thought himself quite Germanized in 1859. He even deluded himself with the idea that he read it as though it were English, which proved that he knew little about it; but whatever success he had in his own experiment interested him less than his contact with German education.

He had revolted at the American school and university; he had instantly rejected the German university; and as his last experience of education he tried the German high school. The experiment was hazardous. In 1858 Berlin was a poor, keen-witted, provincial town, simple, dirty, uncivilized, and in most respects disgusting. Life was primitive beyond what an American boy could have imagined. Overridden by military methods and bureaucratic pettiness, Prussia was only beginning to free her hands from internal bonds. Apart from discipline, activity scarcely existed. The future Kaiser Wilhelm I, regent for his insane brother King Friedrich Wilhelm IV, seemed to pass his time looking at the passers-by from the window of his modest palace on the Linden. German manners, even at Court, were sometimes brutal, and German thoroughness at school was apt to be routine. Bismarck himself was then struggling to begin a career against the inertia of the German system. The condition of Germany was a scandal and nuisance to every earnest German, all whose energies were turned to reforming it from top to bottom; and Adams walked into a great public school to get educated, at precisely the time when the Germans wanted most to get rid of the education they were forced to follow. As an episode in the search for education, this adventure smacked of Heine.

The school system has doubtless changed, and at all events the schoolmasters are probably long ago dead; the story has no longer a practical value, and had very little even at the time; one could at least say in defence of the German school that it was neither very brutal nor very immoral. The head-master was excellent in his Prussian way, and the other instructors were not worse than in other schools; it was their system that struck the systemless American with horror. The arbitrary training given to the memory was stupefying; the strain that the memory endured was a form of torture; and the feats that the boys performed, without complaint, were pitiable. No other faculty than the memory seemed to be recognized. Least of all was any use made of reason, either analytic, synthetic, or dogmatic. The German government did not encourage reasoning.

All State education is a sort of dynamo machine for polarizing the popular mind; for turning and holding its lines of force in the direction supposed to be most effective for State purposes. The German machine was terribly efficient. Its effect on the children was pathetic. The Friedrichs-Wilhelm-Werdersches Gymnasium was an old building in the heart of Berlin which served the educational needs of the small tradesmen or bourgeoisie of the neighborhood; the children were Berliner-kinder if ever there were such, and of a class suspected of sympathy and concern in the troubles of 1848. None was noble or connected with good society. Personally they were rather sympathetic than not, but as the objects of education they were proofs of nearly all the evils that a bad system could give. Apparently Adams, in his rigidly illogical pursuit, had at last reached his ideal of a viciously logical education. The boys' physique showed it first, but their physique could not be wholly charged to the school. German food was bad at best, and a diet of sauerkraut, sausage, and beer could never be good; but it was not the food alone that made their faces white and their flesh flabby. They never breathed fresh air; they had never heard of a playground; in all Berlin not a cubic inch of oxygen was admitted in winter into an inhabited building; in the school every room was tightly closed and had no ventilation; the air was foul beyond all decency; but when the American opened a window in the five minutes between hours, he violated the rules and was invariably rebuked. As long as cold weather lasted, the windows were shut. If the boys had a holiday, they were apt to be taken on long tramps in the Thiergarten or elsewhere, always ending in over-fatigue, tobacco-smoke, sausages, and beer. With this, they were required to prepare daily lessons that would have quickly broken down strong men of a healthy habit, and which they could learn only because their minds were morbid. The German university had seemed a failure, but the German high school was something very near an indictable nuisance.

Before the month of April arrived, the experiment of German education had reached this point. Nothing was left of it except the ghost of the Civil Law shut up in the darkest of closets, never to gibber again before any one who could repeat the story. The derisive Jew laughter of Heine ran through the university and everything else in Berlin. Of course, when one is twenty years old, life is bound to be full, if only of Berlin beer, although German student life was on the whole the thinnest of beer, as an American looked on it, but though nothing except small fragments remained of the education that had been so promising -- or promised -- this is only what most often happens in life, when by-products turn out to be more valuable than staples. The German university and German law were failures; German society, in an American sense, did not exist, or if it existed, never showed itself to an American; the German theatre, on the other hand, was excellent, and German opera, with the ballet, was almost worth a journey to Berlin; but the curious and perplexing result of the total failure of German education was that the student's only clear gain -- his single step to a higher life -- came from time wasted; studies neglected; vices indulged; education reversed; -- it came from the despised beer-garden and music-hall; and it was accidental, unintended, unforeseen.

When his companions insisted on passing two or three afternoons in the week at music-halls, drinking beer, smoking German tobacco, and looking at fat German women knitting, while an orchestra played dull music, Adams went with them for the sake of the company, but with no presence of enjoyment; and when Mr. Apthorp gently protested that he exaggerated his indifference, for of course he enjoyed Beethoven, Adams replied simply that he loathed Beethoven; and felt a slight surprise when Mr. Apthorp and the others laughed as though they thought it humor. He saw no humor in it. He supposed that, except musicians, every one thought Beethoven a bore, as every one except mathematicians thought mathematics a bore. Sitting thus at his beer-table, mentally impassive, he was one day surprised to notice that his mind followed the movement of a Sinfonie. He could not have been more astonished had he suddenly read a new language. Among the marvels of education, this was the most marvellous. A prison-wall that barred his senses on one great side of life, suddenly fell, of its own accord, without so much as his knowing when it happened. Amid the fumes of coarse tobacco and poor beer, surrounded by the commonest of German Haus-frauen, a new sense burst out like a flower in his life, so superior to the old senses, so bewildering, so astonished at its own existence, that he could not credit it, and watched it as something apart, accidental, and not to be trusted. He slowly came to admit that Beethoven had partly become intelligible to him, but he was the more inclined to think that Beethoven must be much overrated as a musician, to be so easily followed. This could not be called education, for he had never so much as listened to the music. He had been thinking of other things. Mere mechanical repetition of certain sounds had stuck to his unconscious mind. Beethoven might have this power, but not Wagner, or at all events not the Wagner later than "Tannhauser." Near forty years passed before he reached the "Gotterdammerung."

One might talk of the revival of an atrophied sense -- the mechanical reaction of a sleeping consciousness -- but no other sense awoke. His sense of line and color remained as dull as ever, and as far as ever below the level of an artist. His metaphysical sense did not spring into life, so that his mind could leap the bars of German expression into sympathy with the idealities of Kant and Hegel. Although he insisted that his faith in German thought and literature was exalted, he failed to approach German thought, and he shed never a tear of emotion over the pages of Goethe and Schiller. When his father rashly ventured from time to time to write him a word of common sense, the young man would listen to no sense at all, but insisted that Berlin was the best of educations in the best of Germanies; yet, when, at last, April came, and some genius suggested a tramp in Thuringen, his heart sang like a bird; he realized what a nightmare he had suffered, and he made up his mind that, wherever else he might, in the infinities of space and time, seek for education, it should not be again in Berlin.

Chapter VI. Rome (1859-1860)

THE tramp in Thuringen lasted four-and-twenty hours. By the end of the first walk, his three companions -- John Bancroft, James J. Higginson, and B. W. Crowninshield, all Boston and Harvard College like himself -- were satisfied with what they had seen, and when they sat down to rest on the spot where Goethe had written --

"Warte nur! balde

Rubest du auch!" --

the profoundness of the thought and the wisdom of the advice affected them so strongly that they hired a wagon and drove to Weimar the same night. They were all quite happy and lighthearted in the first fresh breath of leafless spring, and the beer was better than at Berlin, but they were all equally in doubt why they had come to Germany, and not one of them could say why they stayed. Adams stayed because he did not want to go home, and he had fears that his father's patience might be exhausted if he asked to waste time elsewhere.

They could not think that their education required a return to Berlin. A few days at Dresden in the spring weather satisfied them that Dresden was a better spot for general education than Berlin, and equally good for reading Civil Law. They were possibly right. There was nothing to study in Dresden, and no education to be gained, but the Sistine Madonna and the Correggios were famous; the theatre and opera were sometimes excellent, and the Elbe was prettier than the Spree. They could always fall back on the language. So he took a room in the household of the usual small government clerk with the usual plain daughters, and continued the study of the language. Possibly one might learn something more by accident, as one had learned something of Beethoven. For the next eighteen months the young man pursued accidental education, since he could pursue no other; and by great good fortune, Europe and America were too busy with their own affairs to give much attention to his. Accidental education had every chance in its favor, especially because nothing came amiss.

Perhaps the chief obstacle to the youth's education, now that he had come of age, was his honesty; his simple-minded faith in his intentions. Even after Berlin had become a nightmare, he still persuaded himself that his German education was a success. He loved, or thought he loved the people, but the Germany he loved was the eighteenth-century which the Germans were ashamed of, and were destroying as fast as they could. Of the Germany to come, he knew nothing. Military Germany was his abhorrence. What he liked was the simple character; the good-natured sentiment; the musical and metaphysical abstraction; the blundering incapacity of the German for practical affairs. At that time everyone looked on Germany as incapable of competing with France, England or America in any sort of organized energy. Germany had no confidence in herself, and no reason to feel it. She had no unity, and no reason to want it. She never had unity. Her religious and social history, her economical interests, her military geography, her political convenience, had always tended to eccentric rather than concentric motion. Until coal-power and railways were created, she was mediaeval by nature and geography, and this was what Adams, under the teachings of Carlyle and Lowell, liked.

He was in a fair way to do himself lasting harm, floundering between worlds passed and worlds coming, which had a habit of crushing men who stayed too long at the points of contact. Suddenly the Emperor Napoleon declared war on Austria and raised a confused point of morals in the mind of Europe. France was the nightmare of Germany, and even at Dresden one looked on the return of Napoleon to Leipsic as the most likely thing in the world. One morning the government clerk, in whose family Adams was staying, rushed into his room to consult a map in order that he might measure the distance from Milan to Dresden. The third Napoleon had reached Lombardy, and only fifty or sixty years had passed since the first Napoleon had begun his military successes from an Italian base.

An enlightened young American, with eighteenth-century tastes capped by fragments of a German education and the most excellent intentions, had to make up his mind about the moral value of these conflicting forces. France was the wicked spirit of moral politics, and whatever helped France must be so far evil. At that time Austria was another evil spirit. Italy was the prize they disputed, and for at least fifteen hundred years had been the chief object of their greed. The question of sympathy had disturbed a number of persons during that period. The question of morals had been put in a number of cross-lights. Should one be Guelph or Ghibelline? No doubt, one was wiser than one's neighbors who had found no way of settling this question since the days of the cave-dwellers, but ignorance did better to discard the attempt to be wise, for wisdom had been singularly baffled by the problem. Better take sides first, and reason about it for the rest of life.

Not that Adams felt any real doubt about his sympathies or wishes. He had not been German long enough for befogging his mind to that point, but the moment was decisive for much to come, especially for political morals. His morals were the highest, and he clung to them to preserve his self-respect; but steam and electricity had brought about new political and social concentrations, or were making them necessary in the line of his moral principles -- freedom, education, economic development and so forth -- which required association with allies as doubtful as Napoleon III, and robberies with violence on a very extensive scale. As long as he could argue that his opponents were wicked, he could join in robbing and killing them without a qualm; but it might happen that the good were robbed. Education insisted on finding a moral foundation for robbery. He could hope to begin life in the character of no animal more moral than a monkey unless he could satisfy himself when and why robbery and murder were a virtue and duty. Education founded on mere self-interest was merely Guelph and Ghibelline over again -- Machiavelli translated into American.

Luckily for him he had a sister much brighter than he ever was -- though he thought himself a rather superior person -- who after marrying Charles Kuhn, of Philadelphia, had come to Italy, and, like all good Americans and English, was hotly Italian. In July, 1859, she was at Thun in Switzerland, and there Henry Adams joined them. Women have, commonly, a very positive moral sense; that which they will, is right; that which they reject, is wrong; and their will, in most cases, ends by settling the moral. Mrs. Kuhn had a double superiority. She not only adored Italy, but she cordially disliked Germany in all its varieties. She saw no gain in helping her brother to be Germanized, and she wanted him much to be civilized. She was the first young woman he was ever intimate with -- quick, sensitive, wilful, or full of will, energetic, sympathetic and intelligent enough to supply a score of men with ideas -- and he was delighted to give her the reins -- to let her drive him where she would. It was his first experiment in giving the reins to a woman, and he was so much pleased with the results that he never wanted to take them back. In after life he made a general law of experience -- no woman had ever driven him wrong; no man had ever driven him right.

Nothing would satisfy Mrs. Kuhn but to go to the seat of war as soon as the armistice was declared. Wild as the idea seemed, nothing was easier. The party crossed the St. Gothard and reached Milan, picturesque with every sort of uniform and every sign of war. To young Adams this first plunge into Italy passed Beethoven as a piece of accidental education. Like music, it differed from other education in being, not a means of pursuing life, but one of the ends attained. Further, on these lines, one could not go. It had but one defect -- that of attainment. Life had no richer impression to give; it offers barely half-a-dozen such, and the intervals seem long. Exactly what they teach would puzzle a Berlin jurist; yet they seem to have an economic value, since most people would decline to part with even their faded memories except at a valuation ridiculously extravagant. They were also what men pay most for; but one's ideas become hopelessly mixed in trying to reduce such forms of education to a standard of exchangeable value, and, as in political economy, one had best disregard altogether what cannot be stated in equivalents. The proper equivalent of pleasure is pain, which is also a form of education.

Not satisfied with Milan, Mrs. Kuhn insisted on invading the enemy's country, and the carriage was chartered for Innsbruck by way of the Stelvio Pass. The Valtellina, as the carriage drove up it, showed war. Garibaldi's Cacciatori were the only visible inhabitants. No one could say whether the pass was open, but in any case no carriage had yet crossed. At the inns the handsome young officers in command of the detachments were delighted to accept invitations to dinner and to talk all the evening of their battles to the charming patriot who sparkled with interest and flattery, but not one of them knew whether their enemies, the abhorred Austrian Jagers, would let the travellers through their lines. As a rule, gaiety was not the character failing in any party that Mrs. Kuhn belonged to, but when at last, after climbing what was said to be the finest carriage-pass in Europe, the carriage turned the last shoulder, where the glacier of the Ortler Spitze tumbled its huge mass down upon the road, even Mrs. Kuhn gasped when she was driven directly up to the barricade and stopped by the double line of sentries stretching on either side up the mountains, till the flash of the gun barrels was lost in the flash of the snow. For accidental education the picture had its value. The earliest of these pictures count for most, as first impressions must, and Adams never afterwards cared much for landscape education, except perhaps in the tropics for the sake of the contrast. As education, that chapter, too, was read, and set aside.

The handsome blond officers of the Jagers were not to be beaten in courtesy by the handsome young olive-toned officers of the Cacciatori. The eternal woman as usual, when she is young, pretty, and engaging, had her way, and the barricade offered no resistance. In fifteen minutes the carriage was rolling down to Mals, swarming with German soldiers and German fleas, worse than the Italian; and German language, thought, and atmosphere, of which young Adams, thanks to his glimpse of Italy, never again felt quite the old confident charm.

Yet he could talk to his cabman and conscientiously did his cathedrals, his Rhine, and whatever his companions suggested. Faithful to his self-contracted scheme of passing two winters in study of the Civil Law, he went back to Dresden with a letter to the Frau Hofrathin von Reichenbach, in whose house Lowell and other Americans had pursued studies more or less serious. In those days, "The Initials" was a new book. The charm which its clever author had laboriously woven over Munich gave also a certain reflected light to Dresden. Young Adams had nothing to do but take fencing-lessons, visit the galleries and go to the theatre; but his social failure in the line of "The Initials," was humiliating and he succumbed to it. The Frau Hofrathin herself was sometimes roused to huge laughter at the total discomfiture and helplessness of the young American in the face of her society. Possibly an education may be the wider and the richer for a large experience of the world; Raphael Pumpelly and Clarence King, at about the same time, were enriching their education by a picturesque intimacy with the manners of the Apaches and Digger Indians. All experience is an arch, to build upon. Yet Adams admitted himself unable to guess what use his second winter in Germany was to him, or what he expected it to be. Even the doctrine of accidental education broke down. There were no accidents in Dresden. As soon as the winter was over, he closed and locked the German door with a long breath of relief, and took the road to Italy. He had then pursued his education, as it pleased him, for eighteen months, and in spite of the infinite variety of new impressions which had packed themselves into his mind, he knew no more, for his practical purposes, than the day he graduated. He had made no step towards a profession. He was as ignorant as a schoolboy of society. He was unfit for any career in Europe, and unfitted for any career in America, and he had not natural intelligence enough to see what a mess he had thus far made of his education.

By twisting life to follow accidental and devious paths, one might perhaps find some use for accidental and devious knowledge, but this had been no part of Henry Adams's plan when he chose the path most admired by the best judges, and followed it till he found it led nowhere. Nothing had been further from his mind when he started in November, 1858, than to become a tourist, but a mere tourist, and nothing else, he had become in April, 1860, when he joined his sister in Florence. His father had been in the right. The young man felt a little sore about it. Supposing his father asked him, on his return, what equivalent he had brought back for the time and money put into his experiment! The only possible answer would be: "Sir, I am a tourist! "

The answer was not what he had meant it to be, and he was not likely to better it by asking his father, in turn, what equivalent his brothers or cousins or friends at home had got out of the same time and money spent in Boston. All they had put into the law was certainly thrown away, but were they happier in science? In theory one might say, with some show of proof, that a pure, scientific education was alone correct; yet many of his friends who took it, found reason to complain that it was anything but a pure, scientific world in which they lived.

Meanwhile his father had quite enough perplexities of his own, without seeking more in his son's errors. His Quincy district had sent him to Congress, and in the spring of 1860 he was in the full confusion of nominating candidates for the Presidential election in November. He supported Mr. Seward. The Republican Party was an unknown force, and the Democratic Party was torn to pieces. No one could see far into the future. Fathers could blunder as well as sons, and, in 1860, every one was conscious of being dragged along paths much less secure than those of the European tourist. For the time, the young man was safe from interference, and went on his way with a light heart to take whatever chance fragments of education God or the devil was pleased to give him, for he knew no longer the good from the bad.

He had of both sorts more than he knew how to use. Perhaps the most useful purpose he set himself to serve was that of his pen, for he wrote long letters, during the next three months, to his brother Charles, which his brother caused to be printed in the Boston Courier; and the exercise was good for him. He had little to say, and said it not very well, but that mattered less. The habit of expression leads to the search for something to express. Something remains as a residuum of the commonplace itself, if one strikes out every commonplace in the expression. Young men as a rule saw little in Italy, or anywhere else, and in after life when Adams began to learn what some men could see, he shrank into corners of shame at the thought that he should have betrayed his own inferiority as though it were his pride, while he invited his neighbors to measure and admire; but it was still the nearest approach he had yet made to an intelligent act.

For the rest, Italy was mostly an emotion and the emotion naturally centred in Rome. The American parent, curiously enough, while bitterly hostile to Paris, seemed rather disposed to accept Rome as legitimate education, though abused; but to young men seeking education in a serious spirit, taking for granted that everything had a cause, and that nature tended to an end, Rome was altogether the most violent vice in the world, and Rome before 1870 was seductive beyond resistance. The month of May, 1860, was divine. No doubt other young men, and occasionally young women, have passed the month of May in Rome since then, and conceive that the charm continues to exist. Possibly it does -- in them -- but in 1860 the lights and shadows were still mediaeval, and mediaeval Rome was alive; the shadows breathed and glowed, full of soft forms felt by lost senses. No sand-blast of science had yet skinned off the epidermis of history, thought, and feeling. The pictures were uncleaned, the churches unrestored, the ruins unexcavated. Mediaeval Rome was sorcery. Rome was the worst spot on earth to teach nineteenth-century youth what to do with a twentieth-century world. One's emotions in Rome were one's private affair, like one's glass of absinthe before dinner in the Palais Royal; they must be hurtful, else they could not have been so intense; and they were surely immoral, for no one, priest or politician, could honestly read in the ruins of Rome any other certain lesson than that they were evidence of the just judgments of an outraged God against all the doings of man. This moral unfitted young men for every sort of useful activity; it made Rome a gospel of anarchy and vice; the last place under the sun for educating the young; yet it was, by common consent, the only spot that the young -- of either sex and every race -- passionately, perversely, wickedly loved.

Boys never see a conclusion; only on the edge of the grave can man conclude anything; but the first impulse given to the boy is apt to lead or drive him for the rest of his life into conclusion after conclusion that he never dreamed of reaching. One looked idly enough at the Forum or at St. Peter's, but one never forgot the look, and it never ceased reacting. To a young Bostonian, fresh from Germany, Rome seemed a pure emotion, quite free from economic or actual values, and he could not in reason or common sense foresee that it was mechanically piling up conundrum after conundrum in his educational path, which seemed unconnected but that he had got to connect; that seemed insoluble but had got to be somehow solved. Rome was not a beetle to be dissected and dropped; not a bad French novel to be read in a railway train and thrown out of the window after other bad French novels, the morals of which could never approach the immorality of Roman history. Rome was actual; it was England; it was going to be America. Rome could not be fitted into an orderly, middle-class, Bostonian, systematic scheme of evolution. No law of progress applied to it. Not even time-sequences -- the last refuge of helpless historians -- had value for it. The Forum no more led to the Vatican than the Vatican to the Forum. Rienzi, Garibaldi, Tiberius Gracchus, Aurelian might be mixed up in any relation of time, along with a thousand more, and never lead to a sequence. The great word Evolution had not yet, in 1860, made a new religion of history, but the old religion had preached the same doctrine for a thousand years without finding in the entire history of Rome anything but flat contradiction.

Of course both priests and evolutionists bitterly denied this heresy, but what they affirmed or denied in 1860 had very little importance indeed for 1960. Anarchy lost no ground meanwhile. The problem became only the more fascinating. Probably it was more vital in May, 1860, than it had been in October, 1764, when the idea of writing the Decline and Fall of the city first started to the mind of Gibbon, "in the close of the evening, as I sat musing in the Church of the Zoccolanti or Franciscan Friars, while they were singing Vespers in the Temple of Jupiter, on the ruins of the Capitol." Murray's Handbook had the grace to quote this passage from Gibbon's "Autobiography," which led Adams more than once to sit at sunset on the steps of the Church of Santa Maria di Ara Coeli, curiously wondering that not an inch had been gained by Gibbon -- or all the historians since -- towards explaining the Fall. The mystery remained unsolved; the charm remained intact. Two great experiments of Western civilization had left there the chief monuments of their failure, and nothing proved that the city might not still survive to express the failure of a third.

The young man had no idea what he was doing. The thought of posing for a Gibbon never entered his mind. He was a tourist, even to the depths of his sub-consciousness, and it was well for him that he should be nothing else, for even the greatest of men cannot sit with dignity, "in the close of evening, among the ruins of the Capitol," unless they have something quite original to say about it. Tacitus could do it; so could Michael Angelo; and so, at a pinch, could Gibbon, though in figure hardly heroic; but, in sum, none of them could say very much more than the tourist, who went on repeating to himself the eternal question: -- Why! Why!! Why!!! -- as his neighbor, the blind beggar, might do, sitting next him, on the church steps. No one ever had answered the question to the satisfaction of any one else; yet every one who had either head or heart, felt that sooner or later he must make up his mind what answer to accept. Substitute the word America for the word Rome, and the question became personal.

Perhaps Henry learned something in Rome, though he never knew it, and never sought it. Rome dwarfs teachers. The greatest men of the age scarcely bore the test of posing with Rome for a background. Perhaps Garibaldi -- possibly even Cavour -- could have sat "in the close of the evening, among the ruins of the Capitol," but one hardly saw Napoleon III there, or Palmerston or Tennyson or Longfellow. One morning, Adams happened to be chatting in the studio of Hamilton Wilde, when a middle-aged Englishman came in, evidently excited, and told of the shock he had just received, when riding near the Circus Maximus, at coming unexpectedly on the guillotine, where some criminal had been put to death an hour or two before. The sudden surprise had quite overcome him; and Adams, who seldom saw the point of a story till time had blunted it, listened sympathetically to learn what new form of grim horror had for the moment wiped out the memory of two thousand years of Roman bloodshed, or the consolation, derived from history and statistics, that most citizens of Rome seemed to be the better for guillotining. Only by slow degrees, he grappled the conviction that the victim of the shock was Robert Browning; and, on the background of the Circus Maximus, the Christian martyrs flaming as torches, and the morning's murderer on the block, Browning seemed rather in place, as a middle-aged gentlemanly English Pippa Passes; while afterwards, in the light of Belgravia dinner-tables, he never made part of his background except by effacement. Browning might have sat with Gibbon, among the ruins, and few Romans would have smiled.

Yet Browning never revealed the poetic depths of Saint Francis; William Story could not touch the secret of Michael Angelo, and Mommsen hardly said all that one felt by instinct in the lives of Cicero and Caesar. They taught what, as a rule, needed no teaching, the lessons of a rather cheap imagination and cheaper politics. Rome was a bewildering complex of ideas, experiments, ambitions, energies; without her, the Western world was pointless and fragmentary; she gave heart and unity to it all; yet Gibbon might have gone on for the whole century, sitting among the ruins of the Capitol, and no one would have passed, capable of telling him what it meant. Perhaps it meant nothing.

So it ended; the happiest month of May that life had yet offered, fading behind the present, and probably beyond the past, somewhere into abstract time, grotesquely out of place with the Berlin scheme or a Boston future. Adams explained to himself that he was absorbing knowledge. He would have put it better had he said that knowledge was absorbing him. He was passive. In spite of swarming impressions he knew no more when he left Rome than he did when he entered it. As a marketable object, his value was less. His next step went far to convince him that accidental education, whatever its economical return might be, was prodigiously successful as an object in itself. Everything conspired to ruin his sound scheme of life, and to make him a vagrant as well as pauper. He went on to Naples, and there, in the hot June, heard rumors that Garibaldi and his thousand were about to attack Palermo. Calling on the American Minister, Chandler of Pennsylvania, he was kindly treated, not for his merit, but for his name, and Mr. Chandler amiably consented to send him to the seat of war as bearer of despatches to Captain Palmer of the American sloop of war Iroquois. Young Adams seized the chance, and went to Palermo in a government transport filled with fleas, commanded by a charming Prince Caracciolo.

He told all about it to the Boston Courier; where the narrative probably exists to this day, unless the files of the Courier have wholly perished; but of its bearing on education the Courier did not speak. He himself would have much liked to know whether it had any bearing whatever, and what was its value as a post-graduate course. Quite apart from its value as life attained, realized, capitalized, it had also a certain value as a lesson in something, though Adams could never classify the branch of study. Loosely, the tourist called it knowledge of men, but it was just the reverse; it was knowledge of one's ignorance of men. Captain Palmer of the Iroquois, who was a friend of the young man's uncle, Sydney Brooks, took him with the officers of the ship to make an evening call on Garibaldi, whom they found in the Senate House towards sunset, at supper with his picturesque and piratic staff, in the full noise and color of the Palermo revolution. As a spectacle, it belonged to Rossini and the Italian opera, or to Alexandre Dumas at the least, but the spectacle was not its educational side. Garibaldi left the table, and, sitting down at the window, had a few words of talk with Captain Palmer and young Adams. At that moment, in the summer of 1860, Garibaldi was certainly the most serious of the doubtful energies in the world; the most essential to gauge rightly. Even then society was dividing between banker and anarchist. One or the other, Garibaldi must serve. Himself a typical anarchist, sure to overshadow Europe and alarm empires bigger than Naples, his success depended on his mind; his energy was beyond doubt.

Adams had the chance to look this sphinx in the eyes, and, for five minutes, to watch him like a wild animal, at the moment of his greatest achievement and most splendid action. One saw a quiet-featured, quiet-voiced man in a red flannel shirt; absolutely impervious; a type of which Adams knew nothing. Sympathetic it was, and one felt that it was simple; one suspected even that it might be childlike, but could form no guess of its intelligence. In his own eyes Garibaldi might be a Napoleon or a Spartacus; in the hands of Cavour he might become a Condottiere; in the eyes of history he might, like the rest of the world, be only the vigorous player in the game he did not understand. The student was none the wiser.

This compound nature of patriot and pirate had illumined Italian history from the beginning, and was no more intelligible to itself than to a young American who had no experience in double natures. In the end, if the "Autobiography" tells truth, Garibaldi saw and said that he had not understood his own acts; that he had been an instrument; that he had served the purposes of the class he least wanted to help; yet in 1860 he thought himself the revolution anarchic, Napoleonic, and his ambition was unbounded. What should a young Bostonian have made of a character like this, internally alive with childlike fancies, and externally quiet, simple, almost innocent; uttering with apparent conviction the usual commonplaces of popular politics that all politicians use as the small change of their intercourse with the public; but never betraying a thought?

Precisely this class of mind was to be the toughest problem of Adams's practical life, but he could never make anything of it. The lesson of Garibaldi, as education, seemed to teach the extreme complexity of extreme simplicity; but one could have learned this from a glow-worm. One did not need the vivid recollection of the low-voiced, simple-mannered, seafaring captain of Genoese adventurers and Sicilian brigands, supping in the July heat and Sicilian dirt and revolutionary clamor, among the barricaded streets of insurgent Palermo, merely in order to remember that simplicity is complex.

Adams left the problem as he found it, and came north to stumble over others, less picturesque but nearer. He squandered two or three months on Paris. From the first he had avoided Paris, and had wanted no French influence in his education. He disapproved of France in the lump. A certain knowledge of the language one must have; enough to order dinner and buy a theatre ticket; but more he did not seek. He disliked the Empire and the Emperor particularly, but this was a trifle; he disliked most the French mind. To save himself the trouble of drawing up a long list of all that he disliked, he disapproved of the whole, once for all, and shut them figuratively out of his life. France was not serious, and he was not serious in going there.

He did this in good faith, obeying the lessons his teachers had taught him; but the curious result followed that, being in no way responsible for the French and sincerely disapproving them, he felt quite at liberty to enjoy to the full everything he disapproved. Stated thus crudely, the idea sounds derisive; but, as a matter of fact, several thousand Americans passed much of their time there on this understanding. They sought to take share in every function that was open to approach, as they sought tickets to the opera, because they were not a part of it. Adams did like the rest. All thought of serious education had long vanished. He tried to acquire a few French idioms, without even aspiring to master a subjunctive, but he succeeded better in acquiring a modest taste for Bordeaux and Burgundy and one or two sauces; for the Trois Freres Provencaux and Voisin's and Philippe's and the Cafe Anglais; for the Palais Royal Theatre, and the Varietes and the Gymnase; for the Brohans and Bressant, Rose Cheri and Gil Perez, and other lights of the stage. His friends were good to him. Life was amusing. Paris rapidly became familiar. In a month or six weeks he forgot even to disapprove of it; but he studied nothing, entered no society, and made no acquaintance. Accidental education went far in Paris, and one picked up a deal of knowledge that might become useful; perhaps, after all, the three months passed there might serve better purpose than the twenty-one months passed elsewhere; but he did not intend it -- did not think it -- and looked at it as a momentary and frivolous vacation before going home to fit himself for life. Therewith, after staying as long as he could and spending all the money he dared, he started with mixed emotions but no education, for home.

Chapter VII. Treason (1860-1861)

WHEN, forty years afterwards, Henry Adams looked back over his adventures in search of knowledge, he asked himself whether fortune or fate had ever dealt its cards quite so wildly to any of his known antecessors as when it led him to begin the study of law and to vote for Abraham Lincoln on the same day.

He dropped back on Quincy like a lump of lead; he rebounded like a football, tossed into space by an unknown energy which played with all his generation as a cat plays with mice. The simile is none too strong. Not one man in America wanted the Civil War, or expected or intended it. A small minority wanted secession. The vast majority wanted to go on with their occupations in peace. Not one, however clever or learned, guessed what happened. Possibly a few Southern loyalists in despair might dream it as an impossible chance; but none planned it.

As for Henry Adams, fresh from Europe and chaos of another sort, he plunged at once into a lurid atmosphere of politics, quite heedless of any education or forethought. His past melted away. The prodigal was welcomed home, but not even his father asked a malicious question about the Pandects. At the utmost, he hinted at some shade of prodigality by quietly inviting his son to act as private secretary during the winter in Washington, as though any young man who could afford to throw away two winters on the Civil Law could afford to read Blackstone for another winter without a master. The young man was beyond satire, and asked only a pretext for throwing all education to the east wind. November at best is sad, and November at Quincy had been from earliest childhood the least gay of seasons. Nowhere else does the uncharitable autumn wreak its spite so harshly on the frail wreck of the grasshopper summer; yet even a Quincy November seemed temperate before the chill of a Boston January.

This was saying much, for the November of 1860 at Quincy stood apart from other memories as lurid beyond description. Although no one believed in civil war, the air reeked of it, and the Republicans organized their clubs and parades as Wide-Awakes in a form military in all things except weapons. Henry reached home in time to see the last of these processions, stretching in ranks of torches along the hillside, file down through the November night; to the Old House, where Mr. Adams, their Member of Congress, received them, and, let them pretend what they liked, their air was not that of innocence.

Profoundly ignorant, anxious, and curious, the young man packed his modest trunk again, which had not yet time to be unpacked, and started for Washington with his family. Ten years had passed since his last visit, but very little had changed. As in 1800 and 1850, so in 1860, the same rude colony was camped in the same forest, with the same unfinished Greek temples for work rooms, and sloughs for roads. The Government had an air of social instability and incompleteness that went far to support the right of secession in theory as in fact; but right or wrong, secession was likely to be easy where there was so little to secede from. The Union was a sentiment, but not much more, and in December, 1860, the sentiment about the Capitol was chiefly hostile, so far as it made itself felt. John Adams was better off in Philadelphia in 1776 than his great-grandson Henry in 1860 in Washington.

Patriotism ended by throwing a halo over the Continental Congress, but over the close of the Thirty-sixth Congress in 1860-61, no halo could be thrown by any one who saw it. Of all the crowd swarming in Washington that winter, young Adams was surely among the most ignorant and helpless, but he saw plainly that the knowledge possessed by everybody about him was hardly greater than his own. Never in a long life did he seek to master a lesson so obscure. Mr. Sumner was given to saying after Oxenstiern: "Quantula sapientia mundus regitur!" Oxenstiern talked of a world that wanted wisdom; but Adams found himself seeking education in a world that seemed to him both unwise and ignorant. The Southern secessionists were certainly unbalanced in mind -- fit for medical treatment, like other victims of hallucination -- haunted by suspicion, by idees fixes, by violent morbid excitement; but this was not all. They were stupendously ignorant of the world. As a class, the cotton-planters were mentally one-sided, ill-balanced, and provincial to a degree rarely known. They were a close society on whom the new fountains of power had poured a stream of wealth and slaves that acted like oil on flame. They showed a young student his first object-lesson of the way in which excess of power worked when held by inadequate hands.

This might be a commonplace of 1900, but in 1860 it was paradox. The Southern statesmen were regarded as standards of statesmanship, and such standards barred education. Charles Sumner's chief offence was his insistence on Southern ignorance, and he stood a living proof of it. To this school, Henry Adams had come for a new education, and the school was seriously, honestly, taken by most of the world, including Europe, as proper for the purpose, although the Sioux Indians would have taught less mischief. From such contradictions among intelligent people, what was a young man to learn?

He could learn nothing but cross-purpose. The old and typical Southern gentleman developed as cotton-planter had nothing to teach or to give, except warning. Even as example to be avoided, he was too glaring in his defiance of reason, to help the education of a reasonable being. No one learned a useful lesson from the Confederate school except to keep away from it. Thus, at one sweep, the whole field of instruction south of the Potomac was shut off; it was overshadowed by the cotton planters, from whom one could learn nothing but bad temper, bad manners, poker, and treason.

Perforce, the student was thrown back on Northern precept and example; first of all, on his New England surroundings. Republican houses were few in Washington, and Mr. and Mrs. Adams aimed to create a social centre for New Englanders. They took a house on I Street, looking over Pennsylvania Avenue, well out towards Georgetown -- the Markoe house -- and there the private secretary began to learn his social duties, for the political were confined to committee-rooms and lobbies of the Capitol. He had little to do, and knew not how to do it rightly, but he knew of no one who knew more.

The Southern type was one to be avoided; the New England type was one's self. It had nothing to show except one's own features. Setting aside Charles Sumner, who stood quite alone and was the boy's oldest friend, all the New Englanders were sane and steady men, well-balanced, educated, and free from meanness or intrigue -- men whom one liked to act with, and who, whether graduates or not, bore the stamp of Harvard College. Anson Burlingame was one exception, and perhaps Israel Washburn another; but as a rule the New Englander's strength was his poise which almost amounted to a defect. He offered no more target for love than for hate; he attracted as little as he repelled; even as a machine, his motion seemed never accelerated. The character, with its force or feebleness, was familiar; one knew it to the core; one was it -- had been run in the same mould.

There remained the Central and Western States, but there the choice of teachers was not large and in the end narrowed itself to Preston King, Henry Winter Davis, Owen Lovejoy, and a few other men born with social faculty. Adams took most kindly to Henry J. Raymond, who came to view the field for the New York Times, and who was a man of the world. The average Congressman was civil enough, but had nothing to ask except offices, and nothing to offer but the views of his district. The average Senator was more reserved, but had not much more to say, being always excepting one or two genial natures, handicapped by his own importance.

Study it as one might, the hope of education, till the arrival of the President-elect, narrowed itself to the possible influence of only two men -- Sumner and Seward.

Sumner was then fifty years old. Since his election as Senator in 1851 he had passed beyond the reach of his boy friend, and, after his Brooks injuries, his nervous system never quite recovered its tone; but perhaps eight or ten years of solitary existence as Senator had most to do with his development. No man, however strong, can serve ten years as schoolmaster, priest, or Senator, and remain fit for anything else. All the dogmatic stations in life have the effect of fixing a certain stiffness of attitude forever, as though they mesmerized the subject. Yet even among Senators there were degrees in dogmatism, from the frank South Carolinian brutality, to that of Webster, Benton, Clay, or Sumner himself, until in extreme cases, like Conkling, it became Shakespearian and bouffe -- as Godkin used to call it -- like Malvolio. Sumner had become dogmatic like the rest, but he had at least the merit of qualities that warranted dogmatism. He justly thought, as Webster had thought before him, that his great services and sacrifices, his superiority in education, his oratorical power, his political experience, his representative character at the head of the whole New England contingent, and, above all, his knowledge of the world, made him the most important member of the Senate; and no Senator had ever saturated himself more thoroughly with the spirit and temper of the body.

Although the Senate is much given to admiring in its members a superiority less obvious or quite invisible to outsiders, one Senator seldom proclaims his own inferiority to another, and still more seldom likes to be told of it. Even the greatest Senators seemed to inspire little personal affection in each other, and betrayed none at all. Sumner had a number of rivals who held his judgment in no high esteem, and one of these was Senator Seward. The two men would have disliked each other by instinct had they lived in different planets. Each was created only for exasperating the other; the virtues of one were the faults of his rival, until no good quality seemed to remain of either. That the public service must suffer was certain, but what were the sufferings of the public service compared with the risks run by a young mosquito -- a private secretary -- trying to buzz admiration in the ears of each, and unaware that each would impatiently slap at him for belonging to the other? Innocent and unsuspicious beyond what was permitted even in a nursery, the private secretary courted both.

Private secretaries are servants of a rather low order, whose business is to serve sources of power. The first news of a professional kind, imparted to private secretary Adams on reaching Washington, was that the President-elect, Abraham Lincoln, had selected Mr. Seward for his Secretary of State, and that Seward was to be the medium for communicating his wishes to his followers. Every young man naturally accepted the wishes of Mr. Lincoln as orders, the more because he could see that the new President was likely to need all the help that several million young men would be able to give, if they counted on having any President at all to serve. Naturally one waited impatiently for the first meeting with the new Secretary of State.

Governor Seward was an old friend of the family. He professed to be a disciple and follower of John Quincy Adams. He had been Senator since 1849, when his responsibilities as leader had separated him from the Free Soil contingent, for, in the dry light of the first Free Soil faith, the ways of New York politics Thurlow Weed had not won favor; but the fierce heat which welded the Republican Party in 1856 melted many such barriers, and when Mr. Adams came to Congress in December, 1859, Governor Seward instantly renewed his attitude of family friend, became a daily intimate in the household, and lost no chance of forcing his fresh ally to the front.

A few days after their arrival in December, 1860, the Governor, as he was always called, came to dinner, alone, as one of the family, and the private secretary had the chance he wanted to watch him as carefully as one generally watches men who dispose of one's future. A slouching, slender figure; a head like a wise macaw; a beaked nose; shaggy eyebrows; unorderly hair and clothes; hoarse voice; offhand manner; free talk, and perpetual cigar, offered a new type -- of western New York -- to fathom; a type in one way simple because it was only double -- political and personal; but complex because the political had become nature, and no one could tell which was the mask and which the features. At table, among friends, Mr. Seward threw off restraint, or seemed to throw it off, in reality, while in the world he threw it off, like a politician, for effect. In both cases he chose to appear as a free talker, who loathed pomposity and enjoyed a joke; but how much was nature and how much was mask, he was himself too simple a nature to know. Underneath the surface he was conventional after the conventions of western New York and Albany. Politicians thought it unconventionality. Bostonians thought it provincial. Henry Adams thought it charming. From the first sight, he loved the Governor, who, though sixty years old, had the youth of his sympathies. He noticed that Mr. Seward was never petty or personal; his talk was large; he generalized; he never seemed to pose for statesmanship; he did not require an attitude of prayer. What was more unusual -- almost singular and quite eccentric -- he had some means, unknown to other Senators, of producing the effect of unselfishness.

Superficially Mr. Seward and Mr. Adams were contrasts; essentially they were much alike. Mr. Adams was taken to be rigid, but the Puritan character in all its forms could be supple enough when it chose; and in Massachusetts all the Adamses had been attacked in succession as no better than political mercenaries. Mr. Hildreth, in his standard history, went so far as to echo with approval the charge that treachery was hereditary in the family. Any Adams had at least to be thick-skinned, hardened to every contradictory epithet that virtue could supply, and, on the whole, armed to return such attentions; but all must have admitted that they had invariably subordinated local to national interests, and would continue to do so, whenever forced to choose. C. F. Adams was sure to do what his father had done, as his father had followed the steps of John Adams, and no doubt thereby earned his epithets.

The inevitable followed, as a child fresh from the nursery should have had the instinct to foresee, but the young man on the edge of life never dreamed. What motives or emotions drove his masters on their various paths he made no pretence of guessing; even at that age he preferred to admit his dislike for guessing motives; he knew only his own infantile ignorance, before which he stood amazed, and his innocent good-faith, always matter of simple-minded surprise. Critics who know ultimate truth will pronounce judgment on history; all that Henry Adams ever saw in man was a reflection of his own ignorance, and he never saw quite so much of it as in the winter of 1860-61. Every one knows the story; every one draws what conclusion suits his temper, and the conclusion matters now less than though it concerned the merits of Adam and Eve in the Garden of Eden; but in 1861 the conclusion made the sharpest lesson of life; it was condensed and concentrated education.

Rightly or wrongly the new President and his chief advisers in Washington decided that, before they could administer the Government, they must make sure of a government to administer, and that this chance depended on the action of Virginia. The whole ascendancy of the winter wavered between the effort of the cotton States to drag Virginia out, and the effort of the new President to keep Virginia in. Governor Seward representing the Administration in the Senate took the lead; Mr. Adams took the lead in the House; and as far as a private secretary knew, the party united on its tactics. In offering concessions to the border States, they had to run the risk, or incur the certainty, of dividing their own party, and they took this risk with open eyes. As Seward himself, in his gruff way, said at dinner, after Mr. Adams and he had made their speeches: "If there's no secession now, you and I are ruined."

They won their game; this was their affair and the affair of the historians who tell their story; their private secretaries had nothing to do with it except to follow their orders. On that side a secretary learned nothing and had nothing to learn. The sudden arrival of Mr. Lincoln in Washington on February 23, and the language of his inaugural address, were the final term of the winter's tactics, and closed the private secretary's interest in the matter forever. Perhaps he felt, even then, a good deal more interest in the appearance of another private secretary, of his own age, a young man named John Hay, who lighted on LaFayette Square at the same moment. Friends are born, not made, and Henry never mistook a friend except when in power. From the first slight meeting in February and March, 1861, he recognized Hay as a friend, and never lost sight of him at the future crossing of their paths; but, for the moment, his own task ended on March 4 when Hay's began. The winter's anxieties were shifted upon new shoulders, and Henry gladly turned back to Blackstone. He had tried to make himself useful, and had exerted energy that seemed to him portentous, acting in secret as newspaper correspondent, cultivating a large acquaintance and even haunting ballrooms where the simple, old-fashioned, Southern tone was pleasant even in the atmosphere of conspiracy and treason. The sum was next to nothing for education, because no one could teach; all were as ignorant as himself; none knew what should be done, or how to do it; all were trying to learn and were more bent on asking than on answering questions. The mass of ignorance in Washington was lighted up by no ray of knowledge. Society, from top to bottom, broke down.

From this law there was no exception, unless, perhaps, that of old General Winfield Scott, who happened to be the only military figure that looked equal to the crisis. No one else either looked it, or was it, or could be it, by nature or training. Had young Adams been told that his life was to hang on the correctness of his estimate of the new President, he would have lost. He saw Mr. Lincoln but once; at the melancholy function called an Inaugural Ball. Of course he looked anxiously for a sign of character. He saw a long, awkward figure; a plain, ploughed face; a mind, absent in part, and in part evidently worried by white kid gloves; features that expressed neither self-satisfaction nor any other familiar Americanism, but rather the same painful sense of becoming educated and of needing education that tormented a private secretary; above all a lack of apparent force. Any private secretary in the least fit for his business would have thought, as Adams did, that no man living needed so much education as the new President but that all the education he could get would not be enough.

As far as a young man of anxious temperament could see, no one in Washington was fitted for his duties; or rather, no duties in March were fitted for the duties in April. The few people who thought they knew something were more in error than those who knew nothing. Education was matter of life and death, but all the education in the world would have helped nothing. Only one man in Adams's reach seemed to him supremely fitted by knowledge and experience to be an adviser and friend. This was Senator Sumner; and there, in fact, the young man's education began; there it ended.

Going over the experience again, long after all the great actors were dead, he struggled to see where he had blundered. In the effort to make acquaintances, he lost friends, but he would have liked much to know whether he could have helped it. He had necessarily followed Seward and his father; he took for granted that his business was obedience, discipline, and silence; he supposed the party to require it, and that the crisis overruled all personal doubts. He was thunderstruck to learn that Senator Sumner privately denounced the course, regarded Mr. Adams as betraying the principles of his life, and broke off relations with his family.

Many a shock was Henry Adams to meet in the course of a long life passed chiefly near politics and politicians, but the profoundest lessons are not the lessons of reason; they are sudden strains that permanently warp the mind. He cared little or nothing about the point in discussion; he was even willing to admit that Sumner might be right, though in all great emergencies he commonly found that every one was more or less wrong; he liked lofty moral principle and cared little for political tactics; he felt a profound respect for Sumner himself; but the shock opened a chasm in life that never closed, and as long as life lasted, he found himself invariably taking for granted, as a political instinct, with out waiting further experiment -- as he took for granted that arsenic poisoned -- the rule that a friend in power is a friend lost.

On his own score, he never admitted the rupture, and never exchanged a word with Mr. Sumner on the subject, then or afterwards, but his education -- for good or bad -- made an enormous stride. One has to deal with all sorts of unexpected morals in life, and, at this moment, he was looking at hundreds of Southern gentlemen who believed themselves singularly honest, but who seemed to him engaged in the plainest breach of faith and the blackest secret conspiracy, yet they did not disturb his education. History told of little else; and not one rebel defection -- not even Robert E. Lee's -- cost young Adams a personal pang; but Sumner's struck home.

This, then, was the result of the new attempt at education, down to March 4, 1861; this was all; and frankly, it seemed to him hardly what he wanted. The picture of Washington in March, 1861, offered education, but not the kind of education that led to good. The process that Matthew Arnold described as wandering between two worlds, one dead, the other powerless to be born, helps nothing. Washington was a dismal school. Even before the traitors had flown, the vultures descended on it in swarms that darkened the ground, and tore the carrion of political patronage into fragments and gobbets of fat and lean, on the very steps of the White House. Not a man there knew what his task was to be, or was fitted for it; every one without exception, Northern or Southern, was to learn his business at the cost of the public. Lincoln, Seward, Sumner, and the rest, could give no help to the young man seeking education; they knew less than he; within six weeks they were all to be taught their duties by the uprising of such as he, and their education was to cost a million lives and ten thousand million dollars, more or less, North and South, before the country could recover its balance and movement. Henry was a helpless victim, and, like all the rest, he could only wait for he knew not what, to send him he knew not where.

With the close of the session, his own functions ended. Ceasing to be private secretary he knew not what else to do but return with his father and mother to Boston in the middle of March, and, with childlike docility, sit down at a desk in the law-office of Horace Gray in Court Street, to begin again: "My Lords and Gentlemen"; dozing after a two o'clock dinner, or waking to discuss politics with the future Justice. There, in ordinary times, he would have remained for life, his attempt at education in treason having, like all the rest, disastrously failed.

Chapter VIII. Diplomacy (1861)

HARDLY a week passed when the newspapers announced that President Lincoln had selected Charles Francis Adams as his Minister to England. Once more, silently, Henry put Blackstone back on its shelf. As Friar Bacon's head sententiously announced many centuries before: Time had passed! The Civil Law lasted a brief day; the Common Law prolonged its shadowy existence for a week. The law, altogether, as path of education, vanished in April, 1861, leaving a million young men planted in the mud of a lawless world, to begin a new life without education at all. They asked few questions, but if they had asked millions they would have got no answers. No one could help. Looking back on this moment of crisis, nearly fifty years afterwards, one could only shake one's white beard in silent horror. Mr. Adams once more intimated that he thought himself entitled to the services of one of his sons, and he indicated Henry as the only one who could be spared from more serious duties. Henry packed his trunk again without a word. He could offer no protest. Ridiculous as he knew himself about to be in his new role, he was less ridiculous than his betters. He was at least no public official, like the thousands of improvised secretaries and generals who crowded their jealousies and intrigues on the President. He was not a vulture of carrion -- patronage. He knew that his father's appointment was the result of Governor Seward's personal friendship; he did not then know that Senator Sumner had opposed it, or the reasons which Sumner alleged for thinking it unfit; but he could have supplied proofs enough had Sumner asked for them, the strongest and most decisive being that, in his opinion, Mr. Adams had chosen a private secretary far more unfit than his chief. That Mr. Adams was unfit might well be, since it was hard to find a fit appointment in the list of possible candidates, except Mr. Sumner himself; and no one knew so well as this experienced Senator that the weakest of all Mr. Adams's proofs of fitness was his consent to quit a safe seat in Congress for an exceedingly unsafe seat in London with no better support than Senator Sumner, at the head of the Foreign Relations Committee, was likely to give him. In the family history, its members had taken many a dangerous risk, but never before had they taken one so desperate.

The private secretary troubled himself not at all about the unfitness of any one; he knew too little; and, in fact, no one, except perhaps Mr. Sumner, knew more. The President and Secretary of State knew least of all. As Secretary of Legation the Executive appointed the editor of a Chicago newspaper who had applied for the Chicago Post-Office; a good fellow, universally known as Charley Wilson, who had not a thought of staying in the post, or of helping the Minister. The Assistant Secretary was inherited from Buchanan's time, a hard worker, but socially useless. Mr. Adams made no effort to find efficient help; perhaps he knew no name to suggest; perhaps he knew too much of Washington, but he could hardly have hoped to find a staff of strength in his son.

The private secretary was more passive than his father, for he knew not where to turn. Sumner alone could have smoothed his path by giving him letters of introduction, but if Sumner wrote letters, it was not with the effect of smoothing paths. No one, at that moment, was engaged in smoothing either paths or people. The private secretary was no worse off than his neighbors except in being called earlier into service. On April 13 the storm burst and rolled several hundred thousand young men like Henry Adams into the surf of a wild ocean, all helpless like himself, to be beaten about for four years by the waves of war. Adams still had time to watch the regiments form ranks before Boston State House in the April evenings and march southward, quietly enough, with the air of business they wore from their cradles, but with few signs or sounds of excitement. He had time also to go down the harbor to see his brother Charles quartered in Fort Independence before being thrown, with a hundred thousand more, into the furnace of the Army of the Potomac to get educated in a fury of fire. Few things were for the moment so trivial in importance as the solitary private secretary crawling down to the wretched old Cunard steamer Niagara at East Boston to start again for Liverpool. This time the pitcher of education had gone to the fountain once too often; it was fairly broken; and the young man had got to meet a hostile world without defence -- or arms.

The situation did not seem even comic, so ignorant was the world of its humors; yet Minister Adams sailed for England, May 1, 1861, with much the same outfit as Admiral Dupont would have enjoyed if the Government had sent him to attack Port Royal with one cabin-boy in a rowboat. Luckily for the cabin-boy, he was alone. Had Secretary Seward and Senator Sumner given to Mr. Adams the rank of Ambassador and four times his salary, a palace in London, a staff of trained secretaries, and personal letters of introduction to the royal family and the whole peerage, the private secretary would have been cabin-boy still, with the extra burden of many masters; he was the most fortunate person in the party, having for master only his father who never fretted, never dictated, never disciplined, and whose idea of American diplomacy was that of the eighteenth century. Minister Adams remembered how his grandfather had sailed from

Mount Wollaston in midwinter, 1778, on the little frigate Boston, taking his eleven-year-old son John Quincy with him, for secretary, on a diplomacy of adventure that had hardly a parallel for success. He remembered how John Quincy, in 1809, had sailed for Russia, with himself, a baby of two years old, to cope with Napoleon and the Czar Alexander single-handed, almost as much of an adventurer as John Adams before him, and almost as successful. He thought it natural that the Government should send him out as an adventurer also, with a twenty-three-year-old son, and he did not even notice that he left not a friend behind him. No doubt he could depend on Seward, but on whom could Seward depend? Certainly not on the Chairman of the Committee of Foreign Relations. Minister Adams had no friend in the Senate; he could hope for no favors, and he asked none. He thought it right to play the adventurer as his father and grandfather had done before him, without a murmur. This was a lofty view, and for him answered his objects, but it bore hard on cabin-boys, and when, in time, the young man realized what had happened, he felt it as a betrayal. He modestly thought himself unfit for the career of adventurer, and judged his father to be less fit than himself. For the first time America was posing as the champion of legitimacy and order. Her representatives should know how to play their role; they should wear the costume; but, in the mission attached to Mr. Adams in 1861, the only rag of legitimacy or order was the private secretary, whose stature was not sufficient to impose awe on the Court and Parliament of Great Britain.

One inevitable effect of this lesson was to make a victim of the scholar and to turn him into a harsh judge of his masters. If they overlooked him, he could hardly overlook them, since they stood with their whole weight on his body. By way of teaching him quickly, they sent out their new Minister to Russia in the same ship. Secretary Seward had occasion to learn the merits of Cassius M. Clay in the diplomatic service, but Mr. Seward's education profited less than the private secretary's, Cassius Clay as a teacher having no equal though possibly some rivals. No young man, not in Government pay, could be asked to draw, from such lessons, any confidence in himself, and it was notorious that, for the next two years, the persons were few indeed who felt, or had reason to feel, any sort of confidence in the Government; fewest of all among those who were in it. At home, for the most part, young men went to the war, grumbled and died; in England they might grumble or not; no one listened.

Above all, the private secretary could not grumble to his chief. He knew surprisingly little, but that much he did know. He never labored so hard to learn a language as he did to hold his tongue, and it affected him for life. The habit of reticence -- of talking without meaning -- is never effaced. He had to begin it at once. He was already an adept when the party landed at Liverpool, May 13, 1861, and went instantly up to London: a family of early Christian martyrs about to be flung into an arena of lions, under the glad eyes of Tiberius Palmerston. Though Lord Palmerston would have laughed his peculiar Palmerston laugh at figuring as Tiberius, he would have seen only evident resemblance in the Christian martyrs, for he had already arranged the ceremony.

Of what they had to expect, the Minister knew no more than his son. What he or Mr. Seward or Mr. Sumner may have thought is the affair of history and their errors concern historians. The errors of a private secretary concerned no one but himself, and were a large part of his education. He thought on May 12 that he was going to a friendly Government and people, true to the anti-slavery principles which had been their steadiest profession. For a hundred years the chief effort of his family had aimed at bringing the Government of England into intelligent cooperation with the objects and interests of America. His father was about to make a new effort, and this time the chance of success was promising. The slave States had been the chief apparent obstacle to good understanding. As for the private secretary himself, he was, like all Bostonians, instinctively English. He could not conceive the idea of a hostile England. He supposed himself, as one of the members of a famous anti-slavery family, to be welcome everywhere in the British Islands.

On May 13, he met the official announcement that England recognized the belligerency of the Confederacy. This beginning of a new education tore up by the roots nearly all that was left of Harvard College and Germany. He had to learn -- the sooner the better -- that his ideas were the reverse of truth; that in May, 1861, no one in England -- literally no one -- doubted that Jefferson Davis had made or would make a nation, and nearly all were glad of it, though not often saying so. They mostly imitated Palmerston who, according to Mr. Gladstone, "desired the severance as a diminution of a dangerous power, but prudently held his tongue." The sentiment of anti-slavery had disappeared. Lord John Russell, as Foreign Secretary, had received the rebel emissaries, and had decided to recognize their belligerency before the arrival of Mr. Adams in order to fix the position of the British Government in advance. The recognition of independence would then become an understood policy; a matter of time and occasion.

Whatever Minister Adams may have felt, the first effect of this shock upon his son produced only a dullness of comprehension -- a sort of hazy inability to grasp the missile or realize the blow. Yet he realized that to his father it was likely to be fatal. The chances were great that the whole family would turn round and go home within a few weeks. The horizon widened out in endless waves of confusion. When he thought over the subject in the long leisure of later life, he grew cold at the idea of his situation had his father then shown himself what Sumner thought him to be -- unfit for his post. That the private secretary was unfit for his -- trifling though it were -- was proved by his unreflecting confidence in his father. It never entered his mind that his father might lose his nerve or his temper, and yet in a subsequent knowledge of statesmen and diplomats extending over several generations, he could not certainly point out another who could have stood such a shock without showing it. He passed this long day, and tedious journey to London, without once thinking of the possibility that his father might make a mistake. Whatever the Minister thought, and certainly his thought was not less active than his son's, he showed no trace of excitement. His manner was the same as ever; his mind and temper were as perfectly balanced; not a word escaped; not a nerve twitched.

The test was final, for no other shock so violent and sudden could possibly recur. The worst was in full sight. For once the private secretary knew his own business, which was to imitate his father as closely as possible and hold his tongue. Dumped thus into Maurigy's Hotel at the foot of Regent Street, in the midst of a London season, without a friend or even an acquaintance, he preferred to laugh at his father's bewilderment before the waiter's "'amhandheggsir" for breakfast, rather than ask a question or express a doubt. His situation, if taken seriously, was too appalling to face. Had he known it better, he would only have thought it worse.

Politically or socially, the outlook was desperate, beyond retrieving or contesting. Socially, under the best of circumstances, a newcomer in London society needs years to establish a position, and Minister Adams had not a week or an hour to spare, while his son had not even a remote chance of beginning. Politically the prospect looked even worse, and for Secretary Seward and Senator Sumner it was so; but for the Minister, on the spot, as he came to realize exactly where he stood, the danger was not so imminent. Mr. Adams was always one of the luckiest of men, both in what he achieved and in what he escaped. The blow, which prostrated Seward and Sumner, passed over him. Lord John Russell had acted -- had probably intended to act -- kindly by him in forestalling his arrival. The blow must have fallen within three months, and would then have broken him down. The British Ministers were a little in doubt still -- a little ashamed of themselves -- and certain to wait the longer for their next step in proportion to the haste of their first.

This is not a story of the diplomatic adventures of Charles Francis Adams, but of his son Henry's adventures in search of an education, which, if not taken too seriously, tended to humor. The father's position in London was not altogether bad; the son's was absurd. Thanks to certain family associations, Charles Francis Adams naturally looked on all British Ministers as enemies; the only public occupation of all Adamses for a hundred and fifty years at least, in their brief intervals of quarrelling with State Street, had been to quarrel with Downing Street; and the British Government, well used to a liberal unpopularity abroad, even when officially rude liked to be personally civil. All diplomatic agents are liable to be put, so to speak, in a corner, and are none the worse for it. Minister Adams had nothing in especial to complain of; his position was good while it lasted, and he had only the chances of war to fear. The son had no such compensations. Brought over in order to help his father, he could conceive no way of rendering his father help, but he was clear that his father had got to help him. To him, the Legation was social ostracism, terrible beyond anything he had known. Entire solitude in the great society of London was doubly desperate because his duties as private secretary required him to know everybody and go with his father and mother everywhere they needed escort. He had no friend, or even enemy, to tell him to be patient. Had any one done it, he would surely have broken out with the reply that patience was the last resource of fools as well as of sages; if he was to help his father at all, he must do it at once, for his father would never so much need help again. In fact he never gave his father the smallest help, unless it were as a footman, clerk, or a companion for the younger children.

He found himself in a singular situation for one who was to be useful. As he came to see the situation closer, he began to doubt whether secretaries were meant to be useful. Wars were too common in diplomacy to disturb the habits of the diplomat. Most secretaries detested their chiefs, and wished to be anything but useful. At the St. James's Club, to which the Minister's son could go only as an invited guest, the most instructive conversation he ever heard among the young men of his own age who hung about the tables, more helpless than himself, was: "Quel chien de pays!" or, "Que tu es beau aujourd'hui, mon cher!" No one wanted to discuss affairs; still less to give or get information. That was the affair of their chiefs, who were also slow to assume work not specially ordered from their Courts. If the American Minister was in trouble to-day, the Russian Ambassador was in trouble yesterday, and the Frenchman would be in trouble to-morrow. It would all come in the day's work. There was nothing professional in worry. Empires were always tumbling to pieces and diplomats were always picking them up.

This was his whole diplomatic education, except that he found rich veins of jealousy running between every chief and his staff. His social education was more barren still, and more trying to his vanity. His little mistakes in etiquette or address made him writhe with torture. He never forgot the first two or three social functions he attended: one an afternoon at Miss Burdett Coutts's in Stratton Place, where he hid himself in the embrasure of a window and hoped that no one noticed him; another was a garden-party given by the old anti-slavery Duchess Dowager of Sutherland at Chiswick, where the American Minister and Mrs. Adams were kept in conversation by the old Duchess till every one else went away except the young Duke and his cousins, who set to playing leap-frog on the lawn. At intervals during the next thirty years Henry Adams continued to happen upon the Duke, who, singularly enough, was always playing leap-frog. Still another nightmare he suffered at a dance given by the old Duchess Dowager of Somerset, a terrible vision in castanets, who seized him and forced him to perform a Highland fling before the assembled nobility and gentry, with the daughter of the Turkish Ambassador for partner. This might seem humorous to some, but to him the world turned to ashes.

When the end of the season came, the private secretary had not yet won a private acquaintance, and he hugged himself in his solitude when the story of the battle of Bull Run appeared in the Times. He felt only the wish to be more private than ever, for Bull Run was a worse diplomatic than military disaster. All this is history and can be read by public schools if they choose; but the curious and unexpected happened to the Legation, for the effect of Bull Run on them was almost strengthening. They no longer felt doubt. For the next year they went on only from week to week, ready to leave England at once, and never assuming more than three months for their limit. Europe was waiting to see them go. So certain was the end that no one cared to hurry it.

So far as a private secretary could see, this was all that saved his father. For many months he looked on himself as lost or finished in the character of private secretary; and as about to begin, without further experiment, a final education in the ranks of the Army of the Potomac where he would find most of his friends enjoying a much pleasanter life than his own. With this idea uppermost in his mind, he passed the summer and the autumn, and began the winter. Any winter in London is a severe trial; one's first winter is the most trying; but the month of December, 1861, in Mansfield Street, Portland Place, would have gorged a glutton of gloom.

One afternoon when he was struggling to resist complete nervous depression in the solitude of Mansfield Street, during the absence of the Minister and Mrs. Adams on a country visit, Reuter's telegram announcing the seizure of Mason and Slidell from a British mail-steamer was brought to the office. All three secretaries, public and private were there -- nervous as wild beasts under the long strain on their endurance -- and all three, though they knew it to be not merely their order of departure -- not merely diplomatic rupture -- but a declaration of war -- broke into shouts of delight. They were glad to face the end. They saw it and cheered it! Since England was waiting only for its own moment to strike, they were eager to strike first.

They telegraphed the news to the Minister, who was staying with Monckton Milnes at Fryston in Yorkshire. How Mr. Adams took it, is told in the "Lives" of Lord Houghton and William E. Forster who was one of the Fryston party. The moment was for him the crisis of his diplomatic career; for the secretaries it was merely the beginning of another intolerable delay, as though they were a military outpost waiting orders to quit an abandoned position. At the moment of sharpest suspense, the Prince Consort sickened and died. Portland Place at Christmas in a black fog was never a rosy landscape, but in 1861 the most hardened Londoner lost his ruddiness. The private secretary had one source of comfort denied to them -- he should not be private secretary long.

He was mistaken -- of course! He had been mistaken at every point of his education, and, on this point, he kept up the same mistake for nearly seven years longer, always deluded by the notion that the end was near. To him the Trent Affair was nothing but one of many affairs which he had to copy in a delicate round hand into his books, yet it had one or two results personal to him which left no trace on the Legation records. One of these, and to him the most important, was to put an end forever to the idea of being "useful." Hitherto, as an independent and free citizen, not in the employ of the Government, he had kept up his relations with the American press. He had written pretty frequently to Henry J. Raymond, and Raymond had used his letters in the New York Times. He had also become fairly intimate with the two or three friendly newspapers in London, the Daily News, the Star, the weekly Spectator; and he had tried to give them news and views that should have a certain common character, and prevent clash. He had even gone down to Manchester to study the cotton famine, and wrote a long account of his visit which his brother Charles had published in the Boston Courier. Unfortunately it was printed with his name, and instantly came back upon him in the most crushing shape possible -- that of a long, satirical leader in the London Times. Luckily the Times did not know its victim to be a part, though not an official, of the Legation, and lost the chance to make its satire fatal; but he instantly learned the narrowness of his escape from old Joe Parkes, one of the traditional busy-bodies of politics, who had haunted London since 1830, and who, after rushing to the Times office, to tell them all they did not know about Henry Adams, rushed to the Legation to tell Adams all he did not want to know about the Times. For a moment Adams thought his "usefulness" at an end in other respects than in the press, but a day or two more taught him the value of obscurity. He was totally unknown; he had not even a club; London was empty; no one thought twice about the Times article; no one except Joe Parkes ever spoke of it; and the world had other persons -- such as President Lincoln, Secretary Seward, and Commodore Wilkes -- for constant and favorite objects of ridicule. Henry Adams escaped, but he never tried to be useful again. The Trent Affair dwarfed individual effort. His education at least had reached the point of seeing its own proportions. "Surtout point de zele!" Zeal was too hazardous a profession for a Minister's son to pursue, as a volunteer manipulator, among Trent Affairs and rebel cruisers. He wrote no more letters and meddled with no more newspapers, but he was still young, and felt unkindly towards the editor of the London Times.

Mr. Delane lost few opportunities of embittering him, and he felt little or no hope of repaying these attentions; but the Trent Affair passed like a snowstorm, leaving the Legation, to its surprise, still in place. Although the private secretary saw in this delay -- which he attributed to Mr. Seward's good sense -- no reason for changing his opinion about the views of the British Government, he had no choice but to sit down again at his table, and go on copying papers, filing letters, and reading newspaper accounts of the incapacity of Mr. Lincoln and the brutality of Mr. Seward -- or vice versa. The heavy months dragged on and winter slowly turned to spring without improving his position or spirits. Socially he had but one relief; and, to the end of life, he never forgot the keen gratitude he owed for it. During this tedious winter and for many months afterwards, the only gleams of sunshine were on the days he passed at Walton-on-Thames as the guest of Mr. and Mrs. Russell Sturgis at Mount Felix.

His education had unfortunately little to do with bankers, although old George Peabody and his partner, Junius Morgan, were strong allies. Joshua Bates was devoted, and no one could be kinder than Thomas Baring, whose little dinners in Upper Grosvenor Street were certainly the best in London; but none offered a refuge to compare with Mount Felix, and, for the first time, the refuge was a liberal education. Mrs. Russell Sturgis was one of the women to whom an intelligent boy attaches himself as closely as he can. Henry Adams was not a very intelligent boy, and he had no knowledge of the world, but he knew enough to understand that a cub needed shape. The kind of education he most required was that of a charming woman, and Mrs. Russell Sturgis, a dozen years older than himself, could have good-naturedly trained a school of such, without an effort, and with infinite advantage to them. Near her he half forgot the anxieties of Portland Place. During two years of miserable solitude, she was in this social polar winter, the single source of warmth and light.

Of course the Legation itself was home, and, under such pressure, life in it could be nothing but united. All the inmates made common cause, but this was no education. One lived, but was merely flayed alive. Yet, while this might be exactly true of the younger members of the household, it was not quite so with the Minister and Mrs. Adams. Very slowly, but quite steadily, they gained foothold. For some reason partly connected with American sources, British society had begun with violent social prejudice against Lincoln, Seward, and all the Republican leaders except Sumner. Familiar as the whole tribe of Adamses had been for three generations with the impenetrable stupidity of the British mind, and weary of the long struggle to teach it its own interests, the fourth generation could still not quite persuade itself that this new British prejudice was natural. The private secretary suspected that Americans in New York and Boston had something to do with it. The Copperhead was at home in Pall Mall. Naturally the Englishman was a coarse animal and liked coarseness. Had Lincoln and Seward been the ruffians supposed, the average Englishman would have liked them the better. The exceedingly quiet manner and the unassailable social position of Minister Adams in no way conciliated them. They chose to ignore him, since they could not ridicule him. Lord John Russell set the example. Personally the Minister was to be kindly treated; politically he was negligible; he was there to be put aside. London and Paris imitated Lord John. Every one waited to see Lincoln and his hirelings disappear in one vast debacle. All conceived that the Washington Government would soon crumble, and that Minister Adams would vanish with the rest.

This situation made Minister Adams an exception among diplomats. European rulers for the most part fought and treated as members of one family, and rarely had in view the possibility of total extinction; but the Governments and society of Europe, for a year at least, regarded the Washington Government as dead, and its Ministers as nullities. Minister Adams was better received than most nullities because he made no noise. Little by little, in private, society took the habit of accepting him, not so much as a diplomat, but rather as a member of opposition, or an eminent counsel retained for a foreign Government. He was to be received and considered; to be cordially treated as, by birth and manners, one of themselves. This curiously English way of getting behind a stupidity gave the Minister every possible advantage over a European diplomat. Barriers of race, language, birth, habit, ceased to exist. Diplomacy held diplomats apart in order to save Governments, but Earl Russell could not hold Mr. Adams apart. He was undistinguishable from a Londoner. In society few Londoners were so widely at home. None had such double personality and corresponding double weight.

The singular luck that took him to Fryston to meet the shock of the Trent Affair under the sympathetic eyes of Monckton Milnes and William E. Forster never afterwards deserted him. Both Milnes and Forster needed support and were greatly relieved to be supported. They saw what the private secretary in May had overlooked, the hopeless position they were in if the American Minister made a mistake, and, since his strength was theirs, they lost no time in expressing to all the world their estimate of the Minister's character. Between them the Minister was almost safe.

One might discuss long whether, at that moment, Milnes or Forster were the more valuable ally, since they were influences of different kinds. Monckton Milnes was a social power in London, possibly greater than Londoners themselves quite understood, for in London society as elsewhere, the dull and the ignorant made a large majority, and dull men always laughed at Monckton Milnes. Every bore was used to talk familiarly about "Dicky Milnes," the "cool of the evening"; and of course he himself affected social eccentricity, challenging ridicule with the indifference of one who knew himself to be the first wit in London, and a maker of men -- of a great many men. A word from him went far. An invitation to his breakfast-table went farther. Behind his almost Falstaffian mask and laugh of Silenus, he carried a fine, broad, and high intelligence which no one questioned. As a young man he had written verses, which some readers thought poetry, and which were certainly not altogether prose. Later, in Parliament he made speeches, chiefly criticised as too good for the place and too high for the audience. Socially, he was one of two or three men who went everywhere, knew everybody, talked of everything, and had the ear of Ministers; but unlike most wits, he held a social position of his own that ended in a peerage, and he had a house in Upper Brook Street to which most clever people were exceedingly glad of admission. His breakfasts were famous, and no one liked to decline his invitations, for it was more dangerous to show timidity than to risk a fray. He was a voracious reader, a strong critic, an art connoisseur in certain directions, a collector of books, but above all he was a man of the world by profession, and loved the contacts -- perhaps the collisions -- of society. Not even Henry Brougham dared do the things he did, yet Brougham defied rebuff. Milnes was the good-nature of London; the Gargantuan type of its refinement and coarseness; the most universal figure of May Fair.

Compared with him, figures like Hayward, or Delane, or Venables, or Henry Reeve were quite secondary, but William E. Forster stood in a different class. Forster had nothing whatever to do with May Fair. Except in being a Yorkshireman he was quite the opposite of Milnes. He had at that time no social or political position; he never had a vestige of Milnes's wit or variety; he was a tall, rough, ungainly figure, affecting the singular form of self-defense which the Yorkshiremen and Lancashiremen seem to hold dear -- the exterior roughness assumed to cover an internal, emotional, almost sentimental nature. Kindly he had to be, if only by his inheritance from a Quaker ancestry, but he was a Friend one degree removed. Sentimental and emotional he must have been, or he could never have persuaded a daughter of Dr. Arnold to marry him. Pure gold, without a trace of base metal; honest, unselfish, practical; he took up the Union cause and made himself its champion, as a true Yorkshireman was sure to do, partly because of his Quaker anti-slavery convictions, and partly because it gave him a practical opening in the House. As a new member, he needed a field.

Diffidence was not one of Forster's weaknesses. His practical sense and his personal energy soon established him in leadership, and made him a powerful champion, not so much for ornament as for work. With such a manager, the friends of the Union in England began to take heart. Minister Adams had only to look on as his true champions, the heavy-weights, came into action, and even the private secretary caught now and then a stray gleam of encouragement as he saw the ring begin to clear for these burly Yorkshiremen to stand up in a prize-fight likely to be as brutal as ever England had known. Milnes and Forster were not exactly light-weights, but Bright and

Cobden were the hardest hitters in England, and with them for champions the Minister could tackle even Lord Palmerston without much fear of foul play.

In society John Bright and Richard Cobden were never seen, and even in Parliament they had no large following. They were classed as enemies of order, -- anarchists, -- and anarchists they were if hatred of the so-called established orders made them so. About them was no sort of political timidity. They took bluntly the side of the Union against Palmerston whom they hated. Strangers to London society, they were at home in the American Legation, delightful dinner-company, talking always with reckless freedom. Cobden was the milder and more persuasive; Bright was the more dangerous to approach; but the private secretary delighted in both, and nourished an ardent wish to see them talk the same language to Lord John Russell from the gangway of the House.

With four such allies as these, Minister Adams stood no longer quite helpless. For the second time the British Ministry felt a little ashamed of itself after the Trent Affair, as well it might, and disposed to wait before moving again. Little by little, friends gathered about the Legation who were no fair-weather companions. The old anti-slavery, Exeter Hall, Shaftesbury clique turned out to be an annoying and troublesome enemy, but the Duke of Argyll was one of the most valuable friends the Minister found, both politically and socially, and the Duchess was as true as her mother. Even the private secretary shared faintly in the social profit of this relation, and never forgot dining one night at the Lodge, and finding himself after dinner engaged in instructing John Stuart Mill about the peculiar merits of an American protective system. In spite of all the probabilities, he convinced himself that it was not the Duke's claret which led him to this singular form of loquacity; he insisted that it was the fault of Mr. Mill himself who led him on by assenting to his point of view. Mr. Mill took no apparent pleasure in dispute, and in that respect the Duke would perhaps have done better; but the secretary had to admit that though at other periods of life he was sufficiently and even amply snubbed by Englishmen, he could never recall a single occasion during this trying year, when he had to complain of rudeness.

Friendliness he found here and there, but chiefly among his elders; not among fashionable or socially powerful people, either men or women; although not even this rule was quite exact, for Frederick Cavendish's kindness and intimate relations made Devonshire House almost familiar, and Lyulph Stanley's ardent Americanism created a certain cordiality with the Stanleys of Alderley whose house was one of the most frequented in London. Lorne, too, the future Argyll, was always a friend. Yet the regular course of society led to more literary intimacies. Sir Charles Trevelyan's house was one of the first to which young Adams was asked, and with which his friendly relations never ceased for near half a century, and then only when death stopped them. Sir Charles and Lady Lyell were intimates. Tom Hughes came into close alliance. By the time society began to reopen its doors after the death of the Prince Consort, even the private secretary occasionally saw a face he knew, although he made no more effort of any kind, but silently waited the end. Whatever might be the advantages of social relations to his father and mother, to him the whole business of diplomacy and society was futile. He meant to go home.

Chapter IX. Foes or Friends (1862)

OF the year 1862 Henry Adams could never think without a shudder. The war alone did not greatly distress him; already in his short life he was used to seeing people wade in blood, and he could plainly discern in history, that man from the beginning had found his chief amusement in bloodshed; but the ferocious joy of destruction at its best requires that one should kill what one hates, and young Adams neither hated nor wanted to kill his friends the rebels, while he wanted nothing so much as to wipe England off the earth. Never could any good come from that besotted race! He was feebly trying to save his own life. Every day the British Government deliberately crowded him one step further into the grave. He could see it; the Legation knew it; no one doubted it; no one thought of questioning it. The Trent Affair showed where Palmerston and Russell stood. The escape of the rebel cruisers from Liverpool was not, in a young man's eyes, the sign of hesitation, but the proof of their fixed intention to intervene. Lord Russell's replies to Mr. Adams's notes were discourteous in their indifference, and, to an irritable young private secretary of twenty-four, were insolent in their disregard of truth. Whatever forms of phrase were usual in public to modify the harshness of invective, in private no political opponent in England, and few political friends, hesitated to say brutally of Lord John Russell that he lied. This was no great reproach, for, more or less, every statesman lied, but the intensity of the private secretary's rage sprang from his belief that Russell's form of defence covered intent to kill. Not for an instant did the Legation draw a free breath. The suspense was hideous and unendurable.

The Minister, no doubt, endured it, but he had support and consideration, while his son had nothing to think about but his friends who were mostly dying under McClellan in the swamps about Richmond, or his enemies who were exulting in Pall Mall. He bore it as well as he could till midsummer, but, when the story of the second Bull Run appeared, he could bear it no longer, and after a sleepless night, walking up and down his room without reflecting that his father was beneath him, he announced at breakfast his intention to go home into the army. His mother seemed to be less impressed by the announcement than by the walking over her head, which was so unlike her as to surprise her son. His father, too, received the announcement quietly. No doubt they expected it, and had taken their measures in advance. In those days, parents got used to all sorts of announcements from their children. Mr. Adams took his son's defection as quietly as he took Bull Run; but his son never got the chance to go. He found obstacles constantly rising in his path. The remonstrances of his brother Charles, who was himself in the Army of the Potomac, and whose opinion had always the greatest weight with Henry, had much to do with delaying action; but he felt, of his own accord, that if he deserted his post in London, and found the Capuan comforts he expected in Virginia where he would have only bullets to wound him, he would never forgive himself for leaving his father and mother alone to be devoured by the wild beasts of the British amphitheatre. This reflection might not have stopped him, but his father's suggestion was decisive. The Minister pointed out that it was too late for him to take part in the actual campaign, and that long before next spring they would all go home together.

The young man had copied too many affidavits about rebel cruisers to miss the point of this argument, so he sat down again to copy some more. Consul Dudley at Liverpool provided a continuous supply. Properly, the affidavits were no business of the private secretary, but practically the private secretary did a second secretary's work, and was glad to do it, if it would save Mr. Seward the trouble of sending more secretaries of his own selection to help the Minister. The work was nothing, and no one ever complained of it; not even Moran, the Secretary of Legation after the departure of Charley Wilson, though he might sit up all night to copy. Not the work, but the play exhausted. The effort of facing a hostile society was bad enough, but that of facing friends was worse. After terrific disasters like the seven days before Richmond and the second Bull Run, friends needed support; a tone of bluff would have been fatal, for the average mind sees quickest through a bluff; nothing answers but candor; yet private secretaries never feel candid, however much they feel the reverse, and therefore they must affect candor; not always a simple act when one is exasperated, furious, bitter, and choking with tears over the blunders and incapacity of one's Government. If one shed tears, they must be shed on one's pillow. Least of all, must one throw extra strain on the Minister, who had all he could carry without being fretted in his family. One must read one's Times every morning over one's muffin without reading aloud -- "Another disastrous Federal Defeat"; and one might not even indulge in harmless profanity. Self-restraint among friends required much more effort than keeping a quiet face before enemies. Great men were the worst blunderers. One day the private secretary smiled, when standing with the crowd in the throne-room while the endless procession made bows to the royal family, at hearing, behind his shoulder, one Cabinet Minister remark gaily to another: "So the Federals have got another licking!" The point of the remark was its truth. Even a private secretary had learned to control his tones and guard his features and betray no joy over the "lickings" of an enemy -- in the enemy's presence.

London was altogether beside itself on one point, in especial; it created a nightmare of its own, and gave it the shape of Abraham Lincoln. Behind this it placed another demon, if possible more devilish, and called it Mr. Seward. In regard to these two men, English society seemed demented. Defence was useless; explanation was vain; one could only let the passion exhaust itself. One's best friends were as unreasonable as enemies, for the belief in poor Mr. Lincoln's brutality and Seward's ferocity became a dogma of popular faith. The last time Henry Adams saw Thackeray, before his sudden death at Christmas in 1863, was in entering the house of Sir Henry Holland for an evening reception. Thackeray was pulling on his coat downstairs, laughing because, in his usual blind way, he had stumbled into the wrong house and not found it out till he shook hands with old Sir Henry, whom he knew very well, but who was not the host he expected. Then his tone changed as he spoke of his -- and Adams's -- friend, Mrs. Frank Hampton, of South Carolina, whom he had loved as Sally Baxter and painted as Ethel Newcome. Though he had never quite forgiven her marriage, his warmth of feeling revived when he heard that she had died of consumption at Columbia while her parents and sister were refused permission to pass through the lines to see her. In speaking of it, Thackeray's voice trembled and his eyes filled with tears. The coarse cruelty of Lincoln and his hirelings was notorious. He never doubted that the Federals made a business of harrowing the tenderest feelings of women -- particularly of women -- in order to punish their opponents. On quite insufficient evidence he burst into violent reproach. Had Adams carried in his pocket the proofs that the reproach was unjust, he would have gained nothing by showing them. At that moment Thackeray, and all London society with him, needed the nervous relief of expressing emotion; for if Mr. Lincoln was not what they said he -- was what were they?

For like reason, the members of the Legation kept silence, even in private, under the boorish Scotch jibes of Carlyle. If Carlyle was wrong, his diatribes would give his true measure, and this measure would be a low one, for Carlyle was not likely to be more sincere or more sound in one thought than in another. The proof that a philosopher does not know what he is talking about is apt to sadden his followers before it reacts on himself. Demolition of one's idols is painful, and Carlyle had been an idol. Doubts cast on his stature spread far into general darkness like shadows of a setting sun. Not merely the idols fell, but also the habit of faith. If Carlyle, too, was a fraud, what were his scholars and school?

Society as a rule was civil, and one had no more reason to complain than every other diplomatist has had, in like conditions, but one's few friends in society were mere ornament. The Legation could not dream of contesting social control. The best they could do was to escape mortification, and by this time their relations were good enough to save the Minister's family from that annoyance. Now and then, the fact could not be wholly disguised that some one had refused to meet -- or to receive -- the Minister; but never an open insult, or any expression of which the Minister had to take notice. Diplomacy served as a buffer in times of irritation, and no diplomat who knew his business fretted at what every diplomat -- and none more commonly than the English -- had to expect; therefore Henry Adams, though not a diplomat and wholly unprotected, went his way peacefully enough, seeing clearly that society cared little to make his acquaintance, but seeing also no reason why society should discover charms in him of which he was himself unconscious. He went where he was asked; he was always courteously received; he was, on the whole, better treated than at Washington; and he held his tongue.

For a thousand reasons, the best diplomatic house in London was Lord Palmerston's, while Lord John Russell's was one of the worst. Of neither host could a private secretary expect to know anything. He might as well have expected to know the Grand Lama. Personally Lord Palmerston was the last man in London that a cautious private secretary wanted to know. Other Prime Ministers may perhaps have lived who inspired among diplomatists as much distrust as Palmerston, and yet between Palmerston's word and Russell's word, one hesitated to decide, and gave years of education to deciding, whether either could be trusted, or how far. The Queen herself in her famous memorandum of August 12, 1850, gave her opinion of Palmerston in words that differed little from words used by Lord John Russell, and both the Queen and Russell said in substance only what Cobden and Bright said in private. Every diplomatist agreed with them, yet the diplomatic standard of trust seemed to be other than the parliamentarian No professional diplomatists worried about falsehoods. Words were with them forms of expression which varied with individuals, but falsehood was more or less necessary to all. The worst liars were the candid. What diplomatists wanted to know was the motive that lay beyond the expression. In the case of Palmerston they were unanimous in warning new colleagues that they might expect to be sacrificed by him to any momentary personal object. Every new Minister or Ambassador at the Court of St. James received this preliminary lesson that he must, if possible, keep out of Palmerston's reach. The rule was not secret or merely diplomatic. The Queen herself had emphatically expressed the same opinion officially. If Palmerston had an object to gain, he would go down to the House of Commons and betray or misrepresent a foreign Minister, without concern for his victim. No one got back on him with a blow equally mischievous -- not even the Queen -- for, as old Baron Brunnow described him: "C'est une peau de rhinocere!" Having gained his point, he laughed, and his public laughed with him, for the usual British -- or American -- public likes to be amused, and thought it very amusing to see these beribboned and bestarred foreigners caught and tossed and gored on the horns of this jovial, slashing, devil-may-care British bull.

Diplomatists have no right to complain of mere lies; it is their own fault, if, educated as they are, the lies deceive them; but they complain bitterly of traps. Palmerston was believed to lay traps. He was the enfant terrible of the British Government. On the other hand, Lady Palmerston was believed to be good and loyal. All the diplomats and their wives seemed to think so, and took their troubles to her, believing that she would try to help them. For this reason among others, her evenings at home -- Saturday Reviews, they were called -- had great vogue. An ignorant young

American could not be expected to explain it. Cambridge House was no better for entertaining than a score of others. Lady Palmerston was no longer young or handsome, and could hardly at any age have been vivacious. The people one met there were never smart and seldom young; they were largely diplomatic, and diplomats are commonly dull; they were largely political, and politicians rarely decorate or beautify an evening party; they were sprinkled with literary people, who are notoriously unfashionable; the women were of course ill-dressed and middle-aged; the men looked mostly bored or out of place; yet, beyond a doubt, Cambridge House was the best, and perhaps the only political house in London, and its success was due to Lady Palmerston, who never seemed to make an effort beyond a friendly recognition. As a lesson in social education, Cambridge House gave much subject for thought. First or last, one was to know dozens of statesmen more powerful and more agreeable than Lord Palmerston; dozens of ladies more beautiful and more painstaking than Lady Palmerston; but no political house so successful as Cambridge House. The world never explains such riddles. The foreigners said only that Lady Palmerston was " sympathique."

The small fry of the Legations were admitted there, or tolerated, without a further effort to recognize their existence, but they were pleased because rarely tolerated anywhere else, and there they could at least stand in a corner and look at a bishop or even a duke. This was the social diversion of young Adams. No one knew him -- not even the lackeys. The last Saturday evening he ever attended, he gave his name as usual at the foot of the staircase, and was rather disturbed to hear it shouted up as "Mr. Handrew Hadams!" He tried to correct it, and the footman shouted more loudly: "Mr. Hanthony Hadams!" With some temper he repeated the correction, and was finally announced as "Mr. Halexander Hadams," and under this name made his bow for the last time to Lord Palmerston who certainly knew no better.

Far down the staircase one heard Lord Palmerston's laugh as he stood at the door receiving his guests, talking probably to one of his henchmen, Delane, Borthwick, or Hayward, who were sure to be near. The laugh was singular, mechanical, wooden, and did not seem to disturb his features. "Ha! . . . Ha! . . . Ha!" Each was a slow, deliberate ejaculation, and all were in the same tone, as though he meant to say: "Yes! . . . Yes! . . . Yes!" by way of assurance. It was a laugh of 1810 and the Congress of Vienna. Adams would have much liked to stop a moment and ask whether William Pitt and the Duke of Wellington had laughed so; but young men attached to foreign Ministers asked no questions at all of Palmerston and their chiefs asked as few as possible. One made the usual bow and received the usual glance of civility; then passed on to Lady Palmerston, who was always kind in manner, but who wasted no remarks; and so to Lady Jocelyn with her daughter, who commonly had something friendly to say; then went through the diplomatic corps, Brunnow, Musurus, Azeglio, Apponyi, Van de Weyer, Bille, Tricoupi, and the rest, finally dropping into the hands of some literary accident as strange there as one's self. The routine varied little. There was no attempt at entertainment. Except for the desperate isolation of these two first seasons, even secretaries would have found the effort almost as mechanical as a levee at St. James's Palace.

Lord Palmerston was not Foreign Secretary; he was Prime Minister, but he loved foreign affairs and could no more resist scoring a point in diplomacy than in whist. Ministers of foreign powers, knowing his habits, tried to hold him at arms'-length, and, to do this, were obliged to court the actual Foreign Secretary, Lord John Russell, who, on July 30, 1861, was called up to the House of Lords as an earl. By some process of personal affiliation, Minister Adams succeeded in persuading himself that he could trust Lord Russell more safely than Lord Palmerston. His son, being young and ill-balanced in temper, thought there was nothing to choose. Englishmen saw little difference between them, and Americans were bound to follow English experience in English character. Minister Adams had much to learn, although with him as well as with his son, the months of education began to count as aeons.

Just as Brunnow predicted, Lord Palmerston made his rush at last, as unexpected as always, and more furiously than though still a private secretary of twenty-four. Only a man who had been young with the battle of Trafalgar could be fresh and jaunty to that point, but Minister Adams was not in a position to sympathize with octogenarian youth and found himself in a danger as critical as that of his numerous predecessors. It was late one after noon in June, 1862, as the private secretary returned, with the Minister, from some social function, that he saw his father pick up a note from his desk and read it in silence. Then he said curtly: "Palmerston wants a quarrel!" This was the point of the incident as he felt it. Palmerston wanted a quarrel; he must not be gratified; he must be stopped. The matter of quarrel was General Butler's famous woman-order at New Orleans, but the motive was the belief in President Lincoln's brutality that had taken such deep root in the British mind. Knowing Palmerston's habits, the Minister took for granted that he meant to score a diplomatic point by producing this note in the House of Commons. If he did this at once, the Minister was lost; the quarrel was made; and one new victim to Palmerston's passion for popularity was sacrificed.

The moment was nervous -- as far as the private secretary knew, quite the most critical moment in the records of American diplomacy -- but the story belongs to history, not to education, and can be read there by any one who cares to read it. As a part of Henry Adams's education it had a value distinct from history. That his father succeeded in muzzling Palmerston without a public scandal, was well enough for the Minister, but was not enough for a private secretary who liked going to Cambridge House, and was puzzled to reconcile contradictions. That Palmerston had wanted a quarrel was obvious; why, then, did he submit so tamely to being made the victim of the quarrel? The correspondence that followed his note was conducted feebly on his side, and he allowed the United States Minister to close it by a refusal to receive further communications from him except through Lord Russell. The step was excessively strong, for it broke off private relations as well as public, and cost even the private secretary his invitations to Cambridge House. Lady Palmerston tried her best, but the two ladies found no resource except tears. They had to do with American Minister perplexed in the extreme. Not that Mr. Adams lost his temper, for he never felt such a weight of responsibility, and was never more cool; but he could conceive no other way of protecting his Government, not to speak of himself, than to force Lord Russell to interpose. He believed that Palmerston's submission and silence were due to Russell. Perhaps he was right; at the time, his son had no doubt of it, though afterwards he felt less sure. Palmerston wanted a quarrel; the motive seemed evident; yet when the quarrel was made, he backed out of it; for some reason it seemed that he did not want it -- at least, not then. He never showed resentment against Mr. Adams at the time or afterwards. He never began another quarrel. Incredible as it seemed, he behaved like a well-bred gentleman who felt himself in the wrong. Possibly this change may have been due to Lord Russell's remonstrances, but the private secretary would have felt his education in politics more complete had he ever finally made up his mind whether Palmerston was more angry with General Butler, or more annoyed at himself, for committing what was in both cases an unpardonable betise.

At the time, the question was hardly raised, for no one doubted Palmerston's attitude or his plans. The season was near its end, and Cambridge House was soon closed. The Legation had troubles enough without caring to publish more. The tide of English feeling ran so violently against it that one could only wait to see whether General McClellan would bring it relief. The year 1862 was a dark spot in Henry Adams's life, and the education it gave was mostly one that he gladly forgot. As far as he was aware, he made no friends; he could hardly make enemies; yet towards the close of the year he was flattered by an invitation from Monckton Milnes to Fryston, and it was one of many acts of charity towards the young that gave Milnes immortality. Milnes made it his business to be kind. Other people criticised him for his manner of doing it, but never imitated him. Naturally, a dispirited, disheartened private secretary was exceedingly grateful, and never forgot the kindness, but it was chiefly as education that this first country visit had value. Commonly, country visits are much alike, but Monckton Milnes was never like anybody, and his country parties served his purpose of mixing strange elements. Fryston was one of a class of houses that no one sought for its natural beauties, and the winter mists of Yorkshire were rather more evident for the absence of the hostess on account of them, so that the singular guests whom Milnes collected to enliven his December had nothing to do but astonish each other, if anything could astonish such men. Of the five, Adams alone was tame; he alone added nothing to the wit or humor, except as a listener; but they needed a listener and he was useful. Of the remaining four, Milnes was the oldest, and perhaps the sanest in spite of his superficial eccentricities, for Yorkshire sanity was true to a standard of its own, if not to other conventions; yet even Milnes startled a young American whose Boston and Washington mind was still fresh. He would not have been startled by the hard-drinking, horse-racing Yorkshireman of whom he had read in books; but Milnes required a knowledge of society and literature that only himself possessed, if one were to try to keep pace with him. He had sought contact with everybody and everything that Europe could offer. He knew it all from several points of view, and chiefly as humorous.

The second of the party was also of a certain age; a quiet, well-mannered, singularly agreeable gentleman of the literary class. When Milnes showed Adams to his room to dress for dinner, he stayed a moment to say a word about this guest, whom he called Stirling of Keir. His sketch closed with the hint that Stirling was violent only on one point -- hatred of Napoleon III. On that point, Adams was himself sensitive, which led him to wonder how bad the Scotch gentleman might be. The third was a man of thirty or thereabouts, whom Adams had already met at Lady Palmerston's carrying his arm in a sling. His figure and bearing were sympathetic -- almost pathetic -- with a certain grave and gentle charm, a pleasant smile, and an interesting story. He was Lawrence Oliphant, just from Japan, where he had been wounded in the fanatics' attack on the British Legation. He seemed exceptionally sane and peculiarly suited for country houses, where every man would enjoy his company, and every woman would adore him. He had not then published "Piccadilly"; perhaps he was writing it; while, like all the young men about the Foreign Office, he contributed to The Owl.

The fourth was a boy, or had the look of one, though in fact a year older than Adams himself. He resembled in action -- and in this trait, was remotely followed, a generation later, by another famous young man, Robert Louis Stevenson -- a tropical bird, high-crested, long-beaked, quick-moving, with rapid utterance and screams of humor, quite unlike any English lark or nightingale. One could hardly call him a crimson macaw among owls, and yet no ordinary contrast availed. Milnes introduced him as Mr. Algernon Swinburne. The name suggested nothing. Milnes was always unearthing new coins and trying to give them currency. He had unearthed Henry Adams who knew himself to be worthless and not current. When Milnes lingered a moment in Adams's room to add that Swinburne had written some poetry, not yet published, of really extraordinary merit, Adams only wondered what more Milnes would discover, and whether by chance he could discover merit in a private secretary. He was capable of it.

In due course this party of five men sat down to dinner with the usual club manners of ladyless dinner-tables, easy and formal at the same time. Conversation ran first to Oliphant who told his dramatic story simply, and from him the talk drifted off into other channels, until Milnes thought it time to bring Swinburne out. Then, at last, if never before, Adams acquired education. What he had sought so long, he found; but he was none the wiser; only the more astonished. For once, too, he felt at ease, for the others were no less astonished than himself, and their astonishment grew apace. For the rest of the evening Swinburne figured alone; the end of dinner made the monologue only freer, for in 1862, even when ladies were not in the house, smoking was forbidden, and guests usually smoked in the stables or the kitchen; but Monckton Milnes was a licensed libertine who let his guests smoke in Adams's bedroom, since Adams was an American-German barbarian ignorant of manners; and there after dinner all sat -- or lay -- till far into the night, listening to the rush of Swinburne's talk. In a long experience, before or after, no one ever approached it; yet one had heard accounts of the best talking of the time, and read accounts of talkers in all time, among the rest, of Voltaire, who seemed to approach nearest the pattern.

That Swinburne was altogether new to the three types of men-of-the-world before him; that he seemed to them quite original, wildly eccentric, astonishingly gifted, and convulsingly droll, Adams could see; but what more he was, even Milnes hardly dared say. They could not believe his incredible memory and knowledge of literature, classic, mediaeval, and modern; his faculty of reciting a play of Sophocles or a play of Shakespeare, forward or backward, from end to beginning; or Dante, or Villon, or Victor Hugo. They knew not what to make of his rhetorical recitation of his own unpublished ballads -- "Faustine"; the "Four Boards of the Coffin Lid"; the "Ballad of Burdens" -- which he declaimed as though they were books of the Iliad. It was singular that his most appreciative listener should have been the author only of pretty verses like "We wandered by the brook-side," and "She seemed to those that saw them meet"; and who never cared to write in any other tone; but Milnes took everything into his sympathies, including Americans like young Adams whose standards were stiffest of all, while Swinburne, though millions of ages far from them, united them by his humor even more than by his poetry. The story of his first day as a member of Professor Stubbs's household was professionally clever farce, if not high comedy, in a young man who could write a Greek ode or a Provençal chanson as easily as an English quatrain.

Late at night when the symposium broke up, Stirling of Keir wanted to take with him to his chamber a copy of "Queen Rosamund," the only volume Swinburne had then published, which was on the library table, and Adams offered to light him down with his solitary bedroom candle. All the way, Stirling was ejaculating explosions of wonder, until at length, at the foot of the stairs and at the climax of his imagination, he paused, and burst out: "He's a cross between the devil and the Duke of Argyll!"

To appreciate the full merit of this description, a judicious critic should have known both, and Henry Adams knew only one -- at least in person -- but he understood that to a Scotchman the likeness meant something quite portentous, beyond English experience, supernatural, and what the French call moyenageux, or mediaeval with a grotesque turn. That Stirling as well as Milnes should regard Swinburne as a prodigy greatly comforted Adams, who lost his balance of mind at first in trying to imagine that Swinburne was a natural product of Oxford, as muffins and pork-pies of London, at once the cause and effect of dyspepsia. The idea that one has actually met a real genius dawns slowly on a Boston mind, but it made entry at last.

Then came the sad reaction, not from Swinburne whose genius never was in doubt, but from the Boston mind which, in its uttermost flights, was never moyenageux. One felt the horror of Longfellow and Emerson, the doubts of Lowell and the humor of Holmes, at the wild Walpurgis-night of Swinburne's talk. What could a shy young private secretary do about it? Perhaps, in his good nature, Milnes thought that Swinburne might find a friend in Stirling or Oliphant, but he could hardly have fancied Henry Adams rousing in him even an interest. Adams could no more interest Algernon Swinburne than he could interest Encke's comet. To Swinburne he could be no more than a worm. The quality of genius was an education almost ultimate, for one touched there the limits of the human mind on that side; but one could only receive; one had nothing to give -- nothing even to offer.

Swinburne tested him then and there by one of his favorite tests -- Victor Hugo for to him the test of Victor Hugo was the surest and quickest of standards. French poetry is at best a severe exercise for foreigners; it requires extraordinary knowledge of the language and rare refinement of ear to appreciate even the recitation of French verse; but unless a poet has both, he lacks something of poetry. Adams had neither. To the end of his life he never listened to a French recitation with pleasure, or felt a sense of majesty in French verse; but he did not care to proclaim his weakness, and he tried to evade Swinburne's vehement insistence by parading an affection for Alfred de Musset. Swinburne would have none of it; de Musset was unequal; he did not sustain himself on the wing.

Adams would have given a world or two, if he owned one, to sustain himself on the wing like de Musset, or even like Hugo; but his education as well as his ear was at fault, and he succumbed. Swinburne tried him again on Walter Savage Landor. In truth the test was the same, for Swinburne admired in Landor's English the qualities that he felt in Hugo's French; and Adams's failure was equally gross, for, when forced to despair, he had to admit that both Hugo and Landor bored him. Nothing more was needed. One who could feel neither Hugo nor Landor was lost.

The sentence was just and Adams never appealed from it. He knew his inferiority in taste as he might know it in smell. Keenly mortified by the dullness of his senses and instincts, he knew he was no companion for Swinburne; probably he could be only an annoyance; no number of centuries could ever educate him to Swinburne's level, even in technical appreciation; yet he often wondered whether there was nothing he had to offer that was worth the poet's acceptance. Certainly such mild homage as the American insect would have been only too happy to bring, had he known how, was hardly worth the acceptance of any one. Only in France is the attitude of prayer possible; in England it became absurd. Even Monckton Milnes, who felt the splendors of Hugo and Landor, was almost as helpless as an American private secretary in personal contact with them. Ten years afterwards Adams met him at the Geneva Conference, fresh from Paris, bubbling with delight at a call he had made on Hugo: "I was shown into a large room," he said, "with women and men seated in chairs against the walls, and Hugo at one end throned. No one spoke. At last Hugo raised his voice solemnly, and uttered the words: 'Quant a moi, je crois en Dieu!' Silence followed. Then a woman responded as if in deep meditation: 'Chose sublime! un Dieu qui croft en Dieu!'"

With the best of will, one could not do this in London; the actors had not the instinct of the drama; and yet even a private secretary was not wholly wanting in instinct. As soon as he reached town he hurried to Pickering's for a copy of "Queen Rosamund," and at that time, if Swinburne was not joking, Pickering had sold seven copies. When the "Poems and Ballads" came out, and met their great success and scandal, he sought one of the first copies from Moxon. If he had sinned and doubted at all, he wholly repented and did penance before "Atalanta in Calydon," and would have offered Swinburne a solemn worship as Milnes's female offered Hugo, if it would have pleased the poet. Unfortunately it was worthless.

The three young men returned to London, and each went his own way. Adams's interest in making friends was something desperate, but "the London season," Milnes used to say, "is a season for making acquaintances and losing friends"; there was no intimate life. Of Swinburne he saw no more till Monckton Milnes summoned his whole array of Frystonians to support him in presiding at the dinner of the Authors' Fund, when Adams found himself seated next to Swinburne, famous then, but no nearer. They never met again. Oliphant he met oftener; all the world knew and loved him; but he too disappeared in the way that all the world knows. Stirling of Keir, after one or two efforts, passed also from Adams's vision into Sir William Stirling-Maxwell. The only record of his wonderful visit to Fryston may perhaps exist still in the registers of the St. James's Club, for immediately afterwards Milnes proposed Henry Adams for membership, and unless his memory erred, the nomination was seconded by Tricoupi and endorsed by Laurence Oliphant and Evelyn Ashley. The list was a little singular for variety, but on the whole it suggested that the private secretary was getting on.

Chapter X. Political Morality (1862)

ON Moran's promotion to be Secretary, Mr. Seward inquired whether Minister Adams would like the place of Assistant Secretary for his son. It was the first -- and last -- office ever offered him, if indeed he could claim what was offered in fact to his father. To them both, the change seemed useless. Any young man could make some sort of Assistant Secretary; only one, just at that moment, could make an Assistant Son. More than half his duties were domestic; they sometimes required long absences; they always required independence of the Government service. His position was abnormal. The British Government by courtesy allowed the son to go to Court as Attache, though he was never attached, and after five or six years' toleration, the decision was declared irregular. In the Legation, as private secretary, he was liable to do Secretary's work. In society, when official, he was attached to the Minister; when unofficial, he was a young man without any position at all. As the years went on, he began to find advantages in having no position at all except that of young man. Gradually he aspired to become a gentleman; just a member of society like the rest. The position was irregular; at that time many positions were irregular; yet it lent itself to a sort of irregular education that seemed to be the only sort of education the young man was ever to get.

Such as it was, few young men had more. The spring and summer of 1863 saw a great change in Secretary Seward's management of foreign affairs. Under the stimulus of danger, he too got education. He felt, at last, that his official representatives abroad needed support. Officially he could give them nothing but despatches, which were of no great value to any one; and at best the mere weight of an office had little to do with the public. Governments were made to deal with Governments, not with private individuals or with the opinions of foreign society. In order to affect European opinion, the weight of American opinion had to be brought to bear personally, and had to be backed by the weight of American interests. Mr. Seward set vigorously to work and sent over every important American on whom he could lay his hands. All came to the Legation more or less intimately, and Henry Adams had a chance to see them all, bankers or bishops, who did their work quietly and well, though, to the outsider, the work seemed wasted and the "influential classes" more indurated with prejudice than ever. The waste was only apparent; the work all told in the end, and meanwhile it helped education.

Two or three of these gentlemen were sent over to aid the Minister and to cooperate with him. The most interesting of these was Thurlow Weed, who came to do what the private secretary himself had attempted two years before, with boyish ignorance of his own powers. Mr. Weed took charge of the press, and began, to the amused astonishment of the secretaries, by making what the Legation had learned to accept as the invariable mistake of every amateur diplomat; he wrote letters to the London Times. Mistake or not, Mr. Weed soon got into his hands the threads of management, and did quietly and smoothly all that was to be done. With his work the private secretary had no connection; it was he that interested. Thurlow Weed was a complete American education in himself. His mind was naturally strong and beautifully balanced; his temper never seemed ruffled; his manners were carefully perfect in the style of benevolent simplicity, the tradition of Benjamin Franklin. He was the model of political management and patient address; but the trait that excited enthusiasm in a private secretary was his faculty of irresistibly conquering confidence. Of all flowers in the garden of education, confidence was becoming the rarest; but before Mr. Weed went away, young Adams followed him about not only obediently -- for obedience had long since become a blind instinct -- but rather with sympathy and affection, much like a little dog.

The sympathy was not due only to Mr. Weed's skill of management, although Adams never met another such master, or any one who approached him; nor was the confidence due to any display of professions, either moral or social, by Mr. Weed. The trait that astounded and confounded cynicism was his apparent unselfishness. Never, in any man who wielded such power, did Adams meet anything like it. The effect of power and publicity on all men is the aggravation of self, a sort of tumor that ends by killing the victim's sympathies; a diseased appetite, like a passion for drink or perverted tastes; one can scarcely use expressions too strong to describe the violence of egotism it stimulates; and Thurlow Weed was one of the exceptions; a rare immune. He thought apparently not of himself, but of the person he was talking with. He held himself naturally in the background. He was not jealous. He grasped power, but not office. He distributed offices by handfuls without caring to take them. He had the instinct of empire: he gave, but he did not receive. This rare superiority to the politicians he controlled, a trait that private secretaries never met in the politicians themselves, excited Adams's wonder and curiosity, but when he tried to get behind it, and to educate himself from the stores of Mr. Weed's experience, he found the study still more fascinating. Management was an instinct with Mr. Weed; an object to be pursued for its own sake, as one plays cards; but he appeared to play with men as though they were only cards; he seemed incapable of feeling himself one of them. He took them and played them for their face-value; but once, when he had told, with his usual humor, some stories of his political experience which were strong even for the Albany lobby, the private secretary made bold to ask him outright: "Then, Mr. Weed, do you think that no politician can be trusted? " Mr. Weed hesitated for a moment; then said in his mild manner: "I never advise a young man to begin by thinking so."

This lesson, at the time, translated itself to Adams in a moral sense, as though Mr. Weed had said: "Youth needs illusions !" As he grew older he rather thought that Mr. Weed looked on it as a question of how the game should be played. Young men most needed experience. They could not play well if they trusted to a general rule. Every card had a relative value. Principles had better be left aside; values were enough. Adams knew that he could never learn to play politics in so masterly a fashion as this: his education and his nervous system equally forbade it, although he admired all the more the impersonal faculty of the political master who could thus efface himself and his temper in the game. He noticed that most of the greatest politicians in history had seemed to regard men as counters. The lesson was the more interesting because another famous New Yorker came over at the same time who liked to discuss the same problem. Secretary Seward sent William M. Evarts to London as law counsel, and Henry began an acquaintance with Mr. Evarts that soon became intimate. Evarts was as individual as Weed was impersonal; like most men, he cared little for the game, or how it was played, and much for the stakes, but he played it in a large and liberal way, like Daniel Webster, "a great advocate employed in politics." Evarts was also an economist of morals, but with him the question was rather how much morality one could afford. "The world can absorb only doses of truth," he said; "too much would kill it." One sought education in order to adjust the dose.

The teachings of Weed and Evarts were practical, and the private secretary's life turned on their value. England's power of absorbing truth was small. Englishmen, such as Palmerston, Russell, Bethell, and the society represented by the Times and Morning Post, as well as the Tories represented by Disraeli, Lord Robert Cecil, and the Standard, offered a study in education that sickened a young student with anxiety. He had begun -- contrary to Mr. Weed's advice -- by taking their bad faith for granted. Was he wrong? To settle this point became the main object of the diplomatic education so laboriously pursued, at a cost already stupendous, and promising to become ruinous. Life changed front, according as one thought one's self dealing with honest men or with rogues.

Thus far, the private secretary felt officially sure of dishonesty. The reasons that satisfied him had not altogether satisfied his father, and of course his father's doubts gravely shook his own convictions, but, in practice, if only for safety, the Legation put little or no confidence in Ministers, and there the private secretary's diplomatic education began. The recognition of belligerency, the management of the Declaration of Paris, the Trent Affair, all strengthened the belief that Lord Russell had started in May, 1861, with the assumption that the Confederacy was established; every step he had taken proved his persistence in the same idea; he never would consent to put obstacles in the way of recognition; and he was waiting only for the proper moment to interpose. All these points seemed so fixed -- so self-evident -- that no one in the Legation would have doubted or even discussed them except that Lord Russell obstinately denied the whole charge, and persisted in assuring

Minister Adams of his honest and impartial neutrality. With the insolence of youth and zeal, Henry Adams jumped at once to the conclusion that Earl Russell -- like other statesmen -- lied;

and, although the Minister thought differently, he had to act as though Russell were false. Month by month the demonstration followed its mathematical stages; one of the most perfect educational courses in politics and diplomacy that a young man ever had a chance to pursue. The most costly tutors in the world were provided for him at public expense -- Lord Palmerston, Lord Russell, Lord Westbury, Lord Selborne, Mr. Gladstone, Lord Granville, and their associates, paid by the British Government; William H. Seward, Charles Francis Adams, William Maxwell Evarts, Thurlow Weed, and other considerable professors employed by the American Government; but there was only one student to profit by this immense staff of teachers. The private secretary alone sought education.

To the end of his life he labored over the lessons then taught. Never was demonstration more tangled. Hegel's metaphysical doctrine of the identity of opposites was simpler and easier to understand. Yet the stages of demonstration were clear. They began in June, 1862, after the escape of one rebel cruiser, by the remonstrances of the Minister against the escape of "No. 290," which was imminent. Lord Russell declined to act on the evidence. New evidence was sent in every few days, and with it, on July 24, was included Collier's legal opinion: "It appears difficult to make out a stronger case of infringement of the Foreign Enlistment Act, which, if not enforced on this occasion, is little better than a dead letter." Such language implied almost a charge of collusion with the rebel agents -- an intent to aid the Confederacy. In spite of the warning, Earl Russell let the ship, four days afterwards, escape.

Young Adams had nothing to do with law; that was business of his betters. His opinion of law hung on his opinion of lawyers. In spite of Thurlow Weed's advice, could one afford to trust human nature in politics ? History said not. Sir Robert Collier seemed to hold that Law agreed with History. For education the point was vital. If one could not trust a dozen of the most respected private characters in the world, composing the Queen's Ministry, one could trust no mortal man.

Lord Russell felt the force of this inference, and undertook to disprove it. His effort lasted till his death. At first he excused himself by throwing the blame on the law officers. This was a politician's practice, and the lawyers overruled it. Then he pleaded guilty to criminal negligence, and said in his "Recollections":-- "I assent entirely to the opinion of the Lord Chief Justice of England that the Alabama ought to have been detained during the four days I was waiting for the opinion of the law officers. But I think that the fault was not that of the commissioners of customs, it was my fault as Secretary of State for Foreign Affairs." This concession brought all parties on common ground. Of course it was his fault! The true issue lay not in the question of his fault, but of his intent. To a young man, getting an education in politics, there could be no sense in history unless a constant course of faults implied a constant motive.

For his father the question was not so abstruse; it was a practical matter of business to be handled as Weed or Evarts handled their bargains and jobs. Minister Adams held the convenient belief that, in the main, Russell was true, and the theory answered his purposes so well that he died still holding it. His son was seeking education, and wanted to know whether he could, in politics, risk trusting any one. Unfortunately no one could then decide; no one knew the facts. Minister Adams died without knowing them. Henry Adams was an older man than his father in 1862, before he learned a part of them. The most curious fact, even then, was that Russell believed in his own good faith and that Argyll believed in it also.

Argyll betrayed a taste for throwing the blame on Bethell, Lord Westbury, then Lord Chancellor, but this escape helped Adams not at all. On the contrary, it complicated the case of Russell. In England, one half of society enjoyed throwing stones at Lord Palmerston, while the other half delighted in flinging mud at Earl Russell, but every one of every party united in pelting Westbury with every missile at hand. The private secretary had no doubts about him, for he never professed to be moral. He was the head and heart of the whole rebel contention, and his opinions on neutrality were as clear as they were on morality. The private secretary had nothing to do with him, and regretted it, for Lord Westbury's wit and wisdom were great; but as far as his authority went he affirmed the law that in politics no man should be trusted.

Russell alone insisted on his honesty of intention and persuaded both the Duke and the Minister to believe him. Every one in the Legation accepted his assurances as the only assertions they could venture to trust. They knew he expected the rebels to win in the end, but they believed he would not actively interpose to decide it. On that -- on nothing else -- they rested their frail hopes of remaining a day longer in England. Minister Adams remained six years longer in England; then returned to America to lead a busy life till he died in 1886 still holding the same faith in Earl Russell, who had died in 1878. In 1889, Spencer Walpole published the official life of Earl Russell, and told a part of the story which had never been known to the Minister and which astounded his son, who burned with curiosity to know what his father would have said of it.

The story was this: The Alabama escaped, by Russell's confessed negligence, on July 28, 1862. In America the Union armies had suffered great disasters before Richmond and at the second Bull Run, August 29-30, followed by Lee's invasion of Maryland, September 7, the news of which, arriving in England on September 14, roused the natural idea that the crisis was at hand. The next news was expected by the Confederates to announce the fall of Washington or Baltimore. Palmerston instantly, September 14, wrote to Russell: "If this should happen, would it not be time for us to consider whether in such a state of things England and France might not address the contending parties and recommend an arrangement on the basis of separation?"

This letter, quite in the line of Palmerston's supposed opinions, would have surprised no one, if it had been communicated to the Legation; and indeed, if Lee had captured Washington, no one could have blamed Palmerston for offering intervention. Not Palmerston's letter but Russell's reply, merited the painful attention of a young man seeking a moral standard for judging politicians: --

GOTHA, September, 17, 1862

MY DEAR PALMERSTON:--

Whether the Federal army is destroyed or not, it is clear that it is driven back to Washington and has made no progress in subduing the insurgent States. Such being the case, I agree with you that the time is come for offering mediation to the United States Government with a view to the recognition of the independence of the Confederates. I agree further that in case of failure, we ought ourselves to recognize the Southern States as an independent State. For the purpose of taking so important a step, I think we must have a meeting of the Cabinet. The 23d or 30th would suit me for the meeting.

We ought then, if we agree on such a step, to propose it first to France, and then on the part of England and France, to Russia and other powers, as a measure decided upon by us.

We ought to make ourselves safe in Canada, not by sending more troops there, but by concentrating those we have in a few defensible posts before the winter sets in. . . .

Here, then, appeared in its fullest force, the practical difficulty in education which a mere student could never overcome; a difficulty not in theory, or knowledge, or even want of experience, but in the sheer chaos of human nature. Lord Russell's course had been consistent from the first, and had all the look of rigid determination to recognize the Southern Confederacy "with a view" to breaking up the Union. His letter of September 17 hung directly on his encouragement of the Alabama and his protection of the rebel navy; while the whole of his plan had its root in the Proclamation of Belligerency, May 13, 1861. The policy had every look of persistent forethought, but it took for granted the deliberate dishonesty of three famous men: Palmerston, Russell, and Gladstone. This dishonesty, as concerned Russell, was denied by Russell himself, and disbelieved by Argyll, Forster, and most of America's friends in England, as well as by Minister Adams. What the Minister would have thought had he seen this letter of September 17, his son would have greatly liked to know, but he would have liked still more to know what the Minister would have thought of Palmerston's answer, dated September 23: --

. . . It is evident that a great conflict is taking place to the northwest of Washington, and its issue must have a great effect on the state of affairs. If the Federals sustain a great defeat, they may be at once ready for mediation, and the iron should be struck while it is hot. If, on the other hand, they should have the best of it, we may wait a while and see what may follow. . .

The roles were reversed. Russell wrote what was expected from Palmerston, or even more violently; while Palmerston wrote what was expected from Russell, or even more temperately. The private secretary's view had been altogether wrong, which would not have much surprised even him, but he would have been greatly astonished to learn that the most confidential associates of these men knew little more about their intentions than was known in the Legation. The most trusted member of the Cabinet was Lord Granville, and to him Russell next wrote. Granville replied at once decidedly opposing recognition of the Confederacy, and Russell sent the reply to Palmerston, who returned it October 2, with the mere suggestion of waiting for further news from America. At the same time Granville wrote to another member of the Cabinet, Lord Stanley of Alderley, a letter published forty years afterwards in Granville's "Life" (I, 442) to the private secretary altogether the most curious and instructive relic of the whole lesson in politics:

. . . I have written to Johnny my reasons for thinking it decidedly premature. I, however, suspect you will settle to do so. Pam., Johnny, and Gladstone would be in favor of it, and probably Newcastle. I do not know about the others. It appears to me a great mistake. . . .

Out of a Cabinet of a dozen members, Granville, the best informed of them all, could pick only three who would favor recognition. Even a private secretary thought he knew as much as this, or more. Ignorance was not confined to the young and insignificant, nor were they the only victims of blindness. Granville's letter made only one point clear. He knew of no fixed policy or conspiracy. If any existed, it was confined to Palmerston, Russell, Gladstone, and perhaps

Newcastle. In truth, the Legation knew, then, all that was to be known, and the true fault of education was to suspect too much.

By that time, October 3, news of Antietam and of Lee's retreat into Virginia had reached London. The Emancipation Proclamation arrived. Had the private secretary known all that Granville or Palmerston knew, he would surely have thought the danger past, at least for a time, and any man of common sense would have told him to stop worrying over phantoms. This healthy lesson would have been worth much for practical education, but it was quite upset by the sudden rush of a new actor upon the stage with a rhapsody that made Russell seem sane, and all education superfluous.

This new actor, as every one knows, was William Ewart Gladstone, then Chancellor of the Exchequer. If, in the domain of the world's politics, one point was fixed, one value ascertained, one element serious, it was the British Exchequer; and if one man lived who could be certainly counted as sane by overwhelming interest, it was the man who had in charge the finances of England. If education had the smallest value, it should have shown its force in Gladstone, who was educated beyond all record of English training. From him, if from no one else, the poor student could safely learn.

Here is what he learned! Palmerston notified Gladstone, September 24, of the proposed intervention: "If I am not mistaken, you would be inclined to approve such a course." Gladstone replied the next day: "He was glad to learn what the Prime Minister had told him; and for two reasons especially he desired that the proceedings should be prompt: the first was the rapid progress of the Southern arms and the extension of the area of Southern feeling; the second was the risk of violent impatience in the cotton-towns of Lancashire such as would prejudice the dignity and disinterestedness of the proffered mediation."

Had the puzzled student seen this letter, he must have concluded from it that the best educated statesman England ever produced did not know what he was talking about, an assumption which all the world would think quite inadmissible from a private secretary -- but this was a trifle. Gladstone having thus arranged, with Palmerston and Russell, for intervention in the American war, reflected on the subject for a fortnight from September 25 to October 7, when he was to speak on the occasion of a great dinner at Newcastle. He decided to announce the Government's policy with all the force his personal and official authority could give it. This decision was no sudden impulse; it was the result of deep reflection pursued to the last moment. On the morning of October 7, he entered in his diary: "Reflected further on what I should say about Lancashire and America, for both these subjects are critical." That evening at dinner, as the mature fruit of his long study, he deliberately pronounced the famous phrase:--

. . . We know quite well that the people of the Northern States have not yet drunk of the cup -- they are still trying to hold it far from their lips -- which all the rest of the world see they nevertheless must drink of. We may have our own opinions about slavery; we may be for or against the South; but there is no doubt that Jefferson Davis and other leaders of the South have made an army; they are making, it appears, a navy; and they have made, what is more than either, they have made a nation. . . .

Looking back, forty years afterwards, on this episode, one asked one's self painfully whet sort of a lesson a young man should have drawn, for the purposes of his education, from this world-famous teaching of a very great master. In the heat of passion at the moment, one drew some harsh moral conclusions: Were they incorrect? Posed bluntly as rules of conduct, they led to the worst possible practices. As morals, one could detect no shade of difference between Gladstone and Napoleon except to the advantage of Napoleon. The private secretary saw none; he accepted the teacher in that sense; he took his lesson of political morality as learned, his notice to quit as duly served, and supposed his education to be finished.

Every one thought so, and the whole City was in a turmoil. Any intelligent education ought to end when it is complete. One would then feel fewer hesitations and would handle a surer world. The old-fashioned logical drama required unity and sense; the actual drama is a pointless puzzle, without even an intrigue. When the curtain fell on Gladstone's speech, any student had the right to suppose the drama ended; none could have affirmed that it was about to begin; that one's painful lesson was thrown away.

Even after forty years, most people would refuse to believe it; they would still insist that Gladstone, Russell, and Palmerston were true villains of melodrama. The evidence against Gladstone in special seemed overwhelming. The word "must" can never be used by a responsible Minister of one Government towards another, as Gladstone used it. No one knew so well as he that he and his own officials and friends at Liverpool were alone "making" a rebel navy, and that Jefferson Davis had next to nothing to do with it. As Chancellor of the Exchequer he was the Minister most interested in knowing that Palmerston, Russell, and himself were banded together by mutual pledge to make the Confederacy a nation the next week, and that the Southern leaders had as yet no hope of "making a nation" but in them. Such thoughts occurred to every one at the moment and time only added to their force. Never in the history of political turpitude had any brigand of modern civilization offered a worse example. The proof of it was that it outraged even Palmerston, who immediately put up Sir George Cornewall Lewis to repudiate the Chancellor of the Exchequer, against whom he turned his press at the same time. Palmerston had no notion of letting his hand be forced by Gladstone.

Russell did nothing of the kind; if he agreed with Palmerston, he followed Gladstone. Although he had just created a new evangel of non-intervention for Italy, and preached it like an apostle, he preached the gospel of intervention in America as though he were a mouthpiece of the Congress of Vienna. On October 13, he issued his call for the Cabinet to meet, on October 23, for discussion of the "duty of Europe to ask both parties, in the most friendly and conciliatory terms, to agree to a suspension of arms." Meanwhile Minister Adams, deeply perturbed and profoundly anxious, would betray no sign of alarm, and purposely delayed to ask explanation. The howl of anger against Gladstone became louder every day, for every one knew that the Cabinet was called for October 23, and then could not fail to decide its policy about the United States. Lord Lyons put off his departure for America till October 25 expressly to share in the conclusions to be discussed on October 23. When Minister Adams at last requested an interview, Russell named October 23 as the day. To the last moment every act of Russell showed that, in his mind, the intervention was still in doubt.

When Minister Adams, at the interview, suggested that an explanation was due him, he watched Russell with natural interest, and reported thus:

. . . His lordship took my allusion at once, though not without a slight indication of embarrassment. He said that Mr. Gladstone had been evidently much misunderstood. I must have seen in the newspapers the letters which contained his later explanations. That he had certain opinions in regard to the nature of the struggle in America, as on all public questions, just as other Englishmen had, was natural enough. And it was the fashion here for public men to express such as they held in their public addresses. Of course it was not for him to disavow anything on the part of Mr. Gladstone; but he had no idea that in saying what he had, there was a serious intention to justify any of the inferences that had been drawn from it of a disposition in the Government now to adopt a new policy. . . .

A student trying to learn the processes of politics in a free government could not but ponder long on the moral to be drawn from this "explanation" of Mr. Gladstone by Earl Russell. The point set for study as the first condition of political life, was whether any politician could be believed or trusted. The question which a private secretary asked himself, in copying this despatch of October 24, 1862, was whether his father believed, or should believe, one word of Lord Russell's "embarrassment." The "truth" was not known for thirty years, but when published, seemed to be the reverse of Earl Russell's statement. Mr. Gladstone's speech had been drawn out by Russell's own policy of intervention and had no sense except to declare the "disposition in the Government now to adopt" that new policy. Earl Russell never disavowed Gladstone, although Lord Palmerston and Sir George Cornewall Lewis instantly did so. As far as the curious student could penetrate the mystery, Gladstone exactly expressed Earl Russell's intent.

As political education, this lesson was to be crucial; it would decide the law of life. All these gentlemen were superlatively honorable; if one could not believe them, Truth in politics might be ignored as a delusion. Therefore the student felt compelled to reach some sort of idea that should serve to bring the case within a general law. Minister Adams felt the same compulsion. He bluntly told Russell that while he was "willing to acquit" Gladstone of "any deliberate intention to bring on the worst effects," he was bound to say that Gladstone was doing it quite as certainly as if he had one; and to this charge, which struck more sharply at Russell's secret policy than at Gladstone's public defence of it, Russell replied as well as he could: --

. . . His lordship intimated as guardedly as possible that Lord Palmerston and other members of the Government regretted the speech, and`Mr. Gladstone himself was not disinclined to correct, as far as he could, the misinterpretation which had been made of it. It was still their intention to adhere to the rule of perfect neutrality in the struggle, and to let it come to its natural end without the smallest interference, direct or otherwise. But he could not say what circumstances might happen from month to month in the future. I observed that the policy he mentioned was satisfactory to us, and asked if I was to understand him as saying that no change of it was now proposed. To which he gave his assent. . . .

Minister Adams never knew more. He retained his belief that Russell could be trusted, but that Palmerston could not. This was the diplomatic tradition, especially held by the Russian diplomats. Possibly it was sound, but it helped in no way the education of a private secretary. The cat's-paw theory offered no safer clue, than the frank, old-fashioned, honest theory of villainy. Neither the one nor the other was reasonable.

No one ever told the Minister that Earl Russell, only a few hours before, had asked the Cabinet to intervene, and that the Cabinet had refused. The Minister was led to believe that the Cabinet meeting was not held, and that its decision was informal. Russell's biographer said that, "with this memorandum [of Russell's, dated October 13] the Cabinet assembled from all parts of the country on October 23; but . . . members of the Cabinet doubted the policy of moving, or moving at that time." The Duke of Newcastle and Sir George Grey joined Granville in opposition. As far as known, Russell and Gladstone stood alone. "Considerations such as these prevented the matter being pursued any further."

Still no one has distinctly said that this decision was formal; perhaps the unanimity of opposition made the formal Cabinet unnecessary; but it is certain that, within an hour or two before or after this decision, "his lordship said [to the United States Minister] that the policy of the Government was to adhere to a strict neutrality and to leave this struggle to settle itself." When Mr. Adams, not satisfied even with this positive assurance, pressed for a categorical answer: "I asked him if I was to understand that policy as not now to be changed; he said: Yes!"

John Morley's comment on this matter, in the "Life of Gladstone," forty years afterwards, would have interested the Minister, as well as his private secretary: "If this relation be accurate," said Morley of a relation officially published at the time, and never questioned, "then the Foreign Secretary did not construe strict neutrality as excluding what diplomatists call good offices." For a vital lesson in politics, Earl Russell's construction of neutrality mattered little to the student, who asked only Russell's intent, and cared only to know whether his construction had any other object than to deceive the Minister.

In the grave one can afford to be lavish of charity, and possibly Earl Russell may have been honestly glad to reassure his personal friend Mr. Adams; but to one who is still in the world even if not of it, doubts are as plenty as days. Earl Russell totally deceived the private secretary, whatever he may have done to the Minister. The policy of abstention was not settled on October 23. Only the next day, October 24, Gladstone circulated a rejoinder to G. C. Lewis, insisting on the duty of England, France, and Russia to intervene by representing, "with moral authority and force, the opinion of the civilized world upon the conditions of the case." Nothing had been decided. By some means, scarcely accidental, the French Emperor was led to think that his influence might turn the scale, and only ten days after Russell's categorical "Yes!" Napoleon officially invited him to say "No!" He was more than ready to do so. Another Cabinet meeting was called for November 11, and this time Gladstone himself reports the debate:

Nov. 11. We have had our Cabinet to-day and meet again tomorrow. I am afraid we shall do little or nothing in the business of America. But I will send you definite intelligence. Both Lords Palmerston and Russell are right.

Nov. 12. The United States affair has ended and not well. Lord Russell rather turned tail. He gave way without resolutely fighting out his battle. However, though we decline for the moment, the answer is put upon grounds and in terms which leave the matter very open for the future.

Nov. 13. I think the French will make our answer about America public; at least it is very possible. But I hope they may not take it as a positive refusal, or at any rate that they may themselves act in the matter. It will be clear that we concur with them, that the war should cease. Palmerston gave to Russell's proposal a feeble and half-hearted support.

Forty years afterwards, when every one except himself, who looked on at this scene, was dead, the private secretary of 1862 read these lines with stupor, and hurried to discuss them with John Hay, who was more astounded than himself. All the world had been at cross-purposes, had misunderstood themselves and the situation, had followed wrong paths, drawn wrong conclusions, had known none of the facts. One would have done better to draw no conclusions at all. One's diplomatic education was a long mistake.

These were the terms of this singular problem as they presented themselves to the student of diplomacy in 1862: Palmerston, on September 14, under the impression that the President was about to be driven from Washington and the Army of the Potomac dispersed, suggested to Russell that in such a case, intervention might be feasible. Russell instantly answered that, in any case, he wanted to intervene and should call a Cabinet for the purpose. Palmerston hesitated; Russell insisted; Granville protested. Meanwhile the rebel army was defeated at Antietam, September 17, and driven out of Maryland. Then Gladstone, October 7, tried to force Palmerston's hand by treating the intervention as a fait accompli. Russell assented, but Palmerston put up Sir George Cornewall Lewis to contradict Gladstone and treated him sharply in the press, at the very moment when Russell was calling a Cabinet to make Gladstone's words good. On October 23, Russell assured Adams that no change in policy was now proposed. On the same day he had proposed it, and was voted down. Instantly Napoleon III appeared as the ally of Russell and Gladstone with a proposition which had no sense except as a bribe to Palmerston to replace America, from pole to pole, in her old dependence on Europe, and to replace England in her old sovereignty of the seas, if Palmerston would support France in Mexico. The young student of diplomacy, knowing Palmerston, must have taken for granted that Palmerston inspired this motion and would support it; knowing Russell and his Whig antecedents, he would conceive that Russell must oppose it; knowing Gladstone and his lofty principles, he would not doubt that Gladstone violently denounced the scheme. If education was worth a straw, this was the only arrangement of persons that a trained student would imagine possible, and it was the arrangement actually assumed by nine men out of ten, as history. In truth, each valuation was false. Palmerston never showed favor to the scheme and gave it only "a feeble and half-hearted support." Russell gave way without resolutely fighting out "his battle." The only resolute, vehement, conscientious champion of Russell, Napoleon, and Jefferson Davis was Gladstone.

Other people could afford to laugh at a young man's blunders, but to him the best part of life was thrown away if he learned such a lesson wrong. Henry James had not yet taught the world to read a volume for the pleasure of seeing the lights of his burning-glass turned on alternate sides of the same figure. Psychological study was still simple, and at worst -- or at best -- English character was never subtle. Surely no one would believe that complexity was the trait that confused the student of Palmerston, Russell, and Gladstone. Under a very strong light human nature will always appear complex and full of contradictions, but the British statesman would appear, on the whole, among the least complex of men.

Complex these gentlemen were not. Disraeli alone might, by contrast, be called complex, but Palmerston, Russell, and Gladstone deceived only by their simplicity. Russell was the most interesting to a young man because his conduct seemed most statesmanlike. Every act of Russell, from April, 1861, to November, 1862, showed the clearest determination to break up the Union. The only point in Russell's character about which the student thought no doubt to be possible was its want of good faith. It was thoroughly dishonest, but strong. Habitually Russell said one thing and did another. He seemed unconscious of his own contradictions even when his opponents pointed them out, as they were much in the habit of doing, in the strongest language. As the student watched him deal with the Civil War in America, Russell alone showed persistence, even obstinacy, in a definite determination, which he supported, as was necessary, by the usual definite falsehoods. The young man did not complain of the falsehoods; on the contrary, he was vain of his own insight in detecting them; but he was wholly upset by the idea that Russell should think himself true.

Young Adams thought Earl Russell a statesman of the old school, clear about his objects and unscrupulous in his methods -- dishonest but strong. Russell ardently asserted that he had no objects, and that though he might be weak he was above all else honest. Minister Adams leaned to Russell personally and thought him true, but officially, in practice, treated him as false. Punch, before 1862, commonly drew Russell as a schoolboy telling lies, and afterwards as prematurely senile, at seventy. Education stopped there. No one, either in or out of England, ever offered a rational explanation of Earl Russell.

Palmerston was simple -- so simple as to mislead the student altogether -- but scarcely more consistent. The world thought him positive, decided, reckless; the record proved him to be cautious, careful, vacillating. Minister Adams took him for pugnacious and quarrelsome; the "Lives" of Russell, Gladstone, and Granville show him to have been good-tempered, conciliatory, avoiding quarrels. He surprised the Minister by refusing to pursue his attack on General Butler. He tried to check Russell. He scolded Gladstone. He discouraged Napoleon. Except Disraeli none of the English statesmen were so cautious as he in talking of America. Palmerston told no falsehoods; made no professions; concealed no opinions; was detected in no double-dealing. The most mortifying failure in Henry Adams's long education was that, after forty years of confirmed dislike, distrust, and detraction of Lord Palmerston, he was obliged at last to admit himself in error, and to consent in spirit -- for by that time he was nearly as dead as any of them -- to beg his pardon.

Gladstone was quite another story, but with him a student's difficulties were less because they were shared by all the world including Gladstone himself. He was the sum of contradictions. The highest education could reach, in this analysis, only a reduction to the absurd, but no absurdity that a young man could reach in 1862 would have approached the level that Mr. Gladstone admitted, avowed, proclaimed, in his confessions of 1896, which brought all reason and all hope of education to a still-stand: --

I have yet to record an undoubted error, the most singular and palpable, I may add the least excusable of them all, especially since it was committed so late as in the year 1862 when I had outlived half a century . . . I declared in the heat of the American struggle that Jefferson Davis had made a nation. . . . Strange to say, this declaration, most unwarrantable to be made by a Minister of the Crown with no authority other than his own, was not due to any feeling of partisanship for the South or hostility to the North. . . . I really, though most strangely, believed that it was an act of friendliness to all America to recognize that the struggle was virtually at an end. . . . That my opinion was founded upon a false estimate of the facts was the very least part of my fault. I did not perceive the gross impropriety of such an utterance from a Cabinet Minister of a power allied in blood and language, and bound to loyal neutrality; the case being further exaggerated by the fact that we were already, so to speak, under indictment before the world for not (as was alleged) having strictly enforced the laws of neutrality in the matter of the cruisers. My offence was indeed only a mistake, but one of incredible grossness, and with such consequences of offence and alarm attached to it, that my failing to perceive them justly exposed me to very severe blame. It illustrates vividly that incapacity which my mind so long retained, and perhaps still exhibits, an incapacity of viewing subjects all round. . . .

Long and patiently -- more than patiently -- sympathetically, did the private secretary, forty years afterwards in the twilight of a life of study, read and re-read and reflect upon this confession. Then, it seemed, he had seen nothing correctly at the time. His whole theory of conspiracy -- of policy -- of logic and connection in the affairs of man, resolved itself into "incredible grossness." He felt no rancor, for he had won the game; he forgave, since he must admit, the "incapacity of viewing subjects all round" which had so nearly cost him life and fortune; he was willing even to believe. He noted, without irritation, that Mr. Gladstone, in his confession, had not alluded to the understanding between Russell, Palmerston, and himself; had even wholly left out his most "incredible" act, his ardent support of Napoleon's policy, a policy which even Palmerston and Russell had supported feebly, with only half a heart. All this was indifferent. Granting, in spite of evidence, that Gladstone had no set plan of breaking up the Union; that he was party to no conspiracy; that he saw none of the results of his acts which were clear to every one else; granting in short what the English themselves seemed at last to conclude -- that Gladstone was not quite sane; that Russell was verging on senility; and that Palmerston had lost his nerve -- what sort of education should have been the result of it? How should it have affected one's future opinions and acts?

Politics cannot stop to study psychology. Its methods are rough; its judgments rougher still. All this knowledge would not have affected either the Minister or his son in 1862. The sum of the individuals would still have seemed, to the young man, one individual -- a single will or intention -- bent on breaking up the Union "as a diminution of a dangerous power." The Minister would still have found his interest in thinking Russell friendly and Palmerston hostile. The individual would still have been identical with the mass. The problem would have been the same; the answer equally obscure. Every student would, like the private secretary, answer for himself alone.

Chapter XI. The Battle of the Rams (1863)

MINISTER ADAMS troubled himself little about what he did not see of an enemy. His son, a nervous animal, made life a terror by seeing too much. Minister Adams played his hand as it came, and seldom credited his opponents with greater intelligence than his own. Earl Russell suited him; perhaps a certain personal sympathy united them; and indeed Henry Adams never saw Russell without being amused by his droll likeness to John Quincy Adams. Apart from this shadowy personal relation, no doubt the Minister was diplomatically right; he had nothing to lose and everything to gain by making a friend of the Foreign Secretary, and whether Russell were true or false mattered less, because, in either case, the American Legation could act only as though he were false. Had the Minister known Russell's determined effort to betray and ruin him in October, 1862, he could have scarcely used stronger expressions than he did in 1863. Russell must have been greatly annoyed by Sir Robert Collier's hint of collusion with the rebel agents in the Alabama Case, but he hardened himself to hear the same innuendo repeated in nearly every note from the Legation. As time went on, Russell was compelled, though slowly, to treat the

American Minister as serious. He admitted nothing so unwillingly, for the nullity or fatuity of the Washington Government was his idee fixe; but after the failure of his last effort for joint intervention on November 12, 1862, only one week elapsed before he received a note from Minister Adams repeating his charges about the Alabama, and asking in very plain language for redress. Perhaps Russell's mind was naturally slow to understand the force of sudden attack, or perhaps age had affected it; this was one of the points that greatly interested a student, but young men have a passion for regarding their elders as senile, which was only in part warranted in this instance by observing that Russell's generation were mostly senile from youth. They had never got beyond 1815 Both Palmerston and Russell were in this case. Their senility was congenital, like Gladstone's Oxford training and High Church illusions, which caused wild eccentricities in his judgment. Russell could not conceive that he had misunderstood and mismanaged Minister Adams from the start, and when after November 12 he found himself on the defensive, with Mr Adams taking daily a stronger tone, he showed mere confusion and helplessness.

Thus, whatever the theory, the action of diplomacy had to be the same. Minister Adams was obliged to imply collusion between Russell and the rebels. He could not even stop at criminal negligence. If, by an access of courtesy, the Minister were civil enough to admit that the escape of the Alabama had been due to criminal negligence, he could make no such concession in regard to the ironclad rams which the Lairds were building; for no one could be so simple as to believe that two armored ships-of-war could be built publicly, under the eyes of the Government, and go to sea like the Alabama, without active and incessant collusion. The longer Earl Russell kept on his mask of assumed ignorance, the more violently in the end, the Minister would have to tear it off. Whatever Mr. Adams might personally think of Earl Russell, he must take the greatest possible diplomatic liberties with him if this crisis were allowed to arrive.

As the spring of 1863 drew on, the vast field cleared itself for action. A campaign more beautiful -- better suited for training the mind of a youth eager for training -- has not often unrolled itself for study, from the beginning, before a young man perched in so commanding a position. Very slowly, indeed, after two years of solitude, one began to feel the first faint flush of new and imperial life. One was twenty-five years old, and quite ready to assert it; some of one's friends were wearing stars on their collars; some had won stars of a more enduring kind. At moments one's breath came quick. One began to dream the sensation of wielding unmeasured power. The sense came, like vertigo, for an instant, and passed, leaving the brain a little dazed, doubtful, shy. With an intensity more painful than that of any Shakespearean drama, men's eyes were fastened on the armies in the field. Little by little, at first only as a shadowy chance of what might be, if things could be rightly done, one began to feel that, somewhere behind the chaos in Washington power was taking shape; that it was massed and guided as it had not been before. Men seemed to have learned their business -- at a cost that ruined -- and perhaps too late. A private secretary knew better than most people how much of the new power was to be swung in London, and almost exactly when; but the diplomatic campaign had to wait for the military campaign to lead. The student could only study.

Life never could know more than a single such climax. In that form, education reached its limits. As the first great blows began to fall, one curled up in bed in the silence of night, to listen with incredulous hope. As the huge masses struck, one after another, with the precision of machinery, the opposing mass, the world shivered. Such development of power was unknown. The magnificent resistance and the return shocks heightened the suspense. During the July days

Londoners were stupid with unbelief. They were learning from the Yankees how to fight.

An American saw in a flash what all this meant to England, for one's mind was working with the acceleration of the machine at home; but Englishmen were not quick to see their blunders. One had ample time to watch the process, and had even a little time to gloat over the repayment of old scores. News of Vicksburg and Gettysburg reached London one Sunday afternoon, and it happened that Henry Adams was asked for that evening to some small reception at the house of Monckton Milnes. He went early in order to exchange a word or two of congratulation before the rooms should fill, and on arriving he found only the ladies in the drawing-room; the gentlemen were still sitting over their wine. Presently they came in, and, as luck would have it, Delane of the Times came first. When Milnes caught sight of his young American friend, with a whoop of triumph he rushed to throw both arms about his neck and kiss him on both cheeks. Men of later birth who knew too little to realize the passions of 1863 -- backed by those of 1813 -- and reenforced by those of 1763 -- might conceive that such publicity embarrassed a private secretary who came from Boston and called himself shy; but that evening, for the first time in his life, he happened not to be thinking of himself. He was thinking of Delane, whose eye caught his, at the moment of Milnes's embrace. Delane probably regarded it as a piece of Milnes's foolery; he had never heard of young Adams, and never dreamed of his resentment at being ridiculed in the Times; he had no suspicion of the thought floating in the mind of the American Minister's son, for the British mind is the slowest of all minds, as the files of the Times proved, and the capture of Vicksburg had not yet penetrated Delane's thick cortex of fixed ideas. Even if he had read Adams's thought, he would have felt for it only the usual amused British contempt for all that he had not been taught at school. It needed a whole generation for the Times to reach Milnes's standpoint.

Had the Minister's son carried out the thought, he would surely have sought an introduction to Delane on the spot, and assured him that he regarded his own personal score as cleared off -- sufficiently settled, then and there -- because his father had assumed the debt, and was going to deal with Mr. Delane himself. "You come next!" would have been the friendly warning. For nearly a year the private secretary had watched the board arranging itself for the collision between the Legation and Delane who stood behind the Palmerston Ministry. Mr. Adams had been steadily strengthened and reenforced from Washington in view of the final struggle. The situation had changed since the Trent Affair. The work was efficiently done; the organization was fairly complete. No doubt, the Legation itself was still as weakly manned and had as poor an outfit as the Legations of Guatemala or Portugal. Congress was always jealous of its diplomatic service, and the Chairman of the Committee of Foreign Relations was not likely to press assistance on the Minister to England. For the Legation not an additional clerk was offered or asked. The Secretary, the Assistant Secretary, and the private secretary did all the work that the Minister did not do. A clerk at five dollars a week would have done the work as well or better, but the Minister could trust no clerk; without express authority he could admit no one into the Legation; he strained a point already by admitting his son. Congress and its committees were the proper judges of what was best for the public service, and if the arrangement seemed good to them, it was satisfactory to a private secretary who profited by it more than they did. A great staff would have suppressed him. The whole Legation was a sort of improvised, volunteer service, and he was a volunteer with the rest. He was rather better off than the rest, because he was invisible and unknown. Better or worse, he did his work with the others, and if the secretaries made any remarks about Congress, they made no complaints, and knew that none would have received a moment's attention.

If they were not satisfied with Congress, they were satisfied with Secretary Seward. Without appropriations for the regular service, he had done great things for its support. If the Minister had no secretaries, he had a staff of active consuls; he had a well-organized press; efficient legal support; and a swarm of social allies permeating all classes. All he needed was a victory in the field, and Secretary Stanton undertook that part of diplomacy. Vicksburg and Gettysburg cleared the board, and, at the end of July, 1863, Minister Adams was ready to deal with Earl Russell or Lord Palmerston or Mr. Gladstone or Mr. Delane, or any one else who stood in his way; and by the necessity of the case, was obliged to deal with all of them shortly.

Even before the military climax at Vicksburg and Gettysburg, the Minister had been compelled to begin his attack; but this was history, and had nothing to do with education. The private secretary copied the notes into his private books, and that was all the share he had in the matter, except to talk in private.

No more volunteer services were needed; the volunteers were in a manner sent to the rear; the movement was too serious for skirmishing. All that a secretary could hope to gain from the affair was experience and knowledge of politics. He had a chance to measure the motive forces of men; their qualities of character; their foresight; their tenacity of purpose.

In the Legation no great confidence was felt in stopping the rams. Whatever the reason, Russell seemed immovable. Had his efforts for intervention in September, 1862, been known to the Legation in September, 1863 the Minister must surely have admitted that Russell had, from the first, meant to force his plan of intervention on his colleagues. Every separate step since April, 1861, led to this final coercion. Although Russell's hostile activity of 1862 was still secret -- and remained secret for some five-and-twenty years -- his animus seemed to be made clear by his steady refusal to stop the rebel armaments. Little by little, Minister Adams lost hope. With loss of hope came the raising of tone, until at last, after stripping Russell of every rag of defence and excuse, he closed by leaving him loaded with connivance in the rebel armaments, and ended by the famous sentence: "It would be superfluous in me to point out to your lordship that this is war!"

What the Minister meant by this remark was his own affair; what the private secretary understood by it, was a part of his education. Had his father ordered him to draft an explanatory paragraph to expand the idea as he grasped it, he would have continued thus:--

"It would be superfluous: 1st. Because Earl Russell not only knows it already, but has meant it from the start. 2nd Because it is the only logical and necessary consequence of his unvarying action. 3d. Because Mr. Adams is not pointing out to him that 'this is war,' but is pointing it out to the world, to complete the record."

This would have been the matter-of-fact sense in which the private secretary copied into his books the matter-of-fact statement with which, without passion or excitement, the Minister announced that a state of war existed. To his copying eye, as clerk, the words, though on the extreme verge of diplomatic propriety, merely stated a fact, without novelty, fancy, or rhetoric. The fact had to be stated in order to make clear the issue. The war was Russell's war--Adams only accepted it.

Russell's reply to this note of September 5 reached the Legation on September 8, announcing at last to the anxious secretaries that "instructions have been issued which will prevent the departure of the two ironclad vessels from Liverpool." The members of the modest Legation in Portland Place accepted it as Grant had accepted the capitulation of Vicksburg. The private secretary conceived that, as Secretary Stanton had struck and crushed by superior weight the rebel left on the Mississippi, so Secretary Seward had struck and crushed the rebel right in England, and he never felt a doubt as to the nature of the battle. Though Minister Adams should stay in office till he were ninety, he would never fight another campaign of life and death like this; and though the private secretary should covet and attain every office in the gift of President or people, he would never again find education to compare with the life-and-death alternative of this two-year-and-a-half struggle in London, as it had racked and thumb-screwed him in its shifting phases; but its practical value as education turned on his correctness of judgment in measuring the men and their forces. He felt respect for Russell as for Palmerston because they represented traditional England and an English policy, respectable enough in itself, but which, for four generations, every Adams had fought and exploited as the chief source of his political fortunes. As he understood it, Russell had followed this policy steadily, ably, even vigorously, and had brought it to the moment of execution. Then he had met wills stronger than his own, and, after persevering to the last possible instant, had been beaten. Lord North and George Canning had a like experience. This was only the idea of a boy, but, as far as he ever knew, it was also the idea of his Government. For once, the volunteer secretary was satisfied with his Government. Commonly the self-respect of a secretary, private or public, depends on, and is proportional to, the severity of his criticism, but in this case the English campaign seemed to him as creditable to the State Department as the Vicksburg campaign to the War Department, and more decisive. It was well planned, well prepared, and well executed. He could never discover a mistake in it. Possibly he was biassed by personal interest, but his chief reason for trusting his own judgment was that he thought himself to be one of only half a dozen persons who knew something about it. When others criticised Mr. Seward, he was rather indifferent to their opinions because he thought they hardly knew what they were talking about, and could not be taught without living over again the London life of 1862. To him Secretary Seward seemed immensely strong and steady in leadership; but this was no discredit to Russell or Palmerston or Gladstone. They, too, had shown power, patience and steadiness of purpose. They had persisted for two years and a half in their plan for breaking up the Union, and had yielded at last only in the jaws of war. After a long and desperate struggle, the American Minister had trumped their best card and won the game.

Again and again, in after life, he went back over the ground to see whether he could detect error on either side. He found none. At every stage the steps were both probable and proved. All the more he was disconcerted that Russell should indignantly and with growing energy, to his dying day, deny and resent the axiom of Adams's whole contention, that from the first he meant to break up the Union. Russell affirmed that he meant nothing of the sort; that he had meant nothing at all; that he meant to do right; that he did not know what he meant. Driven from one defence after another, he pleaded at last, like Gladstone, that he had no defence. Concealing all he could conceal -- burying in profound secrecy his attempt to break up the Union in the autumn of 1862 -- he affirmed the louder his scrupulous good faith. What was worse for the private secretary, to the total derision and despair of the lifelong effort for education, as the final result of combined practice, experience, and theory -- he proved it.

Henry Adams had, as he thought, suffered too much from Russell to admit any plea in his favor; but he came to doubt whether this admission really favored him. Not until long after Earl Russell's death was the question reopened. Russell had quitted office in 1866; he died in 1878; the biography was published in 1889. During the Alabama controversy and the Geneva Conference in 1872, his course as Foreign Secretary had been sharply criticised, and he had been compelled to see England pay more than L3,000,000 penalty for his errors. On the other hand, he brought forward -- or his biographer for him -- evidence tending to prove that he was not consciously dishonest, and that he had, in spite of appearances, acted without collusion, agreement, plan, or policy, as far as concerned the rebels. He had stood alone, as was his nature. Like Gladstone, he had thought himself right.

In the end, Russell entangled himself in a hopeless ball of admissions, denials, contradictions, and resentments which led even his old colleagues to drop his defence, as they dropped Gladstone's; but this was not enough for the student of diplomacy who had made a certain theory his law of life, and wanted to hold Russell up against himself; to show that he had foresight and persistence of which he was unaware. The effort became hopeless when the biography in 1889 published papers which upset all that Henry Adams had taken for diplomatic education; yet he sat down once more, when past sixty years old, to see whether he could unravel the skein.

Of the obstinate effort to bring about an armed intervention, on the lines marked out by Russell's letter to Palmerston from Gotha, 17 September, 1862, nothing could be said beyond Gladstone's plea in excuse for his speech in pursuance of the same effort, that it was "the most singular and palpable error," "the least excusable," "a mistake of incredible grossness," which passed defence; but while Gladstone threw himself on the mercy of the public for his speech, he attempted no excuse for Lord Russell who led him into the "incredible grossness" of announcing the Foreign Secretary's intent. Gladstone's offence, "singular and palpable," was not the speech alone, but its cause -- the policy that inspired the speech. "I weakly supposed . . . I really, though most strangely, believed that it was an act of friendliness." Whatever absurdity Gladstone supposed, Russell supposed nothing of the sort. Neither he nor Palmerston "most strangely believed" in any proposition so obviously and palpably absurd, nor did Napoleon delude himself with philanthropy. Gladstone, even in his confession, mixed up policy, speech, motives, and persons, as though he were trying to confuse chiefly himself.

There Gladstone's activity seems to have stopped. He did not reappear in the matter of the rams. The rebel influence shrank in 1863, as far as is known, to Lord Russell alone, who wrote on September 1 that he could not interfere in any way with those vessels, and thereby brought on himself Mr. Adams's declaration of war on September 5. A student held that, in this refusal, he was merely following his policy of September, 1862, and of every step he had taken since 1861.

The student was wrong. Russell proved that he had been feeble, timid, mistaken, senile, but not dishonest. The evidence is convincing. The Lairds had built these ships in reliance on the known opinion of the law-officers that the statute did not apply, and a jury would not convict. Minister Adams replied that, in this case, the statute should be amended, or the ships stopped by exercise of the political power. Bethell rejoined that this would be a violation of neutrality; one must preserve the status quo. Tacitly Russell connived with Laird, and, had he meant to interfere, he was bound to warn Laird that the defect of the statute would no longer protect him, but he allowed the builders to go on till the ships were ready for sea. Then, on September 3, two days before Mr. Adams's "superfluous" letter, he wrote to Lord Palmerston begging for help; "The conduct of the gentlemen who have contracted for the two ironclads at Birkenhead is so very suspicious," -- he began, and this he actually wrote in good faith and deep confidence to Lord Palmerston, his chief, calling "the conduct" of the rebel agents "suspicious" when no one else in Europe or America felt any suspicion about it, because the whole question turned not on the rams, but on the technical scope of the Foreign Enlistment Act, -- "that I have thought it necessary to direct that they should be detained," not, of course, under the statute, but on the ground urged by the American Minister, of international obligation above the statute. "The Solicitor General has been consulted and concurs in the measure as one of policy though not of strict law. We shall thus test the law, and, if we have to pay damages, we have satisfied the opinion which prevails here as well as in America that that kind of neutral hostility should not be allowed to go on without some attempt to stop it."

For naivete that would be unusual in an unpaid attache of Legation, this sudden leap from his own to his opponent's ground, after two years and a half of dogged resistance, might have roused Palmerston to inhuman scorn, but instead of derision, well earned by Russell's old attacks on himself, Palmerston met the appeal with wonderful loyalty. "On consulting the law officers he found that there was no lawful ground for meddling with the ironclads," or, in unprofessional language, that he could trust neither his law officers nor a Liverpool jury; and therefore he suggested buying the ships for the British Navy. As proof of "criminal negligence" in the past, this suggestion seemed decisive, but Russell, by this time, was floundering in other troubles of negligence, for he had neglected to notify the American Minister. He should have done so at once, on September 3. Instead he waited till September 4, and then merely said that the matter was under "serious and anxious consideration." This note did not reach the Legation till three o'clock on the afternoon of September 5 -- after the "superfluous" declaration of war had been sent. Thus, Lord Russell had sacrificed the Lairds: had cost his Ministry the price of two ironclads, besides the Alabama Claims -- say, in round numbers, twenty million dollars -- and had put himself in the position of appearing to yield only to a threat of war. Finally he wrote to the Admiralty a letter which, from the American point of view, would have sounded youthful from an Eton schoolboy: --

September 14, 1863.

MY DEAR DUKE: --

It is of the utmost importance and urgency that the ironclads building at Birkenhead should not go to America to break the blockade. They belong to Monsieur Bravay of Paris. If you will offer to buy them on the part of the Admiralty you will get money's worth if he accepts your offer; and if he does not, it will be presumptive proof that they are already bought by the Confederates. I should state that we have suggested to the Turkish Government to buy them; but you can easily settle that matter with the Turks. . . .

The hilarity of the secretaries in Portland Place would have been loud had they seen this letter and realized the muddle of difficulties into which Earl Russell had at last thrown himself under the impulse of the American Minister; but, nevertheless, these letters upset from top to bottom the results of the private secretary's diplomatic education forty years after he had supposed it complete. They made a picture different from anything he had conceived and rendered worthless his whole painful diplomatic experience.

To reconstruct, when past sixty, an education useful for any practical purpose, is no practical problem, and Adams saw no use in attacking it as only theoretical. He no longer cared whether he understood human nature or not; he understood quite as much of it as he wanted; but he found in the "Life of Gladstone" (II, 464) a remark several times repeated that gave him matter for curious thought. "I always hold," said Mr. Gladstone, "that politicians are the men whom, as a rule, it is most difficult to comprehend"; and he added, by way of strengthening it: "For my own part, I never have thus understood, or thought I understood, above one or two."

Earl Russell was certainly not one of the two.

Henry Adams thought he also had understood one or two; but the American type was more familiar. Perhaps this was the sufficient result of his diplomatic education; it seemed to be the whole.

Chapter XII. Eccentricity (1863)

KNOWLEDGE of human nature is the beginning and end of political education, but several years of arduous study in the neighborhood of Westminster led Henry Adams to think that knowledge of English human nature had little or no value outside of England. In Paris, such a habit stood in one's way; in America, it roused all the instincts of native jealousy. The English mind was one-sided, eccentric, systematically unsystematic, and logically illogical. The less one knew of it, the better.

This heresy, which scarcely would have been allowed to penetrate a Boston mind -- it would, indeed, have been shut out by instinct as a rather foolish exaggeration -- rested on an experience which Henry Adams gravely thought he had a right to think conclusive -- for him. That it should be conclusive for any one else never occurred to him, since he had no thought of educating anybody else. For him -- alone -- the less English education he got, the better!

For several years, under the keenest incitement to watchfulness, he observed the English mind in contact with itself and other minds. Especially with the American the contact was interesting because the limits and defects of the American mind were one of the favorite topics of the European. From the old-world point of view, the American had no mind; he had an economic thinking-machine which could work only on a fixed line. The American mind exasperated the European as a buzz-saw might exasperate a pine forest. The English mind disliked the French mind because it was antagonistic, unreasonable, perhaps hostile, but recognized it as at least a thought. The American mind was not a thought at all; it was a convention, superficial, narrow, and ignorant; a mere cutting instrument, practical, economical, sharp, and direct.

The English themselves hardly conceived that their mind was either economical, sharp, or direct; but the defect that most struck an American was its enormous waste in eccentricity. Americans needed and used their whole energy, and applied it with close economy; but English society was eccentric by law and for sake of the eccentricity itself.

The commonest phrase overheard at an English club or dinner-table was that So-and-So "is quite mad." It was no offence to So-and-So; it hardly distinguished him from his fellows; and when applied to a public man, like Gladstone, it was qualified by epithets much more forcible. Eccentricity was so general as to become hereditary distinction. It made the chief charm of English society as well as its chief terror.

The American delighted in Thackeray as a satirist, but Thackeray quite justly maintained that he was not a satirist at all, and that his pictures of English society were exact and good-natured. The American, who could not believe it, fell back on Dickens, who, at all events, had the vice of exaggeration to extravagance, but Dickens's English audience thought the exaggeration rather in manner or style, than in types. Mr. Gladstone himself went to see Sothern act Dundreary, and laughed till his face was distorted -- not because Dundreary was exaggerated, but because he was ridiculously like the types that Gladstone had seen -- or might have seen -- in any club in Pall Mall. Society swarmed with exaggerated characters; it contained little else.

Often this eccentricity bore all the marks of strength; perhaps it was actual exuberance of force, a birthmark of genius. Boston thought so. The Bostonian called it national character -- native vigor -- robustness -- honesty -- courage. He respected and feared it. British self-assertion, bluff, brutal, blunt as it was, seemed to him a better and nobler thing than the acuteness of the Yankee or the polish of the Parisian. Perhaps he was right.

These questions of taste, of feeling, of inheritance, need no settlement. Every one carries his own inch-rule of taste, and amuses himself by applying it, triumphantly, wherever he travels. Whatever others thought, the cleverest Englishmen held that the national eccentricity needed correction, and were beginning to correct it. The savage satires of Dickens and the gentler ridicule of Matthew Arnold against the British middle class were but a part of the rebellion, for the middle class were no worse than their neighbors in the eyes of an American in 1863; they were even a very little better in the sense that one could appeal to their interests, while a university man, like Gladstone, stood outside of argument. From none of them could a young American afford to borrow ideas.

The private secretary, like every other Bostonian, began by regarding British eccentricity as a force. Contact with it, in the shape of Palmerston, Russell, and Gladstone, made him hesitate; he saw his own national type -- his father, Weed, Evarts, for instance -- deal with the British, and show itself certainly not the weaker; certainly sometimes the stronger. Biassed though he were, he could hardly be biassed to such a degree as to mistake the effects of force on others, and while -- labor as he might -- Earl Russell and his state papers seemed weak to a secretary, he could not see that they seemed strong to Russell's own followers. Russell might be dishonest or he might be merely obtuse -- the English type might be brutal or might be only stupid -- but strong, in either case, it was not, nor did it seem strong to Englishmen.

Eccentricity was not always a force; Americans were deeply interested in deciding whether it was always a weakness. Evidently, on the hustings or in Parliament, among eccentricities, eccentricity was at home; but in private society the question was not easy to answer. That English society was infinitely more amusing because of its eccentricities, no one denied. Barring the atrocious insolence and brutality which Englishmen and especially Englishwomen showed to each other -- very rarely, indeed, to foreigners -- English society was much more easy and tolerant than American. One must expect to be treated with exquisite courtesy this week and be totally forgotten the next, but this was the way of the world, and education consisted in learning to turn one's back on others with the same unconscious indifference that others showed among themselves. The smart of wounded vanity lasted no long time with a young man about town who had little vanity to smart, and who, in his own country, would have found himself in no better position. He had nothing to complain of. No one was ever brutal to him. On the contrary, he was much better treated than ever he was likely to be in Boston -- let alone New York or Washington -- and if his reception varied inconceivably between extreme courtesy and extreme neglect, it merely proved that he had become, or was becoming, at home. Not from a sense of personal griefs or disappointments did he labor over this part of the social problem, but only because his education was becoming English, and the further it went, the less it promised.

By natural affinity the social eccentrics commonly sympathized with political eccentricity. The English mind took naturally to rebellion -- when foreign -- and it felt particular confidence in the Southern Confederacy because of its combined attributes -- foreign rebellion of English blood -- which came nearer ideal eccentricity than could be reached by Poles, Hungarians, Italians or Frenchmen. All the English eccentrics rushed into the ranks of rebel sympathizers, leaving few but well-balanced minds to attach themselves to the cause of the Union. None of the English leaders on the Northern side were marked eccentrics. William E. Forster was a practical, hard-headed Yorkshireman, whose chief ideals in politics took shape as working arrangements on an economical base. Cobden, considering the one-sided conditions of his life, was remarkably well balanced. John Bright was stronger in his expressions than either of them, but with all his self-assertion he stuck to his point, and his point was practical. He did not, like Gladstone, box the compass of thought; "furiously earnest," as Monckton Milnes said, "on both sides of every question"; he was rather, on the whole, a consistent conservative of the old Commonwealth type, and seldom had to defend inconsistencies. Monckton Milnes himself was regarded as an eccentric, chiefly by those who did not know him, but his fancies and hobbies were only ideas a little in advance of the time; his manner was eccentric, but not his mind, as any one could see who read a page of his poetry. None of them, except Milnes, was a university man. As a rule, the Legation was troubled very little, if at all, by indiscretions, extravagances, or contradictions among its English friends. Their work was largely judicious, practical, well considered, and almost too cautious. The "cranks" were all rebels, and the list was portentous. Perhaps it might be headed by old Lord Brougham, who had the audacity to appear at a July 4th reception at the Legation, led by Joe Parkes, and claim his old credit as "Attorney General to Mr. Madison." The Church was rebel, but the dissenters were mostly with the Union. The universities were rebel, but the university men who enjoyed most public confidence -- like Lord Granville, Sir George Cornewall Lewis, Lord Stanley, Sir George Grey -- took infinite pains to be neutral for fear of being thought eccentric. To most observers, as well as to the Times, the Morning Post, and the Standard, a vast majority of the English people seemed to follow the professional eccentrics; even the emotional philanthropists took that direction; Lord Shaftesbury and Carlyle, Fowell Buxton, and Gladstone, threw their sympathies on the side which they should naturally have opposed, and did so for no reason except their eccentricity; but the "canny" Scots and Yorkshiremen were cautious.

This eccentricity did not mean strength. The proof of it was the mismanagement of the rebel interests. No doubt the first cause of this trouble lay in the Richmond Government itself. No one understood why Jefferson Davis chose Mr. Mason as his agent for London at the same time that he made so good a choice as Mr. Slidell for Paris. The Confederacy had plenty of excellent men to send to London, but few who were less fitted than Mason. Possibly Mason had a certain amount of common sense, but he seemed to have nothing else, and in London society he counted merely as one eccentric more. He enjoyed a great opportunity; he might even have figured as a new Benjamin Franklin with all society at his feet; he might have roared as lion of the season and made the social path of the American Minister almost impassable; but Mr. Adams had his usual luck in enemies, who were always his most valuable allies if his friends only let them alone. Mason was his greatest diplomatic triumph. He had his collision with Palmerston; he drove Russell off the field; he swept the board before Cockburn; he overbore Slidell; but he never lifted a finger against Mason, who became his bulwark of defence.

Possibly Jefferson Davis and Mr. Mason shared two defects in common which might have led them into this serious mistake. Neither could have had much knowledge of the world, and both must have been unconscious of humor. Yet at the same time with Mason, President Davis sent out Slidell to France and Mr. Lamar to Russia. Some twenty years later, in the shifting search for the education he never found, Adams became closely intimate at Washington with Lamar, then Senator from Mississippi, who had grown to be one of the calmest, most reasonable and most amiable Union men in the United States, and quite unusual in social charm. In 1860 he passed for the worst of Southern fire-eaters, but he was an eccentric by environment, not by nature; above all his Southern eccentricities, he had tact and humor; and perhaps this was a reason why Mr. Davis sent him abroad with the others, on a futile mission to St. Petersburg. He would have done better in London, in place of Mason. London society would have delighted in him; his stories would have won success; his manners would have made him loved; his oratory would have swept every audience; even Monckton Milnes could never have resisted the temptation of having him to breakfast between Lord Shaftesbury and the Bishop of Oxford.

Lamar liked to talk of his brief career in diplomacy, but he never spoke of Mason. He never alluded to Confederate management or criticised Jefferson Davis's administration. The subject that amused him was his English allies. At that moment -- the early summer of 1863 -- the rebel party in England were full of confidence, and felt strong enough to challenge the American Legation to a show of power. They knew better than the Legation what they could depend upon: that the law officers and commissioners of customs at Liverpool dared not prosecute the ironclad ships; that Palmerston, Russell, and Gladstone were ready to recognize the Confederacy; that the Emperor Napoleon would offer them every inducement to do it. In a manner they owned Liverpool and especially the firm of Laird who were building their ships. The political member of the Laird firm was Lindsay, about whom the whole web of rebel interests clung -- rams, cruisers, munitions, and Confederate loan; social introductions and parliamentary tactics. The firm of Laird, with a certain dignity, claimed to be champion of England's navy; and public opinion, in the summer of 1863, still inclined towards them.

Never was there a moment when eccentricity, if it were a force, should have had more value to the rebel interest; and the managers must have thought so, for they adopted or accepted as their champion an eccentric of eccentrics; a type of 1820; a sort of Brougham of Sheffield, notorious for poor judgment and worse temper. Mr. Roebuck had been a tribune of the people, and, like tribunes of most other peoples, in growing old, had grown fatuous. He was regarded by the friends of the Union as rather a comical personage -- a favorite subject for Punch to laugh at -- with a bitter tongue and a mind enfeebled even more than common by the political epidemic of egotism. In all England they could have found no opponent better fitted to give away his own case. No American man of business would have paid him attention; yet, the Lairds, who certainly knew their own affairs best, let Roebuck represent them and take charge of their interests.

With Roebuck's doings, the private secretary had no concern except that the Minister sent him down to the House of Commons on June 30, 1863, to report the result of Roebuck's motion to recognize the Southern Confederacy. The Legation felt no anxiety, having Vicksburg already in its pocket, and Bright and Forster to say so; but the private secretary went down and was admitted under the gallery on the left, to listen, with great content, while John Bright, with astonishing force, caught and shook and tossed Roebuck, as a big mastiff shakes a wiry, ill-conditioned, toothless, bad-tempered Yorkshire terrier. The private secretary felt an artistic sympathy with Roebuck, for, from time to time, by way of practice, Bright in a friendly way was apt to shake him too, and he knew how it was done. The manner counted for more than the words. The scene was interesting, but the result was not in doubt.

All the more sharply he was excited, near the year 1879, in Washington, by hearing Lamar begin a story after dinner, which, little by little, became dramatic, recalling the scene in the House of Commons. The story, as well as one remembered, began with Lamar's failure to reach St. Petersburg at all, and his consequent detention in Paris waiting instructions. The motion to recognize the Confederacy was about to be made, and, in prospect of the debate, Mr. Lindsay collected a party at his villa on the Thames to bring the rebel agents into relations with Roebuck. Lamar was sent for, and came. After much conversation of a general sort, such as is the usual object or resource of the English Sunday, finding himself alone with Roebuck, Lamar, by way of showing interest, bethought himself of John Bright and asked Roebuck whether he expected Bright to take part in the debate: "No, sir!" said Roebuck sententiously; "Bright and I have met before. It was the old story -- the story of the sword-fish and the whale! No, sir! Mr. Bright will not cross swords with me again!"

Thus assured, Lamar went with the more confidence to the House on the appointed evening, and was placed under the gallery, on the right, where he listened to Roebuck and followed the debate with such enjoyment as an experienced debater feels in these contests, until, as he said, he became aware that a man, with a singularly rich voice and imposing manner, had taken the floor, and was giving Roebuck the most deliberate and tremendous pounding he ever witnessed, "until at last," concluded Lamar, "it dawned on my mind that the sword-fish was getting the worst of it."

Lamar told the story in the spirit of a joke against himself rather than against Roebuck; but such jokes must have been unpleasantly common in the experience of the rebel agents. They were surrounded by cranks of the worst English species, who distorted their natural eccentricities and perverted their judgment. Roebuck may have been an extreme case, since he was actually in his dotage, yet this did not prevent the Lairds from accepting his lead, or the House from taking him seriously. Extreme eccentricity was no bar, in England, to extreme confidence; sometimes it seemed a recommendation; and unless it caused financial loss, it rather helped popularity.

The question whether British eccentricity was ever strength weighed heavily in the balance of education. That Roebuck should mislead the rebel agents on so strange a point as that of Bright's courage was doubly characteristic because the Southern people themselves had this same barbaric weakness of attributing want of courage to opponents, and owed their ruin chiefly to such ignorance of the world. Bright's courage was almost as irrational as that of the rebels themselves. Every one knew that he had the courage of a prize-fighter. He struck, in succession, pretty nearly every man in England that could be reached by a blow, and when he could not reach the individual he struck the class, or when the class was too small for him, the whole people of England. At times he had the whole country on his back. He could not act on the defensive; his mind required attack. Even among friends at the dinner-table he talked as though he were denouncing them, or someone else, on a platform; he measured his phrases, built his sentences, cumulated his effects, and pounded his opponents, real or imagined. His humor was glow, like iron at dull heat; his blow was elementary, like the thrash of a whale.

One day in early spring, March 26, 1863, the Minister requested his private secretary to attend a Trades-Union Meeting at St. James's Hall, which was the result of Professor Beesly's patient efforts to unite Bright and the Trades-Unions on an American platform. The secretary went to the meeting and made a report which reposes somewhere on file in the State Department to this day, as harmless as such reports should be; but it contained no mention of what interested young Adams most -- Bright's psychology. With singular skill and oratorical power, Bright managed at the outset, in his opening paragraph, to insult or outrage every class of Englishman commonly considered respectable, and, for fear of any escaping, he insulted them repeatedly under consecutive heads. The rhetorical effect was tremendous:--

"Privilege thinks it has a great interest in the American contest," he began in his massive, deliberate tones; "and every morning with blatant voice, it comes into our streets and curses the American Republic. Privilege has beheld an afflicting spectacle for many years past. It has beheld thirty million of men happy and prosperous, without emperors -- without king (cheers) -- without the surroundings of a court (renewed cheers)--without nobles, except such as are made by eminence in intellect and virtue -- without State bishops and State priests, those vendors of the love that works salvation (cheers) -- without great armies and great navies -- without a great debt and great taxes -- and Privilege has shuddered at what might happen to old Europe if this great experiment should succeed."

An ingenious man, with an inventive mind, might have managed, in the same number of lines, to offend more Englishmen than Bright struck in this sentence; but he must have betrayed artifice and hurt his oratory. The audience cheered furiously, and the private secretary felt peace in his much troubled mind, for he knew how careful the Ministry would be, once they saw Bright talk republican principles before Trades-Unions; but, while he did not, like Roebuck, see reason to doubt the courage of a man who, after quarrelling with the Trades-Unions, quarreled with all the world outside the Trades-Unions, he did feel a doubt whether to class Bright as eccentric or conventional. Every one called Bright "un-English," from Lord Palmerston to William E. Forster; but to an American he seemed more English than any of his critics. He was a liberal hater, and what he hated he reviled after the manner of Milton, but he was afraid of no one. He was almost the only man in England, or, for that matter, in Europe, who hated Palmerston and was not afraid of him, or of the press or the pulpit, the clubs or the bench, that stood behind him. He loathed the whole fabric of sham religion, sham loyalty, sham aristocracy, and sham socialism. He had the British weakness of believing only in himself and his own conventions. In all this, an American saw, if one may make the distinction, much racial eccentricity, but little that was personal. Bright was singularly well poised; but he used singularly strong language.

Long afterwards, in 1880, Adams happened to be living again in London for a season, when James Russell Lowell was transferred there as Minister; and as Adams's relations with Lowell had become closer and more intimate with years, he wanted the new Minister to know some of his old friends. Bright was then in the Cabinet, and no longer the most radical member even there, but he was still a rare figure in society. He came to dinner, along with Sir Francis Doyle and Sir Robert Cunliffe, and as usual did most of the talking. As usual also, he talked of the things most on his mind. Apparently it must have been some reform of the criminal law which the Judges opposed, that excited him, for at the end of dinner, over the wine, he took possession of the table in his old way, and ended with a superb denunciation of the Bench, spoken in his massive manner, as though every word were a hammer, smashing what it struck:--

"For two hundred years, the Judges of England sat on the Bench, condemning to the penalty of death every man, woman, and child who stole property to the value of five shillings; and, during all that time, not one Judge ever remonstrated against the law. We English are a nation of brutes, and ought to be exterminated to the last man."

As the party rose from table and passed into the drawing-room, Adams said to Lowell that Bright was very fine. "Yes!" replied Lowell, " but too violent! "

Precisely this was the point that Adams doubted. Bright knew his Englishmen better than Lowell did -- better than England did. He knew what amount of violence in language was necessary to drive an idea into a Lancashire or Yorkshire head. He knew that no violence was enough to affect a Somersetshire or Wiltshire peasant. Bright kept his own head cool and clear. He was not excited; he never betrayed excitement. As for his denunciation of the English Bench, it was a very old story, not original with him. That the English were a nation of brutes was a commonplace generally admitted by Englishmen and universally accepted by foreigners; while the matter of their extermination could be treated only as unpractical, on their deserts, because they were probably not very much worse than their neighbors. Had Bright said that the French, Spaniards, Germans, or Russians were a nation of brutes and ought to be exterminated, no one would have found fault; the whole human race, according to the highest authority, has been exterminated once already for the same reason, and only the rainbow protects them from a repetition of it. What shocked Lowell was that he denounced his own people.

Adams felt no moral obligation to defend Judges, who, as far as he knew, were the only class of society specially adapted to defend themselves; but he was curious -- even anxious -- as a point of education, to decide for himself whether Bright's language was violent for its purpose. He thought not. Perhaps Cobden did better by persuasion, but that was another matter. Of course, even Englishmen sometimes complained of being so constantly told that they were brutes and hypocrites, although they were told little else by their censors, and bore it, on the whole, meekly; but the fact that it was true in the main troubled the ten-pound voter much less than it troubled Newman, Gladstone, Ruskin, Carlyle, and Matthew Arnold. Bright was personally disliked by his victims, but not distrusted. They never doubted what he would do next, as they did with John Russell, Gladstone, and Disraeli. He betrayed no one, and he never advanced an opinion in practical matters which did not prove to be practical.

The class of Englishmen who set out to be the intellectual opposites of Bright, seemed to an American bystander the weakest and most eccentric of all. These were the trimmers, the political economists, the anti-slavery and doctrinaire class, the followers of de Tocqueville, and of John Stuart Mill. As a class, they were timid -- with good reason -- and timidity, which is high wisdom in philosophy, sicklies the whole cast of thought in action. Numbers of these men haunted London society, all tending to free-thinking, but never venturing much freedom of thought. Like the anti-slavery doctrinaires of the forties and fifties, they became mute and useless when slavery struck them in the face. For type of these eccentrics, literature seems to have chosen Henry Reeve, at least to the extent of biography. He was a bulky figure in society, always friendly, good-natured, obliging, and useful; almost as universal as Milnes and more busy. As editor of the Edinburgh Review he had authority and even power, although the Review and the whole Whig doctrinaire school had begun -- as the French say -- to date; and of course the literary and artistic sharpshooters of 1867 -- like Frank Palgrave -- frothed and foamed at the mere mention of Reeve's name. Three-fourths of their fury was due only to his ponderous manner. London society abused its rights of personal criticism by fixing on every too conspicuous figure some word or phrase that stuck to it. Every one had heard of Mrs. Grote as "the origin of the word grotesque." Every one had laughed at the story of Reeve approaching Mrs. Grote, with his usual somewhat florid manner, asking in his literary dialect how her husband the historian was: "And how is the learned Grotius?" "Pretty well, thank you, Puffendorf!" One winced at the word, as though it were a drawing of Forain.

No one would have been more shocked than Reeve had he been charged with want of moral courage. He proved his courage afterwards by publishing the "Greville Memoirs," braving the displeasure of the Queen. Yet the Edinburgh Review and its editor avoided taking sides except where sides were already fixed. Americanism would have been bad form in the liberal Edinburgh Review; it would have seemed eccentric even for a Scotchman, and Reeve was a Saxon of Saxons. To an American this attitude of oscillating reserve seemed more eccentric than the reckless hostility of Brougham or Carlyle, and more mischievous, for he never could be sure what preposterous commonplace it might encourage.

The sum of these experiences in 1863 left the conviction that eccentricity was weakness. The young American who should adopt English thought was lost. From the facts, the conclusion was correct, yet, as usual, the conclusion was wrong. The years of Palmerston's last Cabinet, 1859 to 1865, were avowedly years of truce -- of arrested development. The British system like the French, was in its last stage of decomposition. Never had the British mind shown itself so decousu -- so unravelled, at sea, floundering in every sort of historical shipwreck. Eccentricities had a free field. Contradictions swarmed in State and Church. England devoted thirty years of arduous labor to clearing away only a part of the debris. A young American in 1863 could see little or nothing of the future. He might dream, but he could not foretell, the suddenness with which the old Europe, with England in its wake, was to vanish in 1870. He was in dead-water, and the parti-colored, fantastic cranks swam about his boat, as though he were the ancient mariner, and they saurians of the prime.

Chapter XIII. The Perfection of Human Society (1864)

MINISTER ADAMS'S success in stopping the rebel rams fixed his position once for all in English society. From that moment he could afford to drop the character of diplomatist, and assume what, for an American Minister in London, was an exclusive diplomatic advantage, the character of a kind of American Peer of the Realm. The British never did things by halves. Once they recognized a man's right to social privileges, they accepted him as one of themselves. Much as Lord Derby and Mr. Disraeli were accepted as leaders of Her Majesty's domestic Opposition, Minister Adams had a rank of his own as a kind of leader of Her Majesty's American Opposition. Even the Times conceded it. The years of struggle were over, and Minister Adams rapidly gained a position which would have caused his father or grandfather to stare with incredulous envy.

This Anglo-American form of diplomacy was chiefly undiplomatic, and had the peculiar effect of teaching a habit of diplomacy useless or mischievous everywhere but in London. Nowhere else in the world could one expect to figure in a role so unprofessional. The young man knew no longer what character he bore. Private secretary in the morning, son in the afternoon, young man about town in the evening, the only character he never bore was that of diplomatist, except when he wanted a card to some great function. His diplomatic education was at an end; he seldom met a diplomat, and never had business with one; he could be of no use to them, or they to him; but he drifted inevitably into society, and, do what he might, his next education must be one of English social life. Tossed between the horns of successive dilemmas, he reached his twenty-sixth birthday without the power of earning five dollars in any occupation. His friends in the army were almost as badly off, but even army life ruined a young man less fatally than London society. Had he been rich, this form of ruin would have mattered nothing; but the young men of 1865 were none of them rich; all had to earn a living; yet they had reached high positions of responsibility and power in camps and Courts, without a dollar of their own and with no tenure of office.

Henry Adams had failed to acquire any useful education; he should at least have acquired social experience. Curiously enough, he failed here also. From the European or English point of view, he had no social experience, and never got it. Minister Adams happened on a political interregnum owing to Lord Palmerston's personal influence from 1860 to 1865; but this political interregnum was less marked than the social still-stand during the same years. The Prince Consort was dead; the Queen had retired; the Prince of Wales was still a boy. In its best days, Victorian society had never been "smart." During the forties, under the influence of Louis Philippe, Courts affected to be simple, serious and middle class; and they succeeded. The taste of Louis Philippe was bourgeois beyond any taste except that of Queen Victoria. Style lingered in the background with the powdered footman behind the yellow chariot, but speaking socially the Queen had no style save what she inherited. Balmoral was a startling revelation of royal taste. Nothing could be worse than the toilettes at Court unless it were the way they were worn. One's eyes might be dazzled by jewels, but they were heirlooms, and if any lady appeared well dressed, she was either a foreigner or "fast." Fashion was not fashionable in London until the Americans and the Jews were let loose. The style of London toilette universal in 1864 was grotesque, like Monckton Milnes on horseback in Rotten Row.

Society of this sort might fit a young man in some degree for editing Shakespeare or Swift, but had little relation with the society of 1870, and none with that of 1900. Owing to other causes, young Adams never got the full training of such style as still existed. The embarrassments of his first few seasons socially ruined him. His own want of experience prevented his asking introductions to the ladies who ruled society; his want of friends prevented his knowing who these ladies were; and he had every reason to expect snubbing if he put himself in evidence. This sensitiveness was thrown away on English society, where men and women treated each others' advances much more brutally than those of strangers, but young Adams was son and private secretary too; he could not be as thick-skinned as an Englishman. He was not alone. Every young diplomat, and most of the old ones, felt awkward in an English house from a certainty that they were not precisely wanted there, and a possibility that they might be told so.

If there was in those days a country house in England which had a right to call itself broad in views and large in tastes, it was Bretton in Yorkshire; and if there was a hostess who had a right to consider herself fashionable as well as charming, it was Lady Margaret Beaumont; yet one morning at breakfast there, sitting by her side -- not for his own merits -- Henry Adams heard her say to herself in her languid and liberal way, with her rich voice and musing manner, looking into her tea-cup: "I don't think I care for foreigners!" Horror-stricken, not so much on his own account as on hers, the young man could only execute himself as gaily as he might: "But Lady Margaret, please make one small exception for me!" Of course she replied what was evident, that she did not call him a foreigner, and her genial Irish charm made the slip of tongue a happy courtesy; but none the less she knew that, except for his momentary personal introduction, he was in fact a foreigner, and there was no imaginable reason why she should like him, or any other foreigner, unless it were because she was bored by natives. She seemed to feel that her indifference needed a reason to excuse itself in her own eyes, and she showed the subconscious sympathy of the Irish nature which never feels itself perfectly at home even in England. She, too, was some shadowy shade un-English.

Always conscious of this barrier, while the war lasted the private secretary hid himself among the herd of foreigners till he found his relations fixed and unchangeable. He never felt himself in society, and he never knew definitely what was meant as society by those who were in it. He saw far enough to note a score of societies which seemed quite independent of each other. The smartest was the smallest, and to him almost wholly strange. The largest was the sporting world, also unknown to him except through the talk of his acquaintances. Between or beyond these lay groups of nebulous societies. His lawyer friends, like Evarts, frequented legal circles where one still sat over the wine and told anecdotes of the bench and bar; but he himself never set eyes on a judge except when his father took him to call on old Lord Lyndhurst, where they found old Lord Campbell, both abusing old Lord Brougham. The Church and the Bishops formed several societies which no secretary ever saw except as an interloper. The Army; the Navy; the Indian Service; the medical and surgical professions; City people; artists; county families; the Scotch, and indefinite other subdivisions of society existed, which were as strange to each other as they were to Adams. At the end of eight or ten seasons in London society he professed to know less about it, or how to enter it, than he did when he made his first appearance at Miss Burdett Coutts's in May, 1861.

Sooner or later every young man dropped into a set or circle, and frequented the few houses that were willing to harbor him. An American who neither hunted nor raced, neither shot nor fished nor gambled, and was not marriageable, had no need to think of society at large. Ninety-nine houses in every hundred were useless to him, a greater bore to him than he to them. Thus the question of getting into -- or getting out of -- society which troubled young foreigners greatly, settled itself after three or four years of painful speculation. Society had no unity; one wandered about in it like a maggot in cheese; it was not a hansom cab, to be got into, or out of, at dinner-time.

Therefore he always professed himself ignorant of society; he never knew whether he had been in it or not, but from the accounts of his future friends, like General Dick Taylor or George Smalley, and of various ladies who reigned in the seventies, he inclined to think that he knew very little about it. Certain great houses and certain great functions of course he attended, like every one else who could get cards, but even of these the number was small that kept an interest or helped education. In seven years he could remember only two that seemed to have any meaning for him, and he never knew what that meaning was. Neither of the two was official; neither was English in interest; and both were scandals to the philosopher while they scarcely enlightened men of the world.

One was at Devonshire House, an ordinary, unpremeditated evening reception. Naturally every one went to Devonshire House if asked, and the rooms that night were fairly full of the usual people. The private secretary was standing among the rest, when Mme. de Castiglione entered, the famous beauty of the Second Empire. How beautiful she may have been, or indeed what sort of beauty she was, Adams never knew, because the company, consisting of the most refined and aristocratic society in the world, instantly formed a lane, and stood in ranks to stare at her, while those behind mounted on chairs to look over their neighbors' heads; so that the lady walked through this polite mob, stared completely out of countenance, and fled the house at once. This was all!

The other strange spectacle was at Stafford House, April 13, 1864, when, in a palace gallery that recalled Paolo Veronese's pictures of Christ in his scenes of miracle, Garibaldi, in his gray capote over his red shirt, received all London, and three duchesses literally worshipped at his feet. Here, at all events, a private secretary had surely caught the last and highest touch of social experience; but what it meant -- what social, moral, or mental development it pointed out to the searcher of truth -- was not a matter to be treated fully by a leader in the Morning Post or even by a sermon in Westminster Abbey. Mme. de Castiglione and Garibaldi covered, between them, too much space for simple measurement; their curves were too complex for mere arithmetic. The task of bringing the two into any common relation with an ordered social system tending to orderly development -- in London or elsewhere -- was well fitted for Algernon Swinburne or Victor Hugo, but was beyond any process yet reached by the education of Henry Adams, who would probably, even then, have rejected, as superficial or supernatural, all the views taken by any of the company who looked on with him at these two interesting and perplexing sights.

From the Court, or Court society, a mere private secretary got nothing at all, or next to nothing, that could help him on his road through life. Royalty was in abeyance. One was tempted to think in these years, 1860-65, that the nicest distinction between the very best society and the second-best, was their attitude towards royalty. The one regarded royalty as a bore, and avoided it, or quietly said that the Queen had never been in society. The same thing might have been said of fully half the peerage. Adams never knew even the names of half the rest; he never exchanged ten words with any member of the royal family; he never knew any one in those years who showed interest in any member of the royal family, or who would have given five shillings for the opinion of any royal person on any subject; or cared to enter any royal or noble presence, unless the house was made attractive by as much social effort as would have been necessary in other countries where no rank existed. No doubt, as one of a swarm, young Adams slightly knew various gilded youth who frequented balls and led such dancing as was most in vogue, but they seemed to set no value on rank; their anxiety was only to know where to find the best partners before midnight, and the best supper after midnight. To the American, as to Arthur Pendennis or

Barnes Newcome, the value of social position and knowledge was evident enough; he valued it at rather more than it was worth to him; but it was a shadowy thing which seemed to vary with every street corner; a thing which had shifting standards, and which no one could catch outright. The half-dozen leaders and beauties of his time, with great names and of the utmost fashion, made some of the poorest marriages, and the least showy careers.

Tired of looking on at society from the outside, Adams grew to loathe the sight of his Court dress; to groan at every announcement of a Court ball; and to dread every invitation to a formal dinner. The greatest social event gave not half the pleasure that one could buy for ten shillings at the opera when Patti sang Cherubino or Gretchen, and not a fourth of the education. Yet this was not the opinion of the best judges. Lothrop Motley, who stood among the very best, said to him early in his apprenticeship that the London dinner and the English country house were the perfection of human society. The young man meditated over it, uncertain of its meaning. Motley could not have thought the dinner itself perfect, since there was not then -- outside of a few bankers or foreigners -- a good cook or a good table in London, and nine out of ten of the dinners that Motley ate came from Gunter's, and all were alike. Every one, especially in young society, complained bitterly that Englishmen did not know a good dinner when they ate it, and could not order one if they were given carte blanche. Henry Adams was not a judge, and knew no more than they, but he heard the complaints, and he could not think that Motley meant to praise the English cuisine.

Equally little could Motley have meant that dinners were good to look at. Nothing could be worse than the toilettes; nothing less artistic than the appearance of the company. One's eyes might be dazzled by family diamonds, but, if an American woman were present, she was sure to make comments about the way the jewels were worn. If there was a well-dressed lady at table, she was either an American or "fast." She attracted as much notice as though she were on the stage. No one could possibly admire an English dinner-table.

Least of all did Motley mean that the taste or the manners were perfect. The manners of English society were notorious, and the taste was worse. Without exception every American woman rose in rebellion against English manners. In fact, the charm of London which made most impression on Americans was the violence of its contrasts; the extreme badness of the worst, making background for the distinction, refinement, or wit of a few, just as the extreme beauty of a few superb women was more effective against the plainness of the crowd. The result was mediaeval, and amusing; sometimes coarse to a degree that might have startled a roustabout, and sometimes courteous and considerate to a degree that suggested King Arthur's Round Table; but this artistic contrast was surely not the perfection that Motley had in his mind. He meant something scholarly, worldly, and modern; he was thinking of his own tastes.

Probably he meant that, in his favorite houses, the tone was easy, the talk was good, and the standard of scholarship was high. Even there he would have been forced to qualify his adjectives. No German would have admitted that English scholarship was high, or that it was scholarship at all, or that any wish for scholarship existed in England. Nothing that seemed to smell of the shop or of the lecture-room was wanted. One might as well have talked of Renan's Christ at the table of the Bishop of London, as talk of German philology at the table of an Oxford don. Society, if a small literary class could be called society, wanted to be amused in its old way. Sydney Smith, who had amused, was dead; so was Macaulay, who instructed if he did not amuse; Thackeray died at Christmas, 1863; Dickens never felt at home, and seldom appeared, in society; Bulwer Lytton was not sprightly; Tennyson detested strangers; Carlyle was mostly detested by them; Darwin never came to town; the men of whom Motley must have been thinking were such as he might meet at Lord Houghton's breakfasts: Grote, Jowett, Milman, or Froude; Browning, Matthew Arnold, or Swinburne; Bishop Wilberforce, Venables, or Hayward; or perhaps Gladstone, Robert Lowe, or Lord Granville. A relatively small class, commonly isolated, suppressed, and lost at the usual London dinner, such society as this was fairly familiar even to a private secretary, but to the literary American it might well seem perfection since he could find nothing of the sort in America. Within the narrow limits of this class, the American Legation was fairly at home; possibly a score of houses, all liberal, and all literary, but perfect only in the eyes of a Harvard College historian. They could teach little worth learning, for their tastes were antiquated and their knowledge was ignorance to the next generation. What was altogether fatal for future purposes, they were only English.

A social education in such a medium was bound to be useless in any other, yet Adams had to learn it to the bottom. The one thing needful for a private secretary, was that he should not only seem, but should actually be, at home. He studied carefully, and practised painfully, what seemed to be the favorite accomplishments of society. Perhaps his nervousness deceived him; perhaps he took for an ideal of others what was only his reflected image; but he conceived that the perfection of human society required that a man should enter a drawing-room where he was a total stranger, and place himself on the hearth-rug, his back to the fire, with an air of expectant benevolence, without curiosity, much as though he had dropped in at a charity concert, kindly disposed to applaud the performers and to overlook mistakes. This ideal rarely succeeded in youth, and towards thirty it took a form of modified insolence and offensive patronage; but about sixty it mellowed into courtesy, kindliness, and even deference to the young which had extraordinary charm both in women and in men. Unfortunately Adams could not wait till sixty for education; he had his living to earn; and the English air of patronage would earn no income for him anywhere else.

After five or six years of constant practice, any one can acquire the habit of going from one strange company to another without thinking much of one's self or of them, as though silently reflecting that "in a world where we are all insects, no insect is alien; perhaps they are human in parts"; but the dreamy habit of mind which comes from solitude in crowds is not fitness for social success except in London. Everywhere else it is injury. England was a social kingdom whose social coinage had no currency elsewhere.

Englishwomen, from the educational point of view, could give nothing until they approached forty years old. Then they become very interesting -- very charming -- to the man of fifty. The young American was not worth the young Englishwoman's notice, and never received it. Neither understood the other. Only in the domestic relation, in the country -- never in society at large -- a young American might accidentally make friends with an Englishwoman of his own age, but it never happened to Henry Adams. His susceptible nature was left to the mercy of American girls, which was professional duty rather than education as long as diplomacy held its own.

Thus he found himself launched on waters where he had never meant to sail, and floating along a stream which carried him far from his port. His third season in London society saw the end of his diplomatic education, and began for him the social life of a young man who felt at home in

England -- more at home there than anywhere else. With this feeling, the mere habit of going to garden-parties, dinners, receptions, and balls had nothing to do. One might go to scores without a sensation of home. One might stay in no end of country houses without forgetting that one was a total stranger and could never be anything else. One might bow to half the dukes and duchesses in England, and feel only the more strange. Hundreds of persons might pass with a nod and never come nearer. Close relation in a place like London is a personal mystery as profound as chemical affinity. Thousands pass, and one separates himself from the mass to attach himself to another, and so make, little by little, a group.

One morning, April 27, 1863, he was asked to breakfast with Sir Henry Holland, the old Court physician who had been acquainted with every American Minister since Edward Everett, and was a valuable social ally, who had the courage to try to be of use to everybody, and who, while asking the private secretary to breakfast one day, was too discreet to betray what he might have learned about rebel doings at his breakfast-table the day before. He had been friendly with the Legation, in the teeth of society, and was still bearing up against the weight of opinion, so that young Adams could not decline his invitations, although they obliged him to breakfast in Brook Street at nine o'clock in the morning, alternately with Mr. James M. Mason. Old Dr. Holland was himself as hale as a hawk, driving all day bare-headed about London, and eating Welsh rarebit every night before bed; he thought that any young man should be pleased to take his early muffin in Brook Street, and supply a few crumbs of war news for the daily peckings of eminent patients. Meekly, when summoned, the private secretary went, and on reaching the front door, this particular morning, he found there another young man in the act of rapping the knocker. They entered the breakfastroom together, where they were introduced to each other, and Adams learned that the other guest was a Cambridge undergraduate, Charles Milnes Gaskell, son of James Milnes Gaskell, the Member for Wenlock; another of the Yorkshire Milneses, from Thornes near Wakefield. Fate had fixed Adams to Yorkshire. By another chance it happened that young Milnes Gaskell was intimate at Cambridge with William Everett who was also about to take his degree. A third chance inspired Mr. Evarts with a fancy for visiting Cambridge, and led William Everett to offer his services as host. Adams acted as courier to Mr. Evarts, and at the end of May they went down for a few days, when William Everett did the honors as host with a kindness and attention that made his cousin sorely conscious of his own social shortcomings. Cambridge was pretty, and the dons were kind. Mr. Evarts enjoyed his visit but this was merely a part of the private secretary's day's work. What affected his whole life was the intimacy then begun with Milnes Gaskell and his circle of undergraduate friends, just about to enter the world.

Intimates are predestined. Adams met in England a thousand people, great and small; jostled against every one, from royal princes to gin-shop loafers; attended endless official functions and private parties; visited every part of the United Kingdom and was not quite a stranger at the Legations in Paris and Rome; he knew the societies of certain country houses, and acquired habits of Sunday-afternoon calls; but all this gave him nothing to do, and was life wasted. For him nothing whatever could be gained by escorting American ladies to drawing-rooms or American gentlemen to levees at St. James's Palace, or bowing solemnly to people with great titles, at Court balls, or even by awkwardly jostling royalty at garden-parties; all this was done for the Government, and neither President Lincoln nor Secretary Seward would ever know enough of their business to thank him for doing what they did not know how to get properly done by their own servants; but for Henry Adams -- not private secretary -- all the time taken up by such duties was wasted. On the other hand, his few personal intimacies concerned him alone, and the chance that made him almost a Yorkshireman was one that must have started under the Heptarchy.

More than any other county in England, Yorkshire retained a sort of social independence of London. Scotland itself was hardly more distinct. The Yorkshire type had always been the strongest of the British strains; the Norwegian and the Dane were a different race from the Saxon. Even Lancashire had not the mass and the cultivation of the West Riding. London could never quite absorb Yorkshire, which, in its turn had no great love for London and freely showed it. To a certain degree, evident enough to Yorkshiremen, Yorkshire was not English -- or was all England, as they might choose to express it. This must have been the reason why young Adams was drawn there rather than elsewhere. Monckton Milnes alone took the trouble to draw him, and possibly Milnes was the only man in England with whom Henry Adams, at that moment, had a chance of calling out such an un-English effort. Neither Oxford nor Cambridge nor any region south of the Humber contained a considerable house where a young American would have been sought as a friend. Eccentricity alone did not account for it. Monckton Milnes was a singular type, but his distant cousin, James Milnes Gaskell, was another, quite as marked, in an opposite sense. Milnes never seemed willing to rest; Milnes Gaskell never seemed willing to move. In his youth one of a very famous group -- Arthur Hallam, Tennyson, Manning, Gladstone, Francis Doyle -- and regarded as one of the most promising; an adorer of George Canning; in Parliament since coming of age; married into the powerful connection of the Wynns of Wynstay; rich according to Yorkshire standards; intimate with his political leaders; he was one of the numerous Englishmen who refuse office rather than make the effort of carrying it, and want power only to make it a source of indolence. He was a voracious reader and an admirable critic; he had forty years of parliamentary tradition on his memory; he liked to talk and to listen; he liked his dinner and, in spite of George Canning, his dry champagne; he liked wit and anecdote; but he belonged to the generation of 1830, a generation which could not survive the telegraph and railway, and which even Yorkshire could hardly produce again. To an American he was a character even more unusual and more fascinating than his distant cousin Lord Houghton.

Mr. Milnes Gaskell was kind to the young American whom his son brought to the house, and Mrs. Milnes Gaskell was kinder, for she thought the American perhaps a less dangerous friend than some Englishman might be, for her son, and she was probably right. The American had the sense to see that she was herself one of the most intelligent and sympathetic women in England; her sister, Miss Charlotte Wynn, was another; and both were of an age and a position in society that made their friendship a compliment as well as a pleasure. Their consent and approval settled the matter. In England, the family is a serious fact; once admitted to it, one is there for life. London might utterly vanish from one's horizon, but as long as life lasted, Yorkshire lived for its friends.

In the year 1857, Mr. James Milnes Gaskell, who had sat for thirty years in Parliament as one of the Members for the borough of Wenlock in Shropshire, bought Wenlock Abbey and the estate that included the old monastic buildings. This new, or old, plaything amused Mrs. Milnes Gaskell. The Prior's house, a charming specimen of fifteenth-century architecture, had been long left to decay as a farmhouse. She put it in order, and went there to spend a part of the autumn of 1864. Young Adams was one of her first guests, and drove about Wenlock Edge and the Wrekin with her, learning the loveliness of this exquisite country, and its stores of curious antiquity. It was a new and charming existence; an experience greatly to be envied -- ideal repose and rural

Shakespearian peace -- but a few years of it were likely to complete his education, and fit him to act a fairly useful part in life as an Englishman, an ecclesiastic, and a contemporary of Chaucer.

Chapter XIV. Dilettantism (1865-1866)

THE campaign of 1864 and the reelection of Mr. Lincoln in November set the American Minister on so firm a footing that he could safely regard his own anxieties as over, and the anxieties of Earl Russell and the Emperor Napoleon as begun. With a few months more his own term of four years would come to an end, and even though the questions still under discussion with England should somewhat prolong his stay, he might look forward with some confidence to his return home in 1865. His son no longer fretted. The time for going into the army had passed. If he were to be useful at all, it must be as a son, and as a son he was treated with the widest indulgence and trust. He knew that he was doing himself no good by staying in London, but thus far in life he had done himself no good anywhere, and reached his twenty-seventh birthday without having advanced a step, that he could see, beyond his twenty-first. For the most part, his friends were worse off than he. The war was about to end and they were to be set adrift in a world they would find altogether strange.

At this point, as though to cut the last thread of relation, six months were suddenly dropped out of his life in England. The London climate had told on some of the family; the physicians prescribed a winter in Italy. Of course the private secretary was detached as their escort, since this was one of his professional functions; and he passed six months, gaining an education as Italian courier, while the Civil War came to its end. As far as other education went, he got none, but he was amused. Travelling in all possible luxury, at some one else's expense, with diplomatic privileges and position, was a form of travel hitherto untried. The Cornice in vettura was delightful; Sorrento in winter offered hills to climb and grottoes to explore, and Naples near by to visit; Rome at Easter was an experience necessary for the education of every properly trained private secretary; the journey north by vettura through Perugia and Sienna was a dream; the Splugen Pass, if not equal to the Stelvio, was worth seeing; Paris had always something to show. The chances of accidental education were not so great as they had been, since one's field of experience had grown large; but perhaps a season at Baden Baden in these later days of its brilliancy offered some chances of instruction, if it were only the sight of fashionable Europe and America on the race-course watching the Duke of Hamilton, in the middle, improving his social advantages by the conversation of Cora Pearl.

The assassination of President Lincoln fell on the party while they were at Rome, where it seemed singularly fitting to that nursery of murderers and murdered, as though America were also getting educated. Again one went to meditate on the steps of the Santa Maria in Ara Coeli, but the lesson seemed as shallow as before. Nothing happened. The travellers changed no plan or movement. The Minister did not recall them to London. The season was over before they returned; and when the private secretary sat down again at his desk in Portland Place before a mass of copy in arrears, he saw before him a world so changed as to be beyond connection with the past. His identity, if one could call a bundle of disconnected memories an identity, seemed to remain; but his life was once more broken into separate pieces; he was a spider and had to spin a new web in some new place with a new attachment.

All his American friends and contemporaries who were still alive looked singularly commonplace without uniforms, and hastened to get married and retire into back streets and suburbs until they could find employment. Minister Adams, too, was going home "next fall," and when the fall came, he was going home "next spring," and when the spring came, President Andrew Johnson was at loggerheads with the Senate, and found it best to keep things unchanged. After the usual manner of public servants who had acquired the habit of office and lost the faculty of will, the members of the Legation in London continued the daily routine of English society, which, after becoming a habit, threatened to become a vice. Had Henry Adams shared a single taste with the young Englishmen of his time, he would have been lost; but the custom of pounding up and down Rotten Row every day, on a hack, was not a taste, and yet was all the sport he shared. Evidently he must set to work; he must get a new education he must begin a career of his own.

Nothing was easier to say, but even his father admitted two careers to be closed. For the law, diplomacy had unfitted him; for diplomacy he already knew too much. Any one who had held, during the four most difficult years of American diplomacy, a position at the centre of action, with his hands actually touching the lever of power, could not beg a post of Secretary at Vienna or Madrid in order to bore himself doing nothing until the next President should do him the honor to turn him out. For once all his advisers agreed that diplomacy was not possible.

In any ordinary system he would have been called back to serve in the State Department, but, between the President and the Senate, service of any sort became a delusion. The choice of career was more difficult than the education which had proved impracticable. Adams saw no road; in fact there was none. All his friends were trying one path or another, but none went a way that he could have taken. John Hay passed through London in order to bury himself in second-rate Legations for years, before he drifted home again to join Whitelaw Reid and George Smalley on the Tribune. Frank Barlow and Frank Bartlett carried Major-Generals' commissions into small law business. Miles stayed in the army. Henry Higginson, after a desperate struggle, was forced into State Street; Charles Adams wandered about, with brevet-brigadier rank, trying to find employment. Scores of others tried experiments more or less unsuccessful. Henry Adams could see easy ways of making a hundred blunders; he could see no likely way of making a legitimate success. Such as it was, his so-called education was wanted nowhere.

One profession alone seemed possible -- the press. In 1860 he would have said that he was born to be an editor, like at least a thousand other young graduates from American colleges who entered the world every year enjoying the same conviction; but in 1866 the situation was altered; the possession of money had become doubly needful for success, and double energy was essential to get money. America had more than doubled her scale. Yet the press was still the last resource of the educated poor who could not be artists and would not be tutors. Any man who was fit for nothing else could write an editorial or a criticism. The enormous mass of misinformation accumulated in ten years of nomad life could always be worked off on a helpless public, in diluted doses, if one could but secure a table in the corner of a newspaper office. The press was an inferior pulpit; an anonymous schoolmaster; a cheap boarding-school but it was still the nearest approach to a career for the literary survivor of a wrecked education. For the press, then, Henry Adams decided to fit himself, and since he could not go home to get practical training, he set to work to do what he could in London.

He knew, as well as any reporter on the New York Herald, that this was not an American way of beginning, and he knew a certain number of other drawbacks which the reporter could not see so clearly. Do what he might, he drew breath only in the atmosphere of English methods and thoughts; he could breathe none other. His mother -- who should have been a competent judge, since her success and popularity in England exceeded that of her husband -- averred that every woman who lived a certain time in England came to look and dress like an Englishwoman, no matter how she struggled. Henry Adams felt himself catching an English tone of mind and processes of thought, though at heart more hostile to them than ever. As though to make him more helpless and wholly distort his life, England grew more and more agreeable and amusing. Minister Adams became, in 1866, almost a historical monument in London; he held a position altogether his own. His old opponents disappeared. Lord Palmerston died in October, 1865; Lord Russell tottered on six months longer, but then vanished from power; and in July, 1866, the conservatives came into office. Traditionally the Tories were easier to deal with than the Whigs, and Minister Adams had no reason to regret the change. His personal relations were excellent and his personal weight increased year by year. On that score the private secretary had no cares, and not much copy. His own position was modest, but it was enough; the life he led was agreeable; his friends were all he wanted, and, except that he was at the mercy of politics, he felt much at ease. Of his daily life he had only to reckon so many breakfasts; so many dinners; so many receptions, balls, theatres, and country-parties; so many cards to be left; so many Americans to be escorted -- the usual routine of every young American in a Legation; all counting for nothing in sum, because, even if it had been his official duty -- which it was not -- it was mere routine, a single, continuous, unbroken act, which led to nothing and nowhere except Portland Place and the grave.

The path that led somewhere was the English habit of mind which deepened its ruts every day. The English mind was like the London drawing-room, a comfortable and easy spot, filled with bits and fragments of incoherent furnitures, which were never meant to go together, and could be arranged in any relation without making a whole, except by the square room. Philosophy might dispute about innate ideas till the stars died out in the sky, but about innate tastes no one, except perhaps a collie dog, has the right to doubt; least of all, the Englishman, for his tastes are his being; he drifts after them as unconsciously as a honey-bee drifts after his flowers, and, in England, every one must drift with him. Most young Englishmen drifted to the race-course or the moors or the hunting-field; a few towards books; one or two followed some form of science; and a number took to what, for want of a better name, they called Art. Young Adams inherited a certain taste for the same pursuit from his father who insisted that he had it not, because he could not see what his son thought he saw in Turner. The Minister, on the other hand, carried a sort of aesthetic rag-bag of his own, which he regarded as amusement, and never called art. So he would wander off on a Sunday to attend service successively in all the city churches built by Sir Christopher Wren; or he would disappear from the Legation day after day to attend coin sales at Sotheby's, where his son attended alternate sales of drawings, engravings, or water-colors. Neither knew enough to talk much about the other's tastes, but the only difference between them was a slight difference of direction. The Minister's mind like his writings showed a correctness of form and line that his son would have been well pleased had he inherited.

Of all supposed English tastes, that of art was the most alluring and treacherous. Once drawn into it, one had small chance of escape, for it had no centre or circumference, no beginning, middle, or end, no origin, no object, and no conceivable result as education. In London one met no corrective. The only American who came by, capable of teaching, was William Hunt, who stopped to paint the portrait of the Minister which now completes the family series at Harvard College. Hunt talked constantly, and was, or afterwards became, a famous teacher, but Henry Adams did not know enough to learn. Perhaps, too, he had inherited or acquired a stock of tastes, as young men must, which he was slow to outgrow. Hunt had no time to sweep out the rubbish of Adams's mind. The portrait finished, he went.

As often as he could, Adams ran over to Paris, for sunshine, and there always sought out Richardson in his attic in the Rue du Bac, or wherever he lived, and they went off to dine at the Palais Royal, and talk of whatever interested the students of the Beaux Arts. Richardson, too, had much to say, but had not yet seized his style. Adams caught very little of what lay in his mind, and the less, because, to Adams, everything French was bad except the restaurants, while the continuous life in England made French art seem worst of all. This did not prove that English art, in 1866, was good; far from it; but it helped to make bric-a-brac of all art, after the manner of England.

Not in the Legation, or in London, but in Yorkshire at Thornes, Adams met the man that pushed him furthest in this English garden of innate disorder called taste. The older daughter of the Milnes Gaskells had married Francis Turner Palgrave. Few Americans will ever ask whether any one has described the Palgraves, but the family was one of the most describable in all England at that day. Old Sir Francis, the father, had been much the greatest of all the historians of early England, the only one who was un-English; and the reason of his superiority lay in his name, which was Cohen, and his mind which was Cohen also, or at least not English. He changed his name to Palgrave in order to please his wife. They had a band of remarkable sons: Francis Turner, Gifford, Reginald, Inglis; all of whom made their mark. Gifford was perhaps the most eccentric, but his "Travels" in Arabia were famous, even among the famous travels of that generation. Francis Turner -- or, as he was commonly called, Frank Palgrave -- unable to work off his restlessness in travel like Gifford, and stifled in the atmosphere of the Board of Education, became a critic. His art criticisms helped to make the Saturday Review a terror to the British artist. His literary taste, condensed into the "Golden Treasury," helped Adams to more literary education than he ever got from any taste of his own. Palgrave himself held rank as one of the minor poets; his hymns had vogue. As an art-critic he was too ferocious to be liked; even Holman Hunt found his temper humorous; among many rivals, he may perhaps have had a right to claim the much-disputed rank of being the most unpopular man in London; but he liked to teach, and asked only for a docile pupil. Adams was docile enough, for he knew nothing and liked to listen. Indeed, he had to listen, whether he liked or not, for Palgrave's voice was strident, and nothing could stop him. Literature, painting, sculpture, architecture were open fields for his attacks, which were always intelligent if not always kind, and when these failed, he readily descended to meaner levels. John Richard Green, who was Palgrave's precise opposite, and whose Irish charm of touch and humor defended him from most assaults, used to tell with delight of Palgrave's call on him just after he had moved into his new Queen Anne house in Kensington Square: "Palgrave called yesterday, and the first thing he said was, 'I've counted three anachronisms on your front doorstep.' "

Another savage critic, also a poet, was Thomas Woolner, a type almost more emphatic than Palgrave in a society which resounded with emphasis. Woolner's sculpture showed none of the rough assertion that Woolner himself showed, when he was not making supernatural effort to be courteous, but his busts were remarkable, and his work altogether was, in Palgrave's clamorous opinion, the best of his day. He took the matter of British art -- or want of art -- seriously, almost ferociously, as a personal grievance and torture; at times he was rather terrifying in the anarchistic wrath of his denunciation. as Henry Adams felt no responsibility for English art, and had no American art to offer for sacrifice, he listened with enjoyment to language much like Carlyle's, and accepted it without a qualm. On the other hand, as a third member of this critical group, he fell in with Stopford Brooke whose tastes lay in the same direction, and whose expression was modified by clerical propriety. Among these men, one wandered off into paths of education much too devious and slippery for an American foot to follow. He would have done better to go on the race-track, as far as concerned a career.

Fortunately for him he knew too little ever to be an art-critic, still less an artist. For some things ignorance is good, and art is one of them. He knew he knew nothing, and had not the trained eye or the keen instinct that trusted itself; but he was curious, as he went on, to find out how much others knew. He took Palgrave's word as final about a drawing of Rembrandt or Michael Angelo, and he trusted Woolner implicitly about a Turner; but when he quoted their authority to any dealer, the dealer pooh-poohed it, and declared that it had no weight in the trade. If he went to a sale of drawings or paintings, at Sotheby's or Christie's, an hour afterwards, he saw these same dealers watching Palgrave or Woolner for a point, and bidding over them. He rarely found two dealers agree in judgment. He once bought a water-color from the artist himself out of his studio, and had it doubted an hour afterwards by the dealer to whose place he took it for framing He was reduced to admit that he could not prove its authenticity; internal evidence was against it.

One morning in early July, 1867, Palgrave stopped at the Legation in Portland Place on his way downtown, and offered to take Adams to Sotheby's, where a small collection of old drawings was on show. The collection was rather a curious one, said to be that of Sir Anthony Westcomb, from Liverpool, with an undisturbed record of a century, but with nothing to attract notice. Probably none but collectors or experts examined the portfolios. Some dozens of these were always on hand, following every sale, and especially on the lookout for old drawings, which became rarer every year. Turning rapidly over the numbers, Palgrave stopped at one containing several small drawings, one marked as Rembrandt, one as Rafael; and putting his finger on the Rafael, after careful examination; "I should buy this," he said; "it looks to me like one of those things that sell for five shillings one day, and fifty pounds the next." Adams marked it for a bid, and the next morning came down to the auction. The numbers sold slowly, and at noon he thought he might safely go to lunch. When he came back, half an hour afterwards, the drawing was gone. Much annoyed at his own stupidity, since Palgrave had expressly said he wanted the drawing for himself if he had not in a manner given it to Adams, the culprit waited for the sale to close, and then asked the clerk for the name of the buyer. It was Holloway, the art-dealer, near Covent Garden, whom he slightly knew. Going at once to the shop he waited till young Holloway came in, with his purchases under his arm, and without attempt at preface, he said: "You bought to-day, Mr. Holloway, a number that I wanted. Do you mind letting me have it?" Holloway took out the parcel, looked over the drawings, and said that he had bought the number for the sake of the Rembrandt, which he thought possibly genuine; taking that out, Adams might have the rest for the price he paid for the lot -- twelve shillings.

Thus, down to that moment, every expert in London had probably seen these drawings. Two of them -- only two -- had thought them worth buying at any price, and of these two, Palgrave chose the Rafael, Holloway the one marked as Rembrandt. Adams, the purchaser of the Rafael, knew nothing whatever on the subject, but thought he might credit himself with education to the value of twelve shillings, and call the drawing nothing. Such items of education commonly came higher.

He took the drawing to Palgrave. It was closely pasted to an old, rather thin, cardboard mount, and, on holding it up to the window, one could see lines on the reverse. "Take it down to Reed at the British Museum," said Palgrave; "he is Curator of the drawings, and, if you ask him, he will have it taken off the mount." Adams amused himself for a day or two by searching Rafael's works for the figure, which he found at last in the Parnasso, the figure of Horace, of which, as it happened -- though Adams did not know it -- the British Museum owned a much finer drawing. At last he took the dirty, little, unfinished red-chalk sketch to Reed whom he found in the Curator's room, with some of the finest Rafael drawings in existence, hanging on the walls. "Yes!" said Mr Reed; "I noticed this at the sale; but it's not Rafael!" Adams, feeling himself incompetent to discuss this subject, reported the result to Palgrave, who said that Reed knew nothing about it. Also this point lay beyond Adams's competence; but he noted that Reed was in the employ of the British Museum as Curator of the best -- or nearly the best -- collection in the world, especially of Rafaels, and that he bought for the Museum. As expert he had rejected both the Rafael and the Rembrandt at first-sight, and after his attention was recalled to the Rafael for a further opinion he rejected it again.

A week later, Adams returned for the drawing, which Mr. Reed took out of his drawer and gave him, saying with what seemed a little doubt or hesitation: "I should tell you that the paper shows a water-mark, which I kind the same as that of paper used by Marc Antonio." A little taken back by this method of studying art, a method which even a poor and ignorant American might use as well as Rafael himself, Adams asked stupidly: "Then you think it genuine?" "Possibly!" replied Reed; "but much overdrawn."

Here was expert opinion after a second revise, with help of water-marks! In Adams's opinion it was alone worth another twelve shillings as education; but this was not all. Reed continued: "The lines on the back seem to be writing, which I cannot read, but if you will take it down to the manuscript-room, they will read it for you."

Adams took the sheet down to the keeper of the manuscripts and begged him to read the lines. The keeper, after a few minutes' study, very obligingly said he could not: "It is scratched with an artist's crayon, very rapidly, with many unusual abbreviations and old forms. If any one in Europe can read it, it is the old man at the table yonder, Libri! Take it to him!"

This expert broke down on the alphabet! He could not even judge a manuscript; but Adams had no right to complain, for he had nothing to pay, not even twelve shillings, though he thought these experts worth more, at least for his education. Accordingly he carried his paper to Libri, a total stranger to him, and asked the old man, as deferentially as possible, to tell him whether the lines had any meaning. Had Adams not been an ignorant person he would have known all about Libri, but his ignorance was vast, and perhaps was for the best. Libri looked at the paper, and then looked again, and at last bade him sit down and wait. Half an hour passed before he called Adams back and showed him these lines:--

"Or questo credo ben che una elleria

Te offende tanto che te offese il core.

Perche sei grande nol sei in tua volia;

Tu vedi e gia non credi il tuo valore;

Passate gia son tutte gelosie;

Tu sei di sasso; non hai piu dolore."

As far as Adams could afterwards recall it, this was Libri's reading, but he added that the abbreviations were many and unusual; that the writing was very ancient; and that the word he read as "elleria" in the first line was not Italian at all.

By this time, one had got too far beyond one's depth to ask questions. If Libri could not read Italian, very clearly Adams had better not offer to help him. He took the drawing, thanked everybody, and having exhausted the experts of the British Museum, took a cab to Woolner's studio, where he showed the figure and repeated Reed's opinion. Woolner snorted: "Reed's a fool!" he said; "he knows nothing about it; there maybe a rotten line or two, but the drawing's all right."

For forty years Adams kept this drawing on his mantelpiece, partly for its own interest, but largely for curiosity to see whether any critic or artist would ever stop to look at it. None ever did, unless he knew the story. Adams himself never wanted to know more about it. He refused to seek further light. He never cared to learn whether the drawing was Rafael's, or whether the verse were Rafael's, or whether even the water-mark was Rafael's. The experts -- some scores of them including the British Museum, -- had affirmed that the drawing was worth a certain moiety of twelve shillings. On that point, also, Adams could offer no opinion, but he was clear that his education had profited by it to that extent -- his amusement even more.

Art was a superb field for education, but at every turn he met the same old figure, like a battered and illegible signpost that ought to direct him to the next station but never did. There was no next station. All the art of a thousand -- or ten thousand -- years had brought England to stuff which Palgrave and Woolner brayed in their mortars; derided, tore in tatters, growled at, and howled at, and treated in terms beyond literary usage. Whistler had not yet made his appearance in London, but the others did quite as well. What result could a student reach from it? Once, on returning to London, dining with Stopford Brooke, some one asked Adams what impression the Royal Academy Exhibition made on him. With a little hesitation, he suggested that it was rather a chaos, which he meant for civility; but Stopford Brooke abruptly met it by asking whether chaos were not better than death. Truly the question was worth discussion. For his own part, Adams inclined to think that neither chaos nor death was an object to him as a searcher of knowledge -- neither would have vogue in America -- neither would help him to a career. Both of them led him away from his objects, into an English dilettante museum of scraps, with nothing but a wall-paper to unite them in any relation of sequence. Possibly English taste was one degree more fatal than English scholarship, but even this question was open to argument. Adams went to the sales and bought what he was told to buy; now a classical drawing by Rafael or Rubens; now a water-color by Girtin or Cotman, if possible unfinished because it was more likely to be a sketch from nature; and he bought them not because they went together -- on the contrary, they made rather awkward spots on the wall as they did on the mind -- but because he could afford to buy those, and not others. Ten pounds did not go far to buy a Michael Angelo, but was a great deal of money to a private secretary. The effect was spotty, fragmentary, feeble; and the more so because the British mind was constructed in that way -- boasted of it, and held it to be true philosophy as well as sound method.

What was worse, no one had a right to denounce the English as wrong. Artistically their mind was scrappy, and every one knew it, but perhaps thought itself, history, and nature, were scrappy, and ought to be studied so. Turning from British art to British literature, one met the same dangers. The historical school was a playground of traps and pitfalls. Fatally one fell into the sink of history -- antiquarianism. For one who nourished a natural weakness for what was called history, the whole of British literature in the nineteenth century was antiquarianism or anecdotage, for no one except Buckle had tried to link it with ideas, and commonly Buckle was regarded as having failed. Macaulay was the English historian. Adams had the greatest admiration for Macaulay, but he felt that any one who should even distantly imitate Macaulay would perish in self-contempt. One might as well imitate Shakespeare. Yet evidently something was wrong here, for the poet and the historian ought to have different methods, and Macaulay's method ought to be imitable if it were sound; yet the method was more doubtful than the style. He was a dramatist; a painter; a poet, like Carlyle. This was the English mind, method, genius, or whatever one might call it; but one never could quite admit that the method which ended in Froude and Kinglake could be sound for America where passion and poetry were eccentricities. Both Froude and Kinglake, when one met them at dinner, were very agreeable, very intelligent; and perhaps the English method was right, and art fragmentary by essence. History, like everything else, might be a field of scraps, like the refuse about a Staffordshire iron-furnace. One felt a little natural reluctance to decline and fall like Silas Wegg on the golden dust-heap of British refuse; but if one must, one could at least expect a degree from Oxford and the respect of the Athenaeum Club.

While drifting, after the war ended, many old American friends came abroad for a holiday, and among the rest, Dr. Palfrey, busy with his "History of New England." Of all the relics of childhood, Dr. Palfrey was the most sympathetic, and perhaps the more so because he, too, had wandered into the pleasant meadows of antiquarianism, and had forgotten the world in his pursuit of the New England Puritan. Although America seemed becoming more and more indifferent to the Puritan except as a slightly rococo ornament, he was only the more amusing as a study for the Monkbarns of Boston Bay, and Dr. Palfrey took him seriously, as his clerical education required. His work was rather an Apologia in the Greek sense; a justification of the ways of God to Man, or, what was much the same thing, of Puritans to other men; and the task of justification was onerous enough to require the occasional relief of a contrast or scapegoat. When Dr. Palfrey happened on the picturesque but unpuritanic figure of Captain John Smith, he felt no call to beautify Smith's picture or to defend his moral character; he became impartial and penetrating. The famous story of Pocahontas roused his latent New England scepticism. He suggested to Adams, who wanted to make a position for himself, that an article in the North American Review on Captain John Smith's relations with Pocahontas would attract as much attention, and probably break as much glass, as any other stone that could be thrown by a beginner. Adams could suggest nothing better. The task seemed likely to be amusing. So he planted himself in the British Museum and patiently worked over all the material he could find, until, at last, after three or four months of labor, he got it in shape and sent it to Charles Norton, who was then editing the North American. Mr. Norton very civilly and even kindly accepted it. The article appeared in January, 1867.

Surely, here was something to ponder over, as a step in education; something that tended to stagger a sceptic! In spite of personal wishes, intentions, and prejudices; in spite of civil wars and diplomatic education; in spite of determination to be actual, daily, and practical, Henry Adams found himself, at twenty-eight, still in English society, dragged on one side into English dilettantism, which of all dilettantism he held the most futile; and, on the other, into American antiquarianism, which of all antiquarianism he held the most foolish. This was the result of five years in London. Even then he knew it to be a false start. He had wholly lost his way. If he were ever to amount to anything, he must begin a new education, in a new place, with a new purpose.

Chapter XV. Darwinism (1867-1868)

POLITICS, diplomacy, law, art, and history had opened no outlet for future energy or effort, but a man must do something, even in Portland Place, when winter is dark and winter evenings are exceedingly long. At that moment Darwin was convulsing society. The geological champion of Darwin was Sir Charles Lyell, and the Lyells were intimate at the Legation. Sir Charles constantly said of Darwin, what Palgrave said of Tennyson, that the first time he came to town, Adams should be asked to meet him, but neither of them ever came to town, or ever cared to meet a young American, and one could not go to them because they were known to dislike intrusion. The only Americans who were not allowed to intrude were the half-dozen in the Legation. Adams was content to read Darwin, especially his "Origin of Species" and his "Voyage of the Beagle." He was a Darwinist before the letter; a predestined follower of the tide; but he was hardly trained to follow Darwin's evidences. Fragmentary the British mind might be, but in those days it was doing a great deal of work in a very un-English way, building up so many and such vast theories on such narrow foundations as to shock the conservative, and delight the frivolous. The atomic theory; the correlation and conservation of energy; the mechanical theory of the universe; the kinetic theory of gases, and Darwin's Law of Natural Selection, were examples of what a young man had to take on trust. Neither he nor any one else knew enough to verify them; in his ignorance of mathematics, he was particularly helpless; but this never stood in his way. The ideas were new and seemed to lead somewhere -- to some great generalization which would finish one's clamor to be educated. That a beginner should understand them all, or believe them all, no one could expect, still less exact. Henry Adams was Darwinist because it was easier than not, for his ignorance exceeded belief, and one must know something in order to contradict even such triflers as Tyndall and Huxley.

By rights, he should have been also a Marxist but some narrow trait of the New England nature seemed to blight socialism, and he tried in vain to make himself a convert. He did the next best thing; he became a Comteist, within the limits of evolution. He was ready to become anything but quiet. As though the world had not been enough upset in his time, he was eager to see it upset more. He had his wish, but he lost his hold on the results by trying to understand them.

He never tried to understand Darwin; but he still fancied he might get the best part of Darwinism from the easier study of geology; a science which suited idle minds as well as though it were history. Every curate in England dabbled in geology and hunted for vestiges of Creation. Darwin hunted only for vestiges of Natural Selection, and Adams followed him, although he cared nothing about Selection, unless perhaps for the indirect amusement of upsetting curates. He felt, like nine men in ten, an instinctive belief in Evolution, but he felt no more concern in Natural than in unnatural Selection, though he seized with greediness the new volume on the "Antiquity of Man" which Sir Charles Lyell published in 1863 in order to support Darwin by wrecking the Garden of Eden. Sir Charles next brought out, in 1866, a new edition of his "Principles," then the highest text-book of geology; but here the Darwinian doctrine grew in stature. Natural Selection led back to Natural Evolution, and at last to Natural Uniformity. This was a vast stride. Unbroken Evolution under uniform conditions pleased every one -- except curates and bishops; it was the very best substitute for religion; a safe, conservative practical, thoroughly Common-Law deity. Such a working system for the universe suited a young man who had just helped to waste five or ten thousand million dollars and a million lives, more or less, to enforce unity and uniformity on people who objected to it; the idea was only too seductive in its perfection; it had the charm of art. Unity and Uniformity were the whole motive of philosophy, and if Darwin, like a true Englishman, preferred to back into it -- to reach God a posteriori -- rather than start from it, like Spinoza, the difference of method taught only the moral that the best way of reaching unity was to unite. Any road was good that arrived. Life depended on it. One had been, from the first, dragged hither and thither like a French poodle on a string, following always the strongest pull, between one form of unity or centralization and another. The proof that one had acted wisely because of obeying the primordial habit of nature flattered one's self-esteem. Steady, uniform, unbroken evolution from lower to higher seemed easy. So, one day when Sir Charles came to the Legation to inquire about getting his "Principles" properly noticed in America, young Adams found nothing simpler than to suggest that he could do it himself if Sir Charles would tell him what to say. Youth risks such encounters with the universe before one succumbs to it, yet even he was surprised at Sir Charles's ready assent, and still more so at finding himself, after half an hour's conversation, sitting down to clear the minds of American geologists about the principles of their profession. This was getting on fast; Arthur Pendennis had never gone so far.

The geologists were a hardy class, not likely to be much hurt by Adams's learning, nor did he throw away much concern on their account. He undertook the task chiefly to educate, not them, but himself, and if Sir Isaac Newton had, like Sir Charles Lyell, asked him to explain for Americans his last edition of the "Principia," Adams would have jumped at the chance. Unfortunately the mere reading such works for amusement is quite a different matter from studying them for criticism. Ignorance must always begin at the beginning. Adams must inevitably have begun by asking Sir Isaac for an intelligible reason why the apple fell to the ground. He did not know enough to be satisfied with the fact. The Law of Gravitation was so-and-so, but what was Gravitation? and he would have been thrown quite off his base if Sir Isaac had answered that he did not know.

At the very outset Adams struck on Sir Charles's Glacial Theory or theories. He was ignorant enough to think that the glacial epoch looked like a chasm between him and a uniformitarian world. If the glacial period were uniformity, what was catastrophe? To him the two or three labored guesses that Sir Charles suggested or borrowed to explain glaciation were proof of nothing, and were quite unsolid as support for so immense a superstructure as geological uniformity. If one were at liberty to be as lax in science as in theology, and to assume unity from the start, one might better say so, as the Church did, and not invite attack by appearing weak in evidence. Naturally a young man, altogether ignorant, could not say this to Sir Charles Lyell or

Sir Isaac Newton; but he was forced to state Sir Charles's views, which he thought weak as hypotheses and worthless as proofs. Sir Charles himself seemed shy of them. Adams hinted his heresies in vain. At last he resorted to what he thought the bold experiment of inserting a sentence in the text, intended to provoke correction. "The introduction [by Louis Agassiz] of this new geological agent seemed at first sight inconsistent with Sir Charles's argument, obliging him to allow that causes had in fact existed on the earth capable of producing more violent geological changes than would be possible in our own day." The hint produced no effect. Sir Charles said not a word; he let the paragraph stand; and Adams never knew whether the great Uniformitarian was strict or lax in his uniformitarian creed; but he doubted.

Objections fatal to one mind are futile to another, and as far as concerned the article, the matter ended there, although the glacial epoch remained a misty region in the young man's Darwinism. Had it been the only one, he would not have fretted about it; but uniformity often worked queerly and sometimes did not work as Natural Selection at all. Finding himself at a loss for some single figure to illustrate the Law of Natural Selection, Adams asked Sir Charles for the simplest case of uniformity on record. Much to his surprise Sir Charles told him that certain forms, like Terebratula, appeared to be identical from the beginning to the end of geological time. Since this was altogether too much uniformity and much too little selection, Adams gave up the attempt to begin at the beginning, and tried starting at the end -- himself. Taking for granted that the vertebrates would serve his purpose, he asked Sir Charles to introduce him to the first vertebrate. Infinitely to his bewilderment, Sir Charles informed him that the first vertebrate was a very respectable fish, among the earliest of all fossils, which had lived, and whose bones were still reposing, under Adams's own favorite Abbey on Wenlock Edge.

By this time, in 1867 Adams had learned to know Shropshire familiarly, and it was the part of his diplomatic education which he loved best. Like Catherine Olney in "Northanger Abbey," he yearned for nothing so keenly as to feel at home in a thirteenth-century Abbey, unless it were to haunt a fifteenth-century Prior's House, and both these joys were his at Wenlock. With companions or without, he never tired of it. Whether he rode about the Wrekin, or visited all the historical haunts from Ludlow Castle and Stokesay to Boscobel and Uriconium; or followed the Roman road or scratched in the Abbey ruins, all was amusing and carried a flavor of its own like that of the Roman Campagna; but perhaps he liked best to ramble over the Edge on a summer afternoon and look across the Marches to the mountains of Wales. The peculiar flavor of the scenery has something to do with absence of evolution; it was better marked in Egypt: it was felt wherever time-sequences became interchangeable. One's instinct abhors time. As one lay on the slope of the Edge, looking sleepily through the summer haze towards Shrewsbury or Cader Idris or Caer Caradoc or Uriconium, nothing suggested sequence. The Roman road was twin to the railroad; Uriconium was well worth Shrewsbury; Wenlock and Buildwas were far superior to Bridgnorth. The shepherds of Caractacus or Offa, or the monks of Buildwas, had they approached where he lay in the grass, would have taken him only for another and tamer variety of Welsh thief. They would have seen little to surprise them in the modern landscape unless it were the steam of a distant railway. One might mix up the terms of time as one liked, or stuff the present anywhere into the past, measuring time by Falstaff's Shrewsbury clock, without violent sense of wrong, as one could do it on the Pacific Ocean; but the triumph of all was to look south along the Edge to the abode of one's earliest ancestor and nearest relative, the ganoid fish, whose name, according to Professor Huxley, was Pteraspis, a cousin of the sturgeon, and whose kingdom, according to Sir Roderick Murchison, was called Siluria. Life began and ended there.

Behind that horizon lay only the Cambrian, without vertebrates or any other organism except a few shell-fish. On the further verge of the Cambrian rose the crystalline rocks from which every trace of organic existence had been erased.

That here, on the Wenlock Edge of time, a young American, seeking only frivolous amusement, should find a legitimate parentage as modern as though just caught in the Severn below, astonished him as much as though he had found Darwin himself. In the scale of evolution, one vertebrate was as good as another. For anything he, or any one else, knew, nine hundred and ninety nine parts of evolution out of a thousand lay behind or below the Pteraspis . To an American in search of a father, it mattered nothing whether the father breathed through lungs, or walked on fins, or on feet. Evolution of mind was altogether another matter and belonged to another science, but whether one traced descent from the shark or the wolf was immaterial even in morals. This matter had been discussed for ages without scientific result. La Fontaine and other fabulists maintained that the wolf, even in morals, stood higher than man; and in view of the late civil war, Adams had doubts of his own on the facts of moral evolution:--

"Tout bien considere, je te soutiens en somme,

Que scelerat pour scelerat,

Il vaut mieux etre un loup qu'un homme."

It might well be! At all events, it did not enter into the problem of Pteraspis, for it was quite certain that no complete proof of Natural Selection had occurred back to the time of Pteraspis, and that before Pteraspis was eternal void. No trace of any vertebrate had been found there; only starfish, shell-fish, polyps, or trilobites whose kindly descendants he had often bathed with, as a child on the shores of Quincy Bay.

That Pteraspis and shark were his cousins, great-uncles, or grandfathers, in no way troubled him, but that either or both of them should be older than evolution itself seemed to him perplexing; nor could he at all simplify the problem by taking the sudden back-somersault into Quincy Bay in search of the fascinating creature he had called a horseshoe, whose huge dome of shell and sharp spur of tail had so alarmed him as a child. In Siluria, he understood, Sir Roderick Murchison called the horseshoe a Limulus , which helped nothing. Neither in the Limulus nor in the Terebratula , nor in the Cestracion Philippi ,any more than in the Pteraspis, could one conceive an ancestor, but, if one must, the choice mattered little. Cousinship had limits but no one knew enough to fix them. When the vertebrate vanished in Siluria, it disappeared instantly and forever. Neither vertebra nor scale nor print reappeared, nor any trace of ascent or descent to a lower type. The vertebrate began in the Ludlow shale, as complete as Adams himself -- in some respects more so -- at the top of the column of organic evolution: and geology offered no sort of proof that he had ever been anything else. Ponder over it as he might, Adams could see nothing in the theory of Sir Charles but pure inference, precisely like the inference of Paley, that, if one found a watch, one inferred a maker. He could detect no more evolution in life since the Pteraspis than he could detect it in architecture since the Abbey. All he could prove was change. Coal-power alone asserted evolution -- of power -- and only by violence could be forced to assert selection of type.

All this seemed trivial to the true Darwinian, and to Sir Charles it was mere defect in the geological record. Sir Charles labored only to heap up the evidences of evolution; to cumulate them till the mass became irresistible. With that purpose, Adams gladly studied and tried to help Sir Charles, but, behind the lesson of the day, he was conscious that, in geology as in theology, he could prove only Evolution that did not evolve; Uniformity that was not uniform; and Selection that did not select. To other Darwinians -- except Darwin -- Natural Selection seemed a dogma to be put in the place of the Athanasian creed; it was a form of religious hope; a promise of ultimate perfection. Adams wished no better; he warmly sympathized in the object; but when he came to ask himself what he truly thought, he felt that he had no Faith; that whenever the next new hobby should be brought out, he should surely drop off from Darwinism like a monkey from a perch; that the idea of one Form, Law, Order, or Sequence had no more value for him than the idea of none; that what he valued most was Motion, and that what attracted his mind was Change.

Psychology was to him a new study, and a dark corner of education. As he lay on Wenlock Edge, with the sheep nibbling the grass close about him as they or their betters had nibbled the grass -- or whatever there was to nibble -- in the Silurian kingdom of Pteraspis, he seemed to have fallen on an evolution far more wonderful than that of fishes. He did not like it; he could not account for it; and he determined to stop it. Never since the days of his Limulus ancestry had any of his ascendants thought thus. Their modes of thought might be many, but their thought was one. Out of his millions of millions of ancestors, back to the Cambrian mollusks, every one had probably lived and died in the illusion of Truths which did not amuse him, and which had never changed. Henry Adams was the first in an infinite series to discover and admit to himself that he really did not care whether truth was, or was not, true. He did not even care that it should be proved true, unless the process were new and amusing. He was a Darwinian for fun.

From the beginning of history, this attitude had been branded as criminal -- worse than crime -- sacrilege! Society punished it ferociously and justly, in self-defence. Mr. Adams, the father, looked on it as moral weakness; it annoyed him; but it did not annoy him nearly so much as it annoyed his son, who had no need to learn from Hamlet the fatal effect of the pale cast of thought on enterprises great or small. He had no notion of letting the currents of his action be turned awry by this form of conscience. To him, the current of his time was to be his current, lead where it might. He put psychology under lock and key; he insisted on maintaining his absolute standards; on aiming at ultimate Unity. The mania for handling all the sides of every question, looking into every window, and opening every door, was, as Bluebeard judiciously pointed out to his wives, fatal to their practical usefulness in society. One could not stop to chase doubts as though they were rabbits. One had no time to paint and putty the surface of Law, even though it were cracked and rotten. For the young men whose lives were cast in the generation between 1867 and 1900, Law should be Evolution from lower to higher, aggregation of the atom in the mass, concentration of multiplicity in unity, compulsion of anarchy in order; and he would force himself to follow wherever it led, though he should sacrifice five thousand millions more in money, and a million more lives.

As the path ultimately led, it sacrificed much more than this; but at the time, he thought the price he named a high one, and he could not foresee that science and society would desert him in paying it. He, at least, took his education as a Darwinian in good faith. The Church was gone, and Duty was dim, but Will should take its place, founded deeply in interest and law. This was the result of five or six years in England; a result so British as to be almost the equivalent of an Oxford degree.

Quite serious about it, he set to work at once. While confusing his ideas about geology to the apparent satisfaction of Sir Charles who left him his field-compass in token of it, Adams turned resolutely to business, and attacked the burning question of specie payments. His principles assured him that the honest way to resume payments was to restrict currency. He thought he might win a name among financiers and statesmen at home by showing how this task had been done by England, after the classical suspension of 1797-1821. Setting himself to the study of this perplexed period, he waded as well as he could through a morass of volumes, pamphlets, and debates, until he learned to his confusion that the Bank of England itself and all the best British financial writers held that restriction was a fatal mistake, and that the best treatment of a debased currency was to let it alone, as the Bank had in fact done. Time and patience were the remedies.

The shock of this discovery to his financial principles was serious; much more serious than the shock of the Terebratula and Pteraspis to his principles of geology. A mistake about Evolution was not fatal; a mistake about specie payments would destroy forever the last hope of employment in State Street. Six months of patient labor would be thrown away if he did not publish, and with it his whole scheme of making himself a position as a practical man-of-business. If he did publish, how could he tell virtuous bankers in State Street that moral and absolute principles of abstract truth, such as theirs, had nothing to do with the matter, and that they had better let it alone? Geologists, naturally a humble and helpless class, might not revenge impertinences offered to their science; but capitalists never forgot or forgave.

With labor and caution he made one long article on British Finance in 1816, and another on the Bank Restriction of 1797-1821, and, doing both up in one package, he sent it to the North American for choice. He knew that two heavy, technical, financial studies thus thrown at an editor's head, would probably return to crush the author; but the audacity of youth is more sympathetic -- when successful -- than his ignorance. The editor accepted both.

When the post brought his letter, Adams looked at it as though he were a debtor who had begged for an extension. He read it with as much relief as the debtor, if it had brought him the loan. The letter gave the new writer literary rank. Henceforward he had the freedom of the press. These articles, following those on Pocahontas and Lyell, enrolled him on the permanent staff of the North American Review . Precisely what this rank was worth, no one could say; but, for fifty years the North American Review had been the stage coach which carried literary Bostonians to such distinction as they had achieved. Few writers had ideas which warranted thirty pages of development, but for such as thought they had, the Review alone offered space. An article was a small volume which required at least three months' work, and was paid, at best, five dollars a page. Not many men even in England or France could write a good thirty-page article, and practically no one in America read them; but a few score of people, mostly in search of items to steal, ran over the pages to extract an idea or a fact, which was a sort of wild game -- a bluefish or a teal -- worth anywhere from fifty cents to five dollars. Newspaper writers had their eye on quarterly pickings. The circulation of the Review had never exceeded three or four hundred copies, and the Review had never paid its reasonable expenses. Yet it stood at the head of American literary periodicals; it was a source of suggestion to cheaper workers; it reached far into societies that never knew its existence; it was an organ worth playing on; and, in the fancy of Henry Adams, it led, in some indistinct future, to playing on a New York daily newspaper.

With the editor's letter under his eyes, Adams asked himself what better he could have done. On the whole, considering his helplessness, he thought he had done as well as his neighbors. No one could yet guess which of his contemporaries was most likely to play a part in the great world. A shrewd prophet in Wall Street might perhaps have set a mark on Pierpont Morgan, but hardly on the Rockefellers or William C. Whitney or Whitelaw Reid. No one would have picked out William McKinley or John Hay or Mark Hanna for great statesmen. Boston was ignorant of the careers in store for Alexander Agassiz and Henry Higginson. Phillips Brooks was unknown; Henry James was unheard; Howells was new; Richardson and LaFarge were struggling for a start. Out of any score of names and reputations that should reach beyond the century, the thirty-years-old who were starting in the year 1867 could show none that was so far in advance as to warrant odds in its favor. The army men had for the most part fallen to the ranks. Had Adams foreseen the future exactly as it came, he would have been no wiser, and could have chosen no better path.

Thus it turned out that the last year in England was the pleasantest. He was already old in society, and belonged to the Silurian horizon. The Prince of Wales had come. Mr. Disraeli, Lord Stanley, and the future Lord Salisbury had thrown into the background the memories of Palmerston and Russell. Europe was moving rapidly, and the conduct of England during the American Civil War was the last thing that London liked to recall. The revolution since 1861 was nearly complete, and, for the first time in history, the American felt himself almost as strong as an Englishman. He had thirty years to wait before he should feel himself stronger. Meanwhile even a private secretary could afford to be happy. His old education was finished; his new one was not begun; he still loitered a year, feeling himself near the end of a very long, anxious, tempestuous, successful voyage, with another to follow, and a summer sea between.

He made what use he could of it. In February, 1868, he was back in Rome with his friend Milnes Gaskell. For another season he wandered on horseback over the campagna or on foot through the Rome of the middle ages, and sat once more on the steps of Ara Coeli, as had become with him almost a superstition, like the waters of the fountain of Trevi. Rome was still tragic and solemn as ever, with its mediaeval society, artistic, literary, and clerical, taking itself as seriously as in the days of Byron and Shelley. The long ten years of accidental education had changed nothing for him there. He knew no more in 1868 than in 1858. He had learned nothing whatever that made Rome more intelligible to him, or made life easier to handle. The case was no better when he got back to London and went through his last season. London had become his vice. He loved his haunts, his houses, his habits, and even his hansom cabs. He loved growling like an Englishman, and going into society where he knew not a face, and cared not a straw. He lived deep into the lives and loves and disappointments of his friends. When at last he found himself back again at Liverpool, his heart wrenched by the act of parting, he moved mechanically, unstrung, but he had no more acquired education than when he first trod the steps of the Adelphi Hotel in November, 1858. He could see only one great change, and this was wholly in years. Eaton Hall no longer impressed his imagination; even the architecture of Chester roused but a sleepy interest; he felt no sensation whatever in the atmosphere of the British peerage, but mainly an habitual dislike to most of the people who frequented their country houses; he had become English to the point of sharing their petty social divisions, their dislikes and prejudices against each other; he took England no longer with the awe of American youth, but with the habit of an old and rather worn suit of clothes. As far as he knew, this was all that Englishmen meant by social education, but in any case it was all the education he had gained from seven years in London.

Chapter XVI. The Press (1868)

AT ten o'clock of a July night, in heat that made the tropical rain-shower simmer, the Adams family and the Motley family clambered down the side of their Cunard steamer into the government tugboat, which set them ashore in black darkness at the end of some North River pier. Had they been Tyrian traders of the year B.C. 1000 landing from a galley fresh from Gibraltar, they could hardly have been stranger on the shore of a world, so changed from what it had been ten years before. The historian of the Dutch, no longer historian but diplomatist, started up an unknown street, in company with the private secretary who had become private citizen, in search of carriages to convey the two parties to the Brevoort House. The pursuit was arduous but successful. Towards midnight they found shelter once more in their native land.

How much its character had changed or was changing, they could not wholly know, and they could but partly feel. For that matter, the land itself knew no more than they. Society in America was always trying, almost as blindly as an earthworm, to realize and understand itself; to catch up with its own head, and to twist about in search of its tail. Society offered the profile of a long, straggling caravan, stretching loosely towards the prairies, its few score of leaders far in advance and its millions of immigrants, negroes, and Indians far in the rear, somewhere in archaic time. It enjoyed the vast advantage over Europe that all seemed, for the moment, to move in one direction, while Europe wasted most of its energy in trying several contradictory movements at once; but whenever Europe or Asia should be polarized or oriented towards the same point, America might easily lose her lead. Meanwhile each newcomer needed to slip into a place as near the head of the caravan as possible, and needed most to know where the leaders could be found. One could divine pretty nearly where the force lay, since the last ten years had given to the great mechanical energies -- coal, iron, steam -- a distinct superiority in power over the old industrial elements -- agriculture, handwork, and learning; but the result of this revolution on a survivor from the fifties resembled the action of the earthworm; he twisted about, in vain, to recover his starting-point; he could no longer see his own trail; he had become an estray; a flotsam or jetsam of wreckage; a belated reveller, or a scholar-gipsy like Matthew Arnold's. His world was dead. Not a Polish Jew fresh from Warsaw or Cracow -- not a furtive Yacoob or Ysaac still reeking of the Ghetto, snarling a weird Yiddish to the officers of the customs -- but had a keener instinct, an intenser energy, and a freer hand than he -- American of Americans, with Heaven knew how many Puritans and Patriots behind him, and an education that had cost a civil war. He made no complaint and found no fault with his time; he was no worse off than the Indians or the buffalo who had been ejected from their heritage by his own people; but he vehemently insisted that he was not himself at fault. The defeat was not due to him, nor yet to any superiority of his rivals. He had been unfairly forced out of the track, and must get back into it as best he could.

One comfort he could enjoy to the full. Little as he might be fitted for the work that was before him, he had only to look at his father and Motley to see figures less fitted for it than he. All were equally survivals from the forties -- bric-a-brac from the time of Louis Philippe; stylists; doctrinaires; ornaments that had been more or less suited to the colonial architecture, but which never had much value in Desbrosses Street or Fifth Avenue. They could scarcely have earned five dollars a day in any modern industry. The men who commanded high pay were as a rule not ornamental. Even Commodore Vanderbilt and Jay Gould lacked social charm. Doubtless the country needed ornament -- needed it very badly indeed -- but it needed energy still more, and capital most of all, for its supply was ridiculously out of proportion to its wants. On the new scale of power, merely to make the continent habitable for civilized people would require an immediate outlay that would have bankrupted the world. As yet, no portion of the world except a few narrow stretches of western Europe had ever been tolerably provided with the essentials of comfort and convenience; to fit out an entire continent with roads and the decencies of life would exhaust the credit of the entire planet. Such an estimate seemed outrageous to a Texan member of Congress who loved the simplicity of nature's noblemen; but the mere suggestion that a sun existed above him would outrage the self-respect of a deep-sea fish that carried a lantern on the end of its nose. From the moment that railways were introduced, life took on extravagance.

Thus the belated reveller who landed in the dark at the Desbrosses Street ferry, found his energies exhausted in the effort to see his own length. The new Americans, of whom he was to be one, must, whether they were fit or unfit, create a world of their own, a science, a society, a philosophy, a universe, where they had not yet created a road or even learned to dig their own iron. They had no time for thought; they saw, and could see, nothing beyond their day's work; their attitude to the universe outside them was that of the deep-sea fish. Above all, they naturally and intensely disliked to be told what to do, and how to do it, by men who took their ideas and their methods from the abstract theories of history, philosophy, or theology. They knew enough to know that their world was one of energies quite new.

All this, the newcomer understood and accepted, since he could not help himself and saw that the American could help himself as little as the newcomer; but the fact remained that the more he knew, the less he was educated. Society knew as much as this, and seemed rather inclined to boast of it, at least on the stump; but the leaders of industry betrayed no sentiment, popular or other. They used, without qualm, whatever instruments they found at hand. They had been obliged, in 1861, to turn aside and waste immense energy in settling what had been settled a thousand years before, and should never have been revived. At prodigious expense, by sheer force, they broke resistance down, leaving everything but the mere fact of power untouched, since nothing else had a solution. Race and thought were beyond reach. Having cleared its path so far, society went back to its work, and threw itself on that which stood first -- its roads. The field was vast; altogether beyond its power to control offhand; and society dropped every thought of dealing with anything more than the single fraction called a railway system. This relatively small part of its task was still so big as to need the energies of a generation, for it required all the new machinery to be created -- capital, banks, mines, furnaces, shops, power-houses, technical knowledge, mechanical population, together with a steady remodelling of social and political habits, ideas, and institutions to fit the new scale and suit the new conditions. The generation between 1865 and 1895 was already mortgaged to the railways, and no one knew it better than the generation itself.

Whether Henry Adams knew it or not, he knew enough to act as though he did. He reached Quincy once more, ready for the new start. His brother Charles had determined to strike for the railroads; Henry was to strike for the press; and they hoped to play into each other's hands. They had great need, for they found no one else to play with. After discovering the worthlessness of a so-called education, they had still to discover the worthlessness of so-called social connection. No young man had a larger acquaintance and relationship than Henry Adams, yet he knew no one who could help him. He was for sale, in the open market. So were many of his friends. All the world knew it, and knew too that they were cheap; to be bought at the price of a mechanic. There was no concealment, no delicacy, and no illusion about it. Neither he nor his friends complained; but he felt sometimes a little surprised that, as far as he knew, no one, seeking in the labor market, ever so much as inquired about their fitness. The want of solidarity between old and young seemed American. The young man was required to impose himself, by the usual business methods, as a necessity on his elders, in order to compel them to buy him as an investment. As Adams felt it, he was in a manner expected to blackmail. Many a young man complained to him in after life of the same experience, which became a matter of curious reflection as he grew old. The labor market of good society was ill-organized.

Boston seemed to offer no market for educated labor. A peculiar and perplexing amalgam Boston always was, and although it had changed much in ten years, it was not less perplexing. One no longer dined at two o'clock; one could no longer skate on Back Bay; one heard talk of Bostonians worth five millions or more as something not incredible. Yet the place seemed still simple, and less restless-minded than ever before. In the line that Adams had chosen to follow, he needed more than all else the help of the press, but any shadow of hope on that side vanished instantly. The less one meddled with the Boston press, the better. All the newspapermen were clear on that point. The same was true of politics. Boston meant business. The Bostonians were building railways. Adams would have liked to help in building railways, but had no education. He was not fit.

He passed three or four months thus, visiting relations, renewing friendships, and studying the situation. At thirty years old, the man who has not yet got further than to study the situation, is lost, or near it. He could see nothing in the situation that could be of use to him. His friends had won no more from it than he. His brother Charles, after three years of civil life, was no better off than himself, except for being married and in greater need of income. His brother John had become a brilliant political leader on the wrong side. No one had yet regained the lost ground of the war.

He went to Newport and tried to be fashionable, but even in the simple life of 1868, he failed as fashion. All the style he had learned so painfully in London was worse than useless in America where every standard was different. Newport was charming, but it asked for no education and gave none. What it gave was much gayer and pleasanter, and one enjoyed it amazingly; but friendships in that society were a kind of social partnership, like the classes at college; not education but the subjects of education. All were doing the same thing, and asking the same question of the future. None could help. Society seemed founded on the law that all was for the best New Yorkers in the best of Newports, and that all young people were rich if they could waltz. It was a new version of the Ant and Grasshopper.

At the end of three months, the only person, among the hundreds he had met, who had offered him a word of encouragement or had shown a sign of acquaintance with his doings, was Edward Atkinson. Boston was cool towards sons, whether prodigals or other, and needed much time to make up its mind what to do for them -- time which Adams, at thirty years old, could hardly spare. He had not the courage or self-confidence to hire an office in State Street, as so many of his friends did, and doze there alone, vacuity within and a snowstorm outside, waiting for Fortune to knock at the door, or hoping to find her asleep in the elevator; or on the staircase, since elevators were not yet in use. Whether this course would have offered his best chance he never knew; it was one of the points in practical education which most needed a clear understanding, and he could never reach it. His father and mother would have been glad to see him stay with them and begin reading Blackstone again, and he showed no very filial tenderness by abruptly breaking the tie that had lasted so long. After all, perhaps Beacon Street was as good as any other street for his objects in life; possibly his easiest and surest path was from Beacon Street to State Street and back again, all the days of his years. Who could tell? Even after life was over, the doubt could not be determined.

In thus sacrificing his heritage, he only followed the path that had led him from the beginning. Boston was full of his brothers. He had reckoned from childhood on outlawry as his peculiar birthright. The mere thought of beginning life again in Mount Vernon Street lowered the pulsations of his heart. This is a story of education -- not a mere lesson of life -- and, with education, temperament has in strictness nothing to do, although in practice they run close together. Neither by temperament nor by education was he fitted for Boston. He had drifted far away and behind his companions there; no one trusted his temperament or education; he had to go.

Since no other path seemed to offer itself, he stuck to his plan of joining the press, and selected Washington as the shortest road to New York, but, in 1868, Washington stood outside the social pale. No Bostonian had ever gone there. One announced one's self as an adventurer and an office-seeker, a person of deplorably bad judgment, and the charges were true. The chances of ending in the gutter were, at best, even. The risk was the greater in Adams's case, because he had no very clear idea what to do when he got there. That he must educate himself over again, for objects quite new, in an air altogether hostile to his old educations, was the only certainty; but how he was to do it -- how he was to convert the idler in Rotten Row into the lobbyist of the Capital -- he had not an idea, and no one to teach him. The question of money is rarely serious for a young American unless he is married, and money never troubled Adams more than others; not because he had it, but because he could do without it, like most people in Washington who all lived on the income of bricklayers; but with or without money he met the difficulty that, after getting to Washington in order to go on the press, it was necessary to seek a press to go on. For large work he could count on the North American Review, but this was scarcely a press. For current discussion and correspondence, he could depend on the New York Nation; but what he needed was a New York daily, and no New York daily needed him. He lost his one chance by the death of Henry J. Raymond. The Tribune under Horace Greeley was out of the question both for political and personal reasons, and because Whitelaw Reid had already undertaken that singularly venturesome position, amid difficulties that would have swamped Adams in four-and-twenty hours. Charles A. Dana had made the Sun a very successful as well as a very amusing paper, but had hurt his own social position in doing it; and Adams knew himself well enough to know that he could never please himself and Dana too; with the best intentions, he must always fail as a blackguard, and at that time a strong dash of blackguardism was life to the Sun. As for the New York Herald, it was a despotic empire admitting no personality but that of Bennett. Thus, for the moment, the New York daily press offered no field except the free-trade Holy Land of the Evening Post under William Cullen Bryant, while beside it lay only the elevated plateau of the New Jerusalem occupied by Godkin and the Nation. Much as Adams liked Godkin, and glad as he was to creep under the shelter of the Evening Post and the Nation, he was well aware that he should find there only the same circle of readers that he reached in the North American Review.

The outlook was dim, but it was all he had, and at Washington, except for the personal friendship of Mr. Evarts who was then Attorney General and living there, he would stand in solitude much like that of London in 1861. Evarts did what no one in Boston seemed to care for doing; he held out a hand to the young man. Whether Boston, like Salem, really shunned strangers, or whether Evarts was an exception even in New York, he had the social instinct which Boston had not. Generous by nature, prodigal in hospitality, fond of young people, and a born man-of-the-world, Evarts gave and took liberally, without scruple, and accepted the world without fearing or abusing it. His wit was the least part of his social attraction. His talk was broad and free. He laughed where he could; he joked if a joke was possible; he was true to his friends, and never lost his temper or became ill-natured. Like all New Yorkers he was decidedly not a Bostonian; but he was what one might call a transplanted New Englander, like General Sherman; a variety, grown in ranker soil. In the course of life, and in widely different countries, Adams incurred heavy debts of gratitude to persons on whom he had no claim and to whom he could seldom make return; perhaps half-a-dozen such debts remained unpaid at last, although six is a large number as lives go; but kindness seldom came more happily than when Mr. Evarts took him to Washington in October, 1868.

Adams accepted the hospitality of the sleeper, with deep gratitude, the more because his first struggle with a sleeping-car made him doubt the value -- to him -- of a Pullman civilization; but he was even more grateful for the shelter of Mr. Evarts's house in H Street at the corner of Fourteenth, where he abode in safety and content till he found rooms in the roomless village. To him the village seemed unchanged. Had he not known that a great war and eight years of astonishing movement had passed over it, he would have noticed nothing that betrayed growth. As of old, houses were few; rooms fewer; even the men were the same. No one seemed to miss the usual comforts of civilization, and Adams was glad to get rid of them, for his best chance lay in the eighteenth century.

The first step, of course, was the making of acquaintance, and the first acquaintance was naturally the President, to whom an aspirant to the press officially paid respect. Evarts immediately took him to the White House and presented him to President Andrew Johnson. The interview was brief and consisted in the stock remark common to monarchs and valets, that the young man looked even younger than he was. The younger man felt even younger than he looked. He never saw the President again, and never felt a wish to see him, for Andrew Johnson was not the sort of man whom a young reformer of thirty, with two or three foreign educations, was likely to see with enthusiasm; yet, musing over the interview as a matter of education, long years afterwards, he could not help recalling the President's figure with a distinctness that surprised him. The old-fashioned Southern Senator and statesman sat in his chair at his desk with a look of self-esteem that had its value. None doubted. All were great men; some, no doubt, were greater than others; but all were statesmen and all were supported, lifted, inspired by the moral certainty of rightness. To them the universe was serious, even solemn, but it was their universe, a Southern conception of right. Lamar used to say that he never entertained a doubt of the soundness of the Southern system until he found that slavery could not stand a war. Slavery was only a part of the Southern system, and the life of it all -- the vigor -- the poetry -- was its moral certainty of self. The Southerner could not doubt; and this self-assurance not only gave Andrew Johnson the look of a true President, but actually made him one. When Adams came to look back on it afterwards, he was surprised to realize how strong the Executive was in 1868 -- perhaps the strongest he was ever to see. Certainly he never again found himself so well satisfied, or so much at home.

Seward was still Secretary of State. Hardly yet an old man, though showing marks of time and violence, Mr. Seward seemed little changed in these eight years. He was the same -- with a difference. Perhaps he -- unlike Henry Adams -- had at last got an education, and all he wanted. Perhaps he had resigned himself to doing without it. Whatever the reason, although his manner was as roughly kind as ever, and his talk as free, he appeared to have closed his account with the public; he no longer seemed to care; he asked nothing, gave nothing, and invited no support; he talked little of himself or of others, and waited only for his discharge. Adams was well pleased to be near him in these last days of his power and fame, and went much to his house in the evenings when he was sure to be at his whist. At last, as the end drew near, wanting to feel that the great man -- the only chief he ever served even as a volunteer -- recognized some personal relation, he asked Mr. Seward to dine with him one evening in his rooms, and play his game of whist there, as he did every night in his own house. Mr. Seward came and had his whist, and Adams remembered his rough parting speech: "A very sensible entertainment!" It was the only favor he ever asked of Mr. Seward, and the only one he ever accepted.

Thus, as a teacher of wisdom, after twenty years of example, Governor Seward passed out of one's life, and Adams lost what should have been his firmest ally; but in truth the State Department had ceased to be the centre of his interest, and the Treasury had taken its place. The Secretary of the Treasury was a man new to politics -- Hugh McCulloch -- not a person of much importance in the eyes of practical politicians such as young members of the press meant themselves to become, but they all liked Mr. McCulloch, though they thought him a stop-gap rather than a force. Had they known what sort of forces the Treasury was to offer them for support in the generation to come, they might have reflected a long while on their estimate of McCulloch. Adams was fated to watch the flittings of many more Secretaries than he ever cared to know, and he rather came back in the end to the idea that McCulloch was the best of them, although he seemed to represent everything that one liked least. He was no politician, he had no party, and no power. He was not fashionable or decorative. He was a banker, and towards bankers Adams felt the narrow prejudice which the serf feels to his overerseer; for he knew he must obey, and he knew that the helpless showed only their helplessness when they tempered obedience by mockery. The world, after 1865, became a bankers' world, and no banker would ever trust one who had deserted State Street, and had gone to Washington with purposes of doubtful credit, or of no credit at all, for he could not have put up enough collateral to borrow five thousand dollars of any bank in America. The banker never would trust him, and he would never trust the banker. To him, the banking mind was obnoxious; and this antipathy caused him the more surprise at finding McCulloch the broadest, most liberal, most genial, and most practical public man in Washington.

There could be no doubt of it. The burden of the Treasury at that time was very great. The whole financial system was in chaos; every part of it required reform; the utmost experience, tact, and skill could not make the machine work smoothly. No one knew how well McCulloch did it until his successor took it in charge, and tried to correct his methods. Adams did not know enough to appreciate McCulloch's technical skill, but he was struck at his open and generous treatment of young men. Of all rare qualities, this was, in Adams's experience, the rarest. As a rule, officials dread interference. The strongest often resent it most. Any official who admits equality in discussion of his official course, feels it to be an act of virtue; after a few months or years he tires of the effort. Every friend in power is a friend lost. This rule is so nearly absolute that it may be taken in practice as admitting no exception. Apparent exceptions exist, and McCulloch was one of them.

McCulloch had been spared the gluttonous selfishness and infantile jealousy which are the commoner results of early political education. He had neither past nor future, and could afford to be careless of his company. Adams found him surrounded by all the active and intelligent young men in the country. Full of faith, greedy for work, eager for reform, energetic, confident, capable, quick of study, charmed with a fight, equally ready to defend or attack, they were unselfish, and even -- as young men went -- honest. They came mostly from the army, with the spirit of the volunteers. Frank Walker, Frank Barlow, Frank Bartlett were types of the generation. Most of the press, and much of the public, especially in the West, shared their ideas. No one denied the need for reform. The whole government, from top to bottom, was rotten with the senility of what was antiquated and the instability of what was improvised. The currency was only one example; the tariff was another; but the whole fabric required reconstruction as much as in 1789, for the Constitution had become as antiquated as the Confederation. Sooner or later a shock must come, the more dangerous the longer postponed. The Civil War had made a new system in fact; the country would have to reorganize the machinery in practice and theory.

One might discuss indefinitely the question which branch of government needed reform most urgently; all needed it enough, but no one denied that the finances were a scandal, and a constant, universal nuisance. The tariff was worse, though more interests upheld it. McCulloch had the singular merit of facing reform with large good-nature and willing sympathy -- outside of parties, jobs, bargains, corporations or intrigues -- which Adams never was to meet again.

Chaos often breeds life, when order breeds habit. The Civil War had bred life. The army bred courage. Young men of the volunteer type were not always docile under control, but they were handy in a fight. Adams was greatly pleased to be admitted as one of them. He found himself much at home with them -- more at home than he ever had been before, or was ever to be again -- in the atmosphere of the Treasury. He had no strong party passion, and he felt as though he and his friends owned this administration, which, in its dying days, had neither friends nor future except in them.

These were not the only allies; the whole government in all its branches was alive with them. Just at that moment the Supreme Court was about to take up the Legal Tender cases where Judge Curtis had been employed to argue against the constitutional power of the Government to make an artificial standard of value in time of peace. Evarts was anxious to fix on a line of argument that should have a chance of standing up against that of Judge Curtis, and was puzzled to do it. He did not know which foot to put forward. About to deal with Judge Curtis, the last of the strong jurists of Marshall's school, he could risk no chances. In doubt, the quickest way to clear one's mind is to discuss, and Evarts deliberately forced discussion. Day after day, driving, dining, walking he provoked Adams to dispute his positions. He needed an anvil, he said, to hammer his ideas on.

Adams was flattered at being an anvil, which is, after all, more solid than the hammer; and he did not feel called on to treat Mr. Evarts's arguments with more respect than Mr. Evarts himself expressed for them; so he contradicted with freedom. Like most young men, he was much of a doctrinaire, and the question was, in any event, rather historical or political than legal. He could easily maintain, by way of argument, that the required power had never been given, and that no sound constitutional reason could possibly exist for authorizing the Government to overthrow the standard of value without necessity, in time of peace. The dispute itself had not much value for him, even as education, but it led to his seeking light from the Chief Justice himself. Following up the subject for his letters to the Nation and his articles in the North American Review, Adams grew to be intimate with the Chief Justice, who, as one of the oldest and strongest leaders of the Free Soil Party, had claims to his personal regard; for the old Free Soilers were becoming few. Like all strong-willed and self-asserting men, Mr. Chase had the faults of his qualities. He was never easy to drive in harness, or light in hand. He saw vividly what was wrong, and did not always allow for what was relatively right. He loved power as though he were still a Senator. His position towards Legal Tender was awkward. As Secretary of the Treasury he had been its author; as Chief Justice he became its enemy. Legal Tender caused no great pleasure or pain in the sum of life to a newspaper correspondent, but it served as a subject for letters, and the Chief Justice was very willing to win an ally in the press who would tell his story as he wished it to be read. The intimacy in Mr. Chase's house grew rapidly, and the alliance was no small help to the comforts of a struggling newspaper adventurer in Washington. No matter what one might think of his politics or temper, Mr. Chase was a dramatic figure, of high senatorial rank, if also of certain senatorial faults; a valuable ally.

As was sure, sooner or later, to happen, Adams one day met Charles Sumner on the street, and instantly stopped to greet him. As though eight years of broken ties were the natural course of friendship, Sumner at once, after an exclamation of surprise, dropped back into the relation of hero to the school boy. Adams enjoyed accepting it. He was then thirty years old and Sumner was fifty-seven; he had seen more of the world than Sumner ever dreamed of, and he felt a sort of amused curiosity to be treated once more as a child. At best, the renewal of broken relations is a nervous matter, and in this case it bristled with thorns, for Sumner's quarrel with Mr. Adams had not been the most delicate of his ruptured relations, and he was liable to be sensitive in many ways that even Bostonians could hardly keep in constant mind; yet it interested and fascinated Henry Adams as a new study of political humanity. The younger man knew that the meeting would have to come, and was ready for it, if only as a newspaper need; but to Sumner it came as a surprise and a disagreeable one, as Adams conceived. He learned something -- a piece of practical education worth the effort -- by watching Sumner's behavior. He could see that many thoughts -- mostly unpleasant -- were passing through his mind, since he made no inquiry about any of Adams's family, or allusion to any of his friends or his residence abroad. He talked only of the present. To him, Adams in Washington should have seemed more or less of a critic, perhaps a spy, certainly an intriguer or adventurer, like scores of others; a politician without party; a writer without principles; an office-seeker certain to beg for support. All this was, for his purposes, true. Adams could do him no good, and would be likely to do him all the harm in his power. Adams accepted it all; expected to be kept at arm's length; admitted that the reasons were just. He was the more surprised to see that Sumner invited a renewal of old relations. He found himself treated almost confidentially. Not only was he asked to make a fourth at Sumner's pleasant little dinners in the house on La Fayette Square, but he found himself admitted to the Senator's study and informed of his views, policy and purposes, which were sometimes even more astounding than his curious gaps or lapses of omniscience.

On the whole, the relation was the queerest that Henry Adams ever kept up. He liked and admired Sumner, but thought his mind a pathological study. At times he inclined to think that Sumner felt his solitude, and, in the political wilderness, craved educated society; but this hardly told the whole story. Sumner's mind had reached the calm of water which receives and reflects images without absorbing them; it contained nothing but itself. The images from without, the objects mechanically perceived by the senses, existed by courtesy until the mental surface was ruffled, but never became part of the thought. Henry Adams roused no emotion; if he had roused a disagreeable one, he would have ceased to exist. The mind would have mechanically rejected, as it had mechanically admitted him. Not that Sumner was more aggressively egoistic than other Senators -- Conkling, for instance -- but that with him the disease had affected the whole mind; it was chronic and absolute; while, with other Senators for the most part, it was still acute.

Perhaps for this very reason, Sumner was the more valuable acquaintance for a newspaper-man. Adams found him most useful; perhaps quite the most useful of all these great authorities who were the stock-in-trade of the newspaper business; the accumulated capital of a Silurian age. A few months or years more, and they were gone. In 1868, they were like the town itself, changing but not changed. La Fayette Square was society. Within a few hundred yards of Mr. Clark Mills's nursery monument to the equestrian seat of Andrew Jackson, one found all one's acquaintance as well as hotels, banks, markets and national government. Beyond the Square the country began. No rich or fashionable stranger had yet discovered the town. No literary or scientific man, no artist, no gentleman without office or employment, had ever lived there. It was rural, and its society was primitive. Scarcely a person in it had ever known life in a great city. Mr. Evarts, Mr. Sam Hooper, of Boston, and perhaps one or two of the diplomatists had alone mixed in that sort of world. The happy village was innocent of a club. The one-horse tram on F Street to the Capitol was ample for traffic. Every pleasant spring morning at the Pennsylvania Station, society met to bid good-bye to its friends going off on the single express. The State Department was lodged in an infant asylum far out on Fourteenth Street while Mr. Mullett was constructing his architectural infant asylum next the White House. The value of real estate had not increased since 1800, and the pavements were more impassable than the mud. All this favored a young man who had come to make a name. In four-and-twenty hours he could know everybody; in two days everybody knew him.

After seven years' arduous and unsuccessful effort to explore the outskirts of London society, the Washington world offered an easy and delightful repose. When he looked round him, from the safe shelter of Mr. Evarts's roof, on the men he was to work with -- or against -- he had to admit that nine-tenths of his acquired education was useless, and the other tenth harmful. He would have to begin again from the beginning. He must learn to talk to the Western Congressman, and to hide his own antecedents. The task was amusing. He could see nothing to prevent him from enjoying it, with immoral unconcern for all that had gone before and for anything that might follow. The lobby offered a spectacle almost picturesque. Few figures on the Paris stage were more entertaining and dramatic than old Sam Ward, who knew more of life than all the departments of the Government together, including the Senate and the Smithsonian. Society had not much to give, but what it had, it gave with an open hand. For the moment, politics had ceased to disturb social relations. All parties were mixed up and jumbled together in a sort of tidal slack-water. The Government resembled Adams himself in the matter of education. All that had gone before was useless, and some of it was worse.

Chapter XVII. President Grant (1869)

THE first effect of this leap into the unknown was a fit of low spirits new to the young man's education; due in part to the overpowering beauty and sweetness of the Maryland autumn, almost unendurable for its strain on one who had toned his life down to the November grays and browns of northern Europe. Life could not go on so beautiful and so sad. Luckily, no one else felt it or knew it. He bore it as well as he could, and when he picked himself up, winter had come, and he was settled in bachelor's quarters, as modest as those of a clerk in the Departments, far out on G Street, towards Georgetown, where an old Finn named Dohna, who had come out with the Russian Minister Stoeckel long before, had bought or built a new house. Congress had met. Two or three months remained to the old administration, but all interest centred in the new one. The town began to swarm with office-seekers, among whom a young writer was lost. He drifted among them, unnoticed, glad to learn his work under cover of the confusion. He never aspired to become a regular reporter; he knew he should fail in trying a career so ambitious and energetic; but he picked up friends on the press -- Nordhoff, Murat Halstead, Henry Watterson, Sam Bowles -- all reformers, and all mixed and jumbled together in a tidal wave of expectation, waiting for General Grant to give orders. No one seemed to know much about it. Even Senators had nothing to say. One could only make notes and study finance.

In waiting, he amused himself as he could. In the amusements of Washington, education had no part, but the simplicity of the amusements proved the simplicity of everything else, ambitions, interests, thoughts, and knowledge. Proverbially Washington was a poor place for education, and of course young diplomats avoided or disliked it, but, as a rule, diplomats disliked every place except Paris, and the world contained only one Paris. They abused London more violently than Washington; they praised no post under the sun; and they were merely describing three-fourths of their stations when they complained that there were no theatres, no restaurants, no monde, no demi-monde, no drives, no splendor, and, as Mme. de Struve used to say, no grandezza. This was all true; Washington was a mere political camp, as transient and temporary as a camp-meeting for religious revival, but the diplomats had least reason to complain, since they were more sought for there than they would ever be elsewhere. For young men Washington was in one way paradise, since they were few, and greatly in demand. After watching the abject unimportance of the young diplomat in London society, Adams found himself a young duke in Washington. He had ten years of youth to make up, and a ravenous appetite. Washington was the easiest society he had ever seen, and even the Bostonian became simple, good-natured, almost genial, in the softness of a Washington spring. Society went on excellently well without houses, or carriages, or jewels, or toilettes, or pavements, or shops, or grandezza of any sort; and the market was excellent as well as cheap. One could not stay there a month without loving the shabby town. Even the Washington girl, who was neither rich nor well-dressed nor well-educated nor clever, had singular charm, and used it. According to Mr. Adams the father, this charm dated back as far as Monroe's administration, to his personal knowledge.

Therefore, behind all the processes of political or financial or newspaper training, the social side of Washington was to be taken for granted as three-fourths of existence. Its details matter nothing. Life ceased to be strenuous, and the victim thanked God for it. Politics and reform became the detail, and waltzing the profession. Adams was not alone. Senator Sumner had as private secretary a young man named Moorfield Storey, who became a dangerous example of frivolity. The new Attorney-General, E. R. Hoar, brought with him from Concord a son, Sam Hoar, whose example rivalled that of Storey. Another impenitent was named Dewey, a young naval officer. Adams came far down in the list. He wished he had been higher. He could have spared a world of superannuated history, science, or politics, to have reversed better in waltzing.

He had no adequate notion how little he knew, especially of women, and Washington offered no standard of comparison. All were profoundly ignorant together, and as indifferent as children to education. No one needed knowledge. Washington was happier without style. Certainly Adams was happier without it; happier than he had ever been before; happier than any one in the harsh world of strenuousness could dream of. This must be taken as background for such little education as he gained; but the life belonged to the eighteenth century, and in no way concerned education for the twentieth.

In such an atmosphere, one made no great presence of hard work. If the world wants hard work, the world must pay for it; and, if it will not pay, it has no fault to find with the worker. Thus far, no one had made a suggestion of pay for any work that Adams had done or could do; if he worked at all, it was for social consideration, and social pleasure was his pay. For this he was willing to go on working, as an artist goes on painting when no one buys his pictures. Artists have done it from the beginning of time, and will do it after time has expired, since they cannot help themselves, and they find their return in the pride of their social superiority as they feel it. Society commonly abets them and encourages their attitude of contempt. The society of Washington was too simple and Southern as yet, to feel anarchistic longings, and it never read or saw what artists produced elsewhere, but it good-naturedly abetted them when it had the chance, and respected itself the more for the frailty. Adams found even the Government at his service, and every one willing to answer his questions. He worked, after a fashion; not very hard, but as much as the Government would have required of him for nine hundred dollars a year; and his work defied frivolity. He got more pleasure from writing than the world ever got from reading him, for his work was not amusing, nor was he. One must not try to amuse moneylenders or investors, and this was the class to which he began by appealing. He gave three months to an article on the finances of the United States, just then a subject greatly needing treatment; and when he had finished it, he sent it to London to his friend Henry Reeve, the ponderous editor of the Edinburgh Review. Reeve probably thought it good; at all events, he said so; and he printed it in April. Of course it was reprinted in America, but in England such articles were still anonymous, and the author remained unknown.

The author was not then asking for advertisement, and made no claim for credit. His object was literary. He wanted to win a place on the staff of the Edinburgh Review, under the vast shadow of Lord Macaulay; and, to a young American in 1868, such rank seemed colossal -- the highest in the literary world -- as it had been only five-and-twenty years before. Time and tide had flowed since then, but the position still flattered vanity, though it brought no other flattery or reward except the regular thirty pounds of pay -- fifty dollars a month, measured in time and labor.

The Edinburgh article finished, he set himself to work on a scheme for the North American Review. In England, Lord Robert Cecil had invented for the London Quarterly an annual review of politics which he called the "Session." Adams stole the idea and the name -- he thought he had been enough in Lord Robert's house, in days of his struggle with adversity, to excuse the theft -- and began what he meant for a permanent series of annual political reviews which he hoped to make, in time, a political authority. With his sources of information, and his social intimacies at Washington, he could not help saying something that would command attention. He had the field to himself, and he meant to give himself a free hand, as he went on. Whether the newspapers liked it or not, they would have to reckon with him; for such a power, once established, was more effective than all the speeches in Congress or reports to the President that could be crammed into the Government presses.

The first of these "Sessions" appeared in April, but it could not be condensed into a single article, and had to be supplemented in October by another which bore the title of "Civil Service Reform," and was really a part of the same review. A good deal of authentic history slipped into these papers. Whether any one except his press associates ever read them, he never knew and never greatly cared. The difference is slight, to the influence of an author, whether he is read by five hundred readers, or by five hundred thousand; if he can select the five hundred, he reaches the five hundred thousand. The fateful year 1870 was near at hand, which was to mark the close of the literary epoch, when quarterlies gave way to monthlies; letter-press to illustration; volumes to pages. The outburst was brilliant. Bret Harte led, and Robert Louis Stevenson followed. Guy de Maupassant and Rudyard Kipling brought up the rear, and dazzled the world. As usual, Adams found himself fifty years behind his time, but a number of belated wanderers kept him company, and they produced on each other the effect or illusion of a public opinion. They straggled apart, at longer and longer intervals, through the procession, but they were still within hearing distance of each other. The drift was still superficially conservative. Just as the Church spoke with apparent authority, of the quarterlies laid down an apparent law, and no one could surely say where the real authority, or the real law, lay. Science lid not know. Truths a priori held their own against truths surely relative. According to Lowell, Right was forever on the scaffold, Wrong was forever on the Throne; and most people still thought they believed it. Adams was not the only relic of the eighteenth century, and he could still depend on a certain number of listeners -- mostly respectable, and some rich.

Want of audience did not trouble him; he was well enough off in that respect, and would have succeeded in all his calculations if this had been his only hazard. Where he broke down was at a point where he always suffered wreck and where nine adventurers out of ten make their errors. One may be more or less certain of organized forces; one can never be certain of men. He belonged to the eighteenth century, and the eighteenth century upset all his plans. For the moment, America was more eighteenth century than himself; it reverted to the stone age.

As education -- of a certain sort -- the story had probably a certain value, though he could never see it. One seldom can see much education in the buck of a broncho; even less in the kick of a mule. The lesson it teaches is only that of getting out of the animal's way. This was the lesson that Henry Adams had learned over and over again in politics since 1860.

At least four-fifths of the American people -- Adams among the rest -- had united in the election of General Grant to the Presidency, and probably had been more or less affected in their choice by the parallel they felt between Grant and Washington. Nothing could be more obvious. Grant represented order. He was a great soldier, and the soldier always represented order. He might be as partisan as he pleased, but a general who had organized and commanded half a million or a million men in the field, must know how to administer. Even Washington, who was, in education and experience, a mere cave-dweller, had known how to organize a government, and had found Jeffersons and Hamiltons to organize his departments. The task of bringing the Government back to regular practices, and of restoring moral and mechanical order to administration, was not very difficult; it was ready to do it itself, with a little encouragement. No doubt the confusion, especially in the old slave States and in the currency, was considerable, but, the general disposition was good, and every one had echoed that famous phrase: "Let us have peace."

Adams was young and easily deceived, in spite of his diplomatic adventures, but even at twice his age he could not see that this reliance on Grant was unreasonable. Had Grant been a Congressman one would have been on one's guard, for one knew the type. One never expected from a Congressman more than good intentions and public spirit. Newspaper-men as a rule had no great respect for the lower House; Senators had less; and Cabinet officers had none at all. Indeed, one day when Adams was pleading with a Cabinet officer for patience and tact in dealing with Representatives, the Secretary impatiently broke out: "You can't use tact with a Congressman! A Congressman is a hog! You must take a stick and hit him on the snout!" Adams knew far too little, compared with the Secretary, to contradict him, though he thought the phrase somewhat harsh even as applied to the average Congressman of 1869 -- he saw little or nothing of later ones -- but he knew a shorter way of silencing criticism. He had but to ask: "If a Congressman is a hog, what is a Senator?" This innocent question, put in a candid spirit, petrified any executive officer that ever sat a week in his office. Even Adams admitted that Senators passed belief. The comic side of their egotism partly disguised its extravagance, but faction had gone so far under Andrew Johnson that at times the whole Senate seemed to catch hysterics of nervous bucking without apparent reason. Great leaders, like Sumner and Conkling, could not be burlesqued; they were more grotesque than ridicule could make them; even Grant, who rarely sparkled in epigram, became witty on their account; but their egotism and factiousness were no laughing matter. They did permanent and terrible mischief, as Garfield and Blaine, and even McKinley and John Hay, were to feel. The most troublesome task of a reform President was that of bringing the Senate back to decency.

Therefore no one, and Henry Adams less than most, felt hope that any President chosen from the ranks of politics or politicians would raise the character of government; and by instinct if not by reason, all the world united on Grant. The Senate understood what the world expected, and waited in silence for a struggle with Grant more serious than that with Andrew Johnson. Newspaper-men were alive with eagerness to support the President against the Senate. The newspaper-man is, more than most men, a double personality; and his person feels best satisfied in its double instincts when writing in one sense and thinking in another. All newspaper-men, whatever they wrote, felt alike about the Senate. Adams floated with the stream. He was eager to join in the fight which he foresaw as sooner or later inevitable. He meant to support the Executive in attacking the Senate and taking away its two-thirds vote and power of confirmation, nor did he much care how it should be done, for he thought it safer to effect the revolution in 1870 than to wait till 1920..

With this thought in his mind, he went to the Capitol to hear the names announced which should reveal the carefully guarded secret of Grant's Cabinet. To the end of his life, he wondered at the suddenness of the revolution which actually, within five minutes, changed his intended future into an absurdity so laughable as to make him ashamed of it. He was to hear a long list of

Cabinet announcements not much weaker or more futile than that of Grant, and none of them made him blush, while Grant's nominations had the singular effect of making the hearer ashamed, not so much of Grant, as of himself. He had made another total misconception of life -- another inconceivable false start. Yet, unlikely as it seemed, he had missed his motive narrowly, and his intention had been more than sound, for the Senators made no secret of saying with senatorial frankness that Grant's nominations betrayed his intent as plainly as they betrayed his incompetence. A great soldier might be a baby politician.

Adams left the Capitol, much in the same misty mental condition that he recalled as marking his railway journey to London on May 13, 1861; he felt in himself what Gladstone bewailed so sadly, "the incapacity of viewing things all round." He knew, without absolutely saying it, that Grant had cut short the life which Adams had laid out for himself in the future. After such a miscarriage, no thought of effectual reform could revive for at least one generation, and he had no fancy for ineffectual politics. What course could he sail next? He had tried so many, and society had barred them all! For the moment, he saw no hope but in following the stream on which he had launched himself. The new Cabinet, as individuals, were not hostile. Subsequently Grant made changes in the list which were mostly welcome to a Bostonian -- or should have been -- although fatal to Adams. The name of Hamilton Fish, as Secretary of State, suggested extreme conservatism and probable deference to Sumner. The name of George S. Boutwell, as Secretary of the Treasury, suggested only a somewhat lugubrious joke; Mr. Boutwell could be described only as the opposite of Mr. McCulloch, and meant inertia; or, in plain words, total extinction for any one resembling Henry Adams. On the other hand, the name of Jacob D. Cox, as Secretary of the Interior, suggested help and comfort; while that of Judge Hoar, as Attorney-General, promised friendship. On the whole, the personal outlook, merely for literary purposes, seemed fairly cheerful, and the political outlook, though hazy, still depended on Grant himself. No one doubted that Grant's intention had been one of reform; that his aim had been to place his administration above politics; and until he should actually drive his supporters away, one might hope to support him. One's little lantern must therefore be turned on Grant. One seemed to know him so well, and really knew so little.

By chance it happened that Adam Badeau took the lower suite of rooms at Dohna's, and, as it was convenient to have one table, the two men dined together and became intimate. Badeau was exceedingly social, though not in appearance imposing. He was stout; his face was red, and his habits were regularly irregular; but he was very intelligent, a good newspaper-man, and an excellent military historian. His life of Grant was no ordinary book. Unlike most newspaper-men, he was a friendly critic of Grant, as suited an officer who had been on the General's staff. As a rule, the newspaper correspondents in Washington were unfriendly, and the lobby sceptical. From that side one heard tales that made one's hair stand on end, and the old West Point army officers were no more flattering. All described him as vicious, narrow, dull, and vindictive. Badeau, who had come to Washington for a consulate which was slow to reach him, resorted more or less to whiskey for encouragement, and became irritable, besides being loquacious. He talked much about Grant, and showed a certain artistic feeling for analysis of character, as a true literary critic would naturally do. Loyal to Grant, and still more so to Mrs. Grant, who acted as his patroness, he said nothing, even when far gone, that was offensive about either, but he held that no one except himself and Rawlins understood the General. To him, Grant appeared as an intermittent energy, immensely powerful when awake, but passive and plastic in repose. He said that neither he nor the rest of the staff knew why Grant succeeded; they believed in him because of his success. For stretches of time, his mind seemed torpid. Rawlins and the others would systematically talk their ideas into it, for weeks, not directly, but by discussion among themselves, in his presence. In the end, he would announce the idea as his own, without seeming conscious of the discussion; and would give the orders to carry it out with all the energy that belonged to his nature. They could never measure his character or be sure when he would act. They could never follow a mental process in his thought. They were not sure that he did think.

In all this, Adams took deep interest, for although he was not, like Badeau, waiting for Mrs. Grant's power of suggestion to act on the General's mind in order to germinate in a consulate or a legation, his portrait gallery of great men was becoming large, and it amused him to add an authentic likeness of the greatest general the world had seen since Napoleon. Badeau's analysis was rather delicate; infinitely superior to that of Sam Ward or Charles Nordhoff.

Badeau took Adams to the White House one evening and introduced him to the President and Mrs. Grant. First and last, he saw a dozen Presidents at the White House, and the most famous were by no means the most agreeable, but he found Grant the most curious object of study among them all. About no one did opinions differ so widely. Adams had no opinion, or occasion to make one. A single word with Grant satisfied him that, for his own good, the fewer words he risked, the better. Thus far in life he had met with but one man of the same intellectual or unintellectual type -- Garibaldi. Of the two, Garibaldi seemed to him a trifle the more intellectual, but, in both, the intellect counted for nothing; only the energy counted. The type was pre-intellectual, archaic, and would have seemed so even to the cave-dwellers. Adam, according to legend, was such a man.

In time one came to recognize the type in other men, with differences and variations, as normal; men whose energies were the greater, the less they wasted on thought; men who sprang from the soil to power; apt to be distrustful of themselves and of others; shy; jealous; sometimes vindictive; more or less dull in outward appearance; always needing stimulants, but for whom action was the highest stimulant -- the instinct of fight. Such men were forces of nature, energies of the prime, like the Pteraspis , but they made short work of scholars. They had commanded thousands of such and saw no more in them than in others. The fact was certain; it crushed argument and intellect at once.

Adams did not feel Grant as a hostile force; like Badeau he saw only an uncertain one. When in action he was superb and safe to follow; only when torpid he was dangerous. To deal with him one must stand near, like Rawlins, and practice more or less sympathetic habits. Simple-minded beyond the experience of Wall Street or State Street, he resorted, like most men of the same intellectual calibre, to commonplaces when at a loss for expression: "Let us have peace!" or, "The best way to treat a bad law is to execute it"; or a score of such reversible sentences generally to be gauged by their sententiousness; but sometimes he made one doubt his good faith; as when he seriously remarked to a particularly bright young woman that Venice would be a fine city if it were drained. In Mark Twain, this suggestion would have taken rank among his best witticisms; in Grant it was a measure of simplicity not singular. Robert E. Lee betrayed the same intellectual commonplace, in a Virginian form, not to the same degree, but quite distinctly enough for one who knew the American. What worried Adams was not the commonplace; it was, as usual, his own education. Grant fretted and irritated him, like the Terebratula, as a defiance of first principles. He had no right to exist. He should have been extinct for ages. The idea that, as society grew older, it grew one-sided, upset evolution, and made of education a fraud. That, two thousand years after Alexander the Great and Julius Caesar, a man like Grant should be called -- and should actually and truly be -- the highest product of the most advanced evolution, made evolution ludicrous. One must be as commonplace as Grant's own commonplaces to maintain such an absurdity. The progress of evolution from President Washington to President Grant, was alone evidence enough to upset Darwin.

Education became more perplexing at every phase. No theory was worth the pen that wrote it. America had no use for Adams because he was eighteenth-century, and yet it worshipped Grant because he was archaic and should have lived in a cave and worn skins. Darwinists ought to conclude that America was reverting to the stone age, but the theory of reversion was more absurd than that of evolution. Grant's administration reverted to nothing. One could not catch a trait of the past, still less of the future. It was not even sensibly American. Not an official in it, except perhaps Rawlins whom Adams never met, and who died in September, suggested an American idea.

Yet this administration, which upset Adams's whole life, was not unfriendly; it was made up largely of friends. Secretary Fish was almost kind; he kept the tradition of New York social values; he was human and took no pleasure in giving pain. Adams felt no prejudice whatever in his favor, and he had nothing in mind or person to attract regard; his social gifts were not remarkable; he was not in the least magnetic; he was far from young; but he won confidence from the start and remained a friend to the finish. As far as concerned Mr. Fish, one felt rather happily suited, and one was still better off in the Interior Department with J. D. Cox. Indeed, if Cox had been in the Treasury and Boutwell in the Interior, one would have been quite satisfied as far as personal relations went, while, in the Attorney-General's Office, Judge Hoar seemed to fill every possible ideal, both personal and political.

The difficulty was not the want of friends, and had the whole government been filled with them, it would have helped little without the President and the Treasury. Grant avowed from the start a policy of drift; and a policy of drift attaches only barnacles. At thirty, one has no interest in becoming a barnacle, but even in that character Henry Adams would have been ill-seen. His friends were reformers, critics, doubtful in party allegiance, and he was himself an object of suspicion. Grant had no objects, wanted no help, wished for no champions. The Executive asked only to be let alone. This was his meaning when he said: "Let us have peace! "

No one wanted to go into opposition. As for Adams, all his hopes of success in life turned on his finding an administration to support. He knew well enough the rules of self-interest. He was for sale. He wanted to be bought. His price was excessively cheap, for he did not even ask an office, and had his eye, not on the Government, but on New York. All he wanted was something to support; something that would let itself be supported. Luck went dead against him. For once, he was fifty years in advance of his time.

Chapter XVIII. Free Fight (1869-1870)

THE old New Englander was apt to be a solitary animal, but the young New Englander was sometimes human. Judge Hoar brought his son Sam to Washington, and Sam Hoar loved largely and well. He taught Adams the charm of Washington spring. Education for education, none ever compared with the delight of this. The Potomac and its tributaries squandered beauty. Rock Creek was as wild as the Rocky Mountains. Here and there a negro log cabin alone disturbed the dogwood and the judas-tree, the azalea and the laurel. The tulip and the chestnut gave no sense of struggle against a stingy nature. The soft, full outlines of the landscape carried no hidden horror of glaciers in its bosom. The brooding heat of the profligate vegetation; the cool charm of the running water; the terrific splendor of the June thunder-gust in the deep and solitary woods, were all sensual, animal, elemental. No European spring had shown him the same intermixture of delicate grace and passionate depravity that marked the Maryland May. He loved it too much, as though it were Greek and half human. He could not leave it, but loitered on into July, falling into the Southern ways of the summer village about La Fayette Square, as one whose rights of inheritance could not be questioned. Few Americans were so poor as to question them.

In spite of the fatal deception -- or undeception -- about Grant's political character, Adams's first winter in Washington had so much amused him that he had not a thought of change. He loved it too much to question its value. What did he know about its value, or what did any one know? His father knew more about it than any one else in Boston, and he was amused to find that his father, whose recollections went back to 1820, betrayed for Washington much the same sentimental weakness, and described the society about President Monroe much as his son felt the society about President Johnson. He feared its effect on young men, with some justice, since it had been fatal to two of his brothers; but he understood the charm, and he knew that a life in Quincy or Boston was not likely to deaden it.

Henry was in a savage humor on the subject of Boston. He saw Boutwells at every counter. He found a personal grief in every tree. Fifteen or twenty years afterwards, Clarence King used to amuse him by mourning over the narrow escape that nature had made in attaining perfection. Except for two mistakes, the earth would have been a success. One of these errors was the inclination of the ecliptic; the other was the differentiation of the sexes, and the saddest thought about the last was that it should have been so modern. Adams, in his splenetic temper, held that both these unnecessary evils had wreaked their worst on Boston. The climate made eternal war on society, and sex was a species of crime. The ecliptic had inclined itself beyond recovery till life was as thin as the elm trees. Of course he was in the wrong. The thinness was in himself, not in Boston; but this is a story of education, and Adams was struggling to shape himself to his time. Boston was trying to do the same thing. Everywhere, except in Washington, Americans were toiling for the same object. Every one complained of surroundings, except where, as at Washington, there were no surroundings to complain of. Boston kept its head better than its neighbors did, and very little time was needed to prove it, even to Adams's confusion.

Before he got back to Quincy, the summer was already half over, and in another six weeks the effects of President Grant's character showed themselves. They were startling -- astounding -- terrifying. The mystery that shrouded the famous, classical attempt of Jay Gould to corner gold in September, 1869, has never been cleared up -- at least so far as to make it intelligible to Adams. Gould was led, by the change at Washington, into the belief that he could safely corner gold without interference from the Government. He took a number of precautions, which he admitted; and he spent a large sum of money, as he also testified, to obtain assurances which were not sufficient to have satisfied so astute a gambler; yet he made the venture. Any criminal lawyer must have begun investigation by insisting, rigorously, that no such man, in such a position, could be permitted to plead that he had taken, and pursued, such a course, without assurances which did satisfy him. The plea was professionally inadmissible.

This meant that any criminal lawyer would have been bound to start an investigation by insisting that Gould had assurances from the White House or the Treasury, since none other could have satisfied him. To young men wasting their summer at Quincy for want of some one to hire their services at three dollars a day, such a dramatic scandal was Heaven-sent. Charles and Henry Adams jumped at it like salmon at a fly, with as much voracity as Jay Gould, or his ame damnee Jim Fisk, had ever shown for Erie; and with as little fear of consequences. They risked something; no one could say what; but the people about the Erie office were not regarded as lambs.

The unravelling a skein so tangled as that of the Erie Railway was a task that might have given months of labor to the most efficient District Attorney, with all his official tools to work with. Charles took the railway history; Henry took the so-called Gold Conspiracy; and they went to New York to work it up. The surface was in full view. They had no trouble in Wall Street, and they paid their respects in person to the famous Jim Fisk in his Opera-House Palace; but the New York side of the story helped Henry little. He needed to penetrate the political mystery, and for this purpose he had to wait for Congress to meet. At first he feared that Congress would suppress the scandal, but the Congressional Investigation was ordered and took place. He soon knew all that was to be known; the material for his essay was furnished by the Government.

Material furnished by a government seldom satisfies critics or historians, for it lies always under suspicion. Here was a mystery, and as usual, the chief mystery was the means of making sure that any mystery existed. All Adams's great friends -- Fish, Cox, Hoar, Evarts, Sumner, and their surroundings -- were precisely the persons most mystified. They knew less than Adams did; they sought information, and frankly admitted that their relations with the White House and the Treasury were not confidential. No one volunteered advice. No one offered suggestion. One got no light, even from the press, although press agents expressed in private the most damning convictions with their usual cynical frankness. The Congressional Committee took a quantity of evidence which it dared not probe, and refused to analyze. Although the fault lay somewhere on the Administration, and could lie nowhere else, the trail always faded and died out at the point where any member of the Administration became visible. Every one dreaded to press inquiry. Adams himself feared finding out too much. He found out too much already, when he saw in evidence that Jay Gould had actually succeeded in stretching his net over Grant's closest surroundings, and that Boutwell's incompetence was the bottom of Gould's calculation. With the conventional air of assumed confidence, every one in public assured every one else that the President himself was the savior of the situation, and in private assured each other that if the President had not been caught this time, he was sure to be trapped the next, for the ways of Wall Street were dark and double. All this was wildly exciting to Adams. That Grant should have fallen, within six months, into such a morass -- or should have let Boutwell drop him into it -- rendered the outlook for the next four years -- probably eight -- possibly twelve -- mysterious, or frankly opaque, to a young man who had hitched his wagon, as Emerson told him, to the star of reform. The country might outlive it, but not he. The worst scandals of the eighteenth century were relatively harmless by the side of this, which smirched executive, judiciary, banks, corporate systems, professions, and people, all the great active forces of society, in one dirty cesspool of vulgar corruption. Only six months before, this innocent young man, fresh from the cynicism of European diplomacy, had expected to enter an honorable career in the press as the champion and confidant of a new Washington, and already he foresaw a life of wasted energy, sweeping the stables of American society clear of the endless corruption which his second Washington was quite certain to breed.

By vigorously shutting one's eyes, as though one were an Assistant Secretary, a writer for the press might ignore the Erie scandal, and still help his friends or allies in the Government who were doing their best to give it an air of decency; but a few weeks showed that the Erie scandal was a mere incident, a rather vulgar Wall Street trap, into which, according to one's point of view Grant had been drawn by Jay Gould, or Jay Gould had been misled by Grant. One could hardly doubt that both of them were astonished and disgusted by the result; but neither Jay Gould nor any other astute American mind -- still less the complex Jew -- could ever have accustomed itself to the incredible and inexplicable lapses of Grant's intelligence; and perhaps, on the whole, Gould was the less mischievous victim, if victims they both were. The same laxity that led Gould into a trap which might easily have become the penitentiary, led the United States Senate, the Executive departments and the Judiciary into confusion, cross-purposes, and ill-temper that would have been scandalous in a boarding-school of girls. For satirists or comedians, the study was rich and endless, and they exploited its corners with happy results, but a young man fresh from the rustic simplicity of London noticed with horror that the grossest satires on the American Senator and politician never failed to excite the laughter and applause of every audience. Rich and poor joined in throwing contempt on their own representatives. Society laughed a vacant and meaningless derision over its own failure. Nothing remained for a young man without position or power except to laugh too.

Yet the spectacle was no laughing matter to him, whatever it might be to the public. Society is immoral and immortal; it can afford to commit any kind of folly, and indulge in any sort of vice; it cannot be killed, and the fragments that survive can always laugh at the dead; but a young man has only one chance, and brief time to seize it. Any one in power above him can extinguish the chance. He is horribly at the mercy of fools and cowards. One dull administration can rapidly drive out every active subordinate. At Washington, in 1869-70, every intelligent man about the Government prepared to go. The people would have liked to go too, for they stood helpless before the chaos; some laughed and some raved; all were disgusted; but they had to content themselves by turning their backs and going to work harder than ever on their railroads and foundries. They were strong enough to carry even their politics. Only the helpless remained stranded in Washington.

The shrewdest statesman of all was Mr. Boutwell, who showed how he understood the situation by turning out of the Treasury every one who could interfere with his repose, and then locking himself up in it, alone. What he did there, no one knew. His colleagues asked him in vain. Not a word could they get from him, either in the Cabinet or out of it, of suggestion or information on matters even of vital interest. The Treasury as an active influence ceased to exist. Mr. Boutwell waited with confidence for society to drag his department out of the mire, as it was sure to do if he waited long enough.

Warned by his friends in the Cabinet as well as in the Treasury that Mr. Boutwell meant to invite no support, and cared to receive none, Adams had only the State and Interior Departments left to serve. He wanted no better than to serve them. Opposition was his horror; pure waste of energy; a union with Northern Democrats and Southern rebels who never had much in common with any

Adams, and had never shown any warm interest about them except to drive them from public life. If Mr. Boutwell turned him out of the Treasury with the indifference or contempt that made even a beetle helpless, Mr. Fish opened the State Department freely, and seemed to talk with as much openness as any newspaper-man could ask. At all events, Adams could cling to this last plank of salvation, and make himself perhaps the recognized champion of Mr. Fish in the New York press. He never once thought of his disaster between Seward and Sumner in 1861. Such an accident could not occur again. Fish and Sumner were inseparable, and their policy was sure to be safe enough for support. No mosquito could be so unlucky as to be caught a second time between a Secretary and a Senator who were both his friends.

This dream of security lasted hardly longer than that of 1861. Adams saw Sumner take possession of the Department, and he approved; he saw Sumner seize the British mission for Motley, and he was delighted; but when he renewed his relations with Sumner in the winter of 1869-70, he began slowly to grasp the idea that Sumner had a foreign policy of his own which he proposed also to force on the Department. This was not all. Secretary Fish seemed to have vanished. Besides the Department of State over which he nominally presided in the Infant Asylum on Fourteenth Street, there had risen a Department of Foreign Relations over which Senator Sumner ruled with a high hand at the Capitol; and, finally, one clearly made out a third Foreign Office in the War Department, with President Grant himself for chief, pressing a policy of extension in the West Indies which no Northeastern man ever approved. For his life, Adams could not learn where to place himself among all these forces. Officially he would have followed the responsible Secretary of State, but he could not find the Secretary. Fish seemed to be friendly towards Sumner, and docile towards Grant, but he asserted as yet no policy of his own. As for Grant's policy, Adams never had a chance to know fully what it was, but, as far as he did know, he was ready to give it ardent support. The difficulty came only when he heard Sumner's views, which, as he had reason to know, were always commands, to be disregarded only by traitors.

Little by little, Sumner unfolded his foreign policy, and Adams gasped with fresh astonishment at every new article of the creed. To his profound regret he heard Sumner begin by imposing his veto on all extension within the tropics; which cost the island of St. Thomas to the United States, besides the Bay of Samana as an alternative, and ruined Grant's policy. Then he listened with incredulous stupor while Sumner unfolded his plan for concentrating and pressing every possible American claim against England, with a view of compelling the cession of Canada to the United States.

Adams did not then know -- in fact, he never knew, or could find any one to tell him -- what was going on behind the doors of the White House. He doubted whether Mr. Fish or Bancroft Davis knew much more than he. The game of cross-purposes was as impenetrable in Foreign Affairs as in the Gold Conspiracy. President Grant let every one go on, but whom he supported, Adams could not be expected to divine. One point alone seemed clear to a man -- no longer so very young -- who had lately come from a seven years' residence in London. He thought he knew as much as any one in Washington about England, and he listened with the more perplexity to Mr. Sumner's talk, because it opened the gravest doubts of Sumner's sanity. If war was his object, and Canada were worth it, Sumner's scheme showed genius, and Adams was ready to treat it seriously; but if he thought he could obtain Canada from England as a voluntary set-off to the Alabama Claims, he drivelled. On the point of fact, Adams was as peremptory as Sumner on the point of policy, but he could only wonder whether Mr. Fish would dare say it. When at last Mr.

Fish did say it, a year later, Sumner publicly cut his acquaintance. Adams was the more puzzled because he could not believe Sumner so mad as to quarrel both with Fish and with Grant. A quarrel with Seward and Andrew Johnson was bad enough, and had profited no one; but a quarrel with General Grant was lunacy. Grant might be whatever one liked, as far as morals or temper or intellect were concerned, but he was not a man whom a light-weight cared to challenge for a fight; and Sumner, whether he knew it or not, was a very light weight in the Republican Party, if separated from his Committee of Foreign Relations. As a party manager he had not the weight of half-a-dozen men whose very names were unknown to him.

Between these great forces, where was the Administration and how was one to support it? One must first find it, and even then it was not easily caught. Grant's simplicity was more disconcerting than the complexity of a Talleyrand. Mr. Fish afterwards told Adams, with the rather grim humor he sometimes indulged in, that Grant took a dislike to Motley because he parted his hair in the middle. Adams repeated the story to Godkin, who made much play with it in the Nation, till it was denied. Adams saw no reason why it should be denied. Grant had as good a right to dislike the hair as the head, if the hair seemed to him a part of it. Very shrewd men have formed very sound judgments on less material than hair -- on clothes, for example, according to Mr. Carlyle, or on a pen, according to Cardinal de Retz -- and nine men in ten could hardly give as good a reason as hair for their likes or dislikes. In truth, Grant disliked Motley at sight, because they had nothing in common; and for the same reason he disliked Sumner. For the same reason he would be sure to dislike Adams if Adams gave him a chance. Even Fish could not be quite sure of Grant, except for the powerful effect which wealth had, or appeared to have, on Grant's imagination.

The quarrel that lowered over the State Department did not break in storm till July, 1870, after Adams had vanished, but another quarrel, almost as fatal to Adams as that between Fish and Sumner, worried him even more. Of all members of the Cabinet, the one whom he had most personal interest in cultivating was Attorney General Hoar. The Legal Tender decision, which had been the first stumbling-block to Adams at Washington, grew in interest till it threatened to become something more serious than a block; it fell on one's head like a plaster ceiling, and could not be escaped. The impending battle between Fish and Sumner was nothing like so serious as the outbreak between Hoar and Chief Justice Chase. Adams had come to Washington hoping to support the Executive in a policy of breaking down the Senate, but he never dreamed that he would be required to help in breaking down the Supreme Court. Although, step by step, he had been driven, like the rest of the world, to admit that American society had outgrown most of its institutions, he still clung to the Supreme Court, much as a churchman clings to his bishops, because they are his only symbol of unity; his last rag of Right. Between the Executive and the Legislature, citizens could have no Rights; they were at the mercy of Power. They had created the Court to protect them from unlimited Power, and it was little enough protection at best. Adams wanted to save the independence of the Court at least for his lifetime, and could not conceive that the Executive should wish to overthrow it.

Frank Walker shared this feeling, and, by way of helping the Court, he had promised Adams for the North American Review an article on the history of the Legal Tender Act, founded on a volume just then published by Spaulding, the putative father of the legal-tender clause in 1861. Secretary Jacob D. Cox, who alone sympathized with reform, saved from Boutwell's decree of banishment such reformers as he could find place for, and he saved Walker for a time by giving him the Census of 1870. Walker was obliged to abandon his article for the North American in order to devote himself to the Census. He gave Adams his notes, and Adams completed the article.

He had not toiled in vain over the Bank of England Restriction. He knew enough about Legal Tender to leave it alone. If the banks and bankers wanted fiat money, fiat money was good enough for a newspaper-man; and if they changed about and wanted "intrinsic" value, gold and silver came equally welcome to a writer who was paid half the wages of an ordinary mechanic. He had no notion of attacking or defending Legal Tender; his object was to defend the Chief Justice and the Court. Walker argued that, whatever might afterwards have been the necessity for legal tender, there was no necessity for it at the time the Act was passed. With the help of the Chief Justice's recollections, Adams completed the article, which appeared in the April number of the North American. Its ferocity was Walker's, for Adams never cared to abandon the knife for the hatchet, but Walker reeked of the army and the Springfield Republican, and his energy ran away with Adams's restraint. The unfortunate Spaulding complained loudly of this treatment, not without justice, but the article itself had serious historical value, for Walker demolished every shred of Spaulding's contention that legal tender was necessary at the time; and the Chief Justice told his part of the story with conviction. The Chief Justice seemed to be pleased. The Attorney General, pleased or not, made no sign. The article had enough historical interest to induce Adams to reprint it in a volume of Essays twenty years afterwards; but its historical value was not its point in education. The point was that, in spite of the best intentions, the plainest self-interest, and the strongest wish to escape further trouble, the article threw Adams into opposition. Judge Hoar, like Boutwell, was implacable.

Hoar went on to demolish the Chief Justice; while Henry Adams went on, drifting further and further from the Administration. He did this in common with all the world, including Hoar himself. Scarcely a newspaper in the country kept discipline. The New York Tribune was one of the most criminal. Dissolution of ties in every direction marked the dissolution of temper, and the Senate Chamber became again a scene of irritated egotism that passed ridicule. Senators quarrelled with each other, and no one objected, but they picked quarrels also with the Executive and threw every Department into confusion. Among others they quarrelled with Hoar, and drove him from office.

That Sumner and Hoar, the two New Englanders in great position who happened to be the two persons most necessary for his success at Washington, should be the first victims of Grant's lax rule, must have had some meaning for Adams's education, if Adams could only have understood what it was. He studied, but failed. Sympathy with him was not their weakness. Directly, in the form of help, he knew he could hope as little from them as from Boutwell. So far from inviting attachment they, like other New Englanders, blushed to own a friend. Not one of the whole delegation would ever, of his own accord, try to help Adams or any other young man who did not beg for it, although they would always accept whatever services they had not to pay for. The lesson of education was not there. The selfishness of politics was the earliest of all political education, and Adams had nothing to learn from its study; but the situation struck him as curious -- so curious that he devoted years to reflecting upon it. His four most powerful friends had matched themselves, two and two, and were fighting in pairs to a finish; Sumner-Fish; Chase-Hoar; with foreign affairs and the judiciary as prizes! What value had the fight in education?

Adams was puzzled, and was not the only puzzled bystander. The stage-type of statesman was amusing, whether as Roscoe Conkling or Colonel Mulberry Sellers, but what was his value? The statesmen of the old type, whether Sumners or Conklings or Hoars or Lamars, were personally as honest as human nature could produce. They trod with lofty contempt on other people's jobs, especially when there was good in them. Yet the public thought that Sumner and Conkling cost the country a hundred times more than all the jobs they ever trod on; just as Lamar and the old Southern statesmen, who were also honest in money-matters, cost the country a civil war. This painful moral doubt worried Adams less than it worried his friends and the public, but it affected the whole field of politics for twenty years. The newspapers discussed little else than the alleged moral laxity of Grant, Garfield, and Blaine. If the press were taken seriously, politics turned on jobs, and some of Adams's best friends, like Godkin, ruined their influence by their insistence on points of morals. Society hesitated, wavered, oscillated between harshness and laxity, pitilessly sacrificing the weak, and deferentially following the strong. In spite of all such criticism, the public nominated Grant, Garfield, and Blaine for the Presidency, and voted for them afterwards, not seeming to care for the question; until young men were forced to see that either some new standard must be created, or none could be upheld. The moral law had expired -- like the Constitution.

Grant's administration outraged every rule of ordinary decency, but scores of promising men, whom the country could not well spare, were ruined in saying so. The world cared little for decency. What it wanted, it did not know; probably a system that would work, and men who could work it; but it found neither. Adams had tried his own little hands on it, and had failed. His friends had been driven out of Washington or had taken to fisticuffs. He himself sat down and stared helplessly into the future.

The result was a review of the Session for the July North American into which he crammed and condensed everything he thought he had observed and all he had been told. He thought it good history then, and he thought it better twenty years afterwards; he thought it even good enough to reprint. As it happened, in the process of his devious education, this "Session" of 1869-70 proved to be his last study in current politics, and his last dying testament as a humble member of the press. As such, he stood by it. He could have said no more, had he gone on reviewing every session in the rest of the century. The political dilemma was as clear in 1870 as it was likely to be in 1970 The system of 1789 had broken down, and with it the eighteenth-century fabric of a priori, or moral, principles. Politicians had tacitly given it up. Grant's administration marked the avowal. Nine-tenths of men's political energies must henceforth be wasted on expedients to piece out -- to patch -- or, in vulgar language, to tinker -- the political machine as often as it broke down. Such a system, or want of system, might last centuries, if tempered by an occasional revolution or civil war; but as a machine, it was, or soon would be, the poorest in the world -- the clumsiest -- the most inefficient

Here again was an education, but what it was worth he could not guess. Indeed, when he raised his eyes to the loftiest and most triumphant results of politics -- to Mr. Boutwell, Mr. Conkling or even Mr. Sumner -- he could not honestly say that such an education, even when it carried one up to these unattainable heights, was worth anything. There were men, as yet standing on lower levels -- clever and amusing men like Garfield and Blaine -- who took no little pleasure in making fun of the senatorial demi-gods, and who used language about Grant himself which the North American Review would not have admitted. One asked doubtfully what was likely to become of these men in their turn. What kind of political ambition was to result from this destructive political education?

Yet the sum of political life was, or should have been, the attainment of a working political system. Society needed to reach it. If moral standards broke down, and machinery stopped working, new morals and machinery of some sort had to be invented. An eternity of Grants, or even of Garfields or of Conklings or of Jay Goulds, refused to be conceived as possible. Practical Americans laughed, and went their way. Society paid them to be practical. Whenever society cared to pay Adams, he too would be practical, take his pay, and hold his tongue; but meanwhile he was driven to associate with Democratic Congressmen and educate them. He served David Wells as an active assistant professor of revenue reform, and turned his rooms into a college. The Administration drove him, and thousands of other young men, into active enmity, not only to Grant, but to the system or want of system, which took possession of the President. Every hope or thought which had brought Adams to Washington proved to be absurd. No one wanted him; no one wanted any of his friends in reform; the blackmailer alone was the normal product of politics as of business.

All this was excessively amusing. Adams never had been so busy, so interested, so much in the thick of the crowd. He knew Congressmen by scores and newspaper-men by the dozen. He wrote for his various organs all sorts of attacks and defences. He enjoyed the life enormously, and found himself as happy as Sam Ward or Sunset Cox; much happier than his friends Fish or J. D. Cox, or Chief Justice Chase or Attorney General Hoar or Charles Sumner. When spring came, he took to the woods, which were best of all, for after the first of April, what Maurice de Guerin called "the vast maternity" of nature showed charms more voluptuous than the vast paternity of the United States Senate. Senators were less ornamental than the dogwood or even the judas-tree. They were, as a rule, less good company. Adams astonished himself by remarking what a purified charm was lent to the Capitol by the greatest possible distance, as one caught glimpses of the dome over miles of forest foliage. At such moments he pondered on the distant beauty of St. Peter's and the steps of Ara Coeli.

Yet he shortened his spring, for he needed to get back to London for the season. He had finished his New York "Gold Conspiracy," which he meant for his friend Henry Reeve and the Edinburgh Review. It was the best piece of work he had done, but this was not his reason for publishing it in England. The Erie scandal had provoked a sort of revolt among respectable New Yorkers, as well as among some who were not so respectable; and the attack on Erie was beginning to promise success. London was a sensitive spot for the Erie management, and it was thought well to strike them there, where they were socially and financially exposed. The tactics suited him in another way, for any expression about America in an English review attracted ten times the attention in America that the same article would attract in the North American. Habitually the American dailies reprinted such articles in full. Adams wanted to escape the terrors of copyright, his highest ambition was to be pirated and advertised free of charge, since in any case, his pay was nothing. Under the excitement of chase he was becoming a pirate himself, and liked it.

Chapter XIX. Chaos (1870)

ONE fine May afternoon in 1870 Adams drove again up St. James's Street wondering more than ever at the marvels of life. Nine years had passed since the historic entrance of May, 1861.

Outwardly London was the same. Outwardly Europe showed no great change. Palmerston and Russell were forgotten; but Disraeli and Gladstone were still much alive. One's friends were more than ever prominent. John Bright was in the Cabinet; W. E. Forster was about to enter it; reform ran riot. Never had the sun of progress shone so fair. Evolution from lower to higher raged like an epidemic. Darwin was the greatest of prophets in the most evolutionary of worlds. Gladstone had overthrown the Irish Church; was overthrowing the Irish landlords; was trying to pass an Education Act. Improvement, prosperity, power, were leaping and bounding over every country road. Even America, with her Erie scandals and Alabama Claims, hardly made a discordant note.

At the Legation, Motley ruled; the long Adams reign was forgotten; the rebellion had passed into history. In society no one cared to recall the years before the Prince of Wales. The smart set had come to their own. Half the houses that Adams had frequented, from 1861 to 1865, were closed or closing in 1870. Death had ravaged one's circle of friends. Mrs. Milnes Gaskell and her sister Miss Charlotte Wynn were both dead, and Mr. James Milnes Gaskell was no longer in Parliament. That field of education seemed closed too.

One found one's self in a singular frame of mind -- more eighteenth-century than ever -- almost rococo -- and unable to catch anywhere the cog-wheels of evolution. Experience ceased to educate. London taught less freely than of old. That one bad style was leading to another -- that the older men were more amusing than the younger -- that Lord Houghton's breakfast-table showed gaps hard to fill -- that there were fewer men one wanted to meet -- these, and a hundred more such remarks, helped little towards a quicker and more intelligent activity. For English reforms Adams cared nothing. The reforms were themselves mediaeval. The Education Bill of his friend W. E. Forster seemed to him a guaranty against all education he had use for. He resented change. He would have kept the Pope in the Vatican and the Queen at Windsor Castle as historical monuments. He did not care to Americanize Europe. The Bastille or the Ghetto was a curiosity worth a great deal of money, if preserved; and so was a Bishop; so was Napoleon III. The tourist was the great conservative who hated novelty and adored dirt. Adams came back to London without a thought of revolution or restlessness or reform. He wanted amusement, quiet, and gaiety.

Had he not been born in 1838 under the shadow of Boston State House, and been brought up in the Early Victorian epoch, he would have cast off his old skin, and made his court to Marlborough House, in partnership with the American woman and the Jew banker. Common-sense dictated it; but Adams and his friends were unfashionable by some law of Anglo-Saxon custom -- some innate atrophy of mind. Figuring himself as already a man of action, and rather far up towards the front, he had no idea of making a new effort or catching up with a new world. He saw nothing ahead of him. The world was never more calm. He wanted to talk with Ministers about the Alabama Claims, because he looked on the Claims as his own special creation, discussed between him and his father long before they had been discussed by Government; he wanted to make notes for his next year's articles; but he had not a thought that, within three months, his world was to be upset, and he under it. Frank Palgrave came one day, more contentious, contemptuous, and paradoxical than ever, because Napoleon III seemed to be threatening war with Germany. Palgrave said that "Germany would beat France into scraps" if there was war. Adams thought not. The chances were always against catastrophes. No one else expected great changes in Europe. Palgrave was always extreme; his language was incautious --

violent!

In this year of all years, Adams lost sight of education. Things began smoothly, and London glowed with the pleasant sense of familiarity and dinners. He sniffed with voluptuous delight the coal-smoke of Cheapside and revelled in the architecture of Oxford Street. May Fair never shone so fair to Arthur Pendennis as it did to the returned American. The country never smiled its velvet smile of trained and easy hostess as it did when he was so lucky as to be asked on a country visit. He loved it all -- everything -- had always loved it! He felt almost attached to the Royal Exchange. He thought he owned the St. James's Club. He patronized the Legation.

The first shock came lightly, as though Nature were playing tricks on her spoiled child, though she had thus far not exerted herself to spoil him. Reeve refused the Gold Conspiracy. Adams had become used to the idea that he was free of the Quarterlies, and that his writing would be printed of course; but he was stunned by the reason of refusal. Reeve said it would bring half-a-dozen libel suits on him. One knew that the power of Erie was almost as great in England as in America, but one was hardly prepared to find it controlling the Quarterlies. The English press professed to be shocked in 1870 by the Erie scandal, as it had professed in 1860 to be shocked by the scandal of slavery, but when invited to support those who were trying to abate these scandals, the English press said it was afraid. To Adams, Reeve's refusal seemed portentous. He and his brother and the North American Review were running greater risks every day, and no one thought of fear. That a notorious story, taken bodily from an official document, should scare the Endinburgh Review into silence for fear of Jay Gould and Jim Fisk, passed even Adams's experience of English eccentricity, though it was large.

He gladly set down Reeve's refusal of the Gold Conspiracy to respectability and editorial law, but when he sent the manuscript on to the Quarterly, the editor of the Quarterly also refused it. The literary standard of the two Quarterlies was not so high as to suggest that the article was illiterate beyond the power of an active and willing editor to redeem it. Adams had no choice but to realize that he had to deal in 1870 with the same old English character of 1860, and the same inability in himself to understand it. As usual, when an ally was needed, the American was driven into the arms of the radicals. Respectability, everywhere and always, turned its back the moment one asked to do it a favor. Called suddenly away from England, he despatched the article, at the last moment, to the Westminster Review and heard no more about it for nearly six months.

He had been some weeks in London when he received a telegram from his brother-in-law at the Bagni di Lucca telling him that his sister had been thrown from a cab and injured, and that he had better come on. He started that night, and reached the Bagni di Lucca on the second day. Tetanus had already set in.

The last lesson -- the sum and term of education -- began then. He had passed through thirty years of rather varied experience without having once felt the shell of custom broken. He had never seen Nature -- only her surface -- the sugar-coating that she shows to youth. Flung suddenly in his face, with the harsh brutality of chance, the terror of the blow stayed by him thenceforth for life, until repetition made it more than the will could struggle with; more than he could call on himself to bear. He found his sister, a woman of forty, as gay and brilliant in the terrors of lockjaw as she had been in the careless fun of 1859, lying in bed in consequence of a miserable cab-accident that had bruised her foot. Hour by hour the muscles grew rigid, while the mind remained bright, until after ten days of fiendish torture she died in convulsion.

One had heard and read a great deal about death, and even seen a little of it, and knew by heart the thousand commonplaces of religion and poetry which seemed to deaden one's senses and veil the horror. Society being immortal, could put on immortality at will. Adams being mortal, felt only the mortality. Death took features altogether new to him, in these rich and sensuous surroundings. Nature enjoyed it, played with it, the horror added to her charm, she liked the torture, and smothered her victim with caresses. Never had one seen her so winning. The hot Italian summer brooded outside, over the market-place and the picturesque peasants, and, in the singular color of the Tuscan atmosphere, the hills and vineyards of the Apennines seemed bursting with mid-summer blood. The sick-room itself glowed with the Italian joy of life; friends filled it; no harsh northern lights pierced the soft shadows; even the dying women shared the sense of the Italian summer, the soft, velvet air, the humor, the courage, the sensual fulness of Nature and man. She faced death, as women mostly do, bravely and even gaily, racked slowly to unconsciousness, but yielding only to violence, as a soldier sabred in battle. For many thousands of years, on these hills and plains, Nature had gone on sabring men and women with the same air of sensual pleasure.

Impressions like these are not reasoned or catalogued in the mind; they are felt as part of violent emotion; and the mind that feels them is a different one from that which reasons; it is thought of a different power and a different person. The first serious consciousness of Nature's gesture -- her attitude towards life -- took form then as a phantasm, a nightmare, an insanity of force. For the first time, the stage-scenery of the senses collapsed; the human mind felt itself stripped naked, vibrating in a void of shapeless energies, with resistless mass, colliding, crushing, wasting, and destroying what these same energies had created and labored from eternity to perfect. Society became fantastic, a vision of pantomime with a mechanical motion; and its so-called thought merged in the mere sense of life, and pleasure in the sense. The usual anodynes of social medicine became evident artifice. Stoicism was perhaps the best; religion was the most human; but the idea that any personal deity could find pleasure or profit in torturing a poor woman, by accident, with a fiendish cruelty known to man only in perverted and insane temperaments, could not be held for a moment. For pure blasphemy, it made pure atheism a comfort. God might be, as the Church said, a Substance, but He could not be a Person.

With nerves strained for the first time beyond their power of tension, he slowly travelled northwards with his friends, and stopped for a few days at Ouchy to recover his balance in a new world; for the fantastic mystery of coincidences had made the world, which he thought real, mimic and reproduce the distorted nightmare of his personal horror. He did not yet know it, and he was twenty years in finding it out; but he had need of all the beauty of the Lake below and of the Alps above, to restore the finite to its place. For the first time in his life, Mont Blanc for a moment looked to him what it was -- a chaos of anarchic and purposeless forces -- and he needed days of repose to see it clothe itself again with the illusions of his senses, the white purity of its snows, the splendor of its light, and the infinity of its heavenly peace. Nature was kind; Lake Geneva was beautiful beyond itself, and the Alps put on charms real as terrors; but man became chaotic, and before the illusions of Nature were wholly restored, the illusions of Europe suddenly vanished, leaving a new world to learn.

On July 4, all Europe had been in peace; on July 14, Europe was in full chaos of war. One felt helpless and ignorant, but one might have been king or kaiser without feeling stronger to deal with the chaos. Mr. Gladstone was as much astounded as Adams; the Emperor Napoleon was nearly as stupefied as either, and Bismarck: himself hardly knew how he did it. As education, the out-break of the war was wholly lost on a man dealing with death hand-to-hand, who could not throw it aside to look at it across the Rhine. Only when he got up to Paris, he began to feel the approach of catastrophe. Providence set up no affiches to announce the tragedy. Under one's eyes France cut herself adrift, and floated off, on an unknown stream, towards a less known ocean. Standing on the curb of the Boulevard, one could see as much as though one stood by the side of the Emperor or in command of an army corps. The effect was lurid. The public seemed to look on the war, as it had looked on the wars of Louis XIV and Francis I, as a branch of decorative art. The French, like true artists, always regarded war as one of the fine arts. Louis XIV practiced it; Napoleon I perfected it; and Napoleon III had till then pursued it in the same spirit with singular success. In Paris, in July, 1870, the war was brought out like an opera of Meyerbeer. One felt one's self a supernumerary hired to fill the scene. Every evening at the theatre the comedy was interrupted by order, and one stood up by order, to join in singing the Marseillaise to order. For nearly twenty years one had been forbidden to sing the Marseillaise under any circumstances, but at last regiment after regiment marched through the streets shouting "Marchons!" while the bystanders cared not enough to join. Patriotism seemed to have been brought out of the Government stores, and distributed by grammes per capita. One had seen one's own people dragged unwillingly into a war, and had watched one's own regiments march to the front without sign of enthusiasm; on the contrary, most serious, anxious, and conscious of the whole weight of the crisis; but in Paris every one conspired to ignore the crisis, which every one felt at hand. Here was education for the million, but the lesson was intricate. Superficially Napoleon and his Ministers and marshals were playing a game against Thiers and Gambetta. A bystander knew almost as little as they did about the result. How could Adams prophesy that in another year or two, when he spoke of his Paris and its tastes, people would smile at his dotage?

As soon as he could, he fled to England and once more took refuge in the profound peace of Wenlock Abbey. Only the few remaining monks, undisturbed by the brutalities of Henry VIII -- three or four young Englishmen -- survived there, with Milnes Gaskell acting as Prior. The August sun was warm; the calm of the Abbey was ten times secular; not a discordant sound -- hardly a sound of any sort except the cawing of the ancient rookery at sunset -- broke the stillness; and, after the excitement of the last month, one felt a palpable haze of peace brooding over the Edge and the Welsh Marches. Since the reign of Pterspis, nothing had greatly changed; nothing except the monks. Lying on the turf the ground littered with newspapers, the monks studied the war correspondence. In one respect Adams had succeeded in educating himself; he had learned to follow a campaign.

While at Wenlock, he received a letter from President Eliot inviting him to take an Assistant Professorship of History, to be created shortly at Harvard College. After waiting ten or a dozen years for some one to show consciousness of his existence, even a Terabratula would be pleased and grateful for a compliment which implied that the new President of Harvard College wanted his help; but Adams knew nothing about history, and much less about teaching, while he knew more than enough about Harvard College; and wrote at once to thank President Eliot, with much regret that the honor should be above his powers. His mind was full of other matters. The summer, from which he had expected only amusement and social relations with new people, had ended in the most intimate personal tragedy, and the most terrific political convulsion he had ever known or was likely to know. He had failed in every object of his trip. The Quarterlies had refused his best essay. He had made no acquaintances and hardly picked up the old ones. He sailed from Liverpool, on September 1, to begin again where he had started two years before, but with no longer a hope of attaching himself to a President or a party or a press. He was a free lance and no other career stood in sight or mind. To that point education had brought him.

Yet he found, on reaching home, that he had not done quite so badly as he feared. His article on the Session in the July North American had made a success. Though he could not quite see what partisan object it served, he heard with flattered astonishment that it had been reprinted by the Democratic National Committee and circulated as a campaign document by the hundred thousand copies. He was henceforth in opposition, do what he might; and a Massachusetts Democrat, say what he pleased; while his only reward or return for this partisan service consisted in being formally answered by Senator Timothy Howe, of Wisconsin, in a Republican campaign document, presumed to be also freely circulated, in which the Senator, besides refuting his opinions, did him the honor -- most unusual and picturesque in a Senator's rhetoric -- of likening him to a begonia.

The begonia is, or then was, a plant of such senatorial qualities as to make the simile, in intention, most flattering. Far from charming in its refinement, the begonia was remarkable for curious and showy foliage; it was conspicuous; it seemed to have no useful purpose; and it insisted on standing always in the most prominent positions. Adams would have greatly liked to be a begonia in Washington, for this was rather his ideal of the successful statesman, and he thought about it still more when the Westminster Review for October brought him his article on the Gold Conspiracy, which was also instantly pirated on a great scale. Piratical he was himself henceforth driven to be, and he asked only to be pirated, for he was sure not to be paid; but the honors of piracy resemble the colors of the begonia; they are showy but not useful. Here was a tour de force he had never dreamed himself equal to performing: two long, dry, quarterly, thirty or forty page articles, appearing in quick succession, and pirated for audiences running well into the hundred thousands; and not one person, man or woman, offering him so much as a congratulation, except to call him a begonia.

Had this been all, life might have gone on very happily as before, but the ways of America to a young person of literary and political tastes were such as the so-called evolution of civilized man had not before evolved. No sooner had Adams made at Washington what he modestly hoped was a sufficient success, than his whole family set on him to drag him away. For the first time since 1861 his father interposed; his mother entreated; and his brother Charles argued and urged that he should come to Harvard College. Charles had views of further joint operations in a new field. He said that Henry had done at Washington all he could possibly do; that his position there wanted solidity; that he was, after all, an adventurer; that a few years in Cambridge would give him personal weight; that his chief function was not to be that of teacher, but that of editing the North American Review which was to be coupled with the professorship, and would lead to the daily press. In short, that he needed the university more than the university needed him.

Henry knew the university well enough to know that the department of history was controlled by one of the most astute and ideal administrators in the world -- Professor Gurney -- and that it was Gurney who had established the new professorship, and had cast his net over Adams to carry the double load of mediaeval history and the Review. He could see no relation whatever between himself and a professorship. He sought education; he did not sell it. He knew no history; he knew only a few historians; his ignorance was mischievous because it was literary, accidental, indifferent. On the other hand he knew Gurney, and felt much influenced by his advice. One cannot take one's self quite seriously in such matters; it could not much affect the sum of solar energies whether one went on dancing with girls in Washington, or began talking to boys at Cambridge. The good people who thought it did matter had a sort of right to guide. One could not reject their advice; still less disregard their wishes.

The sum of the matter was that Henry went out to Cambridge and had a few words with President Eliot which seemed to him almost as American as the talk about diplomacy with his father ten years before. "But, Mr. President," urged Adams, "I know nothing about Mediaeval History." With the courteous manner and bland smile so familiar for the next generation of Americans Mr. Eliot mildly but firmly replied, "If you will point out to me any one who knows more, Mr. Adams, I will appoint him." The answer was neither logical nor convincing, but Adams could not meet it without overstepping his privileges. He could not say that, under the circumstances, the appointment of any professor at all seemed to him unnecessary.

So, at twenty-four hours' notice, he broke his life in halves again in order to begin a new education, on lines he had not chosen, in subjects for which he cared less than nothing; in a place he did not love, and before a future which repelled. Thousands of men have to do the same thing, but his case was peculiar because he had no need to do it. He did it because his best and wisest friends urged it, and he never could make up his mind whether they were right or not. To him this kind of education was always false. For himself he had no doubts. He thought it a mistake; but his opinion did not prove that it was one, since, in all probability, whatever he did would be more or less a mistake. He had reached cross-roads of education which all led astray. What he could gain at Harvard College he did not know, but in any case it was nothing he wanted. What he lost at Washington he could partly see, but in any case it was not fortune. Grant's administration wrecked men by thousands, but profited few. Perhaps Mr. Fish was the solitary exception. One might search the whole list of Congress, Judiciary, and Executive during the twenty-five years 1870 to 1895, and find little but damaged reputation. The period was poor in purpose and barren in results.

Henry Adams, if not the rose, lived as near it as any politician, and knew, more or less, all the men in any way prominent at Washington, or knew all about them. Among them, in his opinion, the best equipped, the most active-minded, and most industrious was Abram Hewitt, who sat in Congress for a dozen years, between 1874 and 1886, sometimes leading the House and always wielding influence second to none. With nobody did Adams form closer or longer relations than with Mr. Hewitt, whom he regarded as the most useful public man in Washington; and he was the more struck by Hewitt's saying, at the end of his laborious career as legislator, that he left behind him no permanent result except the Act consolidating the Surveys. Adams knew no other man who had done so much, unless Mr. Sherman's legislation is accepted as an instance of success. Hewitt's nearest rival would probably have been Senator Pendleton who stood father to civil service reform in 1882, an attempt to correct a vice that should never have been allowed to be born. These were the men who succeeded.

The press stood in much the same light. No editor, no political writer, and no public administrator achieved enough good reputation to preserve his memory for twenty years. A number of them achieved bad reputations, or damaged good ones that had been gained in the Civil War. On the whole, even for Senators, diplomats, and Cabinet officers, the period was wearisome and stale.

None of Adams's generation profited by public activity unless it were William C. Whitney, and even he could not be induced to return to it. Such ambitions as these were out of one's reach, but supposing one tried for what was feasible, attached one's self closely to the Garfields, Arthurs, Frelinghuysens, Blaines, Bayards, or Whitneys, who happened to hold office; and supposing one asked for the mission to Belgium or Portugal, and obtained it; supposing one served a term as Assistant Secretary or Chief of Bureau; or, finally, supposing one had gone as sub-editor on the New York Tribune or Times -- how much more education would one have gained than by going to Harvard College? These questions seemed better worth an answer than most of the questions on examination papers at college or in the civil service; all the more because one never found an answer to them, then or afterwards, and because, to his mind, the value of American society altogether was mixed up with the value of Washington.

At first, the simple beginner, struggling with principles, wanted throw off responsibility on the American people, whose bare and toiling shoulders had to carry the load of every social or political stupidity; but the American people had no more to do with it than with the customs of Peking. American character might perhaps account for it, but what accounted for American character? All Boston, all New England, and all respectable New York, including Charles Francis Adams the father and Charles Francis Adams the son, agreed that Washington was no place for a respectable young man. All Washington, including Presidents, Cabinet officers, Judiciary, Senators, Congressmen, and clerks, expressed the same opinion, and conspired to drive away every young man who happened to be there or tried to approach. Not one young man of promise remained in the Government service. All drifted into opposition. The Government did not want them in Washington. Adams's case was perhaps the strongest because he thought he had done well. He was forced to guess it, since he knew no one who would have risked so extravagant a step as that of encouraging a young man in a literary career, or even in a political one; society forbade it, as well as residence in a political capital; but Harvard College must have seen some hope for him, since it made him professor against his will; even the publishers and editors of the North American Review must have felt a certain amount of confidence in him, since they put the Review in his hands. After all, the Review was the first literary power in America, even though it paid almost as little in gold as the United States Treasury. The degree of Harvard College might bear a value as ephemeral as the commission of a President of the United States; but the government of the college, measured by money alone, and patronage, was a matter of more importance than that of some branches of the national service. In social position, the college was the superior of them all put together. In knowledge, she could assert no superiority, since the Government made no claims, and prided itself on ignorance. The service of Harvard College was distinctly honorable; perhaps the most honorable in America; and if Harvard College thought Henry Adams worth employing at four dollars a day, why should Washington decline his services when he asked nothing? Why should he be dragged from a career he liked in a place he loved, into a career he detested, in a place and climate he shunned? Was it enough to satisfy him, that all America should call Washington barren and dangerous? What made Washington more dangerous than New York?

The American character showed singular limitations which sometimes drove the student of civilized man to despair. Crushed by his own ignorance -- lost in the darkness of his own gropings -- the scholar finds himself jostled of a sudden by a crowd of men who seem to him ignorant that there is a thing called ignorance; who have forgotten how to amuse themselves; who cannot even understand that they are bored. The American thought of himself as a restless, pushing, energetic, ingenious person, always awake and trying to get ahead of his neighbors. Perhaps this idea of the national character might be correct for New York or Chicago; it was not correct for Washington. There the American showed himself, four times in five, as a quiet, peaceful, shy figure, rather in the mould of Abraham Lincoln, somewhat sad, sometimes pathetic, once tragic; or like Grant, inarticulate, uncertain, distrustful of himself, still more distrustful of others, and awed by money. That the American, by temperament, worked to excess, was true; work and whiskey were his stimulants; work was a form of vice; but he never cared much for money or power after he earned them. The amusement of the pursuit was all the amusement he got from it; he had no use for wealth. Jim Fisk alone seemed to know what he wanted; Jay Gould never did. At Washington one met mostly such true Americans, but if one wanted to know them better, one went to study them in Europe. Bored, patient, helpless; pathetically dependent on his wife and daughters; indulgent to excess; mostly a modest, decent, excellent, valuable citizen; the American was to be met at every railway station in Europe, carefully explaining to every listener that the happiest day of his life would be the day he should land on the pier at New York. He was ashamed to be amused; his mind no longer answered to the stimulus of variety; he could not face a new thought. All his immense strength his intense nervous energy, his keen analytic perceptions, were oriented in one direction, and he could not change it. Congress was full of such men; in the Senate, Sumner was almost the only exception; in the Executive, Grant and Boutwell were varieties of the type -- political specimens -- pathetic in their helplessness to do anything with power when it came to them. They knew not how to amuse themselves; they could not conceive how other people were amused. Work, whiskey, and cards were life. The atmosphere of political Washington was theirs -- or was supposed by the outside world to be in their control -- and this was the reason why the outside world judged that Washington was fatal even for a young man of thirty-two, who had passed through the whole variety of temptations, in every capital of Europe, for a dozen years; who never played cards, and who loathed whiskey.

Chapter XX. Failure (1871)

FAR back in childhood, among its earliest memories, Henry Adams could recall his first visit to Harvard College. He must have been nine years old when on one of the singularly gloomy winter afternoons which beguiled Cambridgeport, his mother drove him out to visit his aunt, Mrs. Everett. Edward Everett was then President of the college and lived in the old President's House on Harvard Square. The boy remembered the drawing-room, on the left of the hall door, in which Mrs. Everett received them. He remembered a marble greyhound in the corner. The house had an air of colonial self-respect that impressed even a nine-year-old child.

When Adams closed his interview with President Eliot, he asked the Bursar about his aunt's old drawing-room, for the house had been turned to base uses. The room and the deserted kitchen adjacent to it were to let. He took them. Above him, his brother Brooks, then a law student, had rooms, with a private staircase. Opposite was J. R. Dennett, a young instructor almost as literary as Adams himself, and more rebellious to conventions. Inquiry revealed a boarding-table, somewhere in the neighborhood, also supposed to be superior in its class. Chauncey Wright, Francis Wharton, Dennett, John Fiske, or their equivalents in learning and lecture, were seen there, among three or four law students like Brooks Adams. With these primitive arrangements, all of them had to be satisfied. The standard was below that of Washington, but it was, for the moment, the best.

For the next nine months the Assistant Professor had no time to waste on comforts or amusements. He exhausted all his strength in trying to keep one day ahead of his duties. Often the stint ran on, till night and sleep ran short. He could not stop to think whether he were doing the work rightly. He could not get it done to please him, rightly or wrongly, for he never could satisfy himself what to do.

The fault he had found with Harvard College as an undergraduate must have been more or less just, for the college was making a great effort to meet these self-criticisms, and had elected President Eliot in 1869 to carry out its reforms. Professor Gurney was one of the leading reformers, and had tried his hand on his own department of History. The two full Professors of History -- Torrey and Gurney, charming men both -- could not cover the ground. Between Gurney's classical courses and Torrey's modern ones, lay a gap of a thousand years, which Adams was expected to fill. The students had already elected courses numbered 1, 2, and 3, without knowing what was to be taught or who was to teach. If their new professor had asked what idea was in their minds, they must have replied that nothing at all was in their minds, since their professor had nothing in his, and down to the moment he took his chair and looked his scholars in the face, he had given, as far as he could remember, an hour, more or less, to the Middle Ages.

Not that his ignorance troubled him! He knew enough to be ignorant. His course had led him through oceans of ignorance; he had tumbled from one ocean into another till he had learned to swim; but even to him education was a serious thing. A parent gives life, but as parent, gives no more. A murderer takes life, but his deed stops there. A teacher affects eternity; he can never tell where his influence stops. A teacher is expected to teach truth, and may perhaps flatter himself that he does so, if he stops with the alphabet or the multiplication table, as a mother teaches truth by making her child eat with a spoon; but morals are quite another truth and philosophy is more complex still. A teacher must either treat history as a catalogue, a record, a romance, or as an evolution; and whether he affirms or denies evolution, he falls into all the burning faggots of the pit. He makes of his scholars either priests or atheists, plutocrats or socialists, judges or anarchists, almost in spite of himself. In essence incoherent and immoral, history had either to be taught as such -- or falsified.

Adams wanted to do neither. He had no theory of evolution to teach, and could not make the facts fit one. He had no fancy for telling agreeable tales to amuse sluggish-minded boys, in order to publish them afterwards as lectures. He could still less compel his students to learn the Anglo-Saxon Chronicle and the Venerable Bede by heart. He saw no relation whatever between his students and the Middle Ages unless it were the Church, and there the ground was particularly dangerous. He knew better than though he were a professional historian that the man who should solve the riddle of the Middle Ages and bring them into the line of evolution from past to present, would be a greater man than Lamarck or Linnaeus; but history had nowhere broken down so pitiably, or avowed itself so hopelessly bankrupt, as there. Since Gibbon, the spectacle was almost a scandal. History had lost even the sense of shame. It was a hundred years behind the experimental sciences. For all serious purpose, it was less instructive than Walter Scott and Alexandre Dumas.

All this was without offence to Sir Henry Maine, Tyler, McLennan, Buckle, Auguste Comte, and the various philosophers who, from time to time, stirred the scandal, and made it more scandalous. No doubt, a teacher might make some use of these writers or their theories; but Adams could fit them into no theory of his own. The college expected him to pass at least half his time teaching the boys a few elementary dates and relations, that they might not be a disgrace to the university. This was formal; and he could frankly tell the boys that, provided they passed their examinations, they might get their facts where they liked, and use the teacher only for questions. The only privilege a student had that was worth his claiming, was that of talking to the professor, and the professor was bound to encourage it. His only difficulty on that side was to get them to talk at all. He had to devise schemes to find what they were thinking about, and induce them to risk criticism from their fellows. Any large body of students stifles the student. No man can instruct more than half-a-dozen students at once. The whole problem of education is one of its cost in money.

The lecture system to classes of hundreds, which was very much that of the twelfth century, suited Adams not at all. Barred from philosophy and bored by facts, he wanted to teach his students something not wholly useless. The number of students whose minds were of an order above the average was, in his experience, barely one in ten; the rest could not be much stimulated by any inducements a teacher could suggest. All were respectable, and in seven years of contact, Adams never had cause to complain of one; but nine minds in ten take polish passively, like a hard surface; only the tenth sensibly reacts.

Adams thought that, as no one seemed to care what he did, he would try to cultivate this tenth mind, though necessarily at the expense of the other nine. He frankly acted on the rule that a teacher, who knew nothing of his subject, should not pretend to teach his scholars what he did not know, but should join them in trying to find the best way of learning it. The rather pretentious name of historical method was sometimes given to this process of instruction, but the name smacked of German pedagogy, and a young professor who respected neither history nor method, and whose sole object of interest was his students' minds, fell into trouble enough without adding to it a German parentage.

The task was doomed to failure for a reason which he could not control. Nothing is easier than to teach historical method, but, when learned, it has little use. History is a tangled skein that one may take up at any point, and break when one has unravelled enough; but complexity precedes evolution. The Pteraspis grins horribly from the closed entrance. One may not begin at the beginning, and one has but the loosest relative truths to follow up. Adams found himself obliged to force his material into some shape to which a method could be applied. He could think only of law as subject; the Law School as end; and he took, as victims of his experiment, half-a-dozen highly intelligent young men who seemed willing to work. The course began with the beginning, as far as the books showed a beginning in primitive man, and came down through the Salic Franks to the Norman English. Since no textbooks existed, the professor refused to profess, knowing no more than his students, and the students read what they pleased and compared their results. As pedagogy, nothing could be more triumphant. The boys worked like rabbits, and dug holes all over the field of archaic society; no difficulty stopped them; unknown languages yielded before their attack, and customary law became familiar as the police court; undoubtedly they learned, after a fashion, to chase an idea, like a hare, through as dense a thicket of obscure facts as they were likely to meet at the bar; but their teacher knew from his own experience that his wonderful method led nowhere, and they would have to exert themselves to get rid of it in the Law School even more than they exerted themselves to acquire it in the college. Their science had no system, and could have none, since its subject was merely antiquarian. Try as hard as he might, the professor could not make it actual.

What was the use of training an active mind to waste its energy? The experiments might in time train Adams as a professor, but this result was still less to his taste. He wanted to help the boys to a career, but not one of his many devices to stimulate the intellectual reaction of the student's mind satisfied either him or the students. For himself he was clear that the fault lay in the system, which could lead only to inertia. Such little knowledge of himself as he possessed warranted him in affirming that his mind required conflict, competition, contradiction even more than that of the student. He too wanted a rank-list to set his name upon. His reform of the system would have begun in the lecture-room at his own desk. He would have seated a rival assistant professor opposite him, whose business should be strictly limited to expressing opposite views. Nothing short of this would ever interest either the professor or the student; but of all university freaks, no irregularity shocked the intellectual atmosphere so much as contradiction or competition between teachers. In that respect the thirteenth-century university system was worth the whole teaching of the modern school.

All his pretty efforts to create conflicts of thought among his students failed for want of system. None met the needs of instruction. In spite of President Eliot's reforms and his steady, generous, liberal support, the system remained costly, clumsy and futile. The university -- as far as it was represented by Henry Adams -- produced at great waste of time and money results not worth reaching.

He made use of his lost two years of German schooling to inflict their results on his students, and by a happy chance he was in the full tide of fashion. The Germans were crowning their new emperor at Versailles, and surrounding his head with a halo of Pepins and Merwigs, Othos and Barbarossas. James Bryce had even discovered the Holy Roman Empire. Germany was never so powerful, and the Assistant Professor of History had nothing else as his stock in trade. He imposed Germany on his scholars with a heavy hand. He was rejoiced; but he sometimes doubted whether they should be grateful. On the whole, he was content neither with what he had taught nor with the way he had taught it. The seven years he passed in teaching seemed to him lost.

The uses of adversity are beyond measure strange. As a professor, he regarded himself as a failure. Without false modesty he thought he knew what he meant. He had tried a great many experiments, and wholly succeeded in none. He had succumbed to the weight of the system. He had accomplished nothing that he tried to do. He regarded the system as wrong; more mischievous to the teachers than to the students; fallacious from the beginning to end. He quitted the university at last, in 1877, with a feeling. that, if it had not been for the invariable courtesy and kindness shown by every one in it, from the President to the injured students, he should be sore at his failure.

These were his own feelings, but they seemed not to be felt in the college. With the same perplexing impartiality that had so much disconcerted him in his undergraduate days, the college insisted on expressing an opposite view. John Fiske went so far in his notice of the family in "Appleton's Cyclopedia," as to say that Henry had left a great reputation at Harvard College; which was a proof of John Fiske's personal regard that Adams heartily returned; and set the kind expression down to camaraderie. The case was different when President Eliot himself hinted that Adams's services merited recognition. Adams could have wept on his shoulder in hysterics, so grateful was he for the rare good-will that inspired the compliment; but he could not allow the college to think that he esteemed himself entitled to distinction. He knew better, and his was among the failures which were respectable enough to deserve self-respect. Yet nothing in the vanity of life struck him as more humiliating than that Harvard College, which he had persistently criticised, abused, abandoned, and neglected, should alone have offered him a dollar, an office, an encouragement, or a kindness. Harvard College might have its faults, but at least it redeemed America, since it was true to its own.

The only part of education that the professor thought a success was the students. He found them excellent company. Cast more or less in the same mould, without violent emotions or sentiment, and, except for the veneer of American habits, ignorant of all that man had ever thought or hoped, their minds burst open like flowers at the sunlight of a suggestion. They were quick to respond; plastic to a mould; and incapable of fatigue. Their faith in education was so full of pathos that one dared not ask them what they thought they could do with education when they got it. Adams did put the question to one of them, and was surprised at the answer: "The degree of Harvard College is worth money to me in Chicago." This reply upset his experience; for the degree of Harvard College had been rather a drawback to a young man in Boston and Washington. So far as it went, the answer was good, and settled one's doubts. Adams knew no better, although he had given twenty years to pursuing the same education, and was no nearer a result than they. He still had to take for granted many things that they need not -- among the rest, that his teaching did them more good than harm. In his own opinion the greatest good he could do them was to hold his tongue. They needed much faith then; they were likely to need more if they lived long.

He never knew whether his colleagues shared his doubts about their own utility. Unlike himself, they knew more or less their business. He could not tell his scholars that history glowed with social virtue; the Professor of Chemistry cared not a chemical atom whether society was virtuous or not. Adams could not pretend that mediaeval society proved evolution; the Professor of Physics smiled at evolution. Adams was glad to dwell on the virtues of the Church and the triumphs of its art: the Professor of Political Economy had to treat them as waste of force. They knew what they had to teach; he did not. They might perhaps be frauds without knowing it; but he knew certainly nothing else of himself. He could teach his students nothing; he was only educating himself at their cost.

Education, like politics, is a rough affair, and every instructor has to shut his eyes and hold his tongue as though he were a priest. The students alone satisfied. They thought they gained something. Perhaps they did, for even in America and in the twentieth century, life could not be wholly industrial. Adams fervently hoped that they might remain content; but supposing twenty years more to pass, and they should turn on him as fiercely as he had turned on his old instructors -- what answer could he make? The college had pleaded guilty, and tried to reform. He had pleaded guilty from the start, and his reforms had failed before those of the college.

The lecture-room was futile enough, but the faculty-room was worse. American society feared total wreck in the maelstrom of political and corporate administration, but it could not look for help to college dons. Adams knew, in that capacity, both Congressmen and professors, and he preferred Congressmen. The same failure marked the society of a college. Several score of the best- educated, most agreeable, and personally the most sociable people in America united in Cambridge to make a social desert that would have starved a polar bear. The liveliest and most agreeable of men -- James Russell Lowell, Francis J. Child, Louis Agassiz, his son Alexander, Gurney, John Fiske, William James and a dozen others, who would have made the joy of London or Paris -- tried their best to break out and be like other men in Cambridge and Boston, but society called them professors, and professors they had to be. While all these brilliant men were greedy for companionship, all were famished for want of it. Society was a faculty-meeting without business. The elements were there; but society cannot be made up of elements -- people who are expected to be silent unless they have observations to make -- and all the elements are bound to remain apart if required to make observations.

Thus it turned out that of all his many educations, Adams thought that of school-teacher the thinnest. Yet he was forced to admit that the education of an editor, in some ways, was thinner still. The editor had barely time to edit; he had none to write. If copy fell short, he was obliged to scribble a book-review on the virtues of the Anglo-Saxons or the vices of the Popes; for he knew more about Edward the Confessor or Boniface VIII than he did about President Grant. For seven years he wrote nothing; the Review lived on his brother Charles's railway articles. The editor could help others, but could do nothing for himself. As a writer, he was totally forgotten by the time he had been an editor for twelve months. As editor he could find no writer to take his place for politics and affairs of current concern. The Review became chiefly historical. Russell Lowell and Frank Palgrave helped him to keep it literary. The editor was a helpless drudge whose successes, if he made any, belonged to his writers; but whose failures might easily bankrupt himself. Such a Review may be made a sink of money with captivating ease. The secrets of success as an editor were easily learned; the highest was that of getting advertisements. Ten pages of advertising made an editor a success; five marked him as a failure. The merits or demerits of his literature had little to do with his results except when they led to adversity.

A year or two of education as editor satiated most of his appetite for that career as a profession. After a very slight experience, he said no more on the subject. He felt willing to let any one edit, if he himself might write. Vulgarly speaking, it was a dog's life when it did not succeed, and little better when it did. A professor had at least the pleasure of associating with his students; an editor lived the life of an owl. A professor commonly became a pedagogue or a pedant; an editor became an authority on advertising. On the whole, Adams preferred his attic in Washington. He was educated enough. Ignorance paid better, for at least it earned fifty dollars a month.

With this result Henry Adams's education, at his entry into life, stopped, and his life began. He had to take that life as he best could, with such accidental education as luck had given him; but he held that it was wrong, and that, if he were to begin again, he would do it on a better system. He thought he knew nearly what system to pursue. At that time Alexander Agassiz had not yet got his head above water so far as to serve for a model, as he did twenty or thirty years afterwards; but the editorship of the North American Review had one solitary merit; it made the editor acquainted at a distance with almost every one in the country who could write or who could be the cause of writing. Adams was vastly pleased to be received among these clever people as one of themselves, and felt always a little surprised at their treating him as an equal, for they all had education; but among them, only one stood out in extraordinary prominence as the type and model of what Adams would have liked to be, and of what the American, as he conceived, should have been and was not.

Thanks to the article on Sir Charles Lyell, Adams passed for a friend of geologists, and the extent of his knowledge mattered much less to them than the extent of his friendship, for geologists were as a class not much better off than himself, and friends were sorely few. One of his friends from earliest childhood, and nearest neighbor in Quincy, Frank Emmons, had become a geologist and joined the Fortieth Parallel Survey under Government. At Washington in the winter of 1869-70, Emmons had invited Adams to go out with him on one of the field-parties in summer. Of course when Adams took the Review he put it at the service of the Survey, and regretted only that he could not do more. When the first year of professing and editing was at last over, and his July North American appeared, he drew a long breath of relief, and took the next train for the West. Of his year's work he was no judge. He had become a small spring in a large mechanism, and his work counted only in the sum; but he had been treated civilly by everybody, and he felt at home even in Boston. Putting in his pocket the July number of the North American, with a notice of the Fortieth Parallel Survey by Professor J. D. Whitney, he started for the plains and the Rocky Mountains.

In the year 1871, the West was still fresh, and the Union Pacific was young. Beyond the Missouri River, one felt the atmosphere of Indians and buffaloes. One saw the last vestiges of an old education, worth studying if one would; but it was not that which Adams sought; rather, he came out to spy upon the land of the future. The Survey occasionally borrowed troopers from the nearest station in case of happening on hostile Indians, but otherwise the topographers and geologists thought more about minerals than about Sioux. They held under their hammers a thousand miles of mineral country with all its riddles to solve, and its stores of possible wealth to mark. They felt the future in their hands.

Emmons's party was out of reach in the Uintahs, but Arnold Hague's had come in to Laramie for supplies, and they took charge of Adams for a time. Their wanderings or adventures matter nothing to the story of education. They were all hardened mountaineers and surveyors who took everything for granted, and spared each other the most wearisome bore of English and Scotch life, the stories of the big game they killed. A bear was an occasional amusement; a wapiti was a constant necessity; but the only wild animal dangerous to man was a rattlesnake or a skunk. One shot for amusement, but one had other matters to talk about.

Adams enjoyed killing big game, but loathed the labor of cutting it up; so that he rarely unslung the little carbine he was in a manner required to carry. On the other hand, he liked to wander off alone on his mule, and pass the day fishing a mountain stream or exploring a valley. One morning when the party was camped high above Estes Park, on the flank of Long's Peak, he borrowed a rod, and rode down over a rough trail into Estes Park, for some trout. The day was fine, and hazy with the smoke of forest fires a thousand miles away; the park stretched its

English beauties off to the base of its bordering mountains in natural landscape and archaic peace; the stream was just fishy enough to tempt lingering along its banks. Hour after hour the sun moved westward and the fish moved eastward, or disappeared altogether, until at last when the fisherman cinched his mule, sunset was nearer than he thought. Darkness caught him before he could catch his trail. Not caring to tumble into some fifty-foot hole, he "allowed" he was lost, and turned back. In half-an-hour he was out of the hills, and under the stars of Estes Park, but he saw no prospect of supper or of bed.

Estes Park was large enough to serve for a bed on a summer night for an army of professors, but the supper question offered difficulties. There was but one cabin in the Park, near its entrance, and he felt no great confidence in finding it, but he thought his mule cleverer than himself, and the dim lines of mountain crest against the stars fenced his range of error. The patient mule plodded on without other road than the gentle slope of the ground, and some two hours must have passed before a light showed in the distance. As the mule came up to the cabin door, two or three men came out to see the stranger.

One of these men was Clarence King on his way up to the camp. Adams fell into his arms. As with most friendships, it was never a matter of growth or doubt. Friends are born in archaic horizons; they were shaped with the Pteraspis in Siluria; they have nothing to do with the accident of space. King had come up that day from Greeley in a light four-wheeled buggy, over a trail hardly fit for a commissariat mule, as Adams had reason to know since he went back in the buggy. In the cabin, luxury provided a room and one bed for guests. They shared the room and the bed, and talked till far towards dawn.

King had everything to interest and delight Adams. He knew more than Adams did of art and poetry; he knew America, especially west of the hundredth meridian, better than any one; he knew the professor by heart, and he knew the Congressman better than he did the professor. He knew even women; even the American woman; even the New York woman, which is saying much. Incidentally he knew more practical geology than was good for him, and saw ahead at least one generation further than the text-books. That he saw right was a different matter. Since the beginning of time no man has lived who is known to have seen right; the charm of King was that he saw what others did and a great deal more. His wit and humor; his bubbling energy which swept every one into the current of his interest; his personal charm of youth and manners; his faculty of giving and taking, profusely, lavishly, whether in thought or in money as though he were Nature herself, marked him almost alone among Americans. He had in him something of the Greek -- a touch of Alcibiades or Alexander. One Clarence King only existed in the world.

A new friend is always a miracle, but at thirty-three years old, such a bird of paradise rising in the sage-brush was an avatar. One friend in a lifetime is much; two are many; three are hardly possible. Friendship needs a certain parallelism of life, a community of thought, a rivalry of aim. King, like Adams, and all their generation, was at that moment passing the critical point of his career. The one, coming from the west, saturated with the sunshine of the Sierras, met the other, drifting from the east, drenched in the fogs of London, and both had the same problems to handle -- the same stock of implements -- the same field to work in; above all, the same obstacles to overcome.

As a companion, King's charm was great, but this was not the quality that so much attracted

Adams, nor could he affect even distant rivalry on this ground. Adams could never tell a story, chiefly because he always forgot it; and he was never guilty of a witticism, unless by accident. King and the Fortieth Parallel influenced him in a way far more vital. The lines of their lives converged, but King had moulded and directed his life logically, scientifically, as Adams thought American life should be directed. He had given himself education all of a piece, yet broad. Standing in the middle of his career, where their paths at last came together, he could look back and look forward on a straight line, with scientific knowledge for its base. Adams's life, past or future, was a succession of violent breaks or waves, with no base at all. King's abnormal energy had already won him great success. None of his contemporaries had done so much, single-handed, or were likely to leave so deep a trail. He had managed to induce Congress to adopt almost its first modern act of legislation. He had organized, as a civil -- not military -- measure, a Government Survey. He had paralleled the Continental Railway in Geology; a feat as yet unequalled by other governments which had as a rule no continents to survey. He was creating one of the classic scientific works of the century. The chances were great that he could, whenever he chose to quit the Government service, take the pick of the gold and silver, copper or coal, and build up his fortune as he pleased. Whatever prize he wanted lay ready for him -- scientific social, literary, political -- and he knew how to take them in turn. With ordinary luck he would die at eighty the richest and most many-sided genius of his day.

So little egoistic he was that none of his friends felt envy of his extraordinary superiority, but rather grovelled before it, so that women were jealous of the power he had over men; but women were many and Kings were one. The men worshipped not so much their friend, as the ideal American they all wanted to be. The women were jealous because, at heart, King had no faith in the American woman; he loved types more robust.

The young men of the Fortieth Parallel had Californian instincts; they were brothers of Bret Harte. They felt no leanings towards the simple uniformities of Lyell and Darwin; they saw little proof of slight and imperceptible changes; to them, catastrophe was the law of change; they cared little for simplicity and much for complexity; but it was the complexity of Nature, not of New York or even of the Mississippi Valley. King loved paradox; he started them like rabbits, and cared for them no longer, when caught or lost; but they delighted Adams, for they helped, among other things, to persuade him that history was more amusing than science. The only question left open to doubt was their relative money value.

In Emmons's camp, far up in the Uintahs, these talks were continued till the frosts became sharp in the mountains. History and science spread out in personal horizons towards goals no longer far away. No more education was possible for either man. Such as they were, they had got to stand the chances of the world they lived in; and when Adams started back to Cambridge, to take up again the humble tasks of schoolmaster and editor he was harnessed to his cart. Education, systematic or accidental, had done its worst. Henceforth, he went on, submissive.

Chapter XXI. Twenty Years After (1892)

ONCE more! this is a story of education, not of adventure! It is meant to help young men -- or such as have intelligence enough to seek help -- but it is not meant to amuse them. What one did -- or did not do -- with one's education, after getting it, need trouble the inquirer in no way; it is a personal matter only which would confuse him. Perhaps Henry Adams was not worth educating;

most keen judges incline to think that barely one man in a hundred owns a mind capable of reacting to any purpose on the forces that surround him, and fully half of these react wrongly. The object of education for that mind should be the teaching itself how to react with vigor and economy. No doubt the world at large will always lag so far behind the active mind as to make a soft cushion of inertia to drop upon, as it did for Henry Adams; but education should try to lessen the obstacles, diminish the friction, invigorate the energy, and should train minds to react, not at haphazard, but by choice, on the lines of force that attract their world. What one knows is, in youth, of little moment; they know enough who know how to learn. Throughout human history the waste of mind has been appalling, and, as this story is meant to show, society has conspired to promote it. No doubt the teacher is the worst criminal, but the world stands behind him and drags the student from his course. The moral is stentorian. Only the most energetic, the most highly fitted, and the most favored have overcome the friction or the viscosity of inertia, and these were compelled to waste three-fourths of their energy in doing it.

Fit or unfit, Henry Adams stopped his own education in 1871, and began to apply it for practical uses, like his neighbors. At the end of twenty years, he found that he had finished, and could sum up the result. He had no complaint to make against man or woman. They had all treated him kindly; he had never met with ill-will, ill-temper, or even ill-manners, or known a quarrel. He had never seen serious dishonesty or ingratitude. He had found a readiness in the young to respond to suggestion that seemed to him far beyond all he had reason to expect. Considering the stock complaints against the world, he could not understand why he had nothing to complain of.

During these twenty years he had done as much work, in quantity, as his neighbors wanted; more than they would ever stop to look at, and more than his share. Merely in print, he thought altogether ridiculous the number of volumes he counted on the shelves of public libraries. He had no notion whether they served a useful purpose; he had worked in the dark; but so had most of his friends, even the artists, none of whom held any lofty opinion of their success in raising the standards of society, or felt profound respect for the methods or manners of their time, at home or abroad, but all of whom had tried, in a way, to hold the standard up. The effort had been, for the older generation, exhausting, as one could see in the Hunts; but the generation after 1870 made more figure, not in proportion to public wealth or in the census, but in their own self-assertion. A fair number of the men who were born in the thirties had won names -- Phillips Brooks; Bret Harte; Henry James; H. H. Richardson; John La Farge; and the list might be made fairly long if it were worth while; but from their school had sprung others, like Augustus St. Gaudens, McKim, Stanford White, and scores born in the forties, who counted as force even in the mental inertia of sixty or eighty million people. Among all these Clarence King, John Hay, and Henry Adams had led modest existences, trying to fill in the social gaps of a class which, as yet, showed but thin ranks and little cohesion. The combination offered no very glittering prizes, but they pursued it for twenty years with as much patience and effort as though it led to fame or power, until, at last, Henry Adams thought his own duties sufficiently performed and his account with society settled. He had enjoyed his life amazingly, and would not have exchanged it for any other that came in his way; he was, or thought he was, perfectly satisfied with it; but for reasons that had nothing to do with education, he was tired; his nervous energy ran low; and, like a horse that wears out, he quitted the race-course, left the stable, and sought pastures as far as possible from the old. Education had ended in 1871; life was complete in 1890; the rest mattered so little!

As had happened so often, he found himself in London when the question of return imposed its verdict on him after much fruitless effort to rest elsewhere. The time was the month of January, 1892; he was alone, in hospital, in the gloom of midwinter. He was close on his fifty-fourth birthday, and Pall Mall had forgotten him as completely as it had forgotten his elders. He had not seen London for a dozen years, and was rather amused to have only a bed for a world and a familiar black fog for horizon. The coal-fire smelt homelike; the fog had a fruity taste of youth; anything was better than being turned out into the wastes of Wigmore Street. He could always amuse himself by living over his youth, and driving once more down Oxford Street in 1858, with life before him to imagine far less amusing than it had turned out to be.

The future attracted him less. Lying there for a week he reflected on what he could do next. He had just come up from the South Seas with John La Farge, who had reluctantly crawled away towards New York to resume the grinding routine of studio-work at an age when life runs low. Adams would rather, as choice, have gone back to the east, if it were only to sleep forever in the trade-winds under the southern stars, wandering over the dark purple ocean, with its purple sense of solitude and void. Not that he liked the sensation, but that it was the most unearthly he had felt. He had not yet happened on Rudyard Kipling's "Mandalay," but he knew the poetry before he knew the poem, like millions of wanderers, who have perhaps alone felt the world exactly as it is. Nothing attracted him less than the idea of beginning a new education. The old one had been poor enough; any new one could only add to its faults. Life had been cut in halves, and the old half had passed away, education and all, leaving no stock to graft on.

The new world he faced in Paris and London seemed to him fantastic Willing to admit it real in the sense of having some kind of existence outside his own mind, he could not admit it reasonable. In Paris, his heart sank to mere pulp before the dismal ballets at the Grand Opera and the eternal vaudeville at the old Palais Royal; but, except for them, his own Paris of the Second Empire was as extinct as that of the first Napoleon. At the galleries and exhibitions, he was racked by the effort of art to be original, and when one day, after much reflection, John La Farge asked whether there might not still be room for something simple in art, Adams shook his head. As he saw the world, it was no longer simple and could not express itself simply. It should express what it was; and this was something that neither Adams nor La Farge understood.

Under the first blast of this furnace-heat, the lights seemed fairly to go out. He felt nothing in common with the world as it promised to be. He was ready to quit it, and the easiest path led back to the east; but he could not venture alone, and the rarest of animals is a companion. He must return to America to get one. Perhaps, while waiting, he might write more history, and on the chance as a last resource, he gave orders for copying everything he could reach in archives, but this was mere habit. He went home as a horse goes back to his stable, because he knew nowhere else to go.

Home was Washington. As soon as Grant's administration ended, in 1877, and Evarts became Secretary of State, Adams went back there, partly to write history, but chiefly because his seven years of laborious banishment, in Boston, convinced him that, as far as he had a function in life, it was as stable-companion to statesmen, whether they liked it or not. At about the same time, old George Bancroft did the same thing, and presently John Hay came on to be Assistant Secretary of State for Mr. Evarts, and stayed there to write the "Life" of Lincoln. In 1884 Adams joined him in employing Richardson to build them adjoining houses on La Fayette Square. As far as Adams had a home this was it. To the house on La Fayette Square he must turn, for he had no other status -- no position in the world.

Never did he make a decision more reluctantly than this of going back to his manger. His father and mother were dead. All his family led settled lives of their own. Except for two or three friends in Washington, who were themselves uncertain of stay, no one cared whether he came or went, and he cared least. There was nothing to care about. Every one was busy; nearly every one seemed contented. Since 1871 nothing had ruffled the surface of the American world, and even the progress of Europe in her side-way track to dis-Europeaning herself had ceased to be violent. After a dreary January in Paris, at last when no excuse could be persuaded to offer itself for further delay, he crossed the channel and passed a week with his old friend, Milnes Gaskell, at Thornes, in Yorkshire, while the westerly gales raved a warning against going home. Yorkshire in January is not an island in the South Seas. It has few points of resemblance to Tahiti; not many to Fiji or Samoa; but, as so often before, it was a rest between past and future, and Adams was grateful for it.

At last, on February 3, he drove, after a fashion, down the Irish Channel, on board the Teutonic. He had not crossed the Atlantic for a dozen years, and had never seen an ocean steamer of the new type. He had seen nothing new of any sort, or much changed in France or England. The railways made quicker time, but were no more comfortable. The scale was the same. The Channel service was hardly improved since 1858, or so little as to make no impression. Europe seemed to have been stationary for twenty years. To a man who had been stationary like Europe, the Teutonic was a marvel. That he should be able to eat his dinner through a week of howling winter gales was a miracle. That he should have a deck stateroom, with fresh air, and read all night, if he chose, by electric light, was matter for more wonder than life had yet supplied, in its old forms. Wonder may be double -- even treble. Adams's wonder ran off into figures. As the Niagara was to the Teutonic -- as 1860 was to 1890 -- so the Teutonic and 1890 must be to the next term -- and then? Apparently the question concerned only America. Western Europe offered no such conundrum. There one might double scale and speed indefinitely without passing bounds.

Fate was kind on that voyage. Rudyard Kipling, on his wedding trip to America, thanks to the mediation of Henry James, dashed over the passenger his exuberant fountain of gaiety and wit -- as though playing a garden hose on a thirsty and faded begonia. Kipling could never know what peace of mind he gave, for he could hardly ever need it himself so much; and yet, in the full delight of his endless fun and variety; one felt the old conundrum repeat itself. Somehow, somewhere, Kipling and the American were not one, but two, and could not be glued together. The American felt that the defect, if defect it were, was in himself; he had felt it when he was with Swinburne, and, again, with Robert Louis Stevenson, even under the palms of Vailima; but he did not carry self-abasement to the point of thinking himself singular. Whatever the defect might be, it was American; it belonged to the type; it lived in the blood. Whatever the quality might be that held him apart, it was English; it lived also in the blood; one felt it little if at all, with Celts, and one yearned reciprocally among Fiji cannibals. Clarence King used to say that it was due to discord between the wave-lengths of the man-atoms; but the theory offered difficulties in measurement. Perhaps, after all, it was only that genius soars; but this theory, too, had its dark corners. All through life, one had seen the American on his literary knees to the European; and all through many lives back for some two centuries, one had seen the European snub or patronize the American; not always intentionally, but effectually. It was in the nature of things. Kipling neither snubbed nor patronized; he was all gaiety and good-nature; but he would have been first to feel what one meant. Genius has to pay itself that unwilling self-respect.

Towards the middle of February, 1892, Adams found himself again in Washington. In Paris and London he had seen nothing to make a return to life worth while; in Washington he saw plenty of reasons for staying dead. Changes had taken place there; improvements had been made; with time -- much time -- the city might become habitable according to some fashionable standard; but all one's friends had died or disappeared several times over, leaving one almost as strange as in Boston or London. Slowly, a certain society had built itself up about the Government; houses had been opened and there was much dining; much calling; much leaving of cards; but a solitary man counted for less than in 1868. Society seemed hardly more at home than he. Both Executive and Congress held it aloof. No one in society seemed to have the ear of anybody in Government. No one in Government knew any reason for consulting any one in society. The world had ceased to be wholly political, but politics had become less social. A survivor of the Civil War -- like George Bancroft, or John Hay -- tried to keep footing, but without brilliant success. They were free to say or do what they liked; but no one took much notice of anything said or done.

A presidential election was to take place in November, and no one showed much interest in the result. The two candidates were singular persons, of whom it was the common saying that one of them had no friends; the other, only enemies. Calvin Brice, who was at that time altogether the wittiest and cleverest member of the Senate, was in the habit of describing Mr. Cleveland in glowing terms and at great length, as one of the loftiest natures and noblest characters of ancient or modern time; "but," he concluded, "in future I prefer to look on at his proceedings from the safe summit of some neighboring hill." The same remark applied to Mr. Harrison. In this respect, they were the greatest of Presidents, for, whatever harm they might do their enemies, was as nothing when compared to the mortality they inflicted on their friends. Men fled them as though they had the evil eye. To the American people, the two candidates and the two parties were so evenly balanced that the scales showed hardly a perceptible difference. Mr. Harrison was an excellent President, a man of ability and force; perhaps the best President the Republican Party had put forward since Lincoln's death; yet, on the whole, Adams felt a shade of preference for President Cleveland, not so much personally as because the Democrats represented to him the last remnants of the eighteenth century; the survivors of Hosea Biglow's Cornwallis; the sole remaining protestants against a banker's Olympus which had become, for five-and-twenty years, more and more despotic over Esop's frog-empire. One might no longer croak except to vote for King Log, or -- failing storks -- for Grover Cleveland; and even then could not be sure where King Banker lurked behind. The costly education in politics had led to political torpor. Every one did not share it. Clarence King and John Hay were loyal Republicans who never for a moment conceived that there could be merit in other ideals. With King, the feeling was chiefly love of archaic races; sympathy with the negro and Indian and corresponding dislike of their enemies; but with Hay, party loyalty became a phase of being, a little like the loyalty of a highly cultivated churchman to his Church. He saw all the failings of the party, and still more keenly those of the partisans; but he could not live outside. To Adams a Western Democrat or a Western Republican, a city Democrat or a city Republican, a W. C. Whitney or a J. G. Blaine, were actually the same man, as far as their usefulness to the objects of King, Hay, or Adams was concerned. They graded themselves as friends or enemies not as Republicans or Democrats. To Hay, the difference was that of being respectable or not.

Since 1879, King, Hay, and Adams had been inseparable. Step by step, they had gone on in the closest sympathy, rather shunning than inviting public position, until, in 1892, none of them held any post at all. With great effort, in Hayes's administration, all King's friends, including Abram Hewitt and Carl Schurz, had carried the bill for uniting the Surveys and had placed King at the head of the Bureau; but King waited only to organize the service, and then resigned, in order to seek his private fortune in the West. Hay, after serving as Assistant Secretary of State under Secretary Evarts during a part of Hayes's administration, then also insisted on going out, in order to write with Nicolay the "Life" of Lincoln. Adams had held no office, and when his friends asked the reason, he could not go into long explanations, but preferred to answer simply that no President had ever invited him to fill one. The reason was good, and was also conveniently true, but left open an awkward doubt of his morals or capacity. Why had no President ever cared to employ him? The question needed a volume of intricate explanation. There never was a day when he would have refused to perform any duty that the Government imposed on him, but the American Government never to his knowledge imposed duties. The point was never raised with regard to him, or to any one else. The Government required candidates to offer; the business of the Executive began and ended with the consent or refusal to confer. The social formula carried this passive attitude a shade further. Any public man who may for years have used some other man's house as his own, when promoted to a position of patronage commonly feels himself obliged to inquire, directly or indirectly, whether his friend wants anything; which is equivalent to a civil act of divorce, since he feels awkward in the old relation. The handsomest formula, in an impartial choice, was the grandly courteous Southern phrase of Lamar: "Of course Mr. Adams knows that anything in my power is at his service." A la disposicion de Usted! The form must have been correct since it released both parties. He was right; Mr. Adams did know all about it; a bow and a conventional smile closed the subject forever, and every one felt flattered.

Such an intimate, promoted to power, was always lost. His duties and cares absorbed him and affected his balance of mind. Unless his friend served some political purpose, friendship was an effort. Men who neither wrote for newspapers nor made campaign speeches, who rarely subscribed to the campaign fund, and who entered the White House as seldom as possible, placed themselves outside the sphere of usefulness, and did so with entirely adequate knowledge of what they were doing. They never expected the President to ask for their services, and saw no reason why he should do so. As for Henry Adams, in fifty years that he knew Washington, no one would have been more surprised than himself had any President ever asked him to perform so much of a service as to cross the square. Only Texan Congressmen imagined that the President needed their services in some remote consulate after worrying him for months to find one.

In Washington this law or custom is universally understood, and no one's character necessarily suffered because he held no office. No one took office unless he wanted it; and in turn the outsider was never asked to do work or subscribe money. Adams saw no office that he wanted, and he gravely thought that, from his point of view, in the long run, he was likely to be a more useful citizen without office. He could at least act as audience, and, in those days, a Washington audience seldom filled even a small theatre. He felt quite well satisfied to look on, and from time to time he thought he might risk a criticism of the players; but though he found his own position regular, he never quite understood that of John Hay. The Republican leaders treated Hay as one of themselves; they asked his services and took his money with a freedom that staggered even a hardened observer; but they never needed him in equivalent office. In Washington Hay was the only competent man in the party for diplomatic work. He corresponded in his powers of usefulness exactly with Lord Granville in London, who had been for forty years the saving grace of every Liberal administration in turn. Had usefulness to the public service been ever a question, Hay should have had a first-class mission under Hayes; should have been placed in the Cabinet by Garfield, and should have been restored to it by Harrison. These gentlemen were always using him; always invited his services, and always took his money.

Adams's opinion of politics and politicians, as he frankly admitted, lacked enthusiasm, although never, in his severest temper, did he apply to them the terms they freely applied to each other; and he explained everything by his old explanation of Grant's character as more or less a general type; but what roused in his mind more rebellion was the patience and good-nature with which Hay allowed himself to be used. The trait was not confined to politics. Hay seemed to like to be used, and this was one of his many charms; but in politics this sort of good-nature demands supernatural patience. Whatever astonishing lapses of social convention the politicians betrayed, Hay laughed equally heartily, and told the stories with constant amusement, at his own expense. Like most Americans, he liked to play at making Presidents, but, unlike most, he laughed not only at the Presidents he helped to make, but also at himself for laughing.

One must be rich, and come from Ohio or New York, to gratify an expensive taste like this. Other men, on both political flanks, did the same thing, and did it well, less for selfish objects than for the amusement of the game; but Hay alone lived in Washington and in the centre of the Ohio influences that ruled the Republican Party during thirty years. On the whole, these influences were respectable, and although Adams could not, under any circumstances, have had any value, even financially, for Ohio politicians, Hay might have much, as he showed, if they only knew enough to appreciate him. The American politician was occasionally an amusing object; Hay laughed, and, for want of other resource, Adams laughed too; but perhaps it was partly irritation at seeing how President Harrison dealt his cards that made Adams welcome President Cleveland back to the White House.

At all events, neither Hay nor King nor Adams had much to gain by reelecting Mr. Harrison in 1892, or by defeating him, as far as he was concerned; and as far as concerned Mr. Cleveland, they seemed to have even less personal concern. The whole country, to outward appearance, stood in much the same frame of mind. Everywhere was slack-water. Hay himself was almost as languid and indifferent as Adams. Neither had occupation. Both had finished their literary work. The "Life" of Lincoln had been begun, completed, and published hand in hand with the "History" of Jefferson and Madison, so that between them they had written nearly all the American history there was to write. The intermediate period needed intermediate treatment; the gap between James Madison and Abraham Lincoln could not be judicially filled by either of them. Both were heartily tired of the subject, and America seemed as tired as they. What was worse, the redeeming energy of Americans which had generally served as the resource of minds otherwise vacant, the creation of new force, the application of expanding power, showed signs of check. Even the year before, in 1891, far off in the Pacific, one had met everywhere in the East a sort of stagnation -- a creeping paralysis -- complaints of shipping and producers -- that spread throughout the whole southern hemisphere. Questions of exchange and silver-production loomed large. Credit was shaken, and a change of party government might shake it even in Washington. The matter did not concern Adams, who had no credit, and was always richest when the rich were poor; but it helped to dull the vibration of society.

However they studied it, the balance of profit and loss, on the last twenty years, for the three friends, King, Hay, and Adams, was exceedingly obscure in 1892. They had lost twenty years, but what had they gained? They often discussed the question. Hay had a singular faculty for remembering faces, and would break off suddenly the thread of his talk, as he looked out of the window on La Fayette Square, to notice an old corps commander or admiral of the Civil War, tottering along to the club for his cards or his cocktail: "There is old Dash who broke the rebel lines at Blankburg! Think of his having been a thunderbolt of war!" Or what drew Adams's closer attention: "There goes old Boutwell gambolling like the gambolling kid!" There they went! Men who had swayed the course of empire as well as the course of Hay, King, and Adams, less valued than the ephemeral Congressman behind them, who could not have told whether the general was a Boutwell or Boutwell a general. Theirs was the highest known success, and one asked what it was worth to them. Apart from personal vanity, what would they sell it for? Would any one of them, from President downwards, refuse ten thousand a year in place of all the consideration he received from the world on account of his success?

Yet consideration had value, and at that time Adams enjoyed lecturing Augustus St. Gaudens, in hours of depression, on its economics: "Honestly you must admit that even if you don't pay your expenses you get a certain amount of advantage from doing the best work. Very likely some of the really successful Americans would be willing you should come to dinner sometimes, if you did not come too often, while they would think twice about Hay, and would never stand me." The forgotten statesman had no value at all; the general and admiral not much; the historian but little; on the whole, the artist stood best, and of course, wealth rested outside the question, since it was acting as judge; but, in the last resort, the judge certainly admitted that consideration had some value as an asset, though hardly as much as ten -- or five -- thousand a year.

Hay and Adams had the advantage of looking out of their windows on the antiquities of La Fayette Square, with the sense of having all that any one had; all that the world had to offer; all that they wanted in life, including their names on scores of title-pages and in one or two biographical dictionaries; but this had nothing to do with consideration, and they knew no more than Boutwell or St. Gaudens whether to call it success. Hay had passed ten years in writing the "Life" of Lincoln, and perhaps President Lincoln was the better for it, but what Hay got from it was not so easy to see, except the privilege of seeing popular book-makers steal from his book and cover the theft by abusing the author. Adams had given ten or a dozen years to Jefferson and Madison, with expenses which, in any mercantile business, could hardly have been reckoned at less than a hundred thousand dollars, on a salary of five thousand a year; and when he asked what return he got from this expenditure, rather more extravagant in proportion to his means than a racing-stable, he could see none whatever. Such works never return money. Even Frank Parkman never printed a first edition of his relatively cheap and popular volumes, numbering more than seven hundred copies, until quite at the end of his life. A thousand copies of a book that cost twenty dollars or more was as much as any author could expect; two thousand copies was a visionary estimate unless it were canvassed for subscription. As far as Adams knew, he had but three serious readers -- Abram Hewitt, Wayne McVeagh, and Hay himself. He was amply satisfied with their consideration, and could dispense with that of the other fifty-nine million, nine hundred and ninety-nine thousand, nine hundred and ninety-seven; but neither he nor Hay was better off in any other respect, and their chief title to consideration was their right to look out of their windows on great men, alive or dead, in La Fayette Square, a privilege which had nothing to do with their writings.

The world was always good-natured; civil; glad to be amused; open-armed to any one who amused it; patient with every one who did not insist on putting himself in its way, or costing it money; but this was not consideration, still less power in any of its concrete forms, and applied as well or better to a comic actor. Certainly a rare soprano or tenor voice earned infinitely more applause as it gave infinitely more pleasure, even in America; but one does what one can with one's means, and casting up one's balance sheet, one expects only a reasonable return on one's capital. Hay and Adams had risked nothing and never played for high stakes. King had followed the ambitious course. He had played for many millions. He had more than once come close to a great success, but the result was still in doubt, and meanwhile he was passing the best years of his life underground. For companionship he was mostly lost.

Thus, in 1892, neither Hay, King, nor Adams knew whether they had attained success, or how to estimate it, or what to call it; and the American people seemed to have no clearer idea than they. Indeed, the American people had no idea at all; they were wandering in a wilderness much more sandy than the Hebrews had ever trodden about Sinai; they had neither serpents nor golden calves to worship. They had lost the sense of worship; for the idea that they worshipped money seemed a delusion. Worship of money was an old-world trait; a healthy appetite akin to worship of the Gods, or to worship of power in any concrete shape; but the American wasted money more recklessly than any one ever did before; he spent more to less purpose than any extravagant court aristocracy; he had no sense of relative values, and knew not what to do with his money when he got it, except use it to make more, or throw it away. Probably, since human society began, it had seen no such curious spectacle as the houses of the San Francisco millionaires on Nob Hill. Except for the railway system, the enormous wealth taken out of the ground since 1840, had disappeared. West of the Alleghenies, the whole country might have been swept clean, and could have been replaced in better form within one or two years. The American mind had less respect for money than the European or Asiatic mind, and bore its loss more easily; but it had been deflected by its pursuit till it could turn in no other direction. It shunned, distrusted, disliked, the dangerous attraction of ideals, and stood alone in history for its ignorance of the past.

Personal contact brought this American trait close to Adams's notice. His first step, on returning to Washington, took him out to the cemetery known as Rock Creek, to see the bronze figure which St. Gaudens had made for him in his absence. Naturally every detail interested him; every line; every touch of the artist; every change of light and shade; every point of relation; every possible doubt of St. Gaudens's correctness of taste or feeling; so that, as the spring approached, he was apt to stop there often to see what the figure had to tell him that was new; but, in all that it had to say, he never once thought of questioning what it meant. He supposed its meaning to be the one commonplace about it -- the oldest idea known to human thought. He knew that if he asked an Asiatic its meaning, not a man, woman, or child from Cairo to Kamtchatka would have needed more than a glance to reply. From the Egyptian Sphinx to the Kamakura Daibuts; from Prometheus to Christ; from Michael Angelo to Shelley, art had wrought on this eternal figure almost as though it had nothing else to say. The interest of the figure was not in its meaning, but in the response of the observer. As Adams sat there, numbers of people came, for the figure seemed to have become a tourist fashion, and all wanted to know its meaning. Most took it for a portrait-statue, and the remnant were vacant-minded in the absence of a personal guide. None felt what would have been a nursery-instinct to a Hindu baby or a Japanese jinricksha-runner. The only exceptions were the clergy, who taught a lesson even deeper. One after another brought companions there, and, apparently fascinated by their own reflection, broke out passionately against the expression they felt in the figure of despair, of atheism, of denial. Like the others, the priest saw only what he brought. Like all great artists, St. Gaudens held up the mirror and no more. The American layman had lost sight of ideals; the American priest had lost sight of faith. Both were more American than the old, half-witted soldiers who denounced the wasting, on a mere grave, of money which should have been given for drink.

Landed, lost, and forgotten, in the centre of this vast plain of self-content, Adams could see but one active interest, to which all others were subservient, and which absorbed the energies of some sixty million people to the exclusion of every other force, real or imaginary. The power of the railway system had enormously increased since 1870. Already the coal output of 160,000,000 tons closely approached the 180,000,000 of the British Empire, and one held one's breath at the nearness of what one had never expected to see, the crossing of courses, and the lead of American energies. The moment was deeply exciting to a historian, but the railway system itself interested one less than in 1868, since it offered less chance for future profit. Adams had been born with the railway system; had grown up with it; had been over pretty nearly every mile of it with curious eyes, and knew as much about it as his neighbors; but not there could he look for a new education. Incomplete though it was, the system seemed on the whole to satisfy the wants of society better than any other part of the social machine, and society was content with its creation, for the time, and with itself for creating it. Nothing new was to be done or learned there, and the world hurried on to its telephones, bicycles, and electric trams. At past fifty, Adams solemnly and painfully learned to ride the bicycle.

Nothing else occurred to him as a means of new life. Nothing else offered itself, however carefully he sought. He looked for no change. He lingered in Washington till near July without noticing a new idea. Then he went back to England to pass his summer on the Deeside. In October he returned to Washington and there awaited the reelection of Mr. Cleveland, which led to no deeper thought than that of taking up some small notes that happened to be outstanding. He had seen enough of the world to be a coward, and above all he had an uneasy distrust of bankers. Even dead men allow themselves a few narrow prejudices.

Chapter XXII. Chicago (1893)

DRIFTING in the dead-water of the fin-de-siecle -- and during this last decade every one talked, and seemed to feel fin-de-siecle -- where not a breath stirred the idle air of education or fretted the mental torpor of self-content, one lived alone. Adams had long ceased going into society. For years he had not dined out of his own house, and in public his face was as unknown as that of an extinct statesman. He had often noticed that six months' oblivion amounts to newspaper-death, and that resurrection is rare. Nothing is easier, if a man wants it, than rest, profound as the grave.

His friends sometimes took pity on him, and came to share a meal or pass a night on their passage south or northwards, but existence was, on the whole, exceedingly solitary, or seemed so to him. Of the society favorites who made the life of every dinner- table and of the halls of Congress -- Tom Reed, Bourke Cockran, Edward Wolcott -- he knew not one. Although Calvin Brice was his next neighbor for six years, entertaining lavishly as no one had ever entertained before in Washington, Adams never entered his house. W. C. Whitney rivalled Senator Brice in hospitality, and was besides an old acquaintance of the reforming era, but Adams saw him as little as he saw his chief, President Cleveland, or President Harrison or Secretary Bayard or

Blaine or Olney. One has no choice but to go everywhere or nowhere. No one may pick and choose between houses, or accept hospitality without returning it. He loved solitude as little as others did; but he was unfit for social work, and he sank under the surface.

Luckily for such helpless animals as solitary men, the world is not only good-natured but even friendly and generous; it loves to pardon if pardon is not demanded as a right. Adams's social offences were many, and no one was more sensitive to it than himself; but a few houses always remained which he could enter without being asked, and quit without being noticed. One was John Hay's; another was Cabot Lodge's; a third led to an intimacy which had the singular effect of educating him in knowledge of the very class of American politician who had done most to block his intended path in life. Senator Cameron of Pennsylvania had married in 1880 a young niece of Senator John Sherman of Ohio, thus making an alliance of dynastic importance in politics, and in society a reign of sixteen years, during which Mrs. Cameron and Mrs. Lodge led a career, without precedent and without succession, as the dispensers of sunshine over Washington. Both of them had been kind to Adams, and a dozen years of this intimacy had made him one of their habitual household, as he was of Hay's. In a small society, such ties between houses become political and social force. Without intention or consciousness, they fix one's status in the world. Whatever one's preferences in politics might be, one's house was bound to the Republican interest when sandwiched between Senator Cameron, John Hay, and Cabot Lodge, with Theodore Roosevelt equally at home in them all, and Cecil Spring-Rice to unite them by impartial variety. The relation was daily, and the alliance undisturbed by power or patronage, since Mr. Harrison, in those respects, showed little more taste than Mr. Cleveland for the society and interests of this particular band of followers, whose relations with the White House were sometimes comic, but never intimate.

In February, 1893, Senator Cameron took his family to South Carolina, where he had bought an old plantation at Coffin's Point on St. Helena Island, and Adams, as one of the family, was taken, with the rest, to open the new experience. From there he went on to Havana, and came back to Coffin's Point to linger till near April. In May the Senator took his family to Chicago to see the Exposition, and Adams went with them. Early in June, all sailed for England, and at last, in the middle of July, all found themselves in Switzerland, at Prangins, Chamounix, and Zermatt. On July 22 they drove across the Furka Pass and went down by rail to Lucerne.

Months of close contact teach character, if character has interest; and to Adams the Cameron type had keen interest, ever since it had shipwrecked his career in the person of President Grant. Perhaps it owed life to Scotch blood; perhaps to the blood of Adam and Eve, the primitive strain of man; perhaps only to the blood of the cottager working against the blood of the townsman; but whatever it was, one liked it for its simplicity. The Pennsylvania mind, as minds go, was not complex; it reasoned little and never talked; but in practical matters it was the steadiest of all American types; perhaps the most efficient; certainly the safest.

Adams had printed as much as this in his books, but had never been able to find a type to describe, the two great historical Pennsylvanians having been, as every one had so often heard, Benjamin Franklin of Boston and Albert Gallatin of Geneva. Of Albert Gallatin, indeed, he had made a voluminous study and an elaborate picture, only to show that he was, if American at all, a New Yorker, with a Calvinistic strain -- rather Connecticut than Pennsylvanian. The true Pennsylvanian was a narrower type; as narrow as the kirk; as shy of other people's narrowness as a Yankee; as self-limited as a Puritan farmer. To him, none but Pennsylvanians were white. Chinaman, negro, Dago, Italian, Englishman, Yankee -- all was one in the depths of Pennsylvanian consciousness. The mental machine could run only on what it took for American lines. This was familiar, ever since one's study of President Grant in 1869; but in 1893, as then, the type was admirably strong and useful if one wanted only to run on the same lines. Practically the Pennsylvanian forgot his prejudices when he allied his interests. He then became supple in action and large in motive, whatever he thought of his colleagues. When he happened to be right -- which was, of course, whenever one agreed with him -- he was the strongest American in America. As an ally he was worth all the rest, because he understood his own class, who were always a majority; and knew how to deal with them as no New Englander could. If one wanted work done in Congress, one did wisely to avoid asking a New Englander to do it. A Pennsylvanian not only could do it, but did it willingly, practically, and intelligently.

Never in the range of human possibilities had a Cameron believed in an Adams -- or an Adams in a Cameron -- but they had curiously enough, almost always worked together. The Camerons had what the Adamses thought the political vice of reaching their objects without much regard to their methods. The loftiest virtue of the Pennsylvania machine had never been its scrupulous purity or sparkling professions. The machine worked on coarse means on coarse interests, but its practical success had been the most curious subject of study in American history. When one summed up the results of Pennsylvanian influence, one inclined to think that Pennsylvania set up the Government in 1789; saved it in 1861; created the American system; developed its iron and coal power; and invented its great railways. Following up the same line, in his studies of American character, Adams reached the result -- to him altogether paradoxical -- that Cameron's qualities and defects united in equal share to make him the most useful member of the Senate.

In the interest of studying, at last, a perfect and favorable specimen of this American type which had so persistently suppressed his own, Adams was slow to notice that Cameron strongly influenced him, but he could not see a trace of any influence which he exercised on Cameron. Not an opinion or a view of his on any subject was ever reflected back on him from Cameron's mind; not even an expression or a fact. Yet the difference in age was trifling, and in education slight. On the other hand, Cameron made deep impression on Adams, and in nothing so much as on the great subject of discussion that year -- the question of silver.

Adams had taken no interest in the matter, and knew nothing about it, except as a very tedious hobby of his friend Dana Horton; but inevitably, from the moment he was forced to choose sides, he was sure to choose silver. Every political idea and personal prejudice he ever dallied with held him to the silver standard, and made a barrier between him and gold. He knew well enough all that was to be said for the gold standard as economy, but he had never in his life taken politics for a pursuit of economy. One might have a political or an economical policy; one could not have both at the same time. This was heresy in the English school, but it had always been law in the American. Equally he knew all that was to be said on the moral side of the question, and he admitted that his interests were, as Boston maintained, wholly on the side of gold; but, had they been ten times as great as they were, he could not have helped his bankers or croupiers to load the dice and pack the cards to make sure his winning the stakes. At least he was bound to profess disapproval -- or thought he was. From early childhood his moral principles had struggled blindly with his interests, but he was certain of one law that ruled all others -- masses of men invariably follow interests in deciding morals. Morality is a private and costly luxury. The morality of the silver or gold standards was to be decided by popular vote, and the popular vote would be decided by interests; but on which side lay the larger interest? To him the interest was political; he thought it probably his last chance of standing up for his eighteenth-century principles, strict construction, limited powers, George Washington, John Adams, and the rest. He had, in a half-hearted way, struggled all his life against State Street, banks, capitalism altogether, as he knew it in old England or new England, and he was fated to make his last resistance behind the silver standard.

For him this result was clear, and if he erred, he erred in company with nine men out of ten in Washington, for there was little difference on the merits. Adams was sure to learn backwards, but the case seemed entirely different with Cameron, a typical Pennsylvanian, a practical politician, whom all the reformers, including all the Adamses, had abused for a lifetime for subservience to moneyed interests and political jobbery. He was sure to go with the banks and corporations which had made and sustained him. On the contrary, he stood out obstinately as the leading champion of silver in the East. The reformers, represented by the Evening Post and Godkin, whose personal interests lay with the gold standard, at once assumed that Senator Cameron had a personal interest in silver, and denounced his corruption as hotly as though he had been convicted of taking a bribe.

More than silver and gold, the moral standard interested Adams. His own interests were with gold, but he supported silver; the Evening Post's and Godkin's interests were with gold, and they frankly said so, yet they avowedly pursued their interests even into politics; Cameron's interests had always been with the corporations, yet he supported silver. Thus morality required that Adams should be condemned for going against his interests; that Godkin was virtuous in following his interests; and that Cameron was a scoundrel whatever he did.

Granting that one of the three was a moral idiot, which was it: -- Adams or Godkin or Cameron? Until a Council or a Pope or a Congress or the newspapers or a popular election has decided a question of doubtful morality, individuals are apt to err, especially when putting money into their own pockets; but in democracies, the majority alone gives law. To any one who knew the relative popularity of Cameron and Godkin, the idea of a popular vote between them seemed excessively humorous; yet the popular vote in the end did decide against Cameron, for Godkin.

The Boston moralist and reformer went on, as always, like Dr. Johnson, impatiently stamping his foot and following his interests, or his antipathies; but the true American, slow to grasp new and complicated ideas, groped in the dark to discover where his greater interest lay. As usual, the banks taught him. In the course of fifty years the banks taught one many wise lessons for which an insect had to be grateful whether it liked them or not; but of all the lessons Adams learned from them, none compared in dramatic effect with that of July 22, 1893, when, after talking silver all the morning with Senator Cameron on the top of their travelling-carriage crossing the Furka Pass, they reached Lucerne in the afternoon, where Adams found letters from his brothers requesting his immediate return to Boston because the community was bankrupt and he was probably a beggar.

If he wanted education, he knew no quicker mode of learning a lesson than that of being struck on the head by it; and yet he was himself surprised at his own slowness to understand what had struck him. For several years a sufferer from insomnia, his first thought was of beggary of nerves, and he made ready to face a sleepless night, but although his mind tried to wrestle with the problem how any man could be ruined who had, months before, paid off every dollar of debt he knew himself to owe, he gave up that insoluble riddle in order to fall back on the larger principle that beggary could be no more for him than it was for others who were more valuable members of society, and, with that, he went to sleep like a good citizen, and the next day started for Quincy where he arrived August 7.

As a starting-point for a new education at fifty-five years old, the shock of finding one's self suspended, for several months, over the edge of bankruptcy, without knowing how one got there, or how to get away, is to be strongly recommended. By slow degrees the situation dawned on him that the banks had lent him, among others, some money -- thousands of millions were -- as bankruptcy -- the same -- for which he, among others, was responsible and of which he knew no more than they. The humor of this situation seemed to him so much more pointed than the terror, as to make him laugh at himself with a sincerity he had been long strange to. As far as he could comprehend, he had nothing to lose that he cared about, but the banks stood to lose their existence. Money mattered as little to him as to anybody, but money was their life. For the first time he had the banks in his power; he could afford to laugh; and the whole community was in the same position, though few laughed. All sat down on the banks and asked what the banks were going to do about it. To Adams the situation seemed farcical, but the more he saw of it, the less he understood it. He was quite sure that nobody understood it much better. Blindly some very powerful energy was at work, doing something that nobody wanted done. When Adams went to his bank to draw a hundred dollars of his own money on deposit, the cashier refused to let him have more than fifty, and Adams accepted the fifty without complaint because he was himself refusing to let the banks have some hundreds or thousands that belonged to them. Each wanted to help the other, yet both refused to pay their debts, and he could find no answer to the question which was responsible for getting the other into the situation, since lenders and borrowers were the same interest and socially the same person. Evidently the force was one; its operation was mechanical; its effect must be proportional to its power; but no one knew what it meant, and most people dismissed it as an emotion -- a panic -- that meant nothing.

Men died like flies under the strain, and Boston grew suddenly old, haggard, and thin. Adams alone waxed fat and was happy, for at last he had got hold of his world and could finish his education, interrupted for twenty years. He cared not whether it were worth finishing, if only it amused; but he seemed, for the first time since 1870, to feel that something new and curious was about to happen to the world. Great changes had taken place since 1870 in the forces at work; the old machine ran far behind its duty; somewhere -- somehow -- it was bound to break down, and if it happened to break precisely over one's head, it gave the better chance for study.

For the first time in several years he saw much of his brother Brooks in Quincy, and was surprised to find him absorbed in the same perplexities. Brooks was then a man of forty-five years old; a strong writer and a vigorous thinker who irritated too many Boston conventions ever to suit the atmosphere; but the two brothers could talk to each other without atmosphere and were used to audiences of one. Brooks had discovered or developed a law of history that civilization followed the exchanges, and having worked it out for the Mediterranean was working it out for the Atlantic. Everything American, as well as most things European and Asiatic, became unstable by this law, seeking new equilibrium and compelled to find it. Loving paradox, Brooks, with the advantages of ten years' study, had swept away much rubbish in the effort to build up a new line of thought for himself, but he found that no paradox compared with that of daily events. The facts were constantly outrunning his thoughts. The instability was greater than he calculated; the speed of acceleration passed bounds. Among other general rules he laid down the paradox that, in the social disequilibrium between capital and labor, the logical outcome was not collectivism, but anarchism; and Henry made note of it for study.

By the time he got back to Washington on September 19, the storm having partly blown over, life had taken on a new face, and one so interesting that he set off to Chicago to study the Exposition again, and stayed there a fortnight absorbed in it. He found matter of study to fill a hundred years, and his education spread over chaos. Indeed, it seemed to him as though, this year, education went mad. The silver question, thorny as it was, fell into relations as simple as words of one syllable, compared with the problems of credit and exchange that came to complicate it; and when one sought rest at Chicago, educational game started like rabbits from every building, and ran out of sight among thousands of its kind before one could mark its burrow. The Exposition itself defied philosophy. One might find fault till the last gate closed, one could still explain nothing that needed explanation. As a scenic display, Paris had never approached it, but the inconceivable scenic display consisted in its being there at all -- more surprising, as it was, than anything else on the continent, Niagara Falls, the Yellowstone Geysers, and the whole railway system thrown in, since these were all natural products in their place; while, since Noah's Ark, no such Babel of loose and ill joined, such vague and ill-defined and unrelated thoughts and half-thoughts and experimental outcries as the Exposition, had ever ruffled the surface of the Lakes.

The first astonishment became greater every day. That the Exposition should be a natural growth and product of the Northwest offered a step in evolution to startle Darwin; but that it should be anything else seemed an idea more startling still; and even granting it were not -- admitting it to be a sort of industrial, speculative growth and product of the Beaux Arts artistically induced to pass the summer on the shore of Lake Michigan -- could it be made to seem at home there? Was the American made to seem at home in it? Honestly, he had the air of enjoying it as though it were all his own; he felt it was good; he was proud of it; for the most part, he acted as though he had passed his life in landscape gardening and architectural decoration. If he had not done it himself, he had known how to get it done to suit him, as he knew how to get his wives and daughters dressed at Worth's or Paquin's. Perhaps he could not do it again; the next time he would want to do it himself and would show his own faults; but for the moment he seemed to have leaped directly from Corinth and Syracuse and Venice, over the heads of London and New York, to impose classical standards on plastic Chicago. Critics had no trouble in criticising the classicism, but all trading cities had always shown traders' taste, and, to the stern purist of religious faith, no art was thinner than Venetian Gothic. All trader's taste smelt of bric-a-brac; Chicago tried at least to give her taste a look of unity.

One sat down to ponder on the steps beneath Richard Hunt's dome almost as deeply as on the steps of Ara Coeli, and much to the same purpose. Here was a breach of continuity -- a rupture in historical sequence! Was it real, or only apparent? One's personal universe hung on the answer, for, if the rupture was real and the new American world could take this sharp and conscious twist towards ideals, one's personal friends would come in, at last, as winners in the great American chariot-race for fame. If the people of the Northwest actually knew what was good when they saw it, they would some day talk about Hunt and Richardson, La Farge and St. Gaudens,

Burnham and McKim, and Stanford White when their politicians and millionaires were otherwise forgotten. The artists and architects who had done the work offered little encouragement to hope it; they talked freely enough, but not in terms that one cared to quote; and to them the Northwest refused to look artistic. They talked as though they worked only for themselves; as though art, to the Western people, was a stage decoration; a diamond shirt-stud; a paper collar; but possibly the architects of Paestum and Girgenti had talked in the same way, and the Greek had said the same thing of Semitic Carthage two thousand years ago.

Jostled by these hopes and doubts, one turned to the exhibits for help, and found it. The industrial schools tried to teach so much and so quickly that the instruction ran to waste. Some millions of other people felt the same helplessness, but few of them were seeking education, and to them helplessness seemed natural and normal, for they had grown up in the habit of thinking a steam-engine or a dynamo as natural as the sun, and expected to understand one as little as the other. For the historian alone the Exposition made a serious effort. Historical exhibits were common, but they never went far enough; none were thoroughly worked out. One of the best was that of the Cunard steamers, but still a student hungry for results found himself obliged to waste a pencil and several sheets of paper trying to calculate exactly when, according to the given increase of power, tonnage, and speed, the growth of the ocean steamer would reach its limits. His figures brought him, he thought, to the year 1927; another generation to spare before force, space, and time should meet. The ocean steamer ran the surest line of triangulation into the future, because it was the nearest of man's products to a unity; railroads taught less because they seemed already finished except for mere increase in number; explosives taught most, but needed a tribe of chemists, physicists, and mathematicians to explain; the dynamo taught least because it had barely reached infancy, and, if its progress was to be constant at the rate of the last ten years, it would result in infinite costless energy within a generation. One lingered long among the dynamos, for they were new, and they gave to history a new phase. Men of science could never understand the ignorance and naiveté; of the historian, who, when he came suddenly on a new power, asked naturally what it was; did it pull or did it push? Was it a screw or thrust? Did it flow or vibrate? Was it a wire or a mathematical line? And a score of such questions to which he expected answers and was astonished to get none.

Education ran riot at Chicago, at least for retarded minds which had never faced in concrete form so many matters of which they were ignorant. Men who knew nothing whatever -- who had never run a steam-engine, the simplest of forces -- who had never put their hands on a lever -- had never touched an electric battery -- never talked through a telephone, and had not the shadow of a notion what amount of force was meant by a watt or an ampere or an erg, or any other term of measurement introduced within a hundred years -- had no choice but to sit down on the steps and brood as they had never brooded on the benches of Harvard College, either as student or professor, aghast at what they had said and done in all these years, and still more ashamed of the childlike ignorance and babbling futility of the society that let them say and do it. The historical mind can think only in historical processes, and probably this was the first time since historians existed, that any of them had sat down helpless before a mechanical sequence. Before a metaphysical or a theological or a political sequence, most historians had felt helpless, but the single clue to which they had hitherto trusted was the unity of natural force.

Did he himself quite know what he meant? Certainly not! If he had known enough to state his problem, his education would have been complete at once. Chicago asked in 1893 for the first time the question whether the American people knew where they were driving. Adams answered, for one, that he did not know, but would try to find out. On reflecting sufficiently deeply, under the shadow of Richard Hunt's architecture, he decided that the American people probably knew no more than he did; but that they might still be driving or drifting unconsciously to some point in thought, as their solar system was said to be drifting towards some point in space; and that, possibly, if relations enough could be observed, this point might be fixed. Chicago was the first expression of American thought as a unity; one must start there.

Washington was the second. When he got back there, he fell headlong into the extra session of Congress called to repeal the Silver Act. The silver minority made an obstinate attempt to prevent it, and most of the majority had little heart in the creation of a single gold standard. The banks alone, and the dealers in exchange, insisted upon it; the political parties divided according to capitalistic geographical lines, Senator Cameron offering almost the only exception; but they mixed with unusual good-temper, and made liberal allowance for each others' actions and motives. The struggle was rather less irritable than such struggles generally were, and it ended like a comedy. On the evening of the final vote, Senator Cameron came back from the Capitol with Senator Brice, Senator Jones, Senator Lodge, and Moreton Frewen, all in the gayest of humors as though they were rid of a heavy responsibility. Adams, too, in a bystander's spirit, felt light in mind. He had stood up for his eighteenth century, his Constitution of 1789, his George Washington, his Harvard College, his Quincy, and his Plymouth Pilgrims, as long as any one would stand up with him. He had said it was hopeless twenty years before, but he had kept on, in the same old attitude, by habit and taste, until he found himself altogether alone. He had hugged his antiquated dislike of bankers and capitalistic society until he had become little better than a crank. He had known for years that he must accept the regime, but he had known a great many other disagreeable certainties -- like age, senility, and death -- against which one made what little resistance one could. The matter was settled at last by the people. For a hundred years, between 1793 and 1893, the American people had hesitated, vacillated, swayed forward and back, between two forces, one simply industrial, the other capitalistic, centralizing, and mechanical. In 1893, the issue came on the single gold standard, and the majority at last declared itself, once for all, in favor of the capitalistic system with all its necessary machinery. All one's friends, all one's best citizens, reformers, churches, colleges, educated classes, had joined the banks to force submission to capitalism; a submission long foreseen by the mere law of mass. Of all forms of society or government, this was the one he liked least, but his likes or dislikes were as antiquated as the rebel doctrine of State rights. A capitalistic system had been adopted, and if it were to be run at all, it must be run by capital and by capitalistic methods; for nothing could surpass the nonsensity of trying to run so complex and so concentrated a machine by Southern and Western farmers in grotesque alliance with city day-laborers, as had been tried in 1800 and 1828, and had failed even under simple conditions.

There, education in domestic politics stopped. The rest was question of gear; of running machinery; of economy; and involved no disputed principle. Once admitted that the machine must be efficient, society might dispute in what social interest it should be run, but in any case it must work concentration. Such great revolutions commonly leave some bitterness behind, but nothing in politics ever surprised Henry Adams more than the ease with which he and his silver friends slipped across the chasm, and alighted on the single gold standard and the capitalistic system with its methods; the protective tariff; the corporations and trusts; the trades-unions and socialistic paternalism which necessarily made their complement; the whole mechanical consolidation of force, which ruthlessly stamped out the life of the class into which Adams was born, but created monopolies capable of controlling the new energies that America adored.

Society rested, after sweeping into the ash-heap these cinders of a misdirected education. After this vigorous impulse, nothing remained for a historian but to ask -- how long and how far!

Chapter XXIII. Silence (1894-1898)

The convulsion of 1893 left its victims in dead-water, and closed much education. While the country braced itself up to an effort such as no one had thought within its powers, the individual crawled as he best could, through the wreck, and found many values of life upset. But for connecting the nineteenth and twentieth centuries, the four years, 1893 to 1897, had no value in the drama of education, and might be left out. Much that had made life pleasant between 1870 and 1890 perished in the ruin, and among the earliest wreckage had been the fortunes of Clarence King. The lesson taught whatever the bystander chose to read in it; but to Adams it seemed singularly full of moral, if he could but understand it. In 1871 he had thought King's education ideal, and his personal fitness unrivalled. No other young American approached him for the combination of chances -- physical energy, social standing, mental scope and training, wit, geniality, and science, that seemed superlatively American and irresistibly strong. His nearest rival was Alexander Agassiz, and, as far as their friends knew, no one else could be classed with them in the running. The result of twenty years' effort proved that the theory of scientific education failed where most theory fails -- for want of money. Even Henry Adams, who kept himself, as he thought, quite outside of every possible financial risk, had been caught in the cogs, and held for months over the gulf of bankruptcy, saved only by the chance that the whole class of millionaires were more or less bankrupt too, and the banks were forced to let the mice escape with the rats; but, in sum, education without capital could always be taken by the throat and forced to disgorge its gains, nor was it helped by the knowledge that no one intended it, but that all alike suffered. Whether voluntary or mechanical the result for education was the same. The failure of the scientific scheme, without money to back it, was flagrant.

The scientific scheme in theory was alone sound, for science should be equivalent to money; in practice science was helpless without money. The weak holder was, in his own language, sure to be frozen out. Education must fit the complex conditions of a new society, always accelerating its movement, and its fitness could be known only from success. One looked about for examples of success among the educated of one's time -- the men born in the thirties, and trained to professions. Within one's immediate acquaintance, three were typical: John Hay, Whitelaw Reid, and William C. Whitney; all of whom owed their free hand to marriage, education serving only for ornament, but among whom, in 1893, William C. Whitney was far and away the most popular type.

Newspapers might prate about wealth till commonplace print was exhausted, but as matter of habit, few Americans envied the very rich for anything the most of them got out of money. New York might occasionally fear them, but more often laughed or sneered at them, and never showed them respect. Scarcely one of the very rich men held any position in society by virtue of his wealth, or could have been elected to an office, or even into a good club. Setting aside the few, like Pierpont Morgan, whose social position had little to do with greater or less wealth, riches were in New York no object of envy on account of the joys they brought in their train, and

Whitney was not even one of the very rich; yet in his case the envy was palpable. There was reason for it. Already in 1893 Whitney had finished with politics after having gratified every ambition, and swung the country almost at his will; he had thrown away the usual objects of political ambition like the ashes of smoked cigarettes; had turned to other amusements, satiated every taste, gorged every appetite, won every object that New York afforded, and, not yet satisfied, had carried his field of activity abroad, until New York no longer knew what most to envy, his horses or his houses. He had succeeded precisely where Clarence King had failed.

Barely forty years had passed since all these men started in a bunch to race for power, and the results were fixed beyond reversal; but one knew no better in 1894 than in 1854 what an American education ought to be in order to count as success. Even granting that it counted as money, its value could not be called general. America contained scores of men worth five millions or upwards, whose lives were no more worth living than those of their cooks, and to whom the task of making money equivalent to education offered more difficulties than to Adams the task of making education equivalent to money. Social position seemed to have value still, while education counted for nothing. A mathematician, linguist, chemist, electrician, engineer, if fortunate might average a value of ten dollars a day in the open market. An administrator, organizer, manager, with mediaeval qualities of energy and will, but no education beyond his special branch, would probably be worth at least ten times as much. Society had failed to discover what sort of education suited it best. Wealth valued social position and classical education as highly as either of these valued wealth, and the women still tended to keep the scales even. For anything Adams could see he was himself as contented as though he had been educated; while Clarence King, whose education was exactly suited to theory, had failed; and Whitney, who was no better educated than Adams, had achieved phenomenal success.

Had Adams in 1894 been starting in life as he did in 1854, he must have repeated that all he asked of education was the facile use of the four old tools: Mathematics, French, German, and Spanish. With these he could still make his way to any object within his vision, and would have a decisive advantage over nine rivals in ten. Statesman or lawyer, chemist or electrician, priest or professor, native or foreign, he would fear none.

King's breakdown, physical as well as financial, brought the indirect gain to Adams that, on recovering strength, King induced him to go to Cuba, where, in January, 1894, they drifted into the little town of Santiago. The picturesque Cuban society, which King knew well, was more amusing than any other that one had yet discovered in the whole broad world, but made no profession of teaching anything unless it were Cuban Spanish or the danza; and neither on his own nor on King's account did the visitor ask any loftier study than that of the buzzards floating on the trade-wind down the valley to Dos Bocas, or the colors of sea and shore at sunrise from the height of the Gran Piedra; but, as though they were still twenty years old and revolution were as young as they, the decaying fabric, which had never been solid, fell on their heads and drew them with it into an ocean of mischief. In the half-century between 1850 and 1900, empires were always falling on one's head, and, of all lessons, these constant political convulsions taught least. Since the time of Rameses, revolutions have raised more doubts than they solved, but they have sometimes the merit of changing one's point of view, and the Cuban rebellion served to sever the last tie that attached Adams to a Democratic administration. He thought that President Cleveland could have settled the Cuban question, without war, had he chosen to do his duty, and this feeling, generally held by the Democratic Party, joined with the stress of economical needs and the gold standard to break into bits the old organization and to leave no choice between parties. The new American, whether consciously or not, had turned his back on the nineteenth century before he was done with it; the gold standard, the protective system, and the laws of mass could have no other outcome, and, as so often before, the movement, once accelerated by attempting to impede it, had the additional, brutal consequence of crushing equally the good and the bad that stood in its way.

The lesson was old -- so old that it became tedious. One had studied nothing else since childhood, and wearied of it. For yet another year Adams lingered on these outskirts of the vortex, among the picturesque, primitive types of a world which had never been fairly involved in the general motion, and were the more amusing for their torpor. After passing the winter with King in the West Indies, he passed the summer with Hay in the Yellowstone, and found there little to study. The Geysers were an old story; the Snake River posed no vital statistics except in its fordings; even the Tetons were as calm as they were lovely; while the wapiti and bear, innocent of strikes and corners, laid no traps. In return the party treated them with affection. Never did a band less bloody or bloodthirsty wander over the roof of the continent. Hay loved as little as Adams did, the labor of skinning and butchering big game; he had even outgrown the sedate, middle-aged, meditative joy of duck-shooting, and found the trout of the Yellowstone too easy a prey. Hallett Phillips himself, who managed the party loved to play Indian hunter without hunting so much as a fieldmouse; Iddings the geologist was reduced to shooting only for the table, and the guileless prattle of Billy Hofer alone taught the simple life. Compared with the Rockies of 1871, the sense of wildness had vanished; one saw no possible adventures except to break one's neck as in chasing an aniseed fox. Only the more intelligent ponies scented an occasional friendly and sociable bear.

When the party came out of the Yellowstone, Adams went on alone to Seattle and Vancouver to inspect the last American railway systems yet untried. They, too, offered little new learning, and no sooner had he finished this debauch of Northwestern geography than with desperate thirst for exhausting the American field, he set out for Mexico and the Gulf, making a sweep of the Caribbean and clearing up, in these six or eight months, at least twenty thousand miles of American land and water.

He was beginning to think, when he got back to Washington in April, 1895, that he knew enough about the edges of life -- tropical islands, mountain solitudes, archaic law, and retrograde types. Infinitely more amusing and incomparably more picturesque than civilization, they educated only artists, and, as one's sixtieth year approached, the artist began to die; only a certain intense cerebral restlessness survived which no longer responded to sensual stimulants; one was driven from beauty to beauty as though art were a trotting-match. For this, one was in some degree prepared, for the old man had been a stage-type since drama began; but one felt some perplexity to account for failure on the opposite or mechanical side, where nothing but cerebral action was needed.

Taking for granted that the alternative to art was arithmetic, plunged deep into statistics, fancying that education would find the surest bottom there; and the study proved the easiest he had ever approached. Even the Government volunteered unlimited statistics, endless columns of figures, bottomless averages merely for the asking. At the Statistical Bureau, Worthington Ford supplied any material that curiosity could imagine for filling the vast gaps of ignorance, and methods for applying the plasters of fact. One seemed for a while to be winning ground, and one's averages projected themselves as laws into the future. Perhaps the most perplexing part of the study lay in the attitude of the statisticians, who showed no enthusiastic confidence in their own figures. They should have reached certainty, but they talked like other men who knew less. The method did not result faith. Indeed, every increase of mass -- of volume and velocity -- seemed to bring in new elements, and, at last, a scholar, fresh in arithmetic and ignorant of algebra, fell into a superstitious terror of complexity as the sink of facts. Nothing came out as it should. In principle, according to figures, any one could set up or pull down a society. One could frame no sort of satisfactory answer to the constructive doctrines of Adam Smith, or to the destructive criticisms of Karl Marx or to the anarchistic imprecations of Elisee Reclus. One revelled at will in the ruin of every society in the past, and rejoiced in proving the prospective overthrow of every society that seemed possible in the future; but meanwhile these societies which violated every law, moral, arithmetical, and economical, not only propagated each other, but produced also fresh complexities with every propagation and developed mass with every complexity.

The human factor was worse still. Since the stupefying discovery of Pteraspis in 1867, nothing had so confused the student as the conduct of mankind in the fin-de-siecle. No one seemed very much concerned about this world or the future, unless it might be the anarchists, and they only because they disliked the present. Adams disliked the present as much as they did, and his interest in future society was becoming slight, yet he was kept alive by irritation at finding his life so thin and fruitless. Meanwhile he watched mankind march on, like a train of pack-horses on the Snake River, tumbling from one morass into another, and at short intervals, for no reason but temper, falling to butchery, like Cain. Since 1850, massacres had become so common that society scarcely noticed them unless they summed up hundreds of thousands, as in Armenia; wars had been almost continuous, and were beginning again in Cuba, threatening in South Africa, and possible in Manchuria; yet impartial judges thought them all not merely unnecessary, but foolish -- induced by greed of the coarsest class, as though the Pharaohs or the Romans were still robbing their neighbors. The robbery might be natural and inevitable, but the murder seemed altogether archaic.

At one moment of perplexity to account for this trait of Pteraspis, or shark, which seemed to have survived every moral improvement of society, he took to study of the religious press. Possibly growth m human nature might show itself there. He found no need to speak unkindly of it; but, as an agent of motion, he preferred on the whole the vigor of the shark, with its chances of betterment; and he very gravely doubted, from his aching consciousness of religious void, whether any large fraction of society cared for a future life, or even for the present one, thirty years hence. Not an act, or an expression, or an image, showed depth of faith or hope.

The object of education, therefore, was changed. For many years it had lost itself in studying what the world had ceased to care for; if it were to begin again, it must try to find out what the mass of mankind did care for, and why. Religion, politics, statistics, travel had thus far led to nothing. Even the Chicago Fair had only confused the roads. Accidental education could go no further, for one's mind was already littered and stuffed beyond hope with the millions of chance images stored away without order in the memory. One might as well try to educate a gravel-pit. The task was futile, which disturbed a student less than the discovery that, in pursuing it, he was becoming himself ridiculous. Nothing is more tiresome than a superannuated pedagogue.

For the moment he was rescued, as often before, by a woman. Towards midsummer, 1895, Mrs. Cabot Lodge bade him follow her to Europe with the Senator and her two sons. The study of history is useful to the historian by teaching him his ignorance of women; and the mass of this ignorance crushes one who is familiar enough with what are called historical sources to realize how few women have ever been known. The woman who is known only through a man is known wrong, and excepting one or two like Mme. de Sevigne, no woman has pictured herself. The American woman of the nineteenth century will live only as the man saw her; probably she will be less known than the woman of the eighteenth; none of the female descendants of Abigail Adams can ever be nearly so familiar as her letters have made her; and all this is pure loss to history, for the American woman of the nineteenth century was much better company than the American man; she was probably much better company than her grandmothers. With Mrs. Lodge and her husband, Senator since 1893, Adams's relations had been those of elder brother or uncle since 1871 when Cabot Lodge had left his examination-papers on Assistant Professor Adams's desk, and crossed the street to Christ Church in Cambridge to get married. With Lodge himself, as scholar, fellow instructor, co-editor of the North American Review, and political reformer from 1873 to 1878, he had worked intimately, but with him afterwards as politician he had not much relation; and since Lodge had suffered what Adams thought the misfortune of becoming not only a Senator but a Senator from Massachusetts -- a singular social relation which Adams had known only as fatal to friends -- a superstitious student, intimate with the laws of historical fatality, would rather have recognized him only as an enemy; but apart from this accident he valued Lodge highly, and in the waste places of average humanity had been greatly dependent on his house. Senators can never be approached with safety, but a Senator who has a very superior wife and several superior children who feel no deference for Senators as such, may be approached at times with relative impunity while they keep him under restraint.

Where Mrs. Lodge summoned, one followed with gratitude, and so it chanced that in August one found one's self for the first time at Caen, Coutances, and Mont-Saint-Michel in Normandy. If history had a chapter with which he thought himself familiar, it was the twelfth and thirteenth centuries; yet so little has labor to do with knowledge that these bare playgrounds of the lecture system turned into green and verdurous virgin forests merely through the medium of younger eyes and fresher minds. His German bias must have given his youth a terrible twist, for the Lodges saw at a glance what he had thought unessential because un-German. They breathed native air in the Normandy of 1200, a compliment which would have seemed to the Senator lacking in taste or even in sense when addressed to one of a class of men who passed life in trying to persuade themselves and the public that they breathed nothing less American than a blizzard; but this atmosphere, in the touch of a real emotion, betrayed the unconscious humor of the senatorial mind. In the thirteenth century, by an unusual chance, even a Senator became natural, simple, interested, cultivated, artistic, liberal -- genial.

Through the Lodge eyes the old problem became new and personal; it threw off all association with the German lecture-room. One could not at first see what this novelty meant; it had the air of mere antiquarian emotion like Wenlock Abbey and Pteraspis; but it expelled archaic law and antiquarianism once for all, without seeming conscious of it; and Adams drifted back to Washington with a new sense of history. Again he wandered south, and in April returned to Mexico with the Camerons to study the charms of pulque and Churriguerresque architecture. In May he ran through Europe again with Hay, as far south as Ravenna. There came the end of the passage. After thus covering once more, in 1896, many thousand miles of the old trails, Adams went home October, with every one else, to elect McKinley President and start the world anew.

For the old world of public men and measures since 1870, Adams wept no tears. Within or without, during or after it, as partisan or historian, he never saw anything to admire in it, or anything he wanted to save; and in this respect he reflected only the public mind which balanced itself so exactly between the unpopularity of both parties as to express no sympathy with either. Even among the most powerful men of that generation he knew none who had a good word to say for it. No period so thoroughly ordinary had been known in American politics since Christopher Columbus first disturbed the balance of American society; but the natural result of such lack of interest in public affairs, in a small society like that of Washington, led an idle bystander to depend abjectly on intimacy of private relation. One dragged one's self down the long vista of Pennsylvania Avenue, by leaning heavily on one's friends, and avoiding to look at anything else. Thus life had grown narrow with years, more and more concentrated on the circle of houses round La Fayette Square, which had no direct or personal share in power except in the case of Mr. Blaine whose tumultuous struggle for existence held him apart. Suddenly Mr. McKinley entered the White House and laid his hand heavily on this special group. In a moment the whole nest so slowly constructed, was torn to pieces and scattered over the world. Adams found himself alone. John Hay took his orders for London. Rockhill departed to Athens. Cecil Spring-Rice had been buried in Persia. Cameron refused to remain in public life either at home or abroad, and broke up his house on the Square. Only the Lodges and Roosevelts remained, but even they were at once absorbed in the interests of power. Since 1861, no such social convulsion had occurred.

Even this was not quite the worst. To one whose interests lay chiefly in foreign affairs, and who, at this moment, felt most strongly the nightmare of Cuban, Hawaiian, and Nicaraguan chaos, the man in the State Department seemed more important than the man in the White House. Adams knew no one in the United States fit to manage these matters in the face of a hostile Europe, and had no candidate to propose; but he was shocked beyond all restraints of expression to learn that the President meant to put Senator John Sherman in the State Department in order to make a place for Mr. Hanna in the Senate. Grant himself had done nothing that seemed so bad as this to one who had lived long enough to distinguish between the ways of presidential jobbery, if not between the jobs. John Sherman, otherwise admirably fitted for the place, a friendly influence for nearly forty years, was notoriously feeble and quite senile, so that the intrigue seemed to Adams the betrayal of an old friend as well as of the State Department. One might have shrugged one's shoulders had the President named Mr. Hanna his Secretary of State, for Mr. Hanna was a man of force if not of experience, and selections much worse than this had often turned out well enough; but John Sherman must inevitably and tragically break down.

The prospect for once was not less vile than the men. One can bear coldly the jobbery of enemies, but not that of friends, and to Adams this kind of jobbery seemed always infinitely worse than all the petty money bribes ever exploited by the newspapers. Nor was the matter improved by hints that the President might call John Hay to the Department whenever John Sherman should retire. Indeed, had Hay been even unconsciously party to such an intrigue, he would have put an end, once for all, to further concern in public affairs on his friend's part; but even without this last disaster, one felt that Washington had become no longer habitable. Nothing was left there but solitary contemplation of Mr. McKinley's ways which were not likely to be more amusing than the ways of his predecessors; or of senatorial ways, which offered no novelty of what the French language expressively calls embetement; or of poor Mr. Sherman's ways which would surely cause anguish to his friends. Once more, one must go!

Nothing was easier! On and off, one had done the same thing since the year 1858, at frequent intervals, and had now reached the month of March, 1897; yet, as the whole result of six years' dogged effort to begin a new education, one could not recommend it to the young. The outlook lacked hope. The object of travel had become more and more dim, ever since the gibbering ghost of the Civil Law had been locked in its dark closet, as far back as 1860. Noah's dove had not searched the earth for resting-places so carefully, or with so little success. Any spot on land or water satisfies a dove who wants and finds rest; but no perch suits a dove of sixty years old, alone and uneducated, who has lost his taste even for olives. To this, also, the young may be driven, as education, end the lesson fails in humor; but it may be worth knowing to some of them that the planet offers hardly a dozen places where an elderly man can pass a week alone without ennui, and none at all where he can pass a year.

Irritated by such complaints, the world naturally answers that no man of sixty should live, which is doubtless true, though not original. The man of sixty, with a certain irritability proper to his years, retorts that the world has no business to throw on him the task of removing its carrion, and that while he remains he has a right to require amusement -- or at least education, since this costs nothing to any one -- and that a world which cannot educate, will not amuse, and is ugly besides, has even less right to exist than he. Both views seem sound; but the world wearily objects to be called by epithets what society always admits in practice; for no one likes to be told that he is a bore, or ignorant, or even ugly; and having nothing to say in its defence, it rejoins that, whatever license is pardonable in youth, the man of sixty who wishes consideration had better hold his tongue. This truth also has the defect of being too true. The rule holds equally for men of half that age Only the very young have the right to betray their ignorance or ill-breeding. Elderly people commonly know enough not to betray themselves.

Exceptions are plenty on both sides, as the Senate knew to its acute suffering; but young or old, women or men, seemed agreed on one point with singular unanimity; each praised silence in others. Of all characteristics in human nature, this has been one of the most abiding. Mere superficial gleaning of what, in the long history of human expression, has been said by the fool or unsaid by the wise, shows that, for once, no difference of opinion has ever existed on this. "Even a fool," said the wisest of men, "when he holdeth his peace, is counted wise," and still more often, the wisest of men, when he spoke the highest wisdom, has been counted a fool. They agreed only on the merits of silence in others. Socrates made remarks in its favor, which should have struck the Athenians as new to them; but of late the repetition had grown tiresome. Thomas Carlyle vociferated his admiration of it. Matthew Arnold thought it the best form of expression; and Adams thought Matthew Arnold the best form of expression in his time. Algernon Swinburne called it the most noble to the end. Alfred de Vigny's dying wolf remarked: --

"A voir ce que l'on fut sur terre et ce qu'on laisse,

Seul le silence est grand; tout le reste est faiblesse."

"When one thinks what one leaves in the world when one dies,

Only silence is strong, -- all the rest is but lies."

Even Byron, whom a more brilliant era of genius seemed to have decided to be but an indifferent poet, had ventured to affirm that --

"The Alp's snow summit nearer heaven is seen

Than the volcano's fierce eruptive crest;"

with other verses, to the effect that words are but a "temporary torturing flame"; of which no one knew more than himself. The evidence of the poets could not be more emphatic: --

"Silent, while years engrave the brow!

Silent, -- the best are silent now!"

Although none of these great geniuses had shown faith in silence as a cure for their own ills or ignorance, all of them, and all philosophy after them, affirmed that no man, even at sixty, had ever been known to attain knowledge; but that a very few were believed to have attained ignorance, which was in result the same. More than this, in every society worth the name, the man of sixty had been encouraged to ride this hobby -- the Pursuit of Ignorance in Silence -- as though it were the easiest way to get rid of him. In America the silence was more oppressive than the ignorance; but perhaps elsewhere the world might still hide some haunt of futilitarian silence where content reigned -- although long search had not revealed it -- and so the pilgrimage began anew!

The first step led to London where John Hay was to be established. One had seen so many American Ministers received in London that the Lord Chamberlain himself scarcely knew more about it; education could not be expected there; but there Adams arrived, April 21, 1897, as though thirty-six years were so many days, for Queen Victoria still reigned and one saw little change in St. James's Street. True, Carlton House Terrace, like the streets of Rome, actually squeaked and gibbered with ghosts, till one felt like Odysseus before the press of shadows, daunted by a "bloodless fear"; but in spring London is pleasant, and it was more cheery than ever in May, 1897, when every one was welcoming the return of life after the long winter since 1893. One's fortunes, or one's friends' fortunes, were again in flood.

This amusement could not be prolonged, for one found one's self the oldest Englishman in England, much too familiar with family jars better forgotten, and old traditions better unknown. No wrinkled Tannhauser, returning to the Wartburg, needed a wrinkled Venus to show him that he was no longer at home, and that even penitence was a sort of impertinence. He slipped away to Paris, and set up a household at St. Germain where he taught and learned French history for nieces who swarmed under the venerable cedars of the Pavillon d'Angouleme, and rode about the green forest-alleys of St. Germain and Marly. From time to time Hay wrote humorous laments, but nothing occurred to break the summer-peace of the stranded Tannhauser, who slowly began to feel at home in France as in other countries he had thought more homelike. At length, like other dead Americans, he went to Paris because he could go nowhere else, and lingered there till the Hays came by, in January, 1898; and Mrs. Hay, who had been a stanch and strong ally for twenty years, bade him go with them to Egypt.

Adams cared little to see Egypt again, but he was glad to see Hay, and readily drifted after him to the Nile. What they saw and what they said had as little to do with education as possible, until one evening, as they were looking at the sun set across the Nile from Assouan, Spencer Eddy brought them a telegram to announce the sinking of the Maine in Havana Harbor. This was the greatest stride in education since 1865, but what did it teach? One leant on a fragment of column in the great hall at Karnak and watched a jackal creep down the debris of ruin. The jackal's ancestors had surely crept up the same wall when it was building. What was his view about the value of silence? One lay in the sands and watched the expression of the Sphinx. Brooks Adams had taught him that the relation between civilizations was that of trade. Henry wandered, or was storm-driven, down the coast. He tried to trace out the ancient harbor of Ephesus. He went over to Athens, picked up Rockhill, and searched for the harbor of Tiryns; together they went on to Constantinople and studied the great walls of Constantine and the greater domes of Justinian. His hobby had turned into a camel, and he hoped, if he rode long enough in silence, that at last he might come on a city of thought along the great highways of exchange.

Chapter XXIV. Indian Summer (1898-1899)

The summer of the Spanish War began the Indian summer of life to one who had reached sixty years of age, and cared only to reap in peace such harvest as these sixty years had yielded. He had reason to be more than content with it. Since 1864 he had felt no such sense of power and momentum, and had seen no such number of personal friends wielding it. The sense of solidarity counts for much in one's contentment, but the sense of winning one's game counts for more; and in London, in 1898, the scene was singularly interesting to the last survivor of the Legation of 1861. He thought himself perhaps the only person living who could get full enjoyment of the drama. He carried every scene of it, in a century and a half since the Stamp Act, quite alive in his mind -- all the interminable disputes of his disputatious ancestors as far back as the year 1750 -- as well as his own insignificance in the Civil War, every step in which had the object of bringing England into an American system. For this they had written libraries of argument and remonstrance, and had piled war on war, losing their tempers for life, and souring the gentle and patient Puritan nature of their descendants, until even their private secretaries at times used language almost intemperate; and suddenly, by pure chance, the blessing fell on Hay. After two hundred years of stupid and greedy blundering, which no argument and no violence affected, the people of England learned their lesson just at the moment when Hay would otherwise have faced a flood of the old anxieties. Hay himself scarcely knew how grateful he should be, for to him the change came almost of course. He saw only the necessary stages that had led to it, and to him they seemed natural; but to Adams, still living in the atmosphere of Palmerston and John Russell, the sudden appearance of Germany as the grizzly terror which, in twenty years effected what Adamses had tried for two hundred in vain -- frightened England into America's arms -- seemed as melodramatic as any plot of Napoleon the Great. He could feel only the sense of satisfaction at seeing the diplomatic triumph of all his family, since the breed existed, at last realized under his own eyes for the advantage of his oldest and closest ally.

This was history, not education, yet it taught something exceedingly serious, if not ultimate, could one trust the lesson. For the first time in his life, he felt a sense of possible purpose working itself out in history. Probably no one else on this earthly planet -- not even Hay -- could have come out on precisely such extreme personal satisfaction, but as he sat at Hay's table, listening to any member of the British Cabinet, for all were alike now, discuss the Philippines as a question of balance of power in the East, he could see that the family work of a hundred and fifty years fell at once into the grand perspective of true empire-building, which Hay's work set off with artistic skill. The roughness of the archaic foundations looked stronger and larger in scale for the refinement and certainty of the arcade. In the long list of famous American Ministers in London, none could have given the work quite the completeness, the harmony, the perfect ease of Hay.

Never before had Adams been able to discern the working of law in history, which was the reason of his failure in teaching it, for chaos cannot be taught; but he thought he had a personal property by inheritance in this proof of sequence and intelligence in the affairs of man -- a property which no one else had right to dispute; and this personal triumph left him a little cold towards the other diplomatic results of the war. He knew that Porto Rico must be taken, but he would have been glad to escape the Philippines. Apart from too intimate an acquaintance with the value of islands in the South Seas, he knew the West Indies well enough to be assured that, whatever the American people might think or say about it, they would sooner or later have to police those islands, not against Europe, but for Europe, and America too. Education on the outskirts of civilized life teaches not very much, but it taught this; and one felt no call to shoulder the load of archipelagoes in the antipodes when one was trying painfully to pluck up courage to face the labor of shouldering archipelagoes at home. The country decided otherwise, and one acquiesced readily enough since the matter concerned only the public willingness to carry loads; in London, the balance of power in the East came alone into discussion; and in every point of view one had as much reason to be gratified with the result as though one had shared in the danger, instead of being vigorously employed in looking on from a great distance. After all, friends had done the work, if not one's self, and he too serves a certain purpose who only stands and cheers.

In June, at the crisis of interest, the Camerons came over, and took the fine old house of Surrenden Dering in Kent which they made a sort of country house to the Embassy. Kent has charms rivalling those of Shropshire, and, even compared with the many beautiful places scattered along the Welsh border, few are nobler or more genial than Surrenden with its unbroken descent from the Saxons, its avenues, its terraces, its deer-park, its large repose on the Kentish hillside, and its broad outlook over what was once the forest of Anderida. Filled with a constant stream of guests, the house seemed to wait for the chance to show its charms to the American, with whose activity the whole world was resounding; and never since the battle of Hastings could the little telegraph office of the Kentish village have done such work. There, on a hot July 4, 1898, to an expectant group under the shady trees, came the telegram announcing the destruction of the Spanish Armada, as it might have come to Queen Elizabeth in 1588; and there, later in the season, came the order summoning Hay to the State Department.

Hay had no wish to be Secretary of State. He much preferred to remain Ambassador, and his friends were quite as cold about it as he. No one knew so well what sort of strain falls on Secretaries of State, or how little strength he had in reserve against it. Even at Surrenden he showed none too much endurance, and he would gladly have found a valid excuse for refusing. The discussion on both sides was earnest, but the decided voice of the conclave was that, though if he were a mere office-seeker he might certainly decline promotion, if he were a member of the Government he could not. No serious statesman could accept a favor and refuse a service. Doubtless he might refuse, but in that case he must resign. The amusement of making Presidents has keen fascination for idle American hands, but these black arts have the old drawback of all deviltry; one must serve the spirit one evokes, even though the service were perdition to body and soul. For him, no doubt, the service, though hard, might bring some share of profit, but for the friends who gave this unselfish decision, all would prove loss. For one, Adams on that subject had become a little daft. No one in his experience had ever passed unscathed through that malarious marsh. In his fancy, office was poison; it killed -- body and soul -- physically and socially. Office was more poisonous than priestcraft or pedagogy in proportion as it held more power; but the poison he complained of was not ambition; he shared none of Cardinal Wolsey's belated penitence for that healthy stimulant, as he had shared none of the fruits; his poison was that of the will -- the distortion of sight -- the warping of mind -- the degradation of tissue -- the coarsening of taste -- the narrowing of sympathy to the emotions of a caged rat. Hay needed no office in order to wield influence. For him, influence lay about the streets, waiting for him to stoop to it; he enjoyed more than enough power without office; no one of his position, wealth, and political experience, living at the centre of politics in contact with the active party managers, could escape influence. His only ambition was to escape annoyance, and no one knew better than he that, at sixty years of age, sensitive to physical strain, still more sensitive to brutality, vindictiveness, or betrayal, he took office at cost of life.

Neither he nor any of the Surrenden circle made presence of gladness at the new dignity for, with all his gaiety of manner and lightness of wit, he took dark views of himself, none the lighter for their humor, and his obedience to the President's order was the gloomiest acquiescence he had ever smiled. Adams took dark views, too, not so much on Hay's account as on his own, for, while Hay had at least the honors of office, his friends would share only the ennuis of it; but, as usual with Hay, nothing was gained by taking such matters solemnly, and old habits of the Civil War left their mark of military drill on every one who lived through it. He shouldered his pack and started for home. Adams had no mind to lose his friend without a struggle, though he had never known such sort of struggle to avail. The chance was desperate, but he could not afford to throw it away; so, as soon as the Surrenden establishment broke up, on October 17, he prepared for return home, and on November 13, none too gladly, found himself again gazing into La Fayette Square.

He had made another false start and lost two years more of education; nor had he excuse; for, this time, neither politics nor society drew him away from his trail. He had nothing to do with Hay's politics at home or abroad, and never affected agreement with his views or his methods, nor did Hay care whether his friends agreed or disagreed. They all united in trying to help each other to get along the best way they could, and all they tried to save was the personal relation. Even there, Adams would have been beaten had he not been helped by Mrs. Hay, who saw the necessity of distraction, and led her husband into the habit of stopping every afternoon to take his friend off for an hour's walk, followed by a cup of tea with Mrs. Hay afterwards, and a chat with any one who called.

For the moment, therefore, the situation was saved, at least in outward appearance, and Adams could go back to his own pursuits which were slowly taking a direction. Perhaps they had no right to be called pursuits, for in truth one consciously pursued nothing, but drifted as attraction offered itself. The short session broke up the Washington circle, so that, on March 22, Adams was able to sail with the Lodges for Europe and to pass April in Sicily and Rome.

With the Lodges, education always began afresh. Forty years had left little of the Palermo that Garibaldi had shown to the boy of 1860, but Sicily in all ages seems to have taught only catastrophe and violence, running riot on that theme ever since Ulysses began its study on the eye of Cyclops. For a lesson in anarchy, without a shade of sequence, Sicily stands alone and defies evolution. Syracuse teaches more than Rome. Yet even Rome was not mute, and the church of Ara Coeli seemed more and more to draw all the threads of thought to a centre, for every new journey led back to its steps -- Karnak, Ephesus, Delphi, Mycencae, Constantinople, Syracuse -- all lying on the road to the Capitol. What they had to bring by way of intellectual riches could not yet be discerned, but they carried camel-loads of moral; and New York sent most of all, for, in forty years, America had made so vast a stride to empire that the world of 1860 stood already on a distant horizon somewhere on the same plane with the republic of Brutus and Cato, while schoolboys read of Abraham Lincoln as they did of Julius Caesar. Vast swarms of Americans knew the Civil War only by school history, as they knew the story of Cromwell or Cicero, and were as familiar with political assassination as though they had lived under Nero. The climax of empire could be seen approaching, year after year, as though Sulla were a President or McKinley a Consul.

Nothing annoyed Americans more than to be told this simple and obvious -- in no way unpleasant -- truth; therefore one sat silent as ever on the Capitol; but, by way of completing the lesson, the Lodges added a pilgrimage to Assisi and an interview with St. Francis, whose solution of historical riddles seemed the most satisfactory -- or sufficient -- ever offered; worth fully forty years' more study, and better worth it than Gibbon himself, or even St. Augustine, St. Ambrose, or St. Jerome. The most bewildering effect of all these fresh cross-lights on the old Assistant Professor of 1874 was due to the astonishing contrast between what he had taught then and what he found himself confusedly trying to learn five-and-twenty years afterwards -- between the twelfth century of his thirtieth and that of his sixtieth years. At Harvard College, weary of spirit in the wastes of Anglo-Saxon law, he had occasionally given way to outbursts of derision at shedding his life-blood for the sublime truths of Sac and Soc: --

    HIC JACET

    HOMUNCULUS SCRIPTOR

    DOCTOR BARBARICUS

     HENRICUS ADAMS

    ADAE FILIUS ET EVAE

    PRIMO EXPLICUIT

     SOCNAM

The Latin was as twelfth-century as the law, and he meant as satire the claim that he had been first to explain the legal meaning of Sac and Soc, although any German professor would have scorned it as a shameless and presumptuous bid for immortality; but the whole point of view had vanished in 1900. Not he, but Sir Henry Maine and Rudolph Sohm, were the parents or creators of Sac and Soc. Convinced that the clue of religion led to nothing, and that politics led to chaos, one had turned to the law, as one's scholars turned to the Law School, because one could see no other path to a profession.

The law had proved as futile as politics or religion, or any other single thread spun by the human spider; it offered no more continuity than architecture or coinage, and no more force of its own. St. Francis expressed supreme contempt for them all, and solved the whole problem by rejecting it altogether. Adams returned to Paris with a broken and contrite spirit, prepared to admit that his life had no meaning, and conscious that in any case it no longer mattered. He passed a summer of solitude contrasting sadly with the last at Surrenden; but the solitude did what the society did not -- it forced and drove him into the study of his ignorance in silence. Here at last he entered the practice of his final profession. Hunted by ennui, he could no longer escape, and, by way of a summer school, he began a methodical survey -- a triangulation -- of the twelfth century. The pursuit had a singular French charm which France had long lost -- a calmness, lucidity, simplicity of expression, vigor of action, complexity of local color, that made Paris flat. In the long summer days one found a sort of saturated green pleasure in the forests, and gray infinity of rest in the little twelfth-century churches that lined them, as unassuming as their own mosses, and as sure of their purpose as their round arches; but churches were many and summer was short, so that he was at last driven back to the quays and photographs. For weeks he lived in silence.

His solitude was broken in November by the chance arrival of John La Farge. At that moment, contact with La Farge had a new value. Of all the men who had deeply affected their friends since 1850 John La Farge was certainly the foremost, and for Henry Adams, who had sat at his feet since 1872, the question how much he owed to La Farge could be answered only by admitting that he had no standard to measure it by. Of all his friends La Farge alone owned a mind complex enough to contrast against the commonplaces of American uniformity, and in the process had vastly perplexed most Americans who came in contact with it. The American mind -- the Bostonian as well as the Southern or Western -- likes to walk straight up to its object, and assert or deny something that it takes for a fact; it has a conventional approach, a conventional analysis, and a conventional conclusion, as well as a conventional expression, all the time loudly asserting its unconventionality. The most disconcerting trait of John La Farge was his reversal of the process. His approach was quiet and indirect; he moved round an object, and never separated it from its surroundings; he prided himself on faithfulness to tradition and convention; he was never abrupt and abhorred dispute. His manners and attitude towards the universe were the same, whether tossing in the middle of the Pacific Ocean sketching the trade-wind from a whale-boat in the blast of sea-sickness, or drinking the cha-no-yu in the formal rites of Japan, or sipping his cocoanut cup of kava in the ceremonial of Samoan chiefs, or reflecting under the sacred bo-tree at Anaradjpura.

One was never quite sure of his whole meaning until too late to respond, for he had no difficulty in carrying different shades of contradiction in his mind. As he said of his friend Okakura, his thought ran as a stream runs through grass, hidden perhaps but always there; and one felt often uncertain in what direction it flowed, for even a contradiction was to him only a shade of difference, a complementary color, about which no intelligent artist would dispute. Constantly he repulsed argument: "Adams, you reason too much!" was one of his standing reproaches even in the mild discussion of rice and mangoes in the warm night of Tahiti dinners. He should have blamed Adams for being born in Boston. The mind resorts to reason for want of training, and Adams had never met a perfectly trained mind.

To La Farge, eccentricity meant convention; a mind really eccentric never betrayed it. True eccentricity was a tone -- a shade -- a nuance -- and the finer the tone, the truer the eccentricity. Of course all artists hold more or less the same point of view in their art, but few carry it into daily life, and often the contrast is excessive between their art and their talk. One evening Humphreys Johnston, who was devoted to La Farge, asked him to meet Whistler at dinner. La Farge was ill -- more ill than usual even for him -- but he admired and liked Whistler, and insisted on going. By chance, Adams was so placed as to overhear the conversation of both, and had no choice but to hear that of Whistler, which engrossed the table. At that moment the Boer War was raging, and, as every one knows, on that subject Whistler raged worse than the Boers. For two hours he declaimed against England -- witty, declamatory, extravagant, bitter, amusing, and noisy; but in substance what he said was not merely commonplace -- it was true! That is to say, his hearers, including Adams and, as far as he knew, La Farge, agreed with it all, and mostly as a matter of course; yet La Farge was silent, and this difference of expression was a difference of art. Whistler in his art carried the sense of nuance and tone far beyond any point reached by La Farge, or even attempted; but in talk he showed, above or below his color-instinct, a willingness to seem eccentric where no real eccentricity, unless perhaps of temper, existed.

This vehemence, which Whistler never betrayed in his painting, La Farge seemed to lavish on his glass. With the relative value of La Farge's glass in the history of glass-decoration, Adams was too ignorant to meddle, and as a rule artists were if possible more ignorant than he; but whatever it was, it led him back to the twelfth century and to Chartres where La Farge not only felt at home, but felt a sort of ownership. No other American had a right there, unless he too were a member of the Church and worked in glass. Adams himself was an interloper, but long habit led La Farge to resign himself to Adams as one who meant well, though deplorably Bostonian; while Adams, though near sixty years old before he knew anything either of glass or of Chartres, asked no better than to learn, and only La Farge could help him, for he knew enough at least to see that La Farge alone could use glass like a thirteenth-century artist. In Europe the art had been dead for centuries, and modern glass was pitiable. Even La Farge felt the early glass rather as a document than as a historical emotion, and in hundreds of windows at Chartres and Bourges and Paris, Adams knew barely one or two that were meant to hold their own against a color-scheme so strong as his. In conversation La Farge's mind was opaline with infinite shades and refractions of light, and with color toned down to the finest gradations. In glass it was insubordinate; it was renaissance; it asserted his personal force with depth and vehemence of tone never before seen. He seemed bent on crushing rivalry.

Even the gloom of a Paris December at the Elysee Palace Hotel was somewhat relieved by this companionship, and education made a step backwards towards Chartres, but La Farge's health became more and more alarming, and Adams was glad to get him safely back to New York, January 15, 1900, while he himself went at once to Washington to find out what had become of Hay. Nothing good could be hoped, for Hay's troubles had begun, and were quite as great as he had foreseen. Adams saw as little encouragement as Hay himself did, though he dared not say so. He doubted Hay's endurance, the President's firmness in supporting him, and the loyalty of his party friends; but all this worry on Hay's account fretted him not nearly so much as the Boer War did on his own. Here was a problem in his political education that passed all experience since the Treason winter of 1860-61! Much to his astonishment, very few Americans seemed to share his point of view; their hostility to England seemed mere temper; but to Adams the war became almost a personal outrage. He had been taught from childhood, even in England, that his forbears and their associates in 1776 had settled, once for all, the liberties of the British free colonies, and he very strongly objected to being thrown on the defensive again, and forced to sit down, a hundred and fifty years after John Adams had begun the task, to prove, by appeal to law and fact, that George Washington was not a felon, whatever might be the case with George III. For reasons still more personal, he declined peremptorily to entertain question of the felony of John Adams. He felt obliged to go even further, and avow the opinion that if at any time England should take towards Canada the position she took towards her Boer colonies, the United States would be bound, by their record, to interpose, and to insist on the application of the principles of 1776. To him the attitude of Mr. Chamberlain and his colleagues seemed exceedingly un-American, and terribly embarrassing to Hay.

Trained early, in the stress of civil war, to hold his tongue, and to help make the political machine run somehow, since it could never be made to run well, he would not bother Hay with theoretical objections which were every day fretting him in practical forms. Hay's chance lay in patience and good-temper till the luck should turn, and to him the only object was time; but as political education the point seemed vital to Adams, who never liked shutting his eyes or denying an evident fact. Practical politics consists in ignoring facts, but education and politics are two different and often contradictory things. In this case, the contradiction seemed crude.

With Hay's politics, at home or abroad, Adams had nothing whatever to do. Hay belonged to the New York school, like Abram Hewitt, Evarts, W. C. Whitney, Samuel J. Tilden -- men who played the game for ambition or amusement, and played it, as a rule, much better than the professionals, but whose aims were considerably larger than those of the usual player, and who felt no great love for the cheap drudgery of the work. In return, the professionals felt no great love for them, and set them aside when they could. Only their control of money made them inevitable, and even this did not always carry their points. The story of Abram Hewitt would offer one type of this statesman series, and that of Hay another. President Cleveland set aside the one; President Harrison set aside the other. "There is no politics in it," was his comment on Hay's appointment to office. Hay held a different opinion and turned to McKinley whose judgment of men was finer than common in Presidents. Mr. McKinley brought to the problem of American government a solution which lay very far outside of Henry Adams's education, but which seemed to be at least practical and American. He undertook to pool interests in a general trust into which every interest should be taken, more or less at its own valuation, and whose mass should, under his management, create efficiency. He achieved very remarkable results. How much they cost was another matter; if the public is ever driven to its last resources and the usual remedies of chaos, the result will probably cost more.

Himself a marvellous manager of men, McKinley found several manipulators to help him, almost as remarkable as himself, one of whom was Hay; but unfortunately Hay's strength was weakest and his task hardest. At home, interests could be easily combined by simply paying their price; but abroad whatever helped on one side, hurt him on another. Hay thought England must be brought first into the combine; but at that time Germany, Russia, and France were all combining against England, and the Boer War helped them. For the moment Hay had no ally, abroad or at home, except Pauncefote, and Adams always maintained that Pauncefote alone pulled him through.

Yet the difficulty abroad was far less troublesome than the obstacles at home. The Senate had grown more and more unmanageable, even since the time of Andrew Johnson, and this was less the fault of the Senate than of the system. "A treaty of peace, in any normal state of things," said Hay, "ought to be ratified with unanimity in twenty-four hours. They wasted six weeks in wrangling over this one, and ratified it with one vote to spare. We have five or six matters now demanding settlement. I can settle them all, honorably and advantageously to our own side; and I am assured by leading men in the Senate that not one of these treaties, if negotiated, will pass the Senate. I should have a majority in every case, but a malcontent third would certainly dish every one of them. To such monstrous shape has the original mistake of the Constitution grown in the evolution of our politics. You must understand, it is not merely my solution the Senate will reject. They will reject, for instance, any treaty, whatever, on any subject, with England. I doubt if they would accept any treaty of consequence with Russia or Germany. The recalcitrant third would be differently composed, but it would be on hand. So that the real duties of a Secretary of State seem to be three: to fight claims upon us by other States; to press more or less fraudulent claims of our own citizens upon other countries; to find offices for the friends of Senators when there are none. Is it worth while -- for me -- to keep up this useless labor?"

To Adams, who, like Hay, had seen a dozen acquaintances struggling with the same enemies, the question had scarcely the interest of a new study. He had said all he had to say about it in a dozen or more volumes relating to the politics of a hundred years before. To him, the spectacle was so familiar as to be humorous. The intrigue was too open to be interesting. The interference of the German and Russian legations, and of the Clan-na-Gael, with the press and the Senate was innocently undisguised. The charming Russian Minister, Count Cassini, the ideal of diplomatic manners and training, let few days pass without appealing through the press to the public against the government. The German Minister, Von Holleben, more cautiously did the same thing, and of course every whisper of theirs was brought instantly to the Department. These three forces, acting with the regular opposition and the natural obstructionists, could always stop action in the Senate. The fathers had intended to neutralize the energy of government and had succeeded, but their machine was never meant to do the work of a twenty-million horse-power society in the twentieth century, where much work needed to be quickly and efficiently done. The only defence of the system was that, as Government did nothing well, it had best do nothing; but the Government, in truth, did perfectly well all it was given to do; and even if the charge were true, it applied equally to human society altogether, if one chose to treat mankind from that point of view. As a matter of mechanics, so much work must be done; bad machinery merely added to friction.

Always unselfish, generous, easy, patient, and loyal, Hay had treated the world as something to be taken in block without pulling it to pieces to get rid of its defects; he liked it all: he laughed and accepted; he had never known unhappiness and would have gladly lived his entire life over again exactly as it happened. In the whole New York school, one met a similar dash of humor and cynicism more or less pronounced but seldom bitter. Yet even the gayest of tempers succumbs at last to constant friction The old friend was rapidly fading. The habit remained, but the easy intimacy, the careless gaiety, the casual humor, the equality of indifference, were sinking into the routine of office; the mind lingered in the Department; the thought failed to react; the wit and humor shrank within the blank walls of politics, and the irritations multiplied. To a head of bureau, the result seemed ennobling.

Although, as education, this branch of study was more familiar and older than the twelfth century, the task of bringing the two periods into a common relation was new. Ignorance required that these political and social and scientific values of the twelfth and twentieth centuries should be correlated in some relation of movement that could be expressed in mathematics, nor did one care in the least that all the world said it could not be done, or that one knew not enough mathematics even to figure a formula beyond the schoolboy $s = gt^2/2$. If Kepler and Newton could take liberties with the sun and moon, an obscure person in a remote wilderness like La Fayette Square could take liberties with Congress, and venture to multiply half its attraction into the square of its time. He had only to find a value, even infinitesimal, for its attraction at any given time. A historical formula that should satisfy the conditions of the stellar universe weighed heavily on his mind; but a trifling matter like this was one in which he could look for no help from anybody -- he could look only for derision at best.

All his associates in history condemned such an attempt as futile and almost immoral -- certainly hostile to sound historical system. Adams tried it only because of its hostility to all that he had taught for history, since he started afresh from the new point that, whatever was right, all he had ever taught was wrong. He had pursued ignorance thus far with success, and had swept his mind clear of knowledge. In beginning again, from the starting-point of Sir Isaac Newton, he looked about him in vain for a teacher. Few men in Washington cared to overstep the school conventions, and the most distinguished of them, Simon Newcomb, was too sound a mathematician to treat such a scheme seriously. The greatest of Americans, judged by his rank in science, Willard Gibbs, never came to Washington, and Adams never enjoyed a chance to meet him. After Gibbs, one of the most distinguished was Langley, of the Smithsonian, who was more accessible, to whom Adams had been much in the habit of turning whenever he wanted an outlet for his vast reservoirs of ignorance. Langley listened with outward patience to his disputatious questionings; but he too nourished a scientific passion for doubt, and sentimental attachment for its avowal. He had the physicist's heinous fault of professing to know nothing between flashes of intense perception. Like so many other great observers, Langley was not a mathematician, and like most physicists, he believed in physics. Rigidly denying himself the amusement of philosophy, which consists chiefly in suggesting unintelligible answers to insoluble problems, he still knew the problems, and liked to wander past them in a courteous temper, even bowing to them distantly as though recognizing their existence, while doubting their respectability. He generously let others doubt what he felt obliged to affirm; and early put into Adams's hands the "Concepts of Modern Science," a volume by Judge Stallo, which had been treated for a dozen years by the schools with a conspiracy of silence such as inevitably meets every revolutionary work that upsets the stock and machinery of instruction. Adams read and failed to understand; then he asked questions and failed to get answers.

Probably this was education. Perhaps it was the only scientific education open to a student sixty-odd years old, who asked to be as ignorant as an astronomer. For him the details of science meant nothing: he wanted to know its mass. Solar heat was not enough, or was too much. Kinetic atoms led only to motion; never to direction or progress. History had no use for multiplicity; it needed unity; it could study only motion, direction, attraction, relation. Everything must be made to move together; one must seek new worlds to measure; and so, like Rasselas, Adams set out once more, and found himself on May 12 settled in rooms at the very door of the Trocadero.

Chapter XXV. The Dynamo and the Virgin (1900)

UNTIL the Great Exposition of 1900 closed its doors in November, Adams haunted it, aching to absorb knowledge, and helpless to find it. He would have liked to know how much of it could have been grasped by the best-informed man in the world. While he was thus meditating chaos, Langley came by, and showed it to him. At Langley's behest, the Exhibition dropped its superfluous rags and stripped itself to the skin, for Langley knew what to study, and why, and how; while Adams might as well have stood outside in the night, staring at the Milky Way. Yet Langley said nothing new, and taught nothing that one might not have learned from Lord Bacon, three hundred years before; but though one should have known the "Advancement of Science" as well as one knew the "Comedy of Errors," the literary knowledge counted for nothing until some teacher should show how to apply it. Bacon took a vast deal of trouble in teaching King James I and his subjects, American or other, towards the year 1620, that true science was the development or economy of forces; yet an elderly American in 1900 knew neither the formula nor the forces; or even so much as to say to himself that his historical business in the Exposition concerned only the economies or developments of force since 1893, when he began the study at Chicago.

Nothing in education is so astonishing as the amount of ignorance it accumulates in the form of inert facts. Adams had looked at most of the accumulations of art in the storehouses called Art Museums; yet he did not know how to look at the art exhibits of 1900. He had studied Karl Marx and his doctrines of history with profound attention, yet he could not apply them at Paris. Langley, with the ease of a great master of experiment, threw out of the field every exhibit that did not reveal a new application of force, and naturally threw out, to begin with, almost the whole art exhibit. Equally, he ignored almost the whole industrial exhibit. He led his pupil directly to the forces. His chief interest was in new motors to make his airship feasible, and he taught Adams the astonishing complexities of the new Daimler motor, and of the automobile, which, since 1893, had become a nightmare at a hundred kilometres an hour, almost as destructive as the electric tram which was only ten years older; and threatening to become as terrible as the locomotive steam-engine itself, which was almost exactly Adams's own age.

Then he showed his scholar the great hall of dynamos, and explained how little he knew about electricity or force of any kind, even of his own special sun, which spouted heat in inconceivable volume, but which, as far as he knew, might spout less or more, at any time, for all the certainty he felt in it. To him, the dynamo itself was but an ingenious channel for conveying somewhere the heat latent in a few tons of poor coal hidden in a dirty engine-house carefully kept out of sight; but to Adams the dynamo became a symbol of infinity. As he grew accustomed to the great gallery of machines, he began to feel the forty-foot dynamos as a moral force, much as the early Christians felt the Cross. The planet itself seemed less impressive, in its old-fashioned, deliberate, annual or daily revolution, than this huge wheel, revolving within arm's length at some vertiginous speed, and barely murmuring -- scarcely humming an audible warning to stand a hair's-breadth further for respect of power -- while it would not wake the baby lying close against its frame. Before the end, one began to pray to it; inherited instinct taught the natural expression of man before silent and infinite force. Among the thousand symbols of ultimate energy the dynamo was not so human as some, but it was the most expressive.

Yet the dynamo, next to the steam-engine, was the most familiar of exhibits. For Adams's objects its value lay chiefly in its occult mechanism. Between the dynamo in the gallery of machines and the engine-house outside, the break of continuity amounted to abysmal fracture for a historian's objects. No more relation could he discover between the steam and the electric current than between the Cross and the cathedral. The forces were interchangeable if not reversible, but he could see only an absolute fiat in electricity as in faith. Langley could not help him. Indeed, Langley seemed to be worried by the same trouble, for he constantly repeated that the new forces were anarchical, and especially that he was not responsible for the new rays, that were little short of parricidal in their wicked spirit towards science. His own rays, with which he had doubled the solar spectrum, were altogether harmless and beneficent; but Radium denied its God -- or, what was to Langley the same thing, denied the truths of his Science. The force was wholly new.

A historian who asked only to learn enough to be as futile as Langley or Kelvin, made rapid progress under this teaching, and mixed himself up in the tangle of ideas until he achieved a sort of Paradise of ignorance vastly consoling to his fatigued senses. He wrapped himself in vibrations and rays which were new, and he would have hugged Marconi and Branly had he met them, as he hugged the dynamo; while he lost his arithmetic in trying to figure out the equation between the discoveries and the economies of force. The economies, like the discoveries, were absolute, supersensual, occult; incapable of expression in horse-power. What mathematical equivalent could he suggest as the value of a Branly coherer? Frozen air, or the electric furnace, had some scale of measurement, no doubt, if somebody could invent a thermometer adequate to the purpose; but X-rays had played no part whatever in man's consciousness, and the atom itself had figured only as a fiction of thought. In these seven years man had translated himself into a new universe which had no common scale of measurement with the old. He had entered a supersensual world, in which he could measure nothing except by chance collisions of movements imperceptible to his senses, perhaps even imperceptible to his instruments, but perceptible to each other, and so to some known ray at the end of the scale. Langley seemed prepared for anything, even for an indeterminable number of universes interfused -- physics stark mad in metaphysics.

Historians undertake to arrange sequences, -- called stories, or histories -- assuming in silence a relation of cause and effect. These assumptions, hidden in the depths of dusty libraries, have been astounding, but commonly unconscious and childlike; so much so, that if any captious critic were to drag them to light, historians would probably reply, with one voice, that they had never supposed themselves required to know what they were talking about. Adams, for one, had toiled in vain to find out what he meant. He had even published a dozen volumes of American history for no other purpose than to satisfy himself whether, by severest process of stating, with the least possible comment, such facts as seemed sure, in such order as seemed rigorously consequent, he could fix for a familiar moment a necessary sequence of human movement. The result had satisfied him as little as at Harvard College. Where he saw sequence, other men saw something quite different, and no one saw the same unit of measure. He cared little about his experiments and less about his statesmen, who seemed to him quite as ignorant as himself and, as a rule, no more honest; but he insisted on a relation of sequence, and if he could not reach it by one method, he would try as many methods as science knew. Satisfied that the sequence of men led to nothing and that the sequence of their society could lead no further, while the mere sequence of time was artificial, and the sequence of thought was chaos, he turned at last to the sequence of force; and thus it happened that, after ten years' pursuit, he found himself lying in the Gallery of Machines at the Great Exposition of 1900, his historical neck broken by the sudden irruption of forces totally new.

Since no one else showed much concern, an elderly person without other cares had no need to betray alarm. The year 1900 was not the first to upset schoolmasters. Copernicus and Galileo had broken many professorial necks about 1600; Columbus had stood the world on its head towards 1500; but the nearest approach to the revolution of 1900 was that of 310, when Constantine set up the Cross. The rays that Langley disowned, as well as those which he fathered, were occult, supersensual, irrational; they were a revelation of mysterious energy like that of the Cross; they were what, in terms of mediaeval science, were called immediate modes of the divine substance.

The historian was thus reduced to his last resources. Clearly if he was bound to reduce all these forces to a common value, this common value could have no measure but that of their attraction on his own mind. He must treat them as they had been felt; as convertible, reversible, interchangeable attractions on thought. He made up his mind to venture it; he would risk translating rays into faith. Such a reversible process would vastly amuse a chemist, but the chemist could not deny that he, or some of his fellow physicists, could feel the force of both. When Adams was a boy in Boston, the best chemist in the place had probably never heard of Venus except by way of scandal, or of the Virgin except as idolatry; neither had he heard of dynamos or automobiles or radium; yet his mind was ready to feel the force of all, though the rays were unborn and the women were dead.

Here opened another totally new education, which promised to be by far the most hazardous of all. The knife-edge along which he must crawl, like Sir Lancelot in the twelfth century, divided two kingdoms of force which had nothing in common but attraction. They were as different as a magnet is from gravitation, supposing one knew what a magnet was, or gravitation, or love. The force of the Virgin was still felt at Lourdes, and seemed to be as potent as X-rays; but in America neither Venus nor Virgin ever had value as force -- at most as sentiment. No American had ever been truly afraid of either.

This problem in dynamics gravely perplexed an American historian. The Woman had once been supreme; in France she still seemed potent, not merely as a sentiment, but as a force. Why was she unknown in America? For evidently America was ashamed of her, and she was ashamed of herself, otherwise they would not have strewn fig-leaves so profusely all over her. When she was a true force, she was ignorant of fig-leaves, but the monthly-magazine-made American female had not a feature that would have been recognized by Adam. The trait was notorious, and often humorous, but any one brought up among Puritans knew that sex was sin. In any previous age, sex was strength. Neither art nor beauty was needed. Every one, even among Puritans, knew that neither Diana of the Ephesians nor any of the Oriental goddesses was worshipped for her beauty. She was goddess because of her force; she was the animated dynamo; she was reproduction -- the greatest and most mysterious of all energies; all she needed was to be fecund. Singularly enough, not one of Adams's many schools of education had ever drawn his attention to the opening lines of Lucretius, though they were perhaps the finest in all Latin literature, where the poet invoked Venus exactly as Dante invoked the Virgin: --

"Quae quondam rerum naturam sola gubernas."

The Venus of Epicurean philosophy survived in the Virgin of the Schools: --

"Donna, sei tanto grande, e tanto vali,

Che qual vuol grazia, e a te non ricorre,

Sua disianza vuol volar senz' ali."

All this was to American thought as though it had never existed. The true American knew something of the facts, but nothing of the feelings; he read the letter, but he never felt the law. Before this historical chasm, a mind like that of Adams felt itself helpless; he turned from the Virgin to the Dynamo as though he were a Branly coherer. On one side, at the Louvre and at Chartres, as he knew by the record of work actually done and still before his eyes, was the highest energy ever known to man, the creator four-fifths of his noblest art, exercising vastly more attraction over the human mind than all the steam-engines and dynamos ever dreamed of; and yet this energy was unknown to the American mind. An American Virgin would never dare command; an American Venus would never dare exist.

The question, which to any plain American of the nineteenth century seemed as remote as it did to Adams, drew him almost violently to study, once it was posed; and on this point Langleys were as useless as though they were Herbert Spencers or dynamos. The idea survived only as art. There one turned as naturally as though the artist were himself a woman. Adams began to ponder, asking himself whether he knew of any American artist who had ever insisted on the power of sex, as every classic had always done; but he could think only of Walt Whitman; Bret Harte, as far as the magazines would let him venture; and one or two painters, for the flesh-tones. All the rest had used sex for sentiment, never for force; to them, Eve was a tender flower, and Herodias an unfeminine horror. American art, like the American language and American education, was as far as possible sexless. Society regarded this victory over sex as its greatest triumph, and the historian readily admitted it, since the moral issue, for the moment, did not concern one who was studying the relations of unmoral force. He cared nothing for the sex of the dynamo until he could measure its energy.

Vaguely seeking a clue, he wandered through the art exhibit, and, in his stroll, stopped almost every day before St. Gaudens's General Sherman, which had been given the central post of honor. St. Gaudens himself was in Paris, putting on the work his usual interminable last touches, and listening to the usual contradictory suggestions of brother sculptors. Of all the American artists who gave to American art whatever life it breathed in the seventies, St. Gaudens was perhaps the most sympathetic, but certainly the most inarticulate. General Grant or Don Cameron had scarcely less instinct of rhetoric than he. All the others -- the Hunts, Richardson, John La Farge, Stanford White -- were exuberant; only St. Gaudens could never discuss or dilate on an emotion, or suggest artistic arguments for giving to his work the forms that he felt. He never laid down the law, or affected the despot, or became brutalized like Whistler by the brutalities of his world. He required no incense; he was no egoist; his simplicity of thought was excessive; he could not imitate, or give any form but his own to the creations of his hand. No one felt more strongly than he the strength of other men, but the idea that they could affect him never stirred an image in his mind.

This summer his health was poor and his spirits were low. For such a temper, Adams was not the best companion, since his own gaiety was not folle; but he risked going now and then to the studio on Mont Parnasse to draw him out for a stroll in the Bois de Boulogne, or dinner as pleased his moods, and in return St. Gaudens sometimes let Adams go about in his company.

Once St. Gaudens took him down to Amiens, with a party of Frenchmen, to see the cathedral. Not until they found themselves actually studying the sculpture of the western portal, did it dawn on Adams's mind that, for his purposes, St. Gaudens on that spot had more interest to him than the cathedral itself. Great men before great monuments express great truths, provided they are not taken too solemnly. Adams never tired of quoting the supreme phrase of his idol Gibbon, before the Gothic cathedrals: "I darted a contemptuous look on the stately monuments of supersition." Even in the footnotes of his history, Gibbon had never inserted a bit of humor more human than this, and one would have paid largely for a photograph of the fat little historian, on the background of Notre Dame of Amiens, trying to persuade his readers -- perhaps himself -- that he was darting a contemptuous look on the stately monument, for which he felt in fact the respect which every man of his vast study and active mind always feels before objects worthy of it; but besides the humor, one felt also the relation. Gibbon ignored the Virgin, because in 1789 religious monuments were out of fashion. In 1900 his remark sounded fresh and simple as the green fields to ears that had heard a hundred years of other remarks, mostly no more fresh and certainly less simple. Without malice, one might find it more instructive than a whole lecture of Ruskin. One sees what one brings, and at that moment Gibbon brought the French Revolution. Ruskin brought reaction against the Revolution. St. Gaudens had passed beyond all. He liked the stately monuments much more than he liked Gibbon or Ruskin; he loved their dignity; their unity; their scale; their lines; their lights and shadows; their decorative sculpture; but he was even less conscious than they of the force that created it all -- the Virgin, the Woman -- by whose genius "the stately monuments of superstition" were built, through which she was expressed. He would have seen more meaning in Isis with the cow's horns, at Edfoo, who expressed the same thought. The art remained, but the energy was lost even upon the artist.

Yet in mind and person St. Gaudens was a survival of the 1500; he bore the stamp of the Renaissance, and should have carried an image of the Virgin round his neck, or stuck in his hat, like Louis XI. In mere time he was a lost soul that had strayed by chance to the twentieth century, and forgotten where it came from. He writhed and cursed at his ignorance, much as Adams did at his own, but in the opposite sense. St. Gaudens was a child of Benvenuto Cellini, smothered in an American cradle. Adams was a quintessence of Boston, devoured by curiosity to think like Benvenuto. St. Gaudens's art was starved from birth, and Adams's instinct was blighted from babyhood. Each had but half of a nature, and when they came together before the Virgin of Amiens they ought both to have felt in her the force that made them one; but it was not so. To Adams she became more than ever a channel of force; to St. Gaudens she remained as before a channel of taste.

For a symbol of power, St. Gaudens instinctively preferred the horse, as was plain in his horse and Victory of the Sherman monument. Doubtless Sherman also felt it so. The attitude was so American that, for at least forty years, Adams had never realized that any other could be in sound taste. How many years had he taken to admit a notion of what Michael Angelo and Rubens were driving at? He could not say; but he knew that only since 1895 had he begun to feel the Virgin or Venus as force, and not everywhere even so. At Chartres -- perhaps at Lourdes -- possibly at Cnidos if one could still find there the divinely naked Aphrodite of Praxiteles -- but otherwise one must look for force to the goddesses of Indian mythology. The idea died out long ago in the German and English stock. St. Gaudens at Amiens was hardly less sensitive to the force of the female energy than Matthew Arnold at the Grande Chartreuse. Neither of them felt goddesses as power -- only as reflected emotion, human expression, beauty, purity, taste, scarcely even as sympathy. They felt a railway train as power, yet they, and all other artists, constantly complained that the power embodied in a railway train could never be embodied in art. All the steam in the world could not, like the Virgin, build Chartres.

Yet in mechanics, whatever the mechanicians might think, both energies acted as interchangeable force on man, and by action on man all known force may be measured. Indeed, few men of science measured force in any other way. After once admitting that a straight line was the shortest distance between two points, no serious mathematician cared to deny anything that suited his convenience, and rejected no symbol, unproved or unproveable, that helped him to accomplish work. The symbol was force, as a compass-needle or a triangle was force, as the mechanist might prove by losing it, and nothing could be gained by ignoring their value. Symbol or energy, the Virgin had acted as the greatest force the Western world ever felt, and had drawn man's activities to herself more strongly than any other power, natural or supernatural, had ever done; the historian's business was to follow the track of the energy; to find where it came from and where it went to; its complex source and shifting channels; its values, equivalents, conversions. It could scarcely be more complex than radium; it could hardly be deflected, diverted, polarized, absorbed more perplexingly than other radiant matter. Adams knew nothing about any of them, but as a mathematical problem of influence on human progress, though all were occult, all reacted on his mind, and he rather inclined to think the Virgin easiest to handle.

The pursuit turned out to be long and tortuous, leading at last to the vast forests of scholastic science. From Zeno to Descartes, hand in hand with Thomas Aquinas, Montaigne, and Pascal, one stumbled as stupidly as though one were still a German student of 1860. Only with the instinct of despair could one force one's self into this old thicket of ignorance after having been repulsed a score of entrances more promising and more popular. Thus far, no path had led anywhere, unless perhaps to an exceedingly modest living. Forty-five years of study had proved to be quite futile for the pursuit of power; one controlled no more force in 1900 than in 1850, although the amount of force controlled by society had enormously increased. The secret of education still hid itself somewhere behind ignorance, and one fumbled over it as feebly as ever. In such labyrinths, the staff is a force almost more necessary than the legs; the pen becomes a sort of blind-man's dog, to keep him from falling into the gutters. The pen works for itself, and acts like a hand, modelling the plastic material over and over again to the form that suits it best. The form is never arbitrary, but is a sort of growth like crystallization, as any artist knows too well; for often the pencil or pen runs into side-paths and shapelessness, loses its relations, stops or is bogged. Then it has to return on its trail, and recover, if it can, its line of force. The result of a year's work depends more on what is struck out than on what is left in; on the sequence of the main lines of thought, than on their play or variety. Compelled once more to lean heavily on this support, Adams covered more thousands of pages with figures as formal as though they were algebra, laboriously striking out, altering, burning, experimenting, until the year had expired, the Exposition had long been closed, and winter drawing to its end, before he sailed from Cherbourg, on January 19, 1901, for home.

Chapter XXVI. Twilight (1901)

WHILE the world that thought itself frivolous, and submitted meekly to hearing itself decried as vain, fluttered through the Paris Exposition, jogging the futilities of St. Gaudens, Rodin, and Besnard, the world that thought itself serious, and showed other infallible marks of coming mental paroxysm, was engaged in weird doings at Peking and elsewhere such as startled even itself. Of all branches of education, the science of gauging people and events by their relative importance defies study most insolently. For three or four generations, society has united in withering with contempt and opprobrium the shameless futility of Mme. de Pompadour and Mme. du Barry; yet, if one bid at an auction for some object that had been approved by the taste of either lady, one quickly found that it were better to buy half-a-dozen Napoleons or Frederics, or Maria Theresas, or all the philosophy and science of their time, than to bid for a cane-bottomed chair that either of these two ladies had adorned. The same thing might be said, in a different sense, of Voltaire; while, as every one knows, the money-value of any hand-stroke of Watteau or Hogarth, Nattier or Sir Joshua, is out of all proportion to the importance of the men. Society seemed to delight in talking with solemn conviction about serious values, and in paying fantastic prices for nothing but the most futile. The drama acted at Peking, in the summer of 1900, was, in the eyes of a student, the most serious that could be offered for his study, since it brought him suddenly to the inevitable struggle for the control of China, which, in his view, must decide the control of the world; yet, as a money-value, the fall of China was chiefly studied in Paris and London as a calamity to Chinese porcelain. The value of a Ming vase was more serious than universal war.

The drama of the Legations interested the public much as though it were a novel of Alexandre Dumas, but the bearing of the drama on future history offered an interest vastly greater. Adams knew no more about it than though he were the best-informed statesman in Europe. Like them all, he took for granted that the Legations were massacred, and that John Hay, who alone championed China's "administrative entity," would be massacred too, since he must henceforth look on, in impotence, while Russia and Germany dismembered China, and shut up America at home. Nine statesmen out of ten, in Europe, accepted this result in advance, seeing no way to prevent it. Adams saw none, and laughed at Hay for his helplessness.

When Hay suddenly ignored European leadership, took the lead himself, rescued the Legations and saved China, Adams looked on, as incredulous as Europe, though not quite so stupid, since, on that branch of education, he knew enough for his purpose. Nothing so meteoric had ever been done in American diplomacy. On returning to Washington, January 30, 1901, he found most of the world as astonished as himself, but less stupid than usual. For a moment, indeed, the world had been struck dumb at seeing Hay put Europe aside and set the Washington Government at the head of civilization so quietly that civilization submitted, by mere instinct of docility, to receive and obey his orders; but, after the first shock of silence, society felt the force of the stroke through its fineness, and burst into almost tumultuous applause. Instantly the diplomacy of the nineteenth century, with all its painful scuffles and struggles, was forgotten, and the American blushed to be told of his submissions in the past. History broke in halves.

Hay was too good an artist not to feel the artistic skill of his own work, and the success reacted on his health, giving him fresh life, for with him as with most men, success was a tonic, and depression a specific poison; but as usual, his troubles nested at home. Success doubles strain. President McKinley's diplomatic court had become the largest in the world, and the diplomatic relations required far more work than ever before, while the staff of the Department was little more efficient, and the friction in the Senate had become coagulated. Hay took to studying the "Diary" of John Quincy Adams eighty years before, and calculated that the resistance had increased about ten times, as measured by waste of days and increase of effort, although Secretary of State J. Q. Adams thought himself very hardly treated. Hay cheerfully noted that it was killing him, and proved it, for the effort of the afternoon walk became sometimes painful.

For the moment, things were going fairly well, and Hay's unruly team were less fidgety, but Pauncefote still pulled the whole load and turned the dangerous corners safely, while Cassini and Holleben helped the Senate to make what trouble they could, without serious offence, and the Irish, after the genial Celtic nature, obstructed even themselves. The fortunate Irish, thanks to their sympathetic qualities, never made lasting enmities; but the Germans seemed in a fair way to rouse ill-will and even ugly temper in the spirit of politics, which was by no means a part of Hay's plans. He had as much as he could do to overcome domestic friction, and felt no wish to alienate foreign powers. Yet so much could be said in favor of the foreigners that they commonly knew why they made trouble, and were steady to a motive. Cassini had for years pursued, in Peking as in Washington, a policy of his own, never disguised, and as little in harmony with his chief as with Hay; he made his opposition on fixed lines for notorious objects; but Senators could seldom give a reason for obstruction. In every hundred men, a certain number obstruct by instinct, and try to invent reasons to explain it afterwards. The Senate was no worse than the board of a university; but incorporators as a rule have not made this class of men dictators on purpose to prevent action. In the Senate, a single vote commonly stopped legislation, or, in committee, stifled discussion.

Hay's policy of removing, one after another, all irritations, and closing all discussions with foreign countries, roused incessant obstruction, which could be overcome only by patience and bargaining in executive patronage, if indeed it could be overcome at all. The price actually paid was not very great except in the physical exhaustion of Hay and Pauncefote, Root and McKinley. No serious bargaining of equivalents could be attempted; Senators would not sacrifice five dollars in their own States to gain five hundred thousand in another; but whenever a foreign country was willing to surrender an advantage without an equivalent, Hay had a chance to offer the Senate a treaty. In all such cases the price paid for the treaty was paid wholly to the Senate, and amounted to nothing very serious except in waste of time and wear of strength. "Life is so gay and horrid!" laughed Hay; "the Major will have promised all the consulates in the service; the Senators will all come to me and refuse to believe me dis-consulate; I shall see all my treaties slaughtered, one by one, by the thirty-four per cent of kickers and strikers; the only mitigation I can foresee is being sick a good part of the time; I am nearing my grand climacteric, and the great culbute is approaching."

He was thinking of his friend Blaine, and might have thought of all his predecessors, for all had suffered alike, and to Adams as historian their sufferings had been a long delight -- the solitary picturesque and tragic element in politics -- incidentally requiring character-studies like Aaron Burr and William B. Giles, Calhoun and Webster and Sumner, with Sir Forcible Feebles like James M. Mason and stage exaggerations like Roscoe Conkling. The Senate took the place of

Shakespeare, and offered real Brutuses and Bolingbrokes, Jack Cades, Falstaffs, and Malvolios -- endless varieties of human nature nowhere else to be studied, and none the less amusing because they killed, or because they were like schoolboys in their simplicity. "Life is so gay and horrid!" Hay still felt the humor, though more and more rarely, but what he felt most was the enormous complexity and friction of the vast mass he was trying to guide. He bitterly complained that it had made him a bore -- of all things the most senatorial, and to him the most obnoxious. The old friend was lost, and only the teacher remained, driven to madness by the complexities and multiplicities of his new world.

To one who, at past sixty years old, is still passionately seeking education, these small, or large, annoyances had no great value except as measures of mass and motion. For him the practical interest and the practical man were such as looked forward to the next election, or perhaps, in corporations, five or ten years. Scarcely half-a-dozen men in America could be named who were known to have looked a dozen years ahead; while any historian who means to keep his alignment with past and future must cover a horizon of two generations at least. If he seeks to align himself with the future, he must assume a condition of some sort for a world fifty years beyond his own. Every historian -- sometimes unconsciously, but always inevitably -- must have put to himself the question: How long could such-or-such an outworn system last? He can never give himself less than one generation to show the full effects of a changed condition. His object is to triangulate from the widest possible base to the furthest point he thinks he can see, which is always far beyond the curvature of the horizon.

To the practical man, such an attempt is idiotic, and probably the practical man is in the right to-day; but, whichever is right -- if the question of right or wrong enters at all into the matter -- the historian has no choice but to go on alone. Even in his own profession few companions offer help, and his walk soon becomes solitary, leading further and further into a wilderness where twilight is short and the shadows are dense. Already Hay literally staggered in his tracks for weariness. More worn than he, Clarence King dropped. One day in the spring he stopped an hour in Washington to bid good-bye, cheerily and simply telling how his doctors had condemned him to Arizona for his lungs. All three friends knew that they were nearing the end, and that if it were not the one it would be the other; but the affectation of readiness for death is a stage role, and stoicism is a stupid resource, though the only one. Non doles, Paete! One is ashamed of it even in the acting.

The sunshine of life had not been so dazzling of late but that a share of it flickered out for Adams and Hay when King disappeared from their lives; but Hay had still his family and ambition, while Adams could only blunder back alone, helplessly, wearily, his eyes rather dim with tears, to his vague trail across the darkening prairie of education, without a motive, big or small, except curiosity to reach, before he too should drop, some point that would give him a far look ahead. He was morbidly curious to see some light at the end of the passage, as though thirty years were a shadow, and he were again to fall into King's arms at the door of the last and only log cabin left in life. Time had become terribly short, and the sense of knowing so little when others knew so much, crushed out hope.

He knew not in what new direction to turn, and sat at his desk, idly pulling threads out of the tangled skein of science, to see whether or why they aligned themselves. The commonest and oldest toy he knew was the child's magnet, with which he had played since babyhood, the most familiar of puzzles. He covered his desk with magnets, and mapped out their lines of force by compass. Then he read all the books he could find, and tried in vain to makes his lines of force agree with theirs. The books confounded him. He could not credit his own understanding. Here was literally the most concrete fact in nature, next to gravitation which it defied; a force which must have radiated lines of energy without stop, since time began, if not longer, and which might probably go on radiating after the sun should fall into the earth, since no one knew why -- or how -- or what it radiated -- or even whether it radiated at all. Perhaps the earliest known of all natural forces after the solar energies, it seemed to have suggested no idea to any one until some mariner bethought himself that it might serve for a pointer. Another thousand years passed when it taught some other intelligent man to use it as a pump, supply-pipe, sieve, or reservoir for collecting electricity, still without knowing how it worked or what it was. For a historian, the story of Faraday's experiments and the invention of the dynamo passed belief; it revealed a condition of human ignorance and helplessness before the commonest forces, such as his mind refused to credit. He could not conceive but that some one, somewhere, could tell him all about the magnet, if one could but find the book -- although he had been forced to admit the same helplessness in the face of gravitation, phosphorescence, and odors; and he could imagine no reason why society should treat radium as revolutionary in science when every infant, for ages past, had seen the magnet doing what radium did; for surely the kind of radiation mattered nothing compared with the energy that radiated and the matter supplied for radiation. He dared not venture into the complexities of chemistry, or microbes, so long as this child's toy offered complexities that befogged his mind beyond X-rays, and turned the atom into an endless variety of pumps endlessly pumping an endless variety of ethers. He wanted to ask Mme. Curie to invent a motor attachable to her salt of radium, and pump its forces through it, as Faraday did with a magnet. He figured the human mind itself as another radiating matter through which man had always pumped a subtler fluid.

In all this futility, it was not the magnet or the rays or the microbes that troubled him, or even his helplessness before the forces. To that he was used from childhood. The magnet in its new relation staggered his new education by its evidence of growing complexity, and multiplicity, and even contradiction, in life. He could not escape it; politics or science, the lesson was the same, and at every step it blocked his path whichever way he turned. He found it in politics; he ran against it in science; he struck it in everyday life, as though he were still Adam in the Garden of Eden between God who was unity, and Satan who was complexity, with no means of deciding which was truth. The problem was the same for McKinley as for Adam, and for the Senate as for Satan. Hay was going to wreck on it, like King and Adams.

All one's life, one had struggled for unity, and unity had always won. The National Government and the national unity had overcome every resistance, and the Darwinian evolutionists were triumphant over all the curates; yet the greater the unity and the momentum, the worse became the complexity and the friction. One had in vain bowed one's neck to railways, banks, corporations, trusts, and even to the popular will as far as one could understand it -- or even further; the multiplicity of unity had steadily increased, was increasing, and threatened to increase beyond reason. He had surrendered all his favorite prejudices, and foresworn even the forms of criticism -- except for his pet amusement, the Senate, which was a tonic or stimulant necessary to healthy life; he had accepted uniformity and Pteraspis and ice age and tramways and telephones; and now -- just when he was ready to hang the crowning garland on the brow of a completed education -- science itself warned him to begin it again from the beginning.

Maundering among the magnets he bethought himself that once, a full generation earlier, he had begun active life by writing a confession of geological faith at the bidding of Sir Charles Lyell, and that it might be worth looking at if only to steady his vision. He read it again, and thought it better than he could do at sixty-three; but elderly minds always work loose. He saw his doubts grown larger, and became curious to know what had been said about them since 1870. The Geological Survey supplied stacks of volumes, and reading for steady months; while, the longer he read, the more he wondered, pondered, doubted what his delightful old friend Sir Charles Lyell would have said about it.

Truly the animal that is to be trained to unity must be caught young. Unity is vision; it must have been part of the process of learning to see. The older the mind, the older its complexities, and the further it looks, the more it sees, until even the stars resolve themselves into multiples; yet the child will always see but one. Adams asked whether geology since 1867 had drifted towards unity or multiplicity, and he felt that the drift would depend on the age of the man who drifted.

Seeking some impersonal point for measure, he turned to see what had happened to his oldest friend and cousin the ganoid fish, the Pteraspis of Ludlow and Wenlock, with whom he had sported when geological life was young; as though they had all remained together in time to act the Mask of Comus at Ludlow Castle, and repeat "how charming is divine philosophy!" He felt almost aggrieved to find Walcott so vigorously acting the part of Comus as to have flung the ganoid all the way off to Colorado and far back into the Lower Trenton limestone, making the Pteraspis as modern as a Mississippi gar-pike by spawning an ancestry for him, indefinitely more remote, in the dawn of known organic life. A few thousand feet, more or less, of limestone were the liveliest amusement to the ganoid, but they buried the uniformitarian alive, under the weight of his own uniformity. Not for all the ganoid fish that ever swam, would a discreet historian dare to hazard even in secret an opinion about the value of Natural Selection by Minute Changes under Uniform Conditions, for he could know no more about it than most of his neighbors who knew nothing; but natural selection that did not select -- evolution finished before it began -- minute changes that refused to change anything during the whole geological record - survival of the highest order in a fauna which had no origin -- uniformity under conditions which had disturbed everything else in creation -- to an honest-meaning though ignorant student who needed to prove Natural Selection and not assume it, such sequence brought no peace. He wished to be shown that changes in form caused evolution in force; that chemical or mechanical energy had by natural selection and minute changes, under uniform conditions, converted itself into thought. The ganoid fish seemed to prove -- to him -- that it had selected neither new form nor new force, but that the curates were right in thinking that force could be increased in volume or raised in intensity only by help of outside force. To him, the ganoid was a huge perplexity, none the less because neither he nor the ganoid troubled Darwinians, but the more because it helped to reveal that Darwinism seemed to survive only in England. In vain he asked what sort of evolution had taken its place. Almost any doctrine seemed orthodox. Even sudden conversions due to mere vital force acting on its own lines quite beyond mechanical explanation, had cropped up again. A little more, and he would be driven back on the old independence of species.

What the ontologist thought about it was his own affair, like the theologist's views on theology, for complexity was nothing to them; but to the historian who sought only the direction of thought and had begun as the confident child of Darwin and Lyell in 1867, the matter of direction seemed vital. Then he had entered gaily the door of the glacial epoch, and had surveyed a universe of unities and uniformities. In 1900 he entered a far vaster universe, where all the old roads ran about in every direction, overrunning, dividing, subdividing, stopping abruptly, vanishing slowly, with side-paths that led nowhere, and sequences that could not be proved. The active geologists had mostly become specialists dealing with complexities far too technical for an amateur, but the old formulas still seemed to serve for beginners, as they had served when new.

So the cause of the glacial epoch remained at the mercy of Lyell and Croll, although Geikie had split up the period into half-a-dozen intermittent chills in recent geology and in the northern hemisphere alone, while no geologist had ventured to assert that the glaciation of the southern hemisphere could possibly be referred to a horizon more remote. Continents still rose wildly and wildly sank, though Professor Suess of Vienna had written an epoch-making work, showing that continents were anchored like crystals, and only oceans rose and sank. Lyell's genial uniformity seemed genial still, for nothing had taken its place, though, in the interval, granite had grown young, nothing had been explained, and a bewildering system of huge overthrusts had upset geological mechanics. The textbooks refused even to discuss theories, frankly throwing up their hands and avowing that progress depended on studying each rock as a law to itself.

Adams had no more to do with the correctness of the science than the gar-pike or the Port Jackson shark, for its correctness in no way concerned him, and only impertinence could lead him to dispute or discuss the principles of any science; but the history of the mind concerned the historian alone, and the historian had no vital concern in anything else, for he found no change to record in the body. In thought the Schools, like the Church, raised ignorance to a faith and degraded dogma to heresy. Evolution survived like the trilobites without evolving, and yet the evolutionists held the whole field, and had even plucked up courage to rebel against the Cossack ukase of Lord Kelvin forbidding them to ask more than twenty million years for their experiments. No doubt the geologists had always submitted sadly to this last and utmost violence inflicted on them by the Pontiff of Physical Religion in the effort to force unification of the universe; they had protested with mild conviction that they could not state the geological record in terms of time; they had murmured Ignoramus under their breath; but they had never dared to assert the Ignorabimus that lay on the tips of their tongues.

Yet the admission seemed close at hand. Evolution was becoming change of form broken by freaks of force, and warped at times by attractions affecting intelligence, twisted and tortured at other times by sheer violence, cosmic, chemical, solar, supersensual, electrolytic -- who knew what? -- defying science, if not denying known law; and the wisest of men could but imitate the Church, and invoke a "larger synthesis" to unify the anarchy again. Historians have got into far too much trouble by following schools of theology in their efforts to enlarge their synthesis, that they should willingly repeat the process in science. For human purposes a point must always be soon reached where larger synthesis is suicide.

Politics and geology pointed alike to the larger synthesis of rapidly increasing complexity; but still an elderly man knew that the change might be only in himself. The admission cost nothing. Any student, of any age, thinking only of a thought and not of his thought, should delight in turning about and trying the opposite motion, as he delights in the spring which brings even to a tired and irritated statesman the larger synthesis of peach-blooms, cherry-blossoms, and dogwood, to prove the folly of fret. Every schoolboy knows that this sum of all knowledge never saved him from whipping; mere years help nothing; King and Hay and Adams could neither of them escape floundering through the corridors of chaos that opened as they passed to the end; but they could at least float with the stream if they only knew which way the current ran. Adams would have liked to begin afresh with the Limulus and Lepidosteus in the waters of Braintree, side by side with Adamses and Quincys and Harvard College, all unchanged and unchangeable since archaic time; but what purpose would it serve? A seeker of truth -- or illusion -- would be none the less restless, though a shark!

Chapter XXVII. Teufelsdrockh (1901)

INEVITABLE Paris beckoned, and resistance became more and more futile as the store of years grew less; for the world contains no other spot than Paris where education can be pursued from every side. Even more vigorously than in the twelfth century, Paris taught in the twentieth, with no other school approaching it for variety of direction and energy of mind. Of the teaching in detail, a man who knew only what accident had taught him in the nineteenth century, could know next to nothing, since science had got quite beyond his horizon, and mathematics had become the only necessary language of thought; but one could play with the toys of childhood, including Ming porcelain, salons of painting, operas and theatres, beaux-arts and Gothic architecture, theology and anarchy, in any jumble of time; or totter about with Joe Stickney, talking Greek philosophy or recent poetry, or discussing the charm of youth and the Seine with Bay Lodge and his exquisite young wife. Paris remained Parisian in spite of change, mistress of herself though China fell. Scores of artists -- sculptors and painters, poets and dramatists, workers in gems and metals, designers in stuffs and furniture -- hundreds of chemists, physicists, even philosophers, philologists, physicians, and historians -- were at work, a thousand times as actively as ever before, and the mass and originality of their product would have swamped any previous age, as it very nearly swamped its own; but the effect was one of chaos, and Adams stood as helpless before it as before the chaos of New York. His single thought was to keep in front of the movement, and, if necessary, lead it to chaos, but never fall behind. Only the young have time to linger in the rear.

The amusements of youth had to be abandoned, for not even pugilism needs more staying-power than the labors of the pale-faced student of the Latin Quarter in the haunts of Montparnasse or Montmartre, where one must feel no fatigue at two o'clock in the morning in a beer- garden even after four hours of Mounet Sully at the Theatre Francais. In those branches, education might be called closed. Fashion, too, could no longer teach anything worth knowing to a man who, holding open the door into the next world, regarded himself as merely looking round to take a last glance of this. The glance was more amusing than any he had known in his active life, but it was more -- infinitely more -- chaotic and complex.

Still something remained to be done for education beyond the chaos, and as usual the woman helped. For thirty years or there-abouts, he had been repeating that he really must go to Baireuth. Suddenly Mrs. Lodge appeared on the horizon and bade him come. He joined them, parents and children, alert and eager and appreciative as ever, at the little old town of Rothenburg-on-the Taube, and they went on to the Baireuth festival together.

Thirty years earlier, a Baireuth festival would have made an immense stride in education, and the spirit of the master would have opened a vast new world. In 1901 the effect was altogether different from the spirit of the master. In 1876 the rococo setting of Baireuth seemed the correct atmosphere for Siegfried and Brunhilde, perhaps even for Parsifal. Baireuth was out of the world, calm, contemplative, and remote. In 1901 the world had altogether changed, and Wagner had become a part of it, as familiar as Shakespeare or Bret Harte. The rococo element jarred. Even the Hudson and the Susquehanna -- perhaps the Potomac itself -- had often risen to drown out the gods of Walhalla, and one could hardly listen to the "Gotterdammerung" in New York, among throngs of intense young enthusiasts, without paroxysms of nervous excitement that toned down to musical philistinism at Baireuth, as though the gods were Bavarian composers. New York or Paris might be whatever one pleased -- venal, sordid, vulgar -- but society nursed there, in the rottenness of its decay, certain anarchistic ferments, and thought them proof of art. Perhaps they were; and at all events, Wagner was chiefly responsible for them as artistic emotion. New York knew better than Baireuth what Wagner meant, and the frivolities of Paris had more than once included the rising of the Seine to drown out the Etoile or Montmartre, as well as the sorcery of ambition that casts spells of enchantment on the hero. Paris still felt a subtile flattery in the thought that the last great tragedy of gods and men would surely happen there, while no one could conceive of its happening at Baireuth, or would care if it did. Paris coquetted with catastrophe as though it were an old mistress -- faced it almost gaily as she had done so often, for they were acquainted since Rome began to ravage Europe; while New York met it with a glow of fascinated horror, like an inevitable earthquake, and heard Ternina announce it with conviction that made nerves quiver and thrill as they had long ceased to do under the accents of popular oratory proclaiming popular virtue. Flattery had lost its charm, but the Fluch-motif went home.

Adams had been carried with the tide till Brunhilde had become a habit and Ternina an ally. He too had played with anarchy; though not with socialism, which, to young men who nourished artistic emotions under the dome of the Pantheon, seemed hopelessly bourgeois, and lowest middle-class. Bay Lodge and Joe Stickney had given birth to the wholly new and original party of Conservative Christian Anarchists, to restore true poetry under the inspiration of the "Gotterdammerung." Such a party saw no inspiration in Baireuth, where landscape, history, and audience were -- relatively -- stodgy, and where the only emotion was a musical dilettantism that the master had abhorred.

Yet Baireuth still amused even a conservative Christian anarchist who cared as little as "Grane, mein Ross," whether the singers sang false, and who came only to learn what Wagner had supposed himself to mean. This end attained as pleased Frau Wagner and the Heiliger Geist, he was ready to go on; and the Senator, yearning for sterner study, pointed to a haven at Moscow. For years Adams had taught American youth never to travel without a Senator who was useful even in America at times, but indispensable in Russia where, in 1901, anarchists, even though conservative and Christian, were ill-seen.

This wing of the anarchistic party consisted rigorously of but two members, Adams and Bay Lodge. The conservative Christian anarchist, as a party, drew life from Hegel and Schopenhauer rightly understood. By the necessity of their philosophical descent, each member of the fraternity denounced the other as unequal to his lofty task and inadequate to grasp it. Of course, no third member could be so much as considered, since the great principle of contradiction could be expressed only by opposites; and no agreement could be conceived, because anarchy, by definition, must be chaos and collision, as in the kinetic theory of a perfect gas. Doubtless this law of contradiction was itself agreement, a restriction of personal liberty inconsistent with freedom; but the "larger synthesis" admitted a limited agreement provided it were strictly confined to the end of larger contradiction. Thus the great end of all philosophy -- the "larger synthesis" -- was attained, but the process was arduous, and while Adams, as the older member, assumed to declare the principle, Bay Lodge necessarily denied both the assumption and the principle in order to assure its truth.

Adams proclaimed that in the last synthesis, order and anarchy were one, but that the unity was chaos. As anarchist, conservative and Christian, he had no motive or duty but to attain the end; and, to hasten it, he was bound to accelerate progress; to concentrate energy; to accumulate power; to multiply and intensify forces; to reduce friction, increase velocity and magnify momentum, partly because this was the mechanical law of the universe as science explained it; but partly also in order to get done with the present which artists and some others complained of; and finally -- and chiefly -- because a rigorous philosophy required it, in order to penetrate the beyond, and satisfy man's destiny by reaching the largest synthesis in its ultimate contradiction.

Of course the untaught critic instantly objected that this scheme was neither conservative, Christian, nor anarchic, but such objection meant only that the critic should begin his education in any infant school in order to learn that anarchy which should be logical would cease to be anarchic. To the conservative Christian anarchist, the amiable doctrines of Kropotkin were sentimental ideas of Russian mental inertia covered with the name of anarchy merely to disguise their innocence; and the outpourings of Elisee Reclus were ideals of the French ouvrier, diluted with absinthe, resulting in a bourgeois dream of order and inertia. Neither made a pretence of anarchy except as a momentary stage towards order and unity. Neither of them had formed any other conception of the universe than what they had inherited from the priestly class to which their minds obviously belonged. With them, as with the socialist, communist, or collectivist, the mind that followed nature had no relation; if anarchists needed order, they must go back to the twelfth century where their thought had enjoyed its thousand years of reign. The conservative Christian anarchist could have no associate, no object, no faith except the nature of nature itself; and his "larger synthesis" had only the fault of being so supremely true that even the highest obligation of duty could scarcely oblige Bay Lodge to deny it in order to prove it. Only the self-evident truth that no philosophy of order -- except the Church -- had ever satisfied the philosopher reconciled the conservative Christian anarchist to prove his own.

Naturally these ideas were so far in advance of the age that hardly more people could understand them than understood Wagner or Hegel; for that matter, since the time of Socrates, wise men have been mostly shy of claiming to understand anything; but such refinements were Greek or German, and affected the practical American but little. He admitted that, for the moment, the darkness was dense. He could not affirm with confidence, even to himself, that his "largest synthesis" would certainly turn out to be chaos, since he would be equally obliged to deny the chaos. The poet groped blindly for an emotion. The play of thought for thought's sake had mostly ceased. The throb of fifty or a hundred million steam horse-power, doubling every ten years, and already more despotic than all the horses that ever lived, and all the riders they ever carried, drowned rhyme and reason. No one was to blame, for all were equally servants of the power, and worked merely to increase it; but the conservative Christian anarchist saw light.

Thus the student of Hegel prepared himself for a visit to Russia in order to enlarge his "synthesis" -- and much he needed it! In America all were conservative Christian anarchists; the faith was national, racial, geographic. The true American had never seen such supreme virtue in any of the innumerable shades between social anarchy and social order as to mark it for exclusively human and his own. He never had known a complete union either in Church or State or thought, and had never seen any need for it. The freedom gave him courage to meet any contradiction, and intelligence enough to ignore it. Exactly the opposite condition had marked Russian growth. The Czar's empire was a phase of conservative Christian anarchy more interesting to history than all the complex variety of American newspapers, schools, trusts, sects, frauds, and Congressmen. These were Nature -- pure and anarchic as the conservative Christian anarchist saw Nature -- active, vibrating, mostly unconscious, and quickly reacting on force; but, from the first glimpse one caught from the sleeping-car window, in the early morning, of the Polish Jew at the accidental railway station, in all his weird horror, to the last vision of the Russian peasant, lighting his candle and kissing his ikon before the railway Virgin in the station at St. Petersburg, all was logical, conservative, Christian and anarchic. Russia had nothing in common with any ancient or modern world that history knew; she had been the oldest source of all civilization in Europe, and had kept none for herself; neither Europe nor Asia had ever known such a phase, which seemed to fall into no line of evolution whatever, and was as wonderful to the student of Gothic architecture in the twelfth century, as to the student of the dynamo in the twentieth. Studied in the dry light of conservative Christian anarchy, Russia became luminous like the salt of radium; but with a negative luminosity as though she were a substance whose energies had been sucked out -- an inert residuum -- with movement of pure inertia. From the car window one seemed to float past undulations of nomad life -- herders deserted by their leaders and herds -- wandering waves stopped in their wanderings -- waiting for their winds or warriors to return and lead them westward; tribes that had camped, like Khirgis, for the season, and had lost the means of motion without acquiring the habit of permanence. They waited and suffered. As they stood they were out of place, and could never have been normal. Their country acted as a sink of energy like the Caspian Sea, and its surface kept the uniformity of ice and snow. One Russian peasant kissing an ikon on a saint's day, in the Kremlin, served for a hundred million. The student had no need to study Wallace, or re-read Tolstoy or Tourguenieff or Dostoiewski to refresh his memory of the most poignant analysis of human inertia ever put in words; Gorky was more than enough: Kropotkin answered every purpose.

The Russian people could never have changed -- could they ever be changed? Could inertia of race, on such a scale, be broken up, or take new form? Even in America, on an infinitely smaller scale, the question was old and unanswered. All the so-called primitive races, and some nearer survivals, had raised doubts which persisted against the most obstinate convictions of evolution. The Senator himself shook his head, and after surveying Warsaw and Moscow to his content, went on to St. Petersburg to ask questions of Mr. de Witte and Prince Khilkoff. Their conversation added new doubts; for their efforts had been immense, their expenditure enormous, and their results on the people seemed to be uncertain as yet, even to themselves. Ten or fifteen years of violent stimulus seemed resulting in nothing, for, since 1898, Russia lagged.

The tourist-student, having duly reflected, asked the Senator whether he should allow three generations, or more, to swing the Russian people into the Western movement. The Senator seemed disposed to ask for more. The student had nothing to say. For him, all opinion founded on fact must be error, because the facts can never be complete, and their relations must be always infinite. Very likely, Russia would instantly become the most brilliant constellation of human progress through all the ordered stages of good; but meanwhile one might give a value as movement of inertia to the mass, and assume a slow acceleration that would, at the end of a generation, leave the gap between east and west relatively the same. This result reached, the Lodges thought their moral improvement required a visit to Berlin; but forty years of varied emotions had not deadened Adams's memories of Berlin, and he preferred, at any cost, to escape new ones. When the Lodges started for Germany, Adams took steamer for Sweden and landed happily, in a day or two, at Stockholm.

Until the student is fairly sure that his problem is soluble, he gains little by obstinately insisting on solving it. One might doubt whether Mr. de Witte himself, or Prince Khilkoff, or any Grand Duke, or the Emperor, knew much more about it than their neighbors; and Adams was quite sure that, even in America, he should listen with uncertain confidence to the views of any Secretary of the Treasury, or railway president, or President of the United States whom he had ever known, that should concern the America of the next generation. The mere fact that any man should dare to offer them would prove his incompetence to judge. Yet Russia was too vast a force to be treated as an object of unconcern. As inertia, if in no other way, she represented three-fourths of the human race, and her movement might be the true movement of the future, against the hasty and unsure acceleration of America. No one could yet know what would best suit humanity, and the tourist who carried his La Fontaine in mind, caught himself talking as bear or as monkey according to the mirror he held before him. "Am I satisfied? " he asked: --

"Moi? pourquoi non?

N'ai-je pas quatre pieds aussi bien que les autres?

Mon portrait jusqu'ici ne m'a rien reproche;

Mais pour mon frere l'ours, on ne l'a qu'ebauche;

Jamais, s'il me veut croire, il ne se fera peindre."

Granting that his brother the bear lacked perfection in details, his own figure as monkey was not necessarily ideal or decorative, nor was he in the least sure what form it might take even in one generation. He had himself never ventured to dream of three. No man could guess what the Daimler motor and X-rays would do to him; but so much was sure; the monkey and motor were terribly afraid of the bear; how much,- only a man close to their foreign departments knew. As the monkey looked back across the Baltic from the safe battlements of Stockholm, Russia looked more portentous than from the Kremlin.

The image was that of the retreating ice-cap -- a wall of archaic glacier, as fixed, as ancient, as eternal, as the wall of archaic ice that blocked the ocean a few hundred miles to the northward, and more likely to advance. Scandinavia had been ever at its mercy. Europe had never changed. The imaginary line that crossed the level continent from the Baltic to the Black Sea, merely extended the northern barrier-line. The Hungarians and Poles on one side still struggled against the Russian inertia of race, and retained their own energies under the same conditions that caused inertia across the frontier. Race ruled the conditions; conditions hardly affected race; and yet no one could tell the patient tourist what race was, or how it should be known. History offered a feeble and delusive smile at the sound of the word; evolutionists and ethnologists disputed its very existence; no one knew what to make of it; yet, without the clue, history was a nursery tale.

The Germans, Scandinavians, Poles and Hungarians, energetic as they were, had never held their own against the heterogeneous mass of inertia called Russia, and trembled with terror whenever Russia moved. From Stockholm one looked back on it as though it were an ice-sheet, and so had Stockholm watched it for centuries. In contrast with the dreary forests of Russia and the stern streets of St. Petersburg, Stockholm seemed a southern vision, and Sweden lured the tourist on. Through a cheerful New England landscape and bright autumn, he rambled northwards till he found himself at Trondhjem and discovered Norway. Education crowded upon him in immense masses as he triangulated these vast surfaces of history about which he had lectured and read for a life-time. When the historian fully realizes his ignorance -- which sometimes happens to Americans -- he becomes even more tiresome to himself than to others, because his naivete is irrepressible. Adams could not get over his astonishment, though he had preached the Norse doctrine all his life against the stupid and beer-swilling Saxon boors whom Freeman loved, and who, to the despair of science, produced Shakespeare. Mere contact with Norway started voyages of thought, and, under their illusions, he took the mail steamer to the north, and on September 14, reached Hammerfest.

Frivolous amusement was hardly what one saw, through the equinoctial twilight, peering at the flying tourist, down the deep fiords, from dim patches of snow, where the last Laps and reindeer were watching the mail-steamer thread the intricate channels outside, as their ancestors had watched the first Norse fishermen learn them in the succession of time; but it was not the Laps, or the snow, or the arctic gloom, that impressed the tourist, so much as the lights of an electro-magnetic civilization and the stupefying contrast with Russia, which more and more insisted on taking the first place in historical interest. Nowhere had the new forces so vigorously corrected the errors of the old, or so effectively redressed the balance of the ecliptic. As one approached the end -- the spot where, seventy years before, a futile Carlylean Teufelsdrockh had stopped to ask futile questions of the silent infinite -- the infinite seemed to have become loquacious, not to say familiar, chattering gossip in one's ear. An installation of electric lighting and telephones led tourists close up to the polar ice-cap, beyond the level of the magnetic pole; and there the newer Teufelsdrockh sat dumb with surprise, and glared at the permanent electric lights of Hammerfest.

He had good reason -- better than the Teufelsdrockh of 1830, in his liveliest Scotch imagination, ever dreamed, or mortal man had ever told. At best, a week in these dim Northern seas, without means of speech, within the Arctic circle, at the equinox, lent itself to gravity if not to gloom; but only a week before, breakfasting in the restaurant at Stockholm, his eye had caught, across, the neighboring table, a headline in a Swedish newspaper, announcing an attempt on the life of President McKinley, and from Stockholm to Trondhjem, and so up the coast to Hammerfest, day after day the news came, telling of the President's condition, and the doings and sayings of Hay and Roosevelt, until at last a little journal was cried on reaching some dim haven, announcing the President's death a few hours before. To Adams the death of McKinley and the advent of Roosevelt were not wholly void of personal emotion, but this was little in comparison with his depth of wonder at hearing hourly reports from his most intimate friends, sent to him far within the realm of night, not to please him, but to correct the faults of the solar system. The electro-dynamo-social universe worked better than the sun.

No such strange chance had ever happened to a historian before, and it upset for the moment his whole philosophy of conservative anarchy. The acceleration was marvellous, and wholly in the lines of unity. To recover his grasp of chaos, he must look back across the gulf to Russia, and the gap seemed to have suddenly become an abyss. Russia was infinitely distant. Yet the nightmare of the glacial ice-cap still pressed down on him from the hills, in full vision, and no one could look out on the dusky and oily sea that lapped these spectral islands without consciousness that only a day's steaming to the northward would bring him to the ice-barrier, ready at any moment to advance, which obliged tourists to stop where Laps and reindeer and Norse fishermen had stopped so long ago that memory of their very origin was lost. Adams had never before met a ne plus ultra, and knew not what to make of it; but he felt at least the emotion of his Norwegian fishermen ancestors, doubtless numbering hundreds of thousands, jammed with their faces to the sea, the ice on the north, the ice-cap of Russian inertia pressing from behind, and the ice a trifling danger compared with the inertia. From the day they first followed the retreating ice-cap round the North Cape, down to the present moment, their problem was the same.

The new Teufelsdrockh, though considerably older than the old one, saw no clearer into past or future, but he was fully as much perplexed. From the archaic ice-barrier to the Caspian Sea, a long line of division, permanent since ice and inertia first took possession, divided his lines of force, with no relation to climate or geography or soil.

The less a tourist knows, the fewer mistakes he need make, for he will not expect himself to explain ignorance. A century ago he carried letters and sought knowledge; to-day he knows that no one knows; he needs too much and ignorance is learning. He wandered south again, and came out at Kiel, Hamburg, Bremen, and Cologne. A mere glance showed him that here was a Germany new to mankind. Hamburg was almost as American as St. Louis. In forty years, the green rusticity of Dusseldorf had taken on the sooty grime of Birmingham. The Rhine in 1900 resembled the Rhine of 1858 much as it resembled the Rhine of the Salic Franks. Cologne was a railway centre that had completed its cathedral which bore an absent- minded air of a cathedral of Chicago. The thirteenth century, carefully strained-off, catalogued, and locked up, was visible to tourists as a kind of Neanderthal, cave-dwelling, curiosity. The Rhine was more modern than the Hudson, as might well be, since it produced far more coal; but all this counted for little beside the radical change in the lines of force.

In 1858 the whole plain of northern Europe, as well as the Danube in the south, bore evident marks of being still the prehistoric highway between Asia and the ocean. The trade-route followed the old routes of invasion, and Cologne was a resting-place between Warsaw and Flanders. Throughout northern Germany, Russia was felt even more powerfully than France. In 1901 Russia had vanished, and not even France was felt; hardly England or America. Coal alone was felt -- its stamp alone pervaded the Rhine district and persisted to Picardy -- and the stamp was the same as that of Birmingham and Pittsburgh. The Rhine produced the same power, and the power produced the same people -- the same mind -- the same impulse. For a man sixty-three years old who had no hope of earning a living, these three months of education were the most arduous he ever attempted, and Russia was the most indigestible morsel he ever met; but the sum of it, viewed from Cologne, seemed reasonable. From Hammerfest to Cherbourg on one shore of the ocean -- from Halifax to Norfolk on the other -- one great empire was ruled by one great emperor -- Coal. Political and human jealousies might tear it apart or divide it, but the power and the empire were one. Unity had gained that ground. Beyond lay Russia, and there an older, perhaps a surer, power, resting on the eternal law of inertia, held its own.

As a personal matter, the relative value of the two powers became more interesting every year;

for the mass of Russian inertia was moving irresistibly over China, and John Hay stood in its path. As long as de Witte ruled, Hay was safe. Should de Witte fall, Hay would totter. One could only sit down and watch the doings of Mr. de Witte and Mr. de Plehve.

Chapter XXVIII. The Height of Knowledge (1902)

AMERICA has always taken tragedy lightly. Too busy to stop the activity of their twenty-million-horse-power society, Americans ignore tragic motives that would have overshadowed the Middle Ages; and the world learns to regard assassination as a form of hysteria, and death as neurosis, to be treated by a rest-cure. Three hideous political murders, that would have fattened the Eumenides with horror, have thrown scarcely a shadow on the White House.

The year 1901 was a year of tragedy that seemed to Hay to centre on himself. First came, in summer, the accidental death of his son, Del Hay. Close on the tragedy of his son, followed that of his chief, "all the more hideous that we were so sure of his recovery." The world turned suddenly into a graveyard. "I have acquired the funeral habit." "Nicolay is dying. I went to see him yesterday, and he did not know me." Among the letters of condolence showered upon him was one from Clarence King at Pasadena, "heart-breaking in grace and tenderness -- the old King manner"; and King himself "simply waiting till nature and the foe have done their struggle." The tragedy of King impressed him intensely: "There you have it in the face!" he said -- "the best and brightest man of his generation, with talents immeasurably beyond any of his contemporaries; with industry that has often sickened me to witness it; with everything in his favor but blind luck; hounded by disaster from his cradle, with none of the joy of life to which he was entitled, dying at last, with nameless suffering alone and uncared-for, in a California tavern. Ca vous amuse, la vie?"

The first summons that met Adams, before he had even landed on the pier at New York, December 29, was to Clarence King's funeral, and from the funeral service he had no gayer road to travel than that which led to Washington, where a revolution had occurred that must in any case have made the men of his age instantly old, but which, besides hurrying to the front the generation that till then he had regarded as boys, could not fail to break the social ties that had till then held them all together.

Ca vous amuse, la vie? Honestly, the lessons of education were becoming too trite. Hay himself, probably for the first time, felt half glad that Roosevelt should want him to stay in office, if only to save himself the trouble of quitting; but to Adams all was pure loss. On that side, his education had been finished at school. His friends in power were lost, and he knew life too well to risk total wreck by trying to save them.

As far as concerned Roosevelt, the chance was hopeless. To them at sixty-three, Roosevelt at forty-three could not be taken seriously in his old character, and could not be recovered in his new one. Power when wielded by abnormal energy is the most serious of facts, and all Roosevelt's friends know that his restless and combative energy was more than abnormal. Roosevelt, more than any other man living within the range of notoriety, showed the singular primitive quality that belongs to ultimate matter -- the quality that mediaeval theology assigned to God -- he was pure act. With him wielding unmeasured power with immeasurable energy, in the White House, the relation of age to youth -- of teacher to pupil -- was altogether out of place;

and no other was possible. Even Hay's relation was a false one, while Adams's ceased of itself. History's truths are little valuable now; but human nature retains a few of its archaic, proverbial laws, and the wisest courtier that ever lived -- Lucius Seneca himself -- must have remained in some shade of doubt what advantage he should get from the power of his friend and pupil Nero Claudius, until, as a gentleman past sixty, he received Nero's filial invitation to kill himself. Seneca closed the vast circle of his knowledge by learning that a friend in power was a friend lost -- a fact very much worth insisting upon -- while the gray-headed moth that had fluttered through many moth-administrations and had singed his wings more or less in them all, though he now slept nine months out of the twelve, acquired an instinct of self-preservation that kept him to the north side of La Fayette Square, and, after a sufficient habitude of Presidents and Senators, deterred him from hovering between them.

Those who seek education in the paths of duty are always deceived by the illusion that power in the hands of friends is an advantage to them. As far as Adams could teach experience, he was bound to warn them that he had found it an invariable disaster. Power is poison. Its effect on Presidents had been always tragic, chiefly as an almost insane excitement at first, and a worse reaction afterwards; but also because no mind is so well balanced as to bear the strain of seizing unlimited force without habit or knowledge of it; and finding it disputed with him by hungry packs of wolves and hounds whose lives depend on snatching the carrion. Roosevelt enjoyed a singularly direct nature and honest intent, but he lived naturally in restless agitation that would have worn out most tempers in a month, and his first year of Presidency showed chronic excitement that made a friend tremble. The effect of unlimited power on limited mind is worth noting in Presidents because it must represent the same process in society, and the power of self-control must have limit somewhere in face of the control of the infinite.

Here, education seemed to see its first and last lesson, but this is a matter of psychology which lies far down in the depths of history and of science; it will recur in other forms. The personal lesson is different. Roosevelt was lost, but this seemed no reason why Hay and Lodge should also be lost, yet the result was mathematically certain. With Hay, it was only the steady decline of strength, and the necessary economy of force; but with Lodge it was law of politics. He could not help himself, for his position as the President's friend and independent statesman at once was false, and he must be unsure in both relations.

To a student, the importance of Cabot Lodge was great -- much greater than that of the usual Senator -- but it hung on his position in Massachusetts rather than on his control of Executive patronage; and his standing in Massachusetts was highly insecure. Nowhere in America was society so complex or change so rapid. No doubt the Bostonian had always been noted for a certain chronic irritability -- a sort of Bostonitis -- which, in its primitive Puritan forms, seemed due to knowing too much of his neighbors, and thinking too much of himself. Many years earlier William M. Evarts had pointed out to Adams the impossibility of uniting New England behind a New England leader. The trait led to good ends -- such as admiration of Abraham Lincoln and George Washington -- but the virtue was exacting; for New England standards were various, scarcely reconcilable with each other, and constantly multiplying in number, until balance between them threatened to become impossible. The old ones were quite difficult enough -- State Street and the banks exacted one stamp; the old Congregational clergy another; Harvard College, poor in votes, but rich in social influence, a third; the foreign element, especially the Irish, held aloof, and seldom consented to approve any one; the new socialist class, rapidly growing, promised to become more exclusive than the Irish. New power was disintegrating society, and setting independent centres of force to work, until money had all it could do to hold the machine together. No one could represent it faithfully as a whole.

Naturally, Adams's sympathies lay strongly with Lodge, but the task of appreciation was much more difficult in his case than in that of his chief friend and scholar, the President. As a type for study, or a standard for education, Lodge was the more interesting of the two. Roosevelts are born and never can be taught; but Lodge was a creature of teaching -- Boston incarnate -- the child of his local parentage; and while his ambition led him to be more, the intent, though virtuous, was -- as Adams admitted in his own case -- restless. An excellent talker, a voracious reader, a ready wit, an accomplished orator, with a clear mind and a powerful memory, he could never feel perfectly at ease whatever leg he stood on, but shifted, sometimes with painful strain of temper, from one sensitive muscle to another, uncertain whether to pose as an uncompromising Yankee; or a pure American; or a patriot in the still purer atmosphere of Irish, Germans, or Jews; or a scholar and historian of Harvard College. English to the last fibre of his thought -- saturated with English literature, English tradition, English taste -- revolted by every vice and by most virtues of Frenchmen and Germans, or any other Continental standards, but at home and happy among the vices and extravagances of Shakespeare -- standing first on the social, then on the political foot; now worshipping, now banning; shocked by the wanton display of immorality, but practicing the license of political usage; sometimes bitter, often genial, always intelligent -- Lodge had the singular merit of interesting. The usual statesmen flocked in swarms like crows, black and monotonous. Lodge's plumage was varied, and, like his flight, harked back to race. He betrayed the consciousness that he and his people had a past, if they dared but avow it, and might have a future, if they could but divine it.

Adams, too, was Bostonian, and the Bostonian's uncertainty of attitude was as natural to him as to Lodge. Only Bostonians can understand Bostonians and thoroughly sympathize with the inconsequences of the Boston mind. His theory and practice were also at variance. He professed in theory equal distrust of English thought, and called it a huge rag-bag of bric-a-brac, sometimes precious but never sure. For him, only the Greek, the Italian or the French standards had claims to respect, and the barbarism of Shakespeare was as flagrant as to Voltaire; but his theory never affected his practice. He knew that his artistic standard was the illusion of his own mind; that English disorder approached nearer to truth, if truth existed, than French measure or Italian line, or German logic; he read his Shakespeare as the Evangel of conservative Christian anarchy, neither very conservative nor very Christian, but stupendously anarchistic. He loved the atrocities of English art and society, as he loved Charles Dickens and Miss Austen, not because of their example, but because of their humor. He made no scruple of defying sequence and denying consistency -- but he was not a Senator.

Double standards are inspiration to men of letters, but they are apt to be fatal to politicians. Adams had no reason to care whether his standards were popular or not, and no one else cared more than he; but Roosevelt and Lodge were playing a game in which they were always liable to find the shifty sands of American opinion yield suddenly under their feet. With this game an elderly friend had long before carried acquaintance as far as he wished. There was nothing in it for him but the amusement of the pugilist or acrobat. The larger study was lost in the division of interests and the ambitions of fifth-rate men; but foreign affairs dealt only with large units, and made personal relation possible with Hay which could not be maintained with Roosevelt or

Lodge. As an affair of pure education the point is worth notice from young men who are drawn into politics. The work of domestic progress is done by masses of mechanical power -- steam, electric, furnace, or other -- which have to be controlled by a score or two of individuals who have shown capacity to manage it. The work of internal government has become the task of controlling these men, who are socially as remote as heathen gods, alone worth knowing, but never known, and who could tell nothing of political value if one skinned them alive. Most of them have nothing to tell, but are forces as dumb as their dynamos, absorbed in the development or economy of power. They are trustees for the public, and whenever society assumes the property, it must confer on them that title; but the power will remain as before, whoever manages it, and will then control society without appeal, as it controls its stokers and pit-men. Modern politics is, at bottom, a struggle not of men but of forces. The men become every year more and more creatures of force, massed about central power-houses. The conflict is no longer between the men, but between the motors that drive the men, and the men tend to succumb to their own motive forces.

This is a moral that man strongly objects to admit, especially in mediaeval pursuits like politics and poetry, nor is it worth while for a teacher to insist upon it. What he insists upon is only that in domestic politics, every one works for an immediate object, commonly for some private job, and invariably in a near horizon, while in foreign affairs the outlook is far ahead, over a field as wide as the world. There the merest scholar could see what he was doing. For history, international relations are the only sure standards of movement; the only foundation for a map. For this reason, Adams had always insisted that international relation was the only sure base for a chart of history.

He cared little to convince any one of the correctness of his view, but as teacher he was bound to explain it, and as friend he found it convenient. The Secretary of State has always stood as much alone as the historian. Required to look far ahead and round hm, he measures forces unknown to party managers, and has found Congress more or less hostile ever since Congress first sat. The Secretary of State exists only to recognize the existence of a world which Congress would rather ignore; of obligations which Congress repudiates whenever it can; of bargains which Congress distrusts and tries to turn to its advantage or to reject. Since the first day the Senate existed, it has always intrigued against the Secretary of State whenever the Secretary has been obliged to extend his functions beyond the appointment of Consuls in Senators' service.

This is a matter of history which any one may approve or dispute as he will; but as education it gave new resources to an old scholar, for it made of Hay the best schoolmaster since 1865. Hay had become the most imposing figure ever known in the office. He had an influence that no other Secretary of State ever possessed, as he had a nation behind him such as history had never imagined. He needed to write no state papers; he wanted no help, and he stood far above counsel or advice; but he could instruct an attentive scholar as no other teacher in the world could do; and Adams sought only instruction -- wanted only to chart the international channel for fifty years to come; to triangulate the future; to obtain his dimension, and fix the acceleration of movement in politics since the year 1200, as he was trying to fix it in philosophy and physics; in finance and force.

Hay had been so long at the head of foreign affairs that at last the stream of events favored him. With infinite effort he had achieved the astonishing diplomatic feat of inducing the Senate, with only six negative votes, to permit Great Britain to renounce, without equivalent, treaty rights which she had for fifty years defended tooth and nail. This unprecedented triumph in his negotiations with the Senate enabled him to carry one step further his measures for general peace. About England the Senate could make no further effective opposition, for England was won, and Canada alone could give trouble. The next difficulty was with France, and there the Senate blocked advance, but England assumed the task, and, owing to political changes in France, effected the object -- a combination which, as late as 1901, had been visionary. The next, and far more difficult step, was to bring Germany into the combine; while, at the end of the vista, most unmanageable of all, Russia remained to be satisfied and disarmed. This was the instinct of what might be named McKinleyism; the system of combinations, consolidations, trusts, realized at home, and realizable abroad.

With the system, a student nurtured in ideas of the eighteenth century, had nothing to do, and made not the least presence of meddling; but nothing forbade him to study, and he noticed to his astonishment that this capitalistic scheme of combining governments, like railways or furnaces, was in effect precisely the socialist scheme of Jaures and Bebel. That John Hay, of all men, should adopt a socialist policy seemed an idea more absurd than conservative Christian anarchy, but paradox had become the only orthodoxy in politics as in science. When one saw the field, one realized that Hay could not help himself, nor could Bebel. Either Germany must destroy England and France to create the next inevitable unification as a system of continent against continent -- or she must pool interests. Both schemes in turn were attributed to the Kaiser; one or the other he would have to choose; opinion was balanced doubtfully on their merits; but, granting both to be feasible, Hay's and McKinley's statesmanship turned on the point of persuading the Kaiser to join what might be called the Coal-power combination, rather than build up the only possible alternative, a Gun-power combination by merging Germany in Russia. Thus Bebel and Jaures, McKinley and Hay, were partners.

The problem was pretty -- even fascinating -- and, to an old Civil-War private soldier in diplomacy, as rigorous as a geometrical demonstration. As the last possible lesson in life, it had all sorts of ultimate values. Unless education marches on both feet -- theory and practice -- it risks going astray; and Hay was probably the most accomplished master of both then living. He knew not only the forces but also the men, and he had no other thought than his policy.

Probably this was the moment of highest knowledge that a scholar could ever reach. He had under his eyes the whole educational staff of the Government at a time when the Government had just reached the heights of highest activity and influence. Since 1860, education had done its worst, under the greatest masters and at enormous expense to the world, to train these two minds to catch and comprehend every spring of international action, not to speak of personal influence; and the entire machinery of politics in several great countries had little to do but supply the last and best information. Education could be carried no further.

With its effects on Hay, Adams had nothing to do; but its effects on himself were grotesque. Never had the proportions of his ignorance looked so appalling. He seemed to know nothing -- to be groping in darkness -- to be falling forever in space; and the worst depth consisted in the assurance, incredible as it seemed, that no one knew more. He had, at least, the mechanical assurance of certain values to guide him -- like the relative intensities of his Coal-powers, and relative inertia of his Gun-powers -- but he conceived that had he known, besides the mechanics, every relative value of persons, as well as he knew the inmost thoughts of his own Government -- had the Czar and the Kaiser and the Mikado turned schoolmasters, like Hay, and taught him all they knew, he would still have known nothing. They knew nothing themselves. Only by comparison of their ignorance could the student measure his own.

Chapter XXIX. The Abyss of Ignorance (1902)

THE years hurried past, and gave hardly time to note their work. Three or four months, though big with change, come to an end before the mind can catch up with it. Winter vanished; spring burst into flower; and again Paris opened its arms, though not for long. Mr. Cameron came over, and took the castle of Inverlochy for three months, which he summoned his friends to garrison. Lochaber seldom laughs, except for its children, such as Camerons, McDonalds, Campbells and other products of the mist; but in the summer of 1902 Scotland put on fewer airs of coquetry than usual. Since the terrible harvest of 1879 which one had watched sprouting on its stalks on the Shropshire hillsides, nothing had equalled the gloom. Even when the victims fled to Switzerland, they found the Lake of Geneva and the Rhine not much gayer, and Carlsruhe no more restful than Paris; until at last, in desperation, one drifted back to the Avenue of the Bois de Boulogne, and, like the Cuckoo, dropped into the nest of a better citizen. Diplomacy has its uses. Reynolds Hitt, transferred to Berlin, abandoned his attic to Adams, and there, for long summers to come, he hid in ignorance and silence.

Life at last managed of its own accord to settle itself into a working arrangement. After so many years of effort to find one's drift, the drift found the seeker, and slowly swept him forward and back, with a steady progress oceanwards. Such lessons as summer taught, winter tested, and one had only to watch the apparent movement of the stars in order to guess one's declination. The process is possible only for men who have exhausted auto-motion. Adams never knew why, knowing nothing of Faraday, he began to mimic Faraday's trick of seeing lines of force all about him, where he had always seen lines of will. Perhaps the effect of knowing no mathematics is to leave the mind to imagine figures -- images -- phantoms; one's mind is a watery mirror at best; but, once conceived, the image became rapidly simple, and the lines of force presented themselves as lines of attraction. Repulsions counted only as battle of attractions. By this path, the mind stepped into the mechanical theory of the universe before knowing it, and entered a distinct new phase of education.

This was the work of the dynamo and the Virgin of Chartres. Like his masters, since thought began, he was handicapped by the eternal mystery of Force -- the sink of all science. For thousands of years in history, he found that Force had been felt as occult attraction -- love of God and lust for power in a future life. After 1500, when this attraction began to decline, philosophers fell back on some vis a tergo -- instinct of danger from behind, like Darwin's survival of the fittest; and one of the greatest minds, between Descartes and Newton -- Pascal -- saw the master-motor of man in ennui, which was also scientific: "I have often said that all the troubles of man come from his not knowing how to sit still." Mere restlessness forces action. "So passes the whole of life. We combat obstacles in order to get repose, and, when got, the repose is insupportable; for we think either of the troubles we have, or of those that threaten us; and even if we felt safe on every side, ennui would of its own accord spring up from the depths of the heart where it is rooted by nature, and would fill the mind with its venom."

"If goodness lead him not, yet weariness

    May toss him to My breast."

Ennui, like Natural Selection, accounted for change, but failed to account for direction of change. For that, an attractive force was essential; a force from outside; a shaping influence. Pascal and all the old philosophies called this outside force God or Gods. Caring but little for the name, and fixed only on tracing the Force, Adams had gone straight to the Virgin at Chartres, and asked her to show him God, face to face, as she did for St. Bernard. She replied, kindly as ever, as though she were still the young mother of to-day, with a sort of patient pity for masculine dulness: "My dear outcast, what is it you seek? This is the Church of Christ! If you seek him through me, you are welcome, sinner or saint; but he and I are one. We are Love! We have little or nothing to do with God's other energies which are infinite, and concern us the less because our interest is only in man, and the infinite is not knowable to man. Yet if you are troubled by your ignorance, you see how I am surrounded by the masters of the schools! Ask them!"

The answer sounded singularly like the usual answer of British science which had repeated since Bacon that one must not try to know the unknowable, though one was quite powerless to ignore it; but the Virgin carried more conviction, for her feminine lack of interest in all perfections except her own was honester than the formal phrase of science; since nothing was easier than to follow her advice, and turn to Thomas Aquinas, who, unlike modern physicists, answered at once and plainly: "To me," said St. Thomas, "Christ and the Mother are one Force -- Love -- simple, single, and sufficient for all human wants; but Love is a human interest which acts even on man so partially that you and I, as philosophers, need expect no share in it. Therefore we turn to Christ and the Schools who represent all other Force. We deal with Multiplicity and call it God. After the Virgin has redeemed by her personal Force as Love all that is redeemable in man, the Schools embrace the rest, and give it Form, Unity, and Motive."

This chart of Force was more easily studied than any other possible scheme, for one had but to do what the Church was always promising to do -- abolish in one flash of lightning not only man, but also the Church itself, the earth, the other planets, and the sun, in order to clear the air; without affecting mediaeval science. The student felt warranted in doing what the Church threatened -- abolishing his solar system altogether -- in order to look at God as actual; continuous movement, universal cause, and interchangeable force. This was pantheism, but the Schools were pantheist; at least as pantheistic as the Energetik of the Germans; and their deity was the ultimate energy, whose thought and act were one.

Rid of man and his mind, the universe of Thomas Aquinas seemed rather more scientific than that of Haeckel or Ernst Mach. Contradiction for contradiction, Attraction for attraction, Energy for energy, St. Thomas's idea of God had merits. Modern science offered not a vestige of proof, or a theory of connection between its forces, or any scheme of reconciliation between thought and mechanics; while St. Thomas at least linked together the joints of his machine. As far as a superficial student could follow, the thirteenth century supposed mind to be a mode of force directly derived from the intelligent prime motor, and the cause of all form and sequence in the universe -- therefore the only proof of unity. Without thought in the unit, there could be no unity; without unity no orderly sequence or ordered society. Thought alone was Form. Mind and Unity flourished or perished together.

This education startled even a man who had dabbled in fifty educations all over the world; for, if he were obliged to insist on a Universe, he seemed driven to the Church. Modern science guaranteed no unity. The student seemed to feel himself, like all his predecessors, caught, trapped, meshed in this eternal drag-net of religion.

In practice the student escapes this dilemma in two ways: the first is that of ignoring it, as one escapes most dilemmas; the second is that the Church rejects pantheism as worse than atheism, and will have nothing to do with the pantheist at any price. In wandering through the forests of ignorance, one necessarily fell upon the famous old bear that scared children at play; but, even had the animal shown more logic than its victim, one had learned from Socrates to distrust, above all other traps, the trap of logic -- the mirror of the mind. Yet the search for a unit of force led into catacombs of thought where hundreds of thousands of educations had found their end. Generation after generation of painful and honest-minded scholars had been content to stay in these labyrinths forever, pursuing ignorance in silence, in company with the most famous teachers of all time. Not one of them had ever found a logical highroad of escape.

Adams cared little whether he escaped or not, but he felt clear that he could not stop there, even to enjoy the society of Spinoza and Thomas Aquinas. True, the Church alone had asserted unity with any conviction, and the historian alone knew what oceans of blood and treasure the assertion had cost; but the only honest alternative to affirming unity was to deny it; and the denial would require a new education. At sixty-five years old a new education promised hardly more than the old. Possibly the modern legislator or magistrate might no longer know enough to treat as the Church did the man who denied unity, unless the denial took the form of a bomb; but no teacher would know how to explain what he thought he meant by denying unity. Society would certainly punish the denial if ever any one learned enough to understand it. Philosophers, as a rule, cared little what principles society affirmed or denied, since the philosopher commonly held that though he might sometimes be right by good luck on some one point, no complex of individual opinions could possibly be anything but wrong; yet, supposing society to be ignored, the philosopher was no further forward. Nihilism had no bottom. For thousands of years every philosopher had stood on the shore of this sunless sea, diving for pearls and never finding them. All had seen that, since they could not find bottom, they must assume it. The Church claimed to have found it, but, since 1450, motives for agreeing on some new assumption of Unity, broader and deeper than that of the Church, had doubled in force until even the universities and schools, like the Church and State, seemed about to be driven into an attempt to educate, though specially forbidden to do it.

Like most of his generation, Adams had taken the word of science that the new unit was as good as found. It would not be an intelligence -- probably not even a consciousness -- but it would serve. He passed sixty years waiting for it, and at the end of that time, on reviewing the ground, he was led to think that the final synthesis of science and its ultimate triumph was the kinetic theory of gases; which seemed to cover all motion in space, and to furnish the measure of time. So far as he understood it, the theory asserted that any portion of space is occupied by molecules of gas, flying in right lines at velocities varying up to a mile in a second, and colliding with each other at intervals varying up to 17,750,000 times in a second. To this analysis -- if one understood it right -- all matter whatever was reducible, and the only difference of opinion in science regarded the doubt whether a still deeper analysis would reduce the atom of gas to pure motion.

Thus, unless one mistook the meaning of motion, which might well be, the scientific synthesis commonly called Unity was the scientific analysis commonly called Multiplicity. The two things were the same, all forms being shifting phases of motion. Granting this ocean of colliding atoms, the last hope of humanity, what happened if one dropped the sounder into the abyss -- let it go -- frankly gave up Unity altogether? What was Unity? Why was one to be forced to affirm it?

Here everybody flatly refused help. Science seemed content with its old phrase of "larger synthesis," which was well enough for science, but meant chaos for man. One would have been glad to stop and ask no more, but the anarchist bomb bade one go on, and the bomb is a powerful persuader. One could not stop, even to enjoy the charms of a perfect gas colliding seventeen million times in a second, much like an automobile in Paris. Science itself had been crowded so close to the edge of the abyss that its attempts to escape were as metaphysical as the leap, while an ignorant old man felt no motive for trying to escape, seeing that the only escape possible lay in the form of vis a tergo commonly called Death. He got out his Descartes again; dipped into his Hume and Berkeley; wrestled anew with his Kant; pondered solemnly over his Hegel and Schopenhauer and Hartmann; strayed gaily away with his Greeks -- all merely to ask what Unity meant, and what happened when one denied it.

Apparently one never denied it. Every philosopher, whether sane or insane, naturally affirmed it. The utmost flight of anarchy seemed to have stopped with the assertion of two principles, and even these fitted into each other, like good and evil, light and darkness. Pessimism itself, black as it might be painted, had been content to turn the universe of contradictions into the human thought as one Will, and treat it as representation. Metaphysics insisted on treating the universe as one thought or treating thought as one universe; and philosophers agreed, like a kinetic gas, that the universe could be known only as motion of mind, and therefore as unity. One could know it only as one's self; it was psychology.

Of all forms of pessimism, the metaphysical form was, for a historian, the least enticing. Of all studies, the one he would rather have avoided was that of his own mind. He knew no tragedy so heartrending as introspection, and the more, because -- as Mephistopheles said of Marguerite -- he was not the first. Nearly all the highest intelligence known to history had drowned itself in the reflection of its own thought, and the bovine survivors had rudely told the truth about it, without affecting the intelligent. One's own time had not been exempt. Even since 1870 friends by scores had fallen victims to it. Within five-and-twenty years, a new library had grown out of it. Harvard College was a focus of the study; France supported hospitals for it; England published magazines of it. Nothing was easier than to take one's mind in one's hand, and ask one's psychological friends what they made of it, and the more because it mattered so little to either party, since their minds, whatever they were, had pretty nearly ceased to reflect, and let them do what they liked with the small remnant, they could scarcely do anything very new with it. All one asked was to learn what they hoped to do.

Unfortunately the pursuit of ignorance in silence had, by this time, led the weary pilgrim into such mountains of ignorance that he could no longer see any path whatever, and could not even understand a signpost. He failed to fathom the depths of the new psychology, which proved to him that, on that side as on the mathematical side, his power of thought was atrophied, if, indeed, it ever existed. Since he could not fathom the science, he could only ask the simplest of questions: Did the new psychology hold that the IvXn -- soul or mind -- was or was not a unit?

He gathered from the books that the psychologists had, in a few cases, distinguished several personalities in the same mind, each conscious and constant, individual and exclusive. The fact seemed scarcely surprising, since it had been a habit of mind from earliest recorded time, and equally familiar to the last acquaintance who had taken a drug or caught a fever, or eaten a Welsh rarebit before bed; for surely no one could follow the action of a vivid dream, and still need to be told that the actors evoked by his mind were not himself, but quite unknown to all he had ever recognized as self. The new psychology went further, and seemed convinced that it had actually split personality not only into dualism, but also into complex groups, like telephonic centres and systems, that might be isolated and called up at will, and whose physical action might be occult in the sense of strangeness to any known form of force. Dualism seemed to have become as common as binary stars. Alternating personalities turned up constantly, even among one's friends. The facts seemed certain, or at least as certain as other facts; all they needed was explanation.

This was not the business of the searcher of ignorance, who felt himself in no way responsible for causes. To his mind, the compound IvXn took at once the form of a bicycle-rider, mechanically balancing himself by inhibiting all his inferior personalities, and sure to fall into the sub-conscious chaos below, if one of his inferior personalities got on top. The only absolute truth was the sub-conscious chaos below, which every one could feel when he sought it.

Whether the psychologists admitted it or not, mattered little to the student who, by the law of his profession, was engaged in studying his own mind. On him, the effect was surprising. He woke up with a shudder as though he had himself fallen off his bicycle. If his mind were really this sort of magnet, mechanically dispersing its lines of force when it went to sleep, and mechanically orienting them when it woke up -- which was normal, the dispersion or orientation? The mind, like the body, kept its unity unless it happened to lose balance, but the professor of physics, who slipped on a pavement and hurt himself, knew no more than an idiot what knocked him down, though he did know -- what the idiot could hardly do -- that his normal condition was idiocy, or want of balance, and that his sanity was unstable artifice. His normal thought was dispersion, sleep, dream, inconsequence; the simultaneous action of different thought-centres without central control. His artificial balance was acquired habit. He was an acrobat, with a dwarf on his back, crossing a chasm on a slack-rope, and commonly breaking his neck.

By that path of newest science, one saw no unity ahead -- nothing but a dissolving mind -- and the historian felt himself driven back on thought as one continuous Force, without Race, Sex, School, Country, or Church. This has been always the fate of rigorous thinkers, and has always succeeded in making them famous, as it did Gibbon, Buckle, and Auguste Comte. Their method made what progress the science of history knew, which was little enough, but they did at last fix the law that, if history ever meant to correct the errors she made in detail, she must agree on a scale for the whole. Every local historian might defy this law till history ended, but its necessity would be the same for man as for space or time or force, and without it the historian would always remain a child in science.

Any schoolboy could see that man as a force must be measured by motion, from a fixed point. Psychology helped here by suggesting a unit -- the point of history when man held the highest idea of himself as a unit in a unified universe. Eight or ten years of study had led Adams to think he might use the century 1150-1250, expressed in Amiens Cathedral and the Works of Thomas

Aquinas, as the unit from which he might measure motion down to his own time, without assuming anything as true or untrue, except relation. The movement might be studied at once in philosophy and mechanics. Setting himself to the task, he began a volume which he mentally knew as "Mont-Saint-Michel and Chartres: a Study of Thirteenth-Century Unity." From that point he proposed to fix a position for himself, which he could label: "The Education of Henry Adams: a Study of Twentieth-Century Multiplicity." With the help of these two points of relation, he hoped to project his lines forward and backward indefinitely, subject to correction from any one who should know better. Thereupon, he sailed for home.

Chapter XXX. Vis Inertiae (1903)

WASHINGTON was always amusing, but in 1900, as in 1800, its chief interest lay in its distance from New York. The movement of New York had become planetary -- beyond control -- while the task of Washington, in 1900 as in 1800, was to control it. The success of Washington in the past century promised ill for its success in the next.

To a student who had passed the best years of his life in pondering over the political philosophy of Jefferson, Gallatin, and Madison, the problem that Roosevelt took in hand seemed alive with historical interest, but it would need at least another half-century to show its results. As yet, one could not measure the forces or their arrangement; the forces had not even aligned themselves except in foreign affairs; and there one turned to seek the channel of wisdom as naturally as though Washington did not exist. The President could do nothing effectual in foreign affairs, but at least he could see something of the field.

Hay had reached the summit of his career, and saw himself on the edge of wreck. Committed to the task of keeping China "open," he saw China about to be shut. Almost alone in the world, he represented the "open door," and could not escape being crushed by it. Yet luck had been with him in full tide. Though Sir Julian Pauncefote had died in May, 1902, after carrying out tasks that filled an ex-private secretary of 1861 with open-mouthed astonishment, Hay had been helped by the appointment of Michael Herbert as his successor, who counted for double the value of an ordinary diplomat. To reduce friction is the chief use of friendship, and in politics the loss by friction is outrageous. To Herbert and his wife, the small knot of houses that seemed to give a vague unity to foreign affairs opened their doors and their hearts, for the Herberts were already at home there; and this personal sympathy prolonged Hay's life, for it not only eased the effort of endurance, but it also led directly to a revolution in Germany. Down to that moment, the Kaiser, rightly or wrongly, had counted as the ally of the Czar in all matters relating to the East. Holleben and Cassini were taken to be a single force in Eastern affairs, and this supposed alliance gave Hay no little anxiety and some trouble. Suddenly Holleben, who seemed to have had no thought but to obey with almost agonized anxiety the least hint of the Kaiser's will, received a telegram ordering him to pretext illness and come home, which he obeyed within four-and-twenty hours. The ways of the German Foreign Office had been always abrupt, not to say ruthless, towards its agents, and yet commonly some discontent had been shown as excuse; but, in this case, no cause was guessed for Holleben's disgrace except the Kaiser's wish to have a personal representative at Washington. Breaking down all precedent, he sent Speck von Sternburg to counterbalance Herbert.

Welcome as Speck was in the same social intimacy, and valuable as his presence was to Hay, the personal gain was trifling compared with the political. Of Hay's official tasks, one knew no more than any newspaper reporter did, but of one's own diplomatic education the successive steps had become strides. The scholar was studying, not on Hay's account, but on his own. He had seen Hay, in 1898, bring England into his combine; he had seen the steady movement which was to bring France back into an Atlantic system; and now he saw suddenly the dramatic swing of Germany towards the west -- the movement of all others nearest mathematical certainty. Whether the Kaiser meant it or not, he gave the effect of meaning to assert his independence of Russia, and to Hay this change of front had enormous value. The least was that it seemed to isolate Cassini, and unmask the Russian movement which became more threatening every month as the Manchurian scheme had to be revealed.

Of course the student saw whole continents of study opened to him by the Kaiser's coup d'etat. Carefully as he had tried to follow the Kaiser's career, he had never suspected such refinement of policy, which raised his opinion of the Kaiser's ability to the highest point, and altogether upset the centre of statesmanship. That Germany could be so quickly detached from separate objects and brought into an Atlantic system seemed a paradox more paradoxical than any that one's education had yet offered, though it had offered little but paradox. If Germany could be held there, a century of friction would be saved. No price would be too great for such an object; although no price could probably be wrung out of Congress as equivalent for it. The Kaiser, by one personal act of energy, freed Hay's hands so completely that he saw his problems simplified to Russia alone.

Naturally Russia was a problem ten times as difficult. The history of Europe for two hundred years had accomplished little but to state one or two sides of the Russian problem. One's year of Berlin in youth, though it taught no Civil Law, had opened one's eyes to the Russian enigma, and both German and French historians had labored over its proportions with a sort of fascinated horror. Germany, of all countries, was most vitally concerned in it; but even a cave-dweller in La Fayette Square, seeking only a measure of motion since the Crusades, saw before his eyes, in the spring of 1903, a survey of future order or anarchy that would exhaust the power of his telescopes and defy the accuracy of his theodolites.

The drama had become passionately interesting and grew every day more Byzantine; for the Russian Government itself showed clear signs of dislocation, and the orders of Lamsdorf and de Witte were reversed when applied in Manchuria. Historians and students should have no sympathies or antipathies, but Adams had private reasons for wishing well to the Czar and his people. At much length, in several labored chapters of history, he had told how the personal friendliness of the Czar Alexander I, in 1810, saved the fortunes of J. Q. Adams, and opened to him the brilliant diplomatic career that ended in the White House. Even in his own effaced existence he had reasons, not altogether trivial, for gratitude to the Czar Alexander II, whose firm neutrality had saved him some terribly anxious days and nights in 1862; while he had seen enough of Russia to sympathize warmly with Prince Khilkoff's railways and de Witte's industries. The last and highest triumph of history would, to his mind, be the bringing of Russia into the Atlantic combine, and the just and fair allotment of the whole world among the regulated activities of the universe. At the rate of unification since 1840, this end should be possible within another sixty years; and, in foresight of that point, Adams could already finish -- provisionally -- his chart of international unity; but, for the moment, the gravest doubts and ignorance covered the whole field. No one -- Czar or diplomat, Kaiser or Mikado -- seemed to know anything.

Through individual Russians one could always see with ease, for their diplomacy never suggested depth; and perhaps Hay protected Cassini for the very reason that Cassini could not disguise an emotion, and never failed to betray that, in setting the enormous bulk of Russian inertia to roll over China, he regretted infinitely that he should have to roll it over Hay too. He would almost rather have rolled it over de Witte and Lamsdorf. His political philosophy, like that of all Russians, seemed fixed in the single idea that Russia must fatally roll -- must, by her irresistible inertia, crush whatever stood in her way.

For Hay and his pooling policy, inherited from McKinley, the fatalism of Russian inertia meant the failure of American intensity. When Russia rolled over a neighboring people, she absorbed their energies in her own movement of custom and race which neither Czar nor peasant could convert, or wished to convert, into any Western equivalent. In 1903 Hay saw Russia knocking away the last blocks that held back the launch of this huge mass into the China Sea. The vast force of inertia known as China was to be united with the huge bulk of Russia in a single mass which no amount of new force could henceforward deflect. Had the Russian Government, with the sharpest sense of enlightenment, employed scores of de Wittes and Khilkoffs, and borrowed all the resources of Europe, it could not have lifted such a weight; and had no idea of trying.

These were the positions charted on the map of political unity by an insect in Washington in the spring of 1903; and they seemed to him fixed. Russia held Europe and America in her grasp, and Cassini held Hay in his. The Siberian Railway offered checkmate to all possible opposition. Japan must make the best terms she could; England must go on receding; America and Germany would look on at the avalanche. The wall of Russian inertia that barred Europe across the Baltic, would bar America across the Pacific; and Hay's policy of the open door would infallibly fail.

Thus the game seemed lost, in spite of the Kaiser's brilliant stroke, and the movement of Russia eastward must drag Germany after it by its mere mass. To the humble student, the loss of Hay's game affected only Hay; for himself, the game -- not the stakes -- was the chief interest; and though want of habit made him object to read his newspapers blackened -- since he liked to blacken them himself -- he was in any case condemned to pass but a short space of time either in Siberia or in Paris, and could balance his endless columns of calculation equally in either place. The figures, not the facts, concerned his chart, and he mused deeply over his next equation. The Atlantic would have to deal with a vast continental mass of inert motion, like a glacier, which moved, and consciously moved, by mechanical gravitation alone. Russia saw herself so, and so must an American see her; he had no more to do than measure, if he could, the mass. Was volume or intensity the stronger? What and where was the vis nova that could hold its own before this prodigious ice-cap of vis inertiae? What was movement of inertia, and what its laws?

Naturally a student knew nothing about mechanical laws, but he took for granted that he could learn, and went to his books to ask. He found that the force of inertia had troubled wiser men than he. The dictionary said that inertia was a property of matter, by which matter tends, when at rest, to remain so, and, when in motion, to move on in a straight line. Finding that his mind refused to imagine itself at rest or in a straight line, he was forced, as usual, to let it imagine something else; and since the question concerned the mind, and not matter, he decided from personal experience that his mind was never at rest, but moved -- when normal -- about something it called a motive, and never moved without motives to move it. So long as these motives were habitual, and their attraction regular, the consequent result might, for convenience, be called movement of inertia, to distinguish it from movement caused by newer or higher attraction; but the greater the bulk to move, the greater must be the force to accelerate or deflect it.

This seemed simple as running water; but simplicity is the most deceitful mistress that ever betrayed man. For years the student and the professor had gone on complaining that minds were unequally inert. The inequalities amounted to contrasts. One class of minds responded only to habit; another only to novelty. Race classified thought. Class-lists classified mind. No two men thought alike, and no woman thought like a man.

Race-inertia seemed to be fairly constant, and made the chief trouble in the Russian future. History looked doubtful when asked whether race-inertia had ever been overcome without destroying the race in order to reconstruct it; but surely sex-inertia had never been overcome at all. Of all movements of inertia, maternity and reproduction are the most typical, and women's property of moving in a constant line forever is ultimate, uniting history in its only unbroken and unbreakable sequence. Whatever else stops, the woman must go on reproducing, as she did in the Siluria of Pteraspis; sex is a vital condition, and race only a local one. If the laws of inertia are to be sought anywhere with certainty, it is in the feminine mind. The American always ostentatiously ignored sex, and American history mentioned hardly the name of a woman, while English history handled them as timidly as though they were a new and undescribed species; but if the problem of inertia summed up the difficulties of the race question, it involved that of sex far more deeply, and to Americans vitally. The task of accelerating or deflecting the movement of the American woman had interest infinitely greater than that of any race whatever, Russian or Chinese, Asiatic or African.

On this subject, as on the Senate and the banks, Adams was conscious of having been born an eighteenth-century remainder. As he grew older, he found that Early Institutions lost their interest, but that Early Women became a passion. Without understanding movement of sex, history seemed to him mere pedantry. So insistent had he become on this side of his subject that with women he talked of little else, and -- because women's thought is mostly subconscious and particularly sensitive to suggestion -- he tried tricks and devices to disclose it. The woman seldom knows her own thought; she is as curious to understand herself as the man to understand her, and responds far more quickly than the man to a sudden idea. Sometimes, at dinner, one might wait till talk flagged, and then, as mildly as possible, ask one's liveliest neighbor whether she could explain why the American woman was a failure. Without an instant's hesitation, she was sure to answer: "Because the American man is a failure!" She meant it.

Adams owed more to the American woman than to all the American men he ever heard of, and felt not the smallest call to defend his sex who seemed able to take care of themselves; but from the point of view of sex he felt much curiosity to know how far the woman was right, and, in pursuing this inquiry, he caught the trick of affirming that the woman was the superior. Apart from truth, he owed her at least that compliment. The habit led sometimes to perilous personalities in the sudden give-and-take of table-talk. This spring, just before sailing for Europe in May, 1903, he had a message from his sister-in-law, Mrs. Brooks Adams, to say that she and her sister. Mrs. Lodge, and the Senator were coming to dinner by way of farewell; Bay Lodge and his lovely young wife sent word to the same effect; Mrs. Roosevelt joined the party; and Michael Herbert shyly slipped down to escape the solitude of his wife's absence. The party were too intimate for reserve, and they soon fell on Adams's hobby with derision which stung him to pungent rejoinder: "The American man is a failure! You are all failures!" he said. "Has not my sister here more sense than my brother Brooks? Is not Bessie worth two of Bay? Wouldn't we all elect Mrs. Lodge Senator against Cabot? Would the President have a ghost of a chance if Mrs. Roosevelt ran against him? Do you want to stop at the Embassy, on your way home, and ask which would run it best -- Herbert or his wife?" The men laughed a little -- not much! Each probably made allowance for his own wife as an unusually superior woman. Some one afterwards remarked that these half-dozen women were not a fair average. Adams replied that the half-dozen men were above all possible average; he could not lay his hands on another half-dozen their equals.

Gay or serious, the question never failed to stir feeling. The cleverer the woman, the less she denied the failure. She was bitter at heart about it. She had failed even to hold the family together, and her children ran away like chickens with their first feathers; the family was extinct like chivalry. She had failed not only to create a new society that satisfied her, but even to hold her own in the old society of Church or State; and was left, for the most part, with no place but the theatre or streets to decorate. She might glitter with historical diamonds and sparkle with wit as brilliant as the gems, in rooms as splendid as any in Rome at its best; but she saw no one except her own sex who knew enough to be worth dazzling, or was competent to pay her intelligent homage. She might have her own way, without restraint or limit, but she knew not what to do with herself when free. Never had the world known a more capable or devoted mother, but at forty her task was over, and she was left with no stage except that of her old duties, or of Washington society where she had enjoyed for a hundred years every advantage, but had created only a medley where nine men out of ten refused her request to be civilized, and the tenth bored her.

On most subjects, one's opinions must defer to science, but on this, the opinion of a Senator or a Professor, a chairman of a State Central Committee or a Railway President, is worth less than that of any woman on Fifth Avenue. The inferiority of man on this, the most important of all social subjects, is manifest. Adams had here no occasion to deprecate scientific opinion, since no woman in the world would have paid the smallest respect to the opinions of all professors since the serpent. His own object had little to do with theirs. He was studying the laws of motion, and had struck two large questions of vital importance to America -- inertia of race and inertia of sex. He had seen Mr. de Witte and Prince Khilkoff turn artificial energy to the value of three thousand million dollars, more or less, upon Russian inertia, in the last twenty years, and he needed to get some idea of the effects. He had seen artificial energy to the amount of twenty or five-and-twenty million steam horse-power created in America since 1840, and as much more economized, which had been socially turned over to the American woman, she being the chief object of social expenditure, and the household the only considerable object of American extravagance. According to scientific notions of inertia and force, what ought to be the result?

In Russia, because of race and bulk, no result had yet shown itself, but in America the results were evident and undisputed. The woman had been set free -- volatilized like Clerk Maxwell's perfect gas; almost brought to the point of explosion, like steam. One had but to pass a week in Florida, or on any of a hundred huge ocean steamers, or walk through the Place Vendome, or join a party of Cook's tourists to Jerusalem, to see that the woman had been set free; but these swarms were ephemeral like clouds of butterflies in season, blown away and lost, while the reproductive sources lay hidden. At Washington, one saw other swarms as grave gatherings of Dames or Daughters, taking themselves seriously, or brides fluttering fresh pinions; but all these shifting visions, unknown before 1840, touched the true problem slightly and superficially. Behind them, in every city, town, and farmhouse, were myriads of new types -- or type-writers -- telephone and telegraph-girls, shop-clerks, factory-hands, running into millions of millions, and, as classes, unknown to themselves as to historians. Even the schoolmistresses were inarticulate. All these new women had been created since 1840; all were to show their meaning before 1940.

Whatever they were, they were not content, as the ephemera proved; and they were hungry for illusions as ever in the fourth century of the Church; but this was probably survival, and gave no hint of the future. The problem remained -- to find out whether movement of inertia, inherent in function, could take direction except in lines of inertia. This problem needed to be solved in one generation of American women, and was the most vital of all problems of force.

The American woman at her best -- like most other women -- exerted great charm on the man, but not the charm of a primitive type. She appeared as the result of a long series of discards, and her chief interest lay in what she had discarded. When closely watched, she seemed making a violent effort to follow the man, who had turned his mind and hand to mechanics. The typical American man had his hand on a lever and his eye on a curve in his road; his living depended on keeping up an average speed of forty miles an hour, tending always to become sixty, eighty, or a hundred, and he could not admit emotions or anxieties or subconscious distractions, more than he could admit whiskey or drugs, without breaking his neck. He could not run his machine and a woman too; he must leave her; even though his wife, to find her own way, and all the world saw her trying to find her way by imitating him.

The result was often tragic, but that was no new thing in feminine history. Tragedy had been woman's lot since Eve. Her problem had been always one of physical strength and it was as physical perfection of force that her Venus had governed nature. The woman's force had counted as inertia of rotation, and her axis of rotation had been the cradle and the family. The idea that she was weak revolted all history; it was a palaeontological falsehood that even an Eocene female monkey would have laughed at; but it was surely true that, if her force were to be diverted from its axis, it must find a new field, and the family must pay for it. So far as she succeeded, she must become sexless like the bees, and must leave the old energy of inertia to carry on the race.

The story was not new. For thousands of years women had rebelled. They had made a fortress of religion -- had buried themselves in the cloister, in self-sacrifice, in good works -- or even in bad. One's studies in the twelfth century, like one's studies in the fourth, as in Homeric and archaic time, showed her always busy in the illusions of heaven or of hell -- ambition, intrigue, jealousy, magic -- but the American woman had no illusions or ambitions or new resources, and nothing to rebel against, except her own maternity; yet the rebels increased by millions from year to year till they blocked the path of rebellion. Even her field of good works was narrower than in the twelfth century. Socialism, communism, collectivism, philosophical anarchism, which promised paradise on earth for every male, cut off the few avenues of escape which capitalism had opened to the woman, and she saw before her only the future reserved for machine-made, collectivist females.

From the male, she could look for no help; his instinct of power was blind. The Church had known more about women than science will ever know, and the historian who studied the sources of Christianity felt sometimes convinced that the Church had been made by the woman chiefly as her protest against man. At times, the historian would have been almost willing to maintain that the man had overthrown the Church chiefly because it was feminine. After the overthrow of the Church, the woman had no refuge except such as the man created for himself. She was free; she had no illusions; she was sexless; she had discarded all that the male disliked; and although she secretly regretted the discard, she knew that she could not go backward. She must, like the man, marry machinery. Already the American man sometimes felt surprise at finding himself regarded as sexless; the American woman was oftener surprised at finding herself regarded as sexual.

No honest historian can take part with -- or against -- the forces he has to study. To him even the extinction of the human race should be merely a fact to be grouped with other vital statistics. No doubt every one in society discussed the subject, impelled by President Roosevelt if by nothing else, and the surface current of social opinion seemed set as strongly in one direction as the silent undercurrent of social action ran in the other; but the truth lay somewhere unconscious in the woman's breast. An elderly man, trying only to learn the law of social inertia and the limits of social divergence could not compel the Superintendent of the Census to ask every young woman whether she wanted children, and how many; he could not even require of an octogenarian Senate the passage of a law obliging every woman, married or not, to bear one baby -- at the expense of the Treasury -- before she was thirty years old, under penalty of solitary confinement for life; yet these were vital statistics in more senses than all that bore the name, and tended more directly to the foundation of a serious society in the future. He could draw no conclusions whatever except from the birth-rate. He could not frankly discuss the matter with the young women themselves, although they would have gladly discussed it, because Faust was helpless in the tragedy of woman. He could suggest nothing. The Marguerite of the future could alone decide whether she were better off than the Marguerite of the past; whether she would rather be victim to a man, a church, or a machine.

Between these various forms of inevitable inertia -- sex and race -- the student of multiplicity felt inclined to admit that -- ignorance against ignorance -- the Russian problem seemed to him somewhat easier of treatment than the American. Inertia of race and bulk would require an immense force to overcome it, but in time it might perhaps be partially overcome. Inertia of sex could not be overcome without extinguishing the race, yet an immense force, doubling every few years, was working irresistibly to overcome it. One gazed mute before this ocean of darkest ignorance that had already engulfed society. Few centres of great energy lived in illusion more complete or archaic than Washington with its simple-minded standards of the field and farm, its Southern and Western habits of life and manners, its assumptions of ethics and history; but even in Washington, society was uneasy enough to need no further fretting. One was almost glad to act the part of horseshoe crab in Quincy Bay, and admit that all was uniform -- that nothing ever changed -- and that the woman would swim about the ocean of future time, as she had swum in the past, with the gar-fish and the shark, unable to change.

Chapter XXXI. The Grammar of Science (1903)

OF all the travels made by man since the voyages of Dante, this new exploration along the shores of Multiplicity and Complexity promised to be the longest, though as yet it had barely touched two familiar regions -- race and sex. Even within these narrow seas the navigator lost his bearings and followed the winds as they blew. By chance it happened that Raphael Pumpelly helped the winds; for, being in Washington on his way to Central Asia he fell to talking with Adams about these matters, and said that Willard Gibbs thought he got most help from a book called the "Grammar of Science," by Karl Pearson. To Adams's vision, Willard Gibbs stood on the same plane with the three or four greatest minds of his century, and the idea that a man so incomparably superior should find help anywhere filled him with wonder. He sent for the volume and read it. From the time he sailed for Europe and reached his den on the Avenue du Bois until he took his return steamer at Cherbourg on December 26, he did little but try to kind out what Karl Pearson could have taught Willard Gibbs.

Here came in, more than ever, the fatal handicap of ignorance in mathematics. Not so much the actual tool was needed, as the right to judge the product of the tool. Ignorant as one was of the finer values of French or German, and often deceived by the intricacies of thought hidden in the muddiness of the medium, one could sometimes catch a tendency to intelligible meaning even in Kant or Hegel; but one had not the right to a suspicion of error where the tool of thought was algebra. Adams could see in such parts of the "Grammar" as he could understand, little more than an enlargement of Stallo's book already twenty years old. He never found out what it could have taught a master like Willard Gibbs. Yet the book had a historical value out of all proportion to its science. No such stride had any Englishman before taken in the lines of English thought. The progress of science was measured by the success of the "Grammar," when, for twenty years past, Stallo had been deliberately ignored under the usual conspiracy of silence inevitable to all thought which demands new thought-machinery. Science needs time to reconstruct its instruments, to follow a revolution in space; a certain lag is inevitable; the most active mind cannot instantly swerve from its path; but such revolutions are portentous, and the fall or rise of half-a-dozen empires interested a student of history less than the rise of the "Grammar of Science," the more pressingly because, under the silent influence of Langley, he was prepared to expect it.

For a number of years Langley had published in his Smithsonian Reports the revolutionary papers that foretold the overthrow of nineteenth-century dogma, and among the first was the famous address of Sir William Crookes on psychical research, followed by a series of papers on Roentgen and Curie, which had steadily driven the scientific lawgivers of Unity into the open; but Karl Pearson was the first to pen them up for slaughter in the schools. The phrase is not stronger than that with which the "Grammar of Science" challenged the fight: "Anything more hopelessly illogical than the statements with regard to Force and Matter current in elementary textbooks of science, it is difficult to imagine," opened Mr. Pearson, and the responsible author of the "elementary textbook," as he went on to explain, was Lord Kelvin himself. Pearson shut out of science everything which the nineteenth century had brought into it. He told his scholars that they must put up with a fraction of the universe, and a very small fraction at that -- the circle reached by the senses, where sequence could be taken for granted -- much as the deep-sea fish takes for granted the circle of light which he generates. "Order and reason, beauty and benevolence, are characteristics and conceptions which we find solely associated with the mind of man." The assertion, as a broad truth, left one's mind in some doubt of its bearing, for order and beauty seemed to be associated also in the mind of a crystal, if one's senses were to be admitted as judge; but the historian had no interest in the universal truth of Pearson's or Kelvin's or Newton's laws; he sought only their relative drift or direction, and Pearson went on to say that these conceptions must stop: "Into the chaos beyond sense-impressions we cannot scientifically project them." We cannot even infer them: "In the chaos behind sensations, in the 'beyond' of sense-impressions, we cannot infer necessity, order or routine, for these are concepts formed by the mind of man on this side of sense-impressions"; but we must infer chaos: "Briefly chaos is all that science can logically assert of the supersensuous." The kinetic theory of gas is an assertion of ultimate chaos. In plain words, Chaos was the law of nature; Order was the dream of man.

No one means all he says, and yet very few say all they mean, for words are slippery and thought is viscous; but since Bacon and Newton, English thought had gone on impatiently protesting that no one must try to know the unknowable at the same time that every one went on thinking about it. The result was as chaotic as kinetic gas; but with the thought a historian had nothing to do. He sought only its direction. For himself he knew, that, in spite of all the Englishmen that ever lived, he would be forced to enter supersensual chaos if he meant to find out what became of British science -- or indeed of any other science. From Pythagoras to Herbert Spencer, every one had done it, although commonly science had explored an ocean which it preferred to regard as Unity or a Universe, and called Order. Even Hegel, who taught that every notion included its own negation, used the negation only to reach a "larger synthesis," till he reached the universal which thinks itself, contradiction and all. The Church alone had constantly protested that anarchy was not order, that Satan was not God, that pantheism was worse than atheism, and that Unity could not be proved as a contradiction. Karl Pearson seemed to agree with the Church, but every one else, including Newton, Darwin and Clerk Maxwell, had sailed gaily into the supersensual, calling it: --

"One God, one Law, one Element,

And one far-off, divine event,

To which the whole creation moves."

Suddenly, in 1900, science raised its head and denied.

Yet, perhaps, after all, the change had not been so sudden as it seemed. Real and actual, it certainly was, and every newspaper betrayed it, but sequence could scarcely be denied by one who had watched its steady approach, thinking the change far more interesting to history than the thought. When he reflected about it, he recalled that the flow of tide had shown itself at least twenty years before; that it had become marked as early as 1893; and that the man of science must have been sleepy indeed who did not jump from his chair like a scared dog when, in 1898, Mme. Curie threw on his desk the metaphysical bomb she called radium. There remained no hole to hide in. Even metaphysics swept back over science with the green water of the deep-sea ocean and no one could longer hope to bar out the unknowable, for the unknowable was known.

The fact was admitted that the uniformitarians of one's youth had wound about their universe a tangle of contradictions meant only for temporary support to be merged in "larger synthesis," and had waited for the larger synthesis in silence and in vain. They had refused to hear Stallo. They had betrayed little interest in Crookes. At last their universe had been wrecked by rays, and Karl Pearson undertook to cut the wreck loose with an axe, leaving science adrift on a sensual raft in the midst of a supersensual chaos. The confusion seemed, to a mere passenger, worse than that of 1600 when the astronomers upset the world; it resembled rather the convulsion of 310 when the Civitas Dei cut itself loose from the Civitas Romae, and the Cross took the place of the legions; but the historian accepted it all alike; he knew that his opinion was worthless; only, in this case, he found himself on the raft, personally and economically concerned in its drift.

English thought had always been chaos and multiplicity itself, in which the new step of Karl Pearson marked only a consistent progress; but German thought had affected system, unity, and abstract truth, to a point that fretted the most patient foreigner, and to Germany the voyager in strange seas of thought alone might resort with confident hope of renewing his youth. Turning his back on Karl Pearson and England, he plunged into Germany, and had scarcely crossed the Rhine when he fell into libraries of new works bearing the names of Ostwald, Ernst Mach, Ernst Haeckel, and others less familiar, among whom Haeckel was easiest to approach, not only because of being the oldest and clearest and steadiest spokesman of nineteenth-century mechanical convictions, but also because in 1902 he had published a vehement renewal of his faith. The volume contained only one paragraph that concerned a historian; it was that in which Haeckel sank his voice almost to a religious whisper in avowing with evident effort, that the "proper essence of substance appeared to him more and more marvellous and enigmatic as he penetrated further into the knowledge of its attributes -- matter and energy -- and as he learned to know their innumerable phenomena and their evolution." Since Haeckel seemed to have begun the voyage into multiplicity that Pearson had forbidden to Englishmen, he should have been a safe pilot to the point, at least, of a "proper essence of substance" in its attributes of matter and energy: but Ernst Mach seemed to go yet one step further, for he rejected matter altogether, and admitted but two processes in nature -- change of place and interconversion of forms. Matter was Motion -- Motion was Matter -- the thing moved.

A student of history had no need to understand these scientific ideas of very great men; he sought only the relation with the ideas of their grandfathers, and their common direction towards the ideas of their grandsons. He had long ago reached, with Hegel, the limits of contradiction; and Ernst Mach scarcely added a shade of variety to the identity of opposites; but both of them seemed to be in agreement with Karl Pearson on the facts of the supersensual universe which could be known only as unknowable.

With a deep sigh of relief, the traveller turned back to France. There he felt safe. No Frenchman except Rabelais and Montaigne had ever taught anarchy other than as path to order. Chaos would be unity in Paris even if child of the guillotine. To make this assurance mathematically sure, the highest scientific authority in France was a great mathematician, M. Poincare of the Institut, who published in 1902 a small volume called "La Science et l'Hypothese," which purported to be relatively readable. Trusting to its external appearance, the traveller timidly bought it, and greedily devoured it, without understanding a single consecutive page, but catching here and there a period that startled him to the depths of his ignorance, for they seemed to show that M. Poincare was troubled by the same historical landmarks which guided or deluded Adams himself: "[In science] we are led," said M. Poincare, " to act as though a simple law, when other things were equal, must be more probable than a complicated law. Half a century ago one frankly confessed it, and proclaimed that nature loves simplicity. She has since given us too often the lie. To-day this tendency is no longer avowed, and only as much of it is preserved as is indispensable so that science shall not become impossible."

Here at last was a fixed point beyond the chance of confusion with self-suggestion. History and mathematics agreed. Had M. Poincare shown anarchistic tastes, his evidence would have weighed less heavily; but he seemed to be the only authority in science who felt what a historian felt so strongly -- the need of unity in a universe. "Considering everything we have made some approach towards unity. We have not gone as fast as we hoped fifty years ago; we have not always taken the intended road; but definitely we have gained much ground." This was the most clear and convincing evidence of progress yet offered to the navigator of ignorance; but suddenly he fell on another view which seemed to him quite irreconcilable with the first: "Doubtless if our means of investigation should become more and more penetrating, we should discover the simple under the complex; then the complex under the simple; then anew the simple under the complex; and so on without ever being able to foresee the last term."

A mathematical paradise of endless displacement promised eternal bliss to the mathematician, but turned the historian green with horror. Made miserable by the thought that he knew no mathematics, he burned to ask whether M. Poincare knew any history, since he began by begging the historical question altogether, and assuming that the past showed alternating phases of simple and complex -- the precise point that Adams, after fifty years of effort, found himself forced to surrender; and then going on to assume alternating phases for the future which, for the weary Titan of Unity, differed in nothing essential from the kinetic theory of a perfect gas.

Since monkeys first began to chatter in trees, neither man nor beast had ever denied or doubted Multiplicity, Diversity, Complexity, Anarchy, Chaos. Always and everywhere the Complex had been true and the Contradiction had been certain. Thought started by it. Mathematics itself began by counting one -- two -- three; then imagining their continuity, which M. Poincare was still exhausting his wits to explain or defend; and this was his explanation: "In short, the mind has the faculty of creating symbols, and it is thus that it has constructed mathematical continuity which is only a particular system of symbols." With the same light touch, more destructive in its artistic measure than the heaviest-handed brutality of Englishmen or Germans, he went on to upset relative truth itself: "How should I answer the question whether Euclidian Geometry is true? It has no sense! . . . Euclidian Geometry is, and will remain, the most convenient."

Chaos was a primary fact even in Paris -- especially in Paris -- as it was in the Book of Genesis; but every thinking being in Paris or out of it had exhausted thought in the effort to prove Unity, Continuity, Purpose, Order, Law, Truth, the Universe, God, after having begun by taking it for granted, and discovering, to their profound dismay, that some minds denied it. The direction of mind, as a single force of nature, had been constant since history began. Its own unity had created a universe the essence of which was abstract Truth; the Absolute; God! To Thomas Aquinas, the universe was still a person; to Spinoza, a substance; to Kant, Truth was the essence of the "I"; an innate conviction; a categorical imperative; to Poincare, it was a convenience; and to Karl Pearson, a medium of exchange.

The historian never stopped repeating to himself that he knew nothing about it; that he was a mere instrument of measure, a barometer, pedometer, radiometer; and that his whole share in the matter was restricted to the measurement of thought-motion as marked by the accepted thinkers. He took their facts for granted. He knew no more than a firefly about rays -- or about race -- or sex -- or ennui -- or a bar of music -- or a pang of love -- or a grain of musk -- or of phosphorus -- or conscience -- or duty -- or the force of Euclidian geometry -- or non-Euclidian -- or heat -- or light -- or osmosis -- or electrolysis -- or the magnet -- or ether -- or vis inertiae -- or gravitation -- or cohesion -- or elasticity -- or surface tension -- or capillary attraction -- or Brownian motion -- or of some scores, or thousands, or millions of chemical attractions, repulsions or indifferences which were busy within and without him; or, in brief, of Force itself, which, he was credibly informed, bore some dozen definitions in the textbooks, mostly contradictory, and all, as he was assured, beyond his intelligence; but summed up in the dictum of the last and highest science, that Motion seems to be Matter and Matter seems to be Motion, yet "we are probably incapable of discovering" what either is. History had no need to ask what either might be; all it needed to know was the admission of ignorance; the mere fact of multiplicity baffling science. Even as to the fact, science disputed, but radium happened to radiate something that seemed to explode the scientific magazine, bringing thought, for the time, to a standstill; though, in the line of thought-movement in history, radium was merely the next position, familiar and inexplicable since Zeno and his arrow: continuous from the beginning of time, and discontinuous at each successive point. History set it down on the record -- pricked its position on the chart -- and waited to be led, or misled, once more.

The historian must not try to know what is truth, if he values his honesty; for, if he cares for his truths, he is certain to falsify his facts. The laws of history only repeat the lines of force or thought. Yet though his will be iron, he cannot help now and then resuming his humanity or simianity in face of a fear. The motion of thought had the same value as the motion of a cannon-ball seen approaching the observer on a direct line through the air. One could watch its curve for five thousand years. Its first violent acceleration in historical times had ended in the catastrophe of 310. The next swerve of direction occurred towards 1500. Galileo and Bacon gave a still newer curve to it, which altered its values; but all these changes had never altered the continuity. Only in 1900, the continuity snapped.

Vaguely conscious of the cataclysm, the world sometimes dated it from 1893, by the Roentgen rays, or from 1898, by the Curie's radium; but in 1904, Arthur Balfour announced on the part of British science that the human race without exception had lived and died in a world of illusion until the last year of the century. The date was convenient, and convenience was truth.

The child born in 1900 would, then, be born into a new world which would not be a unity but a multiple. Adams tried to imagine it, and an education that would fit it. He found himself in a land where no one had ever penetrated before; where order was an accidental relation obnoxious to nature; artificial compulsion imposed on motion; against which every free energy of the universe revolted; and which, being merely occasional, resolved itself back into anarchy at last. He could not deny that the law of the new multiverse explained much that had been most obscure, especially the persistently fiendish treatment of man by man; the perpetual effort of society to establish law, and the perpetual revolt of society against the law it had established; the perpetual building up of authority by force, and the perpetual appeal to force to overthrow it; the perpetual symbolism of a higher law, and the perpetual relapse to a lower one; the perpetual victory of the principles of freedom, and their perpetual conversion into principles of power; but the staggering problem was the outlook ahead into the despotism of artificial order which nature abhorred. The physicists had a phrase for it, unintelligible to the vulgar: "All that we win is a battle -- lost in advance -- with the irreversible phenomena in the background of nature."

All that a historian won was a vehement wish to escape. He saw his education complete; and was sorry he ever began it. As a matter of taste, he greatly preferred his eighteenth-century education when God was a father and nature a mother, and all was for the best in a scientific universe. He repudiated all share in the world as it was to be, and yet he could not detect the point where his responsibility began or ended.

As history unveiled itself in the new order, man's mind had behaved like a young pearl oyster, secreting its universe to suit its conditions until it had built up a shell of nacre that embodied all its notions of the perfect. Man knew it was true because he made it, and he loved it for the same reason. He sacrificed millions of lives to acquire his unity, but he achieved it, and justly thought it a work of art. The woman especially did great things, creating her deities on a higher level than the male, and, in the end, compelling the man to accept the Virgin as guardian of the man's God. The man's part in his Universe was secondary, but the woman was at home there, and sacrificed herself without limit to make it habitable, when man permitted it, as sometimes happened for brief intervals of war and famine; but she could not provide protection against forces of nature. She did not think of her universe as a raft to which the limpets stuck for life in the surge of a supersensual chaos; she conceived herself and her family as the centre and flower of an ordered universe which she knew to be unity because she had made it after the image of her own fecundity; and this creation of hers was surrounded by beauties and perfections which she knew to be real because she herself had imagined them.

Even the masculine philosopher admired and loved and celebrated her triumph, and the greatest of them sang it in the noblest of his verses: --

"Alma Venus, coeli subter labentia signa

Quae mare navigerum, quae terras frugiferenteis

Concelebras . . . .

Quae quondam rerum naturam sola gubernas,

Nec sine te quidquam dias in luminis oras

Exoritur, neque fit laetum neque amabile quidquam;

Te sociam studeo!"

Neither man nor woman ever wanted to quit this Eden of their own invention, and could no more have done it of their own accord than the pearl oyster could quit its shell; but although the oyster might perhaps assimilate or embalm a grain of sand forced into its aperture, it could only perish in face of the cyclonic hurricane or the volcanic upheaval of its bed. Her supersensual chaos killed her.

Such seemed the theory of history to be imposed by science on the generation born after 1900. For this theory, Adams felt himself in no way responsible. Even as historian he had made it his duty always to speak with respect of everything that had ever been thought respectable -- except an occasional statesman; but he had submitted to force all his life, and he meant to accept it for the future as for the past. All his efforts had been turned only to the search for its channel. He never invented his facts; they were furnished him by the only authorities he could find. As for himself, according to Helmholz, Ernst Mach, and Arthur Balfour, he was henceforth to be a conscious ball of vibrating motions, traversed in every direction by infinite lines of rotation or vibration, rolling at the feet of the Virgin at Chartres or of M. Poincare in an attic at Paris, a centre of supersensual chaos. The discovery did not distress him. A solitary man of sixty-five years or more, alone in a Gothic cathedral or a Paris apartment, need fret himself little about a few illusions more or less. He should have learned his lesson fifty years earlier; the times had long passed when a student could stop before chaos or order; he had no choice but to march with his world.

Nevertheless, he could not pretend that his mind felt flattered by this scientific outlook. Every fabulist has told how the human mind has always struggled like a frightened bird to escape the chaos which caged it; how -- appearing suddenly and inexplicably out of some unknown and unimaginable void; passing half its known life in the mental chaos of sleep; victim even when awake, to its own ill-adjustment, to disease, to age, to external suggestion, to nature's compulsion; doubting its sensations, and, in the last resort, trusting only to instruments and averages -- after sixty or seventy years of growing astonishment, the mind wakes to find itself looking blankly into the void of death. That it should profess itself pleased by this performance was all that the highest rules of good breeding could ask; but that it should actually be satisfied would prove that it existed only as idiocy.

Satisfied, the future generation could scarcely think itself, for even when the mind existed in a universe of its own creation, it had never been quite at ease. As far as one ventured to interpret actual science, the mind had thus far adjusted itself by an infinite series of infinitely delicate adjustments forced on it by the infinite motion of an infinite chaos of motion; dragged at one moment into the unknowable and unthinkable, then trying to scramble back within its senses and to bar the chaos out, but always assimilating bits of it, until at last, in 1900, a new avalanche of unknown forces had fallen on it, which required new mental powers to control. If this view was correct, the mind could gain nothing by flight or by fight; it must merge in its supersensual multiverse, or succumb to it.

Chapter XXXII. Vis Nova (1903-1904)

PARIS after midsummer is a place where only the industrious poor remain, unless they can get away; but Adams knew no spot where history would be better off, and the calm of the Champs Elysees was so deep that when Mr. de Witte was promoted to a powerless dignity, no one whispered that the promotion was disgrace, while one might have supposed, from the silence, that the Viceroy Alexeieff had reoccupied Manchuria as a fulfilment of treaty-obligation. For once, the conspiracy of silence became crime. Never had so modern and so vital a riddle been put before Western society, but society shut its eyes. Manchuria knew every step into war; Japan had completed every preparation; Alexeieff had collected his army and fleet at Port Arthur, mounting his siege guns and laying in enormous stores, ready for the expected attack; from Yokohama to Irkutsk, the whole East was under war conditions; but Europe knew nothing. The banks would allow no disturbance; the press said not a word, and even the embassies were silent. Every anarchist in Europe buzzed excitement and began to collect in groups, but the Hotel Ritz was calm, and the Grand Dukes who swarmed there professed to know directly from the Winter Palace that there would be no war.

As usual, Adams felt as ignorant as the best-informed statesman, and though the sense was familiar, for once he could see that the ignorance was assumed. After nearly fifty years of experience, he could not understand how the comedy could be so well acted. Even as late as November, diplomats were gravely asking every passer-by for his opinion, and avowed none of their own except what was directly authorized at St. Petersburg. He could make nothing of it. He found himself in face of his new problem -- the workings of Russian inertia -- and he could conceive no way of forming an opinion how much was real and how much was comedy had he been in the Winter Palace himself. At times he doubted whether the Grand Dukes or the Czar knew, but old diplomatic training forbade him to admit such innocence.

This was the situation at Christmas when he left Paris. On January 6, 1904, he reached Washington, where the contrast of atmosphere astonished him, for he had never before seen his country think as a world-power. No doubt, Japanese diplomacy had much to do with this alertness, but the immense superiority of Japanese diplomacy should have been more evident in Europe than in America, and in any case, could not account for the total disappearance of Russian diplomacy. A government by inertia greatly disconcerted study. One was led to suspect that Cassini never heard from his Government, and that Lamsdorf knew nothing of his own department; yet no such suspicion could be admitted. Cassini resorted to transparent blague: "Japan seemed infatuated even to the point of war! But what can the Japanese do? As usual, sit on their heels and pray to Buddha!" One of the oldest and most accomplished diplomatists in the service could never show his hand so empty as this if he held a card to play; but he never betrayed stronger resource behind. "If any Japanese succeed in entering Manchuria, they will never get out of it alive." The inertia of Cassini, who was naturally the most energetic of diplomatists, deeply interested a student of race-inertia, whose mind had lost itself in the attempt to invent scales of force.

The air of official Russia seemed most dramatic in the air of the White House, by contrast with the outspoken candor of the President. Reticence had no place there. Every one in America saw that, whether Russia or Japan were victim, one of the decisive struggles in American history was pending, and any presence of secrecy or indifference was absurd. Interest was acute, and curiosity intense, for no one knew what the Russian Government meant or wanted, while war had become a question of days. To an impartial student who gravely doubted whether the Czar himself acted as a conscious force or an inert weight, the straight-forward avowals of Roosevelt had singular value as a standard of measure. By chance it happened that Adams was obliged to take the place of his brother Brooks at the Diplomatic Reception immediately after his return home, and the part of proxy included his supping at the President's table, with Secretary Root on one side, the President opposite, and Miss Chamberlain between them. Naturally the President talked and the guests listened; which seemed, to one who had just escaped from the European conspiracy of silence, like drawing a free breath after stifling. Roosevelt, as every one knew, was always an amusing talker, and had the reputation of being indiscreet beyond any other man of great importance in the world, except the Kaiser Wilhelm and Mr. Joseph Chamberlain, the father of his guest at table; and this evening he spared none. With the usual abuse of the quos ego, common to vigorous statesmen, he said all that he thought about Russians and Japanese, as well as about Boers and British, without restraint, in full hearing of twenty people, to the entire satisfaction of his listener; and concluded by declaring that war was imminent; that it ought to be stopped; that it could be stopped: " I could do it myself; I could stop it to-morrow!" and he went on to explain his reasons for restraint.

That he was right, and that, within another generation, his successor would do what he would have liked to do, made no shadow of doubt in the mind of his hearer, though it would have been folly when he last supped at the White House in the dynasty of President Hayes; but the listener cared less for the assertion of power, than for the vigor of view. The truth was evident enough, ordinary, even commonplace if one liked, but it was not a truth of inertia, nor was the method to be mistaken for inert.

Nor could the force of Japan be mistaken for a moment as a force of inertia, although its aggressive was taken as methodically -- as mathematically -- as a demonstration of Euclid, and Adams thought that as against any but Russians it would have lost its opening. Each day counted as a measure of relative energy on the historical scale, and the whole story made a Grammar of new Science quite as instructive as that of Pearson.

The forces thus launched were bound to reach some new equilibrium which would prove the problem in one sense or another, and the war had no personal value for Adams except that it gave Hay his last great triumph. He had carried on his long contest with Cassini so skillfully that no one knew enough to understand the diplomatic perfection of his work, which contained no error; but such success is complete only when it is invisible, and his victory at last was victory of judgment, not of act. He could do nothing, and the whole country would have sprung on him had he tried. Japan and England saved his "open door" and fought his battle. All that remained for him was to make the peace, and Adams set his heart on getting the peace quickly in hand, for Hay's sake as well as for that of Russia. He thought then that it could be done in one campaign, for he knew that, in a military sense, the fall of Port Arthur must lead to negotiation, and every one felt that Hay would inevitably direct it; but the race was close, and while the war grew every day in proportions, Hay's strength every day declined.

St. Gaudens came on to model his head, and Sargent painted his portrait, two steps essential to immortality which he bore with a certain degree of resignation, but he grumbled when the President made him go to St. Louis to address some gathering at the Exposition; and Mrs. Hay bade Adams go with them, for whatever use he could suppose himself to serve. He professed the religion of World's Fairs, without which he held education to be a blind impossibility; and obeyed Mrs. Hay's bidding the more readily because it united his two educations in one; but theory and practice were put to equally severe test at St. Louis. Ten years had passed since he last crossed the Mississippi, and he found everything new. In this great region from Pittsburgh through Ohio and Indiana, agriculture had made way for steam; tall chimneys reeked smoke on every horizon, and dirty suburbs filled with scrap-iron, scrap-paper and cinders, formed the setting of every town. Evidently, cleanliness was not to be the birthmark of the new American, but this matter of discards concerned the measure of force little, while the chimneys and cinders concerned it so much that Adams thought the Secretary of State should have rushed to the platform at every station to ask who were the people; for the American of the prime seemed to be extinct with the Shawnee and the buffalo.

The subject grew quickly delicate. History told little about these millions of Germans and Slavs, or whatever their race-names, who had overflowed these regions as though the Rhine and the Danube had turned their floods into the Ohio. John Hay was as strange to the Mississippi River as though he had not been bred on its shores, and the city of St. Louis had turned its back on the noblest work of nature, leaving it bankrupt between its own banks. The new American showed his parentage proudly; he was the child of steam and the brother of the dynamo, and already, within less than thirty years, this mass of mixed humanities, brought together by steam, was squeezed and welded into approach to shape; a product of so much mechanical power, and bearing no distinctive marks but that of its pressure. The new American, like the new European, was the servant of the powerhouse, as the European of the twelfth century was the servant of the Church, and the features would follow the parentage.

The St. Louis Exposition was its first creation in the twentieth century, and, for that reason, acutely interesting. One saw here a third-rate town of half-a-million people without history, education, unity, or art, and with little capital -- without even an element of natural interest except the river which it studiously ignored -- but doing what London, Paris, or New York would have shrunk from attempting. This new social conglomerate, with no tie but its steam-power and not much of that, threw away thirty or forty million dollars on a pageant as ephemeral as a stage flat. The world had never witnessed so marvellous a phantasm by night Arabia's crimson sands had never returned a glow half so astonishing, as one wandered among long lines of white palaces, exquisitely lighted by thousands on thousands of electric candles, soft, rich, shadowy, palpable in their sensuous depths; all in deep silence, profound solitude, listening for a voice or a foot-fall or the plash of an oar, as though the Emir Mirza were displaying the beauties of this City of Brass, which could show nothing half so beautiful as this illumination, with its vast, white, monumental solitude, bathed in the pure light of setting suns. One enjoyed it with iniquitous rapture, not because of exhibits but rather because of their want. Here was a paradox like the stellar universe that fitted one's mental faults. Had there been no exhibits at all, and no visitors, one would have enjoyed it only the more.

Here education found new forage. That the power was wasted, the art indifferent, the economic failure complete, added just so much to the interest. The chaos of education approached a dream. One asked one's self whether this extravagance reflected the past or imaged the future; whether it was a creation of the old American or a promise of the new one. No prophet could be believed, but a pilgrim of power, without constituency to flatter, might allow himself to hope. The prospect from the Exposition was pleasant; one seemed to see almost an adequate motive for power; almost a scheme for progress. In another half-century, the people of the central valleys should have hundreds of millions to throw away more easily than in 1900 they could throw away tens; and by that time they might know what they wanted. Possibly they might even have learned how to reach it.

This was an optimist's hope, shared by few except pilgrims of World's Fairs, and frankly dropped by the multitude, for, east of the Mississippi, the St. Louis Exposition met a deliberate conspiracy of silence, discouraging, beyond measure, to an optimistic dream of future strength in American expression. The party got back to Washington on May 24, and before sailing for Europe, Adams went over, one warm evening, to bid good-bye on the garden-porch of the White House. He found himself the first person who urged Mrs. Roosevelt to visit the Exposition for its beauty, and, as far as he ever knew, the last.

He left St. Louis May 22, 1904, and on Sunday, June 5, found himself again in the town of Coutances, where the people of Normandy had built, towards the year 1250, an Exposition which architects still admired and tourists visited, for it was thought singularly expressive of force as well as of grace in the Virgin. On this Sunday, the Norman world was celebrating a pretty church-feast -- the Fete Dieu -- and the streets were filled with altars to the Virgin, covered with flowers and foliage; the pavements strewn with paths of leaves and the spring handiwork of nature; the cathedral densely thronged at mass. The scene was graceful. The Virgin did not shut her costly Exposition on Sunday, or any other day, even to American senators who had shut the St. Louis Exposition to her -- or for her; and a historical tramp would gladly have offered a candle, or even a candle-stick in her honor, if she would have taught him her relation with the deity of the Senators. The power of the Virgin had been plainly One, embracing all human activity; while the power of the Senate, or its deity, seemed -- might one say -- to be more or less ashamed of man and his work. The matter had no great interest as far as it concerned the somewhat obscure mental processes of Senators who could probably have given no clearer idea than priests of the deity they supposed themselves to honor -- if that was indeed their purpose; but it interested a student of force, curious to measure its manifestations. Apparently the Virgin -- or her Son -- had no longer the force to build expositions that one cared to visit, but had the force to close them. The force was still real, serious, and, at St. Louis, had been anxiously measured in actual money-value.

That it was actual and serious in France as in the Senate Chamber at Washington, proved itself at once by forcing Adams to buy an automobile, which was a supreme demonstration because this was the form of force which Adams most abominated. He had set aside the summer for study of the Virgin, not as a sentiment but as a motive power, which had left monuments widely scattered and not easily reached. The automobile alone could unite them in any reasonable sequence, and although the force of the automobile, for the purposes of a commercial traveller, seemed to have no relation whatever to the force that inspired a Gothic cathedral, the Virgin in the twelfth century would have guided and controlled both bag-man and architect, as she controlled the seeker of history. In his mind the problem offered itself as to Newton; it was a matter of mutual attraction, and he knew it, in his own case, to be a formula as precise as $s = gt^2/2$, if he could but experimentally prove it. Of the attraction he needed no proof on his own account; the costs of his automobile were more than sufficient: but as teacher he needed to speak for others than himself. For him, the Virgin was an adorable mistress, who led the automobile and its owner where she would, to her wonderful palaces and chateaux, from Chartres to Rouen, and thence to Amiens and Laon, and a score of others, kindly receiving, amusing, charming and dazzling her lover, as though she were Aphrodite herself, worth all else that man ever dreamed. He never doubted her force, since he felt it to the last fibre of his being, and could not more dispute its mastery than he could dispute the force of gravitation of which he knew nothing but the formula. He was only too glad to yield himself entirely, not to her charm or to any sentimentality of religion, but to her mental and physical energy of creation which had built up these World's Fairs of thirteenth-century force that turned Chicago and St. Louis pale.

"Both were faiths and both are gone," said Matthew Arnold of the Greek and Norse divinities; but the business of a student was to ask where they had gone. The Virgin had not even altogether gone; her fading away had been excessively slow. Her adorer had pursued her too long, too far, and into too many manifestations of her power, to admit that she had any equivalent either of quantity or kind, in the actual world, but he could still less admit her annihilation as energy.

So he went on wooing, happy in the thought that at last he had found a mistress who could see no difference in the age of her lovers. Her own age had no time-measure. For years past, incited by John La Farge, Adams had devoted his summer schooling to the study of her glass at Chartres and elsewhere, and if the automobile had one vitesse more useful than another, it was that of a century a minute; that of passing from one century to another without break. The centuries dropped like autumn leaves in one's road, and one was not fined for running over them too fast. When the thirteenth lost breath, the fourteenth caught on, and the sixteenth ran close ahead. The hunt for the Virgin's glass opened rich preserves. Especially the sixteenth century ran riot in sensuous worship. Then the ocean of religion, which had flooded France, broke into Shelley's light dissolved in star-showers thrown, which had left every remote village strewn with fragments that flashed like jewels, and were tossed into hidden clefts of peace and forgetfulness. One dared not pass a parish church in Champagne or Touraine without stopping to look for its window of fragments, where one's glass discovered the Christ-child in his manger, nursed by the head of a fragmentary donkey, with a Cupid playing into its long ears from the balustrade of a Venetian palace, guarded by a legless Flemish leibwache, standing on his head with a broken halbert; all invoked in prayer by remnants of the donors and their children that might have been drawn by Fouquet or Pinturicchio, in colors as fresh and living as the day they were burned in, and with feeling that still consoled the faithful for the paradise they had paid for and lost. France abounds in sixteenth-century glass. Paris alone contains acres of it, and the neighborhood within fifty miles contains scores of churches where the student may still imagine himself three hundred years old, kneeling before the Virgin's window in the silent solitude of an empty faith, crying his culp, beating his breast, confessing his historical sins, weighed down by the rubbish of sixty-six years' education, and still desperately hoping to understand.

He understood a little, though not much. The sixteenth century had a value of its own, as though the one had become several, and Unity had counted more than Three, though the Multiple still showed modest numbers. The glass had gone back to the Roman Empire and forward to the American continent; it betrayed sympathy with Montaigne and Shakespeare; but the Virgin was still supreme. At Beauvais in the Church of St. Stephen was a superb tree of Jesse, famous as the work of Engrand le Prince, about 1570 or 1580, in whose branches, among the fourteen ancestors of the Virgin, three-fourths bore features of the Kings of France, among them Francis I and Henry II, who were hardly more edifying than Kings of Israel, and at least unusual as sources of divine purity. Compared with the still more famous Tree of Jesse at Chartres, dating from 1150 or thereabouts, must one declare that Engrand le Prince proved progress? and in what direction? Complexity, Multiplicity, even a step towards Anarchy, it might suggest, but what step towards perfection?

One late afternoon, at midsummer, the Virgin's pilgrim was wandering through the streets of Troyes in close and intimate conversation with Thibaut of Champagne and his highly intelligent seneschal, the Sieur de Joinville, when he noticed one or two men looking at a bit of paper stuck in a window. Approaching, he read that M. de Plehve had been assassinated at St. Petersburg. The mad mixture of Russia and the Crusades, of the Hippodrome and the Renaissance, drove him for refuge into the fascinating Church of St. Pantaleon near by. Martyrs, murderers, Caesars, saints and assassins -- half in glass and half in telegram; chaos of time, place, morals, forces and motive -- gave him vertigo. Had one sat all one's life on the steps of Ara Coeli for this? Was assassination forever to be the last word of Progress? No one in the street had shown a sign of protest; he himself felt none; the charming Church with its delightful windows, in its exquisite absence of other tourists, took a keener expression of celestial peace than could have been given it by any contrast short of explosive murder; the conservative Christian anarchist had come to his own, but which was he -- the murderer or the murdered ?

The Virgin herself never looked so winning -- so One -- as in this scandalous failure of her Grace. To what purpose had she existed, if, after nineteen hundred years, the world was bloodier than when she was born? The stupendous failure of Christianity tortured history. The effort for Unity could not be a partial success; even alternating Unity resolved itself into meaningless motion at last. To the tired student, the idea that he must give it up seemed sheer senility. As long as he could whisper, he would go on as he had begun, bluntly refusing to meet his creator with the admission that the creation had taught him nothing except that the square of the hypotenuse of a right-angled triangle might for convenience be taken as equal to something else. Every man with self-respect enough to become effective, if only as a machine, has had to account to himself for himself somehow, and to invent a formula of his own for his universe, if the standard formulas failed. There, whether finished or not, education stopped. The formula, once made, could be but verified.

The effort must begin at once, for time pressed. The old formulas had failed, and a new one had to be made, but, after all, the object was not extravagant or eccentric. One sought no absolute truth. One sought only a spool on which to wind the thread of history without breaking it. Among indefinite possible orbits, one sought the orbit which would best satisfy the observed movement of the runaway star Groombridge, 1838, commonly called Henry Adams. As term of a nineteenth-century education, one sought a common factor for certain definite historical fractions. Any schoolboy could work out the problem if he were given the right to state it in his own terms.

Therefore, when the fogs and frosts stopped his slaughter of the centuries, and shut him up again in his garret, he sat down as though he were again a boy at school to shape after his own needs the values of a Dynamic Theory of History.

Chapter XXXIII. A Dynamic Theory of History (1904)

A DYNAMIC theory, like most theories, begins by begging the question: it defines Progress as the development and economy of Forces. Further, it defines force as anything that does, or helps to do work. Man is a force; so is the sun; so is a mathematical point, though without dimensions or known existence.

Man commonly begs the question again taking for granted that he captures the forces. A dynamic theory, assigning attractive force to opposing bodies in proportion to the law of mass, takes for granted that the forces of nature capture man. The sum of force attracts; the feeble atom or molecule called man is attracted; he suffers education or growth; he is the sum of the forces that attract him; his body and his thought are alike their product; the movement of the forces controls the progress of his mind, since he can know nothing but the motions which impinge on his senses, whose sum makes education.

For convenience as an image, the theory may liken man to a spider in its web, watching for chance prey. Forces of nature dance like flies before the net, and the spider pounces on them when it can; but it makes many fatal mistakes, though its theory of force is sound. The spider-mind acquires a faculty of memory, and, with it, a singular skill of analysis and synthesis, taking apart and putting together in different relations the meshes of its trap. Man had in the beginning no power of analysis or synthesis approaching that of the spider, or even of the honey-bee; he had acute sensibility to the higher forces. Fire taught him secrets that no other animal could learn; running water probably taught him even more, especially in his first lessons of mechanics; the animals helped to educate him, trusting themselves into his hands merely for the sake of their food, and carrying his burdens or supplying his clothing; the grasses and grains were academies of study. With little or no effort on his part, all these forces formed his thought, induced his action, and even shaped his figure.

Long before history began, his education was complete, for the record could not have been started until he had been taught to record. The universe that had formed him took shape in his mind as a reflection of his own unity, containing all forces except himself. Either separately, or in groups, or as a whole, these forces never ceased to act on him, enlarging his mind as they enlarged the surface foliage of a vegetable, and the mind needed only to respond, as the forests did, to these attractions. Susceptibility to the highest forces is the highest genius; selection between them is the highest science; their mass is the highest educator. Man always made, and still makes, grotesque blunders in selecting and measuring forces, taken at random from the heap, but he never made a mistake in the value he set on the whole, which he symbolized as unity and worshipped as God. To this day, his attitude towards it has never changed, though science can no longer give to force a name.

Man's function as a force of nature was to assimilate other forces as he assimilated food. He called it the love of power. He felt his own feebleness, and he sought for an ass or a camel, a bow or a sling, to widen his range of power, as he sough fetish or a planet in the world beyond. He cared little to know its immediate use, but he could afford to throw nothing away which he could conceive to have possible value in this or any other existence. He waited for the object to teach him its use, or want of use, and the process was slow. He may have gone on for hundreds of thousands of years, waiting for Nature to tell him her secrets; and, to his rivals among the monkeys, Nature has taught no more than at their start; but certain lines of force were capable of acting on individual apes, and mechanically selecting types of race or sources of variation. The individual that responded or reacted to lines of new force then was possibly the same individual that reacts on it now, and his conception of the unity seems never to have changed in spite of the increasing diversity of forces; but the theory of variation is an affair of other science than history, and matters nothing to dynamics. The individual or the race would be educated on the same lines of illusion, which, according to Arthur Balfour, had not essentially varied down to the year 1900.

To the highest attractive energy, man gave the name of divine, and for its control he invented the science called Religion, a word which meant, and still means, cultivation of occult force whether in detail or mass. Unable to define Force as a unity, man symbolized it and pursued it, both in himself, and in the infinite, as philosophy and theology; the mind is itself the subtlest of all known forces, and its self-introspection necessarily created a science which had the singular value of lifting his education, at the start, to the finest, subtlest, and broadest training both in analysis and synthesis, so that, if language is a test, he must have reached his highest powers early in his history; while the mere motive remained as simple an appetite for power as the tribal greed which led him to trap an elephant. Hunger, whether for food or for the infinite, sets in motion multiplicity and infinity of thought, and the sure hope of gaining a share of infinite power in eternal life would lift most minds to effort.

He had reached this completeness five thousand years ago, and added nothing to his stock of known forces for a very long time. The mass of nature exercised on him so feeble an attraction that one can scarcely account for his apparent motion. Only a historian of very exceptional knowledge would venture to say at what date between 3000 B.C. and 1000 A.D., the momentum of Europe was greatest; but such progress as the world made consisted in economies of energy rather than in its development; it was proved in mathematics, measured by names like Archimedes, Aristarchus, Ptolemy, and Euclid; or in Civil Law, measured by a number of names which Adams had begun life by failing to learn; or in coinage, which was most beautiful near its beginning, and most barbarous at its close; or it was shown in roads, or the size of ships, or harbors; or by the use of metals, instruments, and writing; all of them economies of force, sometimes more forceful than the forces they helped; but the roads were still travelled by the horse, the ass, the camel, or the slave; the ships were still propelled by sails or oars; the lever, the spring, and the screw bounded the region of applied mechanics. Even the metals were old.

Much the same thing could be said of religious or supernatural forces. Down to the year 300 of the Christian era they were little changed, and in spite of Plato and the sceptics were more apparently chaotic than ever. The experience of three thousand years had educated society to feel the vastness of Nature, and the infinity of her resources of power, but even this increase of attraction had not yet caused economies in its methods of pursuit.

There the Western world stood till the year A.D. 305, when the Emperor Diocletian abdicated; and there it was that Adams broke down on the steps of Ara Coeli, his path blocked by the scandalous failure of civilization at the moment it had achieved complete success. In the year 305 the empire had solved the problems of Europe more completely than they have ever been solved since. The Pax Romana, the Civil Law, and Free Trade should, in four hundred years, have put Europe far in advance of the point reached by modern society in the four hundred years since 1500, when conditions were less simple.

The efforts to explain, or explain away, this scandal had been incessant, but none suited Adams unless it were the economic theory of adverse exchanges and exhaustion of minerals; but nations are not ruined beyond a certain point by adverse exchanges, and Rome had by no means exhausted her resources. On the contrary, the empire developed resources and energies quite astounding. No other four hundred years of history before A.D. 1800 knew anything like it; and although some of these developments, like the Civil Law, the roads, aqueducts, and harbors, were rather economies than force, yet in northwestern Europe alone the empire had developed three energies -- France, England, and Germany -- competent to master the world. The trouble seemed rather to be that the empire developed too much energy, and too fast.

A dynamic law requires that two masses -- nature and man -- must go on, reacting upon each other, without stop, as the sun and a comet react on each other, and that any appearance of stoppage is illusive. The theory seems to exact excess, rather than deficiency, of action and reaction to account for the dissolution of the Roman Empire, which should, as a problem of mechanics, have been torn to pieces by acceleration. If the student means to try the experiment of framing a dynamic law, he must assign values to the forces of attraction that caused the trouble; and in this case he has them in plain evidence. With the relentless logic that stamped Roman thought, the empire, which had established unity on earth, could not help establishing unity in heaven. It was induced by its dynamic necessities to economize the gods.

The Church has never ceased to protest against the charge that Christianity ruined the empire, and, with its usual force, has pointed out that its reforms alone saved the State. Any dynamic theory gladly admits it. All it asks is to find and follow the force that attracts. The Church points out this force in the Cross, and history needs only to follow it. The empire loudly asserted its motive. Good taste forbids saying that Constantine the Great speculated as audaciously as a modern stock-broker on values of which he knew at the utmost only the volume; or that he merged all uncertain forces into a single trust, which he enormously overcapitalized, and forced on the market; but this is the substance of what Constantine himself said in his Edict of Milan in the year 313, which admitted Christianity into the Trust of State Religions. Regarded as an Act of Congress, it runs: "We have resolved to grant to Christians as well as all others the liberty to practice the religion they prefer, in order that whatever exists of divinity or celestial power may help and favor us and all who are under our government." The empire pursued power -- not merely spiritual but physical -- in the sense in which Constantine issued his army order the year before, at the battle of the Milvian Bridge: In hoc signo vinces! using the Cross as a train of artillery, which, to his mind, it was. Society accepted it in the same character. Eighty years afterwards, Theodosius marched against his rival Eugene with the Cross for physical champion; and Eugene raised the image of Hercules to fight for the pagans; while society on both sides looked on, as though it were a boxing-match, to decide a final test of force between the divine powers. The Church was powerless to raise the ideal. What is now known as religion affected the mind of old society but little. The laity, the people, the million, almost to a man, bet on the gods as they bet on a horse.

No doubt the Church did all it could to purify the process, but society was almost wholly pagan in its point of view, and was drawn to the Cross because, in its system of physics, the Cross had absorbed all the old occult or fetish-power. The symbol represented the sum of nature - the Energy of modern science - and society believed it to be as real as X-rays; perhaps it was! The emperors used it like gunpowder in politics; the physicians used it like rays in medicine; the dying clung to it as the quintessence of force, to protect them from the forces of evil on their road to the next life.

Throughout these four centuries the empire knew that religion disturbed economy, for even the cost of heathen incense affected the exchanges; but no one could afford to buy or construct a costly and complicated machine when he could hire an occult force at trifling expense. Fetish-power was cheap and satisfactory, down to a certain point. Turgot and Auguste Comte long ago fixed this stage of economy as a necessary phase of social education, and historians seem now to accept it as the only gain yet made towards scientific history. Great numbers of educated people -- perhaps a majority -- cling to the method still, and practice it more or less strictly; but, until quite recently, no other was known. The only occult power at man's disposal was fetish. Against it, no mechanical force could compete except within narrow limits.

Outside of occult or fetish-power, the Roman world was incredibly poor. It knew but one productive energy resembling a modern machine -- the slave. No artificial force of serious value was applied to production or transportation, and when society developed itself so rapidly in political and social lines, it had no other means of keeping its economy on the same level than to extend its slave-system and its fetish-system to the utmost.

The result might have been stated in a mathematical formula as early as the time of Archimedes, six hundred years before Rome fell. The economic needs of a violently centralizing society forced the empire to enlarge its slave-system until the slave-system consumed itself and the empire too, leaving society no resource but further enlargement of its religious system in order to compensate for the losses and horrors of the failure. For a vicious circle, its mathematical completeness approached perfection. The dynamic law of attraction and reaction needed only a Newton to fix it in algebraic form.

At last, in 410, Alaric sacked Rome, and the slave-ridden, agricultural, uncommercial Western Empire -- the poorer and less Christianized half -- went to pieces. Society, though terribly shocked by the horrors of Alaric's storm, felt still more deeply the disappointment in its new power, the Cross, which had failed to protect its Church. The outcry against the Cross became so loud among Christians that its literary champion, Bishop Augustine of Hippo -- a town between Algiers and Tunis -- was led to write a famous treatise in defence of the Cross, familiar still to every scholar, in which he defended feebly the mechanical value of the symbol -- arguing only that pagan symbols equally failed -- but insisted on its spiritual value in the Civitas Dei which had taken the place of the Civitas Romae in human interest. "Granted that we have lost all we had! Have we lost faith? Have we lost piety? Have we lost the wealth of the inner man who is rich before God? These are the wealth of Christians!" The Civitas Dei, in its turn, became the sum of attraction for the Western world, though it also showed the same weakness in mechanics that had wrecked the Civitas Romae. St. Augustine and his people perished at Hippo towards 430, leaving society in appearance dull to new attraction.

Yet the attraction remained constant. The delight of experimenting on occult force of every kind is such as to absorb all the free thought of the human race. The gods did their work; history has no quarrel with them; they led, educated, enlarged the mind; taught knowledge; betrayed ignorance; stimulated effort. So little is known about the mind -- whether social, racial, sexual or heritable; whether material or spiritual; whether animal, vegetable or mineral -- that history is inclined to avoid it altogether; but nothing forbids one to admit, for convenience, that it may assimilate food like the body, storing new force and growing, like a forest, with the storage. The brain has not yet revealed its mysterious mechanism of gray matter. Never has Nature offered it so violent a stimulant as when she opened to it the possibility of sharing infinite power in eternal life, and it might well need a thousand years of prolonged and intense experiment to prove the value of the motive. During these so-called Middle Ages, the Western mind reacted in many forms, on many sides, expressing its motives in modes, such as Romanesque and Gothic architecture, glass windows and mosaic walls, sculpture and poetry, war and love, which still affect some people as the noblest work of man, so that, even to-day, great masses of idle and ignorant tourists travel from far countries to look at Ravenna and San Marco, Palermo and Pisa, Assisi, Cordova, Chartres, with vague notions about the force that created them, but with a certain surprise that a social mind of such singular energy and unity should still lurk in their shadows.

The tourist more rarely visits Constantinople or studies the architecture of Sancta Sofia, but when he does, he is distinctly conscious of forces not quite the same. Justinian has not the simplicity of Charlemagne. The Eastern Empire showed an activity and variety of forces that classical Europe had never possessed. The navy of Nicephoras Phocas in the tenth century would have annihilated in half an hour any navy that Carthage or Athens or Rome ever set afloat. The dynamic scheme began by asserting rather recklessly that between the Pyramids (B.C. 3000), and the Cross (A.D. 300), no new force affected Western progress, and antiquarians may easily dispute the fact; but in any case the motive influence, old or new, which raised both Pyramids and Cross was the same attraction of power in a future life that raised the dome of Sancta Sofia and the Cathedral at Amiens, however much it was altered, enlarged, or removed to distance in space. Therefore, no single event has more puzzled historians than the sudden, unexplained appearance of at least two new natural forces of the highest educational value in mechanics, for the first time within record of history. Literally, these two forces seemed to drop from the sky at the precise moment when the Cross on one side and the Crescent on the other, proclaimed the complete triumph of the Civitas Dei. Had the Manichean doctrine of Good and Evil as rival deities been orthodox, it would alone have accounted for this simultaneous victory of hostile powers.

Of the compass, as a step towards demonstration of the dynamic law, one may confidently say that it proved, better than any other force, the widening scope of the mind, since it widened immensely the range of contact between nature and thought. The compass educated. This must prove itself as needing no proof.

Of Greek fire and gunpowder, the same thing cannot certainly be said, for they have the air of accidents due to the attraction of religious motives. They belong to the spiritual world; or to the doubtful ground of Magic which lay between Good and Evil. They were chemical forces, mostly explosives, which acted and still act as the most violent educators ever known to man, but they were justly feared as diabolic, and whatever insolence man may have risked towards the milder teachers of his infancy, he was an abject pupil towards explosives. The Sieur de Joinville left a record of the energy with which the relatively harmless Greek fire educated and enlarged the French mind in a single night in the year 1249, when the crusaders were trying to advance on Cairo. The good king St. Louis and all his staff dropped on their knees at every fiery flame that flew by, praying -- "God have pity on us!" and never had man more reason to call on his gods than they, for the battle of religion between Christian and Saracen was trifling compared with that of education between gunpowder and the Cross.

The fiction that society educated itself, or aimed at a conscious purpose, was upset by the compass and gunpowder which dragged and drove Europe at will through frightful bogs of learning. At first, the apparent lag for want of volume in the new energies lasted one or two centuries, which closed the great epochs of emotion by the Gothic cathedrals and scholastic theology. The moment had Greek beauty and more than Greek unity, but it was brief; and for another century or two, Western society seemed to float in space without apparent motion. Yet the attractive mass of nature's energy continued to attract, and education became more rapid than ever before. Society began to resist, but the individual showed greater and greater insistence, without realizing what he was doing. When the Crescent drove the Cross in ignominy from Constantinople in 1453, Gutenberg and Fust were printing their first Bible at Mainz under the impression that they were helping the Cross. When Columbus discovered the West Indies in 1492, the Church looked on it as a victory of the Cross. When Luther and Calvin upset Europe half a century later, they were trying, like St. Augustine, to substitute the Civitas Dei for the Civitas Romae. When the Puritans set out for New England in 1620, they too were looking to found a Civitas Dei in State Street; and when Bunyan made his Pilgrimage in 1678, he repeated St. Jerome. Even when, after centuries of license, the Church reformed its discipline, and, to prove it, burned Giordano Bruno in 1600, besides condemning Galileo in 1630 -- as science goes on repeating to us every day -- it condemned anarchists, not atheists. None of the astronomers were irreligious men; all of them made a point of magnifying God through his works; a form of science which did their religion no credit. Neither Galileo nor Kepler, neither Spinoza nor Descartes, neither Leibnitz nor Newton, any more than Constantine the Great -- if so much -- doubted Unity. The utmost range of their heresies reached only its personality.

This persistence of thought-inertia is the leading idea of modern history. Except as reflected in himself, man has no reason for assuming unity in the universe, or an ultimate substance, or a prime-motor. The a priori insistence on this unity ended by fatiguing the more active -- or reactive -- minds; and Lord Bacon tried to stop it. He urged society to lay aside the idea of evolving the universe from a thought, and to try evolving thought from the universe. The mind should observe and register forces -- take them apart and put them together -- without assuming unity at all. "Nature, to be commanded, must be obeyed." "The imagination must be given not wings but weights." As Galileo reversed the action of earth and sun, Bacon reversed the relation of thought to force. The mind was thenceforth to follow the movement of matter, and unity must be left to shift for itself.

The revolution in attitude seemed voluntary, but in fact was as mechanical as the fall of a feather. Man created nothing. After 1500, the speed of progress so rapidly surpassed man's gait as to alarm every one, as though it were the acceleration of a falling body which the dynamic theory takes it to be. Lord Bacon was as much astonished by it as the Church was, and with reason. Suddenly society felt itself dragged into situations altogether new and anarchic -- situations which it could not affect, but which painfully affected it. Instinct taught it that the universe in its thought must be in danger when its reflection lost itself in space. The danger was all the greater because men of science covered it with "larger synthesis," and poets called the undevout astronomer mad. Society knew better. Yet the telescope held it rigidly standing on its head; the microscope revealed a universe that defied the senses; gunpowder killed whole races that lagged behind; the compass coerced the most imbruted mariner to act on the impossible idea that the earth was round; the press drenched Europe with anarchism. Europe saw itself, violently resisting, wrenched into false positions, drawn along new lines as a fish that is caught on a hook; but unable to understand by what force it was controlled. The resistance was often bloody, sometimes humorous, always constant. Its contortions in the eighteenth century are best studied in the wit of Voltaire, but all history and all philosophy from Montaigne and Pascal to Schopenhauer and Nietzsche deal with nothing else; and still, throughout it all, the Baconian law held good; thought did not evolve nature, but nature evolved thought. Not one considerable man of science dared face the stream of thought; and the whole number of those who acted, like Franklin, as electric conductors of the new forces from nature to man, down to the year 1800, did not exceed a few score, confined to a few towns in western Europe. Asia refused to be touched by the stream, and America, except for Franklin, stood outside.

Very slowly the accretion of these new forces, chemical and mechanical, grew in volume until they acquired sufficient mass to take the place of the old religious science, substituting their attraction for the attractions of the Civitas Dei, but the process remained the same. Nature, not mind, did the work that the sun does on the planets. Man depended more and more absolutely on forces other than his own, and on instruments which superseded his senses. Bacon foretold it: "Neither the naked hand nor the understanding, left to itself, can effect much. It is by instruments and helps that the work is done." Once done, the mind resumed its illusion, and society forgot its impotence; but no one better than Bacon knew its tricks, and for his true followers science always meant self-restraint, obedience, sensitiveness to impulse from without. "Non fingendum aut excogitandum sed inveniendum quid Natura faciat aut ferat."

The success of this method staggers belief, and even to-day can be treated by history only as a miracle of growth, like the sports of nature. Evidently a new variety of mind had appeared. Certain men merely held out their hands -- like Newton, watched an apple; like Franklin, flew a kite; like Watt, played with a tea-kettle -- and great forces of nature stuck to them as though she were playing ball. Governments did almost nothing but resist. Even gunpowder and ordnance, the great weapon of government, showed little development between 1400 and 1800. Society was hostile or indifferent, as Priestley and Jenner, and even Fulton, with reason complained in the most advanced societies in the world, while its resistance became acute wherever the Church held control; until all mankind seemed to draw itself out in a long series of groups, dragged on by an attractive power in advance, which even the leaders obeyed without understanding, as the planets obeyed gravity, or the trees obeyed heat and light.

The influx of new force was nearly spontaneous. The reaction of mind on the mass of nature seemed not greater than that of a comet on the sun; and had the spontaneous influx of force stopped in Europe, society must have stood still, or gone backward, as in Asia or Africa. Then only economies of process would have counted as new force, and society would have been better pleased; for the idea that new force must be in itself a good is only an animal or vegetable instinct. As Nature developed her hidden energies, they tended to become destructive. Thought itself became tortured, suffering reluctantly, impatiently, painfully, the coercion of new method. Easy thought had always been movement of inertia, and mostly mere sentiment; but even the processes of mathematics measured feebly the needs of force.

The stupendous acceleration after 1800 ended in 1900 with the appearance of the new class of supersensual forces, before which the man of science stood at first as bewildered and helpless as, in the fourth century, a priest of Isis before the Cross of Christ.

This, then, or something like this, would be a dynamic formula of history. Any schoolboy knows enough to object at once that it is the oldest and most universal of all theories. Church and State, theology and philosophy, have always preached it, differing only in the allotment of energy between nature and man. Whether the attractive energy has been called God or Nature, the mechanism has been always the same, and history is not obliged to decide whether the Ultimate tends to a purpose or not, or whether ultimate energy is one or many. Every one admits that the will is a free force, habitually decided by motives. No one denies that motives exist adequate to decide the will; even though it may not always be conscious of them. Science has proved that forces, sensible and occult, physical and metaphysical, simple and complex, surround, traverse, vibrate, rotate, repel, attract, without stop; that man's senses are conscious of few, and only in a partial degree; but that, from the beginning of organic existence, his consciousness has been induced, expanded, trained in the lines of his sensitiveness; and that the rise of his faculties from a lower power to a higher, or from a narrower to a wider field, may be due to the function of assimilating and storing outside force or forces. There is nothing unscientific in the idea that, beyond the lines of force felt by the senses, the universe may be -- as it has always been -- either a supersensuous chaos or a divine unity, which irresistibly attracts, and is either life or death to penetrate. Thus far, religion, philosophy, and science seem to go hand in hand. The schools begin their vital battle only there. In the earlier stages of progress, the forces to be assimilated were simple and easy to absorb, but, as the mind of man enlarged its range, it enlarged the field of complexity, and must continue to do so, even into chaos, until the reservoirs of sensuous or supersensuous energies are exhausted, or cease to affect him, or until he succumbs to their excess.

For past history, this way of grouping its sequences may answer for a chart of relations, although any serious student would need to invent another, to compare or correct its errors; but past history is only a value of relation to the future, and this value is wholly one of convenience, which can be tested only by experiment. Any law of movement must include, to make it a convenience, some mechanical formula of acceleration.

Chapter XXXIV. A Law of Acceleration (1904)

IMAGES are not arguments, rarely even lead to proof, but the mind craves them, and, of late more than ever, the keenest experimenters find twenty images better than one, especially if contradictory; since the human mind has already learned to deal in contradictions.

The image needed here is that of a new centre, or preponderating mass, artificially introduced on earth in the midst of a system of attractive forces that previously made their own equilibrium, and constantly induced to accelerate its motion till it shall establish a new equilibrium. A dynamic theory would begin by assuming that all history, terrestrial or cosmic, mechanical or intellectual, would be reducible to this formula if we knew the facts.

For convenience, the most familiar image should come first; and this is probably that of the comet, or meteoric streams, like the Leonids and Perseids; a complex of minute mechanical agencies, reacting within and without, and guided by the sum of forces attracting or deflecting it. Nothing forbids one to assume that the man-meteorite might grow, as an acorn does, absorbing light, heat, electricity -- or thought; for, in recent times, such transference of energy has become a familiar idea; but the simplest figure, at first, is that of a perfect comet -- say that of 1843 -- which drops from space, in a straight line, at the regular acceleration of speed, directly into the sun, and after wheeling sharply about it, in heat that ought to dissipate any known substance, turns back unharmed, in defiance of law, by the path on which it came. The mind, by analogy, may figure as such a comet, the better because it also defies law.

Motion is the ultimate object of science, and measures of motion are many; but with thought as with matter, the true measure is mass in its astronomic sense -- the sum or difference of attractive forces. Science has quite enough trouble in measuring its material motions without volunteering help to the historian, but the historian needs not much help to measure some kinds of social movement; and especially in the nineteenth century, society by common accord agreed in measuring its progress by the coal-output. The ratio of increase in the volume of coal-power may serve as dynamometer.

The coal-output of the world, speaking roughly, doubled every ten years between 1840 and 1900, in the form of utilized power, for the ton of coal yielded three or four times as much power in 1900 as in 1840. Rapid as this rate of acceleration in volume seems, it may be tested in a thousand ways without greatly reducing it. Perhaps the ocean steamer is nearest unity and easiest to measure, for any one might hire, in 1905, for a small sum of money, the use of 30,000 steam-horse-power to cross the ocean, and by halving this figure every ten years, he got back to 234 horse-power for 1835, which was accuracy enough for his purposes. In truth, his chief trouble came not from the ratio in volume of heat, but from the intensity, since he could get no basis for a ratio there. All ages of history have known high intensities, like the iron-furnace, the burning-glass, the blow-pipe; but no society has ever used high intensities on any large scale till now, nor can a mere bystander decide what range of temperature is now in common use. Loosely guessing that science controls habitually the whole range from absolute zero to 3000 degrees Centigrade, one might assume, for convenience, that the ten-year ratio for volume could be used temporarily for intensity; and still there remained a ratio to be guessed for other forces than heat. Since 1800 scores of new forces had been discovered; old forces had been raised to higher powers, as could be measured in the navy-gun; great regions of chemistry had been opened up, and connected with other regions of physics. Within ten years a new universe of force had been revealed in radiation. Complexity had extended itself on immense horizons, and arithmetical ratios were useless for any attempt at accuracy. The force evolved seemed more like explosion than gravitation, and followed closely the curve of steam; but, at all events, the ten-year ratio seemed carefully conservative. Unless the calculator was prepared to be instantly overwhelmed by physical force and mental complexity, he must stop there.

Thus, taking the year 1900 as the starting point for carrying back the series, nothing was easier than to assume a ten-year period of retardation as far back as 1820, but beyond that point the statistician failed, and only the mathematician could help. Laplace would have found it child's-play to fix a ratio of progression in mathematical science between Descartes, Leibnitz, Newton, and himself. Watt could have given in pounds the increase of power between Newcomen's engines and his own. Volta and Benjamin Franklin would have stated their progress as absolute creation of power. Dalton could have measured minutely his advance on Boerhaave. Napoleon I must have had a distinct notion of his own numerical relation to Louis XIV. No one in 1789 doubted the progress of force, least of all those who were to lose their heads by it.

Pending agreement between these authorities, theory may assume what it likes -- say a fifty, or even a five-and-twenty-year period of reduplication for the eighteenth century, for the period matters little until the acceleration itself is admitted. The subject is even more amusing in the seventeenth than in the eighteenth century, because Galileo and Kepler, Descartes, Huygens, and Isaac Newton took vast pains to fix the laws of acceleration for moving bodies, while Lord Bacon and William Harvey were content with showing experimentally the fact of acceleration in knowledge; but from their combined results a historian might be tempted to maintain a similar rate of movement back to 1600, subject to correction from the historians of mathematics.

The mathematicians might carry their calculations back as far as the fourteenth century when algebra seems to have become for the first time the standard measure of mechanical progress in western Europe; for not only Copernicus and Tycho Brahe, but even artists like Leonardo, Michael Angelo, and Albert Durer worked by mathematical processes, and their testimony would probably give results more exact than that of Montaigne or Shakespeare; but, to save trouble, one might tentatively carry back the same ratio of acceleration, or retardation, to the year 1400, with the help of Columbus and Gutenberg, so taking a uniform rate during the whole four centuries (1400-1800), and leaving to statisticians the task of correcting it.

Or better, one might, for convenience, use the formula of squares to serve for a law of mind. Any other formula would do as well, either of chemical explosion, or electrolysis, or vegetable growth, or of expansion or contraction in innumerable forms; but this happens to be simple and convenient. Its force increases in the direct ratio of its squares. As the human meteoroid approached the sun or centre of attractive force, the attraction of one century squared itself to give the measure of attraction in the next.

Behind the year 1400, the process certainly went on, but the progress became so slight as to be hardly measurable. What was gained in the east or elsewhere, cannot be known; but forces, called loosely Greek fire and gunpowder, came into use in the west in the thirteenth century, as well as instruments like the compass, the blow-pipe, clocks and spectacles, and materials like paper; Arabic notation and algebra were introduced, while metaphysics and theology acted as violent stimulants to mind. An architect might detect a sequence between the Church of St. Peter's at Rome, the Amiens Cathedral, the Duomo at Pisa, San Marco at Venice, Sancta Sofia at Constantinople and the churches at Ravenna. All the historian dares affirm is that a sequence is manifestly there, and he has a right to carry back his ratio, to represent the fact, without assuming its numerical correctness. On the human mind as a moving body, the break in acceleration in the Middle Ages is only apparent; the attraction worked through shifting forms of force, as the sun works by light or heat, electricity, gravitation, or what not, on different organs with different sensibilities, but with invariable law.

The science of prehistoric man has no value except to prove that the law went back into indefinite antiquity. A stone arrowhead is as convincing as a steam-engine. The values were as clear a hundred thousand years ago as now, and extended equally over the whole world. The motion at last became infinitely slight, but cannot be proved to have stopped. The motion of Newton's comet at aphelion may be equally slight. To evolutionists may be left the processes of evolution; to historians the single interest is the law of reaction between force and force -- between mind and nature -- the law of progress.

The great division of history into phases by Turgot and Comte first affirmed this law in its outlines by asserting the unity of progress, for a mere phase interrupts no growth, and nature shows innumerable such phases. The development of coal-power in the nineteenth century furnished the first means of assigning closer values to the elements; and the appearance of supersensual forces towards 1900 made this calculation a pressing necessity; since the next step became infinitely serious.

A law of acceleration, definite and constant as any law of mechanics, cannot be supposed to relax its energy to suit the convenience of man. No one is likely to suggest a theory that man's convenience had been consulted by Nature at any time, or that Nature has consulted the convenience of any of her creations, except perhaps the Terebratula. In every age man has bitterly and justly complained that Nature hurried and hustled him, for inertia almost invariably has ended in tragedy. Resistance is its law, and resistance to superior mass is futile and fatal.

Fifty years ago, science took for granted that the rate of acceleration could not last. The world forgets quickly, but even today the habit remains of founding statistics on the faith that consumption will continue nearly stationary. Two generations, with John Stuart Mill, talked of this stationary period, which was to follow the explosion of new power. All the men who were elderly in the forties died in this faith, and other men grew old nursing the same conviction, and happy in it; while science, for fifty years, permitted, or encouraged, society to think that force would prove to be limited in supply. This mental inertia of science lasted through the eighties before showing signs of breaking up; and nothing short of radium fairly wakened men to the fact, long since evident, that force was inexhaustible. Even then the scientific authorities vehemently resisted.

Nothing so revolutionary had happened since the year 300. Thought had more than once been upset, but never caught and whirled about in the vortex of infinite forces. Power leaped from every atom, and enough of it to supply the stellar universe showed itself running to waste at every pore of matter. Man could no longer hold it off. Forces grasped his wrists and flung him about as though he had hold of a live wire or a runaway automobile; which was very nearly the exact truth for the purposes of an elderly and timid single gentleman in Paris, who never drove down the Champs Elysees without expecting an accident, and commonly witnessing one; or found himself in the neighborhood of an official without calculating the chances of a bomb. So long as the rates of progress held good, these bombs would double in force and number every ten years.

Impossibilities no longer stood in the way. One's life had fattened on impossibilities. Before the boy was six years old, he had seen four impossibilities made actual -- the ocean-steamer, the railway, the electric telegraph, and the Daguerreotype; nor could he ever learn which of the four had most hurried others to come. He had seen the coal-output of the United States grow from nothing to three hundred million tons or more. What was far more serious, he had seen the number of minds, engaged in pursuing force -- the truest measure of its attraction -- increase from a few scores or hundreds, in 1838, to many thousands in 1905, trained to sharpness never before reached, and armed with instruments amounting to new senses of indefinite power and accuracy, while they chased force into hiding-places where Nature herself had never known it to be, making analyses that contradicted being, and syntheses that endangered the elements. No one could say that the social mind now failed to respond to new force, even when the new force annoyed it horribly. Every day Nature violently revolted, causing so-called accidents with enormous destruction of property and life, while plainly laughing at man, who helplessly groaned and shrieked and shuddered, but never for a single instant could stop. The railways alone approached the carnage of war; automobiles and fire-arms ravaged society, until an earthquake became almost a nervous relaxation. An immense volume of force had detached itself from the unknown universe of energy, while still vaster reservoirs, supposed to be infinite, steadily revealed themselves, attracting mankind with more compulsive course than all the Pontic Seas or Gods or Gold that ever existed, and feeling still less of retiring ebb.

In 1850, science would have smiled at such a romance as this, but, in 1900, as far as history could learn, few men of science thought it a laughing matter. If a perplexed but laborious follower could venture to guess their drift, it seemed in their minds a toss-up between anarchy and order. Unless they should be more honest with themselves in the future than ever they were in the past, they would be more astonished than their followers when they reached the end. If Karl Pearson's notions of the universe were sound, men like Galileo, Descartes, Leibnitz, and Newton should have stopped the progress of science before 1700, supposing them to have been honest in the religious convictions they expressed. In 1900 they were plainly forced back; on faith in a unity unproved and an order they had themselves disproved. They had reduced their universe to a series of relations to themselves. They had reduced themselves to motion in a universe of motions, with an acceleration, in their own case of vertiginous violence. With the correctness of their science, history had no right to meddle, since their science now lay in a plane where scarcely one or two hundred minds in the world could follow its mathematical processes; but bombs educate vigorously, and even wireless telegraphy or airships might require the reconstruction of society. If any analogy whatever existed between the human mind, on one side, and the laws of motion, on the other, the mind had already entered a field of attraction so violent that it must immediately pass beyond, into new equilibrium, like the Comet of Newton, to suffer dissipation altogether, like meteoroids in the earth's atmosphere. If it behaved like an explosive, it must rapidly recover equilibrium; if it behaved like a vegetable, it must reach its limits of growth; and even if it acted like the earlier creations of energy -- the saurians and sharks -- it must have nearly reached the limits of its expansion. If science were to go on doubling or quadrupling its complexities every ten years, even mathematics would soon succumb. An average mind had succumbed already in 1850; it could no longer understand the problem in 1900.

Fortunately, a student of history had no responsibility for the problem; he took it as science gave it, and waited only to be taught. With science or with society, he had no quarrel and claimed no share of authority. He had never been able to acquire knowledge, still less to impart it; and if he had, at times, felt serious differences with the American of the nineteenth century, he felt none with the American of the twentieth. For this new creation, born since 1900, a historian asked no longer to be teacher or even friend; he asked only to be a pupil, and promised to be docile, for once, even though trodden under foot; for he could see that the new American -- the child of incalculable coal-power, chemical power, electric power, and radiating energy, as well as of new forces yet undetermined -- must be a sort of God compared with any former creation of nature. At the rate of progress since 1800, every American who lived into the year 2000 would know how to control unlimited power. He would think in complexities unimaginable to an earlier mind. He would deal with problems altogether beyond the range of earlier society. To him the nineteenth century would stand on the same plane with the fourth -- equally childlike -- and he would only wonder how both of them, knowing so little, and so weak in force, should have done so much. Perhaps even he might go back, in 1964, to sit with Gibbon on the steps of Ara Coeli.

Meanwhile he was getting education. With that, a teacher who had failed to educate even the generation of 1870, dared not interfere. The new forces would educate. History saw few lessons in the past that would be useful in the future; but one, at least, it did see. The attempt of the American of 1800 to educate the American of 1900 had not often been surpassed for folly; and since 1800 the forces and their complications had increased a thousand times or more. The attempt of the American of 1900 to educate the American of 2000, must be even blinder than that of the Congressman of 1800, except so far as he had learned his ignorance. During a million or two of years, every generation in turn had toiled with endless agony to attain and apply power, all the while betraying the deepest alarm and horror at the power they created. The teacher of 1900, if foolhardy, might stimulate; if foolish, might resist; if intelligent, might balance, as wise and foolish have often tried to do from the beginning; but the forces would continue to educate, and the mind would continue to react. All the teacher could hope was to teach it reaction.

Even there his difficulty was extreme. The most elementary books of science betrayed the inadequacy of old implements of thought. Chapter after chapter closed with phrases such as one never met in older literature: "The cause of this phenomenon is not understood"; "science no longer ventures to explain causes"; "the first step towards a causal explanation still remains to be taken"; "opinions are very much divided"; "in spite of the contradictions involved"; "science gets on only by adopting different theories, sometimes contradictory." Evidently the new American would need to think in contradictions, and instead of Kant's famous four antinomies, the new universe would know no law that could not be proved by its anti-law.

To educate -- one's self to begin with -- had been the effort of one's life for sixty years; and the difficulties of education had gone on doubling with the coal-output, until the prospect of waiting another ten years, in order to face a seventh doubling of complexities, allured one's imagination but slightly. The law of acceleration was definite, and did not require ten years more study except to show whether it held good. No scheme could be suggested to the new American, and no fault needed to be found, or complaint made; but the next great influx of new forces seemed near at hand, and its style of education promised to be violently coercive. The movement from unity into multiplicity, between 1200 and 1900, was unbroken in sequence, and rapid in acceleration. Prolonged one generation longer, it would require a new social mind. As though thought were common salt in indefinite solution it must enter a new phase subject to new laws. Thus far, since five or ten thousand years, the mind had successfully reacted, and nothing yet proved that it would fail to react -- but it would need to jump.

Chapter XXXV. Nunc Age (1905)

NEARLY forty years had passed since the ex-private secretary landed at New York with the ex-Ministers Adams and Motley, when they saw American society as a long caravan stretching out towards the plains. As he came up the bay again, November 5, 1904, an older man than either his father or Motley in 1868, he found the approach more striking than ever -- wonderful -- unlike anything man had ever seen -- and like nothing he had ever much cared to see. The outline of the city became frantic in its effort to explain something that defied meaning. Power seemed to have outgrown its servitude and to have asserted its freedom. The cylinder had exploded, and thrown great masses of stone and steam against the sky. The city had the air and movement of hysteria, and the citizens were crying, in every accent of anger and alarm, that the new forces must at any cost be brought under control. Prosperity never before imagined, power never yet wielded by man, speed never reached by anything but a meteor, had made the world irritable, nervous, querulous, unreasonable and afraid. All New York was demanding new men, and all the new forces, condensed into corporations, were demanding a new type of man -- a man with ten times the endurance, energy, will and mind of the old type -- for whom they were ready to pay millions at sight. As one jolted over the pavements or read the last week's newspapers, the new man seemed close at hand, for the old one had plainly reached the end of his strength, and his failure had become catastrophic. Every one saw it, and every municipal election shrieked chaos. A traveller in the highways of history looked out of the club window on the turmoil of Fifth Avenue, and felt himself in Rome, under Diocletian, witnessing the anarchy, conscious of the compulsion, eager for the solution, but unable to conceive whence the next impulse was to come or how it was to act. The two-thousand-years failure of Christianity roared upward from Broadway, and no Constantine the Great was in sight.

Having nothing else to do, the traveller went on to Washington to wait the end. There Roosevelt was training Constantines and battling Trusts. With the Battle of Trusts, a student of mechanics felt entire sympathy, not merely as a matter of politics or society, but also as a measure of motion. The Trusts and Corporations stood for the larger part of the new power that had been created since 1840, and were obnoxious because of their vigorous and unscrupulous energy. They were revolutionary, troubling all the old conventions and values, as the screws of ocean steamers must trouble a school of herring. They tore society to pieces and trampled it under foot. As one of their earliest victims, a citizen of Quincy, born in 1838, had learned submission and silence, for he knew that, under the laws of mechanics, any change, within the range of the forces, must make his situation only worse; but he was beyond measure curious to see whether the conflict of forces would produce the new man, since no other energies seemed left on earth to breed. The new man could be only a child born of contact between the new and the old energies.

Both had been familiar since childhood, as the story has shown, and neither had warped the umpire's judgment by its favors. If ever judge had reason to be impartial, it was he. The sole object of his interest and sympathy was the new man, and the longer one watched, the less could be seen of him. Of the forces behind the Trusts, one could see something; they owned a complete organization, with schools, training, wealth and purpose; but of the forces behind Roosevelt one knew little; their cohesion was slight; their training irregular; their objects vague. The public had no idea what practical system it could aim at, or what sort of men could manage it. The single problem before it was not so much to control the Trusts as to create the society that could manage the Trusts. The new American must be either the child of the new forces or a chance sport of nature. The attraction of mechanical power had already wrenched the American mind into a crab-like process which Roosevelt was making heroic efforts to restore to even action, and he had every right to active support and sympathy from all the world, especially from the Trusts themselves so far as they were human; but the doubt persisted whether the force that educated was really man or nature -- mind or motion. The mechanical theory, mostly accepted by science, seemed to require that the law of mass should rule. In that case, progress would continue as before.

In that, or any other case, a nineteenth-century education was as useless or misleading as an eighteenth-century education had been to the child of 1838; but Adams had a better reason for holding his tongue. For his dynamic theory of history he cared no more than for the kinetic theory of gas; but, if it were an approach to measurement of motion, it would verify or disprove itself within thirty years. At the calculated acceleration, the head of the meteor-stream must very soon pass perihelion. Therefore, dispute was idle, discussion was futile, and silence, next to good-temper, was the mark of sense. If the acceleration, measured by the development and economy of forces, were to continue at its rate since 1800, the mathematician of 1950 should be able to plot the past and future orbit of the human race as accurately as that of the November meteoroids.

Naturally such an attitude annoyed the players in the game, as the attitude of the umpire is apt to infuriate the spectators. Above all, it was profoundly unmoral, and tended to discourage effort. On the other hand, it tended to encourage foresight and to economize waste of mind. If it was not itself education, it pointed out the economies necessary for the education of the new American. There, the duty stopped.

There, too, life stopped. Nature has educated herself to a singular sympathy for death. On the antarctic glacier, nearly five thousand feet above sea-level, Captain Scott found carcasses of seals, where the animals had laboriously flopped up, to die in peace. "Unless we had actually found these remains, it would have been past believing that a dying seal could have transported itself over fifty miles of rough, steep, glacier-surface," but "the seal seems often to crawl to the shore or the ice to die, probably from its instinctive dread of its marine enemies." In India, Purun Dass, at the end of statesmanship, sought solitude, and died in sanctity among the deer and monkeys, rather than remain with man. Even in America, the Indian Summer of life should be a little sunny and a little sad, like the season, and infinite in wealth and depth of tone -- but never hustled. For that reason, one's own passive obscurity seemed sometimes nearer nature than John Hay's exposure. To the normal animal the instinct of sport is innate, and historians themselves were not exempt from the passion of baiting their bears; but in its turn even the seal dislikes to be worried to death in age by creatures that have not the strength or the teeth to kill him outright.

On reaching Washington, November 14, 1904, Adams saw at a glance that Hay must have rest. Already Mrs. Hay had bade him prepare to help in taking her husband to Europe as soon as the Session should be over, and although Hay protested that the idea could not even be discussed, his strength failed so rapidly that he could not effectually discuss it, and ended by yielding without struggle. He would equally have resigned office and retired, like Purun Dass, had not the President and the press protested; but he often debated the subject, and his friends could throw no light on it. Adams himself, who had set his heart on seeing Hay close his career by making peace in the East, could only urge that vanity for vanity, the crown of peacemaker was worth the cross of martyrdom; but the cross was full in sight, while the crown was still uncertain. Adams found his formula for Russian inertia exasperatingly correct. He thought that Russia should have negotiated instantly on the fall of Port Arthur, January 1, 1905; he found that she had not the energy, but meant to wait till her navy should be destroyed. The delay measured precisely the time that Hay had to spare.

The close of the Session on March 4 left him barely the strength to crawl on board ship, March 18, and before his steamer had reached half her course, he had revived, almost as gay as when he first lighted on the Markoe house in I Street forty-four years earlier. The clouds that gather round the setting sun do not always take a sober coloring from eyes that have kept watch on mortality; or, at least, the sobriety is sometimes scarcely sad. One walks with one's friends squarely up to the portal of life, and bids good-bye with a smile. One has done it so often! Hay could scarcely pace the deck; he nourished no illusions; he was convinced that he should never return to his work, and he talked lightly of the death sentence that he might any day expect, but he threw off the coloring of office and mortality together, and the malaria of power left its only trace in the sense of tasks incomplete.

One could honestly help him there. Laughing frankly at his dozen treaties hung up in the Senate Committee-room like lambs in a butcher's shop, one could still remind him of what was solidly completed. In his eight years of office he had solved nearly every old problem of American statesmanship, and had left little or nothing to annoy his successor. He had brought the great Atlantic powers into a working system, and even Russia seemed about to be dragged into a combine of intelligent equilibrium based on an intelligent allotment of activities. For the first time in fifteen hundred years a true Roman pax was in sight, and would, if it succeeded, owe its virtues to him. Except for making peace in Manchuria, he could do no more; and if the worst should happen, setting continent against continent in arms -- the only apparent alternative to his scheme -- he need not repine at missing the catastrophe.

This rosy view served to soothe disgusts which every parting statesman feels, and commonly with reason. One had no need to get out one's notebook in order to jot down the exact figures on either side. Why add up the elements of resistance and anarchy? The Kaiser supplied him with these figures, just as the Cretic approached Morocco. Every one was doing it, and seemed in a panic about it. The chaos waited only for his landing.

Arrived at Genoa, the party hid itself for a fortnight at Nervi, and he gained strength rapidly as long as he made no effort and heard no call for action. Then they all went on to Nanheim without relapse. There, after a few days, Adams left him for the regular treatment, and came up to Paris. The medical reports promised well, and Hay's letters were as humorous and light-handed as ever. To the last he wrote cheerfully of his progress, and amusingly with his usual light scepticism, of his various doctors; but when the treatment ended, three weeks later, and he came on to Paris, he showed, at the first glance, that he had lost strength, and the return to affairs and interviews wore him rapidly out. He was conscious of it, and in his last talk before starting for London and Liverpool he took the end of his activity for granted. "You must hold out for the peace negotiations," was the remonstrance. "I've not time!" he replied. "You'll need little time!" was the rejoinder. Each was correct.

There it ended! Shakespeare himself could use no more than the commonplace to express what is incapable of expression. "The rest is silence!" The few familiar words, among the simplest in the language, conveying an idea trite beyond rivalry, served Shakespeare, and, as yet, no one has said more. A few weeks afterwards, one warm evening in early July, as Adams was strolling down to dine under the trees at Armenonville, he learned that Hay was dead. He expected it; on Hay's account, he was even satisfied to have his friend die, as we would all die if we could, in full fame, at home and abroad, universally regretted, and wielding his power to the last. One had seen scores of emperors and heroes fade into cheap obscurity even when alive; and now, at least, one had not that to fear for one's friend. It was not even the suddenness of the shock, or the sense of void, that threw Adams into the depths of Hamlet's Shakespearean silence in the full flare of Paris frivolity in its favorite haunt where worldly vanity reached its most futile climax in human history; it was only the quiet summons to follow -- the assent to dismissal. It was time to go. The three friends had begun life together; and the last of the three had no motive -- no attraction -- to carry it on after the others had gone. Education had ended for all three, and only beyond some remoter horizon could its values be fixed or renewed. Perhaps some day -- say 1938, their centenary -- they might be allowed to return together for a holiday, to see the mistakes of their own lives made clear in the light of the mistakes of their successors; and perhaps then, for the first time since man began his education among the carnivores, they would find a world that sensitive and timid natures could regard without a shudder.

THE END

Mont-Saint-Michel and Chartres

Preface

[December, 1904.]

Some old Elizabethan play or poem contains the lines:—

... Who reads me, when I am ashes,

Is my son in wishes . . . .

The relationship, between reader and writer, of son and father, may have existed in Queen Elizabeth's time, but is much too close to be true for ours. The utmost that any writer could hope of his readers now is that they should consent to regard themselves as nephews, and even then he would expect only a more or less civil refusal from most of them. Indeed, if he had reached a certain age, he would have observed that nephews, as a social class, no longer read at all, and that there is only one familiar instance recorded of a nephew who read his uncle. The exception tends rather to support the rule, since it needed a Macaulay to produce, and two volumes to record it. Finally, the metre does not permit it. One may not say: "Who reads me, when I am ashes, is my nephew in wishes."

The same objections do not apply to the word "niece." The change restores the verse, and, to a very great degree, the fact. Nieces have been known to read in early youth, and in some cases may have read their uncles. The relationship, too, is convenient and easy, capable of being anything or nothing, at the will of either party, like a Mohammedan or Polynesian or American marriage. No valid objection can be offered to this choice in the verse. Niece let it be!

The following lines, then, are written for nieces, or for those who are willing, for those, to be nieces in wish. For convenience of travel in France, where hotels, in out-of-the-way places, are sometimes wanting in space as well as luxury, the nieces shall count as one only. As many more may come as like, but one niece is enough for the uncle to talk to, and one niece is much more likely than two to listen. One niece is also more likely than two to carry a kodak and take interest in it, since she has nothing else, except her uncle, to interest her, and instances occur when she takes interest neither in the uncle nor in the journey. One cannot assume, even in a niece, too emotional a nature, but one may assume a kodak.

The party, then, with such variations of detail as may suit its tastes, has sailed from New York, let us say, early in June for an entire summer in France. One pleasant June morning it has landed at Cherbourg or Havre and takes the train across Normandy to Pontorson, where, with the evening light, the tourists drive along the chaussee, over the sands or through the tide, till they stop at Madame Poulard's famous hotel within the Gate of the Mount.

The uncle talks:—

CHAPTER I: SAINT MICHIEL DE LA MER DEL PERIL

The Archangel loved heights. Standing on the summit of the tower that crowned his church, wings upspread, sword uplifted, the devil crawling beneath, and the cock, symbol of eternal vigilance, perched on his mailed foot, Saint Michael held a place of his own in heaven and on earth which seems, in the eleventh century, to leave hardly room for the Virgin of the Crypt at Chartres, still less for the Beau Christ of the thirteenth century at Amiens. The Archangel stands for Church and State, and both militant. He is the conqueror of Satan, the mightiest of all created spirits, the nearest to God. His place was where the danger was greatest; therefore you find him here. For the same reason he was, while the pagan danger lasted, the patron saint of France. So the Normans, when they were converted to Christianity, put themselves under his powerful protection. So he stood for centuries on his Mount in Peril of the Sea, watching across the tremor of the immense ocean,-immensi tremor oceani,-as Louis XI, inspired for once to poetry, inscribed on the collar of the Order of Saint Michael which he created. So soldiers, nobles, and monarchs went on pilgrimage to his shrine; so the common people followed, and still follow, like ourselves.

The church stands high on the summit of this granite rock, and on its west front is the platform, to which the tourist ought first to climb. From the edge of this platform, the eye plunges down, two hundred and thirty-five feet, to the wide sands or the wider ocean, as the tides recede or advance, under an infinite sky, over a restless sea, which even we tourists can understand and feel without books or guides; but when we turn from the western view, and look at the church door, thirty or forty yards from the parapet where we stand, one needs to be eight centuries old to know what this mass of encrusted architecture meant to its builders, and even then one must still learn to feel it. The man who wanders into the twelfth century is lost, unless he can grow prematurely young.

One can do it, as one can play with children. Wordsworth, whose practical sense equalled his intuitive genius, carefully limited us to "a season of calm weather," which is certainly best; but granting a fair frame of mind, one can still "have sight of that immortal sea" which brought us hither from the twelfth century; one can even travel thither and see the children sporting on the shore. Our sense is partially atrophied from disuse, but it is still alive, at least in old people, who alone, as a class, have the time to be young.

One needs only to be old enough in order to be as young as one will. From the top of this Abbey Church one looks across the bay to Avranches, and towards Coutances and the Cotentin,—the Constantinus pagus,—whose shore, facing us, recalls the coast of New England. The relation between the granite of one coast and that of the other may be fanciful, but the relation between the people who live on each is as hard and practical a fact as the granite itself. When one enters the church, one notes first the four great triumphal piers or columns, at the intersection of the nave and transepts, and on looking into M. Corroyer's architectural study which is the chief source of all one's acquaintance with the Mount, one learns that these piers were constructed in 1058. Four out of five American tourists will instantly recall the only date of mediaeval history they ever knew, the date of the Norman Conquest. Eight years after these piers were built, in 1066, Duke William of Normandy raised an army of forty thousand men in these parts, and in northern France, whom he took to England, where they mostly stayed. For a hundred and fifty years, until 1204, Normandy and England were united; the Norman peasant went freely to England with his lord, spiritual or temporal; the Norman woman, a very capable person, followed her husband or her parents; Normans held nearly all the English fiefs; filled the English Church; crowded the English Court; created the English law; and we know that French was still currently spoken in England as late as 1400, or thereabouts, "After the scole of Stratford atte bowe." The aristocratic Norman names still survive in part, and if we look up their origin here we shall generally find them in villages so remote and insignificant that their place can hardly be found on any ordinary map; but the common people had no surnames, and cannot be traced, although for every noble whose name or blood survived in England or in Normandy, we must reckon hundreds of peasants. Since the generation which followed William to England in 1066, we can reckon twenty-eight or thirty from father to son, and, if you care to figure up the sum, you will find that you had about two hundred and fifty million arithmetical ancestors living in the middle of the eleventh century. The whole population of England and northern France may then have numbered five million, but if it were fifty it would not much affect the certainty that, if you have any English blood at all, you have also Norman. If we could go back and live again in all our two hundred and fifty million arithmetical ancestors of the eleventh century, we should find ourselves doing many surprising things, but among the rest we should pretty certainly be ploughing most of the fields of the Cotentin and Calvados; going to mass in every parish church in Normandy; rendering military service to every lord, spiritual or temporal, in all this region; and helping to build the Abbey Church at Mont-Saint-Michel. From the roof of the Cathedral of Coutances over yonder, one may look away over the hills and woods, the farms and fields of Normandy, and so familiar, so homelike are they, one can almost take oath that in this, or the other, or in all, one knew life once and has never so fully known it since.

Never so fully known it since! For we of the eleventh century, hard-headed, close-fisted, grasping, shrewd, as we were, and as Normans are still said to be, stood more fully in the centre of the world's movement than our English descendants ever did. We were a part, and a great part, of the Church, of France, and of Europe. The Leos and Gregories of the tenth and eleventh centuries leaned on us in their great struggle for reform. Our Duke Richard-Sans-Peur, in 966, turned the old canons out of the Mount in order to bring here the highest influence of the time, the Benedictine monks of Monte Cassino. Richard II, grandfather of William the Conqueror, began this Abbey Church in 1020, and helped Abbot Hildebert to build it. When William the Conqueror in 1066 set out to conquer England, Pope Alexander II stood behind him and blessed his banner. From that moment our Norman Dukes cast the Kings of France into the shade. Our activity was not limited to northern Europe, or even confined by Anjou and Gascony. When we stop at Coutances, we will drive out to Hauteville to see where Tancred came from, whose sons Robert and Roger were conquering Naples and Sicily at the time when the Abbey Church was building on the Mount. Normans were everywhere in 1066, and everywhere in the lead of their age. We were a serious race. If you want other proof of it, besides our record in war and in politics, you have only to look at our art. Religious art is the measure of human depth and sincerity; any triviality, any weakness, cries aloud. If this church on the Mount is not proof enough of Norman character, we will stop at Coutances for a wider view. Then we will go to Caen and Bayeux. From there, it would almost be worth our while to leap at once to Palermo. It was in the year 1131 or thereabouts that Roger began the Cathedral at Cefalu and the Chapel Royal at Palermo; it was about the year 1174 that his grandson William began the Cathedral of Monreale. No art—either Greek or Byzantine, Italian or Arab—has ever created two religious types so beautiful, so serious, so impressive, and yet so different, as Mont-Saint-Michel watching over its northern ocean, and Monreale, looking down over its forests of orange and lemon, on Palermo and the Sicilian seas.

Down nearly to the end of the twelfth century the Norman was fairly master of the world in architecture as in arms, although the thirteenth century belonged to France, and we must look for its glories on the Seine and Marne and Loire; but for the present we are in the eleventh century,—tenants of the Duke or of the Church or of small feudal lords who take their names from the neighbourhood,— Beaumont, Carteret, Greville, Percy, Pierpont,—who, at the Duke's bidding, will each call out his tenants, perhaps ten men-at-arms with their attendants, to fight in Brittany, or in the Vexin toward Paris, or on the great campaign for the conquest of England which is to come within ten years,—the greatest military effort that has been made in western

Europe since Charlemagne and Roland were defeated at Roncesvalles three hundred years ago. For the moment, we are helping to quarry granite for the Abbey Church, and to haul it to the Mount, or load it on our boat. We never fail to make our annual pilgrimage to the Mount on the Archangel's Day, October 16. We expect to be called out for a new campaign which Duke William threatens against Brittany, and we hear stories that Harold the Saxon, the powerful Earl of Wessex in England, is a guest, or, as some say, a prisoner or a hostage, at the Duke's Court, and will go with us on the campaign. The year is 1058.

All this time we have been standing on the parvis, looking out over the sea and sands which are as good eleventh-century landscape as they ever were; or turning at times towards the church door which is the pons seclorum, the bridge of ages, between us and our ancestors. Now that we have made an attempt, such as it is, to get our minds into a condition to cross the bridge without breaking down in the effort, we enter the church and stand face to face with eleventh- century architecture; a ground-plan which dates from 1020; a central tower, or its piers, dating from 1058; and a church completed in 1135. France can offer few buildings of this importance equally old, with dates so exact. Perhaps the closest parallel to Mont-Saint- Michel is Saint-Benoit-sur-Loire, above Orleans, which seems to have been a shrine almost as popular as the Mount, at the same time. Chartres was also a famous shrine, but of the Virgin, and the west porch of Chartres, which is to be our peculiar pilgrimage, was a hundred years later than the ground-plan of Mont-Saint-Michel, although Chartres porch is the usual starting-point of northern French art. Queen Matilda's Abbaye-aux-Dames, now the Church of the Trinity, at Caen, dates from 1066. Saint Sernin at Toulouse, the porch of the Abbey Church at Moissac, Notre-Dame-du-Port at Clermont, the Abbey Church at Vezelay, are all said to be twelfth- century. Even San Marco at Venice was new in 1020.

Yet in 1020 Norman art was already too ambitious. Certainly nine hundred years leave their traces on granite as well as on other material, but the granite of Abbot Hildebert would have stood securely enough, if the Abbot had not asked too much from it. Perhaps he asked too much from the Archangel, for the thought of the Archangel's superiority was clearly the inspiration of his plan. The apex of the granite rock rose like a sugar-loaf two hundred and forty feet (73.6 metres) above mean sea-level. Instead of cutting the summit away to give his church a secure rock foundation, which would have sacrificed about thirty feet of height, the Abbot took the apex of the rock for his level, and on all sides built out foundations of masonry to support the walls of his church. The apex of the rock is the floor of the croisee, the intersection of nave and transept. On this solid foundation the Abbot rested the chief weight of the church, which was the central tower, supported by the four great piers which still stand; but from the croisee in the centre westward to the parapet of the platform, the Abbot filled the whole space with masonry, and his successors built out still farther, until some two hundred feet of stonework ends now in a perpendicular wall of eighty feet or more. In this space are several ranges of chambers, but the structure might perhaps have proved strong enough to support the light Romanesque front which was usual in the eleventh century, had not fashions in architecture changed in the great epoch of building, a hundred and fifty years later, when Abbot Robert de Torigny thought proper to reconstruct the west front, and build out two towers on its flanks. The towers were no doubt beautiful, if one may judge from the towers of Bayeux and Coutances, but their weight broke down the vaulting beneath, and one of them fell in 1300. In 1618 the whole facade began to give way, and in 1776 not only the facade but also three of the seven spans of the nave were pulled down. Of Abbot Hildebert's nave, only four arches remain.

Still, the overmastering strength of the eleventh century is stamped on a great scale here, not only in the four spans of the nave, and in the transepts, but chiefly in the triumphal columns of the croisee. No one is likely to forget what Norman architecture was, who takes the trouble to pass once through this fragment of its earliest bloom. The dimensions are not great, though greater than safe construction warranted. Abbot Hildebert's whole church did not exceed two hundred and thirty feet in length in the interior, and the span of the triumphal arch was only about twenty-three feet, if the books can be trusted. The nave of the Abbaye-aux-Dames appears to have about the same width, and probably neither of them was meant to be vaulted. The roof was of timber, and about sixty-three feet high at its apex. Compared with the great churches of the thirteenth century, this building is modest, but its size is not what matters to us. Its style is the starting-point of all our future travels. Here is your first eleventh-century church! How does it affect you?

Serious and simple to excess! is it not? Young people rarely enjoy it. They prefer the Gothic, even as you see it here, looking at us from the choir, through the great Norman arch. No doubt they are right, since they are young: but men and women who have lived long and are tired,—who want rest,—who have done with aspirations and ambition,—whose life has been a broken arch,—feel this repose and self-restraint as they feel nothing else. The quiet strength of these curved lines, the solid support of these heavy columns, the moderate proportions, even the modified lights, the absence of display, of effort, of self-consciousness, satisfy them as no other art does. They come back to it to rest, after a long circle of pilgrimage,—the cradle of rest from which their ancestors started. Even here they find the repose none too deep.

Indeed, when you look longer at it, you begin to doubt whether there is any repose in it at all,—whether it is not the most unreposeful thought ever put into architectural form. Perched on the extreme point of this abrupt rock, the Church Militant with its aspirant Archangel stands high above the world, and seems to threaten heaven itself. The idea is the stronger and more restless because the Church of Saint Michael is surrounded and protected by the world and the society over which it rises, as Duke William rested on his barons and their men. Neither the Saint nor the Duke was troubled by doubts about his mission. Church and State, Soul and Body, God and Man, are all one at Mont-Saint-Michel, and the business of all is to fight, each in his own way, or to stand guard for each other. Neither Church nor State is intellectual, or learned, or even strict in dogma. Here we do not feel the Trinity at all; the Virgin but little; Christ hardly more; we feel only the Archangel and the Unity of God. We have little logic here, and simple faith, but we have energy. We cannot do many things which are done in the centre of civilization, at Byzantium, but we can fight, and we can build a church. No doubt we think first of the church, and next of our temporal lord; only in the last instance do we think of our private affairs, and our private affairs sometimes suffer for it; but we reckon the affairs of Church and State to be ours, too, and we carry this idea very far. Our church on the Mount is ambitious, restless, striving for effect; our conquest of England, with which the Duke is infatuated, is more ambitious still; but all this is a trifle to the outburst which is coming in the next generation; and Saint Michael on his Mount expresses it all.

Taking architecture as an expression of energy, we can some day compare Mont-Saint-Michel with Beauvais, and draw from the comparison whatever moral suits our frame of mind; but you should first note that here, in the eleventh century, the Church, however simple-minded or unschooled, was not cheap. Its self-respect is worth noticing, because it was short-lived in its art. Mont-Saint- Michel, throughout, even up to the delicate and intricate stonework of its cloisters, is built of granite. The crypts and substructures are as well constructed as the surfaces most exposed to view. When we get to Chartres, which is largely a twelfth-century work, you will see that the cathedral there, too, is superbly built, of the hardest and heaviest stone within reach, which has nowhere settled or given way; while, beneath, you will find a crypt that rivals the church above. The thirteenth century did not build so. The great cathedrals after 1200 show economy, and sometimes worse. The world grew cheap, as worlds must.

You may like it all the better for being less serious, less heroic, less militant, and more what the French call bourgeois, just as you may like the style of Louis XV better than that of Louis XIV,— Madame du Barry better than Madame de Montespan,—for taste is free, and all styles are good which amuse; but since we are now beginning with the earliest, in order to step down gracefully to the stage, whatever it is, where you prefer to stop, we must try to understand a little of the kind of energy which Norman art expressed, or would have expressed if it had thought in our modes. The only word which describes the Norman style is the French word naif. Littre says that naif comes from natif, as vulgar comes from vulgus, as though native traits must be simple, and commonness must be vulgar. Both these derivative meanings were strange to the eleventh century. Naivete was simply natural and vulgarity was merely coarse. Norman naivete was not different in kind from the naivete of Burgundy or Gascony or Lombardy, but it was slightly different in expression, as you will see when you travel south. Here at Mont-Saint-Michel we have only a mutilated trunk of an eleventh-century church to judge by. We have not even a facade, and shall have to stop at some Norman village—at Thaon or Ouistreham—to find a west front which might suit the Abbey here, but wherever we find it we shall find something a little more serious, more military, and more practical than you will meet in other Romanesque work, farther south. So, too, the central tower or lantern—the most striking feature of Norman churches—has fallen here at Mont-Saint-Michel, and we shall have to replace it from Cerisy-la-Foret, and Lessay, and Falaise. We shall find much to say about the value of the lantern on a Norman church, and the singular power it expresses. We shall have still more to say of the towers which flank the west front of Norman churches, but these are mostly twelfth-century, and will lead us far beyond Coutances and Bayeux, from fleche to fleche, till we come to the fleche of all fleches, at Chartres.

We shall have a whole chapter of study, too, over the eleventh- century apse, but here at Mont-Saint-Michel, Abbot Hildebert's choir went the way of his nave and tower. He built out even more boldly to the east than to the west, and although the choir stood for some four hundred years, which is a sufficient life for most architecture, the foundations gave way at last, and it fell in 1421, in the midst of the English wars, and remained a ruin until 1450. Then it was rebuilt, a monument of the last days of the Gothic, so that now, standing at the western door, you can look down the church, and see the two limits of mediaeval architecture married together,—the earliest Norman and the latest French. Through the Romanesque arches of 1058, you look into the exuberant choir of latest Gothic, finished in 1521. Although the two structures are some five hundred years apart, they live pleasantly together. The Gothic died gracefully in France. The choir is charming,—far more charming than the nave, as the beautiful woman is more charming than the elderly man. One need not quarrel about styles of beauty, as long as the man and woman are evidently satisfied and love and admire each other still, with all the solidity of faith to hold them up; but, at least, one cannot help seeing, as one looks from the older to the younger style, that whatever the woman's sixteenth- century charm may be, it is not the man's eleventh-century trait of naivete;—far from it! The simple, serious, silent dignity and energy of the eleventh century have gone. Something more complicated stands in their place; graceful, self-conscious, rhetorical, and beautiful as perfect rhetoric, with its clearness, light, and line, and the wealth of tracery that verges on the florid.

The crypt of the same period, beneath, is almost finer still, and even in seriousness stands up boldly by the side of the Romanesque; but we have no time to run off into the sixteenth century: we have still to learn the alphabet of art in France. One must live deep into the eleventh century in order to understand the twelfth, and even after passing years in the twelfth, we shall find the thirteenth in many ways a world of its own, with a beauty not always inherited, and sometimes not bequeathed. At the Mount we can go no farther into the eleventh as far as concerns architecture. We shall have to follow the Romanesque to Caen and so up the Seine to the Ile de France, and across to the Loire and the Rhone, far to the South where its home lay. All the other eleventh-century work has been destroyed here or built over, except at one point, on the level of the splendid crypt we just turned from, called the Gros Piliers, beneath the choir.

There, according to M. Corroyer, in a corner between great constructions of the twelfth century and the vast Merveille of the thirteenth, the old refectory of the eleventh was left as a passage from one group of buildings to the other. Below it is the kitchen of Hildebert. Above, on the level of the church, was the dormitory. These eleventh-century abbatial buildings faced north and west, and are close to the present parvis, opposite the last arch of the nave. The lower levels of Hildebert's plan served as supports or buttresses to the church above, and must therefore be older than the nave; probably older than the triumphal piers of 1058.

Hildebert planned them in 1020, and died after carrying his plans out so far that they could be completed by Abbot Ralph de Beaumont, who was especially selected by Duke William in 1048, "more for his high birth than for his merits." Ralph de Beaumont died in 1060, and was succeeded by Abbot Ranulph, an especial favourite of Duchess Matilda, and held in high esteem by Duke William. The list of names shows how much social importance was attributed to the place. The Abbot's duties included that of entertainment on a great scale. The Mount was one of the most famous shrines of northern Europe. We are free to take for granted that all the great people of Normandy slept at the Mount and, supposing M. Corroyer to be right, that they dined in this room, between 1050, when the building must have been in use, down to 1122 when the new abbatial quarters were built.

How far the monastic rules restricted social habits is a matter for antiquaries to settle if they can, and how far those rules were observed in the case of great secular princes; but the eleventh century was not very strict, and the rule of the Benedictines was always mild, until the Cistercians and Saint Bernard stiffened its discipline toward 1120. Even then the Church showed strong leanings toward secular poetry and popular tastes. The drama belonged to it almost exclusively, and the Mysteries and Miracle plays which were acted under its patronage often contained nothing of religion except the miracle. The greatest poem of the eleventh century was the "Chanson de Roland," and of that the Church took a sort of possession. At Chartres we shall find Charlemagne and Roland dear to the Virgin, and at about the same time, as far away as at Assisi in the Perugian country, Saint Francis himself—the nearest approach the Western world ever made to an Oriental incarnation of the divine essence—loved the French romans, and typified himself in the "Chanson de Roland." With Mont-Saint-Michel, the "Chanson de Roland" is almost one. The "Chanson" is in poetry what the Mount is in architecture. Without the

"Chanson," one cannot approach the feeling which the eleventh century built into the Archangel's church. Probably there was never a day, certainly never a week, during several centuries, when portions of the "Chanson" were not sung, or recited, at the Mount, and if there was one room where it was most at home, this one, supposing it to be the old refectory, claims to be the place.

CHAPTER II: LA CHANSON DE ROLAND

    Molz pelerins qui vunt al Munt
    Enquierent molt e grant dreit unt
    Comment l'igliese fut fundee
    Premierement et estoree.
    Cil qui lor dient de l'estoire
    Que cil demandent en memoire
    Ne l'unt pas bien ainz vunt faillant
    En plusors leus e mespernant.
    Por faire la apertement
    Entendre a cels qui escient
    N'unt de clerzie l'a tornee
    De latin tote et ordenee
    Pars veirs romieus novelement
    Molt en segrei por son convent
    Uns jovencels moine est del Munt
    Deus en son reigne part li dunt.
    Guillaume a non de Saint Paier
    Cen vei escrit en cest quaier.
    El tens Robeirt de Torignie
    Fut cil romanz fait e trove.

Most pilgrims who come to the Mount

Enquire much and are quite right,

How the church was founded

At first, and established.

Those who tell them the story

That they ask, in memory

Have it not well, but fall in error

In many places, and misapprehension.

In order to make it clearly

Intelligible to those who have

No knowledge of letters, it has been turned

From the Latin, and wholly rendered

In Romanesque verses, newly,

Much in secret, for his convent,

By a youth; a monk he is of the Mount.

God in his kingdom grant him part!

William is his name, of Saint Pair

As is seen written in this book.

In the time of Robert of Torigny

Was this roman made and invented.

These verses begin the "Roman du Mont-Saint-Michel," and if the spelling is corrected, they still read almost as easily as Voltaire; more easily than Verlaine; and much like a nursery rhyme; but as tourists cannot stop to clear their path, or smooth away the pebbles, they must be lifted over the rough spots, even when roughness is beauty. Translation is an evil, chiefly because every one who cares for mediaeval architecture cares for mediaeval French, and ought to care still more for mediaeval English. The language of this "Roman" was the literary language of England. William of Saint-Pair was a subject of Henry II, King of England and Normandy; his verses, like those of Richard Coeur-de-Lion, are monuments of English literature. To this day their ballad measure is better suited to English than to French; even the words and idioms are more English than French. Any one who attacks them boldly will find that the "vers romieus" run along like a ballad, singing their own meaning, and troubling themselves very little whether the meaning is exact or not. One's translation is sure to be full of gross blunders, but the supreme blunder is that of translating at all when one is trying to catch not a fact but a feeling. If translate one must, we had best begin by trying to be literal, under protest that it matters not a straw whether we succeed. Twelfth-century art was not precise; still less "precieuse," like Moliere's famous seventeenth-century prudes.

The verses of the young monk, William, who came from the little Norman village of Saint-Pair, near Granville, within sight of the Mount, were verses not meant to be brilliant. Simple human beings like rhyme better than prose, though both may say the same thing, as they like a curved line better than a straight one, or a blue better than a grey; but, apart from the sensual appetite, they chose rhyme in creating their literature for the practical reason that they remembered it better than prose. Men had to carry their libraries in their heads.

These lines of William, beginning his story, are valuable because for once they give a name and a date. Abbot Robert of Torigny ruled at the Mount from 1154 to 1186. We have got to travel again and again between Mont-Saint-Michel and Chartres during these years, but for the moment we must hurry to get back to William the Conqueror and the "Chanson de Roland." William of

Saint-Pair comes in here, out of place, only on account of a pretty description he gave of the annual pilgrimage to the Mount, which is commonly taken to be more or less like what he saw every year on the Archangel's Day, and what had existed ever since the Normans became Christian in 912:—

Li jorz iert clers e sanz grant vent.

Les meschines e les vallez

Chascuns d'els dist verz ou sonnez.

Neis li viellart revunt chantant

De leece funt tuit semblant.

Qui plus ne seit si chante outree

E Dex aie u Asusee.

Cil jugleor la u il vunt

Tuit lor vieles traites unt

Laiz et sonnez vunt vielant.

Li tens est beals la joie est grant.

Cil palefrei e cil destrier

E cil roncin e cil sommier

Qui errouent par le chemin

Que menouent cil pelerin

De totes parz henissant vunt

Por la grant joie que il unt.

Neis par les bois chantouent tuit

Li oiselet grant et petit.

Li buef les vaches vunt muant

Par les forez e repaissant.

Cors e boisines e fresteals

E fleutes e chalemeals

Sonnoent si que les montaignes

En retintoent et les pleignes.

Que esteit dont les plaiseiz

E des forez e des larriz.

En cels par a tel sonneiz

Com si ce fust cers acolliz.

Entor le mont el bois follu

Cil travetier unt tres tendu

Rues unt fait par les chemins.

Plentei i out de divers vins

Pain e pastez fruit e poissons

Oisels obleies veneisons

De totes parz aveit a vendre

Assez en out qui ad que tendre.

The day was clear, without much wind.

The maidens and the varlets

Each of them said verse or song;

Even the old people go singing;

All have a look of joy.

Who knows no more sings HURRAH,

Or GOD HELP, or UP AND ON!

The minstrels there where they go

Have all brought their viols;

Lays and songs playing as they go.

The weather is fine; the joy is great;

The palfreys and the chargers,

And the hackneys and the packhorses

Which wander along the road

That the pilgrims follow,

On all sides neighing go,

For the great joy they feel.

Even in the woods sing all

The little birds, big and small.

The oxen and the cows go lowing

Through the forests as they feed.

Horns and trumpets and shepherd's pipes

And flutes and pipes of reed

Sound so that the mountains

Echo to them, and the plains.

How was it then with the glades

And with the forests and the pastures?

In these there was such sound

As though it were a stag at bay.

About the Mount, in the leafy wood,

The workmen have tents set up;

Streets have made along the roads.

Plenty there was of divers wines,

Bread and pasties, fruit and fish,

Birds, cakes, venison,

Everywhere there was for sale.

Enough he had who has the means to pay.

If you are not satisfied with this translation, any scholar of French will easily help to make a better, for we are not studying grammar or archaeology, and would rather be inaccurate in such matters than not, if, at that price, a freer feeling of the art could be caught. Better still, you can turn to Chaucer, who wrote his Canterbury Pilgrimage two hundred years afterwards:—

Whanne that April with his shoures sote

The droughte of March hath perced to the rote…

Than longen folk to gon on pilgrimages

And palmeres for to seken strange strondes…

And especially, from every shires ende

Of Englelonde, to Canterbury they wende

The holy blisful martyr for to seke,

That hem hath holpen whan that they were seke.

The passion for pilgrimages was universal among our ancestors as far back as we can trace them. For at least a thousand years it was their chief delight, and is not yet extinct. To feel the art of Mont-Saint-Michel and Chartres we have got to become pilgrims again: but, just now, the point of most interest is not the pilgrim so much as the minstrel who sang to amuse him,—the jugleor or jongleur,— who was at home in every abbey, castle or cottage, as well as at every shrine. The jugleor became a jongleur and degenerated into the street-juggler; the minstrel, or menestrier, became very early a word of abuse, equivalent to blackguard; and from the beginning the profession seems to have been socially decried, like that of a music-hall singer or dancer in later times; but in the eleventh century, or perhaps earlier still, the jongleur seems to have been a poet, and to have composed the songs he sang. The immense mass of poetry known as the "Chansons de Geste" seems to have been composed as well as sung by the unnamed Homers of France, and of all spots in the many provinces where the French language in its many dialects prevailed, Mont-Saint-Michel should have been the favourite with the jongleur, not only because the swarms of pilgrims assured him food and an occasional small piece of silver, but also because Saint Michael was the saint militant of all the warriors whose exploits in war were the subject of the "Chansons de Geste." William of Saint- Pair was a priest-poet; he was not a minstrel, and his "Roman" was not a chanson; it was made to read, not to recite; but the "Chanson de Roland" was a different affair.

So it was, too, with William's contemporaries and rivals or predecessors, the monumental poets of Norman-English literature. Wace, whose rhymed history of the Norman dukes, which he called the "Roman de Rou," or "Rollo," is an English classic of the first rank, was a canon of Bayeux when William of Saint-Pair was writing at Mont-Saint-Michel. His rival Benoist, who wrote another famous chronicle on the same subject, was also a historian, and not a singer. In that day literature meant verse; elegance in French prose did not yet exist; but the elegancies of poetry in the twelfth century were as different, in kind, from the grand style of the eleventh, as Virgil was different from Homer.

William of Saint-Pair introduces us to the pilgrimage and to the jongleur, as they had existed at least two hundred years before his time, and were to exist two hundred years after him. Of all our two hundred and fifty million arithmetical ancestors who were going on pilgrimages in the middle of the eleventh century, the two who would probably most interest every one, after eight hundred years have passed, would be William the Norman and Harold the Saxon. Through William of Saint-Pair and Wace and Benoist, and the most charming literary monument of all, the Bayeux tapestry of Queen Matilda, we can build up the story of such a pilgrimage which shall be as historically exact as the battle of Hastings, and as artistically true as the Abbey Church.

According to Wace's "Roman de Rou," when Harold's father, Earl Godwin, died, April 15, 1053, Harold wished to obtain the release of certain hostages, a brother and a cousin, whom Godwin had given to Edward the Confessor as security for his good behaviour, and whom Edward had sent to Duke William for safe-keeping. Wace took the story from other and older sources, and its accuracy is much disputed, but the fact that Harold went to Normandy seems to be certain, and you will see at Bayeux the picture of Harold asking permission of King Edward to make the journey, and departing on horseback, with his hawk and hounds and followers, to take ship at Bosham, near Chichester and Portsmouth. The date alone is doubtful. Common sense seems to suggest that the earliest possible date could not be too early to explain the rash youth of the aspirant to a throne who put himself in the power of a rival in the eleventh century. When that rival chanced to be William the Bastard, not even boyhood could excuse the folly; but Mr. Freeman, the chief authority on this delicate subject, inclined to think that Harold was forty years old when he committed his blunder, and that the year was about 1064. Between 1054 and 1064 the historian is free to choose what year he likes, and the tourist is still freer. To save trouble for the memory, the year 1058 will serve, since this is the date of the triumphal arches of the Abbey Church on the Mount. Harold, in sailing from the neighbourhood of Portsmouth, must have been bound for Caen or Rouen, but the usual west winds drove him eastward till he was thrown ashore on the coast of Ponthieu, between Abbeville and Boulogne, where he fell into the hands of the Count of Ponthieu, from whom he was rescued or ransomed by Duke William of Normandy and taken to Rouen. According to Wace and the "Roman de Rou":—

Guillaume tint Heraut maint jour

  Si com il dut a grant enor.

A maint riche torneiement

  Le fist aller mult noblement.

Chevals e armes li dona

  Et en Bretaigne le mena

Ne sai de veir treiz faiz ou quatre

Quant as Bretons se dut combattre.

William kept Harold many a day,

As was his due in great honour.

To many a rich tournament

Made him go very nobly.

Horses and arms gave him

And into Brittany led him

I know not truly whether three or four times

When he had to make war on the Bretons.

Perhaps the allusion to rich tournaments belongs to the time of Wace rather than to that of Harold a century earlier, before the first crusade, but certainly Harold did go with William on at least one raid into Brittany, and the charming tapestry of Bayeux, which tradition calls by the name of Queen Matilda, shows William's men-at-arms crossing the sands beneath Mont-Saint-Michel, with the Latin legend:—"Et venerunt ad Montem Michaelis. Hic Harold dux trahebat eos de arena. Venerunt ad flumen Cononis." They came to Mont-Saint-Michel, and Harold dragged them out of the quicksands.

They came to the river Couesnon. Harold must have got great fame by saving life on the sands, to be remembered and recorded by the Normans themselves after they had killed him; but this is the affair of historians. Tourists note only that Harold and William came to the Mount:— "Venerunt ad Montem." They would never have dared to pass it, on such an errand, without stopping to ask the help of Saint Michael.

If William and Harold came to the Mount, they certainly dined or supped in the old refectory, which is where we have lain in wait for them. Where Duke William was, his jongleur—jugleor—was not far, and Wace knew, as every one in Normandy seemed to know, who this favourite was,—his name, his character, and his song. To him Wace owed one of the most famous passages in his story of the assault at Hastings, where Duke William and his battle began their advance against the English lines:—

Taillefer qui mult bien chantout

Sor un cheval qui tost alout

Devant le duc alout chantant

De Karlemaigne e de Rollant

E d'Oliver e des vassals

Qui morurent en Rencevals.

Quant il orent chevalchie tant

Qu'as Engleis vindrent apreismant:

"Sire," dist Taillefer, "merci!

Io vos ai longuement servi.

Tot mon servise me devez.

Hui se vos plaist le me rendez.

Por tot guerredon vos require

E si vos veil forment preier

Otreiez mei que io ni faille

Le premier colp de la bataille."

Li dus respondi: "Io l'otrei."

Taillefer who was famed for song,

Mounted on a charger strong,

Rode on before the Duke, and sang

Of Roland and of Charlemagne,

Oliver and the vassals all

Who fell in fight at Roncesvals.

When they had ridden till they saw

The English battle close before:

"Sire," said Taillefer, "a grace!

I have served you long and well;

All reward you owe me still;

To-day repay me if you please.

> For all guerdon I require,
>
> And ask of you in formal prayer,
>
> Grant to me as mine of right
>
> The first blow struck in the fight."
>
> The Duke answered: "I grant."

Of course, critics doubt the story, as they very properly doubt everything. They maintain that the "Chanson de Roland" was not as old as the battle of Hastings, and certainly Wace gave no sufficient proof of it. Poetry was not usually written to prove facts. Wace wrote a hundred years after the battle of Hastings. One is not morally required to be pedantic to the point of knowing more than Wace knew, but the feeling of scepticism, before so serious a monument as Mont-Saint-Michel, is annoying. The "Chanson de Roland" ought not to be trifled with, at least by tourists in search of art. One is shocked at the possibility of being deceived about the starting-point of American genealogy. Taillefer and the song rest on the same evidence that Duke William and Harold and the battle itself rest upon, and to doubt the "Chanson" is to call the very roll of Battle Abbey in question. The whole fabric of society totters; the British peerage turns pale.

Wace did not invent all his facts. William of Malmesbury is supposed to have written his prose chronicle about 1120 when many of the men who fought at Hastings must have been alive, and William expressly said: "Tunc cantilena Rollandi inchoata ut martium viri exemplum pugnaturos accenderet, inclamatoque dei auxilio, praelium consertum." Starting the "Chanson de Roland" to inflame the fighting temper of the men, battle was joined. This seems enough proof to satisfy any sceptic, yet critics still suggest that the "cantilena Rollandi" must have been a Norman "Chanson de Rou," or "Rollo," or at best an earlier version of the "Chanson de Roland"; but no Norman chanson would have inflamed the martial spirit of William's army, which was largely French; and as for the age of the version, it is quite immaterial for Mont-Saint-Michel; the actual version is old enough.

Taillefer himself is more vital to the interest of the dinner in the refectory, and his name was not mentioned by William of Malmesbury. If the song was started by the Duke's order, it was certainly started by the Duke's jongleur, and the name of this jongleur happens to be known on still better authority than that of William of Malmesbury. Guy of Amiens went to England in 1068 as almoner of Queen Matilda, and there wrote a Latin poem on the battle of Hastings which must have been complete within ten years after the battle was fought, for Guy died in 1076. Taillefer, he said, led the Duke's battle:—

> Incisor-ferri mimus cognomine dictus.

"Taillefer, a jongleur known by that name." A mime was a singer, but Taillefer was also an actor:—

> Histrio cor audax nimium quem nobilitabat.

"A jongleur whom a very brave heart ennobled." The jongleur was not noble by birth, but was ennobled by his bravery.

Hortatur Gallos verbis et territat Anglos

Alte projiciens ludit et ense suo.

Like a drum-major with his staff, he threw his sword high in the air and caught it, while he chanted his song to the French, and terrified the English. The rhymed chronicle of Geoffrey Gaimer who wrote about 1150, and that of Benoist who was Wace's rival, added the story that Taillefer died in the melee.

The most unlikely part of the tale was, after all, not the singing of the "Chanson," but the prayer of Taillefer to the Duke:—

"Otreiez mei que io ni faille

Le premier colp de la bataille."

Legally translated, Taillefer asked to be ennobled, and offered to pay for it with his life. The request of a jongleur to lead the Duke's battle seems incredible. In early French "bataille" meant battalion,—the column of attack. The Duke's grant: "Io l'otrei!" seems still more fanciful. Yet Guy of Amiens distinctly confirmed the story: "Histrio cor audax nimium quem nobilitabat"; a stage- player—a juggler—the Duke's singer—whose bravery ennobled him. The Duke granted him—octroya—his patent of nobility on the field.

All this preamble leads only to unite the "Chanson" with the architecture of the Mount, by means of Duke William and his Breton campaign of 1058. The poem and the church are akin; they go together, and explain each other. Their common trait is their military character, peculiar to the eleventh century. The round arch is masculine. The "Chanson" is so masculine that, in all its four thousand lines, the only Christian woman so much as mentioned was Alda, the sister of Oliver and the betrothed of Roland, to whom one stanza, exceedingly like a later insertion, was given, toward the end. Never after the first crusade did any great poem rise to such heroism as to sustain itself without a heroine. Even Dante attempted no such feat.

Duke William's party, then, is to be considered as assembled at supper in the old refectory, in the year 1058, while the triumphal piers of the church above are rising. The Abbot, Ralph of Beaumont, is host; Duke William sits with him on a dais; Harold is by his side "a grant enor"; the Duke's brother, Odo, Bishop of Bayeux, with the other chief vassals, are present; and the Duke's jongleur Taillefer is at his elbow. The room is crowded with soldiers and monks, but all are equally anxious to hear Taillefer sing. As soon as dinner is over, at a nod from the Duke, Taillefer begins:—

Carles li reis nostre emperere magnes

Set anz tuz pleins ad estet en Espaigne

Cunquist la tere tresque en la mer altaigne

Ni ad castel ki devant lui remaigne

Murs ne citez ni est remes a fraindre.

Charles the king, our emperor, the great,

Seven years complete has been in Spain,

Conquered the land as far as the high seas,

Nor is there castle that holds against him,

Nor wall or city left to capture.

The "Chanson" opened with these lines, which had such a direct and personal bearing on every one who heard them as to sound like prophecy. Within ten years William was to stand in England where Charlemagne stood in Spain. His mind was full of it, and of the means to attain it; and Harold was even more absorbed than he by the anxiety of the position. Harold had been obliged to take oath that he would support William's claim to the English throne, but he was still undecided, and William knew men too well to feel much confidence in an oath. As Taillefer sang on, he reached the part of Ganelon, the typical traitor, the invariable figure of mediaeval society. No feudal lord was without a Ganelon. Duke William saw them all about him.

He might have felt that Harold would play the part, but if Harold should choose rather to be Roland, Duke William could have foretold that his own brother, Bishop Odo, after gorging himself on the plunder of half England, would turn into a Ganelon so dangerous as to require a prison for life. When Taillefer reached the battle-scenes, there was no further need of imagination to realize them. They were scenes of yesterday and to-morrow. For that matter, Charlemagne or his successor was still at Aix, and the Moors were still in Spain. Archbishop Turpin of Rheims had fought with sword and mace in Spain, while Bishop Odo of Bayeux was to marshal his men at Hastings, like a modern general, with a staff, but both were equally at home on the field of battle. Verse by verse, the song was a literal mirror of the Mount. The battle of Hastings was to be fought on the Archangel's Day. What happened to Roland at Roncesvalles was to happen to Harold at Hastings, and Harold, as he was dying like Roland, was to see his brother Gyrth die like Oliver. Even Taillefer was to be a part, and a distinguished part, of his chanson. Sooner or later, all were to die in the large and simple way of the eleventh century. Duke William himself, twenty years later, was to meet a violent death at Mantes in the same spirit, and if Bishop Odo did not die in battle, he died, at least, like an eleventh-century hero, on the first crusade. First or last, the whole company died in fight, or in prison, or on crusade, while the monks shrived them and prayed.

Then Taillefer certainly sang the great death-scenes. Even to this day every French school-boy, if he knows no other poetry, knows these verses by heart. In the eleventh century they wrung the heart of every man-at-arms in Europe, whose school was the field of battle and the hand-to-hand fight. No modern singer ever enjoys such power over an audience as Taillefer exercised over these men who were actors as well as listeners. In the melee at Roncesvalles, overborne by innumerable Saracens, Oliver at last calls for help:—

Munjoie escriet e haltement e cler.

Rollant apelet sun ami e sun per;

"Sire compainz a mei kar vus justez.

A grant dulur ermes hoi deserveret." Aoi.

"Montjoie!" he cries, loud and clear,

Roland he calls, his friend and peer;

"Sir Friend! ride now to help me here!

Parted today, great pity were."

Of course the full value of the verse cannot be regained. One knows neither how it was sung nor even how it was pronounced. The assonances are beyond recovering; the "laisse" or leash of verses or assonances with the concluding cry, "Aoi," has long ago vanished from verse or song. The sense is as simple as the "Ballad of Chevy Chase," but one must imagine the voice and acting. Doubtless Taillefer acted each motive; when Oliver called loud and clear, Taillefer's voice rose; when Roland spoke "doulcement et suef," the singer must have sung gently and soft; and when the two friends, with the singular courtesy of knighthood and dignity of soldiers, bowed to each other in parting and turned to face their deaths, Taillefer may have indicated the movement as he sang. The verses gave room for great acting. Hearing Oliver's cry for help, Roland rode up, and at sight of the desperate field, lost for a moment his consciousness:—

As vus Rollant sur sun cheval pasmet

E Olivier ki est a mort nafrez!

Tant ad sainiet li oil li sunt trublet

Ne luinz ne pres ne poet veeir si cler

Que reconuisset nisun hume mortel.

Sun cumpaignun cum il l'ad encuntret

Sil fiert amunt sur l'elme a or gemmet

Tut li detrenchet d'ici que al nasel

Mais en la teste ne l'ad mie adeset.

A icel colp l'ad Rollanz reguardet

Si li demandet dulcement et suef

"Sire cumpainz, faites le vus de gred?

Ja est co Rollanz ki tant vus soelt amer.

Par nule guise ne m'aviez desfiet,"

Dist Oliviers: "Or vus oi jo parler

Io ne vus vei. Veied vus damnedeus!

Ferut vus ai. Kar le me pardunez!"

Rollanz respunt: "Jo n'ai nient de mel.

Jol vus parduins ici e devant deu."

A icel mot l'uns al altre ad clinet.

Par tel amur as les vus desevrez!

There Roland sits unconscious on his horse,

And Oliver who wounded is to death,

So much has bled, his eyes grow dark to him,

Nor far nor near can see so clear

As to recognize any mortal man.

His friend, when he has encountered him,

He strikes upon the helmet of gemmed gold,

splits it from the crown to the nose-piece,

But to the head he has not reached at all.

At this blow Roland looks at him,

Asks him gently and softly:

"Sir Friend, do you it in earnest?

You know 't is Roland who has so loved you.

In no way have you sent to me defiance."

Says Oliver: "Indeed I hear you speak,

I do not see you. May God see and save you!

Strike you I did. I pray you pardon me."

Roland replies: "I have no harm at all.

I pardon you here and before God!"

At this word, one to the other bends himself.

With such affection, there they separate.

No one should try to render this into English—or, indeed, into modern French—verse, but any one who will take the trouble to catch the metre and will remember that each verse in the "leash" ends in the same sound,—aimer, parler, cler, mortel, damnede, mel, deu, suef, nasel,—however the terminal syllables may be spelled, can follow the feeling of the poetry as well as though it were Greek hexameter. He will feel the simple force of the words and action, as he feels Homer. It is the grand style,—the eleventh century:—

Ferut vus ai! Kar le me pardunez!

Not a syllable is lost, and always the strongest syllable is chosen.

Even the sentiment is monosyllabic and curt:—

Ja est co Rollanz ki tant vus soelt amer!

Taillefer had, in such a libretto, the means of producing dramatic effects that the French comedy or the grand opera never approached, and such as made Bayreuth seem thin and feeble. Duke William's barons must have clung to his voice and action as though they were in the very melee, striking at the helmets of gemmed gold. They had all been there, and were to be there again. As the climax approached, they saw the scene itself; probably they had seen it every year, more or less, since they could swing a sword. Taillefer chanted the death of Oliver and of Archbishop Turpin and all the other barons of the rear guard, except Roland, who was left for dead by the Saracens when they fled on hearing the horns of Charlemagne's returning host. Roland came back to consciousness on feeling a Saracen marauder tugging at his sword Durendal. With a blow of his ivory horn—oliphant—he killed the pagan; then feeling death near, he prepared for it. His first thought was for Durendal, his sword, which he could not leave to infidels. In the singular triple repetition which gives more of the same solidity and architectural weight to the verse, he made three attempts to break the sword, with a lament—a plaint—for each. Three times he struck with all his force against the rock; each time the sword rebounded without breaking. The third time—

Rollanz ferit en une pierre bise

Plus en abat que jo ne vus sai dire.

L'espee cruist ne fruisset ne ne briset

Cuntre le ciel amunt est resortie.

Quant veit li quens que ne la fraindrat mie

Mult dulcement la plainst a sei meisme.

"E! Durendal cum ies bele e saintisme!

En l'oret punt asez i ad reliques.

La dent saint Pierre e del sanc seint Basilie

E des chevels mun seignur seint Denisie

Del vestment i ad seinte Marie.

Il nen est dreiz que paien te baillisent.

De chrestiens devez estre servie.

Ne vus ait hum ki facet cuardie!

Mult larges terres de vus averai cunquises

Que Carles tient ki la barbe ad flurie.

E li emperere en est e ber e riches."

Roland strikes on a grey stone,

More of it cuts off than I can tell you.

The sword grinds, but shatters not nor breaks,

Upward against the sky it rebounds.

When the Count sees that he can never break it,

Very gently he mourns it to himself:

"Ah, Durendal, how fair you are and sacred!

In your golden guard are many relics,

The tooth of Saint Peter and blood of Saint Basil,

And hair of my seigneur Saint-Denis,

Of the garment too of Saint Mary.

It is not right that pagans should own you.

By Christians you should be served,

Nor should man have you who does cowardice.

Many wide lands by you I have conquered

That Charles holds, who has the white beard,

And emperor of them is noble and rich."

This "laisse" is even more eleventh-century than the other, but it appealed no longer to the warriors; it spoke rather to the monks. To the warriors, the sword itself was the religion, and the relics were details of ornament or strength. To the priest, the list of relics was more eloquent than the Regent diamond on the hilt and the Kohinoor on the scabbard. Even to us it is interesting if it is understood. Roland had gone on pilgrimage to the Holy Land. He had stopped at Rome and won the friendship of Saint Peter, as the tooth proved; he had passed through Constantinople and secured the help of Saint Basil; he had reached Jerusalem and gained the affection of the Virgin; he had come home to France and secured the support of his "seigneur" Saint Denis; for Roland, like Hugh Capet, was a liege-man of Saint Denis and French to the heart. France, to him, was Saint Denis, and at most the Ile de France, but not Anjou or even Maine. These were countries he had conquered with Durendal:—

Jo l'en cunquis e Anjou e Bretaigne

Si l'en cunquis e Peitou e le Maine

Jo l'en cunquis Normendie la franche

Si l'en cunquis Provence e Equitaigne.

He had conquered these for his emperor Charlemagne with the help of his immediate spiritual lord or seigneur Saint Denis, but the monks knew that he could never have done these feats without the help of Saint Peter, Saint Basil, and Saint Mary the Blessed Virgin, whose relics, in the hilt of his sword, were worth more than any king's ransom. To this day a tunic of the Virgin is the most precious property of the cathedral at Chartres. Either one of Roland's relics would have made the glory of any shrine in Europe, and every monk knew their enormous value and power better than he knew the value of Roland's conquests.

Yet even the religion is martial, as though it were meant for the fighting Archangel and Odo of Bayeux. The relics serve the sword; the sword is not in service of the relics. As the death-scene approaches, the song becomes even more military:—

Co sent Rollanz que la mort le tresprent

Devers la teste sur le quer li descent.

Desuz un pin i est alez curanz

Sur l'erbe verte si est culchiez adenz

Desuz lui met s'espee e l'olifant

Turnat sa teste vers la paiene gent.

Pur co l'ad fait que il voelt veirement

Que Carles diet et trestute sa gent

Li gentils quens quil fut morz cunqueranz.

Then Roland feels that death is taking him;

Down from the head upon the heart it falls.

Beneath a pine he hastens running;

On the green grass he throws himself down;

Beneath him puts his sword and oliphant,

Turns his face toward the pagan army.

For this he does it, that he wishes greatly

That Charles should say and all his men,

The gentle Count has died a conqueror.

Thus far, not a thought or a word strays from the field of war. With a childlike intensity, every syllable bends toward the single idea—

Li gentils quens quil fut morz cunqueranz.

Only then the singer allowed the Church to assert some of its rights:-

Co sent Rollanz de sun tens ni ad plus

Devers Espaigne gist en un pui agut

A l'une main si ad sun piz batut.

"Deus meie culpe vers les tues vertuz

De mes pecchiez des granz e des menuz

Que jo ai fait des l'ure que nez fui

Tresqu'a cest jur que ci sui consouz."
Sun destre guant en ad vers deu tendut
Angle del ciel i descendent a lui. Aoi.
Then Roland feels that his last hour has come
Facing toward Spain he lies on a steep hill,
While with one hand he beats upon his breast:
"Mea culpa, God! through force of thy miracles
Pardon my sins, the great as well as small,
That I have done from the hour I was born
Down to this day that I have now attained."
His right glove toward God he lifted up.
Angels from heaven descend on him. Aoi.
Li quens Rollanz se jut desuz un pin
Envers Espaigne en ad turnet sun vis
De plusurs choses a remembrer li prist
De tantes terres cume li bers cunquist
De dulce France des humes de sun lign
De Carlemagne sun seignur kil nurrit
Ne poet muer men plurt e ne suspirt
Mais lui meisme ne voelt metre en ubli
Claimet sa culpe si priet deu mercit.
"Veire paterne ki unkes ne mentis
Seint Lazarun de mort resurrexis
E Daniel des liuns guaresis
Guaris de mei l'anme de tuz perils

Pur les pecchiez que en ma vie fis."
Sun destre guant a deu en puroffrit
E de sa main seinz Gabriel lad pris
Desur sun braz teneit le chief enclin
Juintes ses mains est alez a sa fin.
Deus li tramist sun angle cherubin
E Seint Michiel de la mer del peril
Ensemble od els Seinz Gabriels i vint
L' anme del cunte portent en pareis.

Count Roland throws himself beneath a pine
And toward Spain has turned his face away.
Of many things he called the memory back,
Of many lands that he, the brave, had conquered,
Of gentle France, the men of his lineage,
Of Charlemagne his lord, who nurtured him;
He cannot help but weep and sigh for these,
But for himself will not forget to care;
He cries his Culpe, he prays to God for grace.
"O God the Father who has never lied,
Who raised up Saint Lazarus from death,
And Daniel from the lions saved,
Save my soul from all the perils
For the sins that in my life I did!"
His right-hand glove to God he proffered;
Saint Gabriel from his hand took it;

Upon his arm he held his head inclined,

Folding his hands he passed to his end.

God sent to him his angel cherubim

And Saint Michael of the Sea in Peril,

Together with them came Saint Gabriel.

The soul of the Count they bear to Paradise.

Our age has lost much of its ear for poetry, as it has its eye for colour and line, and its taste for war and worship, wine and women. Not one man in a hundred thousand could now feel what the eleventh century felt in these verses of the "Chanson," and there is no reason for trying to do so, but there is a certain use in trying for once to understand not so much the feeling as the meaning. The naivete of the poetry is that of the society. God the Father was the feudal seigneur, who raised Lazarus—his baron or vassal—from the grave, and freed Daniel, as an evidence of his power and loyalty; a seigneur who never lied, or was false to his word. God the Father, as feudal seigneur, absorbs the Trinity, and, what is more significant, absorbs or excludes also the Virgin, who is not mentioned in the prayer. To this seigneur, Roland in dying, proffered (puroffrit) his right-hand gauntlet. Death was an act of homage. God sent down his Archangel Gabriel as his representative to accept the homage and receive the glove. To Duke William and his barons nothing could seem more natural and correct. God was not farther away than Charlemagne.

Correct as the law may have been, the religion even at that time must have seemed to the monks to need professional advice. Roland's life was not exemplary. The "Chanson" had taken pains to show that the disaster at Roncesvalles was due to Roland's headstrong folly and temper. In dying, Roland had not once thought of these faults, or repented of his worldly ambitions, or mentioned the name of Alda, his betrothed. He had clung to the memory of his wars and conquests, his lineage, his earthly seigneur Charlemagne, and of "douce France." He had forgotten to give so much as an allusion to Christ. The poet regarded all these matters as the affair of the Church; all the warrior cared for was courage, loyalty, and prowess.

The interest of these details lies not in the scholarship or the historical truth or even the local colour, so much as in the art. The naivete of the thought is repeated by the simplicity of the verse. Word and thought are equally monosyllabic. Nothing ever matched it. The words bubble like a stream in the woods:—

Co sent Rollanz de sun tens ni ad plus.

Try and put them into modern French, and see what will happen:—

Que jo ai fait des l'ure que nez fui.

The words may remain exactly the same, but the poetry will have gone out of them. Five hundred years later, even the English critics had so far lost their sense for military poetry that they professed to be shocked by Milton's monosyllables:—

Whereat he inly raged, and, as they talked,

Smote him into the midriff with a stone

That beat out life.

Milton's language was indeed more or less archaic and Biblical; it was a Puritan affectation; but the "Chanson" in the refectory actually reflected, repeated, echoed, the piers and arches of the Abbey Church just rising above. The verse is built up. The qualities of the architecture reproduce themselves in the song: the same directness, simplicity, absence of self-consciousness; the same intensity of purpose; even the same material; the prayer is granite:—

Guaris de mei l'anme de tuz perils Pur les pecchiez que en ma vie fisi

The action of dying is felt, like the dropping of a keystone into the vault, and if the Romanesque arches in the church, which are within hearing, could speak, they would describe what they are doing in the precise words of the poem:—

Desur sun braz teneit le chief enclin Juintes ses mains est alez a sa fin.

Upon their shoulders have their heads inclined,

Folded their hands, and sunken to their rest.

Many thousands of times these verses must have been sung at the Mount and echoed in every castle and on every battle-field from the Welsh Marches to the shores of the Dead Sea. No modern opera or play ever approached the popularity of the "Chanson." None has ever expressed with anything like the same completeness the society that produced it. Chanted by every minstrel,—known by heart, from beginning to end, by every man and woman and child, lay or clerical,—translated into every tongue,—more intensely felt, if possible, in Italy and Spain than in Normandy and England,—perhaps most effective, as a work of art, when sung by the Templars in their great castles in the Holy Land,—it is now best felt at Mont-Saint- Michel, and from the first must have been there at home. The proof is the line, evidently inserted for the sake of its local effect, which invoked Saint Michael in Peril of the Sea at the climax of Roland's death, and one needs no original documents or contemporary authorities to prove that, when Taillefer came to this invocation, not only Duke William and his barons, but still more Abbot Ranulf and his monks, broke into a frenzy of sympathy which expressed the masculine and military passions of the Archangel better than it accorded with the rules of Saint Benedict.

CHAPTER III: THE MERVEILLE

The nineteenth century moved fast and furious, so that one who moved in it felt sometimes giddy, watching it spin; but the eleventh moved faster and more furiously still. The Norman conquest of England was an immense effort, and its consequences were far-reaching, but the first crusade was altogether the most interesting event in European history. Never has the Western world shown anything like the energy and unity with which she then flung herself on the East, and for the moment made the East recoil. Barring her family quarrels, Europe was a unity then, in thought, will, and object. Christianity was the unit. Mont-Saint-Michel and Byzantium were near each other. The Emperor Constantine and the Emperor Charlemagne were figured as allies and friends in the popular legend. The East was the common enemy, always superior in wealth and numbers, frequently in energy, and sometimes in thought and art. The outburst of the first crusade was splendid even in a military sense, but it was great beyond comparison in its reflection in architecture, ornament, poetry, colour, religion, and philosophy. Its men were astonishing, and its women were worth all the rest.

Mont-Saint-Michel, better than any other spot in the world, keeps the architectural record of that ferment, much as the Sicilian temples keep the record of the similar outburst of Greek energy, art, poetry, and thought, fifteen hundred years before. Of the eleventh century, it is true, nothing but the church remains at the Mount, and, if studied further, the century has got to be sought elsewhere, which is not difficult, since it is preserved in any number of churches in every path of tourist travel. Normandy is full of it; Bayeux and Caen contain little else. At the Mount, the eleventh-century work was antiquated before it was finished. In the year 1112, Abbot Roger II was obliged to plan and construct a new group in such haste that it is said to have been finished in 1122. It extends from what we have supposed to be the old refectory to the parvis, and abuts on the three lost spans of the church, covering about one hundred and twenty feet. As usual there were three levels; a crypt or gallery beneath, known as the Aquilon; a cloister or promenoir above; and on the level of the church a dormitory, now lost. The group is one of the most interesting in France, another pons seclorum, an antechamber to the west portal of Chartres, which bears the same date (i 110-25). It is the famous period of Transition, the glory of the twelfth century, the object of our pilgrimage.

Art is a fairly large field where no one need jostle his neighbour, and no one need shut himself up in a corner; but, if one insists on taking a corner of preference, one might offer some excuse for choosing the Gothic Transition. The quiet, restrained strength of the Romanesque married to the graceful curves and vaulting imagination of the Gothic makes a union nearer the ideal than is often allowed in marriage. The French, in their best days, loved it with a constancy that has thrown a sort of aureole over their fickleness since. They never tired of its possibilities. Sometimes they put the pointed arch within the round, or above it; sometimes they put the round within the pointed. Sometimes a Roman arch covered a cluster of pointed windows, as though protecting and caressing its children; sometimes a huge pointed arch covered a great rose-window spreading across the whole front of an enormous cathedral, with an arcade of Romanesque windows beneath. The French architects felt no discord, and there was none. Even the pure Gothic was put side by side with the pure Roman. You will see no later Gothic than the choir of the Abbey Church above (1450-1521), unless it is the north fleche of Chartres Cathedral (1507-13); and if you will look down the nave, through the triumphal arches, into the pointed choir four hundred years more modern, you can judge whether there is any real discord. For those who feel the art, there is none; the strength and the grace join hands; the man and woman love each other still.

The difference of sex is not imaginary. In 1058, when the triumphal columns were building, and Taillefer sang to William the Bastard and Harold the Saxon, Roland still prayed his "mea culpa" to God the Father and gave not a thought to Alda his betrothed. In the twelfth century Saint Bernard recited "Ave Stella Marts" in an ecstasy of miracle before the image of the Virgin, and the armies of France in battle cried, "Notre-Dame-Saint-Denis-Montjoie." What the Roman could not express flowered into the Gothic; what the masculine mind could not idealize in the warrior, it idealized in the woman; no architecture that ever grew on earth, except the Gothic, gave this effect of flinging its passion against the sky.

When men no longer felt the passion, they fell back on themselves, or lower. The architect returned to the round arch, and even further to the flatness of the Greek colonnade; but this was not the fault of the twelfth or thirteenth centuries. What they had to say they said; what they felt they expressed; and if the seventeenth century forgot it, the twentieth in turn has forgotten the seventeenth. History is only a catalogue of the forgotten. The eleventh century is no worse off than its neighbours. The twelfth is, in architecture, rather better off than the nineteenth. These two rooms, the Aquilon and promenoir, which mark the beginning of the Transition, are, on the whole, more modern than Saint-Sulpice, or Il Gesu at Rome. In the same situation, for the same purposes, any architect would be proud to repeat them to-day.

The Aquilon, though a hall or gallery of importance in its day, seems to be classed among crypts. M. Camille Enlart, in his "Manual of French Archaeology" (p. 252) gives a list of Romanesque and Transition crypts, about one hundred and twenty, to serve as examples for the study. The Aquilon is not one of them, but the crypt of Saint-Denis and that of Chartres Cathedral would serve to teach any over-curious tourist all that he should want to know about such matters.

Photographs such as those of the Monuments Historiques answer all the just purposes of underground travel. The Aquilon is one's first lesson in Transition architecture because it is dated (1112); and the crypt of Saint-Denis serves almost equally well because the Abbe Suger must have begun his plans for it about 1122. Both have the same arcs doubleaux and arcs-formerets, though in opposite arrangement. Both show the first heavy hint at the broken arch. There are no nervures—no rib-vaulting,—and hardly a suggestion of the Gothic as one sees it in the splendid crypt of the Gros Fillers close at hand, except the elaborately intersecting vaults and the heavy columns; but the promenoir above is an astonishing leap in time and art. The promenoir has the same arrangement and columns as the Aquilon, but the vaults are beautifully arched and pointed, with ribs rising directly from the square capitals and intersecting the central spacings, in a spirit which neither you nor I know how to distinguish from the pure Gothic of the thirteenth century, unless it is that the arches are hardly pointed enough; they seem to the eye almost round. The height appears to be about fourteen feet.

The promenoir of Abbot Roger II has an interest to pilgrims who are going on to the shrine of the Virgin, because the date of the promenoir seems to be exactly the same as the date which the Abbe Bulteau assigns for the western portal of Chartres. Ordinarily a date is no great matter, but when one has to run forward and back, with the agility of an electric tram, between two or three fixed points, it is convenient to fix them once for all. The Transition is complete here in the promenoir, which was planned as early as 1115. The subject of vaulting is far too ambitious for summer travel; it is none too easy for a graduate of the Beaux Arts; and few architectural fields have been so earnestly discussed and disputed. We must not touch it. The age of the "Chanson de Roland" itself is not so dangerous a topic. Our vital needs are met, more or less sufficiently, by taking the promenoir at the Mount, the crypt at Saint-Denis, and the western portal at Chartres, as the trinity of our Transition, and roughly calling their date the years 1115-20, To overload the memory with dates is the vice of every schoolmaster and the passion of every second-rate scholar. Tourists want as few dates as possible; what they want is poetry. Yet a singular coincidence, with which every classroom is only too familiar, has made of the years—15 a curiously convenient group, and the year 1115 is as convenient as any for the beginning of the century of Transition. That was the year when Saint Bernard laid the foundations of his Abbey of Clairvaux. Perhaps 1115, or at latest 1117, was the year when Abelard sang love-songs to Heloise in Canon Fulbert's house in the Rue des Chantres, beside the cloister of Notre Dame in Paris. The Abbe Suger, the Abbe Bernard, and the Abbe Abelard are the three interesting men of the French Transition.

The promenoir, then, shall pass for the year 1115, and, as such, is an exceedingly beautiful hall, uniting the splendid calm and seriousness of the Romanesque with the exquisite lines of the Gothic. You will hardly see its equal in the twelfth century. At Angers the great hall of the Bishop's Palace survives to give a point of comparison, but commonly the halls of that date were not vaulted; they had timber roofs, and have perished. The promenoir is about sixty feet long, and divided into two aisles, ten feet wide, by a row of columns. If it were used on great occasions as a refectory, eighty or a hundred persons could have been seated at table, and perhaps this may have been about the scale of the Abbey's needs, at that time. Whatever effort of fancy was needed to place Duke William and Harold in the old refectory of 1058, none whatever is required in order to see his successors in the halls of Roger II. With one exception they were not interesting persons. The exception was Henry II of England and Anjou, and his wife Eleanor of Guienne, who was for a while Regent of Normandy. One of their children was born at Domfront, just beyond Avranches, and the Abbot was asked to be godfather. In 1158, just one hundred years after Duke William's visit, King Henry and his whole suite came to the Abbey, heard mass, and dined in the refectory. "Rex venit ad Montem Sancti Michaelis, audita missa ad magis altare, comedit in Refec-torio cum baronibus suis." Abbot Robert of Torigny was his host, and very possibly William of Saint-Pair looked on. Perhaps he recited parts of his "Roman" before the King. One may be quite sure that when Queen Eleanor came to the Mount she asked the poet to recite his verses, for Eleanor gave law to poets.

One might linger over Abbot Robert of Torigny, who was a very great man in his day, and an especially great architect, but too ambitious. All his work, including the two towers, crumbled and fell for want of proper support. What would correspond to the cathedrals of Noyon and Soissons and the old clocher and fleche of Chartres is lost. We have no choice but to step down into the next century at once, and into the full and perfect Gothic of the great age when the new Chartres was building.

In the year 1203, Philip Augustus expelled the English from Normandy and conquered the province; but, in the course of the war the Duke of Brittany, who was naturally a party to any war that took place under his eyes, happened to burn the town beneath the Abbey, and in doing so, set fire unintentionally to the Abbey itself. The sacrilege shocked Philip Augustus, and the wish to conciliate so powerful a vassal as Saint Michel, or his abbot, led the King of France to give a large sum of money for repairing the buildings. The Abbot Jordan (1191-1212) at once undertook to outdo all his predecessors, and, with an immense ambition, planned the huge pile which covers the whole north face of the Mount, and which has always borne the expressive name of the Merveille.

The general motive of abbatial building was common to them all. Abbeys were large households. The church was the centre, and at Mont-Saint-Michel the summit, for the situation compelled the abbots there to pile one building on another instead of arranging them on a level in squares or parallelograms. The dormitory in any case had to be near a door of the church, because the Rule required constant services, day and night. The cloister was also hard-by the church door, and, at the Mount, had to be on the same level in order to be in open air. Naturally the refectory must be immediately beneath one or the other of these two principal structures, and the hall, or place of meeting for business with the outside world, or for internal administration, or for guests of importance, must be next the refectory. The kitchen and offices would be placed on the lowest stage, if for no other reason, because the magazines were two hundred feet below at the landing-place, and all supplies, including water, had to be hauled up an inclined plane by windlass. To administer such a society required the most efficient management. An abbot on this scale was a very great man, indeed, who enjoyed an establishment of his own, close by, with officers in no small number; for the monks alone numbered sixty, and even these were not enough for the regular church services at seasons of pilgrimage. The Abbot was obliged to entertain scores and hundreds of guests, and these, too, of the highest importance, with large suites. Every ounce of food must be brought from the mainland, or fished from the sea. All the tenants and their farms, their rents and contributions, must be looked after. No secular prince had a more serious task of administration, and none did it so well. Tenants always preferred an abbot or bishop for landlord. The Abbey was the highest administrative creation of the Middle Ages, and when one has made one's pilgrimage to Chartres, one might well devote another summer to visiting what is left of Clairvaux, Citeaux, Cluny, and the other famous monasteries, with Viollet-le-Duc to guide, in order to satisfy one's mind whether, on the whole, such a life may not have had activity as well as idleness.

This is a matter of economics, to be settled with the keepers of more modern hotels, but the art had to suit the conditions, and when Abbot Jordan decided to plaster this huge structure against the side of the Mount, the architect had a relatively simple task to handle. The engineering difficulties alone were very serious; The architectural plan was plain enough. As the Abbot laid his requirements before the architect, he seems to have begun by fixing the scale for a refectory capable of seating two hundred guests at table. Probably no king in Europe fed more persons at his table than this. According to M. Corroyer's plan, the length of the new refectory is one hundred and twenty-three feet (37.5 metres). A row of columns down the centre divides it into two aisles, measuring twelve feet clear, from column to column, across the room. If tables were set the whole length of the two aisles, forty persons could have been easily seated, in four rows, or one hundred and sixty persons. Without crowding, the same space would give room for fifty guests, or two hundred in all.

Once the scale was fixed, the arrangement was easy. Beginning at the lowest possible level, one plain, very solidly built, vaulted room served as foundation for another, loftier and more delicately vaulted; and this again bore another which stood on the level of the church, and opened directly into the north transept. This arrangement was then doubled; and the second set of rooms, at the west end, contained the cellar on the lower level, another great room or hall above it, and the cloister at the church door, also entering into the north transept. Doorways, passages, and stairs unite them all. The two heavy halls on the lowest level are now called the almonry and the cellar, which is a distinction between administrative arrangements that does not concern us.

Architecturally the rooms might, to our untrained eyes, be of the same age with the Aquilon. They are earliest Transition, as far as a tourist can see, or at least they belong to the class of crypts which has an architecture of its own. The rooms that concern us are those immediately above: the so-called Salle des Chevaliers at the west end; and the so-called refectory at the east. Every writer gives these rooms different names, and assigns them different purposes, but whatever they were meant for, they are, as halls, the finest in France; the purest in thirteenth-century perfection.

The Salle des Chevaliers of the Order of Saint Michael created by Louis XI in 1469 was, or shall be for tourist purposes, the great hall that every palace and castle contained, and in which the life of the chateau centred. Planned at about the same time with the Cathedral of Chartres (1195-1210), and before the Abbey Church of Saint-Denis, this hall and its neighbour the refectory, studied together with the cathedral and the abbey, are an exceedingly liberal education for anybody, tourist or engineer or architect, and would make the fortune of an intelligent historian, if such should happen to exist; but the last thing we ask from them is education or instruction. We want only their poetry, and shall have to look for it elsewhere. Here is only the shell—the dead art—and silence. The hall is about ninety feet long, and sixty feet in its greatest width. It has three ranges of columns making four vaulted aisles which seem to rise about twenty-two feet in height. It is warmed by two huge and heavy cheminees or fireplaces in the outside wall, between the windows. It is lighted beautifully, but mostly from above through round windows in the arching of the vaults. The vaulting is a study for wiser men than we can ever be. More than twenty strong round columns, free or engaged, with Romanesque capitals, support heavy ribs, or nervures, and while the two central aisles are eighteen feet wide, the outside aisle, into which the windows open, measures only ten feet in width, and has consequently one of the most sharply pointed vaults we shall ever meet. The whole design is as beautiful a bit of early Gothic as exists, but what would take most time to study, if time were to spare, would be the instinct of the Archangel's presence which has animated his architecture. The masculine, military energy of Saint Michael lives still in every stone. The genius that realized this warlike emotion has stamped his power everywhere, on every centimetre of his work; in every ray of light; on the mass of every shadow; wherever the eye falls; still more strongly on all that the eye divines, and in the shadows that are felt like the lights. The architect intended it all. Any one who doubts has only to step through the doorway in the corner into the refectory. There the architect has undertaken to express the thirteenth-century idea of the Archangel; he has left the twelfth century behind him.

The refectory, which has already served for a measure of the Abbot's scale, is, in feeling, as different as possible from the hall. Six charming columns run down the centre, dividing the room into two vaulted aisles, apparently about twenty-seven feet in height. Wherever the hall was heavy and serious, the refectory was made light and graceful. Hardly a trace of the Romanesque remains. Only the slight, round columns are not yet grooved or fluted, and their round capitals are still slightly severe. Every detail is lightened. The great fireplaces are removed to each end of the room. The most interesting change is in the windows. When you reach Chartres, the great book of architecture will open on the word "Fenestration,"— Fenestre,—a word as ugly as the thing was beautiful; and then, with pain and sorrow, you will have to toil till you see how the architects of 1200 subordinated every other problem to that of lighting their spaces. Without feeling their lights, you can never feel their shadows. These two halls at Mont-Saint-Michel are antechambers to the nave of Chartres; their fenestration, inside and out, controls the whole design. The lighting of the refectory is superb, but one feels its value in art only when it is taken in relation to the lighting of the hall, and both serve as a simple preamble to the romance of the Chartres windows.

The refectory shows what the architect did when, to lighten his effects, he wanted to use every possible square centimetre of light. He has made nine windows; six on the north, two on the east, and one on the south. They are nearly five feet wide, and about twenty feet high. They flood the room. Probably they were intended for glass, and M. Corroyer's volume contains wood-cuts of a few fragments of thirteenth-century glass discovered in his various excavations; but one may take for granted that with so much light, colour was the object intended. The floors would be tiled in colour; the walls would be hung with colour; probably the vaults were painted in colour; one can see it all in scores of illuminated manuscripts. The thirteenth century had a passion for colour, and made a colour-world of its own which we have got to explore.

The two halls remain almost the only monuments of what must be called secular architecture of the early and perfect period of Gothic art (1200-10). Churches enough remain, with Chartres at their head, but all the great abbeys, palaces and chateaux of that day are ruins. Arques, Gaillard, Montargis, Coucy, the old Louvre, Chinon, Angers, as well as Cluny, Clairvaux, Citeaux, Jumieges, Vezelay, Saint-Denis, Poissy, Fontevrault, and a score of other residences, royal or semi-royal, have disappeared wholly, or have lost their residential buildings. When Viollet-le-Duc, under the Second Empire, was allowed to restore one great chateau, he chose the latest, Pierrefonds, built by Louis d'Orleans in 1390. Vestiges of Saint Louis's palace remain at the Conciergerie, but the first great royal residence to be compared with the Merveille is Amboise, dating from about 1500, three centuries later. Civilization made almost a clean sweep of art. Only here, at Mont-Saint-Michel, one may still sit at ease on the stone benches in; the embrasures of the refectory windows, looking over the thirteenth-century ocean and watching the architect as he worked out the details which were to produce or accent his contrasts or harmonies, heighten his effects, or hide his show of effort, and all by means so true, simpler and apparently easy that one seems almost competent to follow him. One learns better in time. One gets to feel that these things were due in part to an instinct that the architect himself might not have been able to explain. The instinct vanishes as time creeps on. The halls at Rouen or at Blois are more easily understood; the Salle des Caryatides of Pierre Lescot at the Louvre, charming as it is, is simpler still; and one feels entirely at home in the Salle des Glaces which filled the ambition of Louis XIV at Versailles.

If any lingering doubt remains in regard to the professional cleverness of the architect and the thoroughness of his study, we had best return to the great hall, and pass through a low door in its extreme outer angle, up a few steps into a little room some thirteen feet square, beautifully vaulted, lighted, warmed by a large stone fireplace, and in the corner, a spiral staircase leading up to another square room above opening directly into the cloister. It is a little library or charter-house. The arrangement is almost too clever for gravity, as is the case with more than one arrangement in the Merveille. From the outside one can see that at this corner the architect had to provide a heavy buttress against a double strain, and he built up from the rock below a square corner tower as support, into which he worked a spiral staircase leading from the cellar up to the cloisters. Just above the level of the great hall he managed to construct this little room, a gem. The place was near and far; it was quiet and central; William of Saint-Pair, had he been still alive, might have written his "Roman" there; monks might have illuminated missals there. A few steps upward brought them to the cloisters for meditation; a few more brought them to the church for prayer. A few steps downward brought them to the great hall, for business, a few steps more led them into the refectory, for dinner. To contemplate the goodness of God was a simple joy when one had such a room to work in; such a spot as the great hall to walk in, when the storms blew; or the cloisters in which to meditate, when the sun shone; such a dining-room as the refectory; and such a view from one's windows over the infinite ocean and the guiles of Satan's quicksands. From the battlements of Heaven, William of Saint-Pair looked down on it with envy.

Of all parts of the Merveille, in summer, the most charming must always have been the cloisters. Only the Abbey of the Mount was rich and splendid enough to build a cloister like this, all in granite, carved in forms as light as though it were wood; with columns arranged in a peculiar triangular order that excited the admiration of Viollet-le-Duc. "One of the most curious and complete cloisters that we have in France," he said; although in France there are many beautiful and curious cloisters. For another reason it has value. The architect meant it to reassert, with all the art and grace he could command, the mastery of love, of thought and poetry, in religion, over the masculine, military energy of the great hall below. The thirteenth century rarely let slip a chance to insist on this moral that love is law. Saint Francis was preaching to the birds in 1215 at Assisi, and the architect built this cloister in 1226 at Mont-Saint-Michel. Both sermons were saturated with the feeling of the time, and both are about equally worth noting, if one aspires to feel the art.

A conscientious student has yet to climb down the many steps, on the outside, and look up at the Merveille from below. Few buildings in France are better worth the trouble. The horizontal line at the roof measures two hundred and thirty-five feet. The vertical line of the buttresses measures in round numbers one hundred feet. To make walls of that height and length stand up at all was no easy matter, as Robert de Torigny had shown; and so the architect buttressed them from bottom to top with twelve long buttresses against the thrust of the interior arches, and three more, bearing against the interior walls. This gives, on the north front, fifteen strong vertical lines in a space of two hundred and thirty-five feet. Between these lines the windows tell their story; the seven long windows of the refectory on one side; the seven rounded windows of the hall on the other. Even the corner tower with the charter-house becomes as simple as the rest. The sum of this impossible wall, and its exaggerated vertical lines, is strength and intelligence at rest.

The whole Mount still kept the grand style; it expressed the unity of Church and State, God and Man, Peace and War, Life and Death, Good and Bad; it solved the whole problem of the universe. The priest and the soldier were both at home here, in 1215 as in 1115 or in 1058; the politician was not outside of it; the sinner was welcome; the poet was made happy in his own spirit, with a sympathy, almost an affection, that suggests a habit of verse in the Abbot as well as in the architect. God reconciles all. The world is an evident, obvious, sacred harmony. Even the discord of war is a detail on which the Abbey refuses to insist. Not till two centuries afterwards did the Mount take on the modern expression of war as a discord in God's providence. Then, in the early years of the fifteenth century, Abbot Pierre le Roy plastered the gate of the chatelet, as you now see it, over the sunny thirteenth-century entrance called Belle Chaise, which had treated mere military construction with a sort of quiet contempt. You will know what a chatelet is when you meet another; it frowns in a spirit quite alien to the twelfth century; it jars on the religion of the place; it forebodes wars of religion; dissolution of society; loss of unity; the end of a world. Nothing is sadder than the catastrophe of Gothic art, religion, and hope.

One looks back on it all as a picture; a symbol of unity; an assertion of God and Man in a bolder, stronger, closer union than ever was expressed by other art; and when the idea is absorbed, accepted, and perhaps partially understood, one may move on.

CHAPTER IV: NORMANDY AND THE ILE DE FRANCE

From Mont-Saint-Michel, the architectural road leads across Normandy, up the Seine to Paris, and not directly through Chartres, which lies a little to the south. In the empire of architecture, Normandy was one kingdom, Brittany another; the Ile de France, with Paris, was a third; Touraine and the valley of the Loire were a fourth and in the centre, the fighting-ground between them all, lay the counties of Chartres and Dreux. Before going to Chartres one should go up the Seine and down the Loire, from Angers to Le Mans, and so enter Chartres from Brittany after a complete circle; but if we set out to do our pleasure on that scale, we must start from the Pyramid of Cheops. We have set out from Mont-Saint-Michel; we will go next to Paris.

The architectural highway lies through Coutances, Bayeux, Caen, Rouen, and Mantes. Every great artistic kingdom solved its architectural problems in its own way, as it did its religious, political, and social problems, and no two solutions were ever quite the same; but among them the Norman was commonly the most practical, and sometimes the most dignified. We can test this rule by the standard of the first town we stop at—Coutances. We can test it equally well at Bayeux or Caen, but Coutances comes first after Mont-Saint-Michel let us begin with it, and state the problems with their Norman solution, so that it may be ready at hand to compare with the French solution, before coming to the solution at Chartres.

The cathedral at Coutances is said to be about the age of the Merveille (1200-50), but the exact dates are unknown, and the work is so Norman as to stand by itself; yet the architect has grappled with more problems than one need hope to see solved in any single church in the tie de France. Even at Chartres, although the two stone fleches are, by exception, completed, they are not of the same age, as they are here. Neither at Chartres nor at Paris, nor at Laon or Amiens or Rheims or Bourges, will you see a central tower to compare with the enormous pile at Coutances. Indeed the architects of France failed to solve this particular church problem, and we-shall leave it behind us in leaving Normandy, although it is the most effective feature of any possible church. "A clocher of that period (circa 1200), built over the croisee of a cathedral, following lines so happy, should be a monument of the greatest beauty; unfortunately we possess not a single one in France. Fire, and the hand of man more than time, have destroyed them all, and we find on our greatest religious edifices no more than bases and fragments of these beautiful constructions. The cathedral of Coutances alone has preserved its central clocher of the thirteenth century, and even there it is not complete; its stone fleche is wanting. As for its style, it belongs to Norman architecture, and diverges widely from the character of French architecture." So says Viollet-le-Duc; but although the great churches for the most part never had central clochers, which, on the scale of Amiens, Bourges, or Beauvais, would have required an impossible mass, the smaller churches frequently carry them still, and they are, like the dome, the most effective features they can carry. They were made to dominate the whole.

No doubt the fleche is wanting at Coutances, but you can supply it in imagination from the two fleches of the western tower, which are as simple and severe as the spear of a man-at-arms. Supply the fleche, and the meaning of the tower cannot be mistaken; it is as military as the "Chanson de Roland"; it is the man-at-arms himself, mounted and ready for battle, spear in rest. The mere seat of the central tower astride of the church, so firm, so fixed, so serious, so defiant, is Norman, like the seat of the Abbey Church on the Mount; and at Falaise, where William the Bastard was born, we shall see a central tower on the church which is William himself, in armour, on horseback, ready to fight for the Church, and perhaps, in his bad moods, against it. Such militant churches were capable of forcing Heaven itself; all of them look as though they had fought at Hastings or stormed Jerusalem. Wherever the Norman central clocher stands, the Church Militant of the eleventh century survives;—not the Church of Mary Queen, but of Michael the Archangel;—not the Church of Christ, but of God the Father—Who never lied!

Taken together with the fleches of the facade, this clocher of Coutances forms a group such as one very seldom sees. The two towers of the facade are something apart, quite by themselves among the innumerable church-towers of the Gothic time. We have got a happy summer before us, merely in looking for these church-towers. There is no livelier amusement for fine weather than in hunting them as though they were mushrooms, and no study in architecture nearly so delightful. No work of man has life like the fleche. One sees it for a greater distance and feels it for a longer time than is possible with any other human structure, unless it be the dome. There is more play of light on the octagonal faces of the fleche as the sun moves around them than can be got out of the square or the cone or any other combination of surfaces. For some reason, the facets of the hexagon or octagon are more pleasing than the rounded surfaces of the cone, and Normandy is said to be peculiarly the home of this particularly Gothic church ornament; yet clochers and fleches are scattered all over France until one gets to look for them on the horizon as though every church in every hamlet were an architectural monument. Hundreds of them literally are so,—Monuments Historiques, -protected by the Government; but when you undertake to compare them, or to decide whether they are more beautiful in Normandy than in the Ile de France, or in Burgundy, or on the Loire or the Charente, you are lost, Even the superiority of the octagon is not evident to every one. Over the little church at Fenioux on the Charente, not very far from La Rochelle, is a conical steeple that an infidel might adore; and if you have to decide between provinces, you must reckon with the decision of architects and amateurs, who seem to be agreed that the first of all filches is at Chartres, the second at Vendome, not far from Blois in Touraine, and the third at Auxerre in Burgundy. The towers of Coutances are not in the list, nor are those at Bayeux nor those at Caen. France is rich in art. Yet the towers of Coutances are in some ways as interesting, if not as beautiful, as the best.

The two stone fleches here, with their octagon faces, do not descend, as in other churches, to their resting-place on a square tower, with the plan of junction more or less disguised; they throw out nests of smaller fleches, and these cover buttressing corner towers, with lines that go directly to the ground. Whether the artist consciously intended it or not, the effect is to broaden the facade and lift it into the air. The facade itself has a distinctly military look, as though a fortress had been altered into a church. A charming arcade at the top has the air of being thrown across in order to disguise the alteration, and perhaps owes much of its charm to the contrast it makes with the severity of military lines. Even the great west window looks like an afterthought; one's instinct asks for a blank wall. Yet, from the ground up to the cross on the spire, one feels the Norman nature throughout, animating the whole, uniting it all, and crowding into it an intelligent variety of original motives that would build a dozen churches of late Gothic. Nothing about it is stereotyped or conventional,—not even the conventionality.

If you have any doubts about this, you have only to compare the photograph of Coutances with the photograph of Chartres; and yet, surely, the facade of Chartres is severe enough to satisfy Saint Bernard himself. With the later fronts of Rheims and Amiens, there is no field for comparison; they have next to nothing in common; yet Coutances is said to be of the same date with Rheims, or nearly so, and one can believe it when one enters the interior. The Normans, as they slowly reveal themselves, disclose most unexpected qualities; one seems to sound subterranean caverns of feeling hidden behind their iron nasals. No other cathedral in France or in Europe has an interior more refined—one is tempted to use even the hard-worn adjective, more tender—or more carefully studied. One test is crucial here and everywhere. The treatment of the apse and choir is the architect's severest standard. This is a subject not to be touched lightly; one to which we shall have to come back in a humble spirit, prepared for patient study, at Chartres; but the choir of Coutances is a cousin to that of Chartres, as the facades are cousins; Coutances like Chartres belongs to Notre Dame and is felt in the same spirit; the church is built for the choir and apse, rather than for the nave and transepts; for the Virgin rather than for the public. In one respect Coutances is even more delicate in the feminine charm of the Virgin's peculiar grace than Chartres, but this was an afterthought of the fourteenth century. The system of chapels radiating about the apse was extended down the nave, in an arrangement "so beautiful and so rare," according to Viollet-le-Duc, that one shall seek far before finding its equal. Among the unexpected revelations of human nature that suddenly astonish historians, one of the least reasonable was the passionate outbreak of religious devotion to the ideal of feminine grace, charity, and love that took place here in Normandy while it was still a part of the English kingdom, and flamed up into almost fanatical frenzy among the most hard-hearted and hard-headed race in Europe.

So in this church, in the centre of this arrangement of apse and chapels with their quite unusual—perhaps quite singular—grace, the four huge piers which support the enormous central tower, offer a tour de force almost as exceptional as the refinement of the chapels. At Mont-Saint-Michel, among the monks, the union of strength and grace was striking, but at Coutances it is exaggerated, like Tristram and Iseult,—a roman of chivalry. The four "enormous" columns of the croisee, carry, as Viollet-le-Duc says, the "enormous octagonal tower,"—like Saint Christopher supporting the Christ- child, before the image of the Virgin, in her honour. Nothing like this can be seen at Chartres, or at any of the later palaces which France built for the pleasure of the Queen of Heaven. We are slipping into the thirteenth century again; the temptation is terrible to feeble minds and tourist natures; but a great mass of twelfth and eleventh-century work remains to be seen and felt. To go back is not so easy as to begin with it; the heavy round arch is like old cognac compared with the champagne of the pointed and fretted spire; one must not quit Coutances without making an excursion to Lessay on the road to Cherbourg, where is a church of the twelfth century, with a square tower and almost untouched Norman interior, that closely repeats the Abbey Church at Mont-Saint- Michel. "One of the most complete models of Romanesque architecture to be found in Normandy," says M. de Caumont. The central clocher will begin a photographic collection of square towers, to replace that which was lost on the Mount; and a second example is near Bayeux, at a small place called Cerisy-la-Foret, where the church matches that on the Mount, according to M. Corroyer; for Cerisy-la- Foret was also an abbey, and the church, built by Richard II, Duke of Normandy, at the beginning of the eleventh century, was larger than that on the Mount. It still keeps its central tower.

All this is intensely Norman, and is going to help very little in France; it would be more useful in England; but at Bayeux is a great cathedral much more to the purpose, with two superb western towers crowned by stone fleches, cousins of those at Coutances, and distinctly related to the twelfth-century fleche at Chartres. "The Normans," says Viollet-le-Duc, "had not that instinct of proportion which the architects of the Ile de France, Beauvais, and Soissons possessed to a high degree; yet the boldness of their constructions, their perfect execution, the elevation of the fleches, had evident influence on the French school properly called, and that influence is felt in the old spire of Chartres." The Norman seemed to show distinction in another respect which the French were less quick to imitate. What they began, they completed. Not one of the great French churches has two stone spires complete, of the same age, while each of the little towns of Coutances, Bayeux, and Caen contains its twin towers and fleches of stone, as solid and perfect now as they were seven hundred years ago. Still another Norman character is worth noting, because this is one part of the influence felt at Chartres. If you look carefully at the two western towers of the Bayeux Cathedral, perhaps you will feel what is said to be the strength of the way they are built up. They rise from their foundation with a quiet confidence of line and support, which passes directly up to the weather-cock on the summit of the fleches. At the plane where the square tower is changed into the octagon spire, you will see the corner turrets and the long intermediate windows which effect the change without disguising it. One can hardly call it a device; it is so simple and evident a piece of construction that it does not need to be explained; yet you will have to carry a photograph of this fleche to Chartres, and from there to Vendome, for there is to be a great battle of fleches about this point of junction, and the Norman scheme is a sort of standing reproach to the French.

Coutances and Bayeux are interesting, but Caen is a Romanesque Mecca. There William the Conqueror dealt with the same architectural problems, and put his solution in his Abbaye-aux-Hommes, which bears the name of Saint Stephen. Queen Matilda put her solution into her Abbaye-aux-Femmes, the Church of the Trinity. One ought particularly to look at the beautiful central clocher of the church at Vaucelles in the suburbs; and one must drive out to Thaon to see its eleventh- century church, with a charming Romanesque blind arcade on the outside, and a little clocher, "the more interesting to us," according to Viollet-le-Duc, "because it bears the stamp of the traditions of defence of the primitive towers which were built over the porches." Even "a sort of chemin de ronde" remains around the clocher, perhaps once provided with a parapet of defence. "C'est la, du reste, un charmant edifice." A tower with stone fleche, which actually served for defence in a famous recorded instance, is that of the church at Secqueville, not far off; this beautiful tower, as charming as anything in Norman art, is known to have served as a fortress in 1105, which gives a valuable date. The pretty old Romanesque front of the little church at Ouistreham, with its portal that seems to come fresh from Poitiers and Moissac, can be taken in, while driving past; but we must on no account fail to make a serious pilgrimage to Saint-Pierre-sur-Dives, where the church-tower and fleche are not only classed among the best in Normandy, but have an exact date, 1145, and a very close relation with Chartres, as will appear. Finally, if for no other reason, at least for interest in Arlette, the tanner's daughter, one must go to Falaise, and look at the superb clocher of Saint-Gervais, which was finished and consecrated by 1135.

Some day, if you like, we can follow this Romanesque style to the south, and on even to Italy where it may be supposed to have been born; but France had an architectural life fully a thousand years old when these twelfth-century churches were built, and was long since artistically, as she was politically, independent. The Normans were new in France, but not the Romanesque architecture; they only took the forms and stamped on them their own character. It is the stamp we want to distinguish, in order to trace up our lines of artistic ancestry. The Norman twelfth-century stamp was not easily effaced. If we have not seen enough of it at Mont-Saint-Michel, Coutances, Bayeux, and Caen, we can go to Rouen, and drive out to Boscherville, and visit the ruined Abbey of Jumieges. Wherever there is a church-tower with a tall fleche, as at Boscherville, Secqueville, Saint-Pierre-sur-Dives, Caen, and Bayeux, Viollet-le- Duc bids notice how the octagonal steeple is fitted on to the square tower. Always the passage from the octagon to the square seems to be quite simply made. The Gothic or Romanesque spire had the advantage that a wooden fleche was as reasonable a covering for it as a stone one, and the Normans might have indulged in freaks of form very easily, if they chose, but they seem never to have thought of it. The nearest approach to the freedom of wooden roofs is not in the lofty fleches, but in the covering of the great square central towers, like Falaise or Vaucelles, a huge four-sided roof which tries to be a fleche, and is as massive as the heavy structure it covers.

The last of the Norman towers that Viollet-le-Duc insists upon is the so-called Clocher de Saint-Romain, the northern tower on the west front of the Cathedral of Rouen. Unfortunately it has lost its primitive octagon fleche if it ever had one, but "the tower remains entire, and," according to Viollet-le-Duc, "is certainly one of the most beautiful in this part of France; it offers a mixture of the two styles of the Ile de France and of Normandy, in which the former element dominates"; it is of the same date as the old tower of Chartres (1140-60), and follows the same interior arrangement; "but here the petty, confused disposition of the Norman towers, with their division into stories of equal height, has been adopted by the French master builder, although in submitting to these local customs he has still thrown over his work the grace and finesse, the study of detail, the sobriety in projections, the perfect harmony between the profiles, sculpture, and the general effect of the whole, which belong to the school he came from. He has managed his voids and solids with especial cleverness, giving the more importance to the voids, and enlarging the scale of his details, as the tower rose in height. These details have great beauty; the construction is executed in materials of small dimensions with the care that the twelfth-century architects put into their building; the profiles project little, and, in spite of their extreme finesse, produce much effect; the buttresses are skilfully planted and profiled. The staircase, which, on the east side, deranges the arrangement of the bays, is a chef-d'oeuvre of architecture." This long panegyric, by Viollet-le-Duc, on French taste at the expense of Norman temper, ought to be read, book in hand, before the Cathedral of Rouen, with photographs of Bayeux to compare. Certain it is that the Normans and the French never talked quite the same language, but it is equally certain that the Norman language, to the English ear, expressed itself quite as clearly as the French, and sometimes seemed to have more to express.

The complaint of the French artist against the Norman is the "mesquin" treatment of dividing his tower into storeys of equal height. Even in the twelfth century and in religious architecture, artists already struggled over the best solution of this particularly American problem of the twentieth century, and when tourists return to New York, they may look at the twenty-storey towers which decorate the city, to see whether the Norman or the French plan has won; but this, at least, will be sure in advance:— the Norman will be the practical scheme which states the facts, and stops; while the French will be the graceful one, which states the beauties, and more or less fits the facts to suit them. Both styles are great: both can sometimes be tiresome.

Here we must take leave of Normandy; a small place, but one which, like Attica or Tuscany, has said a great deal to the world, and even goes on saying things—not often in the famous genre ennuyeux—to this day; for Gustave Flaubert's style is singularly like that of the Tour Saint-Romain and the Abbaye-aux-Hommes. Going up the Seine one might read a few pages of his letters, or of "Madame de Bovary," to see how an old art transmutes itself into a new one, without changing its methods. Some critics have thought that at times Flaubert was mesquin like the Norman tower, but these are, as the French say, the defects of his qualities; we can pass over them, and let our eyes rest on the simplicity of the Norman fleche which pierces the line of our horizon.

The last of Norman art is seen at Mantes, where there is a little church of Gassicourt that marks the farthest reach of the style. In arms as in architecture, Mantes barred the path of Norman conquest; William the Conqueror met his death here in 1087. Geographically Mantes is in the Ile de France, less than forty miles from Paris. Architecturally, it is Paris itself; while, forty miles to the southward, is Chartres, an independent or only feudally dependent country. No matter how hurried the architectural tourist may be, the boundary-line of the Ile de France is not to be crossed without stopping. If he came down from the north or east, he would have equally to stop,—either at Beauvais, or at Laon, or Noyon, or Soissons,—because there is an architectural douane to pass, and one's architectural baggage must be opened. Neither Notre Dame de Paris nor Notre Dame de Chartres is quite intelligible unless one has first seen Notre Dame de Mantes, and studied it in the sacred sources of M. Viollet-le-Duc.

Notre Dame de Mantes is a sister to the Cathedral of Paris, "built at the same time, perhaps by the same architect, and reproducing its general dispositions, its mode of structure, and some of its details"; but the Cathedral of Paris has been greatly altered, so that its original arrangement is quite changed, while the church at Mantes remains practically as it was, when both were new, about the year 1200. As nearly as the dates can be guessed, the cathedral was finished, up to its vaulting, in 1170, and was soon afterwards imitated on a smaller scale at Mantes. The scheme seems to have been unsatisfactory because of defects in the lighting, for the whole system of fenestration had been changed at Paris before 1230, naturally at great cost, since the alterations, according to Viollet-le-Duc (articles "Cathedral" and "Rose," and allusions "Triforium"), left little except the ground-plan unchanged. To understand the Paris design of 1160-70, which was a long advance from the older plans, one must come to Mantes; and, reflecting that the great triumph of Chartres was its fenestration, which must have been designed immediately after 1195, one can understand how, in this triangle of churches only forty or fifty miles apart, the architects, watching each other's experiments, were influenced, almost from day to day, by the failures or successes which they saw The fenestration which the Paris architect planned in 1160-70, and repeated at Mantes, 1190-1200, was wholly abandoned, and a new system introduced, immediately after the success of Chartres in 1210.

As they now stand, Mantes is the oldest. While conscientiously trying to keep as far away as we can from technique, about which we know nothing and should care if possible still less if only ignorance would help us to feel what we do not understand, still the conscience is happier if it gains a little conviction, founded on what it thinks a fact. Even theologians—even the great theologians of the thirteenth century—even Saint Thomas Aquinas himself—did not trust to faith alone, or assume the existence of God; and what Saint Thomas found necessary in philosophy may also be a sure source of consolation in the difficulties of art. The church at Mantes is a very early fact in Gothic art; indeed, it is one of the earliest; for our purposes it will serve as the very earliest of pure Gothic churches, after the Transition, and this we are told to study in its windows.

Before one can get near enough fairly to mark the details of the facade, one sees the great rose window which fills a space nearly twenty-seven feet in width. Gothic fanatics commonly reckon the great rose windows of the thirteenth century as the most beautiful creation of their art, among the details of ornament; and this particular rose is the direct parent of that at Chartres, which is classic like the Parthenon, while both of them served as models or guides for that at Paris which dates from 1220, those in the north and south transepts at Rheims, about 1230, and so on, from parent to child, till the rose faded forever. No doubt there were Romanesque roses before 1200, and we shall see them, but this rose of Mantes is the first Gothic rose of great dimensions, and that from which the others grew; in its simplicity, its honesty, its large liberality of plan, it is also one of the best, if M. Viollet-le-Duc is a true guide; but you will see a hundred roses, first or last, and can choose as you would among the flowers.

More interesting than even the great rose of the portal is the remark that the same rose-motive is carried round the church throughout its entire system of fenestration. As one follows it, on the outside, one sees that all the windows are constructed on the same rose-scheme; but the most curious arrangement is in the choir inside the church. You look up to each of the windows through a sort of tunnel or telescope: an arch enlarging outwards, the roses at the end resembling "oeil-de-boeufs," "oculi." So curious is this arrangement that Viollet-le-Duc has shown it, under the head "Triforium," in drawings and sections which any one can study who likes; its interest to us is that this arrangement in the choir was probably the experiment which proved a failure in Notre Dame at Paris, and led to the tearing-out the old windows and substituting those which still stand. Perhaps the rose did not give enough light, although the church at Mantes seems well lighted, and even at Paris the rose windows remain in the transepts and in one bay of the nave.

All this is introduction to the windows of Chartres, but these three churches open another conundrum as one learns, bit by bit, a few of the questions to be asked of the forgotten Middle Ages. The church towers at Mantes are very interesting, inside and out; they are evidently studied with love and labour by their designer; yet they have no fleches. How happens it that Notre Dame at Paris also has no fleches, although the towers, according to Viollet-le-Duc, are finished in full preparation for them? This double omission on the part of the French architect seems exceedingly strange, because his rival at Chartres finished his fleche just when the architect of Paris and Mantes was finishing his towers (1175-1200). The Frenchman was certainly consumed by jealousy at the triumph never attained on anything like the same scale by any architect of the Ile de France; and he was actually engaged at the time on at least two fleches, close to Paris, one at Saint-Denis, another of Saint-Leu-d'Esserent, which proved the active interest he took in the difficulties conquered at Chartres, and his perfect competence to deal with them.

Indeed, one is tempted to say that these twin churches, Paris and Mantes, are the only French churches of the time (1200) which were left without a fleche. As we go from Mantes to Paris, we pass, about half-way, at Poissy, under the towers of a very ancient and interesting church which has the additional merit of having witnessed the baptism of Saint Louis in 1215. Parts of the church at Poissy go back to the seventh and ninth centuries. The square base of the tower dates back before the time of Hugh Capet, to the Carolingian age, and belongs, like the square tower of Saint- Germain-des-Pres at Paris, to the old defensive military architecture; but it has a later, stone fleche and it has, too, by exception a central octagonal clocher, with a timber fleche which dates from near 1100. Paris itself has not much to show, but in the immediate neighbourhood are a score of early churches with charming fleches, and at Etampes, about thirty-five miles to the south, is an extremely interesting church with an exquisite fleche, which may claim an afternoon to visit. That at Saint-Leu-d'Esserent is a still easier excursion, for one need only drive over from Chantilly a couple of miles. The fascinating old Abbey Church of Saint-Leu looks down over the valley of the Oise, and is a sort of antechamber to Chartres, as far as concerns architecture. Its fleche, built towards 1160,—when that at Chartres was rising,—is unlike any other, and shows how much the French architects valued their lovely French creation. On its octagonal faces, it carries upright batons, or lances, as a device for relieving the severity of the outlines; a device both intelligent and amusing, though it was never imitated. A little farther from Paris, at Senlis, is another fleche, which shows still more plainly the effort of the French architects to vary and elaborate the Chartres scheme. As for Laon, which is interesting throughout, and altogether the most delightful building in the Ile de France, the fleches are gone, but the towers are there, and you will have to study them, before studying those at Chartres, with all the intelligence you have to spare. They were the chef-d'oeuvre of the mediaeval architect, in his own opinion.

All this makes the absence of fleches at Paris and Mantes the more strange. Want of money was certainly not the cause, since the Parisians had money enough to pull their whole cathedral to pieces at the very time when fleches were rising in half the towns within sight of them. Possibly they were too ambitious, and could find no design that seemed to satisfy their ambition. They took pride in their cathedral, and they tried hard to make their shrine of Our Lady rival the great shrine at Chartres. Of course, one must study their beautiful church, but this can be done at leisure, for, as it stands, it is later than Chartres and more conventional. Saint-Germain-des-Pres leads more directly to Chartres; but perhaps the church most useful to know is no longer a church at all, but a part of the Museum of Arts et Metiers,—the desecrated Saint-Martin-des-Champs, a name which shows that it dates from a time when the present Porte-Saint-Martin was far out among fields. The choir of Saint-Martin, which is all that needs noting, is said by M. Enlart to date from about 1150. Hidden in a remnant of old Paris near the Pont Notre Dame, where the student life of the Middle Ages was to be most turbulent and the Latin Quarter most renowned, is the little church of Saint-Julien-le-Pauvre, towards 1170. On the whole, further search in Paris would not greatly help us. If one is to pursue the early centuries, one must go farther afield, for the schools of Normandy and the Ile de France were only two among half a dozen which flourished in the various provinces that were to be united in the kingdom of Saint Louis and his successors. We have not even looked to the south and east, whence the impulse came. The old Carolingian school, with its centre at Aix-la-Chapelle, is quite beyond our horizon. The Rhine had a great Romanesque architecture of its own. One broad architectural tide swept up the Rhone and filled the Burgundian provinces as far as the watershed of the Seine. Another lined the Mediterranean, with a centre at Arles. Another spread up the western rivers, the Charente and the Loire, reaching to Le Mans and touching Chartres. Two more lay in the centre of France, spreading from Perigord and Clermont in Auvergne. All these schools had individual character, and all have charm; but we have set out to go from Mont-Saint-Michel to Chartres in three centuries, the eleventh, twelfth, and thirteenth, trying to get, on the way, not technical knowledge; not accurate information; not correct views either on history, art, or religion; not anything that can possibly be useful or instructive; but only a sense of what those centuries had to say, and a sympathy with their ways of saying it. Let us go straight to Chartres!

CHAPTER V: TOWERS AND PORTALS

For a first visit to Chartres, choose some pleasant morning when the lights are soft, for one wants to be welcome, and the cathedral has moods, at times severe. At best, the Beauce is a country none too gay.

The first glimpse that is caught, and the first that was meant to be caught, is that of the two spires. With all the education that Normandy and the Ile de France can give, one is still ignorant. The spire is the simplest part of the Romanesque or Gothic architecture, and needs least study in order to be felt. It is a bit of sentiment almost pure of practical purpose. It tells the whole of its story at a glance, and its story is the best that architecture had to tell, for it typified the aspirations of man at the moment when man's aspirations were highest. Yet nine persons out of ten—perhaps ninety-nine in a hundred—who come within sight of the two spires of Chartres will think it a jest if they are told that the smaller of the two, the simpler, the one that impresses them least, is the one which they are expected to recognize as the most perfect piece of architecture in the world. Perhaps the French critics might deny that they make any such absolute claim; in that case you can ask them what their exact claim is; it will always be high enough to astonish the tourist.

Astonished or not, we have got to take this southern spire of the Chartres Cathedral as the object of serious study, and before taking it as art, must take it as history. The foundations of this tower— always to be known as the "old tower"—are supposed to have been laid in 1091, before the first crusade. The fleche was probably half a century later (1145-70). The foundations of the new tower, opposite, were laid not before 1110, when also the portal which stands between them, was begun with the three lancet windows above it, but not the rose. For convenience, this old facade—including the portal and the two towers, but not the fleches, and the three lancet windows, but not the rose—may be dated as complete about 1150.

Originally the whole portal—the three doors and the three lancets— stood nearly forty feet back, on the line of the interior foundation, or rear wall of the towers. This arrangement threw the towers forward, free on three sides, as at Poitiers, and gave room for a parvis, before the portal,—a porch, roofed over, to protect the pilgrims who always stopped there to pray before entering the church. When the church was rebuilt after the great fire of 1194, and the architect was required to enlarge the interior, the old portal and lancets were moved bodily forward, to be flush with the front walls of the two towers, as you see the facade to-day; and the facade itself was heightened, to give room for the rose, and to cover the loftier pignon and vaulting behind. Finally, the wooden roof, above the stone vault, was masked by the Arcade of Kings and its railing, completed in the taste of Philip the Hardy, who reigned from 1270 to 1285.

These changes have, of course, altered the values of all the parts. The portal is injured by being thrown into a glare of light, when it was intended to stand in shadow, as you will see in the north and south porches over the transept portals. The towers are hurt by losing relief and shadow; but the old fleche is obliged to suffer the cruellest wrong of all by having its right shoulder hunched up by half of a huge rose and the whole of a row of kings, when it was built to stand free, and to soar above the whole facade from the top of its second storey. One can easily figure it so and replace the lost parts of the old facade, more or less at haphazard, from the front of Noyon.

What an outrage it was you can see by a single glance at the new fleche opposite. The architect of 1500 has flatly refused to submit to such conditions, and has insisted, with very proper self-respect, on starting from the balustrade of the Arcade of Kings as his level. Not even content with that, he has carried up his square tower another lofty storey before he would consent to touch the heart of his problem, the conversion of the square tower into the octagon fleche. In doing this, he has sacrificed once more the old fleche; but his own tower stands free as it should.

At Vendome, when you go there, you will be in a way to appreciate still better what happened to the Chartres fleche; for the clocher at Vendome, which is of the same date,—Viollet-le-Duc says earlier, and Enlart, "after 1130,"—stood and still stands free, like an Italian campanile, which gives it a vast advantage. The tower of Saint-Leu-d'Esserent, also after 1130, stands free, above the second storey. Indeed, you will hardly find, in the long list of famous French spires, another which has been treated with so much indignity as this, the greatest and most famous of all; and perhaps the most annoying part of it is that you must be grateful to the architect of 1195 for doing no worse. He has, on the contrary, done his best to show respect for the work of his predecessor, and has done so well that, handicapped as it is, the old tower still defies rivalry. Nearly three hundred and fifty feet high, or, to be exact, 106.5 metres from the church floor, it is built up with an amount of intelligence and refinement that leaves to unprofessional visitors no chance to think a criticism—much less to express one. Perhaps— when we have seen more—and feel less—who knows?—but certainly not now!

"The greatest and surely the most beautiful monument of this kind that we possess in France," says Viollet-le-Duc; but although an ignorant spectator must accept the architect's decision on a point of relative merit, no one is compelled to accept his reasons, as final. "There is no need to dwell," he continues, "upon the beauty and the grandeur of composition in which the artist has given proof of rare sobriety, where all the effects are obtained, not by ornaments, but by the just and skilful proportion of the different parts. The transition, so hard to adjust, between the square base and the octagon of the fleche, is managed and carried out with an address which has not been surpassed in similar monuments." One stumbles a little at the word "adresse." One never caught one's self using the word in Norman churches. Your photographs of Bayeux or Boscherville or Secqueville will show you at a glance whether the term "adresse" applies to them. Even Vendome would rather be praised for "droiture" than for "adresse."—Whether the word "adresse" means cleverness, dexterity, adroitness, or simple technical skill, the thing itself is something which the French have always admired more than the Normans ever did. Viollet-le-Duc himself seems to be a little uncertain whether to lay most stress on the one or the other quality: "If one tries to appreciate the conception of this tower," quotes the Abbe Bulteau (11,84), "one will see that it is as frank as the execution is simple and skilful. Starting from the bottom, one reaches the summit of the fleche without marked break; without anything to interrupt the general form of the building. This clocher, whose base is broad (pleine), massive, and free from ornament, transforms itself, as it springs, into a sharp spire with eight faces, without its being possible to say where the massive construction ends and the light construction begins."

Granting, as one must, that this concealment of the transition is a beauty, one would still like to be quite sure that the Chartres scheme is the best. The Norman clochers being thrown out, and that at Vendome being admittedly simple, the Clocher de Saint-Jean on the Church of Saint-Germain at Auxerre seems to be thought among the next in importance, although it is only about one hundred and sixty feet in height (forty-nine metres), and therefore hardly in the same class with Chartres. Any photograph shows that the Auxerre spire is also simple; and that at Etampes you have seen already to be of the Vendome rather than of the Chartres type. The clocher at Senlis is more "habile"; it shows an effort to be clever, and offers a standard of comparison; but the mediaeval architects seem to have thought that none of them bore rivalry with Laon for technical skill. One of these professional experts, named Villard de Honnecourt, who lived between 1200 and 1250, left a notebook which you can see in the vitrines of the Bibliotheque Nationale in the Rue Richelieu, and which is the source of most that is known about the practical ideas of mediaeval architects. He came to Chartres, and, standing here before the doors, where we are standing, he made a rough drawing, not of the tower, but of the rose, which was then probably new, since it must have been planned between 1195 and 1200. Apparently the tower did not impress him strongly, for he made no note of it; but on the other hand, when he went to Laon, he became vehement in praise of the cathedral tower there, which must have been then quite new: "I have been in many countries, as you can find in this book. In no place have I ever such a tower seen as that of Laon.—J'ai este en mult de tieres, si cum vus pores trover en cest livre. En aucun liu onques tel tor ne vi com est cele de Loon." The reason for this admiration is the same that Viollet-le-Duc gives for admiring the tower of Chartres—the "adresse" with which the square is changed into the octagon. Not only is the tower itself changed into the fleche without visible junction, under cover of four corner tourelles, of open work, on slender columns, which start as squares; but the tourelles also convert themselves into octagons in the very act of rising, and end in octagon fleches that carry up—or once carried up—the lines of profile to the central fleche that soared above them. Clearly this device far surpassed in cleverness the scheme of Chartres, which was comparatively heavy and structural, the weights being adjusted for their intended work, while the transformation at Laon takes place in the air, and challenges discovery in defiance of one's keenest eyesight. "Regard... how the tourelles pass from one disposition to another, in rising! Meditate on it!"

The fleche of Laon is gone, but the tower and tourelles are still there to show what the architects of the thirteenth century thought their most brilliant achievement. One cannot compare Chartres directly with any of its contemporary rivals, but one can at least compare the old spire with the new one which stands opposite and rises above it. Perhaps you will like the new best. Built at a time which is commonly agreed to have had the highest standard of taste, it does not encourage tourist or artist to insist on setting up standards of his own against it. Begun in 1507, it was finished in 1517. The dome of Saint Peter's at Rome, over which Bramante and Raphael and Michael Angelo toiled, was building at the same time; Leonardo da Vinci was working at Amboise; Jean Bullant, Pierre Lescot, and their patron, Francis I, were beginning their architectural careers. Four hundred years, or thereabouts, separated the old spire from the new one; and four hundred more separate the new one from us. If Viollet-le-Duc, who himself built Gothic spires, had cared to compare his fleches at Clermont-Ferrand with the new fleche at Chartres, he might perhaps have given us a rule where "adresse" ceases to have charm, and where detail becomes tiresome; but in the want of a schoolmaster to lay down a law of taste, you can admire the new fleche as much as you please. Of course, one sees that the lines of the new tower are not clean, like those of the old; the devices that cover the transition from the square to the octagon are rather too obvious; the proportion of the fleche to the tower quite alters the values of the parts; a rigid classical taste might even go so far as to hint that the new tower, in comparison with the old, showed signs of a certain tendency toward a dim and distant vulgarity. There can be no harm in admitting that the new tower is a little wanting in repose for a tower whose business is to counterpoise the very classic lines of the old one; but no law compels you to insist on absolute repose in any form of art; if such a law existed, it would have to deal with

Michael Angelo before it dealt with us. The new tower has many faults, but it has great beauties, as you can prove by comparing it with other late Gothic spires, including those of Viollet-le-Duc. Its chief fault is to be where it is. As a companion to the crusades and to Saint Bernard, it lacks austerity. As a companion to the Virgin of Chartres, it recalls Diane de Poitiers.

In fact, the new tower, which in years is four centuries younger than its neighbour, is in feeling fully four hundred years older. It is self-conscious if not vain; its coiffure is elaborately arranged to cover the effects of age, and its neck and shoulders are covered with lace and jewels to hide a certain sharpness of skeleton. Yet it may be beautiful, still; the poets derided the wrinkles of Diane de Poitiers at the very moment when King Henry II idealized her with the homage of a Don Quixote; an atmosphere of physical beauty and decay hangs about the whole Renaissance.

One cannot push these resemblances too far, even for the twelfth century and the old tower. Exactly what date the old tower represents, as a social symbol, is a question that might be as much disputed as the beauty of Diane de Poitiers, and yet half the interest of architecture consists in the sincerity of its reflection of the society that builds. In mere time, by actual date, the old tower represents the second crusade, and when, in 1150, Saint Bernard was elected chief of that crusade in this very cathedral,— or rather, in the cathedral of 1120, which was burned,—the workmen were probably setting in mortar the stones of the fleche as we now see them; yet the fleche does not represent Saint Bernard in feeling, for Saint Bernard held the whole array of church-towers in horror as signs merely of display, wealth and pride. The fleche rather represents Abbot Suger of Saint-Denis, Abbot Peter the Venerable of Cluny, Abbot Abelard of Saint-Gildas-de-Rhuys, and Queen Eleanor of Guienne, who had married Louis-le-Jeune in 1137; who had taken the cross from Saint Bernard in 1147; who returned from the Holy Land in 1149; and who compelled Saint Bernard to approve her divorce in 1152. Eleanor and Saint Bernard were centuries apart, yet they lived at the same time and in the same church. Speaking exactly, the old tower represents neither of them; the new tower itself is hardly more florid than Eleanor was; perhaps less so, if one can judge from the fashions of the court-dress of her time. The old tower is almost Norman, while Eleanor was wholly Gascon, and Gascony was always florid without being always correct. The new tower, if it had been built in 1150, like the old one, would have expressed Eleanor perfectly, even in height and apparent effort to dwarf its mate, except that Eleanor dwarfed her husband without an effort, and both in art and in history the result lacked harmony.

Be the contrast what it may, it does not affect the fact that no other church in France has two spires that need be discussed in comparison with these. Indeed, no other cathedral of the same class has any spires at all, and this superiority of Chartres gave most of its point to a saying that "with the spires of Chartres, the choir of Beauvais, the nave of Amiens, and the facade of Rheims," one could make a perfect church—for us tourists.

The towers have taken much time, though they are the least religious and least complicated part of church architecture, and in no way essential to the church; indeed, Saint Bernard thought them an excrescence due to pride and worldliness, and this is merely Saint Bernard's way of saying that they were an ornament created to gratify the artistic sense of beauty. Beautiful as they are, one's eyes must drop at last down to the church itself. If the spire symbolizes aspiration, the door symbolizes the way; and the portal of Chartres is the type of French doors; it stands first in the history of Gothic art; and, in the opinion of most Gothic artists, first in the interest of all art, though this is no concern of ours. Here is the Way to Eternal Life as it was seen by the Church and the Art of the first crusade!

The fortune of this monument has been the best attested Miracle de la Vierge in the long list of the Virgin's miracles, for it comes down, practically unharmed, through what may with literal accuracy be called the jaws of destruction and the flames of hell. Built some time in the first half of the twelfth century, it passed, apparently unscathed, through the great fire of 1194 which burnt out the church behind, and even the timber interior of the towers in front of it. Owing to the enormous mass of timber employed in the structure of the great churches, these recurrent fires were as destructive as fire can be made, yet not only the portals with their statuary and carving, but also the lancet windows with their glass, escaped the flames; and, what is almost equally strange, escaped also the hand of the builder afterwards, who, if he had resembled other architects, would have made a new front of his own, but who, with piety unexampled, tenderly took the old stones down, one by one, and replaced them forty feet in advance of their old position. The English wars and the wars of religion brought new dangers, sieges, and miseries; the revolution of 1792 brought actual rapine and waste; boys have flung stones at the saints; architects have wreaked their taste within and without; fire after fire has calcined the church vaults; the worst wrecker of all, the restorer of the nineteenth century, has prowled about it; yet the porch still stands, mutilated but not restored, burned but not consumed, as eloquent a witness to the power and perfections of Our Lady as it was seven hundred years ago, and perhaps more impressive.

You will see portals and porches more or less of the same period elsewhere in many different places,—at Paris, Le Mans, Sens, Autun, Vezelay, Clermont-Ferrand, Moissac, Arles,—a score of them; for the same piety has protected them more than once; but you will see no other so complete or so instructive, and you may search far before you will find another equally good in workmanship. Study of the Chartres portal covers all the rest. The feeling and motive of all are nearly the same, or vary only to suit the character of the patron saint; and the point of all is that this feeling is the architectural child of the first crusade. At Chartres one can read the first crusade in the portal, as at Mont-Saint-Michel in the Aquilon and the promenoir.

The Abbe Bulteau gives reason for assuming the year 1117 as the approximate date of the sculpture about the west portal, and you saw at Mont-Saint-Michel, in the promenoir of Abbot Roger II, an accurately dated work of the same decade; but whatever the date of the plan, the actual work and its spirit belong to 1145 or thereabouts. Some fifty years had passed since the crusaders streamed through Constantinople to Antioch and Jerusalem, and they were daily going and returning. You can see the ideas they brought back with the relics and missals and enamels they bought in Byzantium. Over the central door is the Christ, which might be sculptured after a Byzantine enamel, with its long nimbus or aureole or glory enclosing the whole figure. Over the left door is an Ascension, bearing the same stamp; and over the right door, the seated Virgin, with her crown and her two attendant archangels, is an empress. Here is the Church, the Way, and the Life of the twelfth century that we have undertaken to feel, if not to understand!

First comes the central doorway, and above it is the glory of Christ, as the church at Chartres understood Christ in the year 1150; for the glories of Christ were many, and the Chartres Christ is one. Whatever Christ may have been in other churches, here, on this portal, he offers himself to his flock as the herald of salvation alone. Among all the imagery of these three doorways, there is no hint of fear, punishment, or damnation, and this is the note of the whole time. Before 1200, the Church seems not to have felt the need of appealing habitually to terror; the promise of hope and happiness was enough; even the portal at Autun, which displays a Last Judgment, belonged to Saint Lazarus the proof and symbol of resurrection. A hundred years later, every church portal showed Christ not as Saviour but as Judge, and He presided over a Last Judgment at Bourges and Amiens, and here on the south portal, where the despair of the damned is the evident joy of the artist, if it is not even sometimes a little his jest, which is worse. At Chartres Christ is identified with His Mother, the spirit of love and grace, and His Church is the Church Triumphant.

Not only is fear absent; there is not even a suggestion of pain; there is not a martyr with the symbol of his martyrdom; and what is still more striking, in the sculptured life of Christ, from the Nativity to the Ascension, which adorns the capitals of the columns, the single scene that has been omitted is the Crucifixion. There, as everywhere in this portal, the artists seem actually to have gone out of their way in order to avoid a suggestion of suffering. They have pictured Christ and His Mother in all the other events of their lives; they have represented evangelists; apostles; the twenty-four old men of the Apocalypse; saints, prophets, kings, queens, and princes, by the score; the signs of the zodiac, and even the seven liberal arts: grammar, rhetoric, dialectics, arithmetic, geometry, astronomy, and music; everything is there except misery.

Perhaps Our Lady of Chartres was known to be peculiarly gracious and gentle, and this may partially account also for the extreme popularity of her shrine; but whatever the reason, her church was clearly intended to show only this side of her nature, and to impress it on her Son. You can see it in the grave and gracious face and attitude of the Christ, raising His hand to bless you as you enter His kingdom; in the array of long figures which line the entrance to greet you as you pass; in the expression of majesty and mercy of the Virgin herself on her throne above the southern doorway; never once are you regarded as a possible rebel, or traitor, or a stranger to be treated with suspicion, or as a child to be impressed by fear. Equally distinct, perhaps even more emphatic, is the sculptor's earnestness to make you feel, without direct insistence, that you are entering the Court of the Queen of Heaven who is one with her Son and His Church. The central door always bore the name of the "Royal Door," because it belonged to the celestial majesty of Christ, and naturally bears the stamp of royalty; but the south door belongs to the Virgin and to us. Stop a moment to see how she receives us, remembering, or trying to remember, that to the priests and artists who designed the portal, and to the generations that went on the first and second crusades, the Virgin in her shrine was at least as living, as real, as personal an empress as the Basilissa at Constantinople!

On the lintel immediately above the doorway is a succession of small groups: first, the Annunciation; Mary stands to receive the Archangel Gabriel, who comes to announce to her that she is chosen to be the Mother of God. The second is the Visitation, and in this scene also Mary stands, but she already wears a crown; at least, the Abbe Bulteau says so, although time has dealt harshly with it. Then, in the centre, follows the Nativity; Mary lies on a low bed, beneath, or before, a sort of table or cradle on which lies the Infant, while Saint Joseph stands at the bed's head. Then the angel appears, directing three shepherds to the spot, filling the rest of the space.

In correct theology, the Virgin ought not to be represented in bed, for she could not suffer like ordinary women, but her palace at Chartres is not much troubled by theology, and to her, as empress- mother, the pain of child-birth was a pleasure which she wanted her people to share. The Virgin of Chartres was the greatest of all queens, but the most womanly of women, as we shall see; and her double character is sustained throughout her palace. She was also intellectually gifted in the highest degree. In the upper zone you see her again, at the Presentation in the Temple, supporting the Child Jesus on the altar, while Simeon aids. Other figures bring offerings. The voussures of the arch above contain six archangels, with curious wings, offering worship to the Infant and His Imperial Mother. Below are the signs of the zodiac; the Fishes and the Twins. The rest of the arch is filled by the seven liberal arts, with Pythagoras, Aristotle, Cicero, Euclid, Nicomachus, Ptolemy, and Priscian as their representatives, testifying to the Queen's intellectual superiority.

In the centre sits Mary, with her crown on her head and her Son in her lap, enthroned, receiving the homage of heaven and earth; of all time, ancient and modern; of all thought, Christian and Pagan; of all men, and all women; including, if you please, your homage and mine, which she receives without question, as her due; which she cannot be said to claim, because she is above making claims; she is empress. Her left hand bore a sceptre; her right supported the Child, Who looks directly forward, repeating the Mother's attitude, and raises His right hand to bless, while His left rests on the orb of empire. She and her Child are one.

All this was noble beyond the nobility of man, but its earthly form was inspired by the Empire rather than by the petty royalty of Louis-le-Gros or his pious queen Alix of Savoy. One mark of the period is the long, oval nimbus; another is the imperial character of the Virgin; a third is her unity with the Christ which is the Church. To us, the mark that will distinguish the Virgin of Chartres, or, if you prefer, the Virgin of the Crusades, is her crown and robes and throne. According to M. Rohault de Fleury's "Iconographie de la Sainte Vierge" (11, 62), the Virgin's headdress and ornaments had been for long ages borrowed from the costume of the Empresses of the East in honour of the Queen of Heaven. No doubt the Virgin of Chartres was the Virgin recognized by the Empress Helena, mother of Constantine, and was at least as old as Helena's pilgrimage to Jerusalem in 326. She was not a Western, feudal queen, nor was her Son a feudal king; she typified an authority which the people wanted, and the fiefs feared; the Pax Romana; the omnipotence of God in government. In all Europe, at that time, there was no power able to enforce justice or to maintain order, and no symbol of such a power except Christ and His Mother and the Imperial Crown.

This idea is very different from that which was the object of our pilgrimage to Mont-Saint-Michel; but since all Chartres is to be one long comment upon it, you can lay the history of the matter on the shelf for study at your leisure, if you ever care to study into the weary details of human illusions and disappointments, while here we pray to the Virgin, and absorb ourselves in the art, which is your pleasure and which shall not teach either a moral or a useful lesson. The Empress Mary is receiving you at her portal, and whether you are an impertinent child, or a foolish old peasant-woman, or an insolent prince, or a more insolent tourist, she receives you with the same dignity; in fact, she probably sees very little difference between you. An empress of Russia to-day would probably feel little difference in the relative rank of her subjects, and the Virgin was empress over emperors, patriarchs, and popes. Any one, however ignorant, can feel the sustained dignity of the sculptor's work, which is asserted with all the emphasis he could put into it. Not one of these long figures which line the three doorways but is an officer or official in attendance on the Empress or her Son, and bears the stamp of the Imperial Court. They are mutilated, but, if they have been treated with indignity, so were often their temporal rivals, torn to pieces, trampled on, to say nothing of being merely beheaded or poisoned, in the Sacred Palace and the Hippodrome, without losing that peculiar Oriental dignity of style which seems to drape the least dignified attitudes. The grand air of the twelfth century is something like that of a Greek temple; you can, if you like, hammer every separate stone to pieces, but you cannot hammer out the Greek style. There were originally twenty-four of these statues, and nineteen remain. Beginning at the north end, and passing over the first figure, which carries a head that does not belong to it, notice the second, a king with a long sceptre of empire, a book of law, and robes of Byzantine official splendour. Beneath his feet is a curious woman's head with heavy braids of hair, and a crown. The third figure is a queen, charming as a woman, but particularly well-dressed, and with details of ornament and person elaborately wrought; worth drawing, if one could only draw; worth photographing with utmost care to include the strange support on which she stands: a monkey, two dragons, a dog, a basilisk with a dog's head. Two prophets follow—not so interesting;—prophets rarely interest. Then comes the central bay: two queens who claim particular attention, then a prophet, then a saint next the doorway; then on the southern jamb-shafts, another saint, a king, a queen, and another king. Last comes the southern bay, the Virgin's own, and there stands first a figure said to be a youthful king; then a strongly sculptured saint; next the door a figure called also a king, but so charmingly delicate in expression that the robes alone betray his sex; and who this exquisite young aureoled king may have been who stands so close to the Virgin, at her right hand, no one can now reveal. Opposite him is a saint who may be, or should be, the Prince of the Apostles; then a bearded king with a broken sceptre, standing on two dragons; and, at last, a badly mutilated queen.

These statues are the Eginetan marbles of French art; from them all modern French sculpture dates, or ought to date. They are singularly interesting; as naif as the smile on the faces of the Greek warriors, but no more grotesque than they. You will see Gothic grotesques in plenty, and you cannot mistake the two intentions; the twelfth century would sooner have tempted the tortures of every feudal dungeon in Europe than have put before the Virgin's eyes any figure that could be conceived as displeasing to her. These figures are full of feeling, and saturated with worship; but what is most to our purpose is the feminine side which they proclaim and insist upon. Not only the number of the female figures, and their beauty, but also the singularly youthful beauty of several of the males; the superb robes they wear; the expression of their faces and their figures; the details of hair, stuffs, ornaments, jewels; the refinement and feminine taste of the whole, are enough to startle our interest if we recognize what meaning they had to the twelfth century.

These figures looked stiff and long and thin and ridiculous to enlightened citizens of the eighteenth century, but they were made to fit the architecture; if you want to know what an enthusiast thinks of them, listen to M. Huysmans's "Cathedral." "Beyond a doubt, the most beautiful sculpture in the world is in this place." He can hardly find words to express his admiration for the queens, and particularly for the one on the right of the central doorway. "Never in any period has a more expressive figure been thus wrought by the genius of man; it is the chef-d'oeuvre of infantile grace and holy candour …. She is the elder sister of the Prodigal Son, the one of whom Saint Luke does not speak, but who, if she existed, would have pleaded the cause of the absent, and insisted, with the father, that he should kill the fatted calf at his son's return." The idea is charming if you are the returning son, as many twelfth- century pilgrims must have thought themselves; but, in truth, the figure is that of a queen; an Eleanor of Guienne;

her position there is due to her majesty, which bears witness to the celestial majesty of the Court in which she is only a lady-in-waiting: and she is hardly more humanly fascinating than her brother, the youthful king at the Virgin's right hand, who has nothing of the Prodigal Son, but who certainly has much of Lohengrin, or even—almost—Tristan.

The Abbe Bulteau has done his best to name these statues, but the names would be only in your way. That the sculptor meant them for a Queen of Sheba or a King of Israel has little to do with their meaning in the twelfth century, when the people were much more likely to have named them after the queens and kings they knew. The whole charm lies for us in the twelfth-century humanity of Mary and her Court; not in the scriptural names under which it was made orthodox. Here, in this western portal, it stands as the crusaders of 1100-50 imagined it; but by walking round the church to the porch over the entrance to the north transept, you shall see it again as Blanche of Castile and Saint Louis imagined it, a hundred years later, so that you will know better whether the earthly attributes are exaggerated or untrue.

Porches, like steeples, were rather a peculiarity of French churches, and were studied, varied, one might even say petted, by French architects to an extent hardly attempted elsewhere; but among all the French porches, those of Chartres are the most famous. There are two: one on the north side, devoted to the Virgin; the other, on the south, devoted to the Son, "The mass of intelligence, knowledge, acquaintance with effects, practical experience, expended on these two porches of Chartres," says Viollet-le-Duc, "would be enough to establish the glory of a whole generation of artists." We begin with the north porch because it belonged to the Virgin; and it belonged to the Virgin because the north was cold, bleak, sunless, windy, and needed warmth, peace, affection, and power to protect against the assaults of Satan and his swarming devils. There the all-suffering but the all-powerful Mother received other mothers who suffered like her, but who, as a rule, were not powerful. Traditionally in the primitive church, the northern porch belonged to the women. When they needed help, they came here, because it was the only place in this world or in any other where they had much hope of finding even a reception. See how Mary received them!

The porch extends the whole width of the transept, about one hundred and twenty feet (37.65 metres), divided into three bays some twenty feet deep, and covered with a stone vaulted roof supported on piers outside. Begun toward 1215 under Philip Augustus, the architectural part was finished toward 1225 under Louis VIII; and after his death in 1226, the decorative work and statuary were carried on under the regency of his widow, Blanche of Castile, and through the reign of her son, Saint Louis (1235-70), until about 1275, when the work was completed by Philip the Hardy. A gift of the royal family of France, all the members of the family seem to have had a share in building it, and several of their statues have been supposed to adorn it. The walls are lined—the porch, in a religious sense, is inhabited—by more than seven hundred figures, great and small, all, in one way or another, devoted to the glory of the Queen of Heaven. You will see that a hundred years have converted the Byzantine Empress into a French Queen, as the same years had converted Alix of Savoy into Blanche of Castile; but the note of majesty is the same, and the assertion of power is, if possible, more emphatic.

The highest note is struck at once, in the central bay, over the door, where you see the Coronation of Mary as Queen of Heaven, a favourite subject in art from very early times, and the dominant idea of Mary's church. You see Mary on the left, seated on her throne; on the right, seated on a precisely similar throne, is Christ, Who holds up His right hand apparently to bless, since Mary already bears the crown. Mary bends forward, with her hands raised toward her Son, as though in gratitude or adoration or prayer, but certainly not in an attitude of feudal homage. On either side, an archangel swings a censer.

On the lintel below, on the left, is represented the death of Mary; on the right, Christ carries, in the folds of His mantle, the soul of Mary in the form of a little child, and at the same time blesses the body which is carried away by angels—The Resurrection of Mary.

Below the lintel, supporting it, and dividing the doorway in halves, is the trumeau,—the central pier,—a new part of the portal which was unknown to the western door. Usually in the Virgin's churches, as at Rheims, or Amiens or Paris, the Virgin herself, with her Son in her arms, stands against this pier, trampling on the dragon with the woman's head. Here, not the Virgin with the Christ, but her mother Saint Anne stands, with the infant Virgin in her arms; while beneath is, or was, Saint Joachim, her husband, among his flocks, receiving from the Archangel Gabriel the annunciation.

So at the entrance the Virgin declares herself divinely Queen in her own right; divinely born; divinely resurrected from death, on the third day; seated by divine right on the throne of Heaven, at the right hand of God, the Son, with Whom she is one.

Unless we feel this assertion of divine right in the Queen of Heaven, apart from the Trinity, yet one with It, Chartres is unintelligible. The extreme emphasis laid upon it at the church door shows what the church means within. Of course, the assertion was not strictly orthodox; perhaps, since we are not members of the Church, we might be unnoticed and unrebuked if we start by suspecting that the worship of the Virgin never was strictly orthodox; but Chartres was hers before it ever belonged to the Church, and, like Lourdes in our own time, was a shrine peculiarly favoured by her presence. The mere fact that it was a bishopric had little share in its sanctity. The bishop was much more afraid of Mary than he was of any Church Council ever held.

Critics are doing their best to destroy the peculiar personal interest of this porch, but tourists and pilgrims may be excused for insisting on their traditional rights here, since the porch is singular, even in the thirteenth century, for belonging entirely to them and the royal family of France, subject only to the Virgin. True artists, turned critics, think also less of rules than of values, and no ignorant public can be trusted to join the critics in losing temper judiciously over the date or correctness of a portrait until they knew something of its motives and merits. The public has always felt certain that some of the statues which stand against the outer piers of this porch are portraits, and they see no force in the objection that such decoration was not customary in the Church. Many things at Chartres were not customary in the Church, although the Church now prefers not to dwell on them. Therefore the student returns to Viollet-le-Duc with his usual delight at finding at least one critic whose sense of values is stronger than his sense of rule: "Each statue," he says in his "Dictionary" (111, 166), "possesses its personal character which remains graven on the memory like the recollection of a living being whom one has known .... A large part of the statues in the porches of Notre Dame de Chartres, as well as of the portals of the Cathedrals of Amiens and Rheims, possess these individual qualities, and this it is which explains why these statues produce on the crowd so vivid an impression that it names them, knows them, and attaches to each of them an idea, often a legend."

Probably the crowd did so from the first moment they saw the statues, and with good reason. At all events, they have attached to two of the most individual figures on the north porch, two names, perhaps the best known in France in the year 1226, but which since the year 1300 can have conveyed only the most shadowy meaning to any but pure antiquarians. The group is so beautiful as to be given a plate to itself in the "Monographie" (number 26), as representing Philip Hurepel and his wife Mahaut de Boulogne. So little could any crowd, or even any antiquarian, at any time within six hundred years have been likely to pitch on just these persons to associate with Blanche of Castile in any kind of family unity, that the mere suggestion seems wild; yet Blanche outlived Pierre by nearly twenty years, and her power over this transept and porch ended only with her death as regent in 1252.

Philippe, nicknamed Hurepel,—Boarskin,—was a "fils deFrance," whose father, Philip Augustus, had serious, not to say fatal, difficulties with the Church about the legality of his marriage, and was forced to abandon his wife, who died in 1201, after giving birth to Hurepel in 1200. The child was recognized as legitimate, and stood next to the throne, after his half-brother Louis, who was thirteen years older. Almost at his birth he was affianced to Mahaut, Countess of Boulogne, and the marriage was celebrated in 1216. Rich and strongly connected, Hurepel naturally thought himself—and was—head of the royal family next to the King, and when his half-brother, Louis VIII, died in 1226, leaving only a son, afterwards Saint Louis, a ten-year-old boy, to succeed, Hurepel very properly claimed the guardianship of his infant nephew, and deeply resented being excluded by Queen Blanche from what he regarded— perhaps with justice—as his right. Nearly all the great lords and the members of the royal family sided with him, and entered into a civil war against Blanche, at the moment when these two porches of Chartres were building, between 1228 and 1230. The two greatest leaders of the conspiracy were Hurepel, whom we are expected to recognize on the pier of this porch, and Pierre Mauclerc, of Brittany and Dreux, whom we have no choice but to admit on the trumeau of the other. In those days every great feudal lord was more or less related by blood to the Crown, and although Blanche of Castile was also a cousin as well as queen-mother, they hated her as a Spanish intruder with such hatred as men felt in an age when passions were real.

That these two men should be found here, associated with Blanche in the same work, at the same time, under the same roof, is a fantastic idea, and students can feel in this political difficulty a much stronger objection to admitting Hurepel to Queen Blanche's porch than any supposed rule of Church custom; yet the first privilege of tourist ignorance is the right to see, or try to see, their thirteenth century with thirteenth-century eyes. Passing by the statues of Philip and Mahaut, and stepping inside the church door, almost the first figure that the visitor sees on lifting his eyes to the upper windows of the transept is another figure of Philippe Hurepel, in glass, on his knees, with clasped hands, before an altar; and to prevent possibility of mistake his blazoned coat bears the words: "Phi: Conte de Bolone." Apparently he is the donor, for, in the rose above, he sits in arms on a white horse with a shield bearing the blazon of France. Obliged to make his peace with the Queen in 1230, Hurepel died in 1233 or 1234, while Blanche was still regent, and instantly took his place as of right side by side with Blanche's castles of Castile among the great benefactors of the church.

Beneath the next rose is Mahaut herself, as donor, bearing her husband's arms of France, suggesting that the windows must have been given together, probably before Philip's death in 1233, since Mahaut was married again in 1238, this time to Alfonso of Portugal, who repudiated her in 1249, and left her to die in her own town of Boulogne in 1258. Lastly, in the third window of the series, is her daughter Jeanne,—"Iehenne,"—who was probably born before 1220, and who was married in 1236 to Gaucher de Chatillon, one of the greatest warriors of his time. Jeanne also—according to the Abbe Bulteau (111, 225)—bears the arms of her father and mother; which seems to suggest that she gave this window before her marriage. These three windows, therefore, have the air of dating at least as early as 1233 when Philip Hurepel died, while next them follow two more roses, and the great rose of France, presumably of the same date, all scattered over with the castles of Queen Blanche. The motive of the porch outside is repeated in the glass, as it should be, and as the Saint Anne of the Rose of France, within, repeats the Saint Anne on the trumeau of the portal. The personal stamp of the royal family is intense, but the stamp of the Virgin's personality is intenser still. In the presence of Mary, not only did princes hide their quarrels, but they also put on their most courteous manners and the most refined and even austere address. The Byzantine display of luxury and adornment had vanished. All the figures suggest the sanctity of the King and his sister Isabel; the court has the air of a convent; but the idea of Mary's majesty is asserted through it all. The artists and donors and priests forgot nothing which, in their judgment, could set off the authority, elegance, and refinement of the Queen of Heaven; even the young ladies-in-waiting are there, figured by the twelve Virtues and the fourteen Beatitudes; and, indeed, though men are plenty and some of them are handsome, women give the tone, the charm, and mostly the intelligence. The Court of Mary is feminine, and its charms are Grace and Love; perhaps even more grace than love, in a social sense, if you look at Beauty and Friendship among Beatitudes.

M. Huysmans insists that this sculpture is poor in comparison with his twelfth-century Prodigal Daughter, and I hope you can enter into the spirit of his enthusiasm; but other people prefer the thirteenth-century work, and think it equals the best Greek. Approaching, or surpassing this,—as you like,—is the sculpture you will see at Rheims, of the same period, and perhaps the same hands; but, for our purpose, the Queen of Sheba, here in the right-hand bay, is enough, because you can compare it on the spot with M. Huysmans's figure on the western portal, which may also be a Queen of Sheba, who, as spouse of Solomon, typified the Church, and therefore prefigured Mary herself. Both are types of Court beauty and grace, one from the twelfth century, the other from the thirteenth, and you can prefer which you please; but you want to bear in mind that each, in her time, pleased the Virgin. You can even take for a settled fact that these were the types of feminine beauty and grace which pleased the Virgin beyond all others.

The purity of taste, feeling, and manners which stamps the art of these centuries, as it did the Court of Saint Louis and his mother, is something you will not wholly appreciate till you reach the depravity of the Valois; but still you can see how exquisite the Virgin's taste was, and how pure. You can also see how she shrank from the sight of pain. Here, in the central bay, next to King David, who stands at her right hand, is the great figure of Abraham about to sacrifice Isaac. If there is one subject more revolting than another to a woman who typifies the Mother, it is this subject of Abraham and Isaac, with its compound horror of masculine stupidity and brutality. The sculptor has tried to make even this motive a pleasing one. He has placed Abraham against the column in the correct harshness of attitude, with his face turned aside and up, listening for his orders; but the little Isaac, with hands and feet tied, leans like a bundle of sticks against his father's knee with an expression of perfect faith and confidence, while Abraham's left hand quiets him and caresses the boy's face, with a movement that must have gone straight to Mary's heart, for Isaac always prefigured Christ.

The glory of Mary was not one of terror, and her porch contains no appeal to any emotion but those of her perfect grace. If we were to stay here for weeks, we should find only this idea worked into every detail. The Virgin of the thirteenth century is no longer an Empress; she is Queen Mother,—an idealized Blanche of Castile;—too high to want, or suffer, or to revenge, or to aspire, but not too high to pity, to punish, or to pardon. The women went to her porch for help as naturally as babies to their mother; and the men, in her presence, fell on their knees because they feared her intelligence and her anger.

Not that all the men showed equal docility! We must go next, round the church, to the south porch, which was the gift of Pierre Mauclerc, Comte de Dreux, another member of the royal family, great- grandson of Louis VI, and therefore second cousin to Louis VIII and Philip Hurepel. Philip Augustus, his father's first cousin, married the young man, in 1212, to Alix, heiress of the Duchy of Brittany, and this marriage made him one of the most powerful vassals of the Crown. He joined Philip Hurepel in resisting the regency of Queen Blanche in 1227, and Blanche, after a long struggle, caused him to be deposed in 1230. Pierre was obliged to submit, and was pardoned. Until 1236, he remained in control of the Duchy of Brittany, but then was obliged to surrender his power to his son, and turned his turbulent activity against the infidels in Syria and Egypt, dying in 1250, on his return from Saint Louis's disastrous crusade. Pierre de Dreux was a masculine character,—a bad cleric, as his nickname Mauclerc testified, but a gentleman, a soldier, and a scholar, and, what is more to our purpose, a man of taste. He built the south porch at Chartres, apparently as a memorial of his marriage with Alix in 1212, and the statuary is of the same date with that of the north porch, but, like that, it was not finished when Pierre died in 1250.

One would like to know whether Pierre preferred to take the southern entrance, or whether he was driven there by the royal claim to the Virgin's favour. The southern porch belongs to the Son, as the northern belongs to the Mother. Pierre never showed much deference to women, and probably felt more at his ease under the protection of the Son than of Mary; but in any case he showed as clearly as possible what he thought on this question of persons. To Pierre, Christ was first, and he asserted his opinion as emphatically as Blanche asserted hers.

Which porch is the more beautiful is a question for artists to discuss and decide, if they can. Either is good enough for us, whose pose is ignorance, and whose pose is strictly correct; but apart from its beauty or its art, there is also the question of feeling, of motive, which puts the Porche de Dreux in contrast with the Porche de France, and this is wholly within our competence. At the outset, the central bay displays, above the doorway, Christ, on a throne, raising His hands to show the stigmata, the wounds which were the proof of man's salvation. At His right hand sits the Mother,—without her crown; on His left, in equal rank with the Mother, sits Saint John the Evangelist. Both are in the same attitude of supplication as intercessors; there is no distinction in rank or power between Mary and John, since neither has any power except what Christ gives them. Pierre did not, indeed, put the Mother on her knees before the Son, as you can see her at Amiens and in later churches,—certainly bad taste in Mary's own palace; but he allowed her no distinction which is not her strict right. The angels above and around bear the symbols of the Passion; they are unconscious of Mary's presence; they are absorbed in the perfections of the Son. On the lintel just below is the Last Judgment, where Saint Michael reappears, weighing the souls of the dead which Mary and John above are trying to save from the strict justice of Christ. The whole melodrama of Church terrors appears after the manner of the thirteenth century, on this church door, without regard to Mary's feelings; and below, against the trumeau, stands the great figure of Christ,—the whole Church,—trampling on the lion and dragon. On either side of the doorway stand six great figures of the Apostles asserting themselves as the columns of the Church, and looking down at us with an expression no longer calculated to calm our fears or encourage extravagant hopes. No figure on this porch suggests a portrait or recalls a memory.

Very grand, indeed, is this doorway; dignified, impressive, and masculine to a degree seldom if ever equalled in art; and the left bay rivals it. There, in the tympanum, Christ appears again; standing; bearing on His head the crown royal; alone, except for the two angels who adore, and surrounded only by the martyrs, His witnesses. The right bay is devoted to Saint Nicholas and the Saints Confessors who bear witness to the authority of Christ in faith. Of the twenty-eight great figures, the officers of the royal court, who make thus the strength of the Church beneath Christ, not one is a woman. The masculine orthodoxy of Pierre Mauclerc has spared neither sex nor youth; all are of a maturity which chills the blood, excepting two, whose youthful beauty is heightened by the severity of their surroundings, so that the Abbe Bulteau makes bold even to say that "the two statues of Saint George and of Saint Theodore may be regarded as the most beautiful of our cathedral, perhaps even as the two masterpieces of statuary at the end of the thirteenth century." On that point, let every one follow his taste; but one reflection at least seems to force itself on the mind in comparing these twenty-eight figures. Certainly the sword, however it may compare with the pen in other directions, is in art more powerful than all the pens, or volumes, or crosiers ever made. Your "Golden Legend" and Roman Breviary are here the only guide-books worth consulting, and the stories of young George and Theodore stand there recorded; as their miracle under the walls of Antioch, during the first crusade, is matter of history; but among these magnificent figures one detects at a glance that it is not the religion or sacred purity of the subject, or even the miracles or the sufferings, which inspire passion for Saint George and Saint Theodore, under the Abbe's robe; it is with him, as with the plain boy and girl, simply youth, with lance and sword and shield.

These two figures stand in the outer embrasures of the left bay, where they can be best admired, and perhaps this arrangement shows what Perron de Dreux, as he was commonly called, loved most, in his heart of hearts; but elsewhere, even in this porch, he relaxed his severity, and became at times almost gracious to women. Good judges have, indeed, preferred this porch to the northern one; but, be that as you please, it contains seven hundred and eighty-three figures, large and small, to serve for comparison. Among these, the female element has its share, though not a conspicuous one; and even the Virgin gets her rights, though not beside her Son. To see her, you must stand outside in the square and, with a glass, look at the central pignon, or gable, of the porch. There, just above the point of the arch, you will see Mary on her throne, crowned, wearing her royal robes, and holding the Child on her knees, with the two archangels on either side offering incense. Pierre de Dreux, or some one else, admitted at last that she was Queen Regent, although evidently not eager to do so; and if you turn your glass up to the gable of the transept itself, above the great rose and the colonnade over it, you can see another and a colossal statue of the Virgin, but standing, with the Child on her left arm. She seems to be crowned, and to hold the globe in her right hand; but the Abbe Bulteau says it is a flower. The two archangels are still there. This figure is thought to have been a part of the finishing decoration added by Philip the Fair in 1304.

In theology, Pierre de Dreux seems to show himself a more learned clerk than his cousins of France, and, as an expression of the meaning the church of Mary should externally display, the Porche de Dreux, if not as personal, is as energetic as the Porche de France, or the western portal. As we pass into the Cathedral, under the great Christ, on the trumeau, you must stop to look at Pierre himself. A bridegroom, crowned with flowers on his wedding-day, he kneels in prayer, while two servants distribute bread to the poor. Below, you see him again, seated with his wife Alix before a table with one loaf, assisting at the meal they give to the poor. Pierre kneels to God; he and his wife bow before the Virgin and the poor;— but not to Queen Blanche!

Now let us enter!—

CHAPTER VI: THE VIRGIN OF CHARTRES

We must take ten minutes to accustom our eyes to the light, and we had better use them to seek the reason why we come to Chartres rather than to Rheims or Amiens or Bourges, for the cathedral that fills our ideal. The truth is, there are several reasons; there generally are, for doing the things we like; and after you have studied Chartres to the ground, and got your reasons settled, you will never find an antiquarian to agree with you; the architects will probably listen to you with contempt; and even these excellent priests, whose kindness is great, whose patience is heavenly, and whose good opinion you would so gladly gain, will turn from you with pain, if not with horror. The Gothic is singular in this; one seems easily at home in the Renaissance; one is not too strange in the Byzantine; as for the Roman, it is ourselves; and we could walk blindfolded through every chink and cranny of the Greek mind; all these styles seem modern, when we come close to them; but the Gothic gets away. No two men think alike about it, and no woman agrees with either man. The Church itself never agreed about it, and the architects agree even less than the priests. To most minds it casts too many shadows; it wraps itself in mystery; and when people talk of mystery, they commonly mean fear. To others, the Gothic seems hoary with age and decrepitude, and its shadows mean death. What is curious to watch is the fanatical conviction of the Gothic enthusiast, to whom the twelfth century means exuberant youth, the eternal child of Wordsworth, over whom its immortality broods like the day; it is so simple and yet so complicated; it sees so much and so little; it loves so many toys and cares for so few necessities; its youth is so young, its age so old, and its youthful yearning for old thought is so disconcerting, like the mysterious senility of the baby that—

Deaf and silent, reads the eternal deep,

Haunted forever by the eternal mind.

One need not take it more seriously than one takes the baby itself. Our amusement is to play with it, and to catch its meaning in its smile; and whatever Chartres maybe now, when young it was a smile. To the Church, no doubt, its cathedral here has a fixed and administrative meaning, which is the same as that of every other bishop's seat and with which we have nothing whatever to do. To us, it is a child's fancy; a toy-house to please the Queen of Heaven,— to please her so much that she would be happy in it,—to charm her till she smiled.

The Queen Mother was as majestic as you like; she was absolute; she could be stern; she was not above being angry; but she was still a woman, who loved grace, beauty, ornament,—her toilette, robes, jewels;—who considered the arrangements of her palace with attention, and liked both light and colour; who kept a keen eye on her Court, and exacted prompt and willing obedience from king and archbishops as well as from beggars and drunken priests. She protected her friends and punished her enemies. She required space, beyond what was known in the Courts of kings, because she was liable at all times to have ten thousand people begging her for favours— mostly inconsistent with law—and deaf to refusal. She was extremely sensitive to neglect, to disagreeable impressions, to want of intelligence in her surroundings. She was the greatest artist, as she was the greatest philosopher and musician and theologian, that ever lived on earth, except her Son, Who, at Chartres, is still an Infant under her guardianship. Her taste was infallible; her sentence eternally final. This church was built for her in this spirit of simple-minded, practical, utilitarian faith,—in this singleness of thought, exactly as a little girl sets up a doll-house for her favourite blonde doll. Unless you can go back to your dolls, you are out of place here. If you can go back to them, and get rid for one small hour of the weight of custom, you shall see Chartres in glory.

The palaces of earthly queens were hovels compared with these palaces of the Queen of Heaven at Chartres, Paris, Laon, Noyon, Rheims, Amiens, Rouen, Bayeux, Coutances,—a list that might be stretched into a volume. The nearest approach we have made to a palace was the Merveille at Mont-Saint-Michel, but no Queen had a palace equal to that. The Merveille was built, or designed, about the year 1200; toward the year 1500, Louis XI built a great castle at Loches in Touraine, and there Queen Anne de Bretagne had apartments which still exist, and which we will visit. At Blois you shall see the residence which served for Catherine de Medicis till her death in 1589. Anne de Bretagne was trebly queen, and Catherine de Medicis took her standard of comfort from the luxury of Florence. At Versailles you can see the apartments which the queens of the Bourbon line occupied through their century of magnificence. All put together, and then trebled in importance, could not rival the splendour of any single cathedral dedicated to Queen Mary in the thirteenth century; and of them all, Chartres was built to be peculiarly and exceptionally her delight.

One has grown so used to this sort of loose comparison, this reckless waste of words, that one no longer adopts an idea unless it is driven in with hammers of statistics and columns of figures. With the irritating demand for literal exactness and perfectly straight lines which lights up every truly American eye, you will certainly ask when this exaltation of Mary began, and unless you get the dates, you will doubt the facts. It is your own fault if they are tiresome; you might easily read them all in the "Iconographie de la Sainte Vierge," by M. Rohault de Fleury, published in 1878. You can start at Byzantium with the Empress Helena in 326, or with the Council of Ephesus in 431. You will find the Virgin acting as the patron saint of Constantinople and of the Imperial residence, under as many names as Artemis or Aphrodite had borne. As Godmother [word in Greek] Deipara [word in Greek], Pathfinder [word in Greek], afterwards gave to Murillo the subject of a famous painting, told that once, when he was reciting before her statue the "Ave Maris Stella," and came to the words, "Monstra te esse Matrem," the image, pressing its breast, dropped on the lips of her servant three drops of the milk which had nourished the Saviour. The same miracle, in various forms, was told of many other persons, both saints and sinners; but it made so much impression on the mind of the age that, in the fourteenth century, Dante, seeking in Paradise for some official introduction to the foot of the Throne, found no intercessor with the Queen of Heaven more potent than Saint Bernard. You can still read Bernard's hymns to the Virgin, and even his sermons, if you like. To him she was the great mediator. In the eyes of a culpable humanity, Christ was too sublime, too terrible, too just, but not even the weakest human frailty could fear to approach his Mother. Her attribute was humility; her love and pity were infinite. "Let him deny your mercy who can say that he has ever asked it in vain."

Saint Bernard was emotional and to a certain degree mystical, like Adam de Saint-Victor, whose hymns were equally famous, but the emotional saints and mystical poets were not by any means allowed to establish exclusive rights to the Virgin's favour. Abelard was as devoted as they were, and wrote hymns as well. Philosophy claimed her, and Albert the Great, the head of scholasticism, the teacher of Thomas Aquinas, decided in her favour the question: "Whether the Blessed Virgin possessed perfectly the seven liberal arts." The Church at Chartres had decided it a hundred years before by putting the seven liberal arts next her throne, with Aristotle himself to witness; but Albertus gave the reason: "I hold that she did, for it is written, 'Wisdom has built herself a house, and has sculptured seven columns.' That house is the blessed Virgin; the seven columns are the seven liberal arts. Mary, therefore, had perfect mastery of science." Naturally she had also perfect mastery of economics, and most of her great churches were built in economic centres. The guilds were, if possible, more devoted to her than the monks; the bourgeoisie of Paris, Rouen, Amiens, Laon, spend money by millions to gain her favour. Most surprising of all, the great military class was perhaps the most vociferous. Of all inappropriate haunts for the gentle, courteous, pitying Mary, a field of battle seems to be the worst, if not distinctly blasphemous; yet the greatest French warriors insisted on her leading them into battle, and in the actual melee when men were killing each other, on every battle-field in Europe, for at least five hundred years, Mary was present, leading both sides. The battle-cry of the famous Constable du Guesclin was "Notre-Dame-Guesclin"; "Notre-Dame-Coucy" was the cry of the great Sires de Coucy; "Notre-Dame-Auxerre"; "Notre-Dame-Sancerre"; "Notre- Dame-Hainault"; "Notre-Dame-Gueldres"; "Notre-Dame-Bourbon"; "Notre- Dame-Bearn";—all well-known battle-cries. The King's own battle at one time cried, "Notre-Dame-Saint-Denis-Montjoie"; the Dukes of Burgundy cried, "Notre-Dame-Bourgogne"; and even the soldiers of the Pope were said to cry, "Notre-Dame-Saint-Pierre."

The measure of this devotion, which proves to any religious American mind, beyond possible cavil, its serious and practical reality, is the money it cost. According to statistics, in the single century between 1170 and 1270, the French built eighty cathedrals and nearly five hundred churches of the cathedral class, which would have cost, according to an estimate made in 1840, more than five thousand millions to replace. Five thousand million francs is a thousand million dollars, and this covered only the great churches of a single century. The same scale of expenditure had been going on since the year 1000, and almost every parish in France had rebuilt its church in stone; to this day France is strewn with the ruins of this architecture, and yet the still preserved churches of the eleventh and twelfth centuries, among the churches that belong to the Romanesque and Transition period, are numbered by hundreds until they reach well into the thousands. The share of this capital which was—if one may use a commercial figure—invested in the Virgin cannot be fixed, any more than the total sum given to religious objects between 1000 and 1300; but in a spiritual and artistic sense, it was almost the whole, and expressed an intensity of conviction never again reached by any passion, whether of religion, of loyalty, of patriotism, or of wealth; perhaps never even parallelled by any single economic effort, except in war. Nearly every great church of the twelfth and thirteenth centuries belonged to Mary, until in France one asks for the church of Notre Dame as though it meant cathedral; but, not satisfied with this, she contracted the habit of requiring in all churches a chapel of her own, called in English the "Lady Chapel," which was apt to be as large as the church but was always meant to be handsomer; and there, behind the high altar, in her own private apartment, Mary sat, receiving her innumerable suppliants, and ready at any moment to step up upon the high altar itself to support the tottering authority of the local saint.

Expenditure like this rests invariably on an economic idea. Just as the French of the nineteenth century invested their surplus capital in a railway system in the belief that they would make money by it in this life, in the thirteenth they trusted their money to the Queen of Heaven because of their belief in her power to repay it with interest in the life to come. The investment was based on the power of Mary as Queen rather than on any orthodox Church conception of the Virgin's legitimate station. Papal Rome never greatly loved Byzantine empresses or French queens. The Virgin of Chartres was never wholly sympathetic to the Roman Curia. To this day the Church writers—like the Abbe Bulteau or M. Rohault de Fleury—are singularly shy of the true Virgin of majesty, whether at Chartres or at Byzantium or wherever she is seen. The fathers Martin and Cahier at Bourges alone left her true value. Had the Church controlled her, the Virgin would perhaps have remained prostrate at the foot of the Cross. Dragged by a Byzantine Court, backed by popular insistence and impelled by overpowering self-interest, the Church accepted the Virgin throned and crowned, seated by Christ, the Judge throned and crowned; but even this did not wholly satisfy the French of the thirteenth century who seemed bent on absorbing Christ in His Mother, and making the Mother the Church, and Christ the Symbol.

The Church had crowned and enthroned her almost from the beginning, and could not have dethroned her if it would. In all Christian art— sculpture or mosaic, painting or poetry—the Virgin's rank was expressly asserted. Saint Bernard, like John Comnenus, and probably at the same time (1120-40), chanted hymns to the Virgin as Queen:—

O salutaris Virgo Stella Maris

Generans prolem, Aequitatis solem,

Lucis auctorem, Retinens pudorem,

   Suscipe laudem!

Celi Regina Per quam medicina

Datur aegretis, Gratia devotis,

Gaudium moestis, Mundo lux coelestis,

   Spesque salutis;

Aula regalis, Virgo specialis,

Posce medelam Nobis et tutelam,

Suscipe vota, Precibusque cuncta

> Pelle molesta!
>
> O Saviour Virgin, Star of Sea,
>
> Who bore for child the Son of Justice,
>
> The source of Light, Virgin always
>
> > Hear our praise!
>
> Queen of Heaven who have given
>
> Medicine to the sick, Grace to the devout,
>
> Joy to the sad, Heaven's light to the world
>
> > And hope of salvation;
>
> Court royal, Virgin typical,
>
> Grant us cure and guard,
>
> Accept our vows, and by prayers
>
> > Drive all griefs away!

As the lyrical poet of the twelfth century, Adam de Saint-Victor seems to have held rank higher if possible than that of Saint Bernard, and his hymns on the Virgin are certainly quite as emphatic an assertion of her majesty:—

> Imperatrix supernorum!
>
> Superatrix infernorum!
>
> Eligenda via coeli,
>
> Retinenda spe fideli,
>
> Separatos a te longe
>
> Revocatos ad te junge
>
> > Tuorum collegio!
>
> Empress of the highest,
>
> Mistress over the lowest,
>
> Chosen path of Heaven,

Held fast by faithful hope,

Those separated from you far,

Recalled to you, unite

    In your fold!

To delight in the childish jingle of the mediaeval Latin is a sign of a futile mind, no doubt, and I beg pardon of you and of the Church for wasting your precious summer day on poetry which was regarded as mystical in its age and which now sounds like a nursery rhyme; but a verse or two of Adam's hymn on the Assumption of the Virgin completes the record of her rank, and goes to complete also the documentary proof of her majesty at Chartres:—

Salve, Mater Salvatoris!

  Vas electum! Vas honoris!

    Vas coelestis Gratiae!

Ab aeterno Vas provisum!

  Vas insigne! Vas excisum

    Manu sapientiae!

Salve, Mater pietatis,

  Et totius Trinitatis

    Nobile Triclinium!

Verbi tamen incarnati

  Speciale majestati

    Praeparans hospitium!

O Maria! Stella maris!

  Dignitate singularis,

  Super omnes ordinaries

    Ordines coelestium!

In supremo sita poli

  Nos commenda tuae proli,

Ne terrores sive doli
  Nos supplantent hostium!
Mother of our Saviour, hail!
Chosen vessel! Sacred Grail!
  Font of celestial grace!
From eternity forethought!
By the hand of Wisdom wrought!
  Precious, faultless Vase!
Hail, Mother of Divinity!
Hail, Temple of the Trinity!
  Home of the Triune God!
In whom the Incarnate Word had birth,
The King! to whom you gave on earth
  Imperial abode.
Oh, Maria! Constellation!
Inspiration! Elevation!
Rule and Law and Ordination
  Of the angels' host!
Highest height of God's Creation,
Pray your Son's commiseration,
Lest, by fear or fraud, salvation
  For our souls be lost!

Constantly—one might better say at once, officially, she was addressed in these terms of supreme majesty: "Imperatrix supernorum!" "Coeli Regina!" "Aula regalis!" but the twelfth century seemed determined to carry the idea out to its logical conclusion in defiance of dogma. Not only was the Son absorbed in the Mother, or represented as under her guardianship, but the Father fared no better, and the Holy Ghost followed. The poets regarded the Virgin as the

"Templum Trinitatis"; "totius Trinitatis nobile Triclinium." She was the refectory of the Trinity—the "Triclinium"—because the refectory was the largest room and contained the whole of the members, and was divided in three parts by two rows of columns. She was the "Templum Trinitatis," the Church itself, with its triple aisle. The Trinity was absorbed in her.

This is a delicate subject in the Church, and you must feel it with delicacy, without brutally insisting on its necessary contradictions. All theology and all philosophy are full of contradictions quite as flagrant and far less sympathetic. This particular variety of religious faith is simply human, and has made its appearance in one form or another in nearly all religions; but though the twelfth century carried it to an extreme, and at Chartres you see it in its most charming expression, we have got always to make allowances for what was going on beneath the surface in men's minds, consciously or unconsciously, and for the latent scepticism which lurks behind all faith. The Church itself never quite accepted the full claims of what was called Mariolatry. One may be sure, too, that the bourgeois capitalist and the student of the schools, each from his own point of view, watched the Virgin with anxious interest. The bourgeois had put an enormous share of, his capital into what was in fact an economical speculation, not unlike the South Sea Scheme, or the railway system of our own time; except that in one case the energy was devoted to shortening the road to Heaven; in the other, to shortening the road to Paris; but no serious schoolman could have felt entirely convinced that God would enter into a business partnership with man, to establish a sort of joint- stock society for altering the operation of divine and universal laws. The bourgeois cared little for the philosophical doubt if the economical result proved to be good, but he watched this result with his usual practical sagacity, and required an experience of only about three generations (1200-1300) to satisfy himself that relics were not certain in their effects; that the Saints were not always able or willing to help; that Mary herself could not certainly be bought or bribed; that prayer without money seemed to be quite as efficacious as prayer with money; and that neither the road to Heaven nor Heaven itself had been made surer or brought nearer by an investment of capital which amounted to the best part of the wealth of France. Economically speaking, he became satisfied that his enormous money-investment had proved to be an almost total loss, and the reaction on his mind was as violent as the emotion. For three hundred years it prostrated France. The efforts of the bourgeoisie and the peasantry to recover their property, so far as it was recoverable, have lasted to the present day and we had best take care not to get mixed in those passions.

If you are to get the full enjoyment of Chartres, you must, for the time, believe in Mary as Bernard and Adam did, and feel her presence as the architects did, in every stone they placed, and every touch they chiselled. You must try first to rid your mind of the traditional idea that the Gothic is an intentional expression of religious gloom. The necessity for light was the motive of the Gothic architects. They needed light and always more light, until they sacrificed safety and common sense in trying to get it. They converted their walls into windows, raised their vaults, diminished their piers, until their churches could no longer stand. You will see the limits at Beauvais; at Chartres we have not got so far, but even here, in places where the Virgin wanted it,—as above the high altar,—the architect has taken all the light there was to take. For the same reason, fenestration became the most important part of the Gothic architect's work, and at Chartres was uncommonly interesting because the architect was obliged to design a new system, which should at the same time satisfy the laws of construction and the taste and imagination of Mary. No doubt the first command of the Queen of Heaven was for light, but the second, at least equally imperative, was for colour. Any earthly queen, even though she were not Byzantine in taste, loved colour; and the truest of queens—the only true Queen of Queens—had richer and finer taste in colour than the queens of fifty earthly kingdoms, as you will see when we come to the immense effort to gratify her in the glass of her windows. Illusion for illusion,—granting for the moment that Mary was an illusion,—the Virgin Mother in this instance repaid to her worshippers a larger return for their money than the capitalist has ever been able to get, at least in this world, from any other illusion of wealth which he has tried to make a source of pleasure and profit.

The next point on which Mary evidently insisted was the arrangement for her private apartments, the apse, as distinguished from her throne-room, the choir; both being quite distinct from the hall, or reception-room of the public, which was the nave with its enlargements in the transepts. This arrangement marks the distinction between churches built as shrines for the deity and churches built as halls of worship for the public. The difference is chiefly in the apse, and the apse of Chartres is the most interesting of all apses from this point of view.

The Virgin required chiefly these three things, or, if you like, these four: space, light, convenience; and colour decoration to unite and harmonize the whole. This concerns the interior; on the exterior she required statuary, and the only complete system of decorative sculpture that existed seems to belong to her churches:— Paris, Rheims, Amiens, and Chartres. Mary required all this magnificence at Chartres for herself alone, not for the public. As far as one can see into the spirit of the builders, Chartres was exclusively intended for the Virgin, as the Temple of Abydos was intended for Osiris. The wants of man, beyond a mere roof-cover, and perhaps space to some degree, enter to no very great extent into the problem of Chartres. Man came to render homage or to ask favours. The Queen received him in her palace, where she alone was at home, and alone gave commands.

The artist's second thought was to exclude from his work everything that could displease Mary; and since Mary differed from living queens only in infinitely greater majesty and refinement, the artist could admit only what pleased the actual taste of the great ladies who dictated taste at the Courts of France and England, which surrounded the little Court of the Counts of Chartres. What they were—these women of the twelfth and thirteenth centuries—we shall have to see or seek in other directions; but Chartres is perhaps the most magnificent and permanent monument they left of their taste, and we can begin here with learning certain things which they were not.

In the first place, they were not in the least vague, dreamy, or mystical in a modern sense;—far from it! They seemed anxious only to throw the mysteries into a blaze of light; not so much physical, perhaps,—since they, like all women, liked moderate shadow for their toilettes,—but luminous in the sense of faith. There is nothing about Chartres that you would think mystical, who know your Lohengrin, Siegfried, and Parsifal. If you care to make a study of the whole literature of the subject, read M. Male's "Art Religieux du XIIIe Siecle en France," and use it for a guide-book. Here you need only note how symbolic and how simple the sculpture is, on the portals and porches. Even what seems a grotesque or an abstract idea is no more than the simplest child's personification. On the walls you may have noticed the Ane qui vielle,—the ass playing the lyre; and on all the old churches you can see "bestiaries," as they were called, of fabulous animals, symbolic or not; but the symbolism is as simple as the realism of the oxen at Laon. It gave play to the artist in his effort for variety of decoration, and it amused the people,— probably the Virgin also was not above being amused;—now and then it seems about to suggest what you would call an esoteric meaning, that is to say, a meaning which each one of us can consider private property reserved for our own amusement, and from which the public is excluded; yet, in truth, in the Virgin's churches the public is never excluded, but invited. The Virgin even had the additional charm to the public that she was popularly supposed to have no very marked fancy for priests as such; she was a queen, a woman, and a mother, functions, all, which priests could not perform. Accordingly, she seems to have had little taste for mysteries of any sort, and even the symbols that seem most mysterious were clear to every old peasant-woman in her church. The most pleasing and promising of them all is the woman's figure you saw on the front of the cathedral in Paris; her eyes bandaged; her head bent down; her crown falling; without cloak or royal robe; holding in her hand a guidon or banner with its staff broken in more than one place. On the opposite pier stands another woman, with royal mantle, erect and commanding. The symbol is so graceful that one is quite eager to know its meaning; but every child in the Middle Ages would have instantly told you that the woman with the falling crown meant only the Jewish Synagogue, as the one with the royal robe meant the Church of Christ.

Another matter for which the female taste seemed not much to care was theology in the metaphysical sense. Mary troubled herself little about theology except when she retired into the south transept with Pierre de Dreux. Even there one finds little said about the Trinity, always the most metaphysical subtlety of the Church. Indeed, you might find much amusement here in searching the cathedral for any distinct expression at all of the Trinity as a dogma recognized by Mary.

One cannot take seriously the idea that the three doors, the three portals, and the three aisles express the Trinity, because, in the first place, there was no rule about it; churches might have what portals and aisles they pleased; both Paris and Bourges have five; the doors themselves are not allotted to the three members of the Trinity, nor are the portals; while another more serious objection is that the side doors and aisles are not of equal importance with the central, but mere adjuncts and dependencies, so that the architect who had misled the ignorant public into accepting so black a heresy would have deserved the stake, and would probably have gone to it. Even this suggestion of trinity is wanting in the transepts, which have only one aisle, and in the choir, which has five, as well as five or seven chapels, and, as far as an ignorant mind can penetrate, no triplets whatever. Occasionally, no doubt, you will discover in some sculpture or window, a symbol of the Trinity, but this discovery itself amounts to an admission of its absence as a controlling idea, for the ordinary worshipper must have been at least as blind as we are, and to him, as to us, it would have seemed a wholly subordinate detail. Even if the Trinity, too, is anywhere expressed, you will hardly find here an attempt to explain its metaphysical meaning—not even a mystic triangle.

The church is wholly given up to the Mother and the Son. The Father seldom appears; the Holy Ghost still more rarely. At least, this is the impression made on an ordinary visitor who has no motive to be orthodox; and it must have been the same with the thirteenth-century worshipper who came here with his mind absorbed in the perfections of Mary. Chartres represents, not the Trinity, but the identity of the Mother and Son. The Son represents the Trinity, which is thus absorbed in the Mother. The idea is not orthodox, but this is no affair of ours. The Church watches over its own.

The Virgin's wants and tastes, positive and negative, ought now to be clear enough to enable you to feel the artist's sincerity in trying to satisfy them; but first you have still to convince yourselves of the people's sincerity in employing the artists. This point is the easiest of all, for the evidence is express. In the year 1145 when the old fleche was begun,—the year before Saint Bernard preached the second crusade at Vezelay,—Abbot Haimon, of Saint-Pierre-sur-Dives in Normandy, wrote to the monks of Tutbury Abbey in England a famous letter to tell of the great work which the Virgin was doing in France and which began at the Church of Chartres. "Hujus sacrae institutionis ritus apud Carnotensem ecclesiam est inchoatus." From Chartres it had spread through Normandy, where it produced among other things the beautiful spire which we saw at Saint-Pierre-sur-Dives. "Postremo per totam fere Normanniam longe lateque convaluit ac loca per singula Matri misericordiae dicata praecipue occupavit." The movement affected especially the places devoted to Mary, but ran through all Normandy, far and wide. Of all Mary's miracles, the best attested, next to the preservation of her church, is the building of it; not so much because it surprises us as because it surprised even more the people of the time and the men who were its instruments. Such deep popular movements are always surprising, and at Chartres the miracle seems to have occurred three times, coinciding more or less with the dates of the crusades, and taking the organization of a crusade, as Archbishop Hugo of Rouen described it in a letter to Bishop Thierry of Amiens. The most interesting part of this letter is the evident astonishment of the writer, who might be talking to us to-day, so modern is he:—

The inhabitants of Chartres have combined to aid in the construction of their church by transporting the materials; our Lord has rewarded their humble zeal by miracles which have roused the Normans to imitate the piety of their neighbours ... Since then the faithful of our diocese and of other neighbouring regions have formed associations for the same object; they admit no one into their company unless he has been to confession, has renounced enmities and revenges, and has reconciled himself with his enemies. That done, they elect a chief, under whose direction they conduct their waggons in silence and with humility.

The quarries at Bercheres-l'Eveque are about five miles from Chartres. The stone is excessively hard, and was cut in blocks of considerable size, as you can see for yourselves; blocks which required great effort to transport and lay in place. The work was done with feverish rapidity, as it still shows, but it is the solidest building of the age, and without a sign of weakness yet. The Abbot told, with more surprise than pride, of the spirit which was built into the cathedral with the stone:—Who has ever seen!— Who has ever heard tell, in times past, that powerful princes of the world, that men brought up in honour and in wealth, that nobles, men and women, have bent their proud and haughty necks to the harness of carts, and that, like beasts of burden, they have dragged to the abode of Christ these waggons, loaded with wines, grains, oil, stone, wood, and all that is necessary for the wants of life, or for the construction of the church? But while they draw these burdens, there is one thing admirable to observe; it is that often when a thousand persons and more are attached to the chariots,—so great is the difficulty,—yet they march in such silence that not a murmur is heard, and truly if one did not see the thing with one's eyes, one might believe that among such a multitude there was hardly a person present. When they halt on the road, nothing is heard but the confession of sins, and pure and suppliant prayer to God to obtain pardon. At the voice of the priests who exhort their hearts to peace, they forget all hatred, discord is thrown far aside, debts are remitted, the unity of hearts is established.

But if any one is so far advanced in evil as to be unwilling to pardon an offender, or if he rejects the counsel of the priest who has piously advised him, his offering is instantly thrown from the wagon as impure, and he himself ignominiously and shamefully excluded from the society of the holy. There one sees the priests who preside over each chariot exhort every one to penitence, to confession of faults, to the resolution of better life! There one sees old people, young people, little children, calling on the Lord with a suppliant voice, and uttering to Him, from the depth of the heart, sobs and sighs with words of glory and praise! After the people, warned by the sound of trumpets and the sight of banners, have resumed their road, the march is made with such ease that no obstacle can retard it ... When they have reached the church they arrange the wagons about it like a spiritual camp, and during the whole night they celebrate the watch by hymns and canticles. On each waggon they light tapers and lamps; they place there the infirm and sick, and bring them the precious relics of the Saints for their relief. Afterwards the priests and clerics close the ceremony by processions which the people follow with devout heart, imploring the clemency of the Lord and of his Blessed Mother for the recovery of the sick.

Of course, the Virgin was actually and constantly present during all this labour, and gave her assistance to it, but you would get no light on the architecture from listening to an account of her miracles, nor do they heighten the effect of popular faith. Without the conviction of her personal presence, men would not have been inspired; but, to us, it is rather the inspiration of the art which proves the Virgin's presence, and we can better see the conviction of it in the work than in the words. Every day, as the work went on, the Virgin was present, directing the architects, and it is this direction that we are going to study, if you have now got a realizing sense of what it meant. Without this sense, the church is dead. Most persons of a deeply religious nature would tell you emphatically that nine churches out of ten actually were dead-born, after the thirteenth century, and that church architecture became a pure matter of mechanism and mathematics; but that is a question for you to decide when you come to it; and the pleasure consists not in seeing the death, but in feeling the life.

Now let us look about!

CHAPTER VII: ROSES AND APSES

Like all great churches, that are not mere storehouses of theology, Chartres expressed, besides whatever else it meant, an emotion, the deepest man ever felt,—the struggle of his own littleness to grasp the infinite. You may, if you like, figure in it a mathematic formula of infinity,—the broken arch, our finite idea of space; the spire, pointing, with its converging lines, to unity beyond space; the sleepless, restless thrust of the vaults, telling the unsatisfied, incomplete, overstrained effort of man to rival the energy, intelligence, and purpose of God. Thomas Aquinas and the schoolmen tried to put it in words, but their Church is another chapter. In act, all man's work ends there;—mathematics, physics, chemistry, dynamics, optics, every sort of machinery science may invent,—to this favour come at last, as religion and philosophy did before science was born. All that the centuries can do is to express the idea differently:—a miracle or a dynamo; a dome or a coal-pit; a cathedral or a world's fair; and sometimes to confuse the two expressions together. The world's fair tends more and more vigorously to express the thought of infinite energy; the great cathedrals of the Middle Ages always reflected the industries and interests of a world's fair. Chartres showed it less than Laon or Paris, for Chartres was never a manufacturing town, but a shrine, such as Lourdes, where the Virgin was known to have done miracles, and had been seen in person; but still the shrine turned itself into a market and created valuable industries. Indeed, this was the chief objection which Saint Paul made to Ephesus and Saint

Bernard to the cathedrals. They were in some ways more industrial than religious. The mere masonry and structure made a vast market for labour; the fixed metalwork and woodwork were another; but the decoration was by far the greatest. The wood-carving, the glass windows, the sculpture, inside and out, were done mostly in workshops on the spot, but besides these fixed objects, precious works of the highest perfection filled the church treasuries. Their money value was great then; it is greater now. No world's fair is likely to do better to- day. After five hundred years of spoliation, these objects fill museums still, and are bought with avidity at every auction, at prices continually rising and quality steadily falling, until a bit of twelfth-century glass would be a trouvaille like an emerald; a tapestry earlier than 1600 is not for mere tourists to hope; an enamel, a missal, a crystal, a cup, an embroidery of the Middle Ages belongs only to our betters, and almost invariably, if not to the State, to the rich Jews, whose instinctive taste has seized the whole field of art which rested on their degradation. Royalty and feudality spent their money rather on arms and clothes. The Church alone was universal patron, and the Virgin was the dictator of taste.

With the Virgin's taste, during her regency, critics never find fault. One cannot know its whole magnificence, but one can accept it as a matter of faith and trust, as one accepts all her other miracles without cavilling over small details of fact. The period of eighteenth-century scepticism about such matters and the bourgeois taste of Voltaire and Diderot have long since passed, with the advent of a scientific taste still more miraculous; the whole world of the Virgin's art, catalogued in the "Dictionnaire du Mobilier Francais" in six volumes by Viollet-le-Duc; narrated as history by M. Labarte, M. Molinier, M. Paul Lacroix; catalogued in museums by M. du Sommerard and a score of others, in works almost as costly as the subjects,—all the vast variety of bric-a-brac, useful or ornamental, belonging to the Church, increased enormously by the insatiable, universal, private demands for imagery, in ivory, wood, metal, stone, for every room in every house, or hung about every neck, or stuck on every hat, made a market such as artists never knew before or since, and such as instantly explains to the practical American not only the reason for the Church's tenacity of life, but also the inducements for its plunder. The Virgin especially required all the resources of art, and the highest. Notre Dame of Chartres would have laughed at Notre Dame of Paris if she had detected an economy in her robes; Notre Dame of Rheims or Rouen would have derided Notre Dame of Amiens if she had shown a feminine, domestic, maternal turn toward cheapness. The Virgin was never cheap. Her great ceremonies were as splendid as her rank of Queen in Heaven and on Earth required; and as her procession wound its way along the aisles, through the crowd of her subjects, up to the high altar, it was impossible then, and not altogether easy now, to resist the rapture of her radiant presence. Many a young person, and now and then one who is not in first youth, witnessing the sight in the religious atmosphere of such a church as this, without a suspicion of susceptibility, has suddenly seen what Paul saw on the road to Damascus, and has fallen on his face with the crowd, grovelling at the foot of the Cross, which, for the first time in his life, he feels.

If you want to know what churches were made for, come down here on some great festival of the Virgin, and give yourself up to it; but come alone! That kind of knowledge cannot be taught and can seldom be shared. We are not now seeking religion; indeed, true religion generally comes unsought. We are trying only to feel Gothic art. For us, the world is not a schoolroom or a pulpit, but a stage, and the stage is the highest yet seen on earth. In this church the old Romanesque leaps into the Gothic under our eyes; of a sudden, between the portal and the shrine, the infinite rises into a new expression, always a rare and excellent miracle in thought. The two expressions are nowhere far apart; not further than the Mother from the Son. The new artist drops unwillingly the hand of his father or his grandfather; he looks back, from every corner of his own work, to see whether it goes with the old. He will not part with the western portal or the lancet windows; he holds close to the round columns of the choir; he would have kept the round arch if he could, but the round arch was unable to do the work; it could not rise; so he broke it, lifted the vaulting, threw out flying buttresses, and satisfied the Virgin's wish.

The matter of Gothic vaulting, with its two weak points, the flying buttress and the false, wooden shelter-roof, is the bete noire of the Beaux Arts. The duty of defence does not lie on tourists, who are at best hardly able to understand what it matters whether a wall is buttressed without or within, and whether a roof is single or double. No one objects to the dome of Saint Peter's. No one finds fault with the Pont Neuf. Yet it is true that the Gothic architect showed contempt for facts. Since he could not support a heavy stone vault on his light columns, he built the lightest possible stone vault and protected it with a wooden shelter-roof which constantly burned. The lightened vaults were still too heavy for the walls and columns, so the architect threw out buttress beyond buttress resting on separate foundations, exposed to extreme inequalities of weather, and liable to multiplied chances of accident. The results were certainly disastrous. The roofs burned; the walls yielded.

Flying buttresses were not a necessity. The Merveille had none; the Angevin school rather affected to do without them; Albi had none; Assisi stands up independent; but they did give support wherever the architect wanted it and nowhere else; they were probably cheap; and they were graceful. Whatever expression they gave to a church, at least it was not that of a fortress. Amiens and Albi are different religions. The expression concerns us; the construction concerns the Beaux Arts. The problem of permanent equilibrium which distresses the builder of arches is a technical matter which does not worry, but only amuses, us who sit in the audience and look with delight at the theatrical stage-decoration of the Gothic vault; the astonishing feat of building up a skeleton of stone ribs and vertebrae, on which every pound of weight is adjusted, divided, and carried down from level to level till it touches ground at a distance as a bird would alight. If any stone in any part, from apex to foundation, weathers or gives way, the whole must yield, and the charge for repairs is probably great, but, on the best building the Ecole des Beaux Arts can build, the charge for repairs is not to be wholly ignored, and at least the Cathedral of Chartres, in spite of terribly hard usage, is as solid to-day as when it was built, and as plumb, without crack or crevice. Even the towering fragment at Beauvais, poorly built from the first, which has broken down oftener than most Gothic structures, and seems ready to crumble again whenever the wind blows over its windy plains, has managed to survive, after a fashion, six or seven hundred years, which is all that our generation had a right to ask.

The vault of Beauvais is nearly one hundred and sixty feet high (48 metres), and was cheaply built. The vault of Saint Peter's at Rome is nearly one hundred and fifty feet (45 metres). That of Amiens is one hundred and forty-four feet (44 metres). Rheims, Bourges, and Chartres are nearly the same height; at the entrance, one hundred and twenty-two feet. Paris is one hundred and ten feet. The Abbe Bulteau is responsible for these measurements; but at Chartres, as in several very old churches, the nave slopes down to the entrance, because—as is said—pilgrims came in such swarms that they were obliged to sleep in the church, and the nave had to be sluiced with water to clean it. The true height of Chartres, at the croisee of nave and transept, is as near as possible one hundred and twenty feet (36.55 metres).

The measured height is the least interest of a church. The architect's business is to make a small building look large, and his failures are in large buildings which he makes to look small. One chief beauty of the Gothic is to exaggerate height, and one of its most curious qualities is its success in imposing an illusion of size. Without leaving the heart of Paris any one can study this illusion in the two great churches of Notre Dame and Saint-Sulpice; for Saint-Sulpice is as lofty as Notre Dame in vaulting, and larger in its other dimensions, besides being, in its style, a fine building; yet its Roman arches show, as if they were of the eleventh century, why the long, clean, unbroken, refined lines of the Gothic, curving to points, and leading the eye with a sort of compulsion to the culminating point above, should have made an architectural triumph that carried all Europe off its feet with delight. The world had seen nothing to approach it except, perhaps, in the dome of Sancta Sophia in Constantinople; and the discovery came at a moment when Europe was making its most united and desperate struggle to attain the kingdom of Heaven.

According to Viollet-le-Duc, Chartres was the final triumph of the experiment on a very great scale, for Chartres has never been altered and never needed to be strengthened. The flying buttresses of Chartres answered their purpose, and if it were not a matter of pure construction it would be worth while to read what Viollet-le- Duc says about them (article, "Arcs-boutants"). The vaulting above is heavy, about fifteen inches thick; the buttressing had also to be heavy; and to lighten it, the architect devised an amusing sort of arcades, applied on his outside buttresses. Throughout the church, everything was solid beyond all later custom, so that architects would have to begin by a study of the crypt which came down from the eleventh century so strongly built that it still carries the church without a crack in its walls; but if we went down into it, we should understand nothing; so we will begin, as we did outside, at the front.

A single glance shows what trouble the architect had with the old facade and towers, and what temptation to pull them all down. One cannot quite say that he has spoiled his own church in trying to save what he could of the old, but if he did not quite spoil it, he saved it only by the exercise of an amount of intelligence that we shall never learn enough to feel our incapacity to understand. True ignorance approaches the infinite more nearly than any amount of knowledge can do, and, in our case, ignorance is fortified by a certain element of nineteenth-century indifference which refuses to be interested in what it cannot understand; a violent reaction from the thirteenth century which cared little to comprehend anything except the incomprehensible. The architect at Chartres was required by the Virgin to provide more space for her worshippers within the church, without destroying the old portal and fleche which she loved. That this order came directly from the Virgin, may be taken for granted. At Chartres, one sees everywhere the Virgin, and nowhere any rival authority; one sees her give orders, and architects obey them; but very rarely a hesitation as though the architect were deciding for himself. In his western front, the architect has obeyed orders so literally that he has not even taken the trouble to apologize for leaving unfinished the details which, if he had been responsible for them, would have been his anxious care. He has gone to the trouble of moving the heavy doorways forward, so that the chapels in the towers, which were meant to open on a porch, now open into the nave, and the nave itself has, in appearance, two more spans than in the old church; but the work shows blind obedience, as though he were doing his best to please the Virgin without trying to please himself. Probably he could in no case have done much to help the side aisles in their abrupt collision with the solid walls of the two towers, but he might at least have brought the vaulting of his two new bays, in the nave, down to the ground, and finished it. The vaulting is awkward in these two bays, and yet he has taken great trouble to effect what seems at first a small matter. Whether the great rose window was an afterthought or not can never be known, but any one can see with a glass, and better on the architectural plan, that the vaulting of the main church was not high enough to admit the great rose, and that the architect has had to slope his two tower-spans upward. So great is the height that you cannot see this difference of level very plainly even with a glass, but on the plans it seems to amount to several feet; perhaps a metre. The architect has managed to deceive our eyes, in order to enlarge the rose; but you can see as plainly as though he were here to tell you, that, like a great general, he has concentrated his whole energy on the rose, because the Virgin has told him that the rose symbolized herself, and that the light and splendour of her appearance in the west were to redeem all his awkwardnesses.

Of course this idea of the Virgin's interference sounds to you a mere bit of fancy, and that is an account which may be settled between the Virgin and you; but even twentieth-century eyes can see that the rose redeems everything, dominates everything, and gives character to the whole church.

In view of the difficulties which faced the artist, the rose is inspired genius,—the kind of genius which Shakespeare showed when he took some other man's play, and adapted it. Thus far, it shows its power chiefly by the way it comes forward and takes possession of the west front, but if you want a foot-rule to measure by, you may mark that the old, twelfth-century lancet-windows below it are not exactly in its axis. At the outset, in the original plan of 1090, or thereabouts, the old tower—the southern tower—was given greater width than the northern. Such inequalities were common in the early churches, and so is a great deal of dispute in modern books whether they were accidental or intentional, while no one denies that they are amusing. In these towers the difference is not great,—perhaps fourteen or fifteen inches,—but it caused the architect to correct it, in order to fit his front to the axis of the church, by throwing his entrance six or seven inches to the south, and narrowing to that extent the south door and south lancet. The effect was bad, even then, and went far to ruin the south window; but when, after the fire of 1194, the architect inserted his great rose, filling every inch of possible space between the lancet and the arch of the vault, he made another correction which threw his rose six or seven inches out of axis with the lancets. Not one person in a hundred thousand would notice it, here in the interior, so completely are we under the control of the artist and the Virgin; but it is a measure of the power of the rose.

Looking farther, one sees that the rose-motive, which so dominates the west front, is carried round the church, and comes to another outburst of splendour in the transepts. This leads back to fenestration on a great scale, which is a terribly ambitious flight for tourists; all the more, because here the tourist gets little help from the architect, who, in modern times, has seldom the opportunity to study the subject at all, and accepts as solved the problems of early Gothic fenestration. One becomes pedantic and pretentious at the very sound of the word, which is an intolerable piece of pedantry in itself; but Chartres is all windows, and its windows were as triumphant as its Virgin, and were one of her miracles. One can no more overlook the windows of Chartres than the glass which is in them. We have already looked at the windows of Mantes; we have seen what happened to the windows at Paris. Paris had at one leap risen twenty-five feet higher than Noyon, and even at Noyon, the architect, about 1150, had been obliged to invent new fenestration. Paris and Mantes, twenty years later, made another effort, which proved a failure. Then the architect of Chartres, in 1195, added ten feet more to his vault, and undertook, once for all, to show how a great cathedral should be lighted. As an architectural problem, it passes far beyond our powers of understanding, even when solved; but we can always turn to see what the inevitable Viollet-le-Duc says about its solution at Chartres:—

Toward the beginning of the thirteenth century, the architect of the Cathedral of Chartres sought out entirely new window combinations to light the nave from above. Below, in the side aisles he kept to the customs of the times; that is, he opened pointed windows which did not wholly fill the spaces between the piers; he wanted, or was willing to leave here below, the effect of a wall. But in the upper part of his building we see that he changed the system; he throws a round arch directly across from one pier to the next; then, in the enormous space which remains within each span, he inserts two large pointed windows surmounted by a great rose ... We recognize in this construction of Notre Dame de Chartres a boldness, a force, which contrast with the fumbling of the architects in the Ile de France and Champagne. For the first time one sees at Chartres the builder deal frankly with the clerestory, or upper fenestration, occupying the whole width of the arches, and taking the arch of the vault as the arch of the window. Simplicity of construction, beauty in form, strong workmanship, structure true and solid, judicious choice of material, all the characteristics of good work, unite in this magnificent specimen of architecture at the beginning of the thirteenth century.

Viollet-le-Duc does not call attention to a score of other matters which the architect must have had in his mind, such as the distribution of light, and the relations of one arrangement with another: the nave with the aisles, and both with the transepts, and all with the choir. Following him, we must take the choir separately, and the aisles and chapels of the apse also. One cannot hope to understand all the experiments and refinements of the artist, either in their successes or their failures, but, with diffidence, one may ask one's self whether the beauty of the arrangement, as compared with the original arrangement in Paris, did not consist in retaining the rose-motive throughout, while throwing the whole upper wall into window. Triumphant as the clerestory windows are, they owe their charm largely to their roses, as you see by looking at the same scheme applied on a larger scale on the transept fronts; and then, by taking stand under the croisée, and looking at all in succession as a whole.

The rose window was not Gothic but Romanesque, and needed a great deal of coaxing to feel at home within the pointed arch. At first, the architects felt the awkwardness so strongly that they avoided it wherever they could. In the beautiful facade of Laon, one of the chief beauties is the setting of the rose under a deep round arch. The western roses of Mantes and Paris are treated in the same way, although a captious critic might complain that their treatment is not so effective or so logical. Rheims boldly imprisoned the roses within the pointed arch; but Amiens, toward 1240, took refuge in the same square exterior setting that was preferred, in 1200, here at Chartres; and in the interior of Amiens the round arch of the rose is the last vault of the nave, seen through a vista of pointed vaults, as it is here. All these are supposed to be among the chief beauties of the Gothic facade, although the Gothic architect, if he had been a man of logic, would have clung to his lines, and put a pointed window in his front, as in fact he did at Coutances. He felt the value of the rose in art, and perhaps still more in religion, for the rose was Mary's emblem. One is fairly sure that the great Chartres rose of the west front was put there to please her, since it was to be always before her eyes, the most conspicuous object she would see from the high altar, and therefore the most carefully considered ornament in the whole church, outside the choir. The mere size proves the importance she gave it. The exterior diameter is nearly forty-four feet (13.36 metres). The nave of Chartres is, next perhaps to the nave of Angers, the widest of all Gothic naves; about fifty-three feet (16.31 metres); and the rose takes every inch it can get of this enormous span. The value of the rose, among architects of the time, was great, since it was the only part of the church that Villard de Honnecourt sketched; and since his time, it has been drawn and redrawn, described and commented by generations of architects till it has become as classic as the Parthenon.

Yet this Chartres rose is solid, serious, sedate, to a degree unusual in its own age; it is even more Romanesque than the pure Romanesque roses. At Beauvais you must stop a moment to look at a Romanesque rose on the transept of the Church of Saint-Etienne; Viollet-le-Duc mentions it, with a drawing (article, "Pignon"), as not earlier than the year 1100, therefore about a century earlier than the rose of Chartres; it is not properly a rose, but a wheel of fortune, with figures climbing up and falling over. Another supposed twelfth-century rose is at Etampes, which goes with that of Laon and Saint-Leu-d'Esserent and Mantes. The rose of Chartres is so much the most serious of them all that Viollet-le-Duc has explained it by its material,—the heavy stone of Bercheres;—but the material was not allowed to affect the great transept roses, and the architect made his material yield to his object wherever he thought it worth while. Standing under the central croisee, you can see all three roses by simply turning your head. That on the north, the Rose de France, was built, or planned, between 1200 and 1210, in the reign of Philip Augustus, since the porch outside, which would be a later construction, was begun by 1212. The Rose de France is the same in diameter as the western rose, but lighter, and built of lighter stone. Opposite the Rose de France stands, on the south front, Pierre Mauclerc's Rose de Dreux, of the same date, with the same motive, but even lighter; more like a rose and less like a wheel. All three roses must have been planned at about the same time, perhaps by the same architect, within the same workshop; yet the western rose stands quite apart, as though it had been especially designed to suit the twelfth-century facade and portal which it rules. Whether this was really the artist's idea is a question that needs the artist to answer; but that this is the effect, needs no expert to prove; it stares one in the face. Within and without, one feels that the twelfth-century spirit is respected and preserved with the same religious feeling which obliged the architect to injure his own work by sparing that of his grandfathers.

Conspicuous, then, in the west front are two feelings:—respect for the twelfth-century work, and passion for the rose fenestration; both subordinated to the demand for light. If it worries you to have to believe that these three things are in fact one; that the architect is listening, like the stone Abraham, for orders from the Virgin, while he caresses and sacrifices his child; that Mary and not her architects built this facade; if the divine intention seems to you a needless impertinence, you can soon get free from it by going to any of the later churches, where you will not be forced to see any work but that of the architect's compasses. According to Viollet-le-Duc, the inspiration ceased about 1250, or, as the Virgin would have dated it, on the death of Blanche of Castile in 1252. The work of Chartres, where her own hand is plainly shown, belongs in feeling, if not in execution, to the last years of the twelfth century (1195-1200). The great western rose which gives the motive for the whole decoration and is repeated in the great roses of the transepts, marks the Virgin's will,—the taste and knowledge of "cele qui la rose est des roses," or, if you prefer the Latin of Adam de Saint-Victor, the hand of her who is "Super rosam rosida."

All this is easy; but if you really cannot see the hand of Mary herself in these broad and public courts, which were intended, not for her personal presence, but for the use of her common people, you had better stop here, and not venture into the choir. Great halls seem to have been easy architecture. Naves and transepts were not often failures; facades and even towers and fleches are invariably more or less successful because they are more or less balanced, mathematical, calculable products of reason and thought. The most serious difficulties began only with the choir, and even then did not become desperate until the architect reached the curve of the apse, with its impossible vaultings, its complicated lines, its cross-thrusts, its double problems, internal and external, its defective roofing and unequal lighting. A perfect Gothic apse was impossible; an apse that satisfied perfectly its principal objects was rare; the simplest and cheapest solution was to have no apse at all, and that was the English scheme, which was tried also at Laon; a square, flat wall and window. If the hunt for Norman towers offered a summer's amusement, a hunt for apses would offer an education, but it would lead far out of France. Indeed, it would be simpler to begin at once with Sancta Sophia at Constantinople, San Vitale at Ravenna and Monreale at Palermo, and the churches at Torcello and Murano, and San Marco at Venice; and admit that no device has ever equalled the startling and mystical majesty of the Byzantine half-dome, with its marvellous mosaic Madonna dominating the church, from the entrance, with her imperial and divine presence. Unfortunately, the northern churches needed light, and the northern architects turned their minds to a desperate effort for a new apse.

The scheme of the cathedral at Laon seems to have been rejected unanimously; the bare, flat wall at the end of the choir was an eyesore; it was quite bad enough at the end of the nave, and became annoying at the end of the transepts, so that at Noyon and Soissons the architect, with a keen sense of interior form, had rounded the transept ends; but, though external needs might require a square transept, the unintelligence of the flat wall became insufferable at the east end. Neither did the square choir suit the church ceremonies and processions, or offer the same advantages of arrangement, as the French understood them. With one voice, the French architects seem to have rejected the Laon experiment, and turned back to a solution taken directly from the Romanesque.

[Illustration with caption: SAINT-MARTIN-DES-CHAMPS]

Quite early—in the eleventh century—a whole group of churches had been built in Auvergne,— at Clermont and Issoire, for example,— possibly by one architect, with a circular apse, breaking out into five apsidal chapels. Tourists who get down as far south as Toulouse see another example of this Romanesque apse in the famous Church of Saint Sernin, of the twelfth century; and few critics take offence at one's liking it. Indeed, as far as concerns the exterior, one might even risk thinking it more charming than the exterior of any Gothic apse ever built. Many of these Romanesque apses of the eleventh and twelfth centuries still remain in France, showing themselves in unsuspected parish churches, here and there, but always a surprise for their quiet, unobtrusive grace, making a harmony with the Romanesque tower, if there is one, into which they rise, as at Saint Sernin; but all these churches had only one aisle, and, in the interior, there came invariable trouble when the vaults rose in height. The architect of Chartres, in 1200, could get no direct help from these, or even from Paris which was a beautifully perfect apse, but had no apsidal chapels. The earliest apse that could have served as a suggestion for Chartres—or, at least, as a point of observation for us—was that of the Abbey Church of Saint- Martin-des-Champs, which we went to see in Paris, and which is said to date from about 1150.

Here is a circular choir, surrounded by two rows of columns, irregularly spaced, with circular chapels outside, which seems to have been more or less what the architect of Chartres, for the Virgin's purposes, had set his heart on obtaining. Closely following the scheme of Saint-Martin-des-Champs came the scheme of the Abbey Church at Vezelay, built about 1160-80. Here the vaulting sprang directly from the last arch of the choir, as is shown on the plan, and bearing first on the light columns of the choir, which were evenly spaced, then fell on a row of heavier columns outside, which were also evenly spaced, and came to rest at last on massive piers, between which were five circular chapels. The plan shows at a glance that this arrangement stretched the second row of columns far apart, and that a church much larger than Vezelay would need to space them so much farther apart that the arch uniting them would have to rise indefinitely; while, if beyond this, another aisle were added outside, the piers finally would require impossible vaulting.

[Illustration with caption: VEZELAY]

The problem stood thus when the great cathedrals were undertaken, and the architect of Paris boldly grappled with the double aisle on a scale requiring a new scheme. Here, in spite of the most virtuous resolutions not to be technical, we must attempt a technicality, because without it, one of the most interesting eccentricities of Chartres would be lost. Once more, Viollet-le-Duc:—

As the architect did not want to give the interior bays of the apse spaces between the columns (AA) less than that of the parallel bays (BB), it followed that the first radiating bay gave a first space (LMGH) which was difficult to vault, and a second space (HGEF) which was impossible; for how establish an arch from F to E? Even if round, its key would have risen much higher than the key of the pointed archivolt LM. As the second radiating bay opened out still wider, the difficulty was increased. The builder therefore inserted the two intermediate pillars O and P between the columns of the second aisle (H, G, and I); which he supported, in the outside wall of the church, by one corresponding pier (Q) in the first bay of the apse, and by two similar piers (R and S) in the second bay.

[Illustration with caption: NOTRE DAME DE PARIS]

"There is no need to point out," continued Viollet-le-Duc, as though he much suspected that there might be need of pointing out, "what skill this system showed and how much the art of architecture had already been developed in the Ile de France toward the end of the twelfth century; to what an extent the unity of arrangement and style preoccupied the artists of that province."

In fact, the arrangement seems mathematically and technically perfect. At all events, we know too little to criticize it. Yet one would much like to be told why it was not repeated by any other architect or in any other church. Apparently the Parisians themselves were not quite satisfied with it, since they altered it a hundred years later, in 1296, in order to build out chapels between the piers. As the architects of each new cathedral had, in the interval, insisted on apsidal chapels, one may venture to guess that the Paris scheme hampered the services.

At Chartres the church services are Mary's own tastes; the church is Mary; and the chapels are her private rooms. She was not pleased with the arrangements made for her in her palace at Paris;

they were too architectural; too regular and mathematical; too popular; too impersonal; and she rather abruptly ordered her architect at Chartres to go back to the old arrangement. The apse at Paris was hardly covered with its leading before the architect of Chartres adopted a totally new plan, which, according to Viollet-le-Duc, does him little credit, but which was plainly imposed on him, like the twelfth-century portal. Not only had it nothing of the mathematical correctness and precision of the Paris scheme, easy to understand and imitate, but it carried even a sort of violence—a wrench—in its system, as though the Virgin had said, with her grand Byzantine air:—I will it!

[Illustration with caption: CHARTRES]

"At Chartres," said Viollet-le-Duc, "the choir of the Cathedral presents a plan which does no great honour to its architect. There is want of accord between the circular apse and the parallel sides of the sanctuary; the spacings of the columns of the second collateral are loose (laches); the vaults quite poorly combined; and in spite of the great width of the spaces between the columns of the second aisle, the architect had still to narrow those between the interior columns."

The plan shows that, from the first, the architect must have deliberately rejected the Paris scheme; he must have begun by narrowing the spaces between his inner columns; then, with a sort of violence, he fitted on his second row of columns; and, finally, he showed his motive by constructing an outer wall of an original or unusual shape. Any woman would see at once the secret of all this ingenuity and effort. The Chartres apse, enormous in size and width, is exquisitely lighted. Here, as everywhere throughout the church, the windows give the law, but here they actually take place of law. The Virgin herself saw to the lighting of her own boudoir. According to Viollet-le-Duc, Chartres differs from all the other great cathedrals by being built not for its nave or even for its choir, but for its apse; it was planned not for the people or the court, but for the Queen; not a church but a shrine; and the shrine is the apse where the Queen arranged her light to please herself and not her architect, who had already been sacrificed at the western portal and who had a free hand only in the nave and transepts where the Queen never went, and which, from her own apartment, she did not even see.

[Illustration with caption: LAON]

This is, in effect, what Viollet-le-Duc says in his professional language, which is perhaps—or sounds—more reasonable to tourists, whose imaginations are hardly equal to the effort of fancying a real deity. Perhaps, indeed, one might get so high as to imagine a real Bishop of Laon, who should have ordered his architect to build an enormous hall of religion, to rival the immense abbeys of the day, and to attract the people, as though it were a clubroom. There they were to see all the great sights; church ceremonies; theatricals; political functions; there they were to do business, and frequent society. They were to feel at home in their church because it was theirs, and did not belong to a priesthood or to Rome. Jealousy of Rome was a leading motive of Gothic architecture, and Rome repaid it in full. The Bishop of Laon conceded at least a transept to custom or tradition, but the Archbishop of Bourges abolished even the transept, and the great hall had no special religious expression except in the circular apse with its chapels which Laon had abandoned. One can hardly decide whether Laon or Bourges is the more popular, industrial, political, or, in other words, the less religious; but the Parisians, as the plan of Viollet-le-Duc has shown, were quite as advanced as either, and only later altered their scheme into one that provided chapels for religious service.

[Illustration with caption: BOURGES]

[Illustration with caption: AMIENS]

Amiens and Beauvais have each seven chapels, but only one aisle, so that they do not belong in the same class with the apses of Paris, Bourges, and Chartres, though the plans are worth studying for comparison, since they show how many-sided the problem was, and how far from satisfied the architects were with their own schemes. The most interesting of all, for comparison with Chartres, is Le Mans, where the apsidal chapels are carried to fanaticism, while the vaulting seems to be reasonable enough, and the double aisle successfully managed, if Viollet-le-Duc permits ignorant people to form an opinion on architectural dogma. For our purposes, the architectural dogma may stand, and the Paris scheme may be taken for granted, as alone correct and orthodox; all that Viollet-le-Duc teaches is that the Chartres scheme is unorthodox, not to say heretical; and this is the point on which his words are most interesting.

[Illustration with caption: BEAUVAIS]

The church at Chartres belonged not to the people, not to the priesthood, and not even to Rome; it belonged to the Virgin. "Here the religious influence appears wholly; three large chapels in the apse; four others less pronounced; double aisles of great width round the choir; vast transepts! Here the church ceremonial could display all its pomp; the choir, more than at Paris, more than at Bourges, more than at Soissons, and especially more than at Laon, is the principal object; for it, the church is built."

[Illustration with caption: LE MANS]

One who is painfully conscious of ignorance, and who never would dream of suggesting a correction to anybody, may not venture to suggest an idea of any sort to an architect; but if it were allowed to paraphrase Viollet-le-Duc's words into a more or less emotional or twelfth-century form, one might say, after him, that, compared with Paris or Laon, the Chartres apse shows the same genius that is shown in the Chartres rose; the same large mind that overrules,— the same strong will that defies difficulties. The Chartres apse is as entertaining as all the other Gothic apses together, because it overrides the architect. You may, if you really have no imagination whatever, reject the idea that the Virgin herself made the plan; the feebleness of our fancy is now congenital, organic, beyond stimulant or strychnine, and we shrink like sensitive-plants from the touch of a vision or spirit; but at least one can still sometimes feel a woman's taste, and in the apse of Chartres one feels nothing else.

[Illustration with caption: CHARTRES]

CHAPTER VIII: THE TWELFTH-CENTURY GLASS

At last we are face to face with the crowning glory of Chartres. Other churches have glass,— quantities of it, and very fine,—but we have been trying to catch a glimpse of the glory which stands behind the glass of Chartres, and gives it quality and feeling of its own. For once the architect is useless and his explanations are pitiable; the painter helps still less; and the decorator, unless he works in glass, is the poorest guide of all, while, if he works in glass, he is sure to lead wrong; and all of them may toil until Pierre Mauclerc's stone Christ comes to life, and condemns them among the unpardonable sinners on the southern portal, but neither they nor any other artist will ever create another Chartres. You had better stop here, once for all, unless you are willing to feel that Chartres was made what it is, not by artist, but by the Virgin.

If this imperial presence is stamped on the architecture and the sculpture with an energy not to be mistaken, it radiates through the glass with a light and colour that actually blind the true servant of Mary. One becomes, sometimes, a little incoherent in talking about it; one is ashamed to be as extravagant as one wants to be; one has no business to labour painfully to explain and prove to one's self what is as clear as the sun in the sky; one loses temper in reasoning about what can only be felt, and what ought to be felt instantly, as it was in the twelfth century, even by the truie qui file and the ane qui vielle. Any one should feel it that wishes; any one who does not wish to feel it can let it alone. Still, it may be that not one tourist in a hundred—perhaps not one in a thousand of the English-speaking race—does feel it, or can feel it even when explained to him, for we have lost many senses.

Therefore, let us plod on, laboriously proving God, although, even to Saint Bernard and Pascal, God was incapable of proof; and using such material as the books furnish for help. It is not much. The French have been shockingly negligent of their greatest artistic glory. One knows not even where to seek. One must go to the National Library and beg as a special favour permission to look at the monumental work of M. Lasteyrie, if one wishes to make even a beginning of the study of French glass. Fortunately there exists a fragment of a great work which the Government began, but never completed, upon Chartres; and another, quite indispensable, but not official, upon Bourges; while Viollet-le-Duc's article "Vitrail" serves as guide to the whole. Ottin's book "Le Vitrail" is convenient. Male's volume "L'Art Religieux" is essential. In English, Westlake's "History of Design" is helpful. Perhaps, after reading all that is readable, the best hope will be to provide the best glasses with the largest possible field; and, choosing an hour when the church is empty, take seat about halfway up the nave, facing toward the western entrance with a morning light, so that the glass of the western windows shall not stand in direct sun.

The glass of the three lancets is the oldest in the cathedral. If the portal beneath it, with the sculpture, was built in the twenty or thirty years before 1150, the glass could not be much later. It goes with the Abbe Suger's glass at Saint-Denis, which was surely made as early as 1140-50, since the Abbe was a long time at work on it, before he died in 1152. Their perfection proves, what his biographer asserted, that the Abbe Suger spent many years as well as much money on his windows at Saint-Denis, and the specialists affirm that the three lancets at Chartres are quite as good as what remains of Suger's work. Viollet-le-Duc and M. Paul Durand, the Government expert, are positive that this glass is the finest ever made, as far as record exists; and that the northern lancet representing the Tree of Jesse stands at the head of all glasswork whatever. The windows claim, therefore, to be the most splendid colour decoration the world ever saw, since no other material, neither silk nor gold, and no opaque colour laid on with a brush, can compare with translucent glass, and even the Ravenna mosaics or Chinese porcelains are darkness beside them.

The claim may not be modest, but it is none of ours. Viollet-le-Duc must answer for his own sins, and he chose the lancet window of the Tree of Jesse for the subject of his lecture on glass in general, as the most complete and perfect example of this greatest decorative art. Once more, in following him, one is dragged, in spite of one's self, into technique, and, what is worse, into a colour world whose technique was forgotten five hundred years ago. Viollet-le-Duc tried to recover it. "After studying our best French windows," he cautiously suggests that "one might maintain," as their secret of harmony, that "the first condition for an artist in glass is to know how to manage blue. The blue is the light in windows, and light has value only by opposition." The radiating power of blue is, therefore, the starting-point, and on this matter Viollet-le-Duc has much to say which a student would need to master; but a tourist never should study, or he ceases to be a tourist; and it is enough for us if we know that, to get the value they wanted, the artists hatched their blues with lines, covered their surface with figures as though with screens, and tied their blue within its own field with narrow circlets of white or yellow, which, in their turn, were beaded to fasten the blue still more firmly in its place. We have chiefly to remember the law that blue is light:—

But also it is that luminous colour which gives value to all others. If you compose a window in which there shall be no blue, you will get a dirty or dull (blafard) or crude surface which the eye will instantly avoid; but if you put a few touches of blue among all these tones, you will immediately get striking effects if not skilfully conceived harmony. So the composition of blue glass singularly preoccupied the glassworkers of the twelfth and thirteenth centuries. If there is only one red, two yellows, two or three purples, and two or three greens at the most, there are infinite shades of blue, ... and these blues are placed with a very delicate observation of the effects they should produce on other tones, and other tones on them.

Viollet-le-Duc took the window of the Tree of Jesse as his first illustration of the rule, for the reason that its blue ground is one continuous strip from top to bottom, with the subordinate red on either side, and a border uniting the whole so plainly that no one can fail to see its object or its method.

The blue tone of the principal subject [that is to say, the ground of the Tree of Jesse] has commanded the tonality of all the rest. This medium was necessary to enable the luminous splendour to display its energy. This primary condition had dictated the red ground for the prophets, and the return to the blue on reaching the outside semicircular band. To give full value both to the vigour of the red, and to the radiating transparency of the blue, the ground of the corners is put in emerald green; but then, in the corners themselves, the blue is recalled and is given an additional solidity of value by the delicate ornamentation of the squares.

This translation is very free, but one who wants to know these windows must read the whole article, and read it here in the church, the Dictionary in one hand, and binocle in the other, for the binocle is more important than the Dictionary when it reaches the complicated border which repeats in detail the colour-scheme of the centre:—

The border repeats all the tones allotted to the principal subjects, but by small fragments, so that this border, with an effect both solid and powerful, shall not enter into rivalry with the large arrangements of the central parts.

One would think this simple enough; easily tested on any illuminated manuscript, Arab, Persian, or Byzantine; verified by any Oriental rug, old or new; freely illustrated by any Chinese pattern on a Ming jar, or cloisonne vase; and offering a kind of alphabet for the shop-window of a Paris modiste. A strong red; a strong and a weak yellow; a strong and a weak purple; a strong and a weak green, are all to be tied together, given their values, and held in their places by blue. The thing seems simpler still when it appears that perspective is forbidden, and that these glass windows of the twelfth and thirteenth centuries, like Oriental rugs, imply a flat surface, a wall which must not be treated as open. The twelfth- century glassworker would sooner have worn a landscape on his back than have costumed his church with it; he would as soon have decorated his floors with painted holes as his walls. He wanted to keep the coloured window flat, like a rug hung on the wall.

The radiation of translucent colours in windows cannot be modified by the artist; all his talent consists in profiting by it, according to a given harmonic scheme on a single plane, like a rug, but not according to an effect of aerial perspective. Do what you like, a glass window never does and never can represent anything but a plane surface; its real virtues even exist only on that condition. Every attempt to present several planes to the eye is fatal to the harmony of colour, without producing any illusion in the spectator … Translucid painting can propose as its object only a design supporting as energetically as possible a harmony of colours.

Whether this law is absolute you can tell best by looking at modern glass which is mostly perspective; but, whether you like it or not, the matter of perspective does not enter into a twelfth-century window more than into a Japanese picture, and may be ignored. The decoration of the twelfth century, as far as concerns us, was intended only for one plane, and a window was another form of rug or embroidery or mosaic, hung on the wall for colour,—simple decoration to be seen as a whole. If the Tree of Jesse teaches anything at all, it is that the artist thought first of controlling his light, but he wanted to do it not in order to dim the colours; on the contrary, he toiled, like a jeweller setting diamonds and rubies, to increase their splendour. If his use of blue teaches this lesson, his use of green proves it. The outside border of the Tree of Jesse is a sort of sample which our schoolmaster Viollet-le-Duc sets, from which he requires us to study out the scheme, beginning with the treatment of light, and ending with the value of the emerald green ground in the corners.

Complicated as the border of the Tree of Jesse is, it has its mates in the borders of the two other twelfth-century windows, and a few of the thirteenth-century in the side aisles; but the southern of the three lancets shows how the artists dealt with a difficulty that upset their rule. The border of the southern window does not count as it should; something is wrong with it and a little study shows that the builder, and not the glassworker, was to blame. Owing to his miscalculation—if it was really a miscalculation—in the width of the southern tower, the builder economized six or eight inches in the southern door and lancet, which was enough to destroy the balance between the colour-values, as masses, of the south and north windows. The artist was obliged to choose whether he would sacrifice the centre or the border of his southern window, and decided that the windows could not be made to balance if he narrowed the centre, but that he must balance them by enriching the centre, and sacrificing the border. He has filled the centre with medallions as rich as he could make them, and these he has surrounded with borders, which are also enriched to the utmost; but these medallions with their borders spread across the whole window, and when you search with the binocle for the outside border, you see its pattern clearly only at the top and bottom. On the sides, at intervals of about two feet, the medallions cover and interrupt it; but this is partly corrected by making the border, where it is seen, so rich as to surpass any other in the cathedral, even that of the Tree of Jesse. Whether the artist has succeeded or not is a question for other artists—or for you, if you please—to decide; but apparently he did succeed, since no one has ever noticed the difficulty or the device.

The southern lancet represents the Passion of Christ. Granting to Viollet-le-Duc that the unbroken vertical colour-scheme of the Tree of Jesse made the more effective window, one might still ask whether the medallion-scheme is not the more interesting. Once past the workshop, there can be no question about it; the Tree of Jesse has the least interest of all the three windows. A genealogical tree has little value, artistic or other, except to those who belong in its branches, and the Tree of Jesse was put there, not to please us, but to please the Virgin. The Passion window was also put there to please her, but it tells a story, and does it in a way that has more novelty than the subject. The draughtsman who chalked out the design on the whitened table that served for his sketch-board was either a Greek, or had before him a Byzantine missal, or enamel or ivory. The first medallion on these legendary windows is the lower left-hand one, which begins the story or legend; here it represents Christ after the manner of the Greek Church. In the next medallion is the Last Supper; the fish on the dish is Greek. In the middle of the window, with the help of the binocle, you will see a Crucifixion, or even two, for on the left is Christ on the Cross, and on the right a Descent from the Cross; in this is the figure of man pulling out with pincers the nails which fasten Christ's feet; a figure unknown to Western religious art. The Noli Me Tangere, on the right, near the top, has a sort of Greek character. All the critics, especially M. Paul Durand, have noticed this Byzantine look, which is even more marked in the Suger window at Saint-Denis, so as to suggest that both are by the same hand, and that the hand of a Greek. If the artist was really a Greek, he has done work more beautiful than any left at Byzantium, and very far finer than anything in the beautiful work at Cairo, but although the figures and subjects are more or less Greek, like the sculptures on the portal, the art seems to be French.

Look at the central window! Naturally, there sits the Virgin, with her genealogical tree on her left, and her Son's testimony on her right to prove her double divinity. She is seated in the long halo; as, on the western portal, directly beneath her, her Son is represented in stone. Her crown and head, as well as that of the Child, are fourteenth-century restorations more or less like the original; but her cushioned throne and her robes of imperial state, as well as the flowered sceptre in either hand, are as old as the sculpture of the portal, and redolent of the first crusade. On either side of her, the Sun and the Moon offer praise; her two Archangels, Michael and Gabriel, with resplendent wings, offer not incense as in later times, but the two sceptres of spiritual and temporal power; while the Child in her lap repeats His Mother's action and even her features and expression. At first sight, one would take for granted that all this was pure Byzantium, and perhaps it is; but it has rather the look of Byzantium gallicized, and carried up to a poetic French ideal. At Saint-Denis the little figure of the Abbe Suger at the feet of the Virgin has a very Oriental look, and in the twin medallion the Virgin resembles greatly the Virgin of Chartres, yet, for us, until some specialist shows us the Byzantine original, the work is as thoroughly French as the fleches of the churches.

Byzantine art is altogether another chapter, and, if we could but take a season to study it in Byzantium, we might get great amusement; but the art of Chartres, even in 1100, was French and perfectly French, as the architecture shows, and the glass is even more French than the architecture, as you can detect in many other ways. Perhaps the surest evidence is the glass itself. The men who made it were not professionals but amateurs, who may have had some knowledge of enamelling, but who worked like jewellers, unused to glass, and with the refinement that a reliquary or a crozier required. The cost of these windows must have been extravagant; one is almost surprised that they are not set in gold rather than in lead. The Abbe Suger shirked neither trouble nor expense, and the only serious piece of evidence that this artist was a Greek is given by his biographer who unconsciously shows that the artist cheated him: "He sought carefully for makers of windows and workmen in glass of exquisite quality, especially in that made of sapphires in great abundance that were pulverized and melted up in the glass to give it the blue colour which he delighted to admire." The "materia saphirorum" was evidently something precious,—as precious as crude sapphires would have been,—and the words imply beyond question that the artist asked for sapphires and that Suger paid for them; yet all specialists agree that the stone known as sapphire, if ground, could not produce translucent colour at all. The blue which Suger loved, and which is probably the same as that of these Chartres windows, cannot be made out of sapphires. Probably the "materia saphirorum" means cobalt only, but whatever it was, the glassmakers seem to agree that this glass of 1140-50 is the best ever made. M. Paul Durand in his official report of 1881 said that these windows, both artistically and mechanically, were of the highest class: "I will also call attention to the fact that the glass and the execution of the painting are, materially speaking, of a quality much superior to windows of the thirteenth and fourteenth centuries. Having passed several months in contact with these precious works when I copied them, I was able to convince myself of their superiority in every particular, especially in the upper parts of the three windows." He said that they were perfect and irreproachable. The true enthusiast in glass would in the depths of his heart like to say outright that these three windows are worth more than all that the French have since done in colour, from that day to this; but the matter concerns us chiefly because it shows how French the experiment was, and how Suger's taste and wealth made it possible.

Certain it is, too, that the southern window—the Passion—was made on the spot, or near by, and fitted for the particular space with care proportionate to its cost. All are marked by the hand of the Chartres Virgin. They are executed not merely for her, but by her. At Saint-Denis the Abbe Suger appeared,—it is true that he was prostrate at her feet, but still he appeared. At Chartres no one—no suggestion of a human agency—was allowed to appear; the Virgin permitted no one to approach her, even to adore. She is enthroned above, as Queen and Empress and Mother, with the symbols of exclusive and universal power. Below her, she permitted the world to see the glories of her earthly life;—the Annunciation, Visitation, and Nativity; the Magi; King Herod; the Journey to Egypt; and the single medallion, which shows the gods of Egypt falling from their pedestals at her coming, is more entertaining than a whole picture-gallery of oil paintings.

In all France there exist barely a dozen good specimens of twelfth-century glass. Besides these windows at Chartres and the fragments at Saint-Denis, there are windows at Le Mans and Angers and bits at Vendome, Chalons, Poitiers, Rheims, and Bourges; here and there one happens on other pieces, but the earliest is the best, because the glass-makers were new at the work and spent on it an infinite amount of trouble and money which they found to be unnecessary as they gained experience. Even in 1200 the value of these windows was so well understood, relatively to new ones, that they were preserved with the greatest care. The effort to make such windows was never repeated. Their jewelled perfection did not suit the scale of the vast churches of the thirteenth century. By turning your head toward the windows of the side aisles, you can see the criticism which the later artists passed on the old work. They found it too refined, too brilliant, too jewel-like for the size of the new cathedral; the play of light and colour allowed the eye too little repose; indeed, the eye could not see their whole beauty, and half their value was thrown away in this huge stone setting. At best they must have seemed astray on the bleak, cold, windy plain of Beauce,—homesick for Palestine or Cairo,—yearning for Monreale or Venice,—but this is not our affair, and, under the protection of the Empress Virgin, Saint Bernard himself could have afforded to sin even to drunkenness of colour. With trifling expense of imagination one can still catch a glimpse of the crusades in the glory of the glass. The longer one looks into it, the more overpowering it becomes, until one begins almost to feel an echo of what our two hundred and fifty million arithmetical ancestors, drunk with the passion of youth and the splendour of the Virgin, have been calling to us from Mont-Saint-Michel and Chartres. No words and no wine could revive their emotions so vividly as they glow in the purity of the colours; the limpidity of the blues; the depth of the red; the intensity of the green; the complicated harmonies; the sparkle and splendour of the light; and the quiet and certain strength of the mass.

With too strong direct sun the windows are said to suffer, and become a cluster of jewels—a delirium of coloured light. The lines, too, have different degrees of merit. These criticisms seldom strike a chance traveller, but he invariably makes the discovery that the designs within the medallions are childish. He may easily correct them, if he likes, and see what would happen to the window; but although this is the alphabet of art, and we are past spelling words of one syllable, the criticism teaches at least one lesson. Primitive man seems to have had a natural colour-sense, instinctive like the scent of a dog. Society has no right to feel it as a moral reproach to be told that it has reached an age when it can no longer depend, as in childhood, on its taste, or smell, or sight, or hearing, or memory; the fact seems likely enough, and in no way sinful; yet society always denies it, and is invariably angry about it; and, therefore, one had better not say it. On the other hand, we can leave Delacroix and his school to fight out the battle they began against Ingres and his school, in French art, nearly a hundred years ago, which turned in substance on the same point. Ingres held that the first motive in colour-decoration was line, and that a picture which was well drawn was well enough coloured. Society seemed, on the whole, to agree with him. Society in the twelfth century agreed with Delacroix. The French held then that the first point in colour-decoration was colour, and they never hesitated to put their colour where they wanted it, or cared whether a green camel or a pink lion looked like a dog or a donkey provided they got their harmony or value. Everything except colour was sacrificed to line in the large sense, but details of drawing were conventional and subordinate. So we laugh to see a knight with a blue face, on a green horse, that looks as though drawn by a four-year-old child, and probably the artist laughed, too; but he was a colourist, and never sacrificed his colour for a laugh.

We tourists assume commonly that he knew no better. In our simple faith in ourselves, great hope abides, for it shows an earnestness hardly less than that of the crusaders; but in the matter of colour one is perhaps less convinced, or more open to curiosity. No school of colour exists in our world to-day, while the Middle Ages had a dozen; but it is certainly true that these twelfth-century windows break the French tradition. They had no antecedent, and no fit succession. All the authorities dwell on their exceptional character. One is sorely tempted to suspect that they were in some way an accident; that such an art could not have sprung, in such perfection, out of nothing, had it been really French; that it must have had its home elsewhere—on the Rhine—in Italy—in Byzantium— or in Bagdad.

The same controversy has raged for near two hundred years over the Gothic arch, and everything else mediaeval, down to the philosophy of the schools. The generation that lived during the first and second crusades tried a number of original experiments, besides capturing Jerusalem. Among other things, it produced the western portal of Chartres, with its statuary, its glass, and its fleche, as a by-play; as it produced Abelard, Saint Bernard, and Christian of Troyes, whose acquaintance we have still to make. It took ideas wherever it found them;—from Germany, Italy, Spain, Constantinople, Palestine, or from the source which has always attracted the French mind like a magnet—from ancient Greece. That it actually did take the ideas, no one disputes, except perhaps patriots who hold that even the ideas were original; but to most students the ideas need to be accounted for less than the taste with which they were handled, and the quickness with which they were developed. That the taste was French, you can see in the architecture, or you will see if ever you meet the Gothic elsewhere; that it seized and developed an idea quickly, you have seen in the arch, the fleche, the porch, and the windows, as well as in the glass; but what we do not comprehend, and never shall, is the appetite behind all this; the greed for novelty: the fun of life. Every one who has lived since the sixteenth century has felt deep distrust of every one who lived before it, and of every one who believed in the Middle Ages. True it is that the last thirteenth-century artist died a long time before our planet began its present rate of revolution; it had to come to rest, and begin again; but this does not prevent astonishment that the twelfth-century planet revolved so fast. The pointed arch not only came as an idea into France, but it was developed into a system of architecture and covered the country with buildings on a scale of height never before attempted except by the dome, with an expenditure of wealth that would make a railway system look cheap, all in a space of about fifty years; the glass came with it, and went with it, at least as far as concerns us; but, if you need other evidence, you can consult Renan, who is the highest authority: "One of the most singular phenomena of the literary history of the Middle Ages," says Renan of Averroes, "is the activity of the intellectual commerce, and the rapidity with which books were spread from one end of Europe to the other. The philosophy of Abelard during his lifetime (1100-42) had penetrated to the ends of Italy. The French poetry of the trouveres counted within less than a century translations into German, Swedish, Norwegian, Icelandic, Flemish, Dutch, Bohemian, Italian, Spanish"; and he might have added that England needed no translation, but helped to compose the poetry, not being at that time so insular as she afterwards became. "Such or such a work, composed in Morocco or in Cairo, was known at Paris and at Cologne in less time than it would need in our days for a German book of capital importance to pass the Rhine"; and Renan wrote this in 1852 when German books of capital importance were revolutionizing the literary world.

One is apt to forget the smallness of Europe, and how quickly it could always be crossed. In summer weather, with fair winds, one can sail from Alexandria or from Syria, to Sicily, or even to Spain and France, in perfect safety and with ample room for freight, as easily now as one could do it then, without the aid of steam; but one does not now carry freight of philosophy, poetry, or art. The world still struggles for unity, but by different methods, weapons, and thought. The mercantile exchanges which surprised Renan, and which have puzzled historians, were in ideas. The twelfth century was as greedy for them in one shape as the nineteenth century in another. France paid for them dearly, and repented for centuries; but what creates surprise to the point of incredulity is her hunger for them, the youthful gluttony with which she devoured them, the infallible taste with which she dressed them out. The restless appetite that snatched at the pointed arch, the stone fleche, the coloured glass, the illuminated missal, the chanson and roman and pastorelle, the fragments of Aristotle, the glosses of Avicenne, was nothing compared with the genius which instantly gave form and flower to them all.

This episode merely means that the French twelfth-century artist may be supposed to have known his business, and if he produced a grotesque, or a green-faced Saint, or a blue castle, or a syllogism, or a song, that he did it with a notion of the effect he had in mind. The glass window was to him a whole,—a mass,—and its details were his amusement; for the twelfth-century Frenchman enjoyed his fun, though it was sometimes rather heavy for modern French taste, and less refined than the Church liked. These three twelfth-century windows, like their contemporary portal outside, and the fleche that goes with them, are the ideals of enthusiasts of mediaeval art; they are above the level of all known art, in religious form; they are inspired; they are divine! This is the claim of Chartres and its Virgin. Actually, the French artist, whether architect, sculptor, or painter in glass, did rise here above his usual level. He knew it when he did it, and probably he attributed it, as we do, to the Virgin; for these works of his were hardly fifty years old when the rest of the old church was burned; and already the artist felt the virtue gone out of him. He could not do so well in 1200 as he did in 1150; and the Virgin was not so near.

The proof of it—or, if you prefer to think so, the proof against it—is before our eyes on the wall above the lancet windows. When Villard de Honnecourt came to Chartres, he seized at once on the western rose as his study, although the two other roses were probably there, in all their beauty and lightness. He saw in the western rose some quality of construction which interested him; and, in fact, the western rose is one of the flowers of architecture which reveals its beauties slowly without end; but its chief beauty is the feeling which unites it with the portal, the lancets, and the fleche. The glassworker here in the interior had the same task to perform. The glass of the lancets was fifty years old when the glass for the rose was planned; perhaps it was seventy, for the exact dates are unknown, but it does not matter, for the greater the interval, the more interesting is the treatment. Whatever the date, the glass of the western rose cannot be much earlier or much later than that of the other roses, or that of the choir, and yet you see at a glance that it is quite differently treated. On such matters one must, of course, submit to the opinion of artists, which one does the more readily because they always disagree; but until the artists tell us better, we may please ourselves by fancying that the glass of the rose was intended to harmonize with that of the lancets, and unite it with the thirteenth-century glass of the nave and transepts. Among all the thirteenth-century windows the western rose alone seems to affect a rivalry in brilliancy with the lancets, and carries it so far that the separate medallions and pictures are quite lost,—especially in direct sunshine,—blending in a confused effect of opals, in a delirium of colour and light, with a result like a cluster of stones in jewelry. Assuming as one must, in want of the artist's instruction, that he knew what he wanted to do, and did it, one must take for granted that he treated the rose as a whole, and aimed at giving it harmony with the three precious windows beneath. The effect is that of a single large ornament; a round breastpin, or what is now called a sunburst, of jewels, with three large pendants beneath.

We are ignorant tourists, liable to much error in trying to seek motives in artists who worked seven hundred years ago for a society which thought and felt in forms quite unlike ours, but the medieval pilgrim was more ignorant than we, and much simpler in mind; if the idea of an ornament occurs to us, it certainly occurred to him, and still more to the glassworker whose business was to excite his illusions. An artist, if good for anything, foresees what his public will see; and what his public will see is what he ought to have intended—the measure of his genius. If the public sees more than he himself did, this is his credit; if less, this is his fault. No matter how simple or ignorant we are, we ought to feel a discord or a harmony where the artist meant us to feel it, and when we see a motive, we conclude that other people have seen it before us, and that it must, therefore, have been intended. Neither of the transept roses is treated like this one; neither has the effect of a personal ornament; neither is treated as a jewel. No one knew so well as the artist that such treatment must give the effect of a jewel. The Roses of France and of Dreux bear indelibly and flagrantly the character of France and Dreux; on the western rose is stamped with greater refinement but equal decision the character of a much greater power than either of them.

No artist would have ventured to put up, before the eyes of Mary in Majesty, above the windows so dear to her, any object that she had not herself commanded. Whether a miracle was necessary, or whether genius was enough, is a point of casuistry which you can settle with Albertus Magnus or Saint Bernard, and which you will understand as little when settled as before; but for us, beyond the futilities of unnecessary doubt, the Virgin designed this rose; not perhaps in quite the same perfect spirit in which she designed the lancets, but still wholly for her own pleasure and as her own idea. She placed upon the breast of her Church—which symbolized herself—a jewel so gorgeous that no earthly majesty could bear comparison with it, and which no other heavenly majesty has rivalled. As one watches the light play on it, one is still overcome by the glories of the jewelled rose and its three gemmed pendants; one feels a little of the effect she meant it to produce even on infidels, Moors, and heretics, but infinitely more on the men who feared and the women who adored her;—not to dwell too long upon it, one admits that hers is the only Church. One would admit anything that she should require. If you had only the soul of a shrimp, you would crawl, like the Abbe Suger, to kiss her feet.

Unfortunately she is gone, or comes here now so very rarely that we never shall see her; but her genius remains as individual here as the genius of Blanche of Castile and Pierre de Dreux in the transepts. That the three lancets were her own taste, as distinctly as the Trianon was the taste of Louis XIV, is self-evident. They represent all that was dearest to her; her Son's glory on her right; her own beautiful life in the middle; her royal ancestry on her left: the story of her divine right, thrice-told. The pictures are all personal, like family portraits. Above them the man who worked in 1200 to carry out the harmony, and to satisfy the Virgin's wishes, has filled his rose with a dozen or two little compositions in glass, which reveal their subjects only to the best powers of a binocle. Looking carefully, one discovers at last that this gorgeous combination of all the hues of Paradise contains or hides a Last Judgment—the one subject carefully excluded from the old work, and probably not existing on the south portal for another twenty years. If the scheme of the western rose dates from 1200, as is reasonable to suppose, this Last Judgment is the oldest in the church, and makes a link between the theology of the first crusade, beneath, and the theology of Pierre Mauclerc in the south porch. The churchman is the only true and final judge on his own doctrine, and we neither know nor care to know the facts; but we are as good judges as he of the feeling, and we are at full liberty to feel that such a Last Judgment as this was never seen before or since by churchman or heretic, unless by virtue of the heresy which held that the true Christian must be happy in being damned since such is the will of God. That this blaze of heavenly light was intended, either by the Virgin or by her workmen, to convey ideas of terror or pain, is a notion which the Church might possibly preach, but which we sinners knew to be false in the thirteenth century as well as we know it now. Never in all these seven hundred years has one of us looked up at this rose without feeling it to be Our Lady's promise of Paradise.

Here as everywhere else throughout the church, one feels the Virgin's presence, with no other thought than her majesty and grace. To the Virgin and to her suppliants, as to us, who though outcasts in other churches can still hope in hers, the Last Judgment was not a symbol of God's justice or man's corruption, but of her own infinite mercy. The Trinity judged, through Christ;— Christ loved and pardoned, through her. She wielded the last and highest power on earth and in hell. In the glow and beauty of her nature, the light of her Son's infinite love shone as the sunlight through the glass, turning the Last Judgment itself into the highest proof of her divine and supreme authority. The rudest ruffian of the Middle Ages, when he looked at this Last Judgment, laughed; for what was the Last Judgment to her! An ornament, a plaything, a pleasure! a jewelled decoration which she wore on her breast! Her chief joy was to pardon; her eternal instinct was to love; her deepest passion was pity! On her imperial heart the flames of hell showed only the opaline colours of heaven. Christ the Trinity might judge as much as He pleased, but Christ the Mother would rescue; and her servants could look boldly into the flames.

If you, or even our friends the priests who still serve Mary's shrine, suspect that there is some exaggeration in this language, it will only oblige you to admit presently that there is none; but for the moment we are busy with glass rather than with faith, and there is a world of glass here still to study. Technically, we are done with it. The technique of the thirteenth century comes naturally and only too easily out of that of the twelfth. Artistically, the motive remains the same, since it is always the Virgin; but although the Virgin of Chartres is always the Virgin of Majesty, there are degrees in the assertion of her majesty even here, which affect the art, and qualify its feeling. Before stepping down to the thirteenth century, one should look at these changes of the Virgin's royal presence.

First and most important as record is the stone Virgin on the south door of the western portal, which we studied, with her Byzantine Court; and the second, also in stone, is of the same period, on one of the carved capitals of the portal, representing the Adoration of the Magi. The third is the glass Virgin at the top of the central lancet. All three are undoubted twelfth-century work; and you can see another at Paris, on the same door of Notre Dame, and still more on Abbe Suger's window at Saint-Denis, and, later, within a beautiful grisaille at Auxerre; but all represent the same figure; a Queen, enthroned, crowned, with the symbols of royal power, holding in her lap the infant King whose guardian she is. Without pretending to know what special crown she bears, we can assume, till corrected, that it is the Carlovingian imperial, not the Byzantine. The Trinity nowhere appears except as implied in the Christ. At the utmost, a mystic hand may symbolize the Father. The Virgin as represented by the artists of the twelfth century in the Ile de France and at Chartres seems to be wholly French in spite of the Greek atmosphere of her workmanship. One might almost insist that she is blonde, full in face, large in figure, dazzlingly beautiful, and not more than thirty years of age. The Child never seems to be more than five.

You are equally free to see a Southern or Eastern type in her face, and perhaps the glass suggests a dark type, but the face of the Virgin on the central lancet is a fourteenth-century restoration which may or may not reproduce the original, while all the other Virgins represented in glass, except one, belong to the thirteenth century. The possible exception is a well-known figure called Notre-Dame-de-la-Belle-Verriere in the choir next the south transept. A strange, almost uncanny feeling seems to haunt this window, heightened by the veneration in which it was long held as a shrine, though it is now deserted for Notre-Dame-du-Pilier on the opposite side of the choir. The charm is partly due to the beauty of the scheme of the angels, supporting, saluting, and incensing the Virgin and Child with singular grace and exquisite feeling, but rather that of the thirteenth than of the twelfth century. Here, too, the face of the Virgin is not ancient. Apparently the original glass was injured by time or accident, and the colours were covered or renewed by a simple drawing in oil. Elsewhere the colour is thought to be particularly good, and the window is a favourite mine of motives for artists to exploit, but to us its chief interest is its singular depth of feeling. The Empress Mother sits full-face, on a rich throne and dais, with the Child on her lap, repeating her attitude except that her hands support His shoulders. She wears her crown; her feet rest on a stool, and both stool, rug, robe, and throne are as rich as colour and decoration can make them. At last a dove appears, with the rays of the Holy Ghost. Imperial as the Virgin is, it is no longer quite the unlimited empire of the western lancet. The aureole encircles her head only; she holds no sceptre; the Holy Ghost seems to give her support which she did not need before, while Saint Gabriel and Saint Michael, her archangels, with their symbols of power, have disappeared. Exquisite as the angels are who surround and bear up her throne, they assert no authority. The window itself is not a single composition; the panels below seem inserted later merely to fill up the space; six represent the Marriage of Cana, and the three at the bottom show a grotesque little demon tempting Christ in the Desert. The effect of the whole, in this angle which is almost always dark or filled with shadow, is deep and sad, as though the Empress felt her authority fail, and had come down from the western portal to reproach us for neglect. The face is haunting. Perhaps its force may be due to nearness, for this is the only instance in glass of her descending so low that we can almost touch her, and see what the twelfth century instinctively felt in the features which, even in their beatitude, were serious and almost sad under the austere responsibilities of infinite pity and power.

No doubt the window is very old, or perhaps an imitation or reproduction of one which was much older, but to the pilgrim its interest lies mostly in its personality, and there it stands alone. Although the Virgin reappears again and again in the lower windows,- -as in those on either side of the Belle-Verriere; in the remnant of window representing her miracles at Chartres, in the south aisle next the transept; in the fifteenth-century window of the chapel of Vendome which follows; and in the third window which follows that of Vendome and represents her coronation,—she does not show herself again in all her majesty till we look up to the high windows above. There we shall find her in her splendour on her throne, above the high altar, and still more conspicuously in the Rose of France in the north transept. Still again she is enthroned in the first window of the choir next the north transept. Elsewhere we can see her standing, but never does she come down to us in the full splendour of her presence. Yet wherever we find her at Chartres, and of whatever period, she is always Queen. Her expression and attitude are always calm and commanding. She never calls for sympathy by hysterical appeals to our feelings; she does not even altogether command, but rather accepts the voluntary, unquestioning, unhesitating, instinctive faith, love, and devotion of mankind. She will accept ours, and we have not the heart to refuse it; we have not even the right, for we are her guests.

CHAPTER IX: THE LEGENDARY WINDOWS

One's first visit to a great cathedral is like one's first visit to the British Museum; the only intelligent idea is to follow the order of time, but the museum is a chaos in time, and the cathedral is generally all of one and the same time. At Chartres, after finishing with the twelfth century, everything is of the thirteenth. To catch even an order in time, one must first know what part of the thirteenth-century church was oldest. The books say it was the choir. After the fire of 1194, the pilgrims used the great crypt as a church where services were maintained; but the builders must have begun with the central piers and the choir, because the choir was the only essential part of the church. Nave and transepts might be suppressed, but without a choir the church was useless, and in a shrine, such as Chartres, the choir was the whole church. Toward the choir, then, the priest or artist looks first; and, since dates are useful, the choir must be dated. The same popular enthusiasm, which had broken out in 1145, revived in 1195 to help the rebuilding; and the work was pressed forward with the same feverish haste, so that ten years should have been ample to provide for the choir, if for nothing more; and services may have been resumed there as early as the year 1206; certainly in 1210. Probably the windows were designed and put in hand as soon as the architect gave the measurements, and any one who intended to give a window would have been apt to choose one of the spaces in the apse, in Mary's own presence, next the sanctuary.

The first of the choir windows to demand a date is the Belle- Verriere, which is commonly classed as early thirteenth-century, and may go with the two windows next it, one of which—the so-called Zodiac window—bears a singularly interesting inscription: "COMES TEOBALDUS DAT...AD PRECES COMIXIS PTICENSIS." If Shakespeare could write the tragedy of "King John," we cannot admit ourselves not to have read it, and this inscription might be a part of the play. The "pagus perticensis" lies a short drive to the west, some fifteen or twenty miles on the road to Le Mans, and in history is known as the Comte du Perche, although its memory is now preserved chiefly by its famous breed of Percheron horses. Probably the horse also dates from the crusades, and may have carried Richard Coeur-de-Lion, but in any case the count of that day was a vassal of Richard, and one of his intimate friends, whose memory is preserved forever by a single line in Richard's prison-song:—

Mes compaignons cui j'amoie et cui j'aim,

Ces dou Caheu et ces dou Percherain.

In 1194, when Richard Coeur-de-Lion wrote these verses, the Comte du Perche was Geoffrey III, who had been a companion of Richard on his crusade in 1192, where, according to the Chronicle, "he shewed himself but a timid man"; which seems scarcely likely in a companion of Richard; but it is not of him that the Chartres window speaks, except as the son of Mahaut or Matilda of Champagne who was a sister of Alix of Champagne, Queen of France. The Table shows, therefore, that Geoffroi's son and successor as the Comte du Perche—Thomas— was second cousin of Louis the Lion, known as King Louis VIII of France. They were probably of much the same age.

If this were all, one might carry it in one's head for a while, but the relationship which dominates the history of this period was that of all these great ruling families with Richard Coeur-de-Lion and his brother John, nicknamed Lackland, both of whom in succession were the most powerful Frenchmen in France. The Table shows that their mother Eleanor of Guienne, the first Queen of Louis VII, bore him two daughters, one of whom, Alix, married, about 1164, the Count Thibaut of Chartres and Blois, while the other, Mary, married the great Count of Champagne. Both of them being half-sisters of Coeur- de-Lion and John, their children were nephews or half-nephews, indiscriminately, of all the reigning monarchs, and Coeur-de-Lion immortalized one of them by a line in his prison-song, as he immortalized Le Perche:—

> Je nel di pas de celi de Chartain,
> La mere Loeis.

"Loeis," therefore, or Count Louis of Chatres, was not only nephew of Coeur-de-Lion and John Lackland, but was also, like Count Thomas of Le Perche, a second cousin of Louis VIII. Feudally and personally he was directly attached to Coeur-de-Lion rather than to Philip Augustus.

If society in the twelfth century could follow the effects of these relationships, personal and feudal, it was cleverer than society in the twentieth; but so much is simple: Louis of France, Thibaut of Chartres, and Thomas of Le Perche, were cousins and close friends in the year 1215, and all were devoted to the Virgin of Chartres. Judging from the character of Louis's future queen, Blanche of Castile, their wives were, if possible, more devoted still; and in that year Blanche gave birth to Saint Louis, who seems to have been the most devoted of all.

Meanwhile their favourite uncle, Coeur-de-Lion, had died in the year 1199. Thibaut's great-grandmother, Eleanor of Guienne, died in 1202. King John, left to himself, rapidly accumulated enemies innumerable, abroad and at home. In 1203, Philip Augustus confiscated all the fiefs he held from the French Crown, and in 1204 seized Normandy. John sank rapidly from worse to worst, until at last the English barons rose and forced him to grant their Magna Carta at Runnimede in 1215.

The year 1215 was, therefore, a year to be remembered at Chartres, as at Mont-Saint-Michel; one of the most convenient dates in history. Every one is supposed, even now, to know what happened then, to give another violent wrench to society, like the Norman Conquest in 1066. John turned on the barons and broke them down; they sent to

[Genealogical chart showing the relationships among England,

Champagne and Chartres and France and La Perche.]

France for help, and offered the crown of England to young Louis, whose father, Philip Augustus, called a council which pledged support to Louis. Naturally the Comte du Perche and the Comte de Chartres must have pledged their support, among the foremost, to go with Louis to England. He was then twenty-nine years old; they were probably somewhat younger.

The Zodiac window, with its inscription, was the immediate result.

The usual authority that figures in the histories is Roger of

Wendover, but much the more amusing for our purpose is a garrulous

Frenchman known as the Menestrel de Rheims who wrote some fifty years later. After telling in his delightful thirteenth-century French, how the English barons sent hostages to Louis, "et mes sires Loueys les fit bien gardeir et honourablement," the Menestrel continued:—

Et assembla granz genz par amours, et par deniers, et par lignage. Et fu avec lui li cuens dou Perche, et li cuens de Montfort, et li cuens de Chartres, et li cuens de Monbleart, et mes sires Enjorrans de Couci, et mout d'autre grant seigneur dont je ne parole mie.

The Comte de Chartres, therefore, may be supposed to have gone with the Comte du Perche, and to have witnessed the disaster at Lincoln which took place May 20, 1217, after King John's death:—

Et li cuens dou Perche faisait l'avantgarde, et courut tout leiz des portes; et la garnisons de laienz issi hors et leur coururent sus; et i ot asseiz trait et lancie; et chevaus morz et chevaliers abatuz, et gent a pie morz et navreiz. Et li cuens dou Perche i fu morz par un ribaut qui li leva le pan dou hauberc, et l'ocist d'un coutel; et fu desconfite l'avantgarde par la mort le conte. Et quant mes sires Loueys le sot, si ot graigneur duel qu'il eust onques, car il estoit ses prochains ami de char.

Such language would be spoiled by translation. For us it is enough to know that the "ribaut" who lifted the "pan," or skirt, of the Count's "hauberc" or coat-of-mail, as he sat on his horse refusing to surrender to English traitors, and stabbed him from below with a knife, may have been an invention of the Menestrel; or the knight who pierced with his lance through the visor to the brain, may have been an invention of Roger of Wendover; but in either case, Count Thomas du Perche lost his life at Lincoln, May 20, 1217, to the deepest regret of his cousin Louis the Lion as well as of the Count Thibaut of Chartres, whom he charged to put up a window for him in honour of the Virgin.

The window must have been ordered at once, because Count Thibaut, "le Jeune ou le Lepreux," died himself within a year, April 22, 1218, thus giving an exact date for one of the choir windows. Probably it was one of the latest, because the earliest to be provided would have been certainly those of the central apsidal chapel. According to the rule laid down by Viollet-le-Duc, the windows in which blue strongly predominates, like the Saint Sylvester, are likely to be earlier than those with a prevailing tone of red. We must take for granted that some of these great legendary windows were in place as early as 1210, because, in October of that year, Philip Augustus attended mass here. There are some two dozen of these windows in the choir alone, each of which may well have represented a year's work in the slow processes of that day, and we can hardly suppose that the workshops of 1200 were on a scale such as to allow of more than two to have been in hand at once. Thirty or forty years later, when the Sainte Chapelle was built, the workshops must have been vastly enlarged, but with the enlargement, the glass deteriorated. Therefore, if the architecture were so far advanced in the year 1200 as to allow of beginning work on the glass, in the apse, the year 1225 is none too late to allow for its completion in the choir.

Dates are stupidly annoying;—what we want is not dates but taste;— yet we are uncomfortable without them. Except the Perche window, none of the lower ones in the choir helps at all; but the clere- story is more useful. There they run in pairs, each pair surmounted by a rose. The first pair (numbers 27 and 28) next the north transept, shows the Virgin of France, supported, according to the Abbes Bulteau and Clerval, by the arms of Bishop Reynault de Moucon, who was Bishop of Chartres at the time of the great fire in 1194 and died in 1217. The window number 28 shows two groups of peasants on pilgrimage; below, on his knees, Robert of Berou, as donor: "ROBERTUS DE BEROU: CARN. CANCELLARIUS." The Cartulary of the Cathedral contains an entry (Bulteau, i, 123): "The 26th February, 1216, died Robert de Berou, Chancellor, who has given us a window." The Cartulary mentions several previous gifts of windows by canons or other dignitaries of the Church in the year 1215.

Next follow, or once followed, a pair of windows (numbers 29 and 30) which were removed by the sculptor Bridan, in 1788, in order to obtain light for his statuary below. The donor was "DOMINA JOHANNES BAPTISTA," who, we are told, was Jeanne de Dammartin; and the window was given in memory, or in honour, of her marriage to Ferdinand of Castile in 1237. Jeanne was a very great lady, daughter of the Comte d'Aumale and Marie de Ponthieu. Her father affianced her in 1235 to the King of England, Henry III, and even caused the marriage to be celebrated by proxy, but Queen Blanche broke it off, as she had forbidden, in 1231, that of Yolande of Britanny. She relented so far as to allow Jeanne in 1237 to marry Ferdinand of Castile, who still sits on horseback in the next rose: "REX CASTILLAE." He won the crown of Castile in 1217 and died in 1252, when Queen Jeanne returned to Abbeville and then, at latest, put up this window at Chartres in memory of her husband.

The windows numbers 31 and 32 are the subject of much dispute, but whether the donors were Jean de Chatillon or the three children of Thibaut le Grand of Champagne, they must equally belong to the later series of 1260-70, rather than to the earlier of 1210-20. The same thing is or was true of the next pair, numbers 33 and 34, which were removed in 1773, but the record says that at the bottom of number 34 was the figure of Saint Louis's son, Louis of France, who died in 1260, before his father, who still rides in the rose above.

Thus the north side of the choir shows a series of windows that precisely cover the lifetime of Saint Louis (1215-70). The south side begins, next the apse, with windows numbers 35 and 36, which belong, according to the Comte d'Armancourt, to the family of Montfort, whose ruined castle crowns the hill of Montfort l'Amaury, on the road to Paris, some forty kilometres northeast of Chartres. Every one is supposed to know the story of Simon de Montfort who was killed before Toulouse in 1218. Simon left two sons, Amaury and Simon. The sculptor Bridan put an end also to the window of Amaury, but in the rose, Amaury, according to the Abbes, still rides on a white horse. Amaury's history is well known. He was made Constable of France by Queen Blanche in 1231; went on crusade in 1239; was captured by the infidels, taken to Babylon, ransomed, and in returning to France, died at Otranto in 1241. For that age Amaury was but a commonplace person, totally overshadowed by his brother Simon, who went to England, married King John's daughter Eleanor, and became almost king himself as Earl of Leicester. At your leisure you can read Matthew Paris's dramatic account of him and of his death at the battle of Evesham, August 5, 1265. He was perhaps the last of the very great men of the thirteenth century, excepting Saint Louis himself, who lived a few years longer. M. d'Armancourt insists that it is the great Earl of Leicester who rides with his visor up, in full armour, on a brown horse, in the rose above the windows numbers 37 and 38. In any case, the windows would be later than

1240.

The next pair of windows, numbers 39 and 40, also removed in 1788, still offer, in their rose, the figure of a member of the Courtenay family. Gibbon was so much attracted by the romance of the Courtenays as to make an amusing digression on the subject which does not concern us or the cathedral except so far as it tells us that the Courtenays, like so many other benefactors of Chartres Cathedral, belonged to the royal blood. Louis-le-Gros, who died in 1137, besides his son Louis-le-Jeune, who married Eleanor of Guienne in that year, had a younger son, Pierre, whom he married to Isabel de Courtenay, and who, like Philip Hurepel, took the title of his wife. Pierre had a son, Pierre II, who was a cousin of Philip Augustus, and became the hero of the most lurid tragedy of the time. Chosen Emperor of Constantinople in 1216, to succeed his brothers- in-law Henry and Baldwin, he tried to march across Illyria and Macedonia, from Durazzo opposite Brindisi, with a little army of five thousand men, and instantly disappeared forever. The Epirotes captured him in the summer of 1217, and from that moment nothing is known of his fate.

On the whole, this catastrophe was perhaps the grimmest of all the Shakespearean tragedies of the thirteenth century; and one would like to think that the Chartres window was a memorial of this Pierre, who was a cousin of France and an emperor without empire; but M. d'Armancourt insists that the window was given in memory not of this Pierre, but of his nephew, another Pierre de Courtenay, Seigneur de Conches, who went on crusade with Saint Louis in 1249 to Egypt, and died shortly before the defeat and captivity of the King, on February 8, 1250. His brother Raoul, Seigneur d'Illiers, who died in 1271, is said to be donor of the next window, number 40. The date of the Courtenay windows should therefore be no earlier than the death of Saint Louis in 1270; yet one would like to know what has become of another Courtenay window left by the first Pierre's son- in-law, Gaucher or Gaultier of Bar-sur-Seine, who seems to have been Vicomte de Chartres, and who, dying before Damietta in 1218, made a will leaving to Notre Dame de Chartres thirty silver marks, "de quibus fieri debet miles montatus super equum suum." Not only would this mounted knight on horseback supply an early date for these interesting figures, but would fix also the cost, for a mark contained eight ounces of silver, and was worth ten sous, or half a livre. We shall presently see that Aucassins gave twenty sous, or a livre, for a strong ox, so that the "miles montatus super equum suum" in glass was equivalent to fifteen oxen if it were money of Paris, which is far from certain.

This is an economical problem which belongs to experts, but the historical value of these early evidences is still something,— perhaps still as much as ten sous. All the windows tend to the same conclusion. Even the last pair, numbers 41 and 42, offer three personal clues which lead to the same result:—the arms of Bouchard de Marly who died in 1226, almost at the same time as Louis VIII; a certain Colinus or Colin, "de camera Regis," who was alive in 1225; and Robert of Beaumont in the rose, who seems to be a Beaumont of Le Perche, of whom little or nothing is as yet certainly known. As a general rule, there are two series of windows, one figuring the companions or followers of Louis VIII (1215-26); the other, friends or companions of Saint Louis (1226-70), Queen Blanche uniting both. What helps to hold the sequences in a certain order, is that the choir was complete, and services regularly resumed there, in 1210, while in 1220 the transept and nave were finished and vaulted. For the apside windows, therefore, we will assume, subject to correction, a date from 1200 to 1225 for their design and workmanship; for the transept, 1220 to 1236; and for the nave a general tendency to the actual reign of Saint Louis from 1236 to 1270. Since there is a deal of later glass scattered everywhere among the earlier, the margin of error is great; but by keeping the reign of Louis VIII and its personages distinct from that of Louis IX and his generation, we can be fairly sure of our main facts. Meanwhile the Sainte Chapelle in Paris, wholly built and completed between 1240 and 1248, offers a standard of comparison for the legendary windows.

The choir of Chartres is as long as the nave, and much broader, besides that the apse was planned with seven circular projections which greatly increased the window space, so that the guidebook reckons thirty-seven windows. A number of these are grisailles, and the true amateur of glass considers the grisailles to be as well worth study as the legendary windows. They are a decoration which has no particular concern with churches, and no distinct religious meaning, but, it seems, a religious value which Viollet-le-Duc is at some trouble to explain; and, since his explanation is not very technical, we can look at it, before looking at the legends:—

The colouration of the windows had the advantage of throwing on the opaque walls a veil, or coloured glazing, of extreme delicacy, always assuming that the coloured windows themselves were harmoniously toned. Whether their resources did not permit the artists to adopt a complete system of coloured glass, or whether they wanted to get daylight in purer quality into their interiors,— whatever may have been their reasons,—they resorted to this beautiful grisaille decoration which is also a colouring harmony obtained by the aid of a long experience in the effects of light on translucent surfaces. Many of our churches retain grisaille windows filling either all, or only a part, of their bays. In the latter case, the grisailles are reserved for the side windows which are meant to be seen obliquely, and in that case the coloured glass fills the bays of the fond, the apsidal openings which are meant to be seen in face from a distance. These lateral grisailles are still opaque enough to prevent the solar rays which pass through them from lighting the coloured windows on the reverse side; yet, at certain hours of the day, these solar rays throw a pearly light on the coloured windows which gives them indescribable transparence and refinement of tones. The lateral windows in the choir of the Auxerre Cathedral, half-grisaille, half-coloured, throw on the wholly coloured apsidal window, by this means, a glazing the softness of which one can hardly conceive. The opaline light which comes through these lateral bays, and makes a sort of veil, transparent in the extreme, under the lofty vaulting, is crossed by the brilliant tones of the windows behind, which give the play of precious stones. The solid outlines then seem to waver like objects seen through a sheet of clear water. Distances change their values, and take depths in which the eye gets lost. With every hour of the day these effects are altered, and always with new harmonies which one never tires of trying to understand; but the deeper one's study goes, the more astounded one becomes before the experience acquired by these artists, whose theories on the effects of colour, assuming that they had any, are unknown to us and whom the most kindly-disposed among us treat as simple children.

You can read the rest for yourselves. Grisaille is a separate branch of colour-decoration which belongs with the whole system of lighting and fenetrage, and will have to remain a closed book because the feeling and experience which explained it once are lost, and we cannot recover either. Such things must have been always felt rather than reasoned, like the irregularities in plan of the builders; the best work of the best times shows the same subtlety of sense as the dog shows in retrieving, or the bee in flying, but which tourists have lost. All we can do is to note that the grisailles were intended to have values. They were among the refinements of light and colour with which the apse of Chartres is so crowded that one must be content to feel what one can, and let the rest go.

Understand, we cannot! nothing proves that the greatest artists who ever lived have, in a logical sense, understood! or that omnipotence has ever understood! or that the utmost power of expression has ever been capable of expressing more than the reaction of one energy on another, but not of two on two; and when one sits here, in the central axis of this complicated apse, one sees, in mere light alone, the reaction of hundreds of energies, although time has left only a wreck of what the artist put here. One of the best window spaces is wholly filled up by the fourteenth-century doorway to the chapel of Saint Piat, and only by looking at the two windows which correspond on the north does a curious inquirer get a notion of the probable loss. The same chapel more or less blocks the light of three other principal windows. The sun, the dust, the acids of dripping water, and the other works of time, have in seven hundred years corroded or worn away or altered the glass, especially on the south side. Windows have been darkened by time and mutilated by wilful injury. Scores of the panels are wholly restored, modern reproductions or imitations. Even after all this loss, the glass is probably the best-preserved, or perhaps the only preserved part of the decoration in colour, for we never shall know the colour-decoration of the vaults, the walls, the columns, or the floors. Only one point is fairly sure;—that on festivals, if not at other times, every foot of space was covered in some way or another, throughout the apse, with colour; either paint or tapestry or embroidery or Byzantine brocades and Oriental stuffs or rugs, lining the walls, covering the altars, and hiding the floor. Occasionally you happen upon illuminated manuscripts showing the interiors of chapels with their colour-decoration; but everything has perished here except the glass.

If one may judge from the glass of later centuries, the first impression from the thirteenth-century windows ought to be disappointment. You should find them too effeminate, too soft, too small, and above all not particularly religious. Indeed, except for the nominal subjects of the legends, one sees nothing religious about them; the medallions, when studied with the binocle, turn out to be less religious than decorative. Saint Michael would not have felt at home here, and Saint Bernard would have turned from them with disapproval; but when they were put up, Saint Bernard was long dead, and Saint Michael had yielded his place to the Virgin. This apse is all for her. At its entrance she sat, on either side, in the Belle-Verriere or as Our Lady of the Pillar, to receive the secrets and the prayers of suppliants who wished to address her directly in person; there she bent down to our level, resumed her humanity, and felt our griefs and passions. Within, where the cross-lights fell through the wide columned space behind the high altar, was her withdrawing room, where the decorator and builder thought only of pleasing her. The very faults of the architecture and effeminacy of taste witness the artists' object. If the glassworkers had thought of themselves or of the public or even of the priests, they would have strained for effects, strong masses of colour, and striking subjects to impress the imagination. Nothing of the sort is even suggested. The great, awe-inspiring mosaic figure of the Byzantine half-dome was a splendid religious effect, but this artist had in his mind an altogether different thought. He was in the Virgin's employ; he was decorating her own chamber in her own palace; he wanted to please her; and he knew her tastes, even when she did not give him her personal orders. To him, a dream would have been an order. The salary of the twelfth-century artist was out of all relation with the percentage of a twentieth-century decorator. The artist of 1200 was probably the last who cared little for the baron, not very much for the priest, and nothing for the public, unless he happened to be paid by the guild, and then he cared just to the extent of his hire, or, if he was himself a priest, not even for that. His pay was mostly of a different kind, and was the same as that of the peasants who were hauling the stone from the quarry at Bercheres while he was firing his ovens. His reward was to come when he should be promoted to decorate the Queen of Heaven's palace in the New Jerusalem, and he served a mistress who knew better than he did what work was good and what was bad, and how to give him his right place. Mary's taste was infallible; her knowledge like her power had no limits; she knew men's thoughts as well as acts, and could not be deceived. Probably, even in our own time, an artist might find his imagination considerably stimulated and his work powerfully improved if he knew that anything short of his best would bring him to the gallows, with or without trial by jury; but in the twelfth century the gallows was a trifle; the Queen hardly considered it a punishment for an offence to her dignity. The artist was vividly aware that Mary disposed of hell.

All this is written in full, on every stone and window of this apse, as legible as the legends to any one who cares to read. The artists were doing their best, not to please a swarm of flat-eared peasants or slow-witted barons, but to satisfy Mary, the Queen of Heaven, to whom the Kings and Queens of France were coming constantly for help, and whose absolute power was almost the only restraint recognized by Emperor, Pope, and clown. The colour-decoration is hers, and hers alone. For her the lights are subdued, the tones softened, the subjects selected, the feminine taste preserved. That other great ladies interested themselves in the matter, even down to its technical refinements, is more than likely; indeed, in the central apside chapel, suggesting the Auxerre grisaille that Viollet-le-Duc mentioned, is a grisaille which bears the arms of Castile and Queen Blanche; further on, three other grisailles bear also the famous castles, but this is by no means the strongest proof of feminine taste. The difficulty would be rather to find a touch of certainly masculine taste in the whole apse.

Since the central apside chapel is the most important, we can begin with the windows there, bearing in mind that the subject of the central window was the Life of Christ, dictated by rule or custom. On Christ's left hand is the window of Saint Peter; next him is Saint Paul. All are much restored; thirty-three of the medallions are wholly new. Opposite Saint Peter, at Christ's right hand, is the window of Saint Simon and Saint Jude; and next is the grisaille with the arms of Castile. If these windows were ordered between 1205 and 1210, Blanche, who was born in 1187, and married in 1200, would have been a young princess of twenty or twenty-five when she gave this window in grisaille to regulate and harmonize and soften the lighting of the Virgin's boudoir. The central chapel must be taken to be the most serious, the most studied, and the oldest of the chapels in the church, above the crypt. The windows here should rank in importance next to the lancets of the west front which are only about sixty years earlier. They show fully that difference.

Here one must see for one's self. Few artists know much about it, and still fewer care for an art which has been quite dead these four hundred years. The ruins of Nippur would hardly be more intelligible to the ordinary architect of English tradition than these twelfth- century efforts of the builders of Chartres. Even the learning of Viollet-le-Duc was at fault in dealing with a building so personal as this, the history of which is almost wholly lost. This central chapel must have been meant to give tone to the apse, and it shows with the colour-decoration of a queen's salon, a subject-decoration too serious for the amusement of heretics. One sees at a glance that the subject-decoration was inspired by church-custom, while colour was an experiment and the decorators of this enormous window space were at liberty as colourists to please the Countess of Chartres and the Princess Blanche and the Duchess of Brittany, without much regarding the opinions of the late Bernard of Clairvaux or even Augustine of Hippo, since the great ladies of the Court knew better than the Saints what would suit the Virgin.

The subject of the central window was prescribed by tradition. Christ is the Church, and in this church he and his Mother are one; therefore the life of Christ is the subject of the central window, but the treatment is the Virgin's, as the colours show, and as the absence of every influence but hers, including the Crucifixion, proves officially. Saint Peter and Saint Paul are in their proper place as the two great ministers of the throne who represent the two great parties in western religion, the Jewish and the Gentile. Opposite them, balancing by their family influence the weight of delegated power, are two of Mary's nephews, Simon and Jude; but this subject branches off again into matters so personal to Mary that Simon and Jude require closer acquaintance. One must study a new guidebook—the "Golden Legend," by the blessed James, Bishop of Genoa and member of the order of Dominic, who was born at Varazze or Voragio in almost the same year that Thomas was born at Aquino, and whose "Legenda Aurea," written about the middle of the thirteenth century, was more popular history than the Bible itself, and more generally consulted as authority. The decorators of the thirteenth century got their motives quite outside the Bible, in sources that James of Genoa compiled into a volume almost as fascinating as the "Fioretti of Saint Francis."

According to the "Golden Legend" and the tradition accepted in Jerusalem by pilgrims and crusaders, Mary's family connection was large. It appears that her mother Anne was three times married, and by each husband had a daughter Mary, so that there were three Marys, half-sisters.

Joachim-Anne- Cleophas- -Salome

Joseph-Mary Alpheus-Mary Mary-Zebedee

Christ James Joseph Simon Jude James John the Minor the the Major the Evangelist Apostle Just St. Iago of Compostella

Simon and Jude were, therefore, nephews of Mary and cousins of Christ, whose lives were evidence of the truth not merely of Scripture, but specially of the private and family distinction of their aunt, the Virgin Mother of Christ. They were selected, rather than their brothers, or cousins James and John, for the conspicuous honour of standing opposite Peter and Paul, doubtless by reason of some merit of their own, but perhaps also because in art the two counted as one, and therefore the one window offered two witnesses, which allowed the artist to insert a grisaille in place of another legendary window to complete the chapel on their right. According to Viollet-le-Duc, the grisaille in this position regulates the light and so completes the effect.

If custom prescribed a general rule for the central chapel, it seems to have left great freedom in the windows near by. At Chartres the curved projection that contains the next two windows was not a chapel, but only a window-bay, for the sake of the windows, and, if the artists aimed at pleasing the Virgin, they would put their best work there. At Bourges in the same relative place are three of the best windows in the building:—the Prodigal Son, the New Alliance and the Good Samaritan; all of them full of life, story, and colour, with little reference to a worship or a saint. At Chartres the choice is still more striking, and the windows are also the best in the building, after the twelfth-century glass of the west front. The first, which comes next to Blanche's grisaille in the central chapel, is given to another nephew of Mary and apostle of Christ, Saint

James the Major, whose life is recorded in the proper Bible Dictionaries, with a terminal remark as follows:—

For legends respecting his death and his connections with Spain, see the Roman Breviary, in which the healing of a paralytic and the conversion of Hermogenes are attributed to him, and where it is asserted that he preached the Gospel in Spain, and that his remains were translated to Compostella ... As there is no shadow of foundation for any of the legends here referred to, we pass them by without further notice. Even Baronius shows himself ashamed of them....

If the learned Baronius thought himself required to show shame for all the legends that pass as history, he must have suffered cruelly during his laborious life, and his sufferings would not have been confined to the annals of the Church; but the historical accuracy of the glass windows is not our affair, nor are historians especially concerned in the events of the Virgin's life, whether recorded or legendary. Religion is, or ought to be, a feeling, and the thirteenth-century windows are original documents, much more historical than any recorded in the Bible, since their inspiration is a different thing from their authority. The true life of Saint James or Saint Jude or any other of the apostles, did not, in the opinion of the ladies in the Court of France, furnish subjects agreeable enough to decorate the palace of the Queen of Heaven; and that they were right, any one must feel, who compares these two windows with subjects of dogma. Saint James, better known as Santiago of Compostella, was a compliment to the young Dauphine— before Dauphines existed—the Princess Blanche of Castile, whose arms, or castles, are on the grisaille window next to it. Perhaps she chose him to stand there. Certainly her hand is seen plainly enough throughout the church to warrant suspecting it here. As a nephew, Saint James was dear to the Virgin, but, as a friend to Spain, still more dear to Blanche, and it is not likely that pure accident caused three adjacent windows to take a Spanish tone.

The Saint James in whom the thirteenth century delighted, and whose windows one sees at Bourges, Tours, and wherever the scallop-shell tells of the pilgrim, belongs not to the Bible but to the "Golden Legend." This window was given by the Merchant Tailors whose signature appears at the bottom, in the corners, in two pictures that paint the tailor's shop of Chartres in the first quarter of the thirteenth century. The shop-boy takes cloth from chests for his master to show to customers, and to measure off by his ell. The story of Saint James begins in the lower panel, where he receives his mission from Christ. Above, on the right, he seems to be preaching. On the left appears a figure which tells the reason for the popularity of the story. It is Almogenes, or in the Latin, Hermogenes, a famous magician in great credit among the Pharisees, who has the command of demons, as you see, for behind his shoulder, standing, a little demon is perched, while he orders his pupil Filetus to convert James. Next, James is shown in discussion with a group of listeners. Filetus gives him a volume of false doctrine. Almogenes then further instructs Filetus. James is led away by a rope, curing a paralytic as he goes. He sends his cloak to Filetus to drive away the demon. Filetus receives the cloak, and the droll little demon departs in tears. Almogenes, losing his temper, sends two demons, with horns on their heads and clubs in their hands, to reason with James; who sends them back to remonstrate with Almogenes. The demons then bind Almogenes and bring him before James, who discusses differences with him until Almogenes burns his books of magic and prostrates himself before the Saint. Both are then brought before Herod, and Almogenes breaks a pretty heathen idol, while James goes to prison. A panel comes in here, out of place, showing Almogenes enchanting Filetus, and the demon entering into possession of him. Then Almogenes is seen being very roughly handled by a young

Jew, while the bystanders seem to approve. James next makes Almogenes throw his books of magic into the sea; both are led away to execution, curing the infirm on their way; their heads are cut off; and, at the top, God blesses the orb of the world.

That this window was intended to amuse the Virgin seems quite as reasonable an idea as that it should have been made to instruct the people, or us. Its humour was as humorous then as now, for the French of the thirteenth century loved humour even in churches, as their grotesques proclaim. The Saint James window is a tale of magic, told with the vivacity of a fabliau; but if its motive of amusement seems still a forced idea, we can pass on, at once, to the companion window which holds the best position in the church, where, in the usual cathedral, one expects to find Saint John or some other apostle; or Saint Joseph; or a doctrinal lesson such as that called the New Alliance where the Old and New Testaments are united. The window which the artists have set up here is regarded as the best of the thirteenth-century windows, and is the least religious.

The subject is nothing less than the "Chanson de Roland" in pictures of coloured glass, set in a border worth comparing at leisure with the twelfth-century borders of the western lancets. Even at Chartres, the artists could not risk displeasing the Virgin and the Church by following a wholly profane work like the "Chanson" itself, and Roland had no place in religion. He could be introduced only through Charlemagne, who had almost as little right there as he. The twelfth century had made persistent efforts to get Charlemagne into the Church, and the Church had made very little effort to keep him out; yet by the year 1200, Charlemagne had not been sainted except by the anti-Pope Pascal III in 1165, although there was a popular belief, supported in Spain by the necessary documents, that Pope Calixtus II in 1122 had declared the so-called Chronicle of Archbishop Turpin to be authentic. The Bishop of Chartres in 1200 was very much too enlightened a prelate to accept the Chronicle or Turpin or Charlemagne himself, still less Roland and Thierry, as authentic in sanctity; but if the young and beautiful Dauphine of France, and her cousins of Chartres, and their artists, warmly believed that the Virgin would be pleased by the story of Charlemagne and Roland, the Bishop might have let them have their way in spite of the irregularity. That the window was an irregularity, is plain; that it has always been immensely admired, is certain; and that Bishop Renaud must have given his assent to it, is not to be denied.

The most elaborate account of this window can be found in Male's "Art Religieux" (pp. 444-50). Its feeling or motive is quite another matter, as it is with the statuary on the north porch. The Furriers or Fur Merchants paid for the Charlemagne window, and their signature stands at the bottom, where a merchant shows a fur-lined cloak to his customer. That Mary was personally interested in furs, no authority seems to affirm, but that Blanche and Isabel and every lady of the Court, as well as every king and every count, in that day, took keen interest in the subject, is proved by the prices they paid, and the quantities they wore. Not even the Merchant Tailors had a better standing at Court than the Furriers, which may account for their standing so near the Virgin. Whatever the cause, the Furriers were allowed to put their signature here, side by side with the Tailors, and next to the Princess Blanche. Their gift warranted it. Above the signature, in the first panel, the Emperor Constantine is seen, asleep, in Constantinople, on an elaborate bed, while an angel is giving him the order to seek aid from Charlemagne against the Saracens. Charlemagne appears, in full armour of the year 1200, on horseback. Then Charlemagne, sainted, wearing his halo, converses with two bishops on the subject of a crusade for the rescue of

Constantine. In the next scene, he arrives at the gates of Constantinople where Constantine receives him. The fifth picture is most interesting; Charlemagne has advanced with his knights and attacks the Saracens; the Franks wear coats-of-mail, and carry long, pointed shields; the infidels carry round shields; Charlemagne, wearing a crown, strikes off with one blow of his sword the head of a Saracen emir; but the battle is desperate; the chargers are at full gallop, and a Saracen is striking at Charlemagne with his battle-axe. After the victory has been won, the Emperor Constantine rewards Charlemagne by the priceless gift of three chasses or reliquaries, containing a piece of the true Cross; the Suaire or grave-cloth of the Saviour; and a tunic of the Virgin. Charlemagne then returns to France, and in the next medallion presents the three chasses and the crown of the Saracen king to the church at Aix, which to a French audience meant the Abbey of Saint-Denis. This scene closes the first volume of the story.

The second part opens on Charlemagne, seated between two persons, looking up to heaven at the Milky Way, called then the Way of Saint James, which directs him to the grave of Saint James in Spain. Saint James himself appears to Charlemagne in a dream, and orders him to redeem the tomb from the infidels. Then Charlemagne sets out, with Archbishop Turpin of Rheims and knights. In presence of his army he dismounts and implores the aid of God. Then he arrives before Pampeluna and transfixes with his lance the Saracen chief as he flies into the city. Mounted, he directs workmen to construct a church in honour of Saint James; a little cloud figures the hand of God. Next is shown the miracle of the lances; stuck in the ground at night, they are found in the morning to have burst into foliage, prefiguring martyrdom. Two thousand people perish in battle. Then begins the story of Roland which the artists and donors are so eager to tell, knowing, as they do, that what has so deeply interested men and women on earth, must interest Mary who loves them. You see Archbishop Turpin celebrating mass when an angel appears, to warn him of Roland's fate. Then Roland himself, also wearing a halo, is introduced, in the act of killing the giant Ferragus. The combat of Roland and Ferragus is at the top, out of sequence, as often happens in the legendary windows. Charlemagne and his army are seen marching homeward through the Pyrenees, while Roland winds his horn and splits the rock without being able to break Durendal. Thierry, likewise sainted, brings water to Roland in a helmet. At last Thierry announces Roland's death. At the top, on either side of Roland and Ferragus, is an angel with incense.

The execution of this window is said to be superb. Of the colour, and its relations with that of the Saint James, one needs time and long acquaintance to learn the value. In the feeling, compared with that of the twelfth century, one needs no time in order to see a change. These two windows are as French and as modern as a picture of Lancret; they are pure art, as simply decorative as the decorations of the Grand Opera. The thirteenth century knew more about religion and decoration than the twentieth century will ever learn. The windows were neither symbolic nor mystical, nor more religious than they pretended to be. That they are more intelligent or more costly or more effective is nothing to the purpose, so long as one grants that the combat of Roland and Ferragus, or Roland winding his olifant, or Charlemagne cutting off heads and transfixing Moors, were subjects never intended to teach religion or instruct the ignorant, but to please the Queen of Heaven as they pleased the queens of earth with a roman, not in verse but in colour, as near as possible to decorative perfection. Instinctively one looks to the corresponding bay, opposite, to see what the artists could have done to balance these two great efforts of their art; but the bay opposite is now occupied by the entrance to Saint Piat's chapel and one does not know what changes may have been made in the fourteenth century to rearrange the glass; yet, even as it now stands, the Sylvester window which corresponds to the Charlemagne is, as glass, the strongest in the whole cathedral. In the next chapel, on our left, come the martyrs, with Saint Stephen, the first martyr, in the middle window. Naturally the subject is more serious, but the colour is not differently treated. A step further, and you see the artists returning to their lighter subjects. The stories of Saint Julian and Saint Thomas are more amusing than the plots of half the thirteenth-century romances, and not very much more religious. The subject of Saint Thomas is a pendant to that of Saint James, for Saint Thomas was a great traveller and an architect, who carried Mary's worship to India as Saint James carried it to Spain. Here is the amusement of many days in studying the stories, the colour and the execution of these windows, with the help of the "Monographs" of Chartres and Bourges or the "Golden Legend" and occasional visits to Le Mans, Tours, Clermont Ferrand, and other cathedrals; but, in passing, one has to note that the window of Saint Thomas was given by France, and bears the royal arms, perhaps for Philip Augustus the King; while the window of Saint Julian was given by the Carpenters and Coopers. One feels no need to explain how it happens that the taste of the royal family, and of their tailors, furriers, carpenters, and coopers, should fit so marvellously, one with another, and with that of the Virgin; but one can compare with theirs that taste of the Stone-workers opposite, in the window of Saint Sylvester and Saint Melchiades, whose blues almost kill the Charlemagne itself, and of the Tanners in that of Saint Thomas of Canterbury; or, in the last chapel on the south side, with that of the Shoemakers in the window to Saint Martin, attributed for some reason to a certain Clemens vitrearius Carnutensis, whose name is on a window in the cathedral of Rouen. The name tells nothing, even if the identity could be proved. Clement the glassmaker may have worked on his own account, or for others; the glass differs only in refinements of taste or perhaps of cost. Nicolas Lescine, the canon, or Geoffroi Chardonnel, may have been less rich than the Bakers, and even the Furriers may have not had the revenues of the King; but some controlling hand has given more or less identical taste to all.

What one can least explain is the reason why some windows, that should be here, are elsewhere. In most churches, one finds in the choir a window of doctrine, such as the so-called New Alliance, but here the New Alliance is banished to the nave. Besides the costly Charlemagne and Saint James windows in the apse, the Furriers and Drapers gave several others, and one of these seems particularly suited to serve as companion to Saint Thomas, Saint James, and Saint Julian, so that it is best taken with these while comparing them. It is in the nave, the third window from the new tower, in the north aisle,—the window of Saint Eustace. The story and treatment and beauty of the work would have warranted making it a pendant to Almogenes, in the bay now serving as the door to Saint Piat's chapel, which should have been the most effective of all the positions in the church for a legendary story. Saint Eustace, whose name was Placidas, commanded the guards of the Emperor Trajan. One day he went out hunting with huntsmen and hounds, as the legend in the lower panel of the window begins; a pretty picture of a stag hunt about the year 1200; followed by one still prettier, where the stag, after leaping upon a rock, has turned, and shows a crucifix between his horns, the stag on one side balancing the horse on the other, while Placidas on his knees yields to the miracle of Christ. Then Placidas is baptized as Eustace; and in the centre, you see him with his wife and two children—another charming composition—leaving the city. Four small panels in the corners are said to contain the signatures of the Drapers and Furriers. Above, the story of adventure goes on, showing Eustace bargaining with a shipmaster for his passage; his embarcation with wife and children, and their arrival at some shore, where the two children have landed, and the master drives Eustace after them while he detains the wife. Four small panels here have not been identified, but the legend was no doubt familiar to the Middle Ages, and they knew how Eustace and the children came to a river, where you can see a pink lion carrying off one child, while a wolf, which has seized the other, is attacked by shepherds and dogs. The children are rescued, and the wife reappears, on her knees before her lord, telling of her escape from the shipmaster, while the children stand behind; and then the reunited family, restored to the Emperor's favour, is seen feasting and happy. At last Eustace refuses to offer a sacrifice to a graceful antique idol, and is then shut up, with all his family, in a brazen bull; a fire is kindled beneath it; and, from above, a hand confers the crown of martyrdom.

Another subject, which should have been placed in the apse, stands in a singular isolation which has struck many of the students in this branch of church learning. At Sens, Saint Eustace is in the choir, and by his side is the Prodigal Son. At Bourges also the Prodigal Son is in the choir. At Chartres, he is banished to the north transept, where you will find him in the window next the nave, almost as though he were in disgrace; yet the glass is said to be very fine, among the best in the church, while the story is told with rather more vivacity than usual; and as far as colour and execution go, the window has an air of age and quality higher than the average. At the bottom you see the signature of the corporation of Butchers. The window at Bourges was given by the Tanners. The story begins with the picture showing the younger son asking the father for his share of the inheritance, which he receives in the next panel, and proceeds, on horseback, to spend, as one cannot help suspecting, at Paris, in the Latin Quarter, where he is seen arriving, welcomed by two ladies. No one has offered to explain why Chartres should consider two ladies theologically more correct than one; or why Sens should fix on three, or why Bourges should require six. Perhaps this was left to the artist's fancy; but, before quitting the twelfth century, we shall see that the usual young man who took his share of patrimony and went up to study in the Latin Quarter, found two schools of scholastic teaching, one called Realism, the other Nominalism, each of which in turn the Church had been obliged to condemn. Meanwhile the Prodigal Son is seen feasting with them, and is crowned with flowers, like a new Abelard, singing his songs to Heloise, until his religious capital is exhausted, and he is dragged out of bed, to be driven naked from the house with sticks, in this also 1 resembling Abelard. At Bourges he is gently turned out; at Sens he is dragged away by three devils. Then he seeks service, and is seen knocking acorns from boughs, to feed his employer's swine; but, among the thousands of young men who must have come here directly from the schools, nine in every ten said that he was teaching letters to his employer's children or lecturing to the students of the Latin Quarter. At last he decides to return to his father,—possibly the Archbishop of Paris or the Abbot of Saint-Denis,—who receives him with open arms, and gives him a new robe, which to the ribald student would mean a church living—an abbey, perhaps Saint Gildas-de-Rhuys in Brittany, or elsewhere. The fatted calf is killed, the feast is begun, and the elder son, whom the malicious student would name Bernard, appears in order to make protest. Above, God, on His throne, blesses the globe of the world.

The original symbol of the Prodigal Son was a rather different form of prodigality. According to the Church interpretation, the Father had two sons; the older was the people of the Jews; the younger, the Gentiles. The Father divided his substance between them, giving to the older the divine law, to the younger, the law of nature. The younger went off and dissipated his substance, as one must believe, on Aristotle; but repented and returned when the Father sacrificed the victim—Christ—as the symbol of reunion. That the Synagogue also accepts the sacrifice is not so clear; but the Church clung to the idea of converting the Synagogue as a necessary proof of

Christ's divine character. Not until about the time when this window may have been made, did the new Church, under the influence of Saint Dominic, abandon the Jews and turn in despair to the Gentiles alone.

The old symbolism belonged to the fourth and fifth centuries, and, as told by the Jesuit fathers Martin and Cahier in their "Monograph" of Bourges, it should have pleased the Virgin who was particularly loved by the young, and habitually showed her attachment to them. At Bourges the window stands next the central chapel of the apse, where at Chartres is the entrance to Saint Piat's chapel; but Bourges did not belong to Notre Dame, nor did Sens. The story of the prodigal sons of these years from 1200 to 1230 lends the window a little personal interest that the Prodigal Son of Saint Luke's Gospel could hardly have had even to thirteenth-century penitents. Neither the Church nor the Crown loved prodigal sons. So far from killing fatted calves for them, the bishops in 1209 burned no less than ten in Paris for too great intimacy with Arab and Jew disciples of Aristotle. The position of the Bishop of Chartres between the schools had been always awkward. As for Blanche of Castile, her first son, afterwards Saint Louis, was born in 1215; and after that time no Prodigal Son was likely to be welcomed in any society which she frequented. For her, above all other women on earth or in heaven, prodigal sons felt most antipathy, until, in 1229, the quarrel became so violent that she turned her police on them and beat a number to death in the streets. They retaliated without regard for loyalty or decency, being far from model youth and prone to relapses from virtue, even when forgiven and beneficed.

The Virgin Mary, Queen of Heaven, showed no prejudice against prodigal sons, or even prodigal daughters. She would hardly, of her own accord, have ordered such persons out of her apse, when Saint Stephen at Bourges and Sens showed no such puritanism; yet the Chartres window is put away in the north transept. Even there it still stands opposite the Virgin of the Pillar, on the women's and Queen Blanche's side of the church, and in an excellent position, better seen from the choir than some of the windows in the choir itself, because the late summer sun shines full upon it, and carries its colours far into the apse. This may have been one of the many instances of tastes in the Virgin which were almost too imperial for her official court. Omniscient as Mary was, she knew no difference between the Blanches of Castile and the students of the Latin Quarter. She was rather fond of prodigals, and gentle toward the ladies who consumed the prodigal's substance. She admitted Mary Magdalen and Mary the Gipsy to her society. She fretted little about Aristotle so long as the prodigal adored her, and naturally the prodigal adored her almost to the exclusion of the Trinity. She always cared less for her dignity than was to be wished. Especially in the nave and on the porch, among the peasants, she liked to appear as one of themselves; she insisted on lying in bed, in a stable, with the cows and asses about her, and her baby in a cradle by the bedside, as though she had suffered like other women, though the Church insisted she had not. Her husband, Saint Joseph, was notoriously uncomfortable in her Court, and always preferred to get as near to the door as he could. The choir at Chartres, on the contrary, was aristocratic; every window there had a court quality, even down to the contemporary Thomas a'Becket, the fashionable martyr of good society. Theology was put into the transepts or still further away in the nave where the window of the New Alliance elbows the Prodigal Son. Even to Blanche of Castile, Mary was neither a philanthropist nor theologian nor merely a mother,—she was an absolute Empress, and whatever she said was obeyed, but sometimes she seems to have willed an order that worried some of her most powerful servants.

Mary chose to put her Prodigal into the transept, and one would like to know the reason. Was it a concession to the Bishop or the Queen? Or was it to please the common people that these familiar picture-books, with their popular interest, like the Good Samaritan and the Prodigal Son, were put on the walls of the great public hall? This can hardly be, since the people would surely have preferred the Charlemagne and Saint James to any other. We shall never know; but sitting here in the subdued afternoon light of the apse, one goes on for hours reading the open volumes of colour, and listening to the steady discussion by the architects, artists, priests, princes, and princesses of the thirteenth century about the arrangements of this apse. However strong-willed they might be, each in turn whether priest, or noble, or glassworker, would have certainly appealed to the Virgin and one can imagine the architect still beside us, in the growing dusk of evening, mentally praying, as he looked at the work of a finished day: "Lady Virgin, show me what you like best! The central chapel is correct, I know. The Lady Blanche's grisaille veils the rather strong blue tone nicely, and I am confident it will suit you. The Charlemagne window seems to me very successful, but the Bishop feels not at all easy about it, and I should never have dared put it here if the Lady Blanche had not insisted on a Spanish bay. To balance at once both the subjects and the colour, we have tried the Stephen window in the next chapel, with more red; but if Saint Stephen is not good enough to satisfy you, we have tried again with Saint Julian, whose story is really worth telling you as we tell it; and with him we have put Saint Thomas because you loved him and gave him your girdle. I do not myself care so very much for Saint Thomas of Canterbury opposite, though the Count is wild about it, and the Bishop wants it; but the Sylvester is stupendous in the morning sun. What troubles me most is the first right-hand bay. The princesses would not have let me put the Prodigal Son there, even if it were made for the place. I've nothing else good enough to balance the Charlemagne unless it be the Eustace. Gracious Lady, what ought I to do? Forgive me my blunders, my stupidity, my wretched want of taste and feeling! I love and adore you! All that I am, I am for you! If I cannot please you, I care not for Heaven! but without your help, I am lost!"

Upon my word, you may sit here forever imagining such appeals, and the endless discussions and criticisms that were heard every day, under these vaults, seven hundred years ago. That the Virgin answered the questions is my firm belief, just as it is my conviction that she did not answer them elsewhere. One sees her personal presence on every side. Any one can feel it who will only consent to feel like a child. Sitting here any Sunday afternoon, while the voices of the children of the maitrise are chanting in the choir,—your mind held in the grasp of the strong lines and shadows of the architecture; your eyes flooded with the autumn tones of the glass; your ears drowned with the purity of the voices; one sense reacting upon another until sensation reaches the limit of its range,—you, or any other lost soul, could, if you cared to look and listen, feel a sense beyond the human ready to reveal a sense divine that would make that world once more intelligible, and would bring the Virgin to life again, in all the depths of feeling which she shows here,—in lines, vaults, chapels, colours, legends, chants,— more eloquent than the prayer-book, and more beautiful than the autumn sunlight; and any one willing to try could feel it like the child, reading new thought without end into the art he has studied a hundred times; but what is still more convincing, he could, at will, in an instant, shatter the whole art by calling into it a single motive of his own.

CHAPTER X: THE COURT OF THE QUEEN OF HEAVEN

All artists love the sanctuary of the Christian Church, and all tourists love the rest. The reason becomes clear as one leaves the choir, and goes back to the broad, open hall of the nave. The choir was made not for the pilgrim but for the deity, and is as old as Adam, or perhaps older; at all events old enough to have existed in complete artistic and theological form, with the whole mystery of the Trinity, the Mother and Child, and even the Cross, thousands of years before Christ was born; but the Christian Church not only took the sanctuary in hand, and gave it a new form, more beautiful and much more refined than the Romans or Greeks or Egyptians had ever imagined, but it also added the idea of the nave and transepts, and developed it into imperial splendour. The pilgrim-tourist feels at home in the nave because it was built for him; the artist loves the sanctuary because he built it for God.

Chartres was intended to hold ten thousand people easily, or fifteen thousand when crowded, and the decoration of this great space, though not a wholly new problem, had to be treated in a new way. Sancta Sofia was built by the Emperor Justinian, with all the resources of the Empire, in a single violent effort, in six years, and was decorated throughout with mosaics on a general scheme, with the unity that Empire and Church could give, when they acted together. The Norman Kings of Sicily, the richest princes of the twelfth century, were able to carry out a complete work of the most costly kind, in a single sustained effort from beginning to end, according to a given plan. Chartres was a local shrine, in an agricultural province, not even a part of the royal domain, and its cathedral was the work of society, without much more tie than the Virgin gave it. Socially Chartres, as far as its stone-work goes, seems to have been mostly rural; its decoration, in the porches and transepts, is royal and feudal; in the nave and choir it is chiefly bourgeois. The want of unity is much less surprising than the unity, but it is still evident, especially in the glass. The mosaics of Monreale begin and end; they are a series; their connection is artistic and theological at once; they have unity. The windows of Chartres have no sequence, and their charm is in variety, in individuality, and sometimes even in downright hostility to each other, reflecting the picturesque society that gave them. They have, too, the charm that the world has made no attempt to popularize them for its modern uses, so that, except for the useful little guide- book of the Abbe Clerval, one can see no clue to the legendary chaos; one has it to one's self, without much fear of being trampled upon by critics or Jew dealers in works of art; any Chartres beggar- woman can still pass a summer's day here, and never once be mortified by ignorance of things that every dealer in bric-a-brac is supposed to know.

Yet the artists seem to have begun even here with some idea of sequence, for the first window in the north aisle, next the new tower, tells the story of Noah; but the next plunges into the local history of Chartres, and is devoted to Saint Lubin, a bishop of this diocese who died in or about the year 556, and was, for some reason, selected by the Wine-Merchants to represent them, as their interesting medallions show. Then follow three amusing subjects, charmingly treated: Saint Eustace, whose story has been told; Joseph and his brethren; and Saint Nicholas, the most popular saint of the thirteenth century, both in the Greek and in the Roman Churches. The sixth and last window on the north aisle of the nave is the New Alliance.

Opposite these, in the south aisle, the series begins next the tower with John the Evangelist, followed by Saint Mary Magdalen, given by the Water-Carriers. The third, the Good Samaritan, given by the Shoemakers, has a rival at Sens which critics think even better. The fourth is the Death, Assumption, and Coronation of the Virgin. Then comes the fifteenth-century Chapel of Vendome, to compare the early and later glass. The sixth is, or was, devoted to the Virgin's Miracles at Chartres; but only one complete subject remains.

These windows light the two aisles of the nave and decorate the lower walls of the church with a mass of colour and variety of line still practically intact in spite of much injury; but the windows of the transepts on the same level have almost disappeared, except the Prodigal Son and a border to what was once a Saint Lawrence, on the north; and, on the south, part of a window to Saint Apollinaris of Ravenna, with an interesting hierarchy of angels above:—seraphim and cherubim with six wings, red and blue; Dominations; Powers; Principalities; all, except Thrones.

All this seems to be simple enough, at least to the people for whom the nave was built, and to whom the windows were meant to speak. There is nothing esoteric here; nothing but what might have suited the great hall of a great palace. There is no difference in taste between the Virgin in the choir, and the Water-Carriers by the doorway. Blanche, the young Queen, liked the same colours, legends, and lines that her Grocers and Bakers liked. All equally loved the Virgin. There was not even a social difference. In the choir, Thibaut, the Count of Chartres, immediate lord of the province, let himself be put in a dark corner next the Belle Verriere, and left the Bakers to display their wealth in the most serious spot in the church, the central window of the central chapel, while in the nave and transepts all the lower windows that bear signatures were given by trades, as though that part of the church were abandoned to the commons. One might suppose that the feudal aristocracy would have fortified itself in the clerestory and upper windows, but even there the bourgeoisie invaded them, and you can see, with a glass, the Pastrycooks and Turners looking across at the Weavers and Curriers and Money-Changers, and the "Men of Tours." Beneath the throne of the Mother of God, there was no distinction of gifts; and above it the distinction favoured the commonalty.

Of the seven immense windows above and around the high altar, which are designed as one composition, none was given by a prince or a noble. The Drapers, the Butchers, the Bakers, the Bankers are charged with the highest duties attached to the Virgin's service. Apparently neither Saint Louis, nor his father Louis VIII, nor his mother Blanche, nor his uncle Philippe Hurepel, nor his cousin Saint Ferdinand of Castile, nor his other cousin Pierre de Dreux, nor the Duchess Alix of Brittany, cared whether their portraits or armorial shields were thrust out of sight into corners by Pastrycooks and Teamsters, or took a whole wall of the church to themselves. The only relation that connects them is their common relation to the Virgin, but that is emphatic, and dominates the whole.

It dominates us, too, if we reflect on it, even after seven hundred years that its meaning has faded. When one looks up to this display of splendour in the clerestory, and asks what was in the minds of the people who joined to produce, with such immense effort and at such self-sacrifice, this astonishing effect, the question seems to answer itself like an echo. With only half of an atrophied imagination, in a happy mood we could still see the nave and transepts filled with ten thousand people on their knees, and the Virgin, crowned and robed, seating herself on the embroidered cushion that covered her imperial throne; sparkling with gems; bearing in her right hand the sceptre, and in her lap the infant King; but, in the act of seating herself, we should see her pause a moment to look down with love and sympathy on us,—her people,—who pack the enormous hall, and throng far out beyond the open portals; while, an instant later, she glances up to see that her great lords, spiritual and temporal, the advisers of her judgment, the supports of her authority, the agents of her will, shall be in place; robed, mitred, armed; bearing the symbols of her authority and their office; on horseback, lance in hand; all of them ready at a sign to carry out a sentence of judgment or an errand of mercy; to touch with the sceptre or to strike with the sword; and never err.

There they still stand! unchanged, unfaded, as alive and complete as when they represented the real world, and the people below were the unreal and ephemeral pageant! Then the reality was the Queen of Heaven on her throne in the sanctuary, and her court in the glass; not the queens or princes who were prostrating themselves, with the crowd, at her feet. These people knew the Virgin as well as they knew their own mothers; every jewel in her crown, every stitch of gold-embroidery in her many robes; every colour; every fold; every expression on the perfectly familiar features of her grave, imperial face; every care that lurked in the silent sadness of her power; repeated over and over again, in stone, glass, ivory, enamel, wood; in every room, at the head of every bed, hanging on every neck, standing at every street-corner, the Virgin was as familiar to every one of them as the sun or the seasons; far more familiar than their own earthly queen or countess, although these were no strangers in their daily life; familiar from the earliest childhood to the last agony; in every joy and every sorrow and every danger; in every act and almost in every thought of life, the Virgin was present with a reality that never belonged to her Son or to the Trinity, and hardly to any earthly being, prelate, king, or kaiser; her daily life was as real to them as their own loyalty which brought to her the best they had to offer as the return for her boundless sympathy; but while they knew the Virgin as though she were one of themselves, and because she had been one of themselves, they were not so familiar with all the officers of her court at Chartres; and pilgrims from abroad, like us, must always have looked with curious interest at the pageant.

Far down the nave, next the western towers, the rank began with saints, prophets, and martyrs, of all ages and countries; local, like Saint Lubin; national, like Saint Martin of Tours and Saint Hilary of Poitiers; popular like Saint Nicholas; militant like Saint George; without order; symbols like Abraham and Isaac; the Virgin herself, holding on her lap the Seven Gifts of the Holy Ghost; Christ with the Alpha and Omega; Moses and Saint Augustine; Saint Peter; Saint Mary the Egyptian; Saint Jerome; a whole throne-room of heavenly powers, repeating, within, the pageant carved on the porches and on the portals without. From the croisee in the centre, where the crowd is most dense, one sees the whole almost better than Mary sees it from her high altar, for there all the great rose windows flash in turn, and the three twelfth-century lancets glow on the western sun. When the eyes of the throng are directed to the north, the Rose of France strikes them almost with a physical shock of colour, and, from the south, the Rose of Dreux challenges the Rose of France.

Every one knows that there is war between the two! The thirteenth century has few secrets. There are no outsiders. We are one family as we are one Church. Every man and woman here, from Mary on her throne to the beggar on the porch, knows that Pierre de Dreux detests Blanche of Castile, and that their two windows carry on war across the very heart of the cathedral. Both unite only in asking help from Mary; but Blanche is a woman, alone in the world with young children to protect, and most women incline strongly to suspect that Mary will never desert her. Pierre, with all his masculine strength, is no courtier. He wants to rule by force. He carries the assertion of his sex into the very presence of the Queen of Heaven.

The year happens to be 1230, when the roses may be supposed just finished and showing their whole splendour for the first time. Queen Blanche is forty-three years old, and her son Louis is fifteen. Blanche is a widow these four years, and Pierre a widower since 1221. Both are regents and guardians for their heirs. They have necessarily carried their disputes before Mary. Queen Blanche claims for her son, who is to be Saint Louis, the place of honour at Mary's right hand; she has taken possession of the north porch outside, and of the north transept within, and has filled the windows with glass, as she is filling the porch with statuary. Above is the huge rose; below are five long windows; and all proclaim the homage that France renders to the Queen of Heaven.

The Rose of France shows in its centre the Virgin in her majesty, seated, crowned, holding the sceptre with her right hand, while her left supports the infant Christ-King on her knees; which shows that she, too, is acting as regent for her Son. Round her, in a circle, are twelve medallions; four containing doves; four six-winged angels or Thrones; four angels of a lower order, but all symbolizing the gifts and endowments of the Queen of Heaven. Outside these are twelve more medallions with the Kings of Judah, and a third circle contains the twelve lesser prophets. So Mary sits, hedged in by all the divinity that graces earthly or heavenly kings; while between the two outer circles are twelve quatrefoils bearing on a blue ground the golden lilies of France; and in each angle below the rose are four openings, showing alternately the lilies of Louis and the castles of Blanche. We who are below, the common people, understand that France claims to protect and defend the Virgin of Chartres, as her chief vassal, and that this ostentatious profusion of lilies and castles is intended not in honour of France, but as a demonstration of loyalty to Notre Dame, and an assertion of her rights as Queen Regent of Heaven against all comers, but particularly against Pierre, the rebel, who has the audacity to assert rival rights in the opposite transept.

Beneath the rose are five long windows, very unlike the twelfth-century pendants to the western rose. These five windows blaze with red, and their splendour throws the Virgin above quite into the background. The artists, who felt that the twelfth-century glass was too fine and too delicate for the new scale of the church, have not only enlarged their scale and coarsened their design, but have coarsened their colour-scheme also, discarding blue in order to crush us under the earthly majesty of red. These windows, too, bear the stamp and seal of Blanche's Spanish temper as energetically as though they bore her portrait. The great central figure, the tallest and most commanding in the whole church, is not the Virgin, but her mother Saint Anne, standing erect as on the trumeau of the door beneath, and holding the infant Mary on her left arm. She wears no royal crown, but bears a flowered sceptre. The only other difference between Mary and her mother, that seems intended to strike attention, is that Mary sits, while her mother stands; but as though to proclaim still more distinctly that France supports the royal and divine pretensions of Saint Anne, Queen Blanche has put beneath the figure a great shield blazoned with the golden lilies on an azure ground.

With singular insistence on this motive, Saint Anne has at either hand a royal court of her own, marked as her own by containing only figures from the Old Testament. Standing next on her right is Solomon, her Prime Minister, bringing wisdom in worldly counsel, and trampling on human folly. Beyond Wisdom stands Law, figured by Aaron with the Book, trampling on the lawless Pharaoh. Opposite them, on Saint Anne's left, is David, the energy of State, trampling on a Saul suggesting suspicions of a Saul de Dreux; while last, Melchisedec who is Faith, tramples on a disobedient Nebuchadnezzar Mauclerc.

How can we, the common people, help seeing all this, and much more, when we know that

Pierre de Dreux has been for years in constant strife with the Crown and the Church? He is very valiant and lion-hearted;—so say the chroniclers, priests though they are;—very skilful and experienced in war whether by land or sea; very adroit, with more sense than any other great lord in France; but restless, factious, and regardless of his word. Brave and bold as the day; full of courtesy and "largesse"; but very hard on the clergy; a good Christian but a bad churchman! Certainly the first man of his time, says Michelet! "I have never found any that sought to do me more ill than he," says Blanche, and Joinville gives her very words; indeed, this year, 1230, she has summoned our own Bishop of Chartres among others to Paris in a court of peers, where Pierre has been found guilty of treason and deposed. War still continues, but Pierre must make submission. Blanche has beaten him in politics and in the field! Let us look round and see how he fares in theology and art!

There is his rose—so beautiful that Blanche may well think it seeks to do hers ill! As colour, judge for yourselves whether it holds its own against the flaming self-assertion of the opposite wall! As subject, it asserts flat defiance of the monarchy of Queen Blanche. In the central circle, Christ as King is seated on a royal throne, both arms raised, one holding the golden cup of eternal priesthood, the other, blessing the world. Two great flambeaux burn beside Him. The four Apocalyptic figures surround and worship Him; and in the concentric circles round the central medallion are the angels and the kings in a blaze of colour, symbolizing the New Jerusalem.

All the force of the Apocalypse is there, and so is some of the weakness of theology, for, in the five great windows below, Pierre shows his training in the schools. Four of these windows represent what is called, for want of a better name, the New Alliance; the dependence of the New Testament on the Old; but Pierre's choice in symbols was as masculine as that of Blanche was feminine. In each of the four windows, a gigantic Evangelist strides the shoulders of a colossal Prophet. Saint John rides on Ezekiel; Saint Mark bestrides Daniel; Saint Matthew is on the shoulders of Isaiah; Saint Luke is carried by Jeremiah. The effect verges on the grotesque. The balance of Christ's Church seems uncertain. The Evangelists clutch the Prophets by the hair, and while the synagogue stands firm, the Church looks small, feeble, and vacillating. The new dispensation has not the air of mastery either physical or intellectual; the old gives it all the support it has, and, in the absence of Saint Paul, both old and new seem little concerned with the sympathies of Frenchmen. The synagogue is stronger than the Church, but even the Church is Jew.

That Pierre could ever have meant this is not to be dreamed; but when the true scholar gets thoroughly to work, his logic is remorseless, his art is implacable, and his sense of humour is blighted. In the rose above, Pierre had asserted the exclusive authority of Christ in the New Jerusalem, and his scheme required him to show how the Church rested on the Evangelists below, who in their turn had no visible support except what the Prophets gave them. Yet the artist may have had a reason for weakening the Evangelists, because there remained the Virgin! One dares no more than hint at a motive so disrespectful to the Evangelists; but it is certainly true that, in the central window, immediately beneath the Christ, and His chief support, with the four staggering Evangelists and Prophets on either hand, the Virgin stands, and betrays no sign of weakness.

The compliment is singularly masculine; a kind of twelfth-century flattery that might have softened the anger of Blanche herself, if the Virgin had been her own; but the Virgin of Dreux is not the Virgin of France. No doubt she still wears her royal crown, and her head is circled with the halo; her right hand still holds the flowered sceptre, and her left the infant Christ, but she stands, and Christ is King. Note, too, that she stands directly opposite to her mother Saint Anne in the Rose of France, so as to place her one stage lower than the Virgin of France in the hierarchy. She is the Saint Anne of France, and shows it. "She is no longer," says the official Monograph, "that majestic queen who was seated on a throne, with her feet on the stool of honour; the personages have become less imposing and the heads show the decadence." She is the Virgin of Theology; she has her rights, and no more; but she is not the Virgin of Chartres.

She, too, stands on an altar or pedestal, on which hangs a shield bearing the ermines, an exact counterpart of the royal shield beneath Saint Anne. In this excessive display of armorial bearings— for the two roses above are crowded with them—one likes to think that these great princes had in their minds not so much the thought of their own importance—which is a modern sort of religion—as the thought of their devotion to Mary. The assertion of power and attachment by one is met by the assertion of equal devotion by the other, and while both loudly proclaim their homage to the Virgin, each glares defiance across the church. Pierre meant the Queen of Heaven to know that, in case of need, her left hand was as good as her right, and truer; that the ermines were as well able to defend her as the lilies, and that Brittany would fight her battles as bravely as France. Whether his meaning carried with it more devotion to the Virgin or more defiance to France depends a little on the date of the windows, but, as a mere point of history, every one must allow that Pierre's promise of allegiance was kept more faithfully by Brittany than that of Blanche and Saint Louis has been kept by France.

The date seems to be fixed by the windows themselves. Beneath the Prophets kneel Pierre and his wife Alix, while their two children, Yolande and Jean, stand. Alix died in 1221. Jean was born in 1217. Yolande was affianced in marriage in 1227, while a child, and given to Queen Blanche to be brought up as the future wife of her younger son John, then in his eighth year. When John died, Yolande was contracted to Thibaut of Champagne in 1231, and Blanche is said to have written to Thibaut in consequence: "Sire Thibauld of Champagne, I have heard that you have covenanted and promised to take to wife the daughter of Count Perron of Brittany. Wherefore I charge you, if you do not wish to lose whatever you possess in the kingdom of France, not to do it. If you hold dear or love aught in the said kingdom, do it not." Whether Blanche wrote in these words or not, she certainly prevented the marriage, and Yolande remained single until 1238 when she married the Comte de la Marche, who was, by the way, almost as bitter an enemy of Blanche as Pierre had been; but by that time both Blanche and Pierre had ceased to be regents. Yolande's figure in the window is that of a girl, perhaps twelve or fourteen years old; Jean is younger, certainly not more than eight or ten years of age; and the appearance of the two children shows that the window itself should date between 1225 and 1230, the year when Pierre de Dreux was condemned because he had renounced his homage to King Louis, declared war on him, and invited the King of England into France. As already told, Philippe Hurepel de Boulogne, the Comte de la Marche, Enguerrand de Couci,—nearly all the great nobles,—had been leagued with Pierre de Dreux since Blanche's regency began in 1226.

That these transept windows harmonize at all, is due to the Virgin, not to the donors. At the time they were designed, supposing it to be during Blanche's regency (1226-36), the passions of these donors brought France to momentary ruin, and the Virgin in Blanche's Rose de France, as she looked across the church, could not see a single friend of Blanche. What is more curious, she saw enemies in plenty, and in full readiness for battle. We have seen in the centre of the small rose in the north transept, Philippe Hurepel still waiting her orders; across the nave, in another small rose of the south transept, sits Pierre de Dreux on his horse. The upper windows on the side walls of the choir are very interesting but impossible to see, even with the best glasses, from the floor of the church. Their sequence and dates have already been discussed; but their feeling is shown by the character of the Virgin, who in French territory, next the north transept, is still the Virgin of France, but in Pierre's territory, next the Rose de Dreux, becomes again the Virgin of Dreux, who is absorbed in the Child,—not the Child absorbed in her,—and accordingly the window shows the chequers and ermines.

The figures, like the stone figures outside, are the earliest of French art, before any school of painting fairly existed. Among them, one can see no friend of Blanche. Indeed, outside of her own immediate family and the Church, Blanche had no friend of much importance except the famous Thibaut of Champagne, the single member of the royal family who took her side and suffered for her sake, and who, as far as books tell, has no window or memorial here. One might suppose that Thibaut, who loved both Blanche and the Virgin, would have claimed a place, and perhaps he did; but one seeks him in vain. If Blanche had friends here, they are gone. Pierre de Dreux, lance in hand, openly defies her, and it was not on her brother-in-law Philippe Hurepel that she could depend for defence.

This is the court pageant of the Virgin that shows itself to the people who are kneeling at high mass. We, the public, whoever we are,—Chartrain, Breton, Norman, Angevin, Frenchman, Percherain, or what not,—know our local politics as intimately as our lords do, or even better, for our imaginations are active, and we do not love Blanche of Castile. We know how to read the passions that fill the church. From the north transept Blanche flames out on us in splendid reds and flings her Spanish castles in our face. From the south transept Pierre retorts with a brutal energy which shows itself in the Prophets who serve as battle-chargers and in the Evangelists who serve as knights,—mounted warriors of faith,—whose great eyes follow us across the church and defy Saint Anne and her French shield opposite. Pierre was not effeminate; Blanche was fairly masculine. Between them, as a matter of sex, we can see little to choose; and, in any case, it is a family quarrel; they are all cousins; they are all equals on earth, and none means to submit to any superior except the Virgin and her Son in heaven. The Virgin is not afraid. She has seen many troubles worse than this; she knows how to manage perverse children, and if necessary she will shut them up in a darker room than ever their mothers kept open for them in this world. One has only to look at the Virgin to see!

There she is, of course, looking down on us from the great window above the high altar, where we never forget her presence! Is there a thought of disturbance there? Around the curve of the choir are seven great windows, without roses, filling the whole semicircle and the whole vault, forty-seven feet high, and meant to dominate the nave as far as the western portal, so that we may never forget how Mary fills her church without being disturbed by quarrels, and may understand why Saint Ferdinand and Saint Louis creep out of our sight, close by the Virgin's side, far up above brawls; and why France and Brittany hide their ugly or their splendid passions at the ends of the transepts, out of sight of the high altar where Mary is to sit in state as Queen with the young King on her lap. In an instant she will come, but we have a moment still to look about at the last great decoration of her palace, and see how the artists have arranged it.

Since the building of Sancta Sofia, no artist has had such a chance. No doubt, Rheims and Amiens and Bourges and Beauvais, which are now building, may be even finer, but none of them is yet finished, and all must take their ideas from here. One would like, before looking at it, to think over the problem, as though it were new, and so choose the scheme that would suit us best if the decoration were to be done for the first time. The architecture is fixed; we have to do only with the colour of this mass of seven huge windows, forty-seven feet high, in the clerestory, round the curve of the choir, which close the vista of the church as viewed from the entrance. This vista is about three hundred and thirty feet long. The windows rise above a hundred feet. How ought this vast space to be filled? Should the perpendicular upward leap of the architecture be followed and accented by a perpendicular leap of colour? The decorators of the fifteenth and sixteenth centuries seem to have thought so, and made perpendicular architectural drawings in yellow that simulated gold, and lines that ran with the general lines of the building. Many fifteenth-century windows seem to be made up of florid Gothic details rising in stages to the vault. No doubt critics complained, and still complain, that the monotony of this scheme, and its cheapness of intelligence, were objections; but at least the effect was light, decorative, and safe. The artist could not go far wrong and was still at liberty to do beautiful work, as can be seen in any number of churches scattered broadcast over Europe and swarming in Paris and France. On the other hand, might not the artist disregard the architecture and fill the space with a climax of colour? Could he not unite the Roses of France and Dreux above the high altar in an overpowering outburst of purples and reds? The seventeenth century might have preferred to mass clouds and colours, and Michael Angelo, in the sixteenth, might have known how to do it. What we want is not the feeling of the artist so much as the feeling of Chartres. What shall it be—the jewelled brilliancy of the western windows, or the fierce self-assertion of Pierre Mauclerc, or the royal splendour of Queen Blanche, or the feminine grace and decorative refinement of the Charlemagne and Santiago windows in the apse?

Never again in art was so splendid a problem offered, either before or since, for the artist of Chartres solved it, as he did the whole matter of fenestration, and later artists could only offer variations on his work. You will see them at Bourges and Tours and in scores of thirteenth and fourteenth and fifteenth and sixteenth century churches and windows, and perhaps in some of the twentieth century,—all of them interesting and some of them beautiful,—and far be it from us, mean and ignorant pilgrims of art, to condemn any intelligent effort to vary or improve the effect; but we have set out to seek the feeling, and while we think of art in relation to ourselves, the sermon of Chartres, from beginning to end, teaches and preaches and insists and reiterates and hammers into our torpid minds the moral that the art of the Virgin was not that of her artists but her own. We inevitably think of our tastes; they thought instinctively of hers.

In the transepts, Queen Blanche and Duke Perron, in legal possession of their territory, showed that they were thinking of each other as well as of the Virgin, and claimed loudly that they ought each to be first in the Virgin's favour; and they stand there in place, as the thirteenth century felt them. Subject to their fealty to Mary, the transepts belonged to them, and if Blanche did not, like Pierre, assert Herself and her son on the Virgin's window, perhaps she thought the Virgin would resent Pierre's boldness the more by contrast with her own good taste. So far as is known, nowhere does Blanche appear in person at Chartres; she felt herself too near the Virgin to obtrude a useless image, or she was too deeply religious to ask anything for herself. A queen who was to have two children sainted, to intercede for her at Mary's throne, stood in a solitude almost as unique as that of Mary, and might ignore the raw brutalities of a man-at-arms; but neither she nor Pierre has carried the quarrel into Mary's presence, nor has the Virgin condescended even to seem conscious of their temper. This is the theme of the artist—the purity, the beauty, the grace, and the infinite loftiness of Mary's nature, among the things of earth, and above the clamour of kings.

Therefore, when we, and the crushed crowd of kneeling worshippers around us, lift our eyes at last after the miracle of the mass, we see, far above the high altar, high over all the agitation of prayer, the passion of politics, the anguish of suffering, the terrors of sin, only the figure of the Virgin in majesty, looking down on her people, crowned, throned, glorified, with the infant Christ on her knees. She does not assert herself; probably she intends to be felt rather than feared. Compared with the Greek Virgin, as you see her, for example, at Torcello, the Chartres Virgin is retiring and hardly important enough for the place. She is not exaggerated either in scale, drawing, or colour. She shows not a sign of self-consciousness, not an effort for brilliancy, not a trace of stage effect—hardly even a thought of herself, except that she is at home, among her own people, where she is loved and known as well as she knows them. The seven great windows are one composition; and it is plain that the artist, had he been ordered to make an exhibition of power, could have overwhelmed us with a storm of purple, red, yellows, or given us a Virgin of Passion who would have torn the vault asunder; his ability is never in doubt, and if he has kept true to the spirit of the western portal and the twelfth-century, it is because the Virgin of Chartres was the Virgin of Grace, and ordered him to paint her so. One shudders to think how a single false note—a suggestion of meanness, in this climax of line and colour—would bring the whole fabric down in ruins on the eighteenth-century meanness of the choir below; and one notes, almost bashfully, the expedients of the artists to quiet their effects. So the lines of the seven windows are built up, to avoid the horizontal, and yet not exaggerate the vertical.

The architect counts here for more than the colourist; but the colour, when you study it, suggests the same restraint. Three great windows on the Virgin's right, balanced by three more on her left, show the prophets and precursors of her Son; all architecturally support and exalt the Virgin, in her celestial atmosphere of blue, shot with red, calm in the certainty of heaven. Any one who is prematurely curious to see the difference in treatment between different centuries should go down to the church of Saint Pierre in the lower town, and study there the methods of the Renaissance. Then we can come back to study again the ways of the thirteenth century. The Virgin will wait; she will not be angry; she knows her power; we all come back to her in the end.

Or the Renaissance, if one prefers, can wait equally well, while one kneels with the thirteenth century, and feels the little one still can feel of what it felt. Technically these apsidal windows have not received much notice; the books rarely speak of them; travellers seldom look at them; and their height is such that even with the best glass, the quality of the work is beyond our power to judge. We see, and the artists meant that we should see, only the great lines, the colour, and the Virgin. The mass of suppliants before the choir look up to the light, clear blues and reds of this great space, and feel there the celestial peace and beauty of Mary's nature and abode. There is heaven! and Mary looks down from it, into her church, where she sees us on our knees, and knows each one of us by name. There she actually is—not in symbol or in fancy, but in person, descending on her errands of mercy and listening to each one of us, as her miracles prove, or satisfying our prayers merely by her presence which calms our excitement as that of a mother calms her child. She is there as Queen, not merely as intercessor, and her power is such that to her the difference between us earthly beings is nothing. Her quiet, masculine strength enchants us most. Pierre Mauclerc and Philippe Hurepel and their men-at-arms are afraid of her, and the Bishop himself is never quite at his ease in her presence; but to peasants, and beggars, and people in trouble, this sense of her power and calm is better than active sympathy. People who suffer beyond the formulas of expression—who are crushed into silence, and beyond pain—want no display of emotion—no bleeding heart—no weeping at the foot of the Cross—no hysterics—no phrases! They want to see God, and to know that He is watching over His own. How many women are there, in this mass of thirteenth century suppliants, who have lost children? Probably nearly all, for the death rate is very high in the conditions of medieval life. There are thousands of such women here, for it is precisely this class who come most; and probably every one of them has looked up to Mary in her great window, and has felt actual certainty, as though she saw with her own eyes—there, in heaven, while she looked—her own lost baby playing with the Christ-Child at the Virgin's knee, as much at home as the saints, and much more at home than the kings. Before rising from her knees, every one of these women will have bent down and kissed the stone pavement in gratitude for Mary's mercy. The earth, she says, is a sorry place, and the best of it is bad enough, no doubt, even for Queen Blanche and the Duchess Alix who has had to leave her children here alone; but there above is Mary in heaven who sees and hears me as I see her, and who keeps my little boy till I come; so I can wait with patience, more or less! Saints and prophets and martyrs are all very well, and Christ is very sublime and just, but Mary knows!

It was very childlike, very foolish, very beautiful, and very true,- -as art, at least:—so true that everything else shades off into vulgarity, as you see the Persephone of a Syracusan coin shade off into the vulgarity of a Roman emperor; as though the heaven that lies about us in our infancy too quickly takes colours that are not so much sober as sordid, and would be welcome if no worse than that. Vulgarity, too, has feeling, and its expression in art has truth and even pathos, but we shall have time enough in our lives for that, and all the more because, when we rise from our knees now, we have finished our pilgrimage. We have done with Chartres. For seven hundred years Chartres has seen pilgrims, coming and going more or less like us, and will perhaps see them for another seven hundred years; but we shall see it no more, and can safely leave the Virgin in her majesty, with her three great prophets on either hand, as calm and confident in their own strength and in God's providence as they were when Saint Louis was born, but looking down from a deserted heaven, into an empty church, on a dead faith.

CHAPTER XI: THE THREE QUEENS

After worshipping at the shrines of Saint Michael on his Mount and of the Virgin at Chartres, one may wander far and wide over France, and seldom feel lost; all later Gothic art comes naturally, and no new thought disturbs the perfected form. Yet tourists of English blood and American training are seldom or never quite at home there. Commonly they feel it only as a stage-decoration. The twelfth and thirteenth centuries, studied in the pure light of political economy, are insane. The scientific mind is atrophied, and suffers under inherited cerebral weakness, when it comes in contact with the eternal woman—Astarte, Isis, Demeter, Aphrodite, and the last and greatest deity of all, the Virgin. Very rarely one lingers, with a mild sympathy, such as suits the patient student of human error, willing to be interested in what he cannot understand. Still more rarely, owing to some revival of archaic instincts, he rediscovers the woman. This is perhaps the mark of the artist alone, and his solitary privilege. The rest of us cannot feel; we can only study. The proper study of mankind is woman and, by common agreement since the time of Adam, it is the most complex and arduous. The study of Our Lady, as shown by the art of Chartres, leads directly back to Eve, and lays bare the whole subject of sex.

If it were worth while to argue a paradox, one might maintain that Nature regards the female as the essential, the male as the superfluity of her world. Perhaps the best starting-point for study of the Virgin would be a practical acquaintance with bees, and especially with queen bees. Precisely where the French man may come in, on the genealogical tree of parthenogenesis, one hesitates to say; but certain it is that the French woman, from very early times, has shown qualities peculiar to herself, and that the French woman of the Middle Ages was a masculine character. Almost any book which deals with the social side of the twelfth century has something to say on this subject, like the following page from M. Garreau's volume published in 1899, on the "Social State of France during the Crusades":—

A trait peculiar to this epoch is the close resemblance between the manners of men and women. The rule that such and such feelings or acts are permitted to one sex and forbidden to the other was not fairly settled. Men had the right to dissolve in tears, and women that of talking without prudery .... If we look at their intellectual level, the women appear distinctly superior. They are more serious; more subtle. With them we do not seem dealing with the rude state of civilization that their husbands belong to .... As a rule, the women seem to have the habit of weighing their acts; of not yielding to momentary impressions. While the sense of Christianity is more developed in them than in their husbands, on the other hand they show more perfidy and art in crime .... One might doubtless prove by a series of examples that the maternal influence when it predominated in the education of a son gave him a marked superiority over his contemporaries. Richard Coeur-de-Lion the crowned poet, artist, the king whose noble manners and refined mind in spite of his cruelty exercised so strong an impression on his age, was formed by that brilliant Eleanor of Guienne who, in her struggle with her husband, retained her sons as much as possible within her sphere of influence in order to make party chiefs of them. Our great Saint Louis, as all know, was brought up exclusively by Blanche of Castile; and Joinville, the charming writer so worthy of Saint Louis's friendship, and apparently so superior to his surroundings, was also the pupil of a widowed and regent mother.

The superiority of the woman was not a fancy, but a fact. Man's business was to fight or hunt or feast or make love. The man was also the travelling partner in commerce, commonly absent from home for months together, while the woman carried on the business. The woman ruled the household and the workshop; cared for the economy; supplied the intelligence, and dictated the taste. Her ascendancy was secured by her alliance with the Church, into which she sent her most intelligent children; and a priest or clerk, for the most part, counted socially as a woman. Both physically and mentally the woman was robust, as the men often complained, and she did not greatly resent being treated as a man. Sometimes the husband beat her, dragged her about by the hair, locked her up in the house; but he was quite conscious that she always got even with him in the end. As a matter of fact, probably she got more than even. On this point, history, legend, poetry, romance, and especially the popular fabliaux—invented to amuse the gross tastes of the coarser class— are all agreed, and one could give scores of volumes illustrating it. The greatest men illustrate it best, as one might show almost at hazard. The greatest men of the eleventh, twelfth, and thirteenth centuries were William the Norman; his great grandson Henry II Plantagenet; Saint Louis of France; and, if a fourth be needed, Richard Coeur-de-Lion.

Notoriously all these men had as much difficulty as Louis XIV himself with the women of their family. Tradition exaggerates everything it touches, but shows, at the same time, what is passing in the minds of the society which tradites. In Normandy, the people of Caen have kept a tradition, told elsewhere in other forms, that one day, Duke William,—the Conqueror,— exasperated by having his bastardy constantly thrown in his face by the Duchess Matilda, dragged her by the hair, tied to his horse's tail, as far as the suburb of Vaucelles; and this legend accounts for the splendour of the Abbaye-aux-Dames, because William, the common people believed, afterwards regretted the impropriety, and atoned for it by giving her money to build the abbey. The story betrays the man's weakness. The Abbaye-aux-Dames stands in the same relation to the Abbaye-aux-Hommes that Matilda took towards William. Inferiority there was none; on the contrary, the woman was socially the superior, and William was probably more afraid of her than she of him, if Mr. Freeman is right in insisting that he married her in spite of her having a husband living, and certainly two children. If William was the strongest man in the eleventh century, his great-grandson, Henry II of England, was the strongest man of the twelfth; but the history of the time resounds with the noise of his battles with Queen Eleanor whom he, at last, held in prison for fourteen years. Prisoner as she was, she broke him down in the end. One is tempted to suspect that, had her husband and children been guided by her, and by her policy as peacemaker for the good of Guienne, most of the disasters of England and France might have been postponed for the time; but we can never know the truth, for monks and historians abhor emancipated women,—with good reason, since such women are apt to abhor them,—and the quarrel can never be pacified. Historians have commonly shown fear of women without admitting it, but the man of the Middle Ages knew at least why he feared the woman, and told it openly, not to say brutally. Long after Eleanor and Blanche were dead, Chaucer brought the Wife of Bath on his Shakespearean stage, to explain the woman, and as usual he touched masculine frailty with caustic, while seeming to laugh at woman and man alike:—

"My liege lady! generally," quoth he,

"Women desiren to have soverainetee."

The point was that the Wife of Bath, like Queen Blanche and Queen

Eleanor, not only wanted sovereignty, but won and held it.

That Saint Louis, even when a grown man and king, stood in awe of his mother, Blanche of Castile, was not only notorious but seemed to be thought natural. Joinville recorded it not so much to mark the King's weakness, as the woman's strength; for his Queen, Margaret of Provence, showed the courage which the King had not. Blanche and Margaret were exceedingly jealous of each other. "One day," said Joinville, "Queen Blanche went to the Queen's [Margaret] chamber where her son [Louis IX] had gone before to comfort her, for she was in great danger of death from a bad delivery; and he hid himself behind the Queen [Margaret] to avoid being seen; but his mother perceived him, and taking him by the hand said: 'Come along! you will do no good here!' and put him out of the chamber. Queen Margaret, observing this, and that she was to be separated from her husband, cried aloud: 'Alas! will you not allow me to see my lord either living or dying?'" According to Joinville, King Louis always hid himself when, in his wife's chamber, he heard his mother coming.

The great period of Gothic architecture begins with the coming of Eleanor (1137) and ends with the passing of Blanche (1252). Eleanor's long life was full of energy and passion of which next to nothing is known; the woman was always too slippery for monks or soldiers to grasp.

Eleanor came to Paris, a Queen of fifteen years old, in 1137, bringing Poitiers and Guienne as the greatest dowry ever offered to the French Crown. She brought also the tastes and manners of the South, little in harmony with the tastes and manners of Saint Bernard whose authority at court rivalled her own. The Abbe Suger supported her, but the King leaned toward the Abbe Bernard. What this puritan reaction meant is a matter to be studied by itself, if one can find a cloister to study in; but it bore the mark of most puritan reactions in its hostility to women. As long as the woman remained docile, she ruled, through the Church; but the man feared her and was jealous of her, and she of him. Bernard specially adored the Virgin because she was an example of docile obedience to the Trinity who atoned for the indocility of Eve, but Eve herself remained the instrument of Satan, and French society as a whole showed a taste for Eves.

[Genealogical chart showing the relationships among the three queens.]

Eleanor could hardly be called docile. Whatever else she loved, she certainly loved rule. She shared this passion to the full with her only great successor and rival on the English throne, Queen Elizabeth, and she happened to become Queen of France at the moment when society was turning from worship of its military ideal, Saint Michael, to worship of its social ideal, the Virgin. According to the monk Orderic, men had begun to throw aside their old military dress and manners even before the first crusade, in the days of William Rufus (1087-1100), and to affect feminine fashions. In all ages, priests and monks have denounced the growing vices of society, with more or less reason; but there seems to have been a real outbreak of display at about the time of the first crusade, which set a deep mark on every sort of social expression, even down to the shoes of the statues on the western portal of Chartres:—

A debauched fellow named Robert [said Orderic] was the first, about the time of William Rufus, who introduced the practice of filling the long points of the shoes with tow, and of turning them up like a ram's horn. Hence he got the surname of Cornard; and this absurd fashion was speedily adopted by great numbers of the nobility as a proud distinction and sign of merit. At this time effeminacy was the prevailing vice throughout the world ... They parted their hair from the crown of the head on each side of the forehead, and their locks grew long like women, and wore long shirts and tunics, closely tied with points ... In our days, ancient customs are almost all changed for new fashions. Our wanton youths are sunk in effeminacy ... They insert their toes in things like serpents' tails which present to view the shape of scorpions. Sweeping the dusty ground with the prodigious trains of their robes and mantles, they cover their hands with gloves ...

If you are curious to follow these monkish criticisms on your ancestors' habits, you can read Orderic at your leisure; but you want only to carry in mind the fact that the generation of warriors who fought at Hastings and captured Jerusalem were regarded by themselves as effeminate, and plunged in luxury. "Their locks are curled with hot irons, and instead of wearing caps, they bind their heads with fillets. A knight seldom appears in public with his head uncovered and properly shaved according to the apostolic precept." The effeminacy of the first crusade took artistic shape in the west portal of Chartres and the glass of Saint-Denis, and led instantly to the puritan reaction of Saint Bernard, followed by the gentle asceticism of Queen Blanche and Saint Louis. Whether the pilgrimages to Jerusalem and contact with the East were the cause or only a consequence of this revolution, or whether it was all one,—a result of converting the Northern pagans to peaceful habits and the consequent enrichment of northern Europe,—is indifferent; the fact and the date are enough. The art is French, but the ideas may have come from anywhere, like the game of chess which the pilgrims or crusaders brought home from Syria. In the Oriental game, the King was followed step by step by a Minister whose functions were personal. The crusaders freed the piece from control; gave it liberty to move up or down or diagonally, forwards and backwards; made it the most arbitrary and formidable champion on the board, while the King and the Knight were the most restricted in movement; and this piece they named Queen, and called the Virgin:—

    Li Baudrains traist sa fierge por son paon sauver,

    E cele son aufin qui cuida conquester

    La firge ou le paon, ou faire reculer.

The aufin or dauphin became the Fou of the French game, and the bishop of the English. Baldwin played his Virgin to save his pawn; his opponent played the bishop to threaten either the Virgin or the pawn.

For a hundred and fifty years, the Virgin and Queens ruled French taste and thought so successfully that the French man has never yet quite decided whether to be more proud or ashamed of it. Life has ever since seemed a little flat to him, and art a little cheap. He saw that the woman, in elevating herself, had made him appear ridiculous, and he tried to retaliate with a wit not always sparkling, and too often at his own expense. Sometimes in museums or collections of bric-a-brac, you will see, in an illuminated manuscript, or carved on stone, or cast in bronze, the figure of a man on his hands and knees, bestridden by another figure holding a bridle and a whip; it is Aristotle, symbol of masculine wisdom, bridled and driven by woman. Six hundred years afterwards, Tennyson revived the same motive in Merlin, enslaved not for a time but forever. In both cases the satire justly punished the man. Another version of the same story—perhaps the original—was the Mystery of Adam, one of the earliest Church plays. Gaston Paris says "it was written in England in the twelfth century, and its author had real poetic talent; the scene of the seduction of Eve by the serpent is one of the best pieces of Christian dramaturgy … This remarkable work seems to have been played no longer inside the church, but under the porch":—

Diabolus. Jo vi Adam mais trop est fols.

Eva. Un poi est durs.

Diabolus. Il serra mols.

Il est plus durs qui n'est enfers.

Eva. Il est mult francs.

Diabolus. Ainz est mult sers.

Cure ne volt prendre de sei

Car la prenge sevals de tei.

Tu es fieblette et tendre chose

E es plus fresche que n'est rose.

Tu es plus blanche que crystal

Que neif que chiet sor glace en val.

Mal cuple en fist li Criatur.

Tu es trop tendre e il trop dur.

Mais neporquant tu es plus sage

En grant sens as mis tun corrage

For co fait bon traire a tei.

Parler te voil.

Eva. Ore ja fai.

Devil. Adam I've seen, but he's too rough.

Eve. A little hard!

Devil. He'll soon be soft enough!

Harder than hell he is till now.

Eve. He's very frank!

Devil. Say very low!

To help himself he does not care;

The helping you shall be my share;

For you are tender, gentle, true,

The rose is not so fresh as you;

Whiter than crystal, or than snow

That falls from heaven on ice below.

A sorry mixture God has brewed,

You too tender, he too rude.

But you have much the greater sense,

Your will is all intelligence.

Therefore it is I turn to you.

I want to tell you—

Eve. Do it now!

The woman's greater intelligence was to blame for Adam's fall. Eve was justly punished because she should have known better, while Adam, as the Devil truly said, was a dull animal, hardly worth the trouble of deceiving. Adam was disloyal, too, untrue to his wife after being untrue to his Creator:—

La femme que tu me donas

Ele fist prime icest trespass

Donat le mei e jo mangai.

Or mest vis tornez est a gwai

Mal acontai icest manger.

Jo ai mesfait par ma moiller.

The woman that you made me take

First led me into this mistake.

She gave the apple that I ate

And brought me to this evil state.

Badly for me it turned, I own,

But all the fault is hers alone.

The audience accepted this as natural and proper. They recognized the man as, of course, stupid, cowardly, and traitorous. The men of the baser sort revenged themselves by boorishness that passed with them for wit in the taverns of Arras, but the poets of the higher class commonly took sides with the women. Even Chaucer, who lived after the glamour had faded, and who satirized women to satiety, told their tale in his "Legend of Good Women," with evident sympathy. To him, also, the ordinary man was inferior,—stupid, brutal, and untrue. "Full brittle is the truest," he said:—

For well I wote that Christ himself telleth

That in Israel, as wide as is the lond,

That so great faith in all the loud he ne fond

As in a woman, and this is no lie;

And as for men, look ye, such tyrannie

They doen all day, assay hem who so list,

The truest is full brotell for to trist.

Neither brutality nor wit helped the man much. Even Bluebeard in the end fell a victim to the superior qualities of his last wife, and Scheherazade's wit alone has preserved the memory of her royal husband. The tradition of thirteenth-century society still rules the French stage. The struggle between two strong-willed women to control one weak-willed man is the usual motive of the French drama in the nineteenth century, as it was the whole motive of Partenopeus of Blois, one of the best twelfth-century romans; and Joinville described it, in the middle of the thirteenth, as the leading motive in the court of Saint Louis, with Queen Blanche and Queen Margaret for players, and Saint Louis himself for pawn.

One has only to look at the common, so-called Elzevirian, volume of thirteenth-century nouvelles to see the Frenchman as he saw himself. The story of "La Comtesse de Ponthieu" is the more Shakespearean, but "La Belle Jehanne" is the more natural and lifelike. The plot is the common masculine intrigue against the woman, which was used over and over again before Shakespeare appropriated it in "Much Ado"; but its French development is rather in the line of "All's Well." The fair Jeanne, married to a penniless knight, not at all by her choice, but only because he was a favourite of her father's, was a woman of the true twelfth-century type. She broke the head of the traitor, and when he, with his masculine falseness, caused her husband to desert her, she disguised herself as a squire and followed Sir Robert to Marseilles in search of service in war, for the poor knight could get no other means of livelihood. Robert was the husband, and the wife, in entering his service as squire without pay, called herself John:—

Molt fu mesire Robiers dolans cant il vint a Marselle de cou k'il n'oi parler de nulle chose ki fust ou pais; si dist a Jehan:

—Ke ferons nous? Vous m'aves preste de vos deniers la vostre mierchi, si les vos renderai car je venderai mon palefroi et m'acuiterai a vous.

—Sire, dist Jehans, crees moi se il vous plaist je vous dirai ke nous ferons; jou ai bien enchore c sous de tournois, s'Il vous plaist je venderai nos ii chevaus et en ferai deniers; et je suis li miousdres boulengiers ke vous sacies, si ferai pain francois et je ne douc mie ke je ne gaagne bien et largement mon depens.

—Jehans, dist mesire Robiers, je m'otroi del tout a faire votre volente

Et lendemam vendi Jehans ses .ii. chevaux X livres de tornois, et achata son ble et le fist muire, et achata des corbelles et coumencha a faire pain francois si bon et si bien fait k'il en vendoit plus ke li doi melleur boulengier de la ville, et fist tant dedens les ii ans k'il ot bien c livres de katel. Lors dist Jehans a son segnour:

—Je lo bien que nous louons une tres grant mason et jou akaterai del vin et hierbegerai la bonne gent

—Jehan, dist mesire Robiers, faites a vo volente kar je l'otroi et si me loc molt de vous.

Jehans loua une mason grant et bielle, et si hierbrega la bonne gent et gaegnoit ases a plente, et viestoit son segnour biellement et richement, et avoit mesire Robiers son palefroi et aloit boire et mengier aveukes les plus vallans de la ville, et Jehans li envoioit vins et viandes ke tout cil ki o lui conpagnoient s'en esmervelloient. Si gaegna tant ke dedens .iiii ans il gaegna plus de ccc livres de meuble sains son harnois qui valoit bien .L. livres.

Much was Sir Robert grieved when he came to Marseilles and found that there was no talk of anything doing in the country, and he said to John: "What shall we do? You have lent me your money, I thank you, and will repay you, for I will sell my palfrey and discharge the debt to you."

"Sir," said John, "trust to me, if you please, I will tell you what we will do, I have still a hundred sous, if you please I will sell our two horses and turn them into money, and I am the best baker you ever knew, I will make French bread, and I've no doubt I shall pay my expenses well and make money"

"John," said Sir Robert, "I agree wholly to do whatever you like"

And the next day John sold their two horse for ten pounds, and bought his wheat and had it ground, and bought baskets, and began to make French bread so good and so well made that he sold more of it than the two best bakers in the city, and made so much within two years that he had a good hundred pound property Then he said to his lord "I advise our hiring a very large house, and I will buy wine and will keep lodgings for good society

"John," said Sir Robert, "do what you please, for I grant it, and am greatly pleased with you."

John hired a large and fine house and lodged the best people and gained a great plenty, and dressed his master handsomely and richly, and Sir Robert kept his palfrey and went out to eat and drink with the best people of the city, and John sent them such wines and food that all his companions marvelled at it. He made so much that within four years he gained more than three hundred pounds in money besides clothes, etc, well worth fifty.

The docile obedience of the man to the woman seemed as reasonable to the thirteenth century as the devotion of the woman to the man, not because she loved him, for there was no question of love, but because he was HER man, and she owned him as though he were child. The tale went on to develop her character always in the same sense. When she was ready, Jeanne broke up the establishment at Marseilles, brought her husband back to Hainault, and made him, without knowing her object, kill the traitor and redress her wrongs. Then after seven years' patient waiting, she revealed herself and resumed her place.

If you care to see the same type developed to its highest capacity, go to the theatre the first time some ambitious actress attempts the part of Lady Macbeth. Shakespeare realized the thirteenth-century woman more vividly than the thirteenth-century poets ever did; but that is no new thing to say of Shakespeare. The author of "La Comtesse de Ponthieu" made no bad sketch of the character. These are fictions, but the Chronicles contain the names of women by scores who were the originals of the sketch. The society which Orderic described in Normandy—the generation of the first crusade—produced a great variety of Lady Macbeths. In the country of Evreux, about 1100, Orderic says that "a worse than civil war was waged between two powerful brothers, and the mischief was fomented by the spiteful jealousy of their haughty wives. The Countess Havise of Evreux took offence at some taunts uttered by Isabel de Conches,—wife of Ralph, the Seigneur of Conches, some ten miles from Evreux,—and used all her influence with her husband, Count William, and his barons, to make trouble ... Both the ladies who stirred up these fierce enmities were great talkers and spirited as well as handsome; they ruled their husbands, oppressed their vassals, and inspired terror in various ways. But still their characters were very different. Havise had wit and eloquence, but she was cruel and avaricious. Isabel was generous, enterprising, and gay, so that she was beloved and esteemed by those about her. She rode in knight's armour when her vassals were called to war, and showed as much daring among men- at-arms and mounted knights as Camilla ..." More than three hundred years afterwards, far off in the Vosges, from a village never heard of, appeared a common peasant of seventeen years old, a girl without birth, education, wealth, or claim of any sort to consideration, who made her way to Chinon and claimed from Charles VII a commission to lead his army against the English. Neither the king nor the court had faith in her, and yet the commission was given, and the rank-and-file showed again that the true Frenchman had more confidence in the woman than in the man, no matter what the gossips might say. No one was surprised when Jeanne did what she promised, or when the men burned her for doing it. There were Jeannes in every village. Ridicule was powerless against them. Even Voltaire became what the French call frankly "bete," in trying it.

Eleanor of Guienne was the greatest of all Frenchwomen. Her decision was law, whether in Bordeaux or Poitiers, in Paris or in Palestine, in London or in Normandy; in the court of Louis VII, or in that of Henry II, or in her own Court of Love. For fifteen years she was Queen of France; for fifty she was Queen in England; for eighty or thereabouts she was equivalent to Queen over Guienne. No other Frenchwoman ever had such rule. Unfortunately, as Queen of France, she struck against an authority greater than her own, that of Saint Bernard, and after combating it, with Suger's help, from 1137 until 1152, the monk at last gained such mastery that Eleanor quitted the country and Suger died. She was not a person to accept defeat. She royally divorced her husband and went back to her own kingdom of Guienne. Neither Louis nor Bernard dared to stop her, or to hold her territories from her, but they put the best face they could on their defeat by proclaiming her as a person of irregular conduct. The irregularity would not have stood in their way, if they had dared to stand in hers, but Louis was much the weaker, and made himself weaker still by allowing her to leave him for the sake of Henry of Anjou, a story of a sort that rarely raised the respect in which French kings were held by French society. Probably politics had more to do with the matter than personal attachments, for Eleanor was a great ruler, the equal of any ordinary king, and more powerful than most kings living in 1152. If she deserted France in order to join the enemies of France, she had serious reasons besides love for young Henry of Anjou; but in any case she did, as usual, what pleased her, and forced Louis to pronounce the divorce at a council held at Beaugency, March 18, 1152, on the usual pretext of relationship. The humours of the twelfth century were Shakespearean. Eleanor, having obtained her divorce at Beaugency, to the deep regret of all Frenchmen, started at once for Poitiers, knowing how unsafe she was in any territory but her own. Beaugency is on the Loire, between Orleans and Blois, and Eleanor's first night was at Blois, or should have been; but she was told, on arriving, that Count Thibaut of Blois, undeterred by King Louis's experience, was making plans to detain her, with perfectly honourable views of marriage; and, as she seems at least not to have been in love with Thibaut, she was obliged to depart at once, in the night, to Tours. A night journey on horseback from Blois to Tours in the middle of March can have been no pleasure-trip, even in 1152; but, on arriving at Tours in the morning, Eleanor found that her lovers were still so dangerously near that she set forward at once on the road to Poitiers. As she approached her own territory she learned that Geoffrey of Anjou, the younger brother of her intended husband, was waiting for her at the border, with views of marriage as strictly honourable as those of all the others. She was driven to take another road, and at last got safe to Poitiers.

About no figure in the Middle Ages, man or woman, did so many legends grow, and with such freedom, as about Eleanor, whose strength appealed to French sympathies and whose adventures appealed to their imagination. They never forgave Louis for letting her go. They delighted to be told that in Palestine she had carried on relations of the most improper character, now with a Saracen slave of great beauty; now with Raymond of Poitiers, her uncle, the handsomest man of his time; now with Saladin himself; and, as all this occurred at Antioch in 1147 or 1148, they could not explain why her husband should have waited until 1152 in order to express his unwilling disapproval; but they quoted with evident sympathy a remark attributed to her that she thought she had married a king, and found she had married a monk. To the Frenchman, Eleanor remained always sympathetic, which is the more significant because, in English tradition, her character suffered a violent and incredible change. Although English history has lavished on Eleanor somewhat more than her due share of conventional moral reproof, considering that, from the moment she married Henry of Anjou, May 18, 1152, she was never charged with a breath of scandal, it atoned for her want of wickedness by French standards, in the usual manner of historians, by inventing traits which reflected the moral standards of England. Tradition converted her into the fairy-book type of feminine jealousy and invented for her the legend of the Fair Rosamund and the poison of toads.

For us, both legends are true. They reflected, not perhaps the character of Eleanor, but what the society liked to see acted on its theatre of life. Eleanor's real nature in no way concerns us. The single fact worth remembering was that she had two daughters by Louis VII, as shown in the table; who, in due time, married—Mary, in 1164, married Henry, the great Count of Champagne; Alix, at the same time, became Countess of Chartres by marriage with Thibaut, who had driven her mother from Blois in 1152 by his marital intentions. Henry and Thibaut were brothers whose sister Alix had married Louis VII in 1160, eight years after the divorce. The relations thus created were fantastic, especially for Queen Eleanor, who, besides her two French daughters, had eight children as Queen of England. Her second son, Richard Coeur-de-Lion, born in 1157, was affianced in 1174 to a daughter of Louis VII and Alix, a child only six years old, who was sent to

England to be brought up as future queen. This was certainly Eleanor's doing, and equally certain was it that the child came to no good in the English court. The historians, by exception, have not charged this crime to Queen Eleanor; they charged it to Eleanor's husband, who passed most of his life in crossing his wife's political plans; but with politics we want as little as possible to do. We are concerned with the artistic and social side of life, and have only to notice the coincidence that while the Virgin was miraculously using the power of spiritual love to elevate and purify the people, Eleanor and her daughters were using the power of earthly love to discipline and refine the courts. Side by side with the crude realities about them, they insisted on teaching and enforcing an ideal that contradicted the realities, and had no value for them or for us except in the contradiction.

The ideals of Eleanor and her daughter Mary of Champagne were a form of religion, and if you care to see its evangels, you had best go directly to Dante and Petrarch, or, if you like it better, to Don Quixote de la Mancha. The religion is dead as Demeter, and its art alone survives as, on the whole, the highest expression of man's thought or emotion; but in its day it was almost as practical as it now is fanciful. Eleanor and her daughter Mary and her granddaughter Blanche knew as well as Saint Bernard did, or Saint Francis, what a brute the emancipated man could be; and as though they foresaw the society of the sixteenth and eighteenth centuries, they used every terror they could invent, as well as every tenderness they could invoke, to tame the beasts around them. Their charge was of manners, and, to teach manners, they made a school which they called their Court of Love, with a code of law to which they gave the name of "courteous love." The decisions of this court were recorded, like the decisions of a modern bench, under the names of the great ladies who made them, and were enforced by the ladies of good society for whose guidance they were made. They are worth reading, and any one who likes may read them to this day, with considerable scepticism about their genuineness. The doubt is only ignorance. We do not, and never can, know the twelfth-century woman, or, for that matter, any other woman, but we do know the literature she created; we know the art she lived in, and the religion she professed. We can collect from them some idea why the Virgin Mary ruled, and what she was taken to be, by the world which worshipped her.

Mary of Champagne created the literature of courteous love. She must have been about twenty years old when she married Count Henry and went to live at Troyes, not actually a queen in title, but certainly a queen in social influence. In 1164, Champagne was a powerful country, and Troyes a centre of taste. In Normandy, at the same date, William of Saint Pair and Wace were writing the poetry we know. In Champagne the court poet was Christian of Troyes, whose poems were new when the churches of Noyon and Senlis and Saint Leu d'Esserent, and the fleche of Chartres, and the Leaning Tower of Pisa, were building, at the same time with the Abbey of Vezelay, and before the church at Mantes. Christian died not long after 1175, leaving a great mass of verse, much of which has survived, and which you can read more easily than you can read Dante or Petrarch, although both are almost modern compared with Christian. The quality of this verse is something like the quality of the glass windows— conventional decoration; colours in conventional harmonies; refinement, restraint, and feminine delicacy of taste. Christian has not the grand manner of the eleventh century, and never recalls the masculine strength of the "Chanson de Roland" or "Raoul de Cambrai." Even his most charming story, "Erec et Enide," carries chiefly a moral of courtesy. His is poet-laureate's work, says M. Gaston Paris; the flower of a twelfth-century court and of twelfth-century French; the best example of an admirable language; but not lyric; neither strong, nor deep, nor deeply felt. What we call tragedy is unknown to it. Christian's world is sky-blue and rose, with only enough red to give it warmth, and so flooded with light that even its mysteries count only by the clearness with which they are shown.

Among other great works, before Mary of France came to Troyes Christian had, toward 1160, written a "Tristan," which is lost. Mary herself, he says, gave him the subject of "Lancelot," with the request or order to make it a lesson of "courteous love," which he obeyed. Courtesy has lost its meaning as well as its charm, and you might find the "Chevalier de la Charette" even more unintelligible than tiresome; but its influence was great in its day, and the lesson of courteous love, under the authority of Mary of Champagne, lasted for centuries as the standard of taste. "Lancelot" was never finished, but later, not long after 1174, Christian wrote a "Perceval," or "Conte du Graal," which must also have been intended to please Mary, and which is interesting because, while the "Lancelot" gave the twelfth-century idea of courteous love, the "Perceval" gave the twelfth-century idea of religious mystery. Mary was certainly concerned with both. "It is for this same Mary," says Gaston Paris, "that Walter of Arras undertook his poem of 'Eracle'; she was the object of the songs of the troubadours as well as of their French imitators; for her use also she caused the translations of books of piety like Genesis, or the paraphrase at great length, in verse, of the psalm 'Eructavit.'"

With her theories of courteous love, every one is more or less familiar if only from the ridicule of Cervantes and the follies of Quixote, who, though four hundred years younger, was Lancelot's child; but we never can know how far she took herself and her laws of love seriously, and to speculate on so deep a subject as her seriousness is worse than useless, since she would herself have been as uncertain as her lovers were. Visionary as the courtesy was, the Holy Grail was as practical as any bric-a-brac that has survived of the time. The mystery of Perceval is like that of the Gothic cathedral, illuminated by floods of light, and enlivened by rivers of colour. Unfortunately Christian never told what he meant by the fragment, itself a mystery, in which he narrated the story of the knight who saw the Holy Grail, because the knight, who was warned, as usual, to ask no questions, for once, unlike most knights, obeyed the warning when he should have disregarded it. As knights-errant necessarily did the wrong thing in order to make their adventures possible, Perceval's error cannot be in itself mysterious, nor was the castle in any way mysterious where the miracle occurred, It appeared to him to be the usual castle, and he saw nothing unusual in the manner of his reception by the usual old lord, or in the fact that both seated themselves quite simply before the hall-fire with the usual household. Then, as though it were an everyday habit, the Holy Grail was brought in (Bartsch, "Chrestomathie," 183-85, ed. 1895):—

Et leans avail luminaire

Si grant con l'an le porrait faire

De chandoiles a un ostel.

Que qu'il parloient d'un et d'el,

Uns vallez d'une chambre vint

Qui une blanche lance tint

Ampoigniee par le mi lieu.

Si passa par endroit le feu

Et cil qui al feu se seoient,

Et tuit cil de leans veoient

La lance blanche et le fer blanc.

S'issoit une gote de sang

Del fer de la lance au sommet,

Et jusqu'a la main au vaslet

Coroit cele gote vermoille….

A tant dui autre vaslet vindrent

Qui chandeliers an lors mains tindrent

De fin or ovrez a neel.

Li vaslet estoient moult bel

Qui les chandeliers aportoient.

An chacun chandelier ardoient

Dous chandoiles a tot le mains.

Un graal antre ses dous mains

Une demoiselle tenoit,

Qui avec les vaslets venoit,

Bele et gente et bien acesmee.

Quant cle fu leans antree

Atot le graal qu'ele tint

Une si granz clartez i vint

Qu'ausi perdirent les chandoiles

Lor clarte come les estoiles

Qant li solauz luist et la lune.

Apres celi an revint une

Qui tint un tailleor d'argent.

Le graal qui aloit devant

De fin or esmere estoit,

Pierres precieuses avoit

El graal de maintes menieres

Des plus riches et des plus chieres

Qui en mer ne en terre soient.

Totes autres pierres passoient

Celes del graal sanz dotance.

Tot ainsi con passa la lance

Par devant le lit trespasserent

Et d'une chambre a l'autre alerent.

Et li vaslet les vit passer,

Ni n'osa mire demander

Del graal cui l'an an servoit.

And, within, the hall was bright

As any hall could be with light

Of candles in a house at night.

So, while of this and that they talked,

A squire from a chamber walked,

Bearing a white lance in his hand,

Grasped by the middle, like a wand;

And, as he passed the chimney wide,

Those seated by the fireside,

And all the others, caught a glance

Of the white steel and the white lance.

As they looked, a drop of blood

Down the lance's handle flowed;

Down to where the youth's hand stood.

From the lance-head at the top

They saw run that crimson drop....

Presently came two more squires,

In their hands two chandeliers,

Of fine gold in enamel wrought.

Each squire that the candle brought

Was a handsome chevalier.

There burned in every chandelier

Two lighted candles at the least.

A damsel, graceful and well dressed,

Behind the squires followed fast

Who carried in her hands a graal;

And as she came within the hall

With the graal there came a light So brilliant that the candles all

Lost clearness, as the stars at night

When moon shines, or in day the sun.

After her there followed one

Who a dish of silver bore.

The graal, which had gone before,

Of gold the finest had been made,

With precious stones had been inlaid,

Richest and rarest of each kind

That man in sea or earth could find.

All other jewels far surpassed

Those which the holy graal enchased.

Just as before had passed the lance

They all before the bed advance,

Passing straightway through the hall,

And the knight who saw them pass

Never ventured once to ask

For the meaning of the graal.

The simplicity of this narration gives a certain dramatic effect to the mystery, like seeing a ghost in full daylight, but Christian carried simplicity further still. He seemed either to feel, or to want others to feel, the reality of the adventure and the miracle, and he followed up the appearance of the graal by a solid meal in the style of the twelfth century, such as one expects to find in "Ivanhoe" or the "Talisman." The knight sat down with his host to the best dinner that the county of Champagne afforded, and they ate their haunch of venison with the graal in full view. They drank their Champagne wine of various sorts, out of gold cups:—

Vins clers ne raspez ne lor faut

A copes dorees a boivre;

they sat before the fire and talked till bedtime, when the squires made up the beds in the hall, and brought in supper—dates, figs, nutmegs, spices, pomegranates, and at last lectuaries, suspiciously like what we call jams; and "alexandrine gingerbread"; after which they drank various drinks, with or without spice or honey or pepper; and old moret, which is thought to be mulberry wine, but which generally went with clairet, a colourless grape-juice, or piment. At least, here are the lines, and one may translate them to suit one's self:—

Et li vaslet aparellierent

Les lis et le fruit au colchier

Que il en i ot de moult chier,

Dates, figues, et nois mugates,

Girofles et pomes de grenates,

Et leituaires an la fin,

Et gingenbret alixandrin.

Apres ce burent de maint boivre,

Piment ou n'ot ne miel ne poivre

Et viez more et cler sirop.

The twelfth century had the child's love of sweets and spices and preserved fruits, and drinks sweetened or spiced, whether they were taken for supper or for poetry; the true knight's palate was fresh and his appetite excellent either for sweets or verses or love; the world was young then; Robin Hoods lived in every forest, and Richard Coeur-de-Lion was not yet twenty years old. The pleasant adventures of Robin Hood were real, as you can read in the stories of a dozen outlaws, and men troubled themselves about pain and death much as healthy bears did, in the mountains. Life had miseries enough, but few shadows deeper than those of the imaginative lover, or the terrors of ghosts at night. Men's imaginations ran riot, but did not keep them awake; at least, neither the preserved fruits nor the mulberry wine nor the clear syrup nor the gingerbread nor the Holy Graal kept Perceval awake, but he slept the sound and healthy sleep of youth, and when he woke the next morning, he felt only a mild surprise to find that his host and household had disappeared, leaving him to ride away without farewell, breakfast, or Graal.

Christian wrote about Perceval in 1174 in the same spirit in which the workmen in glass, thirty years later, told the story of Charlemagne. One artist worked for Mary of Champagne; the others for Mary of Chartres, commonly known as the Virgin; but all did their work in good faith, with the first, fresh, easy instinct of colour, light, and line. Neither of the two Maries was mystical, in a modern sense; none of the artists was oppressed by the burden of doubt; their scepticism was as childlike as faith. If one has to make an exception, perhaps the passion of love was more serious than that of religion, and gave to religion the deepest emotion, and the most complicated one, which society knew. Love was certainly a passion; and even more certainly it was, as seen in poets like Dante and Petrarch,—in romans like "Lancelot" and "Aucassin,"—in ideals like the Virgin,—complicated beyond modern conception. For this reason the loss of Christian's "Tristan" makes a terrible gap in art, for Christian's poem would have given the first and best idea of what led to courteous love. The "Tristan" was written before 1160, and belonged to the cycle of Queen Eleanor of England rather than to that of her daughter Mary of Troyes; but the subject was one neither of courtesy nor of France; it belonged to an age far behind the eleventh century, or even the tenth, or indeed any century within the range of French history; and it was as little fitted for Christian's way of treatment as for any avowed burlesque. The original Tristan—critics say—was not French, and neither Tristan nor Isolde had ever a drop of French blood in their veins. In their form as Christian received it, they were Celts or Scots; they came from Brittany, Wales, Ireland, the northern ocean, or farther still. Behind the Welsh Tristan, which passed probably through England to Normandy and thence to France and Champagne, critics detect a far more ancient figure living in a form of society that France could not remember ever to have known. King Marc was a tribal chief of the Stone Age whose subjects loved the forest and lived on the sea or in caves; King Marc's royal hall was a common shelter on the banks of a stream, where every one was at home, and king, queen, knights, attendants, and dwarf slept on the floor, on beds laid down where they pleased; Tristan's weapons were the bow and stone knife; he never saw a horse or a spear; his ideas of loyalty and Isolde's ideas of marriage were as vague as Marc's royal authority; and all were alike unconscious of law, chivalry, or church. The note they sang was more unlike the note of Christian, if possible, than that of Richard Wagner; it was the simplest expression of rude and primitive love, as one could perhaps find it among North American Indians, though hardly so defiant even there, and certainly in the Icelandic Sagas hardly so lawless; but it was a note of real passion, and touched the deepest chords of sympathy in the artificial society of the twelfth century, as it did in that of the nineteenth. The task of the French poet was to tone it down and give it the fashionable dress, the pointed shoes and long sleeves, of the time. "The Frenchman," says Gaston Paris, "is specially interested in making his story entertaining for the society it is meant for; he is 'social'; that is, of the world; he smiles at the adventures he tells, and delicately lets you see that he is not their dupe; he exerts himself to give to his style a constant elegance, a uniform polish, in which a few neatly turned, clever phrases sparkle here and there; above all, he wants to please, and thinks of his audience more than of his subject."

In the twelfth century he wanted chiefly to please women, as Orderic complained; Isolde came out of Brittany to meet Eleanor coming up from Guienne, and the Virgin from the east; and all united in giving law to society. In each case it was the woman, not the man, who gave the law;— it was Mary, not the Trinity; Eleanor, not Louis VII; Isolde, not Tristan. No doubt, the original Tristan had given the law like Roland or Achilles, but the twelfth-century Tristan was a comparatively poor creature. He was in his way a secondary figure in the romance, as Louis VII was to Eleanor and Abelard to Heloise. Every one knows how, about twenty years before Eleanor came to Paris, the poet-professor Abelard, the hero of the Latin Quarter, had sung to Heloise those songs which—he tells us—resounded through Europe as widely as his scholastic fame, and probably to more effect for his renown. In popular notions Heloise was Isolde, and would in a moment have done what Isolde did (Bartsch, 107-08):—

Quaint reis Marcs nus out conjeies

E de sa curt nus out chascez,

As mains ensemble nus preismes

E hors de la sale en eissimes,

A la forest puis en alasmes

E un mult bel liu i trouvames

E une roche, fu cavee,

Devant ert estraite la entree,

Dedans fu voesse ben faite,

Tante bel cum se fust portraite.

When King Marc had banned us both,

And from his court had chased us forth,

Hand in hand each clasping fast

Straight from out the hall we passed;

To the forest turned our face;

Found in it a perfect place,

Where the rock that made a cave

Hardly more than passage gave;

Spacious within and fit for use,

As though it had been planned for us.

At any time of her life, Heloise would have defied society or church, and would—at least in the public's fancy—have taken Abelard by the hand and gone off to the forest much more readily than she went to the cloister; but Abelard would have made a poor figure as Tristan. Abelard and Christian of Troyes were as remote as we are from the legendary Tristan; but Isolde and Heloise, Eleanor and Mary were the immortal and eternal woman. The legend of Isolde, both in the earlier and the later version, seems to have served as a sacred book to the women of the twelfth and thirteenth centuries, and Christian's Isolde surely helped Mary in giving law to the Court of Troyes and decisions in the Court of Love.

Countess Mary's authority lasted from 1164 to 1198, thirty-four years, during which, at uncertain intervals, glimpses of her influence flash out in poetry rather than in prose. Christian began his "Roman de la Charette" by invoking her:—

Puisque ma dame de Chanpaigne

Vialt que romans a faire anpraigne

Si deist et jel tesmoignasse

Que ce est la dame qui passe

Totes celes qui sont vivanz

Si con li funs passe les vanz

Qui vante en Mai ou en Avril

Dirai je: tant com une jame

Vaut de pailes et de sardines

Vaut la contesse de reines?

Christian chose curious similes. His dame surpassed all living rivals as smoke passes the winds that blow in May; or as much as a gem would buy of straws and sardines is the Countess worth in queens. Louis XIV would have thought that Christian might be laughing at him, but court styles changed with their masters. Louis XIV would scarcely have written a prison-song to his sister such as Richard Coeur-de-Lion wrote to Mary of Champagne:—

Ja nus bons pris ne dirat sa raison

Adroitement s'ansi com dolans non;

Mais par confort puet il faire chanson.

Moult ai d'amins, mais povre sont li don;

Honte en avront se por ma reancon

Suix ces deus yvers pris.

Ceu sevent bien mi home et mi baron,

Englois, Normant, Poitevin et Gascon,

Ke je n'avoie si povre compaingnon

Cui je laissasse por avoir au prixon.

Je nel di pas por nulle retraison,

Mais ancor suix je pris.

Or sai ge bien de voir certainement

Ke mors ne pris n'ait amin ne parent,

Cant on me lait por or ne por argent.

Moult m'est de moi, mais plus m'est de ma gent

C'apres ma mort avront reprochier grant

Se longement suix pris.

N'est pas mervelle se j'ai lo cuer dolent

Cant li miens sires tient ma terre en torment.

S'or li menbroit de nostre sairement

Ke nos feismes andui communament,

Bien sai de voir ke ceans longement

Ne seroie pas pris.

Ce sevent bien Angevin et Torain,

Cil bacheler ki or sont fort et sain,

C'ancombreis suix long d'aus en autrui main.

Forment m'amoient, mais or ne m'aimment grain.

De belles armes sont ores veut cil plain,

Por tant ke je suix pris.

Mes compaingnons cui j'amoie et cui j'aim,

Ces dou Caheu et ces dou Percherain,

Me di, chanson, kil ne sont pas certain,

C'onques vers aus n'en oi cuer faus ne vain.

S'il me guerroient, il font moult que villain

Tant com je serai pris.

Comtesse suer, vostre pris soverain

Vos saut et gart cil a cui je me claim

Et par cui je suix pris.

Je n'ou di pas de celi de Chartain

La meire Loweis.

No prisoner can tell his honest thought

Unless he speaks as one who suffers wrong;

But for his comfort he may make a song.

My friends are many, but their gifts are naught.

Shame will be theirs, if, for my ransom, here

I lie another year.

They know this well, my barons and my men,

Normandy, England, Gascony, Poitou,

That I had never follower so low

Whom I would leave in prison to my gain.

I say it not for a reproach to them,

But prisoner I am!

The ancient proverb now I know for sure:

Death and a prison know nor kin nor tie,

Since for mere lack of gold they let me lie.

Much for myself I grieve; for them still more.

After my death they will have grievous wrong

If I am prisoner long.

What marvel that my heart is sad and sore

When my own lord torments my helpless lands!

Well do I know that, if he held his hands,

Remembering the common oath we swore,

I should not here imprisoned with my song,

Remain a prisoner long.

They know this well who now are rich and strong

Young gentlemen of Anjou and Touraine,

That far from them, on hostile bonds I strain.

They loved me much, but have not loved me long.

Their plains will see no more fair lists arrayed,

While I lie here betrayed.

Companions, whom I loved, and still do love,

Geoffroi du Perche and Ansel de Caleux,

Tell them, my song, that they are friends untrue.

Never to them did I false-hearted prove;

But they do villainy if they war on me,

While I lie here, unfree.

Countess sister! your sovereign fame

May he preserve whose help I claim,

Victim for whom am I!

I say not this of Chartres' dame,

Mother of Louis!

Richard's prison-song, one of the chief monuments of English literature, sounds to every ear, accustomed to twelfth-century verse, as charming as when it was household rhyme to

mi ome et mi baron Englois, Normant, Poitevin et Gascon.

Not only was Richard a far greater king than any Louis ever was, but he also composed better poetry than any other king who is known to tourists, and, when he spoke to his sister in this cry of the heart altogether singular among monarchs, he made law and style, above discussion. Whether he meant to reproach his other sister, Alix of Chartres, historians may tell, if they know. If he did, the reproach answered its purpose, for the song was written in 1193; Richard was ransomed and released in 1194; and in 1198 the young Count "Loweis" of Chartres and Blois leagued with the Counts of Flanders, Le Perche, Guines, and Toulouse, against Philip Augustus, in favor of Coeur-de-Lion to whom they rendered homage. In any case, neither Mary nor Alice in 1193 was reigning Countess. Mary was a widow since 1181, and her son Henry was Count in Champagne, apparently a great favourite with his uncle Richard Coeur-de-Lion. The life of this Henry of Champagne was another twelfth-century romance, but can serve no purpose here except to recall the story that his mother, the great Countess Mary, died in 1198 of sorrow for the death of this son, who was then King of Jerusalem, and was killed, in 1197, by a fall from the window of his palace at Acre. Coeur-de-Lion died in 1199. In 1201, Mary's other son, who succeeded Henry,—Count Thibaut III,—died, leaving a posthumous heir, famous in the thirteenth century as Thibaut-le-Grand—the Thibaut of Queen Blanche.

They were all astonishing—men and women—and filled the world, for two hundred years, with their extraordinary energy and genius; but the greatest of all was old Queen Eleanor, who survived her son Coeur-de-Lion, as well as her two husbands,—Louis-le-Jeune and Henry II Plantagenet,—and was left in 1200 still struggling to repair the evils and fend off the dangers they caused. "Queen by the wrath of God," she called herself, and she knew what just claim she had to the rank. Of her two husbands and ten children, little remained except her son John, who, by the unanimous voice of his family, his friends, his enemies, and even his admirers, achieved a reputation for excelling in every form of twelfth-century crime. He was a liar and a traitor, as was not uncommon, but he was thought to be also a coward, which, in that family, was singular. Some redeeming quality he must have had, but none is recorded. His mother saw him running, in his masculine, twelfth-century recklessness, to destruction, and she made a last and a characteristic effort to save him and Guienne by a treaty of amity with the French king, to be secured by the marriage of the heir of France, Louis, to Eleanor's granddaughter, John's niece, Blanche of Castile, then twelve or thirteen years old. Eleanor herself was eighty, and yet she made the journey to Spain, brought back the child to Bordeaux, affianced her to Louis VIII as she had herself been affianced in 1137 to Louis VII, and in May, 1200, saw her married. The French had then given up their conventional trick of attributing Eleanor's acts to her want of morals; and France gave her—as to most women after sixty years old—the benefit of the convention which made women respectable after they had lost the opportunity to be vicious. In French eyes, Eleanor played out the drama according to the rules. She could not save John, but she died in 1202, before his ruin, and you can still see her lying with her husband and her son Richard at Fontevrault in her twelfth-century tomb.

In 1223, Blanche became Queen of France. She was thirty-six years old. Her husband, Louis VIII, was ambitious to rival his father, Philip Augustus, who had seized Normandy in 1203. Louis undertook to seize Toulouse and Avignon. In 1225, he set out with a large army in which, among the chief vassals, his cousin Thibaut of Champagne led a contingent. Thibaut was five-and-twenty years old, and, like Pierre de Dreux, then Duke of Brittany, was one of the most brilliant and versatile men of his time, and one of the greatest rulers. As royal vassal Thibaut owed forty days' service in the field; but his interests were at variance with the King's, and at the end of the term he marched home with his men, leaving the King to fall ill and die in Auvergne, November 8, 1226, and a child of ten years old to carry on the government as Louis IX.

Chartres Cathedral has already told the story twice, in stone and glass; but Thibaut does not appear there, although he saved the Queen. Some member of the royal family must be regent. Queen Blanche took the place, and of course the princes of the blood, who thought it was their right, united against her. At first, Blanche turned violently on Thibaut and forbade him to appear at the coronation at Rheims in his own territory, on November 29, as though she held him guilty of treason; but when the league of great vassals united to deprive her of the regency, she had no choice but to detach at any cost any member of the league, and Thibaut alone offered help. What price she paid him was best known to her; but what price she would be believed to have paid him was as well known to her as what had been said of her grandmother Eleanor when she changed her allegiance in 1152. If the scandal had concerned Thibaut alone, she might have been well content, but Blanche was obliged also to pay desperate court to the papal legate. Every member of her husband's family united against her and libelled her character with the freedom which enlivened and envenomed royal tongues.

Maintes paroles en dit en

Comme d'Iseult et de Tristan.

Had this been all, she would have cared no more than Eleanor or any other queen had cared, for in French drama, real or imaginary, such charges were not very serious and hardly uncomplimentary; but Iseult had never been accused, over and above her arbitrary views on the marriage-contract, of acting as an accomplice with Tristan in poisoning King Marc. French convention required that Thibaut should have poisoned Louis VIII for love of the Queen, and that this secret reciprocal love should control their lives. Fortunately for Blanche she was a devout ally of the Church, and the Church believed evil only of enemies. The legate and the prelates rallied to her support and after eight years of desperate struggle they crushed Pierre Mauclerc and saved Thibaut and Blanche.

For us the poetry is history, and the facts are false. French art starts not from facts, but from certain assumptions as conventional as a legendary window, and the commonest convention is the Woman. The fact, then as now, was Power, or its equivalent in exchange, but Frenchmen, while struggling for the Power, expressed it in terms of Art. They looked on life as a drama,—and on drama as a phase of life—in which the bystanders were bound to assume and accept the regular stage-plot. That the plot might be altogether untrue to real life affected in no way its interest. To them Thibaut and Blanche were bound to act Tristan and Isolde. Whatever they were when off the stage, they were lovers on it. Their loves were as real and as reasonable as the worship of the Virgin. Courteous love was avowedly a form of drama, but not the less a force of society. Illusion for illusion, courteous love, in Thibaut's hands, or in the hands of Dante and Petrarch, was as substantial as any other convention;—the balance of trade, the rights of man, or the Athanasian Creed. In that sense the illusions alone were real; if the Middle Ages had reflected only what was practical, nothing would have survived for us.

Thibaut was Tristan, and is said to have painted his verses on the walls of his chateau. If he did, he painted there, in the opinion of M. Gaston Paris, better poetry than any that was written on paper or parchment, for Thibaut was a great prince and great poet who did in both characters whatever he pleased. In modern equivalents, one would give much to see the chateau again with the poetry on its walls. Provins has lost the verses, but Troyes still keeps some churches and glass of Thibaut's time which hold their own with the best. Even of Thibaut himself, something survives, and though it were only the memories of his seneschal, the famous Sire de Joinville, history and France would be poor without him. With Joinville in hand, you may still pass an hour in the company of these astonishing thirteenth-century men and women:—crusaders who fight, hunt, make love, build churches, put up glass windows to the Virgin, buy missals, talk scholastic philosophy, compose poetry: Blanche, Thibaut, Perron, Joinville, Saint Louis, Saint Thomas, Saint Dominic, Saint Francis—you may know them as intimately as you can ever know a world that is lost; and in the case of Thibaut you may know more, for he is still alive in his poems; he even vibrates with life. One might try a few verses, to see what he meant by courtesy. Perhaps he wrote them for Queen Blanche, but, to whomever he sent them, the French were right in thinking that she ought to have returned his love (edition of 1742):—

Nus hom ne puet ami reconforter

Se cele non ou il a son cuer mis.

Pour ce m'estuet sovent plaindre et plourer

Que mis confors ne me vient, ce m'est vis,

De la ou j'ai tote ma remembrance.

Pour bien amer ai sovent esmaiance

  A dire voir.

Dame, merci! donez moi esperance

  De joie avoir.

Jene puis pas sovent a li parler

  Ne remirer les biaus iex de son vis.

  Ce pois moi que je n'i puis aler

  Car ades est mes cuers ententis.

Ho! bele riens, douce sans conoissance,

  Car me mettez en millor attendance

    De bon espoir!

Dame, merci! donez moi esperance

  De joie avoir.

Aucuns si sont qui me vuelent blamer

  Quant je ne di a qui je suis amis;

  Mais ja, dame, ne saura mon penser

  Nus qui soit nes fors vous cui je le dis

Couardement a pavours a doutance

  Dont puestes vous lors bien a ma semblance

    Mon cuer savoir.

Dame, merci! donez moi esperance

  De joie avoir.

There is no comfort to be found for pain
Save only where the heart has made its home.
Therefore I can but murmur and complain
Because no comfort to my pain has come
From where I garnered all my happiness.
From true love have I only earned distress
  The truth to say.
Grace, lady! give me comfort to possess
  A hope, one day.

Seldom the music of her voice I hear
Or wonder at the beauty of her eyes.
It grieves me that I may not follow there
Where at her feet my heart attentive lies.
Oh, gentle Beauty without consciousness,
Let me once feel a moment's hopefulness,
  If but one ray!
Grace, lady! give me comfort to possess
  A hope, one day.

Certain there are who blame upon me throw
Because I will not tell whose love I seek;
But truly, lady, none my thought shall know,
None that is born, save you to whom I speak
In cowardice and awe and doubtfulness,
That you may happily with fearlessness
  My heart essay.

> Grace, lady! give me comfort to possess
>
> A hope, one day.

Does Thibaut's verse sound simple? It is the simplicity of the thirteenth-century glass—so refined and complicated that sensible people are mostly satisfied to feel, and not to understand. Any blunderer in verse, who will merely look at the rhymes of these three stanzas, will see that simplicity is about as much concerned there as it is with the windows of Chartres; the verses are as perfect as the colours, and the versification as elaborate. These stanzas might have been addressed to Queen Blanche; now see how Thibaut kept the same tone of courteous love in addressing the Queen of Heaven!

> De grant travail et de petit esploit
>
> > Voi ce siegle cargie et encombre
> >
> > Que tant somes plain de maleurte
>
> Ke nus ne pens a faire ce qu'il doit,
>
> > Ains avons si le Deauble trouve
> >
> > Qu'a lui servir chascuns paine et essaie
>
> Et Diex ki ot pour nos ja cruel plaie
>
> > Metons arrier et sa grant dignite;
>
> Molt est hardis qui pour mort ne s'esmaie.
>
> Diex que tout set et tout puet et tout voit
>
> > Nous auroit tost en entre-deus giete
> >
> > Se la Dame plaine de grant bonte
>
> Pardelez lui pour nos ne li prioit
>
> > Si tres douc mot plaisant et savoure
>
> Le grant courous dou grant Signour apaie;
>
> Molt par est fox ki autre amor essai
>
> > K'en cestui n'a barat ne fausete
>
> Ne es autres n'a ne merti ne manaie.
>
> La souris quiert pour son cors garandir

Contre l'yver la noif et le forment
Et nous chaitif nous n'alons rien querant
Quant nous morrons ou nous puissions garir.
Nous ne cherchons fors k'infer le puant;
Or esgardes come beste sauvage
Pourvoit de loin encontre son domage
Et nous n'avons ne sens ne hardement;
Il est avis que plain somes de rage.
Li Deable a getey por nos ravir
Quatre amecons aescbies de torment;
Covoitise lance premierement
Et puis Orguel por sa grant rois emplir
Et Luxure va le batel trainant
Felonie les governe et les nage.
Ensi peschant s'en viegnent au rivage
Dont Diex nous gart par son commandement
En qui sains fons nous feismes homage.
A la Dame qui tous les bien avance
T'en va, chancon s'el te vielt escouter
Onques ne fu nus di millor chaunce.
With travail great, and little cargo fraught,
See how our world is labouring in pain;
So filled we are with love of evil gain
That no one thinks of doing what he ought,
But we all hustle in the Devil's train,

And only in his service toil and pray;
And God, who suffered for us agony,
   We set behind, and treat him with disdain;
   Hardy is he whom death does not dismay.
God who rules all, from whom we can hide nought,
   Had quickly flung us back to nought again
   But that our gentle, gracious, Lady Queen
   Begged him to spare us, and our pardon wrought;
   Striving with words of sweetness to restrain
Our angry Lord, and his great wrath allay.
Felon is he who shall her love betray
   Which is pure truth, and falsehood cannot feign,
While all the rest is lie and cheating play.
The feeble mouse, against the winter's cold,
   Garners the nuts and grain within his cell,
While man goes groping, without sense to tell
Where to seek refuge against growing old.
   We seek it in the smoking mouth of Hell.
With the poor beast our impotence compare!
See him protect his life with utmost care,
   While us nor wit nor courage can compel
To save our souls, so foolish mad we are.
The Devil doth in snares our life enfold;
   Four hooks has he with torments baited well;
   And first with Greed he casts a mighty spell,

And then, to fill his nets, has Pride enrolled,
   And Luxury steers the boat, and fills the sail,
And Perfidy controls and sets the snare;
Thus the poor fish are brought to land, and there
   May God preserve us and the foe repel!
Homage to him who saves us from despair!
To Mary Queen, who passes all compare,
   Go, little song! to her your sorrows tell!
Nor Heaven nor Earth holds happiness so rare.

CHAPTER XII: NICOLETTE AND MARION

C'est d'Aucassins et de Nicolete.

Qui vauroit bons vers oir

Del deport du viel caitiff

De deus biax enfans petis

Nicolete et Aucassins;

Des grans paines qu'il soufri

Et des proueces qu'il fist

For s'amie o le cler vis.

Dox est li cans biax est li dis

Et cortois et bien asis.

Nus hom n'est si esbahis

Tant dolans ni entrepris

De grant mal amaladis

Se il l'oit ne soit garis

Et de joie resbaudis

    Tant par est dou-ce.

This is of Aucassins and Nicolette.

Whom would a good ballad please

By the captive from o'er-seas,

A sweet song in children's praise,

Nicolette and Aucassins;

What he bore for her caress,

What he proved of his prowess

For his friend with the bright face?

The song has charm, the tale has grace,

And courtesy and good address.

No man is in such distress,

Such suffering or weariness,

Sick with ever such sickness,

But he shall, if he hear this,

Recover all his happiness,

    So sweet it is!

This little thirteenth-century gem is called a "chante-fable," a story partly in prose, partly in verse, to be sung according to musical notation accompanying the words in the single manuscript known, and published in facsimile by Mr. F. W. Bourdillon at Oxford in 1896. Indeed, few poems, old or new, have in the last few years been more reprinted, translated, and discussed, than "Aucassins," yet the discussion lacks interest to the idle tourist, and tells him little. Nothing is known of the author or his date. The second line alone offers a hint, but nothing more. "Caitif" means in the first place a captive, and secondly any unfortunate or wretched man. Critics have liked to think that the word means here a captive to the Saracens, and that the poet, like Cervantes three or four hundred years later, may have been a prisoner to the infidels. What the critics can do, we can do. If liberties can be taken with impunity by scholars, we can take the liberty of supposing that the poet was a prisoner in the crusade of Coeur-de-Lion and Philippe-Auguste; that he had recovered his liberty, with his master, in 1194; and that he passed the rest of his life singing to the old Queen Eleanor or to Richard, at Chinon, and to the lords of all the chateaux in Guienne, Poitiers, Anjou, and Normandy, not to mention England. The living was a pleasant one, as the sunny atmosphere of the Southern poetry proves.

Dox est li cans; biax est li dis,

Et cortois et bien asis.

The poet-troubadour who composed and recited "Aucassins" could not have been unhappy, but this is the affair of his private life, and not of ours. What rather interests us is his poetic motive, "courteous love," which gives the tale a place in the direct line between Christian of Troyes, Thibaut-le-Grand, and William of Lorris. Christian of Troyes died in 1175; at least he wrote nothing of a later date, so far as is certainly known. Richard Coeur-de-Lion died in 1199, very soon after the death of his half-sister Mary of Champagne. Thibaut-le-Grand was born in 1201. William of Lorris, who concluded the line of great "courteous" poets, died in 1260 or thereabouts. For our purposes, "Aucassins" comes between Christian of Troyes and William of Lorris; the trouvere or jogleor, who sang, was a "viel caitif" when the Chartres glass was set up, and the Charlemagne window designed, about 1210, or perhaps a little later. When one is not a professor, one has not the right to make inept guesses, and, when one is not a critic, one should not risk confusing a difficult question by baseless assumptions; but even a summer tourist may without offence visit his churches in the order that suits him best; and, for our tour, "Aucassins" follows Christian and goes hand in hand with Blondel and the chatelain de Coucy, as the most exquisite expression of "courteous love." As one of "Aucassins'" German editors says in his introduction: "Love is the medium through which alone the hero surveys the world around him, and for which he contemns everything that the age prized: knightly honour; deeds of arms; father and mother; hell, and even heaven; but the mere promise by his father of a kiss from Nicolette inspires him to superhuman heroism; while the old poet sings and smiles aside to his audience as though he wished them to understand that Aucassins, a foolish boy, must not be judged quite seriously, but that, old as he was himself, he was just as foolish about Nicolette."

Aucassins was the son of the Count of Beaucaire. Nicolette was a young girl whom the Viscount of Beaucaire had redeemed as a captive of the Saracens, and had brought up as a god-daughter in his family. Aucassins fell in love with Nicolette, and wanted to marry her. The action turned on marriage, for, to the Counts of Beaucaire, as to other counts, not to speak of kings, high alliance was not a matter of choice but of necessity, without which they could not defend their lives, let alone their counties; and, to make Aucassins' conduct absolutely treasonable, Beaucaire was at that time surrounded and besieged, and the Count, Aucassins' father, stood in dire need of his son's help. Aucassins refused to stir unless he could have Nicolette. What were honours to him if Nicolette were not to share them. "S'ele estait empereris de Colstentinoble u d'Alemaigne u roine de France u d'Engletere, si aroit il asses peu en li, tant est france et cortoise et de bon aire et entecie de toutes bones teces." To be empress of "Colstentinoble" would be none too good for her, so stamped is she with nobility and courtesy and high-breeding and all good qualities.

So the Count, after a long struggle, sent for his Viscount and threatened to have Nicolette burned alive, and the Viscount himself treated no better, if he did not put a stop to the affair; and the Viscount shut up Nicolette, and remonstrated with Aucassins: "Marry a king's daughter, or a count's! leave Nicolette alone, or you will never see Paradise!" This at once gave Aucassins the excuse for a charming tirade against Paradise, for which, a century or two later, he would properly have been burned together with Nicolette:—

En paradis qu'ai je a faire? Je n'i quier entrer mais que j'aie Nicolete, ma tres douce amie, que j'aim tant. C'en paradis ne vont fors tex gens con je vous dirai. Il i vont ci viel prestre et cil vieil clop et cil manke, qui tote jour et tote nuit cropent devant ces autex et en ces vies cruutes, et ci a ces vies capes ereses et a ces vies tatereles vestues, qui sont nu et decauc et estrumele, qui moeurent de faim et d'esci et de froid et de mesaises. Icil vont en paradis; aveuc ciax n'ai jou que faire; mais en infer voil jou aler. Car en infer vont li bel clerc et li bel cevalier qui sont mort as tornois et as rices gueres, et li bien sergant et li franc home. Aveuc ciax voil jou aler. Et si vont les beles dames cortoises que eles ont ii amis ou iii avec leurs barons. Et si va li ors et li agens et li vairs et li gris; et si i vont herpeor et jogleor et li roi del siecle. Avec ciax voil jou aler mais que j'aie Nicolete, ma tres douce amie, aveuc moi.

In Paradise what have I to do? I do not care to go there unless I may have Nicolette, my very sweet friend, whom I love so much. For to Paradise goes no one but such people as I will tell you of. There go old priests and old cripples and the maimed, who all day and all night crouch before altars and in old crypts, and are clothed with old worn-out capes and old tattered rags; who are naked and footbare and sore; who die of hunger and want and misery. These go to Paradise; with them I have nothing to do; but to Hell I am willing to go. For, to Hell go the fine scholars and the fair knights who die in tournies and in glorious wars; and the good men-at-arms and the well-born. With them I will gladly go. And there go the fair courteous ladies whether they have two or three friends besides their lords. And the gold and silver go there, and the ermines and sables; and there go the harpers and jongleurs, and the kings of the world. With these will I go, if only I may have Nicolette, my very sweet friend, with me.

Three times, in these short extracts, the word "courteous" has already appeared. The story itself is promised as "courteous"; Nicolette is "courteous"; and the ladies who are not to go to heaven are "courteous." Aucassins is in the full tide of courtesy, and evidently a professional, or he never would have claimed a place for harpers and jongleurs with kings and chevaliers in the next world. The poets of "courteous love" showed as little interest in religion as the poets of the eleventh century had shown for it in their poems of war. Aucassins resembled Christian of Troyes in this, and both of them resembled Thibaut, while William of Lorris went beyond them all. The literature of the "siecle" was always unreligious, from the "Chanson de Roland" to the "Tragedy of Hamlet"; to be "papelard" was unworthy of a chevalier; the true knight of courtesy made nothing of defying the torments of hell, as he defied the lance of a rival, the frowns of society, the threats of parents or the terrors of magic; the perfect, gentle, courteous lover thought of nothing but his love. Whether the object of his love were Nicolette of Beaucaire or Blanche of Castile, Mary of Champagne or Mary of Chartres, was a detail which did not affect the devotion of his worship.

So Nicolette, shut up in a vaulted chamber, leaned out at the marble window and sang, while Aucassins, when his father promised that he should have a kiss from Nicolette, went out to make fabulous slaughter of the enemy; and when his father broke the promise, shut himself up in his chamber, and also sang; and the action went on by scenes and interludes, until, one night, Nicolette let herself down from the window, by the help of sheets and towels, into the garden, and, with a natural dislike of wetting her skirts which has delighted every hearer or reader from that day to this, "prist se vesture a l'une main devant et a l'autre deriere si s'escorca por le rousee qu'ele vit grande sor l'erbe si s'en ala aval le gardin"; she raised her skirts with one hand in front and the other behind, for the dew which she saw heavy on the grass, and went off down the garden, to the tower where Aucassins was locked up, and sang to him through a crack in the masonry, and gave him a lock of her hair, and they talked till the friendly night-watch came by and warned her by a sweetly-sung chant, that she had better escape. So she bade farewell to Aucassins, and went on to a breach in the city wall, and she looked through it down into the fosse which was very deep and very steep. So she sang to herself—

Peres rois de maeste

Or ne sai quel part aler.

Se je vois u gaut rame

Ja me mengeront li le

Li lions et li sengler

Dont il i a a plente.

Father, King of Majesty!

Now I know not where to flee.

If I seek the forest free,

Then the lions will eat me,

Wolves and wild boars terribly,

Of which plenty there there be.

The lions were a touch of poetic licence, even for Beaucaire, but the wolves and wild boars were real enough; yet Nicolette feared even them less than she feared the Count, so she slid down what her audience well knew to be a most dangerous and difficult descent, and reached the bottom with many wounds in her hands and feet, "et san en sali bien en xii lius"; so that blood was drawn in a dozen places, and then she climbed up the other side, and went off bravely into the depths of the forest; an uncanny thing to do by night, as you can still see.

Then followed a pastoral, which might be taken from the works of another poet of the same period, whose acquaintance no one can neglect to make—Adam de la Halle, a Picard, of Arras. Adam lived, it is true, fifty years later than the date imagined for Aucassins, but his shepherds and shepherdesses are not so much like, as identical with, those of the Southern poet, and all have so singular an air of life that the conventional courteous knight fades out beside them. The poet, whether bourgeois, professional, noble, or clerical, never much loved the peasant, and the peasant never much loved him, or any one else. The peasant was a class by himself, and his trait, as a class, was suspicion of everybody and all things, whether material, social, or divine. Naturally he detested his lord, whether temporal or spiritual, because the seigneur and the priest took his earnings, but he was never servile, though a serf; he was far from civil; he was commonly gross. He was cruel, but not more so than his betters; and his morals were no worse. The object of oppression on all sides,—the invariable victim, whoever else might escape,—the

French peasant, as a class, held his own—and more. In fact, he succeeded in plundering Church, Crown, nobility, and bourgeoisie, and was the only class in French history that rose steadily in power and well-being, from the time of the crusades to the present day, whatever his occasional suffering may have been; and, in the thirteenth century, he was suffering. When Nicolette, on the morning after her escape, came upon a group of peasants in the forest, tending the Count's cattle, she had reason to be afraid of them, but instead they were afraid of her. They thought at first that she was a fairy. When they guessed the riddle, they kept the secret, though they risked punishment and lost the chance of reward by protecting her. Worse than this, they agreed, for a small present, to give a message to Aucassins if he should ride that way.

Aucassins was not very bright, but when he got out of prison after Nicolette's escape, he did ride out, at his friends' suggestion, and tried to learn what had become of her. Passing through the woods he came upon the same group of shepherds and shepherdesses:—

> Esmeres et Martinet, Fruelins et Johannes, Robecons et
>
> Aubries,—

who might have been living in the Forest of Arden, so like were they to the clowns of Shakespeare. They were singing of Nicolette and her present, and the cakes and knives and flute they would buy with it. Aucassins jumped to the bait they offered him; and they instantly began to play him as though he were a trout:—

"Bel enfant, dix vos i ait!"

"Dix vos benie!" fait cil qui fu plus enparles des autres.

"Bel enfant," fait il, "redites le cancon que vos disiez ore!"

"Nous n'i dirons," fait cil qui plus fu enparles des autres. "Dehait ore qui por vos i cantera, biax sire!"

"Bel enfant!" fait Aucassins, "enne me connissies vos?"

"Oïl! nos savions bien que vos estes Aucassins, nos damoisiax, mais nos ne somes mie a vos, ains somes au conte."

"Bel enfant, si feres, je vos en pri!"

"Os, por le cuer be!" fait cil. "Por quoi canteroie je por vos, s'il ne me seoit! Quant il n'a si rice home en cest pais sans le cors le conte Garin s'il trovait mes bues ne mes vaces ne mes brebis en ses pres n'en sen forment qu'il fust mie tant hardis por les es a crever qu'il les en ossast cacier. Et por quoi canteroie je por vos s'il ne me seoit?"

"Se dix vos ait, bel enfant, si feres! et tenes x sous que j'ai ci en une borse!"

"God bless you, fair child!" said Aucassins.

"God be with you!" replied the one who talked best.

"Fair child!" said he, "repeat the song you were just singing."

"We won't!" replied he who talked best among them. "Bad luck to him who shall sing for you, good sir!"

"Fair child," said Aucassins, "do you know me?"

"Yes! we know very well that you are Aucassins, our young lord; but we are none of yours; we belong to the Count."

"Fair child, indeed you'll do it, I pray you!"

"Listen, for love of God!" said he. "Why should I sing for you if it does not suit me? when there is no man so powerful in this country, except Count Garin, if he found my oxen or my cows or my sheep in his pasture or his close, would not rather risk losing his eyes than dare to turn them out! and why should I sing for you, if it does not suit me!"

"So God help you, good child, indeed you will do it! and take these ten sous that I have here in my purse."

"Sire les deniers prenderons nos, mais je ne vos canterai mie, car j'en ai jure. Mais je le vos conterai se vos voles."

"De par diu!" faits Aucassins. "Encore aim je mix center que nient."

"Sire, the money we will take, but I'll not sing to you, for I've sworn it. But I will tell it you, if you like."

"For God's sake!" said Aucassins; "better telling than nothing!"

Ten sous was no small gift! twenty sous was the value of a strong ox. The poet put a high money-value on the force of love, but he set a higher value on it in courtesy. These boors were openly insolent to their young lord, trying to extort money from him, and threatening him with telling his father; but they were in their right, and Nicolette was in their power. At heart they meant Aucassins well, but they were rude and grasping, and the poet used them in order to show how love made the true lover courteous even to clowns. Aucassins' gentle courtesy is brought out by the boors' greed, as the colours in the window were brought out and given their value by a bit of blue or green. The poet, having got his little touch of colour rightly placed, let the peasants go. "Cil qui fu plus enparles des autres," having been given his way and his money, told Aucassins what he knew of Nicolette and her message; so Aucassins put spurs to his horse and cantered into the forest, singing:—

Se diu plaist le pere fort

Je vos reverai encore

> Suer, douce a-mie!
>
> So please God, great and strong,
>
> I will find you now ere long,
>
> Sister, sweet friend!

But the peasant had singular attraction for the poet. Whether the character gave him a chance for some clever mimicry, which was one of his strong points as a story-teller; or whether he wanted to treat his subjects, like the legendary windows, in pairs; or whether he felt that the forest-scene specially amused his audience, he immediately introduced a peasant of another class, much more strongly coloured, or deeply shadowed. Every one in the audience was—and, for that matter, still would be—familiar with the great forests, the home of half the fairy and nursery tales of Europe, still wild enough and extensive enough to hide in, although they have now comparatively few lions, and not many wolves or wild boars or serpents such as Nicolette feared. Every one saw, without an effort, the young damoiseau riding out with his hound or hawk, looking for game; the lanes under the trees, through the wood, or the thick underbrush before lanes were made; the herdsmen watching their herds, and keeping a sharp look-out for wolves; the peasant seeking lost cattle; the black kiln-men burning charcoal; and in the depths of the rocks or swamps or thickets—the outlaw. Even now, forests like Rambouillet, or Fontainebleau or Compiegne are enormous and wild; one can see Aucassins breaking his way through thorns and branches in search of Nicolette, tearing his clothes and wounding himself "en xl lius u en xxx," until evening approached, and he began to weep for disappointment:—

Il esgarda devant lui enmi la voie si vit un vallet tei que je vos dirai. Grans estoit et mervellex et lais et hidex. Il avoit une grande hure plus noire qu'une carbouclee, et avoit plus de planne paume entre ii ex, et avoit unes grandes joes et un grandisme nez plat, et une grans narines lees et unes grosses levres plus rouges d'unes carbounees, et uns grans dens gaunes et lais et estoit caucies d'uns housiax et d'uns sollers de buef fretes de tille dusque deseure le genol et estoit afules d'une cape a ii envers si estoit apoiies sor une grande macue. Aucassins s'enbati sor lui s'eut grand paor quant il le sorvit…

"Baix frere, dix ti ait!"

"Dix vos benie!" fait cil. "Se dix t'ait, que fais tu ilec?"

"A vos que monte?" fait cil.

"Nient!" fait Aucassins; "je nel vos demant se por bien non."

"Mais pour quoi ploures vos?" fait cil, "et faites si fait doel? Certes se j'estoie ausi rices hom que vos estes, tos li mons ne me feroit mie plorer."

"Ba! me conissies vos!" fait Aucassins.

"Oie! je sai bien que vos estes Aucassins li fix le conte, et se vos me dites por quoi vos plores je vos dirai que je fac ici."

As he looked before him along the way he saw a man such as I will tell you. Tall he was, and menacing, and ugly, and hideous. He had a great mane blacker than charcoal and had more than a full palm- width between his two eyes, and had big cheeks, and a huge flat nose and great broad nostrils, and thick lips redder than raw beef, and large ugly yellow teeth, and was shod with hose and leggings of raw hide laced with bark cord to above the knee, and was muffled in a cloak without lining, and was leaning on a great club. Aucassins came upon him suddenly and had great fear when he saw him.

"Fair brother, good day!" said he.

"God bless you!" said the other.

"As God help you, what do you here?"

"What is that to you?" said the other.

"Nothing!" said Aucassins; "I ask only from good-will."

"But why are you crying!" said the other, "and mounring so loud? Sure, if I were as great a man as you are, nothing on earth would make me cry."

"Bah! you know me?" said Aucassins.

"Yes, I know very well that you are Aucassins, the count's son; and if you will tell me what you are crying for, I will tell you what I am doing here."

Aucassins seemed to think this an equal bargain. All damoiseaux were not as courteous as Aucassins, nor all "varlets" as rude as his peasants; we shall see how the young gentlemen of Picardy treated the peasantry for no offence at all; but Aucassins carried a softer, Southern temper in a happier climate, and, with his invariable gentle courtesy, took no offence at the familiarity with which the ploughman treated him. Yet he dared not tell the truth, so he invented, on the spur of the moment, an excuse;—he has lost, he said, a beautiful white hound. The peasant hooted—

"Os!" fait cil; "por le cuer que cil sires eut en sen ventre! que vos plorastes por un cien puant! Mal dehait ait qui ja mais vos prisera quant il n'a si rice home en ceste tere se vos peres len mandoit x u xv u xx qu'il ne les envoyast trop volontiers et s'en esteroit trop lies. Mais je dois plorer et dol faire?"

"Et tu de quoi frere?"

"Sire je lo vos dirai. J'estoie liues a un rice vilain si cacoie se carue. iiii bues i avoit. Or a iii jors qu il m'avint une grande malaventure que je perdi le mellor de mes bues Roget le mellor de me carue. Si le vois querant. Si ne mengai ne ne bue iii jors a passes. Si n'os aler a le vile c'on me metroit en prison que je ne l'ai de quoi saure. De tot l'avoir du monde n'ai je plus vaillant que vos vees sor le cors de mi. Une lasse mere avoie, si n'avoit plus vaillant que une keutisele, si h a on sacie de desous le dos si gist a pur l'estrain, si m'en poise asses plus que denu. Car avoirs va et viaent; se j'ai or perdu je gaaignerai une autre fois si sorrai mon buef quant je porrai, ne ja por cien n'en plorerai. Et vos plorastes por un cien de longaigne! Mal dehait ait qui mais vos prisera!"

"Certes tu es de bon confort, biax frere! que benois sois tu! Et que valoit tes bues!"

"Sire xx sous m'en demande on, je n'en puis mie abatre une seule maille."

"Or, tien" fait Aucassins, "xx que j'ai ci en me borse, si sol ten buef!"

"Listen!" said he, "By the heart God had in his body, that you should cry for a stinking dog! Bad luck to him who ever prizes you! When there is no man in this land so great, if your father sent to him for ten or fifteen or twenty but would fetch them very gladly, and be only too pleased. But I ought to cry and mourn."

"And—why you, brother?"

"Sir, I will tell you. I was hired out to a rich farmer to drive his plough. There were four oxen. Now three days ago I had a great misfortune, for I lost the best of my oxen, Roget, the best of my team. I am looking to find him. I've not eaten or drunk these three days past. I dare n't go to the town, for they would put me in prison as I've nothing to pay with. In all the world I've not the worth of anything but what you see on my body I've a poor old mother who owned nothing but a feather mattress, and they've dragged it from under her back so she lies on the bare straw, and she troubles me more than myself. For riches come and go if I lose to day, I gain to-morrow; I will pay for my ox when I can, and will not cry for that. And you cry for a filthy dog! Bad luck to him who ever thinks well of you!"

"Truly, you counsel well, good brother! God bless you! And what was your ox worth?"

"Sir, they ask me twenty sous for it. I cannot beat them down a single centime."

"Here are twenty," said Aucassins, "that I have in my purse! Pay for your ox!"

"Sire!" fait il, "grans mercies! et dix vos laist trover ce que vox queres!"

"Sir!" said he; "many thanks! and Go! grant you find what you seek!"

The little episode was thrown in without rhyme or reason to the rapid emotion of the love-story, as though the jongleur were showing his own cleverness and humour, at the expense of his hero, as jongleurs had a way of doing; but he took no such liberties with his heroine. While Aucassins tore through the thickets on horseback, crying aloud, Nicolette had built herself a little hut in the depths of the forest:—

Ele prist des flors de lis

Et de l'erbe du garris

Et de le foille autresi;

Une belle loge en fist,

Ainques tant gente ne vi,

Jure diu qui ne menti

Se par la vient Aucassins

Et il por l'amor de li

Ne si repose un petit

Ja ne sera ses amis

N'ele s'a-mie.

So she twined the lilies' flower,

Roofed with leafy branches o'er,

Made of it a lovely bower,

With the freshest grass for floor

Such as never mortal saw.

By God's Verity, she swore,

Should Aucassins pass her door,

And not stop for love of her,

To repose a moment there,

He should be her love no more,

Nor she his dear!

So night came on, and Nicolette went to sleep, a little distance away from her hut. Aucassins at last came by, and dismounted, spraining his shoulder in doing it. Then he crept into the little hut, and lying on his back, looked up through the leaves to the moon, and sang:—

Estoilete, je te voi,

Que la lune trait a soi.

Nicolete est avcuc toi,

M'amiete o le blond poil.

Je quid que dix le veut avoir

Por la lumiere de soir

Que par li plus clere soit.

Vien, amie, je te proie!

Ou monter vauroie droit,

Que que fust du recaoir.

Que fuisse lassus o toi

Ja te baiseroi estroit.

Se j'estoie fix a roi

S'afferies vos bien a moi

  Suer douce amie!

I can see you, little star,

That the moon draws through the air.

Nicolette is where you are,

My own love with the blonde hair.

I think God must want her near

To shine down upon us here

That the evening be more clear.

Come down, dearest, to my prayer,

Or I climb up where you are!

Though I fell, I would not care.

If I once were with you there

I would kiss you closely, dear!

If a monarch's son I were

You should all my kingdom share,

  Sweet friend, sister!

How Nicolette heard him sing, and came to him and rubbed his shoulder and dressed his wounds as though he were a child; and how in the morning they rode away together, like Tennyson's "Sleeping Beauty,"—

  O'er the hills and far away

    Beyond their utmost purple rim,

    Beyond the night, beyond the day,

singing as they rode, the story goes on to tell or to sing in verse—

Aucassins, li biax, li blons,

  Li gentix, lt amorous,

  Est issous del gaut parfont,

  Entre ses bras ses amors

  Devant lui sor son arcon.

  Les ex li baise et le front,

  Et le bouce et le menton.

  Elle l'a mis a raison.

  "Aucassins, biax amis dox,

  "En quel tere en irons nous?"

  "Douce amie, que sai jou?"

  "Moi ne caut u nous aillons,

  "En forest u en destor

  "Mais que je soie aveuc vous."

  Passent les vaus et les mons,

  Et les viles et les bors

  A la mer vinrent au jor,

  Si descendent u sablon

  Les le rivage.

Aucassins, the brave, the fair,

Courteous knight and gentle lover,

From the forest dense came forth;

In his arms his love he bore

On his saddle-bow before;

Her eyes he kisses and her mouth,

And her forehead and her chin.

She brings him back to earth again:

"Aucassins, my love, my own,

"To what country shall we turn?"

"Dearest angel, what say you?

"I care nothing where we go,

"In the forest or outside,

"While you on my saddle ride."

So they pass by hill and dale,

And the city, and the town,

Till they reach the morning pale,

And on sea-sands set them down,

Hard by the shore.

There we will leave them, for their further adventures have not much to do with our matter. Like all the romans, or nearly all, "Aucassins" is singularly pure and refined. Apparently the ladies of courteous love frowned on coarseness and allowed no licence. Their power must have been great, for the best romans are as free from grossness as the "Chanson de Roland" itself, or the church glass, or the illuminations in the manuscripts; and as long as the power of the Church ruled good society, this decency continued. As far as women were concerned, they seem always to have been more clean than the men, except when men painted them in colours which men liked best.

Perhaps society was actually cleaner in the thirteenth century than in the sixteenth, as Saint Louis was more decent than Francis I, and as the bath was habitual in the twelfth century and exceptional at the Renaissance. The rule held good for the bourgeoisie as well as among the dames cortoises. Christian and Thibaut, "Aucassins" and the "Roman de la Rose," may have expressed only the tastes of high- born ladies, but other poems were avowedly bourgeois, and among the bourgeois poets none was better than Adam de la Halle. Adam wrote also for the court, or at least for Robert of Artois, Saint Louis's nephew, whom he followed to Naples in 1284, but his poetry was as little aristocratic as poetry could well be, and most of it was cynically—almost defiantly—middle-class, as though the weavers of Arras were his only audience, and recognized him and the objects of his satire in every verse. The bitter personalities do not concern us, but, at Naples, to amuse Robert of Artois and his court, Adam composed the first of French comic operas, which had an immense success, and, as a pastoral poem, has it still. The Idyll of Arras was a singular contrast to the Idyll of Beaucaire, but the social value was the same in both; Robin and Marion were a pendant to Aucassins and Nicolette; Robin was almost a burlesque on Aucassins, while Marion was a Northern, energetic, intelligent, pastoral Nicolette.

"Li Gieus de Robin et de Marion" had little or no plot. Adam strung together, on a thread of dialogue and by a group of suitable figures, a number of the favourite songs of his time, followed by the favourite games, and ending with a favourite dance, the "tresca." The songs, the games, and the dances do not concern us, but the dialogue runs along prettily, with an air of Flemish realism, like a picture of Teniers, as unlike that of "courtoisie" as Teniers was to Guido Reni. Underneath it all a tone of satire made itself felt, good-natured enough, but directed wholly against the men.

The scene opens on Marion tending her sheep, and singing the pretty air: "Robin m'aime, Robin ma'a," after which enters a chevalier or esquire, on horseback, and sings: "Je me repairoie du tournoiement." Then follows a dialogue between the chevalier and Marion, with no other object than to show off the charm of Marion against the masculine defects of the knight. Being, like most squires, somewhat slow of ideas in conversation with young women, the gentleman began by asking for sport for his falcon. Has she seen any duck down by the river?

Mais veis tu par chi devant

Vers ceste riviere nul ane?

"Ane," it seems, was the usual word for wild duck, the falcon's prey, and Marion knew it as well as he, but she chose to misunderstand him:—

C'est une bete qui recane;

J'en vis ier iii sur che quemin,

Tous quarchies aler au moulin.

Est che chou que vous demandes?

"It is a beast that brays; I saw three yesterday on the road, all with loads going to the mill. Is that what you ask?" That is not what the squire has asked, and he is conscious that Marion knows it, but he tries again. If she has not seen a duck, perhaps she has seen a heron:—

Hairons, sire? par me foi, non!

Je n'en vi nesun puis quareme

Que j'en vi mengier chies dame Eme

Me taiien qui sorit ches brebis.

"Heron, sir! by my faith, no! I've not seen one since Lent when I saw some eaten at my grandmother's—Dame Emma who owns these sheep." "Hairons," it seems, meant also herring, and this wilful misunderstanding struck the chevalier as carrying jest too far:—

Par foi! or suis j'ou esbaubis!

N'ainc mais je ne fui si gabes!

"On my word, I am silenced! never in my life was I so chaffed!" Marion herself seems to think her joke a little too evident, for she takes up the conversation in her turn, only to conclude that she likes Robin better than she does the knight; he is gayer, and when he plays his musette he starts the whole village dancing. At this, the squire makes a declaration of love with such energy as to spur his horse almost over her:—

Aimi, sire! ostez vo cheval!

A poi que il ne m'a blechie.

Li Robin ne regiete mie

Quand je voie apres se karue.

"Aimi!" is an exclamation of alarm, real or affected: "Dear me, sir! take your horse away! he almost hurt me! Robin's horse never rears when I go behind his plough!" Still the knight persists, and though Marion still tells him to go away, she asks his name, which he says is Aubert, and so gives her the catchword for another song:—"Vos perdes vo paine, sire Aubert!"—which ends the scene with a duo. The second scene begins with a duo of Marion and Robin, followed by her giving a softened account of the chevalier's behaviour, and then they lunch on bread and cheese and apples, and more songs follow, till she sends him to get Baldwin and Walter and Peronette and the pipers, for a dance. In his absence the chevalier returns and becomes very pressing in his attentions, which gives her occasion to sing:-

J'oi Robin flagoler

Au flagol d'argent.

When Robin enters, the knight picks a quarrel with him for not handling properly the falcon which he has caught in the hedge; and Robin gets a severe beating. The scene ends by the horseman carrying off Marion by force; but he soon gets tired of carrying her against her will, and drops her, and disappears once for all.

Certes voirement sui je beste

Quant a ceste beste m'areste.

Adieu, bergiere!

Bete the knight certainly was, and was meant to be, in order to give the necessary colour to Marion's charms. Chevaliers were seldom intellectually brilliant in the mediaeval romans, and even the "Chansons de Geste" liked better to talk of their prowess than of their wit; but Adam de la Halle, who felt no great love for chevaliers, was not satisfied with ridiculing them in order to exalt Marion; his second act was devoted to exalting Marion at the expense of her own boors.

The first act was given up to song; the second, to games and dances. The games prove not to be wholly a success; Marion is bored by them, and wants to dance. The dialogue shows Marion trying constantly to control her clowns and make them decent, as Blanche of Castile had been all her life trying to control her princes, and Mary of Chartres her kings. Robin is a rustic counterpart to Thibaut. He is tamed by his love of Marion, but he has just enough intelligence to think well of himself, and to get himself into trouble without knowing how to get out of it. Marion loves him much as she would her child; she makes only a little fun of him; defends him from the others; laughs at his jealousy; scolds him on occasion; flatters his dancing; sends him on errands, to bring the pipers or drive away the wolf; and what is most to our purpose, uses him to make the other peasants decent. Walter and Baldwin and Hugh are coarse, and their idea of wit is to shock the women or make Robin jealous. Love makes gentlemen even of boors, whether noble or villain, is the constant moral of mediaeval story, and love turns Robin into a champion of decency. When, at last, Walter, playing the jongleur, begins to repeat a particularly coarse fabliau, or story in verse, Robin stops him short—

Ho, Gautier, je n'en voeil plus! fi!

Dites, seres vous tous jours teus!

Vous estes un ors menestreus!

"Ho, Walter! I want no more of that: Shame! Say! are you going to be always like that? You're a dirty beggar!" A fight seems inevitable, but Marion turns it into a dance, and the whole party, led by the pipers, with Robin and Marion at the head of the band, leave the stage in the dance which is said to be still known in Italy as the "tresca." Marion is in her way as charming as Nicolette, but we are less interested in her charm than in her power. Always the woman appears as the practical guide; the one who keeps her head, even in love:—

Elle l'a mis a raison:

"Aucassins, biax amis dox,

En quele tere en irons nous?"

"Douce amie, que sai jou?

Moi ne caut ou nous aillons."

The man never cared; he was always getting himself into crusades, or feuds, or love, or debt, and depended on the woman to get him out. The story was always of Charles VII and Jeanne d'Arc, or Agnes Sorel. The woman might be the good or the evil spirit, but she was always the stronger force. The twelfth and thirteenth centuries were a period when men were at their strongest; never before or since have they shown equal energy in such varied directions, or such intelligence in the direction of their energy; yet these marvels of history,—these Plantagenets; these scholastic philosophers; these architects of Rheims and Amiens; these Innocents, and Robin Hoods and Marco Polos; these crusaders, who planted their enormous fortresses all over the Levant; these monks who made the wastes and barrens yield harvests;—all, without apparent exception, bowed down before the woman.

Explain it who will! We are not particularly interested in the explanation; it is the art we have chased through this French forest, like Aucassins hunting for Nicolette; and the art leads always to the woman. Poetry, like the architecture and the decoration, harks back to the same standard of taste. The specimens of Christian of Troyes, Thibaut, Tristan, Aucassins, and Adam de la Halle were mild admissions of feminine superiority compared with some that were more in vogue. If Thibaut painted his love-verses on the walls of his castle, he put there only what a more famous poet, who may have been his friend, set on the walls of his Chateau of Courteous Love, which, not being made with hands or with stone, but merely with verse, has not wholly perished. The "Roman de la Rose" is the end of true mediaeval poetry and goes with the Sainte-Chapelle in architecture, and three hundred years of more or less graceful imitation or variation on the same themes which followed. Our age calls it false taste, and no doubt our age is right;—every age is right by its own standards as long as its standards amuse it;—but after all, the "Roman de la Rose" charmed Chaucer,—it may well charm you. The charm may not be that of Mont-Saint-Michel or of Roland; it has not the grand manner of the eleventh century, or the jewelled brilliancy of the Chartres lancets, or the splendid self-assertion of the roses: but even to this day it gives out a faint odour of Champagne and Touraine, of Provence and Cyprus. One hears Thibaut and sees Queen Blanche.

Of course, this odour of true sanctity belongs only to the "Roman" of William of Lorris, which dates from the death of Queen Blanche and of all good things, about 1250; a short allegory of courteous love in forty-six hundred and seventy lines. To modern taste, an allegory of forty-six hundred and seventy lines seems to be not so short as it might be; but the fourteenth century found five thousand verses totally inadequate to the subject, and, about 1300, Jean de Meung added eighteen thousand lines, the favourite reading of society for one or two hundred years, but beyond our horizon. The "Roman" of William of Lorris was complete in itself; it had shape; beginning, middle, and end; even a certain realism, action,—almost life!

The Rose is any feminine ideal of beauty, intelligence, purity, or grace,—always culminating in the Virgin,—but the scene is the Court of Love, and the action is avowedly in a dream, without time or place. The poet's tone is very pure; a little subdued; at times sad; and the poem ends sadly; but all the figures that were positively hideous were shut out of the court, and painted on the outside walls:—Hatred; Felony; Covetousness; Envy; Poverty; Melancholy, and Old Age. Death did not appear. The passion for representing death in its horrors did not belong to the sunny atmosphere of the thirteenth century, and indeed jarred on French taste always, though the

Church came to insist on it; but Old Age gave the poet a motive more artistic, foreshadowing Death, and quite sad enough to supply the necessary contrast. The poet who approached the walls of the chateau and saw, outside, all the unpleasant facts of life conspicuously posted up, as though to shut them out of doors, hastened to ask for entrance, and, when once admitted, found a court of ideals. Their names matter little. In the mind of William of Lorris, every one would people his ideal world with whatever ideal figures pleased him, and the only personal value of William's figures is that they represent what he thought the thirteenth- century ideals of a perfect society. Here is Courtesy, with a translation long thought to be by Chaucer:-

Apres se tenoit Cortoisie

Qui moult estoit de tous prisie.

Si n'ere orgueilleuse ne fole.

C'est cele qui a la karole,

La soe merci, m'apela,

Ains que nule, quand je vins la.

Et ne fut ne nice n'umbrage,

Mais sages auques, sans outrage,

De biaus respons et de biaus dis,

Onc nus ne fu par li laidis,

Ne ne porta nului rancune,

Et fu clere comme la lune

Est avers les autres estoiles

Qui ne resemblent que chandoiles.

Faitisse estoit et avenant;

Je ne sai fame plus plaisant.

Ele ert en toutes cors bien digne

D'estre empereris ou roine.

And next that daunced Courtesye,

That preised was of lowe and hye,

For neither proude ne foole was she;

She for to daunce called me,

I pray God yeve hir right good grace,

When I come first into the place.

She was not nyce ne outrageous,

But wys and ware and vertuous;

Of faire speche and of faire answere;

Was never wight mysseid of her,

Ne she bar rancour to no wight.

Clere browne she was, and thereto bright

Of face, of body avenaunt.

I wot no lady so pleasaunt.

She were worthy forto bene

An empresse or crowned quene.

You can read for yourselves the characters, and can follow the simple action which owes its slight interest only to the constant effort of the dreamer to attain his ideal,—the Rose,—and owes its charm chiefly to the constant disappointment and final defeat. An undertone of sadness runs through it, felt already in the picture of Time which foreshadows the end of Love—the Rose—and her court, and with it the end of hope:—

Li tens qui s'en va nuit et jor,

Sans repos prendre et sans sejor,

Et qui de nous se part et emble

Si celeement qu'il nous semble

Qu'il s'arreste ades en un point,

Et il ne s'i arreste point,

Ains ne fine de trespasser,

Que nus ne puet neis penser

Quex tens ce est qui est presens;

S'el demandes as clers lisans,

Aincois que l'en l'eust pense

Seroit il ja trois tens passe;

Li tens qui ne puet sejourner,

Ains vait tous jors sans retorner,

Com l'iaue qui s'avale toute,

N'il n'en retourne arriere goute;

Li tens vers qui noient ne dure,

Ne fer ne chose tant soit dure,

Car il gaste tout et menjue;

Li tens qui tote chose muc,

Qui tout fait croistre et tout norist,

Et qui tout use et tout porrist.

The tyme that passeth nyght and daye,

And restelesse travayleth aye,

And steleth from us so prively,

That to us semeth so sykerly

That it in one poynt dwelleth never,

But gothe so fast, and passeth aye

That there nys man that thynke may

What tyme that now present is;

Asketh at these clerkes this,

For or men thynke it readily

Thre tymes ben ypassed by.

The tyme that may not sojourne

But goth, and may never returne,

As water that down renneth ay,

But never drope retourne may.

There may no thing as time endure,

Metall nor earthly creature:

For alle thing it frette and shall.

The tyme eke that chaungith all,

And all doth waxe and fostered be,

And alle thing distroieth he.

The note of sadness has begun, which the poets were to find so much more to their taste than the note of gladness. From the "Roman de la Rose" to the "Ballade des Dames du Temps jadis" was a short step for the Middle-Age giant Time,—a poor two hundred years. Then Villon woke up to ask what had become of the Roses:—Ou est la tres sage Helois Pour qui fut chastie puis moyne, Pierre Esbaillart a Saint Denis? Pour son amour ot cest essoyne.

Et Jehanne la bonne Lorraine

Qu' Englois brulerent a Rouan;

Ou sont elles, Vierge Souvraine?

Mais ou sont les neiges dantan?

Where is the virtuous Heloise,

For whom suffered, then turned monk,

Pierre Abelard at Saint-Denis?

For his love he bore that pain.

And Jeanne d'Arc, the good Lorraine,

Whom the English burned at Rouen!

Where are they, Virgin Queen?

But where are the snows of spring?

Between the death of William of Lorris and the advent of John of Meung, a short half-century (1250-1300), the Woman and the Rose became bankrupt. Satire took the place of worship. Man, with his usual monkey-like malice, took pleasure in pulling down what he had built up. The Frenchman had made what he called "fausse route." William of Lorris was first to see it, and say it, with more sadness and less bitterness than Villon showed; he won immortality by telling how he, and the thirteenth century in him, had lost himself in pursuing his Rose, and how he had lost the Rose, too, waking up at last to the dull memory of pain and sorrow and death, that "tout porrist." The world had still a long march to make from the Rose of Queen Blanche to the guillotine of Madame du Barry; but the "Roman de la Rose" made epoch. For the first time since Constantine proclaimed the reign of Christ, a thousand years, or so, before Philip the Fair dethroned Him, the deepest expression of social feeling ended with the word: Despair.

CHAPTER XIII: LES MIRACLES DE NOTRE DAME

Vergine Madre, figlia del tuo figlio,

Umile ed alta piu che creatura,

Termine fisso d'eterno consiglio,

Tu sei colei che l'umana natura

Nobilitasti si, che il suo fattore

Non disdegno di farsi sua fattura....

La tua benignita non pur soccorre

A chi dimanda, ma molte fiate

Liberamente al dimandar precorre.

In te misericordia, in te pietate,

In te magnificenza, in te s'aduna

Quantunque in creatura e di bontate.

Vergine bella, che di sol vestita,

Coronata di stelle, al sommo sole

Piacesti si che'n te sua luce ascose;

Amor mi spinge a dir di te parole;

Ma non so 'ncominciar senza tu aita,

E di colui ch'amando in te si pose.

Invoco lei che ben sempre rispose

Chi la chiamo con fede.

Vergine, s'a mercede

Miseria estrema dell' umane cose

Giammai ti volse, al mio prego t'inchina!

Soccorri alia mia guerra,

Bench'i sia terra, e tu del del regina!

Dante composed one of these prayers; Petrarch the other. Chaucer translated Dante's prayer in the "Second Nonnes Tale." He who will may undertake to translate either;—not I! The Virgin, in whom is united whatever goodness is in created being, might possibly, in her infinite grace, forgive the sacrilege; but her power has limits, if not her grace; and the whole Trinity, with the Virgin to aid, had not the power to pardon him who should translate Dante and Petrarch. The prayers come in here, not merely for their beauty,—although the Virgin knows how beautiful they are, whether man knows it or not; but chiefly to show the good faith, the depth of feeling, the intensity of conviction, with which society adored its ideal of human perfection.

The Virgin filled so enormous a space in the life and thought of the time that one stands now helpless before the mass of testimony to her direct action and constant presence in every moment and form of the illusion which men thought they thought their existence. The twelfth and thirteenth centuries believed in the supernatural, and might almost be said to have contracted a miracle-habit, as morbid as any other form of artificial stimulant; they stood, like children, in an attitude of gaping wonder before the miracle of miracles which they felt in their own consciousness; but one can see in this emotion, which is, after all, not exclusively infantile, no special reason why they should have so passionately flung themselves at the feet of the Woman rather than of the Man. Dante wrote in 1300, after the height of this emotion had passed; and Petrarch wrote half a century later still; but so slowly did the vision fade, and so often did it revive, that, to this day, it remains the strongest symbol with which the Church can conjure.

Men were, after all, not wholly inconsequent; their attachment to Mary rested on an instinct of self-preservation. They knew their own peril. If there was to be a future life, Mary was their only hope. She alone represented Love. The Trinity were, or was, One, and could, by the nature of its essence, administer justice alone. Only childlike illusion could expect a personal favour from Christ. Turn the dogma as one would, to this it must logically come. Call the three Godheads by what names one liked, still they must remain One; must administer one justice; must admit only one law. In that law, no human weakness or error could exist; by its essence it was infinite, eternal, immutable. There was no crack and no cranny in the system, through which human frailty could hope for escape. One was forced from corner to corner by a remorseless logic until one fell helpless at Mary's feet.

Without Mary, man had no hope except in atheism, and for atheism the world was not ready. Hemmed back on that side, men rushed like sheep to escape the butcher, and were driven to

Mary; only too happy in finding protection and hope in a being who could understand the language they talked, and the excuses they had to offer. How passionately they worshipped Mary, the Cathedral of Chartres shows; and how this worship elevated the whole sex, all the literature and history of the time proclaim. If you need more proof, you can read more Petrarch; but still one cannot realize how actual Mary was, to the men and women of the Middle Ages, and how she was present, as a matter of course, whether by way of miracle or as a habit of life, throughout their daily existence. The surest measure of her reality is the enormous money value they put on her assistance, and the art that was lavished on her gratification, but an almost equally certain sign is the casual allusion, the chance reference to her, which assumes her presence.

The earliest prose writer in the French language, who gave a picture of actual French life, was Joinville; and although he wrote after the death of Saint Louis and of William of Lorris and Adam de la Halle, in the full decadence of Philip the Fair, toward 1300, he had been a vassal of Thibaut and an intimate friend of Louis, and his memories went back to the France of Blanche's regency. Born in 1224, he must have seen in his youth the struggles of Thibaut against the enemies of Blanche, and in fact his memoirs contain Blanche's emphatic letter forbidding Thibaut to marry Yolande of Brittany. He knew Pierre de Dreux well, and when they were captured by the Saracens at Damietta, and thrown into the hold of a galley, "I had my feet right on the face of the Count Pierre de Bretagne, whose feet, in turn, were by my face." Joinville is almost twelfth-century in feeling. He was neither feminine nor sceptical, but simple. He showed no concern for poetry, but he put up a glass window to the Virgin. His religion belonged to the "Chanson de Roland." When Saint Louis, who had a pleasant sense of humour put to him his favourite religious conundrums, Joinville affected not the least hypocrisy. "Would you rather be a leper or commit a mortal sin?" asked the King. "I would rather commit thirty mortal sins than be a leper," answered Joinville. "Do you wash the feet of the poor on Holy Thursday?" asked the King. "God forbid!" replied Joinville; "never will I wash the feet of such creatures!" Saint Louis mildly corrected his, or rather Thibaut's, seneschal, for these impieties, but he was no doubt used to them, for the soldier was never a churchman. If one asks Joinville what he thinks of the Virgin, he answers with the same frankness:—

Ung jour moi estant devant le roi lui demanday congie d'aller en pelerinage a nostre Dame de Tourtouze [Tortosa in Syria] qui estoit ung veage tres fort requis. Et y avoit grant quantite de pelerins par chacun jour pour ce que c'est le premier autel qui onques fust fait en l'onneur de la Mere de Dieu ainsi qu'on disoit lors. Et y faisoit nostre Dame de grans miracles a merveilles. Entre lesquelz elle en fist ung d'un pouvre homme qui estoit hors de son sens et demoniacle. Car il avoit le maling esperit dedans le corps. Et advint par ung jour qu'il fut amene a icelui autel de nostre Dame de Tourtouze. Et ainsi que ses amys qui l'avoient la amene prioient a nostre Dame qu'elle lui voulsist recouvrer sante et guerison le diable que la pouvre creature avoit ou corps respondit: "Nostre Dame n'est pas ici; elle est en Egipte pour aider au Roi de France et aux Chrestiens qui aujourdhui arrivent en la Terre sainte centre toute paiennie qui sont a cheval." Et fut mis en escript le jour que le deable profera ces motz et fut apporte au legat qui estoit avecques le roi de France; lequel me dist depuis que a celui jour nous estion arrivez en la terre d'Egipte. Et suis bien certain que la bonne Dame Marie nous y eut bien besoin.

This happened in Syria, after the total failure of the crusade in Egypt. The ordinary man, even if he were a priest or a soldier, needed a miraculous faith to persuade him that Our Lady or any other divine power, had helped the crusades of Saint Louis. Few of the usual fictions on which society rested had ever required such defiance of facts; but, at least for a time, society held firm. The thirteenth century could not afford to admit a doubt. Society had staked its existence, in this world and the next, on the reality and power of the Virgin; it had invested in her care nearly its whole capital, spiritual, artistic, intellectual, and economical, even to the bulk of its real and personal estate; and her overthrow would have been the most appalling disaster the Western world had ever known. Without her, the Trinity itself could not stand; the Church must fall; the future world must dissolve. Not even the collapse of the Roman Empire compared with a calamity so serious; for that had created, not destroyed, a faith.

If sceptics there were, they kept silence. Men disputed and doubted about the Trinity, but about the Virgin the satirists Rutebeuf and Adam de la Halle wrote in the same spirit as Saint Bernard and Abelard, Adam de Saint-Victor and the pious monk Gaultier de Coincy. In the midst of violent disputes on other points of doctrine, the disputants united in devotion to Mary; and it was the single redeeming quality about them. The monarchs believed almost more implicitly than their subjects, and maintained the belief to the last. Doubtless the death of Queen Blanche marked the flood-tide at its height; but an authority so established as that of the Virgin, founded on instincts so deep, logic so rigorous, and, above all, on wealth so vast, declined slowly. Saint Louis died in 1270. Two hundred long and dismal years followed, in the midst of wars, decline of faith, dissolution of the old ties and interests, until, toward 1470, Louis XI succeeded in restoring some semblance of solidity to the State; and Louis XI divided his time and his money impartially between the Virgin of Chartres and the Virgin of Paris. In that respect, one can see no difference between him and Saint Louis, nor much between Philippe de Commines and Joinville. After Louis XI, another fantastic century passed, filled with the foulest horrors of history—religious wars; assassinations; Saint Bartholomews; sieges of Chartres; Huguenot leagues and sweeping destruction of religious monuments; Catholic leagues and fanatical reprisals on friends and foes,—the actual dissolution of society in a mass of horrors compared with which even the Albigensian crusade was a local accident, all ending in the reign of the last Valois, Henry III, the weirdest, most fascinating, most repulsive, most pathetic and most pitiable of the whole picturesque series of French kings. If you look into the Journal of Pierre de l'Estoile, under date of January 26,1582, you can read the entry:—

The King and the Queen [Louise de Lorraine], separately, and each accompanied by a good troop [of companions] went on foot from Paris to Chartres on a pilgrimage [voyage] to Notre-Dame-de-dessous-Terre [Our Lady of the Crypt], where a neuvaine was celebrated at the last mass at which the King and Queen assisted, and offered a silver-gilt statue of Notre Dame which weighed a hundred marks [eight hundred ounces], with the object of having lineage which might succeed to the throne.

In the dead of winter, in robes of penitents, over the roughest roads, on foot, the King and Queen, then seven years married, walked fifty miles to Chartres to supplicate the Virgin for children, and back again; and this they did year after year until Jacques Clement put an end to it with his dagger, in 1589, although the Virgin never chose to perform that miracle; but, instead, allowed the House of Valois to die out and sat on her throne in patience while the House of Bourbon was anointed in their place. The only French King ever crowned in the presence of Our Lady of Chartres was Henry IV—a heretic.

The year 1589, which was so decisive for Henry IV in France, marked in England the rise of Shakespeare as a sort of stage-monarch. While in France the Virgin still held such power that kings and queens asked her for favours, almost as instinctively as they had done five hundred years before, in England Shakespeare set all human nature and all human history on the stage, with hardly an allusion to the Virgin's name, unless as an oath. The exceptions are worth noting as a matter of curious Shakespearean criticism, for they are but two, and both are lines in the "First Part of Henry VI," spoken by the Maid of Orleans:—

Christ's mother helps me, else I were too weak!

Whether the "First Part of Henry VI" was written by Shakespeare at all has been a doubt much discussed, and too deep for tourists; but that this line was written by a Roman Catholic is the more likely because no such religious thought recurs in all the rest of Shakespeare's works, dramatic or lyric, unless it is implied in Gaunt's allusion to "the world's ransom, blessed Mary's Son." Thus, while three hundred years caused in England the disappearance of the great divinity on whom the twelfth and thirteenth centuries had lavished all their hopes, and during these three centuries every earthly throne had been repeatedly shaken or shattered, the Church had been broken in halves, faith had been lost, and philosophies overthrown, the Virgin still remained and remains the most intensely and the most widely and the most personally felt, of all characters, divine or human or imaginary, that ever existed among men. Nothing has even remotely taken her place. The only possible exception is the Buddha, Sakya Muni; but to the Western mind, a figure like the Buddha stood much farther away than the Virgin. That of the Christ even to Saint Bernard stood not so near as that of his mother. Abelard expressed the fact in its logical necessity even more strongly than Saint Bernard did:—

Te requirunt vota fidelium,

Ad te corda suspirant omnium,

Tu spes nostra post Deum unica,

Advocata nobis es posita.

Ad judicis matrem confugiunt,

Qui judicis iram effugiunt,

Quae praecari pro eis cogitur,

Quae pro reis mater efficitur.

"After the Trinity, you are our ONLY hope"; spes nostra unica; "you are placed there as our advocate; all of us who fear the wrath of the Judge, fly to the Judge's mother, who is logically compelled to sue for us, and stands in the place of a mother to the guilty." Abelard's logic was always ruthless, and the "cogitur" is a stronger word than one would like to use now, with a priest in hearing. We need not insist on it; but what one must insist on, is the good faith of the whole people,—kings, queens, princes of all sorts, philosophers, poets, soldiers, artists, as well as of the commoners like ourselves, and the poor,—for the good faith of the priests is not important to the understanding, since any class which is sufficiently interested in believing will always believe. In order to feel Gothic architecture in the twelfth and thirteenth centuries, one must feel first and last, around and above and beneath it, the good faith of the public, excepting only Jews and atheists, permeating every portion of it with the conviction of an immediate alternative between heaven and hell, with Mary as the ONLY court in equity capable of overruling strict law.

The Virgin was a real person, whose tastes, wishes, instincts, passions, were intimately known. Enough of the Virgin's literature survives to show her character, and the course of her daily life. We know more about her habits and thoughts than about those of earthly queens. The "Miracles de la Vierge" make a large part, and not the poorest part, of the enormous literature of these two centuries, although the works of Albertus Magnus fill twenty-one folio volumes and those of Thomas Aquinas fill more, while the "Chansons de Geste" and the "Romans," published or unpublished, are a special branch of literature with libraries to themselves. The collection of the Virgin's miracles put in verse by Gaultier de Coincy, monk, prior, and poet, between 1214 and 1233—the precise moment of the Chartres sculpture and glass—contains thirty thousand lines. Another great collection, narrating especially the miracles of the Virgin of Chartres, was made by a priest of Chartres Cathedral about 1240. Separate series, or single tales, have appeared and are appearing constantly, but no general collection has ever been made, although the whole poetic literature of the Virgin could be printed in the space of two or three volumes of scholastic philosophy, and if the Church had cared half as truly for the Virgin as it has for Thomas Aquinas, every miracle might have been collected and published a score of times. The miracles themselves, indeed, are not very numerous. In Gaultier de Coincy's collection they number only about fifty. The Chartres collection relates chiefly to the horrible outbreak of what was called leprosy—the "mal ardent,"—which ravaged the north of France during the crusades, and added intensity to the feelings which brought all society to the Virgin's feet. Recent scholars are cataloguing and classifying the miracles, as far as they survive, and have reduced the number within very moderate limits. As poetry, Gaultier de Coincy's are the best.

Of Gaultier de Coincy and his poetry, Gaston Paris has something to say which is worth quoting:—

It is the most curious, and often the most singular monument of the infantile piety of the Middle Ages. Devotion to Mary is presented in it as a kind of infallible guarantee not only against every sort of evil, but also against the most legitimate consequences of sin and even of crime. In these stories which have revolted the most rational piety, as well as the philosophy of modern times, one must still admit a gentle and penetrating charm; a naiveté; a tenderness and a simplicity of heart, which touch, while they raise a smile. There, for instance, one sees a sick monk cured by the milk that Our Lady herself comes to invite him to draw from her "douce mamelle"; a robber who is in the habit of recommending himself to the Virgin whenever he is going to "embler," is held up by her white hands for three days on the gibbet where he is hung, until the miracle becomes evident, and procures his pardon; an ignorant monk who knows only his Ave Maria, and is despised on that account, when dead reveals his sanctity by five roses which come out of his mouth in honour of the five letters of the name Maria; a nun, who has quitted her convent to lead a life of sin, returns after long years, and finds that the Holy Virgin, to whom, in spite of all, she has never ceased to offer every day her prayer, has, during all this time, filled her place as sacristine, so that no one has perceived her absence.

Gaston Paris inclined to apologize to his "bons bourgeois de Paris" for reintroducing to them a character so doubtful as the Virgin Mary, but, for our studies, the professor's elementary morality is eloquent. Clearly, M. Paris, the highest academic authority in the world, thought that the Virgin could hardly, in his time, say the year 1900, be received into good society in the Latin Quarter. Our own English ancestors, known as Puritans, held the same opinion, and excluded her from their society some four hundred years earlier, for the same reasons which affected M. Gaston Paris. These reasons were just, and showed the respectability of the citizens who held them. In no well-regulated community, under a proper system of police, could the Virgin feel at home, and the same thing may be said of most other saints as well as sinners. Her conduct was at times undignified, as M. Paris complained, She condescended to do domestic service, in order to help her friends, and she would use her needle, if she were in the mood, for the same object. The "Golden Legend" relates that:—

A certain priest, who celebrated every day a mass in honour of the Holy Virgin, was brought up before Saint Thomas of Canterbury who suspended him from his charge, judging him to be short-witted and irresponsible. Now Saint Thomas had occasion to mend his hair-cloth shirt, and while waiting for an opportunity to do so, had hidden it under his bed; so the Virgin appeared to the priest and said to him: "Go find the archbishop and tell him that she, for love of whom you celebrated masses, has herself mended his shirt for him which is under his bed; and tell him that she sends you to him that he may take off the interdict he has imposed on you." And Saint Thomas found that his shirt had in fact been mended. He relieved the priest, begging him to keep the secret of his wearing a hair-shirt.

Mary did some exceedingly unconventional things, and among them the darning Thomas A'Becket's hair-shirt, and the supporting a robber on the gibbet, were not the most singular, yet they seem not to have shocked Queen Blanche or Saint Francis or Saint Thomas Aquinas so much as they shocked M. Gaston Paris and M. Prudhomme. You have still to visit the cathedral at Le Mans for the sake of its twelfth- century glass, and there, in the lower panel of the beautiful, and very early, window of Saint Protais, you will see the full-length figure of a man, lying in bed, under a handsome blanket, watching, with staring eyes, the Virgin, in a green tunic, wearing her royal crown, who is striking him on the head with a heavy hammer and with both hands. The miracle belongs to local history, and is amusing only to show how little the Virgin cared for criticism of her manners or acts. She was above criticism. She made manners. Her acts were laws. No one thought of criticizing, in the style of a normal school, the will of such a queen; but one might treat her with a degree of familiarity, under great provocation, which would startle easier critics than the French, Here is an instance:—

A widow had an only child whom she tenderly loved. On hearing that this son had been taken by the enemy, chained, and put in prison, she burst into tears, and addressing herself to the Virgin, to whom she was especially devoted, she asked her with obstinacy for the release of her son; but when she saw at last that her prayers remained unanswered, she went to the church where there was a sculptured image of Mary, and there, before the image, she said: "Holy Virgin, I have begged you to deliver my son, and you have not been willing to help an unhappy mother! I've implored your patronage for my son, and you have refused it! Very good! just as my son has been taken away from me, so I am going to take away yours, and keep him as a hostage!" Saying this, she approached, took the statue child on the Virgin's breast, carried it home, wrapped it in spotless linen, and locked it up in a box, happy to have such a hostage for her son's return. Now, the following night, the Virgin appeared to the young man, opened his prison doors, and said: "Tell your mother, my child, to return me my Son now that I have returned hers!" The young man came home to his mother and told her of his miraculous deliverance; and she, overjoyed, hastened to go with the little Jesus to the Virgin, saying to her: "I thank you, heavenly lady, for restoring me my child, and in return I restore yours!"

For the exactness of this story in all its details, Bishop James of Voragio could not have vouched, nor did it greatly matter. What he could vouch for was the relation of intimacy and confidence between his people and the Queen of Heaven. The fact, conspicuous above all other historical certainties about religion, that the Virgin was by essence illogical, unreasonable and feminine, is the only fact of any ultimate value worth studying, and starts a number of questions that history has shown itself clearly afraid to touch. Protestant and Catholic differ little in that respect. No one has ventured to explain why the Virgin wielded exclusive power over poor and rich, sinners and saints, alike. Why were all the Protestant churches cold failures without her help? Why could not the Holy Ghost—the spirit of Love and Grace—equally answer their prayers? Why was the Son powerless? Why was Chartres Cathedral in the thirteenth century— like Lourdes to-day— the expression of what is in substance a separate religion? Why did the gentle and gracious Virgin Mother so exasperate the Pilgrim Father? Why was the Woman struck out of the Church and ignored in the State? These questions are not antiquarian or trifling in historical value; they tug at the very heart-strings of all that makes whatever order is in the cosmos. If a Unity exists, in which and toward which all energies centre, it must explain and include Duality, Diversity, Infinity—Sex!

Although certain to be contradicted by every pious churchman, a heretic must insist on thinking that the Mater Dolorosa was the logical Virgin of the Church, and that the Trinity would never have raised her from the foot of the Cross, had not the Virgin of Majesty been imposed, by necessity and public unanimity, on a creed which was meant to be complete without her. The true feeling of the Church was best expressed by the Virgin herself in one of her attested miracles: "A clerk, trusting more in the Mother than in the Son, never stopped repeating the angelic salutation for his only prayer. Once as he said again the 'Ave Maria,' the Lord appeared to him, and said to him: 'My Mother thanks you much for all the Salutations that you make her; but still you should not forget to salute me also: tamen et me salutare memento.'" The Trinity feared absorption in her, but was compelled to accept, and even to invite her aid, because the Trinity was a court of strict law, and, as in the old customary law, no process of equity could be introduced except by direct appeal to a higher power. She was imposed unanimously by all classes, because what man wanted most in the Middle Ages was not merely law or equity, but also and particularly favour. Strict justice, either on earth or in heaven, was the last thing that society cared to face. All men were sinners, and had, at least, the merit of feeling that, if they got their deserts, not one would escape worse than whipping. The instinct of individuality went down through all classes, from the count at the top, to the jugleors and menestreus at the bottom. The individual rebelled against restraint; society wanted to do what it pleased; all disliked the laws which Church and State were trying to fasten on them. They longed for a power above law,—or above the contorted mass of ignorance and absurdity bearing the name of law; but the power which they longed for was not human, for humanity they knew to be corrupt and incompetent from the day of Adam's creation to the day of the Last Judgment. They were all criminals; if not, they would have had no use for the Church and very little for the State; but they had at least the merit of their faults; they knew what they were, and, like children, they yearned for protection, pardon, and love. This was what the Trinity, though omnipotent, could not give. Whatever the heretic or mystic might try to persuade himself, God could not be Love. God was Justice, Order, Unity, Perfection; He could not be human and imperfect, nor could the Son or the Holy Ghost be other than the Father. The Mother alone was human, imperfect, and could love; she alone was Favour, Duality, Diversity. Under any conceivable form of religion, this duality must find embodiment somewhere, and the Middle Ages logically insisted that, as it could not be in the Trinity, either separately or together, it must be in the Mother. If the Trinity was in its essence Unity, the Mother alone could represent whatever was not Unity; whatever was irregular, exceptional, outlawed; and this was the whole human race. The saints alone were safe, after they were sainted. Every one else was criminal, and men differed so little in degree of sin that, in Mary's eyes, all were subjects for her pity and help.

This general rule of favour, apart from law, or the reverse of law, was the mark of Mary's activity in human affairs. Take, for an example, an entire class of her miracles, applying to the discipline of the Church! A bishop ejected an ignorant and corrupt priest from his living, as all bishops constantly had to do. The priest had taken the precaution to make himself Mary's MAN; he had devoted himself to her service and her worship. Mary instantly interfered,— just as Queen Eleanor or Queen Blanche would have done,—most unreasonably, and never was a poor bishop more roughly scolded by an orthodox queen! "Moult airieement," very airily or angrily, she said to him (Bartsch, 1887, p. 363):—

Ce saches tu certainement

Se tu li matinet bien main

Ne rapeles mon chapelain

A son servise et a s'enor,

L'ame de toi a desenor

Ains trente jors departira

Et es dolors d'infer ira.

Now know you this for sure and true,

Unless to-morrow this you do,

—And do it very early too,—

Restore my chaplain to his due,

A much worse fate remains for you!

Within a month your soul shall go

To suffer in the flames below.

The story-teller—himself a priest and prior—caught the lofty trick of manner which belonged to the great ladies of the court, and was inherited by them, even in England, down to the time of Queen Elizabeth, who treated her bishops also like domestic servants;— "matinet bien main!" To the public, as to us, the justice of the rebuke was nothing to the point; but that a friend should exist on earth or in heaven, who dared to browbeat a bishop, caused the keenest personal delight. The legends are clearer on this point than on any other. The people loved Mary because she trampled on conventions; not merely because she could do it, but because she liked to do what shocked every well-regulated authority. Her pity had no limit.

One of the Chartres miracles expresses the same motive in language almost plainer still. A good-for-nothing clerk, vicious, proud, vain, rude, and altogether worthless, but devoted to the Virgin, died, and with general approval his body was thrown into a ditch (Bartsch, 1887, p. 369):—

Mais cele ou sort tote pities

Tote douceurs tote amisties

Et qui les siens onques n'oublie

SON PECHEOR n'oblia mie.

"HER sinner!" Mary would not have been a true queen unless she had protected her own. The whole morality of the Middle Ages stood in the obligation of every master to protect his dependent. The herdsmen of Count Garin of Beaucaire were the superiors of their damoiseau Aucassins, while they felt sure of the Count. Mary was the highest of all the feudal ladies, and was the example for all in loyalty to her own, when she had to humiliate her own Bishop of Chartres for the sake of a worthless brute. "Do you suppose it doesn't annoy me," she said, "to see my friend buried in a common ditch? Take him out at once! I command! tell the clergy it is my order, and that I will never forgive them unless to-morrow morning without delay, they bury my friend in the best place in the cemetery!":—

Cuidies vos donc qu'il ne m'enuit

Quant vos l'aves si adosse

Que mis l'aves en un fosse?

    Metes l'en fors je le comant!

    Di le clergie que je li mant!

    Ne me puet mi repaier

    Se le matin sans delayer

    A grant heneur n'est mis amis

    Ou plus beau leu de l'aitre mis.

Naturally, her order was instantly obeyed. In the feudal regime, disobedience to an order was treason—or even hesitation to obey— when the order was serious; very much as in a modern army, disobedience is not regarded as conceivable. Mary's wish was absolute law, on earth as in heaven. For her, other laws were not made. Intensely human, but always Queen, she upset, at her pleasure, the decisions of every court and the orders of every authority, human or divine; interfered directly in the ordeal; altered the processes of nature; abolished space; annihilated time. Like other queens, she had many of the failings and prejudices of her humanity. In spite of her own origin, she disliked Jews, and rarely neglected a chance to maltreat them. She was not in the least a prude. To her, sin was simply humanity, and she seemed often on the point of defending her arbitrary acts of mercy, by frankly telling the Trinity that if the Creator meant to punish man, He should not have made him. The people, who always in their hearts protested against bearing the responsibility for the Creator's arbitrary creations, delighted to see her upset the law, and reverse the rulings of the Trinity. They idolized her for being strong, physically and in will, so that she feared nothing, and was as helpful to the knight in the melee of battle as to the young mother in child-bed. The only character in which they seemed slow to recognize Mary was that of bourgeoise. The bourgeoisie courted her favour at great expense, but she seemed to be at home on the farm, rather than in the shop. She had very rudimentary knowledge, indeed, of the principles of political economy as we understand them, and her views on the subject of money-lending or banking were so feminine as to rouse in that powerful class a vindictive enmity which helped to overthrow her throne. On the other hand, she showed a marked weakness for chivalry, and one of her prettiest and most twelfth-century miracles is that of the knight who heard mass while Mary took his place in the lists. It is much too charming to lose (Bartsch, 1895, p. 311):—

Un chevalier courtois et sages,

Hardis et de grant vasselages,

Nus mieudres en chevalerie,

Moult amoit la vierge Marie.

Pour son barnage demener

Et son franc cors d'armes pener,

Aloit a son tournoiement

Garnis de son contentement.

Au dieu plaisir ainsi avint

Que quant le jour du tournoi vint

Il se hastoit de chevauchier,

Bien vousist estre en champ premier.

D'une eglise qui pres estoit
Oi les sains que l'on sonnoit
Pour la sainte messe chanter.
Le chevalier sans arrester
S'en est ale droit a l'eglise
Pour escouter le dieu servise.
L'en chantoit tantost hautement
Une messe devotement
De la sainte Vierge Marie;
Puis a on autre comencie.
Le chevalier vien l'escouta,
De bon cuer la dame pria,
Et quant la messe fut finee
La tierce fu recomenciee
Tantost en ce meisme lieu.
"Sire, pour la sainte char dieu!"
Ce li a dit son escuier,
"L'heure passe de tournoier,
Et vous que demourez ici?
Venez vous en, je vous en pri!
Volez vous devenir hermite
Ou papelart ou ypocrite?
Alons en a nostre mestier!"
A knight both courteous and wise
And brave and bold in enterprise.

No better knight was ever seen,
Greatly loved the Virgin Queen.
Once, to contest the tourney's prize
And keep his strength in exercise,
He rode out to the listed field
Armed at all points with lance and shield;
But it pleased God that when the day
Of tourney came, and on his way
He pressed his charger's speed apace
To reach, before his friends, the place,
He saw a church hard by the road
And heard the church-bells sounding loud
To celebrate the holy mass.
Without a thought the church to pass
The knight drew rein, and entered there
To seek the aid of God in prayer.
High and dear they chanted then
A solemn mass to Mary Queen;
Then afresh began again.
Lost in his prayers the good knight stayed;
With all his heart to Mary prayed;
And, when the second one was done,
Straightway the third mass was begun,
Right there upon the self-same place.
"Sire, for mercy of God's grace!"

Whispered his squire in his ear;

"The hour of tournament is near;

Why do you want to linger here?

Is it a hermit to become,

Or hypocrite, or priest of Rome?

Come on, at once! despatch your prayer!

Let us be off to our affair!"

The accent of truth still lingers in this remonstrance of the squire, who must, from all time, have lost his temper on finding his chevalier addicted to "papelardie" when he should have been fighting; but the priest had the advantage of telling the story and pointing the moral. This advantage the priest neglected rarely, but in this case he used it with such refinement and so much literary skill that even the squire might have been patient. With the invariable gentle courtesy of the true knight, the chevalier replied only by soft words:—

"Amis!" ce dist li chevalier,

"Cil tournoie moult noblement

Qui le servise dieu entent."

In one of Milton's sonnets is a famous line which is commonly classed among the noblest verses of the English language:—

"They also serve, who only stand and wait."

Fine as it is, with the simplicity of the grand style, like the "Chanson de Roland" the verse of Milton does not quite destroy the charm of thirteenth-century diction:—

"Friend!" said to him the chevalier,

"He tourneys very nobly too,

Who only hears God's service through!"

No doubt the verses lack the singular power of the eleventh century; it is not worth while to pretend that any verse written in the thirteenth century wholly holds its own against "Roland":—

"Sire cumpain! faites le vus de gred?

Ja est co Rollanz ki tant vos soelt amer!"

The courtesy of Roland has the serious solidity of the Romanesque arch, and that of Lancelot and

Aucassins has the grace of a legendary window; but one may love it, all the same; and one may even love the knight,—papelard though he were,—as he turned back to the altar and remained in prayer until the last mass was ended.

Then they mounted and rode on toward the field, and of course you foresee what had happened. In itself the story is bald enough, but it is told with such skill that one never tires of it. As the chevalier and the squire approached the lists, they met the other knights returning, for the jousts were over; but, to the astonishment of the chevalier, he was greeted by all who passed him with shouts of applause for his marvellous triumph in the lists, where he had taken all the prizes and all the prisoners:—

Les chevaliers ont encontrez,

Qui du tournois sont retournes,

Qui du tout en tout est feru.

S'en avoit tout le pris eu

Le chevalier qui reperoit

Des messes qu' oies avoit.

Les autres qui s'en reperoient

Le saluent et le conjoient

Et distrent bien que onques mes

Nul chevalier ne prist tel fes

D'armes com il ot fet ce jour;

A tousjours en avroit l'onnour.

Moult en i ot qui se rendoient

A lui prisonier, et disoient

"Nous somes vostre prisonier,

Ne nous ne pourrions nier,

Ne nous aiez par armes pris."

Lors ne fu plus cil esbahis,

Car il a entendu tantost

Que cele fu pour lui en l'ost

Pour qui il fu en la chapelle.

His friends, returning from the fight,

On the way there met the knight,

For the jousts were wholly run,

And all the prizes had been won

By the knight who had not stirred

From the masses he had heard.

All the knights, as they came by,

Saluted him and gave him joy,

And frankly said that never yet

Had any knight performed such feat,

Nor ever honour won so great

As he had done in arms that day;

While many of them stopped to say

That they all his prisoners were:

"In truth, your prisoners we are:

We cannot but admit it true:

Taken we were in arms by you!"

Then the truth dawned on him there,

And all at once he saw the light,

That She, by whom he stood in prayer,

—The Virgin,—stood by him in fight!

The moral of the tale belongs to the best feudal times. The knight at once recognized that he had become the liege-man of the Queen, and henceforth must render his service entirely to her. So he called his "barons," or tenants, together, and after telling them what had happened, took leave of them and the "siecle":—

"Moult est ciest tournoiement beaux

Ou ele a pour moi tournoie;

Mes trop l'avroit mal emploie

Se pour lui je ne tournoioie!

Fox seroie se retournoie

A la mondaine vanite.

A dieu promet en verite

Que james ne tournoierai

Fors devant le juge verai

Qui conoit le bon chevalier

Et selonc le fet set jutgier."

Lors prent congie piteusement,

Et maint en plorent tenrement.

D'euls se part, en une abaie

Servi puis la vierge Marie.

"Glorious has the tourney been

Where for me has fought the Queen;

But a disgrace for me it were

If I tourneyed not for her.

Traitor to her should I be,

Returned to worldly vanity.

I promise truly, by God's grace,

Never again the lists to see,

Except before that Judge's face,

Who knows the true knight from the base,

And gives to each his final place."

Then piteously he takes his leave

While in tears his barons grieve.

So he parts, and in an abbey

Serves henceforth the Virgin Mary.

Observe that in this case Mary exacted no service! Usually the legends are told, as in this instance, by priests, though they were told in the same spirit by laymen, as you can see in the poems of Rutebeuf, and they would not have been told very differently by soldiers, if one may judge from Joinville; but commonly the Virgin herself prescribed the kind of service she wished. Especially to the young knight who had, of his own accord, chosen her for his liege, she showed herself as exacting as other great ladies showed themselves toward their Lancelots and Tristans. When she chose, she could even indulge in more or less coquetry, else she could never have appealed to the sympathies of the thirteenth-century knight-errant. One of her miracles told how she disciplined the young men who were too much in the habit of assuming her service in order to obtain selfish objects. A youthful chevalier, much given to tournaments and the other worldly diversions of the siecle, fell in love, after the rigorous obligation of his class, as you know from your Dulcinea del Toboso, with a lady who, as was also prescribed by the rules of courteous love, declined to listen to him. An abbot of his acquaintance, sympathizing with his distress, suggested to him the happy idea of appealing for help to the Queen of Heaven. He followed the advice, and for an entire year shut himself up, and prayed to Mary, in her chapel, that she would soften the heart of his beloved, and bring her to listen to his prayer. At the end of the twelvemonth, fixed as a natural and sufficient proof of his earnestness in devotion, he felt himself entitled to indulge again in innocent worldly pleasures, and on the first morning after his release, he started out on horseback for a day's hunting. Probably thousands of young knights and squires were always doing more or less the same thing, and it was quite usual that, as they rode through the fields or forests, they should happen on a solitary chapel or shrine, as this knight did. He stopped long enough to kneel in it and renew his prayer to the Queen:—

La mere dieu qui maint chetif

A retrait de chetivete

Par sa grant debonnairte

Par sa courtoise courtoisie

Au las qui tant l'apele et prie

Ignelement s'est demonstree,

D'une coronne corronnee

Plaine de pierres precieuses

Si flamboianz si precieuses

Pour pou li euil ne li esluisent.

Si netement ainsi reluisent

Et resplendissent com la raie

Qui en este au matin raie.

Tant par a bel et cler le vis

Que buer fu mez, ce li est vis,

Qui s'i puest assez mirer.

"Cele qui te fait soupirer

Et en si grant erreur t'a mis,"

Fait nostre dame, "biau douz amis,

Est ele plus bele que moi?"

Li chevaliers a tel effroi

De la clarte, ne sai que face;

Ses mains giete devant sa face;

Tel hide a et tel freeur

Chaoir se laisse de freeur;

Mais cele en qui pitie est toute

Li dist: "Amis, or n'aies doute!

Je suis cele, n'en doute mie,

Qui te doi faire avoir t'amie.

Or prens garde que tu feras.

Cele que tu miex ameras

De nous ii auras a amie."

God's Mother who to many a wretch

Has brought relief from wretchedness,

By her infinite goodness,

By her courteous courteousness,

To her suppliant in distress

Came from heaven quickly down;

On her head she bore the crown,

Full of precious stones and gems

Darting splendour, flashing flames,

Till the eye near lost its sight

In the keenness of the light,

As the summer morning's sun

Blinds the eyes it shines upon.

So beautiful and bright her face,

Only to look on her is grace.

"She who has caused you thus to sigh,

And has brought you to this end,"—

Said Our Lady,—"Tell me, friend,

Is she handsomer than I?"

Scared by her brilliancy, the knight

Knows not what to do for fright;

He clasps his hands before his face,

And in his shame and his disgrace

Falls prostrate on the ground with fear;

But she with pity ever near

Tells him:—"Friend, be not afraid!

Doubt not that I am she whose aid

Shall surely bring your love to you;

But take good care what you shall do!

She you shall love most faithfully

Of us two, shall your mistress be."

One is at a loss to imagine what a young gentleman could do, in such a situation, except to obey, with the fewest words possible, the suggestion so gracefully intended. Queen's favours might be fatal gifts, but they were much more fatal to reject than to accept. Whatever might be the preferences of the knight, he had invited his own fate, and in consequence was fortunate to be allowed the option of dying and going to heaven, or dying without going to heaven. Mary was not always so gentle with young men who deserted or neglected her for an earthly rival;—the offence which irritated her most, and occasionally caused her to use language which hardly bears translation into modern English. Without meaning to assert that the Queen of Heaven was jealous as Queen Blanche herself, one must still admit that she was very severe on lovers who showed willingness to leave her service, and take service with any other lady. One of her admirers, educated for the priesthood but not yet in full orders, was obliged by reasons of family interest to quit his career in order to marry. An insult like this was more than Mary could endure, and she gave the young man a lesson he never forgot:—

Ireement li prent a dire

La mere au roi de paradis:

"Di moi, di moi, tu que jadis

M'amoies tant de tout ton coeur.

Pourquoi m'as tu jete puer?

Di moi, di moi, ou est donc cele

Qui plus de moi bone est et bele?...

Pourquoi, pourquoi, las durfeus,

Las engignez, las deceuz,

Me lais pour une lasse fame,

Qui suis du del Royne et Dame?

Enne fais tu trop mauvais change

Qui tu por une fame estrange

Me laisses qui par amors t'amoie

Et ja ou ciel t'apareilloie

En mes chambres un riche lit

Por couchier t'ame a grand delit?

Trop par as faites grant merveilles

S'autrement tost ne te conseilles

Ou ciel serra tes lits deffais

Et en la flamme d'enfer faiz!"

With anger flashing in her eyes

Answers the Queen of Paradise:

"Tell me, tell me! you of old

Loved me once with love untold;

Why now throw me aside?

Tell me, tell me! where a bride

Kinder or fairer have you won?…

Wherefore, wherefore, wretched one,

Deceived, betrayed, misled, undone,

Leave me for a creature mean,

Me, who am of Heaven the Queen?

Can you make a worse exchange,

You that for a woman strange,

Leave me who, with perfect love,

Waiting you in heaven above,

Had in my chamber richly dressed

A bed of bliss your soul to rest?

Terrible is your mistake!

Unless you better council take,

In heaven your bed shall be unmade,

And in the flames of hell be spread."

A mistress who loved in this manner was not to be gainsaid. No earthly love had a chance of holding its own against this unfair combination of heaven and hell, and Mary was as unscrupulous as any other great lady in abusing all her advantages in order to save HER souls. Frenchmen never found fault with abuses of power for what they thought a serious object. The more tyrannical Mary was, the more her adorers adored, and they wholly approved, both in love and in law, the rule that any man who changed his allegiance without permission, did so at his own peril. His life and property were forfeit. Mary showed him too much grace in giving him an option.

Even in anger Mary always remained a great lady, and in the ordinary relations of society her manners were exquisite, as they were, according to Joinville, in the court of Saint Louis, when tempers were not overwrought. The very brutality of the brutal compelled the courteous to exaggerate courtesy, and some of the royal family were as coarse as the king was delicate in manners. In heaven the manners were perfect, and almost as stately as those of Roland and Oliver. On one occasion Saint Peter found himself embarrassed by an affair which the public opinion of the Court of Heaven, although not by any means puritanic, thought more objectionable—in fact, more frankly discreditable—than an honest corrupt job ought to be; and even his influence, though certainly considerable, wholly failed to carry it through the law-court. The case, as reported by Gaultier de Coincy, was this: A very worthless creature of Saint Peter's—a monk of Cologne—who had led a scandalous life, and "ne cremoit dieu, ordre ne roule," died, and in due course of law was tried, convicted, and dragged off by the devils to undergo his term of punishment. Saint Peter could not desert his sinner, though much ashamed of him, and accordingly made formal application to the Trinity for a pardon. The Trinity, somewhat severely, refused. Finding his own interest insufficient, Saint Peter tried to strengthen it by asking the archangels to help him; but the case was too much for them also, and they declined. The brother apostles were appealed to, with the same result; and finally even the saints, though they had so obvious interest in keeping friendly relations with Peter, found public opinion too strong to defy. The case was desperate. The Trinity were—or was—emphatic, and—what was rare in the Middle Ages—every member of the feudal hierarchy sustained its decision. Nothing more could be done in the regular way. Saint Peter was obliged to divest himself of authority, and place himself and his dignity in the hands of the Virgin. Accordingly he asked for an audience, and stated the case to Our Lady. With the utmost grace, she instantly responded:—

"Pierre, Pierre," dit Nostre Dame,

"En moult grand poine et por ceste ame

De mon douz filz me fierai

Tant que pour toi l'en prierai."

La Mere Dieu lors s'est levee,

Devant son filz s'en est alee

Et ses virges toutes apres.

De lui si tint Pierre pres,

Quar sanz doutance bien savoit

Que sa besoigne faite avoit

Puisque cele l'avoit en prise

Ou forme humaine avoit prise.

Quant sa Mere vit li douz Sire

Qui de son doit daigna escrire

Qu'en honourant et pere et mere

En contre lui a chere clere

Se leva moult festivement

Et si li dist moult doucement;

"Bien veigniez vous, ma douce mere,"

Comme douz filz, comme douz pere.

Doucement l'a par la main prise

Et doucement lez lui assise;

Lors li a dit:—"A douce chiere,

Que veus ma douce mere chiere,

Mes amies et mes sereurs?"

"Pierre, Pierre," our Lady said,

"With all my heart I'll give you aid,

And to my gentle Son I'll sue

Until I beg that soul for you."

God's Mother then arose straightway,

And sought her Son without delay;

All her virgins followed her,

And Saint Peter kept him near,

For he knew his task was done

And his prize already won,

Since it was hers, in whom began

The life of God in form of Man.

When our dear Lord, who deigned to write

With his own hand that in his sight

Those in his kingdom held most dear

Father and mother honoured here,—

When He saw His Mother's face

He rose and said with gentle grace:

"Well are you come, my heart's desire!"

Like loving son, like gracious sire;

Took her hand gently in His own;

Gently placed her on His throne,

Wishing her graciously good cheer:—

"What brings my gentle Mother here,

My sister, and my dearest friend?"

One can see Queen Blanche going to beg—or command—a favour of her son, King Louis, and the stately dignity of their address, while Saint Peter and the virgins remain in the antechamber; but, as for Saint Peter's lost soul, the request was a mere form, and the doors of paradise were instantly opened to it, after such brief formalities as should tend to preserve the technical record of the law-court. We tread here on very delicate ground. Gaultier de Coincy, being a priest and a prior, could take liberties which we cannot or ought not to take. The doctrines of the Church are too serious and too ancient to be wilfully misstated, and the doctrines of what is called Mariolatry were never even doctrines of the Church. Yet it is true that, in the hearts of Mary's servants, the Church and its doctrines were at the mercy of Mary's will. Gaultier de Coincy claimed that Mary exasperated the devils by exercising a wholly arbitrary and illegitimate power. Gaultier not merely admitted, but frankly asserted, that this was the fact:—

Font li deables:—"de cest plait,

  Mal por mal, assez miex nous plest

  Que nous aillons au jugement

  Li haut jugeur qui ne ment.

  C'au plait n'au jugement sa mere

  De droit jugier est trop avere;

  Mais dieu nous juge si adroit,

  Plainement nous lest notre droit.

  Sa mere juge en tel maniere

  Qu'elle nous met touz jors arriere

  Quant nous cuidons estre devant.

. . . .

  En ciel et en terre est plus Dame

  Par un petit que Diex ne soit.

  Il l'aimme tant et tant la croit,

  N'est riens qu'elle face ne die

  Qu'il desveile ne contredie.

  Quant qu'elle veut li fait acroire,

  S'elle disoit la pie est noire

  Et l'eue trouble est toute clere:

  Si diroit il voir dit ma mere!"

"In this law-suit," say the devils,

"Since it is a choice of evils,

We had best appeal on high

To the Judge Who does not lie.

What is law to any other,

'T is no use pleading with His Mother;

But God judges us so true

That He leaves us all our due.

His Mother judges us so short

That she throws us out of court

When we ought to win our cause.

. . . .

In heaven and earth she makes more laws

By far, than God Himself can do,

He loves her so, and trusts her so,

There's nothing she can do or say

That He'll refuse, or say her nay.

Whatever she may want is right,

Though she say that black is white,

And dirty water clear as snow:—

My Mother says it, and it's so!"

If the Virgin took the feelings of the Trinity into consideration, or recognized its existence except as her Son, the case has not been reported, or, at all events, has been somewhat carefully kept out of sight by the Virgin's poets. The devils were emphatic in denouncing Mary for absorbing the whole Trinity. In one sharply disputed case in regard to a villain, or labourer, whose soul the Virgin claimed because he had learned the "Ave Maria," the devils became very angry, indeed, and protested vehemently:—

Li lait maufe, li rechinie

Adonc ont ris et eschinie.

C'en font il:—"Merveillans merveille!

Por ce vilain plate oreille

Aprent vo Dame a saluer,

Se nous vorro trestous tuer

Se regarder osons vers s'ame.

De tout le monde vieut estre Dame!

Ains nule dame ne fu tiez.

Il est avis qu'ele soit Diex

Ou qu'ele ait Diex en main bornie.

Nul besoigne n'est fournie,

Ne terrienne ne celestre,

Que toute Dame ne veille estre.

Il est avis que tout soit suen;

Dieu ne deable n'i ont rien."

The ugly demons laugh outright

And grind their teeth with envious spite;

Crying:—"Marvel marvellous!

Because that flat-eared ploughman there

Learned to make your Dame a prayer,

She would like to kill us all

Just for looking toward his soul.

All the world she wants to rule!

No such Dame was ever seen!

She thinks that she is God, I ween,

Or holds Him in her hollow hand.

Not a judgment or command

Or an order can be given

Here on earth or there in heaven,

That she does not want control.

She thinks that she ordains the whole,

And keeps it all for her own profit.

God nor Devil share not of it."

As regards Mary of Chartres, these charges seem to have been literally true, except so far as concerned the "laid maufe" Pierre de Dreux. Gaultier de Coincy saw no impropriety in accepting, as sufficiently exact, the allegations of the devils against the Virgin's abuse of power. Down to the death of Queen Blanche, which is all that concerns us, the public saw no more impropriety in it than Gaultier did. The ugly, envious devils, notorious as students of the Latin Quarter, were perpetually making the same charges against Queen Blanche and her son, without disturbing her authority. No one could conceive that the Virgin held less influence in heaven than the queen mother on earth. Nevertheless there were points in the royal policy and conduct of Mary which thoughtful men even then hesitated to approve. The Church itself never liked to be dragged too far under feminine influence, although the moment it discarded feminine influence it lost nearly everything of any value to it or to the world, except its philosophy. Mary's tastes were too popular; some of the uglier devils said they were too low; many ladies and gentlemen of the "siecle" thought them disreputable, though they dared not say so, or dared say so only by proxy, as in "Aucassins." As usual, one must go to the devils for the exact truth, and in spite of their outcry, the devils admitted that they had no reason to complain of Mary's administration:—

"Les beles dames de grant pris

Qui traynant vont ver et gris,

Roys, roynes, dus et contesses, En enfer vienent a granz presses;

Mais ou ciel vont pres tout a fait

Tort et bocu et contrefait.

Ou ciel va toute la ringaille;

Le grain avons et diex la paille."

"All the great dames and ladies fair

Who costly robes and ermine wear,

Kings, queens, and countesses and lords

Come down to hell in endless hordes;

While up to heaven go the lamed,

The dwarfs, the humpbacks, and the maimed;

To heaven goes the whole riff-raff;

We get the grain and God the chaff."

True it was, although one should not say it jestingly, that the Virgin embarrassed the Trinity; and perhaps this was the reason, behind all the other excellent reasons, why men loved and adored her with a passion such as no other deity has ever inspired; and why we, although utter strangers to her, are not far from getting down on our knees and praying to her still. Mary concentrated in herself the whole rebellion of man against fate; the whole protest against divine law; the whole contempt for human law as its outcome; the whole unutterable fury of human nature beating itself against the walls of its prison-house, and suddenly seized by a hope that in the Virgin man had found a door of escape. She was above law; she took feminine pleasure in turning hell into an ornament; she delighted in trampling on every social distinction in this world and the next. She knew that the universe was as unintelligible to her, on any theory of morals, as it was to her worshippers, and she felt, like them, no sure conviction that it was any more intelligible to the Creator of it. To her, every suppliant was a universe in itself, to be judged apart, on his own merits, by his love for her,—by no means on his orthodoxy, or his conventional standing in the Church, or according to his correctness in defining the nature of the Trinity. The convulsive hold which Mary to this day maintains over human imagination—as you can see at Lourdes—was due much less to her power of saving soul or body than to her sympathy with people who suffered under law,—divine or human,—justly or unjustly, by accident or design, by decree of God or by guile of Devil. She cared not a straw for conventional morality, and she had no notion of letting her friends be punished, to the tenth or any other generation, for the sins of their ancestors or the peccadilloes of Eve.

So Mary filled heaven with a sort of persons little to the taste of any respectable middle-class society, which has trouble enough in making this world decent and pay its bills, without having to continue the effort in another. Mary stood in a Church of her own, so independent that the Trinity might have perished without much affecting her position; but, on the other hand, the Trinity could look on and see her dethroned with almost a breath of relief. Aucassins and the devils of Gaultier de Coincy foresaw her danger. Mary's treatment of respectable and law-abiding people who had no favours to ask, and were reasonably confident of getting to heaven by the regular judgment, without expense, rankled so deeply that three hundred years later the Puritan reformers were not satisfied with abolishing her, but sought to abolish the woman altogether as the cause of all evil in heaven and on earth. The Puritans abandoned the New Testament and the Virgin in order to go back to the beginning, and renew the quarrel with Eve. This is the Church's affair, not ours, and the women are competent to settle it with Church or State, without help from outside; but honest tourists are seriously interested in putting the feeling back into the dead architecture where it belongs.

Mary was rarely harsh to any suppliant or servant, and she took no special interest in humiliating the rich or the learned or the wise. For them, law was made; by them, law was administered; and with their doings Mary never arbitrarily interfered; but occasionally she could not resist the temptation to intimate her opinion of the manner in which the Trinity allowed their—the regular—Church to be administered. She was a queen, and never for an instant forgot it, but she took little thought about her divine rights, if she had any,—and in fact Saint Bernard preferred her without them,—while she was scandalized at the greed of officials in her Son's Court. One day a rich usurer and a very poor old woman happened to be dying in the same town. Gaultier de Coincy did not say, as an accurate historian should, that he was present, nor did he mention names or dates, although it was one of his longest and best stories. Mary never loved bankers, and had no reason for taking interest in this one, or for doing him injury; but it happened that the parish priest was summoned to both death-beds at the same time, and neglected the old pauper in the hope of securing a bequest for his church from the banker. This was the sort of fault that most annoyed Mary in the Church of the Trinity, which, in her opinion, was not cared for as it should be, and she felt it her duty to intimate as much.

Although the priest refused to come at the old woman's summons, his young clerk, who seems to have acted as vicar though not in orders, took pity on her, and went alone with the sacrament to her hut, which was the poorest of poor hovels even for that age:—

Close de piex et de serciaus

Comme une viez souz a porciaus.

Roof of hoops, and wall of logs,

Like a wretched stye for hogs.

There the beggar lay, already insensible or at the last gasp, on coarse thatch, on the ground, covered by an old hempen sack. The picture represented the extremest poverty of the thirteenth century; a hovel without even a feather bed or bedstead, as Aucassins' ploughman described his mother's want; and the old woman alone, dying, as the clerk appeared at the opening:—

Li clers qui fu moult bien apris

Le cors Nostre Seigneur a pris

A l'ostel a la povre fame

S'en vient touz seus mes n'i treuve ame.

Si grant clarte y a veue

Que grant peeur en a eue.

Ou povre lit a la vieillete

Qui couvers iert d'une nateite

Assises voit XII puceles

Si avenans et si tres beles

N'est nus tant penser i seust

Qui raconter le vout peust.

A coutee voist Nostre Dame

Sus le chevez la povre fame

Qui por la mort sue et travaille.

La Mere Dieu d'une tovaille

Qui blanche est plus que fleur de lis

La grant sueur d'entor le vis

A ses blanches mains li essuie.

The clerk, well in these duties taught,

The body of our Saviour brought

Where she lay upon her bed

Without a soul to give her aid.

But such brightness there he saw

As filled his mind with fear and awe.

Covered with a mat of straw

The woman lay; but round and near

A dozen maidens sat, so fair

No mortal man could dream such light,

No mortal tongue describe the sight.

Then he saw that next the bed,

By the poor old woman's head,

As she gasped and strained for breath

In the agony of death,

Sat Our Lady,—bending low,—

While, with napkin white as snow,

She dried the death-sweat on the brow.

The clerk, in terror, hesitated whether to turn and run away, but Our Lady beckoned him to the bed, while all rose and kneeled devoutly to the sacrament. Then she said to the trembling clerk:—

"Friend, be not afraid!

But seat yourself, to give us aid,

Beside these maidens, on the bed."

And when the clerk had obeyed, she continued—

"Or tost, amis!" fait Nostre Dame,

"Confessies ceste bone fame

Et puis apres tout sans freeur

Recevra tost son sauveeur

Qui char et sanc vout en moi prendre."

"Come quickly, friend!" Our Lady says,

"This good old woman now confess

And afterwards without distress

She will at once receive her God

Who deigned in me take flesh and blood."

After the sacrament came a touch of realism that recalls the simple death-scenes that Walter Scott described in his grand twelfth- century manner. The old woman lingered pitiably in her agony:—

Lors dit une des demoiselles

A madame sainte Marie:

"Encore, dame, n'istra mie

Si com moi semble du cors l'ame."

"Bele fille," fait Nostre Dame,

"Traveiller lais un peu le cors,

Aincois que l'ame en isse hors,

Si que puree soil et nete

Aincois qu'en Paradis la mete.

N'est or mestier qui soions plus,

Ralon nous en ou ciel lassus,

Quant tens en iert bien reviendrons

En paradis l'ame emmerrons."

A maiden said to Saint Marie,

"My lady, still it seems to me

The soul will not the body fly."

"Fair child!" Our Lady made reply,

"Still let awhile the body fight

Before the soul shall leave it quite.

So that it pure may be, and cleansed

When it to Paradise ascends.

No longer need we here remain;

We can go back to heaven again;

We will return before she dies,

And take the soul to paradise."

The rest of the story concerned the usurer, whose death-bed was of a different character, but Mary's interest in death-beds of that kind was small. The fate of the usurer mattered the less because she knew too well how easily the banker, in good credit, could arrange with the officials of the Trinity to open the doors of paradise for him. The administration of heaven was very like the administration of France; the Queen Mother saw many things of which she could not wholly approve; but her nature was pity, not justice, and she shut her eyes to much that she could not change. Her miracles, therefore, were for the most part mere evidence of her pity for those who needed it most, and these were rarely the well-to-do people of the siecle, but more commonly the helpless. Every saint performed miracles, and these are standard, not peculiar to any one intermediator; and every saint protected his own friends; but beyond these exhibitions of power, which are more or less common to the whole hierarchy below the Trinity, Mary was the mother of pity and the only hope of despair. One might go on for a volume, studying the character of Mary and the changes that time made in it, from the earliest Byzantine legends down to the daily recorded miracles at Lourdes; no character in history has had so long or varied a development, and none so sympathetic; but the greatest poets long ago plundered that mine of rich motives, and have stolen what was most dramatic for popular use. The Virgin's most famous early miracle seems to have been that of the monk Theophilus, which was what one might call her salvation of Faust. Another Byzantine miracle was an original version of Shylock. Shakespeare and his fellow dramatists plundered the Church legends as freely as their masters plundered the Church treasuries, yet left a mass of dramatic material untouched. Let us pray the Virgin that it may remain untouched, for, although a good miracle was in its day worth much money—so much that the rival shrines stole each other's miracles without decency—one does not care to see one's Virgin put to money- making for Jew theatre-managers. One's two-hundred and fifty million arithmetical ancestors shrink.

For mere amusement, too, the miracle is worth reading of the little Jew child who ignorantly joined in the Christian communion, and was thrown into a furnace by his father in consequence; but when the furnace was opened, the Virgin appeared seated in the midst of the flames, with the little child unharmed in her lap. Better is that called the "Tombeor de Notre Dame," only recently printed; told by some unknown poet of the thirteenth century, and told as well as any of Gaultier de Coincy's. Indeed the "Tombeor de Notre Dame" has had more success in our time than it ever had in its own, as far as one knows, for it appeals to a quiet sense of humour that pleases modern French taste as much as it pleased the Virgin. One fears only to spoil it by translation, but if a translation be merely used as a glossary or footnote, it need not do fatal harm.

The story is that of a tumbler—tombeor, street-acrobat—who was disgusted with the world, as his class has had a reputation for becoming, and who was fortunate enough to obtain admission into the famous monastery of Clairvaux, where Saint Bernard may have formerly been blessed by the Virgin's presence. Ignorant at best, and especially ignorant of letters, music, and the offices of a religious society, he found himself unable to join in the services:—

Car n'ot vescu fors de tumer

Et d'espringier et de baler.

Treper, saillir, ice savoit;

Ne d'autre rien il ne savoit;

Car ne savoit autre lecon

Ne "pater noster" ne chancon

Ne le "credo" ne le salu

Ne rien qui fust a son salu.

For he had learned no other thing

Than to tumble, dance and spring:

Leaping and vaulting, that he knew,

But nothing better could he do.

He could not say his prayers by rote;

Not "Pater noster", not a note,

Not "Ave Mary," nor the creed;

Nothing to help his soul in need.

Tormented by the sense of his uselessness to the society whose bread he ate without giving a return in service, and afraid of being expelled as a useless member, one day while the bells were calling to mass he hid in the crypt, and in despair began to soliloquize before the Virgin's altar, at the same spot, one hopes, where the Virgin had shown herself, or might have shown herself, in her infinite bounty, to Saint Bernard, a hundred years before:—

"Hai," fait il, "con suis trais!

Or dira ja cascuns sa laisse

Et jo suis ci i hues en laisse

Qui ne fas ci fors que broster

Et viandes por nient gaster.

Si ne dirai ne ne ferai?

Par la mere deu, si ferai!

Ja n'en serai ore repris;

Jo ferai ce que j'ai apris;

Si servirai de men mestier

La mere deu en son mostier;

Li autre servent de canter

Et jo servirai de tumer."

Sa cape oste, si se despoille,

Deles l'autel met sa despoille,

Mais por sa char que ne soit nue

Une cotele a retenue

Qui moult estait tenre et alise,

Petit vaut miex d'une chemise,

Si est en pur le cors remes.

Il s'est bien chains et acesmes,

Sa cote caint et bien s'atorne,

Devers l'ymage se retorne

Mout humblement et si l'esgarde:

"Dame," fait il, "en vostre garde

Comant jo et mon cors et m'ame.

Douce reine, douce dame,

Ne despisies ce que jo sai

Car jo me voil metre a l'asai

De vos servir en bone foi

Se dex m'ait sans nul desroi.

Jo ne sai canter ne lire

Mais certes jo vos voil eslire

Tos mes biax gieus a eslicon.

Or soie al fuer de taurecon

Qui trepe et saut devant sa mere.

Dame, qui n'estes mie amere

A cels qui vos servent a droit,

Quelsque jo soie, por vos soit!"

Lors li commence a faire saus

Bas et petits et grans et haus

Primes deseur et puis desos,

Puis se remet sor ses genols,

Devers l'ymage, et si l'encline:

"He!" fait il, "tres douce reine

Par vo pitie, par vo francise,

Ne despisies pas mon servise!"

"Ha!" said he, "how I am ashamed!

To sing his part goes now each priest,

And I stand here, a tethered beast,

Who nothing do but browse and feed

And waste the food that others need.

Shall I say nothing, and stand still?

No! by God's mother, but I will!

She shall not think me here for naught;

At least I'll do what I've been taught!

At least I'll serve in my own way

God's mother in her church to-day.

The others serve to pray and sing;

I will serve to leap and spring."

Then he strips him of his gown,

Lays it on the altar down;
But for himself he takes good care
Not to show his body bare,
But keeps a jacket, soft and thin,
Almost a shirt, to tumble in.
Clothed in this supple woof of maille
His strength and health and form showed well.
And when his belt is buckled fast,
Toward the Virgin turns at last:
Very humbly makes his prayer;
"Lady!" says he, "to your care
I commit my soul and frame.
Gentle Virgin, gentle dame,
Do not despise what I shall do,
For I ask only to please you,
To serve you like an honest man,
So help me God, the best I can.
I cannot chant, nor can I read,
But I can show you here instead,
All my best tricks to make you laugh,
And so shall be as though a calf
Should leap and jump before its dam.
Lady, who never yet could blame
Those who serve you well and true,
All that I am, I am for you."

Then he begins to jump about,

High and low, and in and out,

Straining hard with might and main;

Then, falling on his knees again,

Before the image bows his face:

"By your pity! by your grace!"

Says he, "Ha! my gentle queen,

Do not despise my offering!"

In his earnestness he exerted himself until, at the end of his strength, he lay exhausted and unconscious on the altar steps. Pleased with his own exhibition, and satisfied that the Virgin was equally pleased, he continued these devotions every day, until at last his constant and singular absence from the regular services attracted the curiosity of a monk, who kept watch on him and reported his eccentric exercise to the Abbot.

The mediaeval monasteries seem to have been gently administered. Indeed, this has been made the chief reproach on them, and the excuse for robbing them for the benefit of a more energetic crown and nobility who tolerated no beggars or idleness but their own; at least, it is safe to say that few well-regulated and economically administered modern charities would have the patience of the Abbot of Clairvaux, who, instead of calling up the weak-minded tombeor and sending him back to the world to earn a living by his profession, went with his informant to the crypt, to see for himself what the strange report meant. We have seen at Chartres what a crypt may be, and how easily one might hide in its shadows while mass is said at the altars. The Abbot and his informant hid themselves behind a column in the shadow, and watched the whole performance to its end when the exhausted tumbler dropped unconscious and drenched with perspiration on the steps of the altar, with the words:—

"Dame!" fait il, "ne puis plus ore;

Mais voire je reviendrai encore."

"Lady!" says he, "no more I can,

But truly I'll come back again!"

You can imagine the dim crypt; the tumbler lying unconscious beneath the image of the Virgin; the Abbot peering out from the shadow of the column, and wondering what sort of discipline he could inflict for this unforeseen infraction of rule; when suddenly, before he could decide what next to do, the vault above the altar, of its own accord, opened:—

L'abes esgarde sans atendre

Et vit de la volte descendre

Une dame si gloriouse

Ains nus ne vit si preciouse

Ni si ricement conreee,

N'onques tant bele ne fu nee.

Ses vesteures sont bien chieres

D'or et de precieuses pieres.

Avec li estoient li angle

Del ciel amont, et li arcangle,

Qui entor le menestrel vienent,

Si le solacent et sostienent.

Quant entor lui sont arengie

S'ot tot son cuer asoagie.

Dont s'aprestent de lui servir

Por ce qu'ils volrent deservir

La servise que fait la dame

Qui tant est precieuse geme.

Et la douce reine france

Tenoit une touaille blance,

S'en avente son menestrel

Mout doucement devant l'autel.

La franc dame debonnaire

Le col, le cors, et le viaire

Li avente por refroidier;

Bien s'entremet de lui aidier;

La dame bien s'i abandone;
Li bons hom garde ne s'en done,
Car il ne voit, si ne set mie
Qu'il ait si bele compaignie.
The Abbot strains his eyes to see,
And, from the vaulting, suddenly,
A lady steps,—so glorious,—
Beyond all thought so precious,—
Her robes so rich, so nobly worn,—
So rare the gems the robes adorn,—
As never yet so fair was born.
Along with her the angels were,
Archangels stood beside her there;
Round about the tumbler group
To give him solace, bring him hope;
And when round him in ranks they stood,
His whole heart felt its strength renewed.
So they haste to give him aid
Because their wills are only made
To serve the service of their Queen,
Most precious gem the earth has seen.
And the lady, gentle, true,
Holds in her hand a towel new;
Fans him with her hand divine
Where he lies before the shrine.

The kind lady, full of grace,

Fans his neck, his breast, his face!

Fans him herself to give him air!

Labours, herself, to help him there!

The lady gives herself to it;

The poor man takes no heed of it;

For he knows not and cannot see

That he has such fair company.

Beyond this we need not care to go. If you cannot feel the colour and quality—the union of naivete and art, the refinement, the infinite delicacy and tenderness—of this little poem, then nothing will matter much to you; and if you can feel it, you can feel, without more assistance, the majesty of Chartres.

CHAPTER XIV: ABELARD

Super cuncta, subter cuncta,

Extra cuncta, intra cuncta,

Intra cuncta nec inclusus,

Extra cuncta nec exclusus,

Super cuncta nec elatus,

Subter cuncta nec substratus,

Super totus, praesidendo,

Subter totus, sustinendo,

Extra totus, complectendo,

Intra totus est, implendo.

According to Hildebert, Bishop of Le Mans and Archbishop of Tours, these verses describe God. Hildebert was the first poet of his time; no small merit, since he was contemporary with the "Chanson de Roland" and the first crusade; he was also a strong man, since he was able, as Bishop of Le Mans, to gain great credit by maintaining himself against William the Norman and Fulk of Anjou; and finally he was a prelate of high authority. He lived between 1055 and 1133. Supposing his verses to have been written in middle life, toward the year 1100, they may be taken to represent the accepted doctrine of the Church at the time of the first crusade. They were little more than a versified form of the Latin of Saint Gregory the Great who wrote five-hundred years before: "Ipse manet intra omnia, ipse extra omnia, ipse supra omnia, ipse infra omnia; et superior est per potentiam et inferior per sustentationem; exterior per magnitudinem et interior per subtilitatem; sursum regens, deorsum continens, extra circumdans, interius penetrans; nec alia parte superior, alia inferior, aut alia ex parte exterior atque ex alia manet interior, sed unus idemque totus ubique." According to Saint Gregory, in the sixth century, God was "one and the same and wholly everywhere"; "immanent within everything, without everything, above everything, below everything, sursum regens, dear sum continens"; while according to Archbishop Hildebert in the eleventh century: "God is overall things, under all things; outside all, inside all; within but not enclosed; without but not excluded; above but not raised up; below but not depressed; wholly above, presiding; wholly beneath, sustaining; wholly without, embracing; wholly within, filling." Finally, according to Benedict Spinoza, another five hundred years later still: "God is a being, absolutely infinite; that is to say, a substance made up of an infinity of attributes, each one of which expresses an eternal and infinite essence."

Spinoza was the great pantheist, whose name is still a terror to the orthodox, and whose philosophy is—very properly—a horror to the Church—and yet Spinoza never wrote a line that, to the unguided student, sounds more Spinozist than the words of Saint Gregory and Archbishop Hildebert. If God is everywhere; wholly; presiding, sustaining, embracing and filling, "sursum regens, deorsum continens," He is the only possible energy, and leaves no place for human will to act. A force which is "one and the same and wholly everywhere" is more Spinozist than Spinoza, and is likely to be mistaken for frank pantheism by the large majority of religious minds who must try to understand it without a theological course in a Jesuit college. In the year 1100 Jesuit colleges did not exist, and even the great Dominican and Franciscan schools were far from sight in the future; but the School of Notre Dame at Paris existed, and taught the existence of God much as Archbishop Hildebert described it. The most successful lecturer was William of Champeaux, and to any one who ever heard of William at all, the name instantly calls up the figure of Abelard, in flesh and blood, as he sang to Heloise the songs which he says resounded through Europe. The twelfth century, with all its sparkle, would be dull without Abelard and Heloise. With infinite regret, Heloise must be left out of the story, because she was not a philosopher or a poet or an artist, but only a Frenchwoman to the last millimetre of her shadow. Even though one may suspect that her famous letters to Abelard are, for the most part, by no means above scepticism, she was, by French standards, worth at least a dozen Abelards, if only because she called Saint Bernard a false apostle.

Unfortunately, French standards, by which she must be judged in our ignorance, take for granted that she philosophized only for the sake of Abelard, while Abelard taught philosophy to her not so much because he believed in philosophy or in her as because he believed in himself. To this day, Abelard remains a problem as perplexing as he must have been to Heloise, and almost as fascinating. As the west portal of Chartres is the door through which one must of necessity enter the Gothic architecture of the thirteenth century, so Abelard is the portal of approach to the Gothic thought and philosophy within. Neither art nor thought has a modern equivalent; only Heloise, like Isolde, unites the ages.

The first crusade seems, in perspective, to have rilled the whole field of vision in France at the time; but, in fact, France seethed with other emotions, and while the crusaders set out to scale heaven by force at Jerusalem, the monks, who remained at home, undertook to scale heaven by prayer and by absorption of body and soul in God; the Cistercian Order was founded in 1098, and was joined in 1112 by young Bernard, born in 1090 at Fontaines-les-Dijon, drawing with him or after him so many thousands of young men into the self-immolation of the monastery as carried dismay into the hearts of half the women of France. At the same time—that is, about 1098 or 1100—Abelard came up to Paris from Brittany, with as much faith in logic as Bernard had in prayer or Godfrey of Bouillon in arms, and led an equal or even a greater number of combatants to the conquest of heaven by force of pure reason. None showed doubt. Hundreds of thousands of young men wandered from their provinces, mostly to Palestine, largely to cloisters, but also in great numbers to Paris and the schools, while few ever returned.

Abelard had the advantage of being well-born; not so highly descended as Albertus Magnus and Thomas Aquinas who were to complete his work in the thirteenth century, but, like Bernard, a gentleman born and bred. He was the eldest son of Berenger, Sieur du Pallet, a chateau in Brittany, south of the Loire, on the edge of Poitou. His name was Pierre du Pallet, although, for some unknown reason, he called himself Pierre Abailard, or Abeillard, or Esbaillart, or Beylard; for the spelling was never fixed. He was born in 1079, and when, in 1096, the young men of his rank were rushing off to the first crusade, Pierre, a boy of seventeen, threw himself with equal zeal into the study of science, and, giving up his inheritance or birthright, at last came to Paris to seize a position in the schools. The year is supposed to have been 1100.

The Paris of Abelard's time was astonishingly old; so old that hardly a stone of it can be now pointed out. Even the oldest of the buildings still standing in that quarter—Saint-Julien-le-Pauvre, Saint-Severin, and the tower of the Lycee Henri IV—are more modern; only the old Roman Thermae, now part of the Musee de Cluny, within the walls, and the Abbey Tower of Saint-Germain-des-Pres, outside, in the fields, were standing in the year 1100. Politically, Paris was a small provincial town before the reign of Louis-le-Gros (1108- 37), who cleared its gates of its nearest enemies; but as a school, Paris was even then easily first. Students crowded into it by thousands, till the town is said to have contained more students than citizens. Modern Paris seems to have begun as a university town before it had a university. Students flocked to it from great distances, encouraged and supported by charity, and stimulated by privileges, until they took entire possession of what is still called the Latin Quarter from the barbarous Latin they chattered; and a town more riotous, drunken, and vicious than it became, in the course of time, hardly existed even in the Middle Ages. In 1100, when enthusiasm was fresh and faith in science was strong, the great mass of students came there to study, and, having no regular university organization or buildings, they thronged the cloister of Notre Dame—not our Notre Dame, which dates only from 1163, but the old Romanesque cathedral which stood on the same spot—and there they listened, and retained what they could remember, for they were not encouraged to take notes even if they were rich enough to buy notebooks, while manuscripts were far beyond their means. One valuable right the students seem to have had—that of asking questions and even of disputing with the lecturer provided they followed the correct form of dialectics. The lecturer himself was licensed by the Bishop.

Five thousand students are supposed to have swarmed about the cloister of Notre Dame, across the Petit Pont, and up the hill of Sainte-Genevieve; three thousand are said to have paid fees to Abelard in the days of his great vogue and they seem to have attached themselves to their favourite master as a champion to be upheld against the world. Jealousies ran high, and neither scholars nor masters shunned dispute. Indeed, the only science they taught or knew was the art of dispute—dialectics. Rhetoric, grammar, and dialectics were the regular branches of science, and bold students, who were not afraid of dabbling in forbidden fields, extended their studies to mathematics—"exercitium nefarium," according to Abelard, which he professed to know nothing about but which he studied nevertheless. Abelard, whether pupil or master, never held his tongue if he could help it, for his fortune depended on using it well; but he never used it so well in dialectics or theology as he did, toward the end of his life, in writing a bit of autobiography, so admirably told, so vivid, so vibrating with the curious intensity of his generation, that it needed only to have been written in "Romieu" to be the chief monument of early French prose, as the western portal of Chartres is the chief monument of early French sculpture, and of about the same date. Unfortunately Abelard was a noble scholar, who necessarily wrote and talked Latin, even with Heloise, and, although the Latin was mediaeval, it is not much the better on that account, because, in spite of its quaintness, the naivetes of a young language—the egotism, jealousies, suspicions, boastings, and lamentations of a childlike time—take a false air of outworn Rome and Byzantium, although, underneath, the spirit lives:—

I arrived at last in Paris where for a long time dialectics had specially flourished under William of Champeaux, rightly reckoned the first of my masters in that branch of study. I stayed some time in his school, but, though well received at first, I soon got to be an annoyance to him because I persisted in refuting certain ideas of his, and because, not being afraid to enter into argument against him, I sometimes got the better. This boldness, too, roused the wrath of those fellow students who were classed higher, because I was the youngest and the last comer. This was the beginning of my series of misfortunes which still last; my renown every day increasing, envy was kindled against me in every direction.

This picture of the boy of twenty, harassing the professor, day after day, in his own lecture-room before hundreds of older students, paints Abelard to the life; but one may safely add a few touches that heighten the effect; as that William of Champeaux himself was barely thirty, and that Abelard throughout his career, made use of every social and personal advantage to gain a point, with little scruple either in manner or in sophistry. One may easily imagine the scene. Teachers are always much the same. Pupils and students differ only in degrees of docility. In 1100, both classes began by accepting the foundations of society, as they have to do still; only they then accepted laws of the Church and Aristotle, while now they accept laws of the legislature and of energy. In 1100, the students took for granted that, with the help of Aristotle and syllogisms, they could build out the Church intellectually, as the architects, with the help of the pointed arch, were soon to enlarge it architecturally. They never doubted the certainty of their method. To them words had fixed values, like numbers, and syllogisms were hewn stones that needed only to be set in place, in order to reach any height or support any weight. Every sentence was made to take the form of a syllogism. One must have been educated in a Jesuit or Dominican school in order to frame these syllogisms correctly, but merely by way of illustration one may timidly suggest how the phrases sounded in their simplest form. For example, Plato or other equally good authority deemed substance as that which stands underneath phenomena; the most universal of universals, the ultimate, the highest in order of generalization. The ultimate essence or substance is indivisible; God is substance; God is indivisible. The divine substance is incapable of alteration or accident; all other substance is liable to alteration or accident; therefore, the divine substance differs from all other substance. A substance is a universal; as for example, Humanity, or the Human, is a universal and indivisible; the Man Socrates, for instance, is not a universal, but an individual; therefore, the substance Humanity, being indivisible, must exist entire and undivided in Socrates.

The form of logic most fascinating to youthful minds, as well as to some minds that are only too acute, is the reductio ad absurdum; the forcing an opponent into an absurd alternative or admission; and the syllogism lent itself happily to this use. Socrates abused the weapon and Abelard was the first French master of the art; but neither State nor Church likes to be reduced to an absurdity, and, on the whole, both Socrates and Abelard fared ill in the result. Even now, one had best be civil toward the idols of the forum. Abelard would find most of his old problems sensitive to his touch to-day. Time has settled few or none of the essential points of dispute. Science hesitates, more visibly than the Church ever did, to decide once for all whether unity or diversity is ultimate law; whether order or chaos is the governing rule of the universe, if universe there is; whether anything, except phenomena, exists. Even in matters more vital to society, one dares not speak too loud. Why, and for what, and to whom, is man a responsible agent? Every jury and judge, every lawyer and doctor, every legislator and clergyman has his own views, and the law constantly varies. Every nation may have a different system. One court may hang and another may acquit for the same crime, on the same day; and science only repeats what the Church said to Abelard, that where we know so little, we had better hold our tongues.

According to the latest authorities, the doctrine of universals which convulsed the schools of the twelfth century has never received an adequate answer. What is a species? what is a genus or a family or an order? More or less convenient terms of classification, about which the twelfth century cared very little, while it cared deeply about the essence of classes! Science has become too complex to affirm the existence of universal truths, but it strives for nothing else, and disputes the problem, within its own limits, almost as earnestly as in the twelfth century, when the whole field of human and superhuman activity was shut between these barriers of substance, universals, and particulars. Little has changed except the vocabulary and the method. The schools knew that their society hung for life on the demonstration that God, the ultimate universal, was a reality, out of which all other universal truths or realities sprang. Truth was a real thing, outside of human experience. The schools of Paris talked and thought of nothing else. John of Salisbury, who attended Abelard's lectures about 1136, and became Bishop of Chartres in 1176, seems to have been more surprised than we need be at the intensity of the emotion. "One never gets away from this question," he said. "From whatever point a discussion starts, it is always led back and attached to that. It is the madness of Rufus about Naevia; 'He thinks of nothing else; talks of nothing else, and if Naevia did not exist, Rufus would be dumb.'"

Abelard began it. After his first visit to Paris in 1100, he seems to have passed several years elsewhere, while Guillaume de Champeaux in 1108, retired from the school in the cloister of Notre Dame, and, taking orders, established a class in a chapel near by, afterwards famous as the Abbaye-de-Saint-Victor. The Jardin des Plantes and the Gare d'Orleans now cover the ground where the Abbey stood, on the banks of the Seine outside the Latin Quarter, and not a trace is left of its site; but there William continued his course in dialectics, until suddenly Abelard reappeared among his scholars, and resumed his old attacks. This time Abelard could hardly call himself a student. He was thirty years old, and long since had been himself a teacher; he had attended William's course on dialectics nearly ten years before, and was past master in the art; he had nothing to learn from William in theology, for neither William nor he was yet a theologian by profession. If Abelard went back to school, it was certainly not to learn; but indeed, he himself made little or no pretence of it, and told with childlike candour not only why he went, but also how brilliantly he succeeded in his object:—

I returned to study rhetoric in his school. Among other controversial battles, I succeeded, by the most irrefutable argument, in making him change, or rather ruin his doctrine of universals. His doctrine consisted in affirming the perfect identity of the essence in every individual of the same species, so that according to him there was no difference in the essence but only in the infinite variety of accidents. He then came to amend his doctrine so as to affirm, not the identity any longer, but the absence of distinction—the want of difference—in the essence. And as this question of universals had always been one of the most important questions of dialectics—so important that Porphyry, touching on it in his Preliminaries, did not dare to take the responsibility of cutting the knot, but said, "It is a very grave point,"—Champeaux, who was obliged to modify his idea and then renounce it, saw his course fall into such discredit that they hardly let him make his dialectical lectures, as though dialectics consisted entirely in the question of universals.

Why was this point so "very grave"? Not because it was mere dialectics! The only part of the story that seems grave today is the part that Abelard left out; the part which Saint Bernard, thirty years later put in, on behalf of William. We should be more credulous than twelfth-century monks, if we believed, on Abelard's word in 1135, that in 1110 he had driven out of the schools the most accomplished dialectician of the age by an objection so familiar that no other dialectician was ever silenced by it—whatever may have been the case with theologians—and so obvious that it could not have troubled a scholar of fifteen. William stated a settled doctrine as old as Plato; Abelard interposed an objection as old as Aristotle. Probably Plato and Aristotle had received the question and answer from philosophers ten-thousand years older than themselves. Certainly the whole of philosophy has always been involved in the dispute.

The subject is as amusing as a comedy; so amusing that ten minutes may be well given to playing the scene between William and Abelard, not as it happened, but in a form nearer our ignorance, with liberty to invent arguments for William, and analogies—which are figures intended to serve as fatal weapons if they succeed, and as innocent toys if they fail—such as he never imagined; while Abelard can respond with his true rejoinder, fatal in a different sense. For the chief analogy, the notes of music would serve, or the colours of the solar spectrum, or an energy, such as gravity—but the best is geometrical, because Euclid was as scholastic as William of Champeaux himself, and his axioms are even more familiar to the schoolboy of the twentieth, than to the schoolman of the twelfth century.

In these scholastic tournaments the two champions started from opposite points—one, from the ultimate substance, God—the universal, the ideal, the type—the other from the individual, Socrates, the concrete, the observed fact of experience, the object of sensual perception. The first champion—William in this instance— assumed that the universal was a real thing; and for that reason he was called a realist. His opponent—Abelard—held that the universal was only nominally real; and on that account he was called a nominalist. Truth, virtue, humanity, exist as units and realities, said William. Truth, replied Abelard, is only the sum of all possible facts that are true, as humanity is the sum of all actual human beings. The ideal bed is a form, made by God, said Plato. The ideal bed is a name, imagined by ourselves, said Aristotle. "I start from the universe," said William. "I start from the atom," said Abelard; and, once having started, they necessarily came into collision at some point between the two.

William of Champeaux, lecturing on dialectics or logic, comes to the question of universals, which he says, are substances. Starting from the highest substance, God, all being descends through created substances by stages, until it reaches the substance animality, from which it descends to the substance humanity: and humanity being, like other essences or substances, indivisible, passes wholly into each individual, becoming Socrates, Plato, and Aristotle, much as the divine substance exists wholly and undivided in each member of the Trinity.

Here Abelard interrupts. The divine substance, he says, operates by laws of its own, and cannot be used for comparison. In treating of human substance, one is bound by human limitations. If the whole of humanity is in Socrates, it is wholly absorbed by Socrates, and cannot be at the same time in Plato, or elsewhere. Following his favourite reductio ad absurdum, Abelard turns the idea round, and infers from it that, since Socrates carries all humanity in him, he carries Plato, too; and both must be in the same place, though Socrates is at Athens and Plato in Rome.

The objection is familiar to William, who replies by another commonplace:—

"Mr. Abelard, might I, without offence, ask you a simple matter? Can you give me Euclid's definition of a point?"

"If I remember right it is, 'illud cujus nulla pars est'; that which has no parts."

"Has it existence?"

"Only in our minds."

"Not, then, in God?"

"All necessary truths exist first in God. If the point is a necessary truth, it exists first there."

"Then might I ask you for Euclid's definition of the line?"

"The line is that which has only extension; 'Linea vocatur illa quae solam longitudinem habet.'"
"Can you conceive an infinite straight line?"

"Only as a line which has no end, like the point extended."

"Supposing we imagine a straight line, like opposite rays of the sun, proceeding in opposite directions to infinity—is it real?"

"It has no reality except in the mind that conceives it."

"Supposing we divide that line which has no reality into two parts at its origin in the sun or star, shall we get two infinities?—or shall we say, two halves of the infinite?"

"We conceive of each as partaking the quality of infinity."

"Now, let us cut out the diameter of the sun; or rather—since this is what our successors in the school will do,—let us take a line of our earth's longitude which is equally unreal, and measure a degree of this thing which does not exist, and then divide it into equal parts which we will use as a measure or metre. This metre, which is still nothing, as I understand you, is infinitely divisible into points? and the point itself is infinitely small? Therefore we have the finite partaking the nature of the infinite?"

"Undoubtedly!"

"One step more, Mr. Abelard, if I do not weary you! Let me take three of these metres which do not exist, and place them so that the ends of one shall touch the ends of the others. May I ask what is that figure?"

"I presume you mean it to be a triangle."

"Precisely! and what sort of a triangle?"

"An equilateral triangle, the sides of which measure one metre each."

"Now let me take three more of these metres which do not exist, and construct another triangle which does not exist;—are these two triangles or one triangle?"

"They are most certainly one—a single concept of the only possible equilateral triangle measuring one metre on each face."

"You told us a moment ago that a universal could not exist wholly and exclusively in two individuals at once. Does not the universal by definition—THE equilateral triangle measuring one metre on each face—does it not exist wholly, in its integrity of essence, in each of the two triangles we have conceived?"

"It does—as a conception."

"I thank you! Now, although I fear wearying you, perhaps you will consent to let me add matter to mind. I have here on my desk an object not uncommon in nature, which I will ask you to describe."

"It appears to be a crystal."

"May I ask its shape?"

"I should call it a regular octahedron."

"That is, two pyramids, set base to base? making eight plane surfaces, each a perfect equilateral triangle?"

"Concedo triangula (I grant the triangles)."

"Do you know, perchance, what is this material which seems to give substantial existence to these eight triangles?"

"I do not."

"Nor I! nor does it matter, unless you conceive it to be the work of man?"

"I do not claim it as man's work."

"Whose, then?"

"We believe all actual creation of matter, united with form, to be the work of God."

"Surely not the substance of God himself? Perhaps you mean that this form—this octahedron—is a divine concept."

"I understand such to be the doctrine of the Church."

"Then it seems that God uses this concept habitually to create this very common crystal. One question more, and only one, if you will permit me to come to the point. Does the matter—the material—of which this crystal is made affect in any way the form—the nature, the soul—of the universal equilateral triangle as you see it bounding these eight plane surfaces?"

"That I do not know, and do not think essential to decide. As far as these triangles are individual, they are made so by the will of God, and not by the substance you call triangle. The universal—the abstract right angle, or any other abstract form—is only an idea, a concept, to which reality, individuality, or what we might call energy is wanting. The only true energy, except man's free will, is God."

"Very good, Mr. Abelard! we can now reach our issue. You affirm that, just as the line does not exist in space, although the eye sees little else in space, so the triangle does not exist in this crystal, although the crystal shows eight of them, each perfect. You are aware that on this line which does not exist, and its combination in this triangle which does not exist, rests the whole fabric of mathematics with all its necessary truths. In other words, you know that in this line, though it does not exist, is bound up the truth of the only branch of human knowledge which claims absolute certainty for human processes. You admit that this line and triangle, which are mere figments of our human imagination, not only exist independent of us in the crystal, but are, as we suppose, habitually and invariably used by God Himself to give form to the matter contained within the planes of the crystal. Yet to this line and triangle you deny reality. To mathematical truth, you deny compulsive force. You hold that an equilateral triangle may, to you and all other human individuals, be a right-angled triangle if you choose to imagine it so. Allow me to say, without assuming any claim to superior knowledge, that to me your logic results in a different conclusion. If you are compelled, at one point or another of the chain of being, to deny existence to a substance, surely it should be to the last and feeblest. I see nothing to hinder you from denying your own existence, which is, in fact, impossible to demonstrate. Certainly you are free, in logic, to argue that Socrates and Plato are mere names—that men and matter are phantoms and dreams. No one ever has proved or ever can prove the contrary, Infallibly, a great philosophical school will some day be founded on that assumption. I venture even to recommend it to your acute and sceptical mind; but I cannot conceive how, by any process of reasoning, sensual or supersensual, you can reach the conclusion that the single form of truth which instantly and inexorably compels our submission to its laws—is nothing."

Thus far, all was familiar ground; certainly at least as familiar as the Pons Asinorum; and neither of the two champions had need to feel ruffled in temper by the discussion. The real struggle began only at this point; for until this point was reached, both positions were about equally tenable. Abelard had hitherto rested quietly on the defensive, but William's last thrust obliged him to strike in his turn, and he drew himself up for what, five hundred years later, was called the "Coup de Jarnac":—

"I do not deny," he begins; "on the contrary, I affirm that the universal, whether we call it humanity, or equilateral triangle, has a sort of reality as a concept; that it is something; even a substance, if you insist upon it. Undoubtedly the sum of all individual men results in the concept of humanity. What I deny is that the concept results in the individual. You have correctly stated the essence of the point and the line as sources of our concept of the infinite; what I deny is that they are divisions of the infinite. Universals cannot be divided; what is capable of division cannot be a universal. I admit the force of your analogy in the case of the crystal; but I am obliged to point out to you that, if you insist on this analogy, you will bring yourself and me into flagrant contradiction with the fixed foundations of the Church. If the energy of the triangle gives form to the crystal, and the energy of the line gives reality to the triangle, and the energy of the infinite gives substance to the line, all energy at last becomes identical with the ultimate substance, God Himself. Socrates becomes God in small; Judas is identical with both; humanity is of the divine essence, and exists, wholly and undivided, in each of us. The equilateral triangle we call humanity exists, therefore, entire, identical, in you and me, as a subdivision of the infinite line, space, energy, or substance, which is God. I need not remind you that this is pantheism, and that if God is the only energy, human free will merges in God's free will; the Church ceases to have a reason for existence; man cannot be held responsible for his own acts, either to the Church or to the State; and finally, though very unwillingly, I must, in regard for my own safety, bring the subject to the attention of the Archbishop, which, as you know better than I, will lead to your seclusion, or worse."

Whether Abelard used these precise words is nothing to the point. The words he left on record were equivalent to these. As translated by M. de Remusat from a manuscript entitled: "Glossulae magistri Petri Baelardi super Porphyrium," the phrase runs: "A grave heresy is at the end of this doctrine; for, according to it, the divine substance which is recognized as admitting of no form, is necessarily identical with every substance in particular and with all substance in general." Even had he not stated the heresy so bluntly, his objection necessarily pushed William in face of it. Realism, when pressed, always led to pantheism. William of Champeaux and Bishop or Archbishop Hildebert were personal friends, and Hildebert's divine substance left no more room for human free will than Abelard saw in the geometric analogy imagined for William. Throughout the history of the Church for fifteen hundred years, whenever this theological point has been pressed against churchmen it has reduced them to evasion or to apology. Admittedly, the weak point of realism was its fatally pantheistic term.

Of course, William consulted his friends in the Church, probably Archbishop Hildebert among the rest, before deciding whether to maintain or to abandon his ground, and the result showed that he was guided by their advice. Realism was the Roman arch—the only possible foundation for any Church; because it assumed unity, and any other scheme was compelled to prove it, for a starting-point. Let us see, for a moment, what became of the dialogue, when pushed into theology, in order to reach some of the reasons which reduced William to tacit abandonment of a doctrine he could never have surrendered unless under compulsion. That he was angry is sure, for Abelard, by thus thrusting theology into dialectics, had struck him a full blow; and William knew Abelard well:—

"Ah!" he would have rejoined; "you are quick, M. du Pallet, to turn what I offered as an analogy, into an argument of heresy against my person. You are at liberty to take that course if you choose, though I give you fair warning that it will lead you far. But now I must ask you still another question. This concept that you talk about— this image in the mind of man, of God, of matter; for I know not where to seek it—whether is it a reality or not?"

"I hold it as, in a manner, real."

"I want a categorical answer—Yes or No!"

"Distinguo! (I must qualify.)"

"I will have no qualifications. A substance either is, or not.

Choose!"

To this challenge Abelard had the choice of answering Yes, or of answering no, or of refusing to answer at all. He seems to have done the last; but we suppose him to have accepted the wager of battle, and to answer:—

"Yes, then!"

"Good!" William rejoins; "now let us see how your pantheism differs from mine. My triangle exists as a reality, or what science will call an energy, outside my mind, in God, and is impressed on my mind as it is on a mirror, like the triangle on the crystal, its energy giving form. Your triangle you say is also an energy, but an essence of my mind itself; you thrust it into the mind as an integral part of the mirror; identically the same concept, energy, or necessary truth which is inherent in God. Whatever subterfuge you may resort to, sooner or later you have got to agree that your mind is identical with God's nature as far as that concept is concerned. Your pantheism goes further than mine. As a doctrine of the Real Presence peculiar to yourself, I can commend it to the Archbishop together with your delation of me."

Supposing that Abelard took the opposite course, and answered:—

"No! my concept is a mere sign."

"A sign of what, in God's name!"

"A sound! a word! a symbol! an echo only of my ignorance."

"Nothing, then! So truth and virtue and charity do not exist at all. You suppose yourself to exist, but you have no means of knowing God; therefore, to you God does not exist except as an echo of your ignorance; and, what concerns you most, the Church does not exist except as your concept of certain individuals, whom you cannot regard as a unity, and who suppose themselves to believe in a Trinity which exists only as a sound, or a symbol. I will not repeat your words, M. du Pallet, outside this cloister, because the consequences to you would certainly be fatal; but it is only too clear that you are a materialist, and as such your fate must be decided by a Church Council, unless you prefer the stake by judgment of a secular court."

In truth, pure nominalism—if, indeed, any one ever maintained it— afforded no cover whatever. Nor did Abelard's concept help the matter, although for want of a better refuge, the Church was often driven into it. Conceptualism was a device, like the false wooden roof, to cover and conceal an inherent weakness of construction. Unity either is, or is not. If soldiers, no matter in what number, can never make an army, and worshippers, though in millions, do not make a Church, and all humanity united would not necessarily constitute a State, equally little can their concepts, individual or united, constitute the one or the other. Army, Church, and State, each is an organic whole, complex beyond all possible addition of units, and not a concept at all, but rather an animal that thinks, creates, devours, and destroys. The attempt to bridge the chasm between multiplicity and unity is the oldest problem of philosophy, religion, and science, but the flimsiest bridge of all is the human concept, unless somewhere, within or beyond it, an energy not individual is hidden; and in that case the old question instantly reappears: What is that energy?

Abelard would have done well to leave William alone, but Abelard was an adventurer, and William was a churchman. To win a victory over a churchman is not very difficult for an adventurer, and is always a tempting amusement, because the ambition of churchmen to shine in worldly contests is disciplined and checked by the broader interests of the Church: but the victory is usually sterile, and rarely harms the churchman. The Church cares for its own. Probably the bishops advised William not to insist on his doctrine, although every bishop may have held the same view. William allowed himself to be silenced without a judgment, and in that respect stands almost if not quite alone among schoolmen. The students divined that he had sold himself to the Church, and consequently deserted him. Very soon he received his reward in the shape of the highest dignity open to private ambition—a bishopric. As Bishop of Chalons-sur-Marne he made for himself a great reputation, which does not concern us, although it deeply concerned the unfortunate Abelard, for it happened, either by chance or design, that within a year or two after William established himself at Chalons, young Bernard of Citeaux chose a neighbouring diocese in which to establish a branch of the Cistercian Order, and Bishop William took so keen an interest in the success of Bernard as almost to claim equal credit for it. Clairvaux was, in a manner, William's creation, although not in his diocese, and yet, if there was a priest in all France who fervently despised the schools, it was young Bernard. William of Champeaux, the chief of schoolmen, could never have gained Bernard's affections. Bishop William of Chalons must have drifted far from dialectics into mysticism in order to win the support of Clairvaux, and train up a new army of allies who were to mark Abelard for an easy prey.

Meanwhile Abelard pursued his course of triumph in the schools, and in due time turned from dialectics to theology, as every ambitious teacher could hardly fail to do. His affair with Heloise and their marriage seem to have occupied his time in 1117 or 1118, for they both retired into religious orders in 1119, and he resumed his lectures in 1120. With his passion for rule, he was fatally certain to attempt ruling the Church as he ruled the schools; and, as it was always enough for him that any point should be tender in order that he should press upon it, he instantly and instinctively seized on the most sensitive nerve of the Church system to wrench it into his service. He became a sort of apostle of the Holy Ghost.

That the Trinity is a mystery was a law of theology so absolute as in a degree to hide the law of philosophy that the Trinity was meant as a solution of a greater mystery still. In truth, as a matter of philosophy, the Trinity was intended to explain the eternal and primary problem of the process by which unity could produce diversity. Starting from unity alone, philosophers found themselves unable to stir hand or foot until they could account for duality. To the common, ignorant peasant, no such trouble occurred, for he knew the Trinity in its simpler form as the first condition of life, like time and space and force. No human being was so stupid as not to understand that the father, mother, and child made a trinity, returning into each other, and although every father, every mother, and every child, from the dawn of man's intelligence, had asked why, and had never received an answer more intelligible to them than to philosophers, they never showed difficulty in accepting that trinity as a fact. They might even, in their beneficent blindness, ask the Church why that trinity, which had satisfied the Egyptians for five or ten-thousand years, was not good enough for churchmen. They themselves were doing their utmost, though unconsciously, to identify the Holy Ghost with the Mother, while philosophy insisted on excluding the human symbol precisely because it was human and led back to an infinite series. Philosophy required three units to start from; it posed the equilateral triangle, not the straight line, as the foundation of its deometry. The first straight line, infinite in extension, must be assumed, and its reflection engendered the second, but whence came the third? Under protest, philosophy was compelled to accept the symbol of Father and Son as a matter of faith, but, if the relation of Father and Son were accepted for the two units which reflected each other, what relation expressed the Holy Ghost? In philosophy, the product of two units was not a third unit, but diversity, multiplicity, infinity. The subject was, for that reason, better handled by the Arabs, whose reasoning worked back on the Christian theologians and made the point more delicate still. Common people, like women and children and ourselves, could never understand the Trinity; naturally, intelligent people understood it still less, but for them it did not matter; they did not need to understand it provided their neighbours would leave it alone.

The mass of mankind wanted something nearer to them than either the Father or the Son; they wanted the Mother, and the Church tried, in what seems to women and children and ourselves rather a feeble way, to give the Holy Ghost, as far as possible, the Mother's attributes —Love, Charity, Grace; but in spite of conscientious effort and unswerving faith, the Holy Ghost remained to the mass of Frenchmen somewhat apart, feared rather than loved. The sin against the Holy Ghost was a haunting spectre, for no one knew what else it was.

Naturally the Church, and especially its official theologians, took an instinctive attitude of defence whenever a question on this subject was asked, and were thrown into a flutter of irritation whenever an answer was suggested. No man likes to have his intelligence or good faith questioned, especially if he has doubts about it himself. The distinguishing essence of the Holy Ghost, as a theological substance, was its mystery. That this mystery should be touched at all was annoying to every one who knew the dangers that lurked behind the veil, but that it should be freely handled before audiences of laymen by persons of doubtful character was impossible. Such license must end in discrediting the whole Trinity under pretence of making it intelligible.

Precisely this license was what Abelard took, and on it he chose to insist. He said nothing heretical; he treated the Holy Ghost with almost exaggerated respect, as though other churchmen did not quite appreciate its merits; but he would not let it alone, and the Church dreaded every moment lest, with his enormous influence in the schools, he should raise a new storm by his notorious indiscretion. Yet so long as he merely lectured, he was not molested; only when he began to publish his theology did the Church interfere. Then a council held at Soissons in 1121 abruptly condemned his book in block, without reading it, without specifying its errors, and without hearing his defence; obliged him to throw the manuscript into the fire with his own hands, and finally shut him up in a monastery.

He had invited the jurisdiction by taking orders, but even the Church was shocked by the summary nature of the judgment, which seems to have been quite irregular. In fact, the Church has never known what it was that the council condemned. The latest great work on the Trinity, by the Jesuit Father de Regnon, suggests that Abelard's fault was in applying to the Trinity his theory of concepts.

"Yes!" he says; "the mystery is explained; the key of conceptualism has opened the tabernacle, and Saint Bernard was right in saying that, thanks to Abelard, every one can penetrate it and contemplate it at his ease; 'even the graceless, even the uncircumcised.' Yes! the Trinity is explained, but after the manner of the Sabellians. For to identify the Persons in the terms of human concepts is, in the same stroke, to destroy their 'subsistances propres.'"

Although the Saviour seems to have felt no compunctions about identifying the persons of the Trinity in the terms of human concepts, it is clear that tourists and heretics had best leave the Church to deal with its "subsistances propres," and with its own members, in its own way. In sum, the Church preferred to stand firm on the Roman arch, and the architects seem now inclined to think it was right; that scholastic science and the pointed arch proved to be failures. In the twelfth century the world may have been rough, but it was not stupid. The Council of Soissons was held while the architects and sculptors were building the west porch of Chartres and the Aquilon at Mont-Saint-Michel. Averroes was born at Cordova in 1126; Omar Khayyam died at Naishapur in 1123. Poetry and metaphysics owned the world, and their quarrel with theology was a private, family dispute. Very soon the tide turned decisively in Abelard's favour. Suger, a political prelate, became minister of the King, and in March, 1122, Abbot of Saint-Denis. In both capacities he took the part of Abelard, released him from restraint, and even restored to him liberty of instruction, at least beyond the jurisdiction of the Bishop of Paris. Abelard then took a line of conduct singularly parallel with that of Bernard. Quitting civilized life he turned wholly to religion. "When the agreement," he said, "had been executed by both parties to it, in presence of the King and his ministers, I next retired within the territory of Troyes, upon a desert spot which I knew, and on a piece of ground given me by certain persons, I built, with the consent of the bishop of the diocese, a sort of oratory of reeds and thatch, which I placed under the invocation of the Holy Trinity ... Founded at first in the name of the Holy Trinity, then placed under its invocation, it was called 'Paraclete' in memory of my having come there as a fugitive and in my despair having found some repose in the consolations of divine grace. This denomination was received by many with great astonishment, and some attacked it with violence under pretext that it was not permitted to consecrate a church specially to the Holy Ghost any more than to God the Father, but that, according to ancient usage, it must be dedicated either to the Son alone or to the Trinity."

The spot is still called Paraclete, near Nogent-sur-Seine, in the parish of Quincey about halfway between Fontainebleau and Troyes. The name Paraclete as applied to the Holy Ghost meant the Consoler, the Comforter, the Spirit of Love and Grace; as applied to the oratory by Abelard it meant a renewal of his challenge to theologians, a separation of the Persons in the Trinity, a vulgarization of the mystery; and, as his story frankly says, it was so received by many. The spot was not so remote but that his scholars could follow him, and he invited them to do so. They came in great numbers, and he lectured to them. "In body I was hidden in this spot; but my renown overran the whole world and filled it with my word." Undoubtedly Abelard taught theology, and, in defiance of the council that had condemned him, attempted to define the persons of the Trinity. For this purpose he had fallen on a spot only fifty or sixty miles from Clairvaux where Bernard was inspiring a contrary spirit of religion; he placed himself on the direct line between Clairvaux and its source at Citeaux near Dijon; indeed, if he had sought for a spot as central as possible to the active movement of the Church and the time, he could have hit on none more convenient and conspicuous unless it were the city of Troyes itself, the capital of Champagne, some thirty miles away. The proof that he meant to be aggressive is furnished by his own account of the consequences. Two rivals, he says, one of whom seems to have been Bernard of Clairvaux, took the field against him, "and succeeded in exciting the hostility of certain ecclesiastical and secular authorities, by charging monstrous things, not only against my faith, but also against my manner of life, to such a point as to detach from me some of my principal friends; even those who preserved some affection for me dared no longer display it, for fear. God is my witness that I never heard of the union of an ecclesiastical assembly without thinking that its object was my condemnation." The Church had good reason, for Abelard's conduct defied discipline; but far from showing harshness, the Church this time showed a true spirit of conciliation most creditable to Bernard. Deeply as the Cistercians disliked and distrusted Abelard, they did not violently suppress him, but tacitly consented to let the authorities buy his silence with Church patronage.

The transaction passed through Suger's hands, and offered an ordinary example of political customs as old as history. An abbey in Brittany became vacant; at a hint from the Duke Conan, which may well be supposed to have been suggested from Paris, the monks chose Abelard as their new abbot, and sent some of their number to Suger to request permission for Abelard, who was a monk of Saint-Denis, to become Abbot of Saint-Gildas-de-Rhuys, near Vannes, in Brittany. Suger probably intimated to Abelard, with a certain degree of authority, that he had better accept. Abelard, "struck with terror, and as it were under the menace of a thunderbolt," accepted. Of course the dignity was in effect banishment and worse, and was so understood on all sides. The Abbaye-de-Saint-Gildas-de-Rhuys, though less isolated than Mont-Saint-Michel, was not an agreeable winter residence. Though situated in Abelard's native province of Brittany, only sixty or eighty miles from his birthplace, it was for him a prison with the ocean around it and a singularly wild people to deal with; but he could have endured his lot with contentment, had not discipline or fear or pledge compelled him to hold his tongue. From 1125, when he was sent to Brittany until 1135 when he reappeared in Paris, he never opened his mouth to lecture. "Never, as God is my witness,—never would I have acquiesced in such an offer, had it not been to escape, no matter how, from the vexations with which I was incessantly overwhelmed."

A great career in the Church was thus opened for him against his will, and if he did not die an archbishop it was not wholly the fault of the Church. Already he was a great prelate, the equal in rank of the Abbe Suger, himself, of Saint-Denis; of Peter the Venerable of Cluny; of Bernard of Clairvaux. He was in a manner a peer of the realm. Almost immediately he felt the advantages of the change. Barely two years passed when, in 1127, the Abbe Suger, in reforming his subordinate Abbey of Argenteuil, was obliged to disturb Heloise, then a sister in that congregation. Abelard was warned of the necessity that his wife should be protected, and with the assistance of everyone concerned, he was allowed to establish his wife at the Paraclete as head of a religious sisterhood. "I returned there; I invited Heloise to come there with the nuns of her community; and when they arrived, I made them the entire donation of the oratory and its dependencies ... The bishops cherished her as their daughter; the abbots as their sister; the laymen as their mother." This was merely the beginning of her favour and of his. For ten years they were both of them petted children of the Church.

The formal establishment of Heloise at the Paraclete took place in 1129. In February, 1130, on the death of the Pope at Rome, a schism broke out, and the cardinals elected two popes, one of whom took the name of Innocent II, and appealed for support to France. Suger saw a great political opportunity and used it. The heads of the French Church agreed in supporting Innocent, and the King summoned a Church council at Etampes to declare its adhesion. The council met in the late summer; Bernard of Clairvaux took the lead; Peter the Venerable, Suger of Saint-Denis, and the Abbot of Saint-Gildas-de- Rhuys supported him; Innocent himself took refuge at Cluny in October, and on January 20, 1131, he stopped at the Benedictine Abbey of Morigny. The Chronicle of the monastery, recording the abbots present on this occasion,—the Abbot of Morigny itself, of Feversham; of Saint-Lucien of Beauvais, and so forth,—added especially: "Bernard of Clairvaux, who was then the most famous pulpit orator in France; and Peter Abelard, Abbot of Saint-Gildas, also a monk and the most eminent master of the schools to which the scholars of almost all the Latin races flowed."

Innocent needed popular support; Bernard and Abelard were the two leaders of popular opinion in France. To attach them, Innocent could refuse nothing. Probably Abelard remained with Innocent, but in any case Innocent gave him, at Auxerre, in the following November, a diploma, granting to Heloise, prioress of the Oratory of the Holy Trinity, all rights of property over whatever she might possess, against all assailants; which proves Abelard's favour. At this time he seems to have taken great interest in the new sisterhood. "I made them more frequent visits," he said, "in order to work for their benefit." He worked so earnestly for their benefit that he scandalized the neighbourhood and had to argue at unnecessary length his innocence of evil. He went so far as to express a wish to take refuge among them and to abandon his abbey in Brittany. He professed to stand in terror of his monks; he excommunicated them; they paid no attention to him; he appealed to the Pope, his friend, and Innocent sent a special legate to enforce their submission "in presence of the Count and the Bishops."

Even since that, they would not keep quiet. And quite recently, since the expulsion of those of whom I have spoken, when I returned to the abbey, abandoning myself to the rest of the brothers who inspired me with less distrust, I found them even worse than the others. It was no longer a question of poison; it was the dagger that they now sharpened against my breast. I had great difficulty in escaping from them under the guidance of one of the neighbouring lords. Similar perils menace me still and every day I see the sword raised over my head. Even at table I can hardly breathe ... This is the torture that I endure every moment of the day; I, a poor monk, raised to the prelacy, becoming more miserable in becoming more great, that by my example the ambitious may learn to curb their greed.

With this, the "Story of Calamity" ends. The allusions to Innocent II seem to prove that it was written not earlier than 1132; the confession of constant and abject personal fear suggests that it was written under the shock caused by the atrocious murder of the Prior of Saint-Victor by the nephews of the Archdeacon of Paris, who had also been subjected to reforms. This murder was committed a few miles outside of the walls of Paris, on August 20, 1133. The "Story of Calamity" is evidently a long plea for release from the restraints imposed on its author by his position in the prelacy and the tacit, or possibly the express, contract he had made, or to which he had submitted, in 1125. This plea was obviously written in order to serve one of two purposes:— either to be placed before the authorities whose consent alone could relieve Abelard from his restraints; or to justify him in throwing off the load of the Church, and resuming the profession of schoolman. Supposing the second explanation, the date of the paper would be more or less closely fixed by John of Salisbury, who coming to Paris as a student, in 1136, found Abelard lecturing on the Mont-Sainte- Genevieve; that is to say, not under the license of the Bishop of Paris or his Chancellor, but independently, in a private school of his own, outside the walls. "I attached myself to the Palatine Peripatician who then presided on the hill of Sainte-Genevieve, the doctor illustrious, admired by all. There, at his feet, I received the first elements of the dialectic art, and according to the measure of my poor understanding I received with all the avidity of my soul everything that came from his mouth."

This explanation is hardly reasonable, for no prelate who was not also a temporal lord would have dared throw off his official duties without permission from his superiors. In Abelard's case the only superior to whom he could apply, as Abbot of Saint-Gildas in Brittany, was probably the Pope himself. In the year 1135 the moment was exceedingly favourable for asking privileges. Innocent, driven from Rome a second time, had summoned a council at Pisa for May 30 to help him. Louis-le-Gros and his minister Suger gave at first no support to this council, and were overruled by Bernard of Clairvaux who in a manner drove them into giving the French clergy permission to attend. The principal archbishops, a number of bishops, and sixteen abbots went to Pisa in May, 1135, and some one of them certainly asked Innocent for favours on behalf of Abelard, which the Pope granted.

The proof is a papal bull, dated in 1136, in favour of Heloise, giving her the rank and title of Abbess, accompanied by another giving to the Oratory of the Holy Trinity the rank and name of Monastery of the Paraclete, a novelty in Church tradition so extraordinary or so shocking that it still astounds churchmen. With this excessive mark of favour Innocent could have felt little difficulty in giving Abelard the permission to absent himself from his abbey, and with this permission in his hands Abelard might have lectured on dialectics to John of Salisbury in the summer or autumn of 1136. He did not, as far as known, resume lectures on theology.

Such success might have turned heads much better balanced than that of Abelard. With the support of the Pope and at least one of the most prominent cardinals, and with relations at court with the ministers of Louis-le-Gros, Abelard seemed to himself as strong as Bernard of Clairvaux, and a more popular champion of reform. The year 1137, which has marked a date for so many great points in our travels, marked also the moment of Abelard's greatest vogue. The victory of Aristotle and the pointed arch seemed assured when Suger effected the marriage of the young Prince Louis to the heiress Eleanor of Guienne. The exact moment was stamped on the facade of his exquisite creation, the Abbey Church of Saint-Denis, finished in 1140 and still in part erect. From Saint-Denis to Saint-Sulpice was but a step. Louis-le-Grand seems to stand close in succession to Louis-le-Gros.

Fortunately for tourists, the world, restless though it might be, could not hurry, and Abelard was to know of the pointed arch very little except its restlessness. Just at the apex of his triumph, August 1, 1137, Louis-le-Gros died. Six months afterwards the anti-pope also died, the schism ended, and Innocent II needed Abelard's help no more. Bernard of Clairvaux became Pope and King at once. Both Innocent and Louis-le-Jeune were in a manner his personal creations. The King's brother Henry, next in succession, actually became a monk at Clairvaux not long afterwards. Even the architecture told the same story, for at Saint-Denis, though the arch might simulate a point, the old Romanesque lines still assert as firmly as ever their spiritual control. The fleche that gave the facade a new spirit was not added until 1215, which marks Abelard's error in terms of time.

Once arrived at power, Bernard made short work of all that tried to resist him. During 1139 he seems to have been too busy or too ill to take up the affair of Abelard, but in March, 1140, the attack was opened in a formal letter from William of Saint-Thierry, who was Bernard's closest friend, bringing charges against Abelard before Bernard and the Bishop of Chartres. The charges were simple enough:—

Pierre Abelard seized the moment, when all the masters of ecclesiastical doctrine have disappeared from the scene of the world, to conquer a place apart, for himself, in the schools, and to create there an exclusive domination. He treats Holy Scripture as though it were dialectics. It is a matter with him of personal invention and annual novelties. He is the censor and not the disciple of the faith; the corrector and not the imitator of the authorized masters.

In substance, this is all. The need of action was even simpler. Abelard's novelties were becoming a danger; they affected not only the schools, but also even the Curia at Rome. Bernard must act because there was no one else to act: "This man fears you; he dreads you! if you shut your eyes, whom will he fear? ... The evil has become too public to allow a correction limited to amicable discipline and secret warning." In fact, Abelard's works were flying about Europe in every direction, and every year produced a novelty. One can still read them in M. Cousin's collected edition; among others, a volume on ethics: "Ethica, seu Scito teipsum"; on theology in general, an epitome; a "Dialogus inter Philosophum, Judaeum et Christianum"; and, what was perhaps the most alarming of all, an abstract of quotations from standard authorities, on the principle of the parallel column, showing the fatal contradictions of the authorized masters, and entitled "Sic et Non"! Not one of these works but dealt with sacred matters in a spirit implying that the Essence of God was better understood by Pierre du Pallet than by the whole array of bishops and prelates in Europe! Had Bernard been fortunate enough to light upon the "Story of Calamity," which must also have been in existence, he would have found there Abelard's own childlike avowal that he taught theology because his scholars "said that they did not want mere words; that one can believe only what one understands; and that it is ridiculous to preach to others what one understands no better than they do." Bernard himself never charged Abelard with any presumption equal to this. Bernard said only that "he sees nothing as an enigma, nothing as in a mirror, but looks on everything face to face." If this had been all, even Bernard could scarcely have complained. For several thousand years mankind has stared Infinity in the face without pretending to be the wiser; the pretension of Abelard was that, by his dialectic method, he could explain the Infinite, while all other theologians talked mere words; and by way of proving that he had got to the bottom of the matter, he laid down the ultimate law of the universe as his starting-point: "All that God does," he said, "He wills necessarily and does it necessarily; for His goodness is such that it pushes Him necessarily to do all the good He can, and the best He can, and the quickest He can ... Therefore it is of necessity that God willed and made the world." Pure logic admitted no contingency; it was bound to be necessitarian or ceased to be logical; but the result, as Bernard understood it, was that Abelard's world, being the best and only possible, need trouble itself no more about God, or Church, or man.

Strange as the paradox seems, Saint Bernard and Lord Bacon, though looking at the world from opposite standpoints, agreed in this: that the scholastic method was false and mischievous, and that the longer it was followed, the greater was its mischief. Bernard thought that because dialectics led wrong, therefore faith led right. He saw no alternative, and perhaps in fact there was none. If he had lived a century later, he would have said to Thomas Aquinas what he said to a schoolman of his own day: "If you had once tasted true food,"—if you knew what true religion is,—"how quick you would leave those Jew makers of books (literatoribus judaeis) to gnaw their crusts by themselves!" Locke or Hume might perhaps still have resented a little the "literator judaeus," but Faraday or Clerk-Maxwell would have expressed the same opinion with only the change of a word: "If the twelfth century had once tasted true science, how quick they would have dropped Avicenna and Averroes!" Science admits that Bernard's disbelief in scholasticism was well founded, whatever it may think of his reasons. The only point that remains is personal: Which is the more sympathetic, Bernard or Abelard?

The Church feels no doubt, but is a bad witness. Bernard is not a character to be taken or rejected in a lump. He was many-sided, and even toward Abelard he showed more than one surface. He wanted no unnecessary scandals in the Church; he had too many that were not of his seeking. He seems to have gone through the forms of friendly negotiation with Abelard although he could have required nothing less than Abelard's submission and return to Brittany, and silence; terms which Abelard thought worse than death. On Abelard's refusal, Bernard began his attack. We know, from the "Story of Calamity," what Bernard's party could not have certainly known then,—the abject terror into which the very thought of a council had for twenty years thrown Abelard whenever he was threatened with it; and in 1140 he saw it to be inevitable. He preferred to face it with dignity, and requested to be heard at a council to meet at Sens in June. One cannot admit that he felt the shadow of a hope to escape. At the utmost he could have dreamed of nothing more than a hearing. Bernard's friends, who had a lively fear of his dialectics, took care to shut the door on even this hope. The council was carefully packed and overawed. The King was present; archbishops, bishops, abbots, and other prelates by the score; Bernard acted in person as the prosecuting attorney; the public outside were stimulated to threaten violence. Abelard had less chance of a judicial hearing than he had had at Soissons twenty years before. He acted with a proper sense of their dignity and his own by simply appearing and entering an appeal to Rome. The council paid no attention to the appeal, but passed to an immediate condemnation. His friends said that it was done after dinner; that when the volume of Abelard's "Theology" was produced and the clerk began to read it aloud, after the first few sentences the bishops ceased attention, talked, joked, laughed, stamped their feet, got angry, and at last went to sleep. They were waked only to growl "Damnamus—namus," and so made an end. The story may be true, for all prelates, even in the twelfth century, were not Bernards of Clairvaux or Peters of Cluny; all drank wine, and all were probably sleepy after dinner; while Abelard's writings are, for the most part, exceedingly hard reading. The clergy knew quite well what they were doing; the judgment was certain long in advance, and the council was called only to register it. Political trials were usually mere forms.

The appeal to Rome seems to have been taken seriously by Bernard, which is surprising unless the character of Innocent II inspired his friends with doubts unknown to us. Innocent owed everything to Bernard, while Abelard owed everything to Innocent. The Pope was not in a position to alienate the French Church or the French King. To any one who knows only what is now to be known, Bernard seems to have been sure of the Curia, yet he wrote in a tone of excitement as though he feared Abelard's influence there even more than at home. He became abusive; Abelard was a crawling viper (coluber tortuosus) who had come out of his hole (egressus est de caverna sua), and after the manner of a hydra (in similitudinem hydrae), after having one head cut off at Soissons, had thrown out seven more. He was a monk without rule; a prelate without responsibility; an abbot without discipline; "disputing with boys; conversing with women." The charges in themselves seem to be literally true, and would not in some later centuries have been thought very serious; neither faith nor morals were impugned. On the other hand, Abelard never affected or aspired to be a saint, while Bernard always affected to judge the acts and motives of his fellow-creatures from a standpoint of more than worldly charity. Bernard had no right to Abelard's vices; he claimed to be judged by a higher standard; but his temper was none of the best, and his pride was something of the worst; which gave to Peter the Venerable occasion for turning on him sharply with a rebuke that cut to the bone. "You perform all the difficult religious duties," wrote Peter to the saint who wrought miracles; "you fast; you watch; you suffer; but you will not endure the easy ones—you do not love (non vis levia ferre, ut diligas)."

This was the end of Abelard. Of course the Pope confirmed the judgment, and even hurried to do so in order that he might not be obliged to give Abelard a hearing. The judgment was not severe, as judgments went; indeed, it amounted to little more than an order to keep silence, and, as it happened, was never carried into effect. Abelard, at best a nervous invalid, started for Rome, but stopped at Cluny, perhaps the most agreeable stopping-place in Europe. Personally he seems to have been a favourite of Abbot Peter the Venerable, whose love for Bernard was not much stronger than Abelard's or Suger's. Bernard was an excessively sharp critic, and spared worldliness, or what he thought lack of spirituality, in no prelate whatever; Clairvaux existed for nothing else, politically, than as a rebuke to them all, and Bernard's enmity was their bond of union. Under the protection of Peter the Venerable, the most amiable figure of the twelfth century, and in the most agreeable residence in Europe, Abelard remained unmolested at Cluny, occupied, as is believed, in writing or revising his treatises, in defiance of the council. He died there two years later, April 21, 1142, in full communion, still nominal Abbot of Saint-Gildas, and so distinguished a prelate that Peter the Venerable thought himself obliged to write a charming letter to Heloise at the Paraclete not far away, condoling with her on the loss of a husband who was the Socrates, the Aristotle, the Plato, of France and the West; who, if among logicians he had rivals, had no master; who was the prince of study, learned, eloquent, subtle, penetrating; who overcame everything by the force of reason, and was never so great as when he passed to true philosophy, that of Christ.

All this was in Latin verses, and seems sufficiently strong, considering that Abelard's philosophy had been so recently and so emphatically condemned by the entire Church, including Peter the Venerable himself. The twelfth century had this singular charm of liberty in practice, just as its architecture knew no mathematical formula of precision; but Peter's letter to Heloise went further still, and rang with absolute passion:—

Thus, dear and venerable sister in God, he to whom you are united, after your tie in the flesh, by the better and stronger bond of the divine love; he, with whom, and under whom, you have served the Lord, the Lord now takes, in your place, like another you, and warms in His bosom; and, for the day of His coming, when shall sound the voice of the archangel and the trumpet of God descending from heaven, He keeps him to restore him to you by His grace.

CHAPTER XV: THE MYSTICS

The schoolmen of the twelfth century thought they could reach God by reason; the Council of Sens, guided by Saint Bernard, replied that the effort was futile and likely to be mischievous. The council made little pretence of knowing or caring what method Abelard followed; they condemned any effort at all on that line; and no sooner had Bernard silenced the Abbot of Saint-Gildas for innovation than he turned about and silenced the Bishop of Poitiers for conservatism. Neither in the twelfth nor in any other century could three men have understood alike the meaning of Gilbert de la Poree, who seems to one high authority unworthy of notice and to another, worthy of an elaborate but quite unintelligible commentary. When M. Rousselet and M. Haureau judge so differently of a voluminous writer, the Council at Rheims which censured Bishop Gilbert in 1148 can hardly have been clear in mind. One dare hazard no more than a guess at Gilbert's offence, but the guess is tolerably safe that he, like Abelard, insisted on discussing and analyzing the Trinity. Gilbert seems to have been a rigid realist, and he reduced to a correct syllogism the idea of the ultimate substance—God. To make theology a system capable of scholastic definition he had to suppose, behind the active deity, a passive abstraction, or absolute substance without attributes; and then the attributes—justice, mercy, and the rest— fell into rank as secondary substances. "Formam dei divinitatem appellant." Bernard answered him by insisting with his usual fiery conviction that the Church should lay down the law, once for all, and inscribe it with iron and diamond, that Divinity—Divine Wisdom —is God. In philosophy and science the question seems to be still open. Whether anything ultimate exists—whether substance is more than a complex of elements—whether the "thing in itself" is a reality or a name—is a question that Faraday and Clerk-Maxwell seem to answer as Bernard did, while Haeckel answers it as Gilbert did; but in theology even a heretic wonders how a doubt was possible. The absolute substance behind the attributes seems to be pure Spinoza.

This supposes that the heretic understands what Gilbert or Haeckel meant, which is certainly a mistake; but it is possible that he may see in part what Bernard meant and this is enough if it is all. Abelard's necessitarianism and Gilbert's Spinozism, if Bernard understood them right, were equally impossible theology, and the Church could by no evasion escape the necessity of condemning both. Unfortunately, Bernard could not put his foot down so roughly on the schools without putting it on Aristotle as well; and, for at least sixty years after the Council of Rheims, Aristotle was either tacitly or expressly prohibited.

One cannot stop to explain why Aristotle himself would have been first to forbid the teaching of what was called by his name in the Middle Ages; but you are bound to remember that this period between 1140 and 1200 was that of Transition architecture and art. One must go to Noyon, Soissons, and Laon to study the Church that trampled on the schools; one must recall how the peasants of Normandy and the Chartrain were crusading for the Virgin in 1145, and building her fleches at Chartres and Saint-Pierre-sur-Dives while Bernard was condemning Gilbert at Rheims in 1148; we must go to the poets to see what they all meant by it; but the sum is an emotion—clear and strong as love and much clearer than logic—whose charm lies in its unstable balance. The Transition is the equilibrium between the love of God—which is faith—and the logic of God—which is reason; between the round arch and the pointed. One may not be sure which pleases most, but one need not be harsh toward people who think that the moment of balance is exquisite. The last and highest moment is seen at Chartres, where, in 1200, the charm depends on the constant doubt whether emotion or science is uppermost. At Amiens, doubt ceases; emotion is trained in school; Thomas Aquinas reigns.

Bernard of Clairvaux and Thomas of Aquino were both artists,—very great artists, if the Church pleases,—and one need not decide which was the greater; but between them is a region of pure emotion—of poetry and art—which is more interesting than either. In every age man has been apt to dream uneasily, rolling from side to side, beating against imaginary bars, unless, tired out, he has sunk into indifference or scepticism. Religious minds prefer scepticism. The true saint is a profound sceptic; a total disbeliever in human reason, who has more than once joined hands on this ground with some who were at best sinners. Bernard was a total disbeliever in scholasticism; so was Voltaire. Bernard brought the society of his time to share his scepticism, but could give the society no other intellectual amusement to relieve its restlessness. His crusade failed; his ascetic enthusiasm faded; God came no nearer. If there was in all France, between 1140 and 1200, a more typical Englishman of the future Church of England type than John of Salisbury, he has left no trace; and John wrote a description of his time which makes a picturesque contrast with the picture painted by Abelard, his old master, of the century at its beginning. John weighed Abelard and the schools against Bernard and the cloister, and coolly concluded that the way to truth led rather through Citeaux, which brought him to Chartres as Bishop in 1176, and to a mild scepticism in faith. "I prefer to doubt," he said, "rather than rashly define what is hidden." The battle with the schools had then resulted only in creating three kinds of sceptics:—the disbelievers in human reason; the passive agnostics; and the sceptics proper, who would have been atheists had they dared. The first class was represented by the School of Saint-Victor; the second by John of Salisbury himself; the third, by a class of schoolmen whom he called Cornificii, as though they made a practice of inventing horns of dilemma on which to fix their opponents; as, for example, they asked whether a pig which was led to market was led by the man or the cord. One asks instantly: What cord?—whether Grace, for instance, or Free Will?

Bishop John used the science he had learned in the school only to reach the conclusion that, if philosophy were a science at all, its best practical use was to teach charity—love. Even the early, superficial debates of the schools, in 1100-50, had so exhausted the subject that the most intelligent men saw how little was to be gained by pursuing further those lines of thought. The twelfth century had already reached the point where the seventeenth century stood when Descartes renewed the attempt to give a solid, philosophical basis for deism by his celebrated "Cogito, ergo sum." Although that ultimate fact seemed new to Europe when Descartes revived it as the starting-point of his demonstration, it was as old and familiar as Saint Augustine to the twelfth century, and as little conclusive as any other assumption of the Ego or the Non-Ego. The schools argued, according to their tastes, from unity to multiplicity, or from multiplicity to unity; but what they wanted was to connect the two. They tried realism and found that it led to pantheism. They tried nominalism and found that it ended in materialism. They attempted a compromise in conceptualism which begged the whole question. Then they lay down, exhausted. In the seventeenth century the same violent struggle broke out again, and wrung from Pascal the famous outcry of despair in which the French language rose, perhaps for the last time, to the grand style of the twelfth century. To the twelfth century it belongs; to the century of faith and simplicity; not to the mathematical certainties of Descartes and Leibnitz and Newton, or to the mathematical abstractions of Spinoza. Descartes had proclaimed his famous conceptual proof of God: "I am conscious of myself, and must exist; I am conscious of God and He must exist." Pascal wearily replied that it was not God he doubted, but logic. He was tortured by the impossibility of rejecting man's reason by reason; unconsciously sceptical, he forced himself to disbelieve in himself rather than admit a doubt of God. Man had tried to prove God, and had failed: "The metaphysical proofs of God are so remote (eloignees) from the reasoning of men, and so contradictory (impliquees, far-fetched) that they make little impression; and even if they served to convince some people, it would only be during the instant that they see the demonstration; an hour afterwards they fear to have deceived themselves." Moreover, this kind of proof could lead only to a speculative knowledge, and to know God only in that way was not to know Him at all. The only way to reach God was to deny the value of reason, and to deny reason was scepticism:—

En voyant l'aveuglement et la misere de l'homme et ces contrarietes etonnantes qui se decouvrent dans sa nature, et regardant tout l'univers muet, et l'homme sans lumiere, abandonne a lui-meme et comme egare dans ce recoin de l'umvers, sans savoir qui l'y a mis, ce qu'il y est venu faire, ce qu'il deviendra en mourant, j'entre en effroi comme un homme qu'on aurait porte endormi dans une ile deserte et effroyable, et qui s'eveillerait sans connaitre ou il est et sans avoir aucun moyen d'en sortir. Et sur cela j'admire comment on n'entre pas en desespoir d'un si miserable etat. Je vois d'autres personnes aupres de moi de semblable nature, et je leur demande s'ils sont mieux instruits que moi, et ils me disent que non Et sur cela, ces miserables egares, ayant regarde autour d'eux, et ayant vu quelques objets plaisants, s'y sont donnes et s'y sont attaches Pour moi je n'ai pu m'y arreter ni me reposer dans la societe de ces personnes, en tout semblables a moi, miserables comme moi, impuissants comme moi. Je vois qu'ils ne m'aideraient pas a mourir, je mourrai seul, il faut donc faire comme si j'etais seul or, si j'etais seul, je ne batirais pas des maisons, je ne m'embarrasserais point dans des occupations tumultuaires, je ne chercherais l'estime de personne, mais je tacherais settlement a decouvrir la verite.

Ainsi, considerant combien il y a d'apparence qu'il y a autre chose que ce que je vois, j'ai recherche si ce Dieu dont tout le monde parle n'aurait pas laisse quelques marques de lui. Je regarde de toutes parts et ne vois partout qu' obscuritd. La nature ne m'offre rien que ne soit matiere de doute et d'inquietude. Si je n'y voyais rien qui marquat une divinite, je me determinerais a n'en rien croire. Si je voyais partout les marques d'un Createur, je me reposerais en paix dans la foi. Mais voyant trop pour nier, et trop peu pour m'assurer, je suis dans un etat a plaindre, et ou j'ai souhaite cent fois que si un Dieu soutient la nature, elle le marquat sans Equivoque; et que, si les marques qu'elle en donne sont trompeuses, elle les supprimat tout a fait; qu'elle dit tout ou rien, afin que je visse quel parti je dois suivre.

When I see the blindness and misery of man and the astonishing contradictions revealed in his nature, and observe the whole universe mute, and man without light, abandoned to himself, as though lost in this corner of the universe, without knowing who put him here, or what he has come here to do, or what will become of him in dying, I feel fear like a man who has been carried when asleep into a desert and fearful island, and has waked without knowing where he is and without having means of rescue. And thereupon I wonder how man escapes despair at so miserable an estate. I see others about me, like myself, and I ask them if they are better informed than I, and they tell me no. And then these wretched wanderers, after looking about them and seeing some pleasant object, have given themselves up and attached themselves to it. As for me I cannot stop there, or rest in the company of these persons, wholly like myself, miserable like me, impotent like me. I see that they would not help me to die, I shall die alone, I must then act as though alone, but if I were alone I should not build houses, I should not fret myself with bustling occupations, I should seek the esteem of no one, but I should try only to discover the truth.

So, considering how much appearance there is that something exists other than what I see I have sought whether this God of Whom every one talks may not have left some marks of Himself. I search everywhere, and see only obscurity everywhere. Nature offers me nothing but matter of possible doubt and disquiet. If I saw there nothing to mark a divinity, I should make up my mind to believe nothing of it. If I saw everywhere the marks of a Creator, I should rest in peace in faith. But seeing too much to deny, and too little to affirm, I am in a pitiable state, where I have an hundred times wishes that, if a God supports nature, she would show it without equivocation; and that, if the marks she gives are deceptive, she would suppress them wholly; that she say all or nothing, that I may see my path.

This is the true Prometheus lyric, but when put back in its place it refuses to rest at Port-Royal which has a right to nothing but precision; it has but one real home—the Abbaye-de-Saint-Victor. The mind that recoils from itself can only commit a sort of ecstatic suicide; it must absorb itself in God; and in the bankruptcy of twelfth-century science the Western Christian seemed actually on the point of attainment; he, like Pascal, touched God behind the veil of scepticism.

The schools had already proved one or two points which need never have been discussed again. In essence, religion was love; in no case was it logic. Reason can reach nothing except through the senses; God, by essence, cannot be reached through the senses; if He is to be known at all, He must be known by contact of spirit with spirit, essence with essence; directly; by emotion; by ecstasy; by absorption of our existence in His; by substitution of his spirit for ours. The world had no need to wait five hundred years longer in order to hear this same result reaffirmed by Pascal. Saint Francis of Assisi had affirmed it loudly enough, even if the voice of Saint Bernard had been less powerful than it was. The Virgin had asserted it in tones more gentle, but any one may still see how convincing, who stops a moment to feel the emotion that lifted her wonderful Chartres spire up to God.

The Virgin, indeed, made all easy, for it was little enough she cared for reason or logic. She cared for her baby, a simple matter, which any woman could do and understand. That, and the grace of God, had made her Queen of Heaven. The Trinity had its source in her,— totius Trinitatis nobile Triclinium,—and she was maternity. She was also poetry and art. In the bankruptcy of reason, she alone was real.

So Guillaume de Champeaux, half a century dead, came to life again in another of his creations. His own Abbey of Saint-Victor, where Abelard had carried on imaginary disputes with him, became the dominant school. As far as concerns its logic, we had best pass it by. The Victorians needed logic only to drive away logicians, which was hardly necessary after Bernard had shut up the schools. As for its mysticism, all training is much alike in idea, whether one follows the six degrees of contemplation taught by Richard of Saint- Victor, or the eightfold noble way taught by Gautama Buddha. The theology of the school was still less important, for the Victorians contented themselves with orthodoxy only in the sense of caring as little for dogma as for dialectics; their thoughts were fixed on higher emotions. Not Richard the teacher, but Adam the poet, represents the school to us, and when Adam dealt with dogma he frankly admitted his ignorance and hinted his indifference; he was, as always, conscientious; but he was not always, or often, as cold. His statement of the Trinity is a marvel; but two verses of it are enough:—

Digne loqui de personis

Vim transcendit rationis,

  Excedit ingenia.

Quid sit gigni, quid processus,

Me nescire sum professus,

  Sed fide non dubia.

Qui sic credit, non festinet,

Et a via non declinet

  Insolenter regia.

Servet fidem, formet mores,

Nec attendat ad errors

  Quos damnat Ecclesia.

Of the Trinity to reason

Leads to license or to treason

  Punishment deserving.

What is birth and what procession

Is not mine to make profession,

  Save with faith unswerving.

Thus professing, thus believing,

Never insolently leaving

> The highway of our faith,
>
> Duty weighing, law obeying,
>
> Never shall we wander straying
>
> Where heresy is death.

Such a school took natural refuge in the Holy Ghost and the Virgin, —Grace and Love,—but the Holy Ghost, as usual, profited by it much less than the Virgin. Comparatively little of Adam's poetry is expressly given to the Saint Esprit, and too large a part of this has a certain flavour of dogma:—

> Qui procedis ab utroque
>
>   Genitore Genitoque
>
>   Pariter, Paraclite!
>
> .... Amor Patris, Filiique
>
> Par amborum et utrique
>
>   Compar et consimilis!

> The Holy Ghost is of the Father and of the
>
> Son; neither made nor created nor begotten,
>
>   but proceeding.
>
> The whole three Persons are coeternal
>
>   together; and coequal.

This sounds like a mere versification of the Creed, yet when Adam ceased to be dogmatic and broke into true prayer, his verse added a lofty beauty even to the Holy Ghost; a beauty too serious for modern rhyme:—

> Oh, juvamen oppressorum,
>
> Oh, solamen miserorum,
>
>   Pauperum refugium,
>
> Da contemptum terrenorum!
>
> Ad amorem supernorum

Trahe desiderium!

Consolator et fundator,

Habitator et amator,

Cordium humilium,

Pelle mala, terge sordes,

Et discordes fac Concordes,

Et affer praesidium!

Oh, helper of the heavy-laden,

Oh, solace of the miserable,

Of the poor, the refuge,

Give contempt of earthly pleasures!

To the love of heavenly treasures

Lift our hearts' desire!

Consolation and foundation,

Dearest friend and habitation

Of the lowly-hearted,

Dispel our evil, cleanse our foulness,

And our discords turn to concord,

And bring us succour!

Adam's scholasticism was the most sympathetic form of mediaeval philosophy. Even in prose, the greatest writers have not often succeeded in stating simply and clearly the fact that infinity can make itself finite, or that space can make itself bounds, or that eternity can generate time. In verse, Adam did it as easily as though he were writing any other miracle,—as Gaultier de Coincy told the Virgin's,—and any one who thinks that the task was as easy as it seems, has only to try it and see whether he can render into a modern tongue any single word which shall retain the whole value of the word which Adam has chosen:—

Ne periret homo reus

Redemptorem misit Deus,

Pater unigenitum;

Visitavit quos amavit

Nosque vitae revocavit

Gratia non meritum.

Infinitus et Immensus,

Quem non capit ullus sensus

Nec locorum spatia,

Ex eterno temporalis,

Ex immenso fit localis,

Ut restauret omnia.

To death condemned by awful sentence,

God recalled us to repentance,

Sending His only Son;

Whom He loved He came to cherish;

Whom His justice doomed to perish,

By grace to life he won.

Infinity, Immensity,

Whom no human eye can see

Or human thought contain,

Made of infinity a space,

Made of Immensity a place,

To win us Life again.

The English verses, compared with the Latin, are poor enough, with the canting jingle of a cheap religion and a thin philosophy, but by contrast and comparison they give higher value to the Latin. One feels the dignity and religious quality of Adam's chants the better for trying to give them an equivalent. One would not care to hazard such experiments on poetry of the highest class like that of Dante and Petrarch, but Adam was conventional both in verse and thought, and aimed at obtaining his effects from the skilful use of the Latin sonorities for the purposes of the chant. With dogma and metaphysics he dealt boldly and even baldly as he was required to do, and successfully as far as concerned the ear or the voice; but poetry was hardly made for dogma; even the Trinity was better expressed mathematically than by rhythm. With the stronger emotions, such as terror, Adam was still conventional, and showed that he thought of the chant more than of the feeling and exaggerated the sound beyond the value of the sense. He could never have written the "Dies Irae." He described the shipwreck of the soul in magnificent sounds without rousing an emotion of fear; the raging waves and winds that swept his bark past the abysses and up to the sky were as conventional as the sirens, the dragons, the dogs, and the pirates that lay in wait. The mast nodded as usual; the sails were rent; the sailors ceased work; all the machinery was classical; only the prayer to the Virgin saved the poetry from sinking like the ship; and yet, when chanted, the effect was much too fine to bear translation:—

Ave, Virgo singularis,

Mater nostri Salutaris,

Quae vocaris Stella Maris,

Stella non erratica;

Nos in hujus vitae mari

Non permitte naufragari,

Sed pro nobis Salutari

Tuo semper supplica!

Saevit mare, fremunt venti,

Fluctus surgunt turbulenti;

Navis currit, sed currenti

Tot occurrunt obvia!

Hic sirenes voluptatis,

Draco, canes cum piratis,

Mortem pene desperatis

Haec intentant omnia.

Post abyssos, nunc ad coelum

Furens unda fert phaselum;

Nutat malus, fluit velum,

Nautae cessat opera;

Contabescit in his malis

Homo noster animalis;

Tu nos, Mater spiritalis,

Pereuntes liberal!

Finer still is the famous stanza sung at Easter, in which Christ rises, the Lion of Judah, in the crash of the burst gates of death, at the roar of the Father Lion:—

Sic de Juda, leo fortis,

Fractis portis dirae mortis,

Die surgens tertia,

Rugiente voce patris

Ad supernae sinum matris

Tot revexit spolia.

For terror or ferocity or images of pain, the art of the twelfth century had no use except to give a higher value to their images of love. The figures on the west portal of Chartres are alive with the spirit of Adam's poetry, but it is the spirit of the Virgin. Like Saint Bernard, Adam lavished his affections on Mary, and even more than Saint Bernard he could claim to be her poet-laureate. Bernard was not himself author of the hymn "Stella Maris" which brought him the honour of the Virgin's personal recognition, but Adam was author of a dozen hymns in which her perfections were told with equal fervour, and which were sung at her festivals. Among these was the famous

Salve, Mater Pietatis,

Et totius Trinitatis

Nobile Triclinium!

a compliment so refined and yet so excessive that the Venerable Thomas Cantimpratensis who died a century later, about 1280, related in his "Apiarium" that when "venerabilis Adam" wrote down these lines, Mary herself appeared to him and bent her head in recognition. Although the manuscripts do not expressly mention this miracle, they do contain, at that stanza, a curious note expressing an opinion, apparently authorized by the prior, that, if the Virgin had seen fit to recognize the salutation of the Venerable Adam in this manner, she would have done only what he merited: "ab ea resalutari et regratiari meruit."

Adam's poems are still on the shelves of most Parisian bookshops, as common as "Aucassins" and better known than much poetry of our own time; for the mediaeval Latin rhymes have a delightful sonority and simplicity that keep them popular because they were not made to be read but to be sung. One does not forget their swing:—

Infinitus et Immensus;

or—

Oh, juvamen oppressorum;

or—

Consolatrix miserorum

 Suscitatrix mortuorum.

The organ rolls through them as solemnly as ever it did in the Abbey Church; but in mediaeval art so much more depends on the mass than on the measure—on the dignity than on the detail—that equivalents are impossible. Even Walter Scott was content to translate only three verses of the "Dies Irae." At best, Viollet-le-Duc could reproduce only a sort of modern Gothic; a more or less effaced or affected echo of a lost emotion which the world never felt but once and never could feel again. Adam composed a number of hymns to the Virgin, and, in them all, the feeling counts for more, by far, than the sense. Supposing we choose the simplest and try to give it a modern version, aiming to show, by comparison, the difference of sound; one can perhaps manage to recover a little of the simplicity, but give it the grand style one cannot; or, at least, if any one has ever done both, it is Walter Scott, and merely by placing side by side the "Dies Irae" and his translation of it, one can see at a glance where he was obliged to sacrifice simplicity only to obtain sound:—

Dies irae, dies illa,

 Solvet seclum in favilla,

 Teste David cum Sibylla.

Quantus tremor est futurus,

 Quando judex est venturus,

 Cuncta stride discussurus!

Tuba mirum spargens sonum

 Per sepulchra regionum,

 Coget omnes ante thronum.

That day of wrath, that dreadful day,

When heaven and earth shall pass away,

What power shall be the sinner's stay?

How shall he meet that dreadful day?

When shrivelling like a parched scroll

The flaming heavens together roll;

When louder yet and yet more dread

Swells the high trump that wakes the dead.

As translation the last line is artificial.

The "Dies Irae" does not belong, in spirit, to the twelfth century; it is sombre and gloomy like the Last Judgments on the thirteenth- century portals; it does not love. Adam loved. His verses express the Virgin; they are graceful, tender, fervent, and they hold the same dignity which cannot be translated:—

In hac valle lacrimarum

  Nihil dulce, nihil carum,

  Suspecta sunt omnia;

  Quid hic nobis erit tutum,

  Cum nec ipsa vel virtutum

  Tuta sit victoria!

Caro nobis adversatur,

  Mundus carni suffragatur

  In nostram perniciem;

  Hostis instat, nos infestans,

  Nunc se palam manifestans,

  Nunc occultans rabiem.

Et peccamus et punimur,

  Et diversis irretimur

Laqueis venantium.

O Maria, mater Dei,

Tu, post Deum, summa spei,

Tu dulce refugium;

Tot et tantis irretiti,

Non valemus his reniti

Ne vi nec industria;

Consolatrix miserorum,

Suscitatrix mortuorum,

Mortis rompe retia!

In this valley full of tears,

Nothing softens, nothing cheers,

All is suspected lure;

What safety can we hope for, here,

When even virtue faints for fear

Her victory be not sure!

Within, the flesh a traitor is,

Without, the world encompasses,

A deadly wound to bring.

The foe is greedy for our spoils,

Now clasping us within his coils,

Or hiding now his sting.

We sin, and penalty must pay,

And we are caught, like beasts of prey,

Within the hunter's snares.

Nearest to God! oh Mary Mother!

Hope can reach us from none other,

Sweet refuge from our cares;

We have no strength to struggle longer,

For our bonds are more and stronger

Than our hearts can bear!

You who rest the heavy-laden,

You who lead lost souls to Heaven,

Burst the hunter's snare!

The art of this poetry of love and hope, which marked the mystics, lay of course in the background of shadows which marked the cloister. "Inter vania nihil vanius est homine." Man is an imperceptible atom always trying to become one with God. If ever modern science achieves a definition of energy, possibly it may borrow the figure: Energy is the inherent effort of every multiplicity to become unity. Adam's poetry was an expression of the effort to reach absorption through love, not through fear; but to do this thoroughly he had to make real to himself his own nothingness; most of all, to annihilate pride; for the loftiest soul can comprehend that an atom,—say, of hydrogen,—which is proud of its personality, will never merge in a molecule of water. The familiar verse: "Oh, why should the spirit of mortal be proud?" echoes Adam's epitaph to this day:—

Haeres peccati, natura filius irae,

Exiliique reus nascitur omnis homo.

Unde superbit homo, cujus conceptio culpa,

Nasci poena, labor vita, necesse mori?

Heir of sin, by nature son of wrath,

Condemned to exile, every man is born.

Whence is man's pride, whose conception fault,

Birth pain, life labour, and whose death is sure?

Four concluding lines, not by him, express him even better:—

Hic ego qui jaceo, miser et miserabilis Adam,

Unam pro summo munere posco precem.

Peccavi, fateor; veniam peto; parce fatenti;

Parce, pater: fratres, parcite; parce, Deus!

One does not conceive that Adam insisted so passionately on his sins because he thought them—or himself—important before the Infinite. Chemistry does not consider an atom of oxygen as in itself important, yet if it wishes to get a volume of pure gas, it must separate the elements. The human soul was an atom that could unite with God only as a simple element. The French mystics showed in their mysticism the same French reasonableness; the sense of measure, of logic, of science; the allegiance to form; the transparency of thought, which the French mind has always shown on its surface like a shell of nacre. The mystics were in substance rather more logical than the schoolmen and much more artistic in their correctness of line and scale. At bottom, French saints were not extravagant. One can imagine a Byzantine asserting that no French saint was ever quite saintly. Their aims and ideals were very high, but not beyond reaching and not unreasonable. Drag the French mind as far from line and logic as space permits, the instant it is freed it springs back to the classic and tries to look consequent.

This paradox, that the French mystics were never mystical, runs through all our travels, so obstinately recurring in architecture, sculpture, legend, philosophy, religion, and poetry, that it becomes tiresome; and yet it is an idea that, in spite of Matthew Arnold and many other great critics, never has got lodgment in the English or German mind, and probably never will. Every one who loves travel will hope that it never may. If you are driven to notice it as the most distinctive mark of French art, it is not at all for the purpose of arguing a doubtful law, but only in order to widen the amusement of travel. We set out to travel from Mont-Saint-Michel to Chartres, and no farther; there we stop; but we may still look across the boundary to Assisi for a specimen of Italian Gothic architecture, a scheme of colour decoration, or still better for a mystic to compare with the Bernadines and Victorians. Every one who knows anything of religion knows that the ideal mystic saint of western Europe was Francis of Assisi, and that Francis, though he loved France, was as far as possible from being French; though not in the least French, he was still the finest flower from the French mediaeval garden; and though the French mystics could never have understood him, he was what the French mystics would have liked to be or would have thought they liked to be as long as they knew him to be not one of themselves. As an Italian or as a Spaniard, Francis was in harmony with his world; as a Frenchman, he would have been out of place even at Clairvaux, and still more among his own Cordeliers at the doors of the Sorbonne.

Francis was born in 1186, at the instant when French art was culminating, or about to culminate, in the new cathedrals of Laon and Chartres, on the ruins of scholastic religion and in the full summer of the Courts of Love. He died in 1226, just as Queen Blanche became Regent of France and when the Cathedral of Beauvais was planned. His life precisely covered the most perfect moment of art and feeling in the thousand years of pure and confident Christianity. To an emotional nature like his, life was still a phantasm or "concept" of crusade against real or imaginary enemies of God, with the "Chanson de Roland" for a sort of evangel, and a feminine ideal for a passion. He chose for his mistress "domina nostra paupertas," and the rules of his order of knighthood were as visionary as those of Saint Bernard were practical. "Isti sunt fratres mei milites tabulae rotundae, qui latitant in desertis"; his Knights of the Round Table hid themselves for their training in deserts of poverty, simplicity, humility, innocence of self, absorption in nature, in the silence of God, and, above all, in love and joy incarnate, whose only influence was example. Poverty of body in itself mattered nothing; what Francis wanted was poverty of pride, and the external robe or the bare feet were outward and necessary forms of protection against its outward display. Against riches or against all external and visible vanity, rules and laws could be easily enforced if it were worth while, although the purest humility would be reached only by those who were indifferent and unconscious of their external dress; but against spiritual pride the soul is defenceless, and of all its forms the subtlest and the meanest is pride of intellect. If "nostra domina paupertas" had a mortal enemy, it was not the pride beneath a scarlet robe, but that in a schoolmaster's ferule, and of all schoolmasters the vainest and most pretentious was the scholastic philosopher. Satan was logic. Lord Bacon held much the same opinion. "I reject the syllogism," was the starting-point of his teaching as it was the essence of Saint Francis's, and the reasons of both men were the same though their action was opposite. "Let men please themselves as they will in admiring and almost adoring the human mind, this is certain:—that, as an uneven mirror distorts the rays of objects according to its own figure and section, so the mind ... cannot be trusted ..." Bacon's first object was the same as that of Francis, to humiliate and if possible destroy the pride of human reason; both of them knew that this was their most difficult task, and Francis, who was charity incarnate, lost his self-control whenever he spoke of the schools, and became almost bitter, as though in constant terror of a poison or a cancer. "Praeodorabat etiam tempora non longe ventura in quibus jam praesciebat scientiam inflativam debere esse occasionem ruinae." He foresaw the time not far off when puffed-up science would be the ruin of his "domina paupertas." His struggle with this form of human pride was desperate and tragical in its instant failure. He could not make even his novices understand what he meant. The most impossible task of the mind is to reject in practice the reflex action of itself, as Bacon pointed out, and only the highest training has sometimes partially succeeded in doing it. The schools—ancient, mediaeval, or modern—have almost equally failed, but even the simple rustics who tried to follow Francis could not see why the rule of poverty should extend to the use of a psalter. Over and over again he explained vehemently and dramatically as only an Italian or a Spaniard could, and still they failed to catch a notion of what he meant.

Quum ergo venisset beatus Franciscus ad locum ubi erat ille novitius, dixit ille novitius: "Pater, mihi esset magna consolatio habere psalterium, sed licet generalis illud mihi concesserit, tamen vellem ipsum habere, pater, de conscientia tua." Cui beatus Franciscus respondit: "Carolus imperator, Rolandus et Oliverus et omnes palatini et robusti viri qui potentes fuerunt in proelio, prosequendo infideles cum multa sudore et labore usque ad mortem, habuerunt de illis victoriara memorialiter, et ad ultimum ipsi sancti martyres sunt mortui pro fide Christi in certamine. Nunc autem multi sunt qui sola narratione eorum quae illi fecerunt volunt recipere honorem et humanam laudem. Ita et inter nos sunt multi qui solum recitando et praedicando opera quae sancti fecerunt volunt recipere honorem et laudem; ... postquam habueris psalterium, concupisces et volueris habere breviarium; et postquam habueris breviarium, sedebis in cathedra tanquam magnus prelatus et dices fratri tuo:—Apporta mihi breviarium!"

Haec autem dicens beatus Franciscus cum magno fervore spiritus accepit de cinere et posuit super caput suum, et ducendo manum super caput suum in circuitu sicut ille qui lavat caput, dicebat: "Ego breviarium! ego breviarium!" et sic reiteravit multoties ducendo manum per caput. Et stupefactus et verecundatus est frater ille ... Elapsis autem pluribus mensibus quum esset beatus Franciscus apud locum sanctae Mariae de Portiuncula, juxta cellam post domum in via, praedictus frater iterum locutus est ei de psalterio. Cui beatus Franciscus dixit: "Vade et facias de hoc sicut dicet tibi minister tuus!" Quo audito, frater ille coepit redire per viam unde venerat. Beatus autem Franciscus remanens in via coepit considerare illud quod dixerat illi fratri, et statim clamavit post cum, dicens: "Expecta me, frater! expecta!" Et ivit usque ad eum et ait illi: "Revertere mecum, frater, et ostende mihi locum ubi dixi tibi quod faceres de psalterio sicut diceret minister tuus." Quum ergo pervenissent ad locum, beatus Franciscus genuflexit coram fratre illo, et dixit: "Mea culpa, frater! mea culpa! quia quicunque vult esse frater Minor non debet habere nisi tunicam, sicut regula sibi concedit, et cordam et femoralia et qui manifesta necessitate coguntur calciamenta."

So when Saint Francis happened to come to the place where the novice was, the novice said: "Father, it would be a great comfort to me to have a psalter, but though my general should grant it, still I would rather have it, father, with your knowledge too." Saint Francis answered: "The Emperor Charlemagne, Roland and Oliver, and all the palatines and strong men who were potent in battle, pursuing the infidels with much toil and sweat even to death, triumphed over them memorably [without writing it?], and at last these holy martyrs died in the contest for the faith of Christ. But now there are many who, merely by telling of what those men did, want to receive honour and human praise. So, too, among us are many who, merely by reciting and preaching the works which the saints have done, want to receive honour and praise; ... After you have got the psalter, you will covet and want a breviary; and after getting the breviary, you will sit on your throne like a bishop, and will say to your brother: 'Bring me the breviary!'"

While saying this, Saint Francis with great vehemence took up a handful of ashes and spread it over his bead; and moving his hand about his head in a circle as though washing it, said: "I, breviary! I, breviary!" and so kept on, repeatedly moving his hand about his head; and stupefied and ashamed was that novice. ... But several months afterwards when Saint Francis happened to be near Sta Maria de Portiuncula, by the cell behind the house on the road, the same brother again spoke to him about the psalter. Saint Francis replied: "Go and do about it as your director says." On this the brother turned back, but Saint Francis, standing in the road, began to reflect on what he had said, and suddenly called after him: "Wait for me, brother! wait!" and going after him, said: "Return with me, brother, and show me the place where I told you to do as your director should say, about the psalter." When they had come back to it, Saint Francis bent before the brother, and said: "Mea culpa, brother, mea culpa! because whoever wishes to be a Minorite must have nothing but a tunic, as the rule permits, and the cord, and the loincloth, and what covering is manifestly necessary for the limbs."

So vivid a picture of an actual mediaeval saint stands out upon this simple background as is hardly to be found elsewhere in all the records of centuries, but if the brother himself did not understand it and was so shamed and stupefied by Francis's vehemence, the world could understand it no better; the Order itself was ashamed of Saint Francis because they understood him too well. They hastened to suppress this teaching against science, although it was the life of Francis's doctrine. He taught that the science of the schools led to perdition because it was puffed up with emptiness and pride. Humility, simplicity, poverty were alone true science. They alone led to heaven. Before the tribunal of Christ, the schoolmen would be condemned, "and, with their dark logic (opinionibus tenebrosis) shall be plunged into outer darkness with the spirits of the darkness." They were devilish, and would perish with the devils.

One sees instantly that neither Francis of Assisi nor Bacon of Verulam could have hoped for peace with the schools; twelfth-century ecstasy felt the futility of mere rhetoric quite as keenly as seventeenth-century scepticism was to feel it; and yet when Francis died in 1226 at Assisi, Thomas was just being born at Aquino some two hundred kilometres to the southward. True scholasticism had not begun. Four hundred years seem long for the human mind to stand still— or go backward; the more because the human mind was never better satisfied with itself than when thus absorbed in its mirror; but with that chapter we have nothing to do. The pleasantest way to treat it was that of Saint Francis; half-serious, half-jesting; as though, after all, in the thought of infinity, four hundred years were at most only a serio-comic interlude. At Assisi, once, when a theologian attacked Fra Egidio by the usual formal arraignment in syllogisms, the brother waited until the conclusions were laid down, and then, taking out a flute from the folds of his robe, he played his answer in rustic melodies. The soul of Saint Francis was a rustic melody and the simplest that ever reached so high an expression. Compared with it, Theocritus and Virgil are as modern as Tennyson and ourselves.

All this shows only what Saint Francis was not; to understand what he was and how he goes with Saint Bernard and Saint Victor through the religious idyll of Transition architecture, one must wander about Assisi with the "Floretum" or "Fioretti" in one's hand;—the legends which are the gospel of Francis as the evangels are the gospel of Christ, who was reincarnated in Assisi. We have given a deal of time to showing our own sceptical natures how simple the architects and decorators of Chartres were in their notions of the Virgin and her wants; but French simple-mindedness was already complex compared with Italian. The Virgin was human; Francis was elementary nature itself, like sun and air; he was Greek in his joy of life:—

… Recessit inde et venit inter Cannarium et Mevanium. Et respexit quasdam arbores juxta viam in quibus residebat tanta multitudo avium diversarum quod nunquam in partibus illis visa similis multitudo. In campo insuper juxta praedictas arbores etiam multitudo maxima residebat. Quam multitudinem sanctus Franciscus respiciens et admirans, facto super eum Spiritu Dei, dixit sociis: "Vobis hic me in via exspectantibus, ibo et praedicabo sororibus nostris aviculis." Et intravit in campum ad aves quae residebant in terra. Et statim quum praedicare incepit omnes aves in arboribus residentes descenderunt ad eum et simul cum aliis de campo immobiles perman serunt, quum tamen ipse inter eas iret plurimas tunica contingendo. Et nulla earum penitus movebatur, sicut recitavit frater Jacobus de Massa, sanctus homo, qui omnia supradicta habuit ab ore fratris Massei, qui fuit unus de iis qui tune erant socii sancti patris.

Quibus avibus sanctus Franciscus ait: "Multum tenemini Deo, sorores meas aves, et debetis eum semper et ubique laudare propter liberum quem ubique habetis volatum, propter vestitum duplicatum et triplicatum, propter habitum pictum et ornatum, propter victum sine vestro labore paratum, propter cantum a Creatore vobis intimatum, propter numerum ex Dei benedictione multiplicatum, propter semen vestrum a Deo in area reservatum, propter elementum aeris vobis deputatum. Vos non seminatis neque metitis, et Deus vos pascit; et dedit vobis flumina et fontes ad potandum, montes et colles, saxa et ibices ad refugium, et arbores altes ad nidificandum; et quum nec filare nec texere sciatis, praebet tam vobis quam vestris filiis necessarium indumentum. Unde multum diligit vos Creator qui tot beneficia contulit. Quapropter cavete, sorores mes aviculae, ni sitis ingratae sed semper laudare Deum studete."

… He departed thence and came between Cannara and Bevagna; and near the road he saw some trees on which perched so great a number of birds as never in those parts had been seen the like. Also in the field beyond, near these same trees, a very great multitude rested on the ground. This multitude, Saint Francis seeing with wonder, the spirit of God descending on him he said to his companions: "Wait for me on the road, while I go and preach to our sisters the little birds." And he went into the field where the birds were on the ground. And as soon as he began to preach, all the birds in the trees came down to him and with those in the field stood quite still, even when he went among them touching many with his robe. Not one of them moved, as Brother James of Massa related, a saintly man who had the whole story from the mouth of Brother Masseo who was one of those then with the sainted father.

To these birds, Saint Francis said: "Much are you bound to God, birds, my sisters, and everywhere and always must you praise him for the free flight you everywhere have; for the double and triple covering; for the painted and decorated robe; for the food prepared without your labour; for the song taught you by the Creator; for your number multiplied by God's blessing; for your seed preserved by God in the ark; for the element of air allotted to you. You neither sow nor reap, and God feeds you; and has given you rivers and springs to drink at, mountains and hills, rocks and wild goats for refuge, and high trees for nesting; and though you know neither how to spin nor to weave, He gives both you and your children all the garments you need. Whence much must the Creator love you, Who confers so many blessings. Therefore take care, my small bird sisters, never to be ungrateful, but always strive to praise God."

Fra Ugolino, or whoever wrote from the dictation of Brother James of Massa, after the tradition of Brother Masseo of Marignano reported Saint Francis's sermon in absolute good faith as Saint Francis probably made it and as the birds possibly received it. All were God's creatures, brothers and sisters, and God alone knew or knows whether or how far they understand each other; but Saint Francis, in any case, understood them and believed that they were in sympathy with him. As far as the birds or wolves were concerned, it was no great matter, but Francis did not stop with vertebrates or even with organic forms. "Nor was it surprising," said the "Speculum," "if fire and other creatures sometimes revered and obeyed him; for, as we who were with him very frequently saw, he held them in such affection and so much delighted in them, and his soul was moved by such pity and compassion for them, that he would not see them roughly handled, and talked with them with such evident delight as if they were rational beings":—

Nam quadam vice, quum sederet juxta ignem, ipso nesciente, ignis invasit pannos ejus de lino, sive brachas, juxta genu, quumque sentiret calorem ejus nolebat ipsum extinguere. Socius autem ejus videns comburi pannos ejus cucurrit ad eum volens extinguere ignem; ipse vero prohibuit ei, dicens: "Noli, frater, carissime, noli male facere igni!" Et sic nullo modo voluit quod extingueret ipsum. Ille vero festinanter ivit ad fratrem qui erat guardianus ipsius, et duxit eum ad beatum Franciscum, et statim contra voluntatem beati Francisci, extinxit ignem. Unde quacunque necessitate urgente nunquam voluit extinguere ignem vel lampadem vel candelam, tantum pietate movebatur ad ipsum. Nolebat etiam quod frater projiceret ignem vel lignum fumigantem de loco ad locum sicut solet fieri, sed volebat ut plane poneret ipsum in terra ob reverentiam illius cujus est creatura.

For once when he was sitting by the fire, a spark, without his knowing it, caught his linen drawers and set them burning near the knee, and when he felt the heat he would not extinguish it; but his companion, seeing his clothes on fire, ran to put it out, and he forbade it, saying: "Don't, my dearest brother, don't hurt the fire!" So he utterly refused to let him put it out, and the brother hurried off to get his guardian, and brought him to Saint Francis, and together they put out the fire at once against Saint Francis's will. So, no matter what the necessity, he would never put out fire or a lamp or candle, so strong was his feeling for it; he would not even let a brother throw fire or a smoking log from place to place, as is usual, but wanted it placed gently (piano) on the ground, out of respect for Him Whose creature it is.

The modern tourist, having with difficulty satisfied himself that Saint Francis acted thus in good faith, immediately exclaims that he was a heretic and should have been burned; but, in truth, the immense popular charm of Saint Francis, as of the Virgin, was precisely his heresies. Both were illogical and heretical by essence;—in strict discipline, in the days of the Holy Office, a hundred years later, both would have been burned by the Church, as Jeanne d'Arc was, with infinitely less reason, in 1431. The charm of the twelfth-century Church was that it knew how to be illogical—no great moral authority ever knew it better—when God Himself became illogical. It cared no more than Saint Francis, or Lord Bacon, for the syllogism. Nothing in twelfth-century art is so fine as the air and gesture of sympathetic majesty with which the Church drew aside to let the Virgin and Saint Francis pass and take the lead—for a time. Both were human ideals too intensely realized to be resisted merely because they were illogical. The Church bowed and was silent.

This does not concern us. What the Church thought or thinks is its own affair, and what it chooses to call orthodox is orthodox. We have been trying only to understand what the Virgin and Saint Francis thought, which is matter of fact, not of faith. Saint Francis was even more outspoken than the Virgin. She calmly set herself above dogma, and, with feminine indifference to authority, overruled it. He, having asserted in the strongest terms the principle of obedience, paid no further attention to dogma, but, without the least reticence, insisted on practices and ideas that no Church could possibly permit or avow. Toward the end of his life, his physician cauterized his face for some neuralgic pain:—

Et posito ferro in igne pro coctura fienda, beatus Franciscus volens confortare spiritum suum ne pavesceret, sic locutus est ad ignem: "Frater mi, ignis, nobilis et utilis inter alias creaturas, esto mihi curialis in hac hora quia olim te dilexi et diligam amore illius qui creavit te. Deprecor etiam creatorem nostrum qui nos creavit ut ita tuum calorem temperet ut ipsum sustinere valeam." Et oratione finita signavit ignem signo crucis.

When the iron was put on the fire for making the cotterie, Saint Francis, wishing to encourage himself against fear, spoke thus to the fire: "My brother, fire, noblest and usefullest of creatures, be gentle to me now, because I have loved and will love you with the love of Him who created you. Our Creator, too, Who created us both, I implore so to temper your heat that I may have strength to bear it." And having spoken, he signed the fire with the cross.

With him, this was not merely a symbol. Children and saints can believe two contrary things at the same time, but Saint Francis had also a complete faith of his own which satisfied him wholly. All nature was God's creature. The sun and fire, air and water, were neither more nor less brothers and sisters than sparrows, wolves, and bandits. Even "daemones sunt castalli Domini nostri"; the devils are wardens of our Lord. If Saint Francis made any exception from his univeral law of brotherhood it was that of the schoolmen, but it was never expressed. Even in his passionate outbreak, in the presence of Saint Dominic, at the great Chapter of his Order at Sancta Maria de Portiuncula in 1218, he did not go quite to the length of denying the brotherhood of schoolmen, although he placed them far below the devils, and yet every word of this address seems to sob with the anguish of his despair at the power of the school anti-Christ:—

Quum beatus Franciscus esset in capitulo generali apud Sanctam Mariam de Portiuncula ... et fuerunt ibi quinque millia fratres, quamplures fratres sapientes et scientiati iverunt ad dominum Ostiensem qui erat ibidem, et dixerunt ei: "Domine, volumus ut suadetis fratri Francisco quod sequatur consilium fratrum sapientium et permittat se interdum duci ab eis." Et allegabant regulam sancti Benedicti, Augustini et Bernardi qui docent sic et sic vivere ordinate. Quae omnia quum retulisset cardinalis beato Francisco per modum admoni admonitionis, beatus Franciscus, nihil sibi respondens, cepit ipsum per manum et duxit eum ad fratres congregatos in capitulo, et sic locutus est fratribus in fervore et virtute Spirit us sancti:—

"Fratres mei, fratres mei, Dominus vocavit me per viam simplicitatis et humilitatis, et bane viam ostendit mini in veritate pro me et pro illis qui volunt mini credere et imitari. Et ideo volo quod non nominetis mihi aliquam regulam neque sancti Benedicti neque sancti Augustini neque sancti Bernardi, neque aliquam viam et formam vivendi praeter illam quae mihi a Domino est ostensa misericorditer et donata. Et dixit mihi Dominus quod volebat me esse unum pauperem et stultum idiotam [magnum fatuum] in hoc mundo et noluit nos ducere per viam aliam quam per istam scientiam. Sed per vestram scientiam et sapientiam Deus vos confundet et ego confido in castallis Domini [idest dasmonibus] quod per ipsos puniet vos Deus et adhuc redibitis ad vestrum statum cum vituperio vestro velitis nolitis."

When Saint Francis was at the General Chapter held at Sancta maris de Portiuncula ... and five thousand brothers were present, A number of them who were schoolmen went to Cardinal Hugolino who was there, and said to him: "My lord, we want you to persuade Brother Francis to follow the council of the learned brothers, and sometimes let himself be guided by them." And they suggested the rule of Saint Benedict or Augustine or Bernard who require their congregations to live so and so, by regulation. When the cardinal had repeated all this to Saint Francis by way of counsel, Saint Francis, making no answer, took him by the hand and led him to the brothers assembled in Chapter, and in the fervour and virtue of the Holy Ghost, spoke thus to the brothers:

"My brothers, my brothers, God has called me by way of simplicity and humility, and has shown me in verity this path for me and those who want to believe and follow me; so I want you to talk of no Rule to me, neither Saint Benedict nor Saint Augustine nor Saint Bernard, nor any way or form of Life whatever except that which God has mercifully pointed out and granted to me. And God said that he wanted me to be a pauper [poverello] and an idiot—a great fool—in this world, and would not lead us by any other path of science than this. But by your science and syllogisms God will confound you, and I trust in God's warders, the devils, that through them God shall punish you, and you will yet come back to your proper station with shame, whether you will or no."

The narration continues: "Tunc cardinalis obstupuit valde et nihil respondit. Et omnes fratres plurimum timuerunt."

One feels that the reporter has not exaggerated a word; on the contrary, he softened the scandal, because in his time the Cardinal had gained his point, and Francis was dead. One can hear Francis beginning with some restraint, and gradually carried away by passion till he lost control of himself and his language: "'God told me, with his own words, that he meant me to be a beggar and a great fool, and would not have us on any other terms; and as for your science, I trust in God's devils who will beat you out of it, as you deserve.' And the Cardinal was utterly dumbfounded and answered nothing; and all the brothers were scared to death." The Cardinal Hugolino was a great schoolman, and Dominic was then founding the famous order in which the greatest of all doctors, Albertus Magnus, was about to begin his studies. One can imagine that the Cardinal "obstupuit valde," and that Dominic felt shaken in his scheme of school instruction. For a single instant, in the flash of Francis's passion, the whole mass of five thousand monks in a state of semi- ecstasy recoiled before the impassable gulf that opened between them and the Church.

No one was to blame—no one ever is to blame—because God wanted contradictory things, and man tried to carry out, as he saw them, God's trusts. The schoolmen saw their duty in one direction; Francis saw his in another; and, apparently, when both lines had been carried, after such fashion as might be, to their utmost results, and five hundred years had been devoted to the effort, society declared both to be failures. Perhaps both may some day be revived, for the two paths seem to be the only roads that can exist, if man starts by taking for granted that there is an object to be reached at the end of his journey. The Church, embracing all mankind, had no choice but to march with caution, seeking God by every possible means of intellect and study. Francis, acting only for himself, could throw caution aside and trust implicitly in God, like the children who went on crusade. The two poles of social and political philosophy seem necessarily to be organization or anarchy; man's intellect or the forces of nature. Francis saw God in nature, if he did not see nature in God; as the builders of Chartres saw the Virgin in their apse. Francis held the simplest and most childlike form of pantheism. He carried to its last point the mystical union with God, and its necessary consequence of contempt and hatred for human intellectual processes. Even Saint Bernard would have thought his ideas wanting in that "mesure" which the French mind so much prizes. At the same time we had best try, as innocently as may be, to realize that no final judgment has yet been pronounced, either by the Church or by society or by science, on either or any of these points; and until mankind finally settles to a certainty where it means to go, or whether it means to go anywhere,—what its object is, or whether it has an object,—Saint Francis may still prove to have been its ultimate expression. In that case, his famous chant— the "Cantico del Sole"—will be the last word of religion, as it was probably its first. Here it is—too sincere for translation:—

CANTICO DEL SOLE

… Laudato sie, misignore, con tucte le tue creature spetialmente messor lo frate sole lo quale iorno et allumini noi per loi et ellu e bellu e radiante cum grande splendore de te, altissimo, porta significatione.

Laudato si, misignore, per sora luna e le stelle

in celu lai formate clarite et pretiose et belle.

Laudato si, misignore, per frate vento

et per aere et nubilo et sereno et onne tempo

per lo quale a le tue creature dai sustentamento.

Laudato si, misignore, per sor aqua

la quale e multo utile et humile et pretiosa et casta.

Laudato si, misignore, per frate focu

per lo quale enallumini la nocte

ed ello e bello et jocondo et robustoso et forte.

Laudato si, misignore, per sora nostra matre terra la quale ne sustenta et governa et produce diversi fructi con coloriti flori et herba.......................Laudato si, misignore, per sora nostra morte corporale de la quale nullu homo vivente po skappare guai acquelli ke morrano ne le peccata mortali....

The verses, if verses they are, have little or nothing in common with the art of Saint Bernard or Adam of Saint-Victor. Whatever art they have, granting that they have any, seems to go back to the cave-dwellers and the age of stone. Compared with the naivete of the "Cantico del Sole," the "Chanson de Roland" or the "Iliad" is a triumph of perfect technique. The value is not in the verse. The "Chant of the Sun" is another "Pons Seclorum"—or perhaps rather a "Pons Sanctorum"—over which only children and saints can pass. It is almost a paraphrase of the sermon to the birds. "Thank you, mi signore, for messor brother sun, in especial, who is your symbol; and for sister moon and the stars; and for brother wind and air and sky; and for sister water; and for brother fire; and for mother earth! We are all yours, mi signore! We are your children; your household; your feudal family! but we never heard of a Church. We are all varying forms of the same ultimate energy; shifting symbols of the same absolute unity; but our only unity, beneath you, is nature, not law! We thank you for no human institutions, even for those established in your name; but, with all our hearts we thank you for sister our mother Earth and its fruits and coloured flowers!"

Francis loved them all—the brothers and sisters—as intensely as a child loves the taste and smell of a peach, and as simply; but behind them remained one sister whom no one loved, and for whom, in his first verses, Francis had rendered no thanks. Only on his death-bed he added the lines of gratitude for "our sister death," the long-sought, never-found sister of the schoolmen, who solved all philosophy and merged multiplicity in unity. The solution was at least simple; one must decide for one's self, according to one's personal standards, whether or not it is more sympathetic than that with which we have got lastly to grapple in the works of Saint Thomas Aquinas.

CHAPTER XVI: SAINT THOMAS AQUINAS

Long before Saint Francis's death, in 1226, the French mystics had exhausted their energies and the siecle had taken new heart. Society could not remain forever balancing between thought and act. A few gifted natures could absorb themselves in the absolute, but the rest lived for the day, and needed shelter and safety. So the Church bent again to its task, and bade the Spaniard Dominic arm new levies with the best weapons of science, and flaunt the name of Aristotle on the Church banners along with that of Saint Augustine. The year 1215, which happened to be the date of Magna Charta and other easily fixed events, like the birth of Saint Louis, may serve to mark the triumph of the schools. The pointed arch revelled at Rheims and the Gothic architects reached perfection at Amiens just as Francis died at Assisi and Thomas was born at Aquino. The Franciscan Order itself was swept with the stream that Francis tried to dam, and the great Franciscan schoolman, Alexander Hales, in 1222, four years before the death of Francis, joined the order and began lecturing as though Francis himself had lived only to teach scholastic philosophy.

The rival Dominican champion, Albertus Magnus, began his career a little later, in 1228. Born of the noble Swabian family of Bollstadt, in 1193, he drifted, like other schoolmen, to Paris, and the Rue Maitre Albert, opposite Notre Dame, still records his fame as a teacher there. Thence he passed to a school established by the order at Cologne, where he was lecturing with great authority in 1243 when the general superior of the order brought up from Italy a young man of the highest promise to be trained as his assistant.

Thomas, the new pupil, was born under the shadow of Monte Cassino in 1226 or 1227. His father, the Count of Aquino, claimed descent from the imperial line of Swabia; his mother, from the Norman princes of Sicily; so that in him the two most energetic strains in Europe met. His social rank was royal, and the order set the highest value on it. He took the vows in 1243, and went north at once to help Albertus at Cologne. In 1245, the order sent Albertus back to Paris, and Thomas with him. There he remained till 1248 when he was ordered to Cologne as assistant lecturer, and only four years afterwards, at twenty-five years old, he was made full professor at Paris. His industry and activity never rested till his death in 1274, not yet fifty years old, when he bequeathed to the Church a mass of manuscript that tourists will never know enough to estimate except by weight. His complete works, repeatedly printed, fill between twenty and thirty quarto volumes. For so famous a doctor, this is almost meagre. Unfortunately his greatest work, the "Summa Theologiae," is unfinished—like Beauvais Cathedral.

Perhaps Thomas's success was partly due to his memory which is said to have been phenomenal; for, in an age when cyclopaedias were unknown, a cyclopaedic memory must have counted for half the battle in these scholastic disputes where authority could be met only by authority; but in this case, memory was supported by mind. Outwardly Thomas was heavy and slow in manner, if it is true that his companions called him "the big dumb ox of Sicily"; and in fashionable or court circles he did not enjoy reputation for acute sense of humour. Saint Louis's household offers a picture not wholly clerical, least of all among the King's brothers and sons; and perhaps the dinner-table was not much more used then than now to abrupt interjections of theology into the talk about hunting and hounds; but however it happened, Thomas one day surprised the company by solemnly announcing—"I have a decisive argument against the Manicheans!" No wit or humour could be more to the point— between two saints that were to be—than a decisive argument against enemies of Christ, and one greatly regrets that the rest of the conversation was not reported, unless, indeed, it is somewhere in the twenty-eight quarto volumes; but it probably lacked humour for courtiers.

The twenty-eight quarto volumes must be closed books for us. None but Dominicans have a right to interpret them. No Franciscan—or even Jesuit—understands Saint Thomas exactly or explains him with authority. For summer tourists to handle these intricate problems in a theological spirit would be altogether absurd; but, for us, these great theologians were also architects who undertook to build a Church Intellectual, corresponding bit by bit to the Church Administrative, both expressing—and expressed by—the Church Architectural. Alexander Hales, Albert the Great, Thomas Aquinas, Duns Scotus, and the rest, were artists; and if Saint Thomas happens to stand at their head as type, it is not because we choose him or understand him better than his rivals, but because his order chose him rather than his master Albert, to impose as authority on the Church; and because Pope John XXII canonized him on the ground that his decisions were miracles; and because the Council of Trent placed his "Summa" among the sacred books on their table; and because Innocent VI said that his doctrine alone was sure; and finally, because Leo XIII very lately made a point of declaring that, on the wings of Saint Thomas's genius, human reason has reached the most sublime height it can probably ever attain.

Although the Franciscans, and, later, the Jesuits, have not always shown as much admiration as the Dominicans for the genius of Saint Thomas, and the mystics have never shown any admiration whatever for the philosophy of the schools, the authority of Leo XIII is final, at least on one point and the only one that concerns us. Saint Thomas is still alive and overshadows as many schools as he ever did; at all events, as many as the Church maintains. He has outlived Descartes and Leibnitz and a dozen other schools of philosophy more or less serious in their day. He has mostly outlived Hume, Voltaire, and the militant sceptics. His method is typical and classic; his sentences, when interpreted by the Church, seem, even to an untrained mind, intelligible and consistent; his Church Intellectual remains practically unchanged, and, like the Cathedral of Beauvais, erect, although the storms of six or seven centuries have prostrated, over and over again, every other social or political or juristic shelter. Compared with it, all modern systems are complex and chaotic, crowded with self-contradictions, anomalies, impracticable functions and outworn inheritances; but beyond all their practical shortcomings is their fragmentary character. An economic civilization troubles itself about the universe much as a hive of honey-bees troubles about the ocean, only as a region to be avoided. The hive of Saint Thomas sheltered God and man, mind and matter, the universe and the atom, the one and the multiple, within the walls of an harmonious home.

Theologians, like architects, were supposed to receive their Church complete in all its lines; they were modern judges who interpreted the laws but never invented it. Saint Thomas merely selected between disputed opinions, but he allowed himself to wander very far afield, indeed, in search of opinions to dispute. The field embraced all that existed, or might have existed, or could never exist. The immense structure rested on Aristotle and Saint Augustine at the last, but as a work of art it stood alone, like Rheims or Amiens Cathedral, as though it had no antecedents. Then, although, like Rheims, its style was never meant to suit modern housekeeping and is ill-seen by the Ecole des Beaux Arts, it reveals itself in its great mass and intelligence as a work of extraordinary genius; a system as admirably proportioned as any cathedral and as complete; a success not universal either in art or science.

Saint Thomas's architecture, like any other work of art, is best studied by itself as though he created it outright; otherwise a tourist would never get beyond its threshold. Beginning with the foundation which is God and God's active presence in His Church, Thomas next built God into the walls and towers of His Church, in the Trinity and its creation of mind and matter in time and space; then finally he filled the Church by uniting mind and matter in man, or man's soul, giving to humanity a free will that rose, like the fleche, to heaven. The foundation—the structure—the congregation— are enough for students of art; his ideas of law, ethics, and politics; his vocabulary, his syllogisms, his arrangement are, like the drawings of Villard de Honnecourt's sketch-book, curious but not vital. After the eleventh-century Romanesque Church of Saint Michael came the twelfth-century Transition Church of the Virgin, and all merged and ended at last in the thirteenth-century Gothic Cathedral of the Trinity. One wants to see the end.

The foundation of the Christian Church should be—as the simple deist might suppose—always the same, but Saint Thomas knew better. His foundation was Norman, not French; it spoke the practical architect who knew the mathematics of his art, and who saw that the foundation laid by Saint Bernard, Saint Victor, Saint Francis, the whole mystical, semi-mystical, Cartesian, Spinozan foundation, past or future, could not bear the weight of the structure to be put on it. Thomas began by sweeping the ground clear of them. God must be a concrete thing, not a human thought. God must be proved by the senses like any other concrete thing; "nihil est in intellectu quin prius fuerit in sensu"; even if Aristotle had not affirmed the law, Thomas would have discovered it. He admitted at once that God could not be taken for granted.

The admission, as every boy-student of the Latin Quarter knew, was exceedingly bold and dangerous. The greatest logicians commonly shrank from proving unity by multiplicity. Thomas was one of the greatest logicians that ever lived; the question had always been at the bottom of theology; he deliberately challenged what every one knew to be an extreme peril. If his foundation failed, his Church fell. Many critics have thought that he saw dangers four hundred years ahead. The time came, about 1650-1700, when Descartes, deserting Saint Thomas, started afresh with the idea of God as a concept, and at once found himself charged with a deity that contained the universe; nor did the Cartesians—until Spinoza made it clear—seem able or willing to see that the Church could not accept this deity because the Church required a God who caused the universe. The two deities destroyed each other. One was passive; the other active. Thomas warned Descartes of a logical quicksand which must necessarily swallow up any Church, and which Spinoza explored to the bottom. Thomas said truly that every true cause must be proved as a cause, not merely as a sequence; otherwise they must end in a universal energy or substance without causality—a source.

Whatever God might be to others, to His Church he could not be a sequence or a source. That point had been admitted by William of Champeaux, and made the division between Christians and infidels. On the other hand, if God must be proved as a true cause in order to warrant the Church or the State in requiring men to worship Him as Creator, the student became the more curious—if a churchman, the more anxious—to be assured that Thomas succeeded in his proof, especially since he did not satisfy Descartes and still less Pascal. That the mystics should be dissatisfied was natural enough, since they were committed to the contrary view, but that Descartes should desert was a serious blow which threw the French Church into consternation from which it never quite recovered.

"I see motion," said Thomas: "I infer a motor!" This reasoning, which may be fifty thousand years old, is as strong as ever it was; stronger than some more modern inferences of science; but the average mechanic stated it differently. "I see motion," he admitted: "I infer energy. I see motion everywhere; I infer energy everywhere." Saint Thomas barred this door to materialism by adding: "I see motion; I cannot infer an infinite series of motors: I can only infer, somewhere at the end of the series, an intelligent, fixed motor." The average modern mechanic might not dissent but would certainly hesitate. "No doubt!" he might say; "we can conduct our works as well on that as on any other theory, or as we could on no theory at all; but, if you offer it as proof, we can only say that we have not yet reduced all motion to one source or all energies to one law, much less to one act of creation, although we have tried our best." The result of some centuries of experiment tended to raise rather than silence doubt, although, even in his own day, Thomas would have been scandalized beyond the resources of his Latin had Saint Bonaventure met him at Saint Louis's dinner-table and complimented him, in the King's hearing, on having proved, beyond all Franciscan cavils, that the Church Intellectual had necessarily but one first cause and creator—himself.

The Church Intellectual, like the Church Architectural, implied not one architect, but myriads, and not one fixed, intelligent architect at the end of the series, but a vanishing vista without a beginning at any definite moment; and if Thomas pressed his argument, the twentieth-century mechanic who should attend his conferences at the Sorbonne would be apt to say so. "What is the use of trying to argue me into it? Your inference may be sound logic, but is not proof. Actually we know less about it than you did. All we know is the thing we handle, and we cannot handle your fixed, intelligent prime motor. To your old ideas of form we have added what we call force, and we are rather further than ever from reducing the complex to unity. In fact, if you are aiming to convince me, I will tell you flatly that I know only the multiple, and have no use for unity at all."

In the thirteenth century men did not depend so much as now on actual experiment, but the nominalist said in effect the same thing. Unity to him was a pure concept, and any one who thought it real would believe that a triangle was alive and could walk on its legs. Without proving unity, philosophers saw no way to prove God. They could only fall back on an attempt to prove that the concept of unity proved itself, and this phantasm drove the Cartesians to drop Thomas's argument and assert that "the mere fact of having within us the idea of a thing more perfect than ourselves, proves the real existence of that thing." Four hundred years earlier Saint Thomas had replied in advance that Descartes wanted to prove altogether too much, and Spinoza showed mathematically that Saint Thomas had been in the right. The finest religious mind of the time—Pascal— admitted it and gave up the struggle, like the mystics of Saint- Victor.

Thus some of the greatest priests and professors of the Church, including Duns Scotus himself, seemed not wholly satisfied that Thomas's proof was complete, but most of them admitted that it was the safest among possible foundations, and that it showed, as architecture, the Norman temper of courage and caution. The Norman was ready to run great risks, but he would rather grasp too little than too much; he narrowed the spacing of his piers rather than spread them too wide for safe vaulting. Between Norman blood and Breton blood was a singular gap, as Renan and every other Breton has delighted to point out. Both Abelard and Descartes were Breton. The Breton seized more than he could hold; the Norman took less than he would have liked.

God, then, is proved. What the schools called form, what science calls energy, and what the intermediate period called the evidence of design, made the foundation of Saint Thomas's cathedral. God is an intelligent, fixed prime motor—not a concept, or proved by concepts;—a concrete fact, proved by the senses of sight and touch. On that foundation Thomas built. The walls and vaults of his Church were more complex than the foundation; especially the towers were troublesome. Dogma, the vital purpose of the Church, required support. The most weighty dogma, the central tower of the Norman cathedral, was the Trinity, and between the Breton solution which was too heavy, and the French solution which was too light, the Norman Thomas found a way. Remembering how vehemently the French Church, under Saint Bernard, had protected the Trinity from all interference whatever, one turns anxiously to see what Thomas said about it; and unless one misunderstands him,—as is very likely, indeed, to be the case, since no one may even profess to understand the Trinity,—Thomas treated it as simply as he could. "God, being conscious of Himself, thinks Himself; his thought is Himself, his own reflection in the Verb—the so-called Son." "Est in Deo intelligente seipsum Verbum Dei quasi Deus intellectus." The idea was not new, and as ideas went it was hardly a mystery; but the next step was naif:—God, as a double consciousness, loves Himself, and realizes Himself in the Holy Ghost. The third side of the triangle is love or grace.

Many theologians have found fault with this treatment of the subject, which seemed open to every objection that had been made to Abelard, Gilbert de la Poree, or a thousand other logicians. They commonly asked why Thomas stopped the Deity's self-realizations at love, or inside the triangle, since these realizations were real, not symbolic, and the square was at least as real as any other combination of line. Thomas replied that knowledge and will—the Verb and the Holy Ghost—were alone essential. The reply did not suit every one, even among doctors, but since Saint Thomas rested on this simple assertion, it is no concern of ours to argue the theology. Only as art, one can afford to say that the form is more architectural than religious; it would surely have been suspicious to Saint Bernard. Mystery there was none, and logic little. The concept of the Holy Ghost was childlike; for a pupil of Aristotle it was inadmissible, since it led to nothing and helped no step toward the universe.

Admitting, if necessary, the criticism, Thomas need not admit the blame, if blame there were. Every theologian was obliged to stop the pursuit of logic by force, before it dragged him into paganism and pantheism. Theology begins with the universal,—God,—who must be a reality, not a symbol; but it is forced to limit the process of God's realizations somewhere, or the priest soon becomes a worshipper of God in sticks and stones. Theologians had commonly chosen, from time immemorial, to stop at the Trinity; within the triangle they were wholly realist; but they could not admit that God went on to realize Himself in the square and circle, or that the third member of the Trinity contained multiplicity, because the Trinity was a restless weight on the Church piers, which, like the central tower, constantly tended to fall, and needed to be lightened. Thomas gave it the lightest form possible, and there fixed it.

Then came his great tour-de-force, the vaulting of his broad nave; and, if ignorance is allowed an opinion, even a lost soul may admire the grand simplicity of Thomas's scheme. He swept away the horizontal lines altogether, leaving them barely as a part of decoration. The whole weight of his arches fell, as in the latest Gothic, where the eye sees nothing to break the sheer spring of the nervures, from the rosette on the keystone a hundred feet above down to the church floor. In Thomas's creation nothing intervened between God and his world; secondary causes become ornaments; only two forces, God and man, stood in the Church.

The chapter of Creation is so serious, and Thomas's creation, like every other, is open to so much debate, that no student can allow another to explain it; and certainly no man whatever, either saint or sceptic, can ever yet have understood Creation aright unless divinely inspired; but whatever Thomas's theory was as he meant it, he seems to be understood as holding that every created individual— animal, vegetable, or mineral—was a special, divine act. Whatever has form is created, and whatever is created takes form directly from the will of God, which is also his act. The intermediate universals—the secondary causes—vanish as causes; they are, at most, sequences or relations; all merge in one universal act of will; instantaneous, infinite, eternal.

Saint Thomas saw God, much as Milton saw him, resplendent in

> That glorious form, that light unsufferable,
>
> And that far-beaming blaze of Majesty,
>
> Wherewith he wont, at Heaven's high council-table,
>
> To sit the midst of Trinal Unity;

except that, in Thomas's thought, the council-table was a work-table, because God did not take counsel; He was an act. The Trinity was an infinite possibility of will; nothing within but

> The baby image of the giant mass
>
> Of things to come at large.

Neither time nor space, neither matter nor mind, not even force existed, nor could any intelligence conceive how, even though they should exist, they could be united in the lowest association. A crystal was as miraculous as Socrates. Only abstract force, or what the schoolmen called form, existed undeveloped from eternity, like the abstract line in mathematics.

Fifty or a hundred years before Saint Thomas settled the Church dogma, a monk of Citeaux or some other abbey, a certain Alain of Lille, had written a Latin poem, as abstruse an allegory as the best, which had the merit of painting the scene of man's creation as far as concerned the mechanical process much as Thomas seems to have seen it. M. Haureau has printed an extract (vol. I, p. 352). Alain conceded to the weakness of human thought, that God was working in time and space, or rather on His throne in heaven, when nature, proposing to create a new and improved man, sent Reason and Prudence up to ask Him for a soul to fit the new body. Having passed through various adventures and much scholastic instruction, the messenger Prudence arrived, after having dropped her dangerous friend Reason by the way. The request was respectfully presented to God, and favourably received. God promised the soul, and at once sent His servant Noys—Thought—to the storehouse of ideas, to choose it:—

> Ipse Deus rem prosequitur, producit in actum
>
> Quod pepigit. Vocat ergo Noym quae praepaert illi
>
> Numinis exemplar, humanae mentis Idaeam,

Ad cujus formam formetur spiritus omni

Munere virtutum dives, qui, nube caducae

Carnis odumbratus veletur corporis umbra.

Tunc Noys ad regis praeceptum singula rerum

Vestigans exempla, novam perquirit Idaeam.

Inter tot species, speciem vix invenit illam

Quam petit; offertur tandem quaesita petenti

. Hanc formam Noys ipsa Deo praesentat ut ejus

Formet ad exemplar animam. Tunc ille sigillum

Sumit, ad ipsius formae vestigia formam

Dans animae, vultum qualem deposcit Idaea

Imprimit exemplo; totas usurpat imago

Exemplaris opes, loquiturque figura sigillum.

God Himself pursues the task, and sets in act

What He promised. So He calls Noys to seek

A copy of His will, Idea of the human mind,

To whose form the spirit should be shaped,

Rich in every virtue, which, veiled in garb

Of frail flesh, is to be hidden in a shade of body,

Then Noys, at the King's order, turning one by one

Each sample, seeks the new Idea.

Among so many images she hardly finds that

Which she seeks; at last the sought one appears.

This form Noys herself brings to God for Him

To form a soul to its pattern. He takes the seal,

And gives form to the soul after the model

Of the form itself, stamping on the sample

The figure such as the Idea requires. The seal

Covers the whole field, and the impression expresses the stamp.

The translation is probably full of mistakes; indeed, one is permitted to doubt whether Alain himself accurately understood the process; but in substance he meant that God contained a storehouse of ideas, and stamped each creation with one of these forms. The poets used a variety of figures to help out their logic, but that of the potter and his pot was one of the most common. Omar Khayyam was using it at the same time with Alain of Lille, but with a difference: for his pot seems to have been matter alone, and his soul was the wine it received from God; while Alain's soul seems to have been the form and not the contents of the pot.

The figure matters little. In any case God's act was the union of mind with matter by the same act or will which created both. No intermediate cause or condition intervened; no secondary influence had anything whatever to do with the result. Time had nothing to do with it. Every individual that has existed or shall exist was created by the same instantaneous act, for all time. "When the question regards the universal agent who produces beings and time, we cannot consider him as acting now and before, according to the succession of time." God emanated time, force, matter, mind, as He might emanate gravitation, not as a part of His substance but as an energy of His will, and maintains them in their activity by the same act, not by a new one. Every individual is a part of the direct act; not a secondary outcome. The soul has no father or mother. Of all errors one of the most serious is to suppose that the soul descends by generation. "Having life and action of its own, it subsists without the body; ... it must therefore be produced directly, and since it is not a material substance, it cannot be produced by way of generation; it must necessarily be created by God. Consequently to suppose that the intelligence [or intelligent soul] is the effect of generation is to suppose that it is not a pure and simple substance, but corruptible like the body. It is therefore heresy to say that this soul is transmitted by generation." What is true of the soul should be true of all other form, since no form is a material substance. The utmost possible relation between any two individuals is that God may have used the same stamp or mould for a series of creations, and especially for the less spiritual: "God is the first model for all things. One may also say that, among His creatures some serve as types or models for others because there are some which are made in the image of others"; but generation means sequence, not cause. The only true cause is God. Creation is His sole act, in which no second cause can share." Creation is more perfect and loftier than generation, because it aims at producing the whole substance of the being, though it starts from absolute nothing."

Thomas Aquinas, when he pleased, was singularly lucid, and on this point he was particularly positive. The architect insisted on the controlling idea of his structure. The Church was God, and its lines excluded interference. God and the Church embraced all the converging lines of the universe, and the universe showed none but lines that converged. Between God and man, nothing whatever intervened. The individual was a compound of form, or soul, and matter; but both were always created together, by the same act, out of nothing. "Simpliciter fatendum est animas simul cum corporibus creari et infundi." It must be distinctly understood that souls were not created before bodies, but that they were created at the same time as the bodies they animate. Nothing whatever preceded this union of two substances which did not exist: "Creatio est productio alicujus rei secundum suam totam substantiam, nullo praesupposito, quod sit vel increatum vel ab aliquo creatum." Language can go no further in exclusion of every possible preceding, secondary, or subsequent cause, "Productio universalis entis a Deo non est motus nec mutatio, sed est quaedam simplex emanatio." The whole universe is, so to speak, a simple emanation from God.

The famous junction, then, is made!—that celebrated fusion of the universal with the individual, of unity with multiplicity, of God and nature, which had broken the neck of every philosophy ever invented; which had ruined William of Champeaux and was to ruin Descartes; this evolution of the finite from the infinite was accomplished. The supreme triumph was as easily effected by Thomas Aquinas as it was to be again effected, four hundred years later, by Spinoza. He had merely to assert the fact: "It is so! it cannot be otherwise!" "For the thousandth and hundred-thousandth time;—what is the use of discussing this prime motor, this Spinozan substance, any longer? We know it is there!" that—as Professor Haeckel very justly repeats for the millionth time—is enough.

One point, however, remained undetermined. The Prime Motor and His action stood fixed, and no one wished to disturb Him; but this was not the point that had disturbed William of Champeaux. Abelard's question still remained to be answered. How did Socrates differ from Plato—Judas from John—Thomas Aquinas from Professor Haeckel? Were they, in fact, two, or one? What made an individual? What was God's centimetre measure? The abstract form or soul which existed as a possibility in God, from all time,—was it one or many? To the Church, this issue overshadowed all else, for, if humanity was one and not multiple, the Church, which dealt only with individuals, was lost. To the schools, also, the issue was vital, for, if the soul or form was already multiple from the first, unity was lost; the ultimate substance and prime motor itself became multiple; the whole issue was reopened.

To the consternation of the Church, and even of his own order, Thomas, following closely his masters, Albert and Aristotle, asserted that the soul was measured by matter. "Division occurs in substances in ratio of quantity, as Aristotle says in his 'Physics.' And so dimensional quantity is a principle of individuation." The soul is a fluid absorbed by matter in proportion to the absorptive power of the matter. The soul is an energy existing in matter proportionately to the dimensional quantity of the matter. The soul is a wine, greater or less in quantity according to the size of the cup. In our report of the great debate of 1110, between Champeaux and Abelard, we have seen William persistently tempting Abelard to fall into this admission that matter made the man;—that the universal equilateral triangle became an individual if it were shaped in metal, the matter giving it reality which mere form could not give; and Abelard evading the issue as though his life depended on it. In fact, had Abelard dared to follow Aristotle into what looked like an admission that Socrates and Plato were identical as form and differed only in weight, his life might have been the forfeit. How Saint Thomas escaped is a question closely connected with the same inquiry about Saint Francis of Assisi. A Church which embraced, with equal sympathy, and within a hundred years, the Virgin, Saint Bernard, William of Champeaux and the School of Saint-Victor, Peter the Venerable, Saint Francis of Assisi, Saint Dominic, Saint Thomas Aquinas, and Saint Bonaventure, was more liberal than any modern State can afford to be. Radical contradictions the State may perhaps tolerate, though hardly, but never embrace or profess. Such elasticity long ago vanished from human thought.

Yet only Dominicans believe that the Church adopted this law of individualization, or even assented to it. If M. Jourdain is right, Thomas was quickly obliged to give it another form:—that, though all souls belonged to the same species, they differed in their aptitudes for uniting with particular bodies. "This soul is commensurate with this body, and not with that other one." The idea is double; for either the souls individualized themselves, and Thomas abandoned his doctrine of their instantaneous creation, with the bodies, out of nothing; or God individualized them in the act of creation, and matter had nothing to do with it. The difficulty is no concern of ours, but the great scholars who took upon themselves to explain it made it worse, until at last one gathers only that Saint Thomas held one of three views: either the soul of humanity was individualized by God, or it individualized itself, or it was divided by ratio of quantity, that is, by matter. This amounts to saying that one knows nothing about it, which we knew before and may admit with calmness; but Thomas Aquinas was not so happily placed, between the Church and the schools. Humanity had a form common to itself, which made it what it was. By some means this form was associated with matter; in fact, matter was only known as associated with form. If, then, God, by an instantaneous act, created matter and gave it form according to the dimensions of the matter, innocent ignorance might infer that there was, in the act of God, one world-soul and one world-matter, which He united in different proportions to make men and things. Such a doctrine was fatal to the Church. No greater heresy could be charged against the worst Arab or Jew, and Thomas was so well aware of his danger that he recoiled from it with a vehemence not at all in keeping with his supposed phlegm. With feverish eagerness to get clear of such companions, he denied and denounced, in all companies, in season and out of season, the idea that intellect was one and the same for all men, differing only with the quantity of matter it accompanied. He challenged the adherent of such a doctrine to battle; "let him take the pen if he dares!" No one dared, seeing that even Jews enjoyed a share of common sense and had seen some of their friends burn at the stake not very long before for such opinions, not even openly maintained; while uneducated people, who are perhaps incapable of receiving intellect at all, but for whose instruction and salvation the great work of Saint Thomas and his scholars must chiefly exist, cannot do battle because they cannot understand Thomas's doctrine of matter and form which to them seems frank pantheism.

So it appeared to Duns Scotus also, if one may assert in the Doctor Subtilis any opinion without qualification. Duns began his career only about 1300, after Thomas's death, and stands, therefore, beyond our horizon; but he is still the pride of the Franciscan Order and stands second in authority to the great Dominican alone. In denying Thomas's doctrine that matter individualizes mind, Duns laid himself open to the worse charge of investing matter with a certain embryonic, independent, shadowy soul of its own. Scot's system, compared with that of Thomas, tended toward liberty. Scot held that the excess of power in Thomas's prime motor neutralized the power of his secondary causes, so that these appeared altogether superfluous. This is a point that ought to be left to the Church to decide, but there can be no harm in quoting, on the other hand, the authority of some of Scot's critics within the Church, who have thought that his doctrine tended to deify matter and to keep open the road to Spinoza. Narrow and dangerous was the border-line always between pantheism and materialism, and the chief interest of the schools was in finding fault with each other's paths.

The opinions in themselves need not disturb us, although the question is as open to dispute as ever it was and perhaps as much disputed; but the turn of Thomas's mind is worth study. A century or two later, his passion to be reasonable, scientific, architectural would have brought him within range of the Inquisition. Francis of Assisi was not more archaic and cave-dweller than Thomas of Aquino was modern and scientific. In his effort to be logical he forced his Deity to be as logical as himself, which hardly suited Omnipotence. He hewed the Church dogmas into shape as though they were rough stones. About no dogma could mankind feel interest more acute than about that of immortality, which seemed to be the single point vitally necessary for any Church to prove and define as clearly as light itself. Thomas trimmed down the soul to half its legitimate claims as an immortal being by insisting that God created it from nothing in the same act or will by which He created the body and united the two in time and space. The soul existed as form for the body, and had no previous existence. Logic seemed to require that when the body died and dissolved, after the union which had lasted, at most, only an instant or two of eternity, the soul, which fitted that body and no other, should dissolve with it. In that case the Church dissolved, too, since it had no reason for existence except the soul. Thomas met the difficulty by suggesting that the body's form might take permanence from the matter to which it gave form. That matter should individualize mind was itself a violent wrench of logic, but that it should also give permanence—the one quality it did not possess—to this individual mind seemed to many learned doctors a scandal. Perhaps Thomas meant to leave the responsibility on the Church, where it belonged as a matter not of logic but of revealed truth. At all events, this treatment of mind and matter brought him into trouble which few modern logicians would suspect.

The human soul having become a person by contact with matter, and having gained eternal personality by the momentary union, was finished, and remains to this day for practical purposes unchanged; but the angels and devils, a world of realities then more real than man, were never united with matter, and therefore could not be persons. Thomas admitted and insisted that the angels, being immaterial,—neither clothed in matter, nor stamped on it, nor mixed with it,—were universals; that is, each was a species in himself, a class, or perhaps what would be now called an energy, with no other individuality than he gave himself.

The idea seems to modern science reasonable enough. Science has to deal, for example, with scores of chemical energies which it knows little about except that they always seem to be constant to the same conditions; but every one knows that in the particular relation of mind to matter the battle is as furious as ever. The soul has always refused to live in peace with the body. The angels, too, were always in rebellion. They insisted on personality, and the devils even more obstinately than the angels. The dispute was—and is—far from trifling. Mind would rather ignore matter altogether. In the thirteenth century mind did, indeed, admit that matter was something,—which it quite refuses to admit in the twentieth,—but treated it as a nuisance to be abated. To the pure in spirit one argued in vain that spirit must compromise; that nature compromised; that God compromised; that man himself was nothing but a somewhat clumsy compromise. No argument served. Mind insisted on absolute despotism. Schoolmen as well as mystics would not believe that matter was what it seemed,—if, indeed, it existed;—unsubstantial, shifty, shadowy; changing with incredible swiftness into dust, gas, flame; vanishing in mysterious lines of force into space beyond hope of recovery; whirled about in eternity and infinity by that mind, form, energy, or thought which guides and rules and tyrannizes and is the universe. The Church wanted to be pure spirit; she regarded matter with antipathy as something foul, to be held at arms' length lest it should stain and corrupt the soul; the most she would willingly admit was that mind and matter might travel side by side, like a doubleheaded comet, on parallel lines that never met, with a preestablished harmony that existed only in the prime motor.

Thomas and his master Albert were almost alone in imposing on the Church the compromise so necessary for its equilibrium. The balance of matter against mind was the same necessity in the Church Intellectual as the balance of thrusts in the arch of the Gothic cathedral. Nowhere did Thomas show his architectural obstinacy quite so plainly as in thus taking matter under his protection. Nothing would induce him to compromise with the angels. He insisted on keeping man wholly apart, as a complex of energies in which matter shared equally with mind. The Church must rest firmly on both. The angels differed from other beings below them' precisely because they were immaterial and impersonal. Such rigid logic outraged the spiritual Church.

Perhaps Thomas's sudden death in 1274 alone saved him from the fate of Abelard, but it did not save his doctrine. Two years afterwards, in 1276, the French and English churches combined to condemn it. Etienne Tempier, Bishop of Paris, presided over the French Synod; Robert Kilwardeby, of the Dominican Order, Archbishop of Canterbury, presided over the Council at Oxford. The synods were composed of schoolmen as well as churchmen, and seem to have been the result of a serious struggle for power between the Dominican and Franciscan Orders. Apparently the Church compromised between them by condemning the errors of both. Some of these errors, springing from Alexander Hales and his Franciscan schools, were in effect the foundation of another Church. Some were expressly charged against Brother Thomas. "Contra fratrem Thomam" the councils forbade teaching that—"quia intelligentiae non habent materiam, Deus non potest plures ejusdem speciei facere; et quod materia non est in angelis"; further, the councils struck at the vital centre of Thomas's system—"quod Deus non potest individua multiplicare sub una specie sine materia"; and again in its broadest form,—"quod formae non accipiunt divisionem nisi secundam materiam." These condemnations made a great stir. Old Albertus Magnus, who was the real victim of attack, fought for himself and for Thomas. After a long and earnest effort, the Thomists rooted out opposition in the order, and carried their campaign to Rome. After fifty years of struggle, by use of every method known in Church politics, the Dominican Order, in 1323, caused John XXII to canonize Thomas and in effect affirm his doctrine.

The story shows how modern, how heterodox, how material, how altogether new and revolutionary the system of Saint Thomas seemed at first even in the schools; but that was the affair of the Church and a matter of pure theology. We study only his art. Step by step, stone by stone, we see him build his church-building like a stonemason, "with the care that the twelfth-century architects put into" their work, as Viollet-le-Duc saw some similar architect at Rouen, building the tower of Saint-Romain: "He has thrown over his work the grace and finesse, the study of detail, the sobriety in projections, the perfect harmony," which belongs to his school, and yet he was rigidly structural and Norman. The foundation showed it; the elevation, which is God, developed it; the vaulting, with its balance of thrusts in mind and matter, proved it; but he had still the hardest task in art, to model man.

The cathedral, then, is built, and God is built into it, but, thus far, God is there alone, filling it all, and maintains the equilibrium by balancing created matter separately against created mind. The proportions of the building are superb; nothing so lofty, so large in treatment, so true in scale, so eloquent of multiplicity in unity, has ever been conceived elsewhere; but it was the virtue or the fault of superb structures like Bourges and Amiens and the Church universal that they seemed to need man more than man needed them; they were made for crowds, for thousands and tens of thousands of human beings; for the whole human race, on its knees, hungry for pardon and love. Chartres needed no crowd, for it was meant as a palace of the Virgin, and the Virgin filled it wholly; but the Trinity made their church for no other purpose than to accommodate man, and made man for no other purpose than to fill their church; if man failed to fill it, the church and the Trinity seemed equally failures. Empty, Bourges and Beauvais are cold; hardly as religious as a wayside cross; and yet, even empty, they are perhaps more religious than when filled with cattle and machines. Saint Thomas needed to fill his Church with real men, and although he had created his own God for that special purpose, the task was, as every boy knew by heart, the most difficult that Omnipotence had dealt with.

God, as Descartes justly said, we know! but what is man? The schools answered: Man is a rational animal! So was apparently a dog, or a bee, or a beaver, none of which seemed to need churches. Modern science, with infinite effort, has discovered and announced that man is a bewildering complex of energies, which helps little to explain his relations with the ultimate substance or energy or prime motor whose existence both science and schoolmen admit; which science studies in laboratories and religion worships in churches. The man whom God created to fill his Church, must be an energy independent of God; otherwise God filled his own Church with his own energy. Thus far, the God of Saint Thomas was alone in His Church. The beings He had created out of nothing—Omar's pipkins of clay and shape—stood against the walls, waiting to receive the wine of life, a life of their own.

Of that life, energy, will, or wine,—whatever the poets or professors called it,—God was the only cause, as He was also the immediate cause, and support. Thomas was emphatic on that point. God is the cause of energy as the sun is the cause of colour: "prout sol dicitur causa manifestationis coloris." He not only gives forms to his pipkins, or energies to his agents, but He also maintains those forms in being: "dat formas creaturis agentibus et eas tenet in esse." He acts directly, not through secondary causes, on everything and every one: "Deus in omnibus intime operatur." If, for an instant, God's action, which is also His will, were to stop, the universe would not merely fall to pieces, but would vanish, and must then be created anew from nothing: "Quia non habet radicem in aere, statim cessat lumen, cessante actione solis. Sic autem se habet omnis creatura ad Deum sicut aer ad solem illuminantem." God radiates energy as the sun radiates light, and "the whole fabric of nature would return to nothing" if that radiation ceased even for an instant. Everything is created by one instantaneous, eternal, universal act of will, and by the same act is maintained in being.

Where, then,—in what mysterious cave outside of creation,—could man, and his free will, and his private world of responsibilities and duties, lie hidden? Unless man was a free agent in a world of his own beyond constraint, the Church was a fraud, and it helped little to add that the State was another. If God was the sole and immediate cause and support of everything in His creation, God was also the cause of its defects, and could not—being Justice and Goodness in essence—hold man responsible for His own omissions. Still less could the State or Church do it in His name.

Whatever truth lies in the charge that the schools discussed futile questions by faulty methods, one cannot decently deny that in this case the question was practical and the method vital. Theist or atheist, monist or anarchist must all admit that society and science are equally interested with theology in deciding whether the universe is one or many, a harmony or a discord. The Church and State asserted that it was a harmony, and that they were its representatives. They say so still. Their claim led to singular but unavoidable conclusions, with which society has struggled for seven hundred years, and is still struggling.

Freedom could not exist in nature, or even in God, after the single, unalterable act or will which created. The only possible free will was that of God before the act. Abelard with his rigid logic averred that God had no freedom; being Himself whatever is most perfect, He produced necessarily the most perfect possible world. Nothing seemed more logical, but if God acted necessarily, His world must also be of necessity the only possible product of His act, and the Church became an impertinence, since man proved only fatuity by attempting to interfere. Thomas dared not disturb the foundations of the Church, and therefore began by laying down the law that God— previous to His act—could choose, and had chosen, whatever scheme of creation He pleased, and that the harmony of the actual scheme proved His perfections. Thus he saved God's free will.

This philosophical apse would have closed the lines and finished the plan of his church-choir had the universe not shown some divergencies or discords needing to be explained. The student of the Latin Quarter was then harder to convince than now that God was Infinite Love and His world a perfect harmony, when perfect love and harmony showed them, even in the Latin Quarter, and still more in revealed truth, a picture of suffering, sorrow, and death; plague, pestilence, and famine; inundations, droughts, and frosts; catastrophes world-wide and accidents in corners; cruelty, perversity, stupidity, uncertainty, insanity; virtue begetting vice; vice working for good; happiness without sense, selfishness without gain, misery without cause, and horrors undefined. The students in public dared not ask, as Voltaire did, "avec son hideux sourire," whether the Lisbon earthquake was the final proof of God's infinite goodness, but in private they used the argumentum ad personam divinam freely enough, and when the Church told them that evil did not exist, the ribalds laughed.

Saint Augustine certainly tempted Satan when he fastened the Church to this doctrine that evil is only the privation of good, an amissio boni; and that good alone exists. The point was infinitely troublesome. Good was order, law, unity. Evil was disorder, anarchy, multiplicity. Which was truth? The Church had committed itself to the dogma that order and unity were the ultimate truth, and that the anarchist should be burned. She could do nothing else, and society supported her— still supports her; yet the Church, who was wiser than the State, had always seen that Saint Augustine dealt with only half the question. She knew that evil might be an excess of good as well as absence of it; that good leads to evil, evil to good; and that, as Pascal says, "three degrees of polar elevation upset all jurisprudence; a meridian decides truth; fundamental laws change; rights have epochs. Pleasing Justice! bounded by a river or a mountain! truths on this side the Pyrenees! errors beyond!" Thomas conceded that God Himself, with the best intentions, might be the source of evil, and pleaded only that his action might in the end work benefits. He could offer no proof of it, but he could assume as probable a plan of good which became the more perfect for the very reason that it allowed great liberty in detail.

One hardly feels Saint Thomas here in all his force. He offers suggestion rather than proof;— apology—the weaker because of obvious effort to apologize—rather than defence, for Infinite

Goodness, Justice, and Power; scoffers might add that he invented a new proof ab defectu, or argument for proving the perfection of a machine by the number of its imperfections; but at all events, society has never done better by way of proving its right to enforce morals or unity of opinion. Unless it asserts law, it can only assert force. Rigid theology went much further. In God's providence, man was as nothing. With a proper sense of duty, every solar system should be content to suffer, if thereby the efficiency of the Milky Way were improved. Such theology shocked Saint Thomas, who never wholly abandoned man in order to exalt God. He persistently brought God and man together, and if he erred, the Church rightly pardons him because he erred on the human side. Whenever the path lay through the valley of despair he called God to his aid, as though he felt the moral obligation of the Creator to help His creation.

At best the vision of God, sitting forever at His work-table, willing the existence of mankind exactly as it is, while conscious that, among these myriad arbitrary creations of His will, hardly one in a million could escape temporary misery or eternal damnation, was not the best possible background for a Church, as the Virgin and the Saviour frankly admitted by taking the foreground; but the Church was not responsible for it. Mankind could not admit an anarchical—a dual or a multiple—universe. The world was there, staring them in the face, with all its chaotic conditions, and society insisted on its unity in self-defence. Society still insists on treating it as unity, though no longer affecting logic. Society insists on its free will, although free will has never been explained to the satisfaction of any but those who much wish to be satisfied, and although the words in any common sense implied not unity but duality in creation. The Church had nothing to do with inventing this riddle—the oldest that fretted mankind.

Apart from all theological interferences,—fall of Adam or fault of Eve, Atonement, Justification, or Redemption,—either the universe was one, or it was two, or it was many; either energy was one, seen only in powers of itself, or it was several; either God was harmony, or He was discord. With practical unanimity, mankind rejected the dual or multiple scheme; it insisted on unity. Thomas took the question as it was given him. The unity was full of defects; he did not deny them; but he claimed that they might be incidents, and that the admitted unity might even prove their beneficence. Granting this enormous concession, he still needed a means of bringing into the system one element which vehemently refused to be brought:—that is, man himself, who insisted that the universe was a unit, but that he was a universe; that energy was one, but that he was another energy; that God was omnipotent, but that man was free. The contradiction had always existed, exists still, and always must exist, unless man either admits that he is a machine, or agrees that anarchy and chaos are the habit of nature, and law and order its accident. The agreement may become possible, but it was not possible in the thirteenth century nor is it now. Saint Thomas's settlement could not be a simple one or final, except for practical use, but it served, and it holds good still.

No one ever seriously affirmed the literal freedom of will. Absolute liberty is absence of restraint; responsibility is restraint; therefore, the ideally free individual is responsible only to himself. This principle is the philosophical foundation of anarchism, and, for anything that science has yet proved, may be the philosophical foundation of the universe; but it is fatal to all society and is especially hostile to the State. Perhaps the Church of the thirteenth century might have found a way to use even this principle for a good purpose; certainly, the influence of Saint Bernard was sufficiently unsocial and that of Saint Francis was sufficiently unselfish to conciliate even anarchists of the militant class; but Saint Thomas was working for the Church and the

State, not for the salvation of souls, and his chief object was to repress anarchy. The theory of absolute free will never entered his mind, more than the theory of material free will would enter the mind of an architect. The Church gave him no warrant for discussing the subject in such a sense. In fact, the Church never admitted free will, or used the word when it could be avoided. In Latin, the term used was "liberum arbitrium,"—free choice,—and in French to this day it remains in strictness "libre arbitre" still. From Saint Augustine downwards the Church was never so unscientific as to admit of liberty beyond the faculty of choosing between paths, some leading through the Church and some not, but all leading to the next world; as a criminal might be allowed the liberty of choosing between the guillotine and the gallows, without infringing on the supremacy of the judge.

Thomas started from that point, already far from theoretic freedom. "We are masters of our acts," he began, "in the sense that we can choose such and such a thing; now, we have not to choose our end, but the means that relate to it, as Aristotle says." Unfortunately, even this trenchant amputation of man's free energies would not accord with fact or with logic. Experience proved that man's power of choice in action was very far from absolute, and logic seemed to require that every choice should have some predetermining cause which decided the will to act. Science affirmed that choice was not free,—could not be free,—without abandoning the unity of force and the foundation of law. Society insisted that its choice must be left free, whatever became of science or unity. Saint Thomas was required to illustrate the theory of "liberum arbitrium" by choosing a path through these difficulties, where path there was obviously none.

Thomas's method of treating this problem was sure to be as scientific as the vaulting of a Gothic arch. Indeed, one follows it most easily by translating his school-vocabulary into modern technical terms. With very slight straining of equivalents, Thomas might now be written thus:—

By the term God, is meant a prime motor which supplies all energy to the universe, and acts directly on man as well as on all other creatures, moving him as a mechanical motor might do; but man, being specially provided with an organism more complex than the organisms of other creatures, enjoys an exceptional capacity for reflex action,—a power of reflection,—which enables him within certain limits to choose between paths; and this singular capacity is called free choice or free will. Of course, the reflection is not choice, and though a man's mind reflected as perfectly as the facets of a lighthouse lantern, it would never reach a choice without an energy which impels it to act.

Now let us read Saint Thomas:—

Some kind of an agent is required to determine one's choice; that agent is reflection. Man reflects, then, in order to learn what choice to make between the two acts which offer themselves. But reflection is, in its turn, a faculty of doing opposite things, for we can reflect or not reflect; and we are no further forward than before. One cannot carry back this process infinitely, for in that case one would never decide. The fixed point is not in man, since we meet in him, as a being apart by himself, only the alternative faculties; we must, therefore, recur to the intervention of an exterior agent who shall impress on our will a movement capable of putting an end to its hesitations:—That exterior agent is nothing else than God!

The scheme seems to differ little, and unwillingly, from a system of dynamics as modern as the dynamo. Even in the prime motor, from the moment of action, freedom of will vanished. Creation was not successive; it was one instantaneous thought and act, identical with the will, and was complete and unchangeable from end to end, including time as one of its functions. Thomas was as clear as possible on that point:—"Supposing God wills anything in effect; He cannot will not to will it, because His will cannot change." He wills that some things shall be contingent and others necessary, but He wills in the same act that the contingency shall be necessary. "They are contingent because God has willed them to be so, and with this object has subjected them to causes which are so." In the same way He wills that His creation shall develop itself in time and space and sequence, but He creates these conditions as well as the events. He creates the whole, in one act, complete, unchangeable, and it is then unfolded like a rolling panorama, with its predetermined contingencies.

Man's free choice—liberum arbitrium—falls easily into place as a predetermined contingency. God is the first cause, and acts in all secondary causes directly; but while He acts mechanically on the rest of creation,—as far as is known,—He acts freely at one point, and this free action remains free as far as it extends on that line. Man's freedom derives from this source, but it is simply apparent, as far as he is a cause; it is a reflex action determined by a new agency of the first cause.

However abstruse these ideas may once have sounded, they are far from seeming difficult in comparison with modern theories of energy. Indeed, measured by that standard, the only striking feature of Saint Thomas's motor is its simplicity. Thomas's prime motor was very powerful, and its lines of energy were infinite. Among these infinite lines, a certain group ran to the human race, and, as long as the conduction was perfect, each man acted mechanically. In cases where the current, for any reason, was for a moment checked,—that is to say, produced the effect of hesitation or reflection in the mind,—the current accumulated until it acquired power to leap the obstacle. As Saint Thomas expressed it, the Prime Motor, Who was nothing else than God, intervened to decide the channel of the current. The only difference between man and a vegetable was the reflex action of the complicated mirror which was called mind, and the mark of mind was reflective absorption or choice. The apparent freedom was an illusion arising from the extreme delicacy of the machine, but the motive power was in fact the same—that of God.

This exclusion of what men commonly called freedom was carried still further in the process of explaining dogma. Supposing the conduction to be insufficient for a given purpose; a purpose which shall require perfect conduction? Under ordinary circumstances, in ninety-nine cases out of a hundred, the conductor will be burned out, so to speak; condemned, and thrown away. This is the case with most human beings. Yet there are cases where the conductor is capable of receiving an increase of energy from the prime motor, which enables it to attain the object aimed at. In dogma, this store of reserved energy is technically called Grace. In the strict, theological sense of the word, as it is used by Saint Thomas, the exact, literal meaning of Grace is "a motion which the Prime Motor, as a supernatural cause, produces in the soul, perfecting free will." It is a reserved energy, which comes to aid and reinforce the normal energy of the battery.

To religious minds this scientific inversion of solemn truths seems, and is, sacrilege; but Thomas's numerous critics in the Church have always brought precisely this charge against his doctrine, and are doing so still. They insist that he has reduced God to a mechanism and man to a passive conductor of force. He has left, they say, nothing but God in the universe. The terrible word which annihilates all other philosophical systems against which it is hurled, has been hurled freely against his for six hundred years and more, without visibly affecting the Church; and yet its propriety seems, to the vulgar, beyond reasonable cavil. To Father de Regnon, of the extremely learned and intelligent Society of Jesus, the difference between pantheism and Thomism reduces itself to this: "Pantheism, starting from the notion of an infinite substance which is the plenitude of being, concludes that there can exist no other beings than THE being; no other realities than the absolute reality. Thomism, starting from the efficacy of the first cause, tends to reduce more and more the efficacy of second causes, and to replace it by a passivity which receives without producing, which is determined without determining." To students of architecture, who know equally little about pantheism and about Thomism,—or, indeed, for that matter, about architecture, too,—the quality that rouses most surprise in Thomism is its astonishingly scientific method. The Franciscans and the Jesuits call it pantheism, but science, too, is pantheism, or has till very recently been wholly pantheistic. Avowedly science has aimed at nothing but the reduction of multiplicity to unity, and has excommunicated, as though it were itself a Church, any one who doubted or disputed its object, its method, or its results. The effort is as evident and quite as laborious in modern science, starting as it does from multiplicity, as in Thomas Aquinas, who started from unity; and it is necessarily less successful, for its true aims, as far as it is science and not disguised religion, were equally attained by reaching infinite complexity; but the assertion or assumption of ultimate unity has characterized the Law of Energy as emphatically as it has characterized the definition of God in theology. If it is a reproach to Saint Thomas, it is equally a reproach to Clerk-Maxwell. In truth, it is what men most admire in both—the power of broad and lofty generalization.

Under any conceivable system the process of getting God and man under the same roof—of bringing two independent energies under the same control—required a painful effort, as science has much cause to know. No doubt, many good Christians and some heretics have been shocked at the tour de force by which they felt themselves suddenly seized, bound hand and foot, attached to each other, and dragged into the Church, without consent or consultation. To religious mystics, whose scepticism concerned chiefly themselves and their own existence, Saint Thomas's man seemed hardly worth herding, at so much expense and trouble, into a Church where he was not eager to go. True religion felt the nearness of God without caring to see the mechanism. Mystics like Saint Bernard, Saint Francis, Saint Bonaventure, or Pascal had a right to make this objection, since they got into the Church, so to speak, by breaking through the windows; but society at large accepted and retains Saint Thomas's man much as Saint Thomas delivered him to the Government; a two-sided being, free or unfree, responsible or irresponsible, an energy or a victim of energy, moved by choice or moved by compulsion, as the interests of society seemed for the moment to need. Certainly Saint Thomas lavished no excess of liberty on the man he created, but still he was more generous than the State has ever been. Saint Thomas asked little from man, and gave much; even as much freedom of will as the State gave or now gives; he added immortality hereafter and eternal happiness under reasonable restraints; his God watched over man's temporal welfare far more anxiously than the State has ever done, and assigned him space in the Church which he never can have in the galleries of Parliament or Congress; more than all this, Saint Thomas and his God placed man in the centre of the universe, and made the sun and the stars for his uses. No statute law ever did as much for man, and no social reform ever will try to do it; yet man bitterly complained that he had not his rights, and even in the Church is still complaining, because Saint Thomas set a limit, more or less vague, to what the man was obstinate in calling his freedom of will.

Thus Saint Thomas completed his work, keeping his converging lines clear and pure throughout, and bringing them together, unbroken, in the curves that gave unity to his plan. His sense of scale and proportion was that of the great architects of his age. One might go on studying it for a lifetime. He showed no more hesitation in keeping his Deity in scale than in adjusting man to it. Strange as it sounds, although man thought himself hardly treated in respect to freedom, yet, if freedom meant superiority, man was in action much the superior of God, Whose freedom suffered, from Saint Thomas, under restraints that man never would have tolerated. Saint Thomas did not allow God even an undetermined will; He was pure Act, and as such He could not change. Man alone was allowed, in act, to change direction. What was more curious still, man might absolutely prove his freedom by refusing to move at all; if he did not like his life he could stop it, and habitually did so, or acquiesced in its being done for him; while God could not commit suicide or even cease for a single instant His continuous action. If man had the singular fancy of making himself absurd,—a taste confined to himself but attested by evidence exceedingly strong,—he could be as absurd as he liked; but God could not be absurd. Saint Thomas did not allow the Deity the right to contradict Himself, which is one of man's chief pleasures. While man enjoyed what was, for his purposes, an unlimited freedom to be wicked,— a privilege which, as both Church and State bitterly complained and still complain, he has outrageously abused,—God was Goodness, and could be nothing else. While man moved about his relatively spacious prison with a certain degree of ease, God, being everywhere, could not move. In one respect, at least, man's freedom seemed to be not relative but absolute, for his thought was an energy paying no regard to space or time or order or object or sense; but God's thought was His act and will at once; speaking correctly, God could not think; He is. Saint Thomas would not, or could not, admit that God was Necessity, as Abelard seems to have held, but he refused to tolerate the idea of a divine maniac, free from moral obligation to himself. The atmosphere of Saint Louis surrounds the God of Saint Thomas, and its pure ether shuts out the corruption and pollution to come,—the Valois and Bourbons, the Occams and Hobbes's, the Tudors and the Medicis, of an enlightened Europe.

The theology turns always into art at the last, and ends in aspiration. The spire justifies the church. In Saint Thomas's Church, man's free will was the aspiration to God, and he treated it as the architects of Chartres and Laon had treated their famous fleches. The square foundation-tower, the expression of God's power in act,—His Creation,—rose to the level of the Church facade as a part of the normal unity of God's energy; and then, suddenly, without show of effort, without break, without logical violence, became a many-sided, voluntary, vanishing human soul, and neither Villard de Honnecourt nor Duns Scotus could distinguish where God's power ends and man's free will begins. All they saw was the soul vanishing into the skies. How it was done, one does not care to ask; in a result so exquisite, one has not the heart to find fault with "adresse."

About Saint Thomas's theology we need not greatly disturb ourselves; it can matter now not much, whether he put more pantheism than the law allowed or more materialism than Duns Scotus approved—or less of either—into his universe, since the Church is still on the spot, responsible for its own doctrines; but his architecture is another matter. So scientific and structural a method was never an accident or the property of a single mind even with Aristotle to prompt it. Neither his Church nor the architect's church was a sketch, but a completely studied structure. Every relation of parts, every disturbance of equilibrium, every detail of construction was treated with infinite labour, as the result of two hundred years of experiment and discussion among thousands of men whose minds and whose instincts were acute, and who discussed little else. Science and art were one. Thomas Aquinas would probably have built a better cathedral at Beauvais than the actual architect who planned it; but it is quite likely that the architect might have saved Thomas some of his errors, as pointed out by the Councils of 1276. Both were great artists; perhaps in their professions, the greatest that ever lived; and both must have been great students beyond their practice. Both were subject to constant criticism from men and bodies of men whose minds were as acute and whose learning was as great as their own. If the Archbishop of Canterbury and the Bishop of Paris condemned Thomas, the Bernardines had, for near two hundred years, condemned Beauvais in advance. Both the "Summa Theologiae" and Beauvais Cathedral were excessively modern, scientific, and technical, marking the extreme points reached by Europe on the lines of scholastic science. This is all we need to know. If we like, we can go on to study, inch by inch, the slow decline of the art. The essence of it—the despotic central idea—was that of organic unity both in the thought and the building. From that time, the universe has steadily become more complex and less reducible to a central control. With as much obstinacy as though it were human, it has insisted on expanding its parts; with as much elusiveness as though it were feminine, it has evaded the attempt to impose on it a single will. Modern science, like modern art, tends, in practice, to drop the dogma of organic unity. Some of the mediaeval habit of mind survives, but even that is said to be yielding before the daily evidence of increasing and extending complexity. The fault, then, was not in man, if he no longer looked at science or art as an organic whole or as the expression of unity. Unity turned itself into complexity, multiplicity, variety, and even contradiction. All experience, human and divine, assured man in the thirteenth century that the lines of the universe converged. How was he to know that these lines ran in every conceivable and inconceivable direction, and that at least half of them seemed to diverge from any imaginable centre of unity! Dimly conscious that his Trinity required in logic a fourth dimension, how was the schoolman to supply it, when even the mathematician of to-day can only infer its necessity? Naturally man tended to lose his sense of scale and relation. A straight line, or a combination of straight lines, may have still a sort of artistic unity, but what can be done in art with a series of negative symbols? Even if the negative were continuous, the artist might express at least a negation; but supposing that Omar's kinetic analogy of the ball and the players turned out to be a scientific formula!—supposing that the highest scientific authority, in order to obtain any unity at all, had to resort to the Middle Ages for an imaginary demon to sort his atoms!—how could art deal with such problems, and what wonder that art lost unity with philosophy and science! Art had to be confused in order to express confusion; but perhaps it was truest, so.

Some future summer, when you are older, and when I have left, like Omar, only the empty glass of my scholasticism for you to turn down, you can amuse yourselves by going on with the story after the death of Saint Louis, Saint Thomas, and William of Lorris, and after the failure of Beauvais. The pathetic interest of the drama deepens with every new expression, but at least you can learn from it that your parents in the nineteenth century were not to blame for losing the sense of unity in art. As early as the fourteenth century, signs of unsteadiness appeared, and, before the eighteenth century, unity became only a reminiscence. The old habit of centralizing a strain at one point, and then dividing and subdividing it, and distributing it on visible lines of support to a visible foundation, disappeared in architecture soon after 1500, but lingered in theology two centuries longer, and even, in very old-fashioned communities, far down to our own time; but its values were forgotten, and it survived chiefly as a stock jest against the clergy. The passage between the two epochs is as beautiful as the Slave of Michael Angelo; but, to feel its beauty, you should see it from above, as it came from its radiant source. Truth, indeed, may not exist; science avers it to be only a relation; but what men took for truth stares one everywhere in the eye and begs for sympathy. The architects of the twelfth and thirteenth centuries took the Church and the universe for truths, and tried to express them in a structure which should be final. Knowing by an enormous experience precisely where the strains were to come, they enlarged their scale to the utmost point of material endurance, lightening the load and distributing the burden until the gutters and gargoyles that seem mere ornament, and the grotesques that seem rude absurdities, all do work either for the arch or for the eye; and every inch of material, up and down, from crypt to vault, from man to God, from the universe to the atom, had its task, giving support where support was needed, or weight where concentration was felt, but always with the condition of showing conspicuously to the eye the great lines which led to unity and the curves which controlled divergence; so that, from the cross on the fleche and the keystone of the vault, down through the ribbed nervures, the columns, the windows, to the foundation of the flying buttresses far beyond the walls, one idea controlled every line; and this is true of Saint Thomas's Church as it is of Amiens Cathedral. The method was the same for both, and the result was an art marked by singular unity, which endured and served its purpose until man changed his attitude toward the universe. The trouble was not in the art or the method or the structure, but in the universe itself which presented different aspects as man moved. Granted a Church, Saint Thomas's Church was the most expressive that man has made, and the great Gothic cathedrals were its most complete expression.

Perhaps the best proof of it is their apparent instability. Of all the elaborate symbolism which has been suggested for the Gothic cathedral, the most vital and most perfect may be that the slender nervure, the springing motion of the broken arch, the leap downwards of the flying buttress,—the visible effort to throw off a visible strain,—never let us forget that Faith alone supports it, and that, if Faith fails, Heaven is lost. The equilibrium is visibly delicate beyond the line of safety; danger lurks in every stone. The peril of the heavy tower, of the restless vault, of the vagrant buttress; the uncertainty of logic, the inequalities of the syllogism, the irregularities of the mental mirror,—all these haunting nightmares of the Church are expressed as strongly by the Gothic cathedral as though it had been the cry of human suffering, and as no emotion had ever been expressed before or is likely to find expression again. The delight of its aspirations is flung up to the sky. The pathos of its self-distrust and anguish of doubt is buried in the earth as its last secret. You can read out of it whatever else pleases your youth and confidence; to me, this is all.

THE END

Esther

Chapter I

The new church of St. John's, on Fifth Avenue, was thronged the morning of the last Sunday of October, in the year 1880. Sitting in the gallery, beneath the unfinished frescoes, and looking down the nave, one caught an effect of autumn gardens, a suggestion of chrysanthemums and geraniums, or of October woods, dashed with scarlet oaks and yellow maples. As a display of austerity the show was a failure, but if cheerful content and innocent adornment please the Author of the lilies and roses, there was reason to hope that this first service at St. John's found favor in his sight, even though it showed no victory over the world or the flesh in this part of the United States. The sun came in through the figure of St. John in his crimson and green garments of glass, and scattered more color where colors already rivaled the flowers of a prize show; while huge prophets and evangelists in flowing robes looked down from the red walls on a display of human vanities that would have called out a vehement Lamentation of Jeremiah or Song of Solomon, had these poets been present in flesh as they were in figure.

Solomon was a brilliant but not an accurate observer; he looked at the world from the narrow stand-point of his own temple. Here in New York he could not have truthfully said that all was vanity, for even a more ill-natured satirist than he must have confessed that there was in this new temple to-day a perceptible interest in religion. One might almost have said that religion seemed to be a matter of concern. The audience wore a look of interest, and, even after their first gaze of admiration and whispered criticism at the splendors of their new church, when at length the clergyman entered to begin the service, a ripple of excitement swept across the field of bonnets until there was almost a murmur as of rustling cornfields within the many colored walls of St. John's.

In a remote pew, hidden under a gallery of the transept, two persons looked on with especial interest. The number of strangers who crowded in after them forced them to sit closely together, and their low whispers of comment were unheard by their neighbors. Before the service began they talked in a secular tone.

"Wharton's window is too high-toned," said the man.

"You all said it would be like Aladdin's," murmured the woman.

"Yes, but he throws away his jewels," rejoined the man. "See the big prophet over the arch; he looks as though he wanted to come down—and I think he ought."

"Did Michael Angelo ever take lessons of Mr. Wharton?" asked the woman seriously, looking up at the figures high above the pulpit.

"He was only a prophet," answered her companion, and, looking in another direction, next asked:

"Who is the angel of Paradise, in the dove-colored wings, sliding up the main aisle?"

"That! O, you know her! It is Miss Leonard. She is lovely, but she is only an angel of Paris."

"I never saw her before in my life," he replied; "but I know her bonnet was put on in the Lord's honor for the first time this morning."

"Women should take their bonnets off at the church door, as Mussulmen do their shoes," she answered.

"Don't turn Mahommedan, Esther. To be a Puritan is bad enough. The bonnets match the decorations."

"Pity the transepts are not finished!" she continued, gazing up at the bare scaffolding opposite.

"You are lucky to have any thing finished," he rejoined. "Since Hazard got here every thing is turned upside down; all the plans are changed. He and Wharton have taken the bit in their teeth, and the church committee have got to pay for whatever damage is done."

"Has Mr. Hazard voice enough to fill the church?" she asked.

"Watch him, and see how well he'll do it. Here he comes, and he will hit the right pitch on his first word."

The organ stopped, the clergyman appeared, and the talkers were silent until the litany ended and the organ began again. Under the prolonged rustle of settling for the sermon, more whispers passed.

"He is all eyes," murmured Esther; and it was true that at this distance the preacher seemed to be made up of two eyes and a voice, so slight and delicate was his frame. Very tall, slender and dark, his thin, long face gave so spiritual an expression to his figure that the great eyes seemed to penetrate like his clear voice to every soul within their range.

"Good art!" muttered her companion.

"We are too much behind the scenes," replied she.

"It is a stage, like any other," he rejoined; "there should be an entre-acte and drop-scene. Wharton could design one with a last judgment."

"He would put us into it, George, and we should be among the wicked."

"I am a martyr," answered George shortly.

The clergyman now mounted his pulpit and after a moment's pause said in his quietest manner and clearest voice:

"He that hath ears to hear, let him hear."

An almost imperceptible shiver passed through Esther's figure.

"Wait! he will slip in the humility later," muttered George.

On the contrary, the young preacher seemed bent on letting no trace of humility slip into his first sermon. Nothing could be simpler than his manner, which, if it had a fault, sinned rather on the side of plainness and monotony than of rhetoric, but he spoke with the air of one who had a message to deliver which he was more anxious to give as he received than to add any thing of his own; he meant to repeat it all without an attempt to soften it. He took possession of his flock with a general advertisement that he owned every sheep in it, white or black, and to show that there could be no doubt on the matter, he added a general claim to right of property in all mankind and the universe. He did this in the name and on behalf of the church universal, but there was self-assertion in the quiet air with which he pointed out the nature of his title, and then, after sweeping all human thought and will into his strong-box, shut down the lid with a sharp click, and bade his audience kneel.

The sermon dealt with the relations of religion to society. It began by claiming that all being and all thought rose by slow gradations to God,—ended in Him, for Him—existed only through Him and because of being His.

The form of act or thought mattered nothing. The hymns of David, the plays of Shakespeare, the metaphysics of Descartes, the crimes of Borgia, the virtues of Antonine, the atheism of yesterday and the materialism of to-day, were all emanations of divine thought, doing their appointed work. It was the duty of the church to deal with them all, not as though they existed through a power hostile to the deity, but as instruments of the deity to work out his unrevealed ends. The preacher then went on to criticise the attitude of religion towards science. "If there is still a feeling of hostility between them," he said, "it is no longer the fault of religion. There have been times when the church seemed afraid, but she is so no longer. Analyze, dissect, use your microscope or your spectrum till the last atom of matter is reached; reflect and refine till the last element of thought is made clear; the church now knows with the certainty of science what she once knew only by the certainty of faith, that you will find enthroned behind all thought and matter only one central idea,—that idea which the church has never ceased to embody,—I AM! Science like religion kneels before this mystery; it can carry itself back only to this simple consciousness of existence. I AM is the starting point and goal of metaphysics and logic, but the church alone has pointed out from the beginning that this starting-point is not human but divine. The philosopher says—I am, and the church scouts his philosophy. She answers:—No! you are NOT, you have no existence of your own. You were and are and ever will be only a part of the supreme I AM, of which the church is the emblem."

In this symbolic expression of his right of property in their souls and bodies, perhaps the preacher rose a little above the heads of his audience. Most of his flock were busied with a kind of speculation so foreign to that of metaphysics that they would have been puzzled to explain what was meant by Descartes' famous COGITO ERGO SUM, on which the preacher laid so much stress. They would have preferred to put the fact of their existence on almost any other experience in life, as that "I have five millions," or, "I am the best-dressed woman in the church,—therefore I am somebody." The fact of self-consciousness would not have struck them as warranting a claim even to a good social position, much less to a share in omnipotence; they knew the trait only as a sign of bad manners. Yet there were at least two persons among the glorified chrysanthemums of St. John's Garden this day, who as the sermon closed and the organ burst out again, glanced at each other with a smile as though they had enjoyed their lecture.

"Good!" said the man. "He takes hold."

"I hope he believes it all," said his companion.

"Yes, he has put his life into the idea," replied the man. "Even at college he would have sent us all off to the stake with a sweet smile, for the love of Christ and the glory of the English Episcopal Church."

The crowd soon began to pour slowly out of the building and the two observers were swept along with the rest until at length they found themselves outside, and strolled down the avenue. A voice from behind stopped them.

"Esther!" it called.

Esther turned and greeted the caller as aunt. She was a woman of about fifty, still rather handsome, but with features to which time had given an expression of character and will that harmonized only with a manner a little abrupt and decided. She had the air of a woman who knew her own mind and commonly had her own way.

"Well, Esther, I am glad to see you taking George to church. Has he behaved himself?"

"You are wrong again, Aunt Sarah," said George; "it is I who have been taking Esther to church. I thought it was worth seeing."

"Church is always worth seeing, George, and I hope your friend Mr.

Hazard's sermon has done you good."

"It did me good to see Wharton there," answered George; "he looked as though it were a first representation, and he were in a stage box. Hazard and he ought to have appeared before the curtain, hand in hand, and made little speeches. I felt like calling them out."

"What did you think of it, Esther?" asked her aunt.

"I thought it very entertaining, Aunt Sarah. I felt like a butterfly in a tulip bed. Mr. Hazard's eyes are wonderful."

"I shall never get you two to be reverential," said her aunt sternly. "It was the best sermon I ever heard, and I would like to hear you answer it, George, and make your answer as little scientific as you can."

"Aunt Sarah, I never answered any one in my life, not even you, or Esther, or the man who said that my fossil bird was a crocodile. Why do you want me to answer him?"

"Because I don't believe you can."

"I can't. I am a professor of paleontology at the college, and I answer questions about bones. You must get my colleague who does the metaphysics to answer Hazard's sermon. Hazard and I have had it out fifty times, and discussed the whole subject till night reeled, but we never got within shouting distance of each other. He might as well have stood on the earth, and I on the nearest planet, and bawled across. So we have given it up."

"You mean that you were beaten," rejoined his aunt. "I am glad you feel it, though I always knew it was so. After all, Mr. Hazard has got more saints on his church walls than he will ever see in his audience, though not such pretty ones. I never saw so many lovely faces and dresses together. Esther, how is your father to-day?"

"Not very well, aunt. He wants to see you. Come home with us and help us to amuse him."

So talking, all three walked along the avenue to 42d Street, and turning down it, at length entered one of the houses about half way between the avenues. Up-stairs in a sunny room fitted up as a library and large enough to be handsome, they found the owner, William Dudley, a man of sixty or thereabouts, sitting in an arm-chair before the fire, trying to read a foreign review in which he took no interest. He moved with an appearance of effort, as though he were an invalid, but his voice was strong and his manner cheerful.

"I hoped you would all come. This is an awful moment. Tell me instantly, Sarah; is St. Stephen a success?"

"Immense! St. Stephen and St. Wharton too. The loveliest clergyman, the sweetest church, the highest-toned sermon and the lowest-toned walls," said she. "Even George owns that he has no criticisms to make."

"Aunt Sarah tells the loftiest truth, Uncle William," said the professor; "every Christian emblem about the church is superlatively correct, but paleontologically it is a fraud. Wharton and Hazard did the emblems, and I supplied them with antediluvian beasts which were all right when I drew them, but Wharton has played the devil with them, and I don't believe he knows the difference between a saurian and a crab. I could not recognize one of my own offspring."

"And how did it suit you, Esther?"

"I am charmed," replied his daughter. "Only it certainly does come just a little near being an opera-house. Mr. Hazard looks horribly like Meyerbeer's Prophet. He ordered us about in a fine tenor voice, with his eyes, and told us that we belonged to him, and if we did not behave ourselves he would blow up the church and us in it. I thought every moment we should see his mother come out of the front pews, and have a scene with him. If the organ had played the march, the effect would have been complete, but I felt there was something wanting."

"It was the sexton," said the professor; "he ought to have had a medieval costume. I must tell Wharton to-night to invent one for him. Hazard has asked me to come round to his rooms, because he thinks I am an unprejudiced observer and will tell him the exact truth. Now what am I to say?"

"Tell him," said the aunt, "that he looked like a Christian martyr defying the beasts in the amphitheater, and George, you are one of them. Between you and your Uncle William I wonder how Esther and I keep any religion at all."

"It is not enough to save you, Aunt Sarah," replied the professor. "You might just as well go with us, for if the Church is half right, you haven't a chance."

"Just now I must go with my husband, who is not much better than you," she replied. "He must have his luncheon, church or no church. Good-by."

So she departed, notifying Esther that the next day there was to be at her house a meeting of the executive committee of the children's hospital, which Esther must be careful to attend.

When she was out of the room the professor turned to his uncle and said: "Seriously, Uncle William, I wish you knew Stephen Hazard. He is a pleasant fellow in or out of the pulpit, and would amuse you. If you and Esther will come to tea some afternoon at my rooms, I will get Hazard and Wharton and Aunt Sarah there to meet you."

"Will he preach at me?" asked Mr. Dudley.

"Never in his life," replied the professor warmly. "He is the most rational, unaffected parson in the world. He likes fun as much as you or any other man, and is interested in every thing."

"I will come if Esther will let me," said Mr. Dudley. "What have you to say about it, Esther?"

"I don't think it would hurt you, father. George's building has an elevator."

"I didn't mean that, you watch-dog. I meant to ask whether you wanted to go to George's tea party?"

"I should like it of all things. Mr. Hazard won't hurt me, and I always like to meet Mr. Wharton."

"Then I will ask both of them this evening for some day next week or the week after, and will let you know," said George.

"Is he easily shocked?" asked Mr. Dudley. "Am I to do the old-school

Puritan with him, or what?"

"Stephen Hazard," replied the professor, "is as much a man of the world as you or I. He is only thirty-five; we were at college together, took our degrees together, went abroad at the same time, and to the same German university. He had then more money than I, and traveled longer, went to the East, studied a little of every thing, lived some time in Paris, where he discovered Wharton, and at last some few years ago came home to take a church at Cincinnati, where he made himself a power. I thought he made a mistake in leaving there to come to St. John's, and wrote him so. I thought if he came here he would find that he had no regular community to deal with but just an Arab horde, and that it was nonsense to talk of saving the souls of New Yorkers who have no souls to be saved. But he thought it his duty to take the offer. Aunt Sarah hit it right when she called him a Christian martyr in the amphitheater. At college, we used to call him St. Stephen. He had this same idea that the church was every thing, and that every thing belonged to the church. When I told him that he was a common nuisance, and that I had to work for him like a church-warden, he laughed as though it were a joke, and seriously told me it was all right, and he didn't mind my skepticism at all. I know he was laughing at me this morning, when he made me go to church for the first time in ten years to hear that sermon which not twenty people there understood."

"One always has to pay for one's friend's hobbies," said Mr. Dudley. "I am glad he has had a success. If we keep a church we ought to do it in the best style. What will you give me for my pew?"

"I never sat in a worse," growled Strong.

"I'll not change it then," said Mr. Dudley. "I'll make Esther use it to mortify her pride."

"Better make it over to the poor of the parish," said the professor; "you will get no thanks for it even from them."

Mr. Dudley laughed as though it were no affair of his, and in fact he never sat in his pew, and never expected to do so; he had no taste for church-going. A lawyer in moderate practice, with active interest in public affairs, when the civil war broke out he took a commission as captain in a New York regiment, and, after distinguishing himself, was brought home, a colonel, with a bullet through his body and a saber cut across his head. He recovered his health, or as much of it as a man can expect to recover after such treatment, and went back to the law, but coming by inheritance into a property large enough to make him indifferent to his profession, and having an only child whose mother was long since dead, he amused the rest of his life by spoiling this girl. Esther was now twenty-five years old, and for fifteen years had been absolute mistress of her father's house. Her Aunt Sarah, known in New York as Mrs. John Murray of 53d Street, was the only person of whom she was a little—a very little—afraid. Of her Cousin George she was not in the least afraid, although George Strong spoke with authority in the world when he cared to speak at all. He was rich, and his professorship was little more to him than a way of spending money. He had no parents, and no relations besides the Dudleys and the Murrays. Alone in the world, George Strong looked upon himself as having in Esther a younger sister whom he liked, and a sort of older sister, whom he also liked, in his Aunt Sarah.

When, after lunching with the Dudleys, Professor Strong walked down Fifth Avenue to his club, he looked, to the thousand people whom he passed, like what he was, an intelligent man, with a figure made for action, an eye that hated rest, and a manner naturally sympathetic. His forehead was so bald as to give his face a look of strong character, which a dark beard rather helped to increase. He was a popular fellow, known as George by whole gangs of the roughest miners in Nevada, where he had worked for years as a practical geologist, and it would have been hard to find in America, Europe, or Asia, a city in which some one would not have smiled at the mention of his name, and asked where George was going to turn up next.

He kept his word that evening with his friend Hazard. At nine o'clock he was at the house, next door to St. John's church, where the new clergyman was trying to feel himself at home. In a large library, with book-cases to the ceiling, and books lying in piles on the floor; with pictures, engravings and etchings leaning against the books and the walls, and every sort of literary encumbrance scattered in the way of heedless feet; in the midst of confusion confounded, Mr. Hazard was stretched on a sofa trying to read, but worn out by fatigue and excitement. Though his chaos had not settled into order, it was easy to read his character from his surroundings. The books were not all divinity. There were classics of every kind, even to a collection of Eastern literature; a mass of poetry in all languages; not a few novels; and what was most conspicuous, an elaborate collection of illustrated works on art, Egyptian, Greek, Roman, Medieval, Mexican, Japanese, Indian, and whatever else had come in his way. Add to this a shelf of music, and then—construct the tall, slender, large-eyed, thin-nosed, dark-haired figure lying exhausted on the sofa.

He rose to greet Strong with a laugh like a boy, and cried: "Well, skeptic, how do the heathen rage?"

"The heathen are all right," replied Strong. "The orthodox are the ragers."

"Never mind the orthodox," said Hazard. "I will look after them. Tell me about the Pagans. I felt like St. Paul preaching at Athens the God whom they ignorantly worshiped."

"I took with me the sternest little Pagan I know, my cousin, Esther Dudley," said Strong; "and the only question she asked was whether you believed it all."

"She hit the mark at the first shot," answered Hazard. "I must make them all ask that question. Tell me about your cousin. Who is she? Her name sounds familiar."

"As familiar as Hawthorne," replied Strong. "One of his tales is called after it. Her father comes from a branch of the old Puritan Dudleys, and took a fancy to the name when he met it in Hawthorne's story. You never heard of them before because you have been always away from New York, and when you were here they happened to be away. You know that half a dozen women run this city, and my aunt, Mrs. Murray, is one of the half-dozen. She is training Esther to take her place when she retires. I want you to know my Uncle Dudley and my cousin. I am going to have a little tea-party for them in my rooms, and you must help me with it."

Mr. Hazard asked only to have it put off until the week after the next because of his engagements, and hardly had they fixed the day when another caller appeared.

He was a man of their own age, so quiet and subdued in manner, and so delicate in feature, that he would have been unnoticed in any ordinary group, and shoved aside into a corner. He seemed to face life with an effort; his light-brown eyes had an uneasy look as though they wanted to rest on something that should be less hard and real than what they saw. He was not handsome; his mouth was a little sensual; his yellowish beard was ragged. He was apt to be silent until his shyness wore off, when he became a rapid, nervous talker, full of theories and schemes, which he changed from one day to another, but which were always quite complete and convincing for the moment. At times he had long fits of moodiness and would not open his mouth for days. At other times he sought society and sat up all night talking, planning, discussing, drinking, smoking, living on bread and cheese or whatever happened to be within reach, and sleeping whenever he happened to feel in the humor for it. Rule or method he had none, and his friends had for years given up the attempt to control him. They took it for granted that he would soon kill himself with his ill-regulated existence. Hazard thought that his lungs would give way, and Strong insisted that his brain was the weak spot, and no one ventured to hope that he would long hold out, but he lived on in defiance of them.

"Good evening, Wharton," said the clergyman. "I have been trying to find out from Strong what the heathen think of me. Tell us now the art view of the case. How are you satisfied?"

"Tell me what you were sketching in church," said Strong. "Was it not the new martyrdom of St. Stephen?"

"No," answered Wharton quietly. "It was my own. I found I could not look up; I knew how bad my own work was, and I could not stand seeing it; so I drew my own martyrdom rather than make a scandal by leaving the church."

"Did you hear my sermon?" asked the clergyman.

"I don't remember," answered Wharton vaguely; "what was it about?"

Strong and Hazard broke into a laugh which roused him to the energy of self-defense.

"I never could listen," he said. "It is a slow and stupid faculty. An artist's business is only to see, and to-day I could see nothing but my own things which are all bad. The whole church is bad. It is not altogether worth a bit of Japanese enamel that I have brought round here this evening to show Strong."

He searched first in one pocket, then in another, until he found what he wanted in the pocket of his overcoat, and a warm discussion at once began between him and Strong, who declared that he had a better piece.

"Mine was given me by a Daimio, in Kiusiu," said Strong. "It is the best old bit you ever saw. Come round to my rooms a week from to-morrow at five o'clock in the afternoon, and I will show you all my new japs. The Dudleys are coming to see them, and my aunt Mrs. Murray, and Hazard has promised to come."

"I saw you had Miss Dudley with you at church this morning," said Wharton, still absorbed in study of his enamel, and quite unconscious of his host's evident restlessness.

"Ah! then you could see Miss Dudley!" cried the clergyman, who could not forgive the abrupt dismissal of his own affairs by the two men, and was eager to bring the talk back to his church.

"I can always see Miss Dudley," said Wharton quietly.

"Why?" asked Hazard.

"She is interesting," replied the painter. "She has a style of her own, and I never can quite make up my mind whether to like it or not."

"It is the first time I ever knew you to hesitate before a style," said

Hazard.

"I hesitate before every thing American," replied Wharton, beginning to show a shade of interest in what he was talking of. "I don't know—you don't know—and I never yet met any man who could tell me, whether American types are going to supplant the old ones, or whether they are to come to nothing for want of ideas. Miss Dudley is one of the most marked American types I ever saw."

"What are the signs of the most marked American type you ever saw?" asked Hazard.

"In the first place, she has a bad figure, which she makes answer for a good one. She is too slight, too thin; she looks fragile, willowy, as the cheap novels call it, as though you could break her in halves like a switch. She dresses to suit her figure and sometimes overdoes it. Her features are imperfect. Except her ears, her voice, and her eyes which have a sort of brown depth like a trout brook, she has no very good points."

"Then why do you hesitate?" asked Strong, who was not entirely pleased with this cool estimate of his cousin's person.

"There is the point where the subtlety comes in," replied the painter. "Miss Dudley interests me. I want to know what she can make of life. She gives one the idea of a lightly-sparred yacht in mid-ocean; unexpected; you ask yourself what the devil she is doing there. She sails gayly along, though there is no land in sight and plenty of rough weather coming. She never read a book, I believe, in her life. She tries to paint, but she is only a second rate amateur and will never be any thing more, though she has done one or two things which I give you my word I would like to have done myself. She picks up all she knows without an effort and knows nothing well, yet she seems to understand whatever is said. Her mind is as irregular as her face, and both have the same peculiarity. I notice that the lines of her eyebrows, nose and mouth all end with a slight upward curve like a yacht's sails, which gives a kind of hopefulness and self-confidence to her expression. Mind and face have the same curves."

"Is that your idea of our national type?" asked Strong. "Why don't you put it into one of your saints in the church, and show what you mean by American art?"

"I wish I could," said the artist. "I have passed weeks trying to catch it. The thing is too subtle, and it is not a grand type, like what we are used to in the academies. But besides the riddle, I like Miss Dudley for herself. The way she takes my brutal criticisms of her painting makes my heart bleed. I mean to go down on my knees one of these days, and confess to her that I know nothing about it; only if her style is right, my art is wrong."

"What sort of a world does this new deity of yours belong to?" asked the clergyman.

"Not to yours," replied Wharton quickly. "There is nothing medieval about her. If she belongs to any besides the present, it is to the next world which artists want to see, when paganism will come again and we can give a divinity to every waterfall. I tell you, Hazard, I am sick at heart about our church work; it is a failure. Never till this morning did I feel the whole truth, but the instant I got inside the doors it flashed upon me like St. Paul's great light. The thing does not belong to our time or feelings."

The conversation having thus come round to the subject which Mr. Hazard wanted to discuss, the three men plunged deep into serious talk which lasted till after midnight had struck from the neighboring church.

Chapter II

Punctually the next day at three o'clock, Esther Dudley appeared in her aunt's drawing-room where she found half a dozen ladies chatting, or looking at Mr. Murray's pictures in the front parlor. The lady of the house sat in an arm-chair before the fire in an inner room, talking with two other ladies of the board, one of whom, with an aggressive and superior manner, seemed finding fault with every thing except the Middle Ages and Pericles.

"A tailor who builds a palace to live in," said she, "is a vulgar tailor, and an artist who paints the tailor and his palace as though he were painting a doge of Venice, is a vulgar artist."

"But, Mrs. Dyer," replied her hostess coldly, "I don't believe there was any real difference between a doge of Venice and a doge of New York. They all made fortunes more or less by cheating their neighbors, and when they were rich they wanted portraits. Some one told them to send for Mr. Tizian or Mr. Wharton, and he made of them all the gentlemen there ever were."

Mrs. Dyer frowned a protest against this heresy. "Tizian would have respected his art," said she; "these New York men are making money."

"For my part," said Mrs. Murray as gently as she could, "I am grateful to any one who likes beautiful things and is willing to pay for them, and I hope the artists will make them as beautiful as they can for the money. The number is small."

With this she rose, and moving to the table, called her meeting to order. The ladies seated themselves in a business-like way round about, and listened with masculine gravity to a long written report on the work done or needing to be done at the Children's Hospital. Debate rose on the question of putting in a new kitchen range and renewing the plumbing. Mrs. Dyer took the floor, or the table, very much to herself, dealing severely with the treatment of the late kitchen range, and bringing numerous complaints against the matron, the management and the hospital in general. There was an evident look of weariness on the part of the board when she began, but not until after a two hours' session did she show signs of exhaustion and allow a vote to be taken. The necessary work was then rapidly done, and at last Mrs. Murray, referring in a business-like way to her notes, remarked that she had nothing more to suggest except that Mr. Hazard, the new clergyman at St. John's, should be elected as a member of their visiting committee.

"Do we want more figure-heads there?" asked Mrs. Dyer. "Every day and every hour of Mr. Hazard's time ought to be devoted to his church. What we want is workers. We have no one to look after the children's clothes and go down into the kitchen. All our visitors are good for is to amuse the children for half an hour now and then by telling them stories."

Mrs. Murray explained that the election was rather a matter of custom; that the rector of St. John's always had been a member of their committee, and it would look like a personal slight if they left him off; so the vote was passed and the meeting broke up. When the last echo of rapid talk and leave-taking had ceased, Mrs. Murray sat down again before the fire with the air of one who has tried to keep her temper and has not thoroughly satisfied her ambition.

"Mrs. Dyer is very trying," she said to Esther who stayed after the others went; "but there is always one such woman on every board. I should not care except that she gives me a dreadful feeling that I am like her. I hope I'm not, but I know I am."

"You're not, Aunt Sarah!" replied Esther. "She can stick pins faster and deeper than a dozen such as you. What makes me unhappy is that her spitefulness goes so deep. Her dig at me about telling stories to the children seemed to cut me up by the roots. All I do is to tell them stories."

"I hope she will never make herself useful in that way," rejoined Mrs. Murray grimly. "She would frighten the poor little things into convulsions. Don't let her worry you about usefulness. One of these days you will have to be useful whether you like it or not, and now you are doing enough if you are only ornamental. I know you will hold your tongue at the board meetings, and that is real usefulness."

"Very well, aunt! I can do that. And I can go on cutting out dolls' clothes for the children, though Mrs. Dyer will complain that my dolls are not sufficiently dressed. I wish I did not respect people for despising me."

"If we did not, there would be no Mrs. Dyers," answered her aunt. "She is a terrible woman. I feel always like a sort of dry lamp-wick when she has left me. Never mind! I have something else now to talk about. I want you to make yourself useful in a harder path."

"Not another Charity Board, aunt," said Esther rather piteously.

"Worse!" said Mrs. Murray. "A charity girl! Thirty years ago I had a dear friend who was also a friend of your poor mother's. Her name was Catherine Cortright. She married a man named Brooke, and they went west, and they kept going further and further west until at length they reached Colorado, where she died, leaving one daughter, a child of ten years old. The father married again and had a new family. Very lately he has died, leaving the girl with her stepmother and half-sisters. She is unhappy there; they seem to have brought her up in a strict Presbyterian kind of way, and she does not like it. Mr. Murray is an executor under her father's will, and when she comes of age in a few months, she will have a little independent property. She has asked me to look after her till then, and is coming on at once to make me a visit."

"You are always doing something for somebody," said Esther. "What do you expect her to be, and how long will she stay?"

"I don't expect any thing, my dear, and my heart sinks whenever I think of her. My letters say she is amiable and pretty; but if she is a rattlesnake, I must take her in, and you must help to amuse her."

"I will do all I can," replied Esther. "Don't be low about it. She can't be as bad as Mrs. Dyer even if she is a rattlesnake. If she is pretty, and turns out well, we will make George marry her."

"I wish we might," said her aunt.

Esther went her way and thought no more of the orphan, but Mrs. Murray carried the weight of all New York on her mind. Not the least of her anxieties was the condition of her brother-in-law, Esther's father. He was now a confirmed invalid, grateful for society and amusement, and almost every day he expected his sister-in-law to take him to drive, if the weather was tolerable. The tax was severe, but she bore it with heroism, and his gratitude sustained her. When she came for him the next morning, she found him reading as usual, and waiting for her. "I was just wondering," said he, "whether I could read five minutes longer without a stimulant. Do you know that indiscriminate reading is a fiendish torture. No convict could stand it. I seldom take up a book in these days without thinking how much more amusing it would be to jolt off on a bright day at the head of a funeral procession. Between the two ways of amusing one's-self, I am principled against books."

"You have a very rough way of expressing your tastes," said Mrs. Murray with a shiver, as they got into her carriage. "Do you know, I never could understand the humor of joking about funerals."

"That surprises me," said Mr. Dudley. "A good funeral needs a joke. If mine is not more amusing than my friends', I would rather not go to it. The kind of funeral I am invited to has no sort of charm. Indeed, I don't know that I was ever asked to one that seemed to me to show an elegant hospitality in the host."

"If you can't amuse me better, William, I will drive you home again," said his sister-in-law.

"Not quite yet. I have something more to say on this business of funerals which is just now not a little on my mind."

"Are you joking now, or serious?" asked Mrs. Murray.

"I cannot myself see any humor in what I have to say," replied Mr. Dudley; "but I am told that even professional humorists seldom enjoy jokes at their own expense. The case is this. My doctors, who give me their word of honor that they are not more ignorant than the average of their profession, told me long ago that I might die at any moment. I knew then that I must be quite safe, and thought no more about it. Their first guess was wrong. Instead of going off suddenly and without notice, as a colonel of New York volunteers should, I began last summer to go off by bits, as though I were ashamed to be seen running away. This time the doctors won't say any thing, which alarms me. I have watched myself and them for some weeks until I feel pretty confident that I had better get ready to start. All through life I have been thinking how I could best get out of it, and on the whole I am well enough satisfied with this way, except on Esther's account, and it is about her that I want to consult you."

Mrs. Murray knew her brother-in-law too well to irritate him by condolence or sympathy. She said only: "Why be anxious? Esther can take care of herself. Perhaps she will marry, but if not, she has nothing to fear. The unmarried women nowadays are better off than the married ones."

"Oh!" said Mr. Dudley with his usual air of deep gravity; "it is not she, but her husband who is on my mind. I have hated the fellow all his life. About twice a year I have treacherously stabbed him in the back as he was going out of my own front door. I knew that he would interfere with my comfort if I let him get a footing. After all he was always a poor creature, and did not deserve to live. My conscience does not reproach me. But now, when I am weak, and his ghost rises in an irrepressible manner, and grins at me on my own threshold, I begin to feel a sort of pity, mingled with contempt. I want to show charity to him before I die."

"What on earth do you mean?" asked his sister-in-law with an impatient groan. "For thirty years I have been trying to understand you, and you grow worse every year."

"Now, I am not surprised to hear you say so. Any sympathy for the husband is unusual, no doubt, yet I am not prepared to admit that it is unintelligible. You go too far."

"Take your own way, William. When you are tired, let me know what it is that you think I can do."

"I want you to find the poor fellow, and tell him that I bear him no real ill-will."

"You want me to find a husband for Esther?"

"If you have nothing better to do. I have looked rather carefully through her list of friends, and, taking out the dancing men who don't count, I see nobody who would answer, except perhaps her Cousin George, and to marry him would be cold-blooded. She might as well marry you."

"I have thought a great deal about that match, as you know," replied

Mrs. Murray. "It would not answer. I could get over the cousinship, if

I must, but Esther will want a husband to herself and George is a

vagabond. He could never make her happy."

"George had the ill-luck," said Mr. Dudley, "to inherit a small spark of something almost like genius; and a little weak genius mixed in with a little fortune, goes a long way towards making a jack-o-lantern. Still we won't exaggerate George's genius. After all there is not enough of it to prevent his being the best of the lot."

"He could not hold her a week," said Mrs. Murray; "nor she him."

"I own that on his wedding day he would probably be in Dakota flirting with the bones of a fossil monkey," said Mr. Dudley thoughtfully; "but what better can you suggest?"

"I suggest that you should leave it alone, and let Esther take care of her own husband," replied Mrs. Murray. "Women must take their chance. It is what they are for. Marriage makes no real difference in their lot. All the contented women are fools, and all the discontented ones want to be men. Women are a blunder in the creation, and must take the consequences. If Esther is sensible she will never marry; but no woman is sensible, so she will marry without consulting us."

"You are always eloquent on this subject," said Mr. Dudley. "Why have you never applied for a divorce from poor Murray?"

"Because Mr. Murray happens to be one man in a million," answered she. "Nothing on earth would induce me to begin over again and take such a risk a second time, with life before me. As for bringing about a marriage, I would almost rather bring about a murder."

"Poor Esther!" said he gloomily. "She has been brought up among men, and is not used to harness. If things go wrong she will rebel, and a woman who rebels is lost."

"Esther has known too many good men ever to marry a bad one," she replied.

"I am not sure of that," he answered. "When I am out of the way she will feel lonely, and any man who wants her very much can probably get her. Joking apart, it is there I want your help. Keep an eye on her. Your principles will let you prevent a marriage, even though you are not allowed to make one."

"I hope she will not want my help in either way," said Mrs. Murray; "but if she does, I will remember what you say—though I would rather go out to service at five dollars a week than do this kind of work. Do you know that I have already a girl on my hands? Poor Catherine Brooke's daughter is coming to-morrow from Colorado to be under my care for the next few months till she is of age. She never has been to the East, and I expect to have my hands full."

"If I had known it," said he, "I think I would have selected some wiser woman to look after Esther."

"You are too encouraging," replied Mrs. Murray. "If I talk longer with you I shall have a crying fit. Suppose we change the subject and amuse ourselves in a cheerfuller way."

They finished their drive talking of less personal matters, but Mrs. Murray, after leaving her brother-in-law at his house, went back to her own with spirits depressed to a point as low as any woman past fifty cares to enjoy. She had reason to know that Mr. Dudley was not mistaken about his symptoms, and that not many months could pass before that must happen which he foresaw. He could find some relief in talking and even in jesting about it, but she could only with difficulty keep herself from an outburst of grief. She had every reason to feel keenly. To lose one's oldest friends is a trial that human nature never accustoms itself to bear with satisfaction, even when the loss does not double one's responsibilities; but in this case Mrs. Murray, as she grew old, saw her niece Esther about to come on her hands at the same time when a wild girl from the prairie was on the road to her very door, and she had no sufficient authority to control either of them. For a woman without children of her own, to act this part of matron to an extemporized girls' college might be praise-worthy, but could not bring repose of mind or body.

Mrs. Murray was still wider awake to this truth when she went the next day to the Grand Central Station to wait for the arrival of her Colorado orphan. The Chicago express glided in as gracefully and silently as though it were in quite the best society, and had run a thousand miles or so only for gentle exercise before dining at Delmonico's and passing an evening at the opera. Among the crowd of passengers who passed out were several women whose appearance gave Mrs. Murray a pang of fear, but at length she caught sight of one who pleased her fastidious eye. "I hope it is she," broke from her lips as the girl came towards her, and a moment later her hope was gratified. She drew a breath of relief that made her light-hearted. Whatever faults the girl might have, want of charm was not among them. As she raised her veil, the engine-stoker, leaning from his engine above them, nodded approval. In spite of dust and cinders, the fatigue and exposure of two thousand miles or so of travel, the girl was fresh as a summer morning, and her complexion was like the petals of a sweetbrier rose. Her dark blue woollen dress, evidently made by herself, soothed Mrs. Murray's anxieties more completely than though it had come by the last steamer from the best modiste in Paris.

"Is it possible you have come all the way alone?" she asked, looking about with lurking suspicion of possible lovers still to be revealed.

"Only from Chicago," answered Catherine; "I stopped awhile there to rest, but I had friends to take care of me."

"And you were not homesick or lonely?"

"No! I made friends on the cars. I have been taking care of a sick lady and her three children, who are all on their way to Europe, and wanted to pay my expenses if I would go with them."

"I don't wonder!" said Mrs. Murray with an unusual burst of sympathy.

No sooner had they fairly reached the house than Esther came to see the stranger and found her aunt in high spirits. "She is as natural and sweet as a flower," said Mrs. Murray. "To be sure she has a few Western tricks; she says she stopped awhile at Chicago, and that she has a raft of things in her trunks, and she asks häow, and says äout; but so do half the girls in New York, and I will break her of it in a week so that you will never know she was not educated in Boston and finished in Europe. I was terribly afraid she would wear a linen duster and water-waves."

Catherine became a favorite on the spot. No one could resist her hazel eyes and the curve of her neck, or her pure complexion which had the transparency of a Colorado sunrise. Her good nature was inexhaustible, and she occasionally developed a touch of sentiment which made Mr. Murray assert that she was the most dangerous coquette within his experience. Mr. Murray, who had a sound though uncultivated taste for pretty girls, succumbed to her charms, while George Strong, whose good nature was very like her own, never tired of drawing her out and enjoying her comments on the new life about her.

"What kind of a revolver do you carry?" asked George, gravely, at his first interview with her; "do you like yours heavy, or say a 32 ball?"

"Don't mind him, Catherine," said Mrs. Murray; "he is always making poor jokes."

"Oh, but I'm not strong enough to use heavy shooting-irons," replied Catherine quite seriously. "I had a couple of light ones in my room at home, but father told me I could never hurt any thing with them, and I never did."

"Always missed your man?" asked George.

"I never fired at a man but once. One night I took one of our herders for a thief and shot at him, but I missed, and just got laughed at for a week. That was before we moved down to Denver, where we don't use pistols much."

Strong felt a little doubt whether she was making fun of him or he of her, and she never left him in perfect security on this point.

"What is your name in Sioux, Catherine," he would ask; "Laughing

Strawberry, I suppose, or Jumping Turtle?"

"No!" she answered. "I have a very pretty name in Sioux. They call me the Sage Hen, because I am so quiet. I like it much better than my own name."

Strong was beaten at this game. She capped all his questions for him with an air of such good faith as made him helpless. Whether it were real or assumed, he could not make up his mind. He took a great fancy to the Sage Hen, while she in her turn took a violent liking for Esther, as the extremest contrast to herself. When Esther realized that this product of Colorado was likely to be on her hands for several hours every day, she felt less amused than either Strong or Mr. Murray, for Miss Brooke's conversation, though entertaining as far as it went, had not the charm of variety. It was not long before her visits to Esther's studio became so frequent and so exhausting that Esther became desperate and felt that some relief must at any cost be found. The poor little prairie flower found New York at first exciting; she felt shy and awkward among the swarms of strange people to whose houses Mrs. Murray soon began to take her by way of breaking her in at once to the manners of New York society; and whenever she could escape, she fled to Esther and her quiet studio, with the feelings of a bird to its nest. The only drawback to her pleasure there was that she had nothing to do; her reading seemed to have been entirely in books of a severely moral caste, and in consequence she could not be induced to open so much as a magazine. She preferred to chatter about herself and the people she met. Before a week had passed Esther felt that something must be done to lighten this burden, and it was then that, as we shall see, Mr. Hazard suggested her using Catherine for a model. The idea might not have been so easily accepted under other circumstances, but it seemed for the moment a brilliant one.

As Wharton had said of Esther, she was but a second-rate amateur. Whether there was a living artist whom Wharton would have classed higher than a first-rate amateur is doubtful. On his scale to be second-rate was a fair showing. Esther had studied under good masters both abroad and at home. She had not the patience to be thorough, but who had? She asked this question of Mr. Wharton when he attacked her for bad drawing, and Wharton's answer left on her mind the impression that he was himself the only thorough artist in the world; yet others with whom she talked hinted much the same thing of themselves. Esther at all events painted many canvases and panels, good or bad, some of which had been exhibited and had even been sold, more perhaps owing to some trick of the imagination which she had put into them than to their technical merit. Yet into one work she had put her whole soul, and with success. This was a portrait of her father, which that severe critic liked well enough to hang on the wall of his library, and which was admitted to have merits even by Wharton, though he said that its unusual and rather masculine firmness of handling was due to the subject and could never be repeated.

Catherine was charmed to sit for her portrait. It was touching to see the superstitious reverence with which this prairie child kneeled before whatever she supposed to be learned or artistic. She took it for granted that Esther's painting was wonderful; her only difficulty was to understand how a man so trivial as George Strong, could be a serious professor, in a real university. She thought that Strong's taste for bric-à-brac was another of his jokes. He tried to educate her, and had almost succeeded when, in producing his last and most perfect bit of Japanese lacquer, he said: "This piece, Catherine, is too pure for man. We pray to it." Catherine sat as serious as eternity, but she believed in her heart that he was making fun of her.

In this atmosphere, to sit for her portrait was happiness, because it made her a part of her society. Esther was surprised to find what a difficult model she was, with liquid reflections of eyes, hair and skin that would have puzzled Correggio. Of course she was to be painted as the Sage Hen.

George sent for sage brush, and got a stuffed sage hen, and photographs of sage-plains, to give Esther the local color for her picture.

Chapter III

Once a week, if she could, Esther passed an hour or two with the children at the hospital. This building had accommodations for some twenty-five or thirty small patients, and as it was a private affair, the ladies managed it to please themselves. The children were given all the sunlight that could be got into their rooms and all the toys and playthings they could profitably destroy. As the doctors said that, with most of them, amusement was all they would ever get out of life, an attempt was made to amuse them. One large room was fitted up for the purpose, and the result was so satisfactory that Esther got more pleasure out of it than the children did. Here a crowd of little invalids, playing on the yellow floor or lying on couches, were always waiting to be amused and longing to be noticed, and thought themselves ill-treated if at least one of the regular visitors did not appear every day to hear of their pains and pleasures. Esther's regular task was to tell them a story, and, learning from experience that she could double its effect by illustrating it, she was in the custom of drawing, as she went on, pictures of her kings and queens, fairies, monkeys and lions, with amiable manners and the best moral characters. Thus drawing as she talked, the story came on but slowly, and spread itself over weeks and months of time.

On this Saturday afternoon Esther was at her work in the play-room, surrounded by a dozen or more children, with a cripple, tortured by hip-disease, lying at her side and clinging to her skirt, while a proud princess, with red and white cheeks and voluminous robes, was making life bright with colored crayons and more highly colored adventures, when the door opened and Esther saw the Rev. Stephen Hazard, with her aunt, Mrs. Murray, on the threshold.

Mr. Hazard was not to blame if the scene before him made a sudden and sharp picture on his memory. The autumn sun was coming in at the windows; the room was warm and pleasant to look at; on a wide brick hearth, logs of hickory and oak were burning; two tall iron fire-dogs sat up there on their hind legs and roasted their backs, animals in which the children were expected to take living interest because they had large yellow glass eyes through which the fire sparkled; with this, a group of small invalids whose faces and figures were stamped with the marks of organic disease; and in the center—Esther!

Mr. Hazard had come here this afternoon partly because he thought it his duty, and partly because he wanted to create closer relations with a parishioner so likely to be useful as Mrs. Murray. He was miserable with a cold, and was weak with fatigue. His next sermon was turning out dull and disjointed. His building committee were interfering and quarreling with Wharton. A harsh north-west wind had set his teeth on edge and filled his eyes with dust. Rarely had he found himself in a less spiritual frame of mind than when he entered this room. The contrast was overwhelming. When Esther at first said quite decidedly that nothing would induce her to go on with her story, he felt at once that this was the only thing necessary to his comfort, and made so earnest an appeal that she was forced to relent, though rather ungraciously, with a laughing notice that he must listen very patiently to her sermon as she had listened to his. The half hour which he now passed among kings and queens in tropical islands and cocoanut groves, with giants and talking monkeys, was one of peace and pleasure. He drew so good a monkey on a cocoanut tree that the children shouted with delight, and Esther complained that his competition would ruin her market. She rose at last to go, telling him that she was sorry to seem so harsh, but had she known that his pictures and stories were so much better than hers, she would never have voted to make him a visitor.

Mr. Hazard was flattered. He naturally supposed that a woman must have some fine quality if she could interest Wharton and Strong, two men utterly different in character, and at the same time amuse suffering children, and drag his own mind out of its deepest discouragement, without show of effort or consciousness of charm. In this atmosphere of charity, where all faiths were alike and all professions joined hands, the church and the world became one, and Esther was the best of allies; while to her eyes Mr. Hazard seemed a man of the world, with a talent for drawing and a quick imagination, gentle with children, pleasant with women, and fond of humor. She could not help thinking that if he would but tell pleasant stories in the pulpit, and illustrate them on a celestial blackboard such as Wharton might design, church would be an agreeable place to pass one's Sunday mornings in. As for him, when she went away with her aunt, he returned to his solitary dinner with a mind diverted from its current. He finished his sermon without an effort. He felt a sort of half-conscious hope that Esther would be again a listener, and that he might talk it over with her. The next morning he looked about the church and was disappointed at not seeing her there. This young man was used to flattery; he had been sickened with it, especially by the women of his congregation; he thought there was nothing of this nature against which he was not proof; yet he resented Esther Dudley's neglect to flatter him by coming to his sermon. Her absence was a hint that at least one of his congregation did not care to hear him preach a second time.

Piqued at this indifference to his eloquence and earnestness he went the next afternoon, according to his agreement, to Strong's rooms, knowing that Miss Dudley was to be there, and determined to win her over. The little family party which Strong had got together was intended more for this purpose than for any other, and Strong, willing to do what he could to smooth his friend's path, was glad to throw him in contact with persons from whom he could expect something besides flattery. Strong never conceived it possible that Hazard could influence them, but he thought their influence likely to be serious upon Hazard. He underrated his friend's force of character.

His eyes were soon opened. Catherine Brooke made her first appearance on this occasion, and was greatly excited at the idea of knowing people as intellectual as Mr. Hazard and Mr. Wharton. She thought them a sort of princes, and was still ignorant that such princes were as tyrannical as any in the Almanach de Gotha, and that those who submitted to them would suffer slavery. Her innocent eagerness to submit was charming, and the tyrants gloated over the fresh and radiant victim who was eager to be their slave. They lured her on, by assumed gentleness, in the path of bric-à-brac and sermons.

In her want of experience she appealed to Strong, who had not the air of being their accomplice, but seemed to her a rather weak-minded ally of her own. Strong had seated her by the window, and was teaching her to admire his collections, while Wharton and Hazard were talking with the rest of the party on the other side of the room.

"What kind of an artist is Mr. Wharton?" asked Catherine.

"A sort of superior house-painter," replied Strong. "He sometimes does glazing."

"Nonsense!" said Catherine contemptuously. "I know all about him. Esther has told me. I want to know how good an artist he is. What would they think of him in Paris?"

"That would depend on whether they owned any of his pictures," persisted

Strong. "I think he might be worse. But then I have one of his

paintings, and am waiting to sell it when the market price gets well up.

Do you see it? The one over my desk in the corner. How do you like it?"

"Why does he make it so dark and dismal?" asked Catherine. "I can't make it out."

"That is the charm," he replied. "I never could make it out myself; let's ask him;" and he called across the room: "Wharton, will you explain to Miss Brooke what your picture is about? She wants to know, and you are the only man who can tell her."

Wharton in his grave way came over to them, and first looking sadly at

Miss Brooke, then at the picture, said at length, as though to himself:

"I thought it was good when I did it. I think it is pretty good now.

What criticism do you make, Miss Brooke?"

Catherine was in mortal terror, but stood her ground like a heroine. "I said it seemed to me dark, Mr. Wharton, and I asked why you made it so."

Wharton looked again at the picture and meditated over it. Then he said:

"Do you think it would be improved by being lighter?"

Although Catherine pleaded guilty to this shocking heresy, she did it with so much innocence of manner that, in a few minutes, Wharton was captured by her sweet face, and tried to make her understand his theory that the merit of a painting was not so much in what it explained as in what it suggested. Comments from the by-standers interfered with his success. Hazard especially perplexed Catherine's struggling attention by making fun of Wharton's lecture.

"Your idea of a picture," said he, "must seem to Miss Brooke like my Cincinnati parishioner's idea of a corn-field. I was one day admiring his field of Indian corn, which stretched out into the distance like Lake Erie in a yellow sunset, when the owner, looking at his harvest as solemnly as Wharton is looking at his picture, said that what he liked most was the hogs he could see out of it."

"Well," said Wharton, "the Dutch made a good school out of men like him. Art is equal to any thing. I will paint his hogs for him, slaughtered and hung up by the hind legs, and if I know how to paint, I can put his corn-field into them, like Ostade, and make the butchers glow with emotion."

"Don't believe him, Miss Brooke," said Hazard. "He wants you to do his own work, and if you give in to him you are lost. He covers a canvas with paint and then asks you to put yourself into it. He might as well hold up a looking-glass to you. Any man can paint a beautiful picture if he could persuade Miss Brooke to see herself in it."

"What a pretty compliment," said Esther. "It is more flattering than the picture."

"You can prove its truth, Miss Dudley," said Hazard. "It is easy to show that I am right. Paint Miss Brooke yourself! Give to her the soul of the Colorado plains! Show that beauty of subject is the right ideal! You will annihilate Wharton and do an immortal work."

Hazard's knack of fixing an influence wherever he went had long been the wonder of Strong, but had never surprised or amused him more than now, when he saw Esther, after a moment's hesitation, accept this idea, and begin to discuss with Hazard the pose and surroundings which were to give Catherine Brooke's picture the soul of the Colorado plains. Hazard drew well and had studied art more carefully than most men. He used to say that if he had not a special mission for the church, as a matter of personal taste he should have preferred the studio. He not only got at once into intimate relations with Esther and Catherine, but he established a sort of title in Esther's proposed portrait. Strong laughed to himself at seeing that even Mr. Dudley, who disliked the clergy more than any other form of virtue, was destined to fall a victim to Hazard's tact.

When the clergyman walked away from Strong's rooms that afternoon, he felt, although even to himself he would not have confessed it, a little elated. Instinct has more to do than vanity with such weaknesses, and Hazard's instinct told him that his success, to be lasting, depended largely on overcoming the indifference of people like the Dudleys. If he could not draw to himself and his church the men and women who were strong enough to have opinions of their own, it was small triumph to draw a procession of followers from a class who took their opinions, like their jewelry, machine-made. He felt that he must get a hold on the rebellious age, and that it would not prove rebellious to him. He meant that Miss Dudley should come regularly to church, and on his success in bringing her there, he was half-ready to stake the chances of his mission in life.

So Catherine's portrait was begun at once, when Catherine herself had been barely a week in New York. To please Esther, Mr. Dudley had built for her a studio at the top of his house, which she had fitted up in the style affected by painters, filling it with the regular supply of eastern stuffs, porcelains, and even the weapons which Damascus has the credit of producing; one or two ivory carvings, especially a small Italian crucifix; a lay figure; some Japanese screens, and eastern rugs. Her studio differed little from others, unless that it was cleaner than most; and it contained the usual array of misshapen sketches pinned against the wall, and of spoiled canvases leaning against each other in corners as though they were wall flower beauties pouting at neglect.

Here Catherine Brooke was now enthroned as the light of the prairie, and day after day for three weeks, Esther labored over the portrait with as much perseverance as though Hazard were right in promising that it should make her immortal. The last days of November and the first of December are the best in the year for work, and Esther worked with an energy that surprised her.

She wanted to extort praise from Mr. Wharton, and even felt a slight shade of responsibility towards Mr. Hazard. At first no one was to be admitted to see it while in progress; then an exception was made for Strong and Hazard who came to the house one evening, and in a moment of expansiveness were told that they would be admitted to the studio. They came, and Esther found Mr. Hazard's suggestions so useful that she could not again shut him out. In return she was shamed into going to church with her aunt the following Sunday, where she heard Mr. Hazard preach again. She did not enjoy it, and did not think it necessary to repeat the compliment. "One should not know clergymen," she said in excuse to her father for not liking the sermon; "there is no harm in knowing an actress or opera-singer, but religion is a serious thing." Mr. Hazard did not know how mere a piece of civility her attendance was; he saw only that she was present, that his audience was larger and his success more assured than ever. With this he was well satisfied, and, as he had been used in life always to have his own way, he took it for granted that in this instance he had got it.

The portrait of course did not satisfy Esther. Do what she would, Catherine's features and complexion defied modeling and made the artificial colors seem hard and coarse. The best she could paint was not far from down-right failure. She felt the danger and called Mr. Hazard to her aid. Hazard suggested alterations, and insisted much on what he was pleased to call "values," which were not the values Esther had given. With his help the picture became respectable, as pictures go, although it would not have been with impunity that Tintoret himself had tried to paint the soul of the prairie.

Esther, like most women, was timid, and wanted to be told when she could be bold with perfect safety, while Hazard's grasp of all subjects, though feminine in appearance, was masculine and persistent in reality. To be steadily strong was not in Esther's nature. She was audacious only by starts, and recoiled from her own audacity. Before long, Hazard began to dominate her will. She felt a little uneasy until he had seen and approved her work. More than once he disapproved, and then she had to do it over again. She began at length to be conscious of this impalpable tyranny, and submitted to it only because she felt her own dependence and knew that in a few days more she should be free. If he had been clerical or dogmatic, she might have resented it and the charm would have broken to pieces on the spot, but he was for the time a painter like herself, as much interested in the art, and caring for nothing else.

Towards Christmas the great work was finished, and the same party that had met a month before at Strong's rooms, came together again in Esther's studio to sit upon and judge the portrait they had suggested. Mr. Dudley, with some effort, climbed up from his library; Mrs. Murray again acted as chaperon, and even Mr. Murray, whose fancy for pictures was his only known weakness, came to see what Esther had made of Catherine. The portrait was placed in a light that showed all its best points and concealed as far as possible all its weak ones; and Esther herself poured out tea for the connoisseurs.

To disapprove in such a company was not easy, but Wharton was equal to the task. He never compromised his convictions on such matters even to please his hosts, and in consequence had given offense to most of the picture-owners in the city of New York. He showed little mercy now to Esther, and perhaps his attack might have reduced her courage to despair, had she not found a champion who took her defense wholly on his own shoulders. It happened that Wharton attacked parts of the treatment for which Hazard was responsible, and when Hazard stepped into the lists, avowing that he had advised the work and believed it to be good, Esther was able to retire from the conflict and to leave the two men fighting a pitched battle over the principles of art. Hazard defended and justified every portion of the painting with a vigor and resource quite beyond Esther's means, and such as earned her lively gratitude. When he had reduced Wharton to silence, which was not a difficult task, for Wharton was a poor hand at dispute or argument, and felt rather than talked, Mr. Hazard turned to Esther who gave him a look of gratitude such as she had rarely conferred on any of his sex.

"I think we have ground him to powder at last," said Hazard with his boyish laugh of delight.

"I never knew before what it was to have a defender," said she simply.

Meanwhile Strong, who thought this battle no affair of his, was amusing himself as usual by chaffing Catherine. "I have told my colleague, who professes languages," said he, "that I have a young Sioux in the city, and he is making notes for future conversation with you."

"What will he talk about," asked Catherine; "are all professors as foolish as you?"

"He will be light and airy with you. He asked me what gens you belonged to. I told him I guessed it was the grouse gens. He said he had not been aware that such a totem existed among the Sioux. I replied that, so far as I could ascertain, you were the only surviving member of your family."

"Well, and what am I to say?" asked Catherine.

"Tell him that the Rocky Mountains make it their only business to echo his name," said Strong. "Have you an Indian grandmother?"

"No, but perhaps I could lariat an old aunt for him, if he will like me better for it."

"Aunt will do," said Strong. "Address the old gentleman in Sioux, and call him the 'dove with spectacles.' It will please his soft old heart, and he will take off his spectacles and fall in love with you. There is nothing so frivolous as learning; nothing else knows enough."

"I like him already," said Catherine. "A professor with spectacles is worth more than a Sioux warrior. I will go with him."

"Don't be in a hurry," replied Strong; "it will come to about the same thing in the end. My colleague will only want your head to dry and stuff for his collection."

"If I were a girl again," said Mrs. Murray, who was listening to their conversation, "I would much rather a man should ask for my head than my heart."

"That is what is the matter with all of you," said Strong. "There are Wharton and Esther at it again, quarreling about Catherine's head. Every body disputes about her head, and I am the only one who goes for her heart."

"Mr. Wharton is so stern," pleaded Esther in defense against the charge of quarreling. "A hundred times he has told me that I can't draw; he should have made me learn when he undertook to teach me."

"You might learn more easily now, if you would be patient about it," said Wharton. "You have too much quickness and not enough knowledge."

"I think Mr. Hazard turns his compliments better than you," said Esther. "After one of your speeches I have to catch my breath and think what it means."

"I mean that you ought to be a professional," replied Wharton.

"But if I were able to be a professional, do you think I would be an amateur?" asked Esther. "No! I would decorate a church."

"If that is all your ambition, do it now!" said Wharton. "Come and help me to finish St. John's. I have half a dozen workmen there who are certainly not so good as you."

"What will you give me to do?" asked she.

"I will engage you to paint, under my direction, a large female figure on the transept wall. There are four vacant spaces for which I have made only rough drawings, and you can try your hand on whichever you prefer. You shall be paid like the other artists, and you will find some other women employed there, to keep you company."

"Let me choose the subject," said Mr. Hazard. "I think I have a voice in the matter."

"That depends on your choice," replied Wharton.

"It must be St. Cecilia, of course," said Hazard; "and Miss Brooke must sit again as model."

"Could you not sit yourself as St. George on the dragon?" asked Strong. "I have just received a tertiary dragon from the plains, which I should like to see properly used in the interests of the church."

"Catherine is a better model," answered Esther.

"You've not yet seen my dragon. Let me bring him round to you. With

Hazard on his back, he would fly away with you all into the stars."

"There are dragons enough at St. John's," answered Hazard. "I will ride on none of them."

"You've no sense of the highest art," said Strong. "Science alone is truth. You are throwing away your last chance to reconcile science and religion."

So, after much discussion, it was at last decided that Esther Dudley should begin work at St. John's as a professional decorator under Mr. Wharton's eye, and that her first task should be to paint a standing figure of St. Cecilia, some eight or ten feet high, on the wall of the north transept.

Chapter IV

St. John's church was a pleasant spot for such work. The north transept, high up towards the vault of the roof, was still occupied by a wide scaffold which shut in the painters and shut out the curious, and ran the whole length of its three sides, being open towards the body of the church. When Esther came to inspect her field of labor, she found herself obliged to choose between a space where her painting would be conspicuous from below, and one where, except in certain unusual lights, it could hardly be seen at all. Partly out of delicacy, that she might not seem to crowd Wharton's own work into the darkness; partly out of pure diffidence, Esther chose the least conspicuous space, and there a sort of studio was railed off for her, breast high, within which she was mistress. Wharton, when painting, was at this time engaged at some distance, but on the same scaffolding, near the nave.

The great church was silent with the echoing silence which is audible. Except for a call from workmen below to those at work above, or for the murmur of the painters as they chatted in intervals of rest, or for occasional hammering, which echoed in hollow reverberations, no sound disturbed repose. Here one felt the meaning of retreat and self-absorption, the dignity of silence which respected itself; the presence which was not to be touched or seen. To a simple-minded child like Catherine Brooke, the first effect was as impressive as though she were in the church of St. Mark's. She was overwhelmed by the space and silence, the color and form; and as she came close to Wharton's four great figures of the evangelists and saw how coarsely they were painted, and looked sheer down from them upon the distant church-floor, she thought herself in an older world, and would hardly have felt surprised at finding herself turned into an Italian peasant-girl, and at seeing Michael Angelo and Raphael, instead of Wharton and Esther, walk in at the side door, and proceed to paint her in celestial grandeur and beauty, as the new Madonna of the prairie, over the high altar.

This humility lasted several minutes. Then after glancing steadfastly at

Wharton's figure of John of Patmos which stood next to that which

Esther was to paint, Catherine suddenly broke out:

"Shade of Columbus! You are not going to make me look like that?"

"I suppose I must," replied Esther, mischievously.

"Lean and dingy, in a faded brown blanket?" asked Catherine in evident anguish.

"So Mr. Wharton says," answered Esther, unrelentingly.

"Not if I'm there," rejoined Catherine, this time with an air of calm decision. "I'm no such ornery saint as that."

Henceforth she applied all her energies and feminine charms to the task of preventing this disaster, and her first effort was to make a conquest of Wharton. Esther stood in fear of the painter, who was apt to be too earnest to measure his words with great care. He praised little and found fault much. He broke out in rage with all work that seemed to him weak or sentimental. He required Esther to make her design on the spot that he might see moment by moment what it was coming to, and half a dozen times he condemned it and obliged her to begin anew. Almost every day occurred some scene of discouragement which made Esther almost regret that she had undertaken a task so hard.

Catherine, being encouraged by the idea that Esther was partly struggling for her sake, often undertook to join in the battle and sometimes got roughly handled for her boldness.

"Why can't you let her go her own way, Mr. Wharton, and see what she means to do?" asked Catherine one morning, after a week of unprofitable labor.

"Because she does not come here to go her own way, Miss Brooke, but to go the right way."

"But don't you see that she is a woman, and you are trying to make a man of her?"

"An artist must be man, woman and demi-god," replied Wharton sternly.

"You want me to be Michael Angelo," said Esther, "and I hate him. I don't want to draw as badly as he did."

Wharton gave a little snort of wrath: "I want you to be above your subject, whatever it is. Don't you see? You are trying to keep down on a level with it. That is not the path to Paradise. Put heaven in Miss Brooke's eyes! Heaven is not there now; only earth. She is a flower, if you like. You are the real saint. It is your own paradise that St. Cecilia is singing about. I want to make St. Cecilia glow with your soul, not with Miss Brooke's. Miss Brooke has got no soul yet."

"Neither have I," groaned Esther, making up a little face at Wharton's vehemence.

"No," said Wharton, seized with a gravity as sudden as his outbreak, "I suppose not. A soul is like a bird, and needs a sharp tap on its shell to open it. Never mind! One who has as much feeling for art as you have, must have soul some where."

This sort of lecture might be well enough for Esther, if she had the ability to profit by it, but Catherine had no mind to be thus treated as though she were an early Christian lay-figure. She flushed at hearing herself coolly flung aside like common clay, and her exquisite eyes half filled with tears as she broke out:

"I believe you think I'm a beetle because I come from Colorado! Why may

I not have a soul as well as you?"

Wharton started at this burst of feeling; he felt as though he had really cracked the egg-shell of what he called a soul, in the wrong person; but he was not to be diverted from his lecture. "There, Miss Dudley," he said, "look at her now!" Then, catching a crayon, he continued: "Wait! Let me try it myself!" and began rapidly to draw the girl's features. Quite upset by this unexpected recoil of her attack, Catherine would have liked to escape, but the painter, when the fit was on him, became very imperious, and she dared not oppose his will. When at length he finished his sketch, he had the civility to beg her pardon.

"This is a man's work," said Esther, studying his drawing. "No woman would ever have done it. I don't like it. I prefer her as she is and as I made her."

Wharton himself seemed to be not perfectly satisfied with his own success, for he made no answer to Esther's criticism, and after one glance at his sketch, relapsed into moody silence. Perhaps he felt that what he had drawn was not a St. Cecilia at all, and still less a Catherine Brooke. He had narrowed the face, deepened its lines, made the eyes much stronger and darker, and added at least ten years to Catherine's age, in order to give an expression of passion subsided and heaven attained.

"You have reached Nirvana," said Esther to Catherine, still studying the sketch.

"What is Nirvana?" asked Catherine.

"Ask Mr. Wharton. He has put you there."

"Nirvana is what I mean by Paradise," replied Wharton slowly. "It is eternal life, which, my poet says, consists in seeing God."

"I would not like to look like that," said Catherine in an awe-struck tone. "Do you think this picture will ever be like me?"

"The gods forbid!" said the painter uneasily.

Catherine, who could not take her eyes from this revelation of the possible mysteries in her own existence, mysteries which for the first time seemed to have come so near as to over-shadow her face, now suddenly turned to Wharton and said with irresistible simplicity:

"Mr. Wharton, will you let me have it? I have no money. Will you give it to me?"

"You could not buy it. I will give it to you on one condition," replied

Wharton.

"Don't make it a hard one."

"You shall forget that I said you had no soul."

"Oh!" said Catherine greatly relieved; "if I have one, you were the first to see it."

She carried the sketch away with her, nor has any one caught sight of it since she rolled it up. She refused to show it or talk of it, until even Strong was forced to drop the subject, and leave her to dream in peace of the romance that could give such a light to her eyes.

Strong was one of the few persons allowed to climb up to their perch and see their work. When he next came, Esther told him of Wharton's lecture, and of Catherine's sudden rebellion. Delighted with this new flight of his prairie bird, Strong declared that as they were all bent on taking likenesses of Catherine, he would like to try his own hand at it, and show them how an American Saint ought to look when seen by the light of science. He then set to work with

Esther's pencils, and drew a portrait of Catherine under the figure of a large Colorado beetle, with wings extended. When it was done he pinned it against the wall.

"Now, Esther!" said he. "Take my advice. No one wants European saints over here; they are only clerical bric-à-brac, and what little meaning they ever had is not worth now a tolerable Japanese teapot; but here is a national saint that every one knows; not an American citizen can come into your church from Salt Lake City to Nantucket, who will not say that this is the church for his money; he will believe in your saints, for he knows them. Paint her so!"

"Very well!" said Catherine. "If Mr. Wharton will consent, I have no objection."

Wharton took it with his usual seriousness. "I believe you are right," said he sadly. "I feel more and more that our work is thrown away. If Hazard and the committee will consent, Miss Dudley shall paint what she likes for all me."

No one dared carry die joke so far as to ask Mr. Hazard's consent to canonize this American saint, and Strong after finishing his sketch, and labelling it: "Sta. Catarina 10-Lineata (Colorado)," gave it to Catherine as a companion to Wharton's. For some time she was called the beetle. Wharton's conscience seemed to smite him for his rudeness, and Catherine was promoted to the position of favorite. While Esther toiled over the tiresome draperies of her picture, Catherine would wander off with Wharton on his tours of inspection; she listened to all the discussions, and picked up the meaning of his orders and criticisms; in a short time she began to maintain opinions of her own. Wharton liked to have her near him, and came to get her when she failed to appear at his rounds. They became confidential and sympathetic.

"Are you never homesick for your prairie?" he asked one day.

"Not a bit!" she answered. "I like the East. What is the use of having a world to one's self?"

"What is the use of any thing?" asked Wharton.

"I give it up," she replied. "Does art say that a woman is no use?"

"I know of nothing useful in life," said he, "except what is beautiful or creates beauty. You are beautiful, and ought to be most so on your prairie."

"Am I really beautiful?" asked Catherine with much animation. "No one ever told me so before."

This was coquetry. The young person had often heard of the fact, and, even had she not, her glass told her of it several times a day. She meant only that this was the first time the fact came home to her as a new and exquisite sensation.

"You have the charm of the Colorado hills, and plains," said he. "But you won't keep it here. You will become self-conscious, and self-consciousness is worse than ugliness."

"Nonsense!" said Catherine boldly. "I know more art than you, if that is your notion. Do you suppose girls are so savage in Denver as not to know when they are pretty? Why, the birds are self-conscious! So are horses! So are antelopes! I have seen them often showing off their beauties like New York women, and they are never so pretty as then."

"Don't try it," said he. "If you do, I shall warn you. Tell me, do you think my figure of St. Paul here self-conscious? I lie awake nights for fear I have made him so."

Catherine looked long at the figure and then shook her head. "I could tell you if it were a woman," she said. "All women are more or less alike; but men are quite different, and even the silly ones may have brains somewhere. How can I tell?"

"A grain of self-consciousness would spoil him," said Wharton.

"Then men must be very different from women," she replied. "I will give you leave to paint me on every square inch of the church, walls and roof, and defy you to spoil any charm you think I have, if you will only not make me awkward or silly; and you may make me as self-conscious as Esther's St. Cecilia there, only she calls it modesty."

Catherine was so pulled about and put to such practical uses in art as to learn something by her own weary labors. A quick girl soon picks up ideas when she hears clever men talking about matters which they understand. Esther began to feel a little nervous. Catherine took so kindly to every thing romantic that Wharton began to get power over her. He had a queer imagination of his own, which she could not understand, but which had a sort of fascination for her. She ran errands for him, and became a sort of celestial messenger about the church. As for Wharton, he declared that she stood nearer nature than any woman he knew, and she was in sympathy with his highest emotions. He let her ask innumerable questions, which he answered or not, as happened to suit his mood. He paid no attention to Esther's remonstrances at being deprived of her model, but whenever he wanted Catherine for any purpose, he sent for her, and left Esther to her own resources. Catherine had her own reasons for being docile and for keeping him in good humor. She started with the idea that she did not intend to be painted, if she could help it, as a first century ascetic, without color, and clothed in a hair-cloth wrapper; and having once begun the attempt to carry her own object, she was drawn on without the power to stop.

Her intimacy with Wharton began to make Esther uneasy, so that one day, when Strong came up, and, missing Catherine, asked what had become of her, she consulted him on the subject.

"Catherine has gone off with Mr. Wharton to inspect," she said. "He comes for her or sends for her every day. What can I do about it?"

"Where is the harm?" asked Strong. "If she likes to pass an hour or two doing that sort of thing, I should think it was good for her."

"But suppose she takes a fancy to him?"

"Oh! No woman could marry Wharton," said Strong. "He would forget her too often, and she would lose patience with him before he thought of her again. Give her her head! He will teach her more that is worth her knowing than she would learn in a life-time in Aunt Sarah's parlor."

"I wish I could give her something else to amuse her."

"Well!" replied Strong. "We will invent something." Catherine returned a few minutes later, and he asked her how she got on with the task-master, and whether he had yet recovered her favor.

"Since the beetle turned on him," said Catherine, "we have got on like two little blind mice. He has been as kind to me as though I were his mother; but why is he so mysterious? He will not tell me his history."

"He is the same to us all," said Strong. "Some people think he is ashamed of his origin. He was picked out of the gutters of Cincinnati by some philanthropist and sent abroad for an education. The fact is that he cares no more about his origin than you do for being a Sioux Indian, but he had the misfortune to marry badly in Europe, and hates to talk of it."

"Then he has a wife already, when he is breaking my young heart?" exclaimed Catherine.

"I would like to calm your fears, my poor child," said Strong; "but the truth is that no one knows what has become of his wife. She may be alive, and she may be dead. Do you want me to find out?"

"I am dying to know," said Catherine; "but I will make him tell me all about it one of these days."

"Never!" replied Strong. "He lives only in his art since the collapse of his marriage. He eats and drinks paint."

"Does he really paint so very well?" asked Catherine thoughtfully. "Is he a great genius?"

"Young woman, we are all of us great geniuses. We never say so, because we are as modest as we are great, but just look into my book on fossil batrachians."

"I don't feel the least interest in you or your batrachiums; but I adore

Mr. Wharton."

"What is the good of your adoring Wharton?" asked the professor.

"Short's very good as far as he goes, but the real friend is Codlin, not

Short."

"I shall hate you if you always make fun of me. What do you mean by your

Codlins and Shorts?"

"Did you never read Dickens?" cried Strong.

"I never read a novel in my life, if that is what you are talking about," answered Catherine.

"Ho! Cousin Esther! The Sioux don't read Dickens. You should join the tribe."

"I always told you that sensible people never read," said Esther, hard at work on her painting. "Do you suppose St. Cecilia ever read Dickens or would have liked him if she had?"

"Perhaps not," said Strong. "I take very little stock in saints, and she strikes me as a little of a humbug, your Cecilia; but I would like to know what the effect of the 'Old Curiosity Shop' would be on a full-blooded Indian squaw. Catherine, will you try to read it if I bring you a copy here?"

"May I?" asked Catherine. "You know I was taught to believe that novels are sinful."

Strong stared at her a moment with surprise that any new trait in her could surprise him, and then went on solemnly: "Angel, you are many points too good for this wicked city. If you remain here unperverted, you will injure our trade. I must see to it that your moral tone is lowered. Will you read a novel of this person named Dickens if Mr. Hazard will permit you to do so in his church?"

"If Mr. Hazard says I must, I shall do so with pleasure," replied Catherine with her best company manners; and the Reverend Mr. Hazard, having been taken into Esther's confidence on the subject, decided, after reflection, that Miss Brooke's moral nature would not be hurt by reading Dickens under such circumstances; so the next day Catherine was plunged into a new world of imagination which so absorbed her thoughts that for the time Wharton himself seemed commonplace. High on her scaffolding which looked sheer down into the empty, echoing church, with huge saints and evangelists staring at her from every side, and martyrs admiring each other's beatitude, Catherine, who was already half inclined to think life unreal, fell into a dream within a dream, and wondered which was untrue.

Esther's anxiety about Catherine was for the time put at rest by the professor's little maneuver, but she had some rather more serious cause for disquiet about herself, in regard to which she did not care to consult her cousin or any one else. Wharton and Strong were not the only men who undertook to enliven her path of professional labor. Every day at noon, the Reverend Stephen Hazard visited his church to see how Wharton was coming forward, and this clerical duty was not neglected after Esther joined the work-people. Much as Mr. Hazard had to do, and few men in New York were busier, he never forgot to look in for a moment on the artists, and Esther could not help noticing that this moment tended to lengthen. He had a way of joining Wharton and Catherine on their tour of inspection, and then bringing Catherine back to Esther's workplace, and sitting down for an instant to rest and look at the St. Cecilia. Time passed rapidly, and once or twice it had come over Esther's mind that, for a very busy man, Mr. Hazard seemed to waste a great deal of time. It grew to be a regular habit that between noon and one o'clock, Esther and Catherine entertained the clergyman of the parish.

The strain of standing in a pulpit is great. No human being ever yet constructed was strong enough to offer himself long as a light to humanity without showing the effect on his constitution. Buddhist saints stand for years silent, on one leg, or with arms raised above their heads, but the limbs shrivel, and the mind shrivels with the limbs. Christian saints have found it necessary from time to time to drop their arms and to walk on their legs, but they do it with a sort of apology or defiance, and sometimes do it, if they can, by stealth. One is a saint or one is not; every man can choose the career that suits him; but to be saint and sinner at the same time requires singular ingenuity. For this reason, wise clergymen, whose tastes, though in themselves innocent, may give scandal to others, enjoy their relaxation, so far as they can, in privacy. Mr.

Hazard liked the society of clever men and agreeable women; he was bound to keep an eye on the progress of his own church; he stepped not an inch outside the range of his clerical duty and privilege; yet ill-natured persons, and there were such in his parish, might say that he was carrying on a secular flirtation in his own church under the pretense of doing his duty. Perhaps he felt the risk of running into this peril. He invited no public attention to the manner in which he passed this part of his time, and never alluded to the subject in other company.

To make his incessant attention still more necessary, it happened that Hazard's knowledge and his library were often drawn upon by Wharton and his workmen. Not only was he learned in all matters which pertained to church arrangement and decoration, but his collection of books on the subject was the best in New York, and his library touched the church wall. Wharton had a quantity of his books in constant use, and was incessantly sending to consult about points of doubt. Hazard was bent upon having every thing correct, and complained sadly when he found that his wishes were not regarded. He lectured Wharton on the subject of early Christian art until he saw that Wharton would no longer listen, and then he went off to Miss Dudley, and lectured her.

Esther was not a good subject for instruction of this sort. She cared little for what the early Christians believed, either in religion or art, and she remembered nothing at all of his deep instruction on the inferences to be drawn from the contents of crypts and catacombs. The more earnest he became, the less could she make out his meaning. She could not reconcile herself to draw the attenuated figures and haggard forms of the early martyrs merely because they suited the style of church decoration; and she could see no striking harmony of relation between these ill-looking beings and the Fifth Avenue audience to whom they were supposed to have some moral or sentimental meaning. After one or two hesitating attempts to argue this point, she saw that it was useless, and made up her mind that as a matter of ordinary good manners, the least she could do was to treat Mr. Hazard civilly in his own church, and listen with respect to his lectures on Christian art. She even did her best to obey his wishes in all respects in which she understood them, but here an unexpected and confusing play of cross-purposes came in to mislead her. Wharton suddenly found that Hazard let Miss Dudley have her own way to an extent permitted to no one else. Esther was not conscious that the expression of a feeling or a wish on her part carried any special weight, but there could be no doubt that if Miss Dudley seemed to want any thing very much, Mr. Hazard showed no sense of shame in suddenly forgetting his fixed theories and encouraging her to do what she pleased. This point was settled when she had been some ten days at work trying to satisfy Wharton's demands, which were also Mr. Hazard's, in regard to the character and expression of St. Cecilia. Catherine was so earnest not to be made repulsive, and Esther's own tastes lay so strongly in the same direction, that when it came to the point, she could not force herself to draw such a figure as was required; she held out with a sort of feminine sweetness such as cried aloud for discipline, and there was no doubt that Wharton was quite ready to inflict it. In spite of Catherine, and Esther too, he would have carried his point, had Esther not appealed to Mr. Hazard; but this strenuous purist, who had worried Wharton and the building committee with daily complaints that the character of their work wanted spiritual earnestness, now suddenly, at a word from Miss Dudley, turned about and encouraged her, against Wharton's orders, to paint a figure, which, if it could be seen, which was fortunately not the case, must seem to any one who cared for such matters, out of keeping with all the work which surrounded it.

"Do you know," said Esther to Mr. Hazard, "that Mr. Wharton insists on my painting Catherine as though she were forty years old and rheumatic?"

"I know," he replied, glancing timidly towards the procession of stern and elderly saints and martyrs, finished and unfinished, which seemed to bear up the church walls. "Do you think she would feel at home here if she were younger or prettier?"

"No! Honestly, I don't think she would," said Esther, becoming bold as he became timid. "I will paint Cecilia eighty years old, if Mr. Wharton wants her so. She will have lost her touch on the piano, and her voice will be cracked, but if you choose to set such an example to your choir, I will obey. But I can't ask Catherine to sit for such a figure. I will send out for some old woman, and draw from her."

"I can't spare Miss Brooke," said Hazard hastily. "The church needs her.

Perhaps you can find some middle way with Wharton."

"No! If I am to paint her at all, I must paint her as she is. There is more that is angelic in her face now, if I could only catch it, than there is in all Mr. Wharton's figures put together, and if I am to commit sacrilege, I would rather be untrue to Mr. Wharton, than to her."

"I believe you are right, Miss Dudley. There is a little look of heaven in Miss Brooke's eyes. If you think you can put it into the St. Cecilia, why not try? If the experiment fails you can try again on another plan. After all, the drapery is the only part that needs to be very strictly in keeping."

Thus this despotic clergyman gave way and irritated Wharton, who, having promised to let him decide the dispute, was now suddenly overruled. He shrugged his shoulders and told Esther in private that he had struggled hard to get permission to do what she was doing, but only the sternest, strongest types would satisfy the church then. "It was all I could do to get them down to the thirteenth century," he said; "whenever I begged for beauty of form, they asked me whether I wanted the place to look like a theater."

"You know they're quite right," said Esther. "It has a terribly grotesque air of theater even now."

"It is a theater," growled Wharton. "That is what ails our religion. But it is not the fault of our art, and if you had come here a little earlier, I would have made one more attempt. I would like now, even as it is, to go back to the age of beauty, and put a Madonna in the heart of their church. The place has no heart."

"I never could have given you help enough for that, Mr. Wharton; but what does it matter about my poor Cecilia? She does no harm up here. No one can see her, and after all it is only her features that are modern!"

"No harm at all, but I wish I were a woman like you. Perhaps I could have my own way."

Esther liked to have her own way. She had the instinct of power, but not the love of responsibility, and now that she found herself allowed to violate Wharton's orders and derange his plans, she became alarmed, asked no more favors, stuck closely to her work, and kept Catherine always at her side. She even tried to return on her steps and follow Wharton's wishes, until she was stopped by Catherine's outcry. Then it appeared that Wharton had gone over to her side. Instead of supporting Esther in giving severity to the figure, he wanted it to be the closest possible likeness of Catherine herself. Esther began to think that men were excessively queer and variable; the more she tried to please them, the less she seemed to succeed; but Mr. Wharton certainly took more interest in the St. Cecilia as it advanced towards completion, although it was not in the least the kind of work which he liked or respected.

Mr. Hazard took not so much interest in the painting. His pleasure in visiting their gallery seemed to be of a different sort. As Esther learned to know him better, she found that he was suffering from over-work and responsibility, and that the painters' gallery was a sort of refuge, where he escaped from care, for an entire change of atmosphere and thought. In this light Esther found him a very charming fellow, especially when he was allowed to have his own way without question or argument. He talked well; drew well; wrote well, and in case of necessity could even sing fairly well. He had traveled far and wide, and had known many interesting people. He had a sense of humor, except where his church was concerned. He was well read, especially in a kind of literature of which Esther had heard nothing, the devotional writings of the church, and the poetry of religious expression. Esther liked to pick out plums of poetry, without having to search for them on her own account, and as Hazard liked to talk even better than she to listen, they babbled on pleasantly together while Catherine read novels which Hazard chose for her, and which he selected with the idea of carrying her into the life of the past. There was an atmosphere of romance about her novels, and not about the novels alone.

Chapter V

While this ecclesiastical idyl was painting and singing itself in its own way, blind and deaf to the realities of life, this life moved on in its accustomed course undisturbed by idyls. The morning's task was always finished at one o'clock. At that hour, if the weather was fine, Mr. Dudley commonly stopped at the church door to take them away, and the rest of the day was given up to society. Esther and Catherine drove, made calls, dined out, went to balls, to the theater and opera, without interrupting their professional work. Under Mrs. Murray's potent influence, Catherine glided easily into the current of society and became popular without an effort. She soon had admirers. One young man, of an excellent and very old Dutch family, Mr. Rip Van Dam, took a marked fancy for her. Mr. Van Dam knew nothing of her, except that she was very pretty and came from Colorado where she had been brought up to like horses, and could ride almost any thing that would not buck its saddle off. This was quite enough for Mr. Van Dam whose taste for horses was more decided than for literature or art. He took Catherine to drive when the sleighing was good, and was flattered by her enthusiastic admiration of his beautiful pair of fast trotters. His confidence in her became boundless when he found that she could drive them quite as well as he. His success in winning her affections would have been greater if Catherine had not found his charms incessantly counteracted by the society of the older and more intelligent men, whom she never met at balls, but whom she saw every morning at the church, and whose tastes and talk struck her imagination. She liked Mr. Van Dam, but she laughed at him, which proved a thoughtless mind, for neither artists, clergymen nor professors were likely to marry her, as this young man might perhaps have done, under sufficient encouragement. When, towards the first of

January, Catherine left Mrs. Murray, in order to stay with Esther, for greater convenience in the church work, Mr. Van Dam's attentions rather fell off. He was afraid of Esther, whom he insisted on regarding as clever, although Esther took much care never to laugh at him, for fear of doing mischief.

Catherine learned to play whist in order to amuse Mr. Dudley. They had small dinners, at which Hazard was sometimes present, and more often Strong, until he was obliged to go West to deliver a course of lectures at St. Louis. In spite of Mr. Dudley's supposed dislike for clergymen, he took kindly to Hazard and made no objection to his becoming a tame cat about the house. To make up a table at whist, Hazard did not refuse to take a hand; and said it was a part of his parochial duty. Mr. Dudley laughed and told him that if he performed the rest of his parochial duties equally ill, the parish should give him a year's leave of absence for purposes of study. Mr. Dudley disliked nothing so much as to be treated like an invalid, or to be serious, and Hazard gratified him by laughing at the doctors. They got on wonderfully well together, to the increasing amazement of Esther.

Card-playing and novel-reading were not the only cases in which Mr. Hazard took a liberal view of his functions. His theology belonged to the high-church school, and in the pulpit he made no compromise with the spirit of concession, but in all ordinary matters of indifference or of innocent pleasure he gave the rein to his instincts, and in regard to art he was so full of its relations with religion that he would admit of no divergence between the two. Art and religion might take great liberties with each other, and both be the better for it, as he thought.

His thirteenth-century ideas led him into a curious experiment which was quite in the thirteenth-century spirit. Catherine's insatiable spirit of coquetry was to blame, although it was not with him that she coquetted. Ready enough to try her youthful powers on most men, she had seemed to recognize by instinct that Mr. Hazard did not belong to her. Yet she could not rest satisfied without putting even him to some useful purpose of her own.

During Hazard's visits to the scaffold, he sometimes took up a pencil and drew. Once he drew a sketch of Wharton in the character of a monk with his brush and pallet in his hands. Catherine asked what connection there was between Mr. Wharton and a monastery.

"None!" replied Mr. Hazard; "but I like to think of church work as done by churchmen. In the old days he would have been a monk and would have painted himself among these figures on the walls."

Esther ventured to criticise Wharton's style; she thought it severe, monotonous, and sometimes strained.

"Wharton's real notion of art," said Hazard, "is a volcano. You may be a volcano at rest, or extinct, or in full eruption, but a volcano of some kind you have got to be. In one of his violent moods he once made me go over to Sicily with him, and dragged me to the top of Etna. It fascinated him, and I thought he meant to jump into it and pull me after him, but at that time he was a sort of used-up volcano himself."

"Then there is really something mysterious about his life?" asked

Catherine.

"Only that he made a very unhappy marriage which he dislikes to think about," replied Hazard. "As an artist it did him good, but it ruined his peace and comfort, if he ever had any. He would never have made the mistake, if he had not been more ignorant of the world than any mortal that ever drew breath, but, as I was saying, a volcano was like a rattlesnake to him, and the woman he married was a volcano."

"What has become of her?" asked Esther.

"I have not dared to ask for years. No one seems to know whether she is living or dead."

"Did he leave her?"

"No; she left him. He was to the last fascinated by her, so much so that, after she left him, when I persuaded him to quit Paris, he insisted on going to Avignon and Vaucluse, because Petrarch had been under the same sort of fascination, and Wharton thought himself the only man in the world who could understand Petrarch. If you want to insult him and make him bitterly hate you, tell him that Laura was a married woman with a dozen children."

"Who was Laura?" asked Catherine; "and why should she not have a dozen children?"

"Laura was a beautiful girl with golden hair and a green dress whom Petrarch first saw in a church at Avignon," answered Hazard. "She was painted among the frescoes of the cathedral, as you are being painted now, Miss Brooke; and Petrarch wrote some hundreds of sonnets about her which Wharton undertook to translate, and made me help him. We were both poets then."

"I want to hear those sonnets," said Catherine, quite seriously, as though the likeness between herself and Laura had struck her as the most natural thing in the world. "Can you remember them?"

"I think I could. Don't find fault with me if you dislike the moral. I approve it because, like Petrarch, I am a bit of a churchman, but I don't know what you may think of a lover who begins by putting his mistress on the same footing with his deity and ends by groaning over the time he has thrown away on her."

"Not to her face?" said Esther.

"Worse! He saw her in church and wrote to her face something like this:

    'As sight of God is the eternal life,

  Nor more we ask, nor more to wish we dare,

  So, lady, sight of thee,'

and so on, or words to that effect. Yet after she was dead he said he had wasted his life in loving her. I remember the whole of the sonnet because it cost me two days' labor in the railway between Avignon and Nice. It runs like this:—

'For my lost life lamenting now I go,
    Which I have placed in loving mortal thing,
    Soaring to no high flight, although the wing
Had strength to rise and loftier sweep to show.
Oh! Thou that seest my mean life and low!
    Invisible! Immortal! Heaven's king!
    To this weak, pathless spirit, succor bring,
And on its earthly faults thy grace bestow!
That I, who lived in tempest and in fear,
    May die in port and peace; and if it be
That life was vain, at least let death be dear!
    In these few days that yet remain to me,
And in death's terrors, may thy hand be near!
    Thou knowest that I have no hope but thee!'

In the Italian this is very great poetry, Miss Brooke, and if you don't think it so in my English, try and see if you can do better."

"Very well," said Catherine, coolly. "I've no doubt we can do it just as well as you and Mr. Wharton. Can't we, Esther?"

"You are impudent enough to make St. Cecilia blush," said Esther, who happened to be wondering whether she might dare to put a little blush into the cheeks of the figure on which she was painting. "You never read a word of Italian in your little life."

"No! But you have!" replied Catherine, as though this were final.

"The libretto of Lucia!" said Esther with scorn.

"No matter!" resumed Catherine. "Bring me the books, Mr. Hazard, and I will translate one of those sonnets if I have to shut up Esther in a dark closet."

"Catherine! Don't make me ridiculous!" said Esther; but Catherine was inspired by an idea, and would not be stopped.

"Bring me the volume now, Mr. Hazard! You shall have your sonnet for Sunday's sermon."

"Don't do it, Mr. Hazard!" exhorted Esther solemnly. "It is one of her Colorado jokes. She does not know what a sonnet is. She thinks it some kind of cattle-punching."

"If I do not give you that sonnet," cried Catherine, "I will give you leave to have me painted as much like an old skeleton as Mr. Wharton chooses."

"Done!" said Hazard, who regarded this as at least one point worth gaining. "You shall have the books. I want to see Wharton's triumph."

"But if I do poetry for you," continued Catherine, "you must do painting for me."

"Very well!" said Hazard. "What shall it be?"

"If I am Laura," said Catherine, "I must have a Petrarch. I want you to put him up here on the wall, looking at me, as he did in the church where he first saw me."

"But what will Wharton and the committee say?" replied Hazard, startled at so monstrous a demand.

"I don't believe Mr. Wharton will object," answered Catherine. "He will be flattered. Don't you see? He is to be Petrarch."

"Oh!" cried Hazard, with a stare. "Now I understand. You want me to paint Wharton as a scriptural character looking across to Miss Dudley's Cecilia."

"You are very slow!" said Catherine. "I think you might have seen it without making me tell you."

To a low-church evangelical parson this idea might have seemed inexpressibly shocking, but there was something in it which, after a moment's reflection, rather pleased Hazard. It was the sort of thing which the Florentines did, and there was hardly an early church in Italy about whose walls did not cling the colors of some such old union of art and friendship in the service of religion. Catherine's figure was already there. Why not place Wharton's by its side and honor the artist who had devoted so large a share of his life to the service of the church, with, it must be confessed, a very moderate share of worldly profit. The longer Hazard thought of it, the less he saw to oppose. His tastes were flattered by the idea of doing something with his own hand that should add to the character and meaning of the building. His imagination was so pleased with the notion that at last he gave his consent:—"Very well, Miss Brooke! I will draw a figure for this next vacant space, and carry it as far as I know how. If Wharton objects he can efface it. But Miss Dudley will have to finish it for me, for I can't paint, and Wharton would certainly stop me if I tried."

Although this pretty bargain which seemed so fair, really threw on Esther the whole burden of writing sonnets and painting portraits for the amusement of Catherine and Mr. Hazard, Catherine begged so hard that she at last consented to do her best, and her consent so much delighted Hazard that he instantly searched his books for a model to work from, and as soon as he found one to answer his purpose, he began with Esther's crayons to draw the cartoon of a large figure which was to preserve under the character of St. Luke the memory of Wharton's features. When Wharton came next to inspect Esther's work, he was told that Mr. Hazard wished to try his hand on designing a figure for the vacant space, and he criticised and corrected it as freely as the rest. For such a task Hazard was almost as competent as Wharton, from the moment the idea was once given, and in this dark corner it mattered little whether a conventional saint were more or less correct.

Meanwhile Catherine carried off a copy of Petrarch, and instantly turned it over to Esther, seeming to think it a matter of course that she should do so trifling a matter as a sonnet with ease. "It won't take you five minutes if you put your mind to it," she said. "You can do any thing you like, and any one could make a few rhymes." Esther, willing to please her, tried, and exhausted her patience on the first three lines. Then Catherine told the story to Mr. Dudley, who was so much amused by her ambition that he gave his active aid, and between them they succeeded in helping Esther to make out a sonnet which Mr. Dudley declared to be quite good enough for Hazard. This done, Esther refused to mix further in the matter, and made Catherine learn her verses by heart. The young woman found this no easy task, but when she thought herself perfect she told Mr. Hazard, as she would have told a schoolmaster, that she was ready with her sonnet.

"I have finished the sonnet, Mr. Hazard," she said one morning in a bashful voice, as though she were again at school.

"Where is it, Miss Brooke?"

Then Catherine, drawing herself up, with her hands behind her, began to recite:

"Oh, little bird! singing upon your way,

   Or mourning for your pleasant summer-tide,

   Seeing the night and winter at your side,

The joyous months behind, and sunny day!

If, as you know your own pathetic lay,

   You knew as well the sorrows that I hide,

   Nestling upon my breast, you would divide

Its weary woes, and lift their load away.

I know not that our shares would then be even,

   For she you mourn may yet make glad your sight,

> While against me are banded death and heaven;
>
> But now the gloom of winter and of night
>
> With thoughts of sweet and bitter years for leaven,
>
> Lends to my talk with you a sad delight."

Esther laughed till the tears rolled down her face at the droll effect of these tenderly sentimental verses in Catherine's mouth, but Hazard took it quite seriously and was so much delighted with Catherine's recitation that he insisted on her repeating it to Wharton, who took it even more seriously than he. Hazard knew that the verses were Esther's, and was not disposed to laugh at them. Wharton saw that Catherine came out with new beauties in every rôle she filled, and already wanted to use her as a model for some future frescoed Euterpe. Esther was driven to laugh alone.

Petrarch and Laura are dangerous subjects of study for young people in a church. Wharton and Hazard knew by heart scores of the sonnets, and were fond of repeating verses either in the original or in their own translations, and Esther soon picked up what they let fall, being quick at catching what was thrown to her. She caught verse after verse of Hazard's favorites, and sometimes he could hear her murmuring as she painted:

> "Siccome eterna vita è veder dio,
>
> Nè più si brama, nè bramar piu lice;"

and at such moments he began to think that he was himself Petrarch, and that to repeat to his Laura the next two verses of the sonnet had become the destiny of his life.

So the weeks ran on until, after a month of hard work, the last days of January saw the two figures nearly completed. When in due time the meaning of St. Luke became evident, Esther and Catherine waited in fear to see how Wharton would take the liberty on which they had so rashly ventured. As the likeness came out more strongly, he stopped one morning before it, when Esther, after finishing her own task, was working on Mr. Hazard's design.

"By our lady of love!" said Wharton, with a start and a laugh; "now I see what mischief you three have been at!"

"The church would not have been complete without it," said Esther timidly.

For several minutes Wharton looked in silence at the St. Cecilia and at the figure which now seemed its companion; then he said, turning away: "I shall not be the first unworthy saint the church has canonized."

Esther drew a long breath of relief; Catherine started up, radiant with delight; and thus it happens that on the walls of St. John's, high above the world of vanities beneath them, Wharton stands, and will stand for ages, gazing at Catherine Brooke.

Now that the two saints were nearly finished, Esther became a little depressed. This church life, like a bit of religious Bohemianism and acted poetry, had amused her so greatly that she found her own small studio dull. She could no longer work there without missing the space, the echoes, the company, and above all, the sense of purpose, which she felt on her scaffolding. She complained to Wharton of her feminine want of motive in life.

"I wish I earned my living," she said. "You don't know what it is to work without an object."

"Much of the best work in the world," said he, "has been done with no motive of gain."

"Men can do so many things that women can't," said she. "Men like to work alone. Women cannot work without company. Do you like solitude?"

"I would like to own a private desert," he answered, "and live alone in the middle of it with lions and tigers to eat intruders."

"You need not go so far," said she. "Take my studio!"

"With you and Miss Brooke in the neighborhood? Never!"

"We will let you alone. In a week you will put your head out of the door and say: 'Please come and play jack-straws with me!'"

Catherine was not pleased at the thought that her usefulness was at an end. She had no longer a part to play unless it were that of duenna to Esther, and for this she was not so well fitted as she might have been, had providence thought proper to make her differently. Indeed, Esther's anxiety to do her duty as duenna to Catherine was becoming so sharp that it threatened to interfere with the pleasure of both. Catherine did her best to give her friend trouble.

"Please rub me all out, Mr. Wharton," said she; "and make Esther begin again. I am sure she will do it better the next time."

Wharton was quite ready to find an excuse for pleasing her. If it was at times a little annoying to have two women in his way whom he could not control as easily as ordinary work-people, he had become so used to the restraint as not to feel it often, and not to regard it much. Esther thought he need not distress himself by thinking that he regarded it at all. Had not Catherine been so anxious to appear as the most docile and obedient of hand-maids besides being the best-tempered of prairie creatures, she would long ago have resented his habit of first petting, then scolding, next ignoring, and again flattering her, as his mood happened to prompt. He was more respectful with Esther, and kept out of her way when he was moody, while she made it a rule never to leave her own place of work unless first invited, but Catherine, who was much by his side, got used to ill-treatment which she bore with angelic meekness. When she found herself left forgotten in a corner, or unanswered when she spoke, or unnoticed when she bade him good-morning, she consoled herself with reflecting that after every rudeness, Wharton's regard for her seemed to rise, and he took her more and more into his confidence with every new brutality.

"Some day he will drag you to the altar by the hair," said Esther; "and tell you that his happiness requires you to be his wife."

"I wish he would try," said Catherine with a little look of humor; "but he has one wife already."

"She mysteriously disappeared," replied Esther. "Some day you will find her skeleton, poor thing!"

"Do you think so?" said Catherine gravely. "How fascinating he is! He makes me shiver!"

When Catherine begged to have every thing begun again, Wharton hesitated. Esther's work was not to his taste, but he was not at all sure that she would do equally well if she tried to imitate his own manner.

"You know I wanted Miss Dudley to put more religious feeling and force into her painting," said he, "but you all united and rode me down."

"I will look like a real angel this time," said Catherine. "Now I know what it is you want."

"I am more than half on her side," went on Wharton. "I am not sure that she is wrong. It all comes to this: is religion a struggle or a joy? To me it is a terrible battle, to be won or lost. I like your green dress with the violets. Whose idea was that?"

"Petrarch's. You know I am Laura. St. Cecilia has the dress which Laura wore in church when Petrarch first saw her."

"No!" said Wharton, after another pause, and long study of the two figures. "Decidedly I will not rub you out; but I mean to touch up Petrarch."

"O! You won't spoil the likeness!"

"Not at all! But if I am going to posterity by your side I want some expression in my face. Petrarch was a man of troubles."

"You promise not to change the idea?"

"I promise to look at you as long as you look at me," said Wharton gloomily.

Meanwhile Esther had a talk with Mr. Hazard which left her more in doubt than ever as to what she had best do. He urged her to begin something new and to do it in a more strenuous spirit.

"You are learning from Wharton," said he. "Why should you stop at the very moment when you have most to gain?"

"I am learning nothing but what I knew before," she answered sadly. "He can teach only grand art and I am fit only for trifles."

"Try one more figure!"

Esther shook her head.

"My Cecilia is a failure," she went on. "Mr. Wharton said it would be, and he was right. I should do no better next time, unless I took his design and carried it out exactly as he orders."

"One's first attempt is always an experiment. Try once more!"

"I should only spoil your church. In the middle of your best sermon your audience would see you look up here and laugh."

"You are challenging compliments."

"What I could do nicely would be to paint squirrels and monkeys playing on vines round the choir, or daisies and buttercups in a row, with one tall daisy in each group of five. That is the way for a woman to make herself useful."

"Be serious!"

"I feel more solemn than Mr. Wharton's great figure of John of Patmos. I am going home to burn my brushes and break my palette. What is the use of trying to go forward when one feels iron bars across one's face?"

"Be reasonable, Miss Dudley! If Wharton is willing to teach, why not be willing to learn? You are not to be the judge. If I think your work good, have I not a right to call on you for it?"

"Oh, yes! You have a right to call, and I have a right to refuse. I will paint no more religious subjects. I have not enough soul. My St. Cecilia looks like a nursery governess playing a waltz for white-cravated saints to dance by." There was a tone of real mortification in Esther's voice as she looked once more at the figure on the wall, and felt how weak it seemed by the side of Wharton's masculine work. Then she suddenly changed her mind and did just what he asked: "If Mr. Wharton will consent, I will begin again, and paint it all over."

A woman could easily have seen that she was torn in opposite directions by motives of a very contrary kind, but Mr. Hazard did not speculate on this subject; he was glad to carry his point, and let the matter rest there. It was agreed that the next morning Wharton should decide upon the proper course to be taken, and if he chose to reject her figure, she should begin it again. Esther and Catherine went home, but Esther was ill at ease. That her St. Cecilia did not come up to the level of her ambition was a matter of course, and she was prepared for the disappointment. Whose first attempt in a new style ever paired with its conception? She felt that Mr. Hazard would think her wayward and weak. She could not tell him the real reason of her perplexity. She would have liked to work on patiently under Wharton's orders without a thought of herself, but how could she do so when Hazard was day by day coming nearer and nearer until already their hands almost touched. If she had not liked him, the question could easily have been settled, but she did like him, and when she said this to herself she turned scarlet at the thought that he liked her, and—what should she do?

With a heavy heart she made up her mind that there was but one thing to be done; she must retreat into her own house and bar the doors. If he did not see that such an intimacy was sure to make trouble for him, she, who felt, if she did not see, the gulf that separated them, must teach him better.

Whether she would have held to this wise and prudent course against his entreaties and Wharton's commands will never be known, for the question, which at the moment seemed to her so hard to decide, was already answered by fates which left her no voice in the matter. The next morning when the two girls, rather later than usual, reached the south door of the church where a stern guardian always stood to watch lest wolves entered under pretense of business, they saw a woman standing on the steps and gazing at them as they approached from the avenue. In this they found nothing to surprise them, but as they came face to face with her they noticed that the stranger's dress and features were peculiar and uncommon even in New York, the sink of races. Although the weather was not cold, she wore a fur cap, picturesque but much worn, far from neat, and matching in dirt as in style a sort of Polish or Hungarian capote thrown over her shoulders. Her features were strong, coarse and bloated; her eyes alone were fine. When she suddenly spoke to Esther her voice was rough, like her features; and though Esther had seen too little of life to know what depths of degradation such a face and voice meant, she drew back with some alarm. The woman spoke in French only to ask whether this was the church of St. John. Replying shortly that it was, Esther passed in without waiting for another question; but as she climbed the narrow and rough staircase to her gallery, she said to Catherine who was close behind:

"Somewhere I have seen that woman's eyes."

"So have I!" answered Catherine, in a tone of suppressed excitement so unusual that Esther stopped short on the step and turned round.

"Don't you know where?" asked Catherine without waiting to be questioned.

"Where was it?"

"In my picture! Mr. Wharton gave me her eyes. I am sure that woman is his wife."

"Catherine, you shall go back to Colorado. You have been reading too many novels. You are as romantic as a man."

Catherine did not care whether she were romantic or not; she knew the woman was Wharton's wife.

"Perhaps she means to kill him," she ran on in a blood-curdling tone. "Wouldn't it be like Mr. Wharton to be stabbed to the heart on the steps of a church, just as his great work was done? Do you know I think he would like it. He is dying to be tragic like the Venetians, and have some one write a poem about him." Then after a moment's pause, she added, in the same indifferent tone of voice: "All the same, if he's not there, I mean to go back and look out for him. I'm not going to let that woman kill him if I can help it!"

A warm dispute arose between the two girls which continued after they reached their scaffold and found that Wharton was not there. Esther declared that Catherine should not go back; it was ridiculous and improper; Mr. Wharton would laugh in her face and think her bold and impertinent; the woman was probably a beggar who wanted to see Mr. Hazard; and when all this was of no avail Esther insisted that Catherine should not go alone. Catherine, on her part, declared that she was not afraid of the woman, or of any woman, or man either, or of Mr.

Wharton, and that she meant to walk down the avenue and meet him, and tell him that this person was there. She was on the point of doing what she threatened when they saw Wharton himself cross the church beneath and slowly climb the stairs.

The two girls, dismissing their alarm as easily as they had taken it up, turned to their own affairs again. In a few minutes Wharton appeared on the scaffolding and went to his regular work-place. After a time they saw him coming to their corner. He looked paler than usual and more abstracted, and, what was unusual, he carried a brush in his hand, as though he had broken off his work without thinking what he was doing. He hardly noticed them, but sat down, holding the brush with both hands, though it was wet. For some time he looked at the Cecilia without a word; then he began abruptly:

"You're quite right! It's not good! It's not handled in a large way or in keeping with the work round it. You might do it again much better. But it is you and it is she! I would leave it. I will leave it! If necessary I could in a few days paint it all over and make it harmonize, but I should spoil it. I can draw better and paint better, but I can't make a young girl from Colorado as pure and fresh as that. To me religion is passion. To reach Heaven, you must go through hell, and carry its marks on your face and figure. I can't paint innocence without suggesting sin, but you can, and the church likes it. Put your own sanctity on the wall beside my martyrdom!"

Esther thought it would be civil on her part to say something at this point, but Wharton's remarks seemed to be made to no one in particular, and she was not quite certain that they were meant for her in spite of the words. He did not look at her. She was used to his peculiar moods and soliloquies, and had learned to be silent at such times. She sat silent now, but Catherine, who took greater liberties with him, was bolder.

"Why can't you paint innocence?" she asked.

"I am going to tell you," he replied, with more quickness of manner. "It is to be the subject of my last lecture. Ladies, school must close to-day."

Esther and Catherine glanced at each other. "You are going to send us away?" asked Catherine in a tone of surprise.

"You must go for the present," answered Wharton. "I mean to tell you the reason, and then you will see why I can't paint innocence as you can. As a lecture on art, my life is worth hearing, but don't interrupt the story or you will lose it. Begin by keeping in your mind that twenty years ago I was a ragged boy in the streets of Cincinnati. The drawing master in a public school to which I went, said I had a natural talent for drawing, and taught me all he knew. Then a little purse was made up for me and I was sent to Paris. Not yet twenty years old, I found myself dropped into that great sewer of a city, a shy, ill-clothed, ill-fed, ill-educated boy, knowing no more of the world above me than a fish knows of the birds. For two years I knocked about in a studio till my money was used up, and then I knew enough to be able to earn a few francs to keep me alive. Then I went down to Italy and of course got a fever. I came back at last to Paris, half-fed, dyspeptic and morbid. I had visions, and the worst vision of my life I am going to tell you.

"It was after I had been some years at work and had got already a little reputation among Americans, that I was at my worst. Nothing seemed real. What earned me my first success was an attempt I made to paint the strange figures and fancies which possessed me. I studied nothing but the most extravagant subjects. For a time nothing would satisfy me but to draw from models at moments of intense suffering and at the instant of death. Models of that kind do not offer themselves and are not to be bought. I made friends with the surgeons and got myself admitted to one of the great hospitals. I happened to be there one day when a woman was brought in suffering from an overdose of arsenic. This was the kind of subject I wanted. She was fierce, splendid, a priestess of the oracle! Tortured by agony and clinging to it as though it were a delight! The next day I came back to look for her: she was then exhausted and half dead. She was a superb model, and I took an interest in her. When she grew better I talked with her and found that she was a sort of Parisian Pole with a strange history. She had been living as an actress at one of the small theaters, and had attempted suicide in sheer disgust with life. I had played with the same idea for years. We had both struggled with the world and hated it. Her imagination was more morbid than my own, and in her quieter moments, when her affections were roused, she was wonderfully tender and devoted. When she left the hospital she put herself under my protection. I believe she loved me, and no one had ever loved me before. I know she took possession of me, body and soul. I married her. I would just as willingly have jumped into the Seine with her if she had preferred it. For three months we lived together while I finished the picture which I called the Priestess of Delphi, painted from my drawings of her in her agony. The picture made a great noise in Paris, and brought me some new friends, among the rest one who, I think, really saved me from Charenton. Hazard called at my studio just as my troubles were beginning to tear me to pieces. My wife had the temper of a fury, and all the vices of Paris. Excitement was her passion; she could not stand the quiet of an artist's life; yet her Bohemian instincts came over her only in waves, and when they left her in peace she still had splendid qualities that held me to her. Hazard came in upon us one day in the middle of a terrible scene when she was threatening again to take her own life, and trying, or pretending to try to take mine. When he came in, she disappeared. The next I heard of her, she was back on the stage—lost! I was worn out; my nervous system was all gone. Then Hazard came to my help and took me off with him to the south of Europe. Our first stage was to Avignon and Vaucluse, and there I found how curiously my experience had affected my art. I had learned to adore purity and repose, but I could never get hold of my ideal. Fifty times I tried to draw Laura as I wanted to realize her and every time I failed. I knew the secret of Petrarch and I could not tell it. My wife came between me and my thought. All life took form in my hands as a passion. If I could learn again to paint a child, or any thing that had not the world in its eyes, I should be at peace at last."

As he paused here, and seemed again to be musing over St. Cecilia,

Esther's curiosity made her put in a word,

"And your wife?"—she asked.

"My wife?" he repeated in his abstracted tone, "I never saw her again till this morning when I met her on the steps of the church."

"Then it was your wife?" cried Catherine.

"You saw her?" he asked with a touch of bitterness. "I won't ask what you thought of her."

"I knew her by her eyes," cried Catherine. "I thought she meant to shoot you, and when you came in I was just going to warn you. Now you see, Esther, I was right."

Wharton leaned over and took Catherine's hand. "Thank you," said he. "I believe you are my good angel. But you remind me of what I came to say. The woman is quite capable of that or of any other scandal, and of course Hazard's church must not be exposed to such a risk. I shall come here no longer for the present, neither must you. I am bound to take care of my friends."

"But you!" said Esther. "What are you going to do?"

"I? Nothing! What can I do?"

"Do you mean," said Catherine, with a comical fierceness in her voice as though she wanted herself to take the French actress in hand, "do you mean to let that woman worry you how she likes?"

"The fault was mine," replied Wharton. "I gave her my life. After all she is my wife and I can't help it. I have promised to meet her this afternoon at my studio."

Even to these two girls there was something so helpless in Wharton's ideas of life that they protested against his conduct. Catherine was speechless with inability to understand what he meant. Esther boldly interfered.

"You must do nothing without advice," said she. "Wait till Mr. Hazard comes and consult him. If you can't see him, promise me to go to my uncle, Mr. Murray, and let him take charge of this woman. You will ruin your whole life if you let her into it again."

"It is ruined already," answered Wharton gloomily. "I had that one chance of happiness and I can never have another."

Nevertheless he promised to wait for Hazard, and the two girls obediently bade him good-by. Catherine's eyes were full of tears as he held her hand and begged her pardon for his rudeness. A little romance was passing out of her life. She went down the stairs after Esther without a word. As they left the church they saw the woman on the pavement outside, still walking up and down; Catherine passed her with a glance of repulsion and defiance that made the woman turn and watch her till they disappeared down the avenue.

An hour afterwards a quick step hurried up the stair, and Hazard, evidently much disturbed, appeared on the scaffolding. He found Wharton where the two girls had left him, sitting alone before St. Cecilia, the broken brush still in his hands, and his left hand red with the wet paint. His face was paler than ever, and over the left temple was a large red spot, as though he had been pressing his hands to his forehead. Hazard looked for a moment at the white face, contrasting painfully with its ghastly spot of intense red, and then spoke with assumed indifference:

"So she has turned up again!"

Wharton returned his look with a weak smile which made his face still more horrible, and slowly answered:

"I have worse news than that!"

"More bad news!" said Hazard.

"Tell me what you think," continued Wharton in the same dreamy tone.

"You see that Cecilia there?"

Hazard glanced at the figure and back to Wharton without speaking.

Presently Wharton added with a smile of inexpressible content:

"Well! I love her."

Chapter VI

Esther's regrets on quitting her work at the church lasted not so long as Catherine's, though they were more serious. She had already begun to feel alarmed about her father's condition, and nothing but his positive order had induced her to leave him even for a few hours every day. She had seen that his strength steadily failed; he suffered paroxysms of pain; lost consciousness more than once; and although he insisted to the last on acting as though he were well, his weakness increased until he could no longer sit out a game of whist, but was forced to lie on the sofa in his library where he liked to see every visitor who came to the house. He required that every thing about him should go on as usual, and not only made Esther go regularly to her work, but took keen interest in hearing from her and Catherine all that was said and done at the church. He delighted in laughing at Catherine about her romantic relations with Wharton, but he made no jokes about Mr. Hazard. He thought from the first that this intimacy might be a serious matter for Esther, but he would not again interfere in her affairs, and feared making things worse by noticing them. He watched Hazard sharply, until Esther had the uncomfortable sense of feeling that her father's eyes were never far away from the clergyman when he came to the house. She knew, or fancied she knew, every thought in her father's mind, and his silence embarrassed her more than criticism could have done. She asked herself in vain why her father, disliking the clergy as she knew he did, should suddenly admit a clergyman into his intimacy. In truth, Mr. Dudley looked on himself as no longer having a right to speak; his feelings and prejudices were to be kept out of her life; but he could watch, and the longer he watched, the more intense his interest became.

When Esther and Catherine returned from the church with their account of Wharton's wife, their first act was to tell the story to Mr. Dudley, who lay on his sofa and listened with keen interest.

"I suppose you meant to come back for my revolver," said he to

Catherine, whose little explosions of courage always amused him. "I

think I could almost have crawled round to see you take a shot at your

French friend as she started for you."

"Oh, no!" said Catherine modestly. "I would have given the revolver to Mr. Wharton."

"Don't do it, Catherine! Wharton could not hit the church door with it. Suppose he had shot you instead of the other woman!"

"Of course!" said Catherine reflectively. "He wouldn't know how to use a revolver, would he? I suppose I ought to teach him."

"Better not!" said Mr. Dudley. "Keep him under. You may have to talk with him one of these days, after you have settled your little misunderstanding with his wife."

Catherine took chaff with such gravity that even Mr. Dudley could not always make out whether she was in jest or earnest. She had a quaint, serious way of accepting any sort of challenge and going it better, as Strong expressed it, which left her assailants wholly in the dark. Mr. Dudley wanted to stop any romantic nonsense between her and Wharton, but could never quite make out whether she cared for him or not. Esther thought not.

That evening they all hoped that Hazard would come in to tell them what other scenes had occurred, and, under this little excitement, Mr. Dudley felt strong enough to appear like himself, although he dared not rise from his sofa. At about eight o'clock they were gratified. Mr. Hazard appeared, and was received with such cordiality and intimacy as went far to make him feel himself a member of the family.

"Thank you," said Mr. Dudley. "We have done nothing but run to the watch-tower to see if you were coming. Tell us quickly the ghastly news. We are prepared for the worst."

"If you read Turgenieff," replied Hazard, "you can imagine the kind of experience we have had. I feel as though I had stolen a chapter from one of his stories."

"No matter! Spoil it promptly! We never read any thing."

"May I have first a cup of tea, Miss Dudley? Thank you! That woman has left a taste on my palate that all the tea in China will never wash off. Where shall I begin?"

"Where we left off," said Esther. "We left Mr. Wharton in the church at eleven o'clock, and the woman marching up and down outside."

"At noon I found her there, and knew her at once, though it is ten years since I last saw her. She is a person whom one does not forget. I asked her what she wanted. It seemed that Wharton, in his confusion, had told her to come to his studio without saying where it was; and she was waiting for him to come out again. I gave her the address and sent her away. Then I went up to Wharton whom I found in a strange state of mind; he seemed dazed and showed no interest in the affair. He would not talk of his wife at all until I forced him. At length, after a struggle, as he said that Miss Dudley had told him to go to her uncle, Mr. Murray, I got him into a carriage and we drove to Mr. Murray's office. The upshot was that Mr. Murray and I took the matter into our hands and decided to meet the woman ourselves in his company. At the hour fixed, we went, all three of us, to the studio.

"It needed at least three of us to deal with that one woman. When I saw her in Paris she was still young and handsome, with superb eyes and a kind of eastern tread. You could imagine her, when she did not speak, as Semiramis, Medea, Clytemnestra! Except that when you saw a little more of her, you felt that she was only a heroine of a cheap theater. Wharton could not have been fascinated by her, if, at that time of his life, he had ever known a refined woman or mixed at all in the world; but she certainly had a gypsy charm, and seemed to carry oceans of Sahara and caravans of camels about with her. When she was in one of her furies, it was an echo of the whole Greek drama. This, you must recollect, was ten years ago, and even then she was spoiled by being coarse and melodramatic, but now she is a horror. She suggests nothing but the penitentiary. When she saw that there were three of us, she flew into a whirlwind of passion, and screamed French that I was glad to find I could not wholly understand. Her dialect must come from the worst class of Parisian thieves. I should have been glad to understand less than I did. Every now and then she interrupted this Billingsgate, and seemed to think that her dignity required a loftier style, and she poured out on us whole pages of cheap melodrama. She began by flinging her fur cap and cloak on the floor and striking a stage attitude. She wanted to know who we were; by what right did we mix ourselves in this affair and come between a villain and his victim! Then she turned on Wharton and began gesticulating and throwing herself into contortions like a Maenad, repeating again and again that he was her husband, an 'infâme,' a 'lâche,' and that she would take his life if she were not given her rights. She drew herself up in all her height, and growled in her deepest voice: 'Je vais t'écr-r-r-raser!' Then she changed her tone and sobbed violently that on second thoughts she preferred to kill herself, and finally tore a small stage dagger from her breast and proposed to kill us all and herself too."

"How many did she manage in the end?" asked Mr. Dudley.

"How did Mr. Wharton bear it?" asked Esther.

"Wharton stood it very well," replied Hazard. "He was sitting near her, and now and then she made a rush at him as though she really meant to strike him. He never moved, or spoke, or took his eyes away from her. I think he was overcome by association; he thought himself back in Paris ten years ago."

"Doubtless this excellent woman has faults, owing to a defective education," said Mr. Dudley with his usual dry, half-smile. "We must make allowances for them. I am more curious to know whether she got the better of my astute brother-in-law."

"Mr. Murray took an unfair advantage over her," said Hazard. "He had taken the precaution to post a police officer in the next room, and after the woman had exhausted herself, and I think too had worn off the effects of the brandy she reeked with, he told her that she would go instantly to the police station if she did not behave herself. I think her imagination must have taught her that an American police station might be something very terrible, for in a few minutes she quieted down and was only eager for money."

"I suppose Murray means to terrify this poor creature into a sacrifice of her rights?" said Mr.

Dudley.

"Wharton will have to settle an annuity on her, in order to get her back to Europe and keep her there. In return, she has got to consent to a divorce. Mr. Murray insists on this as his first condition. Wharton began to say that she was his wife, and that he was bound to take care of her, until at last Mr. Murray told him to take himself off or he would have no more to do with the case. So the woman, on receiving some money on the spot, consents to deal with Mr. Murray directly, on his terms, and Wharton leaves town till the papers are drawn up and the woman packed off. He has had a shock which will prevent his working for some time."

"He may not feel like painting saints," said Mr. Dudley, "but I should think he was in good form for painting sinners. Is there no room for a Jezebel in your portrait gallery?"

Mr. Dudley was too weak for late hours and Hazard went away early. As he went he said he would come again to tell them the next chapter, if there was one.

"Be quick about it!" said Mr. Dudley. "I am like the Sultan who cut off his wives' heads because they would not tell him stories fast enough. It is not convenient for me to wait."

To Esther this evening was the last when the stars shone bright and clear. The next morning her glimpse of blue sky had vanished and the rigor of the storm began.

She was waked by the news that in the night her father had been seized by another paroxysm, and that although better, he was excessively weak. He had forbidden his attendants to call her, on the cool calculation that he should probably pull through this attack, and that she would need all her strength for the next. When Esther came down to his room, she found him in a state of complete prostration, so that his doctors had forbidden him to speak or even to listen. They no longer talked with him, but gave their orders to her, and she took charge of the sick-room at once with all its responsibilities and fatigues. After a consultation of very few moments, the physicians told her plainly that there was no hope; her father might linger a short time, but any sudden emotion would kill him on the spot.

During the day he rallied a little and in the evening was stronger. Esther, who had been all day in his room, rested till midnight and then took her regular watch by his side. She knew that there was no hope and that her father himself was only anxious for the end, yet to see him suffer and slowly fade out was terrible. At such moments, tears are forbidden. Esther had been told that she must not give way to agitation, under the risk of killing her father, who lay dozing, half-conscious, with his face turned towards her. Whenever his eyes opened they rested on hers. In the dim light she watched his motions, and it seemed to her that he was also watching hers. She wondered whether he could feel stronger because she was near him. Was he afraid? He, who had never to her knowledge shrunk from any danger, and who in the army had shown reckless indifference even when he supposed his wounds to be mortal, was now watching her as though he feared to have her leave his side. In his extreme weakness, unable to lift his head, his mind evidently beginning to wander, perhaps he felt the need of her companionship, and dreaded solitude and death as she did. For half the night she pondered over this weakening of the will in the face of omnipotence crushing out the last spark of life, and was doubly startled when, the nurse coming to relieve her at six o'clock, she leaned over to kiss her father's forehead and found him looking at her in his old humorous way, while, in a low whisper, speaking slowly, as though he would not yield to the enemy that clutched his heart, he said:

"It's not so bad, Esther, when you come to it."

The tears started into Esther's eyes. It was only with an effort more violent than she had thought was in her power, that she forced herself to smile. Now that she had come to it, she thought it was very bad; worse than any thing she had ever imagined; she wanted to escape, to run away, to get out of life itself, rather than suffer such pain, such terror, such misery of helplessness; but after an instant's pause, her father whispered again, though his voice died away in weakness:

"Laugh, Esther, when you're in trouble! Say something droll! then you're safe. I saw the whole regiment laugh under fire at Gettysburg."

This was more than she could bear, and she had to hurry out of the room. She had fancied him yielding to fear and finding courage in her companionship. Suddenly she became aware that, with death's hand on his throat and a brain reeling in exhaustion, he was trying to teach her how to meet what life had to bring. The lesson was one she could not easily forget.

So she went to her bed, in the cold, gray dawn of a winter's day, with the tears still running down her face. When she woke again the day was already waning, a dripping, wasting thaw, when smoking and soot-defiled snow added sadness to the sad sky. Esther, on opening her eyes, saw Catherine sitting quietly before the fire, reading, or pretending to read. She was keeping guard lest Esther should be disturbed.

"He is no worse," she said, when Esther raised her head. "I was at his door five minutes ago. Mrs. Murray is there and so is the doctor. You are not wanted and they sent word that you were not to be disturbed."

Esther was glad to lie still a few minutes and collect her strength. It was pleasant to look at Catherine, the healthiest and most cheery of girls, after having under one's eyes a long night of terror.

"Professor Strong has been here this morning and I saw him," ran on Catherine. "He sent for me because he would not have you disturbed. He got back from St. Louis last night, and will come round here again this afternoon. Mr. Hazard has been here, too, and says he shall stop again in the evening."

This report required no answer. Esther felt the stronger for knowing that her friends were at her side, and that she could count on their help. Catherine ran on in the same vein.

"Mr. Hazard says that Mr. Wharton has left town and will not return until Mr. Murray sends for him. I think he might have left some message for me, to ask me to be true to him or something, but Mr. Hazard says he just went off to Boston without a word to any body. I have more than half a mind to desert him and go back to Colorado."

"If you leave me now, Catherine—"

"Oh! I don't mean to leave you, but I must earn my living. Let me take my watch with your father to-night! You will think you have struck a professional."

Esther refused, but Catherine did rather more than her share of work notwithstanding, and more than once Mr. Dudley, opening his eyes, found her at the head of his bed and greeted her with a faint smile.

He passed the day without much sign of change. Esther was repeatedly called from his side to see persons whom she could not send away. Her aunt was with her till night. Strong came in and sat with her while she tried to dine. So long as day-light lasted she felt no sense of loneliness or desertion, and her courage remained fairly steady; but when she had sent home her aunt and cousin in order to begin her watch earlier than the previous night, her fears returned, her heart sank, and she begged Catherine to stay with her. The two girls began their watch together. Mr. Dudley seemed pleased to have them with him.

Presently a nurse came with a message that Mr. Hazard was below, and had asked to see Esther for a moment. Mr. Dudley overheard the message, and whispered to his daughter:

"Tell him I am sorry not to see him! Say I am just going out!"

He spoke dreamily, as though half asleep, and Esther, as she leaned over him, trying to catch his words, doubted whether he was quite conscious. He muttered a few more words: "I won't interfere, but the church—." She caught no more, and he dozed off again into silence. After watching him a few moments, Esther beckoned to Catherine to take her chair, and slipped out of the room. She wanted to see Hazard, for, strange as it seemed to her, he had become her most intimate friend, and she could not send him away at such a moment.

She found him at the foot of the stairs, and there they remained standing for a few moments, talking in low tones, by the light of a dim gas-burner.

"I want to help you," he said. "I am used to such scenes and you are not. You need help though you may not ask for it."

She shook her head: "I am a miserable coward," she said; "but we are beyond help now, and I must learn endurance."

"You will over-tax your strength," he urged. "Remember, there is no excitement so great as to stand for the first time in face of eternity, as you are doing."

"I suppose it must be so," she answered. "Every thing seems unreal. I can't even realize my father's illness. Your voice sounds far-off, as though you were calling to me out of the distance and darkness. I hardly know what we are saying, or why we are here. I never felt so before."

"It is over-excitement and fatigue," he replied soothingly. "Do you feel afraid, too?"

"Terribly!" she answered; "I want to run away. But I think death excites almost more than it frightens. My father laughs at it even now."

"I am more concerned about you," continued Hazard. "I can do nothing for him, and you may feel sure that for him all the worst is over. Will you let me stay here on the chance of your needing help?"

"I have already sent away my aunt and George Strong," she said. "Do not feel alarmed about me. Women have more strength than men."

As he left the house, he thought to himself that this woman at least had more strength than most men. He could not forget her pale face, or her dreamy voice and far-off eyes as she had told him her feelings. Most women would have asked him for religious help and consolation. She had gently put his offers aside. She seemed to him like a wandering soul, lost in infinite space, but still floating on, with her quiet air of confidence as though she were a part of nature itself, and felt that all nature moved with her.

"I almost think," said Hazard to himself, "that she could give a lesson in strength to me. It seems rather unnecessary, my offering to give one to her."

Yet Esther felt little like giving strength to any one. As she returned to the sick-room and slipped back into the chair which Catherine quitted, the image of Hazard faded from her mind, and the idea that he could help her, except by his sympathy and friendship, never entered it. After a time her father opened his eyes again and looked at her. She bent over him, and he whispered: "Give me your hand!" She took his hand, and for some time he lay with his eyes open, as though watching her. She could only wonder what was in his mind; perhaps disconnected dreams with intervals of partial consciousness, as now, followed by more vague visions and hurrying phantasms; but she imagined that he had meant not so much to ask for the strength of her hand as to give her the will and courage of his own, and she felt only the wish that he might not doubt her answer to the call. Although he soon dozed again, she did not alter her position, but sat hour after hour, only making way for the nurse who came to give him stimulants which had less and less effect. Her watch ended at two o'clock, when she sent Catherine to bed, but remained herself until the gray dawn had passed and the sun was high in the heavens. She meant her father to know, as long as he knew any thing, that her hand was in his. Not until the doctor assured her that he was no longer conscious, did her long walk into the shadow of death at last end. When Mrs. Murray came, she found Esther still there, her face paler than ever, with dark rings round her eyes, and looking worn and old. As she spoke, her eyes constantly filled with tears, and her nerves were strung up to a tension which made her aunt promptly intervene and insist on her taking rest. Esther obeyed like a worn-out child.

So died William Dudley, and was buried under the ice and snow of winter, while his daughter went on alone to meet the buffets of life. It was in the first days of February that Esther looked about her and seemed to feel that the world had changed. She said to herself that youth was gone. What was she to do with middle-life? At twenty-six to be alone, with no one to interpose as much as a shadow across her path, was a strange sensation; it made her dizzy, as though she were a solitary bird flying through mid-air, and as she looked ahead on her aërial path, could see no tie more human than that which bound her to Andromeda and Orion.

To this moral strain was added the reaction from physical fatigue. For a week or two after her father's death, Esther felt languid, weary and listless. She could not sleep. A voice, a bar of music, the sight of any thing unusual, affected her deeply. She could not get back to her regular interests. First came the funeral with its inevitable depression and fatigue; then came days of vacancy, with no appetite for work and no chance for amusement. She took refuge in trifles, but the needle and scissors are terrible weapons for cutting out and trimming not so much women's dresses as their thoughts. She had never been a reader, and perhaps for that reason her mind had all the more run into regions of fancy and imagination. She caught half an idea in the air, and tossed it for amusement. In these days of unrest she tossed her ideas more rapidly than ever. Most women are more or less mystical by nature, and Esther had a vein of mysticism running through a practical mind.

The only person outside her family whom she saw was Hazard. He was either at the house or in some way near her almost every day. He took charge of the funeral services, and came to make inquiries, to bring messages, or to suggest an occupation, until he was looked upon as one of the household. Once or twice, the week after the funeral, he came in the evening, and asked for a cup of tea. Then Catherine sat by and dozed while Esther talked mysticism with Hazard, who was himself a mystic of the purest water. By this time Esther had learned to look on the physical life, the daily repetition of breakfast and dinner, as the unreal part of existence, and apologized to herself for conceding so much to habit, or put it down to Catherine's account. Her illusions were not serious; perhaps she had for this short instant a flash of truth, and by the light of her father's deathbed, saw life as it is; but, while the mood lasted, nothing seemed real except the imagination, and nothing true but the spiritual. In this atmosphere Hazard was always happy, for he reveled in the voluptuousness of poetry, and found peace in the soul of a dandelion; but to share his subtlest fancies with a woman who could understand and feel them, was to reach a height of poetry that trembled on the verge of realizing heaven. His great eyes shone with the radiance of paradise, and his delicate thin features expressed beatitude, as he discussed with Esther the purity of the soul, the victory of spirit over matter, and the peace of infinite love.

Of her regular occupations Esther kept up only such as were duties, but among them she was true to her little hospital, and went once or twice a week to see the children who clamored for her visits. She went alone, for she liked solitude, and was glad to give Catherine an excuse for escaping to gayer houses and seeing brighter society. About a fortnight after her father's death, one Saturday afternoon when she felt more solitary than ever, and more restless because her long quiet had begun to bring back her strength, she went to the hospital where the children welcomed her with delight. She took her old seat and looked through the yellow eyes of the fire-dogs for inspiration; opened a package and distributed small presents, little Japanese umbrellas, fans, doll's shoes and such small change of popularity; and, at last, obeying the cries for more story, she went on with the history of Princess Lovely in her Cocoanut Island, besieged by whales and defended by talking elephants and monkeys. She had hardly begun when the door opened and again Mr. Hazard entered. This time Esther blushed.

Hazard sat down, and finding that she soon tired of story-telling, he took it up, and gave a chapter of his own which had wild success, so that the children begged for more and more, until five o'clock was past and twilight coming on. As Esther was on foot, Mr. Hazard said he would see her to her door, and they walked away together.

"Do you know that Wharton has come back?" said he as they reached the street. "His affair is settled; the woman sailed yesterday for Europe, and he is to have a divorce. Your uncle has managed it very well."

"Will Mr. Wharton go to work again at the church?" asked Esther.

"He begins at once. He asked me to find out for him whether you would begin with him."

"Did he say whether he wanted me or Catherine?" asked Esther with a laugh.

Hazard laughed in reply. "I think myself he would be satisfied to get Miss Brooke, but you must not underrate your own merits. He wants you both."

"I am afraid he must give us up," said Esther, with a little sigh. "Certainly I can't come, and if he wants Catherine, he will have to come himself and get her; but he will find Catherine not easy to get."

They discussed Wharton and his affairs till they reached Esther's house, and she said: "It is not yet six o'clock. I can give you a cup of tea if you will come in?"

She could not do less than offer him this small hospitality, and yet—Catherine was not at home. They went up to the library, and Esther ordered tea to be brought. She took off her bonnet and cloak, and threw them on a chair. She sat down before the fire, and he stood on the hearth-rug looking at her while she made tea in the twilight. At this moment he was more hopelessly in love than any other Church of England clergyman within the diocese of New York.

"What are then your plans for the future?" he asked, after they had chatted for some time on the subject of Esther's painting. "If you will not return to help us, what do you look forward to doing?"

"I want to take Catherine and go abroad," answered Esther. "If I can get my uncle and aunt to go, we shall start in the spring."

At this announcement Hazard seemed to receive a shock. He turned suddenly to her, his eyes sparkling with passion: "Take me with you! What shall I do without you!" He seized her hand and poured out a torrent of broken protests: "I love you with all my heart and soul! Don't leave me alone in this horrible city! I shall die of disgust if you desert me! You are the only woman I ever loved! Ah! You must love me!"

Esther, trembling, bewildered, carried away by this sudden and violent attack, made at first a feeble effort to withdraw her hand and to gasp a protest, but the traitor within her own breast was worse than the enemy without. For the moment all her wise resolutions were swept away in a wave of tenderness; she seemed to come suddenly on a summer sea, sparkling with hope and sunshine, the dreary sand-banks of her old life vanishing like a dream. She shut her eyes and found herself in his arms. Then in terror at what she had done, she tried again to draw back.

"No, no!" she said rapidly, trying to free herself. "You must not love me! You must let me go!"

"I love you! I adore you! I will never let you go!"

"You must! You do not know what you are doing! Ah! Let me go!"

"Tell me first that you love me!"

"No, no! I am not good enough for you. You must love some one who has her heart in your work."

"Tell me that you love me!" repeated Hazard.

"You do not know me! You must not love me! I shall ruin your life! I shall never satisfy you!"

Hazard caressed her only the more tenderly as he answered with the self-confidence which he put into all he did: "If my calling is so poor a thing that it cannot satisfy both our lives, I will have nothing more to do with it. I have more faith in us both. Promise to love me and I will take care of the rest."

"Ah!" gasped Esther, carried away by her own feelings and the vehemence of his love: "I am getting in deeper and deeper! What shall I do? Do not make me promise!"

"Then I will promise for both!" he said; and poor Esther ceased to struggle.

The same evening at dinner, Mrs. Murray remarked to her husband that she was becoming more and more uneasy about Esther's intimacy with Mr. Hazard.

"People are talking about it," she said. "It is really becoming a matter of public discussion."

"Do you suppose she would accept him?" asked Mr. Murray.

"How can I tell? She would say no, and then very likely do it. She is in the worst sort of a state of mind for an offer of that kind."

"Poor Dudley will rise from his grave," said Mr. Murray.

"He warned me to prevent such a match if I saw it coming," said Mrs. Murray; "but he did nothing to prevent it himself. He thought Esther was going to be very unhappy, and would make some such mistake. I would interfere, but it will only make matters worse. The thing has gone too far now."

"Take her away," said Mr. Murray.

"Where to? If you will go to Europe in the spring, we will take her over and leave her there with Catherine, but she may be married by that time."

"Give her a lecture," said Mr. Murray. "Show her that she is making a stupendous blunder!"

"Better show him!" said Mrs. Murray with a little resentment. "The blunder will be worse for him than for her."

"Explain it to her!" said he. "She has sense. Esther is a good girl, and I won't stand by and see her throw herself away on a church. I will speak to her myself if you don't."

"A nice piece of work you would make of it!" rejoined his wife. "No! If it is to be done, I suppose I must do it, but she will hate me all her life."

"Do it at once, then," said Mr. Murray. "The longer you put it off, the worse she will take it."

"I will talk with her to-morrow," replied Mrs. Murray; and the next day, when she went to take Esther to drive in the afternoon, her niece received her with an embarrassed air and a high color, and said:

"Aunt! I have something to tell you."

"Good heavens!" gasped Mrs. Murray.

"I am engaged to Mr. Hazard."

Chapter VII

The instant Esther felt herself really loved, she met her fate as women will when the shock is once over. Hazard had wanted her to love him, had pursued and caught her. Now when she turned to him and answered his call, she seemed to take possession of him and lift him up. By the time he left her house this Saturday evening, he felt that he had found a soul stronger and warmer than his own, and was already a little afraid of it. Every man who has at last succeeded, after long effort, in calling up the divinity which lies hidden in a woman's heart, is startled to find that he must obey the God he summoned.

Esther herself was more astonished than Hazard at the force of this feeling which swept her away. She suddenly found herself passionately attached to a man, whom, down to the last moment, she had thought she could never marry, and now could no more imagine life without him than she could conceive of loving any one else. For the moment she thought that his profession was nothing to her; she could believe whatever he believed and do whatever he did; and if her love, backed by her will, were not strong enough to make his life her own, she cared little what became of her, and could look with indifference on life itself. So far as she was concerned she thought herself ready to worship Woden or Thor, if he did.

The next morning she could not let him preach without being near him, and she made Catherine go with her to St. John's. They took their seats, not in her own pew but in a corner, where no one should notice them under their veils. The experiment was full of peril, though Esther did not know it. This new excitement, coming so swiftly after a fortnight of exhaustion, threw her back into a state of extreme nervousness. Of course the scene of Saturday evening was followed by a sleepless night, and when Sunday morning came, her very restlessness made her hope that she should find repose and calm within the walls of the church. She went believing that she needed nothing so much as the quieting influence of the service, and she was not disappointed, for her sweetest associations were here, and as she glanced timidly up to the scaffolding where her romance had been acted, she felt at home and happy, in spite of the crowd of people who swarmed about her and separated her from the things she loved. In the background stood the solemn and awful associations of the last few weeks, the mysteries and terrors of death, drawing her from thought of earthly things to visions of another world. Full of these deep feelings, saturated with the elixir of love, Esther succumbed to the first notes of the church music. Tears of peaceful delight stood in her eyes. She glanced up towards her Cecilia on the distant wall, wondering at its childishness. How deep a meaning she could give it now, and how religious a feeling!

She was not conscious of rustling silks or waving feathers; she hardly saw the swarm of fashionable people about her; it seemed to her that her old life had vanished as though she were dead; her soul might have taken shelter in the body of some gray linnet for all that she thought or cared about the vanities of human society. She wanted only to be loved and to love, without being thought of, or noticed; to nestle in her own corner, and let the world go by.

Unluckily the world would not go by. This world which she wanted to keep at arms' length, was at church once for all, and meant to stay there; it felt itself at home, and she, with her exclusive griefs and joys, was the stranger. So long as the music lasted, all was sympathetic enough, but when Mr. Hazard read the service, he seemed far-off and strange. He belonged not to her but to the world; a thousand people had rights of property in him, soul and body, and called their claim religion. What had she to do with it? Parts of the service jarred on her ear. She began to take a bitter pleasure in thinking that she had nothing, not even religious ideas, in common with these people who came between her and her lover. Her fatigue steadily worked on her nerves. By the time the creed was read, she could not honestly feel that she believed a word of it, or could force herself to say that she ever should believe it.

With fading self-confidence she listened to the sermon. It was beautiful, simple, full of feeling and even of passion, but she felt that it was made for her, and she shrank before the thousand people who were thus let into the secret chambers of her heart. It treated of death and its mystery, covering ignorance with a veil of religious hope, and ending with an invocation of infinite love so intense in feeling and expression that, beautiful as it was, Esther forgot its beauties in the fear that the next word would reveal her to the world. This sort of publicity was new to her, and threw her back on herself until religion was forgotten in the alarm. She became more jealous than ever. What business had these strangers with her love? Why should she share it with them? When the service was over, she hurried Catherine away so quickly that they were both at home before the church was fairly empty.

This was the end of her short happiness. She knew that through the church door lay the only road to her duty and peace of mind. To see that the first happy impression had lasted barely half an hour, and instead of bringing peace, had brought irritation, was cause enough to alarm the most courageous young woman who ever rushed into the maelstrom of matrimony.

When they had reached home, she flung herself into a chair and covered her face with her hands.

"Catherine!" said she solemnly; "what am I to do? I don't like church."

"You would like your's amazingly," said Catherine, "if you had ever been to mine."

"Was your's worse?"

"If Mrs. Murray hadn't improved my manners so much, I should smile. Was mine worse? I wish you and Mr. Hazard would try it for a change. Mrs. Dyer would like to see you both undergoing discipline. Never joke about serious matters! You had better hold your tongue and be glad to live in a place where your friends let your soul alone."

"But I can't sit still and hear myself turned into a show! I can't share him with all Fifth Avenue. I want no one else to have him. To see him there devoting himself and me to a stupid crowd of people, who have as much right to him as I have, drives religion out of my head."

Catherine treated this weakness with high contempt.

"I might as well be jealous," said she, "of the people who look at Mr.

Wharton's pictures, or read Petrarch's sonnets in my sweet translation.

Did you ever hear that Laura found fault with Petrarch, or, if she did,

that any one believed she was in earnest?"

"It is not the same thing," said Esther. "He believes in his church more than he does in me. If I can't believe in it, he will have to give me up."

"He, give you up!" said Catherine. "The poor saint! You know he is silly about you."

"He must give me up, if I am jealous of his congregation, and won't believe what he preaches," replied Esther mournfully.

"Why should you care what he preaches?" asked Catherine; "you never heard your aunt troubling her head about what Mr. Murray says when he goes to court."

"She is not forced to go to court with him," said Esther; "nor to be a mother to all the old women in the court-room; nor to say that she believes—believes—believes—when in her heart she doesn't believe a word."

Hazard appeared in the middle of this dispute, and Esther, troubled as she was, could not bear to distress him. She still meant to accept every thing and force herself to follow him in silence; she would go where he led, and never once raise her eyes to look for the horizon. As she said to herself quite seriously, though with a want of reverence that augured ill; "I will go down on my knees and help him, though he turn Bonze and burn incense to Buddha in my very studio!" His presence always soothed her. His gayety and affection never failed to revive her spirits and confidence.

"Wasn't it a good sermon?" said he to Catherine as he came in, with his boyish laugh of triumph. "Give me a little praise! I never got a word of encouragement from you in my life."

"I should as soon think of encouraging a whole herd of Texas cattle," answered Catherine. "What good can my praise do you?"

"You child of nature, don't you know that children of nature like you always grow wild and need no cultivation, but that we artificial flowers can't live without it?"

"I don't know how to cultivate," answered Catherine; "it is Esther you are thinking about."

Having announced this self-evident fact, Catherine walked off and left him to quiet Esther's alarms as he could. As she went she heard him turn to Esther and repeat his prayer that she should be gentle with him and give his sermon a word of praise.

"How can I stop to think whether it is good or not," said Esther, "when I hear you telling all our secrets to our whole visiting list? I could think of nothing but myself, and how I could get away."

"And whose secrets can I tell if not our own?" asked Hazard triumphant.

While he was with her Esther was peaceful and happy, but no sooner had he gone than her terrors began again.

"He will find me out, Catherine, and it will break my heart," she said. "I never knew I had a jealous temper. I am horribly narrow-minded. I'm not fit for him, and I knew it when he asked me. He will hate me when he finds what a wife he has got."

Catherine, who positively declined to recognize Mr. Hazard's superiority of mind over Esther, took this with unshaken fortitude. "If you can stand it, I guess he can," she remarked curtly. "Where do you expect the poor man to get a wife, if all of us say we are not fit for him?"

This view of the case amused Esther for a time, but not for long—the matter was too serious for any treatment but a joke, and joking made it more serious still. Try which way she would there was no escape from her anxiety. Hazard, who had foreseen some trouble from her old associations with loose religious opinion, had taken it for granted, with his usual self-confidence, that from the moment she came within the reach of his faith and took a place by his side she would find no difficulties that he could not easily overcome. "Love is the great magnet of life, and Religion," he said "is Love." Nothing could be simpler than his plan, as he explained to her. She had but to trust herself to him and all was sure to go well. So long as he was with her and could gently thrust aside every idea but that of their own happiness, all went as well as he promised; but unluckily for his plan, Esther had all her life been used to act for herself and to order others rather than take orders of any sort. The more confidently Hazard told her to leave every thing to him, the less it occurred to her to do so. She could no more allow him to come into her life and take charge of her thoughts than to go down into her kitchen and take charge of her cook. He might reason with her by the hour, and quite convince her that nothing was of the least consequence provided it were left entirely in his hands, but the moment he was out of sight she forgot that he was to be the keeper of her conscience, and, without a thought of her dependence, she resumed the charge of her own affairs.

Her first idea was to learn something of theology, in the hope of settling her foolish and ignorant doubts as to her fitness for her new position. No sooner did the thought occur to her than she set to work, like a young divinity student, to fit herself for her new calling. Her father's library contained a number of theological books, but these were of a kind that suited Mr. Dudley's way of thinking rather than that of the early fathers. As Esther knew nothing at all about the subject, except what she had gathered from listening to conversation, one book seemed to her as good as another, provided it dealt with the matter that interested her; but when Hazard came in and found her seated on a sofa, with a pile of these works about her, his hair rose on end, and he was forced gently to take them away under the promise of bringing her others of a more correct kind. These in their turn seemed to her not quite clear, and she asked for others still. He found himself, without warning, on the brink of a theological abyss. Unwilling to worry him; eager to accept whatever he told her he believed, but in despair at each failure to understand what it was, Esther became more and more uncomfortable and terrified.

"What would you do, Catherine, if you were in my place?" she asked.

"Let it alone!" said Catherine. "You didn't ask him to marry you. If he wants you, it's his business to suit himself to you."

"But I must go to his church," said Esther, "and sit at his communion."

"How many people at his church could tell you what they believe?" asked Catherine. "Your religion is just as good as theirs as long as you don't know what it is."

"One learns theology fast when one is engaged to be married," said

Esther with a repentant face.

She was already sorry that she had tried to learn any thing about the subject, for she already knew too much, and yet a terrible fascination impelled her to read on about the nature of the trinity and the authority of tradition, until she lost patience with her own stupidity and burned to know what other people had to say on such matters. It occurred to her that she should like to have a quiet talk with George Strong.

Meanwhile Mrs. Murray, panic-stricken at learning the engagement, had sent at once for George. The messenger reached him on Sunday evening, a few hours after Esther told her aunt. Mystified by the urgent tone of Mrs. Murray's note, Strong came up at once, and found his uncle and aunt alone, after dinner, in their parlor, where Mr. Murray was quietly smoking a cigar, while his wife was holding a book in her hand and looking hard into the fire.

"George!" said his aunt solemnly; "do you know the mischief you and your friends have done?"

Strong stared. "You don't mean to tell me that Catherine has run off with Wharton?" said he. "She can't have done it, for I left Wharton not fifteen minutes ago at the club."

"No, not that! thank Heaven! Though if she hadn't more head than ever he had, that French wife of his might have given her more unhappiness than he is worth. No, it's not that! Catherine is the only sensible creature in the family."

Strong glared into the fire for a moment with a troubled air, and then looked at his aunt again. "No!" said he. "Esther hasn't joined the church. It can't be!"

"Yes!" said Mrs. Murray grimly.

"Caramba!" growled Strong, with a profusion of Spanish gutturals. Then after a moment's reflection, he added: "Poor child! Why should I care?"

"You irritate me more than your uncle does," broke out Mrs. Murray, at last losing patience. "Do you think I should be so distressed if Esther had only joined the church? I should like nothing better. What has happened is very different. She is engaged to Mr. Hazard."

Strong broke into a laugh, and Mr. Murray, with a quiet chuckle of humor, took his cigar out of his mouth to say:

"Let me explain this little matter to you, George! What troubles your aunt is not so much that Esther has joined the church as that she fears the church has joined Esther."

"The church has struck it rich this time;" remarked Strong without a sign of his first alarm. "Now we'll see what they'll make of her."

"The matter is too serious for joking;" said Mrs. Murray. "Either Esther will be unhappy for life, or Mr. Hazard will leave his church, or they will both be miserable whatever they do. I think you are bound to prevent it, since you are the one most to blame for getting them into it."

"I don't want to prevent it;" replied Strong. "It's a case of survival for the fittest. If Hazard can manage to convert Esther, let him do it. If not, let her take him in charge and convert him if she can. I'll not interfere."

"That is just the remark I had the honor to make to your aunt as you came in," said Mr. Murray. "Yesterday I wanted to stop it. To-day I want to leave it alone. They are both of them old enough to manage their own case. It has risen now to the dignity of a great cause, and I will be the devil's advocate."

"You are both of you intolerable," said Mrs. Murray, impatiently. "You talk about the happiness of Esther's life as though it were a game of poker. Tell me, George! what kind of a man is Mr. Hazard at heart?"

"Hazard is a priest at heart," replied Strong. "He has the qualities and faults of his class. I understand how this thing happened. He sees nothing good in the world that he does not instantly covet for the glory of God and the church, and just a bit for his own pleasure. He saw Esther; she struck him as something out of his line, for he is used to young women who work altar-cloths; he found that Wharton and I liked her; he thought that such material was too good for heathen like us; so he fell in love with her himself and means to turn her into a candlestick of the church. I don't mind. Let him try! He has done what he liked with us all his life. I have worked like a dog for him and his church because he was my friend. Now he will see whether he has met his match. I double you up all round on Esther."

"You men are simply brutal!" said his aunt. "Esther will be an unhappy woman all her life, whether she marries him or not, and you sit there and will not raise a finger to help her."

"Let him convert her, I say;" repeated Strong. "What is your objection to that, aunt Sarah?"

"My objection is that the whole family is only a drove of mules," said Mrs. Murray. "Poor Mr. Hazard does not know what he is undertaking."

"Is Esther very much in love?" asked Strong.

"You know her well enough to know that she would never have accepted him if she were not;" replied Mrs. Murray. "He has hunted her down when she was unhappy, and he is going to make her more unhappy still."

"I guess you're right," said Strong, seriously. "The struggle is going to tear both their poor little hearts out; but what can we do about it? None of us are to blame."

"Ah, George!" exclaimed his aunt. "You are the one most to blame. You should have married Esther yourself, and you had not wit enough to see that while you went dancing round the world, as though such women were plenty as your old fossil toads, the only woman you will ever meet who could have made you happy, was slipping through your fingers, and you hadn't the strength to hold her."

"I own it, aunt Sarah!" said George, and this time he spoke seriously enough to satisfy her. "If I could have fallen in love with Esther and she with me, I believe it would have been better for both of us than that she should marry a high-church parson and I go on digging bones; but some things are too obvious. You can't get a spark without some break in your conductor. I was ready enough to fall in love with Esther, but one can't do that kind of thing in cold blood."

"Well," said Mrs. Murray with a sigh. "You have lost her now, and Mr. Hazard will lose her too. You and he and all your friends are a sort of clever children. We are always expecting you to do something worth doing, and it never comes. You are a sort of water-color, worsted-work, bric-à-brac, washed-out geniuses, just big enough and strong enough to want to do something and never carry it through. I am heartily tired of the whole lot of you, and now I must set to work and get these two girls out of your hands."

"Do you mean to break up this engagement?" asked Strong, who was used to his aunt's criticisms and never answered them.

"The engagement will break itself up," replied his aunt. "It will have to be kept private for a few weeks on account of her father's death and her mourning, and you will see that it never will be announced. If I can, I shall certainly do all in my power to break it up."

"You will?" said Strong. "Well! I mean to do just the contrary. If Esther wants Hazard she shall have him, if I can help her. Why not? Hazard is a good fellow, and will make her a good husband. I have no fault to find with him except that he poaches outside his preserves. He has poached this time to some purpose, but if the parish can stand it, I can."

"The parish cannot stand it," said Mrs. Murray. "They are saying very ugly things already about Esther."

"Then it will not hurt my feelings to see Hazard snub his congregation," replied Strong angrily.

The family conclave ended here, and all parties henceforward fixed their eyes intently on the drama. Mrs. Murray waited with a woman's instinct for her moment to come. Strong tried to counteract her influence by bungling efforts to make the lovers' path smooth. Catherine was a sort of cushion against which all the billiard balls of the game knocked themselves in succession, leaving her cool and elastic temper undisturbed. Three more days passed without throwing much new light on the disputed question whether the engagement could last, except that Esther seemed clearly more anxious and restless. Mr. Hazard was with her several hours every day and watched over her with extreme vigilance. Mrs. Murray took her to drive every afternoon and not a glance of Esther's eyes escaped scrutiny. Strong stopped once or twice at the house but had no chance to interfere until on Thursday morning, his aunt told him that Esther was rapidly getting into a state of mind that must soon bring on a crisis.

"She cannot possibly make it do," said Mrs. Murray. "She is worrying herself to death already. Mr. Hazard ought to see that she can't marry him."

"She will marry him," answered Strong coolly. "Three women out of four think they can't marry a man at first, but when they come to parting with him, they learn better."

"He is passably selfish, your Mr. Hazard. If he thought a little more of his parish, he would not want to put over them a woman like Esther who has not a quality suited to the place."

"Her qualities are excellent," contradicted Strong. "Once in harness she will be kind and gentle, a little tender-mouthed perhaps, and apt to shy at first, but thorough-bred. He is quite right to take her if he can get her, and what does his parish expect to do about it?"

"The first thing they will do about it will be to make Esther miserable. They have begun to gossip already. A young man, even though he is a clergyman, can't be seen always in company with a pretty woman, without exciting remark. Only yesterday I was asked point-blank whether my niece was engaged to Mr. Hazard."

"What did you say?"

"I told a lie of course, all the meaner because it was an equivocation. I said that Mr. Hazard had not honored me with any communication on the subject. I score up this first falsehood to his account."

"If you lie no better than that, Aunt Sarah, Hazard's conscience won't trouble him much. When is the engagement to be out?"

"Very soon, at this rate. I thought that Esther, in common decency, could not announce it for a week or two, but every one already suspects it, and she will have to make it public within another week if she means to do so at all. Now that she is her own mistress and lives by herself, she can't have men so much about the house as she might if her father were living."

"Do you seriously think she will break it off?" asked Strong incredulously.

"I feel surer than ever," answered his aunt. "The criticism is going to be bitter, and the longer Esther waits, the more sharply people will talk. I should not wonder if it ended by driving Mr.

Hazard out of the parish. He is not strong enough to shock them much. Then Esther is growing more and more nervous every day because the more she tries to understand, the less she succeeds. Yesterday, when I took her to drive, she was in tears about the atonement, and to-day I suppose she will have gone to bed with a sick headache on account of the Athanasian creed."

"I must talk with her," said Strong. "I think I can make some of those things easier for her."

"You? I thought you laughed at them all."

"So I do, but not because they can't be understood. The trouble is that I think I do understand them. Mystery for mystery science beats religion hollow. I can't open my mouth in my lecture-room without repeating ten times as many unintelligible formulas as ever Hazard is forced to do in his church. I can quiet her mind on that score."

"You had better leave it alone, George! Why should you meddle? Let Mr. Hazard fight his own battles!"

George refused to take this wise advice. He was a tender-hearted fellow and could not bear to see his friends suffer. If Esther loved Hazard and wanted to marry him, she should do so though every dogma of the church stood in her way, and every old woman in the parish shrieked sacrilege. Strong had no respect for the church and no wish to save it trouble, but he believed that Hazard was going blindly under Esther's influence which would sooner or later end by drawing him away from his old forms of belief; and as this was entirely Hazard's affair, if he chose to risk the danger, Strong chose to help him.

"Why not?" said Strong to himself. "It is not a question of earning a living. Both of them are well enough off. If he can turn her into a light of his church, let him do it. If she ends in dragging him out of the church, so much the better. She can't get a better husband, and he can't find a better wife. I mean to see this thing through."

So George strolled round to Esther's house after this interview with his aunt, thinking that he might be able to do good. Being at home there, he went up-stairs unannounced, and finding no one in the library he climbed to the studio, where, on opening the door, he saw Catherine sitting before the fire, looking very much bored. Poor Catherine found it hard to keep up with life in New York. Fresh from the prairie, she had been first saturated with art, and was now plunged in a bottomless ocean of theology. She was glad to see Strong who had in her eyes the advantage of being more practical than the rest of her friends.

"Catherine, how are your sheep?"

"I am glad you have come to look after them," answered Catherine. "I won't be watch-dog much longer. They are too troublesome."

"What mischief are they doing now?"

"Every thing they can think of to worry me. Esther won't eat and can't sleep, and Mr. Hazard won't sleep and can't eat. She tries not to worry him, so she comes down on me with questions and books enough to frighten a professor. Do tell me what to say!"

"Where are your questions?" asked Strong.

"This morning she wanted to know what I thought of apostolic succession. She said she was reading some book by a Dr. Newman. What is apostolic succession?"

"A curious disease, quite common among the poorer classes of Sandwich

Islanders," replied Strong. "No one has ever found a cure for it."

"Don't laugh at us! We do nothing but cry now, except when Mr. Hazard is here, and then we pretend to be happy. When Esther cries, I cry too. That makes her laugh. It's our only joke, and we used to have so many."

"Don't you think it rather a moist joke?" asked Strong. "I take mine dry."

"I can't tell what she will think a joke," replied Catherine. "She asked me to-day what was my idea of heaven, and I said it was reading novels in church. She seemed to think this a rich bonanza of a joke, and laughed herself into hysterics, but I was as serious as Mr. Wharton's apostles."

"You are never so funny as when you are serious. Never be so any more!

Why don't you get her to paint?"

"She won't. I'm rather glad of it, for if she did, I should have to sit for melancholy, or an angel, or something I'm not fitted for by education."

"What shall we do about it?" asked Strong. "Things can't go on in this way."

"I think the engagement had better come out," said Catherine. "The longer it is kept private, the more she will doubt whether she ought to marry a clergyman. What do you think about marrying clergymen? Wouldn't it almost be better to marry a painter, or even a professor?"

"That would be playing it too low down," replied Strong gravely. "I would recommend you to look out for a swell. What has become of your admirer, Mr. Van Dam?"

"Gone!" said Catherine sadly. "Mr. Wharton and he went off together.

There is something about me that scares them all off the ranche."

While they were thus improving each other's minds, the door opened and Esther entered. She was pale and her face had no longer the bright look which Wharton had thought so characteristic, but there was no other sign of trouble about her, and she welcomed her cousin as pleasantly as ever, so that he could hardly believe in the stories he had just heard of her distress.

"Good day, Cousin George," she said. "Thank you for coming to cheer up this poor girl. She needs it. Do take her out and amuse her."

"Come out yourself, Esther. You need it more than she does."

"Aunt Sarah is coming at two o'clock to take me to drive," said Esther.

"Catherine hates driving unless she drives herself."

"I thought you hated it too."

"Oh, I hate nothing now," replied Esther, with a little of her old laugh. "I am learning to like every thing."

"Is that in the marriage service?" asked Strong. "Do you have to begin so high up? Couldn't you start easy, and like a few things first,—me for instance—and let the rest wait?"

"No," she said, "you are to come last. Honestly, I am more afraid of you than of all the rest of the world. If you knew what a bug-bear you are to me, you would be afraid of yourself. Don't make fun of me any more! I know I am horribly funny, but you must take me in earnest. Poor papa's last words to me were: 'Laugh and you're safe!'—but if I laugh now, I'm lost."

"This is the first time I ever met any one honest enough to acknowledge that marriage was so sad a thing. Catherine, if I ask you to marry me, will you turn serious?"

"She will turn serious enough if she does it," said Esther. "You would stay with her a week, and then tell her that you were obliged to see a friend in Japan. She would never see you again, but the newspapers would tell her that you had set out to look for bones in the Milky Way."

"What you say sounds to me as though it had a grain of truth," replied Strong. "That reminds me that I got a letter telling me of a lot of new bones only yesterday, but I must leave them underground till the summer; if by that time I can do any thing for you in Oregon, let me know."

"I want you very much to do something for me now," said Esther. "Will you try to be serious a moment for my sake?"

"I don't know," said Strong. "You ask too much all at once. Where are you coming out?"

"Will you answer me a question? Say yes or no!"

"That depends on the question, Mistress Esther! Old birds are not to be caught in old traps. State your question, as we say in the lecture-room."

"Is religion true?"

"I thought so! Cousin Esther, I love you as much as I love any one in this cold world, but I can't answer your question. I can tell you all about the mound-builders or cave-men, so far as known, but I could not tell you the difference between the bones of a saint and those of a heathen. Ask me something easier! Ask me whether science is true!"

"Is science true?"

"No!"

"Then why do you believe in it?"

"I don't believe in it."

"Then why do you belong to it?"

"Because I want to help in making it truer. Now, Esther, just take this matter coolly! You are bothered, I suppose, by the idea that you can't possibly believe in miracles and mysteries, and therefore can't make a good wife for Hazard. You might just as well make yourself unhappy by doubting whether you would make a good wife to me because you can't believe the first axiom in Euclid. There is no science which does not begin by requiring you to believe the incredible."

"Are you telling me the truth?"

"I tell you the solemn truth that the doctrine of the Trinity is not so difficult to accept for a working proposition as any one of the axioms of physics. The wife of my mathematical colleague, to my knowledge, never even stopped to ask whether it was true that a point had neither length, breadth nor thickness."

Esther pondered a few moments, looking into the fire with a grave face.

Then she went on:

"You are not talking honestly. Why should I dare tell you that your old fossil bones are a humbug, when I would not for the world talk so to Mr. Hazard? You don't care whether geology is true or not."

"Well, no, not much!" said Strong. "I should care more if you told me that my best Japanese lacquer was modern."

"Besides," said Esther; "you have not answered my question. I want to know what you think, and you won't tell me. Oh! don't let me lose faith in you too! I know your opinions. You think the whole church a piece of superstition. I've heard you say so, and I want you to tell me why. You're my cousin and I've a right to your help, but you won't give it."

"You are a desperate little tyrant," said Strong laughing. "You always were. Do you remember how we fought when we were children because you would have your own way? I used to give in then, but I am old now, and obstinate."

"I know that you always ended by making me go your way," replied Esther; "but that was because I never cared much where I went. Now it is a matter of life and death. I can't move a step, or even let our engagement be announced until I feel sure that I shall not be a load on his neck. Do you think I should hesitate to break it off, even if I broke my heart with it, if I thought it was going to bring trouble on him?"

Against this assault jesting was out of the question. Strong was forced out of this line of defense and found himself in an awkward position. Esther, not outwardly excited, but leaning her chin on her hand, and gazing into the fire with a look of set will, had the calmness of despair. Strong was staggered and hesitated.

"The trouble with you is that you start wrong," said he at length. "You need what is called faith, and are trying to get it by reason. It can't be done. Faith is a state of mind, like love or jealousy. You can never reason yourself into it."

"So Mr. Hazard says," rejoined Esther. "He tells me to wait and it will come, but he wants me to go on just as though I were certain of its coming. I can't wait. If it does not come quickly, I must do something desperate. Now tell me what you would do to get faith if the happiness of your whole life hung on it."

Strong rose uneasily from his seat and stood up before the fire. He began to think himself rash for venturing into this arena. He had always believed his cousin to be stronger than Hazard, because Hazard was a clergyman, but he had not hitherto thought her stronger than himself, and he now looked at her carefully, wondering whether he could have managed her. Never in his life had he felt so nearly in love with her as now, under the temptation to try whether she could be made to give up her will to his. This feeling was the stronger because even in his own eyes his conduct so far seemed a little cowardly and ridiculous. He pulled himself up sharply, and, seeing nothing else to be done, he took up the weapons of the church and asserted the tone of authority.

"Every one who marries," he said, "goes it blind, more or less. If you have faith enough in Hazard to believe in him, you have faith enough to accept his church. Faith means submission. Submit!"

"I want to submit," cried Esther piteously, rising in her turn and speaking in accents of real distress and passion. "Why can't some of you make me? For a few minutes at a time I think it done, and then I suddenly find myself more defiant than ever. I want nothing of the church! Why should it trouble me? Why should I submit to it? Why can't it leave me alone?"

"What you want is the Roman church," continued Strong mercilessly. "They know how to deal with pride of will. Millions of men and women have gone through the same struggle, and the church tells them to fix their eyes on a symbol of faith, and if their eyes wander, scourges them for it." As he talked, he took up the little carved ivory crucifix which stood on the mantel-piece among other bits of studio furniture, and holding it up before her, said: "There! How many people do you think, have come to this Christ of yours that has no meaning to you, and in their struggle with doubt, have pressed it against their hearts till it drew blood? Ask it!"

"Is that all?" said Esther, taking the crucifix from his hand and looking curiously at it. Then she silently put it against her heart and pressed it with more and more force, until Strong caught her hand in alarm and pulled it away.

"Come!" said he coolly, as he forced her to give up the crucifix; "my little bluff has failed. I throw up the hand. You must play it out with Hazard."

Chapter VIII

Mr. Hazard was not happy. Like Esther he felt himself getting into a state of mind that threatened to break his spirit. He had been used to ordering matters much as he pleased. His parish at Cincinnati, being his creation, had been managed by him as though he owned it, but at St. John's he found himself less free, and was conscious of incessant criticism. He had been now some months in his new pulpit; his popular success had been marked; St. John's was overflowing with a transient audience, like a theater, to the disgust of regular pew-owners; his personal influence was great; but he felt that it was not yet, and perhaps never could be, strong enough to stand the scandal of his marriage to a woman whose opinions were believed to be radical. On this point he was not left in doubt, for the mere suspicion of his engagement raised a little tempest in the pool. The stricter sect, not without reason, were scandalized. They held to their creed, and the bare mention of Esther Dudley's name called warm protests from their ranks. They flatly said that it would be impossible for Mr. Hazard to make them believe his own doctrine to be sound, if he could wish to enter into such a connection. None but a free-thinker could associate with the set of free-thinkers, artists and other unusual people whose society Mr. Hazard was known to affect, and his marriage to one of them would give the unorthodox a hold on the parish which would end by splitting it.

One of his strongest friends, who had done most to bring him to New York and make his path pleasant, came to him with an account of what was said and thought, softening the expression so as to bear telling.

"You ought to hear about it," said he, "so I tell you; but it is between you and me. I don't ask whether you are engaged to Miss Dudley. For my own pleasure, I wish you may be. If I were thirty years younger I would try for her myself; but we all know that she has very little more religious experience than a white rosebud. I'm not strict myself, I don't mind a little looseness on the creed, but the trouble is that every old woman in the parish knows all about the family. Her father, William Dudley, a great friend of mine as you know, was a man who liked to defy opinion and never hid his contempt for ours. He paid for a pew at St. John's because, he said, society needs still that sort of police. But he has told me a dozen times that he could get more police for his money by giving it to the Roman Catholics. He never entered his pew. His brother-in-law Murray is just as bad, never goes near the church, and is always poking fun at us who do. The professor is a full-fledged German Darwinist, and believes in nothing that I know of, unless it is himself. Esther took to society, and I'm told by my young people that she was one of the best waltzers in town until she gave it up for painting and dinners. Her set never bothered their heads about the church. Of the whole family, Mrs. Murray is the only one who has any weight in the parish, and she has a good deal, but if I know her, she won't approve the match any more than the rest, and you must expect to get the reputation of being unorthodox. Only yesterday old Tarbox told me he thought you were rather weak on the Pentateuch, and the best I could say was that now-a-days we must choose between weak doctrines and weak brains, and of the two, I preferred to let up on the Pentateuch."

All this was the more annoying to Mr. Hazard because his orthodoxy was his strong point. Like most vigorous-minded men, seeing that there was no stopping-place between dogma and negation, he preferred to accept dogma. Of all weaknesses he most disliked timid and half-hearted faith. He would rather have jumped at once to Strong's pure denial, than yield an inch to the argument that a mystery was to be paltered with because it could not be explained. The idea that these gossiping parishioners of his should undertake to question his orthodoxy, tried his temper. He knew that they disliked his intimacy with artists and scientific people, but he was not afraid of his parish, and meant that his parish should be a little afraid of him. He preferred to give them some cause of fault-finding in order to keep them awake. His greatest annoyance came from another side. If such gossip should reach Esther's ears, it would go far towards driving her beyond his control, and he knew that even without this additional alarm, it was with the greatest difficulty he could quiet and restrain her. The threatened disaster was terrible enough when looked at as a mere question of love, but it went much deeper. He was ready to override criticism and trample on remonstrance if he could but succeed in drawing her into the fold, because his lifelong faith, that all human energies belonged to the church, was on trial, and, if it broke down in a test so supreme as that of marriage, the blow would go far to prostrate him forever. What was his religious energy worth if it did not carry him successfully through such stress, when the strongest passion in life was working on its side?

At the hour when Strong was making his disastrous attempt to relieve Esther of her scruples, Mr. Hazard was listening to these exasperating criticisms from his parish. It was his habit to come every day at noon to pass an hour with Esther, and as he entered the house to-day he met Strong leaving it, and asked him to spare the time for a talk the same evening. He wanted Strong's advice and help.

A brace of lovers in lower spirits than Hazard and Esther could not have been easily found in the city of New York or its vicinity this day, and the worst part of their depression was that each was determined to hide it from the other. Esther could not tell him much more than he already knew, and would not throw away her charm over him by adding to his anxieties, while he knew that any thing he could tell her would add to her doubts and perhaps drive her to some sudden and violent step. Luckily they were too much attached to each other to feel the full awkwardness of their attitude.

"It is outrageously pleasant to be with you," he said. "One's conscience revolts against such enjoyment. I wonder whether I should ever get enough."

"I shall never give you a chance," said she. "I shall be strict with you and send you off to your work before you can get tired of me."

"You make me shockingly weary of my work," he answered. "At times I wish I could stop making a labor of religion, and enjoy it a little. How pleasant it would be to go off to Japan together and fill our sketch-books with drawings."

This suggestion came on Esther so suddenly that she forgot herself and gave a little cry of delight. "Oh, are you in earnest?" she said. "It seems to me that I could crawl and swim there if you would go with me."

Then she saw her mistake. Her outburst of pleasure gave him pain. He was displeased with himself for speaking so thoughtlessly, for this idea of escape made both of them conscious of the chasm on whose edge they stood.

"No, I wish I could be in earnest," he answered, "but I have just begun work, and there is no vacation for me. You must keep up my courage. Without your help I shall break down."

If he had thought out in advance some device for distressing her, he could not have succeeded better. She had just time to realize the full strength of her love for him, when he thrust the church between them, and bade her love him for its sake. The delight of wandering through the world by his side flashed on her mind only to show a whole Fifth Avenue congregation as her rival. The conviction that the church was hateful to her and that she could never trust herself to obey or love it, forced itself on her at the very moment when she felt that life was nothing without her lover, and that to give up all the world besides in order to go with him, would be the only happiness she cared to ask of her destiny. The feeling was torture. So long as he remained she controlled it, but when he went away she wrung her hands in despair and asked herself again and again what she could do; whether she was not going mad with the strain of these emotions.

Before she had fairly succeeded in calming herself, her aunt came to take her out for their daily drive. Since her father's death, this drive with her aunt, or a walk with Catherine, had been her only escape from the confinement of the house, and she depended on it more than on food and drink. They went first to some shops where Mrs. Murray had purchases to make, and Esther sat alone in the carriage while her aunt was engaged within in buying whatever household articles were on her list for the day. As Esther, sitting quietly in the corner of the carriage, mechanically watched the passers-by, she saw the familiar figure of Mr. Wharton among them, and, with a sudden movement of her old vivacity, she bent forward, caught his eye, and held out her hand. He stopped before the carriage window, and spoke with more than common cordiality.

"I wanted to come and see you, but I heard you received no one."

"I will always see you," she replied.

Looking more than ever shy and embarrassed he said that he should certainly come as soon as his work would let him, and meanwhile he wanted her to know how glad he was to be able at last to offer his congratulations.

"Congratulations? On what?" said she, beginning to flush scarlet.

Wharton stammered out: "I was this moment told by a lady of your acquaintance that your engagement to Mr. Hazard was formally announced to-day."

Esther grew as pale as she had been red, and answered quietly: "When my engagement to any one is announced, I promise to let you know of it, Mr. Wharton, before the world knows it."

He apologized and passed on. Esther, shrinking back into her corner, struggled in vain to recover from this new blow. Mrs. Murray, on returning, found her in a state of feverish excitement.

"I am being dragged in against my will," said she. "I am beyond my depth. What am I to do?"

"Most women feel so at first," replied her aunt calmly. "Many want to escape. Some are afterwards sorry they didn't."

"Have you heard of this too, and not told me?" asked Esther.

Mrs. Murray had thought too long over the coming trouble to hesitate now that the moment had come. She had watched for the crisis; her mind was made up to take her share of the responsibility; so she now settled herself down to the task. As the thing had to be done, she thought that the shortest agony was the most merciful.

"Yes!" she answered. "Several persons have mentioned it to me, and I have had to profess not to know what they meant."

"What did they say?" asked Esther breathlessly.

"The only one who has talked openly to me about it is your friend Mrs. Dyer. The story came from her, and I believe she invented it. Of course she disapproves. I never knew her to approve."

"What reason does she give?"

"She says that you are an amiable girl, but one given up to worldly pursuits and without a trace of religious principle; the last woman to make a clergyman's wife, though you might do very well for an artist or somebody wicked enough for you, as I gathered her idea. I am told that she amuses herself by adding that she never took Mr. Hazard for a clergyman, and the sooner he quits the pulpit, the better. She is never satisfied without hitting every one she can reach."

"What does she want?" asked Esther.

"I suppose she wants to break off the intimacy. She thinks there is no actual engagement yet, and the surest way to prevent one is to invent one in time."

Esther reflected a few minutes before beginning again.

"Aunt, do you think I am fit to be his wife?"

"It all depends on you," replied Mrs. Murray. "If you feel yourself fit, you are the best person in the world for it. You would be a brand saved from the burning, and it will be a great feather in Mr. Hazard's cap to convert you into a strong church-woman. He could then afford to laugh at Mrs. Dyer, and all the parish would laugh with him."

"Aunt!" said Esther in an awe-struck tone; "I am jealous of the church. I never shall like it."

"Then, Esther, you are doing very wrong to let Mr. Hazard think you can marry him. You will ruin him, and yourself too."

"He has seen how I have struggled," answered Esther with a sort of sob. "I never knew how gentle and patient a man could be until I saw how he helped me. He began by taking all the risk. I told him faithfully that I was not fit for him, and he said that he only asked me to love him. I did love him. I love him so much that if he were a beggar in the street here and wanted me, I would get down and pick up rags with him."

She moaned out this last sentence so piteously that Mrs. Murray's heart bled. "Poor child!" she thought. "It is like crushing a sparrow with a stone. I must do it quickly."

"Tell him all about it, Esther! It is his affair more than yours. If his love is great enough to take you as you are, do your best, and never let him repent it; but you must make him choose between you and his profession."

"I can't do that!" said Esther quickly. "I would rather go on and leave it all to chance."

"If you do," replied Mrs. Murray, "You will only put yourself into his hands. Sooner or later Mr. Hazard must find out that you don't belong to him. Then it will be his duty to make you choose between your will and his. You had better not let yourself be put in such a position. A woman can afford to break an engagement, but she can't afford to be thrown over by a man, not even if he is a clergyman, and that is what Mr. Hazard will have to do to you if you let him go on."

"Oh, I know him better!" broke out Esther. She resented bitterly this cruel charge against her lover, but nevertheless it cut into her quivering nerves until her love seemed to wither under it. The idea that he could ever want to get rid of her was the last drop in her cup of bitterness. Mrs. Murray knew how to crush her sparrow. She needed barely five minutes to do it. From the moment that Esther's feminine pride was involved, the sparrow was dead.

Certainly Hazard had as yet no thought of giving up his prize, but he had reached the first stage of wondering what he should do with it. Naturally sanguine and perhaps a little spoiled by flattery and success, he had taken for granted that Esther would at once absorb her existence in his. He hoped that she would become, like most converts, more zealous than himself. After a week of trial, finding her not only unaffected by his influence but actually slipping more and more from his control, he began to feel an alarm which grew more acute every hour, and brought him for the first time face to face with the possibility of failure. What could he do to overcome this fatal coldness.

With very uneasy feelings he admitted that a step backwards must be taken, and it was for this purpose that he wanted to consult with Strong. Never was the Church blessed with a stranger ally than this freest of free thinkers, who looked at churches very much as he would have looked at a layer of extinct oysters in a buried mud-bank. Strong's notion was that since the Church continued to exist, it probably served some necessary purpose in human economy, though he could himself no more understand the good of it than he could comprehend the use of human existence in any shape. Since men and women were here, idiotic and purposeless as they might be, they had what they chose to call a right to amuse themselves in their own way, and if this way made some happy without hurting others, Strong was ready enough to help. He was as willing to help Hazard as to help Esther, provided the happiness of either seemed to be within reach; and as for forms of faith it seemed to him as easy to believe one thing as another. If Esther believed any thing at all, he could see no reason why she might not believe whatever Hazard wanted.

With all the good-will in the world he came from his club after dinner to Hazard's house. As the way was short he did not even grumble, knowing that he could smoke his cigar as well at one place as at the other. He found Hazard in his library, walking up and down, with more discouragement on his face than Strong had ever seen there before. The old confusion of the room had not quite disappeared; the books were not yet all arranged on their shelves; pictures still leaned against the wall; dust had accumulated on them, and even on the large working table where half-written sermons lay scattered among a mass of notes, circulars, invitations and unanswered letters. It was clear that Mr. Hazard was not an orderly person and needed nothing so much as a wife. Esther would have been little flattered at the remark, now rather common among his older friends, that almost any wife would be better for him than none.

With an echo of his old boyish cordiality he welcomed Strong, gave him the best easy-chair by the fire, and told him to smoke as much as he liked.

"Perhaps a cigar will give you wisdom," he added. "You will need it, for

I want to consult you about Esther."

"Don't!" said Strong laconically.

"Hush!" replied Hazard. "You put me out. I don't consult you because I like it, but because I must. The matter is becoming serious, and I must either consult you or Mrs. Murray. I prefer to begin with you. It's a habit I have."

"At your own risk, then!"

"I suppose I shall have to take whatever risk there is in it," answered Hazard. "I must do something, for if my amiable parishioner, Mrs. Dyer, gets at Esther in her present state of mind, the poor child will work herself into a brain fever. But first tell me one thing! Were you ever in love with Esther yourself!"

"Never!" replied Strong, peacefully. "Esther always told me that I had nothing but chalk and plate-glass in my mind, and could never love or be loved. We have discussed it a good deal. She says I am an old glove that fits well enough but will not cling. Of course it was her business to make me cling and I told her so. No! I never was in love with her, but I have been nearer it these last ten days than ever before. She will come out of her trouble either made or marred, and a year hence I will tell you which."

"Take care," said Hazard. "I have learned to conquer all my passions except jealousy, and that I have never yet tried."

"If she marries you," replied Strong, "that will settle it."

"If she marries me!" broke out Hazard, paying no attention to Strong's quiet assumption that for Esther to be thus married was to be marred. "Do you mean that there is any doubt about it?"

"I supposed that was what you wanted to talk about," answered Strong with some surprise. "Is any thing else the matter?"

"You always put facts in a horribly materialistic way," responded Hazard. "I wanted to consult you about making things easier for her, not about broken engagements."

"Bless your idealistic soul!" said Strong. "I have already tried to help her in that way, and made a shocking piece of work. Has not Esther told you?" and he went on to give his friend an account of the morning's conversation in which his attempt to preach the orthodox faith had suffered disastrous defeat. Hazard listened closely, and at the end sat for some time silent in deep thought. Then he said:

"Esther told me something of this, though I did not get the idea it was so serious. I am glad to know the whole; but you should not have tried to discipline her. Leave the thunders of the church to me."

"What could I do?" asked Strong. "She jammed me close up to the wall. I did not know where to turn. You would have been still less pleased if I had done what she wanted, and given her the whole Agnostic creed."

"I am not quite so sure about that," rejoined Hazard thoughtfully. "I am never afraid of pure atheism; it is the flabby kind of sentimental deism that annoys me, because it is as slippery as air. If you will tell her honestly what your skepticism means, I will risk the consequences."

"Just as you like!" said Strong; "if she attacks me again, I will give her the strongest kind of a dose of what you are pleased to call pure atheism. Not that I mind what it is called. She shall have it crude. Only remember that I prefer to tackle her on the other side."

"Do as you please!" said Hazard. "Now let us come to business. All Esther wants is time. I am as certain as I can be of any thing in this uncertain world, that a few weeks, or at the outside a few months, will quiet all her fears. What I want is to stop this immediate strain which is enough to distract any woman."

"Stop the strain of course!" said Strong. "I want to stop it almost as much as you do, but it looked to me this morning as though what you call strain were a steady drift which pays no sort of heed to our trying to stop it."

"I feel sure it is only nervousness," said Hazard earnestly. "Give her time, quiet and rest! She will come out right."

"Then what is it that I can do?"

"Help me to get her out of New York."

"I will ask my aunt to help you," replied Strong; "but how are we to do it? The earthly paradise is not to be found in this neighborhood in the middle of February."

"Never mind! If you and she will back me, we can do it, and it must be done instantly to be of use. There is no end of parish gossip which must not come to Esther's ears, or it will drive her wild. Take her to Florida, California, or even to Europe if you can! Give me time to smooth things down! If she stays here we shall all be the worse for it."

As usual, Hazard had his way. George consented to do all he asked and even to take Esther away himself if it were necessary. The next morning he appeared soon after breakfast at his aunt's to report Hazard's wishes and to devise the means of satisfying them. Much to his relief, and rather to his astonishment, he found Mrs. Murray disposed to look with favor on the idea. She listened quietly to his story, and after a little reflection, asked:

"Where do you think we had best go?"

"Do you mean to go too?" asked Strong in surprise. "Why should you tear yourself up by the roots to please Hazard?"

"Those two girls can't go alone," said Mrs. Murray; "and as for me, I don't go to please Mr. Hazard. I don't think he is going to be pleased."

"Now what mischief are you brewing, Aunt Sarah? I am Hazard's friend, and bound to see him through. Don't make me a party to any scheme against him!"

"You are not very bright, George, and just now you are rather ridiculous, because you do not in the least know what you are about."

"Go on!" said Strong with irrepressible good nature. "Play out all your trumps and let my suit in!"

"Could you be ready to start for Niagara by to-morrow morning?" asked his aunt.

"To-morrow is Saturday. Yes! I could manage it."

"Could you get some pleasant man to go with you?"

"Not much chance!" he replied. "I might ask Wharton, but he is very busy."

"Try for him! I will send you a note to your club early this evening to say whether I shall want you or not. If I make you go, I shall go too, and take Esther and Catherine."

"I will do any thing you want," said Strong, "on condition that you tell me what you are about."

Mrs. Murray looked at her nephew with a pitying air, and said:

"Any one with common sense might see that Esther's engagement never could come to any thing."

"But you are trying to hold her to it."

"I am trying to do no such thing. I expect Esther to dismiss him; then she will need some change of scene, and I mean to take her away."

"To-day?" asked Strong in alarm.

"To-day or to-morrow! Sooner or later! We have got to be ready for it at any moment. Now do you understand?"

"I think I am beginning to catch on," replied Strong with a grave face.

"I wish I were out of the scrape."

"I told you never to get into it," rejoined his aunt.

"Poor Hazard!" muttered George, wondering whether he could do anything to ward off this last blow from his friend.

Even as he spoke, the crisis was at hand. Mrs. Murray's calculations were exact. While Hazard had been arranging with Strong the plan for getting Esther away from New York, letting the engagement remain private, Esther, in a state of feverish restlessness was wearying Catherine with endless discussion of her trouble. Even Catherine felt that, one way or the other, it was time for this thing to stop. Esther had passed the stage of self-submission, and was in a mutinous mood. She had given up the effort to reconcile herself with her situation, and yet could talk of nothing but Hazard, until Catherine's good-nature was sorely tried.

"I never was such a bore till now," said Esther at length, as though she could not at all understand it. "I could sometimes be quite pleasant. I used to go about the house singing and laughing. Am I going mad?"

"Suppose we go mad together?" said Catherine. "I will if you will."

"Suppose we elope together!" said Esther. "Will you run off with me?"

"Any where but to Colorado," replied Catherine, "I have seen all I want of Colorado."

"We will take our wedding journey together and leave our husbands behind. Let them catch us if they can!" continued Esther, talking rapidly and feverishly.

"It would be rather fun to see Mr. Hazard driving Mr. Van Dam's fast trotters after us," remarked Catherine.

"When shall we go? Can we start now?"

"Don't you think we had better go to bed just now, and elope in the morning?" grumbled Catherine. "They can see us better by daylight."

"I tell you, Catherine, that I am in awful earnest. I mean to go away somewhere, and if you won't go with me, I shall go alone."

"Suppose they catch us?" said Catherine.

"I don't care! I am hopelessly wicked! I can't be respectable and believe the thirty-nine articles. I can't go to church every Sunday or hold my tongue or pretend to be pious."

"Then why don't you tell him so, and let him run away?" asked Catherine.

"Because then he would think it his duty to run," said Esther, "and I don't want to be run away from. Would you like to have the world think you were jilted?"

"How you do torture your poor brain!" said Catherine pityingly. "There! Go to bed now! It is long past midnight. To-morrow I will run you off, and you never shall go to church any more."

Esther was really in a way to alarm her friends. She went to bed as Catherine advised, but her sleep was feverish, as though she had dieted herself on opium. She acted over and over again the scene that lay before her, until her brain felt physically weary, as though it had run all night round and round its narrow chamber. Her head was so tired in the morning that it was a relief to get up and face real life. She dressed herself with uncommon care. She meant to keep her crown even though she threw away her kingdom, and though she should lose a husband, she intended to hold fast her lover. Women have the right to this coquetry with fate. Iphigenia herself, when the priests, who muffled her voice, stretched her on the altar and struck the knife in her throat, tried to charm them with her sad eyes while her saffron blood was flowing, and they saw that she would have charmed them with her voice even when hope had vanished.

The unfortunate Hazard was not precisely an Agamemnon, and would have liked nothing better than to stop the sacrifice which seemed to him much too closely like a triumph over himself. His own throat was the one which felt itself in closest danger of the knife. At noon, as usual, he came in, trying to conceal his anxiety under an appearance of confidence, but Esther's first words routed all his forces and drove him back to his last defense.

"I should not have let you come to-day. I ought to have written to bid you good-by, but it was too hard not to see you once more. I am going away."

"I am going with you," said Hazard quietly.

"No, you are not!" replied Esther. "You are to stay here and attend to your duties. Forget me as soon as you can."

Hazard took this address very good-naturedly, and neither showed nor felt surprise. "You have been tormented by this idea," he said, "and I am glad now to meet it face to face. For us to part is impossible. You and I are one. You cannot get yourself apart from me, though you may make us both unhappy; and even if you go away forever you will still belong to me. I could not release you if I would."

"I don't want to be released," said Esther. "If it were only for that, I would stay with you as long as you would let me. I would do whatever you told me, and never ask a question. But I will not be your evil genius. I will be your good genius or nothing."

"Be my good genius then! What stands in your way?"

"I have tried and failed. Already there is not a woman in your parish who is not saying that I shall ruin you and your career. I would rather die than run the risk of your thinking I had done you harm."

"If I, seeing all this, am willing to take the risk, why should you ally yourself against me with all the petty gossip of a parish?" asked Hazard. "Such talk will stop the moment you say the word.

Let me go out now and announce our engagement! If I did not sometimes shock my parish, I could never manage them."

"But I would rather not be made useful in that way," said Esther with a momentary gleam of humor in her eyes. "No woman wants to be shocking. Now I have a favor to ask of you. It is the last, and I want you to promise to grant it."

"Not if it is to give you up."

"I want you to make it easy for me. I am trying to do right. I am so weak and unhappy after all that has happened that if you are cruel to me, I shall want to die. Be generous! You know I am right. Let me go quietly, and do not torture me!"

She sat down as they were talking. He, sinking into a chair by her side, took both her hands in his, and she did not try to free them. When she made her appeal, he answered as quietly and stubbornly as before: "Never! You are my wife, and my wife you will always be in my eyes. I shall not give you up. I shall not make it easy for you to give me up. I shall make it as hard as I can. I shall prevent it. But I will do anything you like to make our engagement easy, and I came to-day with something to propose."

No doubt, had Hazard taken her at her word and coolly walked away, Esther would have been very unpleasantly surprised. She did not expect him to obey her first orders, nor did she want to hurry the moment of separation, or to part from him with a feeling of bitterness. His presence always soothed and satisfied her, and she had never been calmer than now, when, with her hands in his, she waited for his new suggestion.

"I want you to do me a favor not nearly so great as the one you ask of me," said he. "Give me time! Go abroad, if you think best, but let our engagement stand! Let me come out and join you in the summer. I am ready to see you go where you like, and stay as long as you please, if you take me with you."

Esther reflected for a moment how she should answer. She had thought of this plan and rejected it long before, because it seemed to her to combine all possible objections, and to get rid of none. She knew that neither six months nor six years would make her a fit wife for Hazard, and that it would be dishonest to lure him on by any hope that she could change her nature; but it was not easy to put this in delicate words. At length she answered simply.

"I am almost the last person in the world whom you ought to marry. Time will only make me more unfit."

"Should you think so," he asked quickly, "if I were a lawyer, or a stock broker?"

She colored and withdrew her hands. "No!" she said. "If you were a stock broker I suppose I should be quite satisfied. Now I am low enough, am I not? Don't make me feel more degraded than I am. Let me go off alone and forget me!"

But Hazard continued to press his point with infinite patience and gentle obstinacy, until her powers of resistance were almost worn out. Again and again the tears came into her eyes, and she would have told him gladly to take her and do what he liked with her, if she had not steeled herself with the fixed thought that in this case the whole struggle must begin again, and he would know no better what to do with her than before. He would talk only of their love, attacking her where she could not defend herself, and took almost a pleasure in acknowledging that she was at his mercy.

"Oh, if you want only my love," she said at last with a gesture of despair, "I have lost all my pride. I would like nothing better than to lie down and die in your arms. I will promise to be faithful to you all my life; to go into a convent if you want it; to drown myself, or do any thing but lose your love."

"It is not so very much I ask," he urged. "You fear hurting me by marrying me. Do you ever reflect how much you will hurt me by refusing? Do you know how solitary I am? Not a human being counts for any thing in my life. When I go to my rooms, I am terrified to think how lonely they will seem unless I can keep you in my mind. You are the only woman I ever loved. You are my companion, my ideal, my life. We two souls have wandered about the universe from all eternity waiting to meet each other, and now after we have met and become one, you try to part us."

As he went on with this appeal, he wrought himself into stronger and stronger expression of feeling, while Esther fell back in her chair and covered her face with her hands.

"If I am willing to risk every thing for you, why should you refuse to grant me so small a favor as I ask? Look, Esther! What more can I do? Will you not make a little sacrifice of pride for me? Will you ever find another man to love you as I do?"

"How merciless you are!" sobbed Esther.

"I ask only for time," he hurried on. "To part from you now, in this room, at this moment, forever, is awful! You may go if you will, but I shall follow you. I will never give you up. You are mine—mine—mine!"

His passionate cry of love was more than flesh and blood could bear. With an uncontrollable impulse of self-abandonment Esther held out her hand to him and he seized her in his arms, kissing her passionately again and again, till she tore herself away.

"There, go!" said she, breathlessly. "Go! You are killing me!"

Without waiting an answer, she turned and hurried away to her room, where, flinging herself down, she sobbed till her hysterical passion wore itself out.

Chapter IX

At her usual hour for taking Esther to drive, Mrs. Murray appeared at the house, where she found Catherine looking as little pleased as though she were ordered to return to her native prairie.

"We have sent him off," said she, "and we are clean broke up."

The tears were in her eyes as she thus announced the tragedy which had been acted only an hour or two before, but her coolness more than ever won Mrs. Murray's heart.

"Tell me all that has happened," said she.

"I've told you all I know," replied Catherine. "They had it out here for an hour or more, and then Esther ran up to her room. I've been to the door half a dozen times, and could hear her crying and moaning inside."

Mrs. Murray sat down with a rueful face and a weary sigh, but there was no sign of hesitation or doubt in her manner. The time had come for her to take command, and she did it without fretfulness or unnecessary words.

"You are the only person I know with a head," said she to Catherine. "You have some common sense and can help me. I want to take Esther out of this place within six hours. Can you manage to get every thing ready?"

"I will run it all if you will take care of Esther," replied Catherine.

"I'm not old enough to boss her."

"All you will have to do is to see that your trunks are packed for a week's absence and you are both ready to start by eight o'clock," answered Mrs. Murray. "Do you attend to that and I will look out for the rest. Now wait here a few minutes while I go up and see Esther!"

Catherine wished nothing better than to start any where at the shortest notice. She was tired of the long strain on her sympathies and feelings, and was glad to be made useful in a way that pleased her practical mind. Mrs. Murray went up to Esther's room. All was quiet inside. The storm had spent itself. Knowing that her aunt would come, Esther had made the effort to be herself again, and when Mrs. Murray knocked at the door, the voice that told her to come in was firm and sweet as ever. Esther was getting ready for her drive, and though her eyes, in spite of bathing, were red and swollen, they had no longer the anxious and troubled look of a hunted creature which had so much alarmed Mrs. Murray for the last few days. Her expression was more composed than it had been for weeks. Her love had already become a sorrow rather than a passion, and she would not, for a world of lovers, have gone back to the distress of yesterday.

Mrs. Murray took in the whole situation at a glance and breathed a breath of relief. At length the crisis was past and she had only to save the girl from brooding over her pain. Without waiting for an explanation, she plunged into the torrent of Esther's woes.

"Mr. Murray and I are going to Niagara by the night train. I want you and Catherine to go with us."

"You are an angel!" answered Esther. "Did Catherine tell you how I wanted to run away! You knew it would be so? I will go any where; the further the better; but how can I drag you and poor Uncle John away from town at this season? Can't I go off alone with Catherine?"

"Nonsense!" said her aunt briefly. "I shall be glad to get away from New York. I am tired of it.

Get your trunks packed! Put in your sketching materials, and we will pick you up at eight o'clock. George shall come on to-morrow and pass Sunday with us."

Esther thanked her aunt with effusion. "I am going to show you how well I can behave. Uncle John shall not know that any thing is the matter with me unless you tell him. I won't be contemptible, even if I have got red eyes."

Not five minutes were needed to decide on the new departure. Esther and Catherine found relief and amusement in the bustle of preparation. If Esther was still a little feverish and excited, she was able to throw it off in work. She was no longer an object of pity; it was her uncle and aunt who deserved deepest compassion. What worse shock was possible for an elderly, middle-aged New York lawyer than to return to his house at six o'clock and find that he is to have barely time for his dinner and cigar before being thrust out into the cold and hideous darkness of a February night, in order to travel some four hundred miles through a snow-bound country? It is true that he had received some little warning to arrange his affairs for an absence over Saturday, but at best the blow was a severe one, and he bore it with a silent fortitude which wrung his wife's heart. She was a masterful mistress, but she was good to those who obeyed, and she even showed the weakness of begging him not to go, although in her soul she knew that he must.

"After all, John, you needn't go with us. I can take the girls alone."

"As I understand it, you have engaged my professional services," he replied. "On the whole I prefer prevention to cure. I would rather help Esther to run away, than get her a divorce."

"When I am dead, you shall stay quietly at home and be perfectly happy," she answered, with the venerable device which wives, from earliest history, have used to palliate their own sins.

Nevertheless he felt almost as miserable as his wife, when, wrapped in cloaks and rugs, they left their bright dining room and shuffled down the steps into the outside darkness to their carriage. He expressed opinions about lovers which would have put a quick end to the human race had they been laws of nature. He wished the church would take them all and consign them to its own favorite place of punishment. He had a disagreeable trick of gibing at his wife's orthodoxy on this point, and when she remonstrated at his profanity, he smiled contentedly and said: "There is nothing profane about it. It is sound church doctrine, and I envy you for being able to believe it. You can hope to see them with your own eyes getting their reward, confound them!"

Consoling himself with this pleasing hope, they started off, and in five minutes were at Esther's door. After taking the two girls into the carriage, Mr. Murray became more affable and even gay. By the time the party was established in their sleeping car, he had begun to enjoy himself. He had too often made such journeys, and was too familiar with every thing on the road to be long out of humor, and for once it was amusing to have a pair of pretty girls to take with him. Commonly his best society was some member of the Albany Legislature, and his only conversation was about city charters and railroad legislation. The variety had its charm. Esther was as good as her word. She made a desperate battle to recover her gayety, and the little excitement of a night journey helped the triumph of her pride. Determined that she would not be an object of pity, she made the most of all her chances, pretended to take in earnest her uncle's humorous instructions as to the art of arranging a sleeping berth, and horrified her aunt by letting him induce Catherine and herself to eat hot doughnuts and mince pies on the train. It was outwardly a gay little party which rattled along the bank of the snowy river on their way northward.

The gayety, it is true, was forced. For the first ten minutes Esther felt excited by the sense of flight and the rapid motion which was carrying her she knew not where,—away into the infinite and unknown. What lay before her, beyond the darkness of the moment, she hardly cared. Never again could she go back to the old life, but like a young bird that has lost its mate, she must fly on through the gloom till it end. Unluckily all her thoughts brought her back to Hazard. Even this sense of resembling a bird that flies, it knows not where, recalled to her the sonnet of Petrarch which she had once translated for him, and which, since then, had been always on his lips, although she had never dreamed that it could have such meaning to her. Long after she had established herself in her berth, solitary and wakeful, the verses made rhythm with the beat of the car-wheels:

"Vago augelletto che cantando vai!"

They were already far on their way, flying up the frozen stream of the Hudson, before she was left alone with her thoughts in the noisy quiet of the rushing train. She could not even hope to sleep. Propping herself up against the pillows, she raised the curtain of her window and stared into the black void outside. Nothing in nature could be more mysterious and melancholy than this dark, polar world, beside which a winter storm on the Atlantic was at least exciting. On the ocean the forces of nature have it their own way; nothing comes between man and the elements; but as Esther gazed out into the night, it was not the darkness, or the sense of cold, or the vagrant snow-flakes driving against the window, or the heavy clouds drifting through the sky, or even the ghastly glimmer and reflection of the snow-fields, that, by contrast, made the grave seem cheerful; it was rather the twinkling lights from distant and invisible farm-houses, the vague outlines of barn-yards and fences along doubtful roads, the sudden flash of lamps as the train hurried through unknown stations, or the unfamiliar places where it stopped, while the tap-tap of the train-men's hammers on the wheels beneath sounded like spirit-rappings. These signs of life behind the veil were like the steady lights of shore to the drowning fisherman off the reef outside. Every common-place kerosene lamp whose rays struggled from distant, snow-clad farms, brought a picture of peace and hope to Esther. Not one of these invisible roofs but might shelter some realized romance, some contented love. In so dark and dreary a world, what a mad act it was to fly from the only happiness life offered! What a strange idea to seek safety by refusing the only protection worth having! Love was all in all! Esther had never before felt herself so helpless as in the face of this outer darkness, and if her lover had now been there to claim her, she would have dropped into his arms as unresistingly as a tired child.

As the night wore on, the darkness and desolation became intolerable, and she shut them out, only to find herself suffocated by the imprisonment of her sleeping-berth. Hour after hour dragged on; the little excitement of leaving Albany was long past, and the train was wandering through the dullness of Central New York, when at last a faint suspicion of dim light appeared in the landscape, and Esther returned to her window. If any thing could be drearier than the blackness of night, it was the grayness of dawn, which had all the cold terror of death and all the grim repulsiveness of life joined in an hour of despair. Esther could now see the outlines of farm-houses as the train glided on; snow-laden roofs and sheds; long stretches of field with fences buried to their top rails in sweeping snow-drifts; in the houses, lights showed that toil had begun again; smoke rose from the chimneys; figures moved in the farm-yards; a sleigh could be seen on a decided road; the world became real, prosaic, practical, mechanical, not worth struggling about; a mere colorless, passionless, pleasureless grayness. As the mystery vanished, the pain passed and the brain grew heavy. Esther's eyelids drooped, and she sank at last into a sleep so sound that there was hardly need for Catherine to stand sentry before her berth and frown the car into silence. The sun was high above the horizon; the sky was bright and blue; the snowy landscape flashed with the sparkle of diamonds, when Esther woke, and it was with a cry of pleasure that she felt her spirits answer the sun.

Meanwhile her flight was no secret. As the train that carried her off drew out of the great station into the darkness for its long journey of three thousand miles, two notes were delivered to gentlemen only a few squares away. Strong at his club received one from Mrs. Murray: "We all start for Clifton at nine o'clock. Come to-morrow and bring a companion if you can. We need to be amused." The Reverend Stephen Hazard received the other note, which was still more brief, but long enough to strike him with panic; for it contained two words: "Good-by! Esther."

No sooner did Strong receive his missive than he set himself in active motion. Wharton, who commonly dined at the club, was so near that Strong had only to pass the note over to him. Whether Wharton was still suffering from the shock of his wife's appearance, or disappearance, or whether he was on the look-out for some chance to see again his friend Catherine, or whether he found it pleasanter to take a holiday than to attack his long arrears of work, the idea of running up to Niagara for Sunday happened to strike him as pleasant, and he promised to join Strong at the Erie Station in the morning. Strong knew him too well to count on his keeping the engagement, but could do no more, and they both left the club to make their preparations. Strong had another duty. Before stirring further, he must talk with Hazard. The affair was rapidly taking a shape that might embarrass them both.

Going directly to Hazard's house, he burst into the library, where he found his friend trying to work in spite of the heavy load on his mind. Throwing him Mrs. Murray's note, Strong waited without a word while Hazard read it more eagerly than though it had been a summons to a bishopric. The mysterious good-by, which had arrived but a few minutes before, had upset his nerves, and at first the note which Strong brought reassured him, for he thought that Mrs. Murray was earning out his own wishes and drawing Esther nearer to him.

"Then we have succeeded!" he cried.

"Not much!" said Strong dryly. "It is a genuine flight and escape in all the forms. You are out-generaled and your line of attack is left all in the air."

"I shall follow!" said Hazard, doggedly.

"No good! They are in earnest," replied Strong.

"So am I!" answered the clergyman sharply, while Strong threw himself into a chair, good-natured as ever, and said:

"Come along then! Will you go up with Wharton and me by the early train to-morrow?"

"Yes!" replied Hazard quickly. Then he paused; there were limits to his power and he began to feel them. "No!" he went on. "I can't get away to-morrow. I must wait till Sunday night."

"Better wait altogether," said Strong. "You take the chances against you."

"I told her I should follow her, and I shall," repeated Hazard stiffly. He felt hurt, as though Esther had rebelled against his authority, and he was not well pleased that Strong should volunteer advice.

"Give me my orders then!" said Strong. "Can I do any thing for you?"

"I shall be there on Monday afternoon. Telegraph me if they should decide to leave the place earlier. Try and keep them quiet till I get there!"

"Shall I tell them you are coming?"

"Not for your life!" answered Hazard impatiently. "Do all you can to soothe and quiet her. Hint that in my place you would come. Try to make her hope it, but not fear it."

"I will do all that to the letter," said Strong. "I feel partly responsible for getting you and Esther into this scrape, and am ready to go a long way to pull you through; but this done I stop. If Esther is in earnest, I must stand by her. Is that square?"

Hazard frowned severely and hesitated. "The real struggle is just coming," said he. "If you keep out of the way, I shall win. So far I have never failed with her. My influence over her to-day is greater than ever, or she would not try to run away from it. If you interfere I shall think it unkind and unfriendly."

To this Strong answered pleasantly enough, but as though his mind were quite made up: "I don't mean to interfere if I can help it, but I can't persecute Esther, if it is going to make her unhappy. As it is, I am likely to catch a scoring from my aunt for bringing you down on them, and undoing her work. I wish I were clear of the whole matter and Esther were a pillar of the church."

With this declaration of contingent neutrality, Strong went his way, and as he walked musingly back to his rooms, he muttered to himself that he had done quite as much for Hazard as the case would warrant: "What a trump the girl is, and what a good fight she is making! I believe I am getting to be in love with her myself, and if he gives it up—hum—yes, if he gives it up,—then of course Esther will go abroad and forget it."

Hazard's solitary thoughts were not quite so pointless. The danger of disappointment and defeat roused in him the instinct of martyrdom. He was sure that all mankind would suffer if he failed to get the particular wife he wanted. "It is not a selfish struggle," he thought. "It is a human soul I am trying to save, and I will do it in the teeth of all the powers of darkness. If I can but set right this systematically misguided conscience, the task is done. It is the affair of a moment when once the light comes;—A flash! A miracle! If I cannot wield this fire from Heaven, I am unfit to touch it. Let it burn me up!"

Early the next morning, not a little to their own surprise, Strong and Wharton found themselves dashing over the Erie Road towards Buffalo. They had a long day before them and luckily Wharton was in his best spirits. As for Strong he was always in good spirits. Within the memory of man, well or ill, on sea or shore, in peril or safety, Strong had never been seen unhappy or depressed. He had the faculty of interesting himself without an effort in the doings of his neighbors, and Wharton always had on hand some scheme which was to make an epoch in the history of art. Just now it was a question of a new academy of music which was to be the completest product of architecture, and to combine all the senses in delight. The Grand Opera at Paris was to be tame beside it. Here he was to be tied down by no such restraints as the church imposed on him; he was to have beauty for its own sake and to create the thought of a coming world. His decorations should make a revolution in the universe. Strong entered enthusiastically into his plans, but both agreed that preliminary studies were necessary both for architects and artists. The old world must be ransacked to the depths of Japan and Persia. Before their dinner-hour was reached, they had laid out a scheme of travel and study which would fill a life-time, while the Home of Music in New York was still untouched. After dinner and a cigar, they fought a prodigious battle over the influence of the Aryan races on the philosophy of art, and then, dusk coming on, they went to sleep, and finished an agreeable journey at about midnight.

When at last they drove up to the hotel door in the frosty night, and stamped their feet, chilled by the sleigh-ride from the station, the cataract's near roar and dim outline under the stars did not prevent them from warmly greeting Mr. Murray who sallied out to welcome them and to announce that their supper was waiting. The three women had long since gone to bed, but Mr. Murray staid up to have a chat with the boys. He was in high spirits. He owned that he had enjoyed his trip and was in no hurry to go home. While his nephew and Wharton attacked their supper, he sipped his Scotch whisky, and with the aid of a cigar, enlivened the feast.

"We got over here before three o'clock," said he, "and of course I took them out to drive at once. Esther sat in front with me and we let the horses go. Your aunt thinks I am unsafe with horses and I took some pains to prove that she was right. The girls liked it. They wouldn't have minded being tipped into a snow-bank, but I thought it would be rough on your aunt, so I brought them home safe, gave them a first-rate dinner and sent them off to bed hours ago, sleepy as gods. To-morrow you must take them in hand. I have made to-day what the newspapers call my most brilliant forensic effort, and I'll not risk my reputation again."

"Keep out of our way then!" said Strong. "Wharton and I mean to spill those two girls over the cliff unless Canadian horses know geology."

Esther slept soundly that night while the roar of the waters lulled her slumbers. The sun woke her the next morning to a sense of new life. Her room looked down on the cataract, and she had already taken a fancy to this tremendous, rushing, roaring companion, which thundered and smoked under her window, as though she had tamed a tornado to play in her court-yard. To brush her hair while such a confidant looked on and asked questions, was more than Pallas Athene herself could do, though she looked out forever from the windows of her Acropolis over the Blue Ægean. The sea is capricious, fickle, angry, fawning, violent, savage and wanton; it caresses and raves in a breath, and has its moods of silence, but Esther's huge playmate rambled on with its story, in the same steady voice, never shrill or angry, never silent or degraded by a sign of human failings, and yet so frank and sympathetic that she had no choice but to like it. "Even if it had nothing to tell me, its manners are divine," said Esther to herself as she leaned against the window sash and looked out. "And its dress!" she ran on. "What a complexion, to stand dazzling white and diamonds in the full sunlight!" Yet it was not the manners or the dress of her new friend that most won Esther's heart. Her excitement and the strain of the last month had left her subject to her nerves and imagination. She was startled by a snow-flake, was reckless and timid by turns, and her fancy ran riot in dreams of love and pain. She fell in love with the cataract and turned to it as a confidant, not because of its beauty or power, but because it seemed to tell her a story which she longed to understand. "I think I do understand it," she said to herself as she looked out. "If he could hear it as I do," and of course "he" was Mr. Hazard; "how he would feel it!" She felt tears roll down her face as she listened to the voice of the waters and knew that they were telling her a different secret from any that Hazard could ever hear. "He will think it is the church talking!" Sad as she was, she smiled as she thought that it was Sunday morning, and a ludicrous contrast flashed on her mind between the decorations of St. John's, with its parterre of nineteenth century bonnets, and the huge church which was thundering its gospel under her eyes.

To have Niagara for a rival is no joke. Hazard spoke with no such authority; and Esther's next idea was one of wonder how, after listening here, any preacher could have the confidence to preach again. "What do they know about it?" she asked herself. "Which of them can tell a story like this, or a millionth part of it?" To dilute it in words and translate bits of it for school-girls, or to patronize it by defense or praise, was somewhat as though Esther herself should paint a row of her saints on the cliff under Table Rock. Even to fret about her own love affairs in such company was an impertinence. When eternity, infinity and omnipotence seem to be laughing and dancing in one's face, it is well to treat such visitors civilly, for they come rarely in such a humor.

So much did these thoughts interest and amuse her that she took infinite pains with her toilet in order to honor her colossal host whose own toilet was sparkling with all the jewels of nature, like an Indian prince whose robes are crusted with diamonds and pearls. When she came down to the breakfast-room, Strong, who was alone there, looked up with a start.

"Why, Esther!" he broke out, "take care, or one of these days you will be handsome!"

Catherine too was pretty as a fawn, and was so honestly pleased to meet Wharton again that he expanded into geniality. As for broken hearts, no self-respecting young woman shows such an ornament at any well regulated breakfast-table; they are kept in dark drawers and closets like other broken furniture. Esther had made the deadliest resolution to let no trace of her unhappiness appear before her uncle, and Mr. Murray, who saw no deeper than other men into the heart-problem, was delighted with the gayety of the table, and proud of his own success as a physician for heart complaints. Mrs. Murray, who knew more about her own sex, kept her eye on the two girls with more anxiety than she cared to confess. If any new disaster should happen, the prospect would be desperate, and it was useless to deny that she had taken risks heavy enough to stagger a professional gambler. The breakfast table looked gay and happy enough, and so did the rapids which sparkled and laughed in the distance.

After breakfast the two young women, with much preparation of boots, veils and wraps, went off with Strong and Wharton for a stroll down to the banks of the river. The two older members of the party remained quietly in their parlor, thinking that the young people would get on better by themselves. As the four wandered down the road, Mr. Murray watched them, and noticed the natural way in which Esther joined Strong, while Catherine fell to Wharton. Standing with his hands in his trousers' pockets and his nose close to the window-pane, Mr. Murray looked after them as they disappeared down the bank, and then, without turning round, he made a remark as husbands do, addressed to the universe and intended for his wife.

"I suppose that is what you are driving at."

"What?" asked Mrs. Murray.

"I don't mind George and Esther, but I grudge Catherine to that man Wharton. He may be a good artist, but I think his merits as a husband beneath criticism. I believe every woman would connive at a love affair though the man had half a dozen living wives, and had been hung two or three times for murder."

"I wish Esther were as safe as I think Catherine," said Mrs. Murray. "It would surprise me very much if Catherine took Mr. Wharton now, but if Mr. Hazard were to walk round the corner, I should expect to see Esther run straight into his arms."

"Hazard!" exclaimed Mr. Murray. "I thought he was out of the running and you meant Esther for George."

"I am not a match-maker, and I've no idea that Esther will ever marry George," replied Mrs. Murray with the patience which wives sometimes show to husbands whom they think obtuse.

"Then what is it you want?" asked Mr. Murray, with some signs of rebellion, but still talking to the window-pane, with his hands in his pockets. "You encourage a set of clever men to hang round two pretty girls, and you profess at the same time not to want anything to come of it. That kind of conduct strikes an ordinary mind as inconsistent."

"I want to prevent one unhappy marriage, not to make two," replied his wife. "Girls must have an education, and the only way they can get a good one is from clever men. As for falling in love, they will always do that whether the men are clever or not. They must take the risk."

"And what do you mean to do with them when they are educated?" inquired he.

"I mean them to marry dull, steady men in Wall Street, without any manners, and with their hands in their pockets," answered Mrs. Murray, her severity for once mingled with a touch of sweetness.

"Thank you," replied her husband, at last turning round. "Then that is to be the fruit of all this to-do?"

"I am sure it is quite fruit enough," rejoined she. "The business of educating their husbands will take all the rest of their lives."

Mr. Murray reflected a few minutes, standing with his back to the fire and gazing at his wife. Then he said: "Sarah, you are a clever woman. If you would come into my office and work steadily, you could double my income at the bar; but you need practice; your points are too fine;

you run too many risks, and no male judge would ever support your management of a case. As practice I grant you it is bold and has much to recommend it, but in the law we cannot look so far ahead. Now, why won't you let Esther marry George?"

"I shall practice only before women judges," replied Mrs. Murray, "and I will undertake to say that I never should find one so stupid as not to see that George is not at all the sort of man whom a girl with Esther's notions would marry. If I tried to make her do it, I should be as wrong-headed as some men I know."

"I suppose you don't mean to put yourself in George's way, if he asks her," inquired Mr. Murray rather anxiously.

"My dear husband, there is no use in thinking about George one way or the other. Do put him out of your head! You fancy because Esther seems bright this morning, that she might marry George to-morrow. Now I can see a great deal more of Esther's mind than you, and I tell you that it is all we can do to prevent her from recalling Mr. Hazard, and that if we do prevent it, we shall have to take her abroad for at least two years before she gets over the strain."

At this emphatic announcement that his life was to be for two years a sacrifice to Esther's love-affairs, Mr. Murray retired again to his window and meditated in a more subdued spirit. He knew that protest would avail nothing.

Meanwhile the two girls were already down on the edge of the icy river, talking at first of the scene which lay before their eyes.

"Think what the Greeks would have done with it!" said Wharton. "They would have set Zeus in a throne on Table Rock, firing away his lightnings at Prometheus under the fall."

"Just for a change I rather like our way of sticking advertisements there," said Catherine. "It makes one feel at home."

"A woman feels most the kind of human life in it," said Esther.

"A big, rollicking, Newfoundland dog sort of humanity," said Strong.

"You are all wrong," said Catherine. "The fall is a woman, and she is as self-conscious this morning as if she were at church. Look at the coquetry of the pretty curve where the water falls over, and the lace on the skirt where it breaks into foam! Only a woman could do that and look so pretty when she might just as easily be hideous."

"It is not a woman! It is a man!" broke in Esther vehemently. "No woman ever had a voice like that!" She felt hurt that her cataract should be treated as a self-conscious woman.

"Now, Mr. Wharton!" cried Catherine, appealing to the artist: "Now, you see I'm right, and self-consciousness is sometimes a beauty."

Wharton answered this original observation of nature by a lecture which may be read to more advantage in his printed works. It ended by Catherine requiring him to draw for her the design of a dress which should have the soul of Niagara in its folds, and while he was engaged in this labor, which absorbed Catherine's thoughts and gave her extreme amusement, Esther strolled on with Strong, and for nearly an hour walked up and down the road, or leaned against the rock in sheltered places where the sun was warm. At first they went on talking of the scenery, then Esther wanted to know about the geology, and quickly broke in on Strong's remarks upon this subject by questions which led further and further away from it. The river boiled at their feet; the sun melted the enormous icicles which hung from the precipice behind them; a mass of frozen spray was banked up against the American fall opposite them, making it look like an iceberg, and snow covered every thing except the perpendicular river banks and the dark water. The rainbow hung over the cataract, and the mist rose from the furious waters into the peace of the quiet air.

"You know what has happened?" she asked.

Strong nodded assent. He was afraid to tell her how much he knew.

"Do you think I have done wrong?"

"How can I tell without knowing all your reasons?" he asked. "It looks to me as though you were uncertain of yourself and cared less for him than he for you. If I were in his place I should follow you close up, and refuse to leave you."

Esther gave a little gasp: "You don't think he will do that? if he does, I shall run away again."

"Why run away? if you really want to get rid of him, why not make him run away?"

"Because I don't want to make him run away from me, and because I don't know how. If I could only get him away from his church! All I know about it is that I can't be a clergyman's wife, but the moment that I try to explain why, he proves to me that my reasons are good for nothing."

"Are you sure he's not right?" asked Strong.

"Perfectly sure!" replied Esther earnestly. "I can't reason it out, but I feel it. I believe you could explain it if you would, but when I asked you, in the worst of my trouble, you refused to help me."

"I gave you all the help I could, and I am ready to give you whatever you want more," replied Strong.

"Tell me what you think about religion!"

Strong drew himself together with a perceptible effort: "I think about it as little as possible," said he.

"Do you believe in a God?"

"Not in a personal one."

"Or in future rewards and punishments?"

"Old women's nursery tales!"

"Do you believe in nothing?"

"There is evidence amounting to strong probability, of the existence of two things," said Strong, slowly, and as though in his lecture-room.

"What are they, if you please?"

"Should you know better if I said they were mind and matter?"

"You believe in nothing else?"

"N-N-No!" hesitated Strong.

"Isn't it horrible, your doctrine?"

"What of that, if it's true? I never said it was pleasant."

"Do you expect to convert any one to such a religion?"

"Great Buddha, no! I don't want to convert any one. I prefer almost any kind of religion. No one ever took up this doctrine who could help himself."

Esther pondered deeply for a time. Strong's trick of driving her to do what he wanted was so old a habit that she had learned to distrust it. At last she began again from another side.

"You really mean that this life is every thing, and the future nothing?"

"I never said so. I rather think the church is right in thinking this life nothing and the future every thing."

"But you deny a future life!"

Strong began to feel uncomfortable. He wanted to defend his opinions, and it became irksome to go on making out the strongest case he could against himself.

"Come!" said he: "don't go beyond what I said. I only denied the rewards and punishments. Mind! I'll not say there is a future life, but I don't deny it's possibility."

"You are willing to give us a chance?" said Esther rather sarcastically.

"I don't know that you would call it one," replied Strong satisfied by Esther's irony that he had now gone far enough. "If our minds could get hold of one abstract truth, they would be immortal so far as that truth is concerned. My trouble is to find out how we can get hold of the truth at all."

"My trouble is that I don't think I understand in the least what you mean," replied Esther.

"I thought you knew enough theology for that," said George. "The thing is simple enough. Hazard and I and every one else agree that thought is eternal. If you can get hold of one true thought, you are immortal as far as that thought goes. The only difficulty is that every fellow thinks his thought the true one. Hazard wants you to believe in his, and I don't want you to believe in mine, because I've not got one which I believe in myself."

"Still I don't understand," said Esther. "How can I make myself immortal by taking Mr. Hazard's opinions?"

"Because then the truth is a part of you! if I understand St. Paul, this is sound church doctrine, leaving out the personal part of the Trinity which Hazard insists on tacking to it. Except for the rubbish, I don't think I am so very far away from him," continued Strong, now assuming that he had done what he could to set Esther straight, and going on with the conversation as though it had no longer a personal interest. As he talked, he poked holes in the snow with his stick, as though what he said was for his own satisfaction, and he were turning this old problem over again in his mind to see whether he could find any thing new at the bottom of it. "I can't see that my ideas are so brutally shocking. We may some day catch an abstract truth by the tail, and then we shall have our religion and immortality. We have got far more than half way. Infinity is infinitely more intelligible to you than you are to a sponge. If the soul of a sponge can grow to be the soul of a Darwin, why may we not all grow up to abstract truth? What more do you want?"

As he looked up again, saying these words without thinking of Esther's interest, he was startled to see that this time she was listening with a very different expression in her face. She broke in with a question which staggered him.

"Does your idea mean that the next world is a sort of great reservoir of truth, and that what is true in us just pours into it like raindrops?"

"Well!" said he, alarmed and puzzled: "the figure is not perfectly correct, but the idea is a little of that kind."

"After all I wonder whether that may not be what Niagara has been telling me!" said Esther, and she spoke with an outburst of energy that made Strong's blood run cold.

Chapter X

Strong kept his word about amusing the two girls. They were not allowed the time to make themselves unhappy, restless or discontented. This Sunday afternoon he set out with a pair of the fastest horses to be got in the neighborhood, and if these did not go several times over the cliff, it was, as Strong had said, rather their own good sense than their driver's which held them back. Catherine, who sat by Strong's side, made the matter worse by taking the reins, and a more reckless little Amazon never defied men. Even Strong himself at one moment, when wreck seemed certain, asked her to kindly see to the publication of a posthumous memoir, and Esther declared that although she did not fear death, she disliked Catherine's way of killing her. Catherine paid no attention to such ribaldry, and drove on like Phaeton. Wharton was carried away by the girl's dash and coolness. He wanted to paint her as the charioteer of the cataract. They drove by the whirlpool, and so far and fast that, when Esther found herself that night tossing and feverish in her bed, she could only dream that she was still skurrying over a snow-bound country, aching with jolts and jerks, but unable ever to stop. The next day she was glad to stay quietly in the house and amuse herself with sketching, while the rest of the party crossed the river to get Mr. Murray's sleeping-berth by the night train to New York, and to waste their time and money on the small attractions of the village. Mr. Murray was forced to return to his office. Wharton, who had no right to be here at all, for a score of pressing engagements were calling for instant attention in New York, telegraphed simply that his work would detain him several days longer at Niagara, and he even talked of returning with the others by way of Quebec.

While the rest of the party were attending to their own affairs at the railway station and the telegraph office, Wharton and Catherine strolled down to the little park over the American Fall and looked at the scene from there. Catherine in her furs was prettier than ever; her fresh color was brightened by the red handkerchief she had tied round her neck, and her eyes were more mutinous than usual. As she leaned over the parapet, and looked into the bubbling torrent which leaped into space at her feet, Wharton would have liked to carry her off like the torrent and give her no chance to resist. Yet, reckless as he was, he had still common sense enough to understand that, until he was fairly rid of one wife, he could not expect another to throw herself into his arms, and he awkwardly flitted about her, like a moth about a lantern, unable even to singe his wings in the flame.

"Then it is decided?" he asked. "You are really going abroad?"

"I am really going to take Esther to Europe for at least two years. We want excitement. America is too tame."

"May I come over and see you there?"

"No followers are to be allowed. I have forbidden Esther to think of them. She must devote all her time to art, or I shall be severe with her."

"But I suppose you don't mean to devote all your own time to art."

"I must take care of her," replied Catherine. "Then I have got to write some more sonnets. My hand is getting out in sonnets."

"Paris will spoil you; I shall wish you had never left your prairie," said Wharton sadly.

"It is you that have spoiled me," replied she. "You have made me self-conscious, and I am going abroad to escape your influence."

"Do me a favor when you are there; go to Avignon and Vaucluse; when you come to Petrarch's house, think of me, for there I passed the most hopeless hours of my life."

"No, I will not go there to be sad. Sadness is made only for poetry or painting. It is your affair, not mine. I mean to be gay."

"Try, then!" said Wharton. "See for yourself how far gayety will carry you. My turn will come! We all have to go over that cataract, and you will have to go over with the rest of us."

Catherine peered down into the spray and foam beneath as though she were watching herself fall, and then replied: "I shall stay in the shallowest puddle I can find."

"You will one day learn to give up your own life and follow an ideal," said Wharton.

Catherine laughed at his solemn speech with a boldness that irritated him. "Men are always making themselves into ideals and expecting women to follow them," said she. "You are all selfish. Tell me now honestly, would you not sell yourself and me and all New York, like Faust in the opera, if you could paint one picture like Titian?"

Wharton answered sulkily: "I would like to do it on Faust's conditions."

"I knew it," cried she exultingly.

"If ever the devil, or any one else," continued Wharton, "can get me to say to the passing moment, 'stay, thou art so fair,' he can have me for nothing. By that time I shall be worth nothing."

"Your temper will be much sweeter," interjected Catherine.

"Faust made a bargain that any man would be glad to make," growled Wharton. "It was not till he had no soul worth taking that the devil had a chance to win."

Catherine turned on him suddenly with her eyes full of humor: "Then that is the bargain you offer us women. You want us to take you on condition that we amuse you, and then you tell us that if we do amuse you, it will be because you are no longer worth taking. Thank you! I can amuse myself better. When we come home from Europe, I am going to buy a cattle ranche in Colorado and run it myself. You and Mr. Strong and Mr. Hazard shall come out there and see it. You will want me to take you on wages as cowboys. I mean to have ten thousand head, and when you see them you will say that they are better worth painting than all the saints and naiads round the Mediterranean."

Wharton looked earnestly at her for a moment before replying, and she met his eyes with a laugh that left him helpless. Unless taken seriously, he was beneath the level of average men. At last he closed the talk with a desperate confession of failure.

"If you will not go to Vaucluse, Miss Brooke, go at least to the British Museum in London, and when you are there, take a long look at what are called the Elgin marbles. There you will see Greek warriors killing each other with a smile on their faces. You remind me of them. You are like Achilles who answers his Trojan friend's prayer for life by saying: 'Die, friend; you are no better than others I have killed.' I mean to get Miss Dudley to give me her portrait of you, and I shall paint in, over your head: [Greek: PHILOS THANE KAI SY]; and hang it up in my studio to look at, when I am in danger of feeling happy."

With this they rambled back again towards their friends and ended for the time their struggle for mastery. The morning was soon over; all returned to their hotel, and luncheon followed; a silent meal at which no one seemed bright except Strong, who felt that the burden was beginning to be a heavy one. Had it not been for Strong, not one of the party would have moved out of the house again that day, but the Professor privately ordered a sleigh to the door at three o'clock, and packed his uncle and aunt into it together with Catherine and Wharton. Catherine's love of driving lent her energy, and Mrs. Murray, sadly enough, consented to let her take the reins. As they drove away, Strong stood on the porch and watched them till they had disappeared down the road. The afternoon was cloudy and gray, with flakes of snow dropping occasionally through a despondent air. After the sleigh had gone, Strong still gazed down the road, as though he expected to see something, but the road was bare.

He had stayed at home under the pretense of writing letters, and now returned to the sitting-room, where Esther was sketching from the window a view of the cataract. She went quietly on with her work, while he sat down to write as well as his conscience would allow him; for now that he saw how much good Esther's escape had done her, how quiet she had become again, and how her look of trouble had vanished, leaving only a tender little air of gravity, as she worked in the silence of her memories; and when he thought how violently this serenity was likely to be disturbed, his conscience smote him, he bitterly regretted his interference, and roundly denounced himself for a fool.

"Does Mr. Wharton really care for Catherine?" asked Esther, as she went on with her sketch.

"I guess he thinks he does," answered Strong. "He looks at her as though he would eat her."

"What a pity!"

"He is tough! Don't waste sympathy on him! If she took him, he would make her a slave within a week. As it is, his passion will go into his painting."

"She is a practical young savage," said Esther. "I thought at one time she was dazzled by him, but the moment she saw how unfit she was for such a man, she gave it up without a pang."

"I don't see her unfitness," replied Strong. "She has plenty of beauty, more common sense than he, and some money which would help him amazingly except that he would soon spend it. I should say it was he who wanted fitness, but you can't harness a mustang with a unicorn."

"He wants me to study in Paris," said Esther; "but I mean to go to Rome and Venice. I am afraid to tell him."

"When do you expect to be there?"

"Some time in May, if we can get any one to take us."

"Perhaps I will look you up in the summer. If I do not go to Oregon, I may run over to Germany."

"We shall be terribly homesick," replied Esther.

Silence now followed till Strong finished his letters and looked again at his watch. It was four o'clock. "If he is coming," thought Strong, "it is time he were here; but I would draw him a check for his church if he would stay away." The jingling of sleigh-bells made itself heard on the road below as though to rebuke him, and presently a cry of fright from Esther at the window told that she knew what was before her.

"What shall I do?" she cried breathlessly. "Here he is! I can't see him!

I can't go through that scene again. George! won't you stop him?"

"What under the sun are you afraid of?" said Strong. "He'll not shoot you! If you don't mean to marry him, tell him so, and this time make it clear. Let there be no mistake about it! But don't send him away if you mean to make yourself unhappy afterwards."

"Of course I am going to be unhappy afterwards," groaned Esther. "What do you know about it, George? Do you think I feel about him as you would about a lump of coal? I was just beginning to be quiet and peaceful, and now it must all start up again. Go away! Leave us alone! But not long! If he is not gone within an hour, come back!"

The next instant the door opened and Hazard was shown into the room. His manner at this awkward moment was quiet and self-possessed, as though he had made it the business of his life to chase flying maidens. Having taken his own time, he was not to be thrown off his balance by any ordinary chance. He nodded familiarly to Strong, who left the room as he entered, and walking straight to Esther, held out his hand with a look of entreaty harder for her to resist than any form of reproach.

"I told you that I should follow," he said.

She drew back, raising her hand to check him, and putting on what she intended for a forbidding expression.

"It is my own fault. I should have spoken more plainly," she replied.

Instead of taking up the challenge, Hazard turned to the table where her unfinished drawing lay.

"What a good sketch!" he said, bending over it. "But you have not yet caught the real fall. I never saw an artist that had."

Esther's defense was disconcerted by this attack. Hazard was bent on getting back to his old familiar ground, and she let him take it. Her last hope was that he might be willing to take it, and be made content with it. If she could but persuade him to forget what had passed, and return to the footing of friendship which ought never to have been left! This was what she was made for! Her courage rose as she thought that perhaps this was possible, and as he sat down before the drawing and discussed it, she fancied that her object was already gained, and that this young greyhound at her elbow could be held in a leash and made to obey a sign.

In a few minutes he had taken again his old friendly place, and if she did not treat him with all the old familiarity, he still gained ground enough to warrant him in believing more firmly than ever that she could not resist his influence so long as he was at her side. They ran on together in talk about the drawing, until he felt that he might risk another approach, and his way of doing it was almost too easy and dexterous.

"What you want to get into your picture," he was saying; "is the air, which the fall has, of being something final. You can't go beyond Niagara. The universe seems made for it. Whenever I come here, I find myself repeating our sonnet: 'Siccome eterna vita e veder dio;' for the sight of it suggests eternity and infinite power." Then suddenly putting down the drawing, and looking up to her face, as she stood by his side, he said: "Do you know, I feel now for the first time the beauty of the next two verses:

'So, lady, sight of you, in my despair,

Brings paradise to this brief life and frail.'"

"Hush!" said Esther, raising her hand again; "we are friends now and nothing more."

"Mere friends, are we?" quoted Hazard, with a courageous smile. "No!" he went on quickly. "I love you. I cannot help loving you. There is no friendship about it."

"If you tell me so, I must run away again. I shall leave the room.

Remember! I am terribly serious now."

"If you tell me, honestly and seriously, that you love me no longer and want me to go away, I will leave the room myself," answered Hazard.

"I won't say that unless you force me to it, but I expect you from this time to help me in carrying out what you know is my duty."

"I will promise, on condition that you prove to me first what your duty is."

To come back again to their starting point was not encouraging, and they felt it, but this time Esther was determined to be obeyed even if it cost her a lover as well as a husband. She did not flinch.

"What more proof do you need? I am not fit to be a clergyman's wife. I should be a scandal in the church, and you would have to choose between it and me."

"I know you better," said Hazard calmly. "You will find all your fears vanish if you once boldly face them."

"I have tried," said Esther. "I tried desperately and failed utterly."

"Try once more! Do not turn from all that has been the hope and comfort of men, until you have fairly learned what it is!"

"Is it not enough to know myself?" asked Esther. "Some people are made with faith. I am made without it."

Hazard broke in here in a warmer tone: "I know you better than you know yourself! Do you think that I, whose business it is to witness every day of my life the power of my faith, am going to hesitate before a trifle like your common, daily, matter-of-course fears and doubts, such as have risen and been laid in every mind that was worth being called one, ever since minds existed?"

"Have they always been laid?" asked Esther gravely.

"Always!" answered Hazard firmly; "provided the doubter wanted to lay them. It is a simple matter of will!"

"Would you have gone into the ministry if you had been tormented by them as I am?" she asked.

"I am not afraid to lay bare my conscience to you," he replied becoming cool again, and willing perhaps to stretch his own points of conscience in the effort to control hers. "I suppose the clergyman hardly exists who has not been tormented by doubts. As for myself, if I could have removed my doubts by so simple a step as that of becoming an atheist, I should have done it, no matter what scandal or punishment had followed. I studied the subject thoroughly, and found that for one doubt removed, another was raised, only to reach at last a result more inconceivable than that reached by the church, and infinitely more hopeless besides. What do you gain by getting rid of one incomprehensible only to put a greater one in its place, and throw away your only hope besides? The atheists offer no sort of bargain for one's soul. Their scheme is all loss and no gain. At last both they and I come back to a confession of ignorance; the only difference between us is that my ignorance is joined with a faith and hope."

Esther was staggered by this view of the subject, and had to fall back on her common-places: "But you make me say every Sunday that I believe in things I don't believe at all."

"But I suppose you believe at last in something, do you not?" asked Hazard. "Somewhere there must be common ground for us to stand on; and our church makes very large—I think too large, allowances for difference. For my own part, I accept tradition outright, because I think it wiser to receive a mystery than to weaken faith; but no one exacts such strictness from you. There are scores of clergymen to-day in our pulpits who are in my eyes little better than open skeptics, yet I am not allowed to refuse communion with them. Why should you refuse it with me? You must at last trust in some mysterious and humanly incomprehensible form of words. Even Strong has to do this. Why may you not take mine?"

"I hardly know what to trust in," said Esther sadly.

"Then trust in me."

"I wish I could, but—"

"But what? Tell me frankly where your want of confidence lies."

"I want to tell you, but I'm afraid. This is what has stood between us from the first. If I told you what was on my lips, you would think it an insult. Don't drive me into offending you! If you knew how much I want to keep your friendship, you would not force me to say such things."

"I will not be offended," answered Hazard gayly. "I can stand almost any thing except being told that you no longer love me."

It wrung Esther's heart to throw away a love so pure and devoted. She felt ashamed of her fears and of herself. As he spoke, her ears seemed to hear a running echo: "Mistress, know yourself! Down on your knees, and thank heaven fasting for a good man's love!" She sat some moments silent while he gazed into her face, and her eyes wandered out to the gloomy and cloud-covered cataract. She felt herself being swept over it. Whichever way she moved, she had to look down into an abyss, and leap.

"Spare me!" she said at last. "Why should you drive and force me to take this leap? Are all men so tyrannical with women? You do not quarrel with a man because he cannot give you his whole life."

"I own it!" said Hazard warmly. "I am tyrannical! I want your whole life, and even more. I will be put off with nothing else. Don't you see that I can't retreat? Put yourself in my place! Think how you would act if you loved me as I love you!"

"Ah, be generous!" begged Esther. "It is not my fault if you and your profession are one; and of all things on earth, to be half-married must be the worst torture."

"You are perfectly right," he replied. "My profession and I are one, and this makes my case harder, for I have to fight two battles, one of love, and one of duty. Think for a moment what a struggle it is! I love you passionately. I would like to say to you: 'Take me on your own terms! I will give you my life, as I will take yours.' But how can I? You are trembling on the verge of what I think destruction. If I saw you tossing on the rapids yonder, at the edge of the fall, I could not be more eager to save you. Yet think what self-control I have had to exercise, for though I have felt myself, for weeks, fighting a battle of life and death for a soul much dearer to me than my own, I have gone forward as though I felt no alarm. I have never even spoken to you on the subject. I stood by, believing so entirely in you that I dared let your own nature redeem itself. But now you throw out a challenge, and I have no choice but to meet it. I have got to fight for myself and my profession and you, at the same time."

At last, then, the battle was fairly joined, and desperately as both the lovers had struggled against it, they looked their destiny in the face. With all Esther's love and sympathy for Hazard, and with all the subtle power which his presence had on her will, his last speech was unlucky. Here was what she had feared! She seemed to feel now, what she had only vaguely suspected before, the restraint which would be put upon her the moment she should submit to his will. He had as good as avowed that nothing but the fear of losing her had kept him silent. She fancied that the thunders of the church were already rolling over her head, and that her mind was already slowly shutting itself up under the checks of its new surroundings. Hazard's speech, too, was unlucky in another way. If he had tried not to shock her by taking charge of her soul before she asked for his interference, she had herself made a superhuman effort not to shock him, and never once had she let drop a word that could offend his prejudices. Since the truth must now come out, she was the less anxious to spare his pride because he claimed credit for respecting hers.

"Must you know why I have broken down and run away?" she said at last. "Well! I will tell you. It was because, after a violent struggle with myself, I found I could not enter a church without a feeling of—of hostility. I can only be friendly by staying away from it. I felt as though it were part of a different world. You will be angry with me for saying it, but I never saw you conduct a service without feeling as though you were a priest in a Pagan temple, centuries apart from me. At any moment I half expected to see you bring out a goat or a ram and sacrifice it on the high altar. How could I, with such ideas, join you at communion?"

No wonder that Esther should have hesitated! Her little speech was not meant in ridicule of Hazard, but it stung him to the quick. He started up and walked across the room to the window, where he stood a moment trying to recover his composure.

"What you call Pagan is to me proof of an eternal truth handed down by tradition and divine revelation," he said at length. "But the mere ceremonies need not stand in your way. Surely you can disregard them and feel the truths behind."

"Oh, yes!" answered Esther, plunging still deeper into the morass. "The ceremonies are picturesque and I could get used to them, but the doctrines are more Pagan than the ceremonies. Now I have hurt your feelings enough, and will say no more. What I have said proves that I am not fit to be your wife. Let me go in peace!"

Again Hazard thought a moment with a grave face. Then he said: "Every church is open to the same kind of attack you make on ours. Do you mean to separate yourself from all communion?"

"If you will create a new one that shall be really spiritual, and not cry: 'flesh—flesh—flesh,' at every corner, I will gladly join it, and give my whole life to you and it."

Hazard shook his head: "I can suggest nothing more spiritual than what came from the spirit itself, and has from all time satisfied the purest and most spiritual souls."

"If I could make myself contented with what satisfied them, I would do it for your sake," answered Esther. "It must be that we are in a new world now, for I can see nothing spiritual about the church. It is all personal and selfish. What difference does it make to me whether I worship one person, or three persons, or three hundred, or three thousand. I can't understand how you worship any person at all."

Hazard literally groaned, and his involuntary expression so irritated

Esther that she ran on still more recklessly.

"Do you really believe in the resurrection of the body?" she asked.

"Of course I do!" replied Hazard stiffly.

"To me it seems a shocking idea. I despise and loathe myself, and yet you thrust self at me from every corner of the church as though I loved and admired it. All religion does nothing but pursue me with self even into the next world."

Esther had become very animated in the course of her remarks, and not the less so because she saw Hazard frown and make gestures of impatience as she passed from one sacrilege to another. At last he turned at bay, and broke out:

"Do you think all this is new to me? I know by heart all these criticisms of the church. I have heard them in one form and another ever since I was a boy at school. They are all equally poor and ignorant. They touch no vital point, for they are made by men, like your cousin George Strong, from whom I suppose you got them, who know nothing of the church or its doctrines or its history. I'll not argue over them. Let them go for whatever you may think they are worth. I will only put to you one question and no more. If you answer it against me, I will go away, and never annoy you again. You say the idea of the resurrection is shocking to you. Can you, without feeling still more shocked, think of a future existence where you will not meet once more father or mother, husband or children? surely the natural instincts of your sex must save you from such a creed!"

"Ah!" cried Esther, almost fiercely, and blushing crimson, as though Hazard this time had pierced the last restraint on her self-control: "Why must the church always appeal to my weakness and never to my strength! I ask for spiritual life and you send me back to my flesh and blood as though I were a tigress you were sending back to her cubs. What is the use of appealing to my sex? the atheists at least show me respect enough not to do that!"

At this moment the door opened and Strong entered. It was high time. The scene threatened to become almost violent. As Strong came in, Esther was standing by the fire-place, all her restless features flashing with the excitement of her last speech. Hazard, with his back to the window, was looking at her across the room, his face dark with displeasure. As Strong stepped between them, a momentary silence followed, when not a sound was heard except the low thunder of the falling waters. One would have said that storm was in the air. Suddenly Hazard turned on the unlucky professor and hurled at him the lightning.

"You are the cause of all this! what is your motive?"

Strong looked at him with surprise, but understood in a moment what had happened. Seeing himself destined in any case to be the victim of the coming wrath, he quietly made up his mind to bear the lot of all mediators and inter-meddlers.

"I am afraid you are half right," he answered. "My stupidity may have made matters a little worse."

"What was your motive?" repeated Hazard sternly.

"My motive was to fight your battle for you," replied Strong unruffled; "and I did it clumsily, that's all! I might have known it beforehand."

"Have you been trying to supplant me in order to get yourself in my place?" demanded Hazard, still in the tone of a master.

"No!" replied Strong, half inclined to laugh.

"You will never find happiness there!" continued Hazard, turning to

Esther, and pointing with a sweep of his hand to Strong.

"Esther agrees with you on that point," said Strong, beginning to think it time that this scene should end. "I don't mind telling you, too, that since I have seen her stand out against your persecution, I would give any chance I have of salvation if she would marry me; but you needn't be alarmed about it,—she won't!"

"She will!" broke in Hazard abruptly. "You have betrayed me, and your conduct is all of a piece with your theories." Then turning to Esther, who still stood motionless and silent before the fire, he went on: "I am beaten. You have driven me away, and I will never trouble you again, till, in your days of suffering and anguish you send to me for hope and consolation. Till then—God bless you!"

The silence was awful when his retreating footsteps could no longer be heard. It was peace, but the peace of despair. As the sound of the jangling sleigh-bells slowly receded from the door, and Esther realized that the romance of her life was ended, she clasped her hands together in a struggle to control her tears. Strong walked once or twice up and down the room, buried in thought, then suddenly stopping before her, he said in his straight-forward, practical way:

"Esther, I meant it! you have fought your battle like a heroine. If you will marry me, I will admire and love you more than ever a woman was loved since the world began."

Esther looked at him with an expression that would have been a smile if it had not been infinitely dreary and absent; then she said, simply and finally:

"But George, I don't love you, I love him."

THE END.

Democracy, An American Novel

Chapter I

For reasons which many persons thought ridiculous, Mrs. Lightfoot Lee decided to pass the winter in Washington. She was in excellent health, but she said that the climate would do her good. In New York she had troops of friends, but she suddenly became eager to see again the very small number of those who lived on the Potomac. It was only to her closest intimates that she honestly acknowledged herself to be tortured by ennui. Since her husband's death, five years before, she had lost her taste for New York society; she had felt no interest in the price of stocks, and very little in the men who dealt in them; she had become serious. What was it all worth, this wilderness of men and women as monotonous as the brown stone houses they lived in? In her despair she had resorted to desperate measures. She had read philosophy in the original German, and the more she read, the more she was disheartened that so much culture should lead to nothing--nothing.

After talking of Herbert Spencer for an entire evening with a very literary transcendental commission-merchant, she could not see that her time had been better employed than when in former days she had passed it in flirting with a very agreeable young stock-broker; indeed, there was an evident proof to the contrary, for the flirtation might lead to something--had, in fact, led to marriage; while the philosophy could lead to nothing, unless it were perhaps to another evening of the same kind, because transcendental philosophers are mostly elderly men, usually married, and, when engaged in business, somewhat apt to be sleepy towards evening. Nevertheless Mrs. Lee did her best to turn her study to practical use. She plunged into philanthropy, visited prisons, inspected hospitals, read the literature of pauperism and crime, saturated herself with the statistics of vice, until her mind had nearly lost sight of virtue. At last it rose in rebellion against her, and she came to the limit of her strength. This path, too, seemed to lead nowhere. She declared that she had lost the sense of duty, and that, so far as concerned her, all the paupers and criminals in New York might henceforward rise in their majesty and manage every railway on the continent. Why should she care? What was the city to her? She could find nothing in it that seemed to demand salvation. What gave peculiar sanctity to numbers? Why were a million people, who all resembled each other, any way more interesting than one person? What aspiration could she help to put into the mind of this great million-armed monster that would make it worth her love or respect? Religion? A thousand powerful churches were doing their best, and she could see no chance for a new faith of which she was to be the inspired prophet. Ambition? High popular ideals? Passion for whatever is lofty and pure? The very words irritated her. Was she not herself devoured by ambition, and was she not now eating her heart out because she could find no one object worth a sacrifice?

Was it ambition--real ambition--or was it mere restlessness that made Mrs. Lightfoot Lee so bitter against New York and Philadelphia, Baltimore and Boston, American life in general and all life in particular? What did she want? Not social position, for she herself was an eminently respectable Philadelphian by birth; her father a famous clergyman; and her husband had been equally irreproachable, a descendant of one branch of the Virginia Lees, which had drifted to New York in search of fortune, and had found it, or enough of it to keep the young man there. His widow had her own place in society which no one disputed. Though not brighter than her neighbours, the world persisted in classing her among clever women; she had wealth, or at least enough of it to give her all that money can give by way of pleasure to a sensible woman in an American city; she had her house and her carriage; she dressed well; her table was good, and her furniture was never allowed to fall behind the latest standard of decorative art. She had travelled in Europe, and after several visits, covering some years of time, had returned home, carrying in one hand, as it were, a green-grey landscape, a remarkably pleasing specimen of Corot, and in the other some bales of Persian and Syrian rugs and embroideries, Japanese bronzes and porcelain. With this she declared Europe to be exhausted, and she frankly avowed that she was American to the tips of her fingers; she neither knew nor greatly cared whether America or Europe were best to live in; she had no violent love for either, and she had no objection to abusing both; but she meant to get all that American life had to offer, good or bad, and to drink it down to the dregs, fully determined that whatever there was in it she would have, and that whatever could be made out of it she would manufacture. "I know," said she, "that America produces petroleum and pigs; I have seen both on the steamers; and I am told it produces silver and gold. There is choice enough for any woman."

Yet, as has been already said, Mrs. Lee's first experience was not a success. She soon declared that New York might represent the petroleum or the pigs, but the gold of life was not to be discovered there by her eyes.

Not but that there was variety enough; a variety of people, occupations, aims, and thoughts; but that all these, after growing to a certain height, stopped short. They found nothing to hold them up. She knew, more or less intimately, a dozen men whose fortunes ranged between one million and forty millions. What did they do with their money? What could they do with it that was different from what other men did? After all, it is absurd to spend more money than is enough to satisfy all one's wants; it is vulgar to live in two houses in the same street, and to drive six horses abreast. Yet, after setting aside a certain income sufficient for all one's wants, what was to be done with the rest? To let it accumulate was to own one's failure; Mrs. Lee's great grievance was that it did accumulate, without changing or improving the quality of its owners. To spend it in charity and public works was doubtless praiseworthy, but was it wise? Mrs. Lee had read enough political economy and pauper reports to be nearly convinced that public work should be public duty, and that great benefactions do harm as well as good.

And even supposing it spent on these objects, how could it do more than increase and perpetuate that same kind of human nature which was her great grievance? Her New York friends could not meet this question except by falling back upon their native commonplaces, which she recklessly trampled upon, averring that, much as she admired the genius of the famous traveller, Mr. Gulliver, she never had been able, since she became a widow, to accept the Brobdingnagian doctrine that he who made two blades of grass grow where only one grew before deserved better of mankind than the whole race of politicians. She would not find fault with the philosopher had he required that the grass should be of an improved quality; "but," said she, "I cannot honestly pretend that I should be pleased to see two New York men where I now see one; the idea is too ridiculous; more than one and a half would be fatal to me."

Then came her Boston friends, who suggested that higher education was precisely what she wanted; she should throw herself into a crusade for universities and art-schools. Mrs. Lee turned upon them with a sweet smile; "Do you know," said she, "that we have in New York already the richest university in America, and that its only trouble has always been that it can get no scholars even by paying for them? Do you want me to go out into the streets and waylay boys? If the heathen refuse to be converted, can you give me power over the stake and the sword to compel them to come in? And suppose you can? Suppose I march all the boys in Fifth Avenue down to the university and have them all properly taught Greek and Latin, English literature, ethics, and German philosophy. What then? You do it in Boston. Now tell me honestly what comes of it. I suppose you have there a brilliant society; numbers of poets, scholars, philosophers, statesmen, all up and down Beacon Street. Your evenings must be sparkling. Your press must scintillate. How is it that we New Yorkers never hear of it? We don't go much into your society; but when we do, it doesn't seem so very much better than our own. You are just like the rest of us. You grow six inches high, and then you stop. Why will not somebody grow to be a tree and cast a shadow?"

The average member of New York society, although not unused to this contemptuous kind of treatment from his leaders, retaliated in his blind, common-sense way. "What does the woman want?" he said. "Is her head turned with the Tulieries and Marlborough House? Does she think herself made for a throne? Why does she not lecture for women's rights? Why not go on the stage? If she cannot be contented like other people, what need is there for abusing us just because she feels herself no taller than we are? What does she expect to get from her sharp tongue? What does she know, any way?"

Mrs. Lee certainly knew very little. She had read voraciously and promiscuously one subject after another. Ruskin and Taine had danced merrily through her mind, hand in hand with Darwin and Stuart Mill, Gustave Droz and Algernon Swinburne. She had even laboured over the literature of her own country. She was perhaps, the only woman in New York who knew something of American history. Certainly she could not have repeated the list of Presidents in their order, but she knew that the Constitution divided the goverument into Executive, Legislative, and Judiciary; she was aware that the President, the Speaker, and the Chief Justice were important personages, and instinctively she wondered whether they might not solve her problem; whether they were the shade trees which she saw in her dreams.

Here, then, was the explanation of her restlessness, discontent, ambition,--call it what you will. It was the feeling of a passenger on an ocean steamer whose mind will not give him rest until he has been in the engine-room and talked with the engineer. She wanted to see with her own eyes the action of primary forces; to touch with her own hand the massive machinery of society; to measure with her own mind the capacity of the motive power. She was bent upon getting to the heart of the great American mystery of democracy and government. She cared little where her pursuit might lead her, for she put no extravagant value upon life, having already, as she said, exhausted at least two lives, and being fairly hardened to insensibility in the process. "To lose a husband and a baby," said she, "and keep one's courage and reason, one must become very hard or very soft. I am now pure steel. You may beat my heart with a trip-hammer and it will beat the trip-hammer back again."

Perhaps after exhausting the political world she might try again elsewhere; she did not pretend to say where she might then go, or what she should do; but at present she meant to see what amusement there might be in politics.

Her friends asked what kind of amusement she expected to find among the illiterate swarm of ordinary people who in Washington represented constituencies so dreary that in comparison New York was a New Jerusalem, and Broad Street a grove of Academe. She replied that if Washington society were so bad as this, she should have gained all she wanted, for it would be a pleasure to return,--precisely the feeling she longed for. In her own mind, however, she frowned on the idea of seeking for men. What she wished to see, she thought, was the clash of interests, the interests of forty millions of people and a whole continent, centering at Washington; guided, restrained, controlled, or unrestrained and uncontrollable, by men of ordinary mould; the tremendous forces of government, and the machinery of society, at work. What she wanted, was power.

Perhaps the force of the engine was a little confused in her mind with that of the engineer, the power with the men who wielded it. Perhaps the human interest of politics was after all what really attracted her, and, however strongly she might deny it, the passion for exercising power, for its own sake, might dazzle and mislead a woman who had exhausted all the ordinary feminine resources. But why speculate about her motives? The stage was before her, the curtain was rising, the actors were ready to enter; she had only to go quietly on among the supernumeraries and see how the play was acted and the stage effects were produced; how the great tragedians mouthed, and the stage-manager swore.

Chapter II

On the first of December, Mrs. Lee took the train for Washington, and before five o'clock that evening she was entering her newly hired house on Lafayette Square. She shrugged her shoulders with a mingled expression of contempt and grief at the curious barbarism of the curtains and the wall-papers, and her next two days were occupied with a life-and-death struggle to get the mastery over her surroundings. In this awful contest the interior of the doomed house suffered as though a demon were in it; not a chair, not a mirror, not a carpet, was left untouched, and in the midst of the worst confusion the new mistress sat, calm as the statue of Andrew Jackson in the square under her eyes, and issued her orders with as much decision as that hero had ever shown. Towards the close of the second day, victory crowned her forehead. A new era, a nobler conception of duty and existence, had dawned upon that benighted and heathen residence. The wealth of Syria and Persia was poured out upon the melancholy Wilton carpets; embroidered comets and woven gold from Japan and Teheran depended from and covered over every sad stuff-curtain; a strange medley of sketches, paintings, fans, embroideries, and porcelain was hung, nailed, pinned, or stuck against the wall; finally the domestic altarpiece, the mystical Corot landscape, was hoisted to its place over the parlour fire, and then all was over. The setting sun streamed softly in at the windows, and peace reigned in that redeemed house and in the heart of its mistress.

"I think it will do now, Sybil," said she, surveying the scene.

"It must," replied Sybil. "You haven't a plate or a fan or coloured scarf left. You must send out and buy some of these old negro-women's bandannas if you are going to cover anything else. What is the use? Do you suppose any human being in Washington will like it? They will think you demented."

"There is such a thing as self-respect," replied her sister, calmly.

Sybil--Miss Sybil Ross--was Madeleine Lee's sister. The keenest psychologist could not have detected a single feature quality which they had in common, and for that reason they were devoted friends. Madeleine was thirty, Sybil twenty-four. Madeleine was indescribable; Sybil was transparent. Madeleine was of medium height with a graceful figure, a well-set head, and enough golden-brown hair to frame a face full of varying expression. Her eyes were never for two consecutive hours of the same shade, but were more often blue than grey. People who envied her smile said that she cultivated a sense of humour in order to show her teeth. Perhaps they were right; but there was no doubt that her habit of talking with gesticulation would never have grown upon her unless she had known that her hands were not only beautiful but expressive. She dressed as skilfully as New York women do, but in growing older she began to show symptoms of dangerous unconventionality. She had been heard to express a low opinion of her countrywomen who blindly fell down before the golden calf of Mr. Worth, and she had even fought a battle of great severity, while it lasted, with one of her best-dressed friends who had been invited--and had gone--to Mr. Worth's afternoon tea-parties. The secret was that Mrs. Lee had artistic tendencies, and unless they were checked in time, there was no knowing what might be the consequence. But as yet they had done no harm; indeed, they rather helped to give her that sort of atmosphere which belongs only to certain women; as indescribable as the afterglow; as impalpable as an Indian summer mist; and non-existent except to people who feel rather than reason. Sybil had none of it. The imagination gave up all attempts to soar where she came. A more straightforward, downright, gay, sympathetic, shallow, warm-hearted, sternly practical young woman has rarely touched this planet. Her mind had room for neither grave-stones nor guide-books; she could not have lived in the past or the future if she had spent her days in churches and her nights in tombs. "She was not clever, like Madeleine, thank Heaven." Madeleine was not an orthodox member of the church; sermons bored her, and clergymen never failed to irritate every nerve in her excitable system. Sybil was a simple and devout worshipper at the ritualistic altar; she bent humbly before the Paulist fathers. When she went to a ball she always had the best partner in the room, and took it as a matter of course; but then, she always prayed for one; somehow it strengthened her faith. Her sister took care never to laugh at her on this score, or to shock her religious opinions. "Time enough," said she, "for her to forget religion when religion fails her." As for regular attendance at church, Madeleine was able to reconcile their habits without trouble. She herself had not entered a church for years; she said it gave her unchristian feelings; but Sybil had a voice of excellent quality, well trained and cultivated: Madeleine insisted that she should sing in the choir, and by this little manoeuvre, the divergence of their paths was made less evident. Madeleine did not sing, and therefore could not go to church with Sybil. This outrageous fallacy seemed perfectly to answer its purpose, and Sybil accepted it, in good faith, as a fair working principle which explained itself.

Madeleine was sober in her tastes. She wasted no money. She made no display.

She walked rather than drove, and wore neither diamonds nor brocades. But the general impression she made was nevertheless one of luxury. On the other hand, her sister had her dresses from Paris, and wore them and her ornaments according to all the formulas; she was good-naturedly correct, and bent her round white shoulders to whatever burden the Parisian autocrat chose to put upon them. Madeleine never interfered, and always paid the bills.

Before they had been ten days in Washington, they fell gently into their place and were carried along without an effort on the stream of social life.

Society was kind; there was no reason for its being otherwise. Mrs. Lee and her sister had no enemies, held no offices, and did their best to make themselves popular. Sybil had not passed summers at Newport and winters in New York in vain; and neither her face nor her figure, her voice nor her dancing, needed apology. Politics were not her strong point. She was induced to go once to the Capitol and to sit ten minutes in the gallery of the Senate. No one ever knew what her impressions were; with feminine tact she managed not to betray herself But, in truth, her notion of legislative bodies was vague, floating between her experience at church and at the opera, so that the idea of a performance of some kind was never out of her head. To her mind the Senate was a place where people went to recite speeches, and she naively assumed that the speeches were useful and had a purpose, but as they did not interest her she never went again. This is a very common conception of Congress; many Congressmen share it.

Her sister was more patient and bolder. She went to the Capitol nearly every day for at least two weeks. At the end of that time her interest began to flag, and she thought it better to read the debates every morning in the Congressional Record. Finding this a laborious and not always an instructive task, she began to skip the dull parts; and in the absence of any exciting question, she at last resigned herself to skipping the whole. Nevertheless she still had energy to visit the Senate gallery occasionally when she was told that a splendid orator was about to speak on a question of deep interest to his country. She listened with a little disposition to admire, if she could; and, whenever she could, she did admire. She said nothing, but she listened sharply. She wanted to learn how the machinery of government worked, and what was the quality of the men who controlled it. One by one, she passed them through her crucibles, and tested them by acids and by fire.

A few survived her tests and came out alive, though more or less disfigured, where she had found impurities. Of the whole number, only one retained under this process enough character to interest her.

In these early visits to Congress, Mrs. Lee sometimes had the company of John Carrington, a Washington lawyer about forty years old, who, by virtue of being a Virginian and a distant connection of her husband, called himself a cousin, and took a tone of semi-intimacy, which Mrs. Lee accepted because Carrington was a man whom she liked, and because he was one whom life had treated hardly. He was of that unfortunate generation in the south which began existence with civil war, and he was perhaps the more unfortunate because, like most educated Virginians of the old Washington school, he had seen from the first that, whatever issue the war took, Virginia and he must be ruined. At twenty-two he had gone into the rebel army as a private and carried his musket modestly through a campaign or two, after which he slowly rose to the rank of senior captain in his regiment, and closed his services on the staff of a major-general, always doing scrupulously enough what he conceived to be his duty, and never doing it with enthusiasm. When the rebel armies surrendered, he rode away to his family plantation--not a difficult thing to do, for it was only a few miles from Appomatox--and at once began to study law; then, leaving his mother and sisters to do what they could with the worn-out plantation, he began the practice of law in Washington, hoping thus to support himself and them. He had succeeded after a fashion, and for the first time the future seemed not absolutely dark. Mrs. Lee's house was an oasis to him, and he found himself, to his surprise, almost gay in her company. The gaiety was of a very quiet kind, and Sybil, while friendly with him, averred that he was certainly dull; but this dulness had a fascination for Madeleine, who, having tasted many more kinds of the wine of life than Sybil, had learned to value certain delicacies of age and flavour that were lost upon younger and coarser palates. He talked rather slowly and almost with effort, but he had something of the dignity--others call it stiffness--of the old Virginia school, and twenty years of constant responsibility and deferred hope had added a touch of care that bordered closely on sadness. His great attraction was that he never talked or seemed to think of himself. Mrs. Lee trusted in him by instinct. "He is a type!" said she; "he is my idea of George Washington at thirty."

One morning in December, Carrington entered Mrs. Lee's parlour towards noon, and asked if she cared to visit the Capitol.

"You will have a chance of hearing to-day what may be the last great speech of our greatest statesman," said he; "you should come."

"A splendid sample of our na-tive raw material, sir?" asked she, fresh from a reading of Dickens, and his famous picture of American statesmanship.

"Precisely so," said Carrington; "the Prairie Giant of Peonia, the Favourite Son of Illinois; the man who came within three votes of getting the party nomination for the Presidency last spring, and was only defeated because ten small intriguers are sharper than one big one. The Honourable Silas P.

Ratcliffe, Senator from Illinois; he will be run for the Presidency yet."

"What does the P. stand for?" asked Sybil.

"I don't remember ever to have heard his middle name," said Carrington.

"Perhaps it is Peonia or Prairie; I can't say."

"He is the man whose appearance struck me so much when we were in the Senate last week, is he not? A great, ponderous man, over six feet high, very senatorial and dignified, with a large head and rather good features?" inquired Mrs. Lee.

"The same," replied Carrington. "By all means hear him speak. He is the stumbling-block of the new President, who is to be allowed no peace unless he makes terms with Ratcliffe; and so every one thinks that the Prairie Giant of Peonia will have the choice of the State or Treasury Department. If he takes either it will be the Treasury, for he is a desperate political manager, and will want the patronage for the next national convention."

Mrs. Lee was delighted to hear the debate, and Carrington was delighted to sit through it by her side, and to exchange running comments with her on the speeches and the speakers.

"Have you ever met the Senator?" asked she.

"I have acted several times as counsel before his committees. He is an excellent chairman, always attentive and generally civil."

"Where was he born?"

"The family is a New England one, and I believe respectable. He came, I think, from some place in the Connecticut Valley, but whether Vermont, New Hampshire, or Massachusetts, I don't know."

"Is he an educated man?"

"He got a kind of classical education at one of the country colleges there.

I suspect he has as much education as is good for him. But he went West very soon after leaving college, and being then young and fresh from that hot-bed of abolition, he threw himself into the anti-slavery movement m Illinois, and after a long struggle he rose with the wave. He would not do the same thing now."

"Why not?"

"He is older, more experienced, and not so wise. Besides, he has no longer the time to wait. Can you see his eyes from here? I call them Yankee eyes."

"Don't abuse the Yankees," said Mrs. Lee; "I am half Yankee myself."

"Is that abuse? Do you mean to deny that they have eyes?"

"I concede that there may be eyes among them; but Virginians are not fair judges of their expression."

"Cold eyes," he continued; "steel grey, rather small, not unpleasant in good-humour, diabolic in a passion, but worst when a little suspicious; then they watch you as though you were a young rattle-snake, to be killed when convenient."

"Does he not look you in the face?"

"Yes; but not as though he liked you. His eyes only seem to ask the possible uses you might be put to. Ah, the vice-president has given him the floor; now we shall have it. Hard voice, is it not? like his eyes. Hard manner, like his voice. Hard all through."

"What a pity he is so dreadfully senatorial!" said Mrs. Lee; "otherwise I rather admire him."

"Now he is settling down to his work," continued Carrington. "See how he dodges all the sharp issues. What a thing it is to be a Yankee! What a genius the fellow has for leading a party! Do you see how well it is all done? The new President flattered and conciliated, the party united and given a strong lead. And now we shall see how the President will deal with him. Ten to one on Ratcliffe. Come, there is that stupid ass from Missouri getting up. Let us go."

As they passed down the steps and out into the Avenue, Mrs. Lee turned to Carrington as though she had been reflecting deeply and had at length reached a decision.

"Mr. Carrington," said she, "I want to know Senator Ratcliffe."

"You will meet him to-morrow evening," replied Carrington, "at your senatorial dinner."

The Senator from New York, the Honourable Schuyler Clinton, was an old admirer of Mrs. Lee, and his wife was a cousin of hers, more or less distant. They had lost no time in honouring the letter of credit she thus had upon them, and invited her and her sister to a solemn dinner, as imposing as political dignity could make it. Mr. Carrington, as a connection of hers, was one of the party, and almost the only one among the twenty persons at table who had neither an office, nor a title, nor a constituency.

Senator Clinton received Mrs. Lee and her sister with tender enthusiasm, for they were attractive specimens of his constituents. He pressed their hands and evidently restrained himself only by an effort from embracing them, for the Senator had a marked regard for pretty women, and had made love to every girl with any pretensions to beauty that had appeared in the State of New York for fully half a century. At the same time he whispered an apology in her ear; he regretted so much that he was obliged to forego the pleasure of taking her to dinner; Washington was the only city in America where this could have happened, but it was a fact that ladies here were very great sticklers for etiquette; on the other hand he had the sad consolation that she would be the gainer, for he had allotted to her Lord Skye, the British Minister, "a most agreeable man and not married, as I have the misfortune to be;" and on the other side "I have ventured to place Senator Ratcliffe, of Illinois, whose admirable speech I saw you listening to with such rapt attention yesterday. I thought you might like to know him. Did I do right?"

Madeleine assured him that he had divined her inmost wishes, and he turned with even more warmth of affection to her sister: "As for you, my dear--dear Sybil, what can I do to make your dinner agreeable? If I give your sister a coronet, I am only sorry not to have a diadem for you. But I have done everything in my power. The first Secretary of the Russian Legation, Count Popoff, will take you in; a charming young man, my dear Sybil; and on your other side I have placed the Assistant Secretary of State, whom you know."

And so, after the due delay, the party settled themselves at the dinner-table, and Mrs. Lee found Senator Ratcliffe's grey eyes resting on her face for a moment as they sat down.

Lord Skye was very agreeable, and, at almost any other moment of her life, Mrs. Lee would have liked nothing better than to talk with him from the beginning to the end of her dinner. Tall, slender, bald-headed, awkward, and stammering with his elaborate British stammer whenever it suited his convenience to do so; a sharp observer who had wit which he commonly concealed; a humourist who was satisfied to laugh silently at his own humour; a diplomatist who used the mask of frankness with great effect; Lord Skye was one of the most popular men in Washington. Every one knew that he was a ruthless critic of American manners, but he had the art to combine ridicule with good-humour, and he was all the more popular accordingly. He was an outspoken admirer of American women in everything except their voices, and he did not even shrink from occasionally quizzing a little the national peculiarities of his own countrywomen; a sure piece of flattery to their American cousins. He would gladly have devoted himself to Mrs. Lee, but decent civility required that he should pay some attention to his hostess, and he was too good a diplomatist not to be attentive to a hostess who was the wife of a Senator, and that Senator the chairman of the committee of foreign relations.

The moment his head was turned, Mrs. Lee dashed at her Peonia Giant, who was then consuming his fish, and wishing he understood why the British Minister had worn no gloves, while he himself had sacrificed his convictions by wearing the largest and whitest pair of French kids that could be bought for money on Pennsylvania Avenue. There was a little touch of mortification in the idea that he was not quite at home among fashionable people, and at this instant he felt that true happiness was only to be found among the simple and honest sons and daughters of toil. A certain secret jealousy of the British Minister is always lurking in the breast of every American Senator, if he is truly democratic; for democracy, rightly understood, is the government of the people, by the people, for the benefit of Senators, and there is always a danger that the British Minister may not understand this political principle as he should. Lord Skye had run the risk of making two blunders; of offending the Senator from New York by neglecting his wife, and the Senator from Illinois by engrossing the attention of Mrs. Lee. A young Englishman would have done both, but Lord Skye had studied the American constitution. The wife of the Senator from New York now thought him most agreeable, and at the same moment the Senator from Illinois awoke to the conviction that after all, even in frivolous and fashionable circles, true dignity is in no danger of neglect; an American Senator represents a sovereign state; the great state of Illinois is as big as England--with the convenient omission of Wales, Scotland, Ireland, Canada, India, Australia, and a few other continents and islands; and in short, it was perfectly clear that Lord

Skye was not formidable to him, even in light society; had not Mrs. Lee herself as good as said that no position equalled that of an American Senator?

In ten minutes Mrs. Lee had this devoted statesman at her feet. She had not studied the Senate without a purpose. She had read with unerring instinct one general characteristic of all Senators, a boundless and guileless thirst for flattery, engendered by daily draughts from political friends or dependents, then becoming a necessity like a dram, and swallowed with a heavy smile of ineffable content. A single glance at Mr. Ratcliffe's face showed Madeleine that she need not be afraid of flattering too grossly; her own self-respect, not his, was the only restraint upon her use of this feminine bait.

She opened upon him with an apparent simplicity and gravity, a quiet repose of manner, and an evident consciousness of her own strength, which meant that she was most dangerous.

"I heard your speech yesterday, Mr. Ratcliffe. I am glad to have a chance of telling you how much I was impressed by it. It seemed to me masterly. Do you not find that it has had a great effect?"

"I thank you, madam. I hope it will help to unite the party, but as yet we have had no time to measure its results. That will require several days more." The Senator spoke in his senatorial manner, elaborate, condescending, and a little on his guard.

"Do you know," said Mrs. Lee, turning towards him as though he were a valued friend, and looking deep into his eyes, "Do you know that every one told me I should be shocked by the falling off in political ability at Washington? I did not believe them, and since hearing your speech I am sure they are mistaken. Do you yourself think there is less ability in Congress than there used to be?"

"Well, madam, it is difficult to answer that question. Government is not so easy now as it was formerly. There are different customs. There are many men of fair abilities in public life; many more than there used to be; and there is sharper criticism and more of it."

"Was I right in thinking that you have a strong resemblance to Daniel Webster in your way of speaking? You come from the same neighbourhood, do you not?"

Mrs. Lee here hit on Ratcliffe's weak point; the outline of his head had, in fact, a certain resemblance to that of Webster, and he prided himself upon it, and on a distant relationship to the Expounder of the Constitution; he began to think that Mrs. Lee was a very intelligent person. His modest admission of the resemblance gave her the opportunity to talk of Webster's oratory, and the conversation soon spread to a discussion of the merits of Clay and Calhoun. The Senator found that his neighbour--a fashionable New York woman, exquisitely dressed, and with a voice and manner seductively soft and gentle--had read the speeches of Webster and Calhoun. She did not think it necessary to tell him that she had persuaded the honest Carrington to bring her the volumes and to mark such passages as were worth her reading; but she took care to lead the conversation, and she criticised with some skill and more humour the weak points in Websterian oratory, saying with a little laugh and a glance into his delighted eyes:

"My judgment may not be worth much, Mr. Senator, but it does seem to me that our fathers thought too much of themselves, and till you teach me better I shall continue to think that the passage in your speech of yesterday which began with, 'Our strength lies in this twisted and tangled mass of isolated principles, the hair of the half-sleeping giant of Party,' is both for language and imagery quite equal to anything of Webster's."

The Senator from Illinois rose to this gaudy fly like a huge, two-hundred-pound salmon; his white waistcoat gave out a mild silver reflection as he slowly came to the surface and gorged the hook. He made not even a plunge, not one perceptible effort to tear out the barbed weapon, but, floating gently to her feet, allowed himself to be landed as though it were a pleasure. Only miserable casuists will ask whether this was fair play on Madeleine's part; whether flattery so gross cost her conscience no twinge, and whether any woman can without self-abasement be guilty of such shameless falsehood. She, however, scorned the idea of falsehood. She would have defended herself by saying that she had not so much praised Ratcliffe as depreciated Webster, and that she was honest in her opinion of the old-fashioned American oratory. But she could not deny that she had wilfully allowed the Senator to draw conclusions very different from any she actually held. She could not deny that she had intended to flatter him to the extent necessary for her purpose, and that she was pleased at her success. Before they rose from table the Senator had quite unbent himself; he was talking naturally, shrewdly, and with some humour; he had told her Illinois stories; spoken with extraordinary freedom about his political situation; and expressed the wish to call upon Mrs. Lee, if he could ever hope to find her at home.

"I am always at home on Sunday evenings," said she.

To her eyes he was the high-priest of American politics; he was charged with the meaning of the mysteries, the clue to political hieroglyphics. Through him she hoped to sound the depths of statesmanship and to bring up from its oozy bed that pearl of which she was in search; the mysterious gem which must lie hidden somewhere in politics. She wanted to understand this man; to turn him inside out; to experiment on him and use him as young physiologists use frogs and kittens. If there was good or bad in him, she meant to find its meaning.

And he was a western widower of fifty; his quarters in Washington were in gaunt boarding-house rooms, furnished only with public documents and enlivened by western politicians and office-seekers. In the summer he retired to a solitary, white framehouse with green blinds, surrounded by a few feet of uncared-for grass and a white fence; its interior more dreary still, with iron stoves, oil-cloth carpets, cold white walls, and one large engraving of Abraham Lincoln in the parlour; all in Peonia, Illinois! What equality was there between these two combatants? what hope for him? what risk for her? And yet Madeleine Lee had fully her match in Mr. Silas P. Ratcliffe.

Chapter III

Mrs. Lee soon became popular. Her parlour was a favourite haunt of certain men and women who had the art of finding its mistress at home; an art which seemed not to be within the powers of everybody. Carrington was apt to be there more often than any one else, so that he was looked on as almost a part of the family, and if Madeleine wanted a book from the library, or an extra man at her dinner-table, Carrington was pretty certain to help her to the one or the other. Old Baron Jacobi, the Bulgarian minister, fell madly in love with both sisters, as he commonly did with every pretty face and neat figure. He was a witty, cynical, broken-down Parisian roué, kept in Washington for years past by his debts and his salary; always grumbling because there was no opera, and mysteriously disappearing on visits to New York; a voracious devourer of French and German literature, especially of novels; a man who seemed to have met every noted or notorious personage of the century, and whose mmd was a magazine of amusing information; an excellent musical critic, who was not afraid to criticise Sybil's singing; a connoisseur in bric-à-brac, who laughed at Madeleine's display of odds and ends, and occasionally brought her a Persian plate or a bit of embroidery, which he said was good and would do her credit. This old sinner believed in everything that was perverse and wicked, but he accepted the prejudices of Anglo-Saxon society, and was too clever to obtrude his opinions upon others.

He would have married both sisters at once more willingly than either alone, but as he feelingly said, "If I were forty years younger, mademoiselle, you should not sing to me so calmly." His friend Popoff, an intelligent, vivacious Russian, with very Calmuck features, susceptible as a girl, and passionately fond of music, hung over Sybil's piano by the hour; he brought Russian airs which he taught her to sing, and, if the truth were known, he bored Madeleine desperately, for she undertook to act the part of duenna to her younger sister.

A very different visitor was Mr. C. C. French, a young member of Congress from Connecticut, who aspired to act the part of the educated gentleman in politics, and to purify the public tone. He had reform principles and an unfortunately conceited maimer; he was rather wealthy, rather clever, rather well-educated, rather honest, and rather vulgar. His allegiance was divided between Mrs. Lee and her sister, whom he infuriated by addressing as "Miss Sybil" with patronising familiarity. He was particularly strong in what he called "badinaige," and his playful but ungainly attempts at wit drove Mrs.

Lee beyond the bounds of patience. When in a solemn mood, he talked as though he were practising for the ear of a college debating society, and with a still worse effect on the patience; but with all this he was useful, always bubbling with the latest political gossip, and deeply interested in the fate of party stakes. Quite another sort of person was Mr. Hartbeest Schneidekoupon, a citizen of Philadelphia, though commonly resident in New York, where he had fallen a victim to Sybil's charms, and made efforts to win her young affections by instructing her in the mysteries of currency and protection, to both which subjects he was devoted. To forward these two interests and to watch over Miss Ross's welfare, he made periodical visits to Washington, where he closeted himself with committee-men and gave expensive dinners to members of Congress. Mr. Schneidekoupon was rich, and about thirty years old, tall and thin, with bright eyes and smooth face, elaborate manners and much loquacity. He had the reputation of turning rapid intellectual somersaults, partly to amuse himself and partly to startle society. At one moment he was artistic, and discoursed scientifically about his own paintings; at another he was literary, and wrote a book on "Noble Living," with a humanitarian purpose; at another he was devoted to sport, rode a steeplechase, played polo, and set up a four-in-hand; his last occupation was to establish in Philadelphia the Protective Review, a periodical in the interests of American industry, which he edited himself, as a stepping-stone to Congress, the Cabinet, and the Presidency. At about the same time he bought a yacht, and heavy bets were pending among his sporting friends whether he would manage to sink first his Review or his yacht. But he was an amiable and excellent fellow through all his eccentricities, and he brought to Mrs. Lee the simple outpourings of the amateur politician.

A much higher type of character was Mr. Nathan Gore, of Massachusetts, a handsome man with a grey beard, a straight, sharply cut nose, and a fine, penetrating eye; in his youth a successful poet whose satires made a noise in their day, and are still remembered for the pungency and wit of a few verses; then a deep student in Europe for many years, until his famous "History of Spain in America" placed him instantly at the head of American historians, and made him minister at Madrid, where he remained four years to his entire satisfaction, this being the nearest approach to a patent of nobility and a government pension which the American citizen can attain. A change of administration had reduced him to private life again, and after some years of retirement he was now in Washington, willing to be restored to his old mission. Every President thinks it respectable to have at least one literary man in his pay, and Mr. Gore's prospects were fair for obtaining his object, as he had the active support of a majority of the Massachusetts delegation. He was abominably selfish, colossally egoistic, and not a little vain; but he was shrewd; he knew how to hold his tongue; he could flatter dexterously, and he had learned to eschew satire. Only in confidence and among friends he would still talk freely, but Mrs. Lee was not yet on those terms with him. These were all men, and there was no want of women in Mrs.

Lee's parlour; but, after all, they are able to describe themselves better than any poor novelist can describe them. Generally two currents of conversation ran on together--one round Sybil, the other about Madeleine.

"Mees Ross," said Count Popoff, leading in a handsome young foreigner, "I have your permission to present to you my friend Count Orsini, Secretary of the Italian Legation. Are you at home this afternoon? Count Orsini sings also."

"We are charmed to see Count Orsini. It is well you came so late, for I have this moment come in from making Cabinet calls. They were so queer! I have been crying with laughter for an hour past." "Do you find these calls amusing?" asked Popoff, gravely and diplomatically. "Indeed I do! I went with Julia Schneidekoupon, you know, Madeleine; the Schneidekoupons are descended from all the Kings of Israel, and are prouder than Solomon in his glory. And when we got into the house of some dreadful woman from Heaven knows where, imagine my feelings at overhearing this conversation: 'What may be your family name, ma'am?' 'Schneidekoupon is my name,' replies Julia, very tall and straight. 'Have you any friends whom I should likely know?' 'I think not,' says Julia, severely. 'Wal! I don't seem to remember of ever having heerd the name. But I s'pose it's all right. I like to know who calls.' I almost had hysterics when we got into the street, but Julia could not see the joke at all."

Count Orsini was not quite sure that he himself saw the joke, so he only smiled becomingly and showed his teeth. For simple, childlike vanity and self-consciousness nothing equals an Italian Secretary of Legation at twenty-five. Yet conscious that the effect of his personal beauty would perhaps be diminished by permanent silence, he ventured to murmur presently:

"Do you not find it very strange, this society in America?"

"Society!" laughed Sybil with gay contempt. "There are no snakes in America, any more than in Norway."

"Snakes, mademoiselle!" repeated Orsini, with the doubtful expression of one who is not quite certain whether he shall risk walking on thin ice, and decides to go softly: "Snakes! Indeed they would rather be doves I would call them."

A kind laugh from Sybil strengthened into conviction his hope that he had made a joke in this unknown tongue. His face brightened, his confidence returned; once or twice he softly repeated to himself: "Not snakes; they would be doves!" But Mrs. Lee's sensitive ear had caught Sybil's remark, and detected in it a certain tone of condescension which was not to her taste.

The impassive countenances of these bland young Secretaries of Legation seemed to acquiesce far too much as a matter of course in the idea that there was no society except in the old world. She broke into the conversation with an emphasis that fluttered the dove-cote:

"Society in America? Indeed there is society in America, and very good society too; but it has a code of its own, and new-comers seldom understand it. I will tell you what it is, Mr. Orsini, and you will never be in danger of making any mistake. 'Society' in America means all the honest, kindly-mannered, pleasant-voiced women, and all the good, brave, unassuming men, between the Atlantic and the Pacific. Each of these has a free pass in every city and village, 'good for this generation only,' and it depends on each to make use of this pass or not as it may happen to suit his or her fancy. To this rule there are no exceptions, and those who say 'Abraham is our father' will surely furnish food for that humour which is the staple product of our country."

The alarmed youths, who did not in the least understand the meaning of this demonstration, looked on with a feeble attempt at acquiescence, while Mrs.

Lee brandished her sugar-tongs in the act of transferring a lump of sugar to her cup, quite unconscious of the slight absurdity of the gesture, while Sybil stared in amazement, for it was not often that her sister waved the stars and stripes so energetically. Whatever their silent criticisms might be, however, Mrs. Lee was too much in earnest to be conscious of them, or, indeed, to care for anything but what she was saying. There was a moment's pause when she came to the end of her speech, and then the thread of talk was quietly taken up again where Sybil's incipient sneer had broken it.

Carrington came in. "What have you been doing at the Capitol?" asked Madeleine.

"Lobbying!" was the reply, given in the semi-serious tone of Carrington's humour.

"So soon, and Congress only two days old?" exclaimed Mrs. Lee.

"Madam," rejoined Carrington, with his quietest malice, "Congressmen are like birds of the air, which are caught only by the early worm." "Good afternoon, Mrs. Lee. Miss Sybil, how do you do again? Which of these gentlemen's hearts are you feeding upon now?" This was the refined style of Mr. French, indulging in what he was pleased to term "badinaige." He, too, was on his way from the Capitol, and had come in for a cup of tea and a little human society. Sybil made a face which plainly expressed a longing to inflict on Mr. French some grievous personal wrong, but she pretended not to hear. He sat down by Madeleine, and asked, "Did you see Ratcliffe yesterday?"

"Yes," said Madeleine; "he was here last evening with Mr. Carrington and one or two others."

"Did he say anything about politics?"

"Not a word. We talked mostly about books."

"Books! What does he know about books?"

"You must ask him."

"Well, this is the most ridiculous situation we are all in. No one knows anything about the new President. You could take your oath that everybody is in the dark. Ratcliffe says he knows as little as the rest of us, but it can't be true; he is too old a politician not to have wires in his hand; and only to-day one of the pages of the Senate told my colleague Cutter that a letter sent off by him yesterday was directed to Sam Grimes, of North Bend, who, as every one knows, belongs to the President's particular crowd. --Why, Mr. Schneidekoupon! How do you do? When did you come on?"

"Thank you; this morning," replied Mr. Schneidekoupon, just entering the room. "So glad to see you again, Mrs. Lee. How do you and your sister like Washington? Do you know I have brought Julia on for a visit? I thought I should find her here.

"She has just gone. She has been all the afternoon with Sybil, making calls.

She says you want her here to lobby for you, Mr. Schneidekoupon. Is it true?"

"So I did," replied he, with a laugh, "but she is precious little use. So I've come to draft you into the service."

"Me!"

"Yes; you know we all expect Senator Ratcliffe to be Secretary of the Treasury, and it is very important for us to keep him straight on the currency and the tariff. So I have come on to establish more intimate relations with him, as they say in diplomacy. I want to get him to dine with me at Welckley's, but as I know he keeps very shy of politics I thought my only chance was to make it a ladies' dinner, so I brought on Julia. I shall try and get Mrs. Schuyler Clinton, and I depend upon you and your sister to help Julia out."

"Me! at a lobby dinner! Is that proper?"

"Why not? You shall choose the guests."

"I never heard of such a thing; but it would certainly be amusing. Sybil must not go, but I might."
"Excuse me; Julia depends upon Miss Ross, and will not go to table without her."

"Well," assented Mrs. Lee, hesitatingly, "perhaps if you get Mrs. Clinton, and if your sister is there And who else?"

"Choose your own company."

"I know no one."

"Oh yes; here is French, not quite sound on the tariff, but good for what we want just now. Then we can get Mr. Gore; he has his little hatchet to grind too, and will be glad to help grind ours. We only want two or three more, and I will have an extra man or so to fill up."

"Do ask the Speaker. I want to know him."

"I will, and Carrington, and my Pennsylvania Senator. That will do nobly.

Remember, Welckley's, Saturday at seven."

Meanwhile Sybil had been at the piano, and when she had sung for a time, Orsini was induced to take her place, and show that it was possible to sing without injury to one's beauty. Baron Jacobi came in and found fault with them both. Little Miss Dare--commonly known among her male friends as little Daredevil--who was always absorbed in some flirtation with a Secretary of Legation, came in, quite unaware that Popoff was present, and retired with him into a corner, while Orsini and Jacobi bullied poor Sybil, and fought with each other at the piano; everybody was talking with very little reference to any reply, when at last Mrs. Lee drove them all out of the room: "We are quiet people," said she, "and we dine at half-past six."

Senator Ratcliffe had not failed to make his Sunday evening call upon Mrs.

Lee. Perhaps it was not strictly correct to say that they had talked books all the evening, but whatever the conversation was, it had only confirmed Mr. Ratcliffe's admiration for Mrs. Lee, who, without intending to do so, had acted a more dangerous part than if she had been the most accomplished of coquettes. Nothing could be more fascinating to the weary politician in his solitude than the repose of Mrs. Lee's parlour, and when Sybil sang for him one or two simple airs--she said they were foreign hymns, the Senator being, or being considered, orthodox--Mr. Ratcliffe's heart yearned toward the charming girl quite with the sensations of a father, or even of an elder brother.

His brother senators very soon began to remark that the Prairie Giant had acquired a trick of looking up to the ladies' gallery. One day Mr. Jonathan Andrews, the special correspondent of the New York Sidereal System, a very friendly organ, approached Senator Schuyler Clinton with a puzzled look on his face.

"Can you tell me," said he, "what has happened to Silas P. Ratcliffe? Only a moment ago I was talking with him at his seat on a very important subject, about which I must send his opinions off to New York to-night, when, in the middle of a sentence, he stopped short, got up without looking at me, and left the Senate Chamber, and now I see him in the gallery talking with a lady whose face I don't know."

Senator Clinton slowly adjusted his gold eye-glasses and looked up at the place indicated: "Ah! Mrs. Lightfoot Lee! I think I will say a word to her myself;" and turning his back on the special correspondent, he skipped away with youthful agility after the Senator from Illinois.

"Devil!" muttered Mr. Andrews; "what has got into the old fools?" and in a still less audible murmur as he looked up to Mrs. Lee, then in close conversation with Ratcliffe: "Had I better make an item of that?"

When young Mr. Schneidekoupon called upon Senator Ratcliffe to invite him to the dinner at Welckley's, he found that gentleman overwhelmed with work, as he averred, and very little disposed to converse. No! he did not now go out to dinner. In the present condition of the public business he found it impossible to spare the time for such amusements. He regretted to decline Mr. Schneidekoupon's civility, but there were imperative reasons why he should abstain for the present from social entertainments; he had made but one exception to his rule, and only at the pressing request of his old friend Senator Clinton, and on a very special occasion.

Mr. Schneidekoupon was deeply vexed--the more, he said, because he had meant to beg Mr. and Mrs. Clinton to be of the party, as well as a very charming lady who rarely went into society, but who had almost consented to come.

"Who is that?" inquired the Senator.

"A Mrs. Lightfoot Lee, of New York. Probably you do not know her well enough to admire her as I do; but I think her quite the most intelligent woman I ever met."

The Senator's cold eyes rested for a moment on the young man's open face with a peculiar expression of distrust. Then he solemnly said, in his deepest senatorial tones:

"My young friend, at my time of life men have other things to occupy them than women, however intelligent they may be. Who else is to be of your party?"

Mr. Schneidekoupon named his list.

"And for Saturday evening at seven, did you say?"

"Saturday at seven."

"I fear there is little chance of my attending, but I will not absolutely decline. Perhaps when the moment arrives, I may find myself able to be there. But do not count upon me--do not count upon me. Good day, Mr.

Schneidekoupon."

Schneidekoupon was rather a simple-minded young man, who saw no deeper than his neighbours into the secrets of the universe, and he went off swearing roundly at "the infernal airs these senators give themselves." He told Mrs.

Lee all the conversation, as indeed he was compelled to do under penalty of bringing her to his party under false pretences.

"Just my luck," said he; "here I am forced to ask no end of people to meet a man, who at the same time says he shall probably not come. Why, under the stars, couldn't he say, like other people, whether he was coming or not?

I've known dozens of senators, Mrs. Lee, and they're all like that. They never think of any one but themselves."

Mrs. Lee smiled rather a forced smile, and soothed his wounded feelings; she had no doubt the dinner would be very agreeable whether the Senator were there or not; at any rate she would do all she could to carry it off well, and Sybil should wear her newest dress. Still she was a little grave, and Mr. Schneidekoupon could only declare that she was a trump; that he had told Ratcliffe she was the cleverest woman he ever met, and he might have added the most obliging, and Ratcliffe had only looked at him as though he were a green ape. At all which Mrs. Lee laughed good-naturedly, and sent him away as soon as she could.

When he was gone, she walked up and down the room and thought. She saw the meaning of Ratcliffe's sudden change in tone. She had no more doubt of his coming to the dinner than she had of the reason why he came. And was it possible that she was being drawn into something very near a flirtation with a man twenty years her senior; a politician from Illinois; a huge, ponderous, grey-eyed, bald senator, with a Websterian head, who lived in Peonia? The idea was almost too absurd to be credited; but on the whole the thing itself was rather amusing. "I suppose senators can look out for themselves like other men," was her final conclusion. She thought only of his danger, and she felt a sort of compassion for him as she reflected on the possible consequences of a great, absorbing love at his time of life.

Her conscience was a little uneasy; but of herself she never thought. Yet it is a historical fact that elderly senators have had a curious fascination for young and handsome women. Had they looked out for themselves too? And which parties most needed to be looked after?

When Madeleine and her sister arrived at Welckley's 's the next Saturday evening, they found poor Schneidekoupon in a temper very unbecoming a host.

"He won't come! I told you he wouldn't come!" said he to Madeleine, as he handed her into the house. "If I ever turn communist, it will be for the fun of murdering a senator."

Madeleine consoled him gently, but he continued to use, behind Mr. Clinton's back, language the most offensive and improper towards the Senate, and at last, ringing the bell, he sharply ordered the head waiter to serve dinner.

At that very moment the door opened, and Senator Ratcliffe's stately figure appeared on the threshold. His eye instantly caught Madeleine's, and she almost laughed aloud, for she saw that the Senator was dressed with very unsenatorial neatness; that he had actually a flower in his burton-hole and no gloves!

After the enthusiastic description which Schneidekoupon had given of Mrs.

Lee's charms, he could do no less than ask Senator Ratcliffe to take her in to dinner, which he did without delay. Either this, or the champagne, or some occult influence, had an extraordinary effect upon him. He appeared ten years younger than usual; his face was illuminated; his eyes glowed; he seemed bent on proving his kinship to the immortal Webster by rivalling his convivial powers. He dashed into the conversation; laughed, jested, and ridiculed; told stories in Yankee and Western dialect; gave sharp little sketches of amusing political experiences.

"Never was more surprised in my life," whispered Senator Krebs, of Pennsylvania, across the table to Schneidekoupon. "Hadn't an idea that Ratcliffe was so entertaining."

And Mr. Clinton, who sat by Madeleine on the other side, whispered low into her ear: "I am afraid, my dear Mrs. Lee, that you are responsible for this.

He never talks so to the Senate."

Nay, he even rose to a higher flight, and told the story of President Lincoln's death-bed with a degree of feeling that brought tears into their eyes. The other guests made no figure at all. The Speaker consumed his solitary duck and his lonely champagne in a corner without giving a sign.

Even Mr. Gore, who was not wont to hide his light under any kind of extinguisher, made no attempt to claim the floor, and applauded with enthusiasm the conversation of his opposite neighbour. Ill-natured people might say that Mr. Gore saw in Senator Ratcliffe a possible Secretary of State; be this as it may, he certainly said to Mrs. Clinton, in an aside that was perfectly audible to every one at the table: "How brilliant! what an original mind! what a sensation he would make abroad!" And it was quite true, apart from the mere momentary effect of dinner-table talk, that there was a certain bigness about the man; a keen practical sagacity; a bold freedom of self-assertion; a broad way of dealing with what he knew.

Carrington was the only person at table who looked on with a perfectly cool head, and who criticised in a hostile spirit. Carrington's impression of Ratcliffe was perhaps beginning to be warped by a shade of jealousy, for he was in a peculiarly bad temper this evening, and his irritation was not wholly concealed.

"If one only had any confidence in the man!" he muttered to French, who sat by him.

This unlucky remark set French to thinking how he could draw Ratcliffe out, and accordingly, with his usual happy manner, combining self-conceit and high principles, he began to attack the Senator with some "badinaige" on the delicate subject of Civil Service Reform, a subject almost as dangerous in political conversation at Washington as slavery itself in old days before the war. French was a reformer, and lost no occasion of impressing his views; but unluckily he was a very light weight, and his manner was a little ridiculous, so that even Mrs. Lee, who was herself a warm reformer, sometimes went over to the other side when he talked. No sooner had he now shot his little arrow at the Senator, than that astute man saw his opportunity, and promised himself the pleasure of administering to Mr.

French punishment such as he knew would delight the company. Reformer as Mrs. Lee was, and a little alarmed at the roughness of Ratcliffe's treatment, she could not blame the Prairie Giant, as she ought, who, after knocking poor French down, rolled him over and over in the mud.

"Are you financier enough, Mr. French, to know what are the most famous products of Connecticut?"

Mr. French modestly suggested that he thought its statesmen best answered that description.

"No, sir! even there you're wrong. The showmen beat you on your own ground.

But every child in the union knows that the most famous products of Connecticut are Yankee notions, nutmegs made of wood and clocks that won't go. Now, your Civil Service Reform is just such another Yankee notion; it's a wooden nutmeg; it's a clock with a show case and sham works. And you know it! You are precisely the old-school Connecticut peddler. You have gone about peddling your wooden nutmegs until you have got yourself into Congress, and now you pull them out of your pockets and not only want us to take them at your own price, but you lecture us on our sins if we don't.

Well! we don't mind your doing that at home. Abuse us as much as you like to your constituents. Get as many votes as you can. But don't electioneer here, because we know you intimately, and we've all been a little in the wooden nutmeg business ourselves."

Senator Clinton and Senator Krebs chuckied high approval over this punishment of poor French, which was on the level of their idea of wit. They were all in the nutmeg business, as Ratcliffe said. The victim tried to make head against them; he protested that his nutmegs were genuine; he sold no goods that he did not guarantee; and that this particular article was actually guaranteed by the national conventions of both political parties.

"Then what you want, Mr. French, is a common school education. You need a little study of the alphabet. Or if you won't believe me, ask my brother senators here what chance there is for your Reforms so long as the American citizen is what he "You'll not get much comfort in my State, Mr. French," growled the senator from Pennsylvania, with a sneer; "suppose you come and try."

"Well, well!" said the benevolent Mr. Schuyler Clinton, gleaming benignantly through his gold spectacles; "don't be too hard on French. He means well.

Perhaps he's not very wise, but he does good. I know more about it than any of you, and I don't deny that the thing is all bad. Only, as Mr. Ratcliffe says, the difficulty is in the people, not in us. Go to work on them, French, and let us alone."

French repented of his attack, and contented himself by muttering to Carrington: "What a set of damned old reprobates they are!"

"They are right, though, in one thing," was Carrington's reply: "their advice is good. Never ask one of them to reform anything; if you do, you will be reformed yourself."

The dinner ended as brilliantly as it began, and Schneidekoupon was delighted with his success. He had made himself particularly agreeable to Sybil by confiding in her all his hopes and fears about the tariff and the finances. When the ladies left the table, Ratcliffe could not stay for a cigar; he must get back to his rooms, where he knew several men were waiting for him; he would take his leave of the ladies and hurry away. But when the gentlemen came up nearly an hour afterwards they found Ratcliffe still taking his leave of the ladies, who were delighted at his entertaining conversation; and when at last he really departed, he said to Mrs. Lee, as though it were quite a matter of course: "You are at home as usual to-morrow evening?" Madeleine smiled, bowed, and he went his way.

As the two sisters drove home that night, Madeleine was unusually silent.

Sybil yawned convulsively and then apologized:

"Mr. Schneidekoupon is very nice and good-natured, but a whole evening of him goes a long way; and that horrid Senator Krebs would not say a word, and drank a great deal too much wine, though it couldn't make him any more stupid than he is. I don't think I care for senators." Then, wearily, after a pause: "Well, Maude, I do hope you've got what you wanted. I'm sure you must have had politics enough. Haven't you got to the heart of your great American mystery yet?"

"Pretty near it, I think," said Madeleine, half to herself.

Chapter IV

Sunday evening was stormy, and some enthusiasm was required to make one face its perils for the sake of society. Nevertheless, a few intimates made their appearance as usual at Mrs. Lee's. The faithful Popoff was there, and Miss Dare also ran in to pass an hour with her dear Sybil; but as she passed the whole evening in a corner with Popoff, she must have been disappointed in her object. Carrington came, and Baron Jacobi. Schneidekoupon and his sister dined with Mrs. Lee, and remained after dinner, while Sybil and Julia Schneidekoupon compared conclusions about Washington society. The happy idea also occurred to Mr. Gore that, inasmuch as Mrs. Lee's house was but a step from his hotel, he might as well take the chance of amusement there as the certainty of solitude in his rooms. Finally, Senator Ratcliffe duly made his appearance, and, having established himself with a cup of tea by Madeleine's side, was soon left to enjoy a quiet talk with her, the rest of the party by common consent occupying themselves with each other. Under cover of the murmur of conversation in the room, Mr. Ratcliffe quickiy became confidential.

"I came to suggest that, if you want to hear an interesting debate, you should come up to the Senate to-morrow. I am told that Garrard, of Louisiana, means to attack my last speech, and I shall probably in that case have to answer him. With you for a critic I shall speak better."

"Am I such an amiable critic?" asked Madeleine.

"I never heard that amiable critics were the best," said he; "justice is the soul of good criticism, and it is only justice that I ask and expect from you."

"What good does this speaking do?" inquired she. "Are you any nearer the end of your difficulties by means of your speeches?"

"I hardly know yet. Just now we are in dead water; but this can't last long.

In fact, I am not afraid to tell you, though of course you will not repeat it to any human being, that we have taken measures to force an issue.

Certain gentlemen, myself among the rest, have written letters meant for the President's eye, though not addressed directly to him, and intended to draw out an expression of some sort that will show us what to expect."

"Oh!" laughed Madeleine, "I knew about that a week ago."

"About what?"

"About your letter to Sam Grimes, of North Bend."

"What have you heard about my letter to Sam Grimes, of North Bend?" ejaculated Ratcliffe, a little abruptly.

"Oh, you do not know how admirably I have organised my secret service bureau," said she. "Representative Cutter cross-questioned one of the Senate pages, and obliged him to confess that he had received from you a letter to be posted, which letter was addressed to Mr. Grimes, of North Bend."

"And, of course, he told this to French, and French told you," said Ratcliffe; "I see. If I had known this I would not have let French off so gently last night, for I prefer to tell you my own story without his embellishments. But it was my fault. I should not have trusted a page. Nothing is a secret here long. But one thing that Mr. Cutter did not find out was that several other gentlemen wrote letters at the same time, for the same purpose. Your friend, Mr. Clinton, wrote; Krebs wrote; and one or two members."

"I suppose I must not ask what you said?"

"You may. We agreed that it was best to be very mild and conciliatory, and to urge the President only to give us some indication of his intentions, in order that we might not run counter to them. I drew a strong picture of the effect of the present situation on the party, and hinted that I had no personal wishes to gratify."

"And what do you think will be the result?"

"I think we shall somehow manage to straighten things out," said Ratcliffe.

"The difficulty is only that the new President has little experience, and is suspicious. He thinks we shall intrigue to tie his hands, and he means to tie ours in advance. I don't know him personally, but those who do, and who are fair judges, say that, though rather narrow and obstinate, he is honest enough, and will come round. I have no doubt I could settle it all with him in an hour's talk, but it is out of the question for me to go to him unless I am asked, and to ask me to come would be itself a settlement."

"What, then, is the danger you fear?"

"That he will offend all the important party leaders in order to conciliate unimportant ones, perhaps sentimental ones, like your friend French; that he will make foolish appointments without taking advice. By the way, have you seen French to-day?"

"No," replied Madeleine; "I think he must be sore at your treatment of him last evening. You were very rude to him."

"Not a bit," said Ratcliffe; "these reformers need it. His attack on me was meant for a challenge. I saw it in his manner.

"But is reform really so impossible as you describe it? Is it quite hopeless?"

"Reform such as he wants is utterly hopeless, and not even desirable."

Mrs. Lee, with much earnestness of manner, still pressed her question:

"Surely something can be done to check corruption. Are we for ever to be at the mercy of thieves and ruffians? Is a respectable government impossible in a democracy?"

Her warmth attracted Jacobi's attention, and he spoke across the room. "What is that you say, Mrs. Lee? What is it about corruption?"

All the gentlemen began to listen and gather about them.

"I am asking Senator Ratcliffe," said she, "what is to become of us if corruption is allowed to go unchecked."

"And may I venture to ask permission to hear Mr. Ratcliffe's reply?" asked the baron.

"My reply," said Ratcliffe, "is that no representative government can long be much better or much worse than the society it represents. Purify society and you purify the government. But try to purify the government artificially and you only aggravate failure."

"A very statesmanlike reply," said Baron Jacobi, with a formal bow, but his tone had a shade of mockery. Carrington, who had listened with a darkening face, suddenly turned to the baron and asked him what conclusion he drew from the reply.

"Ah!" exclaimed the baron, with his wickedest leer, "what for is my conclusion good? You Americans believe yourselves to be excepted from the operation of general laws. You care not for experience. I have lived seventy-five years, and all that time in the midst of corruption. I am corrupt myself, only I do have courage to proclaim it, and you others have it not. Rome, Paris, Vienna, Petersburg, London, all are corrupt; only Washington is pure! Well, I declare to you that in all my experience I have found no society which has had elements of corruption like the United States. The children in the street are corrupt, and know how to cheat me.

The cities are all corrupt, and also the towns and the counties and the States' legislatures and the judges. Everywhere men betray trusts both public and private, steal money, run away with public funds. Only in the Senate men take no money. And you gentlemen in the Senate very well declare that your great United States, which is the head of the civilized world, can never learn anything from the example of corrupt Europe. You are right--quite right! The great United States needs not an example. I do much regret that I have not yet one hundred years to live. If I could then come back to this city, I should find myself very content--much more than now. I am always content where there is much corruption, and ma parole d'honneur!"

broke out the old man with fire and gesture, "the United States will then be more corrupt than Rome under Caligula; more corrupt than the Church under Leo X.; more corrupt than France under the Regent!"

As the baron closed his little harangue, which he delivered directly at the senator sitting underneath him, he had the satisfaction to see that every one was silent and listening with deep attention. He seemed to enjoy annoying the senator, and he had the satisfaction of seeing that the senator was visibly annoyed. Ratcliffe looked sternly at the baron and said, with some curtness, that he saw no reason to accept such conclusions.

Conversation flagged, and all except the baron were relieved when Sybil, at Schneidekoupon's request, sat down at the piano to sing what she called a hymn. So soon as the song was over, Ratcliffe, who seemed to have been curiously thrown off his balance by Jacobi's harangue, pleaded urgent duties at his rooms, and retired. The others soon afterwards went off in a body, leaving only Carrington and Gore, who had seated himself by Madeleine, and was at once dragged by her into a discussion of the subject which perplexed her, and for the moment threw over her mind a net of irresistible fascination.

"The baron discomfited the senator," said Gore, with a certain hesitation.

"Why did Ratcliffe let himself be trampled upon in that manner?"

"I wish you would explain why," replied Mrs. Lee; "tell me, Mr. Gore--you who represent cultivation and literary taste hereabouts--please tell me what to think about Baron Jacobi's speech. Who and what is to be believed? Mr.

Ratcliffe seems honest and wise. Is he a corruptionist? He believes in the people, or says he does. Is he telling the truth or not?"

Gore was too experienced in politics to be caught in such a trap as this. He evaded the question. "Mr. Ratcliffe has a practical piece of work to do; his business is to make laws and advise the President; he does it extremely well. We have no other equally good practical politician; it is unfair to require him to be a crusader besides."

"No!" interposed Carrington, curtly; "but he need not obstruct crusades. He need not talk virtue and oppose the punishment of vice."

"He is a shrewd practical politician," replied Gore, "and he feels first the weak side of any proposed political tactics."

With a sigh of despair Madeleine went on: "Who, then, is right? How can we all be right? Half of our wise men declare that the world is going straight to perdition; the other half that it is fast becoming perfect. Both cannot be right. There is only one thing in life," she went on, laughing, "that I must and will have before I die. I must know whether America is right or wrong. Just now this question is a very practical one, for I really want to know whether to believe in Mr. Ratcliffe. If I throw him overboard, everything must go, for he is only a specimen."

"Why not believe in Mr. Ratcliffe?" said Gore; "I believe in him myself, and am not afraid to say so."

Carrington, to whom Ratcliffe now began to represent the spirit of evil, interposed here, and observed that he imagined Mr. Gore had other guides besides, and steadier ones than Ratcliffe, to believe in; while Madeleine, with a certain feminine perspicacity, struck at a much weaker point in Mr.

Gore's armour, and asked point-blank whether he believed also in what Ratcliffe represented: "Do you yourself think democracy the best government, and universal suffrage a success?"

Mr. Gore saw himself pinned to the wall, and he turned at bay with almost the energy of despair:

"These are matters about which I rarely talk in society; they are like the doctrine of a personal God; of a future life; of revealed religion; subjects which one naturally reserves for private reflection. But since you ask for my political creed, you shall have it. I only condition that it shall be for you alone, never to be repeated or quoted as mine. I believe in democracy. I accept it. I will faithfully serve and defend it. I believe in it because it appears to me the inevitable consequence of what has gone before it.

Democracy asserts the fact that the masses are now raised to a higher intelligence than formerly. All our civilisation aims at this mark. We want to do what we can to help it. I myself want to see the result. I grant it is an experiment, but it is the only direction society can take that is worth its taking; the only conception of its duty large enough to satisfy its instincts; the only result that is worth an effort or a risk. Every other possible step is backward, and I do not care to repeat the past. I am glad to see society grapple with issues in which no one can afford to be neutral."

"And supposing your experiment fails," said Mrs. Lee; "suppose society destroys itself with universal suffrage, corruption, and communism."

"I wish, Mrs. Lee, you would visit the Observatory with me some evening, and look at Sirius. Did you ever make the acquaintance of a fixed star? I believe astronomers reckon about twenty millions of them in sight, and an infinite possibility of invisible millions, each one of which is a sun, like ours, and may have satellites like our planet. Suppose you see one of these fixed stars suddenly increase in brightness, and are told that a satellite has fallen into it and is burning up, its career finished, its capacities exhausted? Curious, is it not; but what does it matter? Just as much as the burning up of a moth at your candle."

Madeleine shuddered a little. "I cannot get to the height of your philosophy," said she. "You are wandering among the infinites, and I am finite."

"Not at all! But I have faith; not perhaps in the old dogmas, but in the new ones; faith in human nature; faith in science; faith in the survival of the fittest. Let us be true to our time, Mrs. Lee! If our age is to be beaten, let us die in the ranks. If it is to be victorious, let us be first to lead the column. Anyway, let us not be skulkers or grumblers. There! have I repeated my catechism correctly? You would have it! Now oblige me by forgetting it. I should lose my character at home if it got out. Good night!"

Mrs. Lee duly appeared at the Capitol the next day, as she could not but do after Senator Ratcliffe's pointed request. She went alone, for Sybil had positively refused to go near the Capitol again, and Madeleine thought that on the whole this was not an occasion for enrolling Carrington in her service. But Ratcliffe did not speak. The debate was unexpectedly postponed.

He joined Mrs. Lee in the gallery, however, sat with her as long as she would allow, and became still more confidential, telling her that he had received the expected reply from Grimes, of North Bend, and that it had enclosed a letter written by the President-elect to Mr. Grimes in regard to the advances made by Mr. Ratcliffe and his friends.

"It is not a handsome letter," said he; "indeed, a part of it is positively insulting. I would like to read you one extract from it, and hear your opinion as to how it should be treated." Taking the letter from his pocket, he sought out the passage, and read as follows: "'I cannot lose sight, too, of the consideration that these three Senators' (he means Clinton, Krebs, and me) are popularly considered to be the most influential members of that so-called senatorial ring, which has acquired such general notoriety. While I shall always receive their communications with all due respect, I must continue to exercise complete freedom of action in consulting other political advisers as well as these, and I must in all cases make it my first object to follow the wishes of the people, not always most truly represented by their nominal representatives.' What say you to that precious piece of presidential manners?"

"At least I like his courage," said Mrs. Lee.

"Courage is one thing; common sense is another. This letter is a studied insult. He has knocked me off the track once. He means to do it again. It is a declaration of war. What ought I to do?"

"Whatever is most for the public good," said Madeleine, gravely.

Ratcliffe looked into her face with such undisguised delight--there was so little possibility of mistaking or ignoring the expression of his eyes, that she shrank back with a certain shock. She was not prepared for so open a demonstration. He hardened his features at once, and went on:

"But what is most for the public good?"

"That you know better than I," said Madeleine; "only one thing is clear to me. If you let yourself be ruled by your private feelings, you will make a greater mistake than he. Now I must go, for I have visits to make. The next time I come, Mr. Ratcliffe, you must keep your word better."

When they next met, Ratcliffe read to her a part of his reply to Mr. Grimes, which ran thus: "It is the lot of every party leader to suffer from attacks and to commit errors. It is true, as the President says, that I have been no exception to this law. Believing as I do that great results can only be accomplished by great parties, I have uniformly yielded my own personal opinions where they have failed to obtain general assent. I shall continue to follow this course, and the President may with perfect confidence count upon my disinterested support of all party measures, even though I may not be consulted in originating them."

Mrs. Lee listened attentively, and then said: "Have you never refused to go with your party?"

"Never!" was Ratcliffe's firm reply.

Madeleine still more thoughtfully inquired again: "Is nothing more powerful than party allegiance?"

"Nothing, except national allegiance," replied Ratcliffe, still more firmly.

Chapter V

To tie a prominent statesman to her train and to lead him about like a tame bear, is for a young and vivacious woman a more certain amusement than to tie herself to him and to be dragged about like an Indian squaw. This fact was Madeleine Lee's first great political discovery in Washington, and it was worth to her all the German philosophy she had ever read, with even a complete edition of Herbert Spencer's works into the bargain. There could be no doubt that the honours and dignities of a public career were no fair consideration for its pains. She made a little daily task for herself of reading in succession the lives and letters of the American Presidents, and of their wives, when she could find that there was a trace of the latter's existence. What a melancholy spectacle it was, from George Washington down to the last incumbent; what vexations, what disappointments, what grievous mistakes, what very objectionable manners! Not one of them, who had aimed at high purpose, but had been thwarted, beaten, and habitually insulted! What a gloom lay on the features of those famous chieftains, Calhoun, Clay, and Webster; what varied expression of defeat and unsatisfied desire; what a sense of self-importance and senatorial magniloquence; what a craving for flattery; what despair at the sentence of fate! And what did they amount to, after all?

They were practical men, these! they had no great problems of thought to settle, no questions that rose above the ordinary rules of common morals and homely duty. How they had managed to befog the subject! What elaborate show-structures they had built up, with no result but to obscure the horizon! Would not the country have done better without them? Could it have done worse? What deeper abyss could have opened under the nation's feet, than that to whose verge they brought it?

Madeleine's mind wearied with the monotony of the story. She discussed the subject with Ratcliffe, who told her frankly that the pleasure of politics lay in the possession of power. He agreed that the country would do very well without him. "But here I am," said he, "and here I mean to stay." He had very little sympathy for thin moralising, and a statesmanlike contempt for philosophical politics. He loved power, and he meant to be President.

That was enough.

Sometimes the tragic and sometimes the comic side was uppermost in her mind, and sometimes she did not herself know whether to cry or to laugh.

Washington more than any other city in the world swarms with simple-minded exhibitions of human nature; men and women curiously out of place, whom it would be cruel to ridicule and ridiculous to weep over. The sadder exhibitions are fortunately seldom seen by respectable people; only the little social accidents come under their eyes. One evening Mrs. Lee went to the President's first evening reception. As Sybil flatly refused to face the crowd, and Carrington mildly said that he feared he was not sufficiently reconstructed to appear at home in that august presence, Mrs. Lee accepted Mr. French for an escort, and walked across the Square with him to join the throng that was pouring into the doors of the White House. They took their places in the line of citizens and were at last able to enter the reception-room. There Madeleine found herself before two seemingly mechanical figures, which mIght be wood or wax, for any sign they showed of life. These two figures were the President and his wife; they stood stiff and awkward by the door, both their faces stripped of every sign of intelligence, while the right hands of both extended themselves to the column of visitors with the mechanical action of toy dolls. Mrs. Lee for a moment began to laugh, but the laugh died on her lips. To the President and his wife this was clearly no laughing matter. There they stood, automata, representatives of the society which streamed past them. Madeleine seized Mr. French by the arm.

"Take me somewhere at once," said she, "where I can look at it. Here! in the corner. I had no conception how shocking it was!"

Mr. French supposed she was thinking of the queer-looking men and women who were swarming through the rooms, and he made, after his own delicate notion of humour, some uncouth jests on those who passed by. Mrs. Lee, however, was in no humour to explain or even to listen. She stopped him short:--

"There, Mr. French! Now go away and leave me. I want to be alone for half an hour. Please come for me then." And there she stood, with her eyes fixed on the President and his wife, while the endless stream of humanity passed them, shaking hands.

What a strange and solemn spectacle it was, and how the deadly fascination of it burned the image in upon her mind! What a horrid warning to ambition!

And in all that crowd there was no one besides herself who felt the mockery of this exhibition. To all the others this task was a regular part of the President's duty, and there was nothing ridiculous about it. They thought it a democratic institution, this droll a ping of monarchical forms. To them the deadly dulness of the show was as natural and proper as ever to the courtiers of the Philips and Charleses seemed the ceremonies of the Escurial. To her it had the effect of a nightmare, or of an opium-eater's vision, She felt a sudden conviction that this was to be the end of American society; its realisation and dream at once. She groaned in spirit.

"Yes! at last I have reached the end! We shall grow to be wax images, and our talk will be like the squeaking of toy dolls. We shall all wander round and round the earth and shake hands. No one will have any object in this world, and there will be no other. It is worse than anything in the 'Inferno.' What an awful vision of eternity!"

Suddenly, as through a mist, she saw the melancholy face of Lord Skye approaching. He came to her side, and his voice recalled her to reality.

"Does it amuse you, this sort of thing?" he asked in a vague way.

"We take our amusement sadly, after the manner of our people," she replied; "but it certainly interests me."

They stood for a time in silence, watching the slowly eddying dance of Democracy, until he resumed:

"Whom do you take that man to be--the long, lean one, with a long woman on each arm?"

"That man," she replied, "I take to be a Washington department-clerk, or perhaps a member of Congress from Iowa, with a wife and wife's sister. Do they shock your nobility?"

He looked at her with comical resignation. "You mean to tell me that they are quite as good as dowager-countesses. I grant it. My aristocratic spirit is broken, Mrs. Lee. I will even ask them to dinner if you bid me, and if you will come to meet them. But the last time I asked a member of Congress to dine, he sent me back a note in pencil on my own envelope that he would bring two of his friends with him, very respectable constituents from Yahoo city, or some such place; nature's noblemen, he said."

"You should have welcomed them."

"I did. I wanted to see two of nature's noblemen, and I knew they would probably be pleasanter company than their representative. They came; very respectable persons, one with a blue necktie, the other with a red one: both had diamond pins in their shirts, and were carefully brushed in respect to their hair. They said nothing, ate little, drank less, and were much better behaved than I am. When they went away, they unanimously asked me to stay with them when I visited Yahoo city."

"You will not want guests if you always do that."

"I don't know. I think it was pure ignorance on their part. They knew no better, and they seemed modest enough. My only complaint was that I could get nothing out of them. I wonder whether their wives would have been more amusing."

"Would they be so in England, Lord Skye?"

He looked down at her with half-shut eyes, and drawled: "You know my countrywomen?"

"Hardly at all."

"Then let us discuss some less serious subject."

"Willingly. I have waited for you to explain to me why you have to-night an expression of such melancholy."

"Is that quite friendly, Mrs. Lee? Do I really look melancholy?"

"Unutterably, as I feel. I am consumed with curiosity to know the reason."

The British minister coolly took a complete survey of the whole room, ending with a prolonged stare at the President and his wife, who were still mechanically shaking hands; then he looked back into her face, and said never a word.

She insisted: "I must have this riddle answered. It suffocates me. I should not be sad at seeing these same people at work or at play, if they ever do play; or in a church or a lecture-room. Why do they weigh on me like a horrid phantom here?"

"I see no riddle, Mrs. Lee. You have answered your own question; they are neither at work nor at play."

"Then please take me home at once. I shall have hysterics. The sight of those two suffering images at the door is too mournful to be borne. I am dizzy with looking at these stalking figures. I don't believe they're real.

I wish the house would take fire. I want an earthquake. I wish some one would pinch the President, or pull his wife's hair."

Mrs. Lee did not repeat the experiment of visiting the White House, and indeed for some time afterwards she spoke with little enthusiasm of the presidential office. To Senator Ratcliffe she expressed her opinions strongly. The Senator tried in vain to argue that the people had a right to call upon their chief magistrate, and that he was bound to receive them; this being so, there was no less objectionable way of proceeding than the one which had been chosen. "Who gave the people any such right?" asked Mrs.

Lee. "Where does it come from? What do they want it for? You know better, Mr. Ratcliffe! Our chief magistrate is a citizen like any one else. What puts it into his foolish head to cease being a citizen and to ape royalty?

Our governors never make themselves ridiculous. Why cannot the wretched being content himself with living like the rest of us, and minding his own business? Does he know what a figure of fun he is?" And Mrs. Lee went so far as to declare that she would like to be the President's wife only to put an end to this folly; nothing should ever induce her to go through such a performance; and if the public did not approve of this, Congress might impeach her, and remove her from office; all she demanded was the right to be heard before the Senate in her own defence.

Nevertheless, there was a very general impression in Washington that Mrs.

Lee would like nothing better than to be in the White House. Known to comparatively few people, and rarely discussing even with them the subjects which deeply interested her, Madeleine passed for a clever, intriguing woman who had her own objects to gain. True it is, beyond peradventure, that all residents of Washington may be assumed to be in office or candidates for office; unless they avow their object, they are guilty of an attempt--and a stupid one--to deceive; yet there is a small class of apparent exceptions destined at last to fall within the rule. Mrs. Lee was properly assumed to be a candidate for office. To the Washingtonians it was a matter of course that Mrs. Lee should marry Silas P. Ratcliffe. That he should be glad to get a fashionable and intelligent wife, with twenty or thirty thousand dollars a year, was not surprising. That she should accept the first public man of the day, with a flattering chance for the Presidency--a man still comparatively young and not without good looks--was perfectly natural, and in her undertaking she had the sympathy of all well-regulated Washington women who were not possible rivals; for to them the President's wife is of more consequence than the President; and, indeed, if America only knew it, they are not very far from the truth.

Some there were, however, who did not assent to this good-natured though worldly view of the proposed match. These ladies were severe in their comments upon Mrs. Lee's conduct, and did not hesitate to declare their opinion that she was the calmest and most ambitious minx who had ever come within their observation. Unfortunately it happened that the respectable and proper Mrs. Schuyler Clinton took this view of the case, and made little attempt to conceal her opinion. She was justly indignant at her cousin's gross worldliness, and possible promotion in rank.

"If Madeleine Ross marries that coarse, horrid old Illinois politician,"

said she to her husband, "I never will forgive her so long as I live."

Mr. Clinton tried to excuse Madeleine, and even went so far as to suggest that the difference of age was no greater than in their own case; but his wife trampled ruthlessly on his argument.

"At any rate," said she, "I never came to Washington as a widow on purpose to set my cap for the first candidate for the Presidency, and I never made a public spectacle of my indecent eagerness in the very galleries of the Senate; and Mrs. Lee ought to be ashamed of herself. She is a cold-blooded, heartless, unfeminine cat."

Little Victoria Dare, who babbled like the winds and streams, with utter indifference as to what she said or whom she addressed, used to bring choice bits of this gossip to Mrs. Lee. She always affected a little stammer when she said anything uncommonly impudent, and put on a manner of languid simplicity. She felt keenly the satisfaction of seeing Madeleine charged with her own besetting sins. For years all Washington had agreed that Victoria was little better than one of the wicked; she had done nothing but violate every rule of propriety and scandalise every well-regulated family in the city, and there was no good in her. Yet it could not be denied that Victoria was amusing, and had a sort of irregular fascination; consequently she was universally tolerated. To see Mrs. Lee thrust down to her own level was an unmixed pleasure to her, and she carefully repeated to Madeleine the choice bits of dialogue which she picked up in her wanderings.

"Your cousin, Mrs. Clinton, says you are a ca-ca-cat, Mrs. Lee."

"I don't believe it, Victoria. Mrs. Clinton never said anything of the sort."

"Mrs. Marston says it is because you have caught a ra-ra-rat, and Senator Clinton was only a m-m-mouse!"

Naturally all this unexpected publicity irritated Mrs. Lee not a little, especially when short and vague paragraphs, soon followed by longer and more positive ones, in regard to Senator Ratcliffe's matrimonial prospects, began to appear in newspapers, along with descriptions of herself from the pens of enterprising female correspondents for the press, who had never so much as seen her. At the first sight of one of these newspaper articles, Madeleine fairly cried with mortification and anger. She wanted to leave Washington the next day, and she hated the very thought of Ratcliffe. There was something in the newspaper style so inscrutably vulgar, something so inexplicably revolting to the sense of feminine decency, that she shrank under it as though it were a poisonous spider. But after the first acute shame had passed, her temper was roused, and she vowed that she would pursue her own path just as she had begun, without regard to all the malignity and vulgarity in the wide United States. She did not care to marry Senator Ratcliffe; she liked his society and was flattered by his confidence; she rather hoped to prevent him from ever making a formal offer, and if not, she would at least push it off to the last possible moment; but she was not to be frightened from marrying him by any amount of spitefulness or gossip, and she did not mean to refuse him except for stronger reasons than these. She even went so far in her desperate courage as to laugh at her cousin, Mrs.

Clinton, whose venerable husband she allowed and even encouraged to pay her such public attention and to express sentiments of such youthful ardour as she well knew would inflame and exasperate the excellent lady his wife.

Carrington was the person most unpleasantly affected by the course which this affair had taken. He could no longer conceal from himself the fact that he was as much in love as a dignified Virginian could be. With him, at all events, she had shown no coquetry, nor had she ever either flattered or encouraged him. But Carrington, in his solitary struggle against fate, had found her a warm friend; always ready to assist where assistance was needed, generous with her money in any cause which he was willing to vouch for, full of sympathy where sympathy was more than money, and full of resource and suggestion where money and sympathy failed. Carrington knew her better than she knew herself. He selected her books; he brought the last speech or the last report from the Capitol or the departments; he knew her doubts and her vagaries, and as far as he understood them at all, helped her to solve them.

Carrington was too modest, and perhaps too shy, to act the part of a declared lover, and he was too proud to let it be thought that he wanted to exchange his poverty for her wealth. But he was all the more anxious when he saw the evident attraction which Ratcliffe's strong will and unscrupulous energy exercised over her. He saw that Ratcliffe was steadily pushing his advances; that he flattered all Mrs. Lee's weaknesses by the confidence and deference with which he treated her; and that in a very short time, Madeleine must either marry him or find herself looked upon as a heartless coquette. He had his own reasons for thinking ill of Senator Ratcliffe, and he meant to prevent a marriage; but he had an enemy to deal with not easily driven from the path, and quite capable of routing any number of rivals.

Ratcliffe was afraid of no one. He had not fought his own way in life for nothing, and he knew all the value of a cold head and dogged self-assurance.

Nothing but this robust Americanism and his strong will carried him safely through the snares and pitfalls of Mrs. Lee's society, where rivals and enemies beset him on every hand. He was little better than a schoolboy, when he ventured on their ground, but when he could draw them over upon his own territory of practical life he rarely failed to trample on his assailants.

It was this practical sense and cool will that won over Mrs. Lee, who was woman enough to assume that all the graces were well enough employed in decorating her, and it was enough if the other sex felt her superiority. Men were valuable only in proportion to their strength and their appreciation of women. If the senator had only been strong enough always to control his temper, he would have done very well, but his temper was under a great strain in these times, and his incessant effort to control it in politics made him less watchful in private life. Mrs. Lee's tacit assumption of superior refinement irritated him, and sometimes made him show his teeth like a bull-dog, at the cost of receiving from Mrs. Lee a quick stroke in return such as a well-bred tortoise-shell cat administers to check over-familiarity; innocent to the eye, but drawing blood.

One evening when he was more than commonly out of sorts, after sitting some time in moody silence, he roused himself, and, taking up a book that lay on her table, he glanced at its title and turned over the leaves. It happened by ill luck to be a volume of Darwin that Mrs. Lee had just borrowed from the library of Congress.

"Do you understand this sort of thing?" asked the Senator abruptly, in a tone that suggested a sneer.

"Not very well," replied Mrs. Lee, rather curtly.

"Why do you want to understand it?" persisted the Senator. "What good will it do you?"

"Perhaps it will teach us to be modest," answered Madeleine, quite equal to the occasion.

"Because it says we descend from monkeys?" rejoined the Senator, roughly.

"Do you think you are descended from monkeys?"

"Why not?" said Madeleine.

"Why not?" repeated Ratcliffe, laughing harshly. "I don't like the connection. Do you mean to introduce your distant relations into society?"

"They would bring more amusement into it than most of its present members,"

rejoined Mrs. Lee, with a gentle smile that threatened mischief. But Ratcliffe would not be warned; on the contrary, the only effect of Mrs.

Lee's defiance was to exasperate his ill-temper, and whenever he lost his temper he became senatorial and Websterian. "Such books," he began, "disgrace our civilization; they degrade and stultify our divine nature; they are only suited for Asiatic despotisms where men are reduced to the level of brutes; that they should be accepted by a man like Baron Jacobi, I can understand; he and his masters have nothing to do in the world but to trample on human rights. Mr. Carrington, of course, would approve those ideas; he believes in the divine doctrine of flogging negroes; but that you, who profess philanthropy and free principles, should go with them, is astonishing; it is incredible; it is unworthy of you."

"You are very hard on the monkeys," replied Madeleine, rather sternly, when the Senator's oration was ended. "The monkeys never did you any harm; they are not in public life; they are not even voters; if they were, you would be enthusiastic about their intelligence and virtue. After all, we ought to be grateful to them, for what would men do in this melancholy world if they had not inherited gaiety from the monkeys--as well as oratory."

Ratcliffe, to do him justice, took punishment well, at least when it came from Mrs. Lee's hands, and his occasional outbursts of insubordination were sure to be followed by improved discipline; but if he allowed Mrs. Lee to correct his faults, he had no notion of letting himself be instructed by her friends, and he lost no chance of telling them so. But to do this was not always enough. Whether it were that he had few ideas outside of his own experience, or that he would not trust himself on doubtful ground, he seemed compelled to bring every discussion down to his own level. Madeleine puzzled herself in vain to find out whether he did this because he knew no better, or because he meant to cover his own ignorance.

"The Baron has amused me very much with his account of Bucharest society,"

Mrs. Lee would say: "I had no idea it was so gay."

"I would like to show him our society in Peonia," was Ratcliffe's reply; "he would find a very brilliant circle there of nature's true noblemen."

"The Baron says their politicians are precious sharp chaps," added Mr. French.

"Oh, there are politicians in Bulgaria, are there?" asked the Senator, whose ideas of the Roumanian and Bulgarian neighbourhood were vague, and who had a general notion that all such people lived in tents, wore sheepskins with the wool inside, and ate curds: "Oh, they have politicians there! I would like to see them try their sharpness in the west."

"Really!" said Mrs. Lee. "Think of Attila and his hordes running an Indiana caucus?"

"Anyhow," cried French with a loud laugh, "the Baron said that a set of bigger political scoundrels than his friends couldn't be found in all Illinois."

"Did he say that?" exclaimed Ratcliffe angrily.

"Didn't he, Mrs. Lee? but I don't believe it; do you? What's your candid opinion, Ratcliffe? What you don't know about Illinois politics isn't worth knowing; do you really think those Bulgrascals couldn't run an Illinois state convention?"

Ratcliffe did not like to be chaffed, especially on this subject, but he could not resent French's liberty which was only a moderate return for the wooden nutmeg. To get the conversation away from Europe, from literature, from art, was his great object, and chaff was a way of escape.

Carrington was very well aware that the weak side of the Senator lay in his blind ignorance of morals. He flattered himself that Mrs. Lee must see this and be shocked by it sooner or later, so that nothing more was necessary than to let Ratcliffe expose himself. Without talking very much, Carrington always aimed at drawing him out. He soon found, however, that Ratcliffe understood such tactics perfectly, and instead of injuring, he rather improved his position. At times the man's audacity was startling, and even when Carrington thought him hopelessly entangled, he would sweep away all the hunter's nets with a sheer effort of strength, and walk off bolder and more dangerous than ever.

When Mrs. Lee pressed him too closely, he frankly admitted her charges.

"What you say is in great part true. There is much in politics that disgusts and disheartens; much that is coarse and bad. I grant you there is dishonesty and corruption. We must try to make the amount as small as possible."

"You should be able to tell Mrs. Lee how she must go to work," said Carrington; "you have had experience. I have heard, it seems to me, that you were once driven to very hard measures against corruption."

Ratcliffe looked ill-pleased at this compliment, and gave Carrington one of his cold glances that meant mischief. But he took up the challenge on the spot:--

"Yes, I was, and am very sorry for it. The story is this, Mrs. Lee; and it is well-known to every man, woman, and child in the State of Illinois, so that I have no reason for softening it. In the worst days of the war there was almost a certainty that my State would be carried by the peace party, by fraud, as we thought, although, fraud or not, we were bound to save it. Had Illinois been lost then, we should certainly have lost the Presidential election, and with it probably the Union. At any rate, I believed the fate of the war to depend on the result. I was then Governor, and upon me the responsibility rested. We had entire control of the northern counties and of their returns. We ordered the returning officers in a certain number of counties to make no returns until they heard from us, and when we had received the votes of all the southern counties and learned the precise number of votes we needed to give us a majority, we telegraphed to our northern returning officers to make the vote of their districts such and such, thereby overbalancing the adverse returns and giving the State to us.

This was done, and as I am now senator I have a right to suppose that what I did was approved. I am not proud of the transaction, but I would do it again, and worse than that, if I thought it would save this country from disunion. But of course I did not expect Mr. Carrington to approve it. I believe he was then carrying out his reform principles by bearing arms against the government."

"Yes!" said Carrington drily; "you got the better of me, too. Like the old Scotchman, you didn't care who made the people's wars provided you made its ballots.

Carrington had missed his point. The man who has committed a murder for his country, is a patriot and not an assassin, even when he receives a seat in the Senate as his share of the plunder. Women cannot be expected to go behind the motives of that patriot who saves his country and his election in times of revolution.

Carrington's hostility to Ratcliffe was, however, mild, when compared with that felt by old Baron Jacobi. Why the baron should have taken so violent a prejudice it is not easy to explain, but a diplomatist and a senator are natural enemies, and Jacobi, as an avowed admirer of Mrs. Lee, found Ratcliffe in his way. This prejudiced and immoral old diplomatist despised and loathed an American senator as the type which, to his bleared European eyes, combined the utmost pragmatical self-assurance and overbearing temper with the narrowest education and the meanest personal experience that ever existed in any considerable government. As Baron Jacobi's country had no special relations with that of the United States, and its Legation at Washington was a mere job to create a place for Jacobi to fill, he had no occasion to disguise his personal antipathies, and he considered himself in some degree as having a mission to express that diplomatic contempt for the Senate which his colleagues, if they felt it, were obliged to conceal. He performed his duties with conscientious precision. He never missed an opportunity to thrust the sharp point of his dialectic rapier through the joints of the clumsy and hide-bound senatorial self-esteem. He delighted in skilfully exposing to Madeleine's eyes some new side of Ratcliffe's ignorance. His conversation at such times sparkled with historical allusions, quotations in half a dozen different languages, references to well-known facts which an old man's memory could not recall with precision in all their details, but with which the Honourable Senator was familiarly acquainted, and which he could readily supply. And his Voltairian face leered politely as he listened to Ratcliffe's reply, which showed invariable ignorance of common literature, art, and history. The climax of his triumph came one evening when Ratcliffe unluckily, tempted by some allusion to Molière which he thought he understood, made reference to the unfortunate influence of that great man on the religious opinions of his time. Jacobi, by a flash of inspiration, divined that he had confused Molière with Voltaire, and assuming a manner of extreme suavity, he put his victim on the rack, and tortured him with affected explanations and interrogations, until Madeleine was in a manner forced to interrupt and end the scene. But even when the senator was not to be lured into a trap, he could not escape assault. The baron in such a case would cross the lines and attack him on his own ground, as on one occasion, when Ratcliffe was defending his doctrine of party allegiance, Jacobi silenced him by sneering somewhat thus:

"Your principle is quite correct, Mr. Senator. I, too, like yourself, was once a good party man: my party was that of the Church; I was ultramontane.

Your party system is one of your thefts from our Church; your National Convention is our Oecumenic Council; you abdicate reason, as we do, before its decisions; and you yourself, Mr. Ratcliffe, you are a Cardinal. They are able men, those cardinals; I have known many; they were our best friends, but they were not reformers. Are you a reformer, Mr. Senator?"

Ratcliffe grew to dread and hate the old man, but all his ordinary tactics were powerless against this impenetrable eighteenth century cynic. If he resorted to his Congressional practise of browbeating and dogmatism, the Baron only smiled and turned his back, or made some remark in French which galled his enemy all the more, because, while he did not understand it, he knew well that Madeleine did, and that she tried to repress her smile.

Ratcliffe's grey eyes grew colder and stonier than ever as he gradually perceived that Baron Jacobi was carrying on a set scheme with malignant ingenuity, to drive him out of Madeleine's house, and he swore a terrible oath that he would not be beaten by that monkey-faced foreigner. On the other hand Jacobi had little hope of success: "What can an old man do?" said he with perfect sincerity to Carrington; "If I were forty years younger, that great oaf should not have his own way. Ah! I wish I were young again and we were in Vienna!" From which it was rightly inferred by Carrington that the venerable diplomatist would, if such acts were still in fashion, have coolly insulted the Senator, and put a bullet through his heart.

Chapter VI

In February the weather became warmer and summer-like. In Virginia there comes often at this season a deceptive gleam of summer, slipping in between heavy storm-clouds of sleet and snow; days and sometimes weeks when the temperature is like June; when the earliest plants begin to show their hardy flowers, and when the bare branches of the forest trees alone protest against the conduct of the seasons. Then men and women are languid; life seems, as in Italy, sensuous and glowing with colour; one is conscious of walking in an atmosphere that is warm, palpable, radiant with possibilities; a delicate haze hangs over Arlington, and softens even the harsh white glare of the Capitol; the struggle of existence seems to abate; Lent throws its calm shadow over society; and youthful diplomatists, unconscious of their danger, are lured into asking foolish girls to marry them; the blood thaws in the heart and flows out into the veins, like the rills of sparkling water that trickle from every lump of ice or snow, as though all the ice and snow on earth, and all the hardness of heart, all the heresy and schism, all the works of the devil, had yielded to the force of love and to the fresh warmth of innocent, lamb-like, confiding virtue. In such a world there should be no guile--but there is a great deal of it notwithstanding. Indeed, at no other season is there so much. This is the moment when the two whited sepulchres at either end of the Avenue reek with the thick atmosphere of bargain and sale. The old is going; the new is coming. Wealth, office, power are at auction. Who bids highest? who hates with most venom? who intrigues with most skill? who has done the dirtiest, the meanest, the darkest, and the most, political work? He shall have his reward.

Senator Ratcliffe was absorbed and ill at ease. A swarm of applicants for office dogged his steps and beleaguered his rooms in quest of his endorsement of their paper characters. The new President was to arrive on Monday. Intrigues and combinations, of which the Senator was the soul, were all alive, awaiting this arrival. Newspaper correspondents pestered him with questions. Brother senators called him to conferences. His mind was pre-occupied with his own interests. One might have supposed that, at this instant, nothing could have drawn him away from the political gaming-table, and yet when Mrs. Lee remarked that she was going to Mount Vernon on Saturday with a little party, including the British Minister and an Irish gentleman staying as a guest at the British Legation, the Senator surprised her by expressing a strong wish to join them. He explained that, as the political lead was no longer in his hands, the chances were nine in ten that if he stirred at all he should make a blunder; that his friends expected him to do something when, in fact, nothing could be done; that every preparation had already been made, and that for him to go on an excursion to Mount Vernon, at this moment, with the British Minister, was, on the whole, about the best use he could make of his time, since it would hide him for one day at least.

Lord Skye had fallen into the habit of consulting Mrs. Lee when his own social resources were low, and it was she who had suggested this party to Mount Vernon, with Carrington for a guide and Mr. Gore for variety, to occupy the time of the Irish friend whom Lord Skye was bravely entertaining.

This gentleman, who bore the title of Dunbeg, was a dilapidated peer, neither wealthy nor famous. Lord Skye brought him to call on Mrs. Lee, and in some sort put him under her care. He was young, not ill-looking, quite intelligent, rather too fond of facts, and not quick at humour. He was given to smiling in a deprecatory way, and when he talked, he was either absent or excited; he made vague blunders, and then smiled in deprecation of offence, or his words blocked their own path in their rush. Perhaps his manner was a little ridiculous, but he had a good heart, a good head, and a title. He found favour in the eyes of Sybil and Victoria Dare, who declined to admit other women to the party, although they offered no objection to Mr.

Ratcliffe's admission. As for Lord Dunbeg, he was an enthusiastic admirer of General Washington, and, as he privately intimated, eager to study phases of American society. He was delighted to go with a small party, and Miss Dare secretly promised herself that she would show him a phase.

The morning was warm, the sky soft, the little steamer lay at the quiet wharf with a few negroes lazily watching her preparations for departure.

Carrington, with Mrs. Lee and the young ladies, arrived first, and stood leaning against the rail, waiting the arrival of their companions. Then came Mr. Gore, neatly attired and gloved, with a light spring overcoat; for Mr.

Gore was very careful of his personal appearance, and not a little vain of his good looks. Then a pretty woman, with blue eyes and blonde hair, dressed in black, and leading a little girl by the hand, came on board, and Carrington went to shake hands with her. On his return to Mrs. Lee's side, she asked about his new acquaintance, and he replied with a half-laugh, as though he were not proud of her, that she was a client, a pretty widow, well known in Washington. "Any one at the Capitol would tell you all about her.

She was the wife of a noted lobbyist, who died about two years ago.

Congressmen can refuse nothing to a pretty face, and she was their idea of feminine perfection. Yet she is a silly little woman, too. Her husband died after a very short illness, and, to my great surprise, made me executor under his will. I think he had an idea that he could trust me with his papers, which were important and compromising, for he seems to have had no time to go over them and destroy what were best out of the way. So, you see, I am left with his widow and child to look after. Luckily, they are well provided for."

"Still you have not told me her name." "Her name is Baker--Mrs. Sam Baker. But they are casting off, and Mr.

Ratcliffe will be left behind. I'll ask the captain to wait." About a dozen passengers had arrived, among them the two Earls, with a footman carrying a promising lunch-basket, and the planks were actually hauled in when a carriage dashed up to the whatf, and Mr. Ratcliffe leaped out and hurried on board. "Off with you as quick as you can!" said he to the negro-hands, and in another moment the little steamer had begun her journey, pounding the muddy waters of the Potomac and sending up its small column of smoke as though it were a newly invented incense-burner approaching the temple of the national deity. Ratcliffe explained in great glee how he had barely managed to escape his visitors by telling them that the British Minister was waiting for him, and that he would be back again presently. "If they had known where I was going," said he, "you would have seen the boat swamped with office-seekers. Illinois alone would have brought you to a watery grave." He was in high spirits, bent upon enjoying his holiday, and as they passed the arsenal with its solitary sentry, and the navy-yard, with its one unseaworthy wooden war-steamer, he pointed out these evidences of national grandeur to Lord Skye, threatening, as the last terror of diplomacy, to send him home in an American frigate. They were thus indulging in senatorial humour on one side of the boat, while Sybil and Victoria, with the aid of Mr. Gore and Carrington, were improving Lord Dunbeg's mind on the other.

Miss Dare, finding for herself at last a convenient seat where she could repose and be mistress of the situation, put on a more than usually demure expression and waited with gravity until her noble neighbour should give her an opportunity to show those powers which, as she believed, would supply a phase in his existence. Miss Dare was one of those young persons, sometimes to be found in America, who seem to have no object in life, and while apparently devoted to men, care nothing about them, but find happiness only in violating rules; she made no parade of whatever virtues she had, and her chief pleasure was to make fun of all the world and herself.

"What a noble river!" remarked Lord Dunbeg, as the boat passed out upon the wide stream; "I suppose you often sail on it?"

"I never was here in my life till now," replied the untruthful Miss Dare; "we don't think much of it; it s too small; we're used to so much larger rivers."

"I am afraid you would not like our English rivers then; they are mere brooks compared with this."

"Are they indeed?" said Victoria, with an appearance of vague surprise; "how curious! I don't think I care to be an Englishwoman then. I could not live without big rivers."

Lord Dunbeg stared, and hinted that this was almost unreasonable.

"Unless I were a Countess!" continued Victoria, meditatively, looking at Alexandria, and paying no attention to his lordship; "I think I could manage if I were a C-c-countess. It is such a pretty title!"

"Duchess is commonly thought a prettier one," stammered Dunbeg, much embarrassed. The young man was not used to chaff from women.

"I should be satisfied with Countess. It sounds well. I am surprised that you don't like it." Dunbeg looked about him uneasily for some means of escape but he was barred in. "I should think you would feel an awful responsibility in selecting a Countess. How do you do it?"

Lord Dunbeg nervously joined in the general laughter as Sybil ejaculated:

"Oh, Victoria!" but Miss Dare continued without a smile or any elevation of her monotonous voice:

"Now, Sybil, don't interrupt me, please. I am deeply interested in Lord Dunbeg's conversation. He understands that my interest is purely scientific, but my happiness requires that I should know how Countesses are selected.

Lord Dunbeg, how would you recommend a friend to choose a Countess?"

Lord Dunbeg began to be amused by her impudence, and he even tried to lay down for her satisfaction one or two rules for selecting Countesses, but long before he had invented his first rule, Victoria had darted off to a new subject.

"Which would you rather be, Lord Dunbeg? an Earl or George Washington?"

"George Washington, certainly," was the Earl's courteous though rather bewildered reply.

"Really?" she asked with a languid affectation of surprise; "it is awfully kind of you to say so, but of course you can't mean it."

"Indeed I do mean it."

"Is it possible? I never should have thought it."

"Why not, Miss Dare?"

"You have not the air of wishing to be George Washington."

"May I again ask, why not?"

"Certainly. Did you ever see George Washington?"

"Of course not. He died fifty years before I was born."

"I thought so. You see you don't know him. Now, will you give us an idea of what you imagine General Washington to have looked like?"

Dunbeg gave accordingly a flattering description of General Washington, compounded of Stuart's portrait and Greenough's statue of Olympian Jove with Washington's features, in the Capitol Square. Miss Dare listened with an expression of superiority not unmlxed with patience, and then she enlightened him as follows:

"All you have been saying is perfect stuff--excuse the vulgarity of the expression. When I am a Countess I will correct my language. The truth is that General Washington was a raw-boned country farmer, very hard-featured, very awkward, very illiterate and very dull; very bad tempered, very profane, and generally tipsy after dinner."

"You shock me, Miss Dare!" exclaimed Dunbeg.

"Oh! I know all about General Washington. My grandfather knew him intimately, and often stayed at Mount Vernon for weeks together. You must not believe what you read, and not a word of what Mr. Carrington will say.

He is a Virginian and will tell you no end of fine stories and not a syllable of truth in one of them. We are all patriotic about Washington and like to hide his faults. If I weren't quite sure you would never repeat it, I would not tell you this. The truth is that even when George Washington was a small boy, his temper was so violent that no one could do anything with him. He once cut down all his father's fruit-trees in a fit of passion, and then, just because they wanted to flog him, he threatened to brain his father with the hatchet. His aged wife suffered agonies from him. My grandfather often told me how he had seen the General pinch and swear at her till the poor creature left the room in tears; and how once at Mount Vernon he saw Washington, when quite an old man, suddenly rush at an unoffending visitor, and chase him off the place, beating him all the time over the head with a great stick with knots in it, and all just because he heard the poor man stammer; he never could abide s-s-stammering."

Carrington and Gore burst into shouts of laughter over this description of the Father of his country, but Victoria continued in her gentle drawl to enlighten Lord Dunbeg in regard to other subjects with information equally mendacious, until he decided that she was quite the most eccentric person he had ever met. The boat arrived at Mount Vernon while she was still engaged in a description of the society and manners of America, and especially of the rules which made an offer of marriage necessary. According to her, Lord Dunbeg was in imminent peril; gentlemen, and especially foreigners, were expected, in all the States south of the Potomac, to offer themselves to at least one young lady in every city: "and I had only yesterday," said Victoria, "a letter from a lovely girl in North Carolina, a dear friend of mine, who wrote me that she was right put out because her brothers had called on a young English visitor with shot guns, and she was afraid he wouldn't recover, and, after all, she says she should have refused him."

Meanwhile Madeleine, on the other side of the boat, undisturbed by the laughter that surrounded Miss Dare, chatted soberly and seriously with Lord Skye and Senator Ratcliffe. Lord Skye, too, a little intoxicated by the brilliancy of the morning, broke out into admiration of the noble river, and accused Americans of not appreciating the beauties of their own country.

"Your national mind," said he, "has no eyelids. It requires a broad glare and a beaten road. It prefers shadows which you can cut out with a knife. It doesn't know the beauty of this Virginia winter softness."

Mrs. Lee resented the charge. America, she maintained, had not worn her feelings threadbare like Europe. She had still her story to tell; she was waiting for her Burns and Scott, her Wordsworth and Byron, her Hogarth and Turner. "You want peaches in spring," said she. "Give us our thousand years of summer, and then complain, if you please, that our peach is not as mellow as yours. Even our voices may be soft then," she added, with a significant look at Lord Skye.

"We are at a disadvantage in arguing with Mrs. Lee," said he to Ratcliffe; "when she ends as counsel, she begins as witness. The famous Duchess of Devonshire's lips were not half as convincing as Mrs. Lee's voice."

Ratcliffe listened carefully, assenting whenever he saw that Mrs. Lee wished it. He wished he understood precisely what tones and half-tones, colours and harmonies, were.

They arrived and strolled up the sunny path. At the tomb they halted, as all good Americans do, and Mr. Gore, in a tone of subdued sorrow, delivered a short address--

"It might be much worse if they improved it," he said, surveying its proportions with the æsthetic eye of a cultured Bostonian. "As it stands, this tomb is a simple misfortune which might befall any of us; we should not grieve over it too much. What would our feelings be if a Congressional committee reconstructed it of white marble with Gothic pepper-pots, and gilded it inside on machine-moulded stucco!"

Madeleine, however, insisted that the tomb, as it stood, was the only restless spot about the quiet landscape, and that it contradicted all her ideas about repose in the grave. Ratcliffe wondered what she meant.

They passed on, wandering across the lawn, and through the house. Their eyes, weary of the harsh colours and forms of the city, took pleasure in the worn wainscots and the stained walls. Some of the rooms were still occupied; fires were burning in the wide fire-places. All were tolerably furnished, and there was no uncomfortable sense of repair or newness. They mounted the stairs, and Mrs. Lee fairly laughed when she was shown the room in which General Washington slept, and where he died.

Carrington smiled too. "Our old Virginia houses were mostly like this," said he; "suites of great halls below, and these gaunt barracks above. The Virginia house was a sort of hotel. When there was a race or a wedding, or a dance, and the house was full, they thought nothing of packing half a dozen people in one room, and if the room was large, they stretched a sheet across to separate the men from the women. As for toilet, those were not the mornings of cold baths. With our ancestors a little washing went a long way."

"Do you still live so in Virginia?" asked Madeleine.

"Oh no, it is quite gone. We live now like other country people, and try to pay our debts, which that generation never did. They lived from hand to mouth. They kept a stable-full of horses. The young men were always riding about the country, betting on horse-races, gambling, drinking, fighting, and making love. No one knew exactly what he was worth until the crash came about fifty years ago, and the whole thing ran out."

"Just what happened in Ireland!" said Lord Dunbeg, much interested and full of his article in the Quarterly; "the resemblance is perfect, even down to the houses."

Mrs. Lee asked Carrington bluntly whether he regretted the destruction of this old social arrangement.

"One can't help regretting," said he, "whatever it was that produced George Washington, and a crowd of other men like him. But I think we might produce the men still if we had the same field for them."

"And would you bring the old society back again if you could?" asked she.

"What for? It could not hold itself up. General Washington himself could not save it. Before he died he had lost his hold on Virginia, and his power was gone."

The party for a while separated, and Mrs. Lee found herself alone in the great drawing-room. Presently the blonde Mrs. Baker entered, with her child, who ran about making more noise than Mrs. Washington would have permitted.

Madeleine, who had the usual feminine love of children, called the girl to her and pointed out the shepherds and shepherdesses carved on the white Italian marble of the fireplace; she invented a little story about them to amuse the child, while the mother stood by and at the end thanked the story-teller with more enthusiasm than seemed called for. Mrs. Lee did not fancy her effusive manner, or her complexion, and was glad when Dunbeg appeared at the doorway.

"How do you like General Washington at home?" asked she.

"Really, I assure you I feel quite at home myself," replied Dunbeg, with a more beaming smile than ever. "I am sure General Washington was an Irishman.

I know it from the look of the place. I mean to look it up and write an article about it."

"Then if you have disposed of him," said Madeleine, "I think we will have luncheon, and I have taken the liberty to order it to be served outside."

There a table had been improvised, and Miss Dare was inspecting the lunch, and making comments upon Lord Skye's cuisine and cellar.

"I hope it is very dry champagne," said she, "the taste for sweet champagne is quite awfully shocking."

The young woman knew no more about dry and sweet champagne than of the wine of Ulysses, except that she drank both with equal satisfaction, but she was mimicking a Secretary of the British Legation who had provided her with supper at her last evening party. Lord Skye begged her to try it, which she did, and with great gravity remarked that it was about five per cent. she presumed. This, too, was caught from her Secretary, though she knew no more what it meant than if she had been a parrot.

The luncheon was very lively and very good. When it was over, the gentlemen were allowed to smoke, and conversation fell into a sober strain, which at last threatened to become serious.

"You want half-tones!" said Madeleine to Lord Skye: "are there not half-tones enough to suit you on the walls of this house?"

Lord Skye suggested that this was probably owing to the fact that Washington, belonging, as he did, to the universe, was in his taste an exception to local rules.

"Is not the sense of rest here captivating?" she continued. "Look at that quaint garden, and this ragged lawn, and the great river in front, and the superannuated fort beyond the river! Everything is peaceful, even down to the poor old General's little bed-room. One would like to lie down in it and sleep a century or two. And yet that dreadful Capitol and its office-seekers are only ten miles off."

"No! that is more than I can bear!" broke in Miss Victoria in a stage whisper, "that dreadful Capitol! Why, not one of us would be here without that dreadful Capitol! except, perhaps, myself."

"You would appear very well as Mrs. Washington, Victoria."

"Miss Dare has been so very obliging as to give us her views of General Washington's character this morning," said Dunbeg, "but I have not yet had time to ask Mr. Carrington for his."

"Whatever Miss Dare says is valuable," replied Carrington, "but her strong point is facts."

"Never flatter! Mr. Carrington," drawled Miss Dare; "I do not need it, and it does not become your style. Tell me, Lord Dunbeg, is not Mr. Carrington a little your idea of General Washington restored to us in his prime?"

"After your account of General Washington, Miss Dare, how can I agree with you?"

"After all," said Lord Skye, "I think we must agree that Miss Dare is in the main right about the charms of Mount Vernon. Even Mrs. Lee, on the way up, agreed that the General, who is the only permanent resident here, has the air of being confoundedly bored in his tomb. I don't myself love your dreadful Capitol yonder, but I prefer it to a bucolic life here. And I account in this way for my want of enthusiasm for your great General. He liked no kind of life but this. He seems to have been greater in the character of a home-sick Virginia planter than as General or President. I forgive him his inordinate dulness, for he was not a diplomatist and it was not his business to lie, but he might once in a way have forgotten Mount Vernon."

Dunbeg here burst in with an excited protest; all his words seemed to shove each other aside in their haste to escape first. "All our greatest Englishmen have been home-sick country squires. I am a home-sick country squire myself."

"How interesting!" said Miss Dare under her breath.

Mr. Gore here joined in: "It is all very well for you gentlemen to measure General Washington according to your own private twelve-inch carpenter's rule. But what will you say to us New Englanders who never were country gentlemen at all, and never had any liking for Virginia? What did Washington ever do for us? He never even pretended to like us. He never was more than barely civil to us. I'm not finding fault with him; everybody knows that he never cared for anything but Mount Vernon. For all that, we idolize him. To us he is Morality, Justice, Duty, Truth; half a dozen Roman gods with capital letters. He is austere, solitary, grand; he ought to be deified. I hardly feel easy, eating, drinking, smoking here on his portico without his permission, taking liberties with his house, criticising his bedrooms in his absence. Suppose I heard his horse now trotting up on the other side, and he suddenly appeared at this door and looked at us. I should abandon you to his indignation. I should run away and hide myself on the steamer. The mere thought unmans me."

Ratcliffe seemed amused at Gore's half-serious notions. "You recall to me,"

said he, "my own feelings when I was a boy and was made by my father to learn the Farewell Address by heart. In those days General Washington was a sort of American Jehovah. But the West is a poor school for Reverence. Since coming to Congress I have learned more about General Washington, and have been surprised to find what a narrow base his reputation rests on. A fair military officer, who made many blunders, and who never had more men than would make a full army-corps under his command, he got an enormous reputation in Europe because he did not make himself king, as though he ever had a chance of doing it. A respectable, painstaking President, he was treated by the Opposition with an amount of deference that would have made government easy to a baby, but it worried him to death. His official papers are fairly done, and contain good average sense such as a hundred thousand men in the United States would now write. I suspect that half of his attachment to this spot rose from his consciousness of inferior powers and his dread of responsibility. This government can show to-day a dozen men of equal abilities, but we don't deify them. What I most wonder at in him is not his military or political genius at all, for I doubt whether he had much, but a curious Yankee shrewdness in money matters. He thought himself a very rich man, yet he never spent a dollar foolishly. He was almost the only Virginian I ever heard of, in public life, who did not die insolvent."

During this long speech, Carrington glanced across at Madeleine, and caught her eye. Ratcliffe's criticism was not to her taste. Carrington could see that she thought it unworthy of him, and he knew that it would irritate her.

"I will lay a little trap for Mr. Ratcliffe," thought he to himself; "we will see whether he gets out of it." So Carrington began, and all listened closely, for, as a Virginian, he was supposed to know much about the subject, and his family had been deep in the confidence of Washington himself.

"The neighbours hereabout had for many years, and may have still, some curious stories about General Washington's closeness in money matters. They said he never bought anything by weight but he had it weighed over again, nor by tale but he had it counted, and if the weight or number were not exact, he sent it back. Once, during his absence, his steward had a room plastered, and paid the plasterer's bill. On the General's return, he measured the room, and found that the plasterer had charged fifteen shillings too much. Meanwhile the man had died, and the General made a claim of fifteen shillings on his estate, which was paid. Again, one of his tenants brought him the rent. The exact change of fourpence was required.

The man tendered a dollar, and asked the General to credit him with the balance against the next year's rent. The General refused and made him ride nine miles to Alexandria and back for the fourpence. On the other hand, he sent to a shoemaker in Alexandria to come and measure him for shoes. The man returned word that he did not go to any one's house to take measures, and the General mounted his horse and rode the nine miles to him. One of his rules was to pay at taverns the same sum for his servants' meals as for his own. An inn-keeper brought him a bill of three-and-ninepence for his own breakfast, and three shillings for his servant. He insisted upon adding the extra ninepence, as he did not doubt that the servant had eaten as much as he. What do you say to these anecdotes? Was this meanness or not?"

Ratcliffe was amused. "The stories are new to me," he said. "It is just as I thought. These are signs of a man who thinks much of trifles; one who fusses over small matters. We don't do things in that way now that we no longer have to get crops from granite, as they used to do in New Hampshire when I was a boy."

Carrington replied that it was unlucky for Virginians that they had not done things in that way then: if they had, they would not have gone to the dogs.

Gore shook his head seriously; "Did I not tell you so?" said he. "Was not this man an abstract virtue? I give you my word I stand in awe before him, and I feel ashamed to pry into these details of his life. What is it to us how he thought proper to apply his principles to nightcaps and feather dusters? We are not his body servants, and we care nothing about his infirmities. It is enough for us to know that he carried his rules of virtue down to a pin's point, and that we ought, one and all, to be on our knees before his tomb."

Dunbeg, pondering deeply, at length asked Carrington whether all this did not make rather a clumsy politician of the father of his country.

"Mr. Ratcliffe knows more about politics than I. Ask him," said Carrington.

"Washington was no politician at all, as we understand the word," replied Ratcliffe abruptly. "He stood outside of politics. The thing couldn't be done to-day. The people don't like that sort of royal airs."

"I don't understand!" said Mrs. Lee. "Why could you not do it now?"

"Because I should make a fool of myself;" replied Ratcliffe, pleased to think that Mrs. Lee should put him on a level with Washington. She had only meant to ask why the thing could not be done, and this little touch of Ratcliffe's vanity was inimitable.

"Mr. Ratcliffe means that Washington was too respectable for our time,"

interposed Carrington.

This was deliberately meant to irritate Ratcliffe, and it did so all the more because Mrs. Lee turned to Carrington, and said, with some bitterness:

"Was he then the only honest public man we ever had?"

"Oh no!" replied Carrington cheerfully; "there have been one or two others."

"If the rest of our Presidents had been like him," said Gore, "we should have had fewer ugly blots on our short history."

Ratcliffe was exasperated at Carrington's habit of drawing discussion to this point. He felt the remark as a personal insult, and he knew it to be intended. "Public men," he broke out, "cannot be dressing themselves to-day in Washington's old clothes. If Washington were President now, he would have to learn our ways or lose his next election. Only fools and theorists imagine that our society can be handled with gloves or long poles. One must make one's self a part of it. If virtue won't answer our purpose, we must use vice, or our opponents will put us out of office, and this was as true in Washington's day as it is now, and always will be."

"Come," said Lord Skye, who was beginning to fear an open quarrel; "the conversation verges on treason, and I am accredited to this government. Why not examine the grounds?"

A kind of natural sympathy led Lord Dunbeg to wander by the side of Miss Dare through the quaint old garden. His mind being much occupied by the effort of stowing away the impressions he had just received, he was more than usually absent in his manner, and this want of attention irritated the young lady. She made some comments on flowers; she invented some new species with startling names; she asked whether these were known in Ireland; but Lord Dunbeg was for the moment so vague in his answers that she saw her case was perilous.

"Here is an old sun-dial. Do you have sun-dials in Ireland, Lord Dunbeg?"

"Yes; oh, certainly! What! sun-dials? Oh, yes! I assure you there are a great many sun-dials in Ireland, Miss Dare."

"I am so glad. But I suppose they are only for ornament. Here it is just the other way. Look at this one! they all behave like that. The wear and tear of our sun is too much for them; they don't last. My uncle, who has a place at Long Branch, had five sun-dials in ten years."

"How very odd! But really now, Miss Dare, I don't see how a sun--dial could wear out."

"Don't you? How strange! Don't you see, they get soaked with sunshine so that they can't hold shadow. It's like me, you know. I have such a good time all the time that I can't be unhappy. Do you ever read the Burlington Hawkeye, Lord Dunbeg?"

"I don't remember; I think not. Is it an American serial?" gasped Dunbeg, trying hard to keep pace with Miss Dare in her reckless dashes across country.

"No, not serial at all!" replied Virginia; "but I am afraid you would find it very hard reading. I shouldn't try."

"Do you read it much, Miss Dare?"

"Oh, always! I am not really as light as I seem. But then I have an advantage over you because I know the language."

By this time Dunbeg was awake again, and Miss Dare, satisfied with her success, allowed herself to become more reasonable, until a slight shade of sentiment began to flicker about their path.

The scattered party, however, soon had to unite again. The boat rang its bell for return, they filed down the paths and settled themselves in their old places. As they steamed away, Mrs. Lee watched the sunny hill-side and the peaceful house above, until she could see them no more, and the longer she looked, the less she was pleased with herself. Was it true, as Victoria Dare said, that she could not live in so pure an air? Did she really need the denser fumes of the city? Was she, unknown to herself; gradually becoming tainted with the life about her? or was Ratcliffe right in accepting the good and the bad together, and in being of his time since he was in it? Why was it, she said bitterly to herself; that everything Washington touched, he purified, even down to the associations of his house?

and why is it that everything we touch seems soiled? Why do I feel unclean when I look at Mount Vernon? In spite of Mr. Ratcliffe, is it not better to be a child and to cry for the moon and stars?

The little Baker girl came up to her where she stood, and began playing with her parasol.

"Who is your little friend?" asked Ratcliffe.

Mrs. Lee rather vaguely replied that she was the daughter of that pretty woman in black; she believed her name was Baker.

"Baker, did you say?" repeated Ratcliffe.

"Baker--Mrs. Sam Baker; at least so Mr. Carrington told me; he said she was a client of his."

In fact Ratcliffe soon saw Carrington go up to her and remain by her side during the rest of the trip. Ratcliffe watched them sharply and grew more and more absorbed in his own thoughts as the boat drew nearer and nearer the shore.

Carrington was in high spirits. He thought he had played his cards with unusual success. Even Miss Dare deigned to acknowledge his charms that day.

She declared herself to be the moral image of Martha Washington, and she started a discussion whether Carrington or Lord Dunbeg would best suit her in the rôle of the General.

"Mr. Carrington is exemplary," she said, "but oh, what joy to be Martha Washington and a Countess too!"

Chapter VII

When he reached his rooms that afternoon, Senator Ratcliffe found there, as he expected, a choice company of friends and admirers, who had beguiled their leisure hours since noon by cursing him in every variety of profane language that experience could suggest and impatience stimulate. On his part, had he consulted his own feelings only, he would then and there have turned them out, and locked the doors behind them. So far as silent maledictions were concerned, no profanity of theirs could hold its own against the intensity and deliberation with which, as he found himself approaching his own door, he expressed between his teeth his views in respect to their eternal interests. Nothing could be less suited to his present humour than the society which awaited him in his rooms. He groaned in spirit as he sat down at his writing-table and looked about him. Dozens of office-seekers were besieging the house; men whose patriotic services in the last election called loudly for recognition from a grateful country.

They brought their applications to the Senator with an entreaty that he would endorse and take charge of them. Several members and senators who felt that Ratcliffe had no reason for existence except to fight their battle for patronage, were lounging about his room, reading newspapers, or beguiling their time with tobacco in various forms; at long intervals making dull remarks, as though they were more weary than their constituents of the atmosphere that surrounds the grandest government the sun ever shone upon.

Several newspaper correspondents, eager to barter their news for Ratcliffe's hints or suggestions, appeared from time to time on the scene, and, dropping into a chair by Ratcliffe's desk, whispered with him in mysterious tones.

Thus the Senator worked on, hour after hour, mechanically doing what was required of him, signing papers without reading them, answering remarks without hearing them, hardly looking up from his desk, and appearing immersed in labour. This was his protection against curiosity and garrulity.

The pretence of work was the curtain he drew between himself and the world.

Behind this curtain his mental operations went on, undisturbed by what was about him, while he heard all that was said, and said little or nothing himself. His followers respected this privacy, and left him alone. He was their prophet, and had a right to seclusion. He was their chieftain, and while he sat in his monosyllabic solitude, his ragged tail reclined in various attitudes about him, and occasionally one man spoke, or another swore. Newspapers and tobacco were their resource in periods of absolute silence.

A shade of depression rested on the faces and the voices of Clan Ratcliffe that evening, as is not unusual with forces on the eve of battle. Their remarks came at longer intervals, and were more pointless and random than usual. There was a want of elasticity in their bearing and tone, partly coming from sympathy with the evident depression of their chief; partly from the portents of the time. The President was to arrive within forty-eight hours, and as yet there was no sign that he properly appreciated their services; there were signs only too unmistakeable that he was painfully misled and deluded, that his countenance was turned wholly in another direction, and that all their sacrifices were counted as worthless. There was reason to believe that he came with a deliberate purpose of making war upon Ratcliffe and breaking him down; of refusing to bestow patronage on them, and of bestowing it wherever it would injure them most deeply. At the thought that their honestly earned harvest of foreign missions and consulates, department-bureaus, custom-house and revenue offices, postmasterships, Indian agencies, and army and navy contracts, might now be wrung from their grasp by the selfish greed of a mere accidental intruder--a man whom nobody wanted and every one ridiculed--their natures rebelled, and they felt that such things must not be; that there could be no more hope for democratic government if such things were possible. At this point they invariably became excited, lost their equanimity, and swore. Then they fell back on their faith in Ratcliffe: if any man could pull them through, he could; after all, the President must first reckon with him, and he was an uncommon tough customer to tackle.

Perhaps, however, even their faith in Ratcliffe might have been shaken, could they at that moment have looked into his mind and understood what was passing there. Ratcliffe was a man vastly their superior, and he knew it. He lived in a world of his own and had instincts of refinement. Whenever his affairs went unfavourably, these instincts revived, and for the time swept all his nature with them. He was now filled with disgust and cynical contempt for every form of politics. During long years he had done his best for his party; he had sold himself to the devil, coined his heart's blood, toiled with a dogged persistence that no day-labourer ever conceived; and all for what? To be rejected as its candidate; to be put under the harrow of a small Indiana farmer who made no secret of the intention to "corral" him, and, as he elegantly expressed it, to "take his hide and tallow." Ratcliffe had no great fear of losing his hide, but he felt aggrieved that he should be called upon to defend it, and that this should be the result of twenty years' devotion. Like most men in the same place, he did not stop to cast up both columns of his account with the party, nor to ask himself the question that lay at the heart of his grievance: How far had he served his party and how far himself? He was in no humour for self-analysis: this requires more repose of mind than he could then command. As for the President, from whom he had not heard a whisper since the insolent letter to Grimes, which he had taken care not to show, the Senator felt only a strong impulse to teach him better sense and better manners. But as for political life, the events of the last six months were calculated to make any man doubt its value. He was quite out of sympathy with it. He hated the sight of his tobacco-chewing, newspaper-reading satellites, with their hats tipped at every angle except the right one, and their feet everywhere except on the floor. Their conversation bored him and their presence was a nuisance. He would not submit to this slavery longer. He would have given his Senatorship for a civilized house like Mrs. Lee's, with a woman like Mrs. Lee at its head, and twenty thousand a year for life. He smiled his only smile that evening when he thought how rapidly she would rout every man Jack of his political following out of her parlours, and how meekly they would submit to banishment into a back-office with an oil-cloth carpet and two cane chairs.

He felt that Mrs. Lee was more necessary to him than the Presidency itself; he could not go on without her; he needed human companionship; some Christian comfort for his old age; some avenue of communication with that social world, which made his present surroundings look cold and foul; some touch of that refinement of mind and morals beside which his own seemed coarse. He felt unutterably lonely. He wished Mrs. Lee had asked him home to dinner; but Mrs. Lee had gone to bed with a headache. He should not see her again for a week. Then his mind turned back upon their morning at Mount Vernon, and bethinking himself of Mrs. Sam Baker, he took a sheet of note-paper, and wrote a line to Wilson Keen, Esq., at Georgetown, requesting him to call, if possible, the next morning towards one o'clock at the Senator's rooms on a matter of business. Wilson Keen was chief of the Secret Service Bureau in the Treasury Department, and, as the depositary of all secrets, was often called upon for assistance which he was very good-natured in furnishing to senators, especially if they were likely to be Secretaries of the Treasury.

This note despatched, Mr. Ratcliffe fell back into his reflective mood, which led him apparently into still lower depths of discontent until, with a muttered oath, he swore he could "stand no more of this," and, suddenly rising, he informed his visitors that he was sorry to leave them, but he felt rather poorly and was going to bed; and to bed he went, while his guests departed, each as his business or desires might point him, some to drink whiskey and some to repose.

On Sunday morning Mr. Ratcliffe, as usual, went to church. He always attended morning service--at the Methodist Episcopal Church--not wholly on the ground of religious conviction, but because a large number of his constituents were church-going people and he would not willingly shock their principles so long as he needed their votes. In church, he kept his eyes closely fixed upon the clergyman, and at the end of the sermon he could say with truth that he had not heard a word of it, although the respectable minister was gratified by the attention his discourse had received from the Senator from Illinois, an attention all the more praiseworthy because of the engrossing public cares which must at that moment have distracted the Senator's mind. In this last idea, the minister was right. Mr. Ratcliffe's mind was greatly distracted by public cares, and one of his strongest reasons for going to church at all was that he might get an hour or two of undisturbed reflection. During the entire service he was absorbed in carrying on a series of imaginary conversations with the new President. He brought up in succession every form of proposition which the President might make to him; every trap which could be laid for him; every sort of treatment he might expect, so that he could not be taken by surprise, and his frank, simple nature could never be at a loss. One object, however, long escaped him. Supposing, what was more than probable, that the President's opposition to Ratcliffe's declared friends made it impossible to force any of them into office; it would then be necessary to try some new man, not obnoxious to the President, as a candidate for the Cabinet. Who should this be? Ratcliffe pondered long and deeply, searching out a man who combined the most powerful interests, with the fewest enmities. This subject was still uppermost at the moment when service ended. Ratcliffe pondered over it as he walked back to his rooms. Not until he reached his own door did he come to a conclusion:

Carson would do; Carson of Pennsylvania; the President had probably never heard of him.

Mr. Wilson Keen was waiting the Senator's return, a heavy man with a square face, and good-natured, active blue eyes; a man of few words and those well-considered. The interview was brief. After apologising for breaking in upon Sunday with business, Mr. Ratcliffe excused himself on the ground that so little time was left before the close of the session. A bill now before one of his Committees, on which a report must soon be made, involved matters to which it was believed that the late Samuel Baker, formerly a well-known lobby-agent in Washington, held the only clue. He being dead, Mr. Ratcliffe wished to know whether he had left any papers behind him, and in whose hands these papers were, or whether any partner or associate of his was acquainted with his affairs.

Mr. Keen made a note of the request, merely remarking that he had been very well acquainted with Baker, and also a little with his wife, who was supposed to know his affairs as well as he knew them himself; and who was still in Washington. He thought he could bring the information in a day or two. As he then rose to go, Mr. Ratcliffe added that entire secrecy was necessary, as the interests involved in obstructing the search were considerable, and it was not well to wake them up. Mr. Keen assented and went his way.

All this was natural enough and entirely proper, at least so far as appeared on the surface. Had Mr. Keen been so curious in other people's affairs as to look for the particular legislative measure which lay at the bottom of Mr.

Ratcliffe's inquiries, he might have searched among the papers of Congress a very long time and found himself greatly puzzled at last. In fact there was no measure of the kind. The whole story was a fiction. Mr. Ratcliffe had scarcely thought of Baker since his death, until the day before, when he had seen his widow on the Mount Vernon steamer and had found her in relations with Carrington. Something in Carrington's habitual attitude and manner towards himself had long struck him as peculiar, and this connection with Mrs. Baker had suggested to the Senator the idea that it might be well to have an eye on both. Mrs. Baker was a silly woman, as he knew, and there were old transactions between Ratcliffe and Baker of which she might be informed, but which Ratcliffe had no wish to see brought within Mrs. Lee's ken. As for the fiction invented to set Keen in motion, it was an innocent one. It harmed nobody. Ratcliffe selected this particular method of inquiry because it was the easiest, safest, and most effectual. If he were always to wait until he could afford to tell the precise truth, business would very soon be at a standstill, and his career at an end.

This little matter disposed of; the Senator from Illinois passed his afternoon in calling upon some of his brother senators, and the first of those whom he honoured with a visit was Mr. Krebs, of Pennsylvania. There were many reasons which now made the co-operation of that high-minded statesman essential to Mr. Ratcliffe. The strongest of them was that the Pennsylvania delegation in Congress was well disciplined and could be used with peculiar advantage for purposes of "pressure." Ratcliffe's success in his contest with the new President depended on the amount of "pressure" he could employ. To keep himself in the background, and to fling over the head of the raw Chief Magistrate a web of intertwined influences, any one of which alone would be useless, but which taken together were not to be broken through; to revive the lost art of the Roman retiarius, who from a safe distance threw his net over his adversary, before attacking with the dagger; this was Ratcliffe's intention and towards this he had been directing all his manipulation for weeks past. How much bargaining and how many promises he found it necessary to make, was known to himself alone. About this time Mrs. Lee was a little surprised to find Mr. Gore speaking with entire confidence of having Ratcliffe's support in his application for the Spanish mission, for she had rather imagined that Gore was not a favourite with Ratcliffe. She noticed too that Schneidekoupon had come back again and spoke mysteriously of interviews with Ratcliffe; of attempts to unite the interests of New York and Pennsylvania; and his countenance took on a dark and dramatic expression as he proclaimed that no sacrifice of the principle of protection should be tolerated. Schneidekoupon disappeared as suddenly as he came, and from Sybil's innocent complaints of his spirits and temper, Mrs. Lee jumped to the conclusion that Mr. Ratcliffe, Mr. Clinton, and Mr.

Krebs had for the moment combined to sit heavily upon poor Schneidekoupon, and to remove his disturbing influence from the scene, at least until other men should get what they wanted. These were merely the trifling incidents that fell within Mrs. Lee's observation. She felt an atmosphere of bargain and intrigue, but she could only imagine how far it extended. Even Carrington, when she spoke to him about it, only laughed and shook his head:

"Those matters are private, my dear Mrs. Lee; you and I are not meant to know such things."

This Sunday afternoon Mr. Ratcliffe's object was to arrange the little manoeuvre about Carson of Pennsylvania, which had disturbed him in church.

His efforts were crowned with success. Krebs accepted Carson and promised to bring him forward at ten minutes' notice, should the emergency arise.

Ratcliffe was a great statesman. The smoothness of his manipulation was marvellous. No other man in politics, indeed no other man who had ever been in politics in this country, could--his admirers said--have brought together so many hostile interests and made so fantastic a combination. Some men went so far as to maintain that he would "rope in the President himself before the old man had time to swap knives with him." The beauty of his work consisted in the skill with which he evaded questions of principle. As he wisely said, the issue now involved was not one of principle but of power.

The fate of that noble party to which they all belonged, and which had a record that could never be forgotten, depended on their letting principle alone. Their principle must be the want of principles. There were indeed individuals who said in reply that Ratcliffe had made promises which never could be carried out, and there were almost superhuman elements of discord in the combination, but as Ratcliffe shrewdly rejoined, he only wanted it to last a week, and he guessed his promises would hold it up for that time.

Such was the situation when on Monday afternoon the President-elect arrived in Washington, and the comedy began. The new President was, almost as much as Abraham Lincoln or Franklin Pierce, an unknown quantity in political mathematics. In the national convention of the party, nine months before, after some dozens of fruitless ballots in which Ratcliffe wanted but three votes of a majority, his opponents had done what he was now doing; they had laid aside their principles and set up for their candidate a plain Indiana farmer, whose political experience was limited to stump-speaking in his native State, and to one term as Governor. They had pitched upon him, not because they thought him competent, but because they hoped by doing so to detach Indiana from Ratcliffe's following, and they were so successful that within fifteen minutes Ratcliffe's friends were routed, and the Presidency had fallen upon this new political Buddha.

He had begun his career as a stone-cutter in a quarry, and was, not unreasonably, proud of the fact. During the campaign this incident had, of course, filled a large space in the public mind, or, more exactly, in the public eye. "The Stone-cutter of the Wabash," he was sometimes called; at others "the Hoosier Quarryman," but his favourite appellation was "Old Granite," although this last endearing name, owing to an unfortunate similarity of sound, was seized upon by his opponents, and distorted into "Old Granny." He had been painted on many thousand yards of cotton sheeting, either with a terrific sledge-hammer, smashing the skulls (which figured as paving-stones) of his political opponents, or splitting by gigantic blows a huge rock typical of the opposing party. His opponents in their turn had paraded illuminations representing the Quarryman in the garb of a State's-prison convict breaking the heads of Ratcliffe and other well-known political leaders with a very feeble hammer, or as "Old Granny" in pauper's rags, hopelessly repairing with the same heads the impossible roads which typified the ill-conditioned and miry ways of his party. But these violations of decency and good sense were universally reproved by the virtuous; and it was remarked with satisfaction that the purest and most highly cultivated newspaper editors on his side, without excepting those of Boston itself; agreed with one voice that the Stone-cutter was a noble type of man, perhaps the very noblest that had appeared to adorn this country since the incomparable Washington.

That he was honest, all admitted; that is to say, all who voted for him.

This is a general characteristic of all new presidents. He himself took great pride in his home-spun honesty, which is a quality peculiar to nature's noblemen. Owing nothing, as he conceived, to politicians, but sympathising through every fibre of his unselfish nature with the impulses and aspirations of the people, he affirmed it to be his first duty to protect the people from those vultures, as he called them, those wolves in sheep's clothing, those harpies, those hyenas, the politicians; epithets which, as generally interpreted, meant Ratcliffe and Ratcliffe's friends.

His cardinal principle in politics was hostility to Ratcliffe, yet he was not vindictive. He came to Washington determined to be the Father of his country; to gain a proud immortality and a re-election.

Upon this gentleman Ratcliffe had let loose all the forms of "pressure"

which could be set in motion either in or out of Washington. From the moment when he had left his humble cottage in Southern Indiana, he had been captured by Ratcliffe's friends, and smothered in demonstrations of affection. They had never allowed him to suggest the possibility of ill-feeling. They had assumed as a matter of course that the most cordial attachment existed between him and his party. On his arrival in Washington they systematically cut him off from contact with any influences but their own. This was not a very difficult thing to do, for great as he was, he liked to be told of his greatness, and they made him feel himself a colossus. Even the few personal friends in his company were manipulated with the utmost care, and their weaknesses put to use before they had been in Washington a single day.

Not that Ratcliffe had anything to do with all this underhand and grovelling intrigue. Mr. Ratcliffe was a man of dignity and self-respect, who left details to his subordinates. He waited calmly until the President, recovered from the fatigues of his journey, should begin to feel the effect of a Washington atmosphere. Then on Wednesday morning, Mr. Ratcliffe left his rooms an hour earlier than usual on his way to the Senate, and called at the President's Hotel: he was ushered into a large apartment in which the new Chief Magistrate was holding court, although at sight of Ratcliffe, the other visitors edged away or took their hats and left the room. The President proved to be a hard-featured man of sixty, with a hooked nose and thin, straight, iron-gray hair. His voice was rougher than his features and he received Ratcliffe awkwardly. He had suffered since his departure from Indiana. Out there it had seemed a mere flea-bite, as he expressed it, to brush Ratcliffe aside, but in Washington the thing was somehow different.

Even his own Indiana friends looked grave when he talked of it, and shook their heads. They advised him to be cautious and gain time; to lead Ratcliffe on, and if possible to throw on him the responsibility of a quarrel. He was, therefore, like a brown bear undergoing the process of taming; very ill-tempered, very rough, and at the same time very much bewildered and a little frightened. Ratcliffe sat ten minutes with him, and obtained information in regard to pains which the President had suffered during the previous night, in consequence, as he believed, of an over-indulgence in fresh lobster, a luxury in which he had found a diversion from the cares of state. So soon as this matter was explained and condoled upon, Ratcliffe rose and took leave.

Every device known to politicians was now in full play against the Hoosier Quarryman. State delegations with contradictory requests were poured in upon him, among which that of Massachusetts presented as its only prayer the appointment of Mr. Gore to the Spanish mission. Difficulties were invented to embarrass and worry him. False leads were suggested, and false information carefully mingled with true. A wild dance was kept up under his eyes from daylight to midnight, until his brain reeled with the effort to follow it. Means were also found to convert one of his personal, confidential friends, who had come with him from Indiana and who had more brains or less principle than the others; from him every word of the President was brought directly to Ratcliffe's ear.

Early on Friday morning, Mr. Thomas Lord, a rival of the late Samuel Baker, and heir to his triumphs, appeared in Ratcliffe's rooms while the Senator was consuming his lonely egg and chop. Mr. Lord had been chosen to take general charge of the presidential party and to direct all matters connected with Ratcliffe's interests. Some people might consider this the work of a spy; he looked on it as a public duty. He reported that "Old Granny" had at last shown signs of weakness. Late the previous evening when, according to his custom, he was smoking his pipe in company with his kitchen-cabinet of followers, he had again fallen upon the subject of Ratcliffe, and with a volley of oaths had sworn that he would show him his place yet, and that he meant to offer him a seat in the Cabinet that would make him "sicker than a stuck hog." From this remark and some explanatory hints that followed, it seemed that the Quarryman had abandoned his scheme of putting Ratcliffe to immediate political death, and had now undertaken to invite him into a Cabinet which was to be specially constructed to thwart and humiliate him.

The President, it appeared, warmly applauded the remark of one counsellor, that Ratcliffe was safer in the Cabinet than in the Senate, and that it would be easy to kick him out when the time came.

Ratcliffe smiled grimly as Mr. Lord, with much clever mimicry, described the President's peculiarities of language and manner, but he said nothing and waited for the event. The same evening came a note from the President's private secretary requesting his attendance, if possible, to-morrow, Saturday morning, at ten o'clock. The note was curt and cool. Ratcliffe merely sent back word that he would come, and felt a little regret that the President should not know enough etiquette to understand that this verbal answer was intended as a hint to improve his manners. He did come accordingly, and found the President looking blacker than before. This time there was no avoiding of tender subjects. The President meant to show Ratcliffe by the decision of his course, that he was master of the situation. He broke at once into the middle of the matter: "I sent for you,"

said he, "to consult with you about my Cabinet. Here is a list of the gentlemen I intend to invite into it. You will see that I have got you down for the Treasury. Will you look at the list and say what you think of it?"

Ratcliffe took the paper, but laid it at once on the table without looking at it. "I can have no objection," said he, "to any Cabinet you may appoint, provided I am not included in it. My wish is to remain where I am. There I can serve your administration better than in the Cabinet."

"Then you refuse?" growled the President.

"By no means. I only decline to offer any advice or even to hear the names of my proposed colleagues until it is decided that my services are necessary. If they are, I shall accept without caring with whom I serve."

The President glared at him with an uneasy look. What was to be done next?

He wanted time to think, but Ratcliffe was there and must be disposed of. He involuntarily became more civil: "Mr. Ratcliffe, your refusal would knock everything on the head. I thought that matter was all fixed. What more can I do?"

But Ratcliffe had no mind to let the President out of his clutches so easily, and a long conversation followed, during which he forced his antagonist into the position of urging him to take the Treasury in order to prevent some undefined but portentous mischief in the Senate. All that could be agreed upon was that Ratcliffe should give a positive answer within two days, and on that agreement he took his leave.

As he passed through the corridor, a number of gentlemen were waiting for interviews with the President, and among them was the whole Pennsylvania delegation, "ready for biz," as Mr. Tom Lord remarked, with a wink.

Ratcliffe drew Krebs aside and they exchanged a few words as he passed out.

Ten minutes afterwards the delegation was admitted, and some of its members were a little surprised to hear their spokesman, Senator Krebs, press with extreme earnestness and in their names, the appointment of Josiah B. Carson to a place in the Cabinet, when they had been given to understand that they came to recommend Jared Caldwell as postmaster of Philadelphia. But Pennsylvania is a great and virtuous State, whose representatives have entire confidence in their chief. Not one of them so much as winked.

The dance of democracy round the President now began again with wilder energy. Ratcliffe launched his last bolts. His two-days' delay was a mere cover for bringing new influences to bear. He needed no delay. He wanted no time for reflection. The President had undertaken to put him on the horns of a dilemma; either to force him into a hostile and treacherous Cabinet, or to throw on him the blame of a refusal and a quarrel. He meant to embrace one of the horns and to impale the President on it, and he felt perfect confidence in his own success. He meant to accept the Treasury and he was ready to back himself with a heavy wager to get the government entirely into his own hands within six weeks. His contempt for the Hoosier Stone-cutter was unbounded, and his confidence in himself more absolute than ever.

Busy as he was, the Senator made his appearance the next evening at Mrs.

Lee's, and finding her alone with Sybil, who was occupied with her own little devices, Ratcliffe told Madeleine the story of his week's experience.

He did not dwell on his exploits. On the contrary he quite ignored those elaborate arrangements which had taken from the President his power of volition. His picture presented himself; solitary and unprotected, in the character of that honest beast who was invited to dine with the lion and saw that all the footmarks of his predecessors led into the lion's cave, and none away from it. He described in humorous detail his interviews with the Indiana lion, and the particulars of the surfeit of lobster as given in the President's dialect; he even repeated to her the story told him by Mr. Tom Lord, without omitting oaths or gestures; he told her how matters stood at the moment, and how the President had laid a trap for him which he could not escape; he must either enter a Cabinet constructed on purpose to thwart him and with the certainty of ignominious dismissal at the first opportunity, or he must refuse an offer of friendship which would throw on him the blame of a quarrel, and enable the President to charge all future difficulties to the account of Ratcliffe's "insatiable ambition." "And now, Mrs. Lee," he continued, with increasing seriousness of tone; "I want your advice; what shall I do?"

Even this half revelation of the meanness which distorted politics; this one-sided view of human nature in its naked deformity playing pranks with the interests of forty million people, disgusted and depressed Madeleine's mind. Ratclife spared her nothing except the exposure of his own moral sores. He carefully called her attention to every leprous taint upon his neighbours' persons, to every rag in their foul clothing, to every slimy and fetid pool that lay beside their path. It was his way of bringing his own qualities into relief. He meant that she should go hand in hand with him through the brimstone lake, and the more repulsive it seemed to her, the more overwhelming would his superiority become. He meant to destroy those doubts of his character which Carrington was so carefully fostering, to rouse her sympathy, to stimulate her feminine sense of self-sacrifice.

When he asked this question she looked up at him with an expression of indignant pride, as she spoke:

"I say again, Mr. Ratcliffe, what I said once before. Do whatever is most for the public good."

"And what is most for the public good?"

Madeleine half opened her mouth to reply, then hesitated, and stared silently into the fire before her. What was indeed most for the public good?

Where did the public good enter at all into this maze of personal intrigue, this wilderness of stunted natures where no straight road was to be found, but only the tortuous and aimless tracks of beasts and things that crawl?

Where was she to look for a principle to guide, an ideal to set up and to point at?

Ratcliffe resumed his appeal, and his manner was more serious than ever.

"I am hard pressed, Mrs. Lee. My enemies encompass me about. They mean to ruin me. I honestly wish to do my duty. You once said that personal considerations should have no weight. Very well! throw them away! And now tell me what I should do."

For the first time, Mrs. Lee began to feel his power. He was simple, straightforward, earnest. His words moved her. How should she imagine that he was playing upon her sensitive nature precisely as he played upon the President's coarse one, and that this heavy western politician had the instincts of a wild Indian in their sharpness and quickness of perception; that he divined her character and read it as he read the faces and tones of thousands from day to day? She was uneasy under his eye. She began a sentence, hesitated in the middle, and broke down. She lost her command of thought, and sat dumb-founded. He had to draw her out of the confusion he had himself made.

"I see your meaning in your face. You say that I should accept the duty and disregard the consequences."

"I don't know," said Madeleine, hesitatingly; "Yes, I think that would be my feeling."

"And when I fall a sacrifice to that man's envy and intrigue, what will you think then, Mrs. Lee? Will you not join the rest of the world and say that I overreached myself; and walked into this trap with my eyes open, and for my own objects? Do you think I shall ever be thought better of; for getting caught here? I don't parade high moral views like our friend French. I won't cant about virtue. But I do claim that in my public life I have tried to do right. Will you do me the justice to think so?"

Madeleine still struggled to prevent herself from being drawn into indefinite promises of sympathy with this man. She would keep him at arm's length whatever her sympathies might be. She would not pledge herself to espouse his cause. She turned upon him with an effort, and said that her thoughts, now or at any time, were folly and nonsense, and that the consciousness of right-doing was the only reward any public man had a right to expect.

"And yet you are a hard critic, Mrs. Lee. If your thoughts are what you say, your words are not. You judge with the judgment of abstract principles, and you wield the bolts of divine justice. You look on and condemn, but you refuse to acquit. When I come to you on the verge of what is likely to be the fatal plunge of my life, and ask you only for some clue to the moral principle that ought to guide me, you look on and say that virtue is its own reward. And you do not even say where virtue lies."

"I confess my sins," said Madeleine, meekly and despondently; "life is more complicated than I thought."

"I shall be guided by your advice," said Ratcliffe; "I shall walk into that den of wild beasts, since you think I ought. But I shall hold you to your responsibility. You cannot refuse to see me through dangers you have helped to bring me into."

"No, no!" cried Madeleine, earnestly; "no responsibility. You ask more than I can give."

Ratcliffe looked at her a moment with a troubled and careworn face. His eyes seemed deep sunk in their dark circles, and his voice was pathetic in its intensity. "Duty is duty, for you as well as for me. I have a right to the help of all pure minds. You have no right to refuse it. How can you reject your own responsibility and hold me to mine?"

Almost as he spoke, he rose and took his departure, leaving her no time to do more than murmur again her ineffectual protest. After he was gone, Mrs.

Lee sat long, with her eyes fixed on the fire, reflecting upon what he had said. Her mind was bewildered by the new suggestions which Ratcliffe had thrown out. What woman of thirty, with aspirations for the infinite, could resist an attack like this? What woman with a soul could see before her the most powerful public man of her time, appealing--with a face furrowed by anxieties, and a voice vibrating with only half-suppressed affection--to her for counsel and sympathy, without yielding some response? and what woman could have helped bowing her head to that rebuke of her over-confident judgment, coming as it did from one who in the same breath appealed to that judgment as final? Ratcliffe, too, had a curious instinct for human weaknesses. No magnetic needle was ever truer than his finger when he touched the vulnerable spot in an opponent's mind. Mrs. Lee was not to be reached by an appeal to religious sentiment, to ambition, or to affection.

Any such appeal would have fallen flat on her ears and destroyed its own hopes. But she was a woman to the very last drop of her blood. She could not be induced to love Ratcliffe, but she might be deluded into sacrificing herself for him. She atoned for want of devotion to God, by devotion to man.

She had a woman's natural tendency towards asceticism, self-extinction, self-abnegation. All through life she had made painful efforts to understand and follow out her duty. Ratcliffe knew her weak point when he attacked her from this side. Like all great orators and advocates, he was an actor; the more effective because of a certain dignified air that forbade familiarity.

He had appealed to her sympathy, her sense of right and of duty, to her courage, her loyalty, her whole higher nature; and while he made this appeal he felt more than half convinced that he was all he pretended to be, and that he really had a right to her devotion. What wonder that she in her turn was more than half inclined to admit that right. She knew him now better than Carrington or Jacobi knew him. Surely a man who spoke as he spoke, had noble instincts and lofty aims? Was not his career a thousand times more important than hers? If he, in his isolation and his cares, needed her assistance, had she an excuse for refusing it? What was there in her aimless and useless life which made it so precious that she could not afford to fling it into the gutter, if need be, on the bare chance of enriching some fuller existence?

Chapter VIII

Of all titles ever assumed by prince or potentate, the proudest is that of the Roman pontiffs: "Servus servorum Dei"--"Servant of the servants of God."

In former days it was not admitted that the devil's servants could by right have any share in government. They were to be shut out, punished, exiled, maimed, and burned. The devil has no servants now; only the people have servants. There may be some mistake about a doctrine which makes the wicked, when a majority, the mouthpiece of God against the virtuous, but the hopes of mankind are staked on it; and if the weak in faith sometimes quail when they see humanity floating in a shoreless ocean, on this plank, which experience and religion long since condemned as rotten, mistake or not, men have thus far floated better by its aid, than the popes ever did with their prettier principle; so that it will be a long time yet before society repents.

Whether the new President and his chief rival, Mr. Silas P. Ratcliffe, were or were not servants of the servants of God, is not material here. Servants they were to some one. No doubt many of those who call themselves servants of the people are no better than wolves in sheep's clothing, or asses in lions' skins. One may see scores of them any day in the Capitol when Congress is in session, making noisy demonstrations, or more usefully doing nothing. A wiser generation will employ them in manual labour; as it is, they serve only themselves. But there are two officers, at least, whose service is real--the President and his Secretary of the Treasury. The Hoosier Quarryman had not been a week in Washington before he was heartily home-sick for Indiana. No maid-of-all-work in a cheap boarding-house was ever more harassed. Everyone conspired against him. His enemies gave him no peace. All Washington was laughing at his blunders, and ribald sheets, published on a Sunday, took delight in printing the new Chief Magistrate's sayings and doings, chronicled with outrageous humour, and placed by malicious hands where the President could not but see them. He was sensitive to ridicule, and it mortified him to the heart to find that remarks and acts, which to him seemed sensible enough, should be capable of such perversion. Then he was overwhelmed with public business. It came upon him in a deluge, and he now, in his despair, no longer tried to control it. He let it pass over him like a wave. His mind was muddied by the innumerable visitors to whom he had to listen. But his greatest anxiety was the Inaugural Address which, distracted as he was, he could not finish, although in another week it must be delivered. He was nervous about his Cabinet; it seemed to him that he could do nothing until he had disposed of Ratcliffe.

Already, thanks to the President's friends, Ratcliffe had become indispensable; still an enemy, of course, but one whose hands must be tied; a sort of Sampson, to be kept in bonds until the time came for putting him out of the way, but in the meanwhile, to be utilized. This point being settled, the President had in imagination begun to lean upon him; for the last few days he had postponed everything till next week, "when I get my Cabinet arranged;" which meant, when he got Ratcliffe's assistance; and he fell into a panic whenever he thought of the chance that Ratcliffe might refuse.

He was pacing his room impatiently on Monday mormng, an hour before the time fixed for Ratcliffe's visit. His feelings still fluctuated violently, and if he recognized the necessity of using Ratcliffe, he was not the less determined to tie Ratcliffe's hands. He must be made to come into a Cabinet where every other voice would be against him. He must be prevented from having any patronage to dispose of. He must be induced to accept these conditions at the start. How present this to him in such a way as not to repel him at once? All this was needless, if the President had only known it, but he thought himself a profound statesman, and that his hand was guiding the destinies of America to his own re-election. When at length, on the stroke of ten o'clock, Ratcliffe entered the room, the President turned to him with nervous eagerness, and almost before offering his hand, said that he hoped Mr. Ratcliffe had come prepared to begin work at once. The Senator replied that, if such was the President's decided wish, he would offer no further opposition. Then the President drew himself up in the attitude of an American Cato, and delivered a prepared address, in which he said that he had chosen the members ot his Cabinet with a careful regard to the public interests; that Mr. Ratcliffe was essential to the combination; that he expected no disagreement on principles, for there was but one principle which he should consider fundamental, namely, that there should be no removals from office except for cause; and that under these circumstances he counted upon Mr. Ratcliffe's assistance as a matter of patriotic duty.

To all this Ratcliffe assented without a word of objection, and the President, more convinced than ever of his own masterly statesmanship, breathed more freely than for a week past. Within ten minutes they were actively at work together, clearing away the mass of accumulated business.

The relief of the Quarryman surprised himself. Ratcliffe lifted the weight of affairs from his shoulders with hardly an effort. He knew everybody and everything. He took most of the President's visitors at once into his own hands and dismissed them with great rapidity. He knew what they wanted; he knew what recommendations were strong and what were weak; who was to be treated with deference and who was to be sent away abruptly; where a blunt refusal was safe, and where a pledge was allowable. The President even trusted him with the unfinished manuscript of the Inaugural Address, which Ratcliffe returned to him the next day with such notes and suggestions as left nothing to be done beyond copying them out in a fair hand. With all this, he proved himself a very agreeable companion. He talked well and enlivened the work; he was not a hard taskmaster, and when he saw that the President was tired, he boldly asserted that there was no more business that could not as well wait a day, and so took the weary Stone-cutter out to drive for a couple of hours, and let him go peacefully to sleep in the carriage. They dined together and Ratcliffe took care to send for Tom Lord to amuse them, for Tom was a wit and a humourist, and kept the President in a laugh. Mr. Lord ordered the dinner and chose the wines. He could be coarse enough to suit even the President's palate, and Ratcliffe was not behindhand. When the new Secretary went away at ten o'clock that night, his chief; who was in high good humour with his dinner, his champagne, and his conversation, swore with some unnecessary granite oaths, that Ratcliffe was "a clever fellow anyhow," and he was glad "that job was fixed."

The truth was that Ratcliffe had now precisely ten days before the new Cabinet could be set in motion, and in these ten days he must establish his authority over the President so firmly that nothing could shake it. He was diligent in good works. Very soon the court began to feel his hand. If a business letter or a written memorial came in, the President found it easy to endorse: "Referred to the Secretary of the Treasury." If a visitor wanted anything for himself or another, the invariable reply came to be: "Just mention it to Mr. Ratcliffe;" or, "I guess Ratcliffe will see to that."

Before long he even made jokes in a Catonian manner; jokes that were not peculiarly witty, but somewhat gruff and boorish, yet significant of a resigned and self-contented mind. One morning he ordered Ratcliffe to take an iron-clad ship of war and attack the Sioux in Montana, seeing that he was in charge of the army and navy and Indians at once, and Jack of all trades; and again he told a naval officer who wanted a court-martial that he had better get Ratcliffe to sit on him for he was a whole court-martial by himself. That Ratcliffe held his chief in no less contempt than before, was probable but not certain, for he kept silence on the subject before the world, and looked solemn whenever the President was mentioned.

Before three days were over, the President, with a little more than his usual abruptness, suddenly asked him what he knew about this fellow Carson, whom the Pennsylvanians were bothering him to put in his Cabinet. Ratcliffe was guarded: he scarcely knew the man; Mr. Carson was not in politics, he believed, but was pretty respectable--for a Pennsylvanian. The President returned to the subject several times; got out his list of Cabinet officers and figured industriously upon it with a rather perplexed face; called Ratcliffe to help him; and at last the "slate" was fairly broken, and Ratcliffe's eyes gleamed when the President caused his list of nominations to be sent to the Senate on the 5th March, and Josiah B. Carson, of Pennsylvania, was promptly confirmed as Secretary of the Interior.

But his eyes gleamed still more humorously when, a few days afterwards, the President gave him a long list of some two score names, and asked him to find places for them. He assented good-naturedly, with a remark that it might be necessary to make a few removals to provide for these cases.

"Oh, well," said the President, "I guess there's just about as many as that had ought to go out anyway. These are friends of mine; got to be looked after. Just stuff 'em in somewhere."

Even he felt a little awkward about it, and, to do him justice, this was the last that was heard about the fundamental rule of his administration.

Removals were fast and furious, until all Indiana became easy in circumstances. And it was not to be denied that, by one means or another, Ratcliffe's friends did come into their fair share of the public money.

Perhaps the President thought it best to wink at such use of the Treasury patronage for the present, or was already a little overawed by his Secretary.

Ratcliffe's work was done. The public had, with the help of some clever intrigue, driven its servants into the traces. Even an Indiana stone-cutter could be taught that his personal prejudices must yield to the public service. What mischief the selfishness, the ambition, or the ignorance of these men might do, was another matter. As the affair stood, the President was the victim of his own schemes. It remained to be seen whether, at some future day, Mr. Ratcliffe would think it worth his while to strangle his chief by some quiet Eastern intrigue, but the time had gone by when the President could make use of either the bow-string or the axe upon him.

All this passed while Mrs. Lee was quietly puzzling her poor little brain about her duty and her responsibility to Ratcliffe, who, meanwhile, rarely failed to find himself on Sunday evenings by her side in her parlour, where his rights were now so well established that no one presumed to contest his seat, unless it were old Jacobi, who from time to time reminded him that he was fallible and mortal. Occasionally, though not often, Mr. Ratcliffe came at other times, as when he persuaded Mrs. Lee to be present at the Inauguration, and to call on the President's wife. Madeleine and Sybil went to the Capitol and had the best places to see and hear the Inauguration, as well as a cold March wind would allow. Mrs. Lee found fault with the ceremony; it was of the earth, earthy, she said. An elderly western farmer, with silver spectacles, new and glossy evening clothes, bony features, and stiff, thin, gray hair, trying to address a large crowd of people, under the drawbacks of a piercing wind and a cold in his head, was not a hero. Sybil's mind was lost in wondering whether the President would not soon die of pneumonia. Even this experience, however, was happy when compared with that of the call upon the President's wife, after which Madeleine decided to leave the new dynasty alone in future. The lady, who was somewhat stout and coarse-featured, and whom Mrs. Lee declared she wouldn't engage as a cook, showed qualities which, seen under that fierce light which beats upon a throne, seemed ungracious. Her antipathy to Ratcliffe was more violent than her husband's, and was even more openly expressed, until the President was quite put out of countenance by it. She extended her hostility to every one who could be supposed to be Ratcliffe's friend, and the newspapers, as well as private gossip, had marked out Mrs. Lee as one who, by an alliance with Ratcliffe, was aiming at supplanting her own rule over the White House.

Hence, when Mrs. Lightfoot Lee was announced, and the two sisters were ushered into the presidential parlour, she put on a coldly patronizing air, and in reply to Madeleine's hope that she found Washington agreeable, she intimated that there was much in Washington which struck her as awful wicked, especially the women; and, looking at Sybil, she spoke of the style of dress in this city which she said she meant to do what she could to put a stop to. She'd heard tell that people sent to Paris for their gowns, just as though America wasn't good enough to make one's clothes! Jacob (all Presidents' wives speak of their husbands by their first names) had promised her to get a law passed against it. In her town in Indiana, a young woman who was seen on the street in such clothes wouldn't be spoken to. At these remarks, made with an air and in a temper quite unmistakable, Madeleine became exasperated beyond measure, and said that "Washington would be pleased to see the President do something in regard to dress-reform—or any other reform;" and with this allusion to the President's ante-election reform speeches, Mrs. Lee turned her back and left the room, followed by Sybil in convulsions of suppressed laughter, which would not have been suppressed had she seen the face of their hostess as the door shut behind them, and the energy with which she shook her head and said: "See if I don't reform you yet, you--jade!"

Mrs. Lee gave Ratcliffe a lively account of this interview, and he laughed nearly as convulsively as Sybil over it, though he tried to pacify her by saying that the President's most intimate friends openly declared his wife to be insane, and that he himself was the person most afraid of her. But

Mrs. Lee declared that the President was as bad as his wife; that an equally good President and President's wife could be picked up in any corner-grocery between the Lakes and the Ohio; and that no inducement should ever make her go near that coarse washerwoman again.

Ratcliffe did not attempt to change Mrs. Lee's opinion. Indeed he knew better than any man how Presidents were made, and he had his own opinions in regard to the process as well as the fabric produced. Nothing Mrs. Lee could say now affected him. He threw off his responsibility and she found it suddenly resting on her own shoulders. When she spoke with indignation of the wholesale removals from office with which the new administration marked its advent to power, he told her the story of the President's fundamental principle, and asked her what she would have him do. "He meant to tie my hands," said Ratcliffe, "and to leave his own free, and I accepted the condition. Can I resign now on such a ground as this?" And Madeleine was obliged to agree that he could not. She had no means of knowing how many removals he made in his own interest, or how far he had outwitted the President at his own game. He stood before her a victim and a patriot. Every step he had taken had been taken with her approval. He was now in office to prevent what evil he could, not to be responsible for the evil that was done; and he honestly assured her that much worse men would come in when he went out, as the President would certainly take good care that he did go out when the moment arrived.

Mrs. Lee had the chance now to carry out her scheme in coming to Washington, for she was already deep in the mire of politics and could see with every advantage how the great machine floundered about, bespattering with mud even her own pure garments. Ratcliffe himself, since entering the Treasury, had begun to talk with a sneer of the way in which laws were made, and openly said that he wondered how government got on at all. Yet he declared still that this particular government was the highest expression of political thought. Mrs. Lee stared at him and wondered whether he knew what thought was. To her the government seemed to have less thought in it than one of Sybil's gowns, for if they, like the government, were monstrously costly, they were at least adapted to their purpose, the parts fitted together, and they were neither awkward nor unwieldy.

There was nothing very encouraging in all this, but it was better than New York. At least it gave her something to look at, and to think about. Even Lord Dunbeg preached practical philanthropy to her by the hour. Ratcliffe, too, was compelled to drag himself out of the rut of machine politics, and to justify his right of admission to her house. There Mr. French discoursed at great length, until the fourth of March sent him home to Connecticut; and he brought more than one intelligent member of Congress to Mrs. Lee's parlour. Underneath the scum floating on the surface of politics, Madeleine felt that there was a sort of healthy ocean current of honest purpose, which swept the scum before it, and kept the mass pure.

This was enough to draw her on. She reconciled herself to accepting the Ratcliffian morals, for she could see no choice. She herself had approved every step she had seen him take. She could not deny that there must be something wrong in a double standard of morality, but where was it? Mr.

Ratcliffe seemed to her to be doing good work with as pure means as he had at hand. He ought to be encouraged, not reviled. What was she that she should stand in judgment?

Others watched her progress with less satisfaction. Mr. Nathan Gore was one of these, for he came in one evening, looking much out of temper, and, sitting down by her side he said he had come to bid good-bye and to thank her for the kindness she had shown him; he was to leave Washington the next morning. She too expressed her warm regret, but added that she hoped he was only going in order to take his passage to Madrid.

He shook his head. "I am going to take my passage," said he, "but not to Madrid. The fates have cut that thread. The President does not want my services, and I can't blame him, for if our situations were reversed, I should certainly not want his. He has an Indiana friend, who, I am told, wanted to be postmaster at Indianapolis, but as this did not suit the politicians, he was bought off at the exorbitant price of the Spanish mission. But I should have no chance even if he were out of the way. The President does not approve of me. He objects to the cut of my overcoat which is unfortunately an English one. He also objects to the cut of my hair. I am afraid that his wife objects to me because I am so happy as to be thought a friend of yours."

Madeleine could only acknowledge that Mr. Gore's case was a bad one. "But after all," said she, "why should politicians be expected to love you literary gentlemen who write history. Other criminal classes are not expected to love their judges."

"No, but they have sense enough to fear them," replied Gore vindictively; "not one politician living has the brains or the art to defend his own cause. The ocean of history is foul with the carcases of such statesmen, dead and forgotten except when some historian fishes one of them up to gibbet it."

Mr. Gore was so much out of temper that after this piece of extravagance he was forced to pause a moment to recover himself. Then he went on:-- "You are perfectly right, and so is the President. I have no business to be meddling in politics. It is not my place. The next time you hear of me, I promise it shall not be as an office-seeker."

Then he rapidly changed the subject, saying that he hoped Mrs. Lee was soon going northward again, and that they might meet at Newport.

"I don't know," replied Madeleine; "the spring is pleasant here, and we shall stay till the warm weather, I think."

Mr. Gore looked grave. "And your politics!" said he; "are you satisfied with what you have seen?"

"I have got so far as to lose the distinction between right and wrong. Isn't that the first step in politics?"

Mr. Gore had no mind even for serious jesting. He broke out into a long lecture which sounded like a chapter of some future history: "But Mrs. Lee, is it possible that you don't see what a wrong path you are on. If you want to know what the world is really doing to any good purpose, pass a winter at Samarcand, at Timbuctoo, but not at Washington. Be a bank-clerk, or a journeyman printer, but not a Congressman. Here you will find nothing but wasted effort and clumsy intrigue."

"Do you think it a pity for me to learn that?" asked Madeleine when his long essay was ended.

"No!" replied Gore, hesitating; "not if you do learn it. But many people never get so far, or only when too late. I shall be glad to hear that you are mistress of it and have given up reforming politics. The Spaniards have a proverb that smells of the stable, but applies to people like you and me:

The man who washes his donkey's head, loses time and soap."

Gore took his leave before Madeleine had time to grasp all the impudence of this last speech. Not until she was fairly in bed that night did it suddenly flash on her mind that Mr. Gore had dared to caricature her as wasting time and soap on Mr. Ratcliffe. At first she was violently angry and then she laughed in spite of herself; there was truth in the portrait. In secret, too, she was the less offended because she half thought that it had depended only on herself to make of Mr. Gore something more than a friend. If she had overheard his parting words to Carrington, she would have had still more reason to think that a little jealousy of Ratcliffe's success sharpened the barb of Gore's enmity.

"Take care of Ratcliffe!" was his farewell; "he is a clever dog. He has set his mark on Mrs. Lee. Look out that he doesn't walk off with her!"

A little startled by this sudden confidence, Carrington could only ask what he could do to prevent it.

"Cats that go ratting, don't wear gloves," replied Gore, who always carried a Spanish proverb in his pocket. Carrington, after painful reflection, could only guess that he wanted Ratcliffe's enemies to show their claws. But how?

Mrs. Lee not long afterwards spoke to Ratcliffe of her regret at Gore's disappointment and hinted at his disgust. Ratcliffe replied that he had done what he could for Gore, and had introduced him to the President, who, after seeing him, had sworn his usual granitic oath that he would sooner send his nigger farm-hand Jake to Spain than that man-milliner. "You know how I stand;" added Ratcliffe; "what more could I do?" And Mrs. Lee's implied reproach was silenced.

If Gore was little pleased with Ratcliffe's conduct, poor Schneidekoupon was still less so. He turned up again at Washington not long after the Inauguration and had a private interview with the Secretary of the Treasury.

What passed at it was known only to themselves, but, whatever it was, Schneidekoupon's temper was none the better for it. From his conversations with Sybil, it seemed that there was some question about appointments in which his protectionist friends were interested, and he talked very openly about Ratcliffe's want of good faith, and how he had promised everything to everybody and had failed to keep a single pledge; if Schneidekoupon's advice had been taken, this wouldn't have happened. Mrs. Lee told Ratcliffe that Schneidekoupon seemed out of temper, and asked the reason. He only laughed and evaded the question, remarking that cattle of this kind were always complaining unless they were allowed to run the whole government; Schneidekoupon had nothing to grumble about; no one had ever made any promises to him. But nevertheless Schneidekoupon confided to Sybil his antipathy to Ratcliffe and solemnly begged her not to let Mrs. Lee fall into his hands, to which Sybil answered tartly that she only wished Mr.

Schneidekoupon would tell her how to help it.

The reformer French had also been one of Ratcliffe's backers in the fight over the Treasury. He remained in Washington a few days after the Inauguration, and then disappeared, leaving cards with P.P.C. in the corner, at Mrs. Lee's door. Rumour said that he too was disappointed, but he kept his own counsel, and, if he really wanted the mission to Belgium, he contented himself with waiting for it. A respectable stage-coach proprietor from Oregon got the place.

As for Jacobi, who was not disappointed, and who had nothing to ask for, he was bitterest of all. He formally offered his congratulations to Ratcliffe on his appointment. This little scene occurred in Mrs. Lee's parlour. The old Baron, with his most suave manner, and his most Voltairean leer, said that in all his experience, and he had seen a great many court intrigues, he had never seen anything better managed than that about the Treasury.

Ratcliffe was furiously angry, and told the Baron outright that foreign ministers who insulted the governments to which they were accredited ran a risk of being sent home.

"Ce serait toujours un pis aller," said Jacobi, seating himself with calmness in Ratcliffe's favourite chair by Mrs. Lee's side.

Madeleine, alarmed as she was, could not help interposing, and hastily asked whether that remark was translatable.

"Ah!" said the Baron; "I can do nothing with your language. You would only say that it was a choice of evils, to go, or to stay."

"We might translate it by saying: 'One may go farther and fare worse,'"

rejoined Madeleine; and so the storm blew over for the time, and Ratcliffe sulkily let the subject drop. Nevertheless the two men never met in Mrs. Lee's parlour without her dreading a personal altercation. Little by little, what with Jacobi's sarcasms and Ratcliffe's roughness, they nearly ceased to speak, and glared at each other like quarrelsome dogs. Madeleine was driven to all kinds of expedients to keep the peace, yet at the same time she could not but be greatly amused by their behaviour, and as their hatred of each other only stimulated their devotion to her, she was content to hold an even balance between them.

Nor were these all the awkward consequences of Ratcliffe's attentions. Now that he was distinctly recognized as an intimate friend of Mrs. Lee's, and possibly her future husband, no one ventured any longer to attack him in her presence, but nevertheless she was conscious in a thousand ways that the atmosphere became more and more dense under the shadow of the Secretary of the Treasury. In spite of herself she sometimes felt uneasy, as though there were conspiracy in the air. One March afternoon she was sitting by her fire, with an English Review in her hand, trying to read the last Symposium on the sympathies of Eternal Punishment, when her servant brought in a card, and Mrs. Lee had barely time to read the name of Mrs. Samuel Baker when that lady followed the servant into the room, forcing the countersign in so effective style that for once Madeleine was fairly disconcerted. Her manner when thus intruded upon, was cool, but in this case, on Carrington's account, she tried to smile courteously and asked her visitor to sit down, which Mrs. Baker was doing without an invitation, very soon putting her hostess entirely at her ease. She was, when seen without her veil, a showy woman verging on forty, decidedly large, tall, over-dressed even in mourning, and with a complexion rather fresher than nature had made it.

There was a geniality in her address, savouring of easy Washington ways, a fruitiness of smile, and a rich southern accent, that explained on the spot her success in the lobby. She looked about her with fine self-possession, and approved Mrs. Lee's surroundings with a cordiality so different from the northern stinginess of praise, that Madeleine was rather pleased than offended. Yet when her eye rested on the Corot, Madeleine's only pride, she was evidently perplexed, and resorted to eye-glasses, in order, as it seemed, to gain time for reflection. But she was not to be disconcerted even by Corot's masterpiece:

"How pretty! Japanese, isn't it? Sea-weeds seen through a fog. I went to an auction yesterday, and do you know I bought a tea-pot with a picture just like that."

Madeleine inquired with extreme interest about the auction, but after learning all that Mrs. Baker had to tell, she was on the point of being reduced to silence, when she bethought herself to mention Carrington. Mrs.

Baker brightened up at once, if she could be said to brighten where there was no sign of dimness:

"Dear Mr. Carrington! Isn't he sweet? I think he's a delicious man. I don't know what I should do without him. Since poor Mr. Baker left me, we have been together all the time. You know my poor husband left directions that all his papers should be burned, and though I would not say so unless you were such a friend of Mr. Carrington's, I reckon it's just as well for some people that he did. I never could tell you what quantities of papers Mr.

Carrington and I have put in the fire; and we read them all too."

Madeleine asked whether this was not dull work.

"Oh, dear, no! You see I know all about it, and told Mr. Carrington the story of every paper as we went on. It was quite amusing, I assure you."

Mrs. Lee then boldly said she had got from Mr. Carrington an idea that Mrs.

Baker was a very skilful diplomatist.

"Diplomatist!" echoed the widow with her genial laugh; "Well! it was as much that as anything, but there's not many diplomatists' wives in this city ever did as much work as I used to do. Why, I knew half the members of Congress intimately, and all of them by sight. I knew where they came from and what they liked best. I could get round the greater part of them, sooner or later."

Mrs. Lee asked what she did with all this knowledge. Mrs. Baker shook her pink-and-white countenance, and almost paralysed her opposite neighbour by a sort of Grande Duchesse wink:

"Oh, my dear! you are new here. If you had seen Washington in war-times and for a few years afterwards, you wouldn't ask that. We had more congressional business than all the other agents put together. Every one came to us then, to get his bill through, or his appropriation watched. We were hard at work all the time. You see, one can't keep the run of three hundred men without some trouble. My husband used to make lists of them in books with a history of each man and all he could learn about him, but I carried it all in my head."

"Do you mean that you could get them all to vote as you pleased?" asked Madeleine.

"Well! we got our bills through," replied Mrs. Baker.

"But how did you do it? did they take bribes?"

"Some of them did. Some of them liked suppers and cards and theatres and all sorts of things. Some of them could be led, and some had to be driven like Paddy's pig who thought he was going the other way. Some of them had wives who could talk to them, and some--hadn't," said Mrs. Baker, with a queer intonation in her abrupt ending.

"But surely," said Mrs. Lee, "many of them must have been above--I mean, they must have had nothing to get hold of; so that you could manage them."

Mrs. Baker laughed cheerfully and remarked that they were very much of a muchness.

"But I can't understand how you did it," urged Madeleine; "now, how would you have gone to work to get a respectable senator's vote--a man like Mr.

Ratcliffe, for instance?"

"Ratcliffe!" repeated Mrs. Baker with a slight elevation of voice that gave way to a patronising laugh. "Oh, my dear! don't mention names. I should get into trouble. Senator Ratcliffe was a good friend of my husband's. I guess Mr. Carrington could have told you that. But you see, what we generally wanted was all right enough. We had to know where our bills were, and jog people's elbows to get them reported in time. Sometimes we had to convince them that our bill was a proper one, and they ought to vote for it. Only now and then, when there was a great deal of money and the vote was close, we had to find out what votes were worth. It was mostly dining and talking, calling them out into the lobby or asking them to supper. I wish I could tell you things I have seen, but I don't dare. It wouldn't be safe. I've told you already more than I ever said to any one else; but then you are so intimate with Mr. Carrington, that I always think of you as an old friend."

Thus Mrs. Baker rippled on, while Mrs. Lee listened with more and more doubt and disgust. The woman was showy, handsome in a coarse style, and perfectly presentable. Mrs. Lee had seen Duchesses as vulgar. She knew more about the practical working of government than Mrs. Lee could ever expect or hope to know. Why then draw back from this interesting lobbyist with such babyish repulsion?

When, after a long, and, as she declared, a most charming call, Mrs. Baker wended her way elsewhere and Madeleine had given the strictest order that she should never be admitted again, Carrington entered, and Madeleine showed him Mrs. Baker's card and gave a lively account of the interview.

"What shall I do with the woman?" she asked; "must I return her card?" But Carrington declined to offer advice on this interesting point. "And she says that Mr. Ratcliffe was a friend of her husband's and that you could tell me about that."

"Did she say so?" remarked Carrington vaguely.

"Yes! and that she knew every one's weak points and could get all their votes."

Carrington expressed no surprise, and so evidently preferred to change the subject, that Mrs. Lee desisted and said no more.

But she determined to try the same experiment on Mr. Ratcliffe, and chose the very next chance that offered. In her most indifferent manner she remarked that Mrs. Sam Baker had called upon her and had initiated her into the mysteries of the lobby till she had become quite ambitious to start on that career.

"She said you were a friend of her husband's," added Madeleine softly.

Ratcliffe's face betrayed no sign.

"If you believe what those people tell you," said he drily, "you will be wiser than the Queen of Sheba."

Chapter IX

Whenever a man reaches the top of the political ladder, his enemies unite to pull him down. His friends become critical and exacting. Among the many dangers of this sort which now threatened Ratcliffe, there was one that, had he known it, might have made him more uneasy than any of those which were the work of senators and congressmen. Carrington entered into an alliance, offensive and defensive, with Sybil. It came about in this wise. Sybil was fond of riding. and occasionally, when Carrington could spare the time, he went as her guide and protector in these country excursions; for every Virginian, however out at elbows, has a horse, as he has shoes or a shirt.

In a thoughtless moment Carrington had been drawn into a promise that he would take Sybil to Arlington. The promise was one that he did not hurry to keep, for there were reasons which made a visit to Arlington anything but a pleasure to him; but Sybil would listen to no excuses, and so it came about that, one lovely March morning, when the shrubs and the trees in the square before the house were just beginning, under the warmer sun, to show signs of their coming wantonness, Sybil stood at the open window waiting for him, while her new Kentucky horse before the door showed what he thought of the delay by curving his neck, tossing his head, and pawing the pavement.

Carrington was late and kept her waiting so long, that the mignonette and geraniums, which adorned the window, suffered for his slowness, and the curtain tassels showed signs of wilful damage. Nevertheless he arrived at length, and they set out together, choosing the streets least enlivened by horse-cars and provision-carts, until they had crept through the great metropolis of Georgetown and come upon the bridge which crosses the noble river just where its bold banks open out to clasp the city of Washington in their easy embrace. Then reaching the Virginia side they cantered gaily up the laurel-margined road, with glimpses of woody defiles, each carrying its trickling stream and rich in promise of summer flowers, while from point to point they caught glorious glimpses of the distant city and river. They passed the small military station on the heights, still dignified by the name of fort, though Sybil silently wondered how a fort was possible without fortifications, and complained that there was nothing more warlike than a "nursery of telegraph poles." The day was blue and gold; everything smiled and sparkled in the crisp freshness of the morning. Sybil was in bounding spirits, and not at all pleased to find that her companion became moody and abstracted as they went on. "Poor Mr. Carrington!" thought she to herself, "he is so nice; but when he puts on that solemn air, one might as well go to sleep. I am quite certain no nice woman will ever marry him if he looks like that;" and her practical mind ran off among all the girls of her acquaintance, in search of one who would put up with Carrington's melancholy face. She knew his devotion to her sister, but had long ago rejected this as a hopeless chance. There was a simplicity about Sybil's way of dealing with life, which had its own charm. She never troubled herself about the impossible or the unthinkable. She had feelings, and was rather quick in her sympathies and sorrows, but she was equally quick in getting over them, and she expected other people to do likewise. Madeleine dissected her own feelings and was always wondering whether they were real or not; she had a habit of taking off her mental clothing, as she might take off a dress, and looking at it as though it belonged to some one else, and as though sensations were manufactured like clothes. This seems to be one of the easier ways of deadening sorrow, as though the mind could teach itself to lop off its feelers. Sybil particularly disliked this self-inspection. In the first place she did not understand it, and in the second her mind was all feelers, and amputation was death. She could no more analyse a feeling than doubt its existence, both which were habits of her sister.

How was Sybil to know what was passing in Carrington's mind? He was thinking of nothing in which she supposed herself interested. He was troubled with memories of civil war and of associations still earlier, belonging to an age already vanishing or vanished; but what could she know about civil war who had been almost an infant at the time? At this moment, she happened to be interested in the baffle of Waterloo, for she was reading "Vanity Fair," and had cried as she ought for poor little Emmy, when her husband, George Osborne, lay dead on the field there, with a bullet through his heart. But how was she to know that here, only a few rods before her, lay scores and hundreds of George Osbornes, or his betters, and in their graves the love and hope of many Emmys, not creatures of the imagination, but flesh and blood, like herself? To her, there was no more in those associations which made Carrington groan in the silence of his thoughts, than if he had been old Kaspar, and she the little Wilhelmine. What was a skull more or less to her? What concern had she in the famous victory?

Yet even Sybil was startled as she rode through the gate and found herself suddenly met by the long white ranks of head-stones, stretching up and down the hill-sides by thousands, in order of baffle; as though Cadmus had reversed his myth, and had sown living men, to come up dragons' teeth. She drew in her horse with a shiver and a sudden impulse to cry. Here was something new to her. This was war--wounds, disease, death. She dropped her voice and with a look almost as serious as Carrington's, asked what all these graves meant. When Carrington told her, she began for the first time to catch some dim notion why his face was not quite as gay as her own. Even now this idea was not very precise, for he said little about himself, but at least she grappled with the fact that he had actually, year after year, carried arms against these men who lay at her feet and who had given their lives for her cause. It suddenly occurred to her as a new thought that perhaps he himself might have killed one of them with his own hand. There was a strange shock in this idea. She felt that Carrington was further from her. He gained dignity in his rebel isolation. She wanted to ask him how he could have been a traitor, and she did not dare. Carrington a traitor!

Carrington killing her friends! The idea was too large to grasp. She fell back on the simpler task of wondering how he had looked in his rebel uniform.

They rode slowly round to the door of the house and dismounted, after he had with some difficulty found a man to hold their horses. From the heavy brick porch they looked across the superb river to the raw and incoherent ugliness of the city, idealised into dreamy beauty by the atmosphere, and the soft background of purple hills behind. Opposite them, with its crude "thus saith the law" stamped on white dome and fortress-like walls, rose the Capitol.

Carrington stood with her a short time while they looked at the view; then said he would rather not go into the house himself, and sat down on the steps while she strolled alone through the rooms. These were bare and gaunt, so that she, with her feminine sense of fitness, of course considered what she would do to make them habitable. She had a neat fancy for furniture, and distributed her tones and half tones and bits of colour freely about the walls and ceilings, with a high-backed chair here, a spindle-legged sofa there, and a claw-footed table in the centre, until her eye was caught by a very dirty deal desk, on which stood an open book, with an inkstand and some pens. On the leaf she read the last entry: "Eli M. Grow and lady, Thermopyle Centre." Not even the graves outside had brought the horrors of war so near.

What a scourge it was! This respectable family turned out of such a lovely house, and all the pretty old furniture swept away before a horde of coarse invaders "with ladies." Did the hosts of Attila write their names on visiting books in the temple of Vesta and the house of Sallust? What a new terror they would have added to the name of the scourge of God! Sybil returned to the portico and sat down by Carrington on the steps.

"How awfully sad it is!" said she; "I suppose the house was prettily furnished when the Lees lived here? Did you ever see it then?"

Sybil was not very profound, but she had sympathy, and at this moment Carrington felt sorely in need of comfort. He wanted some one to share his feelings, and he turned towards her hungry for companionship.

"The Lees were old family friends of mine," said he. "I used to stay here when I was a boy, even as late as the spring of 1861. The last time I sat here, it was with them. We were wild about disunion and talked of nothing else. I have been trying to recall what was said then. We never thought there would be war, and as for coercion, it was nonsense. Coercion, indeed!

The idea was ridiculous. I thought so, too, though I was a Union man and did not want the State to go out. But though I felt sure that Virginia must suffer, I never thought we could be beaten. Yet now I am sitting here a pardoned rebel, and the poor Lees are driven away and their place is a grave-yard."

Sybil became at once absorbed in the Lees and asked many questions, all which Carrington gladly answered. He told her how he had admired and followed General Lee through the war. "We thought he was to be our Washington, you know; and perhaps he had some such idea himself;" and then, when Sybil wanted to hear about the baffles and the fighting, he drew a rough map on the gravel path to show her how the two lines had run, only a few miles away; then he told her how he had carried his musket day after day over all this country, and where he had seen his battles. Sybil had everything to learn; the story came to her with all the animation of real life, for here under her eyes were the graves of her own champions, and by her side was a rebel who had stood under our fire at Malvern Hill and at South Mountain, and who was telling her how men looked and what they thought in face of death. She listened with breathless interest, and at last summoned courage to ask in an awestruck tone whether Carrington had ever killed any one himself. She was relieved, although a little disappointed, when he said that he believed not; he hoped not; though no private who has discharged a musket in baffle can be quite sure where the bullet went. "I never tried to kill any one," said he, "though they tried to kill me incessantly." Then Sybil begged to know how they had tried to kill him, and he told her one or two of those experiences, such as most soldiers have had, when he had been fired upon and the balls had torn his clothes or drawn blood. Poor Sybil was quite overcome, and found a deadly fascination in the horror. As they sat together on the steps with the glorious view spread before them, her attention was so closely fixed on his story that she saw neither the view nor even the carriages of tourists who drove up, looked about, and departed, envying Carrington his occupation with the lovely girl.

She was in imagination rushing with him down the valley of Virginia on the heels of our flying army, or gloomily toiling back to the Potomac after the bloody days at Gettysburg, or watching the last grand debâcle on the road from Richmond to Appomattox. They would have sat there till sunset if Carrington had not at length insisted that they must go, and then she rose slowly with a deep sigh and undisguised regret.

As they rode away, Carrington, whose thoughts were not devoted to his companion so entirely as they should have been, ventured to say that he wished her sister had come with them, but he found that his hint was not well received.

Sybil emphatically rejected the idea: "I'm very glad she didn't come. If she had, you would have talked with her all the time, and I should have been left to amuse myself. You would have been discussing things, and I hate discussions. She would have been hunting for first principles, and you would have been running about, trying to catch some for her. Besides, she is coming herself some Sunday with that tiresome Mr. Ratcliffe. I don't see what she finds in that man to amuse her. Her taste is getting to be demoralised in Washington. Do you know, Mr. Carrington, I'm not clever or serious, like Madeleine, and I can't read laws, and hate politics, but I've more common sense than she has, and she makes me cross with her. I understand now why young widows are dangerous, and why they're burned at their husband's funerals in India. Not that I want to have Madeleine burned, for she's a dear, good creature, and I love her better than anything in the world; but she will certainly do herself some dreadful mischief one of these days; she has the most extravagant notions about self-sacrifice and duty; if she hadn't luckily thought of taking charge of me, she would have done some awful thing long ago, and if I could only be a little wicked, she would be quite happy all the rest of her life in reforming me; but now she has got hold of that Mr. Ratcliffe, and he is trying to make her think she can reform him, and if he does, it's all up with us. Madeleine will just go and break her heart over that odious, great, coarse brute, who only wants her money."

Sybil delivered this little oration with a degree of energy that went to Carrington's heart. She did not often make such sustained efforts, and it was clear that on this subject she had exhausted her whole mind. Carrington was delighted, and urged her on. "I dislike Mr. Ratcliffe as much as you do;--more perhaps. So does every one who knows much about him. But we shall only make the matter worse if we interfere. What can we do?"

"That is just what I tell everybody," resumed Sybil. "There is Victoria Dare always telling me I ought to do something; and Mr. Schneidekoupon too; just as though I could do anything. Madeleine has done nothing but get into mischief here. Half the people think her worldly and ambitious. Only last night that spiteful old woman, Mrs. Clinton, said to me: 'Your sister is quite spoiled by Washington. She is more wild for power than any human being I ever saw.' I was dreadfully angry and told her she was quite mistaken--Madeleine was not the least spoiled. But I couldn't say that she was not fond of power, for she is; but not in the way Mrs. Clinton meant.

You should have seen her the other evening when Mr. Ratcliffe said about some matter of public business that he would do whatever she thought right; she spoke up quite sharply for her, with a scornful little laugh, and said that he had better do what he thought right. He looked for a moment almost angry, and muttered something about women's being incomprehensible. He is always trying to tempt her with power. She might have had long ago all the power he could give her, but I can see, and he sees too, that she always keeps him at arm's length. He doesn't like it, but he expects one of these days to find a bribe that will answer. I wish we had never come to Washington. New York is so much nicer and the people there are much more amusing; they dance ever so much better and send one flowers all the time, and then they never talk about first principles. Maude had her hospitals and paupers and training school, and got along very well. It was so safe. But when I say so to her, she only smiles in a patronising kind of way, and tells me that I shall have as much of Newport as I want; just as though I were a child, and not a woman of twenty-five. Poor Maude! I can't stay with her if she marries Mr. Ratcliffe, and it would break my heart to leave her with that man. Do you think he would beat her? Does he drink? I would almost rather be beaten a little, if I cared for a man, than be taken out to Peonia. Oh, Mr. Carrington! you are our only hope. She will listen to you.

Don't let her marry that dreadful politician."

To all this pathetic appeal, some parts of which were as liffle calculated to please Carrington as Ratcliffe himself, Carrington answered that he was ready to do all in his power but that Sybil must tell him when and how to act.

"Then, it's a bargain," said she; "whenever I want you, I shall call on you for help, and you shall prevent the marriage."

"Alliance offensive and defensive," said he, laughing; "war to the knife on Ratcliffe. We will have his scalp if necessary, but I rather think he will soon commit hari-kari himself if we leave him alone."

"Madeleine will like him all the better if he does anything Japanese,"

replied Sybil, with great seriousness; "I wish there was more Japanese bric-à-brac here, or any kind of old pots and pans to talk about. A little art would be good for her. What a strange place this is, and how people do stand on their heads in it! Nobody thinks like anyone else. Victoria Dare says she is trying on principle not to be good, because she wants to keep some new excitements for the next world. I'm sure she practices as she preaches. Did you see her at Mrs. Clinton's last night. She behaved more outrageously than ever. She sat on the stairs all through supper, looking like a demure yellow cat with two bouquets in her paws--and I know Lord Dunbeg sent one of them;--and she actually let Mr. French feed her with ice-cream from a spoon. She says she was showing Lord Dunbeg a phase, and that he is going to put it into his article on American Manners and Customs in the Quarterly, but I don't think it's nice, do you, Mr. Carrington? I wish Madeleine had her to take care of. She would have enough to do then, I can tell her."

And so, gently prattling, Miss Sybil returned to the city, her alliance with Carrington completed; and it was a singular fact that she never again called him dull. There was henceforward a look of more positive pleasure and cordiality on her face when he made his appearance wherever she might be; and the next time he suggested a horseback excursion she instantly agreed to go, although aware that she had promised a younger gentleman of the diplomatic body to be at home that same afternoon, and the good fellow swore polyglot oaths on being turned away from her door.

Mr. Ratcliffe knew nothing of this conspiracy against his peace and prospects. Even if he had known it, he might only have laughed, and pursued his own path without a second thought. Yet it was certain that he did not think Carrington's enmity a thing to be overlooked, and from the moment of his obtaining a clue to its cause, he had begun to take precautions against it. Even in the middle of the contest for the Treasury, he had found time to listen to Mr. Wilson Keens report on the affairs of the late Samuel Baker.

Mr. Keen came to him with a copy of Baker's will and with memoranda of remarks made by the unsuspecting Mrs. Baker; "from which it appears," said he, "that Baker, having no time to put his affairs in order, left special directions that his executors should carefully destroy all papers that might be likely to compromise individuals."

"What is the executor's name?" interrupted Ratcliffe.

"The executor's name is--John Carrington," said Keen, methodically referring to his copy of the will.

Ratcliffe's face was impassive, but the inevitable, "I knew it," almost sprang to his lips. He was rather pleased at the instinct which had led him so directly to the right trail.

Keen went on to say that from Mrs. Baker's conversation it was certain that the testator's directions had been carried out, and that the great bulk of these papers had been burned.

"Then it will be useless to press the inquiry further," said Ratcliffe; "I am much obliged to you for your assistance," and he turned the conversation to the condition of Mr. Keen's bureau in the Treasury department.

The next time Ratcliffe saw Mrs. Lee, after his appointment to the Treasury was confirmed, he asked her whether she did not think Carrington very well suited for public service, and when she warmly assented, he said it had occurred to him to offer the place of Solicitor of the Treasury to Mr.

Carrington, for although the actual salary might not be very much more than he earned by his private practice, the incidental advantages to a Washington lawyer were considerable; and to the Secretary it was especially necessary to have a solicitor in whom he could place entire confidence. Mrs. Lee was pleased by this motion of Ratcliffe's, the more because she had supposed that Ratcliffe had no liking for Carrington. She doubted whether Carrington would accept the place, but she hoped that it might modify his dislike for Ratcliffe, and she agreed to sound him on the subject. There was something a little compromising in thus allowing herself to appear as the dispenser of Mr. Ratcliffe's patronage, but she dismissed this objection on the ground that Carrington's interests were involved, and that it was for him to judge whether he should take the place or not. Perhaps the world would not be so charitable if the appointment were made. What then? Mrs. Lee asked herself the question and did not feel quite at ease.

So far as Carrington was concerned, she might have dismissed her doubts.

There was not a chance of his taking the place, as very soon appeared. When she spoke to him on the subject, and repeated what Ratcliffe had said, his face flushed, and he sat for some moments in silence. He never thought very rapidly, but now the ideas seemed to come so fast as to bewilder his mind.

The situation flashed before his eyes like electric sparks. His first impression was that Ratcliffe wanted to buy him; to tie his tongue; to make him run, like a fastened dog, under the waggon of the Secretary of the Treasury. His second notion was that Ratcliffe wanted to put Mrs. Lee under obligations, in order to win her regard; and, again, that he wanted to raise himself in her esteem by posing as a friend of honest administration and unassisted virtue. Then suddenly it occurred to him that the scheme was to make him appear jealous and vindictive; to put him in an attitude where any reason he might give for declining would bear a look of meanness, and tend to separate him from Mrs. Lee. Carrington was so absorbed by these thoughts, and his mind worked so slowly, that he failed to hear one or two remarks addressed to him by Mrs. Lee, who became a little alarmed, under the impression that he was unexpectedly paralyzed.

When at length he heard her and attempted to frame an answer, his embarrassment increased. He could only stammer that he was sorry to be obliged to decline, but this office was one he could not undertake.

If Madeleine felt a little relieved by this decision, she did not show it.

From her manner one might have supposed it to be her fondest wish that Carrington should be

Solicitor of the Treasury. She cross-questioned him with obstinacy. Was not the offer a good one? --and he was obliged to confess that it was. Were the duties such as he could not perform? Not at all! there was nothing in the duties which alarmed him. Did he object to it because of his southern prejudices against the administration? Oh, no! he had no political feeling to stand in his way. What, then, could be his reason for refusing?

Carrington resorted again to silence, until Mrs. Lee, a little impatiently, asked whether it was possible that his personal dislike to Racliffe could blind him so far as to make him reject so fair a proposal. Carrington, finding himself more and more uncomfortable, rose restlessly from his chair and paced the room. He felt that Ratclife had fairly out-generaled him, and he was at his wits' end to know what card he could play that would not lead directly into Ratcliffe's trump suit. To refuse such an offer was hard enough at best, for a man who wanted money and professional advancement as he did, but to injure himself and help Ratcliffe by this refusal, was abominably hard. Nevertheless, he was obliged to admit that he would rather not take a position so directly under Ratcliffe's control. Madeleine said no more, but he thought she looked annoyed, and he felt himself in an intolerably painful situation. He was not certain that she herself might not have had some share in proposing the plan, and that his refusal might not have some mortifying consequences for her. What must she think of him, then?

At this very moment he would have given his right arm for a word of real affection from Mrs. Lee. He adored her. He would willingly enough have damned himself for her. There was no sacrifice he would not have made to bring her nearer to him. In his upright, quiet, simple kind of way, he immolated himself before her. For months his heart had ached with this hopeless passion. He recognized that it was hopeless. He knew that she would never love him, and, to do her justice, she never had given him reason to suppose that it was in her power to love him, r any man. And here he stood, obliged to appear ungrateful and prejudiced, mean and vindictive, in her eyes. He took his seat again, looking so unutterably dejected, his patient face so tragically mournful, that Madeleine, after a while, began to see the absurd side of the matter, and presently burst into a laugh "Please do not look so frightfully miserable!" said she; "I did not mean to make you unhappy. After all, what does it matter? You have a perfect right to refuse, and, for my part, I have not the least wish to see you accept."

On this, Carrington brightened, and declared that if she thought him right in declining, he cared for nothing else. It was only the idea of hurting her feelings that weighed on his mind. But in saying this, he spoke in a tone that implied a deeper feeling, and made Mrs. Lee again look grave and sigh.

"Ah, Mr. Carrington," she said, "this world will not run as we want. Do you suppose the time will ever come when every one will be good and happy and do just what they ought? I thought this offer might possibly take one anxiety off your shoulders. I am sorry now that I let myself be led into making it."

Carrington could not answer her. He dared not trust his voice. He rose to go, and as she held out her hand, he suddenly raised it to his lips, and so left her. She sat for a moment with tears in her eyes after he was gone. She thought she knew all that was in his mind, and with a woman's readiness to explain every act of men by their consuming passions for her own sex, she took it as a matter of course that jealousy was the whole cause of Carrington's hostility to Ratcliffe, and she pardoned it with charming alacrity. "Ten years ago, I could have loved him," she thought to herself, and then, while she was half smiling at the idea, suddenly another thought flashed upon her, and she threw her hand up before her face as though some one had struck her a blow. Carrington had reopened the old wound.

When Ratcliffe came to see her again, which he did very shortly afterwards, glad of so good an excuse, she told him of Carrington's refusal, adding only that he seemed unwilling to accept any position that had a political character. Ratcliffe showed no sign of displeasure; he only said, in a benignant tone, that he was sorry to be unable to do something for so good a friend of hers; thus establishing, at all events, his claim on her gratitude. As for Carrington, the offer which Ratcliffe had made was not intended to be accepted, and Carrington could not have more embarrassed the secretary than by closing with it. Ratcliffe's object had been to settle for his own satisfaction the question of Carrington's hostility, for he knew the man well enough to feel sure that in any event he would act a perfectly straightforward part. If he accepted, he would at least be true to his chief. If he refused, as Ratcliffe expected, it would be a proof that some means must be found of getting him out of the way. In any case the offer was a new thread in the net that Mr. Ratcliffe flattered himself he was rapidly winding about the affections and ambitions of Mrs. Lee. Yet he had reasons of his own for thinking that Carrington, more easily than any other man, could cut the meshes of this net if he chose to do so, and therefore that it would be wiser to postpone action until Carrington were disposed of.

Without a moment's delay he made inquiries as to all the vacant or eligible offices in the gift of the government outside his own department. Very few of these would answer his purpose. He wanted some temporary law business that would for a time take its holder away to a distance, say to Australia or Central Asia, the further the better; it must be highly paid, and it must be given in such a way as not to excite suspicion that Ratcliffe was concerned in the matter. Such an office was not easily found. There is little law business in Central Asia, and at this moment there was not enough to require a special agent in Australia. Carrington could hardly be induced to lead an expedition to the sources of the Nile in search of business merely to please Mr. Ratcliffe, nor could the State Department offer encouragement to a hope that government would pay the expenses of such an expedition. The best that Ratcliffe could do was to select the place of counsel to the Mexican claims-commission which was soon to meet in the city of Mexico, and which would require about six months' absence. By a little management he could contrive to get the counsel sent away in advance of the commission, in order to work up a part of the case on the spot. Ratcliffe acknowledged that Mexico was too near, but he drily remarked to himself that if Carrington could get back in time to dislodge him after he had once got a firm hold on Mrs. Lee, he would never try to run another caucus.

The point once settled in his own mind, Ratcliffe, with his usual rapidity of action, carried his scheme into effect. In this there was little difficulty. He dropped in at the office of the Secretary of State within eight-and-forty hours after his last conversation with Mrs. Lee. During these early days of every new administration, the absorbing business of government relates principally to appointments. The Secretary of the Treasury was always ready to oblige his colleagues in the Cabinet by taking care of their friends to any reasonable extent. The Secretary of State was not less courteous. The moment he understood that Mr. Ratcliffe had a strong wish to secure the appointment of a certain person as counsel to the Mexican claims-commission, the Secretary of State professed readiness to gratify him, and when he heard who the proposed person was, the suggestion was hailed with pleasure, for Carrington was well known and much liked at the Department, and was indeed an excellent man for the place. Ratcliffe hardly needed to promise an equivalent. The business was arranged in ten minutes.

"I only need say," added Ratcliffe, "that if my agency in the affair is known, Mr. Carrington will certainly refuse the place, for he is one of your old-fashioned Virginia planters, proud as Lucifer, and willing to accept nothing by way of favour. I will speak to your Assistant Secretary about it, and the recommendation shall appear to come from him."

The very next day Carrington received a private note from his old friend, the Assistant Secretary of State, who was overjoyed to do him a kindness.

The note asked him to call at the Department at his earliest convenience. He went, and the Assistant Secretary announced that he had recommended Carrington's appointment as counsel to the Mexican claims-commission, and that the Secretary had approved the recommendation. "We want a Southern man, a lawyer with a little knowledge of international law, one who can go at once, and, above all, an honest man. You fit the description to a hair; so pack your trunk as soon as you like."

Carrington was startled. Coming as it did, this offer was not only unobjectionable, but tempting. It was hard for him even to imagine a reason for hesitation. From the first he felt that he must go, and yet to go was the very last thing he wanted to do. That he should suspect Ratcliffe to be at the bottom of this scheme of banishment was a matter of course, and he instantly asked whether any influence had been used in his favour; but the Assistant Secretary so stoutly averred that the appointment was made on his recommendation alone, as to block all further inquiry. Technically this assertion was exact, and it made Carrington feel that it would be base ingratitude on his part not to accept a favour so handsomely offered.

Yet he could not make up his mind to acceptance. He begged four and twenty hours' delay, in order, as he said, to see whether he could arrange his affairs for a six months' absence, although he knew there would be no difficulty in his doing so. He went away and sat in his office alone, gloomily wondering what he could do, although from the first he saw that the situation was only too clear, and there could not be the least dark corner of a doubt to crawl into. Six months ago he would have jumped at this offer.

What had happened within six months to make it seem a disaster?

Mrs. Lee! There was the whole story. To go away now was to give up Mrs. Lee, and probably to give her up to Ratcliffe. Carrington gnashed his teeth when he thought how skilfully Ratcliffe was playing his cards. The longer he reflected, the more certain he felt that Ratcliffe was at the bottom of this scheme to get rid of him; and yet, as he studied the situation, it occurred to him that after all it was possible for Ratcliffe to make a blunder. This Illinois politician was clever, and understood men; but a knowledge of men is a very different thing from a knowledge of women. Carrington himself had no great experience in the article of women, but he thought he knew more than Ratcliffe, who was evidently relying most on his usual theory of political corruption as applied to feminine weaknesses, and who was only puzzled at finding how high a price Mrs. Lee set on herself. If Ratcliffe were really at the bottom of the scheme for separating

Carrington from her, it could only be because he thought that six months, or even six weeks, would be enough to answer his purpose. And on reaching this point in his reflections, Carrington suddenly rose, lit a cigar, and walked up and down his room steadily for the next hour, with the air of a general arranging a plan of campaign, or a lawyer anticipating his opponent's line of argument.

On one point his mind was made up. He would accept. If Ratcliffe really had a hand in this move, he should be gratified. If he had laid a trap, he should be caught in it. And when the evening came, Carrington took his hat and walked off to call upon Mrs. Lee.

He found the sisters alone and quietly engaged in their occupations.

Madeleine was dramatically mending an open-work silk stocking, a delicate and difficult task which required her whole mind. Sybil was at the piano as usual, and for the first time since he had known her, she rose when he came in, and, taking her work-basket, sat down to share in the conversation. She meant to take her place as a woman, henceforward. She was tired of playing girl. Mr. Carrington should see that she was not a fool.

Carrington plunged at once into his subject, and announced the offer made to him, at which Madeleine expressed delight, and asked many questions. What was the pay? How soon must he go? How long should he be away? Was there danger from the climate? and finally she added, with a smile, "What am I to say to Mr. Ratcliffe if you accept this offer after refusing his?" As for Sybil, she made one reproachful exclamation: "Oh, Mr. Carrington!" and sank back into silence and consternation. Her first experiment at taking a stand of her own in the world was not encouraging. She felt betrayed.

Nor was Carrington gay. However modest a man may be, only an idiot can forget himself entirely in pursuing the moon and the stars. In the bottom of his soul, he had a lingering hope that when he told his story, Madeleine might look up with a change of expression, a glance of unpremeditated regard, a little suffusion of the eyes, a little trembling of the voice. To see himself relegated to Mexico with such cheerful alacrity by the woman he loved was not the experience he would have chosen. He could not help feeling that his hopes were disposed of, and he watched her with a painful sinking of the heart, which did not lead to lightness of conversation. Madeleine herself felt that her expressions needed to be qualified, and she tried to correct her mistake. What should she do without a tutor? she said. He must let her have a list of books to read while he was away; they were themselves going north in the middle of May, and Carrington would be back by the time they returned in December. After all, they should see as little of him during the summer if he were in Virginia as if he were in Mexico.

Carrington gloomily confessed that he was very unwilling to go; that he wished the idea had never been suggested; that he should be perfectly happy if for any reason the scheme broke down; but he gave no explanation of his feeling, and Madeleine had too much tact to press for one. She contented herself by arguing against it, and talking as vivaciously as she could. Her heart really bled for him as she saw his face grow more and more pathetic in its quiet expression of disappointment. But what could she say or do? He sat till after ten o'clock; he could not tear himself away. He felt that this was the end of his pleasure in life; he dreaded the solitude of his thoughts. Mrs. Lee's resources began to show signs of exhaustion. Long pauses intervened between her remarks; and at length Carrington, with a superhuman effort, apologized for inflicting himself upon her so unmercifully. If she knew, he said, how he dreaded being alone, she would forgive him. Then he rose to go, and, in taking leave, asked Sybil if she was inclined to ride the next day; if so, he was at her service. Sybil's face brightened as she accepted the invitation.

Mrs. Lee, a day or two afterwards, did mention Carrington's appointment to Mr. Ratcliffe, and she told Carrington that the Secretary certainly looked hurt and mortified, but showed it only by almost instantly changing the subject.

Chapter X

The next morning Carrington called at the Department and announced his acceptance of the post. He was told that his instructions would be ready in about a fortnight, and that he would be expected to start as soon as he received them; in the meanwhile, he must devote himself to the study of a mass of papers in the Department. There was no trifling allowable here.

Carrington had to set himself vigorously to work. This did not, however, prevent him from keeping his appointment with Sybil, and at four o'clock they started together, passing out into the quiet shadows of Rock Creek, and seeking still lanes through the woods where their horses walked side by side, and they themselves could talk without the risk of criticism from curious eyes. It was the afternoon of one of those sultry and lowering spring days when life germinates rapidly, but as yet gives no sign, except perhaps some new leaf or flower pushing its soft head up against the dead leaves that have sheltered it. The two riders had something of the same sensation, as though the leafless woods and the laurel thickets, the warm, moist air and the low clouds, were a protection and a soft shelter. Somewhat to Carrington's surprise, he found that it was pleasant to have Sybil's company. He felt towards her as to a sister--a favourite sister.

She at once attacked him for abandoning her and breaking his treaty so lately made, and he tried to gain her sympathy by saying that if she knew how much he was troubled, she would forgive him. Then when Sybil asked whether he really must go and leave her without any friend whom she could speak to, his feelings got the better of him: he could not resist the temptation to confide all his troubles in her, since there was no one else in whom he could confide. He told her plainly that he was in love with her sister.

"You say that love is nonsense, Miss Ross. I tell you it is no such thing.

For weeks and months it is a steady physical pain, an ache about the heart, never leaving one, by night or by day; a long strain on one's nerves like toothache or rheumatism, not intolerable at any one instant, but exhausting by its steady drain on the strength. It is a disease to be borne with patience, like any other nervous complaint, and to be treated with counter-irritants. My trip to Mexico will be good for it, but that is not the reason why I must go."

Then he told her all his private circumstances; the ruin which the war had brought on him and his family; how, of his two brothers, one had survived the war only to die at home, a mere wreck of disease, privation, and wounds; the other had been shot by his side, and bled slowly to death in his arms during the awful carnage in the Wilderness; how his mother and two sisters were struggling for a bare subsistence on a wretched Virginian farm, and how all his exertions barely kept them from beggary.

"You have no conception of the poverty to which our southern women are reduced since the war," said he; "they are many of them literally without clothes or bread." The fee he should earn by going to Mexico would double his income this year. Could he refuse? Had he a right to refuse? And poor Carrington added, with a groan, that if he alone were in question, he would sooner be shot than go.

Sybil listened with tears in her eyes. She never before had seen a man show suffering. The misery she had known in life had been more or less veiled to her and softened by falling on older and friendly shoulders. She now got for the first time a clear view of Carrington, apart from the quiet exterior in which the man was hidden. She felt quite sure, by a sudden flash of feminine inspiration, that the curious look of patient endurance on his face was the work of a single night when he had held his brother in his arms, and knew that the blood was draining drop by drop from his side, in the dense, tangled woods, beyond the reach of help, hour after hour, till the voice failed and the limbs grew stiff and cold. When he had finished his story, she was afraid to speak. She did not know how to show her sympathy, and she could not bear to seem unsympathetic. In her embarrassment she fairly broke down and could only dry her eyes in silence.

Having once got this weight of confidence off his mind, Carrington felt comparatively gay and was ready to make the best of things. He laughed at himself to drive away the tears of his pretty companion, and obliged her to take a solemn pledge never to betray him. "Of course your sister knows it all," he said; "but she must never know that I told you, and I never would tell any one but you."

Sybil promised faithfully to keep his confidence to herself, and she went on to defend her sister.

"You must not blame Madeleine," said she; "if you knew as well as I do what she has been through, you would not think her cold. You do know how suddenly her husband died, after only one day's illness, and what a nice fellow he was. She was very fond of him, and his death seemed to stun her. We hardly knew what to make of it, she was so quiet and natural. Then just a week later her little child died of diphtheria, suffering horribly, and she wild with despair because she could not relieve it. After that, she was almost insane; indeed, I have always thought she was quite insane for a time. I know she was excessively violent and wanted to kill herself, and I never heard any one rave as she did about religion and resignation and God. After a few weeks she became quiet and stupid and went about like a machine; and at last she got over it, but has never been what she was before. You know she was a rather fast New York girl before she married, and cared no more about politics and philanthropy than I do. It was a very late thing, all this stuff. But she is not really hard, though she may seem so. It is all on the surface. I always know when she is thinking about her husband or child, because her face gets rigid; she looks then as she used to look after her child died, as though she didn't care what became of her and she would just as lieve kill herself as not. I don't think she will ever let herself love any one again. She has a horror of it. She is much more likely to go in for ambition, or duty, or self-sacrifice."

They rode on for a while in silence, Carrington perplexed by the problem how two harmless people such as Madeleine and he could have been made by a beneficent Providence the sport of such cruel tortures; and Sybil equally interested in thinking what sort of a brother-in-law Carrington would make; on the whole, she thought she liked him better as he was. The silence was only broken by Carrington's bringing the conversation back to its starting-point: "Something must be done to keep your sister out of Ratcliffe's power. I have thought about it till I am tired. Can you make no suggestion?"

No! Sybil was helpless and dreadfully alarmed. Mr. Ratcliffe came to the house as often as he could, and seemed to tell Madeleine everything that was going on in politics, and ask her advice, and Madeleine did not discourage him. "I do believe she likes it, and thinks she can do some good by it. I don't dare speak to her about it. She thinks me a child still, and treats me as though I were fifteen. What can I do?"

Carrington said he had thought of speaking to Mrs. Lee himself, but he did not know what to say, and if he offended her, he might drive her directly into Ratcliffe's arms. But Sybil thought she would not be offended if he went to work in the right way. "She will stand more from you than from any one else. Tell her openly that you--that you love her," said Sybil with a burst of desperate courage; "she can't take offence at that; and then you can say almost anything."

Carrington looked at Sybil with more admiration than he had ever expected to feel for her, and began to think that he might do worse than to put himself under her orders. After all, she had some practical sense, and what was more to the point, she was handsomer than ever, as she sat erect on her horse, the rich colour rushing up under the warm skin, at the impropriety of her speech. "You are certainly right," said he; "after all, I have nothing to lose. Whether she marries Ratcliffe or not, she will never marry me, I suppose."

This speech was a cowardly attempt to beg encouragement from Sybil, and met with the fate it deserved, for Sybil, highly flattered at Carrington's implied praise, and bold as a lioness now that it was Carrington's fingers, and not her own, that were to go into the fire, gave him on the spot a feminine view of the situation that did not encourage his hopes. She plainly said that men seemed to take leave of their senses as soon as women were concerned; for her part, she could not understand what there was in any woman to make such a fuss about; she thought most women were horrid; men were ever so much nicer; "and as for Madeleine, whom all of you are ready to cut each other's throats about, she's a dear, good sister, as good as gold, and I love her with all my heart, but you wouldn't like her, any of you, if you married her; she has always had her own way, and she could not help taking it; she never could learn to take yours; both of you would be unhappy in a week; and as for that old Mr. Ratcliffe, she would make his life a burden--and I hope she will," concluded Sybil with a spiteful little explosion of hatred.

Carrington could not help being amused by Sybil's way of dealing with affairs of the heart. Emboldened by encouragement, she went on to attack him pitilessly for going down on his knees before her sister, "just as though you were not as good as she is," and openly avowed that, if she were a man, she would at least have some pride. Men like this kind of punishment.

Carrington did not attempt to defend himself; he even courted Sybil's attack. They both enjoyed their ride through the bare woods, by the rippling spring streams, under the languid breath of the moist south wind. It was a small idyll, all the more pleasant because there was gloom before and behind it. Sybil's irrepressible gaiety made Carrington doubt whether, after all, life need be so serious a matter. She had animal spirits in plenty, and it needed an effort for her to keep them down, while Carrington's spirits were nearly exhausted after twenty years of strain, and he required a greater effort to hold himself up. There was every reason why he should be grateful to Sybil for lending to him from her superfluity. He enjoyed being laughed at by her. Suppose Madeleine Lee did refuse to marry him! What of it?

"Pooh!" said Sybil; "you men are all just alike. How can you be so silly?

Madeleine and you would be intolerable together. Do find some one who won't be solemn!"

They laid out their little plot against Madeleine and elaborated it carefully, both as to what Carrington should say and how he should say it, for Sybil asserted that men were too stupid to be trusted even in making a declaration of love, and must be taught, like little children to say their prayers. Carrington enjoyed being taught how to make a declaration of love.

He did not ask where Sybil had learned so much about men's stupidity. He thought perhaps Schneidekoupon could have thrown light on the subject. At all events, they were so busily occupied with their schemes and lessons, that they did-not-reach home till Madeleine had become anxious lest they had met with some accident. The long dusk had become darkness before she heard the clatter of hoofs on the asphalt pavement, and she went down to the door to scold them for their delay. Sybil only laughed at her, and said it was all Mr. Carrington's fault: he had lost his way, and she had been forced to find it for him.

Ten days more passed before their plan was carried into effect. April had come. Carrington's work was completed and he was ready to start on his journey. Then at last he appeared one evening at Mrs. Lee's at the very moment when Sybil, as chance would have it, was going out to pass an hour or two with her friend Victoria Dare a few doors away. Carrington felt a little ashamed as she went. This kind of conspiracy behind Mrs. Lee's back was not to his taste.

He resolutely sat down, and plunged at once into his subject. He was almost ready to go, he said; he had nearly completed his work in the Department, and he was assured that his instructions and papers would be ready in two days more; he might not have another chance to see Mrs. Lee so quietly again, and he wanted to take his leave now, for this was what lay most heavily on his mind; he should have gone willingly and gladly if it had not been for uneasiness about her; and yet he had till now been afraid to speak openly on the subject. Here he paused for a moment as though to invite some reply.

Madeleine laid down her work with a look of regret though not of annoyance, and said frankly and instantly that he had been too good a friend to allow of her taking offence at anything he could say; she would not pretend to misunderstand him. "My affairs," she added with a shade of bitterness, "seem to have become public property, and I would rather have some voice in discussing them myself than to know they are discussed behind my back."

This was a sharp thrust at the very outset, but Carrington turned it aside and went quietly on:

"You are frank and loyal, as you always are. I will be so too. I can't help being so. For months I have had no other pleasure than in being near you.

For the first time in my life I have known what it is to forget my own affairs in loving a woman who seems to me without a fault, and for one solitary word from whom I would give all I have in life, and perhaps itself."

Madeleine flushed and bent towards him with an earnestness of manner that repeated itself in her tone.

"Mr. Carrington, I am the best friend you have on earth. One of these days you will thank me with your whole soul for refusing to listen to you now.

You do not know how much misery I am saving you. I have no heart to give.

You want a young, fresh life to help yours; a gay, lively temperament to enliven your despondency; some one still young enough to absorb herself in you and make all her existence yours. I could not do it. I can give you nothing. I have done my best to persuade myself that some day I might begin life again with the old hopes and feelings, but it is no use. The fire is burned out. If you married me, you would destroy yourself You would wake up some day, and find the universe dust and ashes."

Carrington listened in silence. He made no attempt to interrupt or to contradict her. Only at the end he said with a little bitterness: "My own life is worth so much to the world and to me, that I suppose it would be wrong to risk it on such a venture; but I would risk it, nevertheless, if you gave me the chance. Do you think me wicked for tempting Providence? I do not mean to annoy you with entreaties. I have a little pride left, and a great deal of respect for you. Yet I think, in spite of all you have said or can say, that one disappointed life may be as able to find happiness and repose in another, as to get them by sucking the young life-blood of a fresh soul."

To this speech, which was unusually figurative for Carrington, Mrs. Lee could find no ready answer. She could only reply that Carrington's life was worth quite as much as his neighbour's, and that it was worth so much to her, if not to himself, that she would not let him wreck it.

Carrington went on: "Forgive my talking in this way. I do not mean to complain. I shall always love you just as much, whether you care for me or not, because you are the only woman I have ever met, or am ever likely to meet, who seems to me perfect."

If this was Sybil's teaching, she had made the best of her time.

Carrington's tone and words pierced through all Mrs. Lee's armour as though they were pointed with the most ingenious cruelty, and designed to torture her. She felt hard and small before him. Life for life, his had been, and was now, far less bright than hers, yet he was her superior. He sat there, a true man, carrying his burden calmly, quietly, without complaint, ready to face the next shock of life with the same endurance he had shown against the rest. And he thought her perfect! She felt humiliated that any brave man should say to her face that he thought her perfect! She! perfect! In her contrition she was half ready to go down at his feet and confess her sins; her hysterical dread of sorrow and suffering, her narrow sympathies, her feeble faith, her miserable selfishness, her abject cowardice. Every nerve in her body tingled with shame when she thought what a miserable fraud she was; what a mass of pretensions unfounded, of deceit ingrained. She was ready to hide her face in her hands. She was disgusted, outraged with her own image as she saw it, contrasted with Carrington's single word: Perfect!

Nor was this the worst. Carrington was not the first man who had thought her perfect. To hear this word suddenly used again, which had never been uttered to her before except by lips now dead and gone, made her brain reel. She seemed to hear her husband once more telling her that she was perfect. Yet against this torture, she had a better defence. She had long since hardened herself to bear these recollections, and they steadied and strengthened her.

She had been called perfect before now, and what had come of it? Two graves, and a broken life! She drew herself up with a face now grown quite pale and rigid. In reply to Carrington, she said not a word, but only shook her head slightly without looking at him.

He went on: "After all, it is not my own happiness I am thinking of but yours. I never was vain enough to think that I was worth your love, or that I could ever win it. Your happiness is another thing. I care so much for that as to make me dread going away, for fear that you may yet find yourself entangled in this wretched political life here, when, perhaps if I stayed, I might be of some use."

"Do you really think, then, that I am going to fall a victim to Mr.

Ratcliffe?" asked Madeleine, with a cold smile.

"Why not?" replied Carrington, in a similar tone. "He can put forward a strong claim to your sympathy and help, if not to your love. He can offer you a great field of usefulness which you want. He has been very faithful to you. Are you quite sure that even now you can refuse him without his complaining that you have trifled with him?"

"And are you quite sure," added Mrs. Lee, evasively, "that you have not been judging him much too harshly? I think I know him better than you. He has many good qualities, and some high ones. What harm can he do me? Supposing even that he did succeed in persuading me that my life could be best used in helping his, why should I be afraid of it?"

"You and I," said Carrington, "are wide apart in our estimates of Mr.

Ratcliffe. To you, of course, he shows his best side. He is on his good behaviour, and knows that any false step will ruin him. I see in him only a coarse, selfish, unprincipled politician, who would either drag you down to his own level, or, what is more likely, would very soon disgust you and make your life a wretched self-immolation before his vulgar ambition, or compel you to leave him. In either case you would be the victim. You cannot afford to make another false start in life. Reject me! I have not a word to say against it. But be on your guard against giving your existence up to him."

"Why do you think so ill of Mr. Ratcliffe?" asked Madeleine; "he always speaks highly of you. Do you know anything against him that the world does not?"

"His public acts are enough to satisfy me," replied Carrington, evading a part of the question. "You know that I have never had but one opinion about him."

There was a pause in the conversation. Both parties felt that as yet no good had come of it. At length Madeleine asked, "What would you have me do? Is it a pledge you want that I will under no circumstances marry Mr. Ratcliffe?"

"Certainly not," was the answer; "you know me better than to think I would ask that. I only want you to take time and keep out of his influence until your mind is fairly made up. A year hence I feel certain that you will think of him as I do."

"Then you will allow me to marry him if I find that you are mistaken," said Mrs. Lee, with a marked tone of sarcasm.

Carrington looked annoyed, but he answered quietly, "What I fear is his influence here and now. What I would like to see you do is this: go north a month earlier than you intended, and without giving him time to act. If I were sure you were safely in Newport, I should feel no anxiety."

"You seem to have as bad an opinion of Washington as Mr. Gore," said Madeleine, with a contemptuous smile. "He gave me the same advice, though he was afraid to tell me why. I am not a child. I am thirty years old, and have seen something of the world. I am not afraid, like Mr. Gore, of Washington malaria, or, like you, of Mr. Ratcliffe's influence. If I fall a victim I shall deserve my fate, and certainly I shall have no cause to complain of my friends. They have given me advice enough for a lifetime."

Carrington's face darkened with a deeper shade of regret. The turn which the conversation had taken was precisely what he had expected, and both Sybil and he had agreed that Madeleine would probably answer just in this way.

Nevertheless, he could not but feel acutely the harm he was doing to his own interests, and it was only by a sheer effort of the will that he forced himself to a last and more earnest attack.

"I know it is an impertinence," he said; "I wish it were in my power to show how much it costs me to offend you. This is the first time you ever had occasion to be offended. If I were to yield to the fear of your anger and were to hold my tongue now, and by any chance you were to wreck your life on this rock, I should never forgive myself the cowardice. I should always think I might have done something to prevent it. This is probably the last time I shall have the chance to talk openly with you, and I implore you to listen to me. I want nothing for myself If I knew I should never see you again, I would still say the same thing. Leave Washington! Leave it now!

--at once! --without giving more than twenty-four hours' notice! Leave it without letting Mr. Ratcliffe see you again in private! Come back next winter if you please, and then accept him if you think proper. I only pray you to think long about it and decide when you are not here."

Madeleine's eyes flashed, and she threw aside her embroidery with an impatient gesture: "No! Mr. Carrington! I will not be dictated to! I will carry out my own plans! I do not mean to marry Mr. Ratcliffe. If I had meant it, I should have done it before now. But I will not run away from him or from myself. It would be unladylike, undignified, cowardly."

Carrington could say no more. He had come to the end of his lesson. A long silence ensued and then he rose to go. "Are you angry with me?" said she in a softer tone.

"I ought to ask that question," said he. "Can you forgive me? I am afraid not. No man can say to a woman what I have said to you, and be quite forgiven. You will never think of me again as you would have done if I had not spoken. I knew that before I did it. As for me, I can only go on with my old life. It is not gay, and will not be the gayer for our talk to-night."

Madeleine relented a little: "Friendships like ours are not so easily broken," she said. "Do not do me another injustice. You will see me again before you go?"

He assented and bade good-night. Mrs. Lee, weary and disturbed in mind, hastened to her room. "When Miss Sybil comes in, tell her that I am not very well, and have gone to bed," were her instructions to her maid, and Sybil thought she knew the cause of this headache.

But before Carrington's departure he had one more ride with Sybil, and reported to her the result of the interview, at which both of them confessed themselves much depressed. Carrington expressed some hope that Madeleine meant, after a sort, to give a kind of pledge by saying that she had no intention of marrying Mr. Ratcliffe, but Sybil shook her head emphatically:

"How can a woman tell whether she is going to accept a man until she is asked?" said she with entire confidence, as though she were stating the simplest fact in the world. Carrington looked puzzled, and ventured to ask whether women did not generally make up their minds beforehand on such an interesting point; but Sybil overwhelmed him with contempt: "What good will they do by making up their minds, I should like to know? of course they would go and do the opposite. Sensible women don't pretend to make up their minds, Mr. Carrington. But you men are so stupid, and you can't understand in the least."

Carrington gave it up, and went back to his stale question: Could Sybil suggest any other resource? and Sybil sadly confessed that she could not. So far as she could see, they must trust to luck, and she thought it was cruel for Mr. Carrington to go away and leave her alone without help. He had promised to prevent the marriage.

"One thing more I mean to do," said Carrington: "and here everything will depend on your courage and nerve. You may depend upon it that Mr. Ratcliffe will offer himself before you go north. He does not suspect you of making trouble, and he will not think about you in any way if you let him alone and keep quiet. When he does offer himself you will know it; at least your sister will tell you if she has accepted him. If she refuses him point blank, you will have nothing to do but to keep her steady. If you see her hesitating, you must break in at any cost, and use all your influence to stop her. Be bold, then, and do your best. If everything fails and she still clings to him, I must play my last card, or rather you must play it for me.

I shall leave with you a sealed letter which you are to give her if everything else fails. Do it before she sees Ratcliffe a second time. See that she reads it and, if necessary, make her read it, no matter when or where. No one else must know that it exists, and you must take as much care of it as though it were a diamond. You are not to know what is in it; it must be a complete secret. Do you understand?"

Sybil thought she did, but her heart sank. "When shall you give me this letter?" she asked.

"The evening before I start, when I come to bid good-bye; probably next Sunday. This letter is our last hope. If, after reading that, she does not give him up, you will have to pack your trunk, my dear Sybil, and find a new home, for you can never live with them."

He had never before called her by her first name, and it pleased her to hear it now, though she generally had a strong objection to such familiarities.

"Oh, I wish you were not going!" she exclaimed tearfully. "What shall I do when you are gone?"

At this pitiful appeal, Carrington felt a sudden pang. He found that he was not so old as he had thought. Certainly he had grown to like her frank honesty and sound common sense, and he had at length discovered that she was handsome, with a very pretty figure. Was it not something like a flirtation he had been carrying on with this young person for the last month? A glimmering of suspicion crossed his mind, though he got rid of it as quickly as possible. For a man of his age and sobriety to be in love with two sisters at once was impossible; still more impossible that Sybil should care for him.

As for her, however, there was no doubt about the matter. She had grown to depend upon him, and she did it with all the blind confidence of youth. To lose him was a serious disaster. She had never before felt the sensation, and she thought it most disagreeable. Her youthful diplomatists and admirers could not at all fill Carrington's place. They danced and chirruped cheerfully on the hollow crust of society, but they were wholly useless when one suddenly fell through and found oneself struggling in the darkness and dangers beneath. Young women, too, are apt to be flattered by the confidences of older men; they have a keen palate for whatever savours of experience and adventure. For the first time in her life, Sybil had found a man who gave some play to her imagination; one who had been a rebel, and had grown used to the shocks of fate, so as to walk with calmness into the face of death, and to command or obey with equal indifference. She felt that he would tell her what to do when the earthquake came, and would be at hand to consult, which is in a woman's eyes the great object of men's existence, when trouble comes. She suddenly conceived that Washington would be intolerable without him, and that she should never get the courage to fight Mr. Ratcliffe alone, or, if she did, she should make some fatal mistake.

They finished their ride very soberly. She began to show a new interest in all that concerned him, and asked many questions about his sisters and their plantation. She wanted to ask him whether she could not do something to help them, but this seemed too awkward. On his part he made her promise to write him faithfully all that took place, and this request pleased her, though she knew his interest was all on her sister's account.

The following Sunday evening when he came to bid good-bye, it was still worse. There was no chance for private talk. Ratcliffe was there, and several diplomatists, including old Jacobi, who had eyes like a cat and saw every motion of one's face. Victoria Dare was on the sofa, chattering with Lord Dunbeg; Sybil would rather have had any ordinary illness, even to the extent of a light case of scarlet fever or small-pox than let her know what was the matter. Carrington found means to get Sybil into another room for a moment and to give her the letter he had promised. Then he bade her good-bye, and in doing so he reminded her of her promise to write, pressing her hand and looking into her eyes with an earnestness that made her heart beat faster, although she said to herself that his interest was all about her sister; as it was--mostly. The thought did not raise her spirits, but she went through with her performance like a heroine. Perhaps she was a little pleased to see that he parted from Madeleine with much less apparent feeling. One would have said that they were two good friends who had no troublesome sentiment to worry them. But then every eye in the room was watching this farewell, and speculating about it. Ratcliffe looked on with particular interest and was a little perplexed to account for this too fraternal cordiality. Could he have made a miscalculation? or was there something behind? He himself insisted upon shaking hands genially with Carrington and wished him a pleasant journey and a successful one.

That night, for the first time since she was a child, Sybil actually cried a little after she went to bed, although it is true that her sentiment did not keep her awake. She felt lonely and weighed down by a great responsibility.

For a day or two afterwards she was nervous and restless. She would not ride, or make calls, or see guests. She tried to sing a little, and found it tiresome. She went out and sat for hours in the Square, where the spring sun was shining warm and bright on the prancing horse of the great Andrew Jackson. She was a little cross, too, and absent, and spoke so often about Carrington that at last Madeleine was struck by sudden suspicion, and began to watch her with anxious care.

Tuesday night, after this had gone on for two days, Sybil was in Madeleine's room, where she often stayed to talk while her sister was at her toilet.

This evening she threw herself listlessly on the couch, and within five minutes again quoted Carrington. Madeleine turned from the glass before which she was sitting, and looked her steadily in the face.

"Sybil," said she, "this is the twenty-fourth time you have mentioned Mr.

Carrington since we sat down to dinner. I have waited for the round number to decide whether I should take any notice of it or not? what does it mean, my child? Do you care for Mr. Carrington?"

"Oh, Maude!" exclaimed Sybil reproachfully, flushing so violently that, even by that dim light, her sister could not but see it.

Mrs. Lee rose and, crossing the room, sat down by Sybil who was lying on the couch and turned her face away. Madeleine put her arms round her neck and kissed her.

"My poor--poor child!" said she pityingly. "I never dreamed of this! What a fool I have been! How could I have been so thoughtless! Tell me!" she added, with a little hesitation; "has he--does he care for you?"

"No! no!" cried Sybil, fairly breaking down into a burst of tears; "no! he loves you! nobody but you! he never gave a thought to me. I don't care for him so very much," she continued, drying her tears; "only it seems so lonely now he is gone."

Mrs. Lee remained on the couch, with her arm round her sister's neck, silent, gazing into vacancy, the picture of perplexity and consternation.

The situation was getting beyond her control.

Chapter XI

In the middle of April a sudden social excitement started the indolent city of Washington to its feet. The Grand-Duke and Duchess of Saxe-Baden-Hombourg arrived in America on a tour of pleasure, and in due course came on to pay their respects to the Chief Magistrate of the Union. The newspapers hastened to inform their readers that the Grand-Duchess was a royal princess of England, and, in the want of any other social event, every one who had any sense of what was due to his or her own dignity, hastened to show this august couple the respect which all republicans who have a large income derived from business, feel for English royalty. New York gave a dinner, at which the most insignificant person present was worth at least a million dollars, and where the gentlemen who sat by the Princess entertained her for an hour or two by a calculation of the aggregate capital represented. New York also gave a ball at which the Princess appeared in an ill-fitting black silk dress with mock lace and jet ornaments, among several hundred toilets that proclaimed the refined republican simplicity of their owners at a cost of various hundred thousand dollars. After these hospitalities the Grand-ducal pair came on to Washington, where they became guests of Lord Skye, or, more properly, Lord Skye became their guest, for he seemed to consider that he handed the Legation over to them, and he told Mrs. Lee, with true British bluntness of speech, that they were a great bore and he wished they had stayed in Saxe-Baden-Hombourg, or wherever they belonged, but as they were here, he must be their lackey. Mrs. Lee was amused and a little astonished at the candour with which he talked about them, and she was instructed and improved by his dry account of the Princess, who, it seemed, made herself disagreeable by her airs of royalty; who had suffered dreadfully from the voyage; and who detested America and everything American; but who was, not without some show of reason, jealous of her husband, and endured endless sufferings, though with a very bad grace, rather than lose sight of him.

Not only was Lord Skye obliged to turn the Legation into an hotel, but in the full enthusiasm of his loyalty he felt himself called upon to give a ball. It was, he said, the easiest way of paying off all his debts at once, and if the Princess was good for nothing else, she could be utilized as a show by way of "promoting the harmony of the two great nations." In other words, Lord Skye meant to exhibit the Princess for his own diplomatic benefit, and he did so. One would have thought that at this season, when Congress had adjourned, Washington would hardly have afforded society enough to fill a ball-room, but this, instead of being a drawback, was an advantage. It permitted the British Minister to issue invitations without limit. He asked not only the President and his Cabinet, and the judges, and the army, and the navy, and all the residents of Washington who had any claim to consideration, but also all the senators, all the representatives in Congress, all the governors of States with their staffs, if they had any, all eminent citizens and their families throughout the Union and Canada, and finally every private individual, from the North Pole to the Isthmus of Panama, who had ever shown him a civility or was able to control interest enough to ask for a card. The result was that Baltimore promised to come in a body, and Philadelphia was equally well-disposed; New York provided several scores of guests, and Boston sent the governor and a delegation; even the well-known millionaire who represented California in the United States Senate was irritated because, his invitation having been timed to arrive just one day too late, he was prevented from bringing his family across the continent with a choice party in a director's car, to enjoy the smiles of royalty in the halls of the British lion. It is astonishing what efforts freemen will make in a just cause.

Lord Skye himself treated the whole affair with easy contempt. One afternoon he strolled into Mrs. Lee's parlour and begged her to give him a cup of tea.

He said he had got rid of his menagerie for a few hours by shunting it off upon the German Legation, and he was by way of wanting a little human society. Sybil, who was a great favourite with him, entreated to be told all about the ball, but he insisted that he knew no more than she did. A man from New York had taken possession of the Legation, but what he would do with it was not within the foresight of the wisest; from the talk of the young members of his Legation, Lord Skye gathered that the entire city was to be roofed in and forty millions of people expected, but his own concern in the affair was limited to the flowers he hoped to receive.

"All young and beautiful women," said he to Sybil, "are to send me flowers.

I prefer Jacqueminot roses, but will accept any handsome variety, provided they are not wired. It is diplomatic etiquette that each lady who sends me flowers shall reserve at least one dance for me. You will please inscribe this at once upon your tablets, Miss Ross."

To Madeleine this ball was a godsend, for it came just in time to divert Sybil's mind from its troubles. A week had now passed since that revelation of Sybil's heart which had come like an earthquake upon Mrs. Lee. Since then Sybil had been nervous and irritable, all the more because she was conscious of being watched. She was in secret ashamed of her own conduct, and inclined to be angry with Carrington, as though he were responsible for her foolishness; but she could not talk with Madeleine on the subject without discussing Mr. Ratcliffe, and Carrington had expressly forbidden her to attack Mr. Ratcliffe until it was clear that Ratcliffe had laid himself open to attack. This reticence deceived poor Mrs. Lee, who saw in her sister's moods only that unrequited attachment for which she held herself solely to blame. Her gross negligence in allowing Sybil to be improperly exposed to such a risk weighed heavily on her mind. With a saint's capacity for self-torment, Madeleine wielded the scourge over her own back until the blood came. She saw the roses rapidly fading from Sybil's cheeks, and by the help of an active imagination she discovered a hectic look and symptoms of a cough. She became fairly morbid on the subject, and fretted herself into a fever, upon which Sybil sent, on her own responsibility, for the medical man, and Madeleine was obliged to dose herself with quinine. In fact, there was much more reason for anxiety about her than for her anxiety about Sybil, who, barring a little youthful nervousness in the face of responsibility, was as healthy and comfortable a young woman as could be shown in America, and whose sentiment never cost her five minutes' sleep, although her appetite may have become a shade more exacting than before. Madeleine was quick to notice this, and surprised her cook by making daily and almost hourly demands for new and impossible dishes, which she exhausted a library of cookery-books to discover.

Lord Skye's ball and Sybil's interest in it were a great relief to Madeleine's mind, and she now turned her whole soul to frivolity. Never, since she was seventeen, had she thought or talked so much about a ball, as now about this ball to the Grand-Duchess. She wore out her own brain in the effort to amuse Sybil. She took her to call on the Princess; she would have taken her to call on the Grand Lama had he come to Washington. She instigated her to order and send to Lord Skye a mass of the handsomest roses New York could afford. She set her at work on her dress several days before there was any occasion for it, and this famous costume had to be taken out, examined, criticised, and discussed with unending interest. She talked about the dress, and the

Princess, and the ball, till her tongue clove to the roof of her mouth, and her brain refused to act. From morning till night, for one entire week, she ate, drank, breathed, and dreamt of the ball. Everything that love could suggest or labour carry out, she did, to amuse and occupy her sister.

She knew that all this was only temporary and palliative, and that more radical measures must be taken to secure Sybil's happiness. On this subject she thought in secret until both head and heart ached. One thing and one thing only was clear: if Sybil loved Carrington, she should have him. How Madeleine expected to bring about this change of heart in Carrington, was known only to herself. She regarded men as creatures made for women to dispose of, and capable of being transferred like checks, or baggage-labels, from one woman to another, as desired. The only condition was that he should first be completely disabused of the notion that he could dispose of himself. Mrs. Lee never doubted that she could make Carrington fall in love with Sybil provided she could place herself beyond his reach. At all events, come what might, even though she had to accept the desperate alternative offered by Mr. Ratcliffe, nothing should be allowed to interfere with Sybil's happiness. And thus it was, that, for the first time, Mrs. Lee began to ask herself whether it was not better to find the solution of her perplexities in marriage.

Would she ever have been brought to this point without the violent pressure of her sister's supposed interests? This is one of those questions which wise men will not ask, because it is one which the wisest man or woman cannot answer. Upon this theme, an army of ingenious authors have exhausted their ingenuity in entertaining the public, and their works are to be found at every book-stall. They have decided that any woman will, under the right conditions, marry any man at any time, provided her "higher nature" is properly appealed to. Only with regret can a writer forbear to moralize on this subject. "Beauty and the Beast," "Bluebeard," "Auld Robin Gray," have the double charm to authors of being very pleasant to read, and still easier to dilute with sentiment. But at least ten thousand modern writers, with Lord Macaulay at their head, have so ravaged and despoiled the region of fairy-stories and fables, that an allusion even to the "Arabian Nights" is no longer decent. The capacity of women to make unsuitable marriages must be considered as the corner-stone of society.

Meanwhile the ball had, in truth, very nearly driven all thought of Carrington out of Sybil's mind. The city filled again. The streets swarmed with fashionable young men and women from the provinces of New York, Philadelphia, and Boston, who gave Sybil abundance of occupation. She received bulletins of the progress of affairs. The President and his wife had consented to be present, out of their high respect for Her Majesty the Queen and their desire to see and to be seen. All the Cabinet would accompany the Chief Magistrate. The diplomatic corps would appear in uniform; so, too, the officers of the army and navy; the Governor-General of Canada was coming, with a staff. Lord Skye remarked that the Governor-General was a flat.

The day of the ball was a day of anxiety to Sybil, although not on account of Mr. Ratcliffe or of Mr. Carrington, who were of trifling consequence compared with the serious problem now before her. The responsibility of dressing both her sister and herself fell upon Sybil, who was the real author of all Mrs. Lee's millinery triumphs when they now occurred, except that Madeleine managed to put character into whatever she wore, which Sybil repudiated on her own account. On this day Sybil had reasons for special excitement. All winter two new dresses, one especially a triumph of Mr.

Worth's art, had lain in state upstairs, and Sybil had waited in vain for an occasion that should warrant the splendour of these garments.

One afternoon in early June of the preceding summer, Mr. Worth had received a letter on the part of the reigning favourite of the King of Dahomey, directing him to create for her a ball-dress that should annihilate and utterly destroy with jealousy and despair the hearts of her seventy-five rivals; she was young and beautiful; expense was not a consideration. Such were the words of her chamberlain. All that night, the great genius of the nineteenth century tossed wakefully on his bed revolving the problem in his mind. Visions of flesh-coloured tints shot with blood-red perturbed his brain, but he fought against and dismissed them; that combination would be commonplace in Dahomey. When the first rays of sunlight showed him the reflection of his careworn face in the plate-glass mirrored ceiling, he rose and, with an impulse of despair, flung open the casements. There before his blood-shot eyes lay the pure, still, new-born, radiant June morning. With a cry of inspiration the great man leaned out of the casement and rapidly caught the details of his new conception. Before ten o'clock he was again at his bureau in Paris. An imperious order brought to his private room every silk, satin, and gauze within the range of pale pink, pale crocus, pale green, silver and azure. Then came chromatic scales of colour; combinations meant to vulgarise the rainbow; sinfonies and fugues; the twittering of birds and the great peace of dewy nature; maidenhood in her awakening innocence; "The Dawn in June." The Master rested content.

A week later came an order from Sybil, including "an entirely original ball-dress,--unlike any other sent to America." Mr. Worth pondered, hesitated; recalled Sybil's figure; the original pose of her head; glanced anxiously at the map, and speculated whether the New York Herald had a special correspondent at Dahomey; and at last, with a generosity peculiar to great souls, he duplicated for "Miss S. Ross, New York, U.S. America," the order for "L'Aube, Mois de Juin."

The Schneidekoupons and Mr. French, who had reappeared in Washington, came to dine with Mrs. Lee on the evening of the ball, and Julia Schneidekoupon sought in vain to discover what Sybil was going to wear. "Be happy, my dear, in your ignorance!" said Sybil; "the pangs of envy will rankle soon enough."

An hour later her room, except the fireplace, where a wood fire was gently smouldering, became an altar of sacrifice to the Deity of Dawn in June. Her bed, her low couch, her little tables, her chintz arm-chairs, were covered with portions of the divinity, down to slippers and handkerchief, gloves and bunches of fresh roses. When at length, after a long effort, the work was complete, Mrs. Lee took a last critical look at the result, and enjoyed a glow of satisfaction. Young, happy, sparkling with consciousness of youth and beauty, Sybil stood, Hebe Anadyomene, rising from the foam of soft creplisse which swept back beneath the long train of pale, tender, pink silk, fainting into breadths of delicate primrose, relieved here and there by facings of June green--or was it the blue of early morning? --or both?

suggesting unutterable freshness. A modest hint from her maid that "the girls," as women-servants call each other in American households, would like to offer their share of incense at the shrine, was amiably met, and they were allowed a glimpse of the divinity before she was enveloped in wraps. An admiring group, huddled in the doorway, murmured approval, from the leading "girl," who was the cook, a coloured widow of some sixty winters, whose admiration was irrepressible, down to a New England spinster whose Anabaptist conscience wrestled with her instincts, and who, although disapproving of "French folks," paid in her heart that secret homage to their gowns and bonnets which her sterner lips refused. The applause of this audience has, from generation to generation, cheered the hearts of myriads of young women starting out on their little adventures, while the domestic laurels flourish green and fresh for one half hour, until they wither at the threshold of the ball-room.

Mrs. Lee toiled long and earnestly over her sister's toilet, for had not she herself in her own day been the best-dressed girl in New York?--at least, she held that opinion, and her old instincts came to life again whenever Sybil was to be prepared for any great occasion. Madeleine kissed her sister affectionately, and gave her unusual praise when the "Dawn in June" was complete. Sybil was at this moment the ideal of blooming youth, and Mrs. Lee almost dared to hope that her heart was not permanently broken, and that she might yet survive until Carrington could be brought back. Her own toilet was a much shorter affair, but Sybil was impatient long before it was concluded; the carriage was waiting, and she was obliged to disappoint her household by coming down enveloped in her long opera-cloak, and hurrying away.

When at length the sisters entered the reception-room at the British Legation, Lord Skye rebuked them for not having come early to receive with him. His Lordship, with a huge riband across his breast, and a star on his coat, condescended to express himself vigorously on the subject of the "Dawn in June." Schneidekoupon, who was proud of his easy use of the latest artistic jargon, looked with respect at Mrs. Lee's silver-gray satin and its Venetian lace, the arrangement of which had been conscientiously stolen from a picture in the Louvre, and he murmured audibly, "Nocturne in silver-gray!"--then, turning to Sybil--"and you? Of course! I see! A song without words!" Mr. French came up and, in his most fascinating tones, exclaimed, "Why, Mrs. Lee, you look real handsome to-night!" Jacobi, after a close scrutiny, said that he took the liberty of an old man in telling them that they were both dressed absolutely without fault. Even the Grand-Duke was struck by Sybil, and made Lord Skye introduce him, after which ceremony he terrified her by asking the pleasure of a waltz. She disappeared from Madeleine's view, not to be brought back again until Dawn met dawn.

The ball was, as the newspapers declared, a brilliant success. Every one who knows the city of Washington will recollect that, among some scores of magnificent residences which our own and foreign governments have built for the comfort of cabinet officers, judges, diplomatists, vice-presidents, speakers, and senators, the British Legation is by far the most impressive.

Combining in one harmonious whole the proportions of the Pitti Palace with the decoration of the Casa d'Oro and the dome of an Eastern Mosque, this architectural triumph offers extraordinary resources for society. Further description is unnecessary, since anyone may easily refer back to the New York newspapers of the following morning, where accurate plans of the house on the ground floor, will be found; while the illustrated newspapers of the same week contain excellent sketches of the most pleasing scenic effects, as well as of the ball-room and of the Princess smiling graciously from her throne. The lady just behind the Princess on her left, is Mrs. Lee, a poor likeness, but easily distinguishable from the fact that the artist, for his own objects, has made her rather shorter, and the Princess rather taller, than was strictly correct, just as he has given the Princess a gracious smile, which was quite different from her actual expression. In short, the artist is compelled to exhibit the world rather as we would wish it to be, than as it was or is, or, indeed, is like shortly to become. The strangest part of his picture is, however, the fact that he actually did see Mrs. Lee where he has put her, at the Princess's elbow, which was almost the last place in the room where any one who knew Mrs. Lee would have looked for her.

The explanation of this curious accident shall be given immediately, since the facts are not mentioned in the public reports of the ball, which only said that, "close behind her Royal Highness the Grand-Duchess, stood our charming and aristocratic countrywoman, Mrs. Lightfoot Lee, who has made so great a sensation in Washington this winter, and whose name public rumour has connected with that of the Secretary of the Treasury. To her the Princess appeared to address most of her conversation."

The show was a very pretty one, and on a pleasant April evening there were many places less agreeable to be in than this. Much ground outside had been roofed over, to make a ball-room, large as an opera-house, with a daïs and a sofa in the centre of one long side, and another daïs with a second sofa immediately opposite to it in the centre of the other long side. Each daïs had a canopy of red velvet, one bearing the Lion and the Unicorn, the other the American Eagle. The Royal Standard was displayed above the Unicorn; the Stars-and-Stripes, not quite so effectively, waved above the Eagle. The Princess, being no longer quite a child, found gas trying to her complexion, and compelled Lord Skye to illuminate her beauty by one hundred thousand wax candles, more or less, which were arranged to be becoming about the Grand-ducal throne, and to be showy and unbecoming about the opposite institution across the way.

The exact facts were these. It had happened that the Grand-Duchess, having been necessarily brought into contact with the President, and particularly with his wife, during the past week, had conceived for the latter an antipathy hardly to be expressed in words. Her fixed determination was at any cost to keep the Presidential party at a distance, and it was only after a stormy scene that the Grand-Duke and Lord Skye succeeded in extorting her consent that the President should take her to supper. Further than this she would not go. She would not speak to "that woman," as she called the President's wife, nor be in her neighbourhood. She would rather stay in her own room all the evening, and she did not care in the least what the Queen would think of it, for she was no subject of the Queen's. The case was a hard one for Lord Skye, who was perplexed to know, from this point of view, why he was entertaining the Princess at all; but, with the help of the Grand-Duke and Lord Dunbeg, who was very active and smiled deprecation with some success, he found a way out of it; and this was the reason why there were two thrones in the ball-room, and why the British throne was lighted with such careful reference to the Princess's complexion. Lord Skye immolated himself in the usual effort of British and American Ministers, to keep the two great powers apart. He and the Grand-Duke and Lord Dunbeg acted as buffers with watchful diligence, dexterity, and success. As one resource, Lord Skye had bethought himself of Mrs. Lee, and he told the Princess the story of Mrs. Lee's relations with the President's wife, a story which was no secret in Washington, for, apart from Madeleine's own account, society was left in no doubt of the light in which Mrs. Lee was regarded by the mistress of the White House, whom Washington ladies were now in the habit of drawing out on the subject of Mrs. Lee, and who always rose to the bait with fresh vivacity, to the amusement and delight of Victoria Dare and other mischief-makers.

"She will not trouble you so long as you can keep Mrs. Lee in your neighbourhood," said Lord

Skye, and the Princess accordingly seized upon Mrs. Lee and brandished her, as though she were a charm against the evil eye, in the face of the President's party. She made Mrs. Lee take a place just behind her as though she were a lady-in-waiting. She even graciously permitted her to sit down, so near that their chairs touched. Whenever "that woman" was within sight, which was most of the time, the Princess directed her conversation entirely to Mrs. Lee and took care to make it evident. Even before the Presidential party had arrived, Madeleine had fallen into the Princess's grasp, and when the Princess went forward to receive the President and his wife, which she did with a bow of stately and distant dignity, she dragged Madeleine closely by her side. Mrs. Lee bowed too; she could not well help it; but was cut dead for her pains, with a glare of contempt and hatred. Lord Skye, who was acting as cavalier to the President's wife, was panic-stricken, and hastened to march his democratic potentate away, under pretence of showing her the decorations. He placed her at last on her own throne, where he and the Grand-Duke relieved each other in standing guard at intervals throughout the evening. When the Princess followed with the President, she compelled her husband to take Mrs. Lee on his arm and conduct her to the British throne, with no other object than to exasperate the President's wife, who, from her elevated platform, looked down upon the cortège with a scowl.

In all this affair Mrs. Lee was the principal sufferer. No one could relieve her, and she was literally penned in as she sat. The Princess kept up an incessant fire of small conversation, principally complaint and fault-finding, which no one dared to interrupt. Mrs. Lee was painfully bored, and after a time even the absurdity of the thing ceased to amuse her.

She had, too, the ill-luck to make one or two remarks which appealed to some hidden sense of humour in the Princess, who laughed and, in the style of royal personages, gave her to understand that she would like more amusement of the same sort. Of all things in life, Mrs. Lee held this kind of court-service in contempt, for she was something more than republican--a little communistic at heart, and her only serious complaint of the President and his wife was that they undertook to have a court and to ape monarchy.

She had no notion of admitting social superiority in any one, President or Prince, and to be suddenly converted into a lady-in-waiting to a small German Grand-Duchess, was a terrible blow. But what was to be done? Lord Skye had drafted her into the service and she could not decently refuse to help him when he came to her side and told her, with his usual calm directness, what his difficulties were, and how he counted upon her to help him out.

The same play went on at supper, where there was a royal-presidential table, which held about two dozen guests, and the two great ladies presiding, as far apart as they could be placed. The Grand-Duke and Lord Skye, on either side of the President's wife, did their duty like men, and were rewarded by receiving from her much information about the domestic arrangements of the White House. The President, however, who sat next the Princess at the opposite end, was evidently depressed, owing partly to the fact that the Princess, in defiance of all etiquette, had compelled Lord Dunbeg to take Mrs. Lee to supper and to place her directly next the President. Madeleine tried to escape, but was stopped by the Princess, who addressed her across the President and in a decided tone asked her to sit precisely there. Mrs.

Lee looked timidly at her neighbour, who made no sign, but ate his supper in silence only broken by an occasional reply to a rare remark. Mrs. Lee pitied him, and wondered what his wife would say when they reached home. She caught Ratcliffe's eye down the table, watching her with a smile; she tried to talk fluently with Dunbeg; but not until supper was long over and two o'clock was at hand; not until the Presidential party, under all the proper formalities, had taken their leave of the Grand-ducal party; not until Lord Skye had escorted them to their carriage and returned to say that they were gone, did the Princess loose her hold upon Mrs. Lee and allow her to slip away into obscurity.

Meanwhile the ball had gone on after the manner of balls. As Madeleine sat in her enforced grandeur she could watch all that passed. She had seen Sybil whirling about with one man after another, amid a swarm of dancers, enjoying herself to the utmost and occasionally giving a nod and a smile to her sister as their eyes met. There, too, was Victoria Dare, who never appeared flurried even when waltzing with Lord Dunbeg, whose education as a dancer had been neglected. The fact was now fully recognized that Victoria was carrying on a systematic flirtation with Dunbeg, and had undertaken as her latest duty the task of teaching him to waltz. His struggles and her calmness in assisting them commanded respect. On the opposite side of the room, by the republican throne, Mrs. Lee had watched Mr. Ratcliffe standing by the President, who appeared unwilling to let him out of arm's length and who seemed to make to him most of his few remarks. Schneidekoupon and his sister were mixed in the throng, dancing as though England had never countenanced the heresy of free-trade. On the whole, Mrs. Lee was satisfied.

If her own sufferings were great, they were not without reward. She studied all the women in the ball-room, and if there was one prettier than Sybil, Madeleine's eyes could not discover her. If there was a more perfect dress, Madeleine knew nothing of dressing. On these points she felt the confidence of conviction. Her calm would have been complete, had she felt quite sure that none of Sybil's gaiety was superficial and that it would not be followed by reaction. She watched nervously to see whether her face changed its gay expression, and once she thought it became depressed, but this was when the Grand-Duke came up to claim his waltz, and the look rapidly passed away when they got upon the floor and his Highness began to wheel round the room with a precision and momentum that would have done honour to a regiment of Life Guards. He seemed pleased with his experiment, for he was seen again and again careering over the floor with Sybil until Mrs. Lee herself became nervous, for the Princess frowned.

After her release Madeleine lingered awhile in the ball-room to speak with her sister and to receive congratulations. For half an hour she was a greater belle than Sybil. A crowd of men clustered about her, amused at the part she had played in the evening's entertainment and full of compliments upon her promotion at Court. Lord Skye himself found time to offer her his thanks in a more serious tone than he generally affected. "You have suffered much," said he, "and I am grateful." Madeleine laughed as she answered that her sufferings had seemed nothing to her while she watched his. But at last she became weary of the noise and glare of the ball-room, and, accepting the arm of her excellent friend Count Popoff, she strolled with him back to the house. There at last she sat down on a sofa in a quiet window-recess where the light was less strong and where a convenient laurel spread its leaves in front so as to make a bower through which she could see the passers-by without being seen by them except with an effort. Had she been a younger woman, this would have been the spot for a flirtation, but Mrs. Lee never flirted, and the idea of her flirting with Popoff would have seemed ludicrous to all mankind.

He did not sit down, but was leaning against the angle of the wall, talking with her, when suddenly Mr. Ratcliffe appeared and took the seat by her side with such deliberation and apparent sense of property that Popoff incontinently turned and fled. No one knew where the Secretary came from, or how he learned that she was there. He made no explanation and she took care to ask for none. She gave him a highly-coloured account of her evening's service as lady-in-waiting, which he matched by that of his own trials as gentleman-usher to the President, who, it seemed, had clung desperately to his old enemy in the absence of any other rock to clutch at.

Ratcliffe looked the character of Prime Minister sufficiently well at this moment. He would have held his own, at a pinch, in any Court, not merely in Europe but in India or China, where dignity is still expected of gentlemen.

Excepting for a certain coarse and animal expression about the mouth, and an indefinable coldness in the eye, he was a handsome man and still in his prime. Every one remarked how much he was improved since entering the Cabinet. He had dropped his senatorial manner. His clothes were no longer congressional, but those of a respectable man, neat and decent. His shirts no longer protruded in the wrong places, nor were his shirt-collars frayed or soiled. His hair did not stray over his eyes, ears, and coat, like that of a Scotch terrier, but had got itself cut. Having overheard Mrs. Lee express on one occasion her opinion of people who did not take a cold bath every morning, he had thought it best to adopt this reform, although he would not have had it generally known, tot it savoured ot caste. He made an effort not to be dictatorial and to forget that he had been the Prairie Giant, the bully of the Senate. In short, what with Mrs. Lee's influence and what with his emancipation from the Senate chamber with its code of bad manners and worse morals, Mr. Ratcliffe was fast becoming a respectable member of society whom a man who had never been in prison or in politics might safely acknowledge as a friend.

Mr. Ratcliffe was now evidently bent upon being heard. After charting for a time with some humour on the President's successes as a man of fashion, he changed the subject to the merits of the President as a statesman, and little by little as he spoke he became serious and his voice sank into low and confidential tones. He plainly said that the President's incapacity had now become notorious among his followers; that it was only with difficulty his Cabinet and friends could prevent him from making a fool of himself fifty times a day; that all the party leaders who had occasion to deal with him were so thoroughly disgusted that the Cabinet had to pass its time in trying to pacify them; while this state of things lasted, Ratcliffe's own influence must be paramount; he had good reason to know that if the Presidential election were to take place this year, nothing could prevent his nomination and election; even at three years' distance the chances in his favour were at least two to one; and after this exordium he went on in a low tone with increasing earnestness, while Mrs. Lee sat motionless as the statue of Agrippina, her eyes fixed on the ground:

"I am not one of those who are happy in political life. I am a politician because I cannot help myself; it is the trade I am fittest for, and ambition is my resource to make it tolerable. In politics we cannot keep our hands clean. I have done many things in my political career that are not defensible. To act with entire honesty and self-respect, one should always live in a pure atmosphere, and the atmosphere of politics is impure.

Domestic life is the salvation of many public men, but I have for many years been deprived of it. I have now come to that point where increasing responsibilities and temptations make me require help. I must have it. You alone can give it to me. You are kind, thoughtful, conscientious, high-minded, cultivated, fitted better than any woman I ever saw, for public duties. Your place is there. You belong among those who exercise an influence beyond their time. I only ask you to take the place which is yours."

This desperate appeal to Mrs. Lee's ambition was a calculated part of Ratcliffe's scheme. He was well aware that he had marked high game, and that in proportion to this height must be the power of his lure. Nor was he embarrassed because Mrs. Lee sat still and pale with her eyes fixed on the ground and her hands twisted together in her lap. The eagle that soars highest must be longer in descending to the ground than the sparrow or the partridge. Mrs. Lee had a thousand things to think about in this brief time, and yet she found that she could not think at all; a succession of mere images and fragments of thought passed rapidly over her mind, and her will exercised no control upon their order or their nature. One of these fleeting reflections was that in all the offers of marriage she had ever heard, this was the most unsentimental and businesslike. As for his appeal to her ambition, it fell quite dead upon her ear, but a woman must be more than a heroine who can listen to flattery so evidently sincere, from a man who is pre-eminent among men, without being affected by it. To her, however, the great and overpowering fact was that she found herself unable to retreat or escape; her tactics were disconcerted, her temporary barriers beaten down.

The offer was made. What should she do with it?

She had thought for months on this subject without being able to form a decision; what hope was there that she should be able to decide now, in a ball-room, at a minute's notice? When, as occasionally happens, the conflicting sentiments, prejudices, and passions of a lifetime are compressed into a single instant, they sometimes overcharge the mind and it refuses to work. Mrs. Lee sat still and let things take their course; a dangerous expedient, as thousands of women have learned, for it leaves them at the mercy of the strong will, bent upon mastery.

The music from the ball-room did not stop. Crowds of persons passed by their retreat. Some glanced in, and not one of these felt a doubt what was going on there. An unmistakeable atmosphere of mystery and intensity surrounded tfle pair. Ratcliffe's eyes were fixed upon Mrs. Lee, and hers on the ground. Neither seemed to speak or to stir. Old Baron Jacobi, who never failed to see everything, saw this as he went by, and ejaculated a foreign oath of frightful import. Victoria Dare saw it and was devoured by curiosity to such a point as to be hardly capable of containing herself.

After a silence which seemed interminable, Ratcliffe went on: "I do not speak of my own feelings because I know that unless compelled by a strong sense of duty, you will not be decided by any devotion of mine. But I honestly say that I have learned to depend on you to a degree I can hardly express; and when I think of what I should be without you, life seems to me so intolerably dark that I am ready to make any sacrifice, to accept any conditions that will keep you by my side."

Meanwhile Victoria Dare, although deeply interested in what Dunbeg was telling her, had met Sybil and had stopped a single second to whisper in her ear: "You had better look after your sister, in the window, behind the laurel with Mr. Ratcliffe!" Sybil was on Lord Skye's arm, enjoying herself amazingly, though the night was far gone, but when she caught Victoria's words, the expression of her face wholly changed. All the anxieties and terrors of the last fortnight, came back upon it. She dragged Lord Skye across the hall and looked in upon her sister. One glance was enough.

Desperately frightened but afraid to hesitate, she went directly up to Madeleine who was still sitting like a statue, listening to Ratcliffe's last words. As she hurriedly entered, Mrs. Lee, looking up, caught sight of her pale face, and started from her seat.

"Are you ill, Sybil?" she exclaimed; "is anything the matter?"

"A little--fatigued," gasped Sybil; "I thought you might be ready to go home."

"I am," cried Madeleine; "I am quite ready. Good evening, Mr. Ratcliffe. I will see you to-morrow. Lord Skye, shall I take leave of the Princess?"

"The Princess retired half an hour ago," replied Lord Skye, who saw the situation and was quite ready to help Sybil; "let me take you to the dressing-room and order your carriage." Mr. Ratcliffe found himself suddenly left alone, while Mrs. Lee hurried away, torn by fresh anxieties. They had reached the dressing-room and were nearly ready to go home, when Victoria Dare suddenly dashed in upon them, with an animation of manner very unusual in her, and, seizing Sybil by the hand, drew her into an adjoining room and shut the door. "Can you keep a secret?" said she abruptly.

"What!" said Sybil, looking at her with open-mouthed interest; "you don't mean--are you really--tell me, quick!"

"Yes!" said Victoria relapsing into composure; "I am engaged!"

"To Lord Dunbeg?"

Victoria nodded, and Sybil, whose nerves were strung to the highest pitch by excitement, flattery, fatigue, perplexity, and terror, burst into a paroxysm of laughter, that startled even the calm Miss Dare.

"Poor Lord Dunbeg! don't be hard on him, Victoria!" she gasped when at last she found breath; "do you really mean to pass the rest of your life in Ireland? Oh, how much you will teach them!"

"You forget, my dear," said Victoria, who had placidly enthroned herself on the foot of a bed, "that I am not a pauper. I am told that Dunbeg Castle is a romantic summer residence, and in the dull season we shall of course go to London or somewhere. I shall be civil to you when you come over. Don't you think a coronet will look well on me?"

Sybil burst again into laughter so irrepressible and prolonged that it puzzled even poor Dunbeg, who was impatiently pacing the corridor outside.

It alarmed Madeleine, who suddenly opened the door. Sybil recovered herself, and, her eyes streaming with tears, presented Victoria to her sister:

"Madeleine, allow me to introduce you to the Countess Dunbeg!"

But Mrs. Lee was much too anxious to feel any interest in Lady Dunbeg. A sudden fear struck her that Sybil was going into hysterics because Victoria's engagement recalled her own disappointment. She hurried her sister away to the carriage.

Chapter XII

They drove home in silence, Mrs. Lee disturbed with anxieties and doubts, partly caused by her sister, partly by Mr. Ratcliffe; Sybil divided between amusement at Victoria's conquest, and alarm at her own boldness in meddling with her sister's affairs. Desperation, however, was stronger than fear. She made up her mind that further suspense was not to be endured; she would fight her baffle now before another hour was lost; surely no time could be better. A few moments brought them to their door. Mrs. Lee had told her maid not to wait for them, and they were alone. The fire was still alive on Madeleine's hearth, and she threw more wood upon it. Then she insisted that Sybil must go to bed at once. But Sybil refused; she felt quite well, she said, and not in the least sleepy; she had a great deal to talk about, and wanted to get it off her mind. Nevertheless, her feminine regard for the "Dawn in June" led her to postpone what she had to say until with Madeleine's help she had laid the triumph of the ball carefully aside; then, putting on her dressing-gown, and hastily plunging Carrington's letter into her breast, like a concealed weapon, she hurried back to Madeleine's room and established herself in a chair before the fire. There, after a moment's pause, the two women began their long-deferred trial of strength, in which the match was so nearly equal as to make the result doubtful; for, if Madeleine were much the cleverer, Sybil in this case knew much better what she wanted, and had a clear idea how she meant to gain it, while Madeleine, unsuspicious of attack, had no plan of defence at all.

"Madeleine," began Sybil, solemnly, and with a violent palpitation of the heart, "I want you to tell me something."

"What is it, my child?" said Mrs. Lee, puzzled, and yet half ready to see that there must be some connection between her sister's coming question and the sudden illness at the ball, which had disappeared as suddenly as it came.

"Do you mean to marry Mr. Ratcliffe?"

Poor Mrs. Lee was quite disconcerted by the directness of the attack. This fatal question met her at every turn. Hardly had she succeeded in escaping trom it at the ball scarcely an hour ago, by a stroke of good fortune for which she now began to see she was indebted to Sybil, and here it was again presented to her face like a pistol. The whole town, then, was asking it.

Ratcliffe's offer must have been seen by half Washington, and her reply was awaited by an immense audience, as though she were a political returning-board. Her disgust was intense, and her first answer to Sybil was a quick inquiry:

"Why do you ask such a question? have you heard anything,--has anyone talked about it to you?"

"No!" replied Sybil; "but I must know; I can see for myself without being told, that Mr. Racliffe is trying to make you marry him. I don't ask out of curiosity; this is something that concerns me nearly as much as it does you yourself. Please tell me! don't treat me like a child any longer! let me know what you are thinking about! I am so tired of being left in the dark!

You have no idea how much this thing weighs on me. Oh, Maude, I shall never be happy again until you trust me about this."

Mrs. Lee felt a little pang of conscience, and seemed suddenly to become conscious of a new coil, tightening about her, in this wretched complication. Unable to see her way, ignorant of her sister's motives, urged on by the idea that Sybil's happiness was involved, she was now charged with want of feeling, and called upon for a direct answer to a plain question.

How could she aver that she did not mean to marry Mr. Ratcliffe? to say this would be to shut the door on all the objects she had at heart. If a direct answer must be given, it was better to say "Yes!" and have it over; better to leap blindly and see what came of it. Mrs. Lee, therefore, with an internal gasp, but with no visible sign of excitement, said, as though she were in a dream:

"Well, Sybil, I will tell you. I would have told you long ago if I had known myself. Yes! I have made up my mind to marry Mr. Ratcliffe!"

Sybil sprang to her feet with a cry: "And have you told him so?" she asked.

"No! you came and interrupted us just as we were speaking. I was glad you did come, for it gives me a little time to think. But I am decided now. I shall tell him to-morrow."

This was not said with the air or one wnose heart beat warmly at the thought of confessing her love. Mrs. Lee spoke mechanically, and almost with an effort. Sybil flung herself with all her energy upon her sister; violently excited, and eager to make herself heard, without waiting for arguments, she broke out into a torrent of entreaties: "Oh, don't, don't, don't! Oh, please, please, don't, my dearest, dearest Maude! unless you want to break my heart, don't marry that man! You can't love him! You can never be happy with him! he will take you away to Peonia, and you will die there! I shall never see you again! He will make you unhappy; he will beat you, I know he will! Oh, if you care for me at all, don't marry him! Send him away! don't see him again! let us go ourselves, now, in the morning train, before he comes back. I'm all ready; I'll pack everything for you; we'll go to Newport; to Europe--anywhere, to be out of his reach!"

With this passionate appeal, Sybil threw herself on her knees by her sister's side, and, clasping her arms around Madeleine's waist, sobbed as though her heart were already broken. Had Carrington seen her then he must have admitted that she had carried out his instructions to the letter. She was quite honest, too, in it all. She meant what she said, and her tears were real tears that had been pent up for weeks. Unluckily, her logic was feeble. Her idea of Mr. Ratcliffe's character was vague, and biased by mere theories of what a Prairie Giant of Peonia should be in his domestic relations. Her idea of Peonia, too, was indistinct. She was haunted by a vision of her sister, sitting on a horse-hair sofa before an air-tight iron stove in a small room with high, bare white walls, a chromolithograph on each, and at her side a marble-topped table surmounted by a glass vase containing funereal dried grasses; the only literature, Frank Leslie's periodical and the New York Ledger, with a strong smell of cooking everywhere prevalent. Here she saw Madeleine receiving visitors, the wives of neighbours and constituents, who told her the Peonia news.

Notwithstanding her ignorant and unreasonable prejudice against western men and women, western towns and prairies, and, in short, everything western, down to western politics and western politicians, whom she perversely asserted to be tue lowest ot all western products, there was still some common sense in Sybil's idea. When that inevitable hour struck for Mr.

Ratcliffe, which strikes sooner or later for all politicians, and an ungrateful country permitted him to pine among his friends in Illinois, what did he propose to do with his wife? Did he seriously suppose that she, who was bored to death by New York, and had been able to find no permanent pleasure in Europe, would live quietly in the romantic village of Peonia? If not, did Mr. Ratcliffe imagine that they could find happiness in the enjoyment of each other's society, and of Mrs. Lee's income, in the excitements of Washington? In the ardour of his pursuit, Mr. Ratcliffe had accepted in advance any conditions which Mrs. Lee might impose, but if he really imagined that happiness and content lay on the purple rim of this sunset, he had more confidence in women and in money than a wider experience was ever likely to justify.

Whatever might be Mr. Ratcliffe's schemes for dealing with these obstacles they could hardly be such as would satisfy Sybil, who, if inaccurate in her theories about Prairie Giants, yet understood women, and especially her sister, much better than Mr. Ratcliffe ever could do. Here she was safe, and it would have been better had she said no more, for Mrs. Lee, though staggered for a moment by her sister's vehemence, was reassured by what seemed the absurdity of her fears. Madeleine rebelled against this hysterical violence of opposition, and became more fixed in her decision.

She scolded her sister in good, set terms--

"Sybil, Sybil! you must not be so violent. Behave like a woman, and not like a spoiled child!"

Mrs. Lee, like most persons who have to deal with spoiled or unspoiled children, resorted to severity, not so much because it was the proper way of dealing with them, as because she knew not what else to do. She was thoroughly uncomfortable and weary. She was not satisfied with herself or with her own motives. Doubt encompassed her on all sides, and her worst opponent was that sister whose happiness had turned the scale against her own judgment.

Nevertheless her tactics answered their object of checking Sybil's vehemence. Her sobs came to an end, and she presently rose with a quieter air.

"Madeleine," said she, "do you really want to marry Mr. Ratcliffe?"

"What else can I do, my dear Sybil? I want to do whatever is for the best. I thought you might be pleased."

"You thought I might be pleased?" cried Sybil in astonishment. "What a strange idea! If you had ever spoken to me about it I should have told you that I hate him, and can't understand how you can abide him. But I would rather marry him myself than see you marry him. I know that you will kill yourself with unhappiness when you have done it. Oh, Maude, please tell me that you won't!" And Sybil began gently sobbing again, while she caressed her sister.

Mrs. Lee was infinitely distressed. To act against the wishes of her nearest friends was hard enough, but to appear harsh and unfeeling to the one being whose happiness she had at heart, was intolerable. Yet no sensible woman, after saying that she meant to marry a man like Mr. Ratcliffe, could throw him over merely because another woman chose to behave like a spoiled child.

Sybil was more childish than Madeleine herself had supposed. She could not even see where her own interest lay. She knew no more about Mr. Ratcliffe and the West than if he were the giant of a fairy-story, and lived at the top of a bean-stalk. She must be treated as a child; with gentleness, affection, forbearance, but with firmness and decision. She must be refused what she asked, for her own good.

Thus it came about that at last Mrs. Lee spoke, with an appearance of decision far from representing her internal tremor.

"Sybil, dear, I have made up my mind to marry Mr. Ratcliffe because there is no other way of making every one happy. You need not be afraid of him. He is kind and generous. Besides, I can take care of myself; and I will take care of you too. Now let us not discuss it any more. It is broad daylight, and we are both tired out."

Sybil grew at once perfectly calm, and standing before her sister, as though their rôles were henceforward to be reversed, said:

"You have really made up your mind, then? Nothing I can say will change it?"

Mrs. Lee, looking at her with more surprise than ever, could not force herself to speak; but she shook her head slowly and decidedly.

"Then," said Sybil, "there is only one thing more I can do. You must read this!" and she drew out Carrington's letter, which she held before Madeleine's face.

"Not now, Sybil!" remonstrated Mrs. Lee, dreading another long struggle. "I will read it after we have had some rest. Go to bed now!"

"I do not leave this room, nor will I ever go to bed until you have read that letter," answered Sybil, seating herself again before the fire with the resolution of Queen Elizabeth; "not if I sit here till you are married. I promised Mr. Carrington that you should read it instantly; it's all I can do now." With a sigh, Mrs. Lee drew up the window-curtain, and in the gray morning light sat down to break the seal and read the following letter:--

"Washington, 2nd April.

"My dear Mrs. Lee, "This letter will only come into your hands in case there should be a necessity for your knowing its contents. Nothing short of necessity would excuse my writing it. I have to ask your pardon for intruding again upon your private affairs. In this case, if I did not intrude, you would have cause for serious complaint against me.

"You asked me the other day whether I knew anything against Mr. Ratcliffe which the world did not know, to account for my low opinion of his character. I evaded your question then. I was bound by professional rules not to disclose facts that came to me under a pledge of confidence. I am going to violate these rules now, only because I owe you a duty which seems to me to override all others.

"I do know facts in regard to Mr. Ratcliffe, which have seemed to me to warrant a very low opinion of his character, and to mark him as unfit to be, I will not say your husband, but even your acquaintance.

"You know that I am executor to Samuel Baker's will. You know who Samuel Baker was. You have seen his wife. She has told you herself that I assisted her in the examination and destruction of all her husband's private papers according to his special death-bed request. One of the first facts I learned from these papers and her explanations, was the following.

"Just eight years ago, the great 'Inter-Oceanic Mail Steamship Company,' wished to extend its service round the world, and, in order to do so, it applied to Congress for a heavy subsidy. The management of this affair was put into the hands of Mr. Baker, and all his private letters to the President of the Company, in press copies, as well as the President's replies, came into my possession. Baker's letters were, of course, written in a sort of cypher, several kinds of which he was in the habit of using. He left among his papers a key to this cypher, but Mrs. Baker could have explained it without that help.

"It appeared from this correspondence that the bill was carried successfully through the House, and, on reaching the Senate, was referred to the appropriate Committee. Its ultimate passage was very doubtful; the end of the session was close at hand; the Senate was very evenly divided, and the Chairman of the Committee was decidedly hostile.

"The Chairman of that Committee was Senator Ratcliffe, always mentioned by Mr. Baker in cypher, and with every precaution. If you care, however, to verify the fact, and to trace the history of the Subsidy Bill through all its stages, together with Mr. Ratcliffe's report, remarks, and votes upon it, you have only to look into the journals and debates for that year.

"At last Mr. Baker wrote that Senator Ratcliffe had put the bill in his pocket, and unless some means could be found of overcoming his opposition, there would be no report, and the bill would never come to a vote. All ordinary kinds of argument and influence had been employed upon him, and were exhausted. In this exigency Baker suggested that the Company should give him authority to see what money would do, but he added that it would be worse than useless to deal with small sums. Unless at least one hundred thousand dollars could be employed, it was better to leave the thing alone.

"The next mail authorized him to use any required amount of money not exceeding one hundred and fifty thousand dollars. Two days later he wrote that the bill was reported, and would pass the Senate within forty-eight hours; and he congratulated the Company on the fact that he had used only one hundred thousand dollars out of its last credit.

"The bill was actually reported, passed, and became law as he foretold, and the Company has enjoyed its subsidy ever since. Mrs. Baker also informed me that to her knowledge her husband gave the sum mentioned, in United States Coupon Bonds, to Senator Ratcliffe.

"This transaction, taken in connection with the tortuousness of his public course, explains the distrust I have always expressed for him. You will, however, understand that all these papers have been destroyed. Mrs. Baker could never be induced to hazard her own comfort by revealing the facts to the public. The officers of the Company in their own interests would never betray the transaction, and their books were undoubtedly so kept as to show no trace of it. If I made this charge against Mr. Ratcliffe, I should be the only sufferer. He would deny and laugh at it. I could prove nothing. I am therefore more directly interested than he is in keeping silence.

"In trusting this secret to you, I rely firmly upon your mentioning it to no one else--not even to your sister. You are at liberty, if you wish, to show this letter to one person only-- to Mr. Ratcliffe himself. That done, you will, I beg, burn it immediately.

"With the warmest good wishes, I am, "Ever most truly yours, "John Carrington."

When Mrs. Lee had finished reading this letter, she remained for some time quite silent, looking out into the square below. The morning had come, and the sky was bright with the fresh April sunlight. She threw open her window, and drew in the soft spring air. She needed all the purity and quiet that nature could give, for her whole soul was in revolt, wounded, mortified, exasperated. Against the sentiment of all her friends she had insisted upon believing in this man; she had wrought herself up to the point of accepting him for her husband; a man who, if law were the same thing as justice, ought to be in a felon's cell; a man who could take money to betray his trust. Her anger at first swept away all bounds. She was impatient for the moment when she should see him again, and tear off his mask. For once she would express all the loathing she felt for the whole pack of political hounds. She would see whether the animal was made like other beings; whether he had a sense of honour; a single clean spot in his mind.

Then it occurred to her that after all there might be a mistake; perhaps Mr.

Ratcliffe could explain the charge away. But this thought only laid bare another smarting wound in her pride. Not only did she believe the charge, but she believed that Mr. Ratcliffe would defend his act. She had been willing to marry a man whom she thought capable of such a crime, and now she shuddered at the idea that this charge might have been brought against her husband, and that she could not dismiss it with instant incredulity, with indignant contempt. How had this happened? how had she got into so foul a complication? When she left New York, she had meant to be a mere spectator in Washington. Had it entered her head that she could be drawn into any project of a second marriage, she never would have come at all, for she was proud of her loyalty to her husband's memory, and second marriages were her abhorrence. In her restlessness and solitude, she had forgotten this; she had only asked whether any life was worth living for a woman who had neither husband nor children. Was the family all that life had to offer? could she find no interest outside the household? And so, led by this will-of-the-wisp, she had, with her eyes open, walked into the quagmire of politics, in spite of remonstrance, in spite of conscience.

She rose and paced the room, while Sybil lay on the couch, watching her with eyes half shut. She grew more and more angry with herself, and as her self-reproach increased, her anger against Ratcliffe faded away. She had no right to be angry with Ratcliffe. He had never deceived her. He had always openly enough avowed that he knew no code of morals in politics; that if virtue did not answer his purpose he used vice. How could she blame him for acts which he had repeatedly defended in her presence and with her tacit assent, on principles that warranted this or any other villainy?

The worst was that this discovery had come on her as a blow, not as a reprieve from execution. At this thought she became furious with herself.

She had not known the recesses of her own heart. She had honestly supposed that Sybil's interests and Sybil's happiness were forcing her to an act of self-sacrifice; and now she saw that in the depths of her soul very different motives had been at work: ambition, thirst for power, restless eagerness to meddle in what did not concern her, blind longing to escape from the torture of watching other women with full lives and satisfied instincts, while her own life was hungry and sad. For a time she had actually, unconscious as she was of the delusion, hugged a hope that a new field of usefulness was open to her; that great opportunities for doing good were to supply the aching emptiness of that good which had been taken away; and that here at last was an object for which there would be almost a pleasure in squandering the rest of existence even if she knew in advance that the experiment would fail. Life was emptier than ever now that this dream was over. Yet the worst was not in that disappointment, but in the discovery of her own weakness and self-deception.

Worn out by long-continued anxiety, excitement and sleeplessness, she was unfit to struggle with the creatures of her own imagination. Such a strain could only end in a nervous crisis, and at length it came:

"Oh, what a vile thing life is!" she cried, throwing up her arms with a gesture of helpless rage and despair. "Oh, how I wish I were dead! how I wish the universe were annihilated!" and she flung herself down by Sybil's side in a frenzy of tears.

Sybil, who had watched all this exhibition in silence, waited quietly for the excitement to pass. There was little to say. She could only soothe.

After the paroxysm had exhausted itself Madeleine lay quiet for a time, until other thoughts began to disturb her. From reproaching herself about Ratcliffe she went on to reproach herself about Sybil, who really looked worn and pale, as though almost overcome by fatigue.

"Sybil," said she, "you must go to bed at once. You are tired out. It was very wrong in me to let you sit up so late. Go now, and get some sleep."

"I am not going to bed till you do, Maude!" replied Sybil, with quiet obstinacy.

"Go, dear! it is all settled. I shall not marry Mr. Ratcliffe. You need not be anxious about it any more."

"Are you very unhappy?"

"Only very angry with myself. I ought to have taken Mr. Carrington's advice sooner."

"Oh, Maude!" exclaimed Sybil, with a sudden explosion of energy; "I wish you had taken him!"

This remark roused Mrs. Lee to new interest: "Why, Sybil," said she, "surely you are not in earnest?"

"Indeed, I am," replied Sybil, very decidedly. "I know you think I am in love with Mr. Carrington myself, but I'm not. I would a great deal rather have him for a brother-in-law, and he is so much the nicest man you know, and you could help his sisters."

Mrs. Lee hesitated a moment, for she was not quite certain whether it was wise to probe a healing wound, but she was anxious to clear this last weight from her mind, and she dashed recklessly forward:

"Are you sure you are telling the truth, Sybil? Why, then, did you say that you cared for him? and why have you been so miserable ever since he went away?"

"Why? I should think it was plain enough why! Because I thought, as every one else did, that you were going to marry Mr. Ratcliffe; and because if you married Mr. Ratcliffe, I must go and live alone; and because you treated me like a child, and never took me into your confidence at all; and because Mr. Carrington was the only person I had to advise me, and after he went away, I was left all alone to fight Mr. Ratcliffe and you both together, without a human soul to help me in case I made a mistake. You would have been a great deal more miserable than I if you had been in my place."

Madeleine looked at her for a moment in doubt. Would this last? did Sybil herself know the depth of her own wound? But what could Mrs. Lee do now?

Perhaps Sybil did deceive herself a little. When this excitement had passed away, perhaps Carrington's image might recur to her mind a little too often for her own comfort. The future must take care of itself. Mrs. Lee drew her sister closer to her, and said: "Sybil, I have made a horrible mistake, and you must forgive me."

Chapter XIII

Not until afternoon did Mrs. Lee reappear. How much she had slept she did not say, and she hardly looked like one whose slumbers had been long or sweet; but if she had slept little, she had made up for the loss by thinking much, and, while she thought, the storm which had raged so fiercely in her breast, more and more subsided into calm. If there was not sunshine yet, there was at least stillness. As she lay, hour after hour, waiting for the sleep that did not come, she had at first the keen mortification of reflecting how easily she had been led by mere vanity into imagining that she could be of use in the world. She even smiled in her solitude at the picture she drew of herself, reforming Ratcliffe, and Krebs, and Schuyler Clinton. The ease with which Ratcliffe alone had twisted her about his finger, now that she saw it, made her writhe, and the thought of what he might have done, had she married him, and of the endless succession of moral somersaults she would have had to turn, chilled her with mortal terror. She had barely escaped being dragged under the wheels of the machine, and so coming to an untimely end. When she thought of this, she felt a mad passion to revenge herself on the whole race of politicians, with Ratcliffe at their head; she passed hours in framing bitter speeches to be made to his face.

Then as she grew calmer, Ratcliffe's sins took on a milder hue; life, after all, had not been entirely blackened by his arts; there was even some good in her experience, sharp though it were. Had she not come to Washington in search of men who cast a shadow, and was not Ratcliffe's shadow strong enough to satisfy her? Had she not penetrated the deepest recesses of politics, and learned how easily the mere possession of power could convert the shadow of a hobby-horse existing only in the brain of a foolish country farmer, into a lurid nightmare that convulsed the sleep of nations? The antics of Presidents and Senators had been amusing--so amusing that she had nearly been persuaded to take part in them. She had saved herself in time.

She had got to the bottom of this business of democratic government, and found out that it was nothing more than government of any other kind. She might have known it by her own common sense, but now that experience had proved it, she was glad to quit the masquerade; to return to the true democracy of life, her paupers and her prisons, her schools and her hospitals. As for Mr. Ratcliffe, she felt no difficulty in dealing with him.

Let Mr. Ratcliffe, and his brother giants, wander on their own political prairie, and hunt for offices, or other profitable game, as they would.

Their objects were not her objects, and to join their company was not her ambition. She was no longer very angry with Mr. Ratcliffe. She had no wish to insult him, or to quarrel with him. What he had done as a politician, he had done according to his own moral code, and it was not her business to judge him; to protect herself was the only right she claimed. She thought she could easily hold him at arm's length, and although, if Carrington had written the truth, they could never again be friends, there need be no difficulty in their remaining acquaintances. If this view of her duty was narrow, it was at least proof that she had learned something from Mr.

Ratcliffe; perhaps it was also proof that she had yet to learn Mr. Ratcliffe himself.

Two o'clock had struck before Mrs. Lee came down from her chamber, and Sybil had not yet made her appearance. Madeleine rang her bell and gave orders that, if Mr. Ratcliffe called she would see him, but she was at home to no one else. Then she sat down to write letters and to prepare for her journey to New York, for she must now hasten her departure in order to escape the gossip and criticism which she saw hanging like an avalanche over her head.

When Sybil at length came down, looking much fresher than her sister, they passed an hour together arranging this and other small matters, so that both of them were again in the best of spirits, and Sybil's face was wreathed in smiles.

A number of visitors came to the door that day, some of them prompted by friendliness and some by sheer curiosity, for Mrs. Lee's abrupt disappearance from the ball had excited remark. Against all these her door was firmly closed. On the other hand, as the afternoon went on, she sent Sybil away, so that she might have the field entirely to herself, and Sybil, relieved of all her alarms, sallied out to interrupt Dunbeg's latest interview with his Countess, and to amuse herself with Victoria's last "phase."

Towards four o'clock the tall form of Mr. Ratcliffe was seen to issue from the Treasury

Department and to descend the broad steps of its western front.

Turning deliberately towards the Square, the Secretary of the Treasury crossed the Avenue and stopping at Mrs. Lee's door, rang the bell. He was immediately admitted. Mrs. Lee was alone in her parlour and rose rather gravely as he entered, but welcomed him as cordially as she could. She wanted to put an end to his hopes at once and to do it decisively, but without hurting his feelings.

"Mr. Ratcliffe," said she, when he was seated- "I am sure you will be better pleased by my speaking instantly and frankly. I could not reply to you last night. I will do so now without delay. What you wish is impossible. I would rather not even discuss it. Let us leave it here and return to our old relations."

She could not force herself to express any sense of gratitude for his affection, or of regret at being obliged to meet it with so little return.

To treat him with tolerable civility was all she thought required of her.

Ratcliffe felt the change of manner. He had been prepared for a struggle, but not to be met with so blunt a rebuff at the start. His look became serious and he hesitated a moment before speaking, but when he spoke at last, it was with a manner as firm and decided as that of Mrs. Lee herself.

"I cannot accept such an answer. I will not say that I have a right to explanation,--I have no rights which you are bound to respect,--but from you I conceive that I may at least ask the favour of one, and that you will not refuse it. Are you willing to tell me your reasons for this abrupt and harsh decision?"

"I do not dispute your right of explanation, Mr. Ratcliffe. You have the right, if you choose to use it, and I am ready to give you every explanation in my power; but I hope you will not insist on my doing so. If I seemed to speak abruptly and harshly, it was merely to spare you the greater annoyance of doubt. Since I am forced to give you pain, was it not fairer and more respectful to you to speak at once? We have been friends. I am very soon going away. I sincerely want to avoid saying or doing anything that would change our relations."

Ratcliffe, however, paid no attention to these words, and gave them no answer. He was much too old a debater to be misled by such trifles, when he needed all his faculties to pin his opponent to the wall. He asked:--

"Is your decision a new one?"

"It is a very old one, Mr. Ratcliffe, which I had let myself lose sight of, for a time. A night's reflection has brought me back to it."

"May I ask why you have returned to it? surely you would not have hesitated without strong reasons."

"I will tell you frankly. If, by appearing to hesitate, I have misled you, I am honestly sorry for it.

I did not mean to do it. My hesitation was owing to the doubt whether my life might not really be best used in aiding you. My decision was owing to the certainty that we are not fitted for each other.

Our lives run in separate grooves. We are both too old to change them."

Ratcliffe shook his head with an air of relief. "Your reasons, Mrs. Lee, are not sound. There is no such divergence in our lives. On the contrary I can give to yours the field it needs, and that it can get in no other way; while you can give to mine everything it now wants. If these are your only reasons I am sure of being able to remove them."

Madeleine looked as though she were not altogether pleased at this idea, and became a little dogmatic. "It is no use our arguing on this subject, Mr.

Ratcliffe. You and I take very different views of life. I cannot accept yours, and you could not practise on mine."

"Show me," said Ratcliffe, "a single example of such a divergence, and I will accept your decision without another word."

Mrs. Lee hesitated and looked at him for an instant as though to be quite sure that he was in earnest. There was an effrontery about this challenge which surprised her, and if she did not check it on the spot, there was no saying how much trouble it might give her. Then unlocking the drawer of the writing-desk at her elbow, she took out Carrington's letter and handed it to Mr. Ratcliffe.

"Here is such an example which has come to my knowledge very lately. I meant to show it to you in any case, but I would rather have waited."

Ratcliffe took the letter which she handed to him, opened it deliberately, looked at the signature, and read. He showed no sign of surprise or disturbance. No one would have imagined that he had, from the moment he saw Carrington's name, as precise a knowledge of what was in this letter as though he had written it himself. His first sensation was only one of anger that his projects had miscarried. How this had happened he could not at once understand, for the idea that Sybil could have a hand in it did not occur to him. He had made up his mind that Sybil was a silly, frivolous girl, who counted for nothing in her sister's actions. He had fallen into the usual masculine blunder of mixing up smartness of intelligence with strength of character. Sybil, without being a metaphysician, willed anything which she willed at all with more energy than her sister did, who was worn out with the effort of life. Mr. Ratcliffe missed this point, and was left to wonder who it was that had crossed his path, and how Carrington had managed to be present and absent, to get a good office in Mexico and to baulk his schemes in Washington, at the same time. He had not given Carrington credit for so much cleverness.

He was violently irritated at the check. Another day, he thought, would have made him safe on this side; and possibly he was right. Had he once succeeded in getting ever so slight a hold on Mrs. Lee he would have told her this story with his own colouring, and from his own point of view, and he fully believed he could do this in such a way as to rouse her sympathy. Now that her mind was prejudiced, the task would be much more difficult; yet he did not despair, for it was his theory that Mrs. Lee, in the depths of her soul, wanted to be at the head of the White House as much as he wanted to be there himself, and that her apparent coyness was mere feminine indecision in the face of temptation. His thoughts now turned upon the best means of giving again the upper hand to her ambition. He wanted to drive Carrington a second time from the field.

Thus it was that, having read the letter once in order to learn what was in it, he turned back, and slowly read it again in order to gain time. Then he replaced it in its envelope, and returned it to Mrs. Lee, who, with equal calmness, as though her interest in it were at an end, tossed it negligently into the fire, where it was reduced to ashes under Ratcliffe's eyes.

He watched it burn for a moment, and then turning to her, said, with his usual composure, "I meant to have told you of that affair myself. I am sorry that Mr. Carrington has thought proper to forestall me. No doubt he has his own motives for taking my character in charge."

"Then it is true!" said Mrs. Lee, a little more quickly than she had meant to speak.

"True in its leading facts; untrue in some of its details, and in the impression it creates. During the Presidential election which took place eight years ago last autumn, there was, as you may remember, a violent contest and a very close vote. We believed (though I was not so prominent in the party then as now), that the result of that election would be almost as important to the nation as the result of the war itself. Our defeat meant that the government must pass into the blood-stained hands of rebels, men whose designs were more than doubtful, and who could not, even if their designs had been good, restrain the violence of their followers. In consequence we strained every nerve. Money was freely spent, even to an amount much in excess of our resources. How it was employed, I will not say.

I do not even know, for I held myself aloof from these details, which fell to the National Central Committee of which I was not a member. The great point was that a very large sum had been borrowed on pledged securities, and must be repaid. The members of the National Committee and certain senators held discussions on the subject, in which I shared. The end was that towards the close of the session the head of the committee, accompanied by two senators, came to me and told me that I must abandon my opposition to the Steamship Subsidy. They made no open avowal of their reasons, and I did not press for one. Their declaration, as the responsible heads of the organization, that certain action on my part was essential to the interests of the party, satisfied me. I did not consider myself at liberty to persist in a mere private opinion in regard to a measure about which I recognized the extreme likelihood of my being in error. I accordingly reported the bill, and voted for it, as did a large majority of the party. Mrs. Baker is mistaken in saying that the money was paid to me. If it was paid at all, of which I have no knowledge except from this letter, it was paid to the representative of the National Committee. I received no money. I had nothing to do with the money further than as I might draw my own conclusions in regard to the subsequent payment of the campaign debt."

Mrs. Lee listened to all this with intense interest. Not until this moment had she really felt as though she had got to the heart of politics, so that she could, like a physician with his stethoscope, measure the organic disease. Now at last she knew why the pulse beat with such unhealthy irregularity, and why men felt an anxiety which they could not or would not explain.

Her interest in the disease overcame her disgust at the foulness of the revelation. To say that the discovery gave her actual pleasure would be doing her injustice; but the excitement of the moment swept away every other sensation. She did not even think of herself. Not until afterwards did she fairly grasp the absurdity of Ratcliffe's wish that in the face of such a story as this, she should still have vanity enough to undertake the reform of politics. And with his aid too! The audacity of the man would have seemed sublime if she had felt sure that he knew the difference between good and evil, between a lie and the truth; but the more she saw of him, the surer she was that his courage was mere moral paralysis, and that he talked about virtue and vice as a man who is colour-blind talks about red and green; he did not see them as she saw them; if left to choose for himself he would have nothing to guide him. Was it politics that had caused this atrophy of the moral senses by disuse? Meanwhile, here she sat face to face with a moral lunatic, who had not even enough sense of humour to see the absurdity of his own request, that she should go out to the shore of this ocean of corruption, and repeat the ancient rôle of King Canute, or Dame Partington with her mop and her pail. What was to be done with such an animal?

The bystander who looked on at this scene with a wider knowledge of facts, might have found entertainment in another view of the subject, that is to say, in the guilelessness ot Madeleine Lee. With all her warnings she was yet a mere baby-in-arms in the face of the great politician. She accepted his story as true, and she thought it as bad as possible; but had Mr.

Ratcliffe's associates now been present to hear his version of it, they would have looked at each other with a smile of professional pride, and would have roundly sworn that he was, beyond a doubt, the ablest man this country had ever produced, and next to certain of being President. They would not, however, have told their own side of the story if they could have helped it, but in talking it over among themselves they might have assumed the facts to have been nearly as follows: that Ratcliffe had dragged them into an enormous expenditure to carry his own State, and with it his own re-election to the Senate; that they had tried to hold him responsible, and he had tried to shirk the responsibility; that there had been warm discussions on the subject; that he himself had privately suggested recourse to Baker, had shaped his conduct accordingly, and had compelled them, in order to save their own credit, to receive the money.

Even if Mrs. Lee had heard this part of the story, though it might have sharpened her indignation against Mr. Ratcliffe, it would not have altered her opinions. As it was, she had heard enough, and with a great effort to control her expression of disgust, she sank back in her chair as Ratcliffe concluded. Finding that she did not speak, he went on:

"I do not undertake to defend this affair. It is the act of my public life which I most regret--not the doing, but the necessity of doing. I do not differ from you in opinion on that point. I cannot acknowledge that there is here any real divergence between us."

"I am afraid," said Mrs. Lee, "that I cannot agree with you."

This brief remark, the very brevity of which carried a barb of sarcasm, escaped from Madeleine's lips before she had fairly intended it. Ratcliffe felt the sting, and it started him from his studied calmness of manner.

Rising from his chair he stood on the hearthrug before Mrs. Lee, and broke out upon her with an oration in that old senatorial voice and style which was least calculated to enlist her sympathies:

"Mrs. Lee," said he, with harsh emphasis and dogmatic tone, "there are conflicting duties in all the transactions of life, except the simplest.

However we may act, do what we may, we must violate some moral obligation.

All that can be asked of us is that we should guide ourselves by what we think the highest. At the time this affair occurred, I was a Senator of the United States. I was also a trusted member of a great political party which I looked upon as identical with the nation. In both capacities I owed duties to my constituents, to the government, to the people. I might interpret these duties narrowly or broadly. I might say: Perish the government, perish the Union, perish this people, rather than that I should soil my hands! Or I might say, as I did, and as I would say again: Be my fate what it may, this glorious Union, the last hope of suffering humanity, shall be preserved."

Here he paused, and seeing that Mrs. Lee, after looking for a time at him, was now regarding the fire, lost in meditation over the strange vagaries of the senatorial mind, he resumed, in another line of argument. He rightly judged that there must be some moral defect in his last remarks, although he could not see it, which made persistence in that direction useless.

"You ought not to blame me--you cannot blame me justly. It is to your sense of justice I appeal. Have I ever concealed from you my opinions on this subject? Have I not on the contrary always avowed them? Did I not here, on this very spot, when challenged once before by this same Carrington, take credit for an act less defensible than this? Did I not tell you then that I had even violated the sanctity of a great popular election and reversed its result? That was my sole act! In comparison with it, this is a trifle! Who is injured by a steamship company subscribing one or ten hundred thousand dollars to a campaign fund? Whose rights are affected by it? Perhaps its stock holders receive one dollar a share in dividends less than they otherwise would. If they do not complain, who else can do so? But in that election I deprived a million people of rights which belonged to them as absolutely as their houses! You could not say that I had done wrong. Not a word of blame or criticism have you ever uttered to me on that account. If there was an offence, you condoned it! You certainly led me to suppose that you saw none. Why are you now so severe upon the smaller crime?"

This shot struck hard. Mrs. Lee visibly shrank under it, and lost her composure. This was the same reproach she had made against herself, and to which she had been able to find no reply. With some agitation she exclaimed:

"Mr. Ratcliffe, pray do me justice! I have tried not to be severe. I have said nothing in the way of attack or blame. I acknowledge that it is not my place to stand in judgment over your acts. I have more reason to blame myself than you, and God knows I have blamed myself bitterly." The tears stood in her eyes as she said these last words, and her voice trembled.

Ratcliffe saw that he had gained an advantage, and, sitting down nearer to her, he dropped his voice and urged his suit still more energetically:

"You did me justice then; why not do it now? You were convinced then that I did the best I could. I have always done so. On the other hand I have never pretended that all my acts could be justified by abstract morality. Where, then, is the divergence between us?"

Mrs. Lee did not undertake to answer this last argument: she only returned to her old ground. "Mr. Ratcliffe," she said, "I do not want to argue this question. I have no doubt that you can overcome me in argument. Perhaps on my side this is a matter of feeling rather than of reason, but the truth is only too evident to me that I am not fitted for politics. I should be a drag upon you. Let me be the judge of my own weakness! Do not insist upon pressing me, further!"

She was ashamed of herself for this appeal to a man whom she could not respect, as though she were a suppliant at his mercy, but she feared the reproach of having deceived him, and she tried pitiably to escape it.

Ratcliffe was only encouraged by her weakness.

"I must insist upon pressing it, Mrs. Lee," replied he, and he became yet more earnest as he went on; "my future is too deeply involved in your decision to allow of my accepting your answer as final. I need your aid.

There is nothing I will not do to obtain it. Do you require affection? mine for you is boundless. I am ready to prove it by a life of devotion. Do you doubt my sincerity? test it in whatever way you please. Do you fear being dragged down to the level of ordinary politicians? so far as concerns myself, my great wish is to have your help in purifying politics. What higher ambition can there be than to serve one's country for such an end?

Your sense of duty is too keen not to feel that the noblest objects which can inspire any woman, combine to point out your course."

Mrs. Lee was excessively uncomfortable, although not in the least shaken.

She began to see that she must take a stronger tone if she meant to bring this importunity to an end, and she answered:--

"I do not doubt your affection or your sincerity, Mr. Ratcliffe. It is myself I doubt. You have been kind enough to give me much of your confidence this winter, and if I do not yet know about politics all that is to be known, I have learned enough to prove that I could do nothing sillier than to suppose myself competent to reform anything. If I pretended to think so, I should be a mere worldly, ambitious woman, such as people think me. The idea of my purifying politics is absurd. I am sorry to speak so strongly, but I mean it. I do not cling very closely to life, and do not value my own very highly, but I will not tangle it in such a way; I will not share the profits of vice; I am not willing to be made a receiver of stolen goods, or to be put in a position where I am perpetually obliged to maintain that immorality is a virtue!"

As she went on she became more and more animated and her words took a sharper edge than she had intended. Ratcliffe felt it, and showed his annoyance. His face grew dark and his eyes looked out at her with their ugliest expression. He even opened his mouth for an angry retort, but controlled himself with an effort, and presently resumed his argument.

"I had hoped," he began more solemnly than ever, "that I should find in you a lofty courage which would disregard such risks. If all tme men and women were to take the tone you have taken, our government would soon perish. If you consent to share my career, I do not deny that you may find less satisfaction than I hope, but you will lead a mere death in life if you place yourself like a saint on a solitary column. I plead what I believe to be your own cause in pleading mine. Do not sacrifice your life!"

Mrs. Lee was in despair. She could not reply what was on her lips, that to marry a murderer or a thief was not a sure way of diminishing crime. She had already said something so much like this that she shrank from speaking more plainly. So she fell back on her old theme.

"We must at all events, Mr. Ratcliffe, use our judgments according to our own consciences. I can only repeat now what I said at first. I am sorry to seem insensible to your expressions towards me, but I cannot do what you wish. Let us maintain our old relations if you will, but do not press me further on this subject."

Ratcliffe grew more and more sombre as he became aware that defeat was staring him in the face. He was tenacious of purpose, and he had never in his life abandoned an object which he had so much at heart as this. He would not abandon it. For the moment, so completely had the fascination of Mrs.

Lee got the control of him, he would rather have abandoned the Presidency itself than her. He really loved her as earnestly as it was in his nature to love anything. To her obstinacy he would oppose an obstinacy greater still; but in the meanwhile his attack was disconcerted, and he was at a loss what next to do. Was it not possible to change his ground; to offer inducements that would appeal even more strongly to feminine ambition and love of display than the Presidency itself? He began again:--

"Is there no form of pledge I can give you? no sacrifice I can make? You dislike politics. Shall I leave political life? I will do anything rather than lose you. I can probably control the appointment of Minister to England. The President would rather have me there than here. Suppose I were to abandon politics and take the English mission. Would that sacrifice not affect you? You might pass four years in London where there would be no politics, and where your social position would be the best in the world; and this would lead to the Presidency almost as surely as the other." Then suddenly, seeing that he was making no headway, he threw off his studied calmness and broke out in an appeal of almost equally studied violence.

"Mrs. Lee! Madeleine! I cannot live without you. The sound of your voice--the touch of your hand--even the rustle of your dress--are like wine to me. For God's sake, do not throw me over!"

He meant to crush opposition by force. More and more vehement as he spoke he actually bent over and tried to seize her hand. She drew it back as though he were a reptile. She was exasperated by this obstinate disregard of her forbearance, this gross attempt to bribe her with office, this flagrant abandonment of even a pretence of public virtue; the mere thought of his touch on her person was more repulsive than a loathsome disease. Bent upon teaching him a lesson he would never forget, she spoke out abruptly, and with evident signs of contempt in her voice and manner:

"Mr. Ratcliffe, I am not to be bought. No rank, no dignity, no consideration, no conceivable expedient would induce me to change my mind.

Let us have no more of this!"

Ratcliffe had already been more than once, during this conversation, on the verge of losing his temper. Naturally dictatorial and violent, only long training and severe experience had taught him self-control, and when he gave way to passion his bursts of fury were still tremendous. Mrs. Lee's evident personal disgust, even more than her last sharp rebuke, passed the bounds of his patience. As he stood before her, even she, high-spirited as she was, and not in a calm frame of mind, felt a momentary shock at seeing how his face flushed, his eyes gleamed, and his hands trembled with rage.

"Ah!" exclaimed he, turning upon her with a harshness, almost a savageness, of manner that startled her still more; "I might have known what to expect!

Mrs. Clinton warned me early. She said then that I should find you a heartless coquette!"

"Mr. Ratcliffe!" exclaimed Madeleine, rising from her chair, and speaking in a warning voice almost as passionate as his own.

"A heartless coquette!" he repeated, still more harshly than before; "she said you would do just this! that you meant to deceive me! that you lived on flattery! that you could never be anything but a coquette, and that if you married me, I should repent it all my life. I believe her now!"

Mrs. Lee's temper, too, was naturally a high one. At this moment she, too, was flaming with anger, and wild with a passionate impulse to annihilate this man. Conscious that the mastery was in her own hands, she could the more easily control her voice, and with an expression of unutterable contempt she spoke her last words to him, words which had been ringing all day in her ears:

"Mr. Ratcliffe! I have listened to you with a great deal more patience and respect than you deserve. For one long hour I have degraded myself by discussing with you the question whether I should marry a man who by his own confession has betrayed the highest trusts that could be placed in him, who has taken money for his votes as a Senator, and who is now in public office by means of a successful fraud of his own, when in justice he should be in a State's prison. I will have no more of this. Understand, once for all, that there is an impassable gulf between your life and mine. I do not doubt that you will make yourself President, but whatever or wherever you are, never speak to me or recognize me again!"

He glared a moment into her face with a sort of blind rage, and seemed about to say more, when she swept past him, and before he realized it, he was alone.

Overmastered by passion, but conscious that he was powerless, Ratcliffe, after a moment's hesitation, left the room and the house. He let himself out, shutting the front door behind him, and as he stood on the pavement old Baron Jacobi, who had special reasons for wishing to know how Mrs. Lee had recovered from the fatigue and excitements of the ball, came up to the spot.

A single glance at Ratcliffe showed him that something had gone wrong in the career of that great man, whose fortunes he always followed with so bitter a sneer of contempt. Impelled by the spirit of evil always at his elbow, the Baron seized this moment to sound the depth of his friend's wound. They met at the door so closely that recognition was inevitable, and Jacobi, with his worst smile, held out his hand, saying at the same moment with diabolic malignity:

"I hope I may offer my felicitations to your Excellency!"

Ratcliffe was glad to find some victim on whom he could vent his rage. He had a long score of humiliations to repay this man, whose last insult was beyond all endurance. With an oath he dashed Jacobi's hand aside, and, grasping his shoulder, thrust him out of the path. The Baron, among whose weaknesses the want of high temper and personal courage was not recorded, had no mind to tolerate such an insult from such a man. Even while Ratcliffe's hand was still on his shoulder he had raised his cane, and before the Secretary saw what was coming, the old man had struck him with all his force full in the face. For a moment Ratcliffe staggered back and grew pale, but the shock sobered him. He hesitated a single instant whether to crush his assailant with a blow, but he felt that for one of his youth and strength, to attack an infirm diplomatist in a public street would be a fatal blunder, and while Jacobi stood, violently excited, with his cane raised ready to strike another blow, Mr. Ratcliffe suddenly turned his back and without a word, hastened away.

When Sybil returned, not long afterwards, she found no one in the parlour.

On going to her sister's room she discovered Madeleine lying on the couch, looking worn and pale, but with a slight smile and a peaceful expression on her face, as though she had done some act which her conscience approved. She called Sybil to her side, and, taking her hand, said:

"Sybil, dearest, will you go abroad with me again?"

"Of course I will," said Sybil; "I will go to the end of the world with you."

"I want to go to Egypt," said Madeleine, still smiling faintly; "democracy has shaken my nerves to pieces. Oh, what rest it would be to live in the Great Pyramid and look out for ever at the polar star!"

Conclusion

SYBIL TO CARRINGTON "May 1st, New York.

"My dear Mr. Carrington, "I promised to write you, and so, to keep my promise, and also because my sister wishes me to tell you about our plans, I send this letter. We have left Washington--for ever, I am afraid--and are going to Europe next month.

You must know that a fortnight ago, Lord Skye gave a great ball to the Grand-Duchess of something-or-other quite unspellable. I never can describe things, but it was all very fine. I wore a lovely new dress, and was a great success, I assure you. So was Madeleine, though she had to sit most of the evening by the Princess--such a dowdy! The Duke danced with me several times; he can't reverse, but that doesn't seem to matter in a Grand-Duke.

Well! things came to a crisis at the end of the evening. I followed your directions, and after we got home gave your letter to Madeleine. She says she has burned it. I don't know what happened afterwards--a tremendous scene, I suspect, but Victoria Dare writes me from Washington that every one is talking about M.'s refusal of Mr. R., and a dreadful thing that took place on our very doorstep between Mr. R. and Baron Jacobi, the day after the ball. She says there was a regular pitched battle, and the Baron struck him over the face with his cane. You know how afraid Madeleine was that they would do something of the sort in our parlour. I'm glad they waited till they were in the street. But isn't it shocking! They say the Baron is to be sent away, or recalled, or something. I like the old gentleman, and for his sake am glad duelling is gone out of fashion, though I don't much believe Mr. Silas P. Ratcliffe could hit anything. The Baron passed through here three days ago on his summer trip to Europe. He left his card on us, but we were out, and did not see him. We are going over in July with the Schneidekoupons, and Mr. Schneidekoupon has promised to send his yacht to the Mediterranean, so that we shall sail about there after finishing the Nile, and see Jerusalem and Gibraltar and Constantinople. I think it will be perfectly lovely. I hate ruins, but I fancy you can buy delicious things in Constantinople. Of course, after what has happened, we can never go back to Washington. I shall miss our rides dreadfully. I read Mr. Browning's 'Last Ride Together,' as you told me; I think it's beautiful and perfectly easy, all but a little. I never could understand a word of him before--so I never tried. Who do you think is engaged? Victoria Dare, to a coronet and a peat-bog, with Lord Dunbeg attached. Victoria says she is happier than she ever was before in any of her other engagements, and she is sure this is the real one. She says she has thirty thousand a year derived from the poor of America, which may just as well go to relieve one of the poor in Ireland.

You know her father was a claim agent, or some such thing, and is said to have made his money by cheating his clients out of their claims. She is perfectly wild to be a countess, and means to make Castle Dunbeg lovely by-and-by, and entertain us all there. Madeleine says she is just the kind to be a great success in London. Madeleine is very well, and sends her kind regards. I believe she is going to add a postscript. I have promised to let her read this, but I don't think a chaperoned letter is much fun to write or receive. Hoping to hear from you soon, "Sincerely yours, "Sybil Ross."

Enclosed was a thin strip of paper containing another message from Sybil, privately inserted at the last moment unknown to Mrs. Lee--

"If I were in your place I would try again after she comes home."

Mrs. Lee's P.S. was very short--

"The bitterest part of all this horrid story is that nine out of ten of our countrymen would say I had made a mistake."

Made in the USA
San Bernardino, CA
11 June 2017